Contents

List of Maps

AN INVITATION TO THE READER

In researching this book, we discovered many wonderful places—hotels, restaurants, shops, and more. We're sure you'll find others. Please tell us about them, so we can share the information with your fellow travelers in upcoming editions. If you were disappointed with a recommendation, we'd love to know that, too. Please write to:

Frommer's Caribbean from $70 a Day, 3rd Edition
Macmillan Travel
1633 Broadway
New York, NY 10019

AN ADDITIONAL NOTE

Please be advised that travel information is subject to change at any time—and this is especially true of prices. We therefore suggest that you write or call ahead for confirmation when making your travel plans. The authors, editors, and publisher cannot be held responsible for the experiences of readers while traveling. Your safety is important to us, however, so we encourage you to stay alert and be aware of your surroundings. Keep a close eye on cameras, purses, and wallets, all favorite targets of thieves and pickpockets.

WHAT THE SYMBOLS MEAN

✪ Frommer's Favorites

Our favorite places and experiences—outstanding for quality, value, or both.

The following abbreviations are used for credit cards:

AE	American Express	MC	MasterCard
DC	Diners Club	V	Visa
DISC	Discover		

The following abbreviations are used in hotel listings:

MAP (Modified American Plan): usually means room, breakfast, and dinner, unless the room rate has been quoted separately, and then it means only breakfast and dinner.
AP (American Plan): includes your room plus three meals.
CP (Continental Plan): includes room and a light breakfast.
EP (European Plan): means room only.

FIND FROMMER'S ONLINE

Arthur Frommer's Budget Travel Online (**www.frommers.com**) offers more than 6,000 pages of up-to-the-minute travel information—including the latest bargains and candid, personal articles updated daily by Arthur Frommer himself. No other Web site offers such comprehensive and timely coverage of the world of travel.

Choosing the Perfect Island: The Best of the Caribbean from $70 a Day

You can hike through national parks and scuba dive along underwater mountains. But perhaps your idea of the perfect Caribbean vacation is to plunk yourself down on a beach and do nothing at all. This guide will show you the best of the islands and prove to you that memorable vacations don't have to cost a fortune. In this chapter, we'll share an opinionated list of our favorite finds and bargains to help you start planning.

For a thumbnail portrait of each island, see "The Islands in Brief" in chapter 2.

1 The Best Destinations for Low-Cost Vacations

Some islands, such as pricey St. Barts or Anguilla, are best left to the rich and famous. If you're not a movie star who commands $18 to $25 million per picture, here are some lovely, less expensive options.

- **Dominica:** This island nation with a British/French-Creole flavor has rugged mountains and lush forests. But it lacks great beaches, which has hindered its development as a resort. That lack of a tourist boom is good news for bargain hunters. If you enjoy lush settings and landscapes, Dominica is for you. The locals are among the friendliest hosts in the West Indies. See chapter 10.
- **The Dominican Republic:** Canadians, whose dollar is weaker in the Caribbean than the Yankee buck, have long flocked to this island nation for its sun, sand, and bargains. It's one of the cheapest destinations in the West Indies. And new resort areas are under development, including the peninsula at Samaná and the Barahona Peninsula, each charging resort prices you haven't seen in 25 years. See chapter 11.
- **Jamaica:** Sure, there's a long list of posh resorts and pricey all-inclusives. But beyond these guarded compounds exists another Jamaica, where the prices are as appealing as a frosty Red Stripe beer. Jamaica is riddled with small inns, and new resort areas are being developed, including along the south coast around Treasure Beach, east of Negril on the long road to Kingston. Even such normally tony areas as Montego Bay are filled with affordable B&Bs and small inns. See chapter 14.

The Caribbean Islands

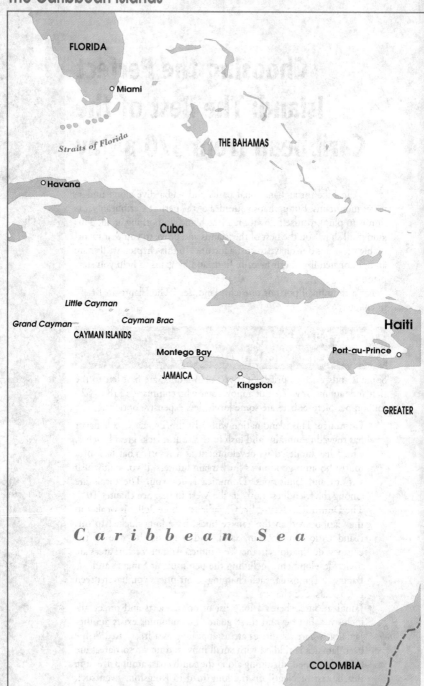

FLORIDA

Miami

Straits of Florida

THE BAHAMAS

Havana

Cuba

Little Cayman

Grand Cayman   Cayman Brac

CAYMAN ISLANDS

Haiti

Port-au-Prince

Montego Bay

JAMAICA   Kingston

GREATER

C a r i b b e a n   S e a

COLOMBIA

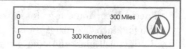

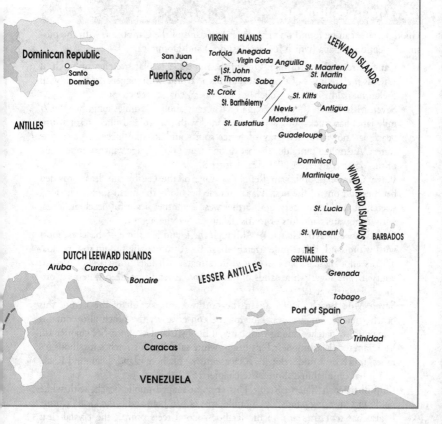

Atlantic

Ocean

TURKS AND CAICOS ISLANDS

Dominican Republic
○ Santo
Domingo

San Juan
○
Puerto Rico

VIRGIN   ISLANDS
Tortola   Anegada
          Virgin Gorda   Anguilla   St. Maarten/
|St. John   St. Martin
St. Thomas   Saba   Barbuda
St. Croix
     St. Barthélemy   St. Kitts
                      Nevis   Antigua
     St. Eustatius   Montserrat

LEEWARD ISLANDS

ANTILLES

Guadeloupe

Dominica
Martinique

WINDWARD ISLANDS

St. Lucia

St. Vincent

THE
GRENADINES

BARBADOS

DUTCH LEEWARD ISLANDS
Aruba   Curaçao
          Bonaire   LESSER ANTILLES

Grenada

Tobago
Port of Spain
○
Trinidad

Caracas

VENEZUELA

- **Puerto Rico:** You can go for broke in Puerto Rico, that's for sure, but you can also find incredible bargains. Ignore those ritzy resorts: Puerto Rico is filled with B&Bs, small inns, and even government-run paradors out in the countryside where you can stay for just a fraction of the price you'd pay along the Condado in San Juan. There's terrific dining at inexpensive roadside kiosks, small cafes, and little family-run dining rooms frequented by locals. See chapter 17.
- **Saba:** Along with Statia, this is a Dutch-held island, but it's like none other in the Caribbean. Only 5 square miles, it's not everyone's cup of tea. But if you can forgo beaches, this volcanic island, ringed with steep cliffs, offers some of the finest diving in the Caribbean. And the hiking is terrific, too. On this beautiful island, the hotels are some of the most affordable in the Caribbean. See chapter 18.
- **St. Eustatius:** Called "Statia" for short, this Dutch-held island is for escapists on a lean budget. It's sleepy, it's undiscovered—and that means great bargains for you. You'll just have to forgo white-sand beaches for some gray- or black-sand ones. It's filled with terrific hiking trails and panoramic dive sites that line the coast, the islanders are friendly, and you can find mom-and-pop hotels charging prices "the way they were." See chapter 19.

2 The Best Beaches

Good beaches can be found on virtually every island of the Caribbean, with the possible exception of Saba (which has rocky shores) and Dominica.

- **Cane Garden Bay** (Tortola): One of the more spectacular stretches of beach, it extends for 1½ miles of white sand and is a favorite with joggers. Its beach with sheltering palms is a living cliché of Caribbean charm. See chapter 7.
- **Seven Mile Beach** (Grand Cayman): It's really about 5½ miles long, but the 7-mile label has stuck. And who cares? Lined with condos and plush resorts, this beach is known for its array of water sports and its translucent aquamarine waters. Australian pines dot the background, and the average winter temperature of the water is a perfect 80°F. See chapter 8.
- **Playa Grande** (Dominican Republic): One of the Caribbean's least crowded beaches and one of the best, Playa Grande lies along the north shore. The long stretch of sand is powdery, and farther west is another beautiful beach at Sosúa, with calm waters and lots of tourist facilities. See chapter 11.
- **Grand Anse Beach** (Grenada): Although the island has some 45 beaches, most with white sand, this 2-mile stretch of sand is reason enough to go to Grenada. There's enough space and so few visitors that you'll likely find a spot just for yourself. The sugar-white sands of Grand Anse extend into deep waters far offshore. See chapter 12.
- **Seven Mile Beach** (Jamaica): In the northwestern section of the island, this beach stretches for 7 miles. Not for the conservative, the beach also contains some nudist "patches" along with bare-all Booby Island offshore. See chapter 14.
- **Le Diamant** (Martinique): This bright white-sand beach stretches for about 6½ miles, much of it undeveloped. It faces a rocky offshore island, Diamond Rock, which has uninhabited shores. See chapter 15.
- **Luquillo Beach** (Puerto Rico): This crescent-shaped public beach, with white sands and towering palms, lies 30 miles east of San Juan and is the local favorite. It also has tent sites and picnic facilities. Coral reefs protect the crystal-clear lagoon. See chapter 17.

- **Trunk Bay** (St. John): Protected by the U.S. National Park Service, this is one of the Caribbean's most popular beaches. A favorite with cruise-ship passengers, it's known for its underwater trail, where markers guide snorkelers along the reef lying just off the white sandy beach. See chapter 25.

3 The Best Snorkeling

While diving in the islands is excellent (see below), you won't need tanks and a regulator to enjoy the abundant sea-life swimming among the Caribbean's colorful coral reefs. All you need is a snorkel, mask, and fins.

- **Bonaire:** Right from their hotels, snorkelers can wade from the shore to the reefs and view an array of coral, including elkhorn barrier, fire and leaf corals, and a range of colorful fish, such as redlip blennies, jewelfish, and parrot fish. The reefs just off Klein Bonaire and Washington/Slagbaai National Park receive rave reviews. See chapter 6.
- **Stingray City** (Grand Cayman): Stingray City has been called the best 12-foot dive (or snorkel) site in the world. In these shallow depths in Grand Cayman's North Sound, more than 30 southern Atlantic stingrays swim freely with snorkelers and divers. See chapter 8.
- **Curaçao Underwater Park** (Curaçao): In contrast to Curaçao's sterile terrain, the marine life that rings the island is rich and spectacular. The best-known snorkeling sites stretch for 12½ miles along its southern coastline—the Curaçao Underwater Park. Sunken shipwrecks, gardens of coral, and millions of fish are your reward. See chapter 9.
- **Buccoo Reef** (Tobago): The shallow, sun-flooded waters off the South American coastline nurture enormous colonies of marine life. Buccoo Reef on Tobago offers many opportunities for snorkeling, and many local entrepreneurs take snorkeling enthusiasts out for junkets on various sailing craft. See chapter 24.
- **Buck Island Reef National Monument** (St. Croix): More than 250 species of fish, as well as a variety of sponges, corals, and crustaceans, have been recorded at this 850-acre island and reef system, 2 miles off St. Croix's north shore. The reef is strictly protected by the National Park Service. See chapter 25.
- **Cane Bay** (St. Croix): One of the island's best diving and snorkeling sites is off this breezy north-shore beach. On a clear day, you can swim out 150 yards and see the Cane Bay Wall, which drops off dramatically to deep waters below. Multicolored fish and elkhorn and brain coral thrive here. See chapter 25.
- **Trunk Bay** (St. John): This self-guided 225-yard-long trail has large underwater signs that identify species of coral and other items of interest. There are freshwater showers, changing rooms, equipment rentals, and a lifeguard on duty. See chapter 25.
- **Leinster Bay** (St. John): With easy access from land or sea, Leinster Bay offers calm, clear, and uncrowded waters, with an abundance of sea life. See chapter 25.
- **Haulover Bay** (St. John): A favorite with locals, this small bay is rougher than Leinster and is often deserted. The snorkeling is dramatic, with ledges, walls, nooks, and sandy areas set close together. At this spot, only about 200 yards separate the Atlantic Ocean from the Caribbean Sea. See chapter 25.
- **Magens Bay** (St. Thomas): On the north shore, Coki Point offers year-round snorkeling, especially around the ledges near Coral World's underwater tower, a favorite with cruise-ship passengers. See chapter 25.

4 The Best Dive Sites

Scuba diving, as everyone knows, is hardly cheap. But if it's your primary reason for visiting the Caribbean, look for a diver's package to get the best deal. Many resorts, including those on Bonaire and the Cayman Islands (the best spots for divers), offer packages that include your room, meals, and limited scuba diving.

If diving is only a sometimes passion, you can stay at a budget hotel and visit a local dive operator. Prices can vary widely, but most one-tank dives cost $45 to $55; two-tank dives, $65 to $75. Full certification courses start at $350.

- **Bonaire:** Here local license plates read "A Diver's Paradise." The highly accessible reefs that surround Bonaire have never suffered from exploitation, poaching, or pollution, and the island's environmentally conscious dive industry will ensure they never do. For the first-timer to the certified diver, the island is one of the world's top underwater environments—it's an underwater mountain created from volcanic eruptions. Diving is possible 24 hours a day. **Captain Don's Habitat Dive Shop** (☎ 800/327-6709) offers some of the most all-around reasonable packages that combine accommodations, meals, and diving. See chapter 6.

- **Virgin Gorda:** Many divers plan their entire vacations around exploring the famed wreck of the HMS *Rhone,* off Salt Island. This royal mail steamer, which went down in 1867, is the most celebrated dive site in the Caribbean. See chapter 7.

- **The Cayman Islands:** Grand Cayman has been called "the best known dive destination in the Caribbean—if not the world," by *Skin Diver* magazine. There are 34 dive operations on Grand Cayman (plus 5 more on Little Cayman, and 3 on Cayman Brac). A full range of professional dive services is available, including equipment sales, rentals, and repairs; instruction at all levels; and underwater photography, video schools, and processing services. Stingray City has become Grand Cayman's most famous dive (and snorkel) site. On Little Cayman, **Sam McCoy's Diving and Fishing Lodge** (☎ 800/626-0496) offers reasonable dive packages that usually include all meals. This resort attracts divers who pursue the sport with a passion. See chapter 8.

- **Saba:** Islanders can't brag about Saba's beaches, but the waters around the island are blessed with some of the Caribbean's richest marine life. It's one of the premier diving locations in the Caribbean, with 38 official dive sites. The unusual setting includes underwater lava flows, black-sand bottoms, very large strands of black coral, millions of fish, and underwater mountaintops. The **Saba Deep Dive Center** (☎ 599/4-63347), one of the best-organized dive outfitters anywhere, offers an assortment of lodgings, many of them affordable choices with charm and a sense of Saban history as part of the package. See chapter 18.

- **Mona Island** (Mayagüez, Puerto Rico): Surrounded by some of the most beautiful coral reefs in the Caribbean, Mona Island has the most pristine, extensive, and well-developed reefs in Puerto Rican waters. The tropical marine ecosystem around Mona includes patch reefs, black coral, spore and groove systems, underwater caverns, deep-water sponges, fringing reefs, and algae reefs. The lush environment attracts octopuses, lobster, queen conch, rays, barracuda, snapper, jack, grunt, angelfish, trunkfish, filefish, butterfly fish, dolphin, parrot fish, tuna, flying fish, and more. The crystal waters afford exceptional horizontal vision for 150 to 200 feet as well as good views down to the shipwrecks that mark the site—including some Hispanic galleons. Five species of whales visit the island's offshore waters. Instead of booking an expensive tour, negotiate with a local fisherman to take you over for a look. See chapter 17.

- **St. Croix:** Increasingly known as a top diving destination, St. Croix hasn't overtaken Grand Cayman yet, but it has a lot going for it. Beach dives, reef dives, wreck dives, nighttime dives, wall dives—it's all here. But none can compete with the underwater trails of the national park at Buck Island, lying off St. Croix's "mainland." Other sites include the drop-offs and coral canyons at Cane Bay and Salt River. Davis Bay is the location of the 12,000-foot-deep Puerto Rico Trench, the fifth-deepest body of water on earth. See chapter 25.

5 The Best Golf Courses—With Greens Fees That Won't Break the Bank

When you see the price of greens fees in the Caribbean, you may want to wait to tee off until you return home. But if you're like many golfers, your passion for the game means that you're willing to splurge to play on a top course. So, in the chapters that follow, we've listed the courses designed by some of the world's most famous golf architects, including Robert Trent Jones (Jr. and Sr.), Pete Dye, Gary Player, and others. In addition, we've found some worthwhile courses where you can play without going broke.

- **Playa Dorado** (Dominican Republic; ☎ 809/320-4340): Normally, playing one of the courses designed by Robert Trent Jones Sr. or Jr. means paying for the privilege and prestige. But there is an exception or two, including this par-72, 18-hole course, a real champion, at Playa Dorado on the north coast of the Dominican Republic. Greens fees are the most reasonable in the Caribbean. If you don't want to play 18 holes, you play 9 holes for less, before enjoying the beach (which is absolutely free). See chapter 11.
- **Ironshore Golf & Country Club** (Montego Bay, Jamaica; ☎ 876/953-2800): Montego Bay is home to some of the world's most legendary courses, notably the championship tee-off spots at Tryall and Half Moon. This excellent privately owned 18-hole, par-72 golf course is not as ritzy as its famous neighbors, but it's quite playable, and the prices are a lot easier on the wallet. See chapter 14 for details on Tryall and Half Moon.
- **Golf de l'Impératrice-Joséphine** (Martinique; ☎ 0596-68-32-81): Robert Trent Jones Sr. created this splendid 18-holer on Martinique, the island's only course. Rolling hills and scenic vistas sweeping down to the sea make for a bucolic setting, and the greens fees are unexpectedly reasonable even though this is a relatively high-priced island. See chapter 15.
- **Bahia Beach Plantation Golf Course** (Puerto Rico; ☎ 787/256-5600): Puerto Rico is the golfing capital of the West Indies, and you'll find its least expensive course only a 30-minute drive east of San Juan. On this 18-hole, par-72 course, the fairways are lined either with palm trees or mangrove swamps—and it's a honey of a spot for tee-off time.
- **Royal St. Kitts Golf Course** (St. Kitts; ☎ 869/465-8339): If you hop over to St. Kitts's neighbor, Nevis, you'll need to win the lottery to play its newly fabled course. But if you stick to St. Kitts, you can play a reasonable game at a reasonable price. This 18-hole, par-72 championship course spreads across 160 acres. You'll have a great game in a scenic setting, designed around seven beautiful ponds. See chapter 20.

6 The Best Adventures That Deliver Bang for Your Buck

- **Going Deep into Harrison's Cave** (Barbados): If you can explore only one cave in the Caribbean, make it Harrison's, one of the finest cave systems in the world. Open to the public since 1981, these limestone caverns are a fairy-tale world of stalagmites, subterranean streams, and stalactites—everything reaching its crescendo with a 40-foot waterfall. See chapter 5.

- **Trekking to a Boiling Lake** (Dominica): The highlight of Dominica National Park, this solfatara lake is like a large cauldron of steaming gray-blue water—a flooded fumarole. It's the world's second-largest boiling lake. Getting here is part of the fun: it's a really arduous climb. The trail (which you should follow only with a guide) takes you through Gtitgou Gorge and along forested mountains until you reach the aptly named Valley of Desolation. After that, it's a rough valley crossing until you ascend to the mysterious lake on the far side. The trick is not to fall through the thin crust that blankets the steaming lava below! See chapter 10.

- **Exploring Luxuriant Guadeloupe:** The mountainous terrain of Basse-Terre island is extraordinarily beautiful. Although the island's coastline is lined with beach resorts and fishing villages, the mountainous interior is a sparsely inhabited region devoted almost completely to a French national forest, Le Parc Naturel de Guadeloupe. Near the park's southernmost boundary stands the 4,812-foot volcanic peak, La Soufrière. The park contains more than 200 miles of hiking trails, allowing physically fit hikers to visit a wealth of gorges, ravines, rivers, and (at points north of La Soufrière) some of the highest waterfalls in the Caribbean. See chapter 13.

- **Discovering the Greatest Sight in the Avian World** (Trinidad): The Caroni Bird Sanctuary, spread across 40 square miles in Trinidad, is without equal in the Caribbean. Home of the national bird of Trinidad & Tobago, the scarlet ibis, this is the world's premier site for birders. Even *Audubon* magazine agrees. Beginning in the late afternoon, fire-engine–red birds arrive by the thousands, settling into roost for the night. As if this weren't enough, snowy egrets and herons fly in to join them in their slumber. The birds arrive in such vast numbers that they look like flaming scarlet and white Christmas tree decorations. See chapter 24.

- **Spending a Day on Buck Island** (off St. Croix): Legendary throughout the Caribbean for its underwater life, Buck Island is riddled with a network of hiking trails. On this 300-acre island surrounded by 550 acres of underwater coral gardens, the snorkeling possibilities are stunning. A circular underwater trail on the island's easternmost side has arrow markers to guide viewers along the inner reef. The elkhorn coral here are among the most massive specimens in the world. See chapter 25.

7 The Friendliest Islands

A few islands are plagued with racial tensions and violent crime, and visitors may not feel welcome. In particular, Jamaica's portside cities (especially Ocho Rios, Kingston, and Montego Bay) are known for crowds of hawkers and peddlers who aggressively pressure tourists to buy unwanted souvenirs. St. Thomas and St. Croix are not very welcoming either, and also have crime problems. And both Puerto Rico and the

Dominican Republic are populous enough to have an urban atmosphere where some visitors might feel anonymous, but many locals there are pretty jaded about the hordes of tourists who arrive each year. So, with these caveats expressed, let's proceed to friendlier oases.

- **Bonaire:** With a tiny population of about 11,000 souls, Bonaire has a small-town atmosphere with a pace slow enough for the most diehard escapist. Residents are usually curious about off-islanders. See chapter 6.
- **Virgin Gorda:** Many locals leave their houses and cars unlocked (though we don't recommend that you become that casual). But, it's the lazy, peaceful life here. Visitors are welcomed into most places with a smile. See chapter 7.
- **Grenada/St. Vincent/the Grenadines:** The islands of the southern Caribbean are English-speaking, music-loving outposts. Locals can be warm and welcoming to North Americans. See chapters 12 and 23.
- **Nevis:** Nevis has a small, intimate feeling. Most accommodations are charming and historic inns, with a British tradition of good manners. See chapter 16.
- **Saba:** The residents here refer to their island as the "Unspoiled Caribbean Queen," because there are no beaches, casinos, or large hotels, and only a handful of bars. The 1,200 shy but cautiously friendly residents follow traditions that were established by the Dutch settlers who first arrived in the 1600s. You'll be very safe here, but expected to behave with dignity and respect for island traditions. See chapter 18.
- **St. John:** St. John remains an unspoiled and relatively safe destination. The locals aren't as jaded about tourism as they are on St. Thomas, and in most places you'll receive a genuine welcome. Many places appreciate your business and want you to return, so they make you feel welcome. See chapter 25.

8 The Best Experiences You Can Have for Free (or Almost)

- **Floating Over to "Treasure Island":** South of Tortola, east of St. John, and accessible only by boat, Norman Island has serviced the needs of smugglers and ruffians since the 1600s, when pirates used its hillocks to spot Spanish galleons to plunder. Legend has it that this was the island that inspired Robert Louis Stevenson's *Treasure Island,* first published in 1883. In a dinghy, you can row into the southernmost cave on the island—with bats overhead and phosphorescent patches. This is where Stevenson's Mr. Fleming, according to legend, took his precious treasure. It was reported that in 1750 treasure from the sunken *Nuestra Señora* was recovered here. The island has a series of other caves whose bottoms are filled with seawater teeming with marine life. Intrepid hikers climb through scrubland to the island's central ridge, Spy Glass Hill, to appreciate the panoramic view of the land and sea, though hiking trails are either nonexistent or poorly maintained. See chapter 7.
- **Calling on the Once-Hostile Caribs** (Dominica): The Carib Indian Reservation, along the eastern coast of Dominica, is home to the once-hostile tribe for whom the Caribbean is named. Reviled by the Spanish invaders because of their cannibalism, the Caribs now live peacefully in half a dozen villages, the largest of which are Bataka, Sineku, and Salybia. See chapter 10.
- **Exploring Two Unspoiled Islands near Guadeloupe:** Marie-Galante (named by Columbus in 1493) and the Iles des Saintes are rarely visited islands near the coast of Guadeloupe. They preserve a raffish, seafaring atmosphere you might

have found in Marseille during the 1930s. Come to sunbathe, explore by bike, and savor the seclusion. See chapter 13.

- **Enjoying Jamaica's People to People Program:** Tell the Jamaica Tourist Board what your interests are—butterflies, reggae, Bible studies, sailing, whatever—and they'll pair you up with Jamaican families who will, without fuss or bother, spend a few hours with you, including you in the normal routine of their lives. Almost 700 Jamaican families participate. There's no cost, but a small gift as a gesture of appreciation is always welcome. Many lasting friendships have formed as a result of this program.

- **Rafting on the Río Grande** (Port Antonio, Jamaica; ☎ **876/993-2778**): Until the late actor Errol Flynn discovered what fun it was, rafting on this river was simply a means of transporting bananas. Now it's the most amusing sport in Jamaica. Propelled by stout bamboo poles, you're guided down the river for 8 miles, viewing a lush backdrop of coconut palms and banana plantations. You're even taken through the Tunnel of Love. See chapter 14.

- **Seeing the Monkeys** (off Palmas del Mar Resort, Humacao, Puerto Rico): Reached from the marina at Palmas del Mar, the 39-acre islet of Cayo Santiago lies off the eastern shore of Puerto Rico. A boat, the *Shagrada*, takes snorkelers and the merely curious over to see an island colony of rhesus monkeys whose ancestors were brought here from India in 1938 for study. Many significant breakthroughs in human medicine have been attributed to observing the behavioral patterns of these rambunctious primates. Passengers aren't allowed to actually go on the island, but you can see the monkeys on the shore, swinging through the trees, playing the mating game, nursing their young, or just going bananas. See chapter 17.

9 The Best Destinations for Serious Shoppers Who Insist on Bargains

Since the American government allows U.S. citizens to take (or send) home more duty-free goods from the U.S. Virgin Islands than from other ports of call, the U.S. Virgin Islands remain the shopping bazaar of the Caribbean. U.S. citizens may carry home $1,200 worth of goods untaxed, as opposed to only $400 to $600 worth of goods from most islands in the Caribbean. (The only exception to this rule is Puerto Rico, where any purchase, regardless of the amount, can be carried tax-free back to the U.S. mainland.)

- **Aruba:** The wisest shoppers on Aruba are the cost-conscious souls who have carefully checked the prices of comparable goods before leaving home. Duty is relatively low (only 3.3%). Much of the European china, jewelry, perfumes, wristwatches, and crystal has a disconcerting habit of reappearing everywhere, so after you determine exactly which brand of watch or china you want, you can comparison-shop. See chapter 4.

- **Barbados:** Bajan shops seem to specialize in all things English. Merchandise includes bone china from British and Irish manufacturers, china, wristwatches, jewelry, and perfumes. Bridgetown's Broad Street is the shopping headquarters of the island, although there are malls along the congested southwestern coast. Duty-free status is extended to anyone showing a passport or ID and an airline ticket with a date of departure from Barbados, and except for cigarettes and tobacco, duty-free items can be hauled off by any buyer as soon as they're paid for. See chapter 5.

- **Cayman Islands:** You can buy tax-free goods at a daunting collection of malls and mini-malls throughout Grand Cayman. Most of these are along the highway that parallels Seven Mile Beach; you'll need a car to shop around. There are also many stores in George Town, which you can explore on foot, poking in and out of some large emporiums in your search for bargains. See chapter 8.

- **Curaçao:** Curaçao has been a mercantile center since the 1700s. In the island's capital, tidy and prosperous Willemstad, hundreds of merchants will be only too happy to cater to your needs. A handful of malls lie on Willemstad's outskirts, but most shops are clustered within a few blocks of the center of town. During seasonal sales, goods might be up to 50% less than comparable prices in the U.S.; most of the year, you'll find luxury goods (porcelain, crystal, watches, and gemstones) priced at about 25% less than in the States. Technically, you'll pay import duties on virtually everything you buy, but rates are so low that you might not even notice. See chapter 9.

- **Dominican Republic:** The island's best buys include handcrafts, amber from Dominican mines, and the distinctive pale-blue semiprecious gemstone known as larimar. However, the amber you buy from a streetside vendor might be nothing more than orange-colored transparent plastic, so buy only from well-established shops. Other charming souvenirs might include a Dominican rocking chair (remember the one JFK used to sit in?), which is sold boxed, in pieces. Shopping malls and souvenir stands abound in Santo Domingo, in Puerto Plata, and along the country's northern coast. See chapter 11.

- **Jamaica:** The shopping was better in Jamaica during the good old days before new taxes added a 10% surcharge. Nevertheless, Jamaica offers a wealth of desirable goods, including flavored rums, Jamaican coffees, handcrafts (such as woodcarvings, woven baskets, and sandals), original paintings and sculpture, and cameras, wristwatches, and VCRs. Unless you're a glutton for handmade souvenirs—available on every beach and street corner—you'd be wise to limit most of your purchases to bona fide merchants and stores. See chapter 14.

- **Puerto Rico:** U.S. citizens don't have to pay any duty on anything—yes, anything—bought in Puerto Rico. Jewelry and watches abound, often at competitive prices, especially in the island's best-stocked area, Old San Juan. Also of great interest are such Puerto Rican handcrafts as charming papier-mâché carnival masks. See chapter 17.

- **St. Thomas:** Charlotte Amalie, the U.S. Virgin Islands' capital, attracts hordes of cruise-ship passengers on a sometimes frantic hunt for bargains, real or imagined. Many of its busiest shops occupy restored warehouses built in the 1700s, and they're stocked with more merchandise than can be found anywhere else in the entire Caribbean. Despite all the fanfare, however, real bargains are hard to come by here. Look for two local publications, *This Week* and *Best Buys;* either might steer you to the type of low-cost merchandise you're seeking. If at all possible, try to avoid shopping when more than one cruise ship is in port—the shopping district is a madhouse on those days. See chapter 25.

- **St. Croix:** This island is the poor stepchild of St. Thomas. You'll see many of the same shops and chains here that you will on St. Thomas. Prices are about the same, but the crowds aren't nearly as bad here. But still, there's much to interest the "born-to-shop" visitor here, and merchandise has never been more wideranging than it is today. Even though most cruise ships call at Frederiksted, a colorful but isolated town near the island's western tip, most shops are in Christiansted, the island's capital. See chapter 25.

10 The Best Reasonably Priced Honeymoon Resorts

More and more couples are exchanging their vows in the Caribbean. Many resorts will arrange everything from the preacher to the flowers, so we've included in the following list some resorts that provide wedding services. For more information about weddings on some of the more popular Caribbean islands, see "Getting Married in the Caribbean" in chapter 2.

- **Falmouth Harbour Beach Apartments** (Antigua; ☎ 268/460-1094): For honeymooners, this beachside complex offers self-sufficient accommodations near the English Harbour of Lord Nelson fame, the most fabled attraction in Antigua and one of the Caribbean's premier sights. With its own small sandy beach, it is an informal, laid-back choice for a honeymoon, with comfortably furnished apartments where you can impress your new partner with your culinary skills. Or, if not that, you can walk over to the Admiral's Inn, one of the most atmospheric restaurants in the West Indies.

- **Jake's** (Calabash Bay, Jamaica; ☎ 800/OUTPOST or 876/965-0552): If you're looking for the perfect honeymoon hideaway, make it Jake's, a 3-hour drive east of Montego Bay's airport. On a cliff by the sea, it's a compound of flamboyant colored cottages offering a lot of pizzazz for little money. It's offbeat, and it's just plain fun, *mon*. What to do in this sleepy backwater? Swim, eat, sleep, snorkel, and do whatever honeymooners do. If you get bored, you can walk up to a cafe called "Trans Love" and catch up on the latest gossip between the rasta men and their girlfriends. See chapter 14.

- **Harmony Marina Suites** (St. Lucia; ☎ 758/452-8756): This property has eight honeymoon suites equipped with double Jacuzzis, four-poster beds, white rattan furniture, and wet bars. The gracious hosts here will arrange your entire wedding for you, complete with champagne, candlelit dinners, and romantic sunset cruises. If you and your spouse decide to get out of bed, you'll have one of the lusher and more beautiful islands in the Caribbean to explore. See chapter 21.

- **Villa Blanca** (St. Thomas; ☎ 340/776-0749): In Charlotte Amalie, Villa Blanca was the former home of the heiress to the Dodge fortune. Now it's the honeymoon bargain of the island, with 12 guest rooms, each with a private balcony and a kitchenette. The "Honeymoon Hideaway" package, for 8 days and 7 nights, costs $875 per couple in winter and only $575 per couple from May 1 to mid-December, including welcome drinks, a bottle of champagne, and flowers.

11 The Best Family Resorts (for Parents Who Don't Want to Blow the Kids' College Fund)

- **Mango Bay Resort** (Virgin Gorda, British Virgin Islands; ☎ 800/223-6510 or 284/495-5652): On the western shore, little villas open right onto the beach, and each has its own fully equipped kitchen (including a dishwasher), plus maid service. Shaded by palm trees and surrounded by wide terraces, the villas can be configured to accommodate both large and small families. An ideal family hideaway. See chapter 7.

- **Calypso Cove** (Grand Cayman; ☎ 345/949-3730): Just off Seven Mile Beach, one of the Caribbean's greatest, this is a bargain on a high-priced island. Both one-bedroom and two-bedroom accommodations are available, with the latter housing as many as six. All accommodations have full kitchens, and such extras as washer and dryer help keep the expenses down. The place is relatively bone bare as to facilities, but restaurants, grocery outlets, and other services are just a short walk away. See chapter 8.

- **Islander Hotel** (St. Lucia; ☎ 758/452-8757): A local entrepreneur who didn't worry too much about architectural finesse built this spartan motel in 1985. A beautiful beach with very gentle surf lies a few steps away, and many of the units contain modest kitchenettes. With your brood in tow, you'll definitely save money if you opt to cook for yourself.
- **Maho Bay** (St. John; ☎ 800/392-9004 or ☎ 340/776-6226): At the edge of a great beach, you'll stay in a network of tent-cottages, with communal showers and a sense of the great outdoors that children adore. See chapter 25.

12   The Best Camping

- **Brewers Bay Campground** (Tortola, British Virgin Islands; ☎ 284/494-3463): At one of the prime snorkeling sites in the BVI, this campground offers you a choice—either a bare site or a prepared one. It's fairly basic here, but it's a safe, clean location. See chapter 7.
- **Anegada Beach Campground** (Anegada; ☎ 284/495-9466): On this remote island you can wander along miles of secluded beaches. At this campground, you get simple accommodations with flush toilets and outdoor showers. There's even a restaurant, although cookout areas are available if you want to barbecue. A cottage is offered for rent. See chapter 7.
- **White Bay Campground** (Jost Van Dyke, British Virgin Islands; ☎ 284/495-9312): At Little Harbour, on this practically deserted island (a former pirate's stamping ground), you get both tent and bare-site options. Running water and flush toilets are available, as are cookout areas. You can wander endlessly without encountering another soul at times. See chapter 7.
- **Cinnamon Bay Campground** (St. John; ☎ 800/539-9998 or 340/776-6330): Directly on the beach, this National Park Service campground is the most complete in the Caribbean. Sleeping in tents, cottages, or bare sites, you're surrounded by thousands of acres of tropical foliage. You can get up in the morning and take a running leap into the warm waters off Cinnamon Bay Beach before breakfast. Bare-siters can make use of a picnic table and grill. There are ample facilities, including a cafeteria, water sports, and bathhouses. See chapter 25.
- **Maho Bay** (St. John; ☎ 800/392-9004 or 340/776-6226): At Maho Bay you can camp close to nature—in style and comfort. Boardwalks and ramps link its three-room tent cottages and lead to the beach. Electric lamps, propane stoves, bathhouses, barbecue areas, water sports, a commissary, even a restaurant—it's all here. See chapter 25.

13   The Best Places to Get Away From It All Without Spending a Fortune

- **Papillote Wilderness Retreat** (Dominica; ☎ 767/448-2287): It's situated in the heart of the Papillote Forest, one of the wildest and least-explored rain forests in the Caribbean. If frequent rain showers don't bother you (and it rains a lot in this incessantly lush region of Dominica), Papillote might provide a suitable escape at a surprisingly reasonable price. See chapter 10.

- **La Sagesse Nature Center** (Grenada; ☎ **473/444-6458**): Even though you're near the airport, the opportunities for exploring the glories of nature are almost unlimited. Trails wind through the neighboring landscape, and ample opportunities for bird-watching are within an easy walk. See chapter 12.
- **La Casa del Francés** (Vieques, off the coast of Puerto Rico; ☎ **787/741-3751**): This house was built in 1905 as the headquarters of a sugar plantation. Since the 1950s it's been an eccentric but very appealing hideaway, though it's not for everyone. The house includes a collection of primitive art objects scattered amid dozens of potted plants and climbing vines. See chapter 17.
- **Blanchisseuse Beach Resort** (Trinidad; ☎ **868/628-3731**): This place lies in the heart of 28 acres of rain forest. You can swim in freshwater springs or in the lagoons of swift-flowing rivers, watch (from afar) the beaches where leatherback turtles lay their eggs, and eat grilled fish caught by local fishers. See chapter 24.

14   The Best Authentic Dining

- **Bourbon Street** (Barbados; ☎ **246/424-4557**): This casual eatery offers the best Cajun flavors on the island, evocative of the Creole tastes of New Orleans. An informal savory cuisine is served in a former private home on a terrace overlooking the sea near many of the southwest coast's budget hotels. Try the shrimp remoulade or the deep-fried oysters with a creamy Tabasco sauce, and the blackened red snapper, and you'll swear you're back on Bourbon Street.
- **North Shore Shell Museum Bar & Restaurant** (Tortola, British Virgin Islands; ☎ **284/495-4714**): The showcase for the culinary talents of Egberth and Mona Donovan, this restaurant succeeds admirably in serving the most authentic island cuisine. Mona is the daughter of the locally famous Mrs. Scatliffe, for decades considered the island's most "authentic" chef. The chefs take the produce of the island when available and shape the foodstuff into all sorts of delectable island fare, ranging from soupsop daiquiris to spicy conch fritters. See chapter 7.
- **Golden Star** (Curaçao; ☎ **599/9-4618741**): It's nothing but a down-home roadside diner, but it's got authentic Antillean grub—all that good stuff like *tia chiki* (goat stew), well-seasoned grilled conch, shrimp Creole, and *keshi yena* (baked Gouda cheese stuffed with spicy meat filling). See chapter 9.
- **Mamma's** (Grenada; ☎ **473/440-1459**): Mamma used to welcome visitors with one of her rum punches and tasty regional cuisine. And we're really talking regional here. When Mamma could get them, she served armadillo or manicou (possum), or even monkey. Regrettably, Mamma isn't with us any more, but daughter Cleo learned all her culinary secrets. Try her fresh seafood such as octopus or crayfish, her callaloo soup, or one of her curries. See chapter 12.
- **Cosmo's Seafood Restaurant & Bar** (Negril, Jamaica; ☎ **876/957-4784**): At a laid-back *bohío* bordering the beach, Cosmo Brown makes Jamaica's best conch soup. His eatery may be rustic, but it's the place to find authentic Jamaican flavor and escape the hotel restaurants with their bland international fare. Fresh fish is your best bet here, and on some nights you can get lobster, curried or grilled. See chapter 14.
- **Chez Mally Edjam** (Martinique; ☎ **0596/78-51-18**): It's said that Martinique chefs serve the Caribbean's zestiest cuisine. If you'd like to find out for yourself, head to this little dive where you'll encounter a virtuosa cook. On the island's northernmost tip, the home is modest—but not the meals. The Creole dishes here are delicacies, with everything from stuffed land crab with hot seasoning to

the best pork curry on the island. Save room for one of her original confitures, tiny portions of fresh island fruit such as guava preserved in vanilla syrup. See chapter 15.

- **Jemma's Seaview Kitchen** (Tobago; ☎ **868/660-4066**): Mrs. Jemma Sealey will feed you well after squeezing some fresh orange or pineapple juice to settle your stomach. She doesn't put on airs—she just serves up the most authentic Tobagonian cuisine on the island. Tucked away on the beach, her place is cheap, good, and may be permanently etched in your memory, especially after you try her kingfish steak dipped in batter and accompanied with a spicy sweet sauce. On some nights, she might serve you a lobster if she has them, or perhaps crab and dumplings. See chapter 24.

- **Eunice's Terrace** (St. Thomas; ☎ **340/775-3975**): It's not the most scenic place on the island, but people flock to Eunice's Terrace anyway for the most authentic Creole dishes on St. Thomas. Pineapple-coconut–fried shrimp, herb-stuffed lobster, callaloo soup, funghi (something like polenta), and plantain are dished out in generous portions—and everything's finished off with sweet potato pie. One or two of Eunice's Queen Mary rum punches will sail you off happily into the afternoon. See chapter 25.

15 The Best Places for Sunset Cocktails

- **Admiral's Inn** (Antigua; ☎ **268/460-1027**): At one of the most atmospheric inns in the Caribbean, you can enjoy your cocktail and watch the sun go down over the loveliest harbor in the West Indies. After the sun sets, you can always play a game of English darts with whatever crew has arrived at the dockyard. See chapter 3.

- **John Moore Bar** (Barbados; ☎ **246/422-2258**): On the waterfront, this is the most famous little bar on Barbados. It's the social center of the island, so you can catch up on the latest gossip while enjoying a rum punch. See chapter 5.

- **Karel's Beach Bar** (Bonaire; ☎ **599/7/8434**): Join the diving set at this Tahitian-styled alfresco bar perched above the sea on stilts right in the center of town. The convivial crowd starts gathering around five o'clock, and on weekends a local band entertains, making it a great place to linger. See chapter 6.

- **Rick's Cafe** (Negril, Jamaica; ☎ **876/957-0380**): Rick's is the premier sunset-watching spot in the Caribbean, almost rivaling the docks at Key West. Watching sunsets here is quite a ritual. The rowdy crowd even toasts Mother Nature with lethal rum drinks, followed by shouts and laughter. Some even applaud at her "handiwork" in getting the sun to set so spectacularly. After the "performance," the rum flows all night. See chapter 14.

- **Frangipani Hotel** (Bequia, the Grenadines; ☎ **784/458-3255**): Any of the watering holes along Admiralty Bay would be lovely for a sundowner, although we give this hotel the edge, since it's where the locals go. A lot of yachties gather here, some of whom fly the skull and crossbones flag. Often you can hear steel bands playing along the shore, and the whole place becomes festive, making you want to linger long after the sun has disappeared. See chapter 23.

- **The Bar at Paradise Point** (St. Thomas; ☎ **340/777-4540**): Head here for your sundowner, and get the bartender to serve you his specialty: a "Bushwacker." Sometimes a one-man steel band is on hand to serenade the sunset watchers, who, after a few of those Painkillers, don't know if the sun has set or not. See chapter 25.

16 The Best Nightspots Without Sky-High Cover Charges

- **Bomba's Surfside Shack** (Tortola; ☎ 284/495-4148): For uninhibited nightlife, this joint, covered with Day-Glo graffiti, rocks until the early hours. Built from the flotsam of a junkyard, it's fun, funky, and wild. The all-you-can-eat barbecue (on some nights) and the live reggae music keep the joint jumping until the early hours. See chapter 7.

- **Palm Court** (in El San Juan Hotel, Isla Verde, Puerto Rico; ☎ 787/791-1000): This is the most beautiful bar in the Caribbean (but not for sunset watching, as it's enclosed). And when you walk through the elegant lobby, you'll feel quite posh. But drink prices are reasonable and you can hear live music on many nights emanating from the adjoining El Chico Bar. There's no finer place for drinking in San Juan. See chapter 17.

- **Cheri's Café** (St. Maarten; ☎ 599/5-53361): This is the local hot spot on this popular island divided between the Netherlands and France. Cheri's is on the Dutch side. *Caribbean Travel and Life* magazine announced it as their readers' pick for the best bar in the West Indies, where the competition is rough. Go here for an inexpensive night of uninhibited fun and revelry. After a few "Straw Hats" (the bartender's specialty), the night is yours. See chapter 22.

- **The Green House** (Charlotte Amalie, St. Thomas; ☎ 340/774-7998): If you must be in Charlotte Amalie at night (there are safer places to be), head here for drinking, dining, and perhaps listening to some of the best music on the island, either live or recorded. What's even better are the two-for-one happy hours including a generous free buffet Monday through Saturday. There's only a modest cover charge when live bands play. See chapter 25.

- **Blue Moon** (St. Croix; ☎ 340/772-2222): This is the hottest dive on the island, holding forth in the capital, Frederiksted. Thursday and Friday are the best nights to show up. It's hip and it's fun—and it also offers good bistro-type food. Live entertainment is often featured, and a convivial crowd—a happy mix of locals and visitors—shows up. See chapter 25.

Planning an Affordable Trip to the Caribbean

This chapter is designed to provide most of the nuts-and-bolts information you'll need before setting off on your island escape. We'll show you how to save money when booking your trip, and how to scout out the best airfares and cruise bargains.

1 The Islands in Brief

The first decision you'll have to make is where to go in the Caribbean. Here is a brief run-down of the region to help get you started. See the following chapters for details.

ANTIGUA Antigua claims to have a different lovely beach for each day of the year. Some British traditions (including a passion for cricket) linger on, though this nation became independent in 1981; its British legacy means that you can see some of the most interesting historic naval sites in the world here. The island has a population of 80,000, mostly descended from the African slaves of plantation owners. Though there are many conservative but very glamorous resorts, we've found some affordable accommodations with charming island atmosphere. Antigua is politically linked to the sparsely inhabited and largely undeveloped island of Barbuda, about 30 miles north. See chapter 3.

ARUBA Until its beaches were "discovered" in the late 1970s, Aruba was an almost-forgotten outpost of Holland, mostly valued for its oil refineries and salt factories. Today it's favored for its unique terrain—an almost lunar landscape of desert, plus spectacular beaches where you can bask under constant sunshine. There's an almost total lack of racial tensions, though its population of 70,000 is culturally diverse, with roots in Holland, Portugal, Spain, Venezuela, India, Pakistan, and Africa. A building boom in the 1980s has transformed this island into a pale version of Las Vegas (it's one of the islands most noted for casinos). Unfortunately, it's next to impossible to find real budget accommodations, though we've scouted out a few for you. See chapter 4.

BARBADOS Cosmopolitan Barbados has the densest population of any island in the Caribbean, a sports tradition that avidly pursues cricket, and many stylish, medium-sized hotels. Its topography varies from rolling hills and savage waves on the eastern (Atlantic) coast, to densely populated flatlands and sheltered beaches in the southwest. Barbados is generally an expensive destination. See chapter 5.

BONAIRE   Bonaire is the place to be for serious divers and birders. The landscape is as dry and inhospitable as anything you'll find in the Caribbean, and the beaches aren't the best, but there's a wealth of rich marine life along the island's miles of off-shore reefs. There's little nightlife or shopping here; most visitors come for diving or nature. A terrific destination for cost-conscious travelers. See chapter 6.

THE BRITISH VIRGIN ISLANDS   Still a British Crown Colony, this lushly forested archipelago contains about 50 mountainous islands (depending on how many rocks, cays, and uninhabited islets you want to include). A superb destination for sailing, the BVI is less densely populated, less developed, and has fewer social problems than its neighbors in the U.S. Virgin Islands. Tortola is the main island, followed in importance by Virgin Gorda. See chapter 7.

THE CAYMAN ISLANDS   Flat and prosperous, this tiny nation of three islands south of Cuba is dependent on Britain for its economic survival. It attracts millionaire expatriates from all over because of its lenient tax and banking laws. The landscapes aren't as lush and lovely as others in the Caribbean—these islands are covered with scrubland and swamp—but they do have great beaches and world-class diving. Many of these beaches are lined with upscale (and horrendously expensive) private homes and condominiums, but we've found some affordable places to stay. See chapter 8.

CURAÇAO   Since much of the island's surface is an arid desert that grows only cactus, its canny Dutch settlers ruled out farming and developed Curaçao into one of the Dutch Empire's busiest trading posts. Until the post–World War II collapse of the oil refineries, Curaçao was a thriving mercantile society with a capital (Willemstad) that somewhat resembled Amsterdam. Tourism began to develop here during the 1980s, and many new hotels—usually in the Dutch colonial style—have been built. Overall, Curaçao is more than just a tourist mecca: It's a well-defined society in its own right. See chapter 9.

DOMINICA   An English-speaking island set midway between Guadeloupe and Martinique, Dominica (Doh-mi-*nee*-kah) is the largest and most mountainous island of the Windwards. A mysterious, rarely visited land of waterfalls, rushing streams, and rain forests, it has only a few beaches, which are mainly lined with black volcanic sand. Some 82,000 people live here, including 2,000 remaining descendants of the Carib Indians. Dominica is one of the poorest islands in the Caribbean, with the misfortune of lying directly in the hurricane belt. But if you like the offbeat and unusual, you may find this the most fascinating island in the Caribbean, with beautiful, lush landscapes to explore—and it's one of the best bargain destinations. See chapter 10.

THE DOMINICAN REPUBLIC   Occupying the eastern two-thirds of Hispaniola (it shares the island with Haiti), this mountainous country is the second-largest in the Caribbean and boasts gorgeous beaches. An endless series of military dictatorships once wreaked havoc on its social fabric, but today there's a more favorable political climate. The "D.R." offers some of the least expensive vacation options in the entire Caribbean, though there are some drawbacks: The contrast between the wealth of foreign tourists and the poverty of locals is especially obvious here, and it's not the safest of the islands. Its crowded capital, Santo Domingo, has a population of two million. The island offers lots of Hispanic color, wonderful *merengue* music, and many opportunities to dance, drink, and party. Unfortunately, the Dominican Republic was hit hard by Hurricane Georges in 1998. See chapter 11.

GRENADA   The southernmost nation of the Windward Islands, Grenada (Gre-*nay*-dah) is one of the lushest in the Caribbean. Extravagantly fertile, it's one of the largest producers of spices in the Western Hemisphere, the result of a gentle climate, rich volcanic soil, and a corps of good-natured islanders. There's a lot of very appealing local color on Grenada, particularly since the political troubles of the 1980s have ended. The beaches are white and sandy, and the populace (a mixture of English expatriates and islanders of African descent) is friendly. Once a British Crown Colony but now independent, the island nation includes Carriacou and Petit Martinique, two smaller islands which have few tourist facilities. Grenada's capital, St. George's, is one of the most raffishly charming towns in the Caribbean. See chapter 12.

GUADELOUPE   It isn't as sophisticated or cosmopolitan as the two outlying islands (St. Barthélemy and the French sector of St. Martin) over which it holds administrative authority. Despite that, there's a lot of natural beauty in this *département* of France. With a relatively low population density (only 340,000 people live here, mostly along the coast), butterfly-shaped Guadeloupe is actually two distinctly different volcanic islands separated by a narrow saltwater strait, the rivière Salée. It's ideal for scenic drives and Creole color, offering any Francophile an unusual insight into the French colonial world. See chapter 13.

JAMAICA   A favorite of North American honeymooners, mountainous Jamaica rises abruptly from the sea 90 miles south of Cuba and about 100 miles west of Haiti. One of the most densely populated nations in the Caribbean, with a vivid sense of its own identity, Jamaica has a tragic history rooted in slavery, and today a legacy of poverty and political turbulence remains. Yet despite that poverty and a regrettable increase in crime and harassment of tourists by vendors in such resort areas as Ocho Rios, Jamaica is one of the most successful predominately-black democracies in the world. The island is large enough to allow the more or less peaceful coexistence of all kinds of people, from expatriate English aristocrats to dyed-in-the-wool Rastafarians. Overall, Jamaica is a fascinating island, with a vibrant culture, a rich musical heritage, and an astounding diversity of landscapes. Many super-expensive resorts line its lovely beaches, fenced off and isolated from the life of the island, but there are countless bargains to be had, too, and we'll round them up for you in chapter 14.

MARTINIQUE   One of the most exotic French-speaking destinations in the Caribbean, Martinique was once the site of a settlement that was demolished by volcanic activity (St. Pierre, which is now only a pale shadow of a once-thriving city). Like Guadeloupe, Martinique is legally and culturally French (certainly many islanders drive with a Gallic panache—read: very badly), although many Creole customs and traditions continue to flourish. The beaches are beautiful, the Creole cuisine is full of flavor and flair, and the island has lots of tropical charm. See chapter 15.

PUERTO RICO   Home to 3.3 million Spanish-speaking people, the Commonwealth of Puerto Rico is under the jurisdiction of the United States. It's one of the Caribbean's most urban islands, with glittering casinos, lots of traffic, a relatively high crime rate, and a more-or-less comfortable mixture of Latin and U.S. cultures. The island's interior is filled with ancient volcanic mountains and lush rain forest; the coastline is ringed with sandy beaches. San Juan, the island's 16th-century capital, contains beautifully preserved Spanish colonial neighborhoods, and the Condado, its beach strip of high-rise hotels, which evokes Miami Beach. Outside of the glitzy resorts are many charming and reasonably priced places to stay, lots of wonderful down-home restaurants, and a host of affordable adventures. See chapter 17.

SABA   Saba is a cone-shaped extinct volcano that rises abruptly and steeply from the watery depths of the Caribbean. There are no beaches to speak of, but the local Dutch- and English-speaking populace has traditionally made a living from fishing, trade, and needlework rather than tourism. Visitors usually come to Saba to dive (which is expensive, but worth it), to visit the rain forest (which is free), and to totally get away

Which Island Is for You?	Vacation Costs	All-Inclusive Resorts	Beaches	Above-Average Food	Campgrounds	Casinos	Condo/Villa Rentals	Family-Friendly	Cruise-Ship Port	Deluxe xxResorts
Antigua	$$$	✔	✔	✔		✔		✔	✔	✔
Aruba	$$	✔	✔	✔		✔	✔	✔	✔	✔
Barbados	$$$	✔	✔	✔			✔	✔	✔	✔
Bonaire	$$		✔							
Cayman Islands	$$$	✔	✔	✔			✔	✔	✔	✔
Curaçao	$$		✔			✔			✔	✔
Dominica	$									
Dominican Republic	$	✔	✔			✔		✔	✔	✔
Grenada	$$		✔					✔	✔	✔
Guadeloupe	$$	✔	✔	✔	✔	✔			✔	
Jamaica	$$	✔	✔	✔	✔		✔	✔	✔	✔
Martinique	$$$	✔	✔	✔	✔	✔			✔	✔
Nevis	$$$		✔	✔						✔
Puerto Rico	$		✔	✔	✔	✔	✔	✔	✔	✔
Saba	$									
St. Croix	$$		✔	✔			✔	✔	✔	✔
St. Eustatius	$		✔							
St. John	$$$		✔	✔	✔		✔	✔		✔
St. Kitts	$$	✔	✔			✔		✔		✔
St. Lucia	$$	✔	✔					✔	✔	✔
St. Martin/St. Maarten	$$$	✔	✔	✔		✔	✔	✔	✔	✔
St. Thomas	$$	✔	✔	✔			✔	✔	✔	✔
St. Vincent	$		✔							
Tobago	$$		✔							✔
Tortola	$$		✔		✔		✔	✔	✔	✔
Trinidad	$		✔							
Virgin Gorda	$$$	✔	✔	✔	✔			✔		✔

Golf	Hiking	Historic Sites	Mountainous Terrain	Music/Entertainment Nightlife	Nonstop Flights from U.S.	Public Transport	Rain Forest	Romantic Getaways	Sailing	Scenic Beauty	Scuba Diving/ Snorkeling	Secret Hideaways	Shopping	Verdant & Lush Terrain	Very Dry Climate
✔	✔	✔			✔			✔	✔	✔	✔	✔			
✔	✔	✔	✔					✔		✔		✔			
✔	✔	✔		✔	✔	✔			✔	✔		✔			
	✔			✔						✔				✔	
✔	✔	✔	✔			✔		✔		✔					
	✔	✔	✔	✔	✔					✔		✔		✔	
	✔	✔	✔			✔	✔			✔		✔		✔	
✔	✔	✔	✔	✔	✔	✔				✔		✔	✔	✔	
✔	✔	✔	✔		✔	✔	✔	✔	✔	✔	✔	✔		✔	
✔	✔	✔	✔		✔	✔		✔	✔	✔			✔		
✔	✔	✔	✔	✔	✔	✔	✔	✔		✔	✔	✔	✔	✔	
✔	✔	✔	✔	✔		✔	✔			✔	✔			✔	
✔	✔	✔	✔					✔		✔		✔		✔	
✔	✔	✔	✔	✔	✔	✔	✔	✔	✔	✔	✔	✔	✔	✔	
	✔		✔							✔	✔	✔		✔	
✔	✔	✔		✔		✔	✔		✔	✔	✔		✔	✔	
	✔														
	✔	✔	✔					✔	✔	✔	✔	✔		✔	
✔	✔	✔						✔		✔		✔			
✔	✔		✔		✔		✔	✔		✔		✔		✔	
✔	✔	✔	✔			✔				✔		✔			
✔	✔	✔	✔	✔	✔			✔				✔			
	✔		✔						✔					✔	
✔	✔			✔	✔		✔								
	✔		✔			✔			✔	✔	✔	✔		✔	
	✔			✔	✔	✔	✔			✔				✔	
	✔		✔			✔		✔	✔	✔	✔	✔		✔	

Web Sites for Divers

For useful information on scuba diving in the Caribbean, check out the Web site of the Professional Association of Diving Instructors (PADI) at **www.padi.com**. This site provides descriptions of dive destinations throughout the Caribbean and a directory of PADI-certified dive operators. *Rodale's Scuba Diving Magazine* also has a helpful Web site at **www.scubadiving.com**. Both sites list dive package specials and display gorgeous color photos of some of the most beautiful dive spots in the world.

---

from it all. Hotel choices are limited, often designed in the traditional Saban style of stone foundations terraced into sloping hillsides with white walls and red roofs. See chapter 18.

ST. EUSTATIUS   Known as "Statia," St. Eustatius is among the poorest islands in the Caribbean, with 8 square miles of arid landscape, beaches that have strong and sometimes dangerous undertows, a population of around 1,700 people, and a sleepy capital, Oranjestad. The island is very committed to maintaining its political and fiscal links to the Netherlands. See chapter 19.

ST. KITTS & NEVIS   These two islands form a single nation although they're separated by a 2-mile strait. St. Kitts (also known as St. Christopher, with 68 square miles) and Nevis (with 36 square miles) both enjoyed some of the richest sugarcane economies of the plantation age, and the boiling rooms and great houses have in many cases been transformed into quaint inns. Both islands possess a very appealing, small-scale charm. See chapter 16 (Nevis) and chapter 20 (St. Kitts).

ST. LUCIA   St. Lucia (*Loo*-sha) is the second-largest of the Windward Islands. A volcanic island with lots of rainfall and great natural beauty, it has both white and black sandy beaches, bubbling sulfur springs, and panoramic mountain scenery. Most tourism is concentrated on the island's northwestern tip, near the capital (Castries), but the arrival of up to 200,000 visitors a year has inevitably altered St. Lucia's old agrarian lifestyle throughout the island. Nevertheless, it remains a beautiful and welcoming place. See chapter 21.

ST. MAARTEN & ST. MARTIN   This "twin nation" of 37 square miles has been divided between the Dutch (St. Maarten) and the French (St. Martin) since 1648. Regardless of how you spell it, it's the same island, although each side of the unguarded border is quite different. The Dutch side contains the island's major airport, and more shops and tourist facilities. St. Martin, whose capital is Marigot, has some of the poshest hotels and the best food on the island. Both sides of the island are modern, urban, and proudly international. Each suffers from traffic jams, a lack of parking space in the capitals, tourist-industry burnout (especially on the Dutch side), and a disturbing increase in crime. See chapter 22.

ST. VINCENT & THE GRENADINES   Despite its natural beauty, this mini-archipelago has only recently emerged from obscurity. It has always been known to divers and yachties, who find its north-to-south string of cays and coral islets some of the most panoramic sailing regions in the world. St. Vincent is by far the largest and most fertile island in the country. Its capital is the sleepy, somewhat dilapidated town of Kingstown. Stretching like a pearl necklace to the south of St. Vincent are some 32 neighbor islands called the Grenadines. These include the boat-building community of Bequia and chic Mustique. Less densely populated islands in the chain include the tiny outposts of Mayreau, Canouan, Palm Island, and Petit St. Vincent, whose sun-blasted surfaces were for the most part covered with scrub until around the late 1960s, when hotel owners planted groves of palms and hardwood trees. See chapter 23.

TRINIDAD & TOBAGO   The southernmost of the West Indies, this two-island nation lies just 7 miles off the coast of Venezuela. Trinidad is the most industrial island in the Caribbean, with oil deposits and a polyglot population derived from India, Pakistan, Venezuela, Africa, and Europe. Known for its calypso music and carnivals, Trinidad is one of the most culturally distinct nations in the Caribbean. It has a rich artistic tradition, a bustling capital (Port-of-Spain), and exotic flora and fauna.

About 20 miles northeast of Trinidad, tiny Tobago is calmer and less heavily forested, with a rather dull capital (Scarborough) and a spectacular array of white-sand beaches. Whereas Trinidad seems to consider tourism as only one of many viable industries, Tobago is absolutely dependent on it. For details on both islands, see chapter 24.

THE U.S. VIRGIN ISLANDS   Formerly Dutch possessions, these islands became part of the United States in 1917. St. Croix is the largest and flattest of the U.S. Virgins, whereas St. Thomas and St. John are more mountainous. St. Thomas and, to a lesser degree, St. Croix, offer all the diversions, facilities, and amusements you'd find on the U.S. mainland, including bars, restaurants, and lots of modern resort hotels. St. Thomas is sometimes referred to as the shopping mall of the Caribbean, and crowds of cruise-ship visitors frequently pass through. Much of the surface of St. John is devoted to a national park, a gift from Laurence Rockefeller. All three islands offer sailing, snorkeling, and unspoiled vistas. Crime is on the increase, however—an unfortunate fly in the ointment of what would otherwise be a corner of paradise. See chapter 25.

2 Visitor Information

All the major islands have tourist representatives who will supply information before you go; we list each one in the "Visitor Information" sections of the individual island chapters. The **Caribbean Tourism Organization,** 80 Broad St., 32nd floor, New York, NY 10004 (☎ **212/635-9530**), can also provide general information.

INFO ON THE WEB

The Internet is a great source of travel information. **Yahoo** (www.yahoo.com), **Excite** (www.excite.com), **Lycos** (www.lycos.com), **Infoseek** (www.infoseek.com), and the other major Internet indexing sites all have subcategories for travel, country/regional information, and culture—click on all three for links to travel-related Web sites.

Other good clearinghouse sites for information are **Microsoft's Expedia** (www.expedia.msn.com), **Travelocity** (www.travelocity.com), the **Internet Travel Network** (www.itn.com), and **TravelWeb** (www.travelweb.com). Another good site is **www.city.net/regions/caribbean**, which will point you toward a wealth of Caribbean travel information on the Web.

Of the many, many online travel magazines, two of the best are **Arthur Frommer's Budget Travel Online** (www.frommers.com), written and updated by the guru of budget travel himself, and **Condé Nast's Epicurious** (www.epicurious.com), based on articles from the company's glossy magazines *Traveler* and *Bon Appétit.*

That covers some of the best general Web sites. As often as possible throughout this chapter, we've included specific Web sites along with phone numbers and addresses. We've also given each hotel and resort's Web site if they have one, so you can see pictures of a property before you make your reservation.

TRAVEL AGENTS

A good travel agent can also provide information and save you plenty of time and money by hunting down the best airfare for your route and arranging for cruise and rental cars. For the time being, most travel agents still charge you nothing for their services—they're paid through commissions from the airlines and other agencies they book for you. However, a number of airlines have begun cutting commissions, and increasingly agents are finding they have to charge you a fee to hold the bottom line— or else unscrupulous agents will only offer you travel options that bag them the juiciest commissions. Shop around and ask hard questions; use this book to become an informed consumer. If you decide to use a travel agent, make sure the agent is a member of the **American Society of Travel Agents (ASTA),** 1101 King St., Alexandria, VA 22314 (☎ **703/739-8739;** www.astanet.com). If you send them a self-addressed stamped envelope, ASTA will mail you its free booklet, *Avoiding Travel Problems.*

3 Entry Requirements & Customs

ENTRY REQUIREMENTS

Even though the Caribbean islands are, for the most part, independent nations and thereby classified as international destinations, passports are not generally required, unless you're coming from Europe. You'll certainly need identification, and a passport is the best form for speeding you through Customs and Immigration, so we recommend carrying one anyway. Other acceptable documents include an ongoing or return ticket, plus a birth certificate (the original or a copy that has been certified by your local registrar of deeds and birth certificates). You will also need some photo ID, such as a driver's license or an expired passport; however, driver's licenses are not acceptable as a sole form of ID.

Visas are usually not required, but some countries may require you to fill out a tourist card (see the individual island chapters for details).

Before leaving home, make two copies of your documents, including your passport and your driver's license, your airline ticket, and any hotel vouchers. If you're on medication, you should also make copies of prescriptions.

CUSTOMS

Each island has specific requirements that will be detailed in the destination chapters that follow. Generally, you're permitted to bring in items intended for your personal use, including tobacco, cameras, film, and a limited supply of liquor—usually 40 ounces. Here's what you can bring home from the islands:

U.S. CUSTOMS The U.S. government generously allows $1,200 worth of duty-free imports every 30 days from the U.S. Virgin Islands; those who go over their exemption are taxed at 5% rather than the usual 10%. The limit is $400 for such international destinations as the French islands of Guadeloupe and Martinique, and $600 for many other islands. If you visit only Puerto Rico, you don't have to go through Customs at all, since the island is a U.S. commonwealth.

Joint Customs declarations are possible for members of a family traveling together. For instance, if you are a husband and wife with two children, your purchases in the U.S. Virgin Islands become duty free up to $4,800! Unsolicited gifts can be sent to friends and relatives at the rate of $100 per day from the U.S. Virgin Islands (or $50 a day from the other islands). U.S. citizens, or returning residents at least 21 years of age, traveling directly or indirectly from the U.S. Virgin Islands, are allowed to bring

What Things Cost in the Caribbean

	Local Phone Call	Average Budget Double Room	Average Budget Lunch	Average Budget Dinner	Coffee	Film
Antigua	10¢	$90	$12	$20	$1	$10
Aruba	25¢	$100	$15	$25	$1	$9
Barbados	25¢	$100	$15	$25	$1.50	$10
Bonaire	9¢	$90	$12	$20	$1	$7
British Virgins	25¢	$75	$10	$18	80¢	$8.50
Cayman Islands	62¢	$110	$15	$25	$1.50	$7.00
Curaçao	25¢	$105	$20	$28	$1.35	$13.50
Dominica	10¢	$75	$8	$15	$1.10	$10
Dominican Republic	10¢	$75	$8	$15	60¢	$7.50
Grenada	10¢	$110	$12	$20	75¢	$13.50
Guadeloupe	60¢	$110	$20	$30	$1.90	$10
Jamaica	11¢	$105	$12	$20	80¢	$10
Martinique	60¢	$110	$20	$30	$1.90	$10
Nevis/St. Kitts	7¢	$95	$12	$18	$1.25	$7
Puerto Rico	25¢	$75	$10	$15	$1.50	$5.50
Saba	15¢	$75	$10	$15	$1	$7
St. Eustacius	25¢	$75	$10	$15	$1	$6.50
St. Lucia	15¢	$125	$12	$18	$1	$7
St. Maarten	30¢	$130	$15	$25	$1.10	$6.50
St. Martin	60¢	$110	$15	$25	$2	$6.50
St. Vincent	15¢	$65	$10	$18	75¢	$8.75
Trinidad/Tobago	23¢	$70	$8	$15	50¢–$1	$7.25
U.S. Virgins	25¢	$85	$12	$18	75¢	$7–$9

in free of duty 1,000 cigarettes, 5 liters of alcohol, and 100 cigars (but not Cuban cigars). Duty-free limitations on articles from other countries are generally 1 liter of alcohol, 200 cigarettes, and 200 cigars.

Collect receipts for all purchases made abroad. You must also declare on your Customs form the nature and value of all gifts received during your stay abroad. It's prudent to carry proof that you purchased expensive cameras or jewelry on the U.S. mainland. If you purchased such an item during an earlier trip abroad, you should carry proof that you have previously paid Customs duty on the item.

Sometimes merchants suggest a false receipt to undervalue your purchase. *Warning:* You could be involved in a sting operation—the merchant might be an informer to U.S. Customs.

If you use any medication that contains controlled substances or requires injection, carry an original prescription or note from your doctor.

For more specifics, write to the **U.S. Customs Service,** 1301 Constitution Ave., P.O. Box 7407, Washington, DC 20044 (☎ **202/927-6724**), and request the free pamphlet *Know Before You Go.*

U.K. CUSTOMS   U.K. citizens returning from a non-EU country such as one of the Caribbean nations have a customs allowance of 200 cigarettes; 50 cigars; 250g of smoking tobacco; 2 liters of still table wine; 1 liter of spirits or strong liqueurs (over 22% volume); 2 liters of fortified wine, sparkling wine, or other liqueurs; 60cc (ml) perfume; 250cc (ml) of toilet water; and £145 worth of all other goods, including gifts and souvenirs. People under age 17 cannot have the tobacco or alcohol allowance. For more information, contact **HM Customs & Excise,** Passenger Enquiry Point, 2nd Floor Wayfarer House, Great South West Road, Feltham, Middlesex, TW14 8NP (☎ **020/8910-3744** or 44/181-910-3744 from outside the U.K.; www.open.gov.uk).

CANADIAN CUSTOMS   For a clear summary of Canadian rules, write for the booklet *I Declare,* issued by **Revenue Canada,** 2265 St. Laurent Blvd., Ottawa K1G 4KE (☎ **613/993-0534**). Canada allows its citizens a $500 exemption, and you're allowed to bring back duty free 200 cigarettes, 2.2 pounds of tobacco, 40 imperial ounces of liquor, and 50 cigars. In addition, you're allowed to mail gifts to Canada from abroad at the rate of Can$60 a day, provided they're unsolicited and don't contain alcohol or tobacco (write on the package "Unsolicited gift, under $60 value"). All valuables should be declared on the Y-38 form before departure from Canada, including serial numbers of valuables you already own, such as expensive foreign cameras. *Note:* The $500 exemption can be used only once a year and only after an absence of 7 days.

4 Money

CASH/CURRENCY

Widely accepted on many of the islands, the **U.S. dollar** is the legal currency of the U.S. Virgin Islands, the British Virgin Islands, and Puerto Rico. Many islands use the **Eastern Caribbean dollar,** even though your hotel bill will most likely be presented in U.S. dollars. French islands use the **French franc,** although many hotels often quote their prices in U.S. dollars. For details, see "Fast Facts" in the individual island chapters.

TRAVELER'S CHECKS

Traveler's checks are something of an anachronism from the days before the ATM made cash accessible at any time. These days, traveler's checks seem less necessary, as most islands have 24-hour ATMs that allow you to withdraw small amounts of cash as needed. However, if you want to avoid ATM service charges, or if you just want the security of knowing you can get a refund in the event that your wallet is stolen, you may want to purchase traveler's checks, which you can do at almost any bank. American Express offers denominations of $10, $20, $50, $100, $500, and $1,000. You'll pay a service charge ranging from 1% to 4%. You can also get **American Express** traveler's checks over the phone by calling ☎ **800/221-7282;** by using this number, Amex gold and platinum cardholders are exempt from the 1% fee. AAA members can obtain checks without a fee at most AAA offices.

Visa offers traveler's checks at **Citibank** locations nationwide and several other participating banks. The service charge ranges from 1½% to 2%; checks come in denominations of $20, $50, $100, $500, and $1,000. **MasterCard** also offers traveler's checks. Call ☎ **800/223-9920** for a location near you.

The U.S. Dollar & the British Pound

The British pound trades at an average of around 61p = $1 U.S. Stated another way, $1.65 U.S. = £1. The chart below gives a rough approximation of conversion rates you're likely to find at the time of your trip, but confirm before you make transactions.

U.S. $	U.K. £	U.S. $	U.K. £
0.25	0.15	15	9.15
0.50	0.31	20	12.20
0.75	0.46	25	15.25
1.00	0.61	50	30.50
2.00	1.22	75	45.75
3.00	1.83	100	61.00
4.00	2.44	150	91.50
5.00	3.05	200	122.00
6.00	3.66	250	152.50
7.00	4.27	300	183.00
8.00	4.88	350	213.50
9.00	5.49	400	244.00
10.00	6.10	500	305.00

If you opt to carry traveler's checks, be sure to keep a record of their serial numbers separate from the checks, so you're ensured a refund in case of loss or theft.

ATMs

ATMs are linked to an international network that most likely includes your bank at home. **Cirrus** (☎ 800/424-7787; www.mastercard.com/atm) and **Plus** (☎ 800/843-7587; www.visa.com/atms) are the two most popular networks; check the back of your ATM card to see which network your bank belongs to. Use the toll-free numbers to locate ATMs in your destination.

If you're traveling abroad, ask your bank for a list of overseas ATMs. Be sure to check the daily withdrawal limit before you depart, and ask whether you need a new PIN to make transactions from abroad.

CREDIT CARDS

Credit cards are invaluable when traveling. They're a safe way to carry money and provide a convenient record of all your expenses. You can also withdraw cash advances from your credit cards at any bank (though you'll start paying hefty interest on the advance the moment you receive the cash, and you won't receive frequent-flyer miles on an airline credit card). At most banks, you don't even need to go to a teller; you can get a cash advance at the ATM if you know your PIN.

Almost every credit-card company has an emergency toll-free number that you can call if your wallet or purse is stolen. They may be able to wire you a cash advance off your credit card immediately, and in many places, they can deliver an emergency credit card in a day or two. The issuing bank's toll-free number is usually on the back of the credit card—though of course that doesn't help you much if the card was stolen.

In that case, call the toll-free information directory at ☎ **800/555-1212. Citicorp Visa's** U.S. emergency number is ☎ **800/336-8472. American Express** cardholders and traveler's check holders should call ☎ **800/221-7282** for all money emergencies. **MasterCard** holders should call ☎ **800/307-7309.**

5 When to Go

WEATHER

The temperature variations in the Caribbean are surprisingly slight, averaging between 75° and 85° Fahrenheit (24°C to 29°C) in both winter and summer, although it can get really chilly, especially in the early morning and at night. The Caribbean winter is usually like a perpetual May. Overall, daytime high temperatures in the mid-80s prevail throughout most of the region, and trade winds make for comfortable days and nights, even without air-conditioning. If you go in summer to get the best bargains, you've got to be prepared for fierce sun.

The humidity and insects can be a problem here year-round. However, more mosquitoes come out during the rainy season, which traditionally occurs from September to December.

The curse of Caribbean weather, the **hurricane season** lasts—officially, at least—from June 1 to November 30. But there's no cause for panic. Satellite forecasts give adequate warnings so that precautions can be taken.

To get a weather report before you go, call the nearest branch of the National Weather Service, listed in your phone directory under the "U.S. Department of Commerce." You can also call **Weather Trak;** for the telephone number for your particular area, call ☎ **900/370-8725** (a taped message gives you the three-digit access code for the place you're interested in; the call costs 95¢ per inquiry). Or you can log onto the Web site of the **Weather Channel** at www.weather.com.

THE "SEASON" & THE "OFF-SEASON"

The Caribbean has become a year-round destination. The "season" runs roughly from mid-December to mid-April. Hotels charge their highest prices during this peak winter period, which is generally the driest time of year. It can be rainy in mountainous areas, however, and you can expect showers especially in December and January on Martinique, Guadeloupe, Dominica, St. Lucia, on the north coast of the Dominican Republic, and in northeast Jamaica.

For a winter vacation, make reservations 2 to 3 months in advance—or earlier for trips at Christmas and in February.

The "off-season" in the Caribbean runs roughly from mid-April to mid-December—it varies from hotel to hotel—and amounts to a summer sale. In most cases, hotels, inns, and condos slash rates to 20% to 60% off their winter tariffs.

Dollar for dollar, you'll spend less money by renting a summer house or self-sufficient unit in the Caribbean than you would on Cape Cod, Fire Island, Laguna Beach, or the coast of Maine. Sailing and water sports are better too, because the West Indies are protected from the Atlantic on their western shores, which border the calm Caribbean Sea. However, you have to be able to take strong sun and heat.

Because there's such a drastic difference in high-season and low-season rates at most hotels, we've included both on every property we review. You'll see the incredible savings you can enjoy if your schedule is flexible enough to wait a couple of months for your fun in the sun!

6 Health & Insurance

STAYING HEALTHY

Vaccinations are not required to enter the Caribbean if you're coming from the United States, Great Britain, or Canada.

If you're staying in a regular Caribbean hotel, few preventive measures are generally needed. Take along an adequate supply of any prescription drugs that you need and a written prescription that uses the generic name of the drug, not the brand name. You may want to pack first-aid cream, insect repellent, aspirin, Band-Aids, and other basic remedies for minor injuries or illnesses.

The Caribbean sun can be brutal. Limit your exposure, especially during the first few days of your trip. Use a sunscreen with a high protection factor and apply it liberally. Wear sunglasses and a hat. And remember that children need more protection than adults do.

Finding a doctor in the Caribbean is not a problem, except perhaps on the smallest islands. Most Caribbean doctors speak English, virtually 100 percent of them. See the "Fast Facts" section in each chapter for specific names or listings of medical help or assistance.

One of the biggest menaces are the "no-see-ums," which appear mainly in the early evening. You can't see these tiny flies, but you sure can "feel-um." Screens can't keep these critters out, so carry your favorite bug repellent.

Mosquitoes are a nuisance, too, but malaria-carrying mosquitoes are confined largely to Haiti and the Dominican Republic. If you're visiting either, consult your doctor for preventive medicine at least 8 weeks before you leave home.

Dengue fever is prevalent in the islands, most prominently on Antigua, St. Kitts, Dominica, and the Dominican Republic. Once thought to have been nearly eliminated, it has made a comeback. To date, no satisfactory treatment has been developed; visitors are advised to avoid mosquito bites—as if that were possible.

Infectious hepatitis has been reported on such islands as Dominica and Haiti. Unless you have been immunized for both hepatitis A and B, consult your doctor about the advisability of getting a gamma-globulin shot before you leave.

SOME PRECAUTIONS   If you suffer from a chronic illness, consult your doctor before your departure. For conditions like epilepsy, diabetes, or heart problems, wear a **Medic Alert Identification Tag** (☎ **800/825-3785;** www.commedicalert.org), which will immediately alert doctors to your condition and give them access to your records through Medic Alert's 24-hour hotline. Membership is $35, plus a $15 annual fee.

Pack prescription medications in your carry-on luggage. Carry written prescriptions in generic, not brand-name form, and dispense all prescription medications from their original labeled vials. Also, bring along copies of your prescriptions in case you lose your pills or run out.

INSURANCE

There are three kinds of travel insurance: trip-cancellation, medical, and lost-luggage coverage.

Trip-cancellation insurance is a good idea if you have paid a large portion of your vacation expenses up front, say, by purchasing a package or a cruise. Trip-cancellation insurance should cost approximately 6% to 8% of the total value of your vacation.

(Don't buy it from the same company from which you've purchased your vacation—talk about putting all your eggs in one basket!)

The other two types of insurance, however, don't make sense for most travelers. Rule number one: Check your existing policies before you buy any additional coverage.

Your existing health insurance should cover you if you get sick on vacation (though if you belong to an HMO, you should check to see whether you are fully covered while you're away from home). If you need hospital treatment, most health insurance plans and HMOs will cover out-of-country hospital visits and procedures, at least to some extent. Most make you pay the bills up front at the time of care, however, and you'll get a refund only after you've returned and filed all the paperwork. Members of **Blue Cross/Blue Shield** can now use their cards at select hospitals in most major cities worldwide (☎ **800/810-BLUE** or www.bluecares.com/blue/bluecard/wwn for a list of hospitals).

Note that **Medicare** covers U.S. citizens traveling only in Mexico and Canada.

Your homeowner's insurance should cover stolen luggage. The airlines are responsible for providing you with $1,250 if they lose your luggage on domestic flights; if you plan to carry anything more valuable than that, keep it in your carry-on bag.

If you do require additional insurance, try one of the following companies: **Access America,** 6600 W. Broad St., Richmond, VA 23230 (☎ 800/284-8300); **Travel Guard International,** 1145 Clark St., Stevens Point, WI 54481 (☎ 800/826-1300); **Travel Insured International, Inc.,** P.O. Box 280568, East Hartford, CT 06128 (☎ 800/243-3174); **Columbus Travel Insurance,** 279 High St., Croydon CR0 1QH (☎ 020/7375-0011 in London; www2.columbusdirect.com/columbusdirect). For medical coverage, try **MEDEX International,** P.O. Box 5375, Timonium, MD 21094-5375 (☎ 888/MEDEX-00 or 410/453-6300; fax 410/453-6301; www.medexassist.com); or **Travel Assistance International** (Worldwide Assistance Services, Inc.), 1133 15th St. NW, Suite 400, Washington, DC 20005 (☎ 800/821-2828 or 202/828-5894; fax 202/828-5896). The **Divers Alert Network** (DAN) (☎ 800/446-2671 or 919/684-2948) insures scuba divers.

7 Tips for Travelers With Special Needs

FOR TRAVELERS WITH DISABILITIES

At times getting around the Caribbean seems only for Olympic athletes, as you traverse rough, steep roads, ascend hills to reach accommodations, wade through sand to the door of your beachfront cottage, get on and off boats in turbulent waters, board small planes with cramped seating, and walk potholed streets even in the larger cities. Wheelchair ramps, TTY phone systems, and the like are in short supply. However, persons with disabilities are visiting the islands in greater numbers every year, and the travel industry, especially the airlines, are beginning to pay attention to their needs. However, such a trip involves careful planning, plus a detailed talk with the hotel of your choice about whether it has facilities equipped for disabled guests.

There are more resources out there than ever before. *A World of Options,* a 658-page book of resources for disabled travelers, covers everything from biking trips to scuba outfitters. It is available from **Mobility International USA,** P.O. Box 10767, Eugene, OR 97440 (☎ **541/343-1284,** voice and TDD; www.miusa.org). Annual membership for Mobility International is $35, which includes their quarterly newsletter, *Over the Rainbow.* In addition, **Twin Peaks Press,** P.O. Box 129, Vancouver, WA 98666 (☎ **360/694-2462**), publishes travel-related books for people with disabilities.

The **Moss Rehab Hospital** (☎ 215/456-9600) has been providing friendly and helpful phone advice and referrals to disabled travelers for years through its **Travel Information Service** (☎ 215/456-9603; www.mossresourcenet.org).

You can join the **Society for the Advancement of Travel for the Handicapped (SATH),** 347 Fifth Ave. Suite 610, New York, NY 10016 (☎ 212/447-7284; fax 212-725-8253; www.sath.org) for $45 annually, $30 for seniors and students, to gain access to their vast network of connections in the travel industry. They provide information sheets on travel destinations, and referrals to tour operators that specialize in traveling with disabilities. Their quarterly magazine, *Open World for Disability and Mature Travel,* is full of good information and resources. A year's subscription is $13.00 ($21 outside the U.S.).

Travelers with disabilities may also want to consider joining a tour that caters specifically to them. One of the best operators is **Flying Wheels Travel,** 143 West Bridge (P.O. Box 382), Owatonna, MN 55060 (☎ 800/535-6790). They offer various escorted tours and cruises, with an emphasis on sports, as well as private tours in mini-vans with lifts. Other reputable specialized tour operators include **Access Adventures** (☎ 716/889-9096), which offers sports-related vacations; **Accessible Journeys** (☎ 800/TINGLES or 610/521-0339), for slow walkers and wheelchair travelers; **The Guided Tour, Inc.** (☎ 215/782-1370); **Wilderness Inquiry** (☎ 800/728-0719 or 612/379-3858); and **Directions Unlimited** (☎ 800/533-5343).

Vision-impaired travelers should contact the **American Foundation for the Blind,** 11 Penn Plaza, Suite 300, New York, NY 10001 (☎ 800/232-5463), for information on traveling with seeing-eye dogs.

FOR GAY & LESBIAN TRAVELERS

Some of the islands are more gay friendly than others. Among the friendly are all the U.S. possessions, notably Puerto Rico, the "gay capital of the Caribbean," which offers gay guest houses, nightclubs, bars, and discos. To a lesser extent, much of St. Thomas, St. John, and St. Croix are welcoming, though they have nowhere near the number of gay-oriented establishments as Puerto Rico.

The French islands—St. Barts, St. Martin, Guadeloupe, and Martinique—are technically an extension of mainland France, and the French have always regarded homosexuality with a certain blasé tolerance. On the other hand, the Dutch islands of Aruba, Bonaire, and Curaçao are quite conservative, so discretion is suggested.

Gay life is fairly secretive in many of the sleepy islands of the Caribbean. It's actively discouraged in places like the Cayman Islands. Homosexuality is illegal in Barbados, and there is often a lack of tolerance there in spite of the large number of gay residents and visitors. Jamaica is the most homophobic island in the Caribbean, with harsh antigay laws, even though there is a large local gay population. One local advised that it's not smart for a white gay man to wander the streets of Jamaica at night. Gay travelers might also note that the Cayman Islands recently refused to allow an all-gay cruise ship to dock on Grand Cayman, and several gay advocacy groups have even called for a boycott on travel to the Caymans in response.

The **International Gay & Lesbian Travel Association (IGLTA),** (☎ 800/448-8550 or 954/776-2626; fax 954/776-3303; www.iglta.org), links travelers with the appropriate gay-friendly service organization or tour specialist. With around 1,200 members, it offers quarterly newsletters, marketing mailings, and a membership directory that's updated quarterly. Membership often includes gay or lesbian businesses but is open to individuals for $150 yearly, plus a $100 administration fee for new members. Members are kept informed of gay and gay-friendly hoteliers, tour operators, and airline and cruise-line representatives. Contact the IGLTA for a list of its member agencies, who will be tied into IGLTA's information resources.

General gay and lesbian travel agencies include **Family Abroad** (☎ **800/999-5500** or 212/459-1800; gay and lesbian); **Above and Beyond Tours** (☎ **800/397-2681;** mainly gay men); and **Yellowbrick Road** (☎ **800/642-2488;** gay and lesbian).

There are also two good, biannual English-language gay guidebooks, both focused on gay men but including information for lesbians as well. You can get the *Spartacus International Gay Guide* or *Odysseus* from most gay and lesbian book stores, or order them from **Giovanni's Room** (☎ **215/923-2960**), or **A Different Light Bookstore** (☎ **800/343-4002** or ☎ 212/989-4850). Both lesbians and gays might want to pick up a copy of *Gay Travel A to Z* ($16). *The Ferrari Guides* (www.q-net.com) is yet another very good series of gay and lesbian guidebooks.

Out and About, 8 W. 19th St. #401, New York, NY 10011 (☎ **800/929-2268** or 212/645-6922), offers guidebooks and a monthly newsletter packed with good information on the global gay and lesbian scene. A year's subscription to the newsletter costs $49. *Our World,* 1104 North Nova Rd., Suite 251, Daytona Beach, FL 32117 (☎ **904/441-5367**), is a slicker monthly magazine promoting and highlighting travel bargains and opportunities. Annual subscription rates are $35 in the US, $45 outside the US.

FOR SENIORS

In general, seniors are treated like all other visitors to the Caribbean, in that there are no special facilities or discounts for them at theaters, museums, and other attractions. It might be possible, however, to negotiate a lower rate off-season at a Caribbean hotel (usually a major hotel as opposed to a small inn). In the high season, everybody is charged virtually the same price unless you book on a package tour deal.

In planning your trip, keep in mind that members of the **American Association of Retired Persons (AARP),** 601 E St. NW, Washington, DC 20049 (☎ **800/424-3410** or 202/434-2277), get discounts on airfares and car rentals. AARP offers members a wide range of special benefits, including *Modern Maturity* magazine and a monthly newsletter.

The National Council of Senior Citizens, 8403 Colesville Rd., Suite 1200, Silver Spring, MD 20910 (☎ **301/578-8800**), a nonprofit organization, offers a newsletter six times a year (partly devoted to travel tips) and discounts on hotel and auto rentals; annual dues are $13 per person or couple.

Mature Outlook, P.O. Box 9390, Des Moines, IA 50306 (☎ **800/336-6330**), began as a travel organization for people over 50, though it now caters to people of all ages. Members receive discounts on hotels and receive a bimonthly magazine. Annual membership is $19.95, which entitles members to discounts and, often, free coupons for discounted merchandise from Sears.

Golden Companions, P.O. Box 5249, Reno, NV 89513 (☎ **702/324-2227**), helps travelers age 45-plus find compatible companions through a personal voice-mail service. Contact them for more information.

The Mature Traveler, a monthly 12-page newsletter on senior citizen travel is a valuable resource. It is available by subscription ($30 a year) from GEM Publishing Group, Box 50400, Reno, NV 89513-0400. GEM also publishes *The Book of Deals,* a collection of more than 1,000 senior discounts on airlines, lodging, tours, and attractions around the country; it's available for $9.95 by calling ☎ **800/460-6676.** Another helpful publication is *101 Tips for the Mature Traveler,* available from **Grand Circle Travel,** 347 Congress St., Suite 3A, Boston, MA 02210 (☎ **800/221-2610** or 617/350-7500; fax 617/346-6700).

Grand Circle Travel is also one of the hundreds of travel agencies specializing in vacations for seniors. Many of these packages, however, are of the tour-bus variety, with free trips thrown in for those who organize groups of 10 or more. Seniors seeking more independent travel should probably consult a regular travel agent. **SAGA International Holidays,** 222 Berkeley St., Boston, MA 02116 (☎ **800/343-0273**), offers inclusive tours and cruises for those 50 and older. SAGA also sponsors the more substantial "Road Scholar Tours" (☎ **800/621-2151**), which are fun-loving but with an educational bent.

8 40 Money-Saving Tips

AIRFARES

1. Always start out by shopping around for air/land packages. Particularly in the Caribbean, a week's stay at even a top-of-the-line resort is often much cheaper if it's arranged as part of a package booked with your airfare. The savings might make a stay at an expensive hotel completely affordable.

2. Try booking through a consolidator, or "bucket shop." See "Finding the Best Airfare," later in this chapter, for recommendations of reputable companies to try.

3. Make sure you're flying into the right airport. On some islands, such as St. Lucia, you can rack up substantial transfer costs by flying into the wrong airport. Whenever an island has more than one international airport, be sure to figure out its position in relation to your hotel and plan your incoming flight accordingly. Taxi costs across the length of a mountainous island can total more than $60.

4. Fly off-season. Airfares plummet from April to late June and from mid-September until about 10 days before Christmas.

5. Shop for the best deal on the Web. See "Finding the Best Airfare," later in this chapter, for tips on how to do this.

ACCOMMODATIONS

6. Find out what "extras" are included in the hotel price. A moderately priced hotel that tacks on charges for everything from beach chairs to snorkel equipment may wind up costing you more than a luxury hotel that includes these extras in its price. And be sure to ask what taxes and surcharges might be tacked on to your final bill.

7. If you're traveling off-season, don't always assume that a large hotel will cost more than an inn with a limited number of amenities. Especially during off-season promotions, a megaresort might be more generous with discounts, add-ons, and packages.

8. An oceanfront room will cost more than a room without a view, so you can save if you can live without seeing the blue waters from your window.

9. If you're traveling with kids, consider housing up to two of your children in your room with you on foldaway beds. Many places offer free accommodations to anyone under 12, under 16, or (in some cases) under 18. We've noted these policies on every hotel we review.

10. Especially if you're traveling in a group of four or more, rent an apartment or villa that has kitchen facilities so you can cook for yourself.

11. If you decide to go in winter, many hotels slash their rates during the "window" that comes during the slow month of January, following right after New Year's when post-holiday business is slow. Sometimes these discounts even match off-season rates!

12. If a hotel is not on the beach, find out if there's a charge to get there. The hotel rates may be lower, but will you wind up spending a lot of time and money to get to the sands every day?

13. In small B&Bs and guest houses, rooms without private bath, although they often have a sink with hot and cold running water, will sometimes save you an average of 40% off the regular rate.

14. Ask if a hotel charges extra for paying with a credit or charge card. Although this is against the bylaws of such lenders as American Express, hoteliers often do it anyway. If you're penalized for plastic, consider bringing enough cash (or, better yet, traveler's checks).

15. If you're an avid golfer, tennis player, or scuba diver, shop around for the best packages without all the frilly stuff.

16. Consider camping. It's not always available on all islands, but on those where it is (St. John's, for example), it may be the way to go.

17. Check the surcharge for either local or long-distance calls, which can be an astonishing 40%. Make your calls outside at a pay phone or the post office.

18. Determine if breakfast is included in the rates, as an extra daily charge can make a big difference in your final bill.

19. If you're going to spend at least a week at a resort, ask about a discount. If they're not full, some hotels might give you the seventh night free.

20. Book the MAP (Modified American Plan), including breakfast and dinner, if it looks good. It'll save a lot over the a la carte menu.

DINING

21. Scan advertisements in local tourist guides and newspapers publicizing specialty buffets and special discounts on meals.

22. Opt for local foods, like fresh fish, chicken, fruit, and vegetables. Most other food is imported at a high cost, and arrives frozen to boot.

23. Stick to rum-based drinks—the island favorite—and watch out for those high price tags on imported booze such as scotch.

24. In most cases, the fixed-price menu or daily specials might be a third cheaper than ordering a la carte.

OUTDOOR ACTIVITIES

25. Enjoy free or cheap activities like hiking through a nature preserve or snorkeling. And, of course, the beach provides you with free amusement all day long!

NIGHTLIFE

26. Scan the local press for reggae concerts, community groups sponsoring "bashes" (all reasonable in price), charity bazaars, whatever. There's always something going on in the Caribbean, and you can learn about island life, too.

27. Hit a bar at happy hour, usually from 5 to 6:30 or even 7pm, when drinks are traditionally discounted 20% to 50%, and hors d'oeuvres are often discounted as well.

SHOPPING

28. Before you leave home, stop by your local discount shops to check the latest prices. Only then can you comparison shop to determine whether you're getting a bargain in a Caribbean discount outlet.

29. Don't be afraid to haggle over a price. Savvy shoppers pride themselves in almost never paying retail for anything. If you think the price is too high, make a lower offer. Sometimes you'll get yes for an answer.

30. If you're traveling as a family, submit a joint declaration to Customs—that is, combine the duty allowance of all members of your group into one bulk package. Even a child gets a duty-free allowance ranging from $400 to $1,200, depending on the island.

31. Buy handcrafted arts and crafts, which in most cases are duty free regardless of the amount you paid.

32. Remember that Puerto Rico has the same tariff barriers as the U.S. mainland. You can take home as many bargains as you find here without paying duty.

33. U.S. Customs allows you to take back home duty free $600 worth of merchandise (per family member) from such islands as Jamaica and Barbados, but only $400 from such islands as St. Barts and Martinique (because these islands are technically part of France).

34. The best deal of all is the U.S. Virgin Islands (St. Thomas, St. Croix, and St. John) where you can bring back $1,200 in duty-free purchases. If you go over the limit, you're charged at a flat rate of 5% up to $1,000 rather than the usual 10% imposed on goods from other countries.

35. Save your big purchases for so-called "duty free" islands as opposed to those that have a heavy sales tax.

TRANSPORTATION

36. Think about whether you can skip a rental car altogether. You might not be as mobile, but your hotel might offer minivan transport that will get you to shops, a local beach, and snorkeling facilities. It's worth asking when you make your reservation.

37. Renting a local taxi for a day's outing might work out to be less expensive than an entire week's rental of a car. See all the sights over a 1- or 2-day period, and plan to relax close to your hotel on other days.

38. If you do rent a car, weekly rentals are more cost-efficient (on a day-to-day basis) than a single day's rental.

39. Rent bikes to get around. Although bicycles are definitely not recommended for nighttime use (Caribbean roads are notoriously dark at night), they can be an invigorating and efficient mode of transportation.

40. Stay at a hotel in one of the beach towns, such as Charlotte Amalie, Christiansted, Montego Bay, or Puerto Rico's Condado or Isla Verde. With dozens of restaurants, bars, and nightclubs nearby, you'll almost never need a car.

9 Package Deals

For popular destinations like the Caribbean, packages are really the smart way to go, because they can save you a ton of money. Especially in the Caribbean, package tours are *not* the same thing as escorted tours. You'll be on your own, but in most cases, a package to the Caribbean will include airfare, hotel, and transportation to and from the airport—and it'll cost you less than just the hotel alone if you booked it yourself. This is really the way to save hundreds and hundreds of dollars! It may not be for you if you want to stay in a more intimate inn or guest house, but if you like resorts, read on.

You'll find an amazing array of packages to popular Caribbean destinations. Some packages offer a better class of hotels than others. Some offer the same hotels for lower prices. Some offer flights on scheduled airlines, while others book charters. In some packages, your choices of accommodations and travel days may be limited. Remember to comparison shop among at least three different operators, and always compare apples to apples.

The best place to start your search is the travel section of your local Sunday newspaper. Also check the ads in the back of national travel magazines like *Travel & Leisure,* *National Geographic Traveler,* and *Condé Nast Traveler.* **Liberty Travel** (☎ **888/271-1584** to be connected with the agent closest to you; www.libertytravel.com), is one of the biggest packagers in the Northeast, and usually boasts a full-page ad in Sunday papers. You won't get much in the way of service, but you will get a good deal. **American Express Vacations** (☎ **800/241-1700;** www.leisureweb.com) is another option. Check out its **Last Minute Travel Bargains** site, offered in conjunction with Continental Airlines (www6.americanexpress.com/travel/lastminutetravel/default.asp), with deeply discounted vacation packages and reduced airline fares that differ from the E-savers bargains that Continental e-mails weekly to subscribers. **Northwest Airlines** offers a similar service. Posted on Northwest's Web site every Wednesday, its **Cyber Saver Bargain Alerts** offer special hotel rates, package deals, and discounted airline fares.

Another good resource is the airlines themselves, which often package their flights together with accommodations. Fly-by-night packagers are uncommon, but they do exist; when you buy your package through an airline, however, you can be pretty sure that the company will still be in business when your departure date arrives. Among the airline packagers, your options include **American Airlines FlyAway Vacations** (☎ **800/321-2121**), **Delta Dream Vacations** (☎ **800/872-7786**), and **US Airways Vacations** (☎ **800/455-0123**).

The biggest hotel chains, casinos, and resorts also offer package deals. If you already know where you want to stay, call the resort itself and ask if they offer land/air packages.

To save time comparing the prices and value of all the package tours out there, consider calling **TourScan, Inc.,** P.O. Box 2367, Darien, CT 06820 (☎ **800/962-2080** or 203/655-8091). Every season, the company computerizes the contents of travel brochures that contain about 10,000 different vacations at 1,600 hotels in the Caribbean, the Bahamas, and Bermuda. TourScan selects the best-value vacation at each hotel and condo. Two catalogs are printed each year, which list a choice of hotels on most of the Caribbean islands in all price ranges. Write to TourScan for their catalogs, the price of which ($4) is credited to any TourScan vacation.

Other tour operators include the following:

Caribbean Concepts Corp., 99 Jericho Turnpike, Jericho, NY 11793 (☎ **800/423-4433** or 516/867-0700), offers low-cost air-and-land packages to the islands, including apartments, hotels, villas, and condo rentals, plus local sightseeing (which can be arranged separately).

Horizon Tours, 1010 Vermont Ave. NW, Suite 202, Washington, DC 20005 (☎ **888/SUN-N-SAND** or 202/393-8390), specializes in good deals for all-inclusive resorts in the Bahamas, Jamaica, Aruba, Puerto Rico, Antigua, and St. Lucia.

Club Med, Club Med Sales, P.O. Box 4460, Scottsdale, AZ 85261-4460 (☎ **800/258-2633**), has various all-inclusive options throughout the Caribbean and the Bahamas.

Globus, 5301 S. Federal Circle, Littleton, CO 80123 (☎ **800/851-0728,** ext. 7518), gives escorted island-hopping expeditions to three or four islands, focusing on the history and culture of the West Indies.

10 Finding the Best Airfare

You shouldn't have to pay a regular fare to the Caribbean. Why? There are so many deals out there—in both summer and winter—that you can certainly find a discount fare. That's especially true if you're willing to plan on the spur of the moment: If a flight is not fully booked, an airline will discount tickets to try to fill it up.

Before you do anything else, read the section above on "Package Deals." But if you decide a package isn't for you (maybe because you'd rather stay in a small inn) and need to book your airfare on your own, read on, and we'll give you lots of money-saving tips.

If you fly in summer, spring, and fall, you're guaranteed substantial reductions on airfares to the Caribbean. You can also ask if it's cheaper to fly Monday through Thursday. And don't forget to consider air-and-land packages, which offer considerably reduced rates.

Most airlines charge different fares according to the season. Peak season, which is winter in the Caribbean, is most expensive; basic season, in the summer, offers the lowest fares. Shoulder season refers to the spring and fall months in between.

- **Keep an eye out for sales.** Check your newspaper for advertised discounts or call the airlines directly and ask if any promotional rates or special fares are available. You'll almost never see a sale during the peak winter vacation months of February and March, or during the Thanksgiving or Christmas seasons; but in periods of low-volume travel, you should find a discounted fare. If your schedule is flexible, ask if you can get a cheaper fare by staying an extra day or by flying midweek. (Many airlines won't volunteer this information.) If you already hold a ticket when a sale breaks, it may even pay to exchange your ticket, which usually incurs a $50 to $75 charge.

   Note, however, that the lowest-priced fares are often nonrefundable, require advance purchase of 1 to 3 weeks and a certain length of stay, and carry penalties for changing dates of travel.

- **Consolidators, also known as "bucket shops," are a good place to find low fares.** Consolidators buy seats in bulk from the airlines and then sell them back to the public at prices below even the airlines' discounted rates. Their small boxed ads usually run in the Sunday travel section of newspapers at the bottom of the page. Before you pay a consolidator, however, ask for a record locator number and confirm your seat with the airline itself. Be prepared to book your ticket with a different consolidator—there are many to choose from—if the airline can't confirm your reservation. Also, be aware that bucket-shop tickets are usually nonrefundable or rigged with stiff cancellation penalties, often as high as 50% to 75% of the ticket price.

   Council Travel (☎ 800/226-8624; www.counciltravel.com) and **STA Travel** (☎ 800/781-4040; www.sta.travel.com) cater especially to young travelers, but their bargain basement prices are available to people of all ages. **Travel Bargains** (☎ 800/AIR-FARE; www.1800airfare.com) was formerly owned by TWA but now offers the deepest discounts on many other airlines, with a 4-day advance purchase. Other reliable consolidators are **1-800-FLY-CHEAP** (www.1800flycheap.com); **TFI Tours International** (☎ 800-745-8000 or 212/736-1140), which serves as a clearinghouse for unused seats; or "rebators" such as **Travel Avenue** (☎ 800/333-3335 or ☎ 312/876-1116) and the **Smart Traveller** (☎ 800/448-3338 in the U.S., or 305/448-3338; www.smarttraveller@juno.com), which rebate part of their commissions to you.

- **Consider a charter flight.** Discounted fares have pared the number available, but they can still be found. Most charter operators advertise and sell their seats through travel agents, thus making these local professionals your best source of information for available flights. Before deciding to take a charter flight, however, check the restrictions on the ticket: You may be asked to purchase a tour package, to pay in advance, to be flexible if the day of departure is changed, to pay a service charge, to fly on an airline you're not familiar with (this usually is not the case), and to pay harsh penalties if you cancel—but be understanding if the charter doesn't fill up and is canceled up to 10 days before departure. Summer charters fill up more quickly than others and are almost sure to fly, but if you decide on a charter flight, seriously consider cancellation and baggage insurance.

- **Join a travel club.** Clubs such as **Moment's Notice** (☎ **718/234-6295**) or **Sears Discount Travel Club** (☎ **800/433-9383,** or 800/255-1487 to join), which supply unsold tickets at discounted prices. You pay an annual membership fee to get the club's hotline number. Of course, you're limited to what's available, so you have to be flexible.

- **Search for the best deal on the Web.** The Web sites highlighted below are worth checking out, especially since all services are free. Always check the lowest published fare, however, before you shop for flights on-line.

  Arthur Frommer's Budget Travel (**www.frommers.com**) offers detailed information on destinations around the world and up-to-the-minute ways to save dramatically on flights, hotels, car rentals, and cruises. Book an entire vacation on-line and research your destination before you leave. Consult the message board to set up "hospitality exchanges" in other countries, to talk with other travelers who have visited a hotel you're considering, or to direct travel questions to Arthur Frommer himself. The newsletter is updated daily to keep you abreast of the latest breaking ways to save, to publicize new hot spots and best buys, and to present veteran readers with fresh, ever-changing approaches to travel.

  Microsoft Expedia (**www.expedia.com**) offers a Fare Tracker that e-mails you weekly with the best airfare deals from your hometown on up to three destinations. The site's Travel Agent will steer you to bargains on hotels and car rentals, and with the help of hotel and airline seat pinpointers, you can book everything right on-line. Before you depart, log on for maps and up-to-date travel information, including weather reports and foreign exchange rates.

  Travelocity (**www.travelocity.com**) is one of the best travel sites out there, especially for finding cheap airfares. In addition to its Personal Fare Watcher, which notifies you via e-mail of the lowest airfares for up to five different destinations, Travelocity will track the three lowest fares for any routes on any dates in minutes. You can book a flight, then find the best hotel or car-rental deals via the SABRE computer reservations system. Click on "Last Minute Deals" for the latest travel bargains.

  The Trip (**www.thetrip.com**) is really geared toward the business traveler, but vacationers-to-be can also use its exceptionally powerful fare-finding engine, which will e-mail you weekly with the best city-to-city airfare deals for as many as 10 routes. The Trip uses the Internet Travel Network, another reputable travel-agent database, to book hotels and restaurants.

Here's a partial list of airlines and their Web sites, where you can not only get on the e-mailing lists but also book flights directly: **Air Jamaica** (www.airjamica.com); **American Airlines** (www.aa.com); **British Airways** (www.british-airways.com); **BWIA** (www.bwee.com); **Canadian Airlines International** (www.cdnair.ca); **Continental Airlines** (www.flycontiental.com); **Delta** (www.delta-air.com); and **US Airways** (www.usairways.com).

11   Cruises That Don't Cost a Fortune

Except for peak-season cruises between Christmas and New Year's, forget the prices listed in the cruise-line brochures. Overcapacity and fierce competition have ushered in the age of the discounted fare. There are great bargains out there, enough at times to baffle even the most experienced cruise-line travel specialists. These low prices make cruising the Caribbean a viable money-saving option.

Don't succumb to sticker shock when you look in a cruise line's brochure, because these rates are the maritime equivalent of new car prices: a fiction. The price you'll actually pay will be far less, sometimes from 20% to 50% less. And remember that your cruise fare doesn't just pay for transportation—you also get accommodations, as many as eight (!) meals a day, a packed roster of activities, free use of fitness and entertainment facilities, as well as cabaret, jazz performances, dance bands, and discos.

Cruises typically cost less than comparable land-based vacations. The key word, of course, is "comparable." If you stay at a Motel 6 and eat only at the local burger joint, you'll generally do better on land, though there are a few cruise lines out there that would even give that arrangement a run for their money.

Almost everything is included in the cruise price. But know before you go that even the sweetest cruise-related deal will contain its share of hidden extras, and if you're not careful, you might get some unpleasant surprises when you eventually pay your piper. You'll have to pay extra for your bar and wine tabs, some shore excursions, gambling, tips, the exorbitant cost of any ship-to-shore phone calls or faxes, any special pampering (hairdressers, manicurists/pedicurists, massages, and/or skin treatments), purchases in the shipboard boutiques and at the ports of call, and medical treatments in the ship's infirmary. There may also be the question of port charges, though most lines now include these in their fares (be sure to ask when you book, just to be on the safe side).

BOOKING A CRUISE FOR THE BEST PRICE

How should you book your cruise and get to the port of embarkation before the good times roll? It's best to use a travel agent, particularly one who specializes in cruises. He or she will be able to steer you toward any of the special promotions that come and go as frequently as Caribbean rainstorms, and may also be able to give specific advice on individual ships. To get to the port on time, many cruise lines offer deals that include airfare from your local airport to the cruise-departure point. It's possible to purchase your air ticket on your own and book your cruise ticket separately, but in most cases you'll save money by combining the fares into a package deal.

Here are some travel agencies to consider: **Cruises, Inc.,** 5000 Campuswood Dr. E., Syracuse, NY 13057 (☎ 800/854-0500 or 315/463-9695); **Cruise Fairs of America,** Century Plaza Towers, 2029 Century Park E., Suite 950, Los Angeles, CA 90067 (☎ 800/456-4FUN or 310/556-2925); **The Cruise Company,** 10760 Q St, Omaha, NE 68127 (☎ 800/289-5505 or 402/339-6800); **Kelly Cruises,** 1315 W. 22nd St., Suite 105, Oak Brook, IL 60523 (☎ 800/837-7447 or 630/990-1111); **Hartford Holidays Travel,** 129 Hillside Ave., Williston Park, NY 11596 (☎ 800/ 828-4813 or 516/746-6670); and **Mann Travel** and **Cruises American Express,** 6010 Fairview Rd., Ste. 104, Charlotte, NC 28210 (☎ 800/849-2301 or 704-556-8311). These companies stay tuned to last-minute price wars; cruise lines don't profit if these megaships don't fill up near peak capacity, so sales pop up all the time.

You're likely to sail from Miami, which has become the cruise capital of the world. Other departure ports include San Juan, Port Everglades, New Orleans, Tampa, and (via the Panama Canal) Los Angeles.

For much more detailed information, including specific information about saving money and reviews of each individual ship, pick up a copy of ***Frommer's Caribbean Cruises & Ports of Call.***

DISCOUNT CRUISE LINES

The lines listed in this section offer consistently low-prices. You won't be sailing on those space-age–looking megaships that the major lines are bringing out in packs these days, but some of these ships have the kind of character you don't see in the new ships. Examples? Windjammer's fleet, which consists almost entirely of old sailing ships, or Commodore's *Enchanted Capri*, which was purchased from the former Soviet Union and still sports the hammer and sickle on its life jackets. MTV apparently thought that was pretty darn hip: They held their first Spring Break cruise on board in 1999.

- **American Canadian Caribbean** (☎ 800/556-7450). These tiny, 80- to 100-passenger coastal cruisers make 7- to 12-day excursions through the Caribbean, visiting smaller, more out-of-the-way ports than the big cruise ships and offering an experience that's quiet and completely unpretentious. The line operates three almost identical ships, at least one of which spends part of the winter cruising around the Bahamas, Puerto Rico, the Virgin Islands, the Panama Canal, and the coasts of Central America.

- **Cape Canaveral Cruise Line** (☎ 800/910-SHIP). This line and its one ship, the *Dolphin IV*, offers good value for your cruise dollar, with 2-night quickie cruises—from Florida for a 1-day outing in the Bahamas—that are an excellent opportunity for the first-time cruiser to get his or her feet wet. Don't expect anything that even vaguely resembles the activities and diversions you'll find aboard a larger and more modern ship; the setting is older, less stylish, and less comprehensive, but, on the other hand, prices are cheap, the whole package is almost completely unpretentious, and it can be a great party if your expectations are realistic. Overall, it's a good choice for passengers with limited time and/or money who want to escape the midwinter doldrums.

- **Commodore Cruise Line** (☎ 800/237-5361). Commodore's two ships are both small, solid, not particularly glamorous, but highly seaworthy vessels, and are based year-round in New Orleans. The *Enchanted Isle* sails through the western Caribbean and usually spends 3 full days of its 7 cruise days at sea, occupying the remaining 4 days at ports in Montego Bay, Jamaica; the Cayman Islands; and at either Mexico or Honduras. The *Enchanted Capri* sails 2- and 5-night cruises: The former sails the Gulf of Mexico, visiting no ports, while the latter visits Progreso (a beach resort on the tip of Mexico's Yucatán peninsula) and Cozumel, where passengers can opt for a day excursion to Cancún. Both ships lack state-of-the-art facilities, but their low rates make a Caribbean cruise a reality for many first-time cruisers without a lot of cash. Theme cruises are especially pronounced aboard the *Enchanted Isle,* while the *Enchanted Capri* in very gambling-oriented, particularly on its 2-night sailings. Both ships attract goodly numbers of unattached singles.

- **Premier Cruises** (☎ 800/990-7770). Premier is a budget-minded line operating ships that are oldies and, in most cases, goodies. They offer good value, though they don't boast the state-of-the-art facilities of newer, custom-designed cruise ships at better-financed lines. One of the line's ships, the *Big Red Boat*, is marketed primarily to families and offers an extensive kids' program. It sails year-round from Port Canaveral on alternating 3- and 4-day cruises visiting Nassau and Port Lucaya. The line's best ship, the *Rembrandt*, is a classic ocean liner built in 1959 and until recently sailed as Holland America's *Rotterdam V.* Still boasting its original beautiful decor, the ship sails 10- and 11-night round-trip itineraries from Ft. Lauderdale, December through late-March, visiting ports that, depending on the exact itinerary, include Tortola, St. John, Dominica, St. Croix, San Juan, Grand Cayman, Curaçao, Aruba, and Jamaica. The 842-passenger, 21,010-ton *SeaBreeze* was built in 1958 as Costa's luxury flagship, *Frederico C.*, and today sails 7-night western Caribbean itineraries roundtrip from Ft. Lauderdale, October through June, visiting Cozumel, Belize, Roatan, and Key West.

Premier offers cost-effective—and sometimes free—hotel packages that allow participants to extend their holiday in either Jamaica or Aruba before or after their cruise experience.

- **Regal Cruises** (☎ 800/270-7425). The line's one ship, the *Regal Empress,* is now in its mid-40s, and shows its age despite dedicated efforts to keep it in shape. Nonetheless, it keeps on chugging along, and quirks and all, offers an unpretentious cruise with decent food and entertainment considering its often bargain-basement prices. January through mid-April, the ship offers alternating 4-night, 5-night, and 7-night western Caribbean itineraries, and an 11-night Panama Canal itinerary. Depending on the itinerary, Caribbean port calls include Playa del Carmen/Cozumel, Key West, Grand Cayman, and Roatan (Honduras).

- **Windjammer Barefoot Cruises** (☎ 800/327-2601). Windjammer operates six sailing ships, most of which are faithful renovations of antique schooners or sail-driven private yachts. The company offers a real "yo ho ho and a bottle of rum" kind of cruise, and true to its name, few passengers ever bring more than shorts and T-shirts for their time aboard. From bases as divergent as San Juan, St. Martin, Tortola, Antigua, and Grenada, the ships travel to rarely visited outposts, with special emphasis on the scattered reefs and cays of the Virgin Islands and the Grenadines. Port calls often mean just anchoring off a small beach and shuttling passengers ashore, and the ships often stay in port late into the evening, giving passengers an opportunity to enjoy nightlife ashore.

  Some of the best deals (and some of the most amazing itineraries) are to be had aboard the company's durable but not very exciting supply ship, *Amazing Grace,* a freighter-style vessel that carries provisions and supplies for the company's sailing ships (and carries passengers between ports while it's at it). *Amazing Grace* makes continuous 13-day trips between Freeport, the Bahamas, and Trinidad, stopping frequently en route to supply other ships in the company's fleet. You can sometimes snag a cruise fare aboard this ship for less than $60 per day (plus airfare to and from the port). Cruises aboard the line's sailing ships generally stay in the $800 to $1,100 dollar range for week-long cruises, but if you're able to travel on short notice, a feature on the line's Web site (www.windjammer.com) offers e-mail updates of last-minute bargains, with weeklong cruises often going for under $500.

MAINSTREAM LINES

If you catch them during off-season and book a relatively small, simple cabin, you can often get steeply discounted rates from these lines, which are the main players in the Caribbean cruise industry (and thus are engaged in some fierce competition—meaning good prices for you). In fact, you may be able to get a cruise aboard one of these lines for the same price you'd pay aboard a budget line, but you have to catch a sale. Again, talk to your travel agent, who will be up on the latest deals.

- **Carnival Cruise Lines** (☎ 800/438-6744). Offering affordable vacations on some of the biggest and most brightly decorated ships afloat, Carnival is the boldest, brashest, and most successful mass-market cruise line in the world.

Twelve of its vessels depart for the Caribbean from Miami, Tampa, New Orleans, Port Canaveral, and San Juan, and eight of them specialize in 7-day or longer tours that feature stopovers at selected ports throughout the eastern, western, and southern Caribbean, including St. Lucia, San Juan, Guadeloupe, Grenada, Grand Cayman, and Jamaica; four others offer 3- to 5-day itineraries visiting such ports as Nassau, Key West, Grand Cayman, and Playa del Carmen/Cozumel. Its fleet has many ships, including the megaship *Paradise.* Launched in 1998 and weighing in at 70,367 tons, it's noteworthy as the only completely smoke-free cruise ship in the Caribbean. Most of the company's Caribbean cruises offer good value and feature nonstop activities. Food and party-colored drinks are plentiful, and the overall atmosphere is comparable to a floating theme park. Lots of single passengers opt for this line, as do families attracted by the line's well-run children's program. The average onboard age is a relatively youthful 42, although ages range from 3 to 95.

- **Celebrity Cruises** (☎ 800/437-3111). Celebrity maintains five newly built, stylish, medium to large ships with cruises that last between 7 and 15 nights to ports such as Key West, San Juan, Grand Cayman, St. Thomas, Ocho Rios, Antigua, and Cozumel, Mexico, to name a few. It's classy but not stuffy, several notches above mass-market, and provides an experience that's both elegant and fun—and all for a price that's competitive with lines offering much less. Accommodations are roomy and well-equipped, cuisine is the most refined of any of its competitors, and its service is impeccable.

- **Costa Cruise Lines** (☎ 800/462-6782). Costa, the U.S.-based branch of a cruise line that has thrived in Italy for about a century, maintains hefty to mega-size vessels, two of which offer virtually identical jaunts through the western and eastern Caribbean on alternate weeks, each of them departing from Fort Lauderdale. Ports of call during the eastern Caribbean itineraries of both vessels include stopovers in San Juan, St. Thomas, Serena Cay (a private island off the coast of the Dominican Republic known for its beaches), and Nassau. Itineraries through the western Caribbean include stopovers at Grand Cayman; either Ocho Rios or Montego Bay, Jamaica; Key West; and Cozumel. There's an Italian flavor and lots of Italian design on board here, and an atmosphere of relaxed indulgence.

- **Holland America Line–Westours** (☎ 800/426-0327). Holland America is the most high-toned of the mass-market cruise lines, with nine respectably hefty and good-looking ships, seven of which spend substantial time cruising the Caribbean. They offer solid value, with very few jolts or surprises, and attract a solid, well-grounded clientele of primarily older travelers (so late-night revelers and serious partyers might want to book cruises on other lines, such as Carnival). Cruises stop at deep-water mainstream ports throughout the Caribbean and last for an average of 7 days, but in some cases for 10 days, visiting such ports as Key West, Grand Cayman, St. Maarten, St. Lucia, Curaçao, Barbados, and St. Thomas.

- **Norwegian Cruise Line** (☎ 800/327-7030). Norwegian operates a diverse fleet ranging from the classic though now massively renovated *Norway* (formerly the *France*) to the medium-sized *Norwegian Majesty, Norwegian Wind, Norwegian Dream,* and *Norwegian Sea.* The first three are based throughout the winter in Miami and embark on 7-day jaunts through the eastern and/or western Caribbean. Ships on either itinerary usually spend a day allowing passengers to sun, swim, and surf at the company's private island, Great Stirrup Cay. *Norwegian Dream* follows a year-round 7-day itinerary departing from San Juan, Puerto

Rico, to such ports as Aruba, Curaçao, Tortola, Virgin Gorda, St. Thomas, St. Lucia, Antigua, St. Kitts, and St. Croix. The *Norwegian Sea* sails year-round from Houston, making continuous circuits across the Gulf of Mexico to such Yucatán ports as Cancún and Cozumel, and Honduras's Roatan Bay. On board the ships, NCL administers a snappy, high-energy array of activities and, in many cases, a revolving array of international sports figures for game tips and lectures. Look for yet another NCL ship, the 80,000 ton, 2,000-passenger *Norwegian Sky,* to be added to the company armada in August 1999, likely sailing year-round from Miami on eastern and western Caribbean itineraries.

- **Princess Cruises** (☎ **800/421-0522**). Currently operating 10 megavessels, four of which cruise through Caribbean and Bahamian waters, Princess offers a cruise experience that's one part Carnival- or Royal Caribbean–style party-time fun and one part Celebrity-style classy enjoyment. The *Ocean Princess, Dawn Princess,* and *Sea Princess,* almost identical vessels all built in the late 1990s, offer the bulk of Princess's Caribbean itineraries, with the *Dawn* and *Ocean* running two alternating 7-night southern Caribbean itineraries round-trip from San Juan, while the *Sea* sails 7-night western Caribbean runs round-trip from Fort Lauderdale. Depending on the exact itinerary, ports on the southern Caribbean runs include Curaçao, Isla Magarita (Venezuela), La Guaira/Caracas (Venezuela), Grenada, Dominica, St. Vincent, St. Kitts, St. Thomas, Trinidad, Barbados, Antigua, Martinique, St. Lucia, and St. Maarten. Western Caribbean itineraries visit Ocho Rios (Jamaica), Grand Cayman, Cozumel, and Princess Cays, the line's private island. The *Grand Princess,* at press time the largest cruise ship in the world, sails 7-night eastern Caribbean itineraries round-trip from Fort Lauderdale, visiting St. Thomas, St. Maarten, and Princess Cays. All of the line's ships are stylish and comfortable, though the *Grand* ups it a notch in the style department, offering amazing open deck areas and some really beautiful indoor public areas.
- **Royal Caribbean International (RCI)** (☎ **800/327-6700** or 305/539-6000). RCI leads the industry in the development of megaships. Most of this company's dozen or so vessels weigh in at around 73,000 tons, though at press time it's scheduled to up the ante on the whole industry by launching the just plain unbelievably enormous *Voyager of the Seas,* weighing in at 142,000 tons, carrying 3,114 passengers, and offering such cruise ship firsts as an ice-skating rink and a rock-climbing wall. A mass-market company that has everything down to a science, RCI encourages a house-party theme that's just a little less frenetic than the mood aboard Carnival.

  There are enough onboard activities to suit virtually any taste and age level. Though accommodations are more than adequate, they are not upscale, and tend to be a bit more cramped than the industry norm. Using either Miami, Fort Lauderdale, or San Juan as their home port, Royal Caribbean ships call regularly at St. Thomas, San Juan, Ocho Rios, St. Maarten, Grand Cayman, St. Croix, Curaçao, and one or the other of the line's private beaches—one in the Bahamas, the other along an isolated peninsula in northern Haiti. Most of the company's cruises last 7 days, although some weekend jaunts from San Juan to St. Thomas are available for 3 nights, and some Panama Canal crossings last for 11 and 12 nights.

MORE WAYS TO CUT CRUISE COSTS

BE FLEXIBLE WITH DATES & ITINERARIES   Cruise discounters can often get you some amazing fares, but you'll have to take what they've got. (They usually negotiate those fares by reserving cabins in bulk from the cruise lines.)

DON'T CRUISE ALONE   When booking a cabin, you'll pay a premium for traveling alone. Most ships impose a supplement of between 125% and 200% of the per-person price for single occupancy of a double cabin. To avoid this penalty, you could let the cruise line match you with a (same-sex) stranger in a shared cabin. Some devoted party lines like Carnival will put up to four single cruisers in a quad cabin at bargain-basement prices. You'll lose your privacy, but you'll love the price.

You could also tap into the "singles" and "senior singles" phone network run by **The Cruise Line, Inc.,** 150 NW 168th St., North Miami Beach, FL 33169 (☎ **800/ 777-0707**). When you call this number, you'll hear information geared to general passenger needs before you get to information pertinent to the solo traveler.

SHARE A CABIN WITH FAMILY OR FRIENDS   Many lines offer cabins that can house a total of three and four passengers (sometimes even five)—two in regular beds and two in bunk-style berths which pull down from the ceiling or upper part of the wall. So for families of four or groups of very good friends, if you're willing to be a bit (or a lot) crowded, you can save money by sharing your cabin. The rates for the third and fourth passengers in a cabin, adults or children, are typically half that of the normal adult fare, and are sometimes less than half. Also, look into sharing a suite; most ships have some. Disney Cruise Line, for example, offers mostly family-style suites comfortably accommodating up to five people and with one-and-a-half bathrooms.

BOOK YOUR CRUISE WITH A GROUP   Many cruise lines offer reduced rates to groups occupying at least 8 cabins (some as few as 5 cabins), with two adults in each cabin (for a total of 16 passengers). Based on two people per cabin, typically the 16th person in the group will get a free cruise, and the entire group can split the savings. In general, discounts for this type of group travel can be significant, but are wholly determined by the cruise line and seasonal demand at the time you're booking. Some high-volume cruise agencies may be able to team you up with a "group" of their own devising that they're booking aboard a certain ship; ask about the possibility when you talk to the agency.

READ THE FINE PRINT   You never know what obscure special deals might apply to you. Carnival, for instance, offers really low rates on the *Carnival Destiny* if you book one of the cabins that is one deck directly above the disco (and all the noise it generates at night). The brochure calls them "Night Owl Staterooms," and if you're planning on being in the disco yourself till the wee hours of the night, you might want to consider these cabins, which are discounted at 50% or more than other, quieter cabins in the same category!

TAKE ADVANTAGE OF SAIL-AND-STAY PROMOTIONS   If you want to add a few more days to your vacation, cruise lines often offer good prices for hotels in the cities of embarkation. These days, cruises are departing from ports that are tourist attractions in their own right. You might want to explore Miami before you sail, drive to Disney World from Port Canaveral, or spend a few days in San Juan. Many cruise lines negotiate group hotel discounts for passengers interested in prolonging their vacation. These packages usually include transportation from the hotel to the ship (before the cruise) or from the docks to the hotel (after a cruise).

TAKE ADVANTAGE OF TWO-FERS   Promotions called "two-fers"—2-for-1 deals that let you bring a companion free—come and go like hurricane winds, but if you see one, it's worth considering. A cruise specialist should know if some cut-rate discount for two is being offered at the time you plan to sail. (These deals don't happen during the peak winter season in the Caribbean.) You'll have to negotiate these two-fers carefully, and compare them with various air/sea packages to see if you're indeed getting a discounted deal. If airfare is included for both of you, then go for it. But if airfare has to be booked separately, compare the cost of a two-fer without airfare to an air/sea package for two to see which one is the better deal.

TAKE ADVANTAGE OF SENIOR DISCOUNTS   Don't keep your age a secret. Membership in any of dozens of clubs, such as the AAA or AARP, can afford discounts of anywhere from 5% to 50%. Always ask when you're booking.

12 Getting the Best Value Out of Your Accommodations

WATCH OUT FOR THOSE EXTRAS!

Nearly all islands charge a government tax on hotel rooms, usually 7½ %, but that rate varies from island to island. This tax mounts quickly, so ask if the rate you're quoted includes this room tax. Sometimes the room tax depends on the quality of the hotel; relatively low for a guest house but steeper for a first-class resort. Determine the tax before you accept the rate.

Furthermore, most hotels routinely add 10% to 12% for "service," even if you didn't like the service or didn't see much evidence of it. That means that with tax and service, some bills are 17% or even 25% higher than originally quoted to you! Naturally, you need to determine just how much the hotel, guest house, or inn plans to add to your bill at the end of your stay.

That's not all. Some hotels slip in little hidden extras that mount quickly. For example, it's common for many establishments to quote rates that include a continental breakfast. Should you prefer ham and eggs added to the order, that will mean extra charges. Sometimes if you request special privileges, such as extra towels for the beach or laundry done in a hurry, surcharges mount. It pays to watch those extras.

HOTELS & RESORTS

Many budget travelers assume they can't afford the big hotels and resorts. But there are so many packages out there (see the section "Package Deals," earlier in this chapter) and so many frequent sales, even in winter, that you might be pleasantly surprised.

The rates given in this book are only "rack rates"—that is, the officially posted rate that you'd be given if you just walked in off the street. Almost no one actually pays them! Always ask about packages and discounts. Think of the rates in this book as guidelines to help you comparison shop.

What the Abbreviations Mean

Rate "sheets"—statements of a hotel's room rates—often have these classifications that we've also used in this guide:

MAP (Modified American Plan) usually means room, breakfast, and dinner, unless the room rate has been quoted separately, and then it means only breakfast and dinner.

CP (Continental Plan) includes room and a light breakfast.

EP (European Plan) means room only.

AP (American Plan) includes your room plus three meals a day.

A savvy travel agent can help save you serious money. Some hotels are often quite flexible about their rates, and many offer discounts and upgrades whenever they have a big block of rooms to fill and few reservations. The smaller hotels and inns are not as likely to be generous with discounts, much less upgrades. Even if you book into one of these bigger hotels, ask for the cheaper rooms—that is, those that don't open directly onto the ocean. Caribbean hoteliers charge dearly for the view alone.

ALL-INCLUSIVE RESORTS

The promises are persuasive: "Forget your cash, put your plastic away." Presumably, everything's all paid for in advance at an "all-inclusive" resort. But is it?

The all-inclusives have a reputation for being expensive, and many of them are, especially the giant SuperClubs of Jamaica or even the Sandals properties (unless you book in a slow period or off-season).

In the 1990s, so many competitors entered the all-inclusive game that the term now means different things to the various resorts using that form of marketing. The ideal all-inclusive is just that—a place where everything, even drinks and water sports, is included. But in the most narrow sense it means a room and three meals a day, with drinks, sports, cigarettes, whatever, appearing as extra charges. Of course, when booking it's important to ask and to understand exactly what's included in your so-called all-inclusive. Water-sports programs and offerings vary greatly at the various resorts. Extras might include options for horseback riding or sightseeing on the island.

The all-inclusive market is geared to the active traveler who likes to participate in organized entertainment, a lot of sports, and workouts at fitness centers, and who also likes a lot of food and drink.

If you're single or gay, avoid Sandals. If you have young children, stay away from Hedonism II in Negril, Jamaica, which lives up to its name. Even some Club Meds are targeted more for singles and couples, although many now aggressively pursue the family market. Some Club Meds have Mini Clubs, Baby Clubs, and Teen Clubs at some of their properties, at least during holiday and summer seasons.

This guide doesn't review the high-priced all-inclusives, but does review the resorts that are within the range of the traveler on a budget—for example, only one Sandals in Jamaica (see Montego Bay in chapter 14) falls in our price range. Forget Jamaica's SuperClubs—consider one of the Jack Tar Villages, including those in Jamaica (Montego Bay), the Dominican Republic (north coast), and St. Kitts instead. The Pineapple resort on Antigua is at least moderate in price, a good splurge choice, and most Club Meds fall within the moderate (if not budget) range.

The trick is to look for that special deal and to travel in off-peak periods, which doesn't always mean just from mid-April to mid-December. Discounts are often granted during certain slow periods—called "windows"—for hotels, most often after the New Year's holiday. If you want a winter vacation at an all-inclusive, choose the month of January—not February or the Christmas holidays, when prices are at their all-year high.

One good deal might be **Club Med's "Wild Card,"** geared to singles and couples. You must be 18 or over. Reservations must be made 2 or more weeks prior to departure. One week prior to departure, Club Med advises passengers which "village" on which island they're going to. If this uncertainty doesn't bother you, you can save $150 to $300 per weekly package. The complete per-person Wild Card cost for a week's package is a flat $999 per person. Each package includes round-trip air transportation from New York, double-occupancy accommodations, all meals with complimentary wine and beer (other alcoholic drinks extra), use of all sports facilities except scuba (extra charges), nightly entertainment, and other recreational activities such as boat rides, snorkeling expeditions, and picnics. For more information call ☎ **800/ CLUB-MED.**

Consult a good travel agent for other good deals that might be available.

GUEST HOUSES

An entirely different type of accommodation is the guest house, where most of the Antilleans themselves stay when they travel. In the Caribbean, the term *guest house* can mean anything. Sometimes so-called guest houses are really like simple motels built around swimming pools. Others are small individual cottages, with their own kitchenettes, constructed around a main building in which you'll often find a bar and a restaurant serving local food. Some are surprisingly comfortable, often with private baths and swimming pools. You may or may not have air-conditioning.

For value, the guest house can't be topped. You can always journey over to a big beach resort and use its seaside facilities for only a small charge, perhaps no more than $5. Although bereft of frills, the guest houses we've recommended are clean and safe for families or single women. The cheapest ones are not places where you'd want to spend time, because of their simple, modest furnishings.

COOKING FOR YOURSELF

Particularly if you're a family or a group of friends, a "housekeeping holiday" can be one of the least expensive ways to vacation in the Caribbean. Accommodations with kitchens are now available on nearly all the islands. Some are individual cottages you can rent, others are housed in one building, and some are private homes rented when the owners are away. Many self-catering places have maid service included in the rental, and you're given fresh linen as well.

In the simpler rentals, doing your own cooking and laundry or even your own maid service may not be your idea of a good time in the sun, but it saves money—a lot of money.

The disadvantages to many of these self-catering cottages is that they're in inaccessible places, which may mean you'll need a car. Public transportation on any island in the Caribbean is simply inadequate, if it exists at all.

You have to approach these rental properties with a certain sense of adventure and a do-it-yourself independence. These rentals are not for everybody, but they can make a Caribbean vacation possible for families or other groups on a tight budget.

For a list of agencies to arrange rentals, refer to the hotel sections of the individual island chapters.

PRIVATE APARTMENTS, EFFICIENCIES & COTTAGES

There are lots of private apartments for rent, either with or without maid service. This is more of a no-frills option than a villa or condo. The apartments may not be in buildings with swimming pools, and they may not have a front desk to help you.

Cottages are the most freewheeling way to stay. Most are fairly simple; many open onto a beach, whereas others may be clustered around a communal swimming pool. Many contain no more than a simple bedroom with a small kitchen and bath. For the peak winter season, reservations should be made at least 5 or 6 months in advance.

Dozens of agents throughout the United States and Canada offer these types of rentals; we've noted some in the destination chapters that follow. You can also write to local tourist offices for good suggestions.

Travel experts agree that savings, especially for a family of three to six people, or two or three couples, can range from 50% to 60% of what a hotel would cost. If there are only two in your party, these savings don't apply. However, groceries are sometimes priced 35% to 60% higher than the average on the U.S. mainland because nearly all foodstuffs have to be imported. Even so, preparing your own food will be a lot cheaper than dining at restaurants.

13 Getting Married in the Caribbean

If you yearn to take the plunge on a sun-dappled island, here are some wedding basics on the islands:

ANTIGUA   There is a 24-hour waiting period for marriages on Antigua. A couple appears at the Ministry of Justice in the capital of St. John to complete and sign a declaration before a marriage coordinator and pay a $150 license fee. The coordinator will arrange for a marriage officer to perform a civil ceremony at any of Antigua's hotels or another place the couple selects. The fee for the marriage officer is $50. Several hotels and resorts offer wedding/honeymoon packages. For more information on civil or religious wedding ceremonies, contact the **Antigua Department of Tourism,** 610 Fifth Ave., Suite 311, New York, NY 10020 (☎ **212/541-4117**).

ARUBA   Civil weddings are possible on Aruba only if one of the partners is an Aruban resident. Because of this restriction, the average couple marries elsewhere, then visits Aruba for a honeymoon. For more information about planning a wedding on Aruba, contact the **Aruba Tourism Authority,** 1000 Harbor Blvd., Weehawken, NJ 08707 (☎ **800/TO-ARUBA** or 201/330-0800).

BARBADOS   Couples can now marry the same day they arrive on Barbados, but must first obtain a marriage license from the **Ministry of Home Affairs** (☎ **246/228-8950**). Bring either a passport or a birth certificate and photo ID, $50 (U.S.) in fees, and $12.50 for the revenue stamp that can be obtained at the local post office, a letter from the authorized officiant who will perform the service, plus proof, if applicable, of pertinent deaths or divorces of any former spouse(s). A Roman Catholic wedding on Barbados carries additional requirements. For more information, contact the **Barbados Tourism Authority,** 800 Second Ave., New York, NY 10017 (☎ **800/221-9831** or 212/986-6516).

BONAIRE   Either the bride or groom must have a temporary residency permit, obtained by writing a letter to the governor of the Island Territory of Bonaire, Wilhelminaplein 1, Kralendijk, Bonaire, N.A. (☎ **599/7-5350**). The letter, submitted within 2 months of departure for Bonaire, should request permission to marry on Bonaire, apply for temporary residency, as well as inform the governor of your arrival and departure dates and the date you wish to marry. The partner who applies for residency must be on the island for 7 days prior to the wedding. A special dispensation must be issued by the governor if there is less than a 10-day time period between the announcement of the marriage and actually getting married. In addition, send three passport photos, copies of the bride's and groom's passports, birth certificates, and proof of divorce or in the case of widows and widowers, the death certificate of the deceased spouse.

   If you desire, you can arrange your wedding on Bonaire through **Multro Travel and Tours,** Attn: Mrs. Marvel Tromp, Kaya Amazon 27B (P.O. Box 237), Bonaire, N.A. (☎ **599/7-8334;** fax 599/7-8416), or check with the hotel where you're planning to stay. Some hotels arrange weddings on special request. For further information, contact the **Bonaire Tourist Office** (☎ **800/826-6247** or 212/956-5911).

THE BRITISH VIRGIN ISLANDS   There is no requirement of island residency, but a couple must apply for a license at the attorney general's office, and must stay in the B.V.I. for 3 days while the application is processed. Present a passport or original birth certificate and photo identification, plus certified proof of your marital status, plus any divorce or death certificates that apply to any former spouse(s). Two witnesses must accompany the couple. The fee is $110. Marriages can be performed by the local registrar or by the officiant of your choice. Contact the **Registrar's Office,** P.O. Box 418, Road Town, Tortola, B.V.I. (☎ **284/494-3134** or 284/494-3701).

THE CAYMAN ISLANDS Visitors must first arrange for a marriage officer prior to arriving in the Cayman Islands in order to name the individual who will be officiating on the application. The application for a special marriage license, which costs $200, can be obtained from the **Deputy Secretary's Office,** Third Floor, Government Administration Building, George Town (☎ **345/949-7900**). There is no waiting period. Present a birth certificate plus the embarkation/disembarkation cards issued by the island's immigration authorities, along with divorce decrees or proof of a former spouse's death (if applicable). Complete wedding services and packages are offered by **Cayman Weddings of Grand Cayman,** owned/operated by Cayman marriage officers Vernon and Francine Jackson. For more information, contact them at P.O. Box 678, Grand Cayman (☎ **345/949-8677;** fax 345/949-8237). A brochure, *Getting Married in the Cayman Islands,* is available from **Government Information Services,** Broadcasting House, Grand Cayman (☎ **345/949-8092;** fax 345/949-5936).

CURAÇAO Couples must be on the island 2 days before applying for a marriage license, for which there is a 14-day waiting period. Passport, birth certificate, return ticket, and divorce papers (if applicable) are required. The fee is subject to change, so check in advance. For further information, call the **Curaçao Tourist Board,** 475 Park Ave. S., Suite 2000, New York, NY 10016 (☎ **212/683-7660;** fax 212/683-9337).

JAMAICA In high season, some Jamaican resorts witness several weddings a day. Many of the larger Jamaican resorts can arrange for an officiant, a photographer, and even the wedding cake and champagne. Some resorts, however, will even throw in your wedding with the cost of your honeymoon at the hotel. Both the Jamaican Tourist Board and your hotel will assist you with the paperwork. Participants must reside on Jamaica for 24 hours before the ceremony. Bring birth certificates and affidavits saying you've never been married before, or, if you've been divorced, bring copies of your divorce papers, or in the case of widows and widowers, a copy of the deceased spouses' death certificate. The cost of the license and stamp duty is $200. The cost of the ceremony can range from $50 to $200, depending on how much legwork you want to do yourself. You may apply in person at the **Ministry of National Security and Justice,** 12 Ocean Blvd., Kingston, Jamaica (☎ **876/922-9500**).

PUERTO RICO There are no residency requirements. You'll need parental consent if either party is under 18. Blood tests are required, although a test conducted within 10 days of the ceremony on the U.S. mainland will suffice. A doctor in Puerto Rico must sign the license after conducting an examination of the bride and groom. For complete details, contact the **Commonwealth of Puerto Rico Health Department,** Demographic Register, 171 Quisaueya St., Hato Rey, PR 00917 (☎ **787/767-9120**).

ST. LUCIA Both parties must have remained on the island for 48 hours prior to the ceremony. Present your passport or birth certificate, plus (if either participant has been widowed or divorced) proof of death or divorce from the former spouse(s). Before the ceremony it usually takes about 2 days to process all the paperwork. Fees run around $150 for a lawyer (one is usually needed for the application to the governor-general), $25 for the registrar to perform the ceremony, and $37.75 for the stamp duty and the license. Some resorts and vacation properties also offer wedding packages that include all the necessary arrangements for a single fee. For more information, contact the **St. Lucia Tourist Board,** 800 Second Ave., Suite 400J, New York, NY 10017 (☎ **212/ 867-2950;** fax 212/370-7867).

THE U.S. VIRGIN ISLANDS   No blood tests or physical examinations are necessary, but there is a $25 license fee, a $25 notarized application, and an 8-day waiting period, which is sometimes waived, depending on circumstances. Civil ceremonies before a judge of the territorial court cost $200 each; religious ceremonies performed by clergy are equally valid. Fees and schedules for church weddings must be negotiated directly with the officiant. More information is available from the **U.S. Virgin Islands Division of Tourism,** 1270 Ave. of the Americas, New York, NY 10020 (☎ 212/332-2222).

The guide *Getting Married in the U.S. Virgin Islands* is distributed by U.S.V.I. tourism offices; it gives information on all three islands, including wedding planners, places of worship, florists, and limousine services. The guide also provides a listing of island accommodations that offer in-house wedding services.

Couples can apply for a marriage license for St. Thomas or St. John by contacting the **Territorial Court of the Virgin Islands,** P.O. Box 70, St. Thomas, U.S.V.I. 00804 (☎ 340/774-6680). For weddings on St. Croix, applications are available by contacting the **Territorial Court of the Virgin Islands,** Family Division, P.O. Box 929, Christiansted, St. Croix, USVI 00821 (☎ **340/778-9750**).

14 Saving Money on Car Rentals

Refer to the individual chapter listing for special driving rules (sometimes a local license is required) and for major car-rental companies serving a particular island. In many Caribbean islands, including the U.S. Virgin Islands, driving is on the left.

Car rental rates vary even more than airline fares. The price you pay will depend on the size of the car, where and when you pick it up and drop it off, the length of the rental period, where and how far you drive it, whether you purchase insurance, and a host of other factors. A few key questions could save you hundreds of dollars.

If you decide to rent a car, shop around and ask a lot of questions. The rental firms aren't going to volunteer to save you money, but competition in their industry is fierce. Their reservations clerks are used to being asked for the lowest rate available and most will find it in order to get your business. You may have to try different dates, different pick-up and drop-off points, and different discount offers yourself to find the best deal. It changes constantly. Also, if you're a member of any organization (AARP or AAA, for example), be sure to ask if you're entitled to discounts.

Check the rental firms' Web sites. Most will automatically bring up the lowest available rate, and there are boxes to click if you are an association member or have a discount coupon. **Microsoft Expedia** (www.expedia.com) and **Travelocity** (www. travelocity.com) help you compare prices and locate car rental bargains from various companies nationwide. They will even make your reservation for you once you've found the best deal. See the "Finding the Best Airfare" section earlier in this chapter for more tips about using the Internet.

Most of the companies pad their profits by selling Loss/Damage Waiver (LDW) insurance. You may already be covered by your insurance carrier and credit- or charge-card companies, so check with them before succumbing to the hard sell.

Also, some rental companies will offer to refill your gas tank at "competitive" prices when you return. Some of their come-ons for this service quote the "average" price of a gallon of gasoline in town. Regular gas usually is less expensive in town.

Most also require a minimum age, ranging from 19 to 25, and some also set maximum ages. Others deny cars to anyone with a bad driving record. Ask about rental requirements and restrictions when you book to avoid problems later. You must have a valid credit card to rent a vehicle.

Some travel packages include airfare, accommodations, and a rental car with unlimited mileage. Compare these prices with the cost of booking airline tickets and renting a car separately to see if these offers are good deals.

3 Antigua

Antiguans boast that they have a different beach for every day of the year (which is a bit of an exaggeration). Most of them protected by coral reefs, and with sand often sugar-white, these beaches are reason enough for most visitors to come here. But Antigua is also known for its sailing facilities, centered at historic English Harbour, where Lord Nelson built a base for his English fleet in the late 18th century. The principal "tourist zone" lies north of the capital of St. John in the northwest. Here you'll find some of the best hotels (but not *the* best) and an array of restaurants, beach bars, and water-sports facilities.

Old-timers claim that their island is trying to imitate Miami Beach with its sprawling resorts. To some extent that's true. Some of the Caribbean's largest resort hotels have opened in Antigua, which also means that the island boasts some of the most expensive places to stay in all the West Indies. The island's guest houses, small inns, and B&Bs just haven't kept pace with all the gigantic mega-resorts that sometimes discount their packages dramatically to fill cavernous floors. There's a dearth of really good budget accommodations, but you'll find a number of small, less expensive restaurants, especially in St. John's.

The islands of Antigua, Barbuda, and Redonda form the independent nation of Antigua and Barbuda, within the Commonwealth of Nations. Redonda is an uninhabited rocky islet of less than a square mile located 20 miles southwest of Antigua. Sparsely populated Barbuda is expensive to get to and super-expensive once there. If your fortune approaches that of Bill Gates, the hoteliers will be only too glad to welcome you. Independence has come, but Antigua is still British in many of its traditions.

Rolling, rustic Antigua has as its highest point Boggy Peak, 1,360 feet above sea level. Antigua has a population of about 67,000 and an area of 108 square miles. Stone towers, once sugar mills, dot the landscape, though its inland scenery isn't as dramatic as on St. Kitts. But, oh, those beaches!

The capital is **St. John's,** a large, neatly laid out town, 6 miles from the airport and less than a mile from Deep Water Harbour Terminal, where cruise ships dock. The town is the focal point of commerce and industry, as well as the seat of government and visitor shopping. Trade winds keep the streets fairly cool, as they were built wide just for that purpose. Protected in the throat of a narrow bay, St. John's consists of cobblestone sidewalks, weather-beaten wooden houses, corrugated iron roofs, and louvered Caribbean verandas.

Antigua

Map labels:

Atlantic Ocean

Hodges Bay
Dutchman's Bay
Dickenson Bay
Runaway Beach
Cedar Grove
Long Island
Deep Water Harbour
Fort James
V. C. Bird Airport
Guiana Island
Hawksbill Beaches
Five Islands
St. John's
Pineapple Beach
Long Bay
Indian Town Point
Parham
Devil's Bridge
Darkwood Beach
Jennings
Willikies
Jolly Harbour
Bolans
Megaliths
All Saints
Driftwood Beach
Boggy Peak
Urlings
Potworks Dam
Freetown
Johnson's Point
Old Road
Fig Tree Dr.
Falmouth
Half Moon Bay
Willoughby Bay
Morris Bay
Falmouth Bay
English Harbour
Turner's Beach
Pigeon Point
Mamora Bay
Carlisle Bay
Nelson's Dockyard National Park
Shirley Heights

Caribbean Sea

0   5 Miles
0   5 Kilometers
N

Airport ✈ Beach 🏖 Mountain ▲▲

1   Essentials

VISITOR INFORMATION

Before you leave, you may wish to contact the **Antigua and Barbuda Department of Tourism,** 610 Fifth Ave., Suite 311, New York, NY 10020 (☎ **212/541-4117**); or 25 SE Second Ave., Suite 300, Miami, FL 33131 (☎ **305/381-6762**). There is also a toll-free number to call for information: ☎ **888/268-4227.** Operators are available Monday to Friday 9am to 5pm Eastern standard time.

In **Canada,** contact the Antigua and Barbuda Department of Tourism & Trade, 60 St. Clair Ave. E., Suite 304, Toronto, ON, M4T 1N5 (☎ **416/961-3085**).

In the **United Kingdom,** information is available at Antigua House, 15 Thayer St., London, England W1M 5LD (☎ **020/7486-7073**).

The official Web site is **www.antigua-barbuda.org**.

On the island, the **Antigua and Barbuda Department of Tourism,** at Thames and Long streets in St. John's (☎ **268/462-0480**), is open Monday to Thursday 8am to 4:30pm and Friday 8am to 3pm.

GETTING THERE

Be sure to read the section on package tours in chapter 2 before you book your airline ticket—it can save you a ton of money!

The major airline flying to Antigua's V. C. Bird Airport is **American Airlines** (☎ **800/433-7300** in the U.S.), which offers three daily (morning, afternoon, and evening) nonstop flights to Antigua from its Caribbean hub in San Juan, Puerto Rico; flight time is about 1½ hours. Each of these flights departs late enough in the day to allow easy transfers from other flights. One of these flights from San Juan is the con-tinuation of a nonstop flight from New York's JFK. American also offers lots of package deals.

British Airways (☎ 800/247-9297 in the U.S., or 0345/222-111 in England) offers flights four times a week from London's Gatwick Airport.

Air Canada (☎ 800/422-6232) has regularly scheduled flights from Toronto to Antigua on Saturday only.

The regional carrier **BWIA** (☎ 888/JET-BWIA in the U.S.) is an increasingly popular means of reaching Antigua. From Miami it has four flights weekly, and two flights weekly from Toronto. There are also five flights weekly from Kingston, Jamaica, plus connections from Europe—two flights a week from London and two flights weekly from Frankfurt.

Continental (☎ 800-231-0856 or 268/462-5355) has daily flights out of Newark, New Jersey.

GETTING AROUND

BY TAXI Taxis meet every airplane, and drivers wait outside the major hotels. In fact, if you're going to be on Antigua for a few days, you may find that a particular driver has "adopted" you, although budget travelers will want to avoid this expensive luxury. The typical one-way fare from the airport to St. John's is $12; to English Harbour, it's $25 and up. The government of Antigua fixes the rates, and the taxis have no meters.

While it's costly, the best way to see Antigua is by private taxi whose drivers also act as guides. Most taxi tours are from the St. John's area to English Harbour. Drivers will generally charge $40 for three or four passengers and will usually wait at least 30 min-utes or maybe more while you sightsee around English Harbour. If you split the cost with another couple, it falls within the range of most budgets.

To call a taxi in St. John's, dial ☎ 268/462-0711; after 6pm, 268/462-5190.

BY RENTAL CAR Newly arrived drivers quickly (and ruefully) learn that the island's roads are among the worst, most potholed, and most badly sign-posted in the Caribbean. Considering that you have to *drive on the left* and are often tempted to have one piña colada too many, renting a car on Antigua is usually not a great idea.

If you insist on driving, you must obtain an Antiguan **driver's license,** which costs an overpriced $20. To obtain one, you must produce a valid driver's license from home. Most car-rental firms are authorized to issue you an Antiguan license, which they usually do without a surcharge.

Several different car-rental agencies operate on Antigua, although they're sometimes precariously financed local operations with cars best described as "battered." The best of them are affiliated with major car-rental companies in the United States. **Avis** (☎ 800/331-1212 in the U.S. or 268/462-2840 in Antigua) and **Hertz** (☎ 800/654-3131 in the U.S. or 268/462-6450 in Antigua) are both represented on Antigua, each offering pickup service at the airport. Although not as reliable as the big compa-nies, you can always call a local company and see if they'll make a cheaper deal. The cars might not be as well maintained, but it could be easier on your pocketbook. Try **Anjam Rent-a-car,** Sunset Cove, Dickenson Bay (☎ 268/462-0959), or **J&L Rent-a-Car,** Crosbies (☎ 268/461-7496). The average rental is about $50 a day. But if you're arriving off-season, be firm about wanting a "summer discount"—it's often granted. Of course, the longer you book the car, especially for use over several days, the cheaper the rate is likely to be.

BY MOTORCYCLE & SCOOTER   Of course, you can cut car-rental costs by renting motorcycles or scooters. These are available at **Shipwreck,** English Harbour (☎ **262/460-2711**). Yamaha or Honda motorcycles rent for about $35 per day or $150 per week, with scooters costing from $25 per day or $85 per week. It's about the cheapest self-guided transport on the island if you don't mind the bumpy rides.

BY BUS   Buses are not recommended for the average visitor, although they do exist and are cheap. Service is erratic and undependable along impossibly bumpy roads. Officially, buses operate between St. John's and the villages daily from 5:30am to 6pm, but don't count on it. In St. John's, buses leave from two different "stations"—near the Central Market and near the Botanical Gardens. Most fares are $1.

SPECIAL EVENTS

The **summer carnival** takes place during the week preceding the first Tuesday in August. This festival includes a beauty competition and calypso and steel-band competitions. Carnival envelops the streets in exotic costumes that recall the people's African heritage. The spring highlight is Antigua's annual **sailing week** in late April or early May.

Fast Facts: Antigua

Banking Hours   Banks are usually open Monday to Thursday 8am to 1pm and Friday 8am to 1pm and 3 to 5pm.

Currency   The **Eastern Caribbean dollar (EC$)** is used on these islands. However, nearly all hotels bill you in U.S. dollars, and only certain tiny restaurants present their prices in EC dollars. Make sure you know which dollars are referred to when you inquire about a price. The EC dollar is worth about 37¢ in U.S. currency (EC$2.70 = U.S.$1). Unless otherwise specified, *rates quoted in this chapter are given in U.S. dollars.*

Customs   Arriving visitors are allowed to bring in 200 cigarettes and 1 quart of liquor, plus 6 ounces of perfume.

Documents   A valid passport is preferred when U.S., British, and Canadian nationals are visiting the island. An original birth certificate accompanied by a photo ID is also acceptable, but we recommend that you bring your passport anyway. All arriving visitors must have a departing ticket.

Electricity   Most of the island's electricity is 220 volts AC (60 cycles), meaning that American appliances need transformers. However, the Hodges Bay area and some hotels are supplied with 110 volts AC (60 cycles).

Emergencies   In an emergency, contact the police (☎ **268/462-0125**), the fire department (☎ **268/462-0044**), or an ambulance (☎ **268/462-0251**). In addition, you can also call ☎ **911** or 999 for any type of emergency.

Hospital   The principal medical facility on Antigua is **Holberton Hospital,** on Hospital Rd. (☎ **268/462-0251**).

Language   The official language is English.

Safety   Antigua is generally safe, but that doesn't mean you should go wandering alone at night on the practically deserted streets of St. John's. Don't leave valuables unguarded on the beach.

Taxes & Service Charges   A departure tax of U.S.$20 is imposed, and an 8.5% government tax is added to all hotel bills. Most hotels also add a 10% service charge.

Telecommunications   Telephone calls can be made from hotels or from the office of **Cable & Wireless,** 42–44 St. Mary's St., in St. John's (☎ **268/462-0840**). Faxes and telegrams can also be sent from here.

Time   Antigua is on Atlantic standard time year-round, so it's 1 hour ahead of U.S. Eastern standard time. When daylight savings time takes over in the States, then Antigua's time is the same as in the eastern United States.

Water   Tap water is generally safe to drink here, but many visitors prefer to only drink bottled water.

Weather   The average year-round temperature ranges from 75° to 85°F (24°C to 29°C).

2   Accommodations You Can Afford

Antigua's hotels are among the best and most plentiful in the eastern Caribbean, but you have to hunt for bargains. Check summer closings, which often depend on the caprice of the owners, who may decide to shut down if business isn't good. Incidentally, air-conditioning, except in first-class hotels, isn't as common as some visitors think it should be. Chances are, your hotel will be on a beach. You can also rent an apartment or cottage if you want to cook for yourself.

Remember that an 8.5% government tax and 10% service charge are added to your hotel bill, which makes quite a difference in your final tab.

✪ **The Admiral's Inn.** English Harbour (P.O. Box 713), St. John's, Antigua, W.I. ☎ **800/223-5695** in the U.S. or 268/460-1027. Fax 268/460-1534. www.gray. maine/com/people/ admiralsinn. E-mail: admirals@candw.ag. 15 units. Winter $96–$108 single, $120–$150 double, $154–$166 triple, $250 suite for 2. Off-season $70–$80 single, $84–$100 double, $114–$122 triple, $150 suite. AE, MC, V. Closed Sept to mid-Oct. Take the road southeast from St. John's, following the signs to English Harbour.

Designed in 1785, the year Nelson sailed into the harbor as captain of the HMS *Boreas,* and completed in 1788, the building once here used to house dockyard services. Today this is the site of one of the most atmospheric inns on Antigua. In the heart of Nelson's Dockyard and loaded with West Indian charm, the hostelry is constructed of weathered brick brought from England as ships' ballast. It has a terrace opening onto a centuries-old garden. The ground floor, with brick walls, giant ship beams, and island-made furniture, has a tavern atmosphere, with decorative copper, boat lanterns, old oil paintings, and wrought-iron chandeliers.

There are three types of character-filled accommodations. The lowest rate is for smaller rooms on the top floor, which may get warm during the day in summer but are quiet, with dormer-window views over the yacht-filled harbor. The most expensive are some ground-floor rooms in a tiny brick building—on the site of a provisions warehouse for Nelson's troops—across the courtyard from the main structure. Each of these spacious rooms has a little patio and a garden entry as well as optional air-conditioning. The same superior rate applies to front rooms on the first floor of the main building with views of the lawn and harbor. A medium rate applies to the back rooms on this floor, all of which have air-conditioning. All rooms have ceiling fans and twin beds with good mattresses. The Inn's bathrooms are small and well maintained, with some shelf space, plus an array of medium-sized towels. The Joiner's

Loft is an upstairs suite adjacent to the annex rooms of the inn, with a large living room looking out over the water; there are two bedrooms, two baths, and a full kitchen.

For the inn's restaurant, see below. On Saturday night a steel band plays. Amenities include room service, laundry, baby-sitting, free transportation to two nearby beaches, snorkeling equipment, and Sunfish craft.

✪ **The Catamaran Hotel & Marina.** Falmouth Harbour (P.O. Box 958), St. John's, Antigua, W.I. ☎ **800/223-6510** in the U.S., 800/424-5500 in Canada, or 268/460-1339. 16 units. Winter $55–$110 single, $65–$150 double. Off-season $45–$75 single, $55–$115 double. Extra person $25; children under age 10 $15. AE, MC, V. Closed Sept.

This is a longtime favorite on Antigua. At Falmouth Harbour, a 2-mile drive from English Harbour, the Catamaran opens onto a palm-lined beach. When we first discovered the property years ago, a film crew had taken it over while making a movie about pirates of the West Indies. The management had to post a sign: TODAY'S "PIRATES" MUST WEAR BATHING SUITS ON THE BEACH. It's not as wild around here anymore, and peace and tranquillity prevail.

On the second floor are eight self-contained rooms, each with a four-poster bed, a good queen-size mattress, and a balcony opening onto the water. The most luxurious and spacious rental is called the Captain's Cabin. The standard rooms are quite small but well maintained and comfortable enough, and the efficiencies at water's edge can be rented by one person or two. Each efficiency has a balcony and a kitchen, plus a small bath with somewhat thin towels. Boaters will like the hotel's location at the 30-slip Catamaran Marina. You can purchase supplies at a nearby grocery store, or else enjoy the hotel's own reasonably priced meals at the hotel restaurant and bar. Sport-fishing and diving can be arranged, and the hotel offers Sunfish dinghies and rowboats.

Island Inn. Anchorage Rd. (P.O. Box 1218), St. John's, Antigua, W.I. ☎ **268/462-4065.** Fax 268/462-4066. 10 units. A/C TV. Winter $80 studio for 1; $90 studio for 2. Off-season $75 studio for 1; $80 studio for 2. Extra person $10; children 11 and under stay free in parents' room. AE, DISC, MC, V.

This white concrete building trimmed in green enjoys a well-kept garden setting only a 10-minute walk from the beach at Dickenson Bay. It features self-contained one-bedroom studios with king-size or double beds with good mattresses; they all have ceiling fans, individual balconies, or patios, plus fully equipped kitchenettes. Bathrooms are tiny and absolutely standard, but the plumbing is up-to-date. Locals often use the inn for wedding receptions. There's a swimming pool and a simple and modestly priced restaurant serving low-cost breakfasts and dinners. The food is only standard but generous in servings and most filling. Baby-sitting can be arranged, and room service is available.

Joe Mike's Hotel. Nevis St., St. John's, Antigua, W.I. ☎ **268/462-1142.** Fax 268/462-6056. 12 units. A/C TEL. Year-round $55 single or double. AE, MC, V.

Only a 10-minute drive from the nearest good beach, this clean, fairly comfortable, and cozy hotel is right in the heart of the capital. It's simplicity itself, but the welcome is warm and inviting. This peach-colored building with a porch around the second floor has standard rooms with furnishings that are a bit frayed and mattresses that have seen better days. Bathrooms are mere cubicles with rather thin towels, but at least the plumbing works. It's a comfortable and cozy nest if you don't plan to spend most of your time in your room. In super-expensive Antigua you book in here for value, not style. There's a TV set in the lobby.

Lashings Beach Café & Inn at Sandhaven. Sandhaven, Runaway, St. John's, Antigua, W.I. ☎ **268/462-4438.** Fax 268/462-4491. E-mail: lashings@candw.ag. Year-round $65 single, $95 double, $110 triple, $145 family room, plus 18.5% tax and service. MC, V.

Three miles north of St. John's, Richie Richardson, the island's cricketing legend, has teamed up with close friend, David Folb, an Englishman, to take over this small inn on the beach facing the sea. Located at Dry Hill, this small hotel is a friend of the budget traveler. It's the lazy life here in this secluded spot, and you can see hotel guests finding their favorite spot underneath the palms or ordering a cool rum punch at the beach bar. The interior of this two-story cinder-block structure is a bit spartan, with small guest rooms with concrete floors and ceiling fans. Beds are twins or doubles, but the mattresses were recently upgraded. Bathrooms offer thin towels, and patios or balconies contain plastic furnishings. Traditionally, Antigua's cheapest hotel has been known as the "barracks on the beach," but new management has made improvements. This might be a good bet for high-priced Antigua if you're not the fussy type and you plan to spend most of your time at the beach.

The on-site bar is an island hot spot and can get noisy at night. It's at beach side, as is the restaurant serving fresh lobster or a mug of chili, all at a reasonable price.

Murphy's Place. All Saints Rd. (P.O. Box 491), St. John's, Antigua, W.I. ☎ **268/461-1183.** 6 units. Winter $45 single, $55 double. Off-season $40 single, $50 double. Extra person $15. No credit cards.

A hurricane recently took the roof off this B&B. Everything, including the mattresses, had to be replaced. It should be fully recovered by the time you visit, but make sure to inquire before booking. Mrs. Murphy receives people from all over the world into her modern bungalow home, only 15 minutes from the airport, 10 minutes from a nearby beach, and a 10-minute walk into St. John's. She works hard to keep everything clean, although everything is admittedly simple in decor, with locally made mahogany furniture. You can cook your own meals or eat next door. Units contain a double bed and a small shower and toilet, plus a tiny kitchenette. Each unit has a ceiling fan, and some have TVs. If you're content with simple, modest accommodations, and you plan to spend most of your time on the beach instead of here, this should be a suitable stopover. It's clean and reasonably comfortable, and your wallet will love you!

3 Great Deals on Dining

Many independently operated restaurants serve West Indian food not readily available in the hotel dining rooms. Some dishes, especially the curries, show an East Indian influence, and Caribbean lobster is a specialty.

Although there are expensive items on the menus (see below), most dishes are at the lower end of the price scale. You get such big helpings that one plate of food will fortify most appetites for the day or night.

✪ Big Banana Holding Company. Redcliffe Quay, St. John's. ☎ **268/462-2621.** Main courses $8–$32. AE, DC, MC, V. Mon–Sat 8:30am–midnight. PIZZA.

Some of the best pizza in the eastern Caribbean is served here in what used to be slave quarters, now amid the most stylish shopping and dining emporiums in town, a few steps from the Heritage Quay Jetty. With its ceiling fans and laid-back atmosphere, you almost expect Sydney Greenstreet to stop in for a drink. The frothy libations, coconut or banana crush, are practically desserts. In addition to the zesty pizza, you can order overstuffed baked potatoes, fresh-fruit salad, or conch salad. On Thursday a reggae band entertains from 10pm to 1am.

Hemingway's. Jardine Court, St. Mary's St., St. John's. ☎ **268/462-2763.** EC$24–EC$60 ($8.90–$22.20). AE, MC, V. Mon–Sat 8:30am–11pm. CREOLE/INTERNATIONAL.

Set on the second floor of a building in the heart of St. John's and accented with intricate gingerbread painted in bright tropical colors, this charming cafe attracts a crowd of shoppers and sightseers. It's very busy when a cruise ship docks. From its upper verandas, you can see the landing dock and enjoy the sight of pedestrian traffic in the street below. Menu items include salads, sandwiches, burgers, sautéed fillets of fish, pastries, ice creams, and an array of brightly colored tropical drinks. This is a place for a convenient, casual meal and great value rather than for serious gourmet fare.

Joe Mike's Restaurant. In Joe Mike's Hotel, Nevis St. ☎ **268/462-1142.** Main courses $8–$10. AE, MC, V. Mon–Wed 7am–10pm, Thurs–Sat 7am–11pm. CARIBBEAN.

Popular with the locals, this restaurant is on the ground floor of Joe Mike's Hotel (see above). Hang out here if you'd like to connect with the bustling life of St. John's, at least during the day. People show up for the good food, affordable prices, and happy times. There are daily specials featuring local foods, including fresh fish. Try one of the homemade soups such as pepper pot, which seems to taste different every day depending on what went into it. Cream of pumpkin is a soothing delight too. A specialty of the chef is *ducana* and saltfish. (Ducana is a kind of dumpling made with sweet potatoes, pumpkin, and coconut.) Tuesday to Friday a one-man band entertains at lunchtime.

Pizzas in Paradise. Redcliffe St., Redcliffe Quay, St. John's. ☎ **268/462-2621.** Pizzas, pastas, and main courses $8–$30. AE, DC, MC, V. Mon–Sat 7:30am–"until." PIZZA/CARIBBEAN.

Young islanders, along with cruise-ship passengers and others, gravitate to this spot, which offers excellent pizzas and a satisfying assortment of seafood salads, fruit platters, pastas, and even grilled flying fish sandwiches. All types of subs are also on the menu. The most expensive item on the menu is a mammoth seafood pizza, and it's delectable. Situated in a historic building, this restaurant offers both indoor and outdoor dining. The deck has picnic tables with umbrellas overlooking the town's shops. A large selection of CDs provides background music except on Thursday night, when there's live entertainment.

Redcliffe Tavern. Redcliffe Quay. ☎ **268/461-4557.** Reservations recommended. Main courses $10–$22; lunch from $6.90. AE, DISC, MC, V. Mon–Sat 8am–11pm. CARIBBEAN/INTERNATIONAL.

Owned by Ian Fraser, this waterside restaurant offers an unusual view of some of Antigua's artifacts of yesteryear, including machines used to pump water during the island's plantation era, the combination of which seems to enhance what was built by the British in the 18th century as a warehouse. Don't expect a quiet and isolated romantic evening here—the place is usually crowded. Menu items include plantain-stuffed chicken breasts in a tomato or basil sauce, Brie wrapped in phyllo dough then served in a tomato-raspberry vinaigrette, and steaks with mushrooms or peppercorn sauce. Try the Normandy-style apple tart for dessert.

Russell's. Fort James. ☎ **268/462-5479.** Reservations recommended. Lunch main courses $4–$22; dinner main courses $12–$22. MC, V. Daily noon–3pm and 6–11pm. Hours vary according to the owner's whims during low season. INTERNATIONAL.

Set within a dark-stained wooden house, on a hillside about 20 feet above sea level directly north of St. John's, this restaurant is best known for its bar (which sometimes

features live music) and the potent drinks that sometimes turn this place into a raucous party. The most appealing time to visit is during the cocktail hour, especially
when live music is playing. That's usually every Wednesday to Saturday between 7 and
10pm, although hours and days vary widely according to the availability of local
artists. Rum-based drinks, especially if they're pink and flavored with guava, paw-paw,
and perhaps a touch of cinnamon, are especially popular. Menu items range from the
simple and unpretentious (burgers, salads, and hot dogs) to more ambitious platters
such as grilled wahoo or grouper with hollandaise or butter sauce, Creole-style
snapper, Caribbean lobster, and shrimp.

WORTH A SPLURGE

The Admiral's Inn. In Nelson's Dockyard, English Harbour. ☎ **268/460-1027.** Reserva-
tions recommended, especially for dinner in high season. Main courses $20–$27. AE, MC, V.
Daily 7:30–10am, noon–2:30pm and 7–9:30pm. Closed Sept to mid-Oct. AMERICAN/
CREOLE.

This historic inn (see "Accommodations You Can Afford," above) serves lobster,
seafood, and steaks in a 17th-century setting. The favorite appetizer is pumpkin soup,
which is followed by a choice of four or five main courses daily—perhaps local red
snapper, grilled steak, or lobster. Sometimes the atmosphere is more exciting than the
cuisine, but it is generally reliable and rather good, standard fare. Before dinner, have
a drink in the bar, where you can read the names of sailors carved in wood more than
a century ago. The service is agreeable, and the setting is heavy on atmosphere.

AN AMAZING LUNCH BUFFET

Miller's By the Sea. Fort James. ☎ **268/462-9414.** Lunch main courses EC$40–EC$45
($14.80–$16.65); West Indian lunch buffet EC$35 ($12.95); dinner main courses
EC$50–EC$65 ($18.50–$24.05). AE, DC, MC, V. Daily 7am–2am. CARIBBEAN.

We love this unpretentious place for the live music—usually steel bands—that perform during most lunches and dinners, and the rum punches that everyone seems to
order regardless of the time of day. Priced at EC$8 ($2.95) each, they keep the good
times rolling. This low-slung patio and terrace, mostly open to the breezes, is set a few
steps from the sands of the Fort James Beach, directly north of St. James's. The menu
provides classic West Indian dishes, including funghi, salt fish, salt pork, Creole-style
conch, stewed wahoo, snapper prepared any way you want, and a traditional starch
product, *ducana,* that's concocted from a mixture of coconut, potatoes, and pumpkins
wrapped in a banana leaf and boiled. A medley of most of these appears within the
daily lunch buffet, which is arguably the island's best food value. More international
in their appeal are grilled steaks and Caribbean spiny lobsters.

WHEN YOUR SWEET TOOTH CALLS

At Jolly Harbour, south of St. John's, drop in at the **M&B's Swiss and Sweet,** Jolly
Harbour (☎ **268/462-7716**), for some of the best baked treats on the island, an array
of cakes, pastries, and cookies. If you're going on a picnic, you can buy freshly baked
bread here, along with sandwiches and patties. It's even open on Sunday.

Another choice, **Philton's Bakery Café,** at Gambles Medical Centre, Gambles
(☎ **268/462-9447**), is a European-style bakery that's one of the best places on the
island for afternoon tea. You can relax in the trade winds and enjoy a cup of freshly
brewed espresso while sampling the cafe's locally celebrated chocolate buttered rum
cake. It's worth walking a mile in the hot sun for a taste of this luscious treat. Breakfast and lunches are also served here.

Antigua's Best Beach Bar

As you whiz along the winding road, you spot the initials of ✪ **O.J.,** Crab Hill
(☎ **268/460-0184**), and you think for a moment that O.J. Simpson is hiding out in
Antigua. Not so. O.J. stands for Oliver Joseph, who has returned to his childhood
home after a stint as what he calls a "Toronto suit." His bar lies overlooking the sea
on a half-acre between the deluxe Curtain Bluff and Jolly Harbour, both south of St.
John's along the coastal road. This is the classic cliché of a Caribbean beach bar, with
sea shells, tablecloths in flamboyant prints, plus sea fans and coral from the reefs. Here
in a laid-back atmosphere, you can sample Wadadli beer (the local brew) or ask for
one of the dark Cavalier rums so beloved by Antiguans. The piña coladas made from
home-grown plantains, guava, coconuts, and mangos are the island's best. O.J. even
grows his own herbs used in his chicken, fresh fish, and lobster dishes. If you want to
stay for a big lunch it'll cost around $12 and rarely more than $20 for dinner. The big
resort hotels don't have this kind of atmosphere.

PIZZA, BARBECUE & LUNCH ON THE RUN

Also at Jolly Harbour, you can visit **Al Porto,** Jolly Harbour (☎ **268/462-7695**), for
a selection of some of the best pizzas on the island. If you're frequenting one of the
beaches in the area, this makes an ideal stopover for a fast lunch. They also serve
freshly caught seafood when available and also some tasty pasta dishes. Everything is
offered in a laid-back alfresco setting.

Still at Jolly Harbour, **The Dog Watch Tavern Bar & Grill,** at the Jolly Harbour
Beach Resort (☎ **268/462-6550**), is one of the most popular pub-style bars on the
island, offering great barbecue, drinks, and some mighty fine music most of the time.
It's good for a quick bite or ideal as a rendezvous point to meet a friend over a drink.

Facing Nelson's Dockyard, you can call at **Catherine's Café,** Antigua Slipway
(☎ **268/460-5050**) for lunch on the run. It's cheap and good; light fare, even breakfast, is served on a lovely waterfront terrace facing the historical dockyard.

4 Hitting the Beaches

ON THE CARIBBEAN SIDE

There's a lovely beach of white sand and calm waters at **Pigeon Point** at Falmouth
Harbour, about a 4-minute drive from English Harbour. Because English Harbour is
the major tourist attraction on the island, and the beach is well known, it is likely to
be a bit crowded, especially on days when a cruise ship is in port. The beach is ideal
for snorkelers and swimmers of most ages and abilities.

✪ **Dickenson Bay** in the northwest, directly north of St. John's, has long been one of
the island's finest beaches, with its wide strip of powder-soft sand and blissfully calm
waters. Because this beach is considered relatively safe for families, it often attracts those
with small children in tow. The center point here is the Halcyon Cove Hotel, where water
sports equipment can be rented and you can patronize its drinking or eating facilities.
There are also casual beach bars and beach-bordering eateries here as well. This beach's
shimmering turquoise waters make it especially alluring.

On the north side of Dickenson Bay there are more secluded beaches and some ideal
snorkeling areas along this fan-shaped northern crown of Antigua. Sometimes locals along
the beach will take you to one of the uninhabited offshore islets for a fee—usually to pint-
sized **Prickly Pear Island,** which is enveloped by beautiful coral gardens. Glass-bottom

excursions are often organized to **Paradise Reef,** a mile-long coral garden of stunning beauty lying north of Dickenson Bay. This is also one of the best spots on the island for snorkeling.

If you want to escape from everybody, you can flee to **Johnson's Point,** which is sign-posted between the hamlets of Johnson's Point and Urlings at the very southwestern tip of Antigua below Jolly Harbour. It opens onto the tranquil Caribbean Sea. Don't expect much in the way of facilities. What you'll get instead is a beach of sand so white it appears bleached. The waters here are clear and calm and populated with schools of rainbow-hued tropical fish.

Near Johnson's Point on the southwest coast is idyllic ✪ **Turner's Beach,** almost invari-ably cooled by trade winds, which makes it one of the best places to go for a tan in the tropical sun. It is a beach of fine white sand with gin-clear waters. If the weather is fine and the skies clear (it usually is), you'll have a view of the volcanic island of Montserrat on the horizon.

If you continue directly east of Urlings heading to the hamlet of "Old Road," you'll reach ✪ **Carlisle Bay,** site of one of the island's most celebrated beaches. As one beach buff said, "Snow White must have designed these sands." Against a backdrop of coconut groves, two long beaches are found at the spot where Curtain Bluff, the island's most deluxe hotel, sits, standing on a bluff overlooking this peninsula. It is at this point that the calm Caribbean Sea meets the more turbulent Atlantic. The waters are so blue at times they almost look as if they've had a dye job.

Another popular beach, **Pidgeon Beach,** lies a 5-minute drive from English Harbour on the east coast of Antigua, fronting the Atlantic. This is a favorite spot for locals as well as for visitors to English Harbour and Nelson's Dockyard. The snorkeling is especially good here, but you must bring your own mask and fins as you can't rent them here.

Directly north of Johnson's Point and south of Jolly Harbour in the southwestern part of Antigua is **Driftwood Beach.** With its white sands and calm, clear waters, this beach is quite delightful. However, it is close to all the villas in the rental pool at Jolly Harbour Beach Resort Marina, and may be overcrowded with vacationing hordes.

In the same vicinity is **Darkwood Beach,** lying a 5-minute drive south of Jolly Harbour Marina and the Jolly Harbour Golf Club. Here the shimmering waters are almost crystal blue. The snorkeling is great, and you can generally count on the gentle trade winds for your air-conditioning. Since this is located in a crowded tourist zone, it also is likely to be crowded, almost impossibly so when cruise ships are in port.

Continuing north toward St. John's but cutting west at the turnoff for Five Islands, you'll reach the four secluded **Hawksbill Beaches** on the Five Islands peninsula. The beaches here are filled with white sands with coral reefs ideal for snorkeling. One reader wrote, "If you're not bedazzled by the color of the water from the beach, take off your glasses, give them a good cleaning, and take another look at the incredible array of blues and greens." One of the beaches is for sunbathing and swimming in the buff. The Five Islands Penin-sula is the site of major hotel developments, so, even though it's secluded, the beaches might also be crowded.

ON THE ATLANTIC SIDE

So far we've been on the Caribbean or western side of Antigua, but if you'd like to escape to the eastern side, fronting the Atlantic, you can head for ✪ **Half Moon Bay,** which stretches for nearly a mile of white sand. It is perhaps the most beautiful beach on Antigua. Since it is on the Atlantic side, the surf is likely to be rough at times, although it draws a never-ending stream of snorkelers and windsurfers. Half Moon is now a public park and is an ideal choice for a family outing, as it is completely protected by its reef. The location is a 5-minute drive from Freetown village on the southeast coast. Because of its

---

❓ Did You Know?

Sometimes called the "Black Pineapple," Antigua Black is grown almost exclusively in Antigua. It is acclaimed as the sweetest pineapple in the island. If you don't eat it directly, you can sample its luscious juice in a tropical fruit punch. The pineapple has a much sweeter nectar than those grown in Hawaii and South America.

---

fine pink sand, evocative of Bermuda, this has long been a favorite of ours with its tradewinds and active surf. The Half Moon Bay lies to the east of English Harbour in the vicinity of Mill Reef.

On the far eastern coast of Antigua, directly north of Half Moon Bay and to the east of the little town of Willikies, is **Long Bay,** site of Long Bay Hotel and the Pineapple Beach Club. Patrons of either property are likely to be the major beachbums on this sandy strip. Unlike the beaches previewed above, the stunning coral here lie in water so shallow that you can actually walk to the reefs, although you're not supposed to harm them in any way.

In the same vicinity, **Pineapple Beach** lies a 5-minute drive from the village of Willikies heading east. It opens onto Long Bay and the west coast (Atlantic side) of Antigua. This is a fine white-sand beach, with crystal blue waters that make it ideal for snorkeling. Most beach buffs come here just to relax in the sun on near-perfect sands.

5 Sports & Outdoor Pursuits

Sports such as scuba diving and fishing are very expensive in the Caribbean, often priced outside the realm of the average budget traveler's wallet. Proceed cautiously when booking a program with an outfitter, and always agree upon the cost in advance.

A DAY CRUISE   All major hotel desks can book a day cruise on the 108-foot "pirate ship," the *Jolly Roger,* Redcliffe Quay (☎ 268/462-2064). For $55 to $60 for adults and $30 for children, you're taken sightseeing on a fun-filled day, with drinks and barbecued steak, chicken, or lobster. The *Jolly Roger* is the largest sailing ship in Antiguan waters. Lunch is combined with a snorkeling trip, and there's dancing on the poop deck. Members of the crew teach passengers how to dance calypso. There are daily cruises, lasting 5½ hours, from 9:30am to 3pm. There's also a Saturday night dinner cruise for $40, leaving Heritage Quay in St. John's at 7pm, returning at 11pm. In spite of the high price, many budget travelers book this trip.

GOLF   Antigua doesn't have the golfing facilities of some of the other islands, but its premier course is good. The 18-hole, par-69 **Cedar Valley Golf Club,** Friar's Hill Road (☎ 268/462-0161), is 3 miles east of St. John's, near the airport. The island's largest, with panoramic views of Antigua's northern coast, it was designed by the late Richard Aldridge to fit the contours of the area. Daily greens fees are $35 for 18 holes. Cart fees are $30 for 18 holes, with club rentals going for $10.

SCUBA DIVING, SNORKELING & OTHER WATER SPORTS   Scuba diving is best arranged through **Dive Antigua,** at the Rex Halcyon Cove, Dickenson Bay (☎ 268/462-3483), Antigua's most experienced dive operation. A resort course is offered for $88, with a two-tank dive costing $73. A five-dive package goes for $295, with open-water certification costing $492. All prices include equipment.

Long Bay Hotel, on the northeastern coast of the island at Long Bay (☎ 268/463-2005), is a good location for various water sports: swimming, sailing, waterskiing, and windsurfing. The hotel also has complete scuba facilities. Both beginning snorkelers and all divers are welcomed. You're taken on snorkeling trips by boat to Green Island and Great Bird Island (minimum of four). The shallow side of the double reef across Long Bay is ideal for the novice, and the whole area on the northeastern tip has many reefs of varying depths. A one-afternoon resort course costs $85.

TENNIS   Tennis buffs will find courts at most of the major hotels, and some are lit for night games. If your hotel doesn't have a court, you can find them available at the **Royal Antiguan Resort,** Deep Bay (☎ 268/462-3733), which have eight courts each. If you're not a guest, you'll have to book a court and pay charges that vary from hotel to hotel. Guests of a hotel usually play free. You might also try the **Temo Sports Complex** at Falmouth Bay (☎ 268/463-1781), which offers two floodlit tennis courts.

WINDSURFING   Located at the Lord Nelson Beach Hotel, on Dutchman's Bay, **Windsurfing Antigua** (☎ 268/462-9463) offers windsurfing for the absolute beginner, the intermediate sailor, and the hard-core windsurfer. The outlet guarantees to get beginners to enjoy the sport after a 2-hour introductory lesson for $60. A 1-hour rental costs $20, a half-day $50.

6 Seeing the Sights

IN ST. JOHN'S

In the southern part of St. John's, the **market** is colorful and interesting, especially on Saturday morning from 8am to noon. Vendors busy selling their fruits and vegetables bargain and gossip. The semi–open-air market lies at the lower end of Market Street.

St. John's Cathedral, the Anglican cathedral between Long Street and Newgate Street at Church Lane (☎ 268/461-0082), has had a disastrous history. Originally built in 1683, it was replaced by a stone building in 1745. That was destroyed by an earthquake in 1843. The present pitch-pine interior dates from 1847. The interior was being restored when, in 1973, the structure was badly damaged by another earthquake. The towers and the southern section have been restored.

You can also visit the **Museum of Antigua & Barbuda,** at Market and Church streets (☎ 268/462-1469), which offers exhibits ranging from its prehistoric days up to its independence from Britain in 1981. The most intriguing exhibit is a full-size replica of an Arawak house, the earliest settlers. There are also models of the once-flourishing sugar plantations, along with paintings and historical prints. The museum has been installed in a former courthouse, built in 1750, and it's open Monday to Friday 8:30am to 4pm and Saturday 10am to 1pm, charging no admission.

AROUND THE ISLAND

After leaving St. John's, most visitors head southeast for 11 miles to ✪ **Nelson's Dockyard National Park** (☎ 268/460-1379), one of the biggest attractions of the eastern Caribbean. The park's centerpiece is the restored Georgian naval dockyard, which was used by Admirals Nelson, Rodney, and Hood, and was the home of the British fleet during the Napoleonic Wars. From 1784, Nelson was the commander of the British navy in the Leeward Islands, and he made his headquarters at English Harbour. English ships used the harbor as a refuge from hurricanes as early as 1671.

The era of privateers, pirates, and great sea battles in the 18th century is recaptured in the dockyard's museum. Restored by the Friends of English Harbour, the dockyard is a sort of Caribbean Williamsburg. Its colonial naval buildings stand as they did when Nelson was here (1784 to 1787). However, Nelson never lived at **Admiral House** (☎ **268/463-1379**)—it was built in 1855. The house has been turned into a museum of nautical memorabilia. Displayed are Nelson's telescope and tea caddy, along with maps, prints, and silver trophies. Hours are daily 8am to 6pm, with an admission charge of $2.

The **park** itself is worth exploring. It's filled with sandy beaches and tropical vegetation, including various species of cactus and mangroves. The latter provides shelter for a migrating colony of African cattle egrets. The park contains archaeological sites dating from well before the time of Christ. Nature trails lead you through the vegetation with views of the coastal scenery. **Tours** of the dockyard are given, lasting 15 to 20 minutes; nature walks along the trails can last anywhere from 30 minutes to 5 hours. The entrance fee is $5 for a tour of the dockyard, although the nature trail costs an additional $2.50. Children 12 and under are admitted free. The dockyard and its museum are open daily 9am to 5pm.

Another major attraction is the **Dow's Hill Interpretation Center** (☎ **268/460-2777**), just 2½ miles from the dockyard. The only one of its kind in the Caribbean, it offers multimedia presentations that cover six periods of the island's history, including the era of Amerindian hunters, the era of the British military, and the struggles connected with slavery. A belvedere opens onto a panoramic view of the park. Admission to the center, including the multimedia show, is EC$15 ($5.55). The center is open daily 9am to 5pm.

On a low hill overlooking Nelson's Dockyard, **Clarence House** (☎ **268/463-1026**) was built by English stonemasons to accommodate Prince William Henry, later known as the Duke of Clarence, and even later as William IV. The future king stayed here when he was in command of the *Pegasus* in 1787. At present it's the country home of the governor of Antigua and Barbuda and is open to visitors when His Excellency is not in residence. A caretaker will show you through (it's customary to tip, of course), and you'll see many pieces of furniture on loan from the National Trust. Princess Margaret and Lord Snowdon stayed here on their honeymoon.

On the way back, take ✪ **Fig Tree Drive,** a 20-some-mile circular drive across the main mountain range. It passes through lush tropical hills and fishing villages along the southern coast. You can pick up the road just outside Liberta, north of Falmouth. Winding through a rain forest, it passes thatched villages. Every hamlet has a church and lots of goats and children running about. But don't expect fig trees—*fig* is an Antiguan name for bananas.

About half a mile before reaching St. John's you come to **Fort James,** begun in 1704 as a main lookout post for the port and named after James II.

Parham Church, overlooking Parham Town, was erected in 1840 in the Italian style. Richly adorned with stucco work, it was damaged by an earthquake in 1843. Much of the ceiling was destroyed and very little of the stucco work remains, but the octagonal structure is still worth a visit.

The **Potworks Dam,** holding back the largest artificial lake on Antigua, is surrounded by an area of great natural beauty. The dam has a capacity of a billion gallons of water and provides protection for Antigua in case of a drought.

Betty's Hope, just outside the village of Pares (☎ **268/462-1469**), lies on the route leading east to Long Bay. Antigua's first sugar plantation dates from 1650, and you can tour free Tuesday to Saturday 10am to 4pm. Exhibits trace the sugar era in the visitor's center, and you can also tour two windmills. Plans call for the excavation of the adjacent village, which would be the first dig of a slave village ever in the Caribbean.

Indian Town National Park is at a northeastern point on the island. Over the centuries Atlantic breakers have lashed the rocks and carved a natural bridge known as Devil's Bridge. It's surrounded by numerous blowholes spouting surf.

Cheap Thrills: What to See & Do for Free (Well, Almost) on Antigua

- **Enjoy Beaches, Beaches & More Beaches.** All of Antigua's beaches are open to the public, and they're free. The only time you'll pay is when you want to buy something—perhaps some handcrafts being hawked right on the beach, even a cold beer, and most definitely water sports rentals which can be expensive (so be duly warned). If a cruise ship docks, beaches tend to be crowded on the western or Caribbean side, so head for the Atlantic or eastern side. The waters aren't as tranquil here, but you'll escape the hordes.

- **Explore Indian Town National Park.** An environmentally protected area, Indian Town Point lies at the tip of a deep cove, Indian Town Creek. The area of natural beauty is found at Long Bay, just west of Indian Town Creek at the eastern side of Antigua, fronting the Atlantic. Birders flock here to see some 36 different species. Along the shore a cove called the Devil's Bridge has been created by the ocean pounding against the cliffs. It took eons of time to hollow out this natural bridge across the crashing surf. The water throws up a neat display of foam from time to time. Around Devil's Bridge there is a large, meadowy headland that would make an ideal spot for a picnic. At several blowholes, sprays of water surge violently through vents in the rocky coast. It's a dramatic sight—and it's free. Arm yourself with directions and a good map before starting out. The main highway ends at Long Bay, but several trails lead to the coastline, ideal for hikes. Long Bay is also ideal for snorkeling.

- **Drive Along Fig Tree Drive.** There's no better drive on Antigua, even though the road is bumpy and potholed. It's beautiful, nonetheless, even though it has no fig trees. In Antigua, fig tree is the name for banana (don't ask why). The road is unmarked—in fact, there are almost no road signs on Antigua. But the drive begins at the little coral-built Catholic church just outside the hamlet of Liberta, north of Falmouth. Once here, it's easy to spot. Head southwest going through the island's only rain forest and its hilliest section. The road rises and falls steeply. Of course, you'll see plenty of bananas along with coconut groves and mango trees—a lush tropical setting. The drive descends to the village of Old Road and the Curtain Bluff area.

- **Take in View from Shirley Heights.** The view from here on the southern rim of Antigua is arguably the most famous in the Caribbean. The road here lies

Megaliths, at Greencastle Hill, reached by a long climb, are said to have been set up by human hands for the worship of a sun god and a moon goddess. Some experts believe, however, that the arrangement is an unusual geological formation, a volcanic rockfall.

Antigua Rum Distillery, at Rat Island (☎ **268/462-1072**), turns out fine Cavalier rum. Check at the tourist office about arranging a visit. Established in 1932, the plant is next to Deep Water Harbour.

7 Shopping

Most of the shops are clustered on St. Mary's Street or High Street in St. John's. Some shops are open Monday to Saturday 8:30am to noon and 1 to 4pm, but this rule varies to the east side of English Harbour, all named for General Thomas Shirley, the governor of the British Leeward Islands from 1781 to 1791. While you take in the view you are likely to be entertained by a Rastafarian steel band (who'd like a tip, of course). On the way here, you'll pass signs of former British colonialism—barracks, fortifications, powder magazines, all in picturesque ruins now, remains of a bygone era. A restaurant on the bluff provides light refreshments after you take in that stunning view.

- **Forage in a Fortress.** Once in the 1700s the coastline of the island was ringed with British forts, all in ruins today. Fort buffs can enjoy rummaging through the ruins. Even if there isn't much left to see, the views from these former military strongholds are among the most panoramic in the Caribbean—and you can visit them for free. You can begin at St. John's harbor (the capital), which was once guarded by Fort Barrington on the south and Fort James on the north. Later you can head down to Fort James Bay where you'll find a couple of bars right on the sand, including Russell's Beach Bar, an ideal place to unwind with a beer on Sunday afternoon when it's most active. In the south near English Harbour check out the view from Shirley Heights (see above).

- **Take a Bus to the Market.** If you're staying outside St. John's (highly likely), take a local bus into the city on market day on Saturday morning. It's best between 8am and noon. Hop on the bus and be prepared for anything. Many of the locals with stuff to sell get right on the bus with what they'll be peddling in town at the market. Often their wares are live—chickens, birds, whatever. Sometimes it's luscious fruit or the island's most beautiful flowers, and certainly plenty of handcrafts. Locals will immediately sense you're a foreigner and start bargaining with you before you even get to the market.

- **Shop the Quays.** Even if you don't buy anything, the thrill is in the adventure of shopping two of the Caribbean's most colorful quays, Heritage Quay or Redcliffe Quay, both in St. John's. Sometimes live musicians entertain you as you browse. Heritage Quay sells a little bit of everything—sexy lingerie, T-shirts galore, designer luggage, you name it. At Redcliffe, which was transformed from old dockside warehouses, you can wander and browse among Antiguan handcrafts and clothing, see the latest French fashions, purchase jewelry and pottery, and even have a pizza.

greatly from store to store—Antiguan shopkeepers are an independent lot. Many of them close at noon on Thursday.

There are many duty-free items for sale, including English woolens and linens, and you can also purchase several specialized items made on Antigua, such as original pottery, local straw work, Antiguan rum, and silk-screened, hand-printed local designs on fabrics, as well as mammy bags, floppy foldable hats, and shell curios.

If you want an island-made bead necklace, don't bother to go shopping; just lie on the beach, anywhere, and some "bead lady" will find you.

If you're in St. John's on a Saturday morning, you can attend the **fruit and vegetable market** at the lower end of Market Street. Locally made handcrafts are also offered for sale. And the incredibly sweet and juicy Antiguan black pineapple is worth the trip into town alone.

Begin your bargain shopping jaunt at St. John's at **Redcliffe Quay** on the waterfront at the southern edge of town. Set around landscaped courtyards, all tree-shaded, you'll find nearly three dozen boutiques, many offering specialty items sold nowhere else. Redcliffe Quay was a slave-trading quarter, but after the abolition of slavery the quay was filled with grog shops and merchants selling various wares. Now it has been redeveloped and contains interesting shops in former warehouses, all open Monday to Saturday. Our favorite shop here is called **A Thousand Flowers,** Redcliffe Quay (☎ 268/462-4264), which sells Indonesian batiks, crafted on the island into sundresses, knock-'em-dead shirts, sarongs, and rompers. Various accessories such as necklaces and earrings are also sold. Many of the garments are one-size-fits-all.

Also at Redcliffe Quay, check out the reasonably priced merchandise in **The Pottery Shop** (☎ 268/462-5503), the best place to shop for pottery made on-island, a selection of vases, mugs, personalized plaques, plates, and more. Kids adore **The Toy Shop** (☎ 268/462-0141), with its British toys plus beach games, snorkels, baskets, island crafts, and much more. A unique collection of items from Egypt is sold at **Isis** (☎ 268/461-2066), including silver jewelry, leather, finely woven cotton, and handcrafts from the Nile. If you always like to purchase the local spirits of any island you visit, head for **The Rum Shoppe** (☎ 268/460-6355), which has a full range of the local brew, Antigua Rum Apparel.

The other major shopping complex is **Heritage Quay** at the foot of St. Mary's Street. It's crammed with boutiques, including **Benjies Photo Centre** (☎ 268/462-3619), a Kodak distributor and photofinisher, selling film and brand-name cameras. **Fashiondock** (☎ 268/462-9672) is known for its duty-free prices on Gianni Versace jeans and accessories, plus other Italian styles. **Sunseakers** (☎ 268/462-4523) carries the largest collection of duty-free swimwear in the Caribbean, including Jantzen and Gottex.

Other specialty stores worth seeking out include **Caribelle Batik,** St. Mary's St. (☎ 268/462-2972), an outlet for the Romney Manor workshop on St. Kitts. The Caribelle label consists of batik and tie-dye items such as beach wraps, scarves, and a range of casual wear for women and men. Prices are reasonable. On the same street, **Specialty Shoppe,** St. Mary's St. (☎ 268/462-1198), has a wide array of collectible gifts, including cosmetics, hand carvings from Antigua, and even imported china.

If you're in the market for fashion, check out the offerings of **Rain Boutique,** Lower St. Mary's (☎ 268/462-0118), which has both casual and formal ware, plus a well-chosen collection of hats, scarves, shoes, jewelry, and handbags.

ELSEWHERE ON THE ISLAND

At Falmouth Harbour, **Seahorse Studios, Art Gallery & Gift Shop** (☎ 268/460-1417) specializes in original art and limited edition prints, with lots of seascape renditions. They also carry the pottery of Nancy Nicholson, considered the island's best craftsperson. Batiks, T-shirts, and much more is also sold.

We've saved the best for last. Head for **Harmony Hall,** in Brown's Bay Mill, near Freetown (☎ 268/460-4120), following the signs along the road to Freetown and Half Moon Bay. This old plantation house and sugar mill overlooking Nonsuch Bay dates back to 1843. Much restored, it's ideal for a luncheon stopover or a shopping expedition. It displays an excellent selection of Caribbean arts and crafts. Lunch is served daily from noon to 4pm, featuring Green Island lobster, flying fish, and other specialties. Sunday is barbecue day.

8 Antigua After Dark

Most nightlife revolves around the hotels, unless you want to roam Antigua at night looking for that hot local club. If you're going out for the night, make arrangements to have a taxi pick you up; otherwise, you could be stranded in the wild somewhere. Regrettably, this can be expensive, so make sure you ask your hotel what taxi fare is likely to cost before you set out. Antigua has some of the best steel bands in the Caribbean.

CASINOS

The **Royal Casino,** in the Royal Antiguan Hotel, Deep Bay (☎ **268/462-3733**), has games including blackjack, baccarat, roulette, craps, and slot machines. It's open daily from 6pm until around 2 or 3am, and there's no cover. Other casino action can be found at the **St. James's Club** at Mamora Bay (☎ **268/463-1113**), which has the island's most flamboyant gambling palace, and at **King's Casino** on Heritage Quay (☎ **268/463-1727**). The latter is the only casino in the capital of St. John's itself.

BARS & LOCAL HANGOUTS

Steel bands, limbo dancers, calypso singers, folkloric groups—there's always something going on every night on Antigua. You'd better check with your hotel to find out where the heat is on any given night. The following are usually reliable hot spots:

Ribbit Night Club, in Donovans, Green Bay (☎ **268/462-7996**), is the nicest club on Antigua and attracts mostly locals, ranging from the prime minister to young people who come here to dance. Overlooking Deep Water Harbour and St. John's, it's known for its hot music and dancing 'til the wee hours. You can count on dancing on Friday and Saturday nights, and sometimes special events are staged on Thursday and Sunday as well. Along with international music, you can hear reggae and some of the best steel bands in the Caribbean. There's a EC$10 ($3.70) cover charge on Friday, EC$20 ($7.40) Saturday.

If you're bar-hopping around the island, stop in at the **Bay House,** Tradewinds Hotel, Marble Hill (☎ **268/462-1223**), which has the best mix of both straight and gay singles on the island, mainly because the hotel is always inhabited by British Airways flight attendants. Live reggae is often presented on Wednesday night at **Colombo's** at the Galleon Beach Club in English Harbour (☎ **268/460-1452**).

Fun right on the beach? Try **Millers by the Sea** at Runaway Beach (☎ **268/462-9414**). Live nightly entertainment is presented, and its happy hour, which spills over onto the sands, is the best in town.

The **Crazy Horse Saloon** at Redcliffe Quay (☎ **268/462-7936**) is actually a country-western hangout; if you had doubts, the Wild West memorabilia will convince you. Burgers, jerk pork, lobster (in at least 15 different ways), and Caribbean smoked fish round out the menu, along with seafood and grilled steaks. But Friday is party night, with a live dance band, and Sunday is devoted to a jazz brunch and karaoke.

At English Harbour, action centers around the **Admiral's Inn** (☎ **268/460-1027**), a barefoot-friendly place. In the true British style, a game of darts is always possible. On Thursday and Saturday nights live music is presented, most often a 14-piece steel band of local boys or else a 5-piece string and flute combo. Try one of Norman's daiquiris—the best on the island, and listen to this bartender tell you tall tales about famous guests he's served in the past (everybody from Richard Burton to Prince Charles).

4

Aruba

Honeymooners, sun worshipers, snorkelers, sailors, and weekend gamblers find that the Dutch island of Aruba suits their needs just fine. Forget lush vegetation here—that's impossible with only 17 inches of rainfall annually. Aruba is dry and sunny almost year-round, with clean, exhilarating air like that found in the desert of Palm Springs, California. Along with the very low humidity, trade winds keep the island from becoming uncomfortably hot.

Its own Palm Beach, one of the best in the world, draws tourists in droves, as do its glittering casinos. As you lie back along the 7-mile stretch of white-sand beach, enjoying an 82°F (28°C) daytime temperature, you're not harassed by the locals peddling wares you don't want. There's almost no racial tension and, chances are, you won't get mugged.

Aruba is not the best island for vacationers on a budget. In winter, the large resort hotels and time-share units are expensive; rates begin at around $150 a night. And Aruba does not have the number of inexpensive guest houses or small inns that many other islands do. However, there are numerous package deals, which a good travel agent can help you find (see "Package Deals" in chapter 2). Restaurant tabs can also be high, since all food has to be imported onto desert-dry Aruba, but we've found a few affordable choices for you.

Aruba stands outside the hurricane path. Its coastline on the leeward side is smooth and serene, with sandy beaches; but on the eastern coast, the windward side, the look is rugged and wild, typical of the windswept Atlantic.

1 Essentials

VISITOR INFORMATION

Before leaving home, you can contact the **Aruba Tourism Authority** at the following locations: 1000 Harbor Blvd., Weekhawken, NJ (☎ **201/330-0800;** fax 201/330-8757; e-mail: newjersey@toaruba. com); One Financial Plaza, Suite 136, Fort Lauderdale, FL 33394 (☎ **954/767-6477;** fax 954/767-0432; e-mail: ata.florida@toaruba. com); 199 14th St., N.E., Suite 2008, Atlanta, GA 39309 (☎ **404/ 892-7822;** fax 404/873-2193; e-mail: ata.atlanta@ toaruba.com); 401 Wilmette Ave., Westmont, IL 60559 (☎ **603/663-1363;** fax 630/ 663-1362; e-mail: ata.chicago@ toaruba.com); 1207 North Freeway, Suite 138, Houston, TX 77060 (☎ **281/872-7822;** fax 281/

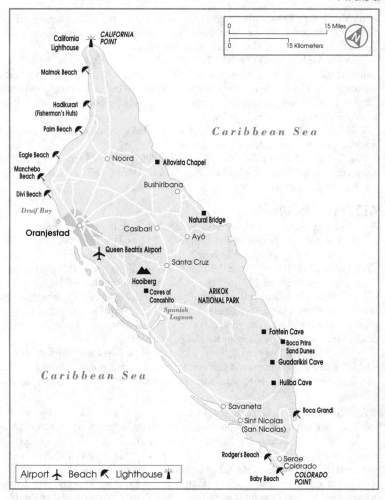

872-7872; e-mail: ata.houston@ toaruba.com); and 86 Bloor St. West, Suite 204, Toronto, Canada M5S 1M5 (☎ **416/975-1950;** fax 416/975-1947; e-mail: ata.canada@toaruba.com).

Once on the island, for information go to the **Aruba Tourism Authority** at L. G. Smith Blvd. 172, Oranjestad (☎ **297/8-23777;** www.aruba.com).

GETTING THERE

On **American Airlines** (☎ **800/433-7300**), Aruba-bound passengers can catch a daily nonstop 4½-hour flight departing New York's JFK airport. From American's hub in San Juan, Puerto Rico, one nonstop flight departs every day for Aruba. American also offers a daily nonstop flight from Miami to Aruba. This service enables vacationers from Chicago, Los Angeles, San Francisco, and Seattle, or wherever, to fly directly to Aruba via the American Airlines Miami hub.

American usually offers a good array of packages on Aruba; ask about these before you book your airfare and hotel separately!

ALM (☎ 800/327-7230) has good connections into Aruba from certain parts of the United States. There are direct flights to Aruba from Atlanta on Thursday and Sunday, and flights leave Miami daily going via Curaçao.

Tiny **Air Aruba** (☎ 800/88-ARUBA), the country's national carrier, boasts several flights weekly. From both Newark and Miami, there is one flight daily to Aruba, leaving Monday to Friday; the frequency increases to two flights daily on Saturday and Sunday. From Tampa, there are daily flights on Thursday to Sunday, and from Baltimore daily flights Friday to Monday.

Continental Airlines (☎ 800/231-0856) also flies to Aruba from Houston, with nonstop service on Saturday and Wednesday.

Air Canada (☎ 800/268-7240 in Canada, or 800/776-3000 in the U.S.) has good connections from Toronto and Québec to Miami. Once in Miami, Canadians and other passengers can fly Air Aruba to the island.

GETTING AROUND

BY TAXI   In Aruba, the taxis are unmetered but rates are fixed, so tell the driver your destination and ask the fare before getting in. The main office is on Sands Street between the bowling center and Taco Bell. A **dispatch office** is located at the Bosabao (☎) 297/8-22116). A ride from the airport to most of the hotels, including those at Palm Beach, costs about $16 to $18 per car, with a maximum of four passengers allowed. Some locals don't tip, although we suggest tipping, especially if the driver has helped you with luggage. Additionally, since it's next to impossible to locate a taxi on some parts of the island, it's a good idea to ask the taxi driver to return to pick you up at a certain time if you're going to a remote destination.

You'll also usually find the English-speaking drivers willing tour guides. Most seem well informed about their island and eager to share it with you. A 1-hour tour (and you don't need much more than that) costs from $30 for a maximum of four passengers.

BY RENTAL CAR   Unlike most Caribbean islands, Aruba makes it easy to rent a car. The roads connecting the major tourist attractions are excellent, and a valid U.S. or Canadian driver's license is accepted by each of the major car-rental companies. The three major U.S. car-rental companies maintain offices on Aruba, and also have airport branches and kiosks at the major hotels. No taxes are imposed on car rentals on Aruba, but insurance can be tricky. Even with the purchase of a collision-damage waiver, a driver is still responsible for the first $300 to $500 worth of damage. (Avis doesn't even offer this waiver, so in the event of an accident—unless you have private insurance—you'll be liable for up to the full value of damage to your car.) Rental rates range between $50 and $70 per day.

Try **Budget Rent-a-Car,** at Divi Aruba Beach Resort, L. G. Smith Blvd. 93 (☎ 800/472-3325 in the U.S., or 297/8-24185); **Hertz,** L. G. Smith Blvd. 142 (☎ 800/654-3001 in the U.S., or 297/8-24545), and **Avis,** Kolibristraat 14 (☎ 800/331-1084 in the U.S., or 297/8-25496). Budget requires that renters be at least 25; Avis, 23; and Hertz, 21.

For a better deal, consider **Hedwina Car Rental,** Bubali 93A (☎ 297/8-76442, or 297/8-30880 at the airport). If you take a car for a week, you sometimes pay for only 5 days. Another agency to consider is **Thrifty Car Rental,** Balashi 65 (☎ 297/8-55300, or 297/8-35335 at the airport), which offers good deals, with many rentals beginning at $42 to $52 per day. You can also rent Jeeps from $65 per day.

BY MOTORCYCLE & MOPED   Since the roads of Aruba are good and the terrain flat, many visitors prefer this form of transport. Mopeds and motorcycles cost an average of $37 to $40 per day. They're available at **George's ScooterRental,** L. G.

Smith Blvd. 136 (☎ **297/8-25975**). **Nelson Motorcycle Rental,** Gasparito 10A, Noord (☎ **297/8-66801**), rents scooters for $25 and motorcycles for $49 to $84.

Melcor Cycle Rental, Bubali 106B (☎ **297/8-75203**), in front of the Adventure Golf Club, rents scooters for $32 per day. You can also rent dirt bikes and street bikes beginning at $45 per day. These are cash prices; a 4% handling charge is assessed if you use a credit or charge card. You can also find rentals at **Semver Cycle Rental,** Noord 22 (☎ **297/8-66851**), where bikes begin at $25 per day.

BY BUS Aruba has excellent bus service, with a round-trip fare between the beach hotels and Oranjestad of $2. Bus schedules are available at the Arubus Office at the central bus station on Zoutmanstraat. Your hotel reception desk will also know the approximate times the buses pass by where you're staying. There's regular daily service from 6am to midnight. Try to have the exact change. For **bus schedules and information,** call the Arubus Co. (☎ **297/8-27089**).

SPECIAL EVENTS
Many visitors come here for the annual pre-Lenten **Carnival,** a month-long festival with events day and night. With music, dancing, parades, costumes, and "jump-ups," Carnival is the highlight of Aruba's winter season.

Fast Facts: Aruba

Banking Hours Banks are open Monday to Friday 8am to noon and 1:30 to 3:45pm.

Currency The currency is the **Aruba florin (AFl),** which is divided into 100 cents. Silver coins are in denominations of 5, 10, 25, and 50 cents and 1 and 2 ½ florins. The 50¢ piece, the square "yotin," is Aruba's best-known coin. The current exchange rate is 1.77 AFl to $1 U.S. (1 AFl is worth about 56¢). U.S. dollars, traveler's checks, and major credit and charge cards are widely accepted throughout the island. *Note:* Unless otherwise stated, *prices quoted in this chapter are in U.S. dollars.*

Documents To enter Aruba, U.S. and Canadian citizens and British subjects may submit a valid passport or a birth certificate. We recommend that you bring a passport whenever you're visiting a foreign country.

Electricity The electricity is 110 volts AC, 60 cycles, the same as in the United States.

Emergencies For the **police,** dial ☎ **11100.** For a **medical emergency,** dial ☎ **74300.** For the **fire** department, call ☎ **115.**

Language The official language is Dutch, but nearly everybody speaks English. Spanish is also widely spoken.

Medical Care To receive medical care, go to the **Horacio Oduber Hospital** on L. G. Smith Boulevard (☎ **297/8-74300;** also the number to call in case of a medical emergency). It's a modern building near Eagle Beach, with excellent medical facilities. Hotels also have medical doctors on call, and there are good dental facilities as well (appointments can be made through your hotel).

Safety Aruba is one of the Caribbean's safer destinations, in spite of its numerous hotels and gambling casinos. Of course, some pickpockets and purse-snatchers are around, so guard your valuables. Never leave them unattended on the beach or even in a locked car.

Taxes and Service   The government of Aruba imposes a 6% room tax, as well as a $20 airport departure tax. At your hotel, you'll have a 15% to 20% service charge added to charges for room, food, and beverages.

Telephones   To call Aruba from the United States, dial **011** (the international access code), then **297** (the country code for Aruba), and then **8** (the area code) and the five-digit local number. Once on Aruba, only the five-digit local number is necessary to call another number on the island.

Time   Aruba is on Atlantic standard time year-round, so most of the year Aruba is 1 hour ahead of Eastern standard time (when it's 10am on Aruba, it's 9am in New York). When daylight saving time is in effect in the United States, clocks in New York and Aruba show the same time.

Water   The water, which comes from the world's second-largest desalination plant, is pure.

2 Accommodations You Can Afford

Most of Aruba's hotels are bustling and self-contained resorts. Unfortunately for the budget traveler, there's a dearth of family or budget hotels. The few guest houses tend to be booked up early in winter by faithful returning visitors. In season, you must make reservations well in advance; don't ever arrive expecting to find a room on the spot—you must have an address to give Immigration when you arrive on Aruba. Don't forget to ask if the 6% room tax and any service charge are included in the rates quoted when you make your reservation.

Andicuri Inn. De La Sallestraat 13, Oranjestad, Aruba. ☎ **297/8-21539.** Fax 297/8-29922. 18 apts. A/C TV TEL. Winter $50 apt. for 1 or 2. Off-season $45 apt. for 1 or 2. 2 children 11 and under stay free in parents' room. MC, V.

If you'd like to stay in the capital, just 5 minutes from the center and only 10 minutes from the nearest good beach, consider this affordable little choice. It offers fully furnished and comfortable apartments, each with a king-size bed with a good mattress, cable TV, and walk-in closet, plus a kitchen with a built-in stove and a small but tidy bath (thin towels, unfortunately). There's little style here, but you get reasonable comfort at a good price. The place is for independent types who don't expect resort-style amenities. For your other diversions, you have to go outside the property.

✪ **Aruba Blue Village Suites.** Cunucu Abao 37, Aruba. ☎ **297/8-78618.** Fax 297/8-70081. 56 suites. Winter $100 junior suite; $111 1-bedroom suite; $140 2-bedroom suite. Off-season $70 junior suite; $88 1-bedroom suite; $105 2-bedroom suite. AE, MC, V.

If you can forgo a beachfront location, you'll find one of Aruba's best deals at this complex. Off-season, it's a sweet bargain if four people share a junior suite or six people share a two-bedroom suite, costing from $16 per person a night. The accommodations are in the typical resort style, plain but comfortable, yet features include cable TV, a safety deposit box, a separate bath with shower, and a fully equipped kitchenette. Some 26 of the suites come with pull-out sofas. The mattresses are firm, and the baths are motel standard but adequate, with decent towels. The complex of single-story apartments lies in a residential area removed from the hotel strip. A free bus service will haul you to the beach, 5 minutes away, and you're close to casinos and nightlife. But many guests stay on the property, enjoying two spacious swimming pools, two large sun terraces, table tennis and other indoor and outdoor games, a children's playground, and bar and barbecue facilities at the pool.

Cactus Apartments. Matadera 5, Aruba. ☎ **297/8-22903.** Fax 297/8-20433. E-mail: cactus.apts@setarnet.aw. 13 apts. A/C TV. Winter $55 apt. for 1 or 2; $65 apt. for 3. Off-season $45 apt. for 1 or 2; $55 apt. for 3. AE, MC, V.

This is a small, inexpensive apartment complex whose mustard-colored exterior blends into the surrounding arid, cactus-dotted landscape. Its oldest section was built in the early 1980s. The nearest beach is 2 miles away, so a car is recommended for anyone who wants to stay here—although owner Jacinto Tromp is happy to tell you how to get around on the island's network of buses and public transport. There's neither a bar nor restaurant on the premises, but the basic and rather small guest rooms contain their own kitchenettes. They also have rather thin mattresses and tiny, shower-only bathrooms (no tub baths) and a rack of rather thin towels. Nevertheless, the place is reasonably comfortable. The nearest beach is 2 miles away. There's a small launderette, a single coin-operated telephone that's shared by all the units, and maid service Monday to Saturday.

Coconut Inn. Noord 31, Aruba. ☎ **297/8-66288.** Fax 297/8-65433. 40 units. A/C TV TEL. Winter $65 studio for 1; $75 studio for 2; $90 double or 1-bedroom suite for 2. Extra person $20. Off-season $50 studio for 1; $55 studio for 2; $70 double or 1-bedroom suite for 2. Rates include breakfast. Extra person $15. MC, V.

Within a 7-minute walk from the landlocked village of Noord, this affordable hotel was built in five yellow-and-white sections between 1975 and 1996. Considering what beachfront hotels a 10-minute drive away charge, its rates are a steal. The location is convenient to supermarkets, and a public bus stops a short walk away. Just remember that you're on a desert island and won't be near the beach. Units come in an array of styles that include relatively cramped studios, as well as conventional rooms and one-bedroom suites, which both contain almost the same amount of floor space. All accommodations are furnished in a somewhat unimaginative motel style, each with a balcony or patio and a kitchenette or at least a microwave and refrigerator. The beds are good, with fairly new mattresses, but the bathrooms are typically small, with not enough room to spread out your stuff. There's no maid service on Sunday. A swimming pool, restaurant, and bar are on the premises.

Mi Cielo Apartments. Italiesstraat 12, Aruba. ☎ **297/8-20021.** Fax 297/8-30076. 7 apts. A/C TV. Winter $55 studio apt. for 1 or 2; $75 1-bedroom apt. Off-season $45 studio apt. for 1 or 2; $65 1-bedroom apt. No credit cards.

Although these incredible rates—at least for Aruba—might not hold indefinitely, Mi Cielo offers one of the island's lowest-priced places to stay. A local lawyer runs the property and there's little on-site management, so this choice is really for self-sufficient types. You're in a good location, however, between beach and town, about a 10-minute walk each way. In this one-story property, the units are absolutely standard, with no frills or style, but each is reasonably comfortable and pleasantly furnished, with firm mattresses, a patio, kitchenette, and a tiny bath with a minimum of towels.

Turibana Plaza. Noord 124, Aruba. ☎ **297/8-67292.** Fax 297/8-62658. www.arubatourism.com/turilhtml. E-mail: turibana@mail.setarnet.aw. 19 apts. A/C TV TEL. Winter $75 apt. for 2; $152.50 apt. for 4. Extra person $15. Off-season $50 apt. for 2; $95. apt for 4. Extra person $10. AE, MC, V.

This modern complex of rather standard apartments is only minutes from the best white, sandy beaches of Aruba as well as some terrific restaurants near Oranjestad. And its prices are among the island's most affordable. For those cooking in, a supermarket is less than a mile away. Because of their low rates, the apartments are booked early in winter, so reserve as far in advance as possible. The medium-size bedrooms have wall-to-wall carpeting and plain, simple furnishings, with a full kitchenette. The mattresses, although not new, are still rather firm, and the bathrooms are well maintained and rather efficient, with adequate shelf space. Some guests like the place so much that they check in for a month. On the ground level is an excellent restaurant. Although the Turibana Plaza isn't a full-service hotel, it does offer daily maid service and laundry facilities.

✪ **Vistalmar Apartments.** Bucutiweg 28, Aruba. ☎ **297/8-28579.** Fax 297/8-22200. 8 apts. A/C. Winter $95 apt. with a car; off-season $55 apt. with a car. No credit cards.

An affordable and intimate place to stay on Aruba, this property doesn't have access to the celebrated beaches, but lies across from the water in a residential section near the airport. It's a fine bargain, however, for not only will you have complimentary use of boats, bikes, picnic coolers, snorkeling equipment, beach towels, and an outdoor grill, you also get a car! The complex of apartments is in two similar buildings, each with a balcony or courtyard offering water views. A little more stylish than some of the more bare-boned apartment units rented on the island, the accommodations here are spacious and furnished for comfort. Your hosts, among the island's more personable, are Aby and Katy Yarzagaray, a font of island information. Aby was born on Aruba and comes from a family which has lived on the island since 1805.

The apartments have a master-size bed with a good mattress, a well-maintained bathroom with a tub and shower, plenty of towels, a separate dressing area, a fully equipped kitchen, and a living room with a sofa that can be turned into an extra bed. There's also a second sleeping room and a sun porch. The seaside sun deck in front of the complex is just 50 yards from the water, and guests can swim from the deck. Upon arrival, guests find complimentary food in the refrigerator. Daily maid service and such thoughtful touches as fresh flowers make this an inviting choice.

WORTH A SPLURGE

The Mill Resort. L. G. Smith Blvd. 330, Palm Beach, Aruba. ☎ **297/8-67700.** Fax 297/ 8-67271. 200 units. A/C TV TEL. Winter $160–$170 single or double with refrigerator; $195–$205 mini-suite with kitchenette for 1 or 2. Off-season $90–$100 single or double with refrigerator; $107–$117 studio or mini-suite with kitchenette for 1 or 2. AE, DC, MC, V.

Opened in 1990 and enlarged in 1994, this complex of two-story concrete buildings with red roofs is set in an arid, rather dusty location inland from the beach but within a 7-minute trek of Eagle Beach (which is used by such megahotels as the Hilton). It's adjacent to a large, modern re-creation of a Dutch windmill, which has become a kitschy Aruban landmark. Units ring a large swimming pool. The room decor is tropical, with white rattan, carpeting or white floor tiles, and pastel-colored curtains and draperies. The rooms and furnishings are standard motel. Mattresses are renewed every two years. The bathrooms, while small, are adequate, with well-maintained plumbing.

This hotel is best for independent types who don't mind exploring Aruba for dining, drinking, and diversions. You'll find very limited bar and restaurant service here, but since most units have kitchenettes (or at least a refrigerator), many guests cook in. There's a launderette, a sauna, a fitness center, an exercise room, a beauty salon, and massage facilities. In many rooms you'll find king-size beds and Jacuzzi-style bathtubs.

Caribbean Town Beach Resort. L. G. Smith Blvd. 2, Aruba. ☎ **800/223-1108** in the U.S., or 297/8-23380. E-mail: cartownres@setarnet.aw. Fax 297/8-33208. 62 units. A/C TV. Winter $102–$123 single; $122–$133 double; $148–$158 1-bedroom studio; $143–$173 2-bedroom apt. Off-season $73–$85 single; $83–$95 double; $93–$103 1-bedroom studio;

$107–$117 2-bedroom apt. Extra person $10; children 11 and under stay free in parents' room. MAP (breakfast and dinner) $35 per person extra. AE, DC, MC, V.

Although it's seen the wear and tear of the years, this longtime favorite has long been known as one of the best moderately priced choices on Aruba. On the south side of Oranjestad, it's really like a motel and is frequented by business travelers. An upgraded and enlarged beach is 200 yards (183 meters) across the street. The bedrooms are a bit dark, and both standard and superior rooms have ceiling fans, balconies, room safes, refrigerators, and microwaves, whereas the studios and apartments offer fuller kitchenettes. New owners have spruced up the bedrooms with new furniture and mattresses and rejuvenated the plumbing.

Three meals a day are provided in the Moonlight Grill, and you can also patronize the open-air Surfside Bar and Grill. A daily happy hour with free snacks and live music draws the budget traveler, and you can eat all the prime rib you want at Friday night's carvery, one of Aruba's best food values. The hotel's beach club has reopened as Havana Beach Club and is now one of the island hot spots.

3 Great Deals on Dining

Regrettably, nearly everything has to be imported, making Aruba one of the higher-priced dining destinations in the Caribbean. But there are some bargains here. The trick is, you have to order from the lower end of the menu and avoid the high-priced fish dishes, which often cost from $25 or more.

Brisas del Mar. Savaneta 222A. ☎ **297/8-47718.** Reservations required. Main courses $12–$32. AE, MC, V. Tues–Sun noon–2:30pm; daily 6:30–9:30pm. SEAFOOD.

A 15-minute drive east of Oranjestad, near the police station, Brisas del Mar is like a place you might encounter in some outpost in Australia. Here, in very simple surroundings right at water's edge, Lucia Rasmijn opened this little hut with an air-conditioned bar where locals gather to drink the day away. The place is often jammed on weekends with many of the same local people, who come here to drink and dance. In back the tables are open to the sea breezes, and nearby you can see the catch of the day, perhaps wahoo, being sliced up and sold to local buyers. Specialties include mixed seafood platter, baby shark, and broiled lobster; you can order meat and poultry dishes as well, including tenderloin steak and broiled chicken. Don't expect subtlety of cuisine. This is the type of food Arubans enjoyed back in the 1950s, and nothing much has changed since then. Most main courses are at the lower end of the price range.

Charlie's Bar and Restaurant. B. v/d Veen Zeppenveldstraat 56 (Main St.), San Nicolas. ☎ **297/8-45086.** Daily soup $4.75; main courses $15–$20. AE, MC, V. Mon–Sat noon–9:30pm. (Bar, Mon–Sat noon–10pm.) SEAFOOD/INTERNATIONAL.

Charlie's is the best reason to visit San Nicolas. The bar dates from 1941 and is the most overly-decorated in the West Indies, sporting an array of memorabilia and local souvenirs. Where roustabouts and roughnecks once brawled, you'll now find tables filled with contented tourists admiring thousands of pennants, banners, and trophies dangling from the high ceiling. Two-fisted drinks are still served, but the menu has improved since the good old days, when San Nicolas was one of the toughest towns in the Caribbean. You can now enjoy freshly made soup, grilled scampi, Creole-style squid, and churrasco. Sirloin steak and red snapper are usually featured. Even so, most patrons come here for the good times and the brew, not necessarily for the food, although it isn't bad. Charlie's is a 25-minute drive east of Oranjestad.

Frankie's Prime Grill. In the Royal Plaza Mall, L.G. Smith Blvd. ☎ **297/8-38471.** Main courses $14.50–$28.50. AE, DC, DISC, MC, V. Mon–Sat noon–4:30pm; daily 6–10:30pm. STEAKS/SEAFOOD.

Come here for hearty steak and seafood, some of it grilled in the *churrasco* style of the Argentinian pampas. You can dine either inside, where it's air-conditioned, or on an outdoor terrace whose views encompass potted palms, the busy street life of downtown Oranjestad, and boats bobbing at anchor in the harbor. Menu items include a wide selection of pastas, including penne with vodka sauce or a spicy *l'arrabiata* sauce; lasagna; filet mignon; barbecue ribs; and a full-fledged mixed grill containing various sausages and cuts of meat. Seafood crêpes, shrimp in garlic sauce, and various preparations of grouper and snapper usually please anyone who prefers fish.

Le Petit Café. Emmastraat 1, Strada Complex II. ☎ **297/8-26577.** Reservations recommended. Main courses $16.50–$32.50; lunch $5.30–$13. AE, DC, MC, V. Mon–Sat 11am–4:30pm and 6–11pm, Sun 6–11pm. CONTINENTAL.

This local hangout's specialty is called Romance on the Stone—meals cooked on hot stones, including steak, chicken, jumbo shrimp, fish, and lobster. Dinner is not for the price-conscious, but lunch offers a wide selection of dishes at reasonable prices. The menu spotlights chicken kebabs with peanut sauce and whatever happens to be the catch of the day. For a quick bite, try one of the salads (chicken, tuna, fruit, and chef) or a sandwich, such as a BLT, club, or steak. Le Petit Café offers indoor-outdoor dining with seating on two floors and also on the terrace.

Mama's & Papa's. Noord 41C. ☎ **297/8-67913.** Main courses $11–$25. AE, DC, MC, V. Mon–Sat 6–11pm. ARUBAN/SPANISH.

Located north of Oranjestad, this small place serves Aruban and Spanish specialties and some West Indian dishes. The cooks here serve the island's best paella. Local favorites include *keshi yena*, a casserole of chicken and cheese, and *kreeft di cay reef*, broiled lobster. Fish selections are served in a variety of sauces including Creole and garlic butter. If you're in the mood for West Indian, try the curried chicken, stewed goat, or conch stew. Most nights a guitar player entertains with music from the 1960s. Desserts include carrot cake and sweet-potato pie.

The Paddock. 13 L.G. Smith Blvd. Oranjestad. ☎ **297/8-32334.** Sandwiches, snacks, and salads $3.70–$5.50; main courses $8.50–$14.50. MC, V. Mon–Thurs 10am–2am, Fri–Sun 10am–3am. INTERNATIONAL.

Set in the heart of Oranjestad, overlooking the harbor and within a short walk of virtually every shop in town, this is a cafe and bistro with a Dutch aesthetic and ambience. Much of the staff is blonde, hip, and European; and no one will mind if you opt for a drink, a cup of tea or coffee, or a snack of sliced sausage and Gouda cheese instead of a full-fledged meal. The menu offers crab, salmon, shrimp, and tuna sandwiches, salads, pita-bread sandwiches stuffed with sliced beef and an herb sauce with plenty of tang, filet mignon encrusted with crushed pepper, fresh poached or sautéed fish, and a glazed tenderloin of pork. Happy hours, when drink prices are reduced, change frequently, but whenever they're offered, the place is as crowded and animated as anything else within the island's capital.

WORTH A SPLURGE

The Waterfront Crabhouse. In the Seaport Market, L. G. Smith Blvd., Oranjestad. ☎ **297/8-35858.** Reservations recommended. Main courses $14–$40; lunch from $7. AE, MC, V. Daily 11am–11pm. SEAFOOD/STEAK.

Set at the most desirable end of a shopping mall in downtown Oranjestad, overlooking a manicured lawn, this restaurant evokes a dining room on the California coast. Amid painted murals of underwater life and rattan furniture, at tables placed both indoors and on a garden terrace, you can enjoy well-prepared seafood. The chef lists "crabs, crabs, crabs" as his specialty, including garlic crabs, Alaska crab legs, and (in season) soft-shell crabs. Stuffed Maine lobster and Cajun grilled shrimp are also served, as are stuffed clams and fried squid with a marinara sauce, and linguine with white or red clam sauce, which can be ordered on the side or as a main course. A wide range of other fish dishes, including yellowfin tuna and swordfish, are grilled over an open fire. All fish served are hook-and-line caught, never from drift nets. The restaurant's steak menu includes a 10-ounce Black Angus filet mignon, as well as the less expensive chopped sirloin smothered in onions.

A GREAT DEAL ON A TWO-FOR-ONE DINNER

Kowloon. Emmastraat 11, Oranjestad. ☎ **297/8-24950.** Reservations recommended. Main courses $17–$20. Set-price *rijsttafel* (rice table), $35 for 2 diners. AE, DISC, MC, V. Daily 11am–10pm. CHINESE/INDONESIAN.

Set within a pair of red-and-black dining rooms that are accented with varnished hardwoods and Chinese lamps, with a view overlooking one of the main thoroughfares of the island's capital, this is a worthy and elegant place offering Hunan, Szechuan, and Shanghai cuisine. It also prepares such Indonesian staples as *nasi goreng* and *bami goreng*, made with rice or noodles and tidbits of pork, vegetables, and shrimp. Two well-prepared specialties include an elaborate *rijsttafel*, where dozens of small dishes of curried vegetables and meats, as well as spicy and sweet accompaniments, are served with rice and a spicy peanut sauce, and a house special seafood that combines fish, scallops, lobster, shrimp, and Szechuan-style black bean sauce.

4 Hitting the Beaches

The western and southern shore, called the **Turquoise Coast,** attracts sun seekers to Aruba. **Palm Beach** and **Eagle Beach** (the latter closer to Oranjestad) are the best beaches. No hotel along the strip owns the beaches, all of which are open to the public (you'll be charged to use any of the hotels' facilities).

Unlike some of the beaches of the Caribbean, those of Aruba are usually litter free. That sign, NO TIRA SUSHI, meaning "no littering," is to be taken seriously. The police impose heavy fines for those caught soiling Aruba's beaches of white sand.

The major resort hotels are built on the southwestern and more tranquil strip of Aruba. In two hours you can wander from the Bushiri Beach Hotel to the Holiday Inn, never taking your feet out of the sand. These beaches open onto calm waters, ideal for swimming. The beaches on the northern, Atlantic side of Aruba, although quite beautiful, face choppy waters and aren't good for swimming except by the most skilled. On this side you'll see crashing white waves that brush against a jagged rock coast.

✪ **Palm Beach** has been heralded as one of the 10 best beaches in the world. This is a superb stretch of wide white sand that fronts such hotels as the Aruba Hilton, the Allegro Resort, and the Holiday Inn. It is the very heartbeat of Aruban tourism. As one hotelier confided, "It puts us on the tourist map." All sorts of activities take place here—not just swimming, but sailing and fishing as well. Regrettably, in the winter months the beach is overcrowded. The waters off this beach are incredibly blue and teeming with neon-yellow fish, along with flame-bright coral reefs. In any given day, billowing rainbow-colored sails add to the picture.

Next to Palm Beach, **Eagle Beach** is also on the southern coast and quite similar to Palm Beach. It fronts a number of time-share units. Because of the gentle surf, swimming conditions here are excellent along miles of white powder sand. Hotels along the strip organize water sports and beach activities.

If you'd like something more private, head for ✪ **Baby Beach** on the island's eastern tip. Bordering a bay that's as tranquil as a wading pool, with waters only 4 to 5 feet deep, this is an ideal place for swimming. The beach is of white powder sand. It is also a great spot for snorkeling. Thatched shaded areas are great for escaping the fierce sun, but there are no facilities other than a refreshment stand. Don't be surprised to encounter a topless bather or two. Locals are fond of this beach (our island friends will be furious at us for telling you about it). You'll spot the Arubans themselves here on weekends, enjoying the relaxed sunbathing and swimming. Baby Beach opens onto a vast lagoon shielded by coral rocks rising about the water. Bring your own towels, lotion, and snorkeling gear. And don't tell anyone about this beach!

Punta Brabo is also called Manchebo Beach, since it borders the grounds of the Manchebo Beach Hotel. This is a broad stretch of white powdery sand, and a favorite for topless sunbathers. (Going topless is not officially sanctioned by the government, but local authorities seem to turn a blind eye to the exhibitionism here.) Actually, Manchebo is part of the greater Eagle Beach (see above), and the hotel is a good refueling stop, as it offers a dive shop and will rent snorkeling gear. It is also set amid 100 acres of gardens, filled with everything from cacti to bougainvillea.

Also worth seeking out is **Hadikurari** (Fishermens' Huts), where the swimming conditions are excellent in very shallow water. The only drawback to this beach of white powder sand are some pebbles and stones at water's edge, so proceed with caution. Next to the Holiday Inn, this beach is known for some of the finest windsurfing on island. It is, in fact, the site of the annual Hi-Winds Pro-Am Windsurfing Competition. Arrangements can be made at Windsurfing Village, bordering the beach. This is also one of the best beaches for a picnic lunch in Aruba; tables are available.

Next to Baby Beach on the eastern tip of the island, **Rodger's Beach** is also filled with white powdery sand, with excellent conditions for swimming. The backdrop isn't scenic, however, as in the distance you can see an oil refinery at the far side of the bay. But the refinery doesn't pollute the waters here. You can admire large and small fish here, all multicolored, along with strange coral formations. The trade winds will keep you cool.

5 Sports & Outdoor Pursuits

DAY CRUISES   Visitors interested in combining a boat ride with a few hours of snorkeling should contact **De Palm Tours,** which has offices in eight of the island's hotels, and its main office at L. G. Smith Blvd. 142, in Oranjestad (☎ **800/766-6016** or 297/8-24400). De Palm Tours offers a 1½-hour glass-bottom boat cruise that visits two coral reefs and the German shipwreck *Antilla* on Thursday and Friday. The cost is $19.50 per person.

DEEP-SEA FISHING   In the deep waters off the coast of Aruba you can test your skill and wits against the big ones—wahoo, marlin, tuna, bonito, and sailfish. **De Palm Tours,** L. G. Smith Blvd. 142, in Oranjestad (☎ 297/8-24400), takes out a maximum of six people (four of whom can fish at the same time) on one of its four boats, which range in length from 27 to 41 feet. Half-day tours, with all equipment included, begin at $250 for up to four people and $30 per person for five or six. The prices are doubled for full-day trips. Boats leave from the docks in Oranjestad. De Palm maintains 11 branches, most of which are in Aruba's major hotels.

GOLF   Visitors can play at the **Aruba Golf Club,** Golfweg 82 (☎ **297/8-42006**), near San Nicolas on the southeastern end of the island. Although it has only 10 greens, they are played from different tees to simulate 18-hole play. Twenty-five different sand traps add an extra challenge. Greens fees are $18 for 18 holes and $10 for 9 holes. The course is open daily from 7:30am to 5pm, although anyone wishing to play 18 holes must begin the rounds before 1pm. Golf carts and clubs can be rented in the pro shop. There's an air-conditioned restaurant and changing rooms with showers on the premises.

Golfers may want to splurge on playing at a more acclaimed course, the **Tierra del Sol Golf Course** (☎ **297/8-67800**). Designed by Robert Trent Jones Jr., it's on the northwest coast, near the California Lighthouse. The 18-hole, par-71, 6,811-yard affair was designed to combine the beauty of the island's indigenous flora, such as the swaying divi-divi tree, with lush greens. Facilities include a restaurant and lounge in the clubhouse and a swimming pool. The course is managed by Golf Hyatt. In winter, greens fees are $130, including golf cart, or $95 after 3pm. Off-season, greens fees are $75, or $55 after 3pm. The course is open daily from 6am to 7pm.

HORSEBACK RIDING De Palm Tours, L. G. Smith Blvd. 142 (☎ **297/ 8-24400**), will make arrangements for you to ride at **Rancho Del Campo** (☎ **297/ 8-50290**). Two rides a day are offered, lasting 3 hours and cutting through a park to a natural pool where you can dismount and cool off with a swim. The price is $45 per person, and the minimum age is 10 years.

TENNIS   If your hotel doesn't have a tennis court, head to the **Aruba Racket Club** (☎ **297/8-60215**), the island's first world-class tennis facility, with eight courts, an exhibition center court, a swimming pool, a bar, a small restaurant, an aerobics center, and a fitness center. The club is open Monday through Saturday from 8am to 11pm and on Sunday from 3 to 8pm. Rates are $10 per hour per court, with lessons going for $20 for a half hour or $35 per hour. The location is part of the Tierra del Sol complex on Aruba's northwest coast, near the California Lighthouse.

SCUBA DIVING & OTHER WATER SPORTS   You can snorkel in rather shallow waters, and scuba divers find stunning marine life with endless varieties of coral as well as tropical fish in infinite hues; at some points visibility is up to 90 feet. The goal of most divers is the German freighter *Antilla,* which was scuttled in the early years of World War II off the northwestern tip of Aruba, not too far from Palm Beach.

Red Sails Sports, Palm Beach (☎ **297/8-61603**), is the best water-sports center on the island. It has an extensive variety of activities, including sailing, waterskiing, and scuba diving. Red Sail dive packages include shipwreck dives as well as exploration of marine reefs all in one day. Guests are first given a poolside resort course in which Red Sail's certified instructors teach procedures that ensure safety during dives. For those who wish to become certified, full PADI certification can be achieved in as little as 4 days for $350. One-tank dives cost $40, two-tank dives cost $65.

Divi Winds Center, J. E. Irausquin Blvd. 41 (☎ **297/8-37841**), near the Tamarind Aruba Beach Resort, is the windsurfing headquarters of the island. Equipment is made by Fanatic and is rented for $15 per hour or $30 per half-day and $45 all day. The resort is on the tranquil (Caribbean) side of the island and doesn't face the fierce Atlantic waves. Sunfish lessons can also be arranged for $45 (private) or $30 (if in a group). Snorkeling gear an also be rented.

6 Seeing the Sights

IN ORANJESTAD

Oranjestad, Aruba's capital, attracts more shoppers than sightseers. The bustling city has a very Caribbean flavor, and it's part Spanish, part Dutch in architecture. Cutting in from the airport, the main thoroughfare, Lloyd G. Smith Boulevard, goes along the waterfront and on to Palm Beach, changing its name along the way to J. E. Irausquin Boulevard. But most visitors cross it heading for **Caya G. F. Betico Croes** and the best duty-free shopping.

After a shopping trip, you might return to the harbor where fishing boats and schooners, many from Venezuela, are moored. Nearly all newcomers to Aruba like to take a picture of the **Schooner Harbor.** Not only does it have colorful boats docked along the quay, but boat people display their wares in open stalls. The local *patois* predominates. A little farther along, at the **fish market,** fresh fish are sold directly from the boats. Also on the sea-side of Oranjestad is Wilhelmina Park, which was named after **Queen Wilhelmina** of the Netherlands. A tropical garden has been planted along the water, and there's a sculpture of the Queen Mother there.

OUT IN THE COUNTRY

If you can lift yourselves from the sands for one afternoon, you might like to drive into the *cunucu*, which in Papiamento means "the countryside." Papiamento is the local dialect, and it's officially recognized as one of the languages of Aruba. The language itself reflects the population diversity of Aruba, as it's a mixture of Spanish and Dutch, plus some African languages and even echoes of the original inhabitants of the Caribbean, the Caribs and the Arawaks. Here in the cunucu, Arubans live in very modest but colorful pastel-washed houses decorated with tropical plants, which require expensive desalinated water to grow. Of course, all visitors venturing into the center of Aruba want to see the strangely shaped **divi-divi tree** with its trade-wind-blown coiffure.

Aruba is studded with rocks, and the most impressive ones are those found at **Ayo** and **Casibari,** northeast of Hooiberg. These stacks of diorite boulders are the size of buildings. The rocks, weighing several thousand tons, are a puzzle to geologists. Ancient Amerindian drawings appear on the rocks at Ayo. At Casibari, you can climb the boulder-strewn terrain to the top for a panoramic view of the island or look at rocks which nature has carved into seats or likenesses of prehistoric birds and animals. You might want to pay special attention to the island's unusual species of lizards and cacti. Casibari is open daily from 9am to 5pm; no admission is charged. There's a lodge at Casibari where you can buy souvenirs, snacks, soft drinks, and beer.

Guides can also point out drawings on the walls and ceiling of the **Caves of Canashito,** south of Hooiberg. While here, you may get to see the giant green parakeets.

Hooiberg is affectionately known as "The Haystack." It's Aruba's most outstanding landmark, and anybody with the stamina can take the steps all the way to the top of this 541-foot-high hill. One Aruban jogs up there every morning. From its location in the center of the island you can see Venezuela on a clear day.

On the jagged, windswept northern coast, the **Natural Bridge** has been carved out of the coral rock by the relentless surf. In a little cafe overlooking the coast you can order snacks. Here you'll also find a souvenir shop with a large selection of trinkets, T-shirts, and wall hangings, all for reasonable prices.

You turn inland for the short trip to **Pirate's Castle** at Bushiribana, which stands on a cliff on the island's windward coast. This is actually a deserted gold mill from the island's now-defunct industry. Another gold mill is in the old ghost town on the west coast, **Balashi.**

You can continue to the village of Noord, known for its **St. Anne's Church,** which has a hand-carved, 17th-century Dutch altar.

EAST TO SAN NICOLAS

Driving along the highway toward the island's southernmost section, more or less paralleling the south coast of Aruba, you may want to stop at the **Spaans Lagoen (Spanish Lagoon),** where legend says pirates used to hide out as they waited to plunder rich cargo ships in the Caribbean. Today this is an ideal place for snorkeling, and you can picnic at tables under the mangrove trees.

On to the east, you'll pass an area called **Savaneta,** where some of the most ancient traces of human habitation have been unearthed. You'll see along here the first oil tanks marking the position of the Lago Oil & Transport Company, the Exxon subsidiary around which the town of San Nicolas developed. A "company town" until the refinery greatly curtailed operations in 1985, San Nicolas, 12 miles from Oranjestad, is called the Aruba Sunrise Side, and tourism has become its main economic engine. In the area are **caves** with Arawak artwork on the walls and a modern innovation, a PGA-approved golf course with sand "greens" and cactus traps.

Boca Grandi, on the windward side of the island, is a favorite windsurfing location; if you prefer quieter waters, you'll find them at **Baby Beach** and **Rodgers Beach,** on Aruba's leeward side. Baby Beach offers the best beach-based snorkeling on the island. Overlooking the latter two beaches is **Seroe Colorado (Colorado Point),** from which it's possible to see the coastline of Venezuela as well as the pounding surf on the windward side. You can climb down the cliffs, and perhaps spot an iguana here and there; protected by law, the once-endangered saurians now proliferate in peace.

Other sights in the San Nicolas area are the **Guadarikiri Cave** and **Fontein Cave,** where you can see the wall drawings, plus the **Huliba** and **Tunnel of Love** caves, with guides and refreshment stands. In spite of its name, the Tunnel of Love cave requires some physical stamina to explore. Filled with steep climbs, its steps are illuminated by hand-held lamps. Wear sturdy shoes and watch your step.

AN UNDERWATER JOURNEY

One of the island's most fun activities is an underwater journey on one of the world's few passenger submarines, operated by ✪ **Atlantis Submarines,** Seaport Village Marina, opposite the Sonesta in Oranjestad (☎ **800/253-0493** or 297/8-36090). Carrying 46 passengers to a depth of up to 150 feet, the underwater ride offers one of the Caribbean's best opportunities for nondivers to witness firsthand the life of a coral reef, with fewer obstacles and dangers than posed by a scuba expedition and without ever getting wet. In 1995 an old Danish fishing vessel was sunk to create a fascinating view for divers and submariners. The submarine organizes four departures from the Oranjestad harbor front every hour on the hour, Tuesday to Sunday from 10am to 2pm (there are no departures on Monday). Each tour includes a 30-minute transit by catamaran to Barcadera Reef, 2 miles southeast of Aruba, a site chosen for the huge variety of its underwater flora and fauna. At the reef, participants are transferred to the submarine for a 1-hour underwater lecture and tour.

Allow 2 hours for the complete experience. The cost is $69 for adults and $32 for children 4 to 16 (no children under 4 are admitted). Advance reservations are essential, either through the concierge of one of the island's hotels or via the telephone number listed above. In either event, a staff member will ask for a credit-card number (and give you a confirmation number) to hold the booking for you.

7 Shopping

Aruba manages to compress the offerings of six continents into the half-mile-long **Caya G. F. Betico Croes,** the main shopping street of Oranjestad. While this is not

Cheap Thrills: What to See & Do for Free
(Well, Almost) on Aruba

- **Wander the Beach Gardens.** Along Palm Beach, all the seaside hotels are set in flowering gardens. This is unusual for Aruba, which is an otherwise barren landscape. Of course, it needs a river of water to keep these gardens blooming, but they take on a special beauty on such a dry island. As you walk along the beach you can wander through garden after garden, watching the tropical mockingbirds feeding on juicy local fruits. You'll also see the black-faced grass quit or the green-throated carib hovering around these flowers and flowering shrubs. If you stop to have a drink at one of the hotel open-air bars, chances are you'll be joined soon by a bananaquit hoping to steal some sugar from you.

- **Enjoy Sunset at Bubali Pond.** This bird sanctuary lies on the north side of Eagle Beach (see above) at Post Chikito. It is south of De Olde Molen, a 19th-century windmill, now turned into a restaurant and the most famous landmark on Aruba. Flocks of birds cluster at the pond, particularly at sunset, making for one of the most memorable sights on Aruba. Mostly they are pelicans, but you can see many other species too, including black olivaceous cormorants and the black-crowned night herons. Great egrets with long, black legs and yellow bills will also delight you, as will spotted sandpipers. You'll even see visitors flying in from Venezuela, especially the large wood stork and the glossy scarlet ibis.

- **Stroll Through Oranjestad.** The old Dutch capital city is incongruous in the Caribbean. You expect to find something like this in the Netherlands, not off the coast of South America. Wander past the tall multicolored houses of Wilhelminastraat, combining carved wooden doors and traditional Dutch tiles with air-open galleries and sloping Aruban-style roofs. At Fort Zoutman, the oldest building on the island, a weekly Bonbini Festival offers up local food,

technically a duty-free port, the duty is so low (3.3%) that articles are attractively priced—and Aruba has no sales tax. You'll find the usual array of Swiss watches; German and Japanese cameras; jewelry; liquor; English bone china and porcelain; Dutch, Swedish, and Danish silver and pewter; French perfume; British woolens; Indonesian specialties; and Madeira embroidery. Delft blue pottery is an especially good buy. Other good buys include Dutch cheese (Edam and Gouda), as well as Dutch chocolate and English cigarettes in the airport departure area.

Philatelists interested in the wealth of colorful and artistic stamps issued in honor of the changed governmental status of Aruba can purchase a complete assortment, as well as other special issues, at the post office in Oranjestad.

The budget shopper might want to stick to one of the major shopping centers instead of the more expensive specialty stores. Aruba has some of the best stocked shopping malls in the Caribbean.

Try **Alhambra Moonlight Shopping Center,** adjacent to the Alhambra Casino, L. G. Smith Blvd. (☎ **297/8-35000**), which has a blend of international shops, outdoor marketplaces, and cafes and restaurants. Merchandise ranges from fine jewelry, crafts, folkloric dancing, and free shows. Oranjestad is also the place to do some duty-free shopping as you browse in the market place for Aruban art and local handcrafts.

- **Spelunk in Former Private Hideouts.** In the San Nicolas area you'll come across underground caves, unusual on a tropical island. At the Guadirikiri Cave, sunlight filters through two inner chambers, providing the perfect photo opportunity for cave explorers. The cave's 100-foot long tunnel is home to hundreds of harmless bats. Nearby, the Fontein Cave is testimony to the island's native population. Still visible drawings by the Arawak Indians decorate the cave's ceilings and are a powerful reminder of the island's indigenous history. Another cave in the area is called the Tunnel of Love, because of its heart-shaped entrance. A 300-foot-long tunnel winds through eerie rock formations and narrow passages. Helmets and flashlights can be rented for $6 from Arubans who are positioned at the entrances to the Guadirikiri and Tunnel of Love Caves.

- **Explore a Desert in the Caribbean.** On the northeastern coast, Arikok National Park is a desert-like ecological preserve. The island's rich crust makes it one of the rare places in the world where you can trace its geological origins with a naked eye. Hiking trails make it easy for visitors to explore the unusual terrain and diverse flora and fauna of the preserve. Iguanas and many species of migratory birds nest in the park, and goats and donkeys graze on nearby brush trees. Some of the island's best examples of early Indian art and artifacts are preserved within its boundaries. Visitors feeling particularly active can try dune sliding with the locals at the nearby Boca Prins dunes. At dusk, parakeets and other birds bid a cacophonous farewell in Jaburibari.

chocolates, and perfume to imported craft items, leather goods, clothing, and lingerie. Its major competitor is **Royal Plaza Mall,** L. G. Smith Blvd. 94 (no phone). For many visitors, this bustling shopping center, across from the cruise-ship terminal, meets all their shopping needs.

It's got a little bit of everything, including outlets for many of the big-name chains of the Caribbean, notably Gandelman's Jewelers and Little Switzerland. You'll also find outlets for other chains, including Tommy Hilfiger and Nautica. There's even an Internet Café, where you can send e-mail and order coffee as well. Finally, check out **Seaport Mall/Seaport Market Place,** L. G. Smith Blvd. 82 (☎ 297/8-24622). Aruba's densest concentration of shopping options is located in the heart of Oranjestad, within a pair of nearly adjacent two-story malls that collectively contain virtually everything an avid shopper could want. Overlooking the harbor of Oranjestad, these malls contain the Crystal Casino and the Seaport Casino, a movie theater with six screens and recently released films from Europe and the U.S. mainland, a convention center, several bars and cafes, and at least 200 purveyors of fashion, gift items, sporting goods, liquors, perfumes, and photographic supplies. Most shops within the complex are open Monday to Saturday from 9am to 6pm, and the bars and cafes usually operate on a Sunday as well. For information on the movie facilities at the **Seaport Cinema,** call (☎ **297/8-30318**).

Notable specialty shops include **Agatha at Les Accessories,** in the Seaport Mall (☎ **297/8-37965**). Agatha Brown, an award-winning American designer, operates this shop, featuring her exclusive designs. Agatha has recently added a stunning Italian knitwear collection, along with a handbag collection (both leather and nylon). Her elegant designer sportswear collection from Chile is not available elsewhere in the Caribbean. She also offers assorted designer collections of swimwear, sportswear, and evening wear. **Aruba Trading Company,** Caya G. F. Betico Croes 12 (☎ **297/ 8-22602**), has the island's best and most moderately priced selection of perfume, sold at prices considerably cheaper than in the U.S. because of the low duty. The company also offers a complete range of other items: cosmetics, shoes, clothing for men and women, liquor, and cigarettes (the smokes and booze can be delivered to your plane). Brand-name perfumes are often discounted here, but you'll have to search the store carefully to find the good buys.

Again, because of the low duty imposed on Aruba, even budget travelers can some-times pick up a good deal on jewelry. Try **Gandelman Jewelers,** Royal Plaza (☎ **297/ 8-34433**), which offers an extensive collection of fine gold jewelry and famous-name timepieces at duty-free prices. Go here if you're in the market for a deluxe watch or some piece of jewelry you'll have for a lifetime. Prices are reasonable, and they're the real thing. There are branch stores in the Americana Aruba Hotel, Airport Departure Hall, Wyndham Hotel, Royal Plaza, and Hyatt Regency Aruba. **Jewelers Warehouse,** in the Seaport Mall (☎ **297/8-36045**), is a popular international jewelry store found near the center of Oranjestad. It carries a complete line of rings, earrings, and bracelets, most of them inexpensive. **Little Switzerland Jewelers,** Caya G. F. Betico Croes 14 (☎ **297/8-21192**), is famous for its duty-free 14- and 18-karat-gold jew-elry and watches. This chain store also carries a big variety of famous-name Swiss watches. Over the years we've gotten some very good buys here in their Omega and Rado watches, which are usually discounted handsomely from stateside prices.

New Amsterdam Store, Caya G. F. Betico Croes 50 (☎ **297/8-21152**), is Aruba's leading department store for linens, with its selection of napkins, place mats, and embroidered tablecloths from as far away as China. It has an extensive line of other merchandise as well, from Delft blue pottery to beachwear and boutique items. **Penha,** Caya G. F. Betico Croes 11–13 (☎ **297/8-24161**), has offered one of the largest selections of top-name perfumes and cosmetics on the island since 1865. A household name on Aruba, it's one of the most dependable stores around. A Tommy Hilfiger boutique has been added to the store, and the men's department on the second floor is the finest in Aruba. Prices are usually lower than in the U.S. Of course, you must know your hometown prices before you'll spot what's a bargain here and what's not.

Finally, there's **Boulevard Book & Drugstore,** in the Seaport Mall (☎ **297/8-27358**), which sells a complete range of goods from the latest paperback books to cos-metics, candies, gifts, toys, high-quality T-shirts and sweatshirts, swimwear, sportswear, and souvenirs. You can also buy stamps, road maps, current magazines, and newspapers.

8 Aruba After Dark

THE CLUB & BAR SCENE

Nongamblers or those who grow tired of the casinos can head for hotels' cocktail lounges and supper clubs. You don't have to be a guest of a hotel to see the shows, but you should make a reservation. Tables at the big shows, especially in season, are likely to be booked early in the day. Usually you can go to one of the major hotel supper clubs and just order drinks.

The Cellar, Kliebstraat 2, Oranjestad (☎ **297/8-28567**), scattered over two floors of a battered-looking building, draws both tourists and locals. Upstairs you will find people dancing to everything from disco to house to *merengue*. Downstairs, the raucous cellar is more for the types who prefer to sit, talk, and people-watch. On weekends The Cellar can get pretty noisy and crowded, but it's a highly appealing place to go if you just want to get away from the casinos and relax with a drink, or perhaps flirt with a new-found friend. It's open until 4am.

Another simpatico place to spend an evening is **Cheers Bar,** L. G. Smith Blvd. 17 (☎ **297/8-30838**), which contains a total of four bars and is convivial, even raucous. The main bar provides cable sports, with a special emphasis on European soccer games. It has an enormous terrace with outside speakers and enough room for you to dance if you like, or to just sit and relax. Its fans appreciate the resident DJ who spins mostly house music during the week, as well as individual requests. Expect particularly animated mobs on Tuesday nights, when women drink for free. Sunday night is *Carnival* night, featuring a live band playing salsa and *merengue*. A full menu of shrimp, fried fish, burgers, and sandwiches is available. The place is open from sundown until 2am weeknights and until 4am on Saturday and Sunday.

Mumbo Jumbo, in the Royal Plaza Mall, L. G. Smith Blvd. (☎ **297/8-33632**), sultry but relaxing, presents an appealing blend of Dutch and Venezuelan style. Expect a cosmopolitan crowd dancing to Latin rhythms. The volume is kept at a decent level for those who prefer not to dance or lose their hearing by the end of the night. This is a great place to come alone if you like, but be careful, because the staff may ask you to join them in a drink or a dance. They offer an array of specialty drinks like the "Mambo Me Crazy" and the "Aruba-Riba." Imagine coconut shells, very colorful straws, and large fruit. Hours are from sunset until between 2 and 3am, depending on the night of the week.

New in 1999, the **Havana Beach Club,** L. G. Smith Blvd. 4 (☎ **297/8-23380**), is a seafront building that functions as a beach club during the day, where chairs and parasols are rented to sunlovers and a swimming pool is available for dips. After 8pm, however, the open-air premises are transformed into one of the island's busiest nightclubs, site of either recorded or live salsa music and lots of high-energy exhibitionism on the dance floor. It's very popular, continuing every night until 5am. The cover ranges from $6 to $8.

CASINOS: LET THE GOOD TIMES ROLL

The casinos of the big hotels along Palm Beach are the liveliest nightspots, and they stay open into the wee hours. In plush gaming parlors, guests try their luck at roulette, craps, blackjack, and, of course, the one-armed bandits. **Excelsior Casino,** J. E. Irausquin Blvd. 230 (☎ **297/8-67777**), wins the prize for all-around action. Its casino doors are open from 8am to 4am. The **Aruba Grand,** J. E. Irausquin Blvd. 79 (☎ **297/8-63900**), opens its games at noon; it stays open until 2am.

The **Casino Masquerade,** at the Radisson Aruba Caribbean Resort & Casino, J. E. Irausquin Blvd. 81, Palm Beach (☎ **297/8-66555**), is one of the newest casinos on Aruba. In the center of the high-rise hotel area, it sits on the lower-level lobby of the hotel and is open from 10am to 4am daily. It offers blackjack, single deck, roulette, Caribbean stud, craps, and "Let It Ride."

One of the island's best casinos is the **Crystal Casino** at the Aruba Sonesta Resort & Casino at Seaport Village (☎ **297/8-36000**). Open daily 24 hours, the 14,000-

square-foot casino offers 11 blackjack tables, 270 slot machines, 4 roulette tables, 3 Caribbean stud-poker tables, 2 craps tables, 1 mini-baccarat table, and 3 baccarat tables. The casino evokes European casinos with its luxurious furnishings, ornate moldings, marble, and crystal chandeliers.

Visitors have a tendency to flock to the newest casinos on the island, and these include those at the **Wyndham Hotel and Resort,** J. E. Irausquin Blvd. 77 (☎ **297/8-64466**), and at the **Hyatt Regency Aruba,** J. E. Irausquin Blvd. 85 (☎ **297/8-61234**). But outdrawing them all is the **Royal Cabana Casino,** at the La Cabana All Suite Beach Resort & Casino, J. E. Irausquin Blvd. 250 (☎ **297/ 8-79000**). It's known for its multi-theme, three-in-one restaurant and for its showcase cabaret theater and nightclub, which features everything from Las Vegas–style revues to female impersonators to comedy series on the weekend. Call to find out what's happening here at the time of your visit and to reserve a table if the action interests you. The largest casino on Aruba, it offers 33 tables and games, plus 320 slot machines.

The Alhambra, J. E. Irausquin Blvd. 47 (☎ **297/8-35000**), a complex of buildings and courtyards designed like an 18th-century Dutch village, contains about a dozen shops selling souvenirs, leather goods, jewelry, and beachwear. From the outside the complex looks Moorish, with serpentine mahogany columns, arches, and domes; the desert setting of Aruba seems appropriate. On the premises you'll find one of the busiest casinos on Aruba (open from 10am till very early in the morning, usually 3am).

Barbados 5

Bajans like to think of their island as "England in the tropics," but endless pink- and white-sand beaches are what really put Barbados on the map. Rich in tradition, Barbados has a grand array of hotels (many of them super-expensive). Although it doesn't offer casinos, it has more than beach life for travelers interested in learning about the local culture, and more sightseeing attractions than most islands of the West Indies.

Afternoon tea remains a tradition at many places, cricket is still the national sport, and many Bajans speak with a British accent. Crime has been on the rise in recent years, although Barbados is a relatively safe destination. The difference between the haves and the have-nots doesn't cause the sometimes-violent clash here that it does on some other islands, such as Jamaica.

Don't rule out Barbados if you're seeking a peaceful island getaway. Although the south coast is known for its nightlife and the west-coast beach strip is completely built up, some of the island remains undeveloped. The east coast is fairly tranquil, and you can often be alone here (but since it faces the Atlantic, the waters aren't tranquil as they are on the Caribbean side). Many escapists, especially Canadians seeking a low-cost place to stay in the winter don't seem to mind the Atlantic waters at all.

Because it's so built-up with hotels and condos, Barbados offers more package deals than most islands. You can often get a steal in the off-season, which lasts from April until mid-December. You don't necessarily have to pay the rack rate (the published or highest rate for individual bookings) at hotels if you'll take the time to shop around. Barbados is filled with bargains, especially along its southern coast directly below Bridgetown. This strip of beachfront isn't the most glamorous, but it's the most reasonable in price. Go back and read the section on "Package Deals" in chapter 2 before you try to book on your own.

1 Essentials

VISITOR INFORMATION

In the **United States,** you can obtain information before you go at these offices: 800 Second Ave., New York, NY 10017 (☎ **800/ 221-9831** or 212/986-6516) or 3440 Wilshire Blvd., Suite 1215, Los

Angeles, CA 90010 (☎ **213/380-2198**). Another outlet is at 158 Alhambra Circle, Suite 1270, Miami, FL 33134 (☎ **305/442-7471**).

In **Canada,** there is an office at 105 Adelaide St. West, Suite 1010, Toronto Ontario M5H 1P9 (☎ **416/214-9880**).

In the **United Kingdom,** the Barbados Tourism Authority is at 263 Tottenham Court Rd., London W1P 0LA (☎ **020/7636-9448**).

On the island, contact the **Barbados Tourism Authority,** Harbour Road (P.O. Box 242), Bridgetown, Barbados, W.I. (☎ **246/427-2623**).

The official Web site is **www.barbados.org**.

GETTING THERE

Before you book your flight, be sure to read the section on package tours in chapter 2—it can save you a bundle!

More than 20 daily flights arrive on Barbados from all over the world. **Grantley Adams International Airport** is on Highway 7, on the southern tip of the island at Long Bay, between Oistins and The Crane (a village). From North America, the four major gateways to Barbados are New York, Miami, Toronto, and San Juan. Flying time to Barbados from New York is 4½ hours, from Miami it's 3½ hours, from Toronto it's 5 hours, and from San Juan, 1½ hours.

American Airlines (☎ **800/433-7300**) has dozens of connections passing through San Juan, plus a daily nonstop flight from New York's JFK to Barbados and one from Miami to Barbados.

Travelers via New York and Miami can opt for nonstop flights offered daily by **BWIA** (☎ **800/538-2942**), the national airline of Trinidad and Tobago. BWIA also offers many flights from Barbados to Trinidad.

Canadians can fly nonstop to Barbados from Toronto. **Air Canada** (☎ **800/268-7240** in Canada or 800/776-3000 in the U.S.) has seven flights per week from Toronto in winter plus one Sunday flight from Montréal year-round. In summer, when demand slackens, there are fewer flights from Toronto.

Barbados is a major hub of the Caribbean-based airline known as **LIAT** (☎ **800/468-0482** in the U.S. and Canada, 246/434-5428 for reservations, or 246/428-0986 at the Barbados airport), which provides generally poor service from Barbados to a handful of neighboring islands, including St. Vincent in the Grenadines, Antigua, and Dominica.

Air Jamaica (☎ **800/523-5585** in the U.S.) has increased service to Barbados from key U.S. feeder markets. Daily inbound and outbound flights link Barbados with Atlanta, Baltimore, Fort Lauderdale, and Miami through the airline's new Montego Bay hub. Additionally, Air Jamaica has added service between Los Angeles and Barbados on Friday and Sunday, and service between Orlando and Barbados is also available Thursday and Sunday but requires an overnight stay in Montego Bay in each direction. Flights out of JFK to Barbados are non-stop Tuesday, Friday, and Sunday.

British Airways (☎ **800/247-9297** in the U.S., or 0345/222-111 in England) offers nonstop service to Barbados from both of London's airports—Heathrow Airport and Gatwick Airport.

GETTING AROUND

BY TAXI   Taxis aren't metered, but rates are fixed by the government. Taxis on the island are identified by the letter Z on their license plates and will carry up to five passengers for the same fare. Taxis are plentiful, and drivers will produce a list of standard rates, which is $20 per hour, subject to change. To call a taxi, dial one of the following services: **Paramount Taxi Service** (☎ **246/429-3718**), **Royal Pavilion Taxi Service** (☎ **246/422-5555**), or **Lyndhurst Taxi Service** (☎ **246/436-2639**).

Barbados

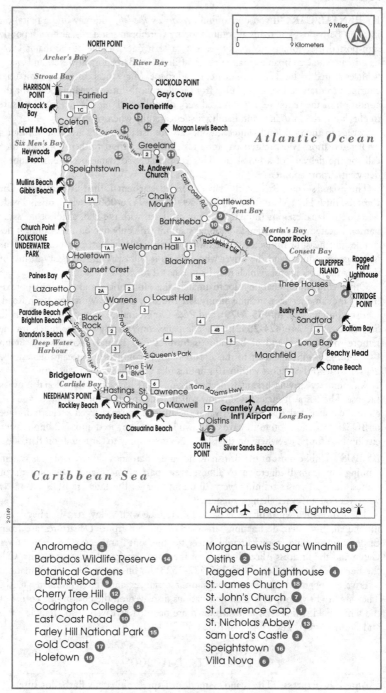

Andromeda ⑧
Barbados Wildlife Reserve ⑭
Botanical Gardens
    Bathsheba ⑨
Cherry Tree Hill ⑫
Codrington College ⑤
East Coast Road ⑩
Farley Hill National Park ⑮
Gold Coast ⑰
Holetown ⑲

Morgan Lewis Sugar Windmill ⑪
Oistins ②
Ragged Point Lighthouse ④
St. James Church ⑱
St. John's Church ⑦
St. Lawrence Gap ①
St. Nicholas Abbey ⑬
Sam Lord's Castle ③
Speightstown ⑯
Villa Nova ⑥

BY RENTAL CAR   If you don't mind *driving on the left,* you may find a rental car ideal on Barbados. The roads are quite good by Caribbean standards, although poorly sign-posted (newcomers invariably get lost, at least once). None of the major U.S.-based car-rental companies maintains an affiliate on Barbados, however, and many vehicles rented by local companies are in bad shape. Many local car-rental companies continue to draw serious complaints from readers, both for overcharging and for the condition of the rental vehicle. Proceed very carefully with rentals here. And be sure to check out the insurance and liability issues carefully when you rent.

Except in the peak mid-winter season, cars are usually readily available without a prior reservation. Most renters pay for a taxi from the airport to their hotel and then call for the delivery of a rental car. This is especially advisable because of frequent delays at airport counters.

The island's most frequently recommended car-rental firm is **National Car Rentals,** Bush Hall, Main Road, St. Michael (☎ **246/426-0603**), which offers a wide selection of Japanese cars (note that it's not affiliated with the U.S. chain of the same name). Located near the island's national stadium (the only one on the island), it lies 3 miles northeast of Bridgetown. Cars will be delivered to almost any location on the island upon request, and the driver who delivers it will carry the necessary forms for the Bajan driver's license, which may be purchased for $5.

Other companies, charging approximately the same prices and offering approximately the same services, include **Sunny Isle Motors,** Dayton, Worthing Main Road, Christ Church (☎ **246/435-7979**), and **P&S Car Rentals,** Pleasant View, Cave Hill, St. Michael (☎ **246/424-2052**). One company conveniently close to hotels on the remote southeastern end of Barbados is **Stoutes Car Rentals,** Kirtons, St. Philip (☎ **246/435-4456**). Closer to the airport than its competitors, it can theoretically deliver a car to the airport within 10 minutes of a call placed when you arrive.

A temporary driving permit is needed if you don't have an International Driver's License. The rental agencies listed below will all issue you a visitor's permit, or you can go to the police desk upon your arrival at the airport. You're charged a registration fee of BD$10 ($5), and you must have your own license. The speed limit is 20mph inside city limits, 45mph elsewhere on the island. No taxes apply to car rentals on Barbados.

BY BUS   Unlike most of the British Windwards, Barbados has a reliable bus system fanning out from Bridgetown to almost every part of the island. On most major routes, there are buses running every 20 minutes or so. Bus fares are BD$1.50 (75¢) wherever you go; exact change is required.

The nationally owned **buses** of Barbados are blue with yellow stripes. They're not numbered, but their destinations are marked on the front. Departures are from Bridgetown, leaving from Fairchild Street for the south and east, and from Lower Green and the Princess Alice Highway for the north going along the west coast. Call the **Barbados Tourist Board** (☎ **246/427-2623**) for bus schedules and information.

Privately operated **minibuses** run shorter distances and travel more frequently. They are bright yellow, with their destinations displayed on the bottom-left corner of the windshield. Minibuses in Bridgetown are boarded at River Road, Temple Yard, and Probyn Street. They, too, cost BD$1.50 (75¢).

Fast Facts: Barbados

American Express   The island's American Express affiliate is **Barbados International Travel Services,** Horizon House, McGregor Street (☎ **246/431-2423**), in the heart of Bridgetown.

Business Hours   Most banks on Barbados are open Monday to Thursday 9am to 3pm and Friday 9am to 1pm and 3 to 5pm. Stores are open Monday to Friday 8am to 4pm and Saturday 8am to noon. Most government offices are open Monday to Friday 8:30am to 4:30pm.

Consulates & High Commissions   The U.S. Consulate is located in the ALICO Building, Cheapside, Bridgetown (☎ **246/431-0225**); the Canadian High Commission at Bishop Court Hill, Pine Road (☎ **246/429-3550**); and the British High Commission at Lower Collymore Rock, St. Michael (☎ **246/436-6694**).

Currency   The **Barbados dollar (BD$)** is the official currency, available in $5, $10, $20, and $100 notes, as well as 10¢, 25¢, and $1 silver coins, plus 1¢ and 5¢ copper coins. The Bajan dollar is worth 50¢ in U.S. currency. Unless otherwise specified, *currency quotations in this chapter are in U.S. dollars.* Most stores take traveler's checks or U.S. dollars. However, it's best to convert your money at banks and pay in Bajan dollars.

Dentist   **Dr. Derek Golding,** with two other colleagues, maintains one of the busiest practices on Barbados. Located at the Beckwith Shopping Mall in Bridgetown (☎ **246/426-3001**), he accepts most emergency dental problems; otherwise, hours are Monday to Saturday 8am to 2:30pm.

Doctor   Your hotel might have a list of doctors on call, although some of the best recommended are **Dr. J. D. Gibling** (☎ **246/432-1772**) and **Dr. Adrian Lorde** or his colleague **Dr. Ahmed Mohamad** (☎ **246/424-8236**), any of whom will pay house calls to patients unable to leave their hotel rooms.

Documents   A U.S. or Canadian citizen coming directly from North America to Barbados for a period not exceeding 3 months must have proof of identity and national status, such as a passport, which is always preferred. A birth certificate (either an original or a certified copy) is also acceptable, provided it's backed up with photo ID, but we recommend that you carry a passport. For stays longer than 3 months, a passport is required. An ongoing or return ticket is also necessary. British subjects need a valid passport.

Electricity   The electricity is 110 volts AC (50 cycles), so at most places you can use your U.S.-made appliances.

Emergencies   In an **emergency,** call ☎ **119.** Other important numbers include the **police** at ☎ **112,** the **fire** department at ☎ **113,** and an **ambulance** at ☎ **115.**

Hospitals   The **Queen Elizabeth Hospital** is on Martinsdale Road in St. Michael (☎ **246/436-6450**). There are several private clinics as well; one of the most expensive and best recommended is the **Bayview Hospital,** St. Paul's Avenue, Bayville, St. Michael (☎ **246/436-5446**).

Language   The Barbadians, or Bajans, as they're called, speak English, but with their own island lilt.

Safety   Crimes against tourists used to be rare, but the U.S. State Department reports rising crime, such as purse snatching, pickpocketing, armed robbery, and even sexual assault upon women. The department advises that you not leave cash or valuables in your hotel room, beware of purse snatchers when walking, exercise caution when walking on the beach or visiting tourist attractions, and be wary of driving in isolated areas of Barbados.

Taxes When you leave, you'll have to pay a BD$25 ($12.50) departure tax. A 7½% government sales tax is added to hotel bills, and a 15% VAT (value added tax) is added to all restaurant meals. For example, if your hotel costs $200 per night, and you are charged $50 per person for a MAP, you are levied a 7½% government tax plus the 10% additional service charge for the $200 room rate, then an additional 15% VAT on the MAP rate. Comprende? Some visitors have viewed these additional charges as "larcenous." They certainly won't make you happy when you go to pay your final bill.

Tipping Most hotels and restaurants add at least a 10% service charge to your bill.

Water Barbados has a pure water supply. It's pumped from underground sources in the coral rock that covers six-sevenths of the island, and it's safe to drink.

Weather Daytime temperatures are in the 75°F to 85°F (24°C to 29°C) range throughout the year.

2 Accommodations You Can Afford

There are bargains to be found, but to find them you'll have to avoid the resorts on fashionable St. James Beach and instead head south from Bridgetown to such places as Hastings and Worthing. The best buys are often self-contained efficiencies or studio apartments where you can do your own cooking. You can usually find good package deals to Barbados, too; see the section "Package Deals" in chapter 2.

Prices in this section, unless otherwise indicated, are in U.S. dollars. Remember that the government hotel tax of 5% and a 10% service charge will be added to your final bill.

Some of the best and least expensive rental deals can be made through **Homar Rentals,** Europa, Sunset Crest, St. James (☎ **246/432-6750;** fax 246/432-7229; www.tropix.com; e-mail: homar@caribsurf.com), which controls 109 apartments. These accommodations are two-apartment bungalows, some on one floor, others in two-story buildings, all constructed from concrete. Furnishings for the most part are basic in a West Indian motif, with rattan pieces or leatherette. There are phones, and some bedrooms have ceiling fans, although TVs must be rented. Daily maid service is provided. Air-conditioning is token-operated at $4.50 for 10 hours. In winter a single or double begins at $85 daily, with off-season prices lowered to $60. An extra person is charged $10, and one child 11 and under stays free in their parents' room. Homar is one of several companies managing the Sunset Crest Resort, privately owned condos where apartments are rented when the owners are off-island. There's a network of two pools, plus a restaurant serving three standard meals a day. The nearby Beach Club also has a pool, a bar, and water-sports equipment for rent.

Atlantis Hotel. Bathsheba, St. Joseph, Barbados, W.I. ☎ **246/433-9445.** 15 units. Winter $40 single; $65 double. Off-season $35 single; $60 double. Extra adult $35 each in winter $30 each off-season; extra child 11 and under $17 each in winter $15 each off-season. Rates include half-board. AE.

This boxy, concrete-sided hotel offers virtues (and drawbacks) not associated with more modern resorts in better-developed regions of Barbados. It's one of the most durable establishments on the island, with a long history of feeding large numbers of lunchtime visitors (reviewed below). It's in an isolated position on Barbados's rocky and turbulent Atlantic coast, where strong currents, winds, and undertows usually make swimming a bad idea. If that doesn't deter you, here are the pluses: The scenery in St. Joseph is among the most beautiful on Barbados; the welcome is warm and the ambience authentically Bajan; and the place is respectable, well known by virtually everyone on the island. The accommodations are clean but simple affairs, with white walls, carpeted floors, wooden furniture, and (in many cases) views and balconies over-looking the surging Atlantic. Mattresses are rather old and lumpy but the diehard devotees of this place rarely complain. Bathrooms are really too tiny, and towels are on the skimpy side. You stay here more for old Bajan atmosphere than for any grand com-fort. Mrs. Enid Maxwell and members of her family are the longtime owners.

✪ **Fairholme.** Maxwell, Christ Church, Barbados, W.I. ☎ **246/428-9425.** Fax 246/420-2389. 31 units. Winter $30 single or double; $55 studio apt. Off-season $28 single or double; $35 studio apt. No credit cards.

Fairholme is a converted plantation house that has been enlarged during the past 20 years with a handful of connected annexes. The main house and its original gardens are just off a major road 6 miles southeast of Bridgetown. The hotel is a 5-minute walk to the beach and across from its neighbor, the Sea Breeze, which has a waterfront cafe and bar that Fairholme guests may use. The older part has 11 double rooms, each with a living-room area and a patio overlooking an orchard and swimming pool. More recently added are 20 Spanish-style studio apartments, all with balcony or patio, built in the old plantation style, with cathedral ceilings, dark beams, and traditional fur-nishings. Bedrooms range from small to medium in size; the mattresses are firm and the baths tend to be tiny but are tidy, with a set of rather thin towels. The restaurant has a reputation for home-cooking—wholesome, nothing fancy, but the ingredients are fresh. Air-conditioning is available only in the studios. (At the reception desk you buy a brass token for $3 that you insert into your air conditioner for around 8 hours of cooling-off time.)

Fleet View Apartments. Tent Bay, Bathsheba, St. Joseph, Barbados, W.I. ☎ **246/433-9445.** 6 apts. Winter $40 studio apt. for 1 or 2; $45 1-bedroom apt. for 1 or 2. Off-season $30 studio apt. for 1 or 2; $35 1-bedroom apt. for 1 or 2. AE.

These apartments are an annex of the Atlantis Hotel. They're simple, and cater to independent-minded guests who don't want the fussiness associated with a traditional hotel or resort. Their last renovation occurred in 1998. Their lack of resort amenities is offset by the surprisingly low rates, and if you have a bicycle or car you can com-pensate for the isolation. Rooms are small and are meant more for sleeping than lin-gering, but the mattresses are relatively new. Don't plan to play football in the tiny bathrooms. Although each unit has a modest kitchen, breakfast is served across the street in the dining room of the Atlantis Hotel, and if you grow tired of cooking, the Atlantis will happily feed you. For more information about the location, refer to the Atlantis listing, below.

Little Bay Hotel. St. Lawrence Gap, Christ Church, Barbados, W.I. ☎ **246/435-7246.** Fax 246/435-8574. 10 units. A/C TV TEL. Winter $100 studio for 1 or 2; $140 1-bedroom apt. for up to 4. Off-season $65 studio for 1 or 2; $85 1-bedroom apt. for up to 4. AE, MC, V.

This small apartment complex consists of an older core, which has been upgraded and renovated by its owners, the Patterson family. It's a peach-colored building with a tiled roof and pleasant, unfrilly accommodations with brick-tile floors, utilitarian furniture, and views over Barbados's well-developed southwestern coastline. Accommodations are a bit small but adequate for one or two guests, though very crowded when four share a unit. Mattresses are firm and comfortable, and the bathrooms are tiny but tidy. There are ample opportunities for affordable drinking, nightclubbing, and dining within a brisk walk (or short drive) of your room. If you cook your meals in-house, you'll have a private kitchenette and access to several grocery stores and mini-marts nearby. No breakfast is served on-site, but Italian dinners are available at Bellini's restaurant, which is vaguely associated with this hotel.

Meridian Inn. Dover, Christ Church, Barbados, W.I. ☎ **246/428-4051.** Fax 246/420-6495. 16 studio apts. A/C. Winter $59 studio apt. for 1 or 2. Off-season $42 studio apt. for 1 or 2. Children under 3 stay free in parents' studio; children 4 and over, $12 per day. AE, MC, V.

Close to shopping, restaurants, and nightclubs, this four-story, white-painted building right on the street is about a minute's walk to a good beach. It offers some of the least-expensive rooms on the island. Admittedly, although clean and comfortable, some of the accommodations evoke Miami motels of the 1960s, although there was a recent refurbishment that installed new mattresses. Units are air-conditioned, with twin beds, kitchenettes, small bathrooms, and private balconies, along with daily maid service. Each has a ceiling fan and a small fridge; TVs can be rented. Phones are in the corridors. There's no room service; baby-sitting can be arranged. On the ground floor a simple restaurant features fresh seafood at both lunch and dinner.

Pegwell Inn. Welches, Christ Church Parish, Barbados, W.I. ☎ **246/428-6150.** 4 units. Winter $15 single; $30 double. Off-season $14 single; $28 double. No credit cards.

This simple but respectable guest house in a one-story, wood-sided building was built during the early 1940s. Rosemary Phillips is devoted to running the island's least expensive accommodations. There's a laundry across the street, a swimming area (Welches Beach, which can be seen across the road), and easy access to such nearby facilities as a bank, restaurants, and shops. Each accommodation is plain as can be; two rooms have two single beds, two rooms have one double bed each, and all rooms have a toilet, a sink, and shower. You're a bit cramped in both the bedrooms and bathrooms, but the mattresses are comfortable.

Rio Guest House. Paradise Village, St. Lawrence Gap, Christ Church, Barbados, W.I. ☎ **246/428-1546.** Fax 246/428-1546. 8 units, 5 with bath; 1 studio. Winter $25 single without bath; $35 single or double with bath; $55 studio. Off-season $20 single without bath; $26 single or double with bath; $45 studio. No credit cards.

Built as a private home in the 1940s, this simple black-and-white–painted guest house is maintained by the resident owner, Mrs. Denise Harding. It features low rates and clean, no-frills bedrooms. None of the single rooms has a private bathroom; there are no private kitchens, except in the studio. Accommodations are small and the mattresses have been used many, many times before but they are still comfortable. Accommodations that have private bathrooms are a bit cramped for shelf space; the communal baths are kept neat and tidy if you have to share. The mini-marts, bars, nightclubs, and hamburger joints of St. Lawrence Gap are within walking distance; Dover Beach is within a 2-minute walk. Guests share a communal kitchen, in which a large refrigerator is divided into compartments, each reserved more or less exclusively for one of the bedrooms, where you can store your munchies.

Southern Surf Beach Apartment. Rockley Beach, Christ Church, Barbados, W.I. ☎ **246/435-6672.** Fax 246/435-6649. 4 "Great House" units, 12 studio apts. A/C. Winter $50–$60 single or double; $70 studio apt. for 2. Off-season $40 single or double; $50 studio apt. for 2. Extra person in apartment $15. MC, V.

Close to the famous Accra Beach at Rockley, this is a good, serviceable choice in a centrally located complex with a swimming pool and garden. It's also convenient for nearby dining, shopping, and entertainment. Four rooms are in the main or Great House, whereas the studio apartments are in a four-story concrete-block building. There are three apartments per floor, each simply but comfortably furnished, with a balcony and beach view. The rooms don't have phones, but there is one for public use in the apartment block, and the only TV is in the office reception area. Rooms in the main house, although not as large, have more of an old-time Bajan feeling, with ceiling fans overhead. The apartment complex renews its mattresses as needed, and keeps the plumbing in a good state in its small but well-maintained bathrooms, which have racks with medium-size towels. Children are housed free in a studio apartment if an extra cot is not needed; otherwise a $15-per-day surcharge applies. Baby-sitting can also be arranged. Southern Surf owns the land between it and the ocean, so there's an unobstructed view of the beach.

Sunhaven Beach Apartment Hotel. Rockley Beach, Christ Church, Barbados, W.I. ☎ **246/435-8905.** Fax 246/435-6621. 9 units, 26 apts. A/C. Winter $60 single; $70 double. $75 1-bedroom apt. for 1, $90 1-bedroom apt. for 2, $105 1-bedroom apt. for 3. Off-season $45 single; $50 double; $50 1-bedroom apt. for 1, $60 1-bedroom apt. for 2, $70 1-bedroom apt. for 3. Children 4 and under stay free in parents' unit; children 5–12, $10 each. MAP (breakfast and dinner) $30 per person extra. AE, DC, MC, V.

This small, rather innocuous-looking complex offers both conventional bedrooms and a larger number of one-bedroom apartments with kitchenettes. It's close to the sands of Rockley Beach, near many fast-food and inexpensive pub-style restaurants. The accommodations are small and a bit dowdy, with functional furniture and dour, floral-patterned carpeting, but if you're traveling with friends or children in tow, it's hard to beat the savings. Each unit has a sea view and a balcony. The mattresses are good and are replaced as needed, and the bathrooms are neatly arranged with some shelf space for your stuff and a good supply of medium-size towels. At one edge of the pool, over-looking the beach, is an open-air restaurant, The Lagoon, serving lunches for around $5 to $10 and dinners for $12.

Time Out Hotel. St. Lawrence Gap, Christ Church, Barbados, WI. ☎ **246/420-5021.** Fax 246/420-5021. E-mail: timeoutgap@caribsurf.com. 76 units. TV TEL. Winter $100–$135 single or double, $115–$150 triple, $130–$165 quad. Off-season $80 single or double, $95 triple, $110 quad. AE, MC, V.

In 1998, new management took over the premises of a faded four-story relic from the 1970s, and radically upgraded the old furniture and amenities. Soon thereafter, on the opposite side of the seafront boulevard, they began building an all-new four-story annex that will double the room count above during the lifetime of this edition. Set across from the site of the original hotel, it will be directly on the surf at Dover Beach. Accommodations here almost always have tile floors, walls, plus vibrant color schemes. Each has a small, unstocked refrigerator, and many contain small balconies. Nearly all the mattresses are new; bathrooms are a bit small, but adequate. On the premises is a whimsical sports bar and restaurant, the Whistling Frog, which is recommended below.

Windsurf Village Hotel. Maxwell Main Rd., Christ Church, Barbados, W.I. ☎ **246/428-9095.** Fax 246/435-6621. 15 units. Winter $60 single or double; $90–$115 studio with kitch-enette for 2; $170 2-bedroom apt. for 4. Off-season $45 single or double; $65–$75 studio with kitchenette for 2; $125 2-bedroom apt. for 4. AE, MC, V.

Although this hotel assumes that windsurfers appreciate proximity to other wind-surfers, many guests who don't have very much interest in the sport have been happy here, too. Designed in a two-story, white-walled format with balconies, with at least two patios for outdoor mingling of guests, it attracts a youngish crowd of sports enthusiasts, as well as older nonparticipants who appreciate the lighthearted setting. The small bedrooms contain white-painted walls, wooden furnishings, ceiling fans, and tile-covered floors. Mattresses are a bit thin, as are the towels in the tiny baths, but it's a grade above college dorm living. Budget travelers like its location amid Barbados's densest concentration of nightclubs, supermarkets, and cheap restaurants, all of which are in the same parish (Christ Church), within an easy walk or drive. It maintains a snack-style restaurant on the beach, with lunches priced at $6 and dinners beginning at $10.

Despite the establishment's name, it doesn't own or rent any Windsurfers. Instead, windsurfing enthusiasts are directed to the water-sports facilities at the nearby Club Mistral.

Woodville Beach Apartments. Hastings, Christ Church, Barbados, W.I. ☎ **246/435-6694.** Fax 246/435-9211. 36 units. TEL. Winter $110–$116 studio apt. for 1 or 2; $145 1-bedroom apt. for 1 or 2; $190 2-bedroom apt. for up to 4. Off-season $85–$90 studio apt. for 1 or 2; $110 1-bedroom apt. for 1 or 2; $130 2-bedroom apt. for up to 4. AE, MC, V.

These apartments, last renovated in 1995, represent one of the best bargains on Barbados and are ideal for families. Directly on a rocky shoreline 2½ miles southeast of Bridgetown, the hotel is in the heart of the village of Hastings. The U-shaped apartment complex is built around a pool terrace overlooking the sea. Functional and minimalist in decor, it's clean and comfortable. The tiny kitchenettes in each accommodation are fully equipped, and a variety of rental units are offered. All have balconies or decks, and some units contain air-conditioning. Bedrooms are small, as are the bathrooms, but the beds are good. Plumbing is kept well-maintained. There are supermarkets, stores, and banks within easy walking distance. Although some athletic guests attempt to swim off the nearby rocks, most walk 5 minutes to the white sands of nearby Rockley (Accra) Beach. A small restaurant is open on the property, serving American and Bajan fare.

WORTH A SPLURGE

✪ **Bagshot House Hotel.** St. Lawrence, Christ Church, Barbados, W.I. ☎ **246/435-6956.** Fax 246/435-9000. 16 units. A/C TEL. Winter $80 single; $120 double. Off-season $55 single; $80 double. Rates include breakfast. AE, CB, DC, DISC, MC, V.

Completely renovated in 1996, this small, family-managed hotel, which has been painted pink since the 1940s, has flowering vines tumbling over the railing of the balconies and an old-fashioned, unhurried kind of charm. The hotel was named after the early 19th-century manor house that once stood on this site. In front, a white-sand beach stretches out before you. Some of the well-kept rooms boast views of the water. In pastel color schemes with wall-to-wall carpeting, the bedrooms range in size from small to spacious. Most have twin beds with excellent mattresses, plus medium-size private bathrooms. A sunbathing deck, which doubles as a kind of living room for the resort, is perched at the edge of a lagoon. A deck-side lounge is decorated with paintings by local artists, and a restaurant, Sand Dollar, is on the premises.

Sea Foam Haciendas. Worthing, Christ Church, Barbados, W.I. ☎ **800/8-BARBADOS** in the U.S. and Canada, or 246/435-7380. Fax 246/435-7384. E-mail: seafoam@ caribsurf.com. 12 suites. A/C TEL. Winter $135 single or double; $185 quad. Off-season $95 single or double; $120 quad. Extra person $15. MC, V.

Centrally located on Worthing Beach, this Spanish-style property lies between the airport and Bridgetown. It's also convenient to supermarkets, banks, a post office, and a small shopping plaza. All the drinking and dining facilities of the St. Lawrence area are close at hand if you don't want to rent a car. Each good-size suite is fully furnished, with two air-conditioned bedrooms with fine mattresses, a modern kitchen with electric stove, and a large refrigerator with a microwave. Each suite also has its own private phone and radio, and there's a wall safe in the master bedroom. Bathrooms are fairly standard and routine, but with enough space to spread out your toilet articles. The open-style kitchen looks into the living and dining room area, which opens onto a large private balcony overlooking the ocean. Because of this place's good value, it enjoys a high repeat clientele.

Silver Sands Resort. Silver Sands, Christ Church, Barbados, W.I. ☎ **800/GO-BAJAN** in the U.S., 800/822-2077 in Canada, or 246/428-6001. Fax 246/428-3758. 106 units. A/C TV. Winter $130 single or double; $140 studio for 2; $170 suite for 2; $180 triple; $190 quad. Off-season $65–$70 single or double; $75 studio for 2; $85 suite for 2; $95 triple; $105 quad. Extra person $10; children 12 and under stay free in parents' room. AE, DC, DISC, MC, V.

This is a beachfront resort of 6 mushroom-colored buildings on 6 acres of handsomely landscaped grounds. Each is well furnished, and, although not particularly stylish, all come with balconies and a number of conveniences, including pay-per-view TV. All the studios have kitchenettes, and the suites come with full kitchens. The least desirable rooms are classified as standards, which are the smallest and almost evoke dormitory living. Studios are suitable for one or two. The one-bedroom suites are the most desirable as they are more spacious and better furnished. Closets are tiny, as are the bathrooms. Mattresses, however, are fairly new throughout, and the towels are in generous supply. The best views of the ocean are on the third floor of the main building. Extra amenities include baby-sitting, and room service is also available. You can dine here or patronize several restaurants nearby. The Sands is a true resort, with two swimming pools, tennis courts, and a water-sports concession. The place may not be for the hopelessly romantic—it's too sterile for that. It's a good, all-around, reliable resort, one of the best in the area, and it charges only a fraction of the price of the megaresorts with their megarates.

3 Great Deals on Dining

Angry Annie's Restaurant & Bar. First St., Holetown, St. James. ☎ **246/432-2119.** Main courses $12.50–$27.50. MC, V. Daily 6pm–10pm (or sometimes after midnight). INTERNATIONAL.

Don't ask "Annie" why she's angry. She might tell you! Annie and Paul Matthews, both of the U.K., run this friendly restaurant. This cozy 34-seat joint is decorated in tropical colors with a circular bar. Rock 'n' roll classics play on the excellent sound system. The dishes are tasty with lots of local flavor. The place is known for ribs, the most savory on the island. We also like their garlic cream potatoes, and their use of local vegetables whenever possible. Angry or not, Annie also turns out excellent pasta dishes, and you can also order fresh fish. Begin with a homemade soup or chicken wings, and then the night is yours, especially if you order such dishes as chicken Kiev or spaghetti bolognese. There's even a take-out service if you'd like to take something back to your studio or apartment.

✪ **Atlantis Hotel.** Bathsheba, St. Joseph. ☎ **246/433-9445.** Reservations required for Sun buffet and 7pm dinner, recommended at all other times. Two-course fixed-price lunch $12.50, fixed-price dinner $15.75; Sun buffet $18.75. AE. Daily 11:30am–3pm, dinner at 7pm (and don't be late). BAJAN.

Harking back to the old-fashioned Barbados of several years ago, the slightly run-down Atlantis Hotel is often filled with both Bajans and visitors. It's located between Cattlewash-on-Sea and Tent Bay on the east coast (Atlantic Ocean). In the sunny, breeze-filled interior, with a sweeping view of the turbulent ocean, Enid I. Maxwell has been welcoming visitors from all over the world ever since she opened the place in 1945. Her copious buffets are one of the best food values on the island. From loaded tables, you can sample such Bajan foods as pumpkin fritters, peas and rice, macaroni and cheese, chow mein, souse, and a Bajan pepperpot. No one ever leaves here hungry.

Barbecue Barn. Rockley, Christ Church. ☎ **246/430-3402.** Main courses $9.50–$12.50. MC, V. Daily 11am–11pm. BAJAN.

This basic restaurant serves simple fare, often to families staying in south-coast hotels. There's a fully stocked self-service salad bar. Try the barbecued chicken as a main course or in a sandwich. The menu also includes roast chicken, burgers, steak, and fried chicken nuggets. Most main courses are served with your choice of potato or spiced rice and garlic bread. A small selection of wines complements your meal.

Bombas. Paynes Bay, St. James. ☎ **246/432-0569.** Main courses $10–$16.50; lunch from $8. MC, V. Daily 11am–11pm. INTERNATIONAL.

Simple and unpretentious though it is, this place is worth a detour. Right on the water at Paynes Bay, it's so inviting that you may adopt it as your local hangout. The avocados on Barbados are said to be "ethereal," and you can find out why here, along with sampling an array of other Bajan specialties and even dishes designed to appeal to the vegetarian market. The drinks here are made with fresh juices and not overly loaded with buckets of sugar. The owners Gaye and Wayne, a Scottish/Bajan couple, are hospitable hosts, chalking up their latest offerings on a blackboard menu. You can visit just for a snack, perhaps enjoying ròti or seasoned flying fish. Their main dishes are certainly worth trying, including the catch of the day, which can be blackened in the Cajun style or deep-fried in crispy batter and chips in the English style. They also make a wicked Bomba curry, or, for a taste of the Highlands of Scotland, will serve you sautéed chicken breast on a bed of saffron rice with a Drambuie-cream sauce.

Café Calabash. St. Nicholas Abbey, on the St. Peter/St. Lucy border. ☎ **246/422-8725.** Creole lunch $5–$18; snacks, traditional English teas from $4. No credit cards. Mon–Fri 10am–4pm. BAJAN/AFTERNOON TEA.

On the site of this Jacobean plantation Great House, this is the most romantic place on Barbados to have afternoon tea or to stop in for a Bajan lunch of Creole fare. Nick Hudson, a restaurateur who became famous islandwide when he operated the restaurant La Cage aux Folles, opened this cafe in 1997. Now you can eat or drink at one of the premier tourist attractions of Barbados. The cafe looks out onto one of the few remaining virgin rain forests in the Caribbean. A typical meal might include one of the local homemade soups such as pumpkin or fish. Sandwiches and burgers are always available, or you can order one of the fresh fish dishes of the day. Barracuda is often featured, as are swordfish and mahi mahi. The cooks also make a mean chicken pot, and wait until you sample some of the island's best banana bread.

Café Sol. St. Lawrence Gap, Christ Church. ☎ **246/435-9531.** Main courses $12–$17. AE, MC, V. Daily 6–11pm. TEX-MEX.

Even though this cafe has a gringo section on the menu, designed for diehard meat-and-potatoes Yankees, most people come for some of the best Tex-Mex food on the island. The burritos and tacos don't get much bigger than here. If you're looking for flavorful and zesty meals, good prices, oversized portions, and enthusiastic service, eat here. Feast on the tostados, fajitas, nachos, and all the good-tasting beef, shrimp, and chicken dishes, each served with rice and beans or fries. As for the non-Mexican burgers, barbecued chicken, hot dogs, and steaks, you can fare better elsewhere. This is a small, comfortable place with an outside bar and patio and a medley of recorded Italian and Mexican music to entertain you.

Crane Beach Hotel. Crane Bay, St. Philip. ☎ **246/423-6220.** Reservations required. Lunch BD$9–BD$45 (U.S.$4.50–$22.50); Sun brunch BD$40 (U.S.$20). AE, DC, MC, V. Daily 7:30am–9:30pm (Sun brunch 12:30–3pm). BAJAN.

On a remote hilltop opening onto the Atlantic Coast, this scenic restaurant serves traditional Bajan specialties as well as a few international dishes. The dinner, costing BD$42 to BD$60 (U.S.$21 to $30), is a little too pricey to be a bargain, but lunches include burgers, sandwiches, and lighter fare kinder to your wallet. Sunday brunch is a real bargain. Served buffet-style, the brunch—"a good tuck-in"—includes soup of the day (hot or cold); Bajan and international dishes, including flying fish and a baked pie made of macaroni, cream, onions, and sweet peppers; a number of side items (rice and peas, candied sweet potatoes, and plantains); an assortment of desserts, including fresh fruit; and a beverage. Either before or after brunch, guests walk down the coral-hewn stairway from the hotel's cantilevered terrace to the pink sandy beach. The restaurant features live entertainment Tuesday and Friday until 10:30pm.

Pizzaz. Hwy. 1, Holetown, St. James. ☎ **246/432-0227.** Pizzas, pastas, and salads $6–$20. MC, V. Sun–Thurs 10am–11pm, Fri–Sat 10am–midnight. PIZZA.

If you're staying at one of the expensive West Coast hotels and get a sudden craving for pizza, head here to this site directly across from the Sunset Crest Beach Club. The place is new but simple. There's an unbelievable $18.50 pizza: the "ridiculous pie," with everything on it. Many pies aren't your typical cheese and tomato concoctions, but come with smoked mozzarella, prosciutto, smoked fish, and sun-dried tomatoes.

Rôti Hut. Worthing, Christ Church. ☎ **246/435-7362.** Snacks and plates $2–$4.60; picnic box $4.25. No credit cards. Mon–Thurs 11am–10pm, Fri–Sat 11am–11pm. ROTIS.

The island's best rôtis are served here at this little Worthing hut, an off-white concrete structure with an enclosed patio for dining. Count on these zesty pastries to be filled with good-tasting and spicy meats, or whatever. The crowd pleaser is the mammoth chicken or beef potato rôti. The locals like their rôtis with bone, but you can order yours without if you wish. You can also order other food items, including beef burgers, fried chicken, and beef or chicken curry with rice. This is also a good place to pick up a picnic box.

T.G.I. Boomers. St. Lawrence Gap, Christ Church. ☎ **246/428-8439.** Main courses $9–$22.50; lunch specials $3.50–$7; American breakfast $6.50; daiquiris $5; Sun buffet $12.50. AE, MC, V. Daily 7:30am–11:30pm. AMERICAN/BAJAN.

Four miles south of Bridgetown near Rockley Beach along Highway 7, T.G.I. Boomers offers some of the best bargain meals on the island. An American/Bajan operation, it has an active bar and a row of tables where food is served, usually along with frothy pastel-colored drinks. The cook prepares a special catch of the day, and the fish is served with soup or salad, rice or baked potato, and a vegetable. You can always count on seafood, steaks, and hamburgers. For lunch, try a daily Bajan special or a jumbo sandwich. Be sure to try one of the 16-ounce daiquiris.

39 Steps. Chattel Plaza, Hastings, Christ Church. ☎ **246/427-0715.** Main courses $14–$17. MC, V. Mon–Fri noon–3pm and 6:30–9:30pm, Sat 6:30–10pm. Closed Sept. INTERNATIONAL.

This south-coast choice, one of the area's most popular, is the best wine bar in Hastings. Diners walk the 39 steps (or however many) to reach this convivial place where performers sometimes entertain on the sax and guitar. It's laid-back and casual, and the food and wine are not only good but affordable. Look to the chalkboard for the tasty favorites of the day. Whenever possible the cooks use fresh, local produce to concoct dishes appealing to a wide cross section, including English pub grub–style pies such as steak and kidney or chicken and mushroom. They also turn out lasagna and other pastas, along with seafood crêpes, shrimp and chicken curry, and blackened fish. The most famous dish of Barbados, flying fish, appears only on the lunch menu. They're not big on vegetables, however, serving only a mixed green salad. This pleasant restaurant and bar has lots of windows and a balcony for outdoor dining.

The Whistling Frog. In the Time Out Hotel, St. Lawrence Gap, Christ Church. ☎ **246/420-5021.** Main courses $10–$25. AE, DC, MC, V. Daily 7am–10:45pm. INTERNATIONAL

The decor of this restaurant is one of the most themed, but also one of the most charming, of the many that line the edges of St. Lawrence Gap. The decor includes lots and lots of images of every kind of frog. (Most of them are adorable, a fact that may or may not jibe with your particular point of view about amphibians.) Menu items manage to elevate bar food to slightly more respectable levels, thanks to stuffed peppers and platters of fresh fish that augment the traditional roster of nachos and burgers that form the basis of sports bar menus throughout the known world. Look for salads, platters of fried fish, and rum-based drinks such as the Time Bomb or Smoothie.

The Waterfront Cafe. The Careenage, Bridgetown. ☎ **246/427-0093.** Reservations required. Main courses BD$20–BD$40 ($10–$20). AE, DC, MC, V. Mon–Sat 10am–midnight. INTERNATIONAL.

In a turn-of-the-century warehouse, this cafe serves international fare with a strong emphasis on Bajan specialties. Try the fresh catch of the day prepared Creole style, peppered steak, or the fish burger made with kingfish or dolphin. For vegetarians, the menu includes such dishes as pasta primavera, vegetable soup, and usually a featured special. This enterprise welcomes both diners and drinkers to its reverberating walls for Creole food, beer, and pastel-colored drinks. Live steel-band music is presented, with a Bajan buffet featured on Tuesday from 7 to 9pm, costing BD$41 ($20.50). If you expect to see the Dixieland bands on Thursday night, you need to make reservations about a week in advance. Jazz is presented on Friday and Saturday.

ALL-YOU-CAN-EAT BARGAINS
The Coach House. Paynes Bay, St. James. ☎ **246/432-1163.** Reservations recommended. Dinner main courses $7–$24; lunch buffet $14. AE, MC, V. Daily noon–2am. BAJAN.

The Coach House is a green-and-white house said to be 200 years old. The atmosphere is a Bajan version of an English pub, with an outdoor garden bar. Businesspeople and sun worshippers from nearby beaches come here to order buffet lunches, where Bajan food is served Sunday to Friday from noon to 3pm. The price is $14 for an all-you-can-eat lunch including local vegetables and salads prepared fresh daily. The best deal here is the bar menu, which ranges from burgers and fries to fried shrimp and flying fish. Dinner is from an a la carte menu with steak, chicken, fish, curried dishes, fresh salads, and a wide range of desserts from cheesecake to banana flambé. Live music is available every night of the week, from top nightclub bands to steel bands. The pub is on the main Bridgetown-Holetown road, just south of Sandy Lane, about 6 miles north of Bridgetown.

The Ship Inn. St. Lawrence Gap, Christ Church. ☎ **246/435-6961.** Reservations recommended for the Captain's Carvery only. Main courses $8–$15; all-you-can-eat carvery meal $15 at lunch, $21 (plus $7.50 for appetizer and dessert) at dinner. MC, V. Sun–Fri noon–3pm and 6:30–10:30pm (last order), Sat 6:30–10:30pm. ENGLISH PUB/BAJAN.

South of Bridgetown between Rockley Beach and Worthing, the Ship Inn is a traditional English-style pub with an attractive, rustic decor of nautical memorabilia. You might just have a tropical drink in the garden bar. Many guests come for darts and to meet friends, and certainly to listen to the live music presented nightly by some of the island's top bands (see "Barbados After Dark," later in this chapter). The Ship Inn serves substantial bar food, such as homemade steak-and-kidney pie, shepherd's pie, and chicken, shrimp, and fish dishes. For more formal dining, visit the Captain's Carvery, where you can have your fill of succulent cuts from prime roasts on a nighttime buffet table, and an array of traditional Bajan food (fillets of flying fish).

Diners can enjoy their repast in a tropical garden. An additional attraction: Top local bands perform in the pub at no extra charge.

WORTH A SPLURGE

Champers. Keswick Centre, Hastings, Christ Church. ☎ **246/435-6644.** Main courses $22–$25; lunch from $15. MC, V. Mon–Sat noon–3pm and 6–10pm. INTERNATIONAL.

The prices here are high, but you're paying for some of the south coast's best seafood, served at this comfortable two-story restaurant on the ocean with picture windows. You can also eat at the four tables and the bar downstairs. Lunch always has some interesting offerings ranging from a vegetable plate to chicken liver pâté. Try one of the freshly made fish chowders or perhaps a well-stuffed sandwich. The best offerings at night are the fresh fish, notably kingfish, barracuda, dolphin, or snapper. Although it's shipped in frozen, an array of meat dishes is also offered, including steaks, lamb, and duck. Several succulent pasta dishes are regularly featured as well.

✪ **Ragmuffins.** First St., St. James. ☎ **246/432-1295.** Main courses $16–$25. AE, MC, V. Tues–Sun 6–10pm. CARIBBEAN.

The only restaurant in Barbados housed in the typical chattel house, this is a real discovery in Holetown. It's a lively, inviting, and most welcoming choice. You get really good food here: A lot of hard-to-please locals recommend it when visitors ask where to go for an authentic island cuisine. The kitchen is within sight of the bar, so you can see what's going into the pots. The broiled T-bones are juicy and perfectly flavored, and there's always an offering of fresh fish. Vegetarians aren't ignored either, and the cooks are always willing to stir-fry some vegetables with noodles. Blackened fish is among one of the finest dishes on the menu, and another highlight is the local version of a spicy West Indian curry. A jerk chicken salad is another delight.

4 Hitting the Beaches

Bajans will tell you that their island has a beach for every day of the year. If you're only visiting for a short time, however, you'll probably be happy with the ones that are easy to find. They're all open to the public—even those in front of the big resort hotels and private homes—and the government requires that there be access to all beaches, via roads along the property line or through the hotel entrance. The beaches on the west, the so-called **Gold Coast,** are the most popular.

WEST COAST

Waters are calm here on the Caribbean Sea side of the island. Major beaches include ✪ **Paynes Bay,** which is reached from the Coach House, south of Holetown. This is a good beach for water sports, especially snorkeling, and there's also a parking area. The beach can get rather crowded, however, but the beautiful bay somehow makes it seem worth the effort to get here.

Directly south of Payne's Bay, at Fresh Water Bay, are three of the best west-coast beaches: **Brighton Beach, Brandon's Beach,** and **Paradise Beach.**

Church Point lies north of St. James Church, opening onto ✪ **Heron Bay,** site of the Colony Club Hotel. This is one of the most scenic bays on Barbados and the swimming is ideal. The beach can get overcrowded, however. There are some shade trees when you've had enough sun. You can also order drinks at the beach terrace operated by the Colony Club.

Mullins Beach, a final west-coast selection, is also recommended. Its blue waters are glassy and attract snorkelers. There's parking on the main road. Again, the beach has some shady areas. At the Mullins Beach Bar, you can order that rum drink.

SOUTH COAST

Beaches here include **Casuarina Beach,** with access from Maxwell Coast Road, going across the property of the Casuarina Beach Hotel. This is one of the wider beaches of Barbados, and we've noticed that it's swept by trade winds even on the hottest days of August. Windsurfers are especially fond of this one. Food and drink can be ordered at the hotel.

✪ **Silver Sands Beach,** to the east of Oistins, is near the southernmost point of Barbados, directly east of South Point Lighthouse and near the Silver Rock Hotel. This white-sand beach is a favorite with many Bajans (who probably want to keep it a secret from as many tourists as possible). Drinks are sold at the Silver Rock Bar.

Sandy Beach, reached from the parking lot on the Worthing main road, has tranquil waters opening onto a lagoon, the epitome of Caribbean charm. This is a family favorite, with lots of screaming and yelling on the weekends especially. Food and drink are sold here.

SOUTHEAST COAST

The southeast coast is the site of the big waves, especially at ✪ **Crane Beach,** a stretch of white-sand set against a backdrop of palms that you've probably seen in all the travel magazines. The beach is spectacular, as Prince Andrew, who has a house overlooking the beach, might agree. It offers excellent body surfing, but at times the waters might be too rough for all but the strongest swimmers. The beach is backed by cliffs, and the Crane Beach Hotel towers above it. This is ocean swimming, not the calm Caribbean, so take precautions.

✪ **Bottom Bay,** north of Sam Lord's Castle Resorts, is one of our all-time Bajan favorites. You park on the top of a cliff, then walk down steps to this much-photographed tropical beach with its grove of coconut palms. There's even a cave. The sand is brilliantly white against the aquamarine sea, a picture-postcard perfect beach paradise.

EAST (ATLANTIC) COAST

There are miles and miles of uncrowded beaches along the east coast, but this is the Atlantic side, and swimming here is potentially dangerous. Many visitors like to visit the beaches here, especially those in the **Bathsheba/Cattlewash** areas, for their rugged grandeur. Waves are extremely high on these beaches, and the bottom tends to be rocky. The currents are also unpredictable. Otherwise, the beaches are ideal for strolling if you don't go into the water.

5 Sports & Outdoor Pursuits

You've come to swim and sunbathe, and both are far preferable on the western coast in the clear, buoyant waters of the Caribbean, although you may also want to visit the surf-pounded Atlantic coast in the east, which is better for the views than for swimming.

WATER SPORTS

DEEP-SEA FISHING The fishing is first-rate in the waters around Barbados, which are rich with dolphin (mahi-mahi), marlin, wahoo, barracuda, and sailfish, to name only the most popular catches. There's also an occasional cobia.

The Dive Shop (Pebbles Beach, Aquatic Gap, St. Michael; ☎ **800/693-3483** or 246/426-9947) can arrange half-day charters for one to six people (all equipment and drinks included), costing $350 per boat. Under the same arrangement, the whole-day jaunt goes for $700.

SNORKELING & SCUBA DIVING   The clear waters off Barbados have a visibility of more than 100 feet most of the year. More than 50 varieties of fish are found on the shallow inside reefs. On night dives, sleeping fish, night anemones, lobsters, moray eels, and octopuses can be seen. On a mile-long coral reef 2 minutes by boat from **Sandy Beach,** sea fans, corals, gorgonias, and reef fish are plentiful. The *J.R.,* a dredge barge sunk as an artificial reef in 1983, is popular with beginners for its coral, fish life, and 20-foot depth. The *Berwyn,* a coral-encrusted tugboat that sank in Carlisle Bay in 1916, attracts photographers because of its variety of reef fish, shallow depth, good light, and visibility.

Asta Reef, with a drop of 80 feet, has coral, sea fans, and reef fish in abundance. It's the site of a Barbados wreck sunk in 1986 as an artificial reef. **Dottins,** the most beautiful reef on the west coast, stretches 5 miles from Holetown to Bridgetown and has numerous dive sites at an average depth of 40 feet and drop-offs of 100 feet. The SS *Stavronika,* a Greek freighter, is a popular dive site for advanced divers. Crippled by fire in 1976, the 360-foot freighter was sunk ¼ mile off the west coast to become an artificial reef in **Folkestone Underwater Park.** The mast is at 40 feet, the deck at 80 feet, and the keel at 140 feet. It's encrusted with coral.

The Dive Shop, Pebbles Beach, Aquatic Gap, St. Michael (☎ **800/693-3483** or ☎ 246/426-9947), offers some of the best scuba diving on Barbados, charging $55 for a one-tank dive and $80 for a two-tank dive. Every day, three dive trips go out to the nearby reefs and wrecks, and in addition, snorkeling trips and equipment rentals are possible. Visitors with reasonable swimming skills who have never dived before can sign up for a resort course. Priced at $70, it includes pool training, safety instructions, and a one-tank open-water dive. The establishment is NAUI- and PADI-certified, and is open daily from 9am to 5pm. Some other dive shops in Barbados that rent or sell snorkeling equipment include the following: **Carib Ocean Divers** (☎ **246/422-4414**) in St. James; **Hazel's Water World,** Bridgetown, St. Michael (☎ **246/426-4043**); and **Explore Sub,** Christ Church, close to Bridgetown (☎ **246/435-6542**). Call for information

Several companies also operate snorkeling cruises to take you to particularly picturesque areas; see "Cruises" under "Seeing the Sights" below.

PARASAILING   The best beaches for this sport are either St. James or Christ Church. **Skyrider Parasail** (☎ **246/435-0570**) will hook you up with this sport. It is found along Bay Street in Bridgetown, but its boat, a 32-foot speedboat, will pick you up at any of several hotels along the west coast if arrangements are made in advance. Rates are $45 per session.

WINDSURFING   Experts say that the windsurfing off Barbados is as good as any this side of Hawaii. Judging from the crowds of 20- to 35-year-olds who flock here, it's true. Windsurfing on Barbados has turned into a very big business between November and April. Thousands of windsurfers from all over the world now come here from as far away as Finland, Argentina, and Japan. The shifting of the trade winds between November and May and the shallow offshore reef off **Silver Sands** create unique conditions of wind and wave swells. This allows windsurfers to reach speeds of up to 50 knots and do complete loops off the waves. Silver Sands is rated the best spot in the Caribbean for advanced windsurfing (skill rating five to six). In other words, one needs skills similar to those of a professional downhill skier to master these conditions.

An outfit set up to handle the demand from the hordes of international windsurfers, **Barbados Windsurfing Club** maintains two branches on the island. Beginners and intermediates usually opt for the branch in Oistins (☎ **246/428-7277**), where winds are constant but where the sea is generally flat and calm. Advanced intermediates and expert windsurfers usually select the branch adjacent to the Silver Sands Hotel, in Christ Church (☎ 246/428-6001), where stronger winds and higher waves allow surfers to combine aspects of windsurfing with the conventional surfing known in Hawaii. The boards and equipment used by both branches of this outfit are provided by the Germany-based Club Mistral. Lessons at either branch cost between $40 and $65 per hour, depending on how many people are in your class. Equipment rents for $25 per hour or $55 to $65 per half-day, depending on where and what you rent. The budget-minded usually opt for the Oistins branch, as prices are less expensive than at the Silver Sands branch.

SPORTS ON DRY LAND

GOLF   Open to all is the 18-hole championship golf course of the **Sandy Lane Hotel,** St. James (☎ 246/432-1311), on the west coast. Greens fees are $135 in winter and $100 in summer for 18 holes, or $90 in winter and $60 in summer for 9 holes. Carts and caddies are available.

HIKING   **Barbados National Trust** (☎ 246/426-2421) offers Sunday morning hikes throughout the year. The program gives participants an opportunity to learn about the natural beauty of Barbados. It attracts more than 300 participants weekly. Led by young Bajans and members of the National Trust, the hikes cover a different area of the island each week. Tour escorts give brief talks on various aspects of the hikes, such as geography, history, geology, and agriculture. The hikes, free and open to participants of all ages, are divided into fast, medium, and slow categories. All the hikes leave promptly at 6am; each is about 5 miles long and takes about 3 hours to complete. There are also hikes at 3:30pm and 5:30pm, the latter conducted only if it is a moonlit night. For information or transportation, contact the Barbados National Trust.

HORSEBACK RIDING   A different view of Barbados is offered by the **Caribbean International Riding Centre,** Auburn, St. Joseph (☎ 246/433-1453). With nearly 40 horses, Mrs. Roachford or one of her daughters offers a variety of trail rides for all levels of experience. The various rides range from the 1-hour trek for $40 to a 2½-hour jaunt for $82.50. You ride through some of the most panoramic parts of Barbados, especially the hilly terrain of the Scotland district. Wild ducks and water lilies, with the rhythm of the Atlantic as background music, are some of nature's sights viewed along the way.

TENNIS   The big hotels have tennis courts that can be reserved even if you're not a guest. In Barbados they still wear the traditional whites, as opposed to the more flamboyant pastels in use elsewhere in the world. **Folkestone Park** at Holetown (☎ 246/422-2314) is a public tennis court available for free. You can also play at **National Tennis Centre,** Sir Garfield Sobers Sports Complex, Wildey St., St. Michael (☎ 246/437-6010), at a cost of $12 per hour. You must make a reservation for this, however. At the **Barbados Squash Club,** Marine House, Christ Church (☎ 246/427-7913), courts can be reserved at the charge of $9 for 45 minutes.

6 Seeing the Sights

Barbados is worth exploring, either in your own car or with a taxi-driver guide. Unlike on so many islands of the Caribbean, the roads are fair and quite passable. They are, however, poorly sign-posted, and newcomers invariably get lost, not only once, but several times. If you get lost, the people in the countryside are generally helpful.

TOURS & CRUISES

ORGANIZED TOURS   Instead of a private taxi, you can book a tour with **Bajan Tours,** Glenayre, Locust Hall, St. George (☎ 246/437-9389), a locally owned and operated tour company. The best bet for the first-timer is the Exclusive Island Tour, costing $56 per person, with departures between 8:30 and 9am, with a return from 3:30 to 4pm daily. It covers all the highlights of the island, including the Barbados Wildlife Reserve, the Chalky Mount Potteries, and the rugged east coast.

On Friday, for the same price, the outfit conducts a Heritage Tour, mainly of the island's major plantations and museums. And Monday through Friday it offers an Eco Tour, which takes in the natural beauty of the island. It, too, costs $56 and leaves at the same time as the above two tours. A full buffet lunch is included in all tours.

CRUISES   Largest of the coastal cruising vessels, the *Bajan Queen* is modeled after a Mississippi riverboat and is the only cruise ship offering table seating and dining on local fare produced fresh from the onboard galley. There's also cover available in case of too much sun or rain. The *Bajan Queen* becomes a showboat by night, with local bands providing music for dancing under the stars. You're treated to a dinner of roast chicken, barbecued steak, and seasoned flying fish with a buffet of fresh side dishes and salads. Cruises are usually sold out, so you should book early to avoid disappointment. Each cruise costs $44.50 and includes transportation to and from your hotel. For reservations, contact **Jolly Roger Cruises,** Shallow Draft, Bridgetown Harbour (☎ 246/436-6424). Cruises are on Wednesday from 6 to 10pm and on Saturday from 5 to 9pm.

The same company also owns two motorized replicas of pirate frigates, the *Jolly Roger I* and the *Jolly Roger II.* One or both of these, depending on demand, departs five mornings a week for daytime snorkeling cruises from 10am to 2pm. Included in the price of $61.50 is an all-you-can-eat buffet, complimentary drinks, and free use of snorkeling equipment, which requires a $20 refundable deposit. There's an onboard boutique on both of these boats. For information, call Jolly Roger Cruises or visit the berth at Bridgetown Harbour. They also operate a fourth boat, *Excellence,* a catamaran running on Monday, Wednesday, and Friday from 9am to 2pm, and on Sunday from 10am to 3pm. The price of $61.50 includes a continental breakfast, a lunch buffet, free drinks, and free snorkeling gear (no deposit), plus inflatable water mattresses. Since it's a catamaran, there are less people, making the ambience more intimate.

Limbo Lady Sailing Cruises, Casamara, Inchmarlow (☎ 246/420-5418) is another touring option. Patrick Gonsalves skippers the classic 44-foot CSY yacht, *Limbo Lady,* and his wife, Yvonne, a singer and guitarist, serenades you on a sunset cruise. Daily lunch cruises are also available, with a stop for swimming and snorkeling (equipment provided). Both lunch and sunset cruises offer a complimentary open bar and transportation to and from your hotel. Lunch cruises lasting 4½ hours cost $63, and 3-hour sunset cruises, including a glass of champagne, go for $52. Moonlight dinner cruises can also be arranged as well as private charters, both local and to neighboring islands (call for more information).

Part cruise ship, part nightclub, the **M/V *Harbour Master*** (☎ 246/430-0900) is one of the island's newest attractions. A 100-foot, four-story coastal vessel, with theme decks, it contains a modern gallery and a trio of bars. It boasts a dance floor and a sit-down restaurant, also offering formal buffets on its Calypso Deck. A bank of TVs for sport buffs is found on the Harbour Master Deck. The showpiece of the vessel is an onboard semi-submersible, which is lowered hydraulically to 6 feet beneath the ship.

This is, in effect, a "boat in a boat," with 30 seats. Lunch and dinner cruises start at $25 per person, although the semi-submersible experience costs another $10.

SUBMERGED SIGHTSEEING   You no longer have to be an experienced diver to see what lives 150 feet below the surface of the sea around Barbados. Now all visitors can view the sea's wonders on sightseeing submarines. The air-conditioned submersibles seat 28 to 48 passengers and make several dives daily from 9am to 4pm. Passengers are transported aboard a ferry boat from the Careenage in downtown Bridgetown to the submarine site, about a mile from the west coast of Barbados. The ride offers a view of the west coast of the island.

The submarines have viewing ports allowing you to see a rainbow of colors, tropical fish, plants, and even a shipwreck that lies upright and intact below the surface. You're taken aboard either *Atlantic I* or *III,* and the cost is $80 to $87.50 for adults, $40 to $43.75 for children. For reservations, contact **Atlantis Submarines (Barbados),** Shallow Draught, Bridgetown (☎ **246/436-8929**).

It's also possible to go cruising over one of the shore reefs to observe marine life. You sit in air-conditioned comfort aboard the *Atlantis Seatrec,* a semi-submersible boat, which gives you a chance to get a snorkeler's view of the reef through large viewing windows. You can also relax on deck as you take in the scenic coastline. The tour costs $35 for adults; children 4 to 12 are charged half fare (not suitable for those 3 or under). A second *Seatrec* tour explores wreckage sites. Divers go down with video cameras to three different wrecks on Carlisle Bay, and the video is transmitted to TV monitors aboard the vessel. The price is the same as for the first tour. For reservations, call the number above.

EXPLORING BRIDGETOWN

Often hot and traffic-clogged, the capital, Bridgetown, merits no more than a morning's shopping jaunt (see the shopping section of this chapter for a rundown of the best stores).

Since some half million visitors arrive on Barbados by cruise ship each year, the government has opened a $6 million **cruise-ship terminal** for them. It offers a variety of shopping options, including 20 duty-free shops, 13 local retail stores, and scads of vendors. Many of the stores stock the arts and crafts of Barbados, and cruise passengers can choose among a range of other products, including jewelry, liquor, china, crystal, electronics, perfume, and leather goods. Some shops sell Barbadian wood carvings and art, as well as locally-made fashions. The interior was designed to re-create an island street scene, with some storefronts appearing as traditional chattel houses in brilliant island colors with street lights, tropical landscaping, benches, and pushcarts.

Begin your tour at the waterfront, called **The Careenage** (the French word for turning vessels on their side for cleaning). This was a haven for clipper ships, and even though today it doesn't have the color of yesteryear, it's still worth exploring.

At **Trafalgar Square,** the long tradition of British colonization is immortalized. The monument here, honoring Lord Nelson, was executed by Sir Richard Westmacott and erected in 1813. The **Public Buildings** on the square are of the great, gray Victorian/Gothic variety that you might expect to find in London. The east wing contains the meeting halls of the Senate and the House of Assembly, with some stained-glass windows representing the sovereigns of England. Look for the "Great Protector" himself, Oliver Cromwell.

Behind the Financial Building, **St. Michael's Cathedral,** east of Trafalgar Square, is the symbol of the Church of England. This Anglican church was built in 1655, but was completely destroyed in a 1780 hurricane. Reconstructed in 1789, it was again damaged by a hurricane in 1831, but was not completely demolished as before. George Washington is said to have worshiped here on his Barbados visit.

The **Synagogue,** Synagogue Lane (☎ **246/426-5792**), is one of the oldest in the western hemisphere and is surrounded by a burial ground of early Jewish settlers. The present building dates from 1833. It was constructed on the site of an even older synagogue, erected by Jews from Brazil in 1654. It's open Monday to Friday 9am to 4pm. A donation is requested.

First made popular in 1870, **cricket** is the national pastime on Barbados. Matches can last from 1 to 5 days. If you'd like to see a local match, watch for announcements in the newspapers or ask at the **Tourist Board,** on Harbour Road (☎ **246/427-2623**). From Bridgetown, you can hail a taxi if you don't have a car and visit **Garrison Savannah,** just south of the capital, which is a frequent venue for cricket matches and horse races.

The **Barbados Gallery of Art,** Bush Hill (☎ **246/228-0149**), in the historic Garrison district, displays the very best Barbadian and Caribbean visual art. Its permanent collection consists of 160 drawings, paintings, and sculptures. The gallery also pays tribute to the memory of the late actress, Claudette Colbert, longtime resident of Barbados. She is memorialized in a beautiful garden here, and the gallery even owns one of her own paintings. Hours are Tuesday to Saturday 10am to 5pm. Admission is $5 for adults Tuesday to Friday and $2 Saturday; for children under 18, $2 Tuesday to Friday, and free Saturday.

The **Barbados Museum,** St. Ann's Garrison, St. Michael (☎ **246/427-0201**), is housed in a former military prison. Extensive collections show the island's development from prehistoric to modern times, as well as fascinating glimpses into the natural environment. There are also fine collections of West Indian maps, decorative arts, and fine arts. The museum sells a variety of quality publications, reproductions (maps, cards, prints), and handcrafts. Its Museum Café is a good place for a snack or light lunch. The museum is open Monday to Saturday 9am to 5pm and Sunday 2 to 6pm. Admission is $5 for adults and $2.50 for children.

Nearby, the russet-red **St. Ann's Fort,** on the fringe of the Savannah, garrisoned British soldiers in 1694. The fort wasn't completed until 1703. The Clock House survived the hurricane of 1831.

INLAND SIGHTS: TROPICAL GARDENS & A SPECTACULAR CAVE

Welchman Hall Gully. Welchman Hall, St. Thomas. ☎ **246/438-6671.** Admission $6 adults, $3 children 6 to 12, free for children 5 and under. Daily 9am–5pm.

This is a lush tropical garden owned by the Barbados National Trust. You'll see some specimens of plants that were here when the English settlers landed in 1627. Many of the plants are labeled—clove, nutmeg, tree fern, and cocoa, among others—and occasionally you'll spot a wild monkey. You'll also view breadfruit trees that are claimed to have descended from the seedlings brought ashore by Captain Bligh, of *Bounty* fame. To get here, take Highway 2 from Bridgetown.

✪ **Harrison's Cave.** Welchman Hall, St. Thomas. ☎ **246/438-6640.** Tour reservations recommended. Admission $8.75 adults, $4.35 children. Daily 8:45am–4pm. Closed Good Friday, Easter Sunday, and Christmas Day.

The beautiful underground world here, the number-one tourist attraction of Barbados, is viewed from aboard an electric tram and trailer. During the tour, visitors see bubbling streams, tumbling cascades, and deep pools, which are subtly lit, while all around stalactites hang overhead like icicles, and stalagmites rise from the floor. Visitors may disembark and get a closer look at this natural phenomenon at the Rotunda Room and the Cascade Pool.

Flower Forest. Richmond Plantation, St. Joseph. ☎ **246/433-8152.** Admission $7 adults, $3.50 children 5 to 16, free for children 4 and under. Daily 9am–5pm.

An old sugar plantation, the Flower Forest stands 850 feet above sea level near the western edge of the "Scotland district," a mile from Harrison's Cave. Set in one of the most scenic parts of Barbados, it's more than just a botanical garden; it's where people and nature came together to create something beautiful. After viewing the grounds, visitors can purchase handcrafts at Best of Barbados.

OTHER HISTORIC SIGHTS

Francia Plantation. St. George, Barbados. ☎ **246/429-0474.** Admission $4.50. Mon–Fri 10am–4pm. On the ABC Hwy., turn east onto Hwy. 4 at the Norman Niles Roundabout (follow the signs to Gun Hill); after going ½ mile, turn left onto Hwy. X (follow the signs to Gun Hill); after another mile, turn right at the Shell gas station and follow Hwy. X past St. George's Parish Church and up the hill for a mile, turning left at the sign to Francia.

A fine family home, this house stands on a wooded hillside overlooking the St. George Valley and is still owned and occupied by descendants of the original owner. You can explore several rooms, including the dining room with family silver and an 18th-century James McCabe bracket clock. On the walls are antique maps and prints, including a map of the West Indies printed in 1522.

Gun Hill Signal Station. Hwy. 4. ☎ **246/429-1358.** Admission $4.60 adults, $2.30 children 13 and under. Mon–Sat 9am–5pm. Take Hwy. 3 from Bridgetown and then go inland from Hwy. 4 toward St. George Church.

One of two such stations owned and operated by the Barbados National Trust, the Gun Hill Signal Station is strategically placed on the highland of St. George and commands a panoramic view from the east to the west. Built in 1818, it was the finest of a chain of signal stations and was also used as an outpost for the British army stationed here at the time. The restored military cookhouse houses a snack bar and gift shop.

Heritage Park & Rum Factory. Foursquare Plantation, St. Philip. ☎ **246/423-6669.** Admission $12. Sun–Thurs 9am–5pm, Fri–Sat 9am–9pm.

After driving through cane fields, you arrive at the first rum distillery to be launched on the island since the 19th century. Inaugurated in 1996, this factory is located in a former molasses and sugar plantation dating back some 350 years. Produced on-site is a white rum, ESA Field, praised by connoisseurs. Adjacent is an admission-free park where Barbadian handcrafts are displayed in the Art Foundry (see "Shopping," below). You'll also find an array of shops and carts selling local foods, handcrafts, and products.

Sunbury Plantation House. 6 Cross Rd., St. Philip. ☎ **246/423-6270.** Admission $6 adults, $3 children. Daily 10am–5pm.

This 300-year-old plantation house is steeped in history, featuring mahogany antiques, old prints, and a unique collection of horse-drawn carriages. This is the only great house in Barbados where all the rooms are open for viewing. An informative tour is given, and later guests can patronize the Courtyard Restaurant and Bar for meals or drinks, and there's also an on-site gift shop. Sunbury also offers a candlelight dinner, at least once a week. This is a five-course meal costing $75, served at a 200-year-old mahogany table. Call the number above to learn when the dinner is offered, to find out more information, or to make reservations.

Tyrol Cot Heritage Village. Codrington Hill, St. Michael. ☎ **246/424-2074.** Admission $5.75 adults, $2.85 children. Mon–Fri 9am–5pm.

If you arrived at the airport, you'll recognize the name of Sir Grantley Adams, the leader of the Bajan movement for independence from Britain. This was once his home, and his wife, Lady Adams, lived in the house until her death in 1990. Once you had to wrangle a highly prized invitation to visit, but it's now open to all who have paid the price of admission. It was built sometime in the mid-1850s from coral stone in a Palladian style. The grounds have been turned into a museum of Bajan life, including small chattel houses where potters and artists work.

SIGHTS AROUND THE ISLAND

In Bathsheba, visit the **Andromeda Botanic Gardens,** Bathsheba, St. Joseph (☎ **246/433-9384**). On a cliff overlooking the town of Bathsheba on the rugged east coast, limestone boulders make for a natural 8-acre rock-garden setting, where thousands of orchids are in bloom in season, along with hundreds of hibiscus and heliconia. Many varieties of ferns, begonias, and other species grow here in splendid profusion. One section, a palm garden, has more than 100 species. A simple guide helps visitors to identify many of the plants. On the grounds you'll occasionally see frogs, herons, lizards, hummingbirds, and sometimes a mongoose or a monkey. With an admission of BD$12 ($6) for adults, BD$6 ($3) for children, the gardens are open daily 9am to 5pm; children 5 and under enter free.

On Cherry Tree Hill, which is on Highway 1, signs point the way to **St. Nicholas Abbey** (☎ 246/422-8725), a Jacobean plantation Great House and sugarcane fields that have been around since about 1650. It was never an abbey—around 1820 an ambitious owner simply christened it as such. More than 200 acres are still cultivated each year. The structure, at least the ground floor, is open to the public Monday to Friday 10am to 3:30pm, charging an admission of $5; children 12 and under enter free. The house is believed to be one of three Jacobean houses in the western hemisphere and is characterized by curved gables. Lt. Col. Stephen Cave, the owner, is descended from the family that purchased the sugar plantation and Great House in 1810. You can lunch or take afternoon tea here (see Café Calabash, above under "Dining").

Across the road from Farley Hill National Park, in northern St. Peter Paris, lies the **Barbados Wildlife Reserve,** St. Peter (☎ 246/422-8826), an operation set in a mahogany forest that's run by the Barbados Primate Research Center in St. Peter. From 10am to 5pm daily, for an admission charge of BD$20 ($10) for adults (half price for children 12 and under), you can stroll through what is primarily a monkey sanctuary and an arboretum. Aside from the uncaged monkeys, you can see wild hares, deer, tortoises, otters, wallabies (which were brought into Barbados), and a variety of tropical birds.

EXPLORING THE GREEN HILLS

Unless you make special efforts to explore the lush interior of this former British colony, most of your time might be confined to the island's densely populated coastal plain. But much of Barbados's true beauty can only be appreciated through treks, tours, or hill climbs through such rarely visited parishes as St. Thomas and St. George (both of which are landlocked) and the Atlantic coast parishes of St. Andrews and St. John (where the rough surf of the Atlantic usually discourages the embarkation of sailing vessels). Until recently, most visitors were requested to restrict their sightseeing in these relatively undeveloped parishes to the sides of the

Cheap Thrills: What to See & Do for Free (Well, Almost) on Barbados

- **Go Native at the Market.** The major markets are found in the center of the main towns of Bridgetown (the capital), Oistins, and Speightstown. To get you in the mood for a taste treat, order a glass of mauby from one of the vendors. This is a refreshing but slightly bitter iced tea made from a tree bark. On our recent rounds we discovered a delightful new way of doing gazpacho: From the mango trees. It's addictive. Every hawker in these markets has something good to eat: One woman was cooking some pumpkin fritters, formed into a ball and fried in butter, and another was luring you to taste her bowl of pepperpot, a meat stew preserved by cassava juice and kept for several days (it dates from the time of the Arawaks). For dessert, seek out a Rastaman pushing an over-sized cart filled with coconut. On command he'll take his machete to a green coconut and whack it off to offer you a cool drink, followed by "the jelly," that soft essence that slithers sweetly down your throat.

- **Journey Into Yesteryear.** The capital of the island known as "Little England" retains its British influence even though independent. Stroll around the city center for a nostalgic look at a time gone by. Relatively small, its heart lies on the north bank of the Careenage in the heart of the old port. Broad Street leads into Trafalgar Square, the city's main drag. Here is a monument to Lord Horatio Nelson, predating the column in London's Trafalgar Square by 27 years. As a 19-year-old lieutenant, Nelson was based in Barbados in 1777. A short walk from Trafalgar, St. Michael's Cathedral was completed in 1789 and makes for a peaceful oasis in the heart of the bustling city. The classier stores are along Broad Street, including Cave Shepherd, the largest department store. Want something esoteric to look up? Head for George Washington House atop Bush Hill in the historic Garrison area south of Bridgetown. Although it's now filled with the offices of Barbados Light & Power Co., this is where in 1751 Washington, long before the American Revolution, stayed with his brother Lawrence, to recover from tuberculosis.

- **Visit a Pirate's Castle.** The finest mansion in Barbados has had a notorious history. Today the property is the site of **Sam Lord's Castle Resorts,** Long Bay at St. Philip (☎ **246/423-7350**), but in 1820 it was the Great House built by one of the island's most notorious scoundrels. According to the legend, Samuel Hall Lord—called "the Regency Rascal"—constructed the estate with money acquired by luring ships to wreck on the jagged but hard-to-detect rocks of Cobbler's Cove Reef. The Great House, still standing today, features double verandas on all sides and magnificent plaster ceilings created by Charles Rutter, who crafted the ceilings of Windsor Castle in England. Many of the original

highways and roads. But a locally owned tour operator, **Highland Outdoor Tours,** Canefield, St. Thomas Parish (☎ **246/438-8069**), conducts a series of tours across privately owned land. With its verdant, rolling hills and many dramatic rock out-croppings, much of the terrain might remind you of a windswept but balmy version of Scotland.

You'll have the option of conducting your tour on horseback, on foot, or as a passenger in a tractor-drawn jitney. Horseback rides and walking tours last anywhere mahogany furniture and gilt mirrors remain intact today. The castle is open to the public daily and charges an admission of only $1.25.

- **Hike a Self-Guided Nature Trail.** In October of 1998 Barbados launched two nature trails that explore the natural history and heritage of Speightstown, once a major sugar port and even today a fishing town with old houses and a bustling waterfront. The **Arbib Nature & Heritage Trail** offers insights into this old Caribbean town as well as the mysterious gully known as "the Whim," and the surrounding districts. The first marked trail is a 4.7-mile trek that traverses the Whim, crosses one of the last working plantations in Barbados (Warleight), and goes all the way to the historic 18th-century Dover Fort, following along white-sand beaches at Heywoods before ending up back in Speightstown. Equally enchanting is the 3.4-mile trail designed for those looking for a more relaxing hike. There are two guided hikes at 9am to 2:30pm on Wednesday, Thursday, and Saturday. The trail begins outside St. Peter's Church in Speightstown. To pre-book a hike and learn more information, call the Barbados National Trust at ☎ **246/ 426-2421.**

- **Tour the Great Houses.** From mid-January through the first week of April, you can tour a different Great House every Wednesday afternoon. You'll get a feeling for the elegant colonial lifestyle once commonplace on Barbados, and see a great array of plantation antiques. Houses include those rarely seen by the public, as well as major attractions such as Francia Plantation house at St. George, owned and occupied today by the descendants of the original owner. For more information on these tours, including how to hook up with one, call ☎ **246/426-2421.**

- **Hike the Rugged East Coast.** Many visitors to Barbados never leave the tranquil waters of the west coast, with its fine, white, sandy beaches, to view the more turbulent east coast. Yet the east coast is far more dramatic. It stretches from the lighthouse at Ragged Point, the easternmost point of Barbados, all the way north along the Atlantic coast to Bathsheba and Pico Tenerife. In all, this is a distance of about 16 miles, and is the island's most panoramic hiking area. Some adventurers hike the entire coast, but if time is limited you can confine your scenic route to a 4-mile stretch from Ragged Point to Consett Bay. Allow at least 2½ hours for this journey along a rough, stony trail. A small picnic facility just north of Bathsheba is a popular spot for Bajan families, especially on Sunday, and you might want to take along your own picnic to join in the fun.

from 2 to 5 hours. As you traverse what used to be some of the most productive sugar plantations in the British Empire, your guide will describe the geology, architecture, and historical references you'll see en route.

All tours depart from the Highland Outdoor Tour Center in the parish of St. Thomas (in north-central Barbados). Transportation to and from your hotel is included in the price of 2-hour horseback tours (from $60), hiking tours (from $30 to $60), and tractor-drawn jitney tours (from $30).

7 Shopping

Cruise passengers generally head for the **Bridgetown Cruise Terminal** at Bridgetown Harbour, which has some 20 duty-free shops, 13 local and regional merchandise shops, and several vendors.

BAJAN HANDCRAFTS & ART

The outstanding Barbados handcraft is black-coral jewelry. Clay pottery is another Bajan craft. We recommend a visit to **Chalky Mount Potteries,** where this special craft originated. Potters turn out different products, some based on designs that are centuries old. The potteries (sign-posted) are found north of Bathsheba on the east coast in the parish of St. Joseph, near Barclay's Park. In shops across the island, you'll also find a selection of locally made vases, pots, pottery mugs, glazed plates, and ornaments.

Wall hangings are made from local grasses and dried flowers, and island crafts-people also turn out straw mats, baskets, and bags with raffia embroidery. Still in its infant stage, leather work is also found on Barbados, particularly handbags, belts, and sandals.

You don't have to pay duty on items made on Barbados.

Articrafts, Broad St., Bridgetown (☎ 246/427-5767), is where John and Rosyln Watson have assembled one of the most impressive displays of Bajan arts and crafts on the island. Roslyn's woven wall hangings are decorated with objects from the island, including sea fans and coral. Straw work, handbags, and pottery items are also sold.

Art Foundry, Heritage Park (☎ 246/418-0714), in a historic factory building, this ground-floor gallery is a partnership between Bajan artist Joscelyn Gardner and R. L. Seale, the rum distiller. It displays some of the finest works of art on Barbados in its ground-floor gallery, while offering changing exhibitions in its upstairs galleries. Gardner's own work is for sale, as she is both a printmaker and an artist in residence.

Best of Barbados, in the Southern Palms, St. Lawrence Gap, Christ Church (☎ 246/420-8040), is part of an island-wide chain of 12 stores. It's the best shop on the island for local products. It was established in 1975 by an English-born painter, Jill Walker, whose prints are best-sellers. They sell coasters, mats, T-shirts, pottery, dolls and games, and cookbooks, among other items. This tasteful shop is around the corner from the entrance to Southern Palms. A more convenient location might be the outlet in Bridgetown at Mall 34, Broad Street (☎ 246/436-1416).

Colours of De Caribbean, the Waterfront Marina, Bridgetown (☎ 246/436-8522), stands next to the Waterfront Café, on the Careenage. This unique store has a very individualized collection of tropical clothing, all made in the West Indies, and jewelry and decorative objects. Original hand-painted and batiked clothing may hold the most interest.

✪ **Earthworks Pottery/The Potter's House Gallery,** Edgehill Heights 2, St. Thomas Parish (☎ 246/425-0223), is one of the artistic highlights of Barbados. Deep in the island's central highlands, Canadian-born Goldie Spieler and her son, David, create whimsical plates, cups, saucers, and bowls, whose blue and green colors emulate the color of the Bajan sea and sky. Many objects are decorated with Antillean-inspired swirls and zigzags and can be shipped virtually anywhere. On the premises is the studio where the objects are crafted and a showroom that sells the output of at least half a dozen other island potters.

The Great House Gallery, at the Bagatelle Restaurant, Hwy. 2A, St. Thomas (☎ 246/421-6767), lies on an airy upper floor of one of the most historic Great Houses on Barbados. This art gallery combines an inventory of artworks with West Indian graciousness. Pieces are displayed on high white walls amid the reflected glow

In case you want to see the world.

At American Express, we're here to make your journey a smooth one. So we have over 1,700 travel service locations in over 130 countries ready to help. What else would you expect from the world's largest travel agency?

do more

Travel

In case you want to be welcomed there.

We're here to see that you're always welcomed at establishments everywhere. That's why millions of people carry the American Express® Card – for peace of mind, confidence, and security, around the world or just around the corner.

do more

To apply, call 1 800 THE-CARD
or visit www.americanexpress.com

Cards

In case you're running low.

We're here to help with more than 190,000 Express Cash locations around the world. In order to enroll, just call American Express at 1 800 CASH-NOW before you start your vacation.

do more

Express
Cash

And in case you'd rather be safe than sorry.

We're here with American Express® Travelers Cheques. They're the safe way to carry money on your vacation, because if they're ever lost or stolen you can get a refund, practically anywhere or anytime. To find the nearest place to buy Travelers Cheques, call 1 800 495-1153. Another way we help you do more.

do more

Travelers Cheques

of an antique mahogany floor: oils and watercolors by Caribbean, Latin American, and British artists.

Pelican Village, Harbour Rd., Bridgetown (☎ 246/426-4391), offers bargains from Bajan artisans. While in Bridgetown, go down to the Pelican Village on Princess Alice Highway, leading down to the city's Deep Water Harbour. A collection of island-made crafts and souvenirs is sold here in a tiny colony of thatch-roofed shops, and you can wander from one to another. Sometimes you can see craftspeople at work. Some of the shops here are gimmicky and repetitive, although interesting items can be found.

The Shell Gallery, Carlton House, St. James (☎ 246/422-2593), has the best collection in the West Indies. Shells for sale come from all over the world. Also offered are hand-painted chinaware, shell jewelry, local pottery and ceramics, and batik and papier-mâché artwork depicting shells and aquatic life.

Walker's Caribbean World, St. Lawrence Gap (☎ 246/428-1183), close to the Southern Palms, offers many locally made items for sale, as well as handcrafts from the Caribbean Basin. Here you can buy the famous Jill Walker prints.

DUTY-FREE SHOPPING

On Barbados you might find duty-free merchandise at prices 20% to 40% lower than in the United States and Canada. But, of course, you've got to be a smart shopper to spot bargains and also be familiar with prices back in your hometown. Duty-free shops have two prices listed on items of merchandise, the local retail price and the local retail price less the government-imposed tax.

Some of the best duty-free buys include cameras (Leica, Rolex, and Fuji), watches (Omega, Piaget, Seiko), crystal (Waterford and Lalique), gold (especially jewelry), bone china (Wedgwood and Royal Doulton), cosmetics and perfumes, and liquor (including locally produced Barbados rum and liqueurs), along with tobacco products and cashmere sweaters, tweeds, and sportswear from Britain.

Cave Shepherd, Broad St., Bridgetown (☎ 246/431-2121), is the best place to shop for duty-free merchandise on Barbados. It has branches at Sunset Crest in Holetown, Da Costas Mall, Grantley Adams International Airport, and the Bridgetown Cruise Terminal. If your time is limited and you want a preview of what's for sale on Barbados, try this outlet, which has the widest selection of goods island-wide. Cave Shepherd is the largest department store on Barbados and one of the most modern in the Caribbean. After you finish shopping, relax in the cool comfort of the Ideal Restaurant, or at the Balcony, overlooking Broad Street and serving vegetarian dishes with a salad bar and beer garden as well.

Little Switzerland, in the Da Costas Mall, Broad St., Bridgetown (☎ 246/431-0030), offers a wide selection of fragrances and cosmetics, plus fine china and crystal. The shop also specializes in watches and jewelry, plus Mont Blanc pens.

A competitor, **Luna Jewelers,** Bay St. at Bedford Ave., Bridgetown (☎ 246/430-0355), sells an appealing but predictable collection of diamonds and precious stones, as well as watches and gift items. But what makes it unusual is its emphasis on art nouveau and art-deco designs set into gold and silver that are crafted on Barbados into alluring designs. Of special note are the pieces that elevate fossilized Bajan coral into a high art form, thanks to careful polishing, gold or silver settings, and in some cases, intricate mosaic-style inlays. The pristine whiteness of these pieces is sometimes highlighted thanks to colored gemstones from India, Brazil, or Guatemala. The establishment is within a 10-minute drive south of Bridgetown, about four buildings from Barbados's Parliament.

Harrison's, 1 Broad St., Bridgetown (☎ 246/431-5500), has 14 branch stores, all selling a wide variety of duty-free merchandise, including china, crystal, jewelry, leather goods, and perfumes—all at fair prices. They also sell some state-of-the-art leather products handcrafted in Colombia. Harrison's is the major competitor to Cave Shepherd on the island, but we'd give the edge to Cave Shepherd.

8 Barbados After Dark

Most of the big resort hotels feature entertainment nightly, often steel band dance music and occasional Bajan floor shows. Sometimes beach barbecues are staged.

For the most authentic Bajan evening possible, head for **Baxters Road in Bridgetown,** where there's always something cooking on Friday and Saturday after 11pm. In fact, if you stick around until dawn, the party's still going strong. The entertainment tends to be spontaneous. Some old-time visitors have compared Baxters Road to the backstreets of New Orleans in the 1930s. If you fall in love with the place, you can "caf crawl" up and down the street, where nearly every bar is run by a Bajan mama. Each place has its own atmosphere. The street is safe, too, since Bajans come here to have fun, not to make trouble.

The most popular "caf" on Baxters Road is **Enid's** (she has a phone, "but it doesn't work"), a little ramshackle establishment where Bajans come to devour fried chicken at 3 in the morning. Her place is open daily from 8:30pm to 8:30am, when the last satisfied customer departs into the blazing morning sun and Enid heads home to get some sleep before the new night begins. Stop in for a Banks beer.

Baku Beach Club, Sunset Crest, St. James (☎ 246/432-1309), is a bar and restaurant, serving as a social focal point for Sunset Crest, with many island residents happily hobnobbing with their friends and colleagues. Happy hour at the bar is from 5 to 6pm and 9 to 10pm nightly, when drinks are half-price. Fish fries, barbecues, or buffets are offered from 7 to 10pm daily, priced at $10 to $12.50. There's live entertainment most nights, including bands and amateur talent shows, and the club recently added a dance floor. The cover charge is $15 for non-diners.

Coach House, Paynes Bay, St. James (☎ 246/432-1163), is a green-and-white house said to be 200 years old. The atmosphere is a Bajan version of an English pub, with an outdoor garden bar. If you visit from 6 to 10:30pm, you can order bar meals, including flying-fish burgers, priced at $8 and up. Live music is presented most nights, featuring everything from steel bands to jazz, pop, and rock. The pub is on the main Bridgetown-Holetown road, just south of Sandy Lane, about 6 miles north of Bridgetown. Live music and an attentive crowd assemble together here nightly from 9pm on. The lunchtime buffet offered Monday to Friday ($14) is popular.

☉ Harbour Lights, Marine's Villa, Upper Bay St., about a mile southeast of Bridgetown (☎ 246/436-7225), is the most popular weekend venue for dancing, drinking, and flirting, on all of Barbados. In a modern seafront building whose oceanfront patio allows dancers the chance to cool off, the place plays reggae, soca, and just about anything else that happens to be popular in the Caribbean at the time. No one under 18 is admitted. Grilled meats and hamburgers are available from a barbecue pit/kiosk on the premises. It's open till the wee hours every night. Monday is beach party night, costing $44 including transportation to and from your hotel, a barbecue buffet, free drinks, and a live band. A cover charge ranging from $12 to $15 is imposed on Wednesday and Friday.

☉ John Moore Bar, on the waterfront, Weston, St. James Parish (☎ 246/422-2258), is the most atmospheric and least pretentious bar on Barbados. Although its namesake (John Moore) died in 1987, the place is owned and managed by Mr. Lamont (Breedy) Addison, who began his tenure here as a teenager. If you think this bar is only a watering hole, think again: It's the nerve center in this waterfront town, filled throughout the day and evening with the widest and most congenial group of residents in the neighborhood. Most visitors opt for a rum punch or beer, but if you're hungry, platters of local fish can be prepared, after a moderate delay.

✪ **Plantation Restaurant and Garden Theatre,** Main Rd. (Hwy. 7), St. Lawrence, Christ Church (☎ **246/428-5048**), is the island's most prominent showcase for evening dinner theater and Caribbean cabaret. Dinner and a show are presented every Wednesday and Friday. Dinner is served at 6:30pm, and a show, *Plantation Tropical Spectacular II,* is presented at 8pm. The show involves plenty of exotic costumes and lots of reggae, calypso, limbo, and Caribbean exoticism. Reserve in advance. This is an expensive evening, so view it as a big splurge. For $61.50 you get the dinner, the show, and transport to and from your hotel. Otherwise, the show costs $30.

1627 and All That, Barbados Museum, Hwy. 7, Garrison, St. Michael (☎ **246/ 428-1627**), effectively combines music with entertainment and dancing. It's the most interesting place on Barbados to visit on a Thursday night. The entertainment combines a cocktail hour, a large buffet of Bajan food, and a historic and cultural presentation. A ticket costing $57.50 includes transportation to and from your hotel. Dinner is served at 7pm, with show time at 6:30pm, concluding at 10pm.

The Ship Inn, St. Lawrence Gap, Christ Church (☎ **246/435-6961**), mentioned above as a restaurant, is now among the leading entertainment centers on the south coast. The pub is the hot spot. Top local bands perform every night of the week, and patrons gather to listen to live reggae, calypso, and Top 40 music. The entrance fee of $5 to the Ship Inn complex is redeemable in food or drink at any of the other bars or restaurants in the complex. That means that guests are actually only paying $2 for the live entertainment.

Frugal travelers can spend an inexpensive Bajan night at one of the island's popular clubs and hangouts, **Bert's Bar,** at the Abbeville Hotel in Worthing, on the Main Road in Christ Church (☎ **246/435-7924**). Bert's is known for serving the best on-island daiquiris.

Sports fans head for **Bubba's Sports Bar,** Rockley Main Rd., Christ Church (☎ **246/435-6217**), which offers a couple of satellite dishes plus a 10-foot video screen. There are also a dozen TVs playing live sports action. The food and drink of choice here is a Bubba burger washed down with a Bank's beer.

A pubby atmosphere attracts fans to **The Boatyard,** Bay Street in Bridgetown (☎ **246/436-2622**), with a DJ and occasional live band music. The longest bar on the island is found at **After Dark,** St. Lawrence Gap, Christ Church (☎ **246/435-6547**), where you can often hear live reggae, soca, Bajan calypso, and jazz.

6 Bonaire

Untrampled by hordes of tourists, Bonaire is one of the world's premier destinations for diving and snorkeling. Unlike some islands, Bonaire isn't just surrounded by coral reefs—it *is* the reef, sitting on the top of a dry, sunny underwater mountain. Its shores are thick with rainbow-hued fish. Powdery white sands and turquoise waters beckon. Spearfishing isn't allowed in its waters, nor is the taking or destruction of any coral or other living animal from the sea.

Bonaire is also a bird-watcher's haven, with 135 species. You'll spot flamingos (which nearly outnumber the sparse human population), as well as big-billed pelican, bright-green parrots, snipes, terns, parakeets, herons, and hummingbirds. Bring binoculars.

This sleepy island doesn't have the glitz of Aruba, its sibling in the Netherlands Antilles (an autonomous part of the Netherlands). In fact, Bonaireans treasure their precious environment and go to great lengths to protect it. Although they eagerly seek tourism, they don't want to create "another Aruba," with its high-rise hotels.

Bonaire has a number of moderately priced inns and hotels and a handful of small guest houses. Budget travelers can also rent an apartment with a kitchen to keep food costs low. Even so, you'll be shocked at grocery-store prices, since everything has to be imported. If you're a serious diver, always book in on a package tour.

Bonaire has a population of about 10,000. Its capital is **Kralendijk.** It's most often reached from its neighbor island of Curaçao, 30 miles west. Like Curaçao, it's desert-like, with a dry and brilliant atmosphere. Only 5 miles wide and 24 miles long, Bonaire is poised in the Caribbean close to the coast of South America and comprises about 112 square miles. Its northern sector is hilly, tapering up to Mount Brandaris, all of 788 feet. However, the southern half, flat as a flapjack, is given over to bays, reefs, beaches, and a salt lake that attracts flamingos.

1 Essentials

VISITOR INFORMATION

Before you go, you can contact the **Bonaire Government Tourist Office** at Adams Unlimited, 10 Rockefeller Plaza, Suite 900, New York, NY 10020 (☎ **800/U-BONAIR** or 212/956-5911).

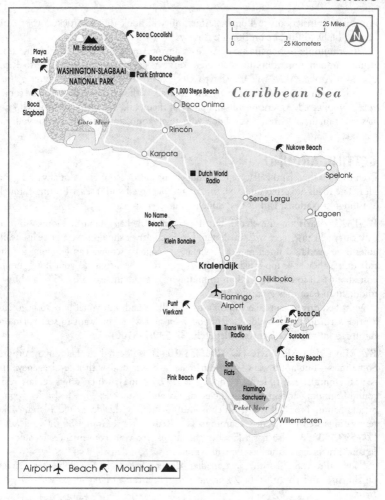

For tourist information on Bonaire, go to the **Bonaire Government Tourist Bureau,** Kaya Libertad Simón Bolivar 12, Kralendijk (☎ **599/7-8322**). Open Monday to Friday from 7:30am to noon and 1:30 to 5pm.

Bonaire's official Web site is **www.bonaire.org**.

GETTING THERE

ALM (☎ **800/327-7230**) is one of your best bets for flying to Bonaire. The airline flies from Miami and Atlanta daily. **Air Aruba** (☎ **800/882-7822**) flies from Newark to Bonaire on Thursday, Saturday, and Sunday. These are direct flights. On Monday, Tuesday, Wednesday, and Friday it has air links to Bonaire via Aruba.

American Airlines (☎ **800/433-7300**) offers one daily nonstop flight to Curaçao from its hub in Miami. These depart late enough in the day (11am) to allow easy connections from cities all over the Northeast. They reach Curaçao early enough to allow immediate transfers on to Bonaire. American will book (but not ticket) your connecting flight to Bonaire on Bonaire Airways.

Other routings to Bonaire are possible on any of American's daily nonstop flights to Aruba through American's hubs in New York, Miami, and San Juan, Puerto Rico. Once on Aruba, ALM will transfer passengers on to Bonaire, usually after a brief touchdown (or change of equipment) on Curaçao. Although these transfers are somewhat complicated, American will set up any of them, and will also offer reduced rates at some Bonairean hotels if you book your reservation simultaneously with your air passage.

GETTING AROUND

Even though the island is flat, renting mopeds or motor scooters is not always a good idea. The roads are often unpaved, pitted, and peppered with rocks. Touring through Washington National Park is best done by van, Jeep, or car.

BY TAXI   Taxis are unmetered, but the government has established rates. All taxicabs carry a license plate with the letters TX. Each driver should have a price list available to be produced upon request. As many as four passengers can go along for the ride unless they have too much luggage. A trip from the airport to your hotel should cost about $10 to $12. From 8pm to midnight fares are increased by 25%, and from midnight to 6am they go up by 50%.

Most taxi drivers can take you on a tour of the island, but you'll have to negotiate a price according to how long a trip you want and what you want to see. For more information, call **Taxi Central Dispatch** (☎ 599/7-8100).

BY RENTAL CAR   Avis (☎ 800/331-1084) is located at Flamingo Airport. Sometimes—but not always—you can make a better deal with a local agency. Try **Avanti Rentals,** Kaya Herman Pop 2 (☎ 599/7-5661), which offers rentals year-round beginning at $46 per day, including tax and insurance. They'll also rent you a Suzuki Samurai for $61 a day, which is ideal for touring this desert-like island. Make reservations well in advance. **Flamingo Car Rental,** Kaya Grandi 86, in Kralendijk (☎ 599/7-8888), also has a kiosk at the airport for your convenience. Its stock of Japanese-made cars, usually a type of Nissan, costs $56 daily.

Your valid U.S., British, or Canadian driver's license is acceptable for driving on Bonaire, and you must be 25 or older to rent a car. *Driving on Bonaire is on the right.*

BY BICYCLE   You might consider renting a bike, although you'll have to contend with the hot sun and powerful trade winds. Nevertheless, much of the island is flat, and if you follow the main road you'll go along the water's edge. The best deals are at **Cycle Bonaire,** Kaya L. D. Gerjharts (☎ 599/7-7558), where you can rent a 21-speed or an 830 Trek for $15 to $20 per day. Rental includes a water bottle, lock, helmet, repair kit, and pump. A map is provided free for a 6-day rental; otherwise, you're charged $5.

SPECIAL EVENTS

The big annual event is the **October Sailing Regatta,** a 5-day festival of racing sponsored by the local tourist bureau. Now an international affair, the event attracts sailors and spectators from around the world, as a flotilla of sailboats and yachts anchor in Kralendijk Bay. If you're planning to visit during regatta days, make sure you have an iron-clad hotel reservation.

Fast Facts: Bonaire

Banking Hours   Banks are usually open Monday to Friday 8:30am to noon and 2 to 4pm.

Currency   Like the other islands of the Netherlands Antilles (Curaçao, St. Maarten, St. Eustatius, and Saba), Bonaire's coin of the realm is the **Netherlands Antillean florin (NAf),** sometimes called a guilder. The official rate is Naf1.77 to the U.S. dollar. However, U.S. dollars are widely accepted, and the rates in this chapter are quoted in U.S. dollars.

Customs   There are no Customs requirements for Bonaire. See chapter 2 for details on what you can bring home.

Documents   U.S. and Canadian citizens don't need a passport to enter Bonaire, although a birth or naturalization certificate or an alien registration card will be required, plus a return ticket. British subjects may carry a British Visitor's Passport, obtainable at post offices on Bonaire, although a valid passport issued in the United Kingdom is preferred. We strongly suggest that you bring your passport whenever you travel to a foreign country anyway.

Electricity   The electricity on Bonaire is slightly different from that used in North America (110–130 volts, 50 cycles, as opposed to U.S. and Canadian voltages of 110 volts, 60 cycles). Adapters and transformers are necessary for North American appliances, but you should still proceed with caution in using any appliance on Bonaire and try to avoid usage if possible because of the erratic current. Be warned, further, that electrical current used to feed or recharge finely calibrated diving equipment should be stabilized with a specially engineered electrical stabilizer. Every dive operation on the island has one of these as part of its standard equipment for visiting divers to use.

Language   English is widely spoken, but you'll also hear Dutch, Spanish, and Papiamento.

Medical Care   The **St. Franciscus Hospital** is at Kayasoeur Bartola 2 in Kralendijk (☎ **599/7-8900**). A plane on standby at the airport takes seriously ill patients to Curaçao for treatment.

Safety   Bonaire is a remarkably safe destination. But remember, any place that attracts tourists also attracts people who prey on them. Safeguard your valuables.

Taxes and Service   The government requires a $5.50-per-person daily room tax on all hotel rooms. Most hotels and guest houses add a 10% service charge in lieu of tipping. Restaurants generally add a service charge of 15% to the bill. Upon leaving Bonaire, you'll be charged an airport departure tax of $10, so don't spend every penny. There's also an inter-island departure tax of $5.75.

Telecommunications   Service for telephone, Telex, telegraph, radio, and TV is available in English. To call Bonaire from the United States, dial **011** (the international access code), then **599** (the country code for Bonaire), and then **7** (the area code) and the four-digit local number.

Once on Bonaire, to call another number on the island only the four-digit local number is necessary.

Time   Bonaire is on Atlantic standard time year-round, 1 hour ahead of Eastern standard time (when it's noon on Bonaire, it's 11am in Miami). When daylight saving time is in effect in the United States, clocks in Miami and Bonaire show the same time.

Water Drinking water is pure and safe. It comes from distilled seawater.

Weather Bonaire is known for its climate, with midday temperatures hovering at 82°F (28°C). The water temperature averages 80°F (27°C). It's warmest in August and September, coolest in January and February. The average rainfall is 22 inches, and December to March are the rainiest months.

2 Accommodations You Can Afford

Hotels, all facing the sea, are low-key, hassle-free, and personally run operations where everybody gets to know everybody else rather quickly.

Taxes and service charges are seldom included in the prices you're quoted, so ask about them when making your reservations.

Avanti Bungalows. Punt Vierkant, Belnem, Bonaire, N.A. ☎ **599/7-8405.** Fax 599/7-8605. www.bonaire.org/happy-holiday/. E-mail: hhh@bonairelive.com. 13 bungalows. A/C TV. Winter $75 1-bedroom bungalow; $100 2-bedroom bungalow; $130 3-bedroom bungalow. Off-season $65 1-bedroom bungalow; $90 2-bedroom bungalow; $120 3-bedroom bungalow. Extra person $15. AE, MC, V.

A block in from Bachelor's Beach, south of the airport, this complex of bungalows is managed by a family business, Happy Holiday Homes. The basic units are comfortable, with the usual amenities including air-conditioning, cable TV, an on-site washer, and a living/dining-room area. There aren't a lot of graceful notes around here; it's pretty much a do-it-yourself affair. The bungalows are in rows of two or three units each, and all have front terraces and gardens. The area is heavily planted with foliage for more privacy. Each unit is furnished differently with a sofa, Venetian blinds, just-adequate tables and chairs, and color-coordinated curtains and bed linens, plus good mattresses. The bedrooms are air-conditioned and the living/dining areas are cooled by ceiling fans. Bathrooms are small but well maintained, with a minimum of rather thin towels. The kitchens are fully furnished, with refrigerators and microwaves. There's no swimming pool.

Blue Iguana. Kaya Prinses Marie 6, Kralendijk, Bonaire, N.A. ☎ or fax **599/7-6855.** 6 rooms, none with private bathroom. Winter $65 single, $80 double. Off-season $55 single, $70 double. Rates include breakfast. No credit cards.

This is the most amusing and funky guest house on Bonaire. It occupies a bright-yellow century-old building about 2 blocks north of the center of Kralendijk, separated from the dusty road by a screen of cactus. It's an artsy, appealingly worn, bohemian place. Its chatelaine is the Curaçao-born, New York artist Laurie Dovale.

The furnishings include a mishmash of family antiques, a mixture of tropical and North European kitsch, and old photographs. Friends of the owner drop in throughout the day offering sightseeing advice. No meals are served other than breakfast, although guests have the run of a communal kitchen that seems straight out of the 1940s. A rear garden is a haven for land turtles, squirrels, seedlings sprouting from coffee cans, and a quartet of iguanas that search out the fruit and table scraps Ms. Dovale prepares for them. Each accommodation has a ceiling fan, funky old furniture, and thin doors that might not keep out the noise from the comfortably cluttered public rooms. Both the bedrooms and the shared bathrooms are small, and the mattresses aren't the newest. The bars and restaurants of Kralendijk are a very short walk away from this appealingly eccentric hotel.

Bonaire Caribbean Club. Tourist Rd., Kralendijk, Bonaire, N.A. ☎ **800/748-8733** or 599/
7-7901. Fax 599/7-7900. www.bonairecaribbeanclub.com. E-mail: info@bonairecaribbeanclub.
com. 20 apts. A/C. Year-round $65–$95 1-bedroom apt.; $110 2-bedroom apt. Apr–July 1
and Nov–Dec 15, guests receive 7th night free. Extra person $9; children 4 and under stay
free in parents' apt. AE, MC, V (5% extra fee for use of charge card).

A mile north of the hotel strip, this Dutch-owned complex rents bungalow apartments, some with their own porches. Some good dive sites lie about a block away,
although the property fronts a coral beach. The nearest good sandy beach, however, is
about 1½ miles away. The apartments are two to a unit in a park setting with gardens
and flowering vines around the porches. The furnishings are simple, with colorful
seat cushions and curtains in a vague tropical motif. All have kitchens and air-
conditioning, and some offer ceiling fans as well, although there are no phones or TVs.
Mattresses are replaced as needed. The bathrooms are cramped, with not enough room
for your stuff. A pool with a mural of underwater life is the big on-site attraction, and
there's a simple restaurant serving breakfast and dinner. Daily maid service is provided
except on Sunday, and baby-sitting can be arranged with advance notice.

Buddy Dive Center. Kaya Gob. N. E. Debrot (P.O. Box 231), Kralendijk, Bonaire, N.A.
☎ **800/786-3483** or 599/7-5080. Fax 599/7-8647. E-mail: info@BuddyDive.com. 4 units,
30 apts. with kitchen. Winter $113 single or double; $170 1-bedroom apt. for 2; $242 2-bed-
room apt. for up to 4; $297 3-bedroom apt. for up to 6. Off-season $110 single or double,
$156 1-bedroom apt. for 2; $220 2-bedroom apt. for up to 4; $272 3-bedroom apt. for up
to 6. Ask about dive packages. AE, MC, V.

On the island's western edge amid a strip of other hotels, many of which are more
expensive, this hotel consists of three buildings. The oldest contains bedrooms but
not apartments. The pair of newer buildings (circa 1992–93) have white concrete
walls, red roofs, and apartments with kitchens, air-conditioning, and TV. As its
name implies, most visitors check in here for the diving opportunities, abundant
off the nearby coast. PADI and NAUI dive options are available on-site. The accommodations are ultra-simple and not particularly large, each outfitted with rattan
furniture and white walls. The apartments also have balconies. Mattresses are firm,
but bathrooms are barely adequate, rather cramped with somewhat thin towels.
There's a pool, although most visitors swim at Buddy Beach, a few steps away. Maid
service is offered only twice a week. Arrangements for rental cars are available on-site.
Each apartment has its own kitchen, and there's also an in-house restaurant, Buddy's
Reef.

Carib Inn. J. A. Abraham Blvd. (P.O. Box 68), Kralendijk, Bonaire, N.A. ☎ **599/7-8819.**
Fax 599/7-5295. E-mail: bruce@caribinn.com. 10 apts. A/C TV. Year-round $89 studio apt.;
$99 efficiency apt.; $119 1-bedroom apt.; $139 2-bedroom apt.; $159 3-bedroom apt. AE,
MC, V.

On the water, this hotel—owned and managed by the American diver Bruce
Bowker—is occupied with dedicated scuba divers drawn to its five-star PADI dive
facility. This is the most intimate little dive resort on Bonaire and remains one of
Bonaire's best values. Eight of its ten rooms have kitchens. All units are equipped with
refrigerators, and maid service is provided daily. The accommodations are furnished in
a tropical rattan, with good beds. The bathrooms have been enlarged and refurbished.
There's no restaurant or bar. Repeat guests are likely to book this place far in advance
in winter.

Cyndany Lodge. J. A. Abraham Blvd. 51, Kralendijk, Bonaire, N.A. ☎ **599/7-7075.**
Fax 599/7-4047. www.bonaire.com. E-mail: cyndanylodge@bonaire.com. 12 units. A/C TV.
Year-round $75 single or double. AE, MC, V.

In a tranquil residential area within a short walk of a good beach, this is a small inn known for its good value. The units are only in the basic motel style, but guests who check in here are more interested in saving money than in fancy resort amenities. Opened in the summer of 1995, this hotel offers bedrooms with either two double beds or one queen size, each with a good mattress. All the accommodations are tiled and feature large bathrooms, refrigerators, and wet bars. The location is behind the landmark Divi Flamingo Beach Resort and near several dive and snorkeling outfitters. It is peaceful, private, and welcoming, somewhat like a Bonaire-style country inn. There is a bar and a restaurant, the latter serving breakfast only.

The Great Escape. Blvd. Europese Economische Gemeenschap 97, Belnem, Bonaire, N.A. ☎ and fax **599/7-7488.** 12 units. A/C. Winter $95–$105 single or double; $120 suite. Off-season $80–$90 single or double; $115 suite. Extra person $30 in winter, $20 off-season. Children stay free in parents' room. Rates include breakfast. AE, MC, V.

About half a mile south of the airport, near Bachelor's Beach, this is one of the newest B&Bs on the island, a welcoming and homey two-story white stone building. The lobby is large and open, and guests gather to watch TV in a lounge on the wide upstairs balcony. Although not noted for any particular style, except for the flowery courtyard with a freshwater swimming pool, the medium-size accommodations range from standard through deluxe to the most expensive of all, a suite. Special budget honeymoon arrangements can be made. The rooms are pleasantly furnished and well maintained and offer a double bed or two twins, each with a good mattress. The suites have two double beds and a pull-out sofa, although all accommodations have both a ceiling fan and air-conditioning. Bathrooms are small. This place is family friendly, with a small playground with a tiny zoo and baby-sitting services. A simple restaurant serves three meals a day.

3 Great Deals on Dining

At the restaurants below, fish dishes are expensive, but most other selections are at the lower end of the price scale.

If you're striking out for Washington-Slagbaai National Park or one of the island's more remote beaches, you can stop at the **Sand Dollar Grocery** at Kaya Gobernador N. Debrot (☎ **599/7-5490**), and rent a cooler for $4.60 to $8.60, plus a $10.60 deposit. Later, you can head for **The Sandwich Factory,** Princess Plaza in Kralendijk (☎ **599/7-7369**). Here you can purchase foot-long hoagies for $7.75 or pizza, hot and spicy chili, hot dogs, and draft beer—in other words, a picnic!

Managerie de la Mer. Kaya Bonaire 4C. ☎ **599/7-2888.** Reservations recommended. Dinner main courses $5.60–$20, lunch main courses $2.25–$11. MC, V. Mon–Fri 11:30am–10pm, Sat–Sun 5:30–11pm. FRENCH/INTERNATIONAL.

This is the island's most amusing restaurant, a little bit of St. Tropez down in the tropics. Joop van der Ligt and Ed de Vuyst have created this amusing place and decorated it with images of Marilyn Monroe, Charlie Chaplin, Laurel and Hardy, and the like. It is decorated in pastel shades of pink, banana, orange, and green, with terrace dining on the water where you can watch the boats and see some fabulous sunsets. At lunch you can have light fare such as omelets, sandwiches, soups, or 10 different freshly made salads. The menu changes frequently but is always based on quality ingredients. At night try one of their tender steaks, or else a pasta or shrimp dish. A specialty that frequently appears is "Blue Chicken," in a blue-cheese sauce. You can also enjoy loin of lamb or salmon. The gazpacho is always a refreshing way to begin a meal. The towering coupe Mont Blanc is the mother of all sundaes.

✪ **Mi Poron.** Kaya Caracas 1. ☎ **599/7-5199.** Reservations recommended. Main courses $6–$10. MC, V. Tues–Sat noon–2pm and 5–10pm, Sun 5–10pm. BONAIRIAN.

This place serves the island's most authentic Antillean cuisine. The konfó or hibachi and karbón or charcoal are still used as the original cooking methods to prepare such mouthwatering dishes as stobá (stew). You can sample all those dishes you've dreamed about here, ranging from tripe soup to okra soup. The conch dishes are delectable, and you can also sample goat specialties. Start your repast with a crab salad of locally smoked marlin. After dinner you can browse through the antique house, with its original artifacts. On the first Sunday of the month there is live mariachi music and a barbecue.

Old Inn. J. A. Abraham Blvd. ☎ **599/7-6666.** Reservations recommended. Main courses $12–$24. MC, V. Thurs–Tues 5–10pm. INDONESIAN/INTERNATIONAL.

Few other restaurants on Bonaire present so strong a Dutch colonial theme. Low-slung and unpretentious, the setting includes plaster walls lined with murals of Indonesian landscapes, with a menu whose unerring specialty is *rijsttafel*, the Indonesian rice dish whose curried flavors are enhanced with at least a dozen condiments and spices served on the side. Also look for *satay* (skewered Indonesian beef), and *nasi goreng*, an Indonesian fried-rice special. Service is attentive by a mostly Dutch-born staff, and prices are reasonable.

t'ankertje. Ceb Hallmund. ☎ **599/7-5216.** Main courses $9–$15 No credit cards. Mon–Fri 5–10pm. INTERNATIONAL.

A winning little choice, this inviting restaurant (pronounced "tan-ker-jay") is across the street from the water in Kralendijk. Open-air tables are set near the ocean. For inspiration, the cooks roam the world—everything from Italian-style pizza to Mexican tacos. Our favorite dish is their Indonesian *satay* with marinated chicken and a delectable peanut sauce. The "Arabian sandwich," similar to a gyro, appears on pita bread stuffed with pork. Your best bet? Look for the daily specials chalked up on a blackboard menu. If it's fresh fish, go for it; otherwise, you can sample what's frozen from the larder—perhaps a blackened sirloin steak or a Wiener schnitzel.

WORTH A SPLURGE

Oasis Bar & Grill. Kaminda Sorobon 64, Lac Bay. ☎ **599/7-8198.** Reservations recommended. Main courses $12–$33. MC, V. Tues–Sun 10am–2pm and 7–10pm. INTERNATIONAL.

At the southern tip of Bonaire, this is a little winner, seating 32 hungry diners. You're likely to share the culinary experience with a flock of hummingbirds in the garden out front. Tall ceilings and plenty of windows open onto views of the tranquil side of the island's windward coastline. If the weather is right, opt for a table on the patio. If you arrive early you can enjoy a tropical fruit punch at the half-moon shape bar. You might begin with either a Greek salad or a Caesar salad. If you're here for lunch, you can select from an array of char-grilled burgers and the like. In the evening, the offers are more elaborate, focusing on such dishes as chicken breast stuffed with feta cheese and spinach or one of the juicy steaks, perhaps a pasta dish. The marlin served here is smoked locally.

Rendez-Vous Restaurant & Espresso Bar. Kaya L. D. Gerharts 3. ☎ **599/7-8454.** Reservations recommended. Main courses $16–$22.30. AE, MC, V. Mon–Fri noon–2pm and Mon–Sat 6–10:30pm. INTERNATIONAL.

This restaurant is known for its renowned chef, Martin Bouwmeester, who prepares some of the island's finest fare. Opt for a table on the terrace of this cafe where you can watch the people of Bonaire parade before you. You can do all this while enjoying an array of both cold or hot appetizers, ranging from locally smoked marlin to escargots in herb butter. Everyone tries to get the recipe for the shrimp bisque. A number of main courses, each well prepared, will tempt you nightly—perhaps the catch of the day baked in puff pastry and served with a creamy white wine sauce or the pork tenderloin medallions stuffed with a nut filling. A touch of the islands appear in the ensemble of fresh salmon and shrimp with a passion fruit sauce. For dessert, save room for the island's most delectable apple strudel.

4 Hitting the Beaches

Sports lovers come to Bonaire for the diving (see below)—not the beaches. For the most part, the beaches are laden with coral and feel gritty to the bare feet. Those on the leeward (the more tranquil side of the island) are often narrow strips. To compensate, some hotels have shipped in extra sand for their guests.

✪ **Pink Beach,** lying south of Kralendijk, the capital, out past Salt Pier, is the island's most desirable beach, in spite of its narrow strip of sand and shallow water. It's aptly named: The sand does have a deep pink color, the result of corals that have been pulverized into sand by the waves. There are no refreshment stands to mar the panoramic setting here. Beach buffs bring their own cooler full of Amstel beer and their own towels, as there is nothing here to rent. It's also wise to bring along an umbrella if you have one, as the few palm trees bordering the dunes offer little protection from the sun. Midday here can get especially hot. It's best to enter the water at the southern end of this beach, as the northern tier has some exposed rock. Pink Beach is also close to Bonaire's large colony of pink flamingos. Many Bonairians flock to this beach on Saturday and Sunday, but during the week you'll virtually have the beach to yourself.

Within Washington-Slagbaai National Park, **Boca Slagbaai** is a highlight for snorkelers. You can spot flamingos wading in the salinja behind the beach. This beach has decent toilets and showers housed in a building from the 19th century. Drinks and snacks are available here. You'll want Tevas or aqua socks for walking along the beach and in the water; the coral beach is rough going on bare feet. This is also a popular site for picnics.

Also in the park, **Playa Funchi** is good for snorkeling but it has almost no sand and no facilities; we found the area surrounding the beach a bit smelly. There is a lagoon on one side where flamingos nest. Iridescent green parrotfish swim right up to the shore here.

A final beach at the national park is **Boca Cocollishi,** a black-sand beach on the northern coast. This is the most windswept beach on Bonaire. The tradewinds will certainly keep you cool as they whip the surf into a frenzy. The color of the water can change quickly from turquoise to midnight blue. The surf is too rough for swimming, although some visitors go wading. Many locals view this more as a place for a beach picnic than a swimming hole.

Lac Bay Beach lies adjacent to Sorobon Resort Beach, a private nudist colony. Lac Bay has an area of mangroves at the north end of the bay and is the best beach for windsurfers. A couple of windsurfing outfitters usually operate on this beach, and there is a bar and cafe at the far end near the entrance to the bay. Lac Bay lies on the southern shore.

Like the island's hotels, many of Bonaire's beaches lie along the island's west coast. One of the more unusual beaches is **Nukove Beach,** a mini-cave in a limestone cliff which features a small white sand beach. A white sand channel that cuts through the dense wall of elkhorn coral near the shore gives divers and snorkelers easy access to the water. Located further north along Bonaire's west coast is ✪ **1,000 Steps Beach,** more challenging to reach than some of the island's other beaches. Sixty-seven steps (although it can feel like 1,000 steps when climbing back up) carved out of the limestone cliff lead down to the beach. This white-sand beach offers a good place to scuba dive and snorkel, with a unique location and view and nearly perfect solitude.

A TRIP TO KLEIN BONAIRE

Bonaire's offshore island, **Klein Bonaire,** which lies just ¾-mile offshore, offers some of the island's most pristine beaches. This 1,500-acre island is flat and rocky. Its vegetation will make you think you're in Arizona. The little island is known for its almost deserted white sandy beaches, of which **No Name Beach** is deservedly the most popular, ideal for both a picnic lunch or a snorkeling adventure. As you enter the waters off the coast here, expect to encounter such friends as the yellowtail snapper, the tiger grouper, the parrot fish or the trumpetfish, and certainly the white mullet. The spotted moray eel might also be seen, but these are rather elusive creatures and will not harm you if you don't touch them. The island is known for its spectacular reefs, 16 sites of which are world-class. They're filled with stunning elkhorn coral as well as large star corals and brain corals. Great varieties of sponges and gorgonians can also be spotted.

Sunset Beach Hotel at Playa Lechi (☎ **599/7-5300**) offers trips to Klein Bonaire daily. You'll be left in the morning for a day of snorkeling, beachcombing, and picnicking, then be picked up later that afternoon. The cost is $35. Other hotels will also arrange a trip to the islet for you, perhaps for the Wednesday barbecue for $48.

5 World-Class Diving

One of the richest reef communities in the entire West Indies, Bonaire has plunging walls that descend to a sand bottom at 130 or so feet. The reefs are home to various coral formations that grow at different depths, ranging from the knobby brain coral at 3 feet to staghorn and elkhorn up to about 10 feet deeper, and gorgonians, giant brain, and others all the way to 40 to 83 feet. Swarms of rainbow-hued tropical fish inhabit the reefs, and the deep reef slope is home to a range of basket sponges, groupers, and moray eels. Most of the diving is done on the leeward side where the ocean usually is lake flat. There are more than 40 dive sites on sharply sloping reefs.

The waters off the coast of Bonaire got an additional attraction in 1984. A rust-bottomed general cargo ship, 80 feet long, was confiscated by the police along with its contraband cargo, about 25,000 pounds of marijuana. Known as the *Hilma Hooker* (familiarly dubbed "The Hooker" by everyone on the island), it sank unclaimed (obviously) and without fanfare one calm day in 90 feet of water. Lying just off the southern shore near the capital, its wreck is now a popular dive site.

The ✪ **Bonaire Marine Park** was created to protect the coral-reef ecosystem off Bonaire. The park incorporates the entire coastline of Bonaire and neighboring **Klein Bonaire.** Scuba diving and snorkeling are all popular here. The park is policed, and services and facilities include a Visitor Information Center at the **Karpata Ecological Center,** lectures, slide presentations, films, and permanent dive-site moorings.

Visitors are asked to respect the marine environment and to refrain from activities that may damage it, including sitting or walking on the coral. All marine life is completely protected. This means there's no fishing or collecting fish, shells, or corals— dead or alive. Spearfishing is forbidden, as is anchoring; all craft must use permanent moorings, except for emergency stops (boats shorter than 12 feet may use a stone anchor). Most recreational activity in the marine park takes place on the island's leeward side and among the reefs surrounding uninhabited Klein Bonaire.

Bonaire has a unique program for divers in that the major hotels offer personalized, close-up encounters with the island's fish and other marine life under the expertise of Bonaire's dive guides.

DIVE SHOPS

Dive I and *Dive II*, at opposite ends of the beachfront of the Divi Flamingo Beach Resort & Casino, J. A. Abraham Boulevard (☎ 599/7-8285), north of Kralendijk, are among the island's most complete scuba facilities. They're open daily from 8am to 12:30pm and 1:30 to 5pm. Both operate out of well-stocked beachfront buildings, rent diving equipment, charge the same prices, and offer the same type of expeditions. A resort course for first-time divers costs $88; for experienced divers, a one-tank dive goes for $55, a two-tank dive for $75.

✪ **Captain Don's Habitat Dive Shop,** Kaya Gobernador N. Debrot 103 (☎ 599/7-8290), is a PADI five-star training facility. The open-air, full-service dive shop includes a classroom, photo/video lab, camera-rental facility, equipment repair, and compressor rooms. Habitat's slogan is "Diving Freedom," and divers can take their tanks and dive anywhere any time of day or night, most often along "The Pike," half a mile of protected reef right in front of the property. The highly qualified staff is here to assist and advise, not to police or dictate dive plans. Diving packages include boat dives, unlimited offshore diving (24 hours a day), unlimited air, tanks, weights, and belt. Some dive packages also include accommodations and meals (see above). If you're not staying at the hotel as part of a dive package, you can visit for a beach dive, costing $21. If you want to rent snorkeling equipment, the charge is $7.45 a day. A half-day of diving, with all equipment included, goes for $37.

Sand Dollar Dive and Photo, at the Sand Dollar Condominium & Beach Club, Kaya Gobernador N. Debrot (☎ 599/7-5252), offers dive packages, PADI and NAUI instruction, and equipment rental and repairs; boat and shore trips with an instructor are available by appointment. The photo shop offers underwater photo and video shoots, PADI specialty courses by appointment, E-6 processing, print developing, and equipment rental and repair. It's open daily from 8:30am to 5:30pm.

6 Other Sports & Outdoor Pursuits

The true beauty on Bonaire is under the sea, where visibility is 100 feet 365 days of the year, and the water temperatures range from 78°F to 82°F (25.5°C to 27.7°C). Many dive sites can be reached directly from the beach, and sailing is another favored pastime. The bird watching is among the best in the Caribbean, and for beachcombers there are acres and acres of driftwood, found along the shore from the salt flats to Lac.

BIRD WATCHING   Bonaire is home to 190 species of birds, 80 of which are indigenous to the island. But most famous are its flamingos, which can number 15,000 during the mating season. For great places to bring your binoculars, see "Seeing the Sights," below.

FISHING   The island's offshore fishing grounds offer some of the best fishing in the Caribbean. A good day's catch might include mackerel, tuna, wahoo, dolphin (mahi-mahi), blue marlin, Amber Jack, grouper, sailfish, or snapper. Bonaire is also one of the best-kept secrets of bonefishing enthusiasts.

Your best bet is Chris Morkos of **Piscatur Fishing Supplies,** Kaya Herman 4, Playa Pabao (☎ 599/7-8774). A native Bonairean, he has been fishing almost since he was born. His company takes a maximum of 6 people on a 42-foot boat with a guide and captain, at a cost of $350 for a half-day or $500 for a whole day, including all tackle and bait. Reef fishing is another popular sport, in boats averaging 15 and 19 feet. A maximum of two people can go out for a half day at $225 or a whole day at $400. For the same price, a maximum of two people can fish for bonefish and tarpon on the island's large salt flats.

HORSEBACK RIDING   Bonaire's fine horse ranches offer private lessons and trail rides. You can usually arrange a day in the saddle through your hotel. You can also call **Kunuku Warahama Ranch** (☎ 599/7-7324), a 165-acre spread that features hour-long trail rides through fields studded with cactus, where you are likely to spot everything from an iguana to a colony of pink flamingos. The cost is $20 for these trail rides.

MOUNTAIN BIKING   Biking on Bonaire can be a rewarding experience; you can explore more than 186 miles of trails and dirt roads where you can venture off the beaten path to enjoy the scenery and contrasting geography. Check with your hotel about arranging a trip. Or else call **Cycle Bonaire,** Kaya L. D. Gerharts 11D (☎ 599/7-7558), which rents 21-speed mountain bikes and arranges half- or full-day excursions costing from $40 to $65, respectively, in addition to the bike rental charges.

SEA KAYAKING   Paddle the protected waters of Lac Bay, or head for the miles of flats and mangroves in the south (the island's nursery) where baby fish and wildlife can be viewed. Kayak rentals are available at **Jive City,** Lac Bay (☎ 599/7-5233), for $10 per hour or $20 per half-day.

✪ **SNORKELING**   Snorkeling gear can be rented at **Carib Inn,** J. A. Abraham Blvd. (☎ 599/7-8819); **Sand Dollar Dive and Photo,** Kaya Gobernador N. Debrot (☎ 599/7-5252), and **Captain Don's Habitat Dive Shop,** Kaya Governador N. Debrot (☎ 599/7-8290).

Bonaire's snorkeling is amazing, and can be accessed easily from many spots. Some of the highlights include **Boca Slagbaai** and **Playa Funchi,** both in Washington-Slagbaai National Park; **1,000 Steps Beach;** and **Klein Bonaire,** the offshore island.

TENNIS   There are two courts at the **Sand Dollar Condominium & Beach Club** at Kaya Governador N. Debrot 79, and there are also courts at the **Divi Flamingo Beach Resort,** J. A. Abraham Blvd. All the courts are lit for night play.

WINDSURFING   Consistent conditions, enjoyed by windsurfers with a wide range of skill levels, make the shallow, calm waters of Lac Bay the island's home to the sport. Call **Bonaire Windsurfing** (☎ 599/7-2288) for details. A half day costs $40.

7 Seeing the Sights

THE CAPITAL

The capital's name, **Kralendijk,** means "coral dike" and is pronounced *KRALL-en-dike,* although most denizens refer to it as *Playa,* Spanish for "beach." A dollhouse town of some 2,500 residents, it's small, neat, pretty, Dutch-clean, and just a bit dull. Its stucco buildings are painted pink and orange, with an occasional lime green. The capital's jetty is lined with island sloops and fishing boats.

Kralendijk nestles in a bay on the west coast, opposite **Klein Bonaire** (Little Bonaire), the uninhabited, low-lying islet a 10-minute boat ride away (see "Hitting the Beaches," above).

The main street of town leads along the beachfront on the harbor. A Protestant church was built in 1834, and **St. Bernard's Roman Catholic Church** has some interesting stained-glass windows.

Cheap Thrills: What to See & Do for Free (Well, Almost) on Bonaire

- **Investigate Washington-Slagbaai National Park.** One of the first national parks in the Caribbean, this land mass is home to some 190 species of birds, thousands of towering Candle cacti, herds of goats, stray donkeys, and lizards and more lizards. The park terrain is varied, and those ambitious enough to climb some of its steep hills are rewarded with panoramic views. You can take your Jeep or car through the park on one of two driving trails, and, of course, the hiking possibilities are seemingly endless. Small hidden beaches with crashing waters by the cliffs provide an ideal place for a picnic.

- **Watch Flamingoes at the Salt Flats.** Bonaire's flamingo population during the breeding season swells to almost 10,000, nearly outnumbering the island's human population. The best place to watch flamingos is at the island's salt ponds in the National Park, at Goto Meer, or at the southern end of the island at the solar salt works. While the solar sanctuary within the salt works requires a special permit for entry, the pink flamingos can be seen from the road. Every day at sunset, the entire flock flies the short 50-mile trip to Venezuela for feeding.

- **Explore Bonaire's Reefs.** Nature has blessed Bonaire with gorgeous coral reefs that start in just inches of water and have dense coral formations in very shallow surf. To a snorkeler, this is an underwater paradise. Most snorkeling on the island is conducted in 15 feet of water or less, and there's plenty to see even at this depth.

- **Mountain Bike Around the Island.** Biking is an ideal way to see Bonaire's hidden beauty off the beaten track. There are more than 300 kilometers of trails on the island, ranging from goat paths to unpaved roads. Other than hiking, this is the only way to explore the wonders of Bonaire's terrestrial natural resources. You can take along a picnic to enjoy at some scenic vista. Along these paths you'll encounter panoramic views of Caribbean flora and wildlife. Ask at the tourist office for a trail map, outlining the most scenic routes. You can find a little cafe for a quick lunch in the town of Rincón or else have a picnic on the windward side of the island, as you're cooled by the trade winds.

- **Spend a Day on an Uninhabited Island.** Tiny, uninhabited Klein Bonaire lies less than a mile west of Kralendijk. It's popular for snorkeling, scuba diving, beaching, and picnicking. Accessible only by boat, Klein Bonaire is home to sea turtles and other indigenous wildlife. See "Hitting the Beaches," earlier in this chapter.

At **Fort Oranje** you'll see a lone cannon dating from the days of Napoleon. If possible, try to get up early to see the **Fish Market** on the waterfront, where you'll see a variety of strange and brilliantly colored fish.

EXPLORING THE BEAUTIFUL NORTH

The road north is one of the most beautiful stretches in the Antilles, with turquoise waters on your left and coral cliffs on your right. You can stop at several points along this road where you'll find paved paths for strolling or bicycling.

After leaving Kralendijk and passing the Sunset Beach Hotel and the desalination plant, you'll come to **Radio Nederland Wereld Omroep (Dutch World Radio).** It's a 13-tower, 300,000-watt transmitting station. Opposite the transmitting station is a lovers' promenade, built by nature and an ideal spot for a picnic.

Continuing, you'll pass the storage tanks of the Bonaire Petroleum Corporation, the road heading to **Gotomeer,** the island's inland sector, with a saltwater lake. Several flamingos prefer this spot to the salt flats in the south.

Down the hill the road leads to a section called **"Dos Pos"** or two wells, which has palm trees and vegetation in contrast to the rest of the island, where only the drought-resistant kibraacha and divi-divi trees, tilted before the constant wind, can grow, along with forests of cacti.

Bonaire's oldest village is **Rincón.** Slaves who used to work in the salt flats in the south once lived here. There are a couple of bars, and the Rincón Ice Cream Parlour makes homemade ice cream in a variety of interesting flavors. Above the bright roofs of the village is the crest of a hill called Para Mira, or "stop and look."

A side path outside Rincón takes you to some Arawak inscriptions supposedly 500 years old. The petroglyph designs are in pink-red dye. At nearby **Boca Onima,** you'll find grotesque grottoes of coral.

Before going back to the capital, you might take a short bypass to **Seroe Largu,** which has a good view of Kralendijk and the sea. Lovers frequent the spot at night.

WASHINGTON-SLAGBAAI NATIONAL PARK

Occupying 15,000 acres of Bonaire's northwestern end, **Washington-Slagbaai National Park** (☎ 599/7-8444) conserves the island's fauna, flora, and landscape, and is a changing vista highlighted by desert-like terrain, secluded beaches, caverns, and a bird sanctuary. The park was once plantation land, producing divi-divi, aloe, and charcoal. It was purchased by the Netherlands Antilles government, and since 1967 part of the land, formerly the Washington plantation, has been a wildlife sanctuary. The southern part of the park, the Slagbaai plantation, was added in 1978.

You can see the park in a few hours, although it takes days to appreciate it fully. Touring the park is easy, with two self-guided routes: a 15-mile "short" route, marked by green arrows, and a 22-mile "long" route, marked by yellow arrows. The trails are well-marked and easy to follow although somewhat rugged (they're gradually being improved). Admission to the park is $5 for adults and $1 for children 11 and under, and can be purchased at the gate. The park is open daily except holidays from 8am to 5pm. No one is allowed to enter after 3pm because there isn't enough time left to explore before closing. Also, be aware when arranging your car rental that only four-wheel-drive vehicles are allowed into the park, because of the poor quality of the mostly unpaved roads, and that the park is sometimes closed to visitors during the rainy season because the roads become impassable.

Whichever route you take, there are a few important stops you should make. Just past the gate is **Salina Mathijs,** a salt flat that's home to flamingos during the rainy season. Beyond the salt flat on the road to the right is **Boca Chikitu,** a white-sand beach and bay. A few miles up the beach lies **Boca Cocolishi,** a two-part black-sand beach. Many a couple has raved about the romantic memories of this beach, perfect for picnics, privacy, and seclusion. Its deep, rough seaward side and calm, shallow basin are separated by a ridge of calcareous algae. The basin and the beach were formed by small pieces of coral, mollusks, and their shells (*cocolishi* means "shells"), thus the "black sand." The basin itself has no current, so it's perfect for snorkeling close to shore, where hermit crabs scuttle through the shallow water and black sands.

The main road leads to **Boca Bartol,** a bay full of living and dead elkhorn coral, seafans, and reef fish. A popular watering hole good for bird-watching is **Poosdi Mangel. Wajaca** is a remote reef, perfect for divers and home to the island's most exciting sea creatures, including turtles, octopuses, and trigger-fish. Immediately inland towers 788-foot **Mount Brandaris,** Bonaire's highest peak, at whose foot is **Bronswinkel Well,** a watering spot for pigeons and parakeets. Some 130 species of birds live in the park, many with such exotic names as bananaquit and black-faced grassquit. Bonaire has few mammals, but you'll see goats and donkeys, perhaps even a wild bull.

TOURING THE SOUTH

Leaving the capital again, you pass another radio transmitter, the **Trans World Radio antennas.** Towering 500 feet in the air, they blast their signals at 810,000 watts, making it one of the hemisphere's most powerful medium-wave radio stations and the most powerful nongovernmental broadcast station in the world. It sends out interdenominational Gospel messages and hymns in 20 languages to places as far away as Eastern Europe and the Middle East.

Later, you arrive at the ✪ **salt flats,** where the island's brilliantly colored pink flamingos live. Bonaire shelters the largest accessible nesting and breeding grounds in the world. The flamingos build high mud mounds to hold their eggs. The best time to see the birds is in spring when they're usually nesting and tending their young. The salt flats were once worked by slaves, and the government has rebuilt some primitive stone huts, bare shelters little more than waist high. The slaves slept in these huts, and returned to their homes in Rincón in the north on weekends. The centuries-old salt pans have been reactivated by the International Salt Company. Near the salt pans you'll see some 30-foot obelisks in white, blue, and orange, built in 1838 to help mariners locate their proper anchorages.

Farther down the coast is the island's oldest lighthouse, **Willemstoren,** built in 1837. Still farther along, **Sorobon Beach** and **Boca Cai** come into view. They're at landlocked Lac Bay, which is ideal for swimming and snorkeling. Conch shells are stacked up on the beach. The water here is so vivid and clear you can see coral 65 to 120 feet down in the reef-protected waters.

ORGANIZED TOURS

Bonaire Sightseeing Tours (☎ 599/7-8778) transports you on tours of the island, both north and south, taking in the flamingos, slave huts, conch shells, Goto Lake, the Amerindian inscriptions, and other sights. Each of these tours lasts 2 hours and costs $17 per person. You can also take a half-day "City and Country Tour," lasting 3 hours and costing from $22 per person, allowing you to see the entire northern section and the southern part as far as the slave huts.

8 Shopping

Kralendijk features an assortment of goods, including gemstone jewelry, wood, leather, sterling, ceramics, liquors, and tobacco priced 25% to 50% less than in the United States and Canada. Prices are often quoted in U.S. dollars. Walk along Kaya Grandi in Kralendijk to sample the merchandise.

Bonaire Art Gallery, Kaya L. D. Gerharts 10, (☎ 599/7-7120), is Bonaire's only art gallery, with an impressive collection of watercolors, oil paintings, acrylics, and photographs (many of underwater scenes). Especially prominent are the artworks of Venezuelan-born Hugo Aguirre. Artworks range in price from $15 to $2,500.

Ki Bo Ke Pakus ("What Do You Want"), in the Divi Flamingo Beach Resort & Casino, J. A. Abraham Blvd. (☎ 599/7-8239), has T-shirts, handbags, and beach wear.

Men might feel especially comfortable in **Little Holland,** in the Harbourside Mall, Kralendijk (☎ 599/7-5670), a masculine-looking enclave that specializes in silk neckties, Nautica shorts and shirts, and most important of all, a sophisticated array of cigars. Crafted, usually by hand, in Cuba, the Dominican Republic, and to a lesser degree, Brazil, they include some of the most prestigious names in cigars, including Montecristos (five different sizes), Cohiba, and Churchills. Be aware that at this writing, it's still illegal to bring Cuban cigars into the mainland U.S.

Littman Jewelers, Kaya Grandi 33 (☎ 599/7-8160), sells Tag Heuer dive watches and also carries Daum French crystal and Lladró Spanish porcelain. Steve and Esther Littman have restored this old house to its original state. Next door, the Littmans have a shop called **Littman's Gifts,** selling standard and hand-painted T-shirts, plus sandals, hats, Gottex swimsuits, gift items, costume jewelry, and toys.

Things Bonaire, Kaya Grandi 38C (☎ 599/7-8423), carries many gift items, including sunglasses, postcards, and locally made shell and driftwood items. They also carry men's and women's swimsuits, shorts, T-shirts, beach towels, guayaberas, caps, hats, and visors.

United Colors of Benetton, Kaya Grandi 49 (☎ 599/7-5107), has invaded Bonaire. Directly imported from Italy, the clothing is often priced 30% lower than in Europe or the United States.

9 Bonaire After Dark

Underwater **slide shows** provide entertainment for both divers and nondivers. The best shows are at **Captain Don's Habitat** (☎ 599/7-8290) (see "World-Class Diving," above). Shows are presented in the hotel bar, Rum-Runner, Thursday night from 7 to 8:30pm.

✪ **Karel's Beach Bar,** on the waterfront (☎ 599/7-8434), is almost Tahitian in its high-ceilinged, open-walled design. This popular bar is perched above the sea on stilts. You can sit at the long rectangular bar with many of the island's dive and boating professionals or select a table near the balustrades overlooking the illuminated surf. On weekends local bands entertain. If you show up for happy hour from 5:30 to 7pm, drink prices are reduced.

Call **Klein Bonaire,** Kaya C. E. B. Hellmund 5 (☎ 599/7-8617), to check to see if they are offering live jazz on the weekends, as they so often do.

We'd nominate the **City Café,** Kaya Isla Riba 3 (no phone) as the island's funkiest bar. Painted in vibrant Caribbean colors of electric blue, scarlet magenta, and banana, this bar is a popular local hangout, but "only for the crazy ones," in the words of one regular. You can also order snack food here.

Disco still lives at **Fantasy Disco,** Kaya L. D. Gerharts 11 (☎ 599/7-6345), the local dance hot spot on the island. Big screen TVs and taped music such as Jamaican reggae or merengue from the Dominican Republic keep the crowd jumping. You might also catch a live performance from one of the island's best bands.

The **Plaza Resort Casino,** J. A. Abraham Blvd. 80 (☎ 599/7-2500), is the larger of Bonaire's two casinos, and usually the noisier and more animated. It glitters, vibrates, and jangles with the sound of slot machines that cover entire walls, and gaming tables offer several games of chance. It's open daily from 6pm to 4am. Jackets and ties aren't required, but shorts after dark are frowned upon.

The island's other casino, the **Divi Flamingo Beach Resort & Casino,** in a former residence on J. A. Abraham Blvd. (☎ **599/7-8285**), promotes itself as "The World's First Barefoot Casino." It offers blackjack, roulette, poker, wheel of fortune, video games, and slot machines. Entrance is free, and it's open Monday to Saturday from 8pm to 2am.

7

The British Virgin Islands

With their small bays and hidden coves, the British Virgin Islands are among the world's loveliest cruising grounds. Strung over the northeastern corner of the Caribbean, about 60 miles east of Puerto Rico, are some 40 islands, including some small uninhabited cays or spits of land. Only three of the British Virgins are of any significant size: Virgin Gorda (the "Fat Virgin"), Tortola ("Dove of Peace"), and Jost Van Dyke. Other islands have such names as Fallen Jerusalem and Ginger. Norman Island is said to have been the inspiration for Robert Louis Stevenson's *Treasure Island*. On Deadman Bay, a rocky cay, Blackbeard marooned 15 pirates and a bottle of rum, which gave rise to the ditty.

There are predictions that mass tourism is on the way, but so far the British Virgins are still a place to escape the world. The good news for budget travelers is that you'll turn up any number of moderately priced or inexpensive hotels and restaurants here. Many of these places have recently opened, so in the pages that follow, we'll introduce you to some hotels, inns, guest houses, restaurants, and taverns that haven't yet appeared in any guidebook. You'll also find some of the best campgrounds in the Caribbean here, although those on St. John in the U.S. Virgin Islands are even better (see chapter 25).

1 Essentials

VISITOR INFORMATION

Before you go, you can obtain information from the **British Virgin Islands Tourist Board,** 370 Lexington Ave., Suite 313, New York, NY 10017 (☎ **212/696-0400**). Other sources are the **British Virgin Islands Information Offices,** 1804 Union St., San Francisco, CA 94123 (☎ **415/775-0344**); 3450 Wilshire Blvd., Suite 108-17, Los Angeles, CA 90010 (☎ **310/287-2200**); and 3390 Peachtree Rd., N.E., Suite 1000, Lenox Towers, Atlanta, GA 30326 (☎ **404/ 240-8018**).

In the United Kingdom, contact the **B.V.I. Information Office,** 110 St. Martin's Lane, London WC2N 4DY (☎ **020/7240-4259**).

The official Web site is **www.bviwelcome.com**.

Once on the islands, you'll find the **B.V.I. Tourist Board** is in the center of Road Town (Tortola), close to the ferry dock, south of Wickhams Cay (☎ **284/494-3134**).

GETTING THERE

BY PLANE There are no direct flights from North America or Europe to the British Virgin Islands, but you can make connections from San Juan and St. Thomas to Tortola's airport on Beef Island. (See chapters 17 and 25 for information on flying to these islands.) Beef Island is connected to Tortola by the one-lane **Queen Elizabeth Bridge.**

Your best bet to reach Tortola is to take **American Eagle** (☎ 800/433-7300 in the U.S.), the most reliable airline in the Caribbean, with at least four daily trips from San Juan to Beef Island/Tortola.

Another choice, if you're on one of Tortola's neighboring islands, is the much less reliable **LIAT** (☎ 800/468-0482 in the U.S. and Canada, 284/495-2577 or 284/495-1187 locally). This Caribbean carrier makes the short hops to Tortola from St. Kitts, Antigua, St. Maarten, St. Thomas, and San Juan in small planes not known for their frequency or careful scheduling. Reservations are made through travel agents or through the larger U.S.-based airlines that connect with LIAT hubs.

BY FERRY You can travel from Charlotte Amalie on St. Thomas in the U.S. Virgin Islands by public ferry to West End and Road Town on Tortola, a 45-minute voyage on Drake's Channel, which runs through the islands. Boats making this run include **Native Son** (☎ 284/495-4617), **Smith's Ferry Service** (☎ 284/495-4495), and **Inter-Island Boat Services** (☎ 284/495-4166). The latter specializes in a somewhat obscure routing—that is, from St. John to the West End on Tortola.

Fast Facts: The British Virgin Islands

Banks Banks are generally open Monday to Thursday 9am to 3pm and Friday 9am to 5pm.

Currency The U.S. dollar is the legal currency, much to the surprise of British travelers.

Customs You can bring items intended for your personal use into the British Virgin Islands. For U.S. residents, the duty-free allowance is only $400, providing you have been out of the country for 48 hours. You can send unsolicited gifts home if they total less than $50 per day to any single address. You don't pay duty on items classified as handcrafts, art, or antiques.

Doctor Thirteen doctors practice on Tortola. One doctor practices on Virgin Gorda. If you need medical help, your hotel will put you in touch with the islands' medical staff.

Documents To enter the British Virgins, visitors need a valid passport or an original birth certificate with a raised seal accompanied by a government-issued photo identification. We always recommend traveling to another country with your passport in hand.

Electricity The electrical current is 110 volts AC (60 cycles), as in the United States.

Embassies & Consulates There are none in the British Virgin Islands.

Hospitals In Road Town, you can go to **Peebles Hospital,** Porter Road (☎ 284/494-3497).

Liquor Laws The legal minimum age for purchasing liquor or drinking alcohol in bars or restaurants is 21.

The British Virgin Islands

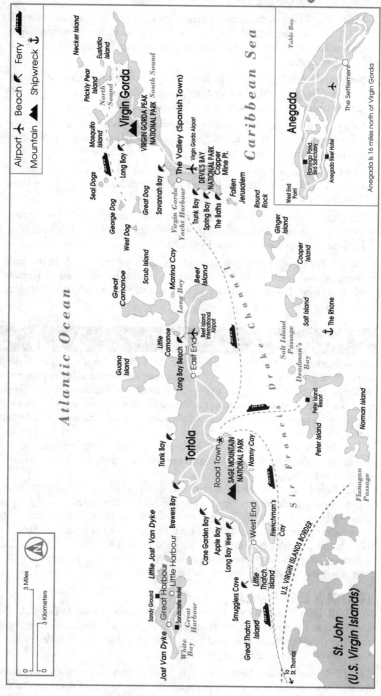

Airport ✈ Beach ⚓ Ferry 🚢
Mountain ▲ Shipwreck ⚓

Atlantic Ocean

Caribbean Sea

Necker Island
Eustatia Island
Prickly Pear Island
Mosquito Island
Virgin Gorda
North Sound
South Sound
Seal Dogs
Long Bay
VIRGIN GORDA PEAK NATIONAL PARK
George Dog
West Dog
Great Dog
Savannah Bay
The Valley (Spanish Town)
Virgin Gorda Yacht Harbour
Virgin Gorda Airport
DEVIL'S BAY NATIONAL PARK
Copper Mine Pt.
Trunk Bay
Spring Bay
The Baths
Fallen Jerusalem
Round Rock
Ginger Island
Cooper Island

Great Camanoe
Scrub Island
Marina Cay
Little Camanoe
Beef Island
Long Bay
Beef Island International Airport
Long Bay Beach
East End
Guana Island
Salt Island
⚓ The Rhone
Salt Island Passage
Deadman's Bay
Peter Island Resort

Drake Channel
S i r F r a n c i s

Tortola
Trunk Bay
Brewers Bay
Cane Garden Bay
Apple Bay
Long Bay West
Road Town ✈
SAGE MOUNTAIN NATIONAL PARK
Nanny Cay
West End
Frenchman's Cay
Little Thatch Island
Smugglers Cove

Great Thatch Island
To St. Thomas
U.S. VIRGIN ISLANDS BORDER
Flanagan Passage

Peter Island
Norman Island

Jost Van Dyke
Little Jost Van Dyke
Sandy Ground
Great Harbour
Sandcastle Hotel
Little Harbour
White Bay
Great Harbour

St. John (U.S. Virgin Islands)

N

0 ─── 3 Miles
0 ─── 3 Kilometers

Table Bay

Anegada
Flamingo Pond Bird Sanctuary
Anegada Reef Hotel
West End Point
The Settlement
Anegada is 16 miles north of Virgin Gorda

Mail Postal rates in the British Virgin Islands are 30¢ for a postcard (airmail) to the U.S. or Canada, and 45¢ for a first-class airmail letter (½ ounce) to the United States or Canada, or 35¢ for a second-class letter (½ ounce) to the United States or Canada.

Newspapers & Magazines The British Virgin Islands has no daily newspaper, but *The Island Sun,* published Wednesday and Friday, is a good source of information on local entertainment, as is *The Beacon,* published on Thursday.

Safety Crime is rare here; in fact, the British Virgin Islands are among the safest places in the Caribbean. Still, you should take all the usual precautions you would anywhere, and don't leave items unattended on the beach.

Taxes There is no sales tax. A government tax of 7% is imposed on all hotel rooms. A $10 departure tax is collected from everyone leaving by air; $5 for those departing by sea.

Telephone You can call the British Virgins from the continental United States by dialing area code **284,** followed by **49,** and then five digits. Once here, omit both the 284 and the 49 to make local calls.

Time The islands operate on Atlantic standard time year-round. In the peak winter season, when it's 6am in the British Virgins, it's only 5am in Florida. However, when Florida and the rest of the East Coast go on daylight saving time, the clocks do not change.

2 Tortola

On the southern shore of this 24-square-mile island, **Road Town** is the capital of the British Virgin Islands. It's the seat of Government House and other administrative buildings, but it seems more like a village. The landfill at **Wickhams Cay,** a 70-acre town center development and marina in the harbor, has brought in a massive yacht-chartering business and has transformed the sleepy capital into more of a bustling center.

The entire southern coast of Tortola, including Road Town, is characterized by rugged mountain peaks. On the northern coast are white sandy beaches, banana trees, mangoes, and clusters of palms.

Beef Island, close to Tortola's eastern end, is the site of the main airport for passengers arriving in the British Virgins. The tiny island is connected to Tortola by the Queen Elizabeth Bridge, which the queen dedicated in 1966. The one-lane bridge spans the 300-foot channel that divides the little island from its bigger neighbor, Tortola. On the north shore of Beef Island is a good beach, Long Bay.

Because Tortola is the gateway to the British Virgin Islands, the information on how to get there is covered at the beginning of this chapter.

TORTOLA ESSENTIALS

VISITOR INFORMATION There is a **B.V.I. Tourist Board Office** (☎ **284/ 494-3134**) at the center of Road Town near the ferry dock. You'll find information about hotels, restaurants, tours, and more. Pick up a copy of *The Welcome Tourist Guide,* which has a useful map of the island.

GETTING AROUND **Taxis** meet every arriving flight. Government regulations prohibit anyone from renting a car at the airport, so visitors must take a taxi to their hotels. The fare from the Beef Island airport to Road Town is $15 for one to three

Tortola

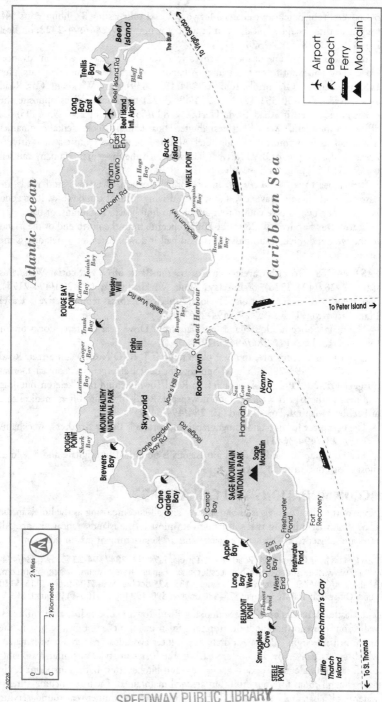

Legend:
- ✈ Airport
- ✦ Beach
- ⛴ Ferry
- ▲ Mountain

Atlantic Ocean

Caribbean Sea

Beef Island
The Bluff
Trellis Bay
Bluff Bay
Long Bay East
Beef Island Rd
Beef Island Int'l. Airport
To Virgin Gorda
East End
Parham Towne
Lambert Rd
Fat Hogs Bay
Buck Island
WHELK POINT
Paraquita Bay
Blackburn Hwy
Brandy Wine Bay
ROUGE BAY POINT
Carrot Bay
Josiah's Bay
Wesley Will
Belle Vue Rd
Baugher's Bay
Road Harbour
To Peter Island →
Trunk Bay
Fahia Hill
Cooper Bay
Lorimers Bay
Road Town
MOUNT HEALTHY NATIONAL PARK
Shark Bay
ROUGH POINT
Skyworld
Joe's Hill Rd
Sea Cow Bay
Nanny Cay
Hannah
Brewers Bay
Cane Garden Bay Rd
Ridge Rd
SAGE MOUNTAIN NATIONAL PARK
Sage Mountain
Cane Garden Bay
Carrot Bay
Freshwater Pond
Fort Recovery
Apple Bay
Zion Hill Rd
Long Bay West
Long Bay
West End
Freshwater Pond
BELMONT POINT
Belmont Pond
Smugglers Cove
STEELE POINT
Little Thatch Island
Frenchman's Cay
To St. Thomas →

2 Miles
2 Kilometers
0

2-0228

passengers. Your hotel can call a taxi for you. A **taxi tour** lasting 2½ hours costs $45 for one to three people. To call a taxi in Road Town, call ☎ **284/494-2322;** on Beef Island dial ☎ **284/495-2378.**

Because of the volume of tourism to Tortola, you should reserve a **car** in advance, especially if you want to rent in winter. A handful of local companies rent cars, plus U.S.-based chains. On Tortola, **Itgo** (☎ **284/494-2639**) is at 1 Wickhams Cay, Road Town. **Avis** (☎ **800/331-1212** or 284/494-3322) maintains offices opposite the police headquarters in Road Town. **Hertz** (☎ **800/654-3001** or 284/495-4405) has offices on the island's West End, near the ferryboat landing dock. Rental companies will usually deliver your car to your hotel. All three companies require a valid driver's license and a temporary B.V.I. driver's license, which the car-rental company can sell you for $10; it's valid for 3 months.

Remember to *drive on the left* in the British fashion. Because island roads are narrow, poorly lit, and have few, if any, lines, driving at night can be risky. It's a good idea to rent a taxi to take you to that difficult-to-find beach, restaurant, or bar.

Scato's Bus Service (☎ **284/494-2365**) operates from the north end of the island to the west end, picking up passengers who hail it down. Fares for a trek across the island are $1 to $3.

FAST FACTS   To cash traveler's checks, try the **Bank of Nova Scotia,** Wickhams Cay (☎ **284/494-2526**), or **Barclays Bank,** Wickhams Cay (☎ **284/494-2171**), both near Road Town on Tortola. The local **American Express** representative is **Travel Plan,** Waterfront Drive (☎ **284/494-2347**).

The main **police** headquarters is on Waterfront Drive near the ferry docks on Sir Olva Georges Plaza (☎ **284/494-3822**).

If you need a **drugstore,** the best place to go is **J. R. O'Neal,** Main Street, Road Town (☎ **284/494-2292**); closed Sunday. For dental emergencies, contact **Dental Surgery** (☎ **284/494-3274**), which is in Road Town, behind the Skeleton Building and next to the *BVI Beacon,* the local newspaper. Road Town also offers medical care at **Peebles Hospital,** Porter Road (☎ **284/494-3497**).

The best place for film and camera repair on Tortola is **Bolo's Brothers,** Wickhams Cay (☎ **284/494-3641**).

The best **map** of the British Virgin Islands is published by Vigilate and is sold at most bookstores in Road Town.

ACCOMMODATIONS YOU CAN AFFORD

None of the island's hotels is as big, splashy, and all-encompassing as the hotels in the U.S. Virgin Islands, and that's just fine with most of the islands' repeat visitors. All rates are subject to a 10% service charge and a 7% government tax on the room.

Castle Maria. P.O. Box 206, Road Town, Tortola, B.V.I. ☎ **284/494-2553.** Fax 284/494-2111. www.islandsonline.com/hotelcastlemaria. E-mail: hotelcastlemaria@caribsurf.com. 31 units. A/C TV TEL. Winter $70–$75 single; $85–$95 double; $96–$105 triple; $115–$130 quad. Off-season $60–$65 single; $75–$80 double; $90–$99 triple; $100–$110 quad. MC, V.

The Castle Maria sits on a hill overlooking Road Town Harbour just a few minutes' walk from downtown. The lush, tropical garden out front is one of the best in the entire British Virgin Islands. An orchard produces avocados, mangoes, and bananas, which guests can enjoy. Rooms are back-to-the-basics in style, but offer reasonable comfort, with balconies, patios, good beds, and kitchenettes. Bathrooms don't really have enough room for your stuff, but are well maintained. Facilities include a freshwater pool, a bar, and a restaurant that serves breakfast and dinner year-round, serving some of the best steaks on island. All the beaches are on the northern side of the island, so guests must take a taxi to them.

✪ **Fort Burt Hotel.** P.O. Box 3380, Fort Burt, Road Town, Tortola, B.V.I. ☎ **284/494-2587.** Fax 284/494-2002. 18 units. A/C TV. Winter $85–$110 single; $95–$120 double; $150–$200 suite with kitchen, $275 suite with private pool but no kitchen. Off-season $75–$100 single; $85–$110 double; $130–$180 suite with kitchen, $255 suite with private pool but no kitchen. AE, MC, V.

Covered with flowering vines, Fort Burt rents rooms but devotes some of its energy to its popular pub and restaurant (reviewed below). Built in 1960 on the ruins of a 17th-century Dutch fort, the rooms are set at a higher elevation than any others in Road Town, offering views from their private terraces to the waterfront below. Simple, sunny, and cozy, they have a colonial charm and freewheeling conviviality. The suites are expensive, but the regular doubles are in our ballpark; they're spacious enough and have recently been refurbished. Most accommodations have tiled floors, double or twin beds with firm mattresses, and furniture that has seen its wear and tear. Baths are quite small but have marble vanities and full tubs. Try for rooms 301 or 306 as these have a circular private pool. There's a pool on the grounds, or in 3 minutes guests can walk to Garden Bay Beach or Smuggler's Cove Beach.

The Jolly Roger Inn. West End, Tortola, B.V.I. ☎ **284/495-4559.** Fax 284/495-4184. 5 units, 2 with private bathroom. Winter $64.35 single without bathroom, $75 single with bathroom; $77 double without bathroom, $86.50 double with bath; $87.75 triple without bathroom, $99 triple with bathroom. Off-season $47 single without bathroom, $57.35 single with bathroom; $58.50 double without bathroom, $70.20 double with bathroom; $64.50 triple without bathroom, $82 triple with bathroom. AE, MC, V. Closed Aug–Sept.

This small harborfront hotel is located at Soper's Hole, only 100 yards from the ferry dock for St. Thomas and St. John. The accommodations are clean and very simple. The small rooms have recently been refurbished with new draperies, bedspreads, firm mattresses, and fresh paint, though only two have a private bathroom. Communal baths are adequate and you're given two medium-size towels. The rooms lack air-conditioning but are breezy. The atmosphere is fun and casual and is definitely laid-back. The hotel can arrange sportfishing charters, sailing, or diving trips. For sailors the hotel also offers a dinghy dock, bag ice, and fax service. The beach at Smuggler's Cove is a 20- to 30-minute walk over the hill.

Maria's by the Sea. P.O. Box 206, Road Town, Tortola, B.V.I. ☎ **284/494-2595.** Fax 284/494-2420. 41 units. A/C TV TEL. Winter $95–$125 single; $110–$125 double. Off-season $80–$110 single; $95–$125 double. AE, DC, MC, V.

This enterprise is centrally located in Road Town with a panoramic view of the harbor, although it's a 10- to 15-minute drive to the nearest beach. The rooms are decorated with rattan furniture and locally created murals. All units include a kitchenette, balcony, a good mattress, and a small private bathroom. The hotel has a freshwater pool, and water sports can be arranged. This business also offers a bar and restaurant serving breakfast, lunch, and dinner.

Rhymer's Beach Hotel. P.O. Box 570, Cane Garden Bay, Tortola, B.V.I. ☎ **284/495-4639.** Fax 284/495-4820. 21 units. A/C TV TEL. Winter $75 single; $80 double. Off-season $40 single; $45 double. Extra person $10. AE, MC, V.

A low-slung pink-sided building, this comfortable, unpretentious mini-resort sits next to a white-sand beach on the island's north shore. The hotel's social center is a wide ground-floor veranda where beach life and restaurant/bar orders merge into one smoothly flowing ritual. The simple accommodations have ceiling fans and basic kitchenettes, plus firm mattresses. Bathrooms are really cramped but well maintained, with a good set of towels. On the premises is a restaurant, a beauty salon, a general store/commissary, and a boutique. Music lovers can head for the bar of the nearby Ole Works Inn, where live music by island star Quito Rhymer is presented.

Sea View Hotel. P.O. Box 59, Road Town, Tortola, B.V.I. ☎ **284/494-2483.** Fax 284/494-4952. E-mail: jumukhal@caribsurf.com. 34 units. TV. Year-round $55 single or double; $76 suite for 2; $135 efficiency apt. with kitchenette for 4. MC, V.

Set at the western perimeter of Road Town, this concrete-sided modern guest house occupies a sloping site that affords a view over the boats bobbing at anchor in Road Town Harbour, but it's a 10-mile ride to the nearest beach. It's about as simple (and inexpensive) a hotel as you're likely to find, with few frills, although all rooms were recently renovated. The efficiency apartments contain a sitting room, a concrete-sided porch, ceiling fans, two bedrooms, and a modest kitchen. The smaller suites have air-conditioning, radios, and a mini-fridge. Mattresses are a bit used but still comfortable, and the bathrooms are very tiny with a set of thin towels. Only breakfast is served, but the bars, sandwich shops, and grocery stores of Road Town are a 5-minute walk away. Maid service and use of a small swimming pool are included in the price.

WORTH A SPLURGE

Lambert Beach Resort. Lambert Beach, Tortola, BVI. ☎ **284/495-2877.** Fax 284/495-2876. E-mail: lambert@caribsurf.com. 38 units. A/C TEL. Jan 5–Apr 15 $100–$170 double, $260 suite. Apr 16–Dec 19 $90–$150 double, $250 suite. Dec 20–Jan 4 $120–$210 double, $320 suite. MC, V.

One of the newest hotels in Tortola (it opened in March of 1998), this resort is a compound of one-story white-walled villas, each with a terra-cotta roof and between 4 and 6 bedrooms. Set a few paces from Lambert Beach, on the island's east end near the airport, the hotel's accommodations have white walls, green-painted furniture, and either balconies or verandas. There is much comfort here, as reflected by the excellent mattresses on the beds, and the tiptop maintenance. Bathrooms, though small, are efficiently arranged with enough room for your stuff. On the premises are two swimming pools, one of which is for children, and an open-air dining pavilion. Included in the rates are use of watersports equipment such as kayaks and snorkeling gear.

Ole Works Inn. P.O. Box 560, Cane Garden Bay, Tortola, B.V.I. ☎ **284/495-4837.** Fax 284/495-9618. 18 units. A/C TEL. Winter $80–$200 single or double, from $165 suite. Off-season $60–$175 single or double, from $140 suite. Rates include continental breakfast. Extra person $25; children 11 and under stay free in parents' room. Rates include breakfast. MC, V. Closed Sept.

Set inland from Cane Garden Bay, this hotel occupies the historic premises of a 300-year-old sugar refinery. It's across the road from a beautiful white-sand beach, and offers terrific music at the rustic indoor/outdoor bar, Quito's Gazebo.

The accommodations are cramped but cozy, outfitted with angular furniture and pastel colors. Many have water views. Each accommodation contains a small refrigerator and ceiling fan. Not all the rooms are the same: Some are built as hillside units with ceiling fans (plus air conditioning), refrigerators, and clock radios. Others are older and smaller. The mattresses are regularly replaced, and though the bathrooms are a bit too small, the housekeeping is good. The most romantic unit is the honeymoon suite in the venerable tower; it's larger than you'd expect. On the premises is a boutique-style art gallery showing watercolors by local artists and souvenirs. There are seven different restaurants on the beach.

The hotel bar is a magnet for lovers of modern calypso music, largely because it's supervised by the hotel owner Quito (Enriquito) Rhymer, who's the most famous living recording star ever produced on Tortola. Quito himself performs several times a week.

Sebastians on the Beach. Little Apple Bay (P.O. Box 441), West End, Tortola, B.V.I. ☎ **284/495-4212.** Fax 284/495-4466. 26 units. Winter $110 single; $120–$190 double. Off-season $75–$140 single; $85–$150 double. Extra person $15; MAP (breakfast and dinner) $35 per person extra. AE, DISC, MC, V.

The hotel is located at Little Apple Bay, about a 15-minute drive from Road Town, on a long beach that offers a view of Jost Van Dyke and some of the best surfing in the B.V.I. The rooms are housed in three buildings, with only one on the beach. All the floral-accented rooms come with rattan furniture and have small refrigerators and private bathrooms; six have air-conditioning, balconies, and porches. You should be careful here about room selection, as accommodations vary considerably, so ask lots of questions. Most sought after are the beachfront rooms, only steps from the surf; they have an airy tropical feeling with tile floors, balconies, patios, and screened jalousies. The rear accommodations on the beach side are less desirable. Not only do they lack views but they are subject to traffic noise. Also, avoid if possible the two bedrooms above the commissary, as they are likely to be noisy. If you're economizing you can opt for one of the dozen rather spartan rooms in the back of the main building, as they are much less expensive. They don't have any view, but they're only a short walk from the beach.

The restaurant overlooks the bay and offers an international menu. On Saturday and Sunday guests can enjoy live entertainment in the bar. The hotel features dive packages along with packages that include a MAP plan, a welcome cocktail, a dozen assorted postcards, a pictorial guide to the B.V.I., and a bottle of rum.

GREAT OFF-SEASON BARGAINS

Between mid-April and mid-December many hotels that might be out of your price range become more affordable. The best discounts are offered at the following properties:

Nanny Cay Resort & Marina. P.O. Box 281, Road Town, Tortola, B.V.I. ☎ **800/74-CHARMS** in the U.S., or 284/494-4895. Fax 284/494-0555. 42 studios. A/C TV TEL. Winter $100–$145 single; $150–$195 double; $175–$220 triple. Off-season $70–$80 single; $100–$145 double; $125–$170 triple. AE, MC, V.

Nanny Cay appeals to yacht owners but offers anyone a great deal in the off-season. This sprawling, somewhat disorganized resort displays great wealth, in the form of hyper-expensive yachts, which lie juxtaposed alongside old, battered, funky West Indian fishing boats. We prefer one of the air-conditioned studios in the two-story wing because they are more spacious and better appointed than the regular hotel bedrooms. Each unit has a ceiling fan, kitchenette, dining table, tile floors, digital clock, and either two queen or two double beds, each with a firm mattress. We prefer rooms 117, 118, and 119 because they are more spacious than the other units and have peaked roofs. Bathrooms are very tiny but efficiently organized with shower stalls instead of tubs. The driving force here is the 180-slip marina, headquarters to at least three yacht-chartering companies, and permanent home to many fishing and pleasure boats. Collectively, the resort sprawls over 25 acres of steamy flatlands, adjacent to a saltwater inlet that's favored because of the protection it offers to sailing craft during storms and hurricanes. Don't expect the spit-and-polish of a fancy resort; this place is artfully and deliberately casual and funky, which seems to be the way folks here want to keep it.

The Pegleg Restaurant, open daily for dinner, offers a richly equipped re-creation of a pirate's lair fashioned from weathered planks. Thick steaks, seafood, a Yankee/

nautical theme, and stiff drinks are the norm. A tennis court, swimming pool, a kiosk for the rental of pedal bikes, a dive shop, and several boating businesses are on the premises.

APARTMENT & VILLA RENTALS

Icis Vacation Villas. P.O. Box 383, Road Town, Tortola, B.V.I. ☎ **284/494-6979.** Fax 284/494-6980. 5 efficiencies, 5 one-bedroom apts., 1 three-bedroom apt. A/C TV. Winter $99–$115 efficiency; $159 1-bedroom apt.; $260 3-bedroom apt. Off-season $69–$79 efficiency; $89–$99 1-bedroom apt.; $179 3-bedroom apt. Children 11 and under stay free in parents' unit. DC, DISC, MC, V.

Just yards from Brewers Bay with its good swimming, these apartment units, although rather basic, are spotlessly maintained. Doors open onto a patio or porch in three white-and-pink concrete buildings in a tropical setting with lots of foliage. The rooms are decorated in summery colors with both air-conditioning and ceiling fans. Each mattress has been recently replaced, and the bathrooms, though small, are very well-maintained. Room service is available upon request, and baby-sitting can be arranged. There are no room phones, but an on-site coin phone is available. The place is in a tranquil part of the island and has a swimming pool.

Mongoose Apartments. P.O. Box 581, Cane Garden Bay, Tortola, B.V.I. ☎ **284/495-4421.** Fax 284/495-9721. 6 one-bedroom apts. Winter $125 apt. for 1 or 2. Off-season, $85 apt. for 1 or 2. Extra person $20; children 12 and under $10. No credit cards.

Just minutes from the beach, in the Cane Garden Bay area, is one of the most reasonably priced apartment units on the island. All the apartments, although simply furnished, have a living room, kitchen, and balcony, a twin sleeper couch in the living room, firm mattresses, and ceiling fans. Two units have TV, although you'll have to rely on the office phone. The apartments are in a U-shaped two-story building. Some of the rooms open onto an ocean view. Each of the small bathrooms has room to spread out your stuff, and is well maintained. The good news is that the complex lies only 100 yards from the beach. There's no restaurant, but a number of choices are close at hand. The owner, Sandra Henley, grows medicinal teas, which guests are invited to try. Baby-sitting can be arranged.

Ronneville Cottages. P.O. Box 2652, Brewers Bay, Tortola, B.V.I. ☎ **284/494-3337.** 2 two-bedroom cottages, 1 three-bedroom/two-bath house. TV. Winter $675 cottage per week; $725 house per week. Off-season $425 cottage per week; $500 house per week. Extra person $25 year-round; children 2 and under stay free with parents. No credit cards.

If you'd like an inexpensive vacation for a week in the Brewers Bay area, this is a good choice, although the cottages are hardly romantic. They're designed for basic beach living; a beach bar serving burgers and the like is only a 5-minute walk away. The cottages are in concrete structures on ground level, and everything is set in tropical foliage with lots of flowers. The units are clean and basic, with ceiling fans in the living rooms and standing fans in the bedrooms. Each unit has a porch or patio and TV. Mattresses are a bit tired but still comfortable, and the efficiently arranged, small bathrooms have a set of rather thin towels. There's no pool, however, and no restaurant. But if you'd like some local cookery, the owner will prepare a dinner with sufficient notice.

CAMPING

✪ **Brewers Bay Campground.** Brewers Bay (P.O. Box 185), Road Town, Tortola, B.V.I. ☎ **284/494-3463.** 20 tents, 20 bare sites. Year-round, $35 tent for 2; $10 bare site for 2. No credit cards. A camp shuttle is sometimes available.

Most camping buffs appreciate this place, located 3 miles from Road Town, for its low costs and for its easy access to some of the best snorkeling off the coast of Tortola. Both tent and bare-site options are available, and both include access to cookout areas, showers with running water and flush toilets, and a simple beachfront bar selling sandwiches, hot dogs, and beer. Dinner can be provided with advance notice, and on Friday nights there's a communal fish fry, followed by a barbecue on Sunday night, each for $10 per person. There's no on-site commissary, but shops in Road Town sell groceries and camping paraphernalia.

GREAT DEALS ON DINING

Cafesito. Romasco Place, Wickham's Cay, Road Town. ☎ **284/494-7412.** Lunch main courses $3.50–$13.50; dinner main courses $11–$19.75. AE, DISC, MC, V. Daily 10:30am–11pm. INTERNATIONAL.

No one will object if you stop into this hip and popular place just for one of their Bahama Mamas, a seductive, mildly psychedelic drink that's deceptively pink and laced with rum. But if you want a meal, there's a full menu of culinary temptations that range from simple rôtis and BLTs to more complicated fare such as coconut-flavored shrimp, pasta with shrimp and lobster-flavored cream sauce, blackened red snapper, and barbecued baby back ribs. There's some kind of live entertainment, usually either a steel band or a calypso band, that performs every Friday, Saturday, and Sunday from 7:30pm till around 11pm (no cover). There's no sea view from this place's terrace, but whenever the drinks are flowing and the music is playing, no one ever really seems to care.

✪ **Capriccio di Mare.** Waterfront Dr., Road Town. ☎ **284/494-5369.** Main courses $6–$13. No credit cards. Daily 8–10:30am and 11am–9pm. ITALIAN.

Small, casual, and laid-back, this local favorite was created by the owners of the upmarket Brandywine Bay restaurant in a moment of whimsy. It's the most authentic-looking Italian *café* in the Virgin Islands. When it opens for breakfast, many locals stop in for an Italian pastry along with a cup of cappuccino. You can come back for lunch or dinner. If it's evening, you might also order the mango Bellini, a variation of the famous cocktail served at Harry's Bar in Venice (it's made with fresh peaches). Begin with such appetizers as *tiapina* (flour tortillas with various toppings), and go on to fresh pastas with succulent sauces, the best pizza on the island, or even well-stuffed sandwiches. We prefer the pizza topped with freshly grilled eggplant. If you arrive on the right night, you might even be treated to lobster ravioli in a rosé sauce. Also try one of their freshly made salads: We go for the *insalata mista* with large, leafy greens and slices of fresh parmesan.

Flying Iguana. At the airport. ☎ **284/495-5277.** Main courses $3–$42; lunch $4–$12. MC, V. Daily 8:30am–10pm. CARIBBEAN/CONTINENTAL.

Don't make a special trip here, but if you're in the vicinity this is a good lunch spot. It also serves tasty dinners as well. Don't be scared off by the $42 price for surf and turf. Most dishes are under $7, and the portions are so big they are a meal unto themselves. This open-air restaurant is painted in vivid Caribbean colors. At lunch order one of the iguana burgers (actually, made with beef), the conch chowder, or one of the spicy conch fritters, along with a selection of sandwiches and pasta. The kitchen shines brighter at dinner, with an array of steak and seafood dishes, filet mignon, and roast duck. Puck, the chef and co-owner, will also prepare pretty much what you want to eat that night—within reason, of course. Just tell him your culinary desires, and he'll try to whip something up for you.

The Jolly Roger. West End. ☎ **284/495-4559.** Main courses $10.95–$19.75; pizzas from $10.25. AE, MC, V. Daily 8–10pm. Closed July–Aug. INTERNATIONAL/SEAFOOD.

The Jolly Roger is located close to the St. Thomas ferry dock and is a favorite watering hole for Tortola's resident yachties. The menu offerings range from burgers and signature pizzas to other island dishes such as rôti. Look for the seafood specials offered daily. The chef cooks island dishes with what he calls "an American twist." The house specialty is homemade key lime pie along with rum-fried banana. On Friday and Saturday nights guests can savor the Caribbean barbecue and on Friday they also can enjoy live music.

Marlene's. Wickhams Cay. ☎ **284/494-4634.** Pâtés $1.50–$2.50; main courses $6.50–$12; breakfast $2.50–$5. No credit cards. Mon–Sat 7:30am–6pm. WEST INDIAN.

This centrally located restaurant—really a take-out joint—provides casual dining with tropical overtones. Marlene's offers Caribbean pâtés—conch, swordfish, chicken, or beef wrapped in pastry dough, then baked or fried. Included among the local fare are rôtis and curries. If you're not in the mood for local creations, you can order baked chicken, steak, or seafood such as lobster and other shellfish. The desserts are made from scratch.

Midtown Restaurant. Main St., Road Town. ☎ **284/494-2764.** Main courses $6–$15. No credit cards. Mon–Sat 7am–10pm, Sun 7am–5pm. CARIBBEAN.

Set in the heart of Road Town, this hangout offers typical local fare such as curried chicken and mutton. The menu also includes soups ranging from conch to pea, along with a boiled cow-foot soup for the more adventurous. Patrons may enjoy other fare including the stewed beef ribs, baked chicken, and a wide selection of fresh seafood, depending on the day's catch. Most dishes come with your choice of fungi, plantains, or Caribbean carrots. If you're staying in an apartment or villa where breakfast isn't served, this is an ideal choice for your morning meal.

✪ North Shore Shell Museum Bar & Restaurant. Main Rd., Carrot Bay. ☎ **284/495-4714.** Dinner $28; breakfast from $5; lunch $4.50–$10. No credit cards. Daily 7am–10pm. WEST INDIAN.

When Egberth and Mona Donovan, both chefs, got married, they naturally decided to open a restaurant to showcase their culinary talents. They have succeeded admirably, serving an authentic island cuisine. Mona learned from her mother, Mrs. Scatliffe, who is the most celebrated local chef in the B.V.I. On the ground floor of this two-story concrete house is a museum of sorts, mainly shells and stuff that washed up on the beach. You can skip it and head instead for the upstairs where good home-cookery awaits you.

If you're in the area for breakfast, by all means drop in to sample the delectable pancakes. They're not your typical offerings, but made with coconut, guava, and mango. At lunch you can sample typical island fare along with some spicy conch fritters. For dinner you can try what was good at the market that day. The best soursop daiquiri on the island will get you in the mood for the evening fare. Tuesday and Saturday are barbecue nights, with chicken, lobster, and ribs featured. After dining, folks hang out for a hoedown, a music fest with such instruments as a ukulele, a washtub, or a gourd maraca.

Paradise Pub. Fort Burt Marina, Harbour Rd. ☎ **284/494-2608.** Reservations recommended. Main courses $8.50–$21. AE, MC, V. Mon–Sat 6am–10pm. INTERNATIONAL.

In a low-slung timbered building on a narrow strip of land between the coastal road and the southern edge of Road Town's harbor, this place has a grange-like interior and a rambling veranda built on piers over the water. Many of the island's sports teams celebrate here after their victories. The pub also attracts the island's "boat people." Available are more than 25 different kinds of beer. If you're here for a meal, you can order

AT&T

AT&T Direct® Service

AT&T Access Numbers

Anguilla+	1-800-872-2881	Cayman Isl.+	1-800-872-2881
Antigua✦	1-800-872-2881	Chile●	800-800-311
Argentina	0-800-555-4288	Colombia	980-11-0010
Aruba	800-8000	Costa Rica	0800-0-114-114
Bahamas	1-800-872-2881	Dom. Rep.+	1-800-872-2881
Barbados+	1-800-872-2881	Dominica+	1-800-872-2881
Bermuda✦	1-800-872-2881	Ecuador▲	999-119
Brazil	000-8010	El Salvador ○	800-1785
Brit. Vir. Isl.+	1-800-872-2881	Grenada✦	1-800-872-2881

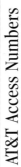

AT&T

AT&T Direct® Service

AT&T Access Numbers

Anguilla+	1-800-872-2881	Cayman Isl.+	1-800-872-2881
Antigua✦	1-800-872-2881	Chile●	800-800-311
Argentina	0-800-555-4288	Colombia	980-11-0010
Aruba	800-8000	Costa Rica	0800-0-114-114
Bahamas	1-800-872-2881	Dom. Rep.+	1-800-872-2881
Barbados+	1-800-872-2881	Dominica+	1-800-872-2881
Bermuda✦	1-800-872-2881	Ecuador▲	999-119
Brazil	000-8010	El Salvador ○	800-1785
Brit. Vir. Isl.+	1-800-872-2881	Grenada✦	1-800-872-2881

Guadeloupe✶	0800-99-00-11	Peru▲	0-800-50000
Guatemala◦✕	99-99-190	Puerto Rico	1 800 CALL ATT
Guyana✓	165	St. Barthélemy	0800-99-00-11
Haiti	183	St. Kitt/Nevis✚	1-800-872-2881
Honduras	800-0-123	St. Lucia✚	1-800-872-2881
Jamaica◦	1-800-872-2881	St. Martin	0800-99-00-11
Martinique✶	0800-99-00-11	St.Pierre/Miquelon	0800-99-00-11
Mexico◆	01-800-288-2872	St. Vincent▽	1-800-872-2881
Montserrat	1-800-872-2881	Trinidad & Tobago	0-800-872-2881
Neth. Antill. 001-800-872-2881		Turks & Calcos ✚	1-800-872-2881
Nicaragua●	174	US Virgin Isl.	1 800 CALL ATT
Panama	109	Venezuela	800-11-120

FOR EASY CALLING WORLDWIDE

1. Just dial the AT&T Access Number for the country you are calling from.
2. Dial the phone number you're calling.   3. Dial your card number.

For access numbers not listed ask any operator for **AT&T Direct®** Service.
In the U.S. call 1-800-331-1140 for a wallet guide listing all worldwide AT&T Access Numbers.

Visit our Web site at: **www.att.com/traveler**

Bold faced countries permit country-to-country calling outside the U.S.
- ✕   Public phones require coin or card deposit.
- ▲   Available from select hotels.
- ▽   Available from public phones.
- ✚   Public phones and select hotels.
- ◆✚   Some public phones and select hotels.
- ✶   When calling from public phones, use phones marked "Lactate."
- ◦   If call does not complete, use 001-800-462-4240.
- ✓   May not be available from every phone/public phone.
- ●   Public phones require local coin payment during call.
-   Collect calling only.
-   Collect calling from public phones.

When placing an international call **from** the U.S., dial 1 800 CALL ATT.

© 6/99 AT&T

Guadeloupe✶	0800-99-00-11	Peru▲	0-800-50000
Guatemala◦✕	99-99-190	Puerto Rico	1 800 CALL ATT
Guyana✓	165	St. Barthélemy	0800-99-00-11
Haiti	183	St. Kitt/Nevis✚	1-800-872-2881
Honduras	800-0-123	St. Lucia✚	1-800-872-2881
Jamaica◦	1-800-872-2881	St. Martin	0800-99-00-11
Martinique✶	0800-99-00-11	St.Pierre/Miquelon	0800-99-00-11
Mexico◆	01-800-288-2872	St. Vincent▽	1-800-872-2881
Montserrat	1-800-872-2881	Trinidad & Tobago	0-800-872-2881
Neth. Antill. 001-800-872-2881		Turks & Calcos ✚	1-800-872-2881
Nicaragua●	174	US Virgin Isl.	1 800 CALL ATT
Panama	109	Venezuela	800-11-120

FOR EASY CALLING WORLDWIDE

1. Just dial the AT&T Access Number for the country you are calling from.
2. Dial the phone number you're calling.   3. Dial your card number.

For access numbers not listed ask any operator for **AT&T Direct®** Service.
In the U.S. call 1-800-331-1140 for a wallet guide listing all worldwide AT&T Access Numbers.

Visit our Web site at: **www.att.com/traveler**

Bold faced countries permit country-to-country calling outside the U.S.
- ✕   Public phones require coin or card deposit.
- ▲   Available from select hotels.
- ▽   Available from public phones.
- ✚   Public phones and select hotels.
- ◆✚   Some public phones and select hotels.
- ✶   When calling from public phones, use phones marked "Lactate."
- ◦   If call does not complete, use 001-800-462-4240.
- ✓   May not be available from every phone/public phone.
- ●   Public phones require local coin payment during call.
-   Collect calling only.
-   Collect calling from public phones.

When placing an international call **from** the U.S., dial 1 800 CALL ATT.

© 6/99 AT&T

It's a big world.

And we've got the network to cover it.

For Travelers who want more than the Official Line

For Travelers Who Want More Than the Official Line

the Unofficial Guide® to Florida with Kids

For Travelers Who Want More Than the Official Line

the Unofficial Guide® to Walt Disney World®

♦ Tips & Warnings
♦ Save Money & Time
♦ All Attractions Candidly Rated & Ranked, Including Disney's New Animal Kingdom

Bob Sehlinger

The Series with More Than **3 Million** Copies Sold!

♦ Tips for Saving Time
Family-Friendly Hotels & R...
Attractions Rated for Each ...

For Travelers Who Want More Than the Official Line

the Unofficial Guide® to Las Vegas

The Series with More Than **3 Million** Copies Sold!

♦ Save Time & Money
♦ Insider Gambling Tips
♦ Casinos & Hotels
Candidly Rated & Ranked

Bob Sehlinger

Also Available:

- The Unofficial Guide to Branson
- The Unofficial Guide to California with Kids
- The Unofficial Guide to Chicago
- The Unofficial Guide to Cruises
- The Unofficial Disney Companion
- The Unofficial Guide to Disneyland
- The Unofficial Guide to the Great Smoky & Blue Ridge Region
- The Unofficial Guide to Miami & the Keys
- Mini-Mickey: The Pocket-Sized Unofficial Guide to Walt Disney World
- The Unofficial Guide to New Orleans
- The Unofficial Guide to New York City
- The Unofficial Guide to San Francisco
- The Unofficial Guide to Skiing in the West
- The Unofficial Guide to Washington, D.C.

Macmillan Publishing USA

Bahamian fritters, Caesar or Greek salad, pasta, four kinds of steaks, and burgers. The chef also prepares a catch of the day, perhaps wahoo. Saturday night offers all-you-can-eat baby-back ribs for $19.95 per person. Happy hour with discounted drinks is 5 to 7pm Monday to Thursday and 11am to 7pm on Friday when hot wings and raw vegetable platters are offered.

✪ **Pusser's Road Town Pub.** Waterfront Dr. and Main St., Road Town. ☎ **284/494-3897.** Reservations recommended. Main courses $7–$19. AE, DISC, MC, V. Daily 10am–10pm. CARIBBEAN/ENGLISH PUB/PIZZAS.

Standing on the waterfront across from the ferry dock, Pusser's serves Caribbean fare, English pub grub, and good pizzas. This is not as fancy or as good as the Pusser's in the West End, but it's a lot more convenient and has faster service. The complete lunch and dinner menu includes English shepherd's pies and deli-style sandwiches. *Gourmet* magazine asked for the recipe for its chicken-and-asparagus pie. John Courage ale is on draft, but the drink to have here is the famous Pusser's Rum, the same blend of five West Indian rums that the Royal Navy has served to its men for more than 300 years. Thursday is nickel beer night.

There's also Pusser's Landing, in the West End, opening onto the water (☎ **284/495-4554**).

✪ **Quito's Gazebo.** Cane Garden Bay. ☎ **284/495-4837.** Main courses $12–$18; lunch platters, sandwiches, and salads $5–$10. AE, MC, V. Mon–Fri 7am–6pm, Fri–Sat 7am–4pm. (Bar, Tues–Sun 11am–midnight.) CONTINENTAL/WEST INDIAN.

Owned by Quito Rhymer, the island's most acclaimed musician, this is the most popular of the several restaurants located along the shoreline of Cane Bay. Quito himself performs after dinner several nights a week. Set directly on the sands of the beach, and designed like an enlarged gazebo, it serves frothy rum-based drinks (ask for the house version of a piña colada, or a Bushwacker made with four different kinds of rum). Lunch is served to a beach-loving crowd, and includes sandwiches, salads, and platters. Evening meals are more elaborate, and might feature conch or pumpkin fritters, mahi-mahi with a wine-butter sauce, a conch dinner with (Callwood) rum sauce, chicken rôti, and steamed local mutton served with a sauce of island tomatoes and pepper. On Friday night for only $16 you can enjoy a buffet—all you want to eat—of barbecue ribs, chicken, rôti, corn on the cob, and Johnny cakes. Dishes have true island flavor and a lot of zest.

Rita's Restaurant. Round-A-Bout, Road Town. ☎ **284/494-6165.** Breakfast $2.50–$8; lunch or dinner $9–$15. No credit cards. Daily 8am–10pm. CARIBBEAN/AMERICAN.

If you're looking for an inexpensive place with a touch of the island, then you may want to stop at Rita's for some local fare. The surroundings are simple, but the atmosphere is lively. Breakfast ranges from the standard American fare to local favorites such as fried fish or saltfish, which is chopped up with a variety of spices and sautéed in butter. Both are served with johnnycakes. The lunch menu includes pea soup, curried chicken, and stewed mutton. For those who want a taste of home, try the barbecued chicken and ribs, sandwiches, or that old standby, spaghetti and meatballs.

Rôti Palace. Abbot Hill, Road Town. ☎ **284/494-4196.** Main courses $6–$15. No credit cards. Mon–Sat 7am–9:30pm. INDIAN.

The best rôtis in the B.V.I. are served here—they're just as good as those in Port-of-Spain, Trinidad. These Indian-style turnovers are stuffed with such good things as potato and peas for vegetarians or curried chicken. Right on the old main street of the island's capital, this is primarily a luncheon stop, although it's also a good choice for an affordable dinner. The breakfast is standard, but the menu gets lively at lunch and dinner, with a wide selection of vegetables and local conch, along with lobster, beef, and chicken dishes, often spicy and tasty. Sea snails are a specialty: They're mixed with onions, garlic, and celery, and spiced with curries, then served in a butter sauce. Ginger beer, along with the usual juices and wines, might accompany your meal.

Scuttlebutt Bar and Grill. In the Prospect Reef Resort, Slaney Hill, Drake's Hwy. ☎ **284/494-3311.** Sandwiches, platters, and salads $5.50–$14. AE, MC, V. Daily 7am–1am. INTERNATIONAL/CARIBBEAN.

This cafe's greatest asset is its location 1 mile west of the center of Road Town beside the smallest and most charming marina. Order your meal at the counter, then carry it to one of the picnic tables, which are sheltered from the sun but not from the breezes off the water. The simple setting here keeps prices down, and the food—especially breakfast when eight different kinds of "rooster omelets" draw the yachters—is plentiful and good. Specialties include beef crêpes and crabmeat salads, sandwiches, burgers, and a house drink that combines several kinds of rum into a lethal combination known as a Painkiller. Upstairs is a more expensive restaurant, Callaloo.

Spaghetti Junction. Waterfront Dr., Road Town. ☎ **284/494-4880.** Main courses $9.75–$22. AE, MC, V. Daily 6–10pm. Closed Mid-Aug to mid-Oct. ITALIAN/SEAFOOD.

Boaters like this funky place. It's located near several marinas on the second floor of a blue-painted building designed to look like a poop deck. There's a nautical mural on the floor, and the gorilla in the toilet is a huge painting and a source of constant amusement. The bar remains open long after the food service has stopped, and there's occasional impromptu dancing late at night. The Italian dishes, although standard, are quite good, including the chicken or veal parmigiana. Beef marsala and several seafood items are also featured. Look for the blackboard specials. The *frutta di mare* (medley of seafood) is always a winner, and it's served in a light cream sauce over angel-hair pasta. The Cajun jambalaya is always a crowd-pleaser.

The Tavern in the Town. Main St. (also entered from Waterfront Dr.), Road Town. ☎ **284/494-2790.** Main courses $14–$20; sandwiches and burgers $3.95–$7.95. No credit cards. Mon–Fri 11:30am–3pm and 5:30–9:30pm. (Bar, Mon–Fri 10:30am–closing; hours vary.) ENGLISH PUB.

Expatriates David and Jackie Cameron run this traditional English pub and beer garden in the center of Road Town. This is a warm and inviting place for either a drink, snack, or full meal. Be sure to check out the daily specials. Burgers are juicy quarter-pounder burgers served on a toasted bun with fried onions and french fries, and you can also order from a selection of sandwiches. Appetizers range from a prawn cocktail to garlic mushrooms. Main dishes are the traditional fish-and-chips, but you can also order honey-dipped chicken or fisherman's pie.

Virgin Queen. Fleming St., Road Town. ☎ **284/494-2310.** Reservations recommended. Main courses $7.50–$16.50; lunch $8.50. MC, V. Mon–Fri 11am–10pm, Sat 6:30–10pm. WEST INDIAN/ENGLISH PUB.

Housed in a cinder-block building, this restaurant offers casual dining in simple surroundings modestly appointed with nautical pictures scattered throughout. The menu includes a wide spectrum of dishes ranging from local fare such as curried chicken to a more international offering of pastas such as the fettuccine served with a tomato-basil sauce, and barbecued chicken and baby-back ribs. Included among the British specialties are shepherd's pie, bangers and mash, and a steak-and-ale pie. Although some dishes are on the pricey side, the portions are substantial, and many dishes, along with the daily specials, are less than $8.

The Wreck of the *Rhone* & Other Top Dive Sites

The one site in the British Virgin Islands that lures divers over from St. Thomas is ✪ **the wreck of the HMS *Rhone,*** which sank in 1867 near the western point of Salt Island. *Skin Diver* magazine called this "the world's most fantastic shipwreck dive." It teems with marine life and coral formations and was featured in the 1977 movie *The Deep,* starring Nick Nolte and Jacqueline Bisset.

Although it's no *Rhone, Chikuzen* is another intriguing dive site off Tortola. It's a 270-foot steel-hulled refrigerator ship, which sank off the island's east end in 1981. The hull, still intact under about 80 feet of water, is now home to a vast array of tropical fish, including yellowtail, barracuda, black-tip sharks, octopus, and drum fish.

The best way for novice and expert divers to see these and other great dive sites is with one of the following outfitters:

Baskin in the Sun, a PADI five-star facility on Tortola (☎ **800/233-7938** in the U.S., or 284/494-2858), is a good choice, with two different locations at the Prospect Reef Resort, near Road Town, and at Soper's Hole, on Tortola's West End. Baskin's most popular trip is the supervised "Half-Day Scuba Diving" experience for $95, catered to beginners, but there are trips for all levels of experience. Daily excursions are scheduled to the HMS *Rhone,* as well as "Painted Walls" (an underwater canyon, the walls of which are formed of brightly colored coral and sponges), and the "Indians" (four pinnacle rocks sticking out of the water, which divers follow 40 feet below the surface).

Underwater Safaris (☎ **284/494-3235**) takes you to all the best sites, including the HMS *Rhone,* "Spyglass Wall," and "Alice in Wonderland." It has two offices: "Safari Base" in Road Town and "Safari Cay" on Cooper Island. Get complete directions and information when you call. The center, connected with The Moorings (see below), offers a complete PADI and NAUI training facility. An introductory resort course and one dive costs $95, and open-water certification, with 4 days of instruction and four open-water dives, goes for $385, plus $40 for the instruction manual. They also rent snorkel gear.

Zodiacs. Wickhams Cay I (at the traffic circle). ☎ **284/494-2177.** Main courses $10–$20; lunch $4–$11.95. AE, MC, V. Daily 8am–10pm. CARIBBEAN/CONTINENTAL.

If you're a foodie who likes to taste authentic flavor regardless of where you land, try this place. Its dishes have true island zest. It's better to stick to the local items and skip the so-called continental dishes. The walls of this West Indian–style restaurant are decorated with murals by local artists. Many drop in for lunch to order the usual array of sandwiches, burgers, and salads. At night the menu is more elaborate. Try the grilled chicken with a tamarind sauce—it's a winner. Mahi-mahi, seafood combos (quite delectable), a stew of the day (often mutton or curried goat), and even such pricey dishes as filet mignon and lobster also tempt you.

WORTH A SPLURGE

Captain's Table. Wickhams Cay II. ☎ **284/494-3885.** Reservations recommended. Main courses $12.50–$27. DC, MC, V. Mon–Fri 11am–3pm and 5–11pm, Sat–Sun 5–9pm. CONTINENTAL.

Set amid a cluster of palm trees on the marina, the Captain's Table offers outdoor dining in an inviting atmosphere. For appetizers you can enjoy selections ranging from gazpacho to escargots. Also included is honey-dipped chicken, which is lightly coated with flour and deep-fried to a golden brown, then served with french fries on the side. For a lighter meal, you may want to try the Cajun chicken over a Caesar salad. For even more substantial appetites, the menu offers dolphin, served sautéed or grilled, along with grilled salmon and lobster. For something unusual, try fillet of Jamaican jerk duck or one of the Asian specialties.

Fort Burt Restaurant and Pub. Fort Burt, Road Town. ☎ **284/494-2587.** Reservations recommended for dinner. English breakfast $8.75; dinner platters $15–$25; lunch sandwiches and platters $5–$8.50. AE, MC, V. Daily 8–10am, noon–3pm, and 6–11pm. (Bar, daily 10am–midnight.) INTERNATIONAL.

This restaurant was built on rocks mortared together in the 17th century with lime and molasses by the Dutch and French. Lunches offer soups, salads, grilled fish, and sandwiches. Dinners are candlelit and more elaborate, with such dishes as fresh asparagus with aïoli sauce, conch fritters, shepherd's pie, baby back ribs, and roast duck with orange-and-tarragon sauce. It's hardly the best food on the island, although quite passable. Chalk it up as a "local favorite."

HITTING THE BEACHES

Beaches are rarely crowded on Tortola unless a cruise ship is in port. If you're not staying on or near one, you can rent a car or a Jeep to reach them, or take a taxi (but arrange for a time to be picked up).

Tortola's finest and most accessible beach is ✪ **Cane Garden Bay,** on Cane Garden Bay Road (see "Over the Mountains to Cane Garden Bay," below), which some beach buffs have compared to St. Thomas's famous Magens Bay Beach. It's directly west of Road Town, up and down some steep hills, but it's worth the effort to get there. This half-moon beach, the most popular in the B.V.I., offers great sands. You can enjoy a nosh when you're famished, as there are some seven places here to eat, none finer than Quito's Gazebo (see above), where owner Quito Rhymer, the local recording star, sings four nights a week. Nothing is more romantic than listening to Quito's love songs drifting out across the sands. Jilly Buffet sings about his days on Cane Garden Bay, sipping a rum and coke (probably a Tequila Sunrise), and watching the sun set. This beach and its lovely bay is beloved by yachties. You can also rent sailboards, Hobie Cats, and kayaks here, and windsurfing is also possible. Beware of big crowds in high season.

Surfers like **Apple Bay,** west of Road Town, along North Shore Road, and a hotel here, Sebastians, caters to them (see "Accommodations You Can Afford," above). The beach is rather narrow but that doesn't diminish activity when the surf is up. Good waves are never guaranteed, but they are most likely in January and February. After enjoying the white sands and view of Jost Van Dyke, you can later enjoy a drink at the Bomba Shack, lying at the water's edge. This dive is infamous for its "Full Moon Parties."

Site of a campground (see "Accommodations You Can Afford," above), **Brewers Bay** is reached along the long, steep Brewers Bay Road. It's ideal for snorkelers and surfers. This clean, white-sand beach is a great place to enjoy walks in the early morning or at sunset. There's also a beach bar here and you can see the ruins of an old sugar mill and rum distillery just past Luck Hill. It is said that if you want to go "truly native," head here, sip a rum punch on the beach, and watch the world go by.

Smugglers Cove, a beach known for the beauty of its sands and its tranquility, lies at the extreme western end of Tortola, opposite the offshore island of Great Thatch and just north of St. John. It's a lovely crescent of white sand, with calm turquoise waters. One of the favorite local beaches, it lies at the end of a bumpy road (Belmont

Road). Once you get here, a little worse for wear after traveling that road, you'll think the crystal clear water and the beautiful palm trees worth the effort. Snorkelers like this beach, which is sometimes called "Lower Belmont Bay."

Long Bay West, reached along Long Bay Road, is one of the most stunning beaches in the B.V.I.—a mile-long stretch of white sand. The approach to it is panoramic: Have your camera ready for the classic beach shot. Joggers can be seen running along the water's edge, and it's also a lovers' walk, particularly at sunset. Even at twilight beach buffs sometimes linger here even after the sun sets, enjoying the waves crashing into the beach. The beach is the site of Long Bay Resort, although it is a public beach and open to all. The resort is located on the northeast side of the beach. Many visitors, even if they're not staying here, like to book a table at the resort's restaurant to enjoy dining overlooking the water,.

East of Tortola, **Long Bay Beach East,** reached along Beef Island Road, is great for swimming, with its white sands glistening in the sun. To get here, cross Queen Elizabeth Bridge and take the dirt road to the left before you come to the airport. From Long Bay you'll have a good view of Little Camanoe, one of the rocky offshore islands around Tortola. You can also see Scrub Island and tiny Marina Cay. Many shell collectors find rich pickings along this beach.

EXPLORING AN ANCIENT RAIN FOREST

No visit to Tortola is complete without a trip to ✪ **Mount Sage,** a national park rising to 1,780 feet. Here you'll find traces of a primeval rain forest, and you can enjoy a picnic while overlooking neighboring islets and cays. Go west from Road Town to reach the mountain.

Before you head out, stop by the tourist office and pick up a brochure called *Sage Mountain National Park.* It has a location map, directions to the forest (where there's a parking lot), and an outline of the main trails through the park.

Covering 92 acres, the park was established in 1964 to protect the remnants of Tortola's original forests not burned or cleared during the island's plantation era. From the parking lot, a trail leads to the main entrance to the park. The two main trails are the Rain Forest Trail and the Mahogany Forest Trail.

OVER THE MOUNTAINS TO CANE GARDEN BAY

If you've decided to risk everything and navigate the roller-coaster hills of the B.V.I., then head to Cane Garden Bay, one of the choicest pieces of real estate on the island, long ago discovered by the sailing crowd. Surrounded by mountains on three sides, its white sandy beach with sheltering palms is a living cliché of Caribbean charm.

Rhymer's, Cane Garden Bay (☎ 284/495-4639), is the place to go for refreshment. Skippers of any kind of craft are likely to stock up on supplies here, but you can also order cold beer and refreshing rum drinks. The beach bar and restaurant is open daily from 8am to 9pm and serves breakfast, lunch, and dinner. On some nights a steel-drum band entertains the mariners. Ice and freshwater showers are available (and you can rent towels). Ask about renting Sunfish and Windsurfers next door. Major credit and charge cards are accepted.

ORGANIZED TOURS

Travel Plan Tours, Romasco Place, Wickhams Cay 1, Road Town (☎ 284/494-2872), will organize 3½-hour tours that touch on the panoramic highlights of Tortola (a minimum of four participants is required) for $25 per person, with a supplement of $5 per person if you want to extend the tour with a bout of hill-climbing in the rain forest. The company also offers 2½-hour snorkeling tours for $28 per person, or full-day (with lunch included) snorkeling tours for $42 per person. A half-day sailing tour

Cheap Thrills: What to See & Do for Free (Well, Almost) in the British Virgins

- **Sample Mango Pancakes.** Head for a place called "North Shore Shell Museum/Home Made Banana Bread," on Main Road at Carrot Bay on Tortola (☎ 284/495-4714). There's no more downhome spot than this. Come for breakfast and look for the special on the chalkboard: mango pancakes (or else coconut, guava, or banana), along with the homemade bread of the day—guava, mango, or banana, each pan-toasted for extra flavor. Ask owner Egbert Donovan to wrap an extra three or four slices for treats later on the beach. Come back at night to hear an ad hoc fungi band with such instruments as a grooved gourd or a metal scratching stick. Enjoy cracked conch or barbecued chicken, and certainly one of those to-die-for guava daiquiris.

- **Visit a Remarkable Tropical Forest.** If you like to explore mountainous landscape that looks no doubt as it did when Columbus first landed, the B.V.I. is filled with wonder. At the Sage Mountain National Park on Tortola you'll see the results of reforestation and the reintroduction of vegetation that's quite remarkable. Although it gets only 100 inches of rain a year, the park nevertheless has the makings of a rain forest.

- **Discover Dead Chest.** For a small fee (to be negotiated), a local boatman will also take you over to Dead Chest Island, part of the Rhone National Marine Park, a half mile south of Peter Island. Dead Chest also has historic appeal, being the reputed island where Blackbeard marooned 15 crew members with only their sea chests and a bottle of rum—hence the ditty, *"yo, ho, ho. . ."*

- **Check Out Treacherous Anegada.** In the overcrowded Caribbean, there is still tiny Anegada, a remote limestone and coral atoll. The population is only 250 so you can often walk for miles without seeing anyone. You'll feel like a modern-day Robinson Crusoe. More than 300 ships have been sent to the bottom of the sea because of the dangerous coral shelf extending out from it. That's more wrecks than anywhere else in the Caribbean. Here's the good news: the entire island is surrounded by white sandy beaches, making it a paradise for divers and snorkelers.

aboard a catamaran that moves from Tortola to either Peter Island or Norman Island costs $50 per person; a full-day tour that goes farther afield to as far away as the Baths at Virgin Gorda and includes lunch costs $80 per person. And if deep-sea fishing appeals to you, a half-day excursion, with equipment, for four fishers and up to two "non-fishing observers" will cost $520.

A **taxi tour** lasting 2½ hours costs $45 for two passengers for 2 hours or $55 for three. To call a taxi in Road Town, dial ☎ **284/494-2322;** on Beef Island, ☎ **284/495-2378.**

SHOPPING

Most of the shops are on Main Street in Road Town.

Caribbean Corner Spice House Co., Soper's Hole (☎ **284/495-9567**), offers the island's finest selection of spices and herbs, along with local handcrafts and botanical skin-care products, most of which you'll find useful in the fierce sun. There's also a selection of Cuban cigars, but Americans will have to smoke them on-island, as

- **Explore the B.V.I.'s Tropical Showcase.** The J. R. O'Neal Botanic Gardens, Botanic Station (☎ 284/494-4997), are free and a gem. This 3-acre park in Road Town was created by the B.V.I. National Parks Trust and is run by local volunteers eager to show you around. Plants are arranged according to habitat in sections reached by landscaped paths radiating from a three-tiered fountain. The orchid house and a small rain forest are reached by crossing a charming lily pond, and other paths lead to a cactus garden and a palm grove. The brilliant scarlet flowers of the aptly named flamboyant tree are just part of what you'll see.

- **Find Hidden Pools in The Baths.** The most celebrated site on Virgin Gorda is The Baths, where giant boulders were brought to the surface eons ago by a vast volcanic eruption. The huge rocks strewn along the beach on the island's southwest shore are granite; it's been suggested they were placed here by some race of giants, but scientists think they were spewed up by volcanic activity. The important thing is not to solve this mystery but to explore the cave-like passages between them and find hidden pools just right for a quick dip.

- **Snorkel Off "Treasure Island."** Across Drake Channel from Tortola lies Norman Isle. Although it used to be a pirate den with treasure ships at anchor, it is now deserted by all except some seabirds and small wild animals. Legend has it that this tiny isle was the inspiration for Robert Louis Stevenson's *Treasure Island,* first published in 1883. You can row a dinghy into the southernmost cave of the island—with bats overhead and phosphorescent patches—where Stevenson's Mr. Fleming supposedly stowed his precious treasure. Norman Isle has a series of other caves whose waters are teeming with marine life. The caves are one of the most well-known snorkeling spots in the B.V.I. Intrepid hikers climb through scrubland to the island's central ridge, Spy Glass Hill. To cut costs ask three or four other people to go in with you and rent a sailboat to go over for a cheap adventure.

U.S. Customs do not allow their importation. **Caribbean Fine Arts Ltd.,** Main St., Road Town (☎ 284/494-4240), has one of the most unusual collections of art from the West Indies. It sells original watercolors and oils, limited-edition serigraphs and sepia photographs, and pottery and primitives. **Caribbean Handprints,** Main St., Road Town (☎ 284/494-3717), features island hand-prints, all hand-done by local craftspeople. **Flamboyance,** Soper's Hole (☎ 284/495-4099), is the best place to shop for perfume. There is also an upscale assortment of quality cosmetics. None of these products is particularly cheap, but since they are hawked without duty you'll save money.

   Fort Wines Gourmet, Main St., Road Town, (☎ 284/494-3036), is a store-cum-cafe and a good place to stock up on a truly gourmet picnic. A decorative and home accessories store, **J. R. O'Neal,** Upper Main St., Road Town (☎ 284/494-2292), across from the Methodist church, has an extensive collection of terra-cotta pottery, and wicker and rattan home furnishings, Mexican glassware, Dhurrie rugs, baskets, ceramics, fine crystal, china, and more, all at good prices.

Bargain hunters also gravitate to **Sea Urchin,** Columbus Centre, Road Town (☎ **284/494-3129**), where you'll find print shirts and shorts, along with stuff for the beach, including T-shirts, cover-ups, bathing suits, and sandals. Good prices in swimwear are also available at **Turtle Dove Boutique,** Fleming St., Road Town (☎ **284/494-3611**), which has a wide international selection. Women can also purchase linen and silk dresses here at reasonable prices.

Pusser's Company Store, Main St. and Waterfront Rd., Road Town (☎ **284/494-2467**), is for nautical memorabilia. There's a long, mahogany-trimmed bar accented with many fine nautical artifacts and a Pusser's Store selling a proprietary line of Pusser's sports and travel clothing and gift items. Pusser's Rum is one of the best-selling items here, or perhaps you'd prefer a Pusser's ceramic flask as a memento.

Sunny Caribbee Herb and Spice Company, Main St., Road Town (☎ **284/494-2178**), in an old West Indian building, was the first hotel on Tortola. Today it's a shop specializing in Caribbean spices, seasonings, teas, condiments, and handcrafts. You can buy two world-famous specialties here: the West Indian hangover cure and the Arawak love potion. A Caribbean cosmetics collection, Sunsations, is also available and includes herbal bath gels, island perfume, and sunshine lotions. With its aroma of spices permeating the air, this factory is an attraction in itself. There's a daily sampling of island products, something different every day—perhaps tea, coffee, sauces, or dips. Right next door is the Sunny Caribbee Gallery, featuring original paintings, prints, wood carvings, and hand-painted furniture, plus crafts from throughout the Caribbean. In the Sunny Caribbee Art Gallery, adjacent to the spice shop, you'll find an extensive collection of original art, prints, metal sculpture, and many other Caribbean crafts.

TORTOLA AFTER DARK

Ask around to find out which hotel has entertainment on any given evening. Steel bands and fungi or scratch bands (African-Caribbean musicians who improvise on locally available instruments) appear regularly, and nonguests are usually welcome. Pick up a copy of *Limin' Times,* an entertainment magazine listing what's happening locally; it's usually available at your hotel.

✪ **Bomba's Surfside Shack,** Cappoon's Bay (☎ **284/495-4148**), is the oldest, most memorable, and most uninhibited nightspot on the island. It sits on a 20-foot-wide strip of unpromising coastline near the West End. It's covered with Day-Glo graffiti and laced into a semblance of coherence with wire and rejected odds and ends of plywood, driftwood, and abandoned rubber tires. Despite its makeshift appearance, the shack has the electronic amplification system to create a really great party. Every month (dates vary) Bomba's stages a full-moon party when free house tea is spiked with hallucinogenic mushrooms. "We don't make it really strong any more," says Bomba Smith, the owner. "But it still gets you plenty high." The tea is free because it's illegal to sell it. The place is also wild on Wednesday and Sunday nights, when there's live music and a $7 all-you-can-eat barbecue. Open daily from 10am to midnight (or later, depending on business).

The Moorings/Mariner Inn, Wickhams Cay (☎ **284/494-2332**), is the preferred watering hole for some upscale yacht owners, but drink prices are low. Open to a view of its own marina and bathed in a dim and flattering light, the place is nautical and relaxed. The two drink specials are Moorings Delight, made with vodka, rum, cointreau, and cream of coconut, or else a Tortola Sunset, made with tequila, orange juice, and cranberry juice. A fungi band sometimes provides a backdrop to the socializing.

Another popular watering hole is **Spyglass Bar,** in the Treasure Isle Hotel, at the eastern end of Road Town (☎ **284/494-2501**). This popular bar is in a little house designed with Haitian gingerbread. The sunken bar on the terrace overlooks the swimming pool and faraway marina facilities of this popular hotel. Bar specialties include Treasure Island rum punch with dark rum, orange juice, strawberry syrup, and apricot brandy, and "Windstorm," made with Galiano, rum, fruit punch, and Seven-Up.

The Bat Cave, Waterfront Dr. at Road Town (☎ **284/494-4880**), on the ground floor of Spaghetti Junction (see above), is one of the newest hot spots. It's a full bar where you can eat spaghetti at tables if the restaurant upstairs is too packed. On Friday night they play "pre-released" music or songs just being released on radio stations. The latest recorded music on the charts is presented to the convivial crowd nightly. On the last Friday of each month the staff throws a big themed costume party—it's an island hit.

De Loose Mongoose, Beef Island (☎ **284/495-2302**), should be near the top of the list of funky beach bars in the Caribbean. Sailors on sailboats or the yachting crowd on their yachts like to drop anchor at this laid-back haven overlooking Trellis Bay near the airport. The bar is set right on the water. You're welcomed into the domain of Michele Gill who runs the bar with her husband, Ken, who is often heard strumming the guitar. Their house specialty is called No-See-Um, named after the pesky biting gnat of the Caribbean, the plague of every sunset watch. Michele says if you drink enough of her potent rum concoction, "these biting insects won't bother you—nothing will!"

Other little island hot spots, worth at least a drop in on a bar-hopping jaunt include **Bing's Drop in Bar,** Fat Hog's Bay in the East End (☎ **284/495-2627**), where the locals gather at night. In winter there's a DJ playing the latest music. At **Jolly Roger,** West End (☎ **284/495-4559**), you can hear local bands or perhaps some from America, playing everything from reggae to blues. On Friday and Saturday nights, starting at 8pm, the joint rocks and rolls. You can count on a jumping dance crowd at **Myett's,** Cane Garden Bay (☎ **284/495-9543**), on Friday and Saturday evenings and also after 3pm on Sunday afternoon when the B.V.I. usually gets pretty dull. Also in Cane Garden Bay, visit **Stanley's Welcome Bar** (☎ **284/495-4520**), where a rowdy fraternity-type crowd gathers on the beach to drink, talk, and drink some more. Finally, check out **Sebastian's,** Apple Bay (☎ **284/495-414**), especially on Saturday and Sunday when you can dance to live music under the stars—at least in the winter season.

3 Virgin Gorda

In 1493, on his second voyage to the New World, Columbus named this island Virgin Gorda, or "fat virgin" (from a distance, the island looks like a reclining woman with a protruding stomach). The second-largest of the British Virgin Islands, Virgin Gorda is 10 miles long and 2 miles wide, with a population of some 1,400. It's 12 miles east of Road Town and 26 miles from St. Thomas.

The island was a fairly desolate agricultural community until Laurence S. Rockefeller established the Little Dix Bay Hotel in the early 1960s, following his success with Caneel Bay on St. John and in the 1950s (see chapter 25). He envisioned a "wilderness beach," where privacy and solitude reign, and he literally put Virgin Gorda on the map. Other major hotels followed in the wake of Little Dix, but you can still find that privacy and solitude.

In 1971 the Virgin Gorda Yacht Harbour opened. Operated by the Little Dix Bay Hotel, it accommodates 120 yachts.

VIRGIN GORDA ESSENTIALS
GETTING THERE   Air St. Thomas (☎ **340/776-2722**) flies to Virgin Gorda daily from St. Thomas. The 40-minute flight costs $68 one-way, $139 round-trip.

Speedy's Fantasy (☎ **284/495-5240**) operates a ferry service between Road Town and Virgin Gorda. Four ferries a day leave from Road Town Monday to Saturday, reduced to two on Sunday. The trip costs $10 one-way or $19 round-trip. From St. Thomas to Virgin Gorda there's service three times a week (on Tuesday, Thursday, and Saturday), costing $31 one-way or $50 round-trip.

GETTING AROUND   Independently operated open-sided **safari buses** run along the main road. Holding up to 14 passengers, these buses charge upwards from $3 per person to transport a passenger, say, from The Valley to The Baths.

If you'd like to rent a car, try one of the local firms, including **Mahogany Rentals,** The Valley, Spanish Town (☎ **284/495-5469**), across from the yacht harbor. A representative will meet you at the airport or ferry dock and do the paperwork there. This company is the least expensive on the island, beginning at around $50 daily for a Suzuki Samurai. An alternative choice is **Andy's Taxi and Jeep Rental** (☎ **284/495-5252**), 7 minutes from the marina in Spanish Town. A representative here will also meet you at the airport of ferry dock for the paperwork. Rates begin at $50 daily.

FAST FACTS   The local **American Express** representative is **Travel Plan Ltd.,** Virgin Gorda Yacht Harbour (☎ **284/494-2347**). You can call the local police station at ☎ **284/495-5222.**

ACCOMMODATIONS YOU CAN AFFORD

Sometimes, particularly in the off-season, you can get a good deal on a villa rental. The best agency for that is **Virgin Gorda Villa Rentals Ltd.,** P.O. Box 63, The Valley, Virgin Gorda, B.V.I. (☎ **284/495-7421;** fax 284/495-7367). The company manages villas throughout the island, most of which are quite expensive. A 5-night minimum stay is required off-season, a 7-night minimum in winter. About the cheapest weekly rentals in winter are $1,150 per week, dropping to $800 per week off-season—plus 19% tax.

✪ **Fischers Cove Beach Hotel.** The Valley (P.O. Box 60), Virgin Gorda, B.V.I. ☎ **284/495-5252.** Fax 284/495-5820. 12 units, 8 studio cottages. A/C. Winter $145–$150 single or double; $170–$285 studio cottage. Off-season $100 single or double; $125–$205 studio cottage. MAP (breakfast and dinner) $40 per person extra. AE, MC, V.

There's swimming at your doorstep in this group of units nestled near the sandy beach of St. Thomas Bay. Erected of native stone, each cottage is self-contained, with one or two bedrooms and a combination living/dining room with a kitchenette. You can stock up on provisions at a food store near the grounds. There are 12 pleasant but simple rooms with views of Drake Channel. Each has its own small private bathroom (hot and cold showers) and private balcony. Beds are comfortable with firm mattresses, but there is nothing special here and nothing to equal any stateside Day's Inn along the highway. Jeep rentals are available, as is a children's playground. Live entertainment is often presented.

Oceanview Hotel. P.O. Box 66, Virgin Gorda, B.V.I. ☎ **284/495-5230.** 12 units. A/C TV. Year-round, $85 single or double. AE, MC, V. Free parking.

This hotel is in a residential neighborhood at the edge of Virgin Gorda's largest settlement, site of the ferryboat arrivals from nearby Tortola. Small, simple, and family-operated, it offers sheetrock- or cinder-block–sided rooms with ceiling fans, a bit of Caribbean style, and very few frills. The nearest beach (Devil's Bay) is within ½ mile, and many guests abandon their rather small rooms to spend many hours outdoors near the sea. Mattresses are a bit worn but not lumpy, and bathrooms are exceedingly small with thin towels. The bars, restaurants, and launderettes of town are a short walk

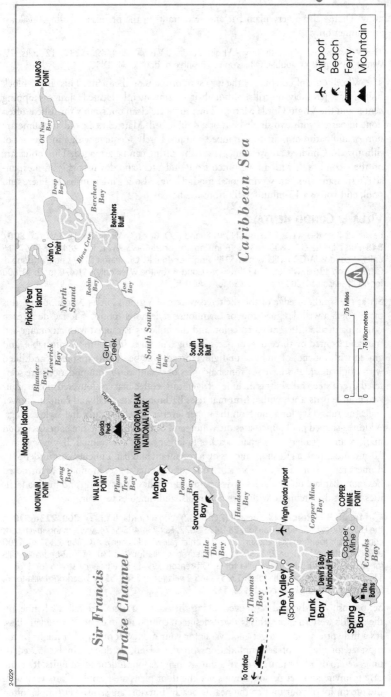

away. There's also a very plain bar and restaurant on the premises, serving breakfast and dinner only.

The Wheelhouse. Spanish Town, Virgin Gorda, B.V.I. ☎ **284/495-5230.** 12 units. TV. Winter $85 single or double. Off-season $70 single or double. AE, DISC, MC, V.

The Wheelhouse offers some of the lowest resort rates on the island. This cinder-block building is definitely no-frills, although it is conveniently located, near a shopping center and the Virgin Gorda Marina. The rooms are clean but simply furnished, often done in pastels with two single beds or a double bed. Mattresses are old and some are lumpy, and bathrooms are too cramped and just barely adequate with a meager set of thin towels. Children are welcome, and baby-sitting can be arranged. The rooms are on the second floor with a long porch front and back, and downstairs is an inexpensive restaurant and bar, serving local food. There's also a garden in back. There's no pool, and you're a 15-minute walk from the beach.

VILLA & CONDO RENTALS

Leverick Bay Resort & Marina. North Sound (P.O. Box 63), Virgin Gorda, B.V.I. ☎ **800/ 848-7081** in the U.S., 800/463-9396 in Canada, or 284/495-7421. Fax 284/495-7367. 16 units, 4 condos. A/C TV TEL. Winter $149 single or double. Off-season $119 single or double. Extra person $36 in winter, $24 off-season. Condos (by the week only): $1,470 for 2, $1,800 for 6 Off-season $1,200 for 2, $1,350 for 6 AE, MC, V.

Set at the southern edge of the sheltered waters of Virgin Gorda's North Sound, this place offers a well-designed row of townhouse-style hotel rooms. The façade of each unit is painted a different pastel color, and the building is capped with an orange-red roof and fronted by three tiers of ocean-facing balconies. It's stylish, comfortable, and graced with touches of architectural gingerbread. The bedrooms are breezy and filled with original art, and have seafront balconies or verandas. Accommodations are scattered over a steep hill. Extras include refrigerators, coffee makers, louvered closets, plus two double beds, each with a firm mattress. Bathrooms are small and contain shower stalls (no tubs). Try for a room on the upper level as they have cathedral-style ceilings. A kidney-shaped pool punctuates the white sand of the beach. The site contains a food market, an art gallery, two small beaches (a larger beach at Savannah Bay is within a 10-minute drive), a gift shop, and its own restaurant and bar. Lunches cost under $10; dinners range from $15 to $25 each. Four condo units are set in modern, red-roofed hexagons flanked on four sides by wraparound porches. A dive shop and marina facilities are on the premises, with surfers, kayaks, and dinghies for rent.

✪ Mango Bay Resort. Mahoe Bay (P.O. 1062), Virgin Gorda, B.V.I. ☎ **800/223-6510** in the U.S., 800/424-5500 in Canada, 284/495-5672. Fax 284/495-5674. www.mangobayresort. com. E-mail: mangobay@caribsurf.com. 12 units (all with kitchen). A/C. Winter $120–$200 efficiency studio for 1 or 2; $250–$470 1-bedroom villa for 2; $330–$770 2-bedroom villa for 4; $500–$850 3-bedroom villa for 6. Off-season $99–$130 efficiency studio for 1 or 2; $179–$290 1-bedroom villa for 2; $235–$465 2 villa for 4; $365–$515 3-bedroom villa for 6. Extra person on foldaway couch $25–$45. AE, MC, V.

Set on lushly landscaped acres overlooking the scattered islets of Drake's Channel on the island's western shore, this is a well-designed compound of eight white-sided villas. It's a little pricey, but you get good value for your money. It offers what might be the most adaptable set of accommodations on the island, as doors can be locked or unlocked to divide or unify each villa into as many as four independent units. It's quite easy to invite another person along since the floor plans are flexible. Costs vary with the proximity of your unit to the nearby beach. Interiors are stylish yet simple, often dominated by the same turquoise as that of the seascape in front of you. We like villas 10 and 11 best; they are just a minute from the surf, and they also contain a spacious porch and an outdoor shower. These accommodations could be in California instead of the British Virgin Islands. With their high ceilings and vibrant colors, units are most inviting. Bedrooms have king or twin beds, each with a firm mattress, and bathrooms are spacious, with a set of fluffy towels. Daily maid service is included. You can cook in, or else dine on site at the quite-good Georgio's Table, serving three meals a day. There's also a bar.

GREAT DEALS ON DINING

Bath and Turtle Pub. Virgin Gorda Yacht Harbour, Spanish Town. ☎ **284/495-5239.** Reservations recommended. Breakfast $4.50–$8.95; lunch main courses $6.75–$9; dinner main courses $9–$20. AE, MC, V. Daily 7am–11pm. INTERNATIONAL.

At the end of the waterfront shopping plaza in Spanish Town sits the most popular pub on Virgin Gorda, packed with locals during happy hour from 4 to 6pm. Even if you don't care about food, you might join the regulars over guava coladas or peach daiquiris. There's live music every Wednesday and Sunday in summer from 8pm to midnight (no cover charge). From its handful of indoor and courtyard tables, you can order fried fish fingers, nachos, very spicy chili, pizzas, fresh pasta, barbecue chicken, steak, lobster, and daily seafood specials such as conch fritters from the simple menu here.

The Crab Hole. South Valley. ☎ **284/495-5307.** Main courses $6–$12. No credit cards. Mon–Sat 9am–9pm. Head south along the road to The Baths, and turn left at the sign to the Crab Hole. WEST INDIAN.

This is a clean and decent West Indian restaurant, far removed from the expense and glitter of such resorts as Little Dix Bay and Biras Creek Estate in the private home of Kenroy and Janet Millington (look for a concrete house surrounded by fields and other simple private dwellings). Order your food from the chalkboard posted above the bar. They have their good days and bad days here, depending on what the market turned up. You might get stewed whelk with a Creole sauce made from local spices or tomatoes, perhaps stewed chicken, and most definitely fried fish. Stewed oxtail is sometimes on the menu, and guests, often hotel workers in the area, drop in for a noonday hamburger.

Mad Dog. The Baths, The Country. ☎ **284/495-5830.** Sandwiches $5; piña coladas $4. No credit cards. Daily 9am–7pm. PIÑA COLADAS/SANDWICHES.

This is a most skillful and charming reconstruction of a West Indian cottage. A wide veranda and the brightly painted 19th-century wooden timbers and clapboards create a cozy and convivial drink and sandwich bar where the piña coladas are absolutely divine. The owner and supervisor of this laid-back corner of heaven is London-born Colin McCullough, a self-described "mad dog," who sailed the B.V.I. for almost 30 years before setting up shop here.

✪ **Pusser's Leverick Bay.** Leverick Bay, North Sound. ☎ **284/495-7369.** Reservations recommended. Main courses $12.95–$24.95; lunch $5.95–$13.95; pizzas from $4.95. AE, MC, V. Daily 8:30am–10pm. CONTINENTAL.

Glass cases containing ship models lend a nautical feel to this restaurant, while dark wooden beams and an antique English bar add just the right touch of quiet elegance. Although there are a few tables inside, the main dining area is on the deck overlooking North Sound. The menu selections range from the very simple to the more elaborate such as tuna encrusted with sesame seed. The real bargains here are the meals served up until 6pm, when dinner begins. The breakfasts are hearty, lunches are filling, and to beat those higher prices at night, opt for an early dinner of pizza, which is served from 11am to 6pm every day.

Thelma's Hideout. The Valley. ☎ **284/495-5646.** Reservations required for dinner. Dinner $13–$15; lunch $8–$9. No credit cards. Daily 7–10am, 11:30am–2:30pm, and (only upon notification before 3pm) 6–10pm. (Bar, daily 11am–midnight.) CARIBBEAN.

Mrs. Thelma King, one of the most outspoken *grandes dames* of Virgin Gorda (she worked in New York City for many years before returning to her native B.V.I.), runs this convivial gathering place for the island's local community. It's located in a concrete house whose angles are softened by ascending tiers of verandas. Food choices include grilled steaks, fish filets, and West Indian stews containing pork, mutton, or chicken. Limeade or mauby are available, but many folks stick to rum or beer. Live music is presented on Saturday night in winter, and every other Saturday off-season.

Top of the Baths. The Valley. ☎ **284/495-5497.** Dinner from $18; sandwiches and salad plates $8–$12.50. AE, MC, V. Daily 8am–10pm. CARIBBEAN.

This aptly named green-and-white restaurant offers a patio with a swimming pool. Here locals gather to enjoy food they grew up on. At lunch you can order an array of appetizers, sandwiches, and salad plates. You're invited to swim in the pool either before or after dining. At night the kitchen turns out good home-style cookery, including fresh fish, plus lobster, chicken, and steaks. Look for one of the daily specials. And save room for a piece of that rum cake! On Sunday a DJ entertains from 10am to 3pm, and occasional live music is presented.

SWIMMING AT THE BATHS & OTHER OUTDOOR PURSUITS

On everyone's to-do list is a visit to ✪ **The Baths,** where house-size boulders form a series of tranquil pools and grottoes flooded with sea water. As these boulders toppled over one another, they formed saltwater grottoes, suitable for exploring. The pools around The Baths are excellent for swimming and snorkeling (equipment can be rented on the beach).

Neighboring The Baths is **Spring Bay,** one of the best of the island's beaches, with white sand, clear water, and good snorkeling. **Trunk Bay** is a wide sand beach reachable by boat or along a rough path from Spring Bay. **Savannah Bay** is a sandy beach north of the yacht harbor, and **Mahoe Bay,** at the Mango Bay Resort, has a gently curving beach with neon-blue water.

Devil's Bay National Park can be reached by a trail from the Baths roundabout. The walk to the secluded coral-sand beach takes about 15 minutes through boulders and dry coastal vegetation.

The Baths and surrounding areas are part of a proposed system of parks and protected areas in the B.V.I. The protected area encompasses 682 acres of land, including sites at Little Fort, Spring Bay, the Baths, and Devil's Bay on the east coast.

DIVING **Kilbrides Sunchaser Scuba,** at the Bitter End Resort at North Sound (☎ **800/932-4286** in the U.S., or 284/495-9638), offers the best diving in the British Virgin Islands, visiting 15 to 20 dive sites, including the wreck of the ill-fated HMS *Rhone* (see the box earlier in this chapter). Prices range from $80 to $90 for a two-tank dive on one of the coral reefs. A one-tank dive in the afternoon costs $60. Equipment, except wet suits, is supplied at no charge, and videos of your dives are available.

HIKING Consider a trek up the stairs and hiking paths that crisscross **Virgin Gorda Peak National Park,** the island's largest stretch of undeveloped land. To reach the best departure point for your uphill trek, drive for about 15 minutes north of The Valley on the only road leading to North Sound (it's very hilly, so a four-wheel-drive vehicle is a very good idea). Stop at the base of the stairway leading steeply uphill. There's a sign pointing to the park.

Depending on your speed, you'll embark on a trek of between 25 and 40 minutes to reach the summit of Gorda Peak, the highest point on the island, where views out over many scattered islets of the Virgin archipelago await you. There's a tower at the summit, which you can climb for enhanced views. Admire the flora and the fauna (birds, lizards, nonvenomous snakes) that you're likely to run across en route. Because the vegetation you'll encounter is not particularly lush, wear protection against the intense noonday sun, and consider bringing a picnic as tables are scattered along the hiking trails.

EXPLORING THE ISLAND

The northern side of Virgin Gorda is mountainous, with Gorda Peak reaching 1,370 feet, the highest spot on the island. However, the southern half is flat, with large boulders appearing at every turn.

Coppermine Point, the site of an abandoned copper mine and smelter at the island's southeastern tip, is an interesting place to visit. Legend has it that the Spanish worked these mines in the 1600s; however, the only authenticated document reveals that the English sank the shafts in 1838 to mine copper.

The best way to see the island if you're over for a day-trip is to call **Andy Flax** at the Fischers Cove Beach Hotel. He runs the **Virgin Gorda Tours Association** (☎ 284/495-5252), which will give you a tour of the island for $20 per person. The tour leaves twice daily, or more often based on demand. You can be picked up at the ferry dock if you give them 24-hours notice.

SHOPPING

There isn't much to buy here. Your best bet is the **Virgin Gorda Craft Shop** at Yacht Harbour (☎ 284/495-5137), which has some good arts and crafts, especially straw items. Some of the more upscale hotels have boutiques, notably the **Bitter End Yacht Club's Reeftique** (☎ 284/494-2745), with its selection of sports clothing, including sundresses and logo wear. You can also purchase a hat here to protect you from the sun. You might also check **Island Silhouette in Flax Plaza,** near Fischer's Cove Beach Hotel (no phone), which has a good selection of resort wear hand-painted by local artists. **Pusser's Company Store,** Leverick Bay (☎ 284/495-7369), sells rum products, sportswear, and gift and souvenir items—a good selection. **Tropical Gift Collections,** The Baths (☎ 284/495-5380), is the best place for local crafts. Here you'll find island spices, bags, and pottery on sale, all at good prices.

VIRGIN GORDA AFTER DARK

There isn't a lot of action at night, unless you want to make some of your own. The **Bath & Turtle Pub,** at Yacht Harbour (☎ 284/495-5239), brings in local bands for dancing on Wednesday and Sunday at 8pm. Most evenings in winter the **Bitter End Yacht Club** (☎ 284/494-2746) has live music. Reached only by boat, this is the best bar on the island. With its dark wood, it evokes an English pub and even serves British brews. Sailors from all over the world (usually rich ones) keep the place lively deep into the night with talk of Lasers and Boston whalers. Call to see what's happening at the time of your visit.

Andy's Chateau de Pirate, at the Fischer's Cove Beach Hotel, The Valley (☎ 284/495-5252), is a sprawling, sparsely-furnished local hangout. It has a simple stage, a very long bar, and huge oceanfront windows which almost never close. The complex also houses the Lobster Pot Restaurant, the Buccaneer Bar, and the nightclub EFX. The Lobster Pot is open from 7am to 10pm. The place is a famous showcase for the island's musical groups, which perform Wednesday to Sunday from 8pm to midnight; lots of people congregate to listen and kibitz. There's a $5 cover charge Friday to Sunday nights.

You might also check out **Pusser's at Leverick Bay** (see above), which has live bands on Saturday night and again on Sunday afternoon.

4 Anegada

The most northerly and isolated of the British Virgins, 30 miles east of Tortola, Anegada has a population of about 250, none of whom has found the legendary treasure from the more than 500 wrecks lying off its notorious Horseshoe Reef. It's different from the other British Virgins in that it's a flat coral-and-limestone atoll. Its highest point reaches 28 feet, and it hardly appears on the horizon if you're sailing to it.

At the northern and western ends of the island are some good beaches, which might be your only reason for coming here. This is a remote little corner of the Caribbean: Be prepared to put up with some inconveniences, such as mosquitoes.

Most of the island has been declared off-limits to settlement and reserved for birds and other wildlife. The B.V.I. National Parks Trust has established a flamingo colony in a bird sanctuary, which is also the protected home of several different varieties of heron as well as ospreys and terns. It has also designated much of the interior of the island as a preserved habitat for Anegada's animal population of some 2,000 wild goats, donkeys, and cattle. Among the endangered species being given a new lease on life is the rock iguana, a fierce-looking but quite-harmless reptile, that can grow to a length of 5 feet and a weight of up to 20 pounds. Though rarely seen, these creatures have called Anegada home for thousands of years. The environment they share with other wildlife has hardly changed in all those years.

You might want to drop in at **Pat's Pottery** (☎ 284/495-8031), where islanders sell some interesting crafts, including dishes, plates, pitchers, and mugs in whimsical folk-art patterns.

ANEGADA ESSENTIALS

GETTING THERE   The only carrier with regular service from Tortola to Anegada, **Clair Aero Service** (☎ 284/495-2271), uses six- to eight-passenger prop planes. It operates four times a week, on Monday, Wednesday, Friday, and Sunday, charging $59 per person round-trip. In addition, **Fly BVI** (☎ 284/495-1747) operates a charter/sightseeing service between Anegada and Beef Island off Tortola. The one-way cost is $125 for two to three passengers.

GETTING AROUND   Limited taxi service is available on the island—not that you'll have many places to go. **Tony's Taxis,** which you'll easily spot when you arrive, will take you around the island. It's also possible to rent **bicycles**—ask around.

ACCOMMODATIONS YOU CAN AFFORD

Also see **Neptune's Treasure** under "Great Deals on Dining," below.

✪ **Anegada Beach Campground.** Anegada, B.V.I. ☎ 284/495-9466. 10 tent sites, 10 bare sites, 2 cottages. Year-round, $36 tent for 2; $7 per person bare site; $100 cottage. No credit cards.

Despite its isolated setting on one of the least developed islands in the British Virgins, this campground boasts amenities that are usually not available at campgrounds on other, better-equipped islands such as Tortola. It lies near waters with many snorkeling options, at the edge of about a dozen miles of secluded beachfront. For those who enjoy completely simple living in a natural setting, this campsite contains a woodsy but relatively elaborate restaurant (which serves dinners priced at $14 to $35 each), access to cookout areas for budgeters who want to barbecue, flush toilets in the restaurant, and outdoor showers whose privacy is assured by artfully woven palm fronds. For tent sites, the management provides a sponge-foam mattress, but campers usually bring their own pillows. The campsite also contains two breezy beach cottages for rent, equipped with a private kitchenette.

GREAT DEALS ON DINING

Neptune's Treasure. Between Pomato and Saltheap points, Anegada, B.V.I. ☎ **284/495-9439** or VHF Channel 16 or 68. www.islandsonline.com. E-mail: neptunetreasure@caribsurf. com. Breakfast from $7–$9; sandwiches $4–$9; fixed-price meals $16–$35. AE, MC, V. Daily 8am–10pm. INTERNATIONAL.

Set near its own 24-slip marina, near the southern tip of the island in the same cluster of buildings that includes the more high-priced Anegada Reef Hotel, this funky and appealing bar and restaurant is known to off-island yacht owners who make it a point to mingle with local residents. Dining is in a spacious indoor area whose focal point is a bar and lots of nautical memorabilia. The drink of choice is a Pink Whoopee, composed of fruit juices and rum. The Soares family and their staff serve platters of swordfish, lobster, fish fingers, chicken, steaks, and ribs; dispense information about local snorkeling sites; and generally maintain order and something approaching a (low-key) party atmosphere.

They also rent four simple bedrooms and about four tents for anyone looking for super-low-cost lodgings. Depending on the season, rooms with private bath rent for $45 to $55 single and $70 to $85 double. Tents share the plumbing facilities of the restaurant and go for $15 a night for one occupant, $25 a night for two. Continental breakfast is included in the rates, and discounts are offered for stays of a week or more.

5 Jost Van Dyke

About 130 people live on the 4 square miles of this mountainous island. On the south shore, White Bay and Great Harbour are good beaches. While there are only a handful of places to stay, there are several dining choices, as it's a popular stopping-over point not only for the yachting set, but also for many cruise ships, including Club Med, Cunard, and often all-gay cruises. So you'll only experience the peace and tranquillity of yesteryear when the cruise ships aren't here.

JOST VAN DYKE ESSENTIALS

GETTING THERE   Take the ferry from either St. Thomas or Tortola. Be warned that departure times can vary widely throughout the year, and at times don't adhere very closely to the printed timetables. Ferries from St. Thomas depart from Red Hook Friday, Saturday, and Sunday, about twice a day. More convenient (and more frequent) are the daily ferryboat shuttles from Tortola's isolated West End. The latter departs three times a day on the 25-minute trip, and costs $8 each way, $15 round-trip. Call the **Jost Van Dyke Ferryboat service** (☎ **284/494-2997**) for information about departures from any of the above-mentioned points. If all else fails, carefully negotiate a transportation fee with one of the handful of privately operated water taxis.

FAST FACTS   You can reach the local police station at ☎ **284/495-9828.**

ACCOMMODATIONS YOU CAN AFFORD

The ✪ **White Bay Campground** (☎ **284/495-9312** on Tortola) rents bare sites costing $15 for three people or equipped tent sites going for $35 for two. Facilities include showers and toilets.

Rudy's Mariner Inn. Great Harbour, Jost Van Dyke, B.V.I. ☎ **284/495-9282,** or 284/ 775-3558 in the U.S.V.I. 5 units. Winter $75–$125 single or double. Off-season $55–$75 single or double. DISC, MC, V.

About as simple as you'd like to get, this place is modesty itself, but it's got a lot of friends who like the hospitality of Rudy George, the owner. It's also one of the best places to eat on the island, with simply prepared and inexpensive food. (Conch always seems to be available, and a catch of the day is featured. Dinner is served daily.) Next to the boat dock at the west end of the harbor, this place is the social gathering point for much of the island: It's also a bar and nightclub of sorts and a ship's commissary. Some of the rooms open onto the water. There's snorkeling from the beach, and fishing and windsurfing can be arranged. It's a true West Indian inn.

GREAT DEALS ON DINING

Abe's by the Sea. Little Harbour. ☎ **284/495-9329.** Reservations recommended for groups of 5 or more. Dinner $12–$30; nightly barbecue $20. MC, V. Daily 8–11am, noon–3pm, and 7–10pm. Take the private motor launch or boat from Tortola; as you approach the east side of the harbor you'll see Abe's on your right. CARIBBEAN.

In this local bar and restaurant, sailors are satisfied with a menu of fish, lobster, conch, and chicken. Prices are low too, and it's money well spent, especially when a fungi band plays for dancing. For the price of the main course, you get peas and rice, coleslaw, plus dessert. On some nights a festive pig roast is served.

✪ **Foxy's Tamarind Bar.** Great Harbour. ☎ **284/495-9258.** Reservations recommended. Dinners $12–$35; lunch $7–$9. AE, MC, V. Daily 9am "until." CARIBBEAN.

Arguably the most famous bar in the B.V.I., this mecca of yachties and other boat people spins entirely around a sixth-generation Jost Van Dyke native, Philicianno ("Foxy") Callwood. He opened the place some three decades ago, and sailors and the world have been coming back ever since. A songwriter and entertainer, Foxy is part of the draw. He creates impromptu calypso—almost in the Jamaican tradition—around his guests. If you're singled out, he'll embarrass you, but all in good fun. He also plays the guitar and takes a profound interest in preserving the island's environment.

Thursday to Saturday a live band entertains. On other evenings, it's rock 'n' roll or perhaps reggae or soca. The food and drink aren't neglected either. Try his Painkiller Punch. During the day flying fish sandwiches, rôtis, and the usual burgers are served, but in the evening it might be freshly caught lobster, spicy steamed shrimp, or even grilled fish, depending on the catch of the day. No lunch is served on Saturday and Sunday.

✪ **Rudy's Mariner's Rendezvous.** Great Harbour. ☎ **284/495-9282.** Reservations required by 6:30pm. Dinner $15–$25. MC, V. Daily 7pm–midnight. WEST INDIAN.

Rudy's, at the western end of Great Harbour, serves good but basic West Indian food and plenty of it. The place looks and feels like a private home with a waterfront terrace for visiting diners. A welcoming drink awaits sailors and landlubbers alike, and the food that follows is simply prepared and inexpensive. Conch always seems to be available, and a catch of the day is featured.

The Cayman Islands

8

Don't go to the Cayman Islands expecting fast-paced excitement. Island life focuses on the sea. Snorkelers will find a paradise, beach lovers will relish the powdery sands of Seven Mile Beach—but party-hungry travelers in search of urban thrills might be disappointed. Come here to relax and get away from it all.

The Caymans, 480 miles due south of Miami, consist of three islands: Grand Cayman, Cayman Brac, and Little Cayman. Despite its name, Grand Cayman is only 22 miles long and 8 miles across at its widest point. The other islands are considerably smaller, of course, and contain very limited tourist facilities, in contrast to well-developed Grand Cayman. George Town on Grand Cayman is the capital, and is therefore the hub of government, banking, and shopping.

English is the official language of the islands, although it's often spoken with an English slur mixed with an American southern drawl and a lilting Welsh accent.

Winter vacations in the Caymans can be pricey affairs. The cost of living here is about 20% higher than in the United States. Because so much food has to be imported from the U.S. mainland, restaurant tabs are second only to the high-priced French islands such as St. Barts and Martinique (we've included tips on how to save on dining costs below). But you can make a trip here affordable. The key is advance planning and visiting the islands between mid-April and mid-December, when room rates are 20% to 40% lower than in winter. And in recent years several low-cost or moderately priced lodgings have opened, many of them with provisions for cooking simple meals.

Gay and lesbian travelers take note: In 1998 the Cayman Islands government turned away Norwegian Cruise Line's *Leeward,* which was carrying 900 gay passengers. The tourism directors of the Caymans claimed that "we cannot count on this group to uphold the standards of appropriate behavior expected of visitors to the Cayman Islands." This decision drew massive protest, but the government refused to change its stance.

1 Essentials

VISITOR INFORMATION

The **Cayman Islands Department of Tourism** has the following offices in the United States: 6100 Blue Lagoon Dr., 6100 Waterford

Bldg., Suite 150, Miami, FL 33126 (☎ **305/266-2300**); 9525 W. Bryn Mawr, Suite 160, Rosemont, IL 60018 (☎ **847/678-6446**); Two Memorial City Plaza, 820 Gessner, Suite 170, Houston, TX 77024 (☎ **713/461-1317**); 3440 Wilshire Blvd., Suite 1202, Los Angeles, CA 90010 (☎ **213/738-1968**); 6100 Blue Lagoon Dr., Suite 150, Miami, FL 33126 (☎ **305/266-2300**); and 420 Lexington Ave., Suite 2733, New York, NY 10170 (☎ **212/682-5582**).

In Canada, contact Earl B. Smith, **Travel Marketing Consultants,** 234 Eglinton Ave. E., Suite 306, Toronto, ON M4P 1K5 (☎ **416/485-1550**).

In the United Kingdom, the contact is **Cayman Islands,** 100 Brompton Rd., London SW3 1EX (☎ **020/7581-9960**).

The official Web site is **www.caymanislands.ky**.

GETTING THERE

The Caymans are easily accessible. Only a handful of nonstop flights are available from the heartland of North America to Grand Cayman, so many visitors use Miami as their gateway. Flying time from Miami is 1 hour 20 minutes; from Houston, 2 hours 45 minutes; from Tampa, 1 hour 40 minutes; and from Atlanta, 3 hours 35 minutes.

Cayman Airways (☎ **800/422-9626** in the U.S. and Canada, or 345/949-2311), offers the most frequent service to Grand Cayman, with three daily flights from Miami, four flights a week from Tampa, three from Orlando, and three nonstop flights a week from Houston and Atlanta. Once in the Caymans, the airline's subsidiary, **Island Air Ltd.** (☎ **345/949-5152**), operates frequent flights between Grand Cayman and Little Cayman and Cayman Brac. Round-trip fares between Grand Cayman and Cayman Brac begin at $154.

American Airlines (☎ **800/433-7300**) operates three daily nonstop flights from Miami and from Raleigh/Durham. **Delta** (☎ **800/221-1212**) flies daily into Grand Cayman from its hub in Atlanta. **Northwest Airlines** (☎ **800/447-4747**) flies to Grand Cayman from Detroit and Memphis via Miami. **US Airways** (☎ **800/428-4322**) flies daily nonstop from Tampa, and offers three flights a week from Pittsburgh and Charlotte.

SPECIAL EVENTS: AHOY, MATEY!

Cayman Islands Pirates' Week is held in late October. It's a national festival in which cutlass-bearing pirates and sassy wenches storm George Town, capture the governor, throng the streets, and stage a costume parade. The celebration, which is held throughout the Caymans, pays tribute to the nation's past and its cultural heritage. For the exact dates, contact the **Pirates Week Festival Administration** (☎ **345/949-5078**).

Fast Facts: The Cayman Islands

Area Code   You can dial the Cayman Islands direct from the United States. The area code is ☎ **345.**

Business Hours   Normally, banks are open Monday to Thursday 9am to 2:30pm and Friday 9am to 1pm and 2:30 to 4:30pm. Shops are usually open Monday to Saturday 9am to 5pm.

Currency   The legal tender is the Cayman Islands dollar (CI$), currently valued at U.S.$1.25 (U.S.$1 equals 80¢ CI$). Canadian, U.S., and British

The Cayman Islands

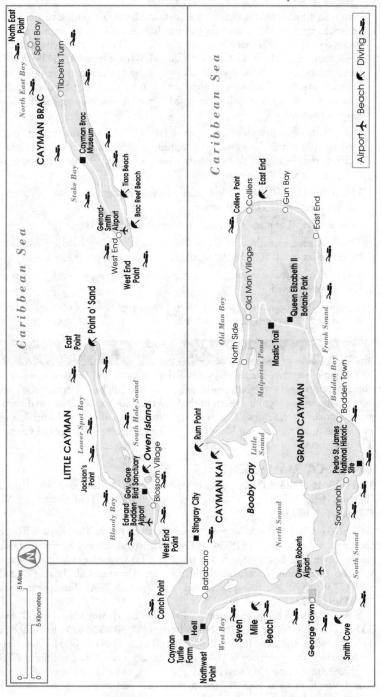

Airport ✈ Beach 🏖 Diving 🤿

Caribbean Sea

CAYMAN BRAC

North East Point
Spot Bay
Tibbetts Turn
North East Bay
Cayman Brac Museum
Stake Bay
Tiara Beach
Gerrard-Smith Airport
Brac Reef Beach
West End
West End Point

LITTLE CAYMAN

Point o' Sand
East Point
Jackson's Point
Lower Spot Bay
South Hole Sound
Bloody Bay
Edward Bodden Airport
Gov Gore Bird Sanctuary
Owen Island
Blossom Village
West End Point

Caribbean Sea

GRAND CAYMAN

Colliers Point
Colliers
East End
Gun Bay
East End
Old Man Bay
Old Man Village
North Side
Malportus Pond
Mastic Trail
Queen Elizabeth II Botanic Park
Frank Sound
Bodden Bay
Bodden Town
Pedro St. James National Historic Site
Savannah
South Sound
Rum Point
Little Sound
Booby Cay
CAYMAN KAI
Stingray City
North Sound
Batabano
Conch Point
Cayman Turtle Farm
Hell
Northwest Point
West Bay
Seven Mile Beach
Owen Roberts Airport
George Town
Smith Cove

0   5 Miles
0   5 Kilometers

currencies are accepted throughout the Cayman Islands, but you'll save money if you exchange your U.S. dollars for Cayman Islands dollars. The Cayman dollar breaks down into 100 cents. Coins come in 1¢, 5¢, 10¢, and 25¢. Bills come in denominations of $1, $5, $10, $25, $50, and $100 (there is no CI$20 bill). Most hotels quote rates in U.S. dollars, although many restaurants quote prices in Cayman Islands dollars, which might lead you to think that food is much cheaper than it is. Unless otherwise noted, *prices in this chapter are in U.S. dollars, rounded off.*

Documents   No passports are required for U.S. or Canadian citizens, but entering visitors must have proof of citizenship (such as a birth certificate) and a return ticket. We suggest that you carry a passport anyway whenever you visit a foreign country.

Electricity   It's 110 volts AC (60 cycles), so American and Canadian appliances will not need adapters or transformers.

Emergencies   For medical or police emergencies, dial ☎ **911** or 555.

Taxes   A government tourist tax of 10% is added to your hotel bill. Also, a departure tax of CI$10 ($12.50) is collected when you leave the Caymans.

Time   U.S. eastern standard time is in effect all year; however, daylight saving time is not observed.

Tipping   Most restaurants add a 10% to 15% charge in lieu of tipping. Hotels also add a 10% service charge to your bill.

2 Grand Cayman

The largest of the three islands and a real diving mecca, Grand Cayman is one of the hottest destinations in the Caribbean. With more than 500 banks, its capital, George Town, is the offshore banking center of the Caribbean. Retirees are drawn to the peace and tranquility of this British Crown Colony, site of a major condominium development. Almost all the Cayman Islands' population of 32,000 live on Grand Cayman. The civil manners of the locals reflect their British heritage.

GRAND CAYMAN ESSENTIALS

VISITOR INFORMATION   The **Department of Tourism** is in the Pavilion Building, Cricket Square (P.O. Box 67), George Town, Grand Cayman, B.W.I. (☎ **345/949-0623**).

GETTING AROUND   All arriving flights are met by taxis. The rates are fixed by the director of civil aviation (☎ **345/949-7811**); typical one-way fares from the airport to Seven Mile Beach range from $10 to $12. Taxis (which can hold five people) will also take visitors on around-the-island tours. **Cayman Cab Team** (☎ **345/947-1173**) offers 24-hour service. You can also call **A.A. Transportation** at ☎ **345/949-7222**.

Several car-rental companies operate on the island, including **Cico Avis** (☎ **800/331-1212** in the U.S., or 345/949-2468), **Budget** (☎ **800/527-0700** in the U.S., or 345/949-5605), and **Ace Hertz** (☎ **800/654-3131** in the U.S., or 345/949-2280). Each will issue the mandatory Cayman Islands driving permit for an additional $7.50. All three require that reservations be made between 6 and 36 hours before pickup. At Avis drivers must be at least 21, and at Hertz, 25. Budget requires that drivers be between 25 and 70 years old. It pays to call around for the lowest rate. Cars generally range in price from $266 to $315 and up per week, including unlimited mileage. An optional collision-damage waiver (CDW) cost from $12 a day. All three rental companies maintain kiosks within walking distance of the airport, although most visitors find it easier to take a taxi to their hotels and then arrange for the cars to be brought to them.

Remember to drive on the left and to reserve your car as far in advance as possible, especially in midwinter.

Soto Scooters Ltd., Seven Mile Beach (☎ **345/945-4652**), located at Coconut Place, offers Honda Elite scooters for $30 daily, or bicycles for $15 daily. It also offers Jeep and car rentals from $50 per day.

FAST FACTS   Island Pharmacy, West Shore Centre, Seven Mile Beach (☎ **345/ 949-8987**), is open Monday to Saturday 8:30am to 5:30pm. The only hospital is **George Town Hospital,** Hospital Road (☎ **345/949-4234**).

In George Town, the **post office** and Philatelic Bureau is on Edward Street (☎ **345/949-2474**), open Monday to Friday 8:30am to 5pm and Saturday 8:30am to noon. There's also a counter at the Seven Mile Beach Post Office, open the same hours.

The **Cable and Wireless,** Anderson Square, George Town, on Grand Cayman (☎ **345/949-7800**), is open Monday to Friday 8:15am to 5pm, Saturday 9am to 1pm, and Sunday 9am to noon.

ACCOMMODATIONS YOU CAN AFFORD

True budget travelers will rent an apartment or condo (shared with friends or families), so they can cut costs by cooking their own meals. Divers will want to find hotels or small resorts that include a half day's dive in their tariffs. Hotels, unlike many Caymanian restaurants, generally quote prices to you in U.S. dollars.

✪ **Adam's Guest House.** Melmac Ave., George Town, Grand Cayman, B.W.I. ☎ **345/ 949-2512.** Fax 345/949-0919. 3 units, 1 apt. A/C TV. Winter $65 single; $75 double; $170 apt. Off-season $55 single; $65 double; $150 apt. $10 per person extra (up to a maximum of 6). MC, V (accepted only for room deposit; pay with cash or traveler's checks).

Tom and Olga Adam advertise their guest house as "the best at the lowest." While it may not be the best place to stay, it's among the best values on the island. This 1950s-style West Indian ranch bungalow is located in a residential area a mile south of George Town, which is a long 4-mile haul from Seven Mile Beach. However, there's excellent snorkeling at Smith Cove Bay, only about a 10-minute walk away, and scuba-diving facilities—five different outfits—lie within a 5-minute stroll. For a restaurant and bar, you can stroll over to the Seaview Hotel, about 5 minutes away. A supermarket and a drugstore are also nearby, as are some breakfast places.

Each no-frills room has a private entrance, twin beds with good mattresses, a small private bathroom with rather thin towels, ceiling fans, and a compact refrigerator, along with a microwave and TV, plus a washer and dryer. The two-bedroom apartment, which can hold up to six, is ideal for families.

The Enterprise Bed & Breakfast. Selkirk Dr., Red Bay (P.O. Box 246), Savannah, Grand Cayman, B.W.I. ☎ **345/947-6009.** Fax 345/947-6010. E-mail: enterprise@firstlink.net. 8 units. A/C TV. Winter $88 single or double; off-season $77 single or double. Rates include American breakfast. AE, MC, V (accepted for deposit only).

A 6-minute drive from the airport, this two-story white frame house is definitely for Trekkies. Posters of captains Kirk and Picard and pals decorate the B&B—hence, its name. Naturally, videos of all *Star Trek* episodes and movies are shown as well. It's about a 10-minute ride from Seven Mile Beach, so you'll want to have a car if you stay here. A very helpful staff will welcome you and explain nearby options for diving, fishing, and snorkeling. The rooms are simply but comfortably furnished, containing such extras as a small refrigerator, kitchenette, bar sink, and microwave. Mattresses are a bit old but still comfortable, and the baths are rather tiny, with skimpy towels, but clean and efficient. There's a laundry nearby, and baby-sitting can be arranged if sufficient notice is given. No smoking.

✪ **Erma Eldemire's Guest House.** S. Church St. (P.O. Box 482), George Town, Grand Cayman, B.W.I. ☎ **345/949-5387.** Fax 345/949-6987. 5 units, 3 apts. A/C. Winter $88 single or double; $121 apt. Off-season $67 single or double; $110 apt. Extra person $10. No credit cards.

This casual and friendly place is owned by Erma Eldemire, an old-time Caymanian, now in her 80s, who established the first guest house on the island. No one knows the island better than dear Mrs. Eldemire, who will not only regale you with tall tales of Caymanian life but might also share her recipe for coconut jelly. About a mile from the center of George Town and ½ mile from great snorkeling at Smith Cove Beach, this rambling West Indian ranch-style house offers small bedrooms and studio apartments. The place is simple yet comfortable and suitable for families. Each unit has a tiny private bathroom with thin towels, air-conditioning, and a ceiling fan. Beds are quite comfortable, the mattresses having been recently replaced. Guests also have access to a refrigerator, toaster oven, hotplate, and coffee maker. The apartments have their own kitchenettes, with maid service Monday to Saturday.

Within walking distance are dive sites, a snorkeling area, the "Cove" (a white sandy beach with crystal-clear water), and a number of restaurants. Seven Mile Beach lies 2 miles away, and the house is 3 miles from the airport. Families or groups might want to use the barbecue pit and the picnic table in the garden. A launderette is nearby. Across the street is a restaurant where you can order breakfast for $6.

Seaview Hotel. S. Church St., George Town, Grand Cayman, B.W.I. ☎ **345/945-0558.** Fax 345/945-0559. E-mail: seadive@condw.ky. 15 units. A/C. Winter $100 single; $110 double. Off-season $80 single; $90 double. Extra person $10. Children 11 and under stay free in parents' room. AE, MC, V.

This seafront property lies on the south side of George Town, about a 10-minute walk from the downtown area or a 10-minute walk to the beach at Smith Cove. It's about a 2- to 3-minute drive to Seven Mile Beach. One of the island's oldest properties, the hotel still retains its '50s-style look. Under new management, it's being improved and upgraded, but is still a tin-roofed wooden hotel. Bright Caribbean fabrics have enlivened some rooms, and 10 accommodations face the ocean in a central veranda style. Rooms range in size from small to medium, but each has a good bed with a firm mattress, plus a tiny but well-maintained private bathroom (with showers instead of tubs). The on-site pool is large and inviting, and there's also an inside restaurant and bar, offering three meals a day, with rather excellent seafood. Boat dives can be arranged.

GREAT CHOICES FOR DIVERS

Coconut Harbour. S. Church St., George Town, Grand Cayman, B.W.I. ☎ **800/552-6281** in the U.S., or 345/949-7468. Fax 345/949-7117. 35 units. A/C TV TEL. Winter $182 double; off-season $174 double. Rates include a continental breakfast. AE, MC, V.

This resort property just south of George Town, with a friendly staff and a convivial crowd, offers one of the best values for divers. There's excellent diving right offshore, and on-site is a full-service dive shop operated by Parrots Landing (which you might check out even if you don't stay here). The clean and comfortable rooms, with kitchenettes, are furnished in a plain Florida-motel style. Upper rooms have balconies overlooking the sea, and lower accommodations open onto patios. There's daily housekeeping. Rooms range from small to medium but there is reasonable comfort here, although the mattresses are a bit thin. Your bathrooms will be like a cubicle, with a shower (no tub), plus meager shelf space, but a generous rack of medium-size towels. The hotel operates an open-air bar, a good place for a drink, and a rather standard restaurant open until 10pm. There's also a large pool.

Sunset House. S. Church St. (P.O. Box 479), George Town, Grand Cayman, B.W.I. ☎ **800/854-4767** in the U.S., or 345/949-7111. Fax 345/949-7101. www.maduro.com. E-mail: sunset@candw.ky. 59 units. A/C TV TEL. Winter $140 single; $145–$200 double, $165–$220 triple, $185–$240 quad. Summer $138 single, $150 double, $175 triple, $185 quad. Year-round from $220 suite. Children 11 and under stay free in parents' room. AE, DC, MC, V.

Of the many homey inns catering to divers, this is another good deal, although it's a better value if you're willing to team up in a triple or a quad instead of a single or double. However, some of the standard rooms are too small, and the furnishings are a bit frayed. Mattresses are well used, but there is reasonable comfort here. At least most of the divers don't seem to mind. Bathrooms are small, with showers and somewhat thin towels. Called a place "for divers by divers," it lies south of George Town on the Ironshore, a craggy limestone shoreline about an 8-minute walk from the beach at Smith Cove. The five light-pink concrete buildings are informally but thoughtfully managed. Many rooms have two doubles or two king-size beds along with a balcony or patio, and a refrigerator can be rented for another $5 a day. The hotel offers two pools—one freshwater, the other saltwater—plus a Jacuzzi. On the premises are a dive shop and the Cathy Church photo school. The Seaharvest restaurant is very casual, serving standard fare, and the thatched-roof seaside "My Bar" is the place to discuss the day's adventures over a tropical drink. Even if you're not a guest, it's one of the best places on the island to go for a sundowner.

WORTH A SPLURGE

Sleep Inn Hotel. West Bat Rd. (P.O. Box 30111), Grand Cayman, B.W.I. ☎ **800/753-3746** or 345/949-9111. Fax 345/949-6699. 121 units. A/C TV TEL. Winter $120–$210 single or double, $170–$240 suite. Off-season, $120–$140 single or double, $170–$190 suite. Rates include buffet breakfast. Children 12 and under stay free in parents' room. AE, DC, DISC, MC, V.

The Sleep Inn is the closest hotel on Seven Mile Beach to the center of George Town. On rather bleak grounds, it lies 250 feet from the sands and about a five-minute drive from the international airport. It's one of the more reasonably priced hotels on the island, with great value for your money, and a good choice for families.

A franchise of Choice Hotels International, it offers both smoking and no-smoking rooms and units that are accessible for persons with disabilities. Furnishings are rather nondescript but very comfortable. The rooms have modern tropical furnishings, TVs with built-in radios and alarm clocks, and a small safe for valuables; the suites contain kitchenettes. Bedrooms have queen-size beds with good mattresses, and the medium-sized bathrooms contain adequate shelf space, separate vanities, and extremely spacious double showers (no tubs). Rooms are a bit small, but very well maintained if you don't mind the impersonal atmosphere here.

Features include the Dive Shop, with a full-service dive and water-sports program, a swimming pool and Jacuzzi, a pool bar, and a pool grill.

Villa & Condo Rentals

Grand Cayman offers a wide choice of condos and villas; renting one can cut your accommodation costs considerably. Most are owned as second or third homes (or purely as untaxed investments) by absentee owners, and are available for short-term rentals by qualified vacationers.

Most places have some kind of kitchen or kitchenette as well as a washing machine and dryer (or access to coin-operated laundry facilities on-site). Some even have barbecue grills in the garden area, so you can stock up at a grocery store for a cookout. You may be able to arrange maid service. Or you can go for a bare-boned rental, even bringing from home your own sheets and towels.

For more deals, you can contact the following condo and villa rentals yourself. Try the **Grape Tree Cocoplum** (☎ **345/949-5640**), **The Retreat at Rum Point** (☎ **345/947-9135**), or the **Victoria House Apartments** (☎ **345/945-4233**).

Calypso Cove. West Bay, Grand Cayman, B.W.I. ☎ or fax **345/949-3730.** 7 units. A/C TV TEL. Winter $100–$145 studio; $145 1-bedroom unit; $220 2-bedroom unit. Off-season $75–$105 studio; $105 1-bedroom unit; $160 2-bedroom unit. Children 11 and under stay free in parents' room. MC, V.

Just a dozen or so steps from the northernmost fringe of Seven Mile Beach, this guest house—renovated in 1998—is run by Sonia and Leif Barkinge. It is often booked by airline employees stopping over on Grand Cayman. They know what a good bargain it is on this high-priced island. It's a condo facility, in two pink concrete-block buildings in West Bay, with three studios for two, two one-bedroom units for up to four, and two two-bedroom/two-bath units housing as many as six. The two-bedroom units are each equipped with a washer and dryer. All accommodations have full kitchens, ceiling fans, and front and back patios, and are furnished in standard style with various combinations of twin, queen-size, and king-size beds and sofa sleepers, all with firm mattresses. Bathrooms are a bit cramped but tidily maintained. There is no pool, restaurant, or bar on the premises, but a number of places are within walking distance.

GREAT DEALS ON DINING

Make sure you understand which currency the menu is printed in. If it's not written on the menu, ask the waiter if the prices are in U.S. dollars or Cayman Island dollars (CI$), as this will make a big difference when you get your final bill.

One of the best places for breakfast is the **Wholesome Bakery & Café,** North Church Street (☎ **345/949-7064**). It's also a good bet if you're planning a picnic, as it does an excellent takeout. Breakfast prices range from CI$1.50 to CI$4.25 ($1.90 to $5.30), with overstuffed sandwiches going for CI$1.75 to CI$3.50 ($2.20 to $4.40). Throughout the day you can order main courses for CI$3.45 to CI$8 ($4.30 to $10). Place your order at the counter. Open Monday to Friday 6:30am to 7pm, Saturday 6:30am to 6pm, and Sunday 6:30am to 4pm.

Billy's Place. N. Church St., George Town. ☎ **345/949-0470.** Main courses CI$12–CI$34 ($15–$42.50); lunch CI$8–CI$24 ($10–$30). AE, MC, V. Mon–Sat 11am–10pm, Sun 6–10pm. JAMAICAN/CARIBBEAN/INDIAN.

Don't come here if you feel like dressing up and hitting the town. But if you like to stay in your T-shirt and shorts and enjoy the laid-back island-style, this is the local favorite. A pink-and-blue house in the Kirk Shopping Center with flowers on both sides and a garden and fountain in front, it's the creation of Jamaican-born Billy MacLaren, a real raconteur. He wanders through the restaurant making sure everything is running smoothly, but he only sits with people he knows. While calypso and reggae rock in the background, you can check out the menu.

The Indian curries are the best on the island, as are the Jamaican-inspired jerk dishes such as chicken and pork. He even serves the island's only "jerk" pizza. Try one of the Indian *pakoras* (vegetable fritters) or tandoori chicken or shrimp. There's very little difference between the lunch and dinner menus except the prices.

Champion House. Eastern Ave. ☎ **345/949-2190.** Reservations recommended. Soups CI$2–CI$4 ($2.50–$5); main courses CI$5–CI$6 ($6.30–$7.50). No credit cards. Sun–Thurs 11:30am–midnight, Fri–Sat 10am–3am. WEST INDIAN.

The Champion House has two grades of restaurants; this particular location is the least expensive. Here you'll get down-home West Indian food such as curried goat and chicken, stewed beef, peppered steak, and barbecued beef and ribs. There's also a variety of fresh seafood, but the West Bay location has a greater selection. The casual and friendly atmosphere has a certain quaint charm about it.

✪ **Chicken! Chicken!** In the West Shore Centre, West Bay Rd., along Seven Mile Beach. ☎ **345/945-2290.** Main courses CI$6.95–CI$9.95 ($8.70–$12.40); lunch specials CI$5.50–CI$5.95 ($6.90–$7.45). AE, MC, V. Daily 11am–10pm. CHICKEN.

The chicken is marinated in a sauce of lemon, lime, rosemary, parsley, garlic, and thyme, and served with fresh vegetables. The dinners include your choice of two side dishes, including garlic-and-herb potatoes, wild-mushroom pilaf, sweet tarragon carrots, potato salad, spinach pesto pasta, and coleslaw. For a slightly different taste, this restaurant serves two kinds of chicken salad (one with ginger, oranges, soy sauce, and water chestnuts). For a finish, they'll bring you the congo square, a chocolate brownie smothered in chocolate, coffee, and rum. This enterprise also offers fixed-price feasts for four or more people, including one for eight for CI$36.95 ($46.20).

✪ **Corita's Copper Kettle.** In Dolphin Center. ☎ **345/949-7078.** Reservations required. Main courses CI$6.75–CI$12 ($8.45–$15); lunch CI$6.50–CI$8.50 ($8.15–$10.65). No credit cards. Mon–Sat 7am–5pm, Sun 7am–3pm. CARIBBEAN/AMERICAN.

This place is generally packed in the mornings, when diners can enjoy a full American breakfast or West Indian breakfast specialties. Included are green bananas served with fried dumplings, fried flying fish, and Corita's Special (ham, melted cheese, egg, and jelly all presented on a fried fritter). For lunch, the menu varies from salads to chicken and beef along with conch, turtle, or lobster prepared as burgers or served up in a hearty stew.

Eats Crocodile Rock Café. In Falls Centre, West Bay Rd. (just north of the Holiday Inn Grand Cayman). ☎ **345/945-5288.** Main courses CI$10–CI$15 ($12.50–$18.75); lunch CI$4.50–CI$7 ($5.65–$8.75). AE, DC, MC, V. Daily 6:30am–11pm. AMERICAN/INTERNATIONAL.

Also called Eats Café, this restaurant has a Hard Rock Café atmosphere, with a bright interior with leopard spots and tiger stripes. It serves hearty fare at reasonable prices. Lunch features salads, sandwiches, and burgers. Dinner spotlights stir-fries including Szechuan teriyaki and mix-and-match pastas (a selection of five with a choice of seafood, tomato, pesto, Alfredo, or meat sauce). Other dishes include black-bean soup, coconut shrimp, and rum-garlic shrimp. Breakfast can also be ordered.

Golden Pagoda. West Bay Rd., along Seven Mile Beach. ☎ **345/949-5475.** Reservations recommended in winter. Main courses CI$7–CI$19 ($8.75–$23.75); buffet lunches CI$7 ($8.75). AE, MC, V. Mon–Fri 11:30am–2:30pm and 6–10pm, Sat–Sun 6–10pm. CHINESE.

Craving Chinese? This friendly restaurant is located in front of the Radisson Resort Grand Cayman on West Bay Road. When you see the sign TAKEE OUTEE, you've found it! In front is a fountain with a modest garden and a small, red bridge that leads to the front door. One house specialty is the mango chicken, a stir-fry dish with mango chutney, water chestnuts, and green peppers. The Hakka-style cooking features such fare as Mongolian beef, butterfly shrimp, Kung Pao chicken, and (the dish that the locals love) sweet-and-sour chicken.

✪ **Liberty's West Bay.** Reverend Blackman Rd., West Bay. ☎ **345/949-3226.** Main courses CI$6.50–CI$24 ($8.15–$30); lunch CI$6.50–CI$18.50 ($8.15–$23.15). MC, V. Daily 11am–4pm and 6–10pm. CAYMANIAN.

Visitors rarely find this local dive in the center of the West Bay shopping area, but it offers some of the best values on the island, especially at its all-you-can-eat dinner buffets on Wednesday, Friday, and Sunday night, which cost CI$14.95 ($18.70). The place is a real dollar-stretcher, and a local patron told us that the food was "real he-man." Presumably by that he meant such regional fare as codfish and ackee (the national dish of Jamaica), curried goat, and zesty oxtail, the latter a mite greasy but good. On many nights a "seafood feast" is offered up, with lobster, shrimp, and the local catch. At lunch you might opt for burgers and sandwiches.

WORTH A SPLURGE

Captain Brians. N. Church St. ☎ **345/949-6163.** Reservations recommended in winter for dinner. Main courses CI$9–CI$20 ($11.25–$25). AE, MC, V. Daily 8am–10pm (last order). Bar open till 1am. CARIBBEAN/ENGLISH.

On a plot of seafront land near the beginning of West Bay Road, this restaurant has developed a loyal following. In a low-slung cottage, whose verandas are vivid shades of pink, blue, and yellow, the place is both an amusingly decorated pub and a Caribbean-inspired dining room open to a view of the harbor. In the pub, you can order such British staples as fish-and-chips or cottage pie, and such drinks as a Snake Bite (equal parts of hard English cider and English lager) or a frothy tropical concoction.

The food is competently prepared and satisfying, though not a lot more. Dining choices include a Caesar salad topped with marinated conch or Cajun chicken, fresh catch of the day, shrimp, pastas, and seafood pastry stuffed with lobster, shrimp, and scallops, all of which are great values for the money. Don't overlook this as a possible site for breakfast, where you can devour *huevos rancheros.*

HITTING THE BEACHES

One of the finest beaches in the Caribbean, Grand Cayman's ✪ **Seven Mile Beach,** which begins north of George Town, has sparkling white sands rimmed with Australian pines and palms. Although it's not actually seven miles long, it is still a honey; 5½ miles of white, white sands stretching all the way to George Town, the capital. There are always lots of sunbathers near the big resorts, but the beach is so big you can always find some room to spread out your towel.

The waters are clear and warm here, with no great tide. Because the beach is on the more tranquil side of Grand Cayman, the water is generally placid and inviting, ideal for families, even those with small children. A sandy bottom slopes gently to deep water. The water's so clear you can generally see what's swimming in it; it's great for snorkelers and swimmers of most ages and abilities.

From one end of the beach to the other, there are hotels and condos, many with beachside bars you can visit. All sorts of water-sports concessions can be found along this beach, including rental of snorkel and diving equipment. You can parasail, take a tour of the waters off the beach, go water skiing, and rent windsurfing equipment, wave runners, paddlecats, and aqua trikes.

Unlike the beaches of Jamaica, this beach is without peddlers. It is also beautifully maintained, so you shouldn't encounter litter.

Although they pale in comparison to Seven Mile Beach, Grand Cayman also has a number of minor beaches. Visit these if you want to escape the crowds. Those on the east and north coasts are also good, filled with white sand. They are protected by an offshore barrier reef, so waters are generally tranquil.

One of our favorites is on the north coast, bordering the **Cayman Kai Beach Resort.** This beach is a Caribbean cliché of charm, with palm trees and beautiful sands. You can snorkel along the reef to Rum Point. The beach is also ideal as a Sunday afternoon picnic spot. There are changing facilities, and Red Sail Sports at Rum Point offers windsurfers, wave runners, sailboats, waterskiing, and even glass-bottom boat tours to see the sting-rays offshore. They also offer scuba diving.

Locals often go to **Smith's Cove,** lying off South Church Street. This is especially popular on Saturday and Sunday. The best windsurfing is just off the beaches of the East End, at Colliers, bordered by Morritt's Tortuga Club.

SPORTS & OUTDOOR PURSUITS

✪ **DIVING**   Grand Cayman is one of the top diving destinations in the world. Coral reefs and coral formations encircle the islands and are filled with lots of marine life—which scuba divers are forbidden to disturb, by the way.

It's easy to dive close to shore here, so boats aren't necessary, but there are plenty of boat diving operations. On certain excursions, we recommend a trip with a qualified divemaster. There are many dive shops for rentals, but they won't rent you scuba gear or supply air unless you have a NAUI or PADI certification card. Hotels also rent diving equipment to their guests, as well as arrange snorkeling and scuba-diving trips.

Universally regarded as the most up-to-date and best-equipped water-sports facility in the Cayman Islands, **Red Sail Sports** maintains its headquarters at the Hyatt Regency Grand Cayman, West Bay Road (☎ **800/255-6425** or 345/949-8745). Other locations are at the Westin Casuarina (☎ **345/949-8732**) and at Rum Point (☎ **345/947-9203**). A two-tank morning dive includes exploration of two different dive sites at depths ranging from 50 to 100 feet, and costs $85. Beginners can take a daily course that costs $120 per person. They have a wide range of offerings, from deep-sea fishing to sailing, diving, and more. Red Sail can also arrange waterskiing for $75 per half-hour (the cost can be divided among several people) and parasailing at $50 per ride.

Established in 1957, the best dive operation in the Caymans is **Bob Soto's Diving Ltd.** (☎ **345/949-2022,** or 800/262-7686 to make reservations). Owned by Ron Kipp, the operation includes full-service dive shops at Treasure Island, the SCUBA Centre on North Church Street, and Soto's Coconut in the Coconut Place Shopping Centre. A full-day resort course, designed to teach the fundamentals of scuba to beginners who know how to swim, costs $99: The morning is spent in the pool and the afternoon is a one-tank dive from a boat. All necessary equipment is included. Certified divers can choose from a wide range of one-tank ($50) and two-tank ($75) boat dives daily on the west, north, and south walls, plus shore diving from the SCUBA Centre. A one-tank night dive costs $50. Nondivers can take advantage of daily snorkel trips ($25), including Stingray City. The staff is helpful and highly professional.

GOLF   It's not cheap, but it's the only game on the island. The **Britannia Golf Club,** next to the Hyatt Regency on West Bay Road (☎ **345/949-8020**), was designed by Jack Nicklaus and is unique in that it incorporates three different courses in one: a 9-hole championship layout, an 18-hole executive setup, and a Cayman course. The last was designed for play with the Cayman ball, which goes about half

Swimming With the Stingrays

The offshore waters of Grand Cayman are home to one of the most unusual (and ephemeral) underwater attractions in the world, ✪ **Stingray City.** Set in the sun-flooded, 12-foot-deep waters of North Sound, about 2 miles east of the island's northwestern tip, the site originated in the mid-1980s when local fishers cleaned their catch and dumped the offal overboard. They quickly noticed scores of stingrays (which usually eat marine crabs) feeding on the debris, a phenomenon that quickly attracted local divers and marine zoologists. Today, between 30 and 50 relatively tame stingrays hover in the waters around the site for daily handouts of squid and ballyhoo from increasing hordes of amateur snorkelers and scuba enthusiasts.

Interestingly, most of the stingrays that feed here are females, the males preferring to remain in deeper waters offshore. To capitalize on the phenomenon, about half a dozen entrepreneurs lead expeditions from points along Seven Mile Beach, traveling around the landmass of Conch Point to the feeding grounds. One well-known outfit is **Treasure Island Divers** (☎ **345/949-4456**), which charges divers $50 and snorkelers $30. Trips are made on Sunday, Wednesday, and Friday at 1:30pm.

Be warned that stingrays possess deeply penetrating and viciously barbed stingers capable of inflicting painful damage to anyone who mistreats them. (Above all, the divers say, never try to grab one by the tail.) Despite the dangers, divers and snorkelers seem amazingly adept at feeding, petting, and stroking the velvet surfaces of these bat-like creatures without unpleasant incidents.

the distance of a regulation ball. Greens fees are a whopping $100 for 18 holes, or $60 for 9 holes. Cart rentals are included, but club rentals cost $20 for 9 holes or $35 for 18 holes.

SNORKEL CRUISES   **Red Sail Sports** (see "Diving," above) has a number of inexpensive ways you can go sailing in Cayman waters, including a glassbottom boat ride costing $25 without snorkeling equipment or $30 with snorkeling equipment. They also offer sunset cruises costing $27.50 or half price for children under 12. A 10am to 2pm sail to Stingray City, with snorkeling equipment and lunch included in the price of $65 per person, leaves once daily. Children under 12 go for half price.

INTO THE DEEP: SUBMARINE DIVES

So scuba diving's not enough for you? You want to see the real undiscovered depths of the ocean? On Grand Cayman, you can take the *Atlantis* reef dive. It's expensive, but it's a unique way to go underwater—and it might be the highlight of your trip.

One of the island's most popular attractions is the ***Atlantis XI,*** Goring Avenue (☎ 345/949-7700), a submersible that's 65 feet long, weighs 80 tons, and was built at a cost of $3 million to carry 48 passengers. You can view the reefs and colorful tropical fish through the 26 large viewpoints 2 feet in diameter, as it cruises at a depth of 100 feet through the maze of coral gardens at a speed of 1½ knots; a guide keeps you informed.

There are two types of dives. The premier dive, *Atlantis* Odyssey, features such high-tech extras as divers communicating with submarine passengers by wireless underwater phone and moving about on underwater scooters. This dive, operated both day and night, costs $82. On the *Atlantis* Expedition dive, you'll experience the reef and see the famous Cayman Wall; this dive lasts 55 minutes and costs $72. Children 4 to 12 are charged half price (no children under 4 allowed). *Atlantis XI* dives Monday to Saturday, and reservations are recommended 3 days in advance.

EXPLORING THE ISLAND

The capital, **George Town,** can easily be explored in an afternoon; stop by for its restaurants and shops (and banks!)—not sights. The town does offer a clock monument to King George V and the oldest government building in use in the Caymans today, the post office on Edward Street. Stamps sold here are avidly sought by collectors.

The island's premier museum, the **Cayman Islands National Museum,** Harbor Drive, in George Town (☎ **345/949-8368**), is in a much-restored old building directly on the water. Today the museum incorporates a gift shop, theater, cafe, and more than 2,000 items portraying the natural, social, and cultural history of the Caymans. Admission is CI$4 ($5) for adults and CI$2 ($2.50) for children 7 to 12 and senior citizens, free for children 6 and under. It's open Monday to Friday 9am to 5pm and Saturday 10am to 2pm (last admission is half an hour prior to closing).

Elsewhere on the island, you might go to **Hell!** That's at the north end of West Bay Beach, a jagged piece of rock named Hell by a former commissioner. There the postmistress will stamp "Hell, Grand Cayman" on your postcard to send back to the U.S.

The ✪ **Cayman Turtle Farm,** Northwest Point (☎ **345/949-3893**), is the only green sea-turtle farm of its kind in the world, and the most popular land-based tourist attraction in the Caymans. Once the islands had a multitude of turtles in the surrounding waters (which is why Columbus called the islands "Las Tortugas"), but today these creatures are sadly few in number (practically extinct elsewhere in the Caribbean), and the green sea turtle has been designated an endangered species. (You cannot bring turtle products into the United States.) The turtle farm has a twofold purpose: to provide the local market with edible turtle meat and to replenish the waters with hatchling and yearling turtles. Visitors today can look at 100 circular concrete tanks in which these sea creatures can be observed in every stage of development; the hope is that one day their population in the sea will regain its former status. Turtles here range in size from 6 ounces to 600 pounds. At a snack bar and restaurant, you can sample turtle dishes (we couldn't bring ourselves to, though). The turtle farm is open daily 8:30am to 5pm. Admission is $6 for adults, $3 for children 6 to 12, free for children 5 and under.

At **Botabano,** on the North Sound, fishers tie up with their catch, much to the delight of photographers. You can buy lobster (in season), fresh fish, and even conch. A large barrier reef protects the sound, which is surrounded on three sides by the island and is a mecca for diving and sports fishing.

If you're driving, you might want to go along **South Sound Road,** which is lined with pines and, in places, old wooden Caymanian houses. After leaving the houses behind, you'll find good spots for a picnic.

On the road again, you reach **Bodden Town,** once the largest settlement on the island. At Gun Square, two cannons commanded the channel through the reef. They are now stuck muzzle-first into the ground.

On the way to the **East End,** just before Old Isaac Village, you'll see the onshore sprays of water shooting up like geysers. These are called "blowholes," and they sound like the roar of a lion.

Old Man Bay is reached by a road that opened in 1983. From here you can travel along the north shore of the island to **Rum Point,** which has a good beach and is a fine place to end the tour. After visiting Rum Point, you can head back toward Old

Cheap Thrills: What to See & Do for Free
(Well, Almost) in the Cayman Islands

- **Stroll Through Historic George Town.** Arm yourself with a map (the tourist office will help you plot a route) and start at the Old Courts Building, now the Cayman Islands National Museum, on Harbour Drive. It has exhibits of the natural and cultural history of the island. To your left as you leave is Panton Square, with three old Cayman houses distinguished by pitched gables and ornate fretwork. On Harbour Drive, past the cruisedock, is Elmslie Memorial Church, built by Captain Rayal Bodden, a well-known shipwright. To the right, by the car park, are old grave markers shaped like houses, with small ones for children. In the churchyard is a War Memorial, and, across the street, the Seamen's Memorial, with names of 153 Caymanians lost at sea. Next to it are the remains of Fort George, built in 1790 for defense against the Spaniards who raided the islands, carrying inhabitants captive to Cuba.

- **View an Underwater Ecosystem.** Snorkeling in the Caymans is one of the reasons to come here, and it's cheap to rent equipment. You have many sites close to shore in calm, shallow waters. Virtually any shoreline in Grand Cayman, and the lesser islands too, offer great opportunities for the snorkeler, often with no boat required. Among the more popular sites are Parrot's Reef and Smith's Cove south of George Town. Lush reefs abound with parrotfish, coral, sea fans, and sponges. Also great for snorkelers is Turtle Farm Reef, a short swim from shore, offering a mini-wall rising from a sandy bottom.

- **Hang Out With the Stingrays.** What has been called "the world's best 12-foot dive" takes place on a sandy seafloor at Grand Cayman's North Sound. Numerous stingrays in the past few years have flocked to this area to accept handouts and greet snorkelers and divers. They "fly" here and there in the water, going up and down, looking for food (their favorite snack is squid, in case you'd like to purchase some to feed these guys). Although not as friendly, schools of yellowtail snappers are also showing up to taste some of the *fruits de*

Man Village, where you can go south along a cross-island road through savannah country that will eventually lead you west to George Town.

On 60 acres of rugged wooded land off Frank Sound Road, North Side, the **Queen Elizabeth II Botanic Park** (☎ **345/947-9462**) offers visitors a short walk through wetland, swamp, dry thicket, mahogany trees, orchids, and bromeliads. You'll likely see chickatees, the fresh-water turtles found only on the Caymans and in Cuba. Occasionally you'll spot the rare Grand Cayman parrot, or if not that, perhaps the anole lizard, with its cobalt-blue throat pouch. Even rarer is the endangered blue iguana. There are six rest stations with visitor information along the trail. The park is open daily from 7:30am to 5:30pm. Admission is CI$6 ($7.50) for adults, CI$3 ($3.75) for children, free for children 5 and under. There's a visitor center with changing exhibitions, plus a canteen for food and refreshments. It's set in a botanic park adjacent to the woodland trail and includes a heritage garden with a re-creation of a traditional Cayman home, garden, and farm; a floral garden with 1½ acres of flowering plants, and a 2-acre lake with three islands, home to many native birds.

mer. As the rays glide in and around, you're treated to close encounters, and can even caress their delicate underbellies.

- **Spend a Day on Seven Mile Beach.** Soaking up the sun on these brilliant white sands must surely rank among the great beach experiences of a lifetime. Even Tom Cruise succumbed to its charm in the movie *The Firm.* Lie back on the powdery white sand, without the annoyance of peddlers, and enjoy one of the few hassle-free experiences left in a troubled world. When you want action, choose one of the restaurants or watersports centers that line this fabled strip.

- **Go to Hell!** Back in the 1930s, the island commissioner, Alan Cardinall, was enthralled with the bleak, forbidding-looking landscape in the West Bay area, and christened it Hell. Word spread and a tourist stop was born. In 1962 the destination became so popular that the Cayman Island government established a district post office here open daily, including Sunday, from 8:30am to 1pm and 2 to 3:30pm. Literally thousands of visitors want to send postcards back home from Hell. The messages go somewhat like this: "We went to Hell and back today." "Greetings from a Hell of a place." Hell is set in an unusual geological formation of weathered and blackened local rock called ironshore. It's a rather bleak place, but then we wouldn't expect Hell to be a Garden of Eden.

- **Sip a Rum Punch at Rum Point.** Rum Point got its name from barrels of rum that once washed ashore here after a shipwreck. Today, it is dreamy and quaint, surrounded by towering causarina trees blowing in the trade winds. Most of these trees have hammocks hanging from their trunks, inviting you to enjoy the leisurely life. With its cays, reefs, mangroves, and shallows, Rum Point is a refuge that extends west and south for 7 miles. The sound's many spits of land and its plentiful lagoons are ideal for snorkeling, swimming, wading, and birding. It you get hungry, drop in to the Wreck Bar for a juicy hamburger.

Mastic Trail is a restored 200-year-old footpath through a 2-million-year-old woodland area in the heart of the island. The trail lies west of Frank Sound Road, about a 45-minute drive from the heart of George Town. Named for the majestic mastic tree, the trail showcases the reserve's natural attractions, including a native mangrove swamp, traditional agriculture, and an ancient woodland area—home to the largest variety of native plant and animal life found in the Cayman Islands. Guided tours, lasting 2½ to 3 hours and limited to eight participants, are offered Monday to Friday at 8:30am and at 3pm, and again on Saturday at 8:30am. Reservations are required, and the cost is $50 per person (expensive, but if you're really into plants you may want to splurge on it). The hike is not recommended for children under 6, the elderly, or persons with physical disabilities. Wear comfortable, sturdy shoes, and carry water and insect repellent. For reservations, call ☎ **345/945-6588** Monday to Friday from 7 to 9am.

Pedro St. James National Historic Site, Savannah (☎ **345/947-3329**), is a restored great house dating from 1780 when only 400 people lived on the island. It outlasted all the hurricanes until 1970 but was destroyed by fire that year. Now it's been rebuilt and is the centerpiece of a new heritage park, with a visitor center and an audio-visual theater with a laser light show. The Great House sits atop a limestone bluff on 7.65 acres of land overlooking a panoramic view of the sea. Guests enter via a $1.5 million Visitors' Center with a landscaped courtyard, a gift shop, and a cafe. Self-guided tours are possible. You can explore the house's wide verandas, rough-hewn timber beams, gabled framework, mahogany floors and staircases, and wide beam wooden ceilings. Guides in 18th-century costumes are on hand to answer questions. Admission is $8 for adults and $4 for children (5 and under free). Hours are daily 9am to 5pm.

SHOPPING

Although duty-free shopping in George Town encompasses silver, china, crystal, Irish linen, French perfumes, British woolen goods, and such local crafts as black-coral jewelry and thatch-woven baskets, there aren't any real bargains. Americans shouldn't purchase turtle products—they cannot be brought into the United States.

Blackbeard's Liquors, which has several locations, the most convenient at The Strand, opposite Foster's Food Fair (☎ 345/949-8763), sells liquors bottled in the Cayman Islands. Try various flavored rums such as banana, coconut, and mango, all based on original recipes.

While on the liquor trail, visit the **Tortuga Rum Company,** Selkirk Plaza (☎ 345/945-7655), which in addition to selling rum is also famous locally for its chocolate rum cake. Other new products include chocolate hazelnut rum truffles and a rum-flavored barbecue sauce, plus three varieties of rum-flavored coffee. Of course, most people come here for a bottle of its premium gold, 151-proof, superb light rum at $8.50 per liter.

Ayurvedic Concepts, Elizabethan Square (☎ 345/949-1769), is one of the most unusual stores in the Cayman Islands. It's been known for its natural herbal remedies, which it has sold since 1930. Some of their products include MindCare, said to calm a "racing mind" and help enhance memory.

For reasonably priced resort wear for men, women, and children, head for **Island Casuals,** Galleria Plaza, West Bay Road (☎ 345/949-8094).

Kayman Kids, Galleria Plaza on West Bay Road (☎ 345/945-2356), sells a vast array of items, mainly children's clothing, plus a large selection of bathing suits for boys and girls. They also sell doll houses designed to look like a typical Caymanian cottage. A lot of specialty gifts are also hawked.

Kirk Freeport Plaza, Cardinal Avenue and Panton Street, George Town (☎ 345/949-7477), is the largest store of its kind on the Caymans, with a treasure trove of gold jewelry, watches, china, crystal, perfumes, and cosmetics. The store holds a Cartier franchise, with items priced 15% to 35% below suggested retail prices stateside. Also stocked are crystal and porcelain from Wedgwood, Waterford, Lladró, and Baccarat, priced 30% to 50% less than recommended retail prices stateside.

Pure Art, S. Church St., George Town (☎ 345/949-9133), is good for some local souvenirs and is your best bet for arts and crafts. One room is devoted to original art, including locally produced Christmas ornaments. Another room stocks art prints and note cards. The shop also carries carvings, ceramics, thatch work, and baskets, plus pottery from the Bodden Town primary school (made by the youngsters there).

Tropical Trader Market & Bazaar, Edward St. (☎ 345/949-6538), is a good bet on an island of overpriced art galleries. You can pick up some typical Caymanian scenes here, not only paintings, but drawings and prints as well, for $15 and up. Local artists painted many of the island scenes in watercolors. The outlet is a true bazaar, selling gold, silver, and black-coral jewelry (the latter among the most inexpensive on the island). You can also purchase watches by Anne Klein, Casio, and Swiss Army, plus Tommy Bahama men's sports clothing. Bags and luggage by Kipling and Tumi are also sold.

An offbeat shopping adventure is found at **Caribbean Charlie's,** Hut Village, 4 miles from Rum Point (☎ 345/947-9452), on the north side of the island in a typical Caymanian settlement. This is the workshop and home of the remarkable Charlie Ebanks, who is known on the island for his brightly painted wooden waurie boards. This game was believed to have been imported to the island by slaves. It is said that everybody from Blackbeard to Ernest Hemingway has enjoyed playing this game. Charlie also makes birdhouses in the shape of the traditional Cayman cottages. One of the few native artisans still on the island, Charlie is aided by his American-born wife, Elaine, who adds bright colors and fanciful designs to his creations.

GRAND CAYMAN AFTER DARK

Lone Star Bar & Grill, West Bay Road (☎ 345/945-5175), is a transplanted corner of the Texas Panhandle. You can enjoy juicy burgers in the dining room or head immediately for the bar in back. Here, beneath murals of Lone Star beauties, you can watch several sports events simultaneously on 15 different TV screens and sip lime and strawberry margaritas. Monday and Thursday are fajita nights, all-you-can-eat affairs at CI$12 ($15), and Tuesday is all-you-can-eat lobster night at CI$34.95 ($43.70). There's a new volleyball court too.

The Planet, about a block inland from West Bay Road (☎ 345/949-7169), adjacent to the island's only cinema, offers the island's largest dance floor, plus the biggest indoor stage and four bars dispensing reasonably priced drinks along with bar food. The mix of locals and tourists form a wide age range—from 18 to 50. Expect a $5 cover.

Sharkey's, Fall Shopping Center, Seven Mile Beach (☎ 345/947-5366), is like *Back to the Future,* filled with rock 'n' roll paraphernalia from the 1950s. Music here ranges from karaoke to the big hits of the 1970s.

3 Cayman Brac

The "middle" island of the group, Cayman Brac is a piece of limestone and coral-based land 12 miles long and a mile wide, about 89 miles east-northeast of Grand Cayman. It was given the name Brac (Gaelic for bluff) by 17th-century Scottish fishers who settled here. The bluff for which the island was named is a towering limestone plateau rising to 140 feet above the sea, covering the eastern half of Cayman Brac. Caymanians refer to the island simply as Brac, and its 1,400 inhabitants, a hospitable bunch of people, are called Brackers.

The big attraction of the bluff are the more than 170 caves honeycombing its limestone height. In the early 18th century, the Caymans were occupied by pirates, and Edward Teach, the infamous Blackbeard, is supposed to have spent quite a bit of time around Cayman Brac. Some of the caves are at the bluff's foot; others can be reached only by climbing over jagged limestone rock. One of the biggest caves is Great Cave, with a number of chambers. Harmless fruit bats cling to the roofs of the caverns.

On the south side of the bluff, you won't see many people, and the only sounds are of the sea crashing against the lava-like shore. The island's herons and wild green parrots are seen here. Most of the Brackers live on the north side, many in traditional wooden seaside cottages, some built by the island's pioneers. The islanders must all have green thumbs, as attested to by the variety of flowers, shrubs, and fruit trees in many of the yards. On Cayman Brac, you'll see poinciana trees, bougainvillea, Cayman orchids, croton, hibiscus, aloe, sea grapes, cactus, and coconut and cabbage palms. The gardeners grow cassava, pumpkins, breadfruit, yams, and sweet potatoes.

There are no actual towns on the island, only settlements, such as Stake Bay (the "capital"), Spot Bay, the Creek, Tibbitt's Turn, the Bight, and West End, where the airport is located.

Flights from Grand Cayman to Cayman Brac are operated on **Cayman Airways** (☎ **800/422-9626** in the U.S., or 345/949-2311). The airline uses relatively large 737 jets carrying 122 passengers each. There is an evening flight here, plus a morning return. The round-trip cost is $104 per person.

The only hospital is the 18-bed **Faith Hospital** (☎ **345/948-2243**).

ACCOMMODATIONS YOU CAN AFFORD

The two major resorts on the island, Brac Reef Beach Resort and Divi Tiara Beach Resort, are pretty high-priced, and the other accommodations here aren't exactly inexpensive.

Brac Airport Inn. P.O. Box 56, Cayman Brac, Cayman Islands, B.W.I. ☎ **800/327-3835** in the U.S., or 345/948-1323. Fax 345/948-1207. E-mail: bracinn@candw.ky. 4 units. A/C TV. Year-round $120–$132 single or double. AE, MC, V. Free parking.

This hotel was conceived and designed as part of the only shopping center on Cayman Brac. It might not be suited to everyone's beach-going fantasy, as it's in a landlocked setting 1½ miles from the sea. But budget travelers sometimes opt for the relatively simple lodging here, then commute to the island's legendary beach and scuba facilities. Technically, guests can enjoy the dining, drinking, and sports facilities of the larger (and better-equipped) Brac Reef Beach Resort, which manages this place. You can arrange dining for around $40 a day (MAP) at the Brac Reef Beach Resort. The bedrooms (each with a radio and ceiling fan) are above the shops, and usually cost around 15% less than equivalent accommodations in more upscale locations. It's in a very simple motel style, with worn mattresses and rather cramped bathrooms.

✪ **Walton's Mango Manor.** Stake Bay (P.O. Box 56), Cayman Brac. ☎ or fax **345/948-0518**. E-mail: waltons@condy.ky. 5 units. A/C. Winter $80–$90 double; off-season $70–$80 double. Rates include breakfast. AE, MC, V.

Unique on Cayman Brac, this is a personalized, small-scale B&B that's more richly decorated and elegant than you might have thought. Originally the home of a sea captain, it was moved to a less exposed location and rebuilt from salvaged materials shortly after the disastrous hurricane of 1932. Set on 3 acres of land on the island's north shore, within a lush garden that's ripe with breadfruit, a hardy species of mango, and a local species of edible fruit known as guenup, it contains such intriguing touches as a banister salvaged from the mast of a 19th-century schooner. The best rooms are on the upper floor, partly because of their narrow balconies that offer views of the sea. The place is very comfortable, with rooms that come in a variety of sizes, each with a firm mattress and a tidy though small bathroom. No meals are served other than the full American breakfasts that are included in the price. Your hosts are Brooklyn-born Lynne Walton and her husband, George.

GREAT DEALS ON DINING

Captain's Table. Brac Caribbean Beach Village, Stake Bay. ☎ **345/948-1418**. Reservations recommended. Main courses $11.25–$22.50; lunch from $12. AE, MC, V. Mon–Sat 11:30am–3pm and 6–9:30pm; Sun noon–3pm. AMERICAN.

The decor is island style, vaguely nautical with oars over and around the bar and pieces of boats forming the restaurant's entryway. In the same building as a scuba shop and the reception desk of the hotel, the restaurant offers both indoor and air-conditioned seating, along with outside dining by the pool. Begin with a captain's cocktail of shrimp and lobster or perhaps conch fritter, then follow with one of the soups such as black bean. Main dishes include everything from the catch of the day, often served pan-fried, to barbecue ribs. At lunch, you can order burgers and sandwiches.

FUN ON & OFF THE BEACH

The biggest attraction is the variety of **water sports**—swimming, fishing, snorkeling, and some of the world's best diving and exploration of coral reefs. There are undersea walls on both the north and south sides of the island, with stunning specimens lining their sides. The big attraction for divers is the M.V. *Tibbetts*, a 330-foot-long Russian frigate resting in 100 feet of water, a relic of the Cold War sunk in September of 1996. It is complete with guns both fore and aft. Hatches into the ship have been barred off to ensure diver safety. Marine life is becoming more pronounced on this relic which now rests in a watery grave far, far from its home. The best dive center is **Peter Hughes Dive Tiara** at the Divi Tiara Beach Resort (☎ **800/367-3484** or 345/945-1553).

History buffs might check out the **Cayman Brac Museum,** in the former Government Administration Building, Stake Bay (☎ **345/948-2622**), which has an interesting collection of Caymanian antiques, including pieces rescued from shipwrecks and items from the 18th century. Open Monday to Friday from 9am to noon and 1 to 4pm, Saturday from 9am to noon, and Sunday from 1 to 4pm. Admission is free.

4 Little Cayman

The smallest of the Cayman Islands is cigar-shaped Little Cayman, 10 miles long and about a mile across at its widest point. It lies about 75 miles northeast of Grand Cayman and some 5 miles from Cayman Brac. The entire island is coral and sand.

The islands of the Caymans are mountaintops of the long-submerged Sierra Maestra Range, which runs north and into Cuba. Coral formed layers over the underwater peaks, eventually forming the islands. Beneath Little Cayman's Bloody Bay is one of the mountain's walls—a stunning sight for snorkelers and scuba divers.

The island seems to have come into its own now that fishing and diving have taken center stage; this is a near-perfect place for such pursuits. The waters around the little island were hailed by the late Jacques Cousteau as one of the three finest diving spots in the world. Fine bonefishing is available just offshore, and a brackish inland pool can be fished for tarpon. Even if you don't dive or fish, you can row 200 yards off Little Cayman to isolated and uninhabited Owen Island, where you can swim from the sandy beach and picnic by a blue lagoon.

There may still be pirate treasure buried on the island, but it's in the dense interior of what is now the largest bird sanctuary in the Caribbean. Little Cayman is also home to a unique species of lizard that predates the iguana.

Blossom Village, the island's "capital," is on the southwest coast.

Most visitors fly from Grand Cayman to Little Cayman. **Cayman Airways** (☎ **800/949-0241** in the U.S., or 345/949-5252 on Grand Cayman) is the reservations agent for Island Air, a charter company that charges $154 round-trip.

ACCOMMODATIONS YOU CAN AFFORD

Paradise Resort. P.O. Box 30, Little Cayman, Cayman Islands, B.W.I. ☎ **345/948-0001.** Fax 345/948-0002. www.paradise.com. E-mail: iggy@candw.ky. 12 units. A/C. Winter $162.50 single; $187.50 double; $212.50 triple. Off-season $150 single; $162.50 double; $187.50 triple. Children 11 and under stay free in parents' room. AE, MC, V.

On this high-priced little island, this resort on the beach is your best deal, and it's also the best choice if you're traveling with family (baby-sitting can be arranged). The style is typically Caymanian, with gingerbread decoration, metal roofs, and porches front and back. Guests prepare their own meals. Bordering the sea are six duplex cottages, each divided into two one-bedroom units. Pullout couches in the living room easily accommodate extra guests, and in addition to air-conditioning, there are ceiling fans. Rooms are small and mattresses are well used, but there is basic comfort here. Bathrooms contain shower stalls. The resort is on the island's south side, near the little airport from which pickup is provided free. A grocery store, boutique, two auto rentals, and a liquor store are all within walking distance, and Paradise Resort offers free bikes. On the premises is the best affordable restaurant on the island, the Hungry Iguana (see below). Diving is arranged through Paradise Divers. Its two-tank dive at $75 is the island's best value.

⭐ **Sam McCoy's Diving and Fishing Lodge.** P.O. Box 12, Little Cayman, Cayman Islands, B.W.I. ☎ **800/626-0496** in the U.S. and Canada, or 345/948-0026. Fax 345/949-0057. 8 units. A/C. Dive packages $536.50 for 3 nights/2 days, and $1,354.50 for 7 nights/6 days, per person, double occupancy. Rates include all meals and all dives. AE, MC, V.

Set on the island's northwestern shore, this hotel reflects the personalities of Sam McCoy and his family, who include their guests in many aspects of their day-to-day lives. There's not really a bar or restaurant in the traditional sense; rather, you'll pour your own drinks (usually from your own bottle) or drink at a beach bar that rises from the sands of Bloody Bay a short walk from the hotel. Light snacks and simple platters are offered at outdoor tables near the main lodge with Sam and his gang, many of whom are associated in one way or another with diving operations on the reefs offshore. The bedrooms are ultra-simple, with few adornments other than beds with a firm mattress, a table and chair, and a ceiling fan. Baths are small with dated plumbing and a rack of thin towels. Maid service is included in the price. There's a pool on the premises, but most visitors opt for dips in the wide blue sea instead, usually taking part in any of the wide choice of scuba explorations offered by Sam and his staff. (Jackson Beach lies nearby.) Picnics can be arranged to the offshore sands of Owens Cay. This is a place built by divers, and intended for divers, even those with children in tow.

GREAT DEALS ON DINING

Birds of Paradise. At Little Cayman Resort. ☎ **345/948-1033.** Reservations recommended for dinner. Breakfast CI$12 ($15); lunch CI$15 ($18.75); dinner CI$25 ($31.25). AE, MC, V. Daily 7:30–8:30am, 12:30–1:30pm, and 6:30–7:30pm. AMERICAN/CONTINENTAL.

The best buffet dinners on the island—the kind your parents might have enjoyed back in the golden 1950s or 1960s—are served at this little spot that caters primarily to hotel guests, but welcomes outsiders. The best night to show up is Tuesday, which features the island's most generous barbecue spread—all the ribs, fish, and Jamaican-inspired jerk chicken you'd want. On other nights, try the prime rib, fresh fish Caribbean style (your best bet), or chicken either Russian style (Kiev) or French style (Cordon Bleu). There's a freshly made salad bar, and homemade desserts are yummy, especially the key lime pie. At night, opt for an outdoor table under the stars.

The Hungry Iguana. Paradise Resort. ☎ **345/948-0007.** Reservations recommended. Lunch CI$7.25–CI$9.95 ($9.05–$12.45); dinner CI$14.95–CI$23.95 ($18.70–$29.95). AE, MC, V. Daily noon–9:30pm. (Bar, Mon–Fri noon–1am, Sat–Sun noon–midnight.) AMERICAN/ CARIBBEAN.

At the beach, you'll spot this place immediately with its mammoth iguana mural. The island's tastiest dishes are served here, a winning combination of standard American fare along with some zesty flavors from the islands south of here. It's the most macho place on the island, especially the sports bar with its satellite TV in the corner, with a sort of TGI Friday's atmosphere. Lunch is the usual burgers and fries along with some well-stuffed sandwiches. We always prefer the grilled chicken salad. Dinner gets a little more elaborate—there's usually a special meat dish of the day, depending on the market (supplies are shipped in once a week by barge). Try one of the seafood platters. The chef always seems willing to prepare you a steak as you like it. Marinated shrimp with rémoulade is a tasty choice as well. To go local, sample the marinated conch salad.

SPORTS & OUTDOOR ACTIVITIES

Established in 1994, the **Governor Gore Bird Sanctuary** is home to some 5,000 pairs of red-footed boobies. As far as it is known, this is the largest colony of such birds in the western hemisphere. The sanctuary, lying near the small airport, is also home to dramatic colonies of snowy egrets and black frigates. Many bird-watchers from the U.S. fly into Little Cayman just to see these bird colonies.

The best fishing is at Bloody Bay, lying off the island's north coast. It is especially noted for its bonefishing and tarpon catches. For fishing, contact Sam McCoy's Diving and Fishing Lodge (see above).

The Bloody Bay Wall is also the best dive site on island, lying just 20 minutes off-shore and reached by boat. The drop here begins at only 20 feet but plunges to more than 1,200 feet. This is one of the great dive spots in the Caymans. For more information about how to enjoy it, call **Paradise Divers** at ☎ **800/450-2084** or 345/948-0004. You can also make arrangements at Sam McCoy's as well (see above).

9

Curaçao

Just 35 miles north of the coast of Venezuela, Curaçao, the "C" of the Dutch ABC islands of the Caribbean, is the most populous in the Netherlands Antilles. It attracts visitors because of its distinctive culture, warm people, duty-free shopping, lively casinos, and water sports. Heading out from its harbor, fleets of tankers carry refined oil to all parts of the world.

The largest of the Netherlands Antilles, Curaçao is 37 miles long and 7 miles across at its widest point. Because of all that early Dutch building, Curaçao is the most important island architecturally in the entire West Indies, with more European flavor than anywhere else in the Caribbean. After leaving the capital, **Willemstad,** you plunge into a strange, desert-like countryside that evokes the American Southwest. The landscape is an amalgam of browns and russets, studded with three-pronged cactus, spiny-leafed aloes, and the divi-divi trees, with their coiffures bent by centuries of trade winds. Classic Dutch-style windmills are in and around Willemstad and in some parts of the countryside. These standard farm models pump water from wells to irrigate vegetation.

Curaçao, together with Bonaire, St. Maarten, St. Eustatius, and Saba, is in the Kingdom of the Netherlands as part of the Netherlands Antilles. Curaçao has its own governmental authority, relying on the Netherlands only for defense and foreign affairs. Its population of 171,000 represents more than 50 nationalities.

Only in the 1990s did tourism become the biggest money earner for this island. As a result, a number of inexpensive or moderately priced hotels, inns, and apartment complexes have opened.

1 Essentials

VISITOR INFORMATION

In the United States, contact the **Curaçao Tourist Board** at 475 Park Ave. S., Suite 2000, New York, NY 10016 (☎ **800/270-3350** or 212/683-7660); or at 330 Biscayne Blvd., Suite 330, Miami, FL 33132 (☎ **305/374-5811**).

The official Web site is **www.curacao-tourism.com**.

On the island, go to the **Curaçao Tourist Board,** Pietermaai (☎ **599/9-616000**).

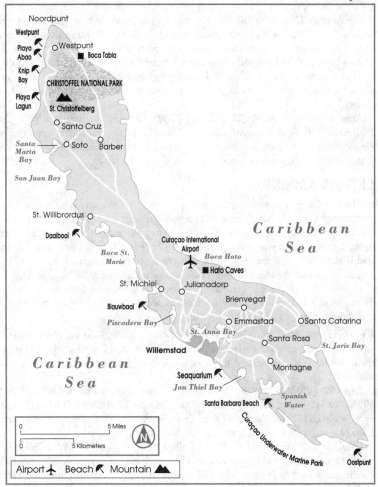

Airport ✈ Beach 🏖 Mountain ▲▲

GETTING THERE

The air routes to **Curaçao International Airport,** Plaza Margareth Abraham (☎ **599/9-682288**), are still firmly linked to those leading to nearby Aruba. In recent years, however, developments at such airlines as American have initiated direct or non-stop routings into Curaçao from such international hubs as Miami.

American Airlines (☎ **800/433-7300**) offers a daily nonstop flight to Curaçao from its hub in Miami, which departs late enough in the day to permit easy connections from cities all over the northeast. Fortunately, it arrives early enough in the day (around 3pm) to allow guests to unpack and enjoy a leisurely dinner the same evening. American also offers flights to Curaçao's neighbor, Aruba, from New York, Miami, and San Juan, Puerto Rico. Once on Aruba, many clients transfer on to Curaçao on any of ALM's many shuttle flights. An American Airlines sales representative can also sell discounted hotel packages if you book your airfare and overnight accommodations simultaneously.

Air Aruba (☎ 800/88ARUBA) flies daily from Newark, New Jersey, to Aruba, with two flights on Saturday and Sunday (one of the Sunday flights stops in Baltimore to pick up passengers). The same airline also offers daily nonstop flights to Aruba from Miami and Tampa, and direct service from Baltimore. On Aruba, regardless of their points of origin, Curaçao-bound passengers either remain on the same plane for its continuation on to Curaçao, or transfer to another aircraft after a brief delay.

Another choice is **ALM** (☎ 800/327-7230), Curaçao's national carrier. It flies 14 times a week from Miami to Curaçao. Although 10 of these flights stop in either Aruba, Bonaire, or Haiti, the others are nonstop. ALM also flies two times a week to Curaçao from Atlanta, usually with a stop in Bonaire en route.

GETTING AROUND

BY TAXI   Since taxis don't have meters, ask your driver to quote you the rate before getting in. Drivers are supposed to carry an official tariff sheet, which they'll produce upon request. Charges go up by 25% after 11pm. Generally there's no need to tip, unless a driver helped you with your luggage. The charge from the airport to Willemstad is about $15, and the cost can be split among four passengers. If a piece of luggage is so big that the trunk lid won't close, you'll be assessed a surcharge of $1.

In town, the best place to get a taxi is on the Otrabanda side of the floating bridge. To summon a cab, call ☎ **599/9-8690747.** Cabbies will usually give you a tour of the island for around $20 per hour for up to four passengers.

BY RENTAL CAR   Since all points of interest on Curaçao are easily accessible by paved roads, you may want to rent a car. U.S., British, and Canadian visitors can use their own licenses, if valid, and *traffic moves on the right.* International road signs are observed.

Avis (☎ 800/331-2112 or 599/9-8681163) and **Budget** (☎ 800/472-3325 or 599/9-8683420) offer some of the lowest rates. **Hertz** (☎ 800/654-3001 in the U.S., or 599/9-8681182) may also offer good deals. Rentals are often cheaper if you reserve from North America at least a week before your departure.

Local car-rental firms include **Rent a Yellow,** Santa Rosa 9 (☎ **599/9-7673777**), whose cars are painted like a yellow cab. The lowest rates are for vehicles without air-conditioning, costing from $33.50 daily, rising to $40 with air-conditioning. Tariffs include tax and insurance.

BY BUS   Some hotels operate a free bus shuttle that will take you from the suburbs to the shopping district of Willemstad. A fleet of DAF yellow buses operates from Wilhelmina Plein, near the shopping center, to most parts of Curaçao. Some limousines function as "C" buses. When you see one listing the destination you're heading for, you can hail it at any of the designated bus stops.

Fast Facts: Curaçao

Banks   Banking hours are Monday to Friday 8:30am to noon and 1:30 to 4:30pm. However, the Banco Popular and the Bank of America remain open during the lunch hour, doing business Monday to Friday 9am to 3pm.

Currency   Whereas Canadian and U.S. dollars are accepted for purchases on the island, the official currency is the **Netherlands Antillean florin (NAf),** also called a guilder, which is divided into 100 NA (Netherlands Antillean) cents. The exchange rate is $1 U.S. to 1.77 NAf (1 NAf = 56¢ U.S.). Shops, hotels, and restaurants usually accept most major U.S. and Canadian credit and charge cards. Rates in this chapter are quoted in U.S. dollars unless otherwise specified.

Documents   To enter Curaçao, U.S. or Canadian citizens need proof of citizenship, such as a birth certificate or a passport, along with a return or continuing airline ticket out of the country. We always recommend carrying your passport when visiting a foreign country. British subjects need a valid passport.

Electricity   The electricity is 110–130 volts AC, 50 cycles, the same as in North America, although many hotels will have transformers if your appliances happen to be European.

Language   Dutch, Spanish, and English are spoken on Curaçao, along with Papiamento, a patois that combines the three major tongues with Amerindian and African dialects.

Medical Care   Medical facilities are well equipped, and the 534-bed **St. Elisabeth Hospital,** Breedestraat 193 (☎ **599/9-462-4900**), near Otrabanda in Willemstad, is one of the most up-to-date facilities in the Caribbean.

Police   The police emergency number is ☎ **114.**

Safety   While Curaçao is not plagued with crime, it would be wise to safeguard your valuables.

Taxes and Service   Curaçao levies a room tax of 7% on accommodations, and most hotels add 12% for room service. There's a departure tax of $12.50 for international flights, $5.65 for flights to other islands in the Netherlands Antilles.

Telephones   To call Curaçao from the United States, dial **011** (the international access code), then **599** (the country code for Curaçao), and then **9** (the area code) and the local number (the number of digits in the local number varies).

Once on Curaçao, to call another number on the island only the local number is necessary; to make calls to an off-island destination, dial **021** and then the area code and number.

Time   Curaçao is on Atlantic standard time year-round, 1 hour ahead of eastern standard time, and the same as eastern daylight saving time.

Water   The water comes from a modern desalination plant and is safe to drink.

Weather   Curaçao has an average temperature of 81°F (22.7°C). Trade winds keep the island fairly cool, and it is flat and arid, with an average rainfall of only 22 inches per year—hardly your idea of a lush, palm-studded tropical island.

2 Accommodations You Can Afford

Your hotel will be in Willemstad or in one of the suburbs, which are 10 to 15 minutes from the shopping center. The bigger hotels often have free shuttle buses running into town, and most of them have their own beaches and pools.

Remember that Curaçao is a bustling commercial center, and the downtown hotels often fill up fast with business travelers and visitors from neighboring countries on a shopping holiday. Therefore, reservations are always important.

When making reservations, ask if the 7% room tax and 12% service charge are included in the price you're quoted.

Hotel Holland. F. D. Rooseveltweg 524, Curaçao, N.A. ☎ **599/9-8688044.** Fax 599/9-688114. 45 units. A/C TV TEL. Year-round $66 single; $79 double; from $117 suite. AE, DC, MC, V.

A 2-minute drive from the airport, the Hotel Holland contains a casino and the Flying Dutchman Bar, a popular gathering place. For a few brief minutes of every day you can see airplanes landing from your perch at the edge of the poolside terrace, where well-prepared breakfasts, lunches, and dinners from the Cockpit Restaurant are served during good weather. This property is the domain of ex-navy frogman Hans Vrolijk and his family. Hans still retains his interest in scuba and arranges dive packages for his guests. The small but comfortably furnished accommodations have VCRs, refrigerators, good beds, and balconies, plus somewhat cramped bathrooms. Laundry, babysitting, and room service are available.

Hotel Seru Coral. Koraal Partier 10, Curaçao, N.A. ☎ **599/9-7678499.** Fax 599/9-7678256. 86 units. A/C TV TEL. $95.20 single studio with kitchen, $100.80 double studio with kitchen; $119.85 single 1-bedroom suite; $129.35 double 1-bedroom suite; $176.40 bungalow for 4; $208.30 2-bedroom suite for 4; $265.45 villa for 6. Children 12 and under stay free in parents' room. Extra bed for one additional occupant $8.50 per day. AE, DC, MC, V.

Built in the early 1990s, this is a landscaped hotel complex whose white-walled buildings are clustered around the edges of a very large circular pool terrace. It lies on Curaçao's eastern edge, about 4 miles from the nearest beach (Santa Barbara Beach), but the inconvenience of reaching the beach is offset by the lavish size of the largest freshwater pool on Curaçao. At least five room configurations are available, allowing groups of travelers to cut their costs to very reasonable levels by sharing. Each has white walls with pastel trim, white tile floors, and a mixture of rattan and wooden furniture, including good beds with firm mattresses and standard bathrooms with stall showers only. Water sports, boat trips, and tennis can be arranged nearby. Families are welcome: On the premises is a child's wading pool, a launderette, a mini-mart, and a bar. Baby-sitting is available.

Landhaus Daniel. Wegnaar, Westpunt, Curaçao, N.A. ☎ **599/9-864-8400.** Fax 599/9-864-8400. 7 units. TV TEL. Winter $45–$55 single or double; off-season $40–$50 single or double. AE, DC, MC, V.

A mile south of Westpunt, near the island's most noteworthy tip, this mustard-colored plantation house is most often frequented by locals because of its on-site restaurant. However, if you don't mind a location away from the beach, it offers the best-value accommodations on the island. The nearest worthwhile beach is Porto Marie or Habitat Curaçao, a 10-minute drive from the hotel.

One floor above the restaurant, management rents very simple but reasonably comfortable bedrooms, each tidily maintained with excellent mattresses and small but well-maintained private bathrooms. All the rooms have ceiling fans, or else guests rely on the trade winds to keep things cool. Only two rooms are air-conditioned. Ask for a room in the main house, as these have more charm than those in the converted slave quarters, which appear like a standard stateside motel and are about half the size of a typical Day's Inn room. This place seems like a youth hostel, with its basic rooms along with a communal TV room. Guests also play billiards and darts.

Otrabanda Hotel & Casino. Breedestraat, Otrabanda, Curaçao, N.A. ☎ **599/9-4627400.** Fax 599/9-627299. 48 units. A/C TV TEL. Winter $105 single; $115 double; $150 suite. Off-season $95 single; $105 double; $140 suite. Rates include breakfast. AE, DISC, MC, V.

This six-story, somewhat anonymous hotel serves both tourists and business travelers in the heart of Willemstad. Although the nearest beach is a 15-minute drive away, there's a pool and lots of diversions, shopping, bars, and inexpensive restaurants within an easy stroll. The bedrooms are simple, spartan, and clean, with white walls, carpets, and wooden furniture. Maintenance is good, and the units are medium in size with carpeted floors, floor-to-ceiling windows, and excellent mattresses. Bathrooms are spacious, with combination shower and tub baths, adequate shelf space, and a generous assortment of medium-size towels. On the premises is the Bay Sight Terrace restaurant and the Pontoon Bar. The ground-floor casino, although not particularly memorable, seems relatively busy.

✪ **Porto Paseo Hotel & Casino.** De Rouvilleweg 47, Willemstad, Curaçao, N.A. ☎ **599/9-4627878.** Fax 599/9-4627969. E-mail: ppaseo@cura.net. 47 units. Year-round $95 single or double, $150 suite for 2 (including breakfast); $110 1- or 2-bedroom apt. (without breakfast). 7-night minimum on apt. rentals. AE, MC.

Set on the Otrabanda side of Willemstad's harbor front, this is one of the capital's most beautiful and stylish restorations of a historic building, and one of the island's best hotel values. Completed in 1992, it incorporates what was originally constructed in the 1870s as the island's first hospital, with a sprawling, pancake-flat garden and clusters of modern, low-rise buildings that each contain between four and five accommodations. One of the centerpieces of the estate is a flagstone-covered courtyard illuminated with streetlamps, and a simple brasserie, the Bon Bini, which is only open for lunch. On the premises is a casino, a bar with views over Santa Ana bay, and a collection of ornamental birds. It all evokes Dutch colonial life of long ago. Bedrooms are severely dignified, airy, and comfortable. Rooms are a bit spartan, showing no decorator's flair, but are tidy and well maintained with decent beds. Each small bathroom has a shower unit (no tub) and suitable shelf space.

BEST DEAL BY THE WEEK

Chogogo Resort. Jan Thiel Bay, Curaçao, N.A. ☎ **599/9-7472844.** Fax 599/9-7472424. www.chogogo.com. E-mail: chogogo@cura.net. 54 units. A/C TV TEL. Year-round rates per week: $487 studio for 1 or 2; $557 1-bedroom apt. for 2–4. 2-bedroom bungalows: $700 for 2; $766 for 3; $870 for 4. Supplemental charges for water and electricity average about $10 a day per unit, depending on usage. MC, V.

Named after a species of local flamingo, and set within an arid landscape between the oceanfront beaches and a shallow saltwater bay (Jan Thiel Bay), southeast of Willemstad, this resort caters mostly to European (mostly Dutch) families who check in for at least a week and prepare their own meals. Contained within several dozen party-colored units of either one or two stories each, the units each contain their own kitchenette, airy, unpretentious furniture, and pale interior colors. There is reasonable comfort here, though the mattresses are a bit thin; bathrooms are small but efficiently organized with shelf space and shower stalls (no tubs). There's a free-form swimming pool on the premises, complete with its own waterfall, a grocery store for the provision of supplies, and both a bar and a restaurant. Don't expect a lot of amenities or services here, as it was conceived for independent travelers looking to escape the pressures of urban life and recover without the help of a social director. The activities revolve around the in-house bar and restaurant and a beach club set up near the reefs, white sands, and marine life of a nearby beach club. Although clean towels are provided daily, apartments are cleaned only three times a week; stays of less than a week are not encouraged.

3 Great Deals on Dining

Although the restaurants reviewed below offer some high-priced dishes—mostly fresh fish—most items are at the lower end of the price scale.

The Cockpit. In the Hotel Holland, F. D. Rooseveltweg 524. ☎ **599/9-8688044.** Reservations required. Main courses $10–$25. AE, DC, MC, V. Daily 7am–10pm. DUTCH/INTERNATIONAL.

This hotel restaurant's decor has an aeronautical flavor, with an airplane cockpit as the focal point. Located on the scrub-bordered road leading to the airport, a few minutes from the landing strips, it serves international cuisine with an emphasis on Dutch and Antillean specialties. Guests enjoy fresh fish in season (served according to Curaçao style), Dutch-style steak, Caribbean curried chicken, split-pea soup, and various pasta dishes, such as shrimp linguine *della mama* served in a lobster sauce and topped with melted cheese. All dishes are accompanied by fresh vegetables and Dutch-style potatoes. No one pretends that the food is gourmet fare—it's robust, hearty, and filled with good country flavor. It's also one of the best dining values on this island, where food prices often climb to dizzying heights. Guests can enjoy their meals outside around the pool or in the cockpit-inspired dining room.

✪ **Golden Star.** Socratesstraat 2. ☎ **599/9-461-8741.** Main courses $7.50–$25.70. AE, DC, MC, V. Daily 9am–1am. CREOLE.

The best place to go on the island for *criollo* (local) food is inland from the coast road leading southeast from St. Anna Bay, at the corner of Dr. Hugenholtzweg and Dr. Maalweg, southeast of Willemstad. Evoking a roadside diner, the air-conditioned restaurant is very simple, but it has a large menu of very tasty Antillean dishes, such as *carco stoba* (conch stew), *bestia chiki* (goatmeat stew), *bakijauw* (salted cod), and *concomber stoba* (stewed meat and marble-size spiny cucumbers). Other specialties include *criollo* shrimp (kiwa) and *sopi carni* (meat stew). Everything is served with a side order of funchi, the cornmeal staple. The place has a large local following with an occasional tourist dropping in.

The Grill King. Water Foort 2–3. ☎ **599/9-4616870.** Main courses $4.50–$26. AE, DC, DISC, MC, V. Mon–Thurs noon–midnight, Fri–Sat noon–12:30am, Sun 5:30pm–midnight. GRILLED MEATS/FISH.

This casual place draws locals and visitors to an open-air site near the harbor with a panoramic view of the passing ships. It's a lively, bustling place, specializing in grilled meats and fish, although there are other choices as well. The grilled steaks are succulent, as is the fresh catch of the day. You can also order pepper steak, a platter full of seafood (shrimp, calamari, conch, and lobster). Savvy foodies often gravitate to the mixed grill with pork, beef, conch, and chicken, all served with fresh vegetables. Burgers are also available, and there's not only a soup of the day but a daily special, often regional. The bar often stays open until 1am, attracting a convivial crowd.

Herbie's Pizza. Santa Rosaweg, Van Engelen. ☎ **599/9-7679533.** Main courses and pizzas $3.50–$19. AE, DC, MC, V. Daily 11am–11pm. PIZZA/ITALIAN.

East of town on Santa Rosaweg, this is the local family favorite for a pizza fix. There's an area for children, with a mini-zoo with monkeys, ducks, rabbits, and parrots. Children's parties are held here every day. In the front is a counter for ordering takeout along with some tables. Beyond is an open-air dining area and a two-story hut. Upstairs is the bar. In addition to pizza, the menu offers a standard repertoire of chicken, fish, and meat dishes, all prepared Italian style from family recipes. There are a number of freshly made pastas, salads, and soups, the menu rounded off nicely with such desserts as egg custards, pies, and tiramisù. Live music is presented on Friday and Saturday nights, so Herbie's becomes a cheap way to spend an evening.

Il Barile. Hanhi Sna 12, Punda. ☎ **599/9-4613025.** Main courses $6–$15. AE, DISC, MC, V. Mon–Sat 8am–8pm. ITALIAN.

Many Italian meals in Curaçao are very expensive, but this winning little two-story trattoria-style place not only offers affordable prices, but serves a very good cuisine. It's really only an informal cafe with an outdoor terrace on the ground floor. Many locals, including some Italians, cite it for its good food. You can drop in for breakfast, stick around for such lunch offerings as burgers and sandwiches, and definitely stay for dinner. It's in the evening when the kitchen shines, turning out a number of pasta dishes, such as linguine al pesto. The fresh basil in the pesto sauce is grown at the owner's home. You can also order an excellent grilled red snapper or shrimp in garlic butter.

Jaanchi's. Westpunt 15. ☎ **599/9-8640126.** Main courses $12–$18; lunch from $10. AE, DC, MC, V. Daily noon–8:30pm. SEAFOOD.

In the village of Westpunt, on the island's western tip, this local dive has made a name for itself by its fried fresh fish. Many locals drive out here for a feast that ranges from shrimp to conch and octopus—each dish prepared according to time-tested traditional recipes. For those with exotic palates, the menu offers a number of very rare regional dishes, even iguana soup! If the spicy local goat doesn't interest you, you can always opt for a good steak instead. Platters are served with rice, french fries, fried bananas, salad, and fungi polenta (a cornmeal bread). The restaurant is built ranch style, offering open-air dining. Birds looking for handouts (breadcrumbs) will often join you at table. On Sunday and holidays there's live music when Jaanchi's becomes rather festive.

Mambo Beach. Seaquarium Beach. ☎ **599/9-461-8999.** Lunch main courses $3.65–$14; dinner main courses $7–$17.10. MC, V. Mon–Fri 10am–1pm; Sat–Sun 10am–3am. INTERNATIONAL.

Set two miles south of Willemstad, on an isolated stretch of sandy beachfront near the Prince's Beach Hotel, this bar and restaurant consists of little more than a wooden deck that's raised above the sand, less than 60 feet from the water's edge. Don't expect a ceiling or a roof to shelter you from a view of the stars, although parasols will shade you at noontime. Although most of the energy at this place is devoted to its restaurant and bar trade, it does an active business every Saturday and Sunday night between 11pm and 3am on the nightlife circuit. Then you'll see up to six Dutch or Caribbean bands at a time, or at least a DJ spinning the kind of tunes that encourage you to shake, rattle, and roll. If there's a cover charge at all, it won't exceed $5.60 per person, and will only apply during the rare super-concert that occurs only a few times a year. If you arrive during mealtimes, menu items at lunch include pastas, pancakes and crêpes, salads, and grilled fish or chicken. Evening meals are more substantial, and often include grilled shark with lobster sauce, tuna with teriyaki sauce, salmon with mayonnaise sauce, shrimp with garlic sauce, and tournedos with sun-dried tomatoes. The food is surprisingly good and excellently prepared with first-rate ingredients.

WORTH A SPLURGE

Martha Koosje Café. Martha Koosje Weg 10. ☎ **599/9-8648235.** Reservations recommended. Main courses $15–$37.40. AE, DC, DISC, MC, V. Daily 5–11pm. CARIBBEAN.

In a 160-year-old estate on the west side of the island, this is a discovery. It's an alfresco dining room decorated with antique furnishings and in full bloom with tropical flora.

The place deserves to be better known, lying at the narrowest part of the island. A Curaçao/Dutch couple, Errol and Simone Caprino, took over from the long-established owners and plan changes. Errol is an actor, so he also offers dinner-the-ater—type entertainment. The bar opens at 5pm, so you can come early for a leisurely drink, enjoying pre-entertainment entertainment by watching the iguanas on the roof being fed. The food has been improved. Today you can begin with pumpkin soup or, even better, fish soup, or perhaps a seafood cocktail. Locals like the grilled steaks served with various sauces, or you can sample conch, shrimp, or grilled red snapper (delectable).

Rodeo Ranch Saloon & Steakhouse. At the Curaçao Seaquarium, in Bapor Kibra. ☎ **599/ 9-4615757.** Reservations recommended. Main courses $15–$34.30. AE, MC, V. Mon–Sat 6pm–midnight, Sun noon–2pm and 6pm–midnight. (Bar, daily 5pm–midnight.) STEAK/ AMERICAN.

East of Willemstad, the Rodeo Ranch is kitschy but a lot of fun. The owners have created a touch of the Old West with a replica of a covered wagon over the entrance and an interior decor of rough-sawn planking, dark woods, and antique wagon wheels. A "sheriff," wearing a 10-gallon hat and a silver star, greets visitors at the door. You'll be presented with a cowhide-covered menu by a cowgirl/waitress. To the sounds of country-western music, you can order dishes such as soup from the kettle, a chuck-wagon choice of potato specials, steak, roast prime rib, and seafood. All steaks are U.S. prime beef, and there's a serve-yourself soup-and-salad bar. You don't have to dress up, and you'll enjoy your meal in air-conditioned comfort. Hot snacks are served at the happy hour from 5 to 7pm.

4 Hitting the Beaches

Its beaches are not as good as Aruba's 7-mile strip of sand (see chapter 4), but Curaçao does have some 38 of them, ranging from hotel sands to secluded coves. Beaches are called *playas* or *bocas.* Playas are larger, classic sandy beaches, whereas bocas are small inlets placed between two large rock formations.

In general the northwest coast is rugged and difficult for swimming, but the more tranquil waters of the west coast are filled with sheltered bays where both swimming and snorkeling are excellent. About 30 minutes from town, in the Willibrordus area on the west side, **Daaibooi** is free, but there are no changing facilities. The shade here is provided by wooden parasols on the beach. Snorkelers are attracted to the sides of the bay here, as the cliffs rise out of the surf. Small rainbow-hued fish are commonplace, and a lot of varying corals cover the rocks. This beach gets very crowded on Sunday with the locals themselves. People dance to music played on local instruments, old men play dominoes, and many families barbecue their food on the beach.

A good private beach on the eastern side of the island is **Santa Barbara Beach,** on land owned by a mining company. It's between the open sea and the island's primary water-sports and recreational area known as **Spanish Water.** On the same land are Table Mountain, a remarkable landmark, and an old phosphate mine. The natural beach has pure-white sand and calm water. A buoy line protects swimmers from boats. Rest rooms, changing rooms, a snack bar, and a terrace are among the amenities. You can rent water bicycles and small motorboats. The beach, open daily from 8am to 6pm, has access to the Curaçao Underwater Park (see "Sports & Outdoor Pursuits," below).

Blauwbaai (Blue Bay) is the largest and most popular beach on Curaçao, with enough white sand for everybody. Along with showers and changing facilities, there are plenty of shady places to retreat from the noonday sun. To reach it, follow the road that goes past the Holiday Beach Hotel, heading in the direction of Juliandorp. Follow the sign that tells you to bear left for Blauwbaai and the fishing village of San Michiel.

Other beaches include: **Westpunt,** known for the gigantic cliffs that frame it, and from which divers jump into the ocean below on Sundays. This is often called the "beach of fishermen," as nets can be seen hanging out to dry and rainbow-hued little boats come and go with the day's catch. This beach tends to be exceptionally hot, and there are no facilities. There are no shade trees, so bring sun protection. Nonetheless, the swimming here is excellent in calm waters. This is not good for snorkeling, however, as the bay is too wide. Many locals bring a picnic basket. This public beach is located on the northwestern tip of the island.

Knip Bay, just south of Westpunt, has a beach at the foot of beautiful turquoise waters. Its white sands and rocky sides make it suitable for snorkeling, swimming, or sunbathing. The beach tends to be crowded on weekends, often with locals. The manzanilla trees in the backdrop of this beach provide some shade, but their fruits are poisonous. Never seek shelter here when it rains, as water dropping off the tree will cause major irritation to your skin. On weekends, live music and dancing make it a lively place. Changing facilities and refreshments are available.

Playa Abao, with crystal turquoise water, is a beach at the northern tip of the island. One of Curaçao's most popular strands, this is often called Playa Grandi, meaning the "Big Beach." It can get very, very hot at midday, but *pergolas* (thatched shade umbrellas) provide some protection. A stairway and ramp lead down to the beach with its excellent white sands. In the parking lot is a snack bar.

Near the large cove at Playa Abao, **Playa Kenepa** is much smaller but gets our nod as one of the island's most beautiful beach strips. It is partially shaded by trees and is a good place for sunbathing and swimming as well as shore diving. There is a 10-minute swim from the beach to a reef where visibility is often 100 feet. Baby sea turtles are often spotted here. On weekends a snack bar is open.

A beach popular with families, **Playa Lagun** lies well concealed in the corner of the village of Lagun, as you approach from Santa Cruz. The narrow cove here is excellent for swimming because of the tranquil, shallow water. Rainbow-hued fish appear everywhere, so the beach is also a favorite with snorkelers. Some concrete huts on the beach provide some shelter from the scorching sun. Fishing boats are based here, adding local color. A snack bar is open on weekends.

Seaquarium Beach charges $2.50 per person admission. It's manmade, lying near the center of Willemstad with complete facilities, including two bars, two restaurants, a water sports shop, as well as beach chair rentals, plus changing facilities and showers. From a meager rubble beach here, a developer made a spacious sandy beach area. Its calm waters make it ideal for swimming, but you have to dive outside the breakwaters.

A word of caution to swimmers: The sea water remains an almost-constant 76°F (24.5°C) year-round, with good underwater visibility, but beware of stepping on the spines of the sea urchins that sometimes abound in these waters. To give temporary first aid for an embedded urchin's spine, try the local remedies of vinegar or lime juice, or as the natives advise, a burning match if you're tough. While the urchin spines are not fatal, they can cause several days of real discomfort.

5 Sports & Outdoor Pursuits

DAY CRUISES   **Taber Tours,** Dokweg (☎ 599/9-7376637), offers a handful of seagoing tours, such as an 8-hour snorkel/barbecue trip to Port Marie, which includes round-trip transportation to excellent reef sites, use of snorkeling equipment, and a barbecue, for a cost of $60 per person. Children 9 and under pay half price.

A less ambitious tour involves a sunset cruise on which wine, cheese, and French bread are served. The 2-hour sailing trip leaves at dusk on Friday only, for a cost of $30 per adult and $20 for children 11 and under.

Travelers looking for a seagoing experience similar to the sailing days of yore should book a trip on the *Insulinde*, Handelskade (☎ 599/9-5601340; beware, this is a cellular phone so the connection might be muffled). This 120-foot traditionally rigged sail clipper is available for day trips and chartering. Every Thursday (or by special arrangement), the ship sails north from its berth beside Willemstad's main pier to the island's northwestern shore. Here, at Porto Marie (also referred to as Boca St. Marie), guests disembark onto the white sands of a beach, beside a private beach house. Included in the $55 per person charge is lunch and use of snorkeling equipment. Advance reservations are necessary. Outbound transit is by sail; the return is by the ship's engines. Departure from the pier is at 8:30am every Thursday; return to the pier is around 6pm the same day. Longer trips to Bonaire or Venezuela are also possible.

On Friday, the *Bounty* (☎ 599/9-560-1887), a 90-foot replica of its famous namesake, departs up the coast to the secluded white sand beach of Porttomarie Bay, returning by nightfall. On Sunday the ship sets out for Klein Curaçao, a desert island that is a favorite of snorkelers. Each Monday the *Bounty* visits Spanish Bay, a coastal community surrounded by terraced hills. The Friday and Sunday trips cost $50, with the Monday cruise going for $30; all prices including a buffet lunch.

DIVING & SNORKELING Most hotels offer their own water-sports programs. However, if your hotel isn't equipped, we suggest that you head for one of the most complete water-sports facilities on Curaçao, **Seascape Dive and Watersports,** at the Four Points Resort Curaçao (☎ 599/9-4625000). Specializing in snorkeling and scuba diving to reefs and underwater wrecks, it operates from a hexagonal kiosk set on stilts above the water, just offshore from the hotel's beach. Open from 8am to 5pm daily, it offers snorkeling excursions for $25 per person in an underwater park offshore from the hotel, waterskiing for $40 per half hour, and rental of jet skis for $50 per half hour. A Sunfish can be rented for $20, and an introductory scuba lesson, conducted by a competent dive instructor with PADI certification, goes for $45; four-dive packages cost $124.

One trip, enthusiastically endorsed by some visitors, departs from the hotel at 7am (when participation warrants). The destination is Little Curaçao, midway between Curaçao and Bonaire. Swimwear is skimpy once you get to the sugar-white sands of the island. Fishing, snorkeling, and the acquisition of a "topless tan" are highlights. The price is $70 per person, and the excursion lasts all day.

They can also arrange deep-sea fishing for $336 for a half-day tour carrying a maximum of six people, $560 for a full-day tour. Drinks and equipment are included, but you'll have to get your hotel to pack your lunch.

Underwater Curaçao, in Bapor Kibrá (☎ 599/9-4618131), has a complete PADI-accredited underwater-sports program. A fully stocked modern dive shop has retail and rental equipment. Individual dives and dive packages are offered, costing $33 per dive for experienced divers. An introductory dive for novices is priced at $65, and a snorkel trip costs only $20, including equipment.

Scuba divers and snorkelers can expect spectacular scenery in waters with visibility often exceeding 100 feet at the ✪ **Curaçao Underwater Park,** which stretches along 12½ miles of Curaçao's southern coastline. Although the park technically begins at

Princess Beach and extends all the way to East Point, the island's most southeasterly tip, some scuba aficionados and island dive operators are aware of other, excellent dive sites outside the official boundaries of this park. Lying beneath the surface of the water are steep walls, at least two shallow wrecks, gardens of soft corals, and more than 30 species of hard corals. Although access from shore is possible at Jan Thiel Bay and Santa Barbara Beach, most people visit the park by boat. For easy and safe mooring, the park has 16 mooring buoys, placed at the best dive and snorkel sites. A snorkel trail with underwater interpretive markers is laid out just east of the Princess Beach Resort & Casino and is accessible from shore. Spearfishing, anchoring in the coral, and taking anything from the reefs, except photographs, are strictly prohibited.

GOLF The **Curaçao Golf and Squash Club,** Wilhelminalaan, in Emmastad (☎ 599/9-7373590), is your best bet. Greens fees are $30, and both clubs and carts can be rented upon demand. The nine-hole course (the only one on the island) is open to nonmembers only in the morning, Friday to Wednesday from 8am to noon. Afternoon tee-offs are reserved for members and for tournaments. Thursday hours for nonmembers are 10am until sundown.

HORSEBACK RIDING At Christoffel National Park, **Rancho Christof** (☎ **599/9-864-0535**), specializes in outdoor horseback riding, private rides along unspoiled trails, riding smooth-gaited "paseo" horses suitable even for nonriders. You can call for reservations daily between 8am and 4pm. Most trail rides cost $49, with departures daily at 9am.

TENNIS Most of the deluxe hotels have tennis courts, but we frugal travelers won't be staying there. So if you want to play tennis, head for the **Santa Catherine Sports Complex** at Club Seru Coral, Koraal Partier 10 (☎ **599/9-767-7028**), where courts cost $20 per hour.

WINDSURFING At Seaquarium Beach you'll find **Top Watersports Curaçao** (☎ **599/9-461-7343**), the best windsurfing center on the island. It offers both rentals and instruction. The cost for windsurfing equipment is $15 per hour, plus a refundable $60 deposit. This is a tranquil section of the coast, which makes it more suitable for beginners.

6 Seeing the Sights

Most cruise-ship passengers see only Willemstad—or, more accurately, the capital's shops—but you may want to get out into the *cunucu*, or countryside, and explore the towering cacti and rolling hills topped by *landhuizen* (plantation houses) built more than 3 centuries ago.

SIGHTSEEING IN WILLEMSTAD

Willemstad was founded as Santa Ana by the Spanish in the 1500s. Dutch traders found a vast natural harbor, a perfect hideaway along the Spanish Main, and they renamed it Willemstad in the 17th century. Not only is Willemstad the capital of Curaçao, it's also the seat of government for the Netherlands Antilles. Today it boasts rows of pastel-colored, red-roofed town houses in the downtown area. After more than a decade of restoration, the historic center of Willemstad and the island's natural harbor, Schottegat, have been inscribed on UNESCO's World Heritage List.

The city grew up on both sides of a canal. It's divided into **Punda** (Old World Dutch ambience and the best shopping) and **Otrabanda** (the contemporary "other side"). Both sections are connected by the **Queen Emma Pontoon Bridge,** a pedestrian walkway. Powered by a diesel engine, it swings open many times every day to let ships from all over the globe pass in and out of the harbor.

The view from the bridge is of the old **gabled houses** in harmonized pastel shades. The bright colors, according to legend, are a holdover from the time when one of the island's early governors is said to have had eye trouble and flat white gave him headaches.

The colonial-style architecture, reflecting the Dutch influence, gives the town a storybook look. The houses, built three or four stories high, are crowned by "step" gables and roofed with orange Spanish tiles. Hemmed in by the sea, a tiny canal, and an inlet, the streets are narrow, and they're crosshatched by still narrower alleyways.

Except for the pastel colors, Willemstad may remind you of old Amsterdam. It has one of the most intriguing townscapes in the Caribbean. Don't let the colors deceive you. The city can be rather dirty, in spite of its fairy-tale appearance.

A **statue of Pedro Luis Brion** dominates the square known as Brionplein right at the Otrabanda end of the pontoon bridge. Born in Curaçao in 1782, he became the island's favorite son and best-known war hero. Under Simón Bolívar, he was an admiral of the fleet and fought for the independence of Venezuela and Colombia.

In addition to the pontoon bridge, the **Queen Juliana Bridge** opened to vehicular traffic in 1973. Spanning the harbor, it rises 195 feet, which makes it the highest bridge in the Caribbean and one of the tallest in the world.

The waterfront originally guarded the mouth of the canal on the eastern or Punda side, but now it has been incorporated into the Plaza Hotel. The task of standing guard has been taken over by **Fort Amsterdam,** site of the Governor's Palace and the 1769 Dutch Reformed church. The church still has a British cannonball embedded in it. The arches leading to the fort were tunneled under the official residence of the governor.

A corner of the fort stands at the intersection of Breedestraat and Handelskade, the starting point for a plunge into the island's major shopping district.

A few minutes' walk from the pontoon bridge, at the north end of Handelskade, is the **Floating Market,** where scores of schooners tie up alongside the canal, a few yards from the main shopping section. Docked boats arrive from Venezuela and Colombia, as well as other West Indian islands, to sell tropical fruits and vegetables—a little bit of everything, in fact, including handcrafts. The modern market under its vast concrete cap has not replaced this unique shopping expedition, which is fun to watch. Either arrive early or stay late to view the panoramic scene.

At some point save time to visit the **Waterfort Arches,** stretching for a quarter mile. They rise 30 feet high and are built of barrel-vaulted 17th-century stone set against the sea. Waterfort offers a chance to explore boutiques, have film developed quickly, cash a traveler's check, or else purchase fruit-flavored ice cream. You can walk through to a breezy terrace on the sea for a local Amstel beer or a choice of restaurants. At night the grand buildings and cobbled walkways are illuminated.

Between the I. H. (Sha) Capriles Kade and Fort Amsterdam, at the corner of Columbusstraat and Hanchi di Snoa, stands the **Mikve Israel-Emanuel Synagogue** (☎ 599/9-4611067), the oldest synagogue building in the western hemisphere. Consecrated on the eve of Passover in 1732, it houses the oldest Jewish congregation in the New World, dating from 1651. A fine example of Dutch colonial architecture, covering about a square block in the heart of Willemstad, it was built in a Spanish-style walled courtyard, with four large portals. Sand covers the sanctuary floor following a Portuguese Sephardic custom, representing the desert where Israelites camped when the Jews passed from slavery to freedom. The highlight of the east wall is the Holy Ark, rising 17 feet, and a raised *banca,* canopied in mahogany, is on the north wall.

Joaño d'Illan led the first Jewish settlers (13 families) to the island in 1651, almost half a century after their expulsion from Portugal by the Inquisition. The settlers came via Amsterdam to Curaçao.

Adjacent to the synagogue courtyard is the **Jewish Cultural Historical Museum,** Kuiperstraat 26–28 (☎ **599/9-461-1633**), housed in two buildings dating back to 1728. They were originally the rabbi's residence and the bathhouse. The 2½-centuries-old *mikvah,* or bath for religious purification purposes, was in constant use until around 1850 when this practice was discontinued and the buildings sold. They have been reacquired and turned into the present museum. On display are a great many ritual, ceremonial, and cultural objects, many of which date back to the 17th and 18th centuries and are still in use by the congregation for holidays and events.

The synagogue and museum are open to visitors Monday to Friday 9 to 11:45am and 2:30 to 4:45pm; if there's a cruise ship in port, also Sunday 9am to noon. Services are Friday at 6:30pm and Saturday at 10am. Visitors are welcome, with appropriate dress required. There's a $2 entrance fee to the museum.

WEST OF WILLEMSTAD

You can walk to the **Curaçao Museum,** Van Leeuwenhoekstraat (☎ **599/ 9-4626051**), from the Queen Emma Pontoon Bridge. The tiny museum was built in 1853 by the Royal Dutch Army Corps of Engineers as a military quarantine hospital for yellow fever victims and was carefully restored in 1946–48 as a fine example of 19th-century Dutch architecture. Equipped with paintings, objets d'art, and antique furniture made in the 19th century by local cabinetmakers, it re-creates the atmosphere of an era gone by. The museum contains a large collection from the Caiquetio tribes, the early inhabitants described by Amerigo Vespucci as 7-foot-tall giants. There's also a reconstruction of a traditional music pavilion in the garden where Curaçao musicians give regular performances. It's open Monday to Saturday 9am to noon and 2 to 5pm and Sunday 10am to 4pm. Admission is $2.50 for adults, $1.25 for children 13 and under.

Opened in 1998, the **Maritime Museum,** Van De Brandhof Straat 7 (☎ **599/ 9-465-2327**), traces the story of Curaçao in various exhibits, beginning with the arrival of the island's original inhabitants in 600 B.C. In the historic Scharloo neighborhood of Willemstad, the museum stands just off the old harbor of St. Ana Bay. Video presentations include the development of Curaçao's harbor and the sad role of the island as one of the largest slave depots in the Caribbean. Five oral histories are also presented, one from a 97-year-old Curaçaoan who served on the cargo vessel *Normandie.* Other exhibits include antique miniatures, 17th-century ship models, and a collection of maps, some dating from the 16th century. Admission is $6 adults and $4 children, and hours are Monday to Saturday 10am to 5pm.

The **Curaçao Underwater Marine Park** (☎ **599/9-4624242**) stretches from the Princess Beach Resort & Casino to the east point of the island, a strip of about 12½ miles of untouched coral reefs. For information on snorkeling, scuba diving, and trips in a glass-bottom boat to view the park, see "Sports & Outdoor Pursuits," above.

The **Country House Museum,** Doktorstuin 27 (☎ **599/9-8642742**), 12 miles west of Willemstad, is a small-scale restoration of a 19th-century manor house that boasts thick stone walls, a thatched roof, and artifacts that represent the old-fashioned methods of agriculture and fishing. It's open Tuesday to Friday 9am to 4pm, and Saturday and Sunday 9am to 5pm. Admission is $2.

En route to Westpunt, you'll come across a seaside cavern known as **Boca Tabla,** one of many such grottoes on this rugged, uninhabited northwest coast.

Cheap Thrills: What to See & Do for Free
(Well, Almost) on Curaçao

- **Stroll Across Curaçao's Golden Gate.** Walking from Punda to Otrobanda (Papiamento for "other side") takes you across the Queen Emma Bridge (circa 1888), which locals hold in the same high regard that citizens of San Francisco do their Golden Gate bridge. This pontoon bridge is affectionately known as the "Swinging Old Lady." It floats open and closed to let maritime traffic enter the harbor. Guarding the harbor-side entrance is a restaurant, Bistro Le Clochard, where you can dine in a former jail or a former rain cistern. From the galleys on top, you can sip a drink at the Harbour Side Terrace, enjoying a panoramic view of Punda across the harbor entrance.

- **Taste the Original and Authentic Curaçao.** When Spaniards landed on the island in the early 16th century, they planted hundreds of Naranja orange trees. But the island's arid climate and sparse rainfall didn't provide good growing conditions for their citrus crop. An inedible, bitter fruit, known locally as the *lahara* orange, was produced. By accident it was discovered that the peel of this orange, when dried in the sun, provided an aromatic oil which families used to make liqueur. Exotic spices were added, and the unique Curaçao liqueur was the result. Today the Curaçao Liqueur Factory still distills and distributes this popular beverage created from the original and very secret recipe. You can take a free tour of the factory at Landhuis Chobolobo and sample the real thing.

- **Browse the Floating Market.** Around the corner from the ferry terminal in Willemstad, on Sha Caprileskade, the Floating Market lies only a few minutes walk from the Queen Emma Pontoon Bridge. Schooners tie up along the Waaigat Canal to sell fresh fish, tropical fruits, produce, herbs, spices, and handcrafts under colorful canopies. You can stop by to sample the wares, take photographs, or just watch the action. You can sample tropical treats such as tamarind juice. Purchase a mango and you'll be treated as graciously as if you bought a whole bushel.

In the Westpunt area, a 45-minute ride from Punda in Willemstad, **Playa Forti** is a stark region characterized by soaring hills and towering cacti, along with 200-year-old Dutch land houses, the former mansions that housed slave owners.

Out toward the western tip of Curaçao in Savonet, a high-wire fence surrounds the entrance to the 4,500-acre **Christoffel National Park** (☎ 599/9-8640363), about a 45-minute drive from the capital. A macadam road gives way to dirt, surrounded on all sides by abundant cactus and bromeliads. In the higher regions you can spot rare orchids. Rising from flat, arid countryside, 1,230-foot-high St. Christoffelberg is the highest point in the Dutch Leewards. Donkeys, wild goats, iguanas, the Curaçao deer, and many species of birds thrive in this preserve, and there are some Arawak paintings on a coral cliff near the two caves.

The park has 20 miles of one-way trail-like roads, with lots of flora and fauna along the way. The shortest trail is about 5 miles long and, because of the rough terrain, takes about 40 minutes to drive through. Various walking trails are available also. One of them will take you to the top of **St. Christoffelberg** in about 1½ hours. (Come early in the morning when it isn't so hot.) The park is open Monday to Saturday 8am

- **Sample Authentic Curaçaoan Food.** At the Old Marshé (The Old Market), which lies behind the post office at De Ruyterkade, you can sample all the famous Antillean dishes of the island at a fraction of the price you'd pay in a restaurant. This is the most boisterous, authentic, and popular local lunch spot on the island. Stop by this famous old market around noon. Family seating is on a first-come, first-served basis. The portions are generous, and most platters of food cost only $4 to $6. You can feast on funchi, their version of the cornmeal-made polenta, goat stew, fried fish, peas and rice, keshi yena, and fried plantains.

- **Watch the Crashing Waves.** At Shete Boka, which means "Seven Inlets" in the local dialect, the islanders have created a new national park, along Westpunt Highway, just past the village of Soto. Here you can hike along the rugged, crag-strewn cliffs where the sea has carved out dramatic caverns. You can also join park rangers for some turtle-monitoring every morning. The showcase of the park is Boka Tabla, one of Curaçao's most spectacular sites. Millions of years of pounding surf have carved out a wide cavern underneath a limestone terrace where you can watch and listen to the surf roll in. A path along the bluff takes you to the edge where you can see waves crashing against the north coast for miles in each direction. Flocks of parakeets emerge in formation, birds of prey such as hawks soar and dip, and seagulls dive-bomb for luckless fish.

- **Hike Through a National Park.** At the western end of the island, Christoffel National Park is centered around Mount Christoffel, the island's highest point at 1,237 feet. A protected wildlife preserve and garden covers 4,500 acres of land. The park consists of three former plantations and offers 20 miles of one-way driving trails through abundant flora and fauna, including divi-divi trees, exotic flowers, and prickly pear cactus. Protected wildlife includes iguanas, rabbits, donkeys, several species of birds, and some 200 white-tail Curaçao deer. Visitors can explore the park on foot, by horseback, by mountain bike, by car, or by jeep.

to 4pm and Sunday 6am to 3pm. Admission is $13.50 for both adults and children, including admission to the museum.

The park also has a museum with varying exhibitions year-round set in an old storehouse leftover from plantation days. Phone to arrange a guided tour. Next door, the park has opened the **National Park Shete Boka** (Seven Bays). It's a turtle sanctuary and contains a cave with pounding waves off the choppy north coast. Admission to this park is $1.50 per person.

NORTH & EAST OF WILLEMSTAD

Just northeast of the capital, **Fort Nassau** was completed in 1797 and christened by the Dutch as Fort Republic. Built high on a hill overlooking the harbor entrance to the south and St. Anna Bay to the north, it was fortified as a second line of defense in case the waterfront gave way. Today diners have replaced soldiers (see "Great Deals on Dining," above).

In addition, the **Curaçao Liqueur Distillery,** Landhuis Chobolobo, Saliña Arriba (☎ **599/9-461-3526**), offers a chance to visit and taste at Chobolobo, the

17th-century *landhuis* where the famous Curaçao liqueur is made. It's made by a secret formula handed down through generations. One of the rewards of a visit here is a free snifter of the liqueur, offered Monday to Friday from 8am to noon and 1 to 5pm.

On Schottegatweg West, northwest of Willemstad, past the oil refineries, lies the **Beth Haim Cemetery,** the oldest Caucasian burial site still in use in the western hemisphere. Meaning "House of Life," the cemetery was consecrated before 1659. On about 3 acres are some 2,500 graves. The carving on some of the 17th- and 18th-century tombstones is exceptional.

Landhuis Brievengat, Brienvengat (☎ **599/9-7378344**), gives visitors a chance to visit a Dutch version of an 18th-century West Indian plantation house. This stately building, in a scrub-dotted landscape on the eastern side of the island, contains a few antiques, high ceilings, and a gallery facing two entrance towers, said to have been used to imprison slaves. It's open daily from 9:15am to 12:15pm and 3 to 6pm; admission is $1.

Hato Caves, F. D. Rooseveltweg (☎ **599/9-8680379**), have been called "mystical." Every hour, professional local guides take visitors through this Curaçao world of stalagmites and stalactites, found in the highest limestone terrace of the island. Actually, they were once old coral reefs, which were formed when the ocean water fell and the landmass was lifted up over the years. Over thousands of years, limestone formations were created, some mirrored in an underground lake. After crossing the lake, you enter the "Cathedral," an underground cavern. The caves are open daily from 10am to 4pm. Admission is $6.25 for adults and $4.75 for children 4 to 11 (free for kids 3 and under).

The **Curaçao Seaquarium,** off Dr. Martin Luther King Boulevard at a site called Bapor Kibrá (☎ **599/9-4616666**), has more than 400 species of fish, crabs, anemones, sponges, and coral displayed and growing in a natural environment. Located a few minutes' walk along the rocky coast from the Princess Beach Resort & Casino, the Seaquarium is open daily from 8:30am to 6pm. Admission is $12.50 for adults, $7 for children 14 and under.

A special feature of the aquarium is a "shark and animal encounter," which costs $55 for divers or $30 for snorkelers. Divers, snorkelers, and experienced swimmers are able to feed, film, and photograph sharks, which are separated from them by a large window with feeding holes. In the Animal-Encounters section, swimmers are able to swim among stingrays, lobsters, tarpons, parrotfish, and other marine life, feeding and photographing these creatures in a controlled environment where safety is always a consideration. The Seaquarium is also home to Curaçao's only full-facility, palm-shaded, white-sand beach.

The *Seaworld Explorer* is a semi-submersible submarine that departs daily at 4:30pm on hour-long journeys into the deep. You're taken on a tour of submerged wrecks off the shores of Curaçao and are treated to close encounters of coral reefs with their rainbow-hued tropical fish. The *Explorer* has a barge top that submerges only 5 or so feet under the water, but the submerged section has wide glass windows allowing passengers underwater views, which can extend for 110 feet or so. Reservations must be made a day in advance by calling ☎ **599/9-5604892.** Adults pay $33; children 11 and under are charged $19.

SIGHTSEEING TOURS

Taber Tours, Dokweg (☎ **599/9-7376637**), offers several tours to points of interest on Curaçao. The tour through Willemstad, to the Curaçao Liqueur distillery, through the residential area and the Bloempot shopping center, and to the Curaçao Museum (admission fee included in the tour price) costs $12.50 for adults, $6.25 for children 11 and under.

The easiest way to go exploring is to take a 1¼-hour **trolley tour,** visiting the highlights of Willemstad. The open-sided cars, pulled by a silent "locomotive," make two tours each week—Monday at 11am and Wednesday at 4pm. The tour begins at Fort Amsterdam near the Queen Emma Pontoon Bridge. The cost is $15.90 for adults or $10.90 for children 2 to 12 (free for children 1 and under). Call ☎ **599/9-4628833** for more information.

7 Shopping

Curaçao is a shopper's paradise. Some 200 shops line the major shopping malls of such streets as Heerenstraat and Breedestraat. Right in the heart of Willemstad, the **Punda** shopping area is a 5-block district. Most stores are open Monday to Saturday from 8am to noon and 2 to 6pm (some, from 8am to 6pm). When cruise ships are in port, stores are also open for a few hours on Sunday and holidays. To avoid the cruise-ship crowds, do your shopping in the morning.

Look for good buys in French perfumes, Dutch Delft blue souvenirs, finely woven Italian silks, Japanese and German cameras, jewelry, silver, Swiss watches, linens, leather goods, liquor, and island-made rum and liqueurs, especially Curaçao liqueur, some of which has a distinctive blue color. The island is famous for its 5-pound "wheels" of Gouda or Edam cheese. It also sells wooden shoes, although we're not sure what you'd do with them. Some of its stores also stock some good buys in intricate lacework imported from Portugal, China, and everywhere between. If you're a street shopper and want something colorful, consider one of the wood carvings or flamboyant paintings from Haiti or the Dominican Republic. Both are hawked by street vendors at any of the main plazas.

Incidentally, Curaçao is not technically a free port, but import levies are low, so its prices are often inexpensive.

Every garment sold in **Bamali,** Breedestraat 2 (☎ **599/9-4612258**), is designed and, in many cases, crafted, by the store owners. Influenced largely by Indonesian patterns, the garments include V-necked cotton pullovers and linen shifts, often in batik prints. Most garments are for women; a few are for men.

Benetton, Madurostraat 4 (☎ **599/9-4614619**), has invaded Curaçao with all its many colors. In July you can stock up on winter wear, and in December make summer purchases. Some items are marked down by about 20% off stateside prices.

Bert Knubben Black Koral Art Studio, in the Princess Beach Resort & Casino, Dr. Martin Luther King Blvd. (☎ **599/9-465-2122**), is a name synonymous with craftsmanship and quality. Although collection of black coral has been made illegal by the Curaçao government, an exception was made for Bert, a diver who has been harvesting corals from the sea and fashioning them into the fine jewelry and objets d'art for more than 35 years. The jewelry is finished with 14-karat gold. Collectors avidly seek out this type of coral, not only because of the craftsmanship in the work, but because it's becoming increasingly rare and may one day not be offered for sale at all.

Boolchand's, Heerenstraat 4B, Punda (☎ **599/9-4612262**), in business since 1930, stands for reliability in electronic equipment. Electronics are a good buy in Curaçao because they're duty free.

Curaçao Creations, Schrijnwerkerstraat 14 (☎ **599/9-4624516**), lying off Breedestraat, is a showcase for authentic Curaçao handcrafts created within the walls of a 150-year-old storefront in Otrobanda. On a narrow side street, it is within easy walking distance of the Queen Emma Bridge, the bus stop, and the cruise-ship terminal. A workshop and souvenir outlet are combined so visitors can watch how their purchases are created. This is one of the few shops on the island to offer authentic, handmade Curaçao crafts; most stores sell imported items.

Kas di Arte Kursou, Breedestraat 126, Otrabanda (☎ 599/9-864-2516), lies in a 19th-century mansion in Otrobanda near the cruise-ship terminal. There are unique souvenirs such as one-of-a-kind T-shirts, all handmade by local artists. The gallery also has changing exhibits of paintings, plus a sculpture gallery.

Little Holland, Braedestraat 37, Punda (☎ 599/9-461-1768), is the main branch of a chain of stores with outlets in Bonaire and Aruba. Men might feel especially comfortable in this masculine-looking enclave that specializes in silk neckties, Nautica shorts and shirts, and most important of all, a sophisticated array of cigars. The chain maintains a second branch, where there's more focus on men's sportswear and neckties than on cigars, at Gomez Place #6, in Punda (☎ 599/9-4611413).

Penha & Sons, Heerenstraat 1 (☎ 599/9-4612266), in the oldest building in town, constructed in 1708, has a history dating to 1865. It has long been known for its perfumes and brand-name clothes.

Two final and rather offbeat shopping selections include **Landhuis Groot Santa Martha,** Santa Martha (☎ 599/9-864-1559), where craftspeople with disabilities fashion unusual handcrafts, some evoking those found in South America, and **Yoqui,** De Rouvilleweg 9A (☎ 599-9-462-7533), which sells an unusual collection of artifacts from the Incas and the Mayan Indians. Most of the objects are made of clay and onyx. There are also contemporary tribal paintings done on leather and bark.

8 Curaçao After Dark

Most nighttime action here spins around the island's **casinos:** the **Sonesta Beach Hotel & Casino,** Piscadera Bay (☎ 599/9-736-8800); **Holiday Beach Hotel & Casino,** Otrabanda, Pater Euwensweg 31 (☎ 599/9-462-5400), **Plaza Hotel & Casino,** Plaza Piar, in Willemstad (☎ 599/9-461-2500), **Porto Paseo Hotel & Casino,** De Rouvilleweg 47 in Willemstad (☎ 599/9-462-7878), and **Princess Beach Resort & Casino,** Martin Luther King Blvd. 8 (☎ 599/9-736-7888).

The **Emerald Casino** at the Sonesta is especially popular, designed to resemble an open-air courtyard. It features 143 slot machines, 6 blackjack tables, 2 roulette wheels, 2 Caribbean stud poker tables, 1 craps table, 1 baccarat table, and 1 mini-baccarat table. The casino at the **Princess Beach Hotel** is the liveliest on the island. These hotel gaming houses usually start their action at 2pm, and some of them remain open until 4am. The Princess Beach serves complimentary drinks.

The historic **Landhuis Brievengat** (see "Seeing the Sights," above), in addition to being a museum with island artifacts, is also the site of Wednesday, Friday, and Sunday night *rijsttafel* parties. They begin at 7:30pm, require an admission fee of $8 (which includes the first drink), and feature heaping portions of *rijsttafel* that begin at $16.50 each. Although the Landhuis itself is not directly connected with the dancing and drinking, there's a platform set up amid the flamboyant trees nearby, and two bands that alternate with one another to provide a happy ambience. Call before going, because the event, especially on Friday nights, is very popular.

The landlocked, flat, and somewhat dusty neighborhood of **Salinja** is now the nightlife capital of Curaçao. Among the best of its nightspots is **Blues,** in the Avila Beach Hotel, Penstraat 130 (☎ 599/9-4614377), a restaurant with a hopping bar. Live music, especially blues, is offered every Thursday and Saturday; no cover.

Studio 99, Lindbergweg, Salinja (☎ 599/9-465-5433), in a sprawling and much-renovated low-slung building set inland from the coast, is located in the heart of the Salinja district and is the tops on Curaçao. The jungle motif is enhanced with masses of coconut palms, a dance floor where rhythms seem to pulsate out of the floor, and a copious bar area where more than a usual number of drinks seem to be tinted blue. Although hours vary with the season and according to the number of foreign visitors on island, it's usually open Wednesday to Sunday from 9:30pm to 2am. The cover is $6 to $7.

Club Façade, Lindbergweg 8 (☎ 599/9-4614640), is located in the Salinja district, and is one of the most popular discos on the island. Spread over several different levels of a modern building, it has a huge bar and three dance floors, and is sometimes filled with balloons. There's live music daily. Open Wednesday to Sunday from 8pm to 3am. The cover is $5 to $10.

10 Dominica

Dominica's meager beaches aren't worth the effort to get here, but its landscape is. Untamed, unspoiled Dominica (pronounced Dom-in-*ee*-ka) is known for clear rivers and waterfalls, hot springs and boiling lakes. According to myth, it has 365 "rivers," one for each day of the year. This is the most rugged of the Caribbean islands, too. Nature lovers will experience a wild Caribbean setting, as well as the rural life that has largely disappeared on the more developed islands. This is, after all, one of the poorest and least developed islands in the Caribbean. Many of Dominica's citizens make a subsistence living from fishing or living off the land. Come here for lush tropical beauty, not fancy beach resorts.

The cost of living here is the lowest of all the West Indies islands. Imported items, of course, carry high price tags, but if you stick to local produce, you can eat well and inexpensively. Hotel rates are very low, but the rooms will be quite basic—spartan but clean.

Dominica, with a population of 71,000, lies in the eastern Caribbean, between Guadeloupe to the north and Martinique to the south. English is the official language, but a French patois is widely spoken. The Caribs, the indigenous people of the Caribbean, live as a community on the northeast of the island. The art and craft of traditional basketry is still practiced and is unique to today's Carib community, whose numbers have dwindled to 3,000.

The mountainous island is 29 miles long and 16 miles wide, with a total land area of 290 square miles, many of which have never been seen by explorers.

Because of the pristine coral reefs, dramatic drop-offs, and shipwrecks found in the crystal-clear waters with visibility of 100 feet plus, scuba diving is becoming increasingly popular, particularly off the west coast, site of Dominica's two dive operations.

Yearly rainfall varies from 50 inches (1.3m) along the dry west coast to as much as 350 inches (8.9m) in the tropical rain forests of the mountainous interior, where downpours are not uncommon.

Clothing is casual, including light summer wear for most of the year. However, take along walking shoes for those trips into the mountains and a sweater for cooler evenings. Bikinis and swimwear should not be worn on the streets of the capital city, in Roseau, or in the villages.

Dominica

Airport ✈ Beach ⚓ Mountain ▲▲

Morne Aux Diables
Hampstead Beach
Hodges Beach
L'Anse Noire
Woodford Hill Bay
Grand Bay
Portsmouth Calibishie
Picard Beach
Melville Hall Airport ✈
Woodford Hill

Caribbean Sea

Colihaut
Morne Diablotin
Marigot

CENTRAL FOREST RESERVE
Carib Indian Reservation

Salisbury

Atlantic Ocean

Mero
Layou River
St. Joseph

Morne Trois Pitons
Rosalie

Mahaut
Canefield Airport ✈
Laudat
Trafalgar
Goodwill
La Plaine

Roseau
Reigate *Boiling Lake*
Castle
Comfort
Pointe Michel

Soufrière

Soufrière Bay Beach ⚓
Scotts Head Beach ⚓
Grand Bay

Botanical Gardens National Park Office **8**
Cabrits National Park **1**
Carib Indian Reservation **3**
Emerald Pool Trail **4**
Morne Trois Pitons National Park **5**
Portsmouth **2**
Sulphur Springs **6**
Titou Gorge and Valley of Desolation **9**
Trafalgar Falls **7**

2-0194

0 ——— 5 Miles
0 ——— 5 Kilometers

1 Essentials

VISITOR INFORMATION

Before you go, you can contact the **Dominica Tourist Office** at 10 E. 21st St., Suite 600, New York, NY 10010 (☎ **212/475-7542**).

In England, contact the Office of the Dominica High Commission London, 1 Collingham Gardens, London SW5 0HW (☎ **020/7370-5194**).

The official Web site is **www.dominica.dm**.

On the island, the **Dominica Tourist Information Office** is on the Old Market Plaza, Roseau, with administrative offices at the National Development Corporation offices, Valley Road (☎ **767/448-2186**). It's open on Monday 8am to 5pm and Tuesday to Friday 8am to 4pm.

Also, there are information bureaus at Melville Hall Airport (☎ **767/445-7051**) and Canefield Airport (☎ **767/449-1242**).

GETTING THERE

BY PLANE There are two airports on Dominica, neither of which is large enough to handle a jet; therefore, there are no direct flights from North America. The **Melville Hall Airport** (☎ **767/445-7100**) is on the northeastern coast, almost diagonally across the island from the capital, Roseau, which is on the southwestern coast. Should you land at Melville Hall, there's a 1½-hour taxi ride into Roseau, a tour across the island through the forest and coastal villages. The fare from Melville Hall to Roseau is

$18 per person, and drivers have the right to gather up at least four passengers in their cabs. Private use of a taxi could cost $50.

The newer **Canefield Airport** (☎ 767/449-1199) is about a 15-minute taxi ride to the north of Roseau. The 2,000-foot airstrip accommodates smaller planes than those that can land at Melville Hall. From here, the typical taxi fare into town is $15. There's also a public bus (with an *H* that precedes the number on the license plate) which charges $2 per person. The buses come every 20 minutes and hold between 15 and 18 passengers.

For many Americans, the easiest way to reach Dominica is to take the daily **American Eagle** (☎ 800/433-7300) flight from San Juan. From Thursday to Sunday there is also a second flight. From Antigua, you can board one of the five daily **LIAT** (☎ 800/468-0482 in the U.S. and Canada, or 767/448-2422) flights to Dominica. Another possibility would be to fly via St. Maarten (see "Essentials" in chapter 22). From there, LIAT offers one nonstop flight daily and two other daily flights with intermediary stops.

It's also possible to fly to Guadeloupe (see "Getting There" in chapter 13) and make a connection to Dominica on **Air Guadeloupe** (☎ 767/448-2181). This airline has two flights a day to Dominica except on Sunday, when there is no morning flight (flying time is 30 minutes).

If you're in Fort-de-France on Martinique, you can take a LIAT flight to Dominica.

Two minor airlines also serve Dominica: **Helen Air** (☎ 767/448-2181) flies in from Barbados and St. Lucia, arriving two times a day at both the Canefield and Melville Hall airports; and **Cardinal Airlines** (☎ 767/449-0600) wings in from the islands of Antigua, Barbados, and Dutch St. Maarten, arriving at Canefield daily.

BY BOAT   The *Caribbean Express* (☎ 596/63-12-11, or 767/448-2181 on Dominica), sailing from the French West Indies, runs between Guadeloupe in the north to Martinique in the south, and Dominica is a port of call along the way. Call for exact schedules. Departures are Friday to Wednesday.

In addition, car-ferries sail from Pointe-à-Pitre on Martinique to Roseau five to seven times a week, depending on demand. For information about schedules, contact **White Church Travel,** 5 Great Marlborough St. in Roseau (☎ 767/448-2181). A one-way fare costs EC$224.50 ($83.05).

GETTING AROUND

Many of the places to stay are found in or very close by Roseau, the capital.

BY TAXI   At either the Melville Hall or Canefield Airports, you can rent a taxi. Prices are regulated by the government (airport fares are covered under "Getting There," above). If you want to see the island by taxi, rates are about $18 per car for each hour of touring, and as many as four passengers can go along at the same time.

BY RENTAL CAR   If you rent a car, a fee of EC$30 ($11.10) is charged to obtain a driver's license, which is available at the airports. There are 310 miles of newly paved roads, and only in a few areas is a four-wheel-drive necessary. *Driving is on the left.*

Most U.S. vacationers reserve their car in advance from the local representative of **Avis,** 4 High St. in Roseau (☎ 800/331-1212 or 767/448-2481), although we've found the service here poor.

There are also a handful of small, usually family-owned car-rental companies, the condition and price of whose vehicles vary widely. Their ranks include **Valley Rent-a-Car,** Goodwill Road in Roseau (☎ 767/448-3233); **Wide Range,** 79 Bath Rd., Roseau (☎ 767/448-2198); and **Best Deal Car Rental,** 15 Hanover St. in Roseau (☎ 767/449-9204).

BY MINIBUS   The public transportation system consists of private minibus service between Roseau and the rest of Dominica. These minibuses, each of which is painted and sometimes garishly decorated according to the tastes of their individual owners, are filled mainly with schoolchildren, workers, and country people who need to come into Roseau. They're identified by the letter *H* preceding their license number. Taxis may be a more reliable means of transport for visitors, but there are hotels at which buses call during the course of the day. Fares range from $1.25 to $3.35.

SPECIAL EVENTS

National Day celebrations on November 3 commemorate Columbus's discovery of Dominica in 1493 and its independence in 1978. Cultural celebrations of the island's traditional dance, music, song, and storytelling begin in mid-October and continue to Community Day, November 4, when people undertake community-based projects.

Fast Facts: Dominica

Banking Hours   Banks are open Monday to Thursday 8am to 3pm and on Friday 8am to 5pm.

Currency   Dominica uses the Eastern Caribbean dollar (EC$), worth about EC$2.60 to $1 U.S. *Prices in this chapter are given in U.S. dollars unless otherwise indicated.*

Customs   Dominica is lenient, allowing you to bring in personal and household effects, plus 200 cigarettes, 50 cigars, and 40 ounces of liquor or wine per person.

Documents   To enter, U.S. and Canadian citizens must have proof of citizenship, such as a passport or birth certificate along with a photo ID (bring the passport). In addition, an ongoing or return ticket must be shown. British visitors should have a valid passport.

Drugstores   The island's best-stocked drugstore is **Jolly's Pharmacy,** with two branches in Roseau at 37 Great George St., and at 12 King George V St. Both branches share the same phone number and hours (☎ **767/448-3388**). They're open Monday to Thursday from 8am to 4:30pm, Friday from 8am to 5pm, and Saturday from 8am to 1:30pm. They also have a 24-hour prescription service available at the same number for after-hours needs.

Electricity   The electricity is 220–240 volts AC (50 cycles), so both adapters and transformers are necessary for North American appliances. It's advisable to take a flashlight with you to Dominica, in case of power outages.

Emergencies   Dial ☎ **999** to reach the police, report a fire, or summon an ambulance.

Hospitals   The island hospital is **Princess Margaret Hospital,** Federation Drive, Goodwill (☎ **767/448-2231**). However, those with serious medical complications may want to forgo a visit to Dominica, as island medical facilities are often inadequate.

Language   English is the official language. Locals often speak a Creole-French patois.

Safety   Although crime is rare here, you should still safeguard your valuables. Never leave them unattended on the beach or left alone in a locked car.

Taxes   A 10% government room tax is added to every hotel accommodation bill, and a 3% tax is tacked onto the price of alcoholic drinks and food items. Anyone who remains on Dominica for more than 24 hours must pay a $12 (U.S.) departure tax.

Telephone & Fax   Dominica maintains phone, telegraph, teletype, Telex, and fax connections with the rest of the world. International direct dialing (IDD) is available, as well as U.S. direct service through AT&T. To call Dominica from another island within the Caribbean, just dial **767,** plus the seven-digit local number.

Time   Dominica is on Atlantic standard time, 1 hour ahead of eastern standard time in the United States. Dominica does not observe daylight saving time, so when the United States changes to daylight time, clocks in Dominica and the U.S. east coast tell the same time.

Tipping   Most hotels and restaurants add a 10% service charge to all bills. Where this charge has not been included, tipping is up to you.

Water   The water is drinkable from the taps and in the high mountain country. Pollution is hardly a problem here.

Weather   Daytime temperatures average between 70°F and 85°F (21°C and 29.4°C). Nights are much cooler, especially in the mountains. The rainy season is June to October, when there can be warnings of hurricane activity. Regrettably, Dominica lies in the "hurricane path," and fierce storms have taken their toll on the island over the years.

2 Accommodations You Can Afford

Anchorage Hotel. Castle Comfort (P.O. Box 34), Roseau, Dominica, W.I. ☎ **767/448-2638.** Fax 767/448-5680. E-mail: anchorage@mail.tod.dm. 32 units. A/C TV TEL. Year-round $86–$103 single; $120–$150 double. MAP (breakfast and dinner) $35 per person extra. Children 11 and under granted 50% reductions. AE, DC, DISC, MC, V.

Recently renovated, the Anchorage is at Castle Comfort, ½ mile south of Roseau. For the active traveler, there is no finer choice, as scuba diving, whale-watching, hiking, fishing, and bird-sighting are given great emphasis here. The Armour family provides small rooms with two double-beds and a shower or bathtub, plus a balcony overlooking a pool. The best rooms open onto views of the Caribbean Sea and contain two double-beds with firm mattresses. The other rooms are more standardized with comfortable twin beds or one double. Recent renovations have much improved this property, and bathrooms are adequate enough with their showers and decent shelf space. Try to see which room you're getting before checking in. In spite of its location at the shore, there's little or no sandy beach available, so guests spend their days around the pool. However, the hotel has its own jetty, you can swim off a pebble beach, and there's a squash court.

The hotel's French and Caribbean cuisine is simple, with an emphasis on fresh fish and vegetables. Nonresidents must ask permission to use the swimming pool, and they can also visit for meals. A West Indian band plays music twice a week for dancing. On Thursday night, there's a buffet accompanied by a live band. Laundry, room service, and baby-sitting are provided.

Floral Gardens. Concord Village (P.O. Box 192), Roseau, Dominica, W.I. ☎ **767/445-7636.** Fax 767/445-7333. 15 units. Year-round $45 single; $60 double; $80 apt. for 2 with kitchenette. AE, MC, V.

Everything about the place pays homage to the surrounding scenic jungles. Situated near the edge of the Carib Indian reservation adjacent to the Layou River, it appeals to hikers, naturalists, birders, and students of Indian culture. It's quietly proud of its allure as a funky, nonstandard hotel, quite different from its larger and more anonymous competitors. The older part is designed vaguely like a tropical version of a Swiss chalet, with latticed windows and flowerboxes. The bedrooms in the newer section are preferable to those in the original house because they're larger, not as noisy, and get more sunlight. Furnishings, including beds with well-worn mattresses, are utterly basic, with small showers that may or may not have hot water, plus rather thin towels. An on-site restaurant serves simple West Indian cuisine to residents and group tours, which sometimes stop in as part of guided jaunts through Dominica. Your host is O. J. Seraphin, a former prime minister. He is ably assisted by his wife, Lily, and as a team they are the most welcoming and dynamic hosts on the island.

✪ **Hummingbird Inn.** Morne Daniel (P.O. Box 1901), Roseau, Dominica, W.I. ☎ or fax **767/449-1042.** www.lexposure.com/dca/hummingbird. E-mail: hummingbird@ cwdom. dm. 10 units. Winter $65 single or double; $110 suite. Off-season $55 single or double; $80–$92 suite. Extra person $20; children 11 and under stay free in parents' room. MAP $20 per person extra. AE, DC, DISC, MC, V.

A short drive from Roseau and the Canefield Airport and a 2-minute walk to the beach, this hilltop retreat is a great little bargain. Opening onto panoramic views, the rooms are in two bungalows. Each has louvered windows and doors to capture the breezes in lieu of air-conditioning. Ceiling fans hum day and night, and you can also retreat to terraces with hammocks. Each accommodation has bedside tables and reading lamps (not always a guarantee on Dominica). The handmade quilts on the beds with excellent mattresses add a homey touch. One four-poster bed, a mammoth wooden affair, is 250 years old. Bathrooms are small, but beautifully maintained. This is a friendly, family-style place, and there are lovely gardens with exotic plants that attract both hummingbirds and iguanas. The local cook is one of the best on the island, and she'll pack a picnic lunch for you. The restaurant is open to nonguests without a reservation. Many diners come here to sample "mountain chicken" (frog).

✪ **Papillote Wilderness Retreat.** Trafalgar Falls Road (P.O. Box 2287), Roseau, Dominica, W.I. ☎ **767/448-2287.** Fax 767/448-2285. www.papillote.dm. E-mail: papillote@ cwdom. dm. 7 units. Year-round $70 single; $85 double; $90 suite; $180 2-bedroom cottage for 4. MAP $35 per person extra. AE, MC, V. Closed Aug 15–Oct 15.

This hotel and restaurant is run by the Jean-Baptistes: Cuthbert, who handles the restaurant, and his wife, Anne Grey, who was a marine scientist. Their place, 4 miles east of Roseau, stands right in the middle of Papillote Forest, at the foothills of Morne Macaque. In this remote setting, they have created a unique rain-forest resort; you can lead an Adam-and-Eve life here, surrounded by exotic fruits, flowers, and herb gardens. The small rooms have a rustic, log-cabin atmosphere. Bedrooms are decorated in a tropical style with local crafts and artifacts, but they are often dark because of the forest. Beds are comfortable though mattresses are on the old side, and bathrooms are just adequate with thin towels. Laundry and room service are available.

Don't expect constantly sunny weather, since this part of the jungle is known for its downpours; however, the rain keeps the orchids, begonias, and brilliantly colored bromeliads lush. The 12 acres of sloping and forested land are pierced with a labyrinth of stone walls and trails, beside which flows a network of freshwater streams, a few of which come from hot mineral springs. Natural hot mineral baths are available, and you'll be directed to a secluded waterfall where you can swim in the river. The

Jean-Baptistes also run a boutique in which they sell Dominican products, including appliquéd quilts made by local artisans. Even if you don't stay here, it's an experience to dine on the thatch-roofed terrace.

WORTH A SPLURGE

Castle Comfort Lodge. Castle Comfort (P.O. Box 2253), Roseau, Dominica, W.I. ☎ **800/ 544-7631** in the U.S., or 767/448-2188. Fax 767/448-6088. 15 units. A/C. Year-round $80–$85 single; $160 double. Rates include half-board. Dive packages available. AE, MC, V.

No one at this diving lodge seems to mind that the setting doesn't include easy access to a sandy beach. Instead, you'll be able to easily go on dives off the calm, rock-fringed waters of Dominica's southwestern leeward shore. The lodge itself is a simple, rustic enclave devoted to enjoying the beauties both below and above the water's surface. It's centered around an open-air living and dining area, and a family-style living room where guests gather every evening to watch superb sunsets. The well-scrubbed accommodations have white walls, wooden tables, chairs, and headboards crowning good beds. The larger and more desirable accommodations open onto the front and are better appointed. Back rooms tend to be small. Mattresses are replaced as needed, and overall the maintenance is rather good, as reflected by the tidily kept and efficiently arranged bathrooms with medium-size towels. The dive operation here is certified by both NAUI and PADI, and cocktail cruises are offered as part of the entertainment. Derek, incidentally, is one of the leading divemasters on Dominica.

Picard Beach Cottage Resort. Picard Beach, Portsmouth, Dominica, W.I. ☎ **767/445-5142.** Fax 767/445-5599. 8 cottages. TEL. Winter $100–$120 cottage for 1; $120–$140 cottage for 2. Off-season 50% reductions. Children 12 and under stay free in parents' room. MAP (breakfast and dinner) $30 per person extra. AE, MC, V.

This is the best deal on the island if you want to stay in a cozy West Indian cottage. Here you'll find eight Dominican-style, stained-wood cottages, built in the 18th century, set on landscaped grounds opening on the beach. Each small building has a veranda, kitchenette, ceiling fan, and phone. There's space in the living and dining area for two single beds. The decor is plain motel style, with flowery bed linens and good mattresses. Bathrooms are small but well kept with a shower (no tub). There's a pool and a restaurant, plus such services as 24-hour security. A dive shop is about a 5-minute walk away. This is a good stop as you explore the northern part of the island.

☉ **Zandoli Inn.** Roche Cassee, Stowe (P.O. Box 2099), Dominica, W.I. ☎ **767/446-3161.** Fax 767/446-3344. www.zandoli.com. E-mail: zandoli@cwdom.dm. 5 units. Year-round $115 single, $125 double. Extra person $40. AE, MC, V.

On the most southerly coast of the island, a 25-minute drive from Roseau, this country inn opened in 1998 and immediately became a hit with discerning guests who want maximum comfort but don't want to pay a lot of money for it. The hamlet of Stowe itself offers the rugged geography and abundant flora for which Dominica is known. The inn is nestled 80 feet above the sea in a secluded 6-acre forest garden. From the balconies and dining terrace, there are panoramas in all directions. Footpaths riddle the property, inviting hikes. The accommodations are spacious, with good beds and balconies opening onto views of either the coastline or the mountains. Each room has a small private bathroom with solar-generated hot water showers, plus a rack of good towels. There are mosquito nets and fans in each room, but no air conditioning, telephone, radio, or TV. Other features include a shaded plunge pool area with a sea view. There's even a star-gazing terrace. As there are a fair number of stairs, it is not wheelchair accessible, nor is it suitable for children under 12. The food is excellent, relying on local ingredients whenever possible.

3 Great Deals on Dining

It's customary to eat at your hotel, although Dominica has a string of independent restaurants. Dress is casual. If you're going out in the evening, always call to make sure your dining choice is actually open, and also that you have proper transportation there and back.

The Almond Tree. In the Castaways Beach Hotel, Mero. ☎ **767/449-6244.** Main courses EC$25–EC$75 ($9.25–$27.75) AE, MC, V. Daily seatings at noon, 2pm, and 6:30pm. ÉCREOLE.

If you're touring north along the coast, consider stopping in for a meal at the Castaways, 11 miles north of Roseau. Nonguests are welcome to eat in the hotel dining room with its waterfront setting. Guests dress in casual resortwear, and enjoy the hospitality of the staff. Here you get the standard cuisine for which Dominica is known, including *crapaud,* or mountain chicken. You can also get *lambi* (conch), as well as island crab mixed with a savory Creole stuffing. Fish and pork dishes are also served. All are garnished with the fruits and vegetables of Dominica's rich soil, including passion fruit. Before dining, try a rum punch in the lounge or beach bar. The service is very laid-back, and you can find better versions of many of these Creole dishes elsewhere, but if you're on this part of the island, a meal here should be generally satisfying.

Calaloo Restaurant. 66 King George V St. ☎ **767/448-3386.** Reservations recommended. Main courses EC$30–EC$65 ($11.10–$24.05); lunch EC$12–EC$45 ($4.45–$16.65). AE, DISC, MC, V. Mon–Sat 8am–10pm, Sun 8am–9pm. WEST INDIAN.

When you enter this restaurant, you'll be greeted by a collection of local art that adorns the walls, including straw mats, paintings, and maps of the route Christopher Columbus used when he sailed the Caribbean. Touted as one of the few remaining original Caribbean restaurants in the region, it offers patrons a taste of the island. Although the dinner prices include three courses, lunch is the best time to find a real bargain. The Calaloo's forte is the mountain chicken (frogs' legs) served in a variety of ways including fried, Creole style, and in a garlic-butter sauce. The menu also features calaloo soup, curried conch, and chicken, baked or fried. For a finale, try one of the homemade desserts.

Floral Gardens Restaurant. In the Floral Gardens Hotel, Concord Rd. ☎ **767/445-7636.** Reservations recommended. Main courses EC$20–EC$45 ($7.40–$16.70). AE, MC, V. Daily 7am–11pm. WEST INDIAN.

Located at the Floral Gardens Hotel about 10 miles from the Melville Hall Airport, this simple eatery specializes in Creole cuisine. For starters, try the pumpkin accras (grated pumpkin mixed with herbs and spices, then deep-fried and served with a pepper sauce) or the calaloo soup (puréed dasheen leaves seasoned with herbs, spices, coconut cream, and bits of crayfish). The main courses include chicken, mountain goat, mutton, rabbit, and seafood such as lobster, codfish, and crab. Save room for dessert such as the banana flambé lit up in Dominica's local rum.

✪ **Forest Bistro.** Soufrière. ☎ **767/448-7104.** Reservations essential. Main courses EC$25–EC$35 ($9.25–$12.95). Daily 11am–9pm. No credit cards. CARIBBEAN.

This bistro is aptly named. It's your best bet if you're hiking, diving, or driving in the Soufrière area of Dominica. Your hosts, Andre and Joyce Charles, extend a warm welcome. On the southwestern coast of Dominica, the bistro is set in a lush tropical section of the island, cozy and secluded, with cliffs as a backdrop and a panoramic vista of the Caribbean from the tables. Cows roam among the acres of lime trees, and the whole place has such a bucolic setting you'd want to go here even if the food wasn't good. But the cuisine is excellent, well prepared, and made whenever possible with the freshest of ingredients, often grown by Andre and Joyce. The restaurant on this 5-acre dairy farm is actually the top floors of the Charles' home. Joyce is a top-notch chef, having worked at some of the island's finest restaurants. Her talent is particularly obvious in her fresh fish dishes. The farm also provides an endless source of refreshing drinks, including lime squash, passion fruit, grapefruit, and fresh coconut water. At lunch you can order some of the island's most delightful soups, either made with peas, pumpkin, callaloo, or papaya. Stick to the fish unless you're a total vegetarian; then you might opt for one of the delicious Creole-style vegetarian dishes such as a savory eggplant.

La Guinguette. Calibishie. ☎ **767/445-7783.** Reservations recommended. Main courses EC$30–EC$60 ($11.10–$22.20). DISC, MC, V. Daily 8am–10pm. FRENCH/CRÉOLE.

Annick Giraud, the owner of this likable restaurant, was born in France and remains a Francophile. Accordingly, the décor here is tastefully outfitted in her national colors of blue, white, and red. You'll find it within a slightly battered wood-sided house on the main street of the hamlet of Calibishie, beside the road that runs between Portsmouth and Marigot. Menu items include both traditional French and West Indian specialties that include calaloo soup, quiche, fish sautéed in wine sauce, crayfish, boeuf bourguignonne, jumbo shrimp sautéed in garlic with Antillean spices, frog's legs (mountain chicken), and a delectable version of chocolate mousse. There's a lot of both French and Caribbean charm here.

Ocean Terrace. In the Anchorage Hotel, Victoria St. ☎ **767/448-2638.** Reservations recommended. Burgers, pastas, soups, and sandwiches EC$6–EC$50 ($2.20–$18.50); 3-course fixed-price meal EC$55 ($20.40). AE, DC, DISC, MC, V. Daily 7am–2:30pm and 7–9:30pm. INTERNATIONAL.

The menu here offers a marriage between international fare and local ingredients. The restaurant dining room serves lunch and dinner as a three-course meal, while a la carte items can be found in the bar downstairs. If you're in the mood to splurge a little, the fixed-price menu includes starters such as black-eyed pea and coconut soup, pâté of chicken and parsley served with a curried-cucumber vinaigrette, and a salad of local fruits and vegetables with fried shrimp in a garlic-wine sauce. For the main course, the selection includes chicken kebabs served with a fresh-fruit chutney and gingered barbecued lamb. Included in the fixed-price menu are a variety of desserts (fresh-fruit soups, served cold, and crêpes, served hot with vanilla ice cream). For a less-expensive meal, it's best to try the bar menu—burgers, sandwiches, and pastas. Also a good bargain here are the breakfasts, which range from EC$3 to EC$27 ($1.10 to $10). You can have as little as a bowl of fresh local fruit or a fuller meal with eggs, bacon, and toast. On Thursday evening a fixed-price barbecue, all you can eat, is featured for EC$50 ($18.50).

✪ **Papillote Wilderness Retreat.** Trafalgar Falls Rd. ☎ **767/448-2287.** Reservations recommended for lunch, required for dinner. Main courses EC$25–EC$60 ($9.25–$22.20). AE, DISC, MC, V. Daily noon–2pm and 7:30–8:30pm. CREOLE/CARIBBEAN.

Previously recommended for its lodgings, the Papillote is an alluring "Garden of Eden" type of restaurant. Even if you're not staying here, come by taxi for lunch—it's only

4 miles east of Roseau. Amid nature trails laced with exotic flowers, century-old trees, and filtered sunlight, you dine overlooking rivers and mountains. The array of healthful food includes flying fish and truly delectable river shrimp known as *bookh*. Frogs legs inevitably appear, as does kingfish. Breadfruit or dasheen puffs merit a try if you've never ordered them, and tropical salads are flavor filled. Favorite dishes here include "the seafood symphony" and "chicken rain forest" (sautéed with orange, papaya, and banana, and wrapped in a banana leaf). Sturdy walking shoes and a bathing suit are often called for. Near the dining terrace is a Jacuzzi-size pool, which is constantly filled with the mineral-rich waters of a hot spring.

✪ **Pearl's Cuisine.** 50 King George V St., Rouseau. ☎ **767/448-8707.** Lunch EC$5–EC$30 ($1.85–$11.10), dinner EC$20–EC$60 ($7.40–$22.20). AE, DC, MC, V. Daily 9am–9pm. CARIBBEAN.

In this restored Creole house in the capital city, Chef Pearl is the hearty empress, and enjoys a certain celebrity in town for her island delicacies. Come here for a true taste of Dominica likely to be unequaled anywhere else. In her antique wooden building with a veranda, she serves up savory fare. Begin with one of her tropical fruit juices, then go on to sample mountain chicken (frogs' legs) or perhaps freshly caught cray-fish. Whenever lobster is available, it's served at dinner any way you want it. She also makes some mean pork chops, and her curried goat will make a man of you, even if you're a woman. Try her rice and spareribs or her codfish and plantains if you want to see what delights the local patronage. What's Pearl's favorite dish? Souse or pickled pigs' feet.

World of Food Restaurant and Bar. In Vena's Hotel, 48 Cork St. ☎ **767/448-3286.** Main courses EC$28–EC$58 ($10.35–$21.45). No credit cards. Daily 7:30am–10:30pm. CREOLE.

If you want to enter this dining room without passing through Vena's Hotel (really a guest house; see "Accommodations You Can Afford," above), come in off Field's Lane. In the 1930s, the garden containing this restaurant belonged to a well-known female novelist, Jean Rhys. Today it's the patio for one of the most charming Creole restaurants in Roseau. Some say that its owner, Vena McDougal, is the best Creole cook in town. You can have a drink at the stone-walled building at the far end of the garden if you want, but many guests select one of the tables in the shadow of a large mango tree. Specialties include steamed fish or fish steak, curried goat, chicken-filled rôti, black pudding, breadfruit puffs, conch, and tee-tee-ree (fried fish cakes). She also makes the best rum punches on the island.

GOOD LUNCH SPOTS

If you're shopping or sightseeing in the capital and you'd like a lunch, you'll find the best selection of sandwiches at **The Blue Max Café,** upstairs over the Prevo Cinemall at Kennedy Avenue (☎ **767/449-8907**). Max serves the best stuffed sandwiches around, especially his honey ham and his pastrami. The sandwich specialty is made with flying fish, and it comes with Creole sauce, vegetables, and hot banana ring peppers. Max's large bar is one of the most popular in town, especially at happy hour. On weekends live music keeps the place jumping. The cafe is also a great place to visit even if you're seeking only a cappuccino or espresso. There is also a selection of delicious desserts, including a fat-free double chocolate cheesecake.

Another local dive worth knowing about when you're out touring the island is **Miranda's Corner,** Mount Joy, Springfield (☎ **767/449-2509**). Miranda serves three meals a day, but you can also drop in just for a snack or a drink. Her place is found as you drive toward Pont Cassee beyond Springfield Plantation. It enjoys a lush setting in the midst of ginger lilies, poinsettias, and anthuriums, plus several homesteads devoted to growing fresh vegetables. It's just as popular as a rum shop and bar as it is as a cafe for dining. What is she likely to serve? "Whatever I feel like," Miranda says. That would mean curried goat or fresh fish, and one of her delectable vegetable soups. She even serves fresh shrimp from her pond. Her rôtis are among the island's best, loaded with flavor. As for prices, she claims, "I just make them up every day, and nobody has ever said I overcharge."

4 Hitting the Beaches

If you demand great beaches as part of your Caribbean vacation, don't come here, for Dominica has some of the worst beaches in the Caribbean. Most of the island's beaches are rocky with gray-black volcanic sand. Some beaches, even though they don't have great sand or shade, nevertheless are still good for diving or snorkeling in the turquoise waters surrounding the island.

The best beach on the island lies on the northwest coast. Here **Picard Beach** stretches for about 2 miles, a strip of grayish sand with palm trees as a backdrop. It is ideal for snorkeling or windsurfing, but not much else. Guests can drop in for food and drink at the Picard Beach Cottage Resort or the Coconut Beach Hotel, both of which lie along this beach.

On the northeast coast, a quartet of beaches are among the island's most beautiful, although neither is ideal for swimming. They are **L'Anse Noire, Hodges Beach, Woodford Hill Bay,** and **Hampstead Beach.** Divers and snorkelers seek them out, although at times their turbulent waters make the pursuit of either of those sports less than ideal. The waters off the coasts of all of these beaches have strong currents, so be duly warned. That island you can see in the distance is Marie Galante, which is an off-shore island of Guadeloupe.

The southwest coast also has some beaches, but the sand here is black and studded with rocks. Nonetheless, snorkelers and scuba divers flock to **Soufrière Bay Beach** and **Scotts Head Beach.** The snorkeling and diving here are excellent because of the gin-clear waters, the sudden drop-offs, and the underwater walls which are stunning. At one point along the coast volcanic vents puff steam into the sea. Divers claim it's like swimming in champagne, and locals have dubbed the spot "Champagne."

Near the hamlet of La Plaine, on the southwest coast, is one final beach, **Bout Sable Bay.** Again, it's not suitable for swimming, but it is a dramatic beach nonetheless, set against towering chalky red cliffs overlooking the turbulent Atlantic. Waters are too churned up for safe swimming.

5 Sports & Outdoor Pursuits

HIKING Wild and untamed Dominica offers very experienced and physically fit hikers some of the most bizarre geological oddities in the Caribbean. Sights include scalding lava covered with a hot, thin, and not-very-stable crust; a boiling lake where mountain streams turn to vapor as they come into contact with super-heated volcanic fissures; and a barren wasteland known as the "Valley of Desolation."

All these attractions are in the 17,000 heavily-forested acres of the ✪ **Morne Trois Pitons National Park,** in the island's south-central region (see "Seeing the Sights," below). You should go with a guide—they're in plentiful supply, waiting for your business in the village of Laudat. Or go to the office of the ✪ **Dominica National**

Park, in the Botanical Gardens in Roseau (☎ **767/448-2401**), or to the Dominica Tourist Board (see "Essentials," above).

Few markers appear en route, but the trek, which includes a real assortment of geological oddities, stretches 6 miles in both directions from Laudat to the Boiling Lake. Hikers bring their lunch and walk cautiously, particularly in districts peppered with bubbling hot springs. Regardless of where you turn, you'll run into streams and waterfalls, the inevitable result of an island whose mountaintops receive up to 400 inches of rainfall a year. Winds on the summits are strong enough to have pushed one recreational climber to her death several years ago, so be careful. Ferns, orchids, trees, and epiphytes create a tangle of underbrush; insect, bird, and reptilian life is profuse.

During your trek, pay a visit to the **Titou Gorge,** a deep and very narrow ravine whose depths were created as lava floes cooled and contracted. On the way there might be views of rare Sisserou and Jacquot parrots, monkeys, and vines whose growth seems to increase visibly on an hourly basis. The hill treks of Dominica have been described as "sometimes easy, sometimes hellish," and if it should happen to rain during your climb (and it rains very frequently on Dominica), your path is likely to become very slippery. But botanists and geologists agree with the assessment of experienced hikers, that climbs through the jungles of Dominica are the most rewarding in the Caribbean.

Locals warn that to proceed along the island's badly marked trails into areas that can be physically treacherous is not a good idea, and climbing alone or even in pairs is not advisable. Forestry officials recommend **Ken's Hinterland Adventure Tours & Taxi Service,** 10A Old St., in Roseau (☎ **767/448-4850**). Depending on their destination and the attractions they feature, treks cost $25 to $50 per person for up to 4 participants and require 4 to 8 hours round-trip. Transportation from Roseau in a minivan to the starting point of your hill climb is usually included in the price.

SCUBA DIVING   Diving holidays in Dominica are becoming more and more popular. The underwater terrain is spectacular. Most of the diving is on the southwestern end of the island, with its dramatic drop-offs, walls, and pinnacles. These volcanic formations are interwoven with cuts, arches, ledges, and overhangs. A myriad of sponges, gorgonians, and corals cloak these ledges. An abundance of invertebrates, reef school fish, and unusual sea creatures such as sea horses, frog-fish, batfish, and flying gunards attract the underwater photographer.

You can discover diving on the island with **Dive Dominica,** in the Castle Comfort Diving Lodge (P.O. Box 2253, Roseau Castle Comfort, Dominica, W.I.; ☎ **767/448-2188**). Open-water certification (both NAUI and PADI) instruction is given. Two diving catamarans (45- and 33-feet long, respectively), plus a handful of other, smaller boats that are used for groups of divers, get you to the dive sites in relative comfort. The dive outfit is closely linked to its on-site hotel, a 15-room lodge where at least 90% of the clientele check in as part of the outfit's dive packages. A 7-night dive package, double occupancy, where breakfasts and dinners are included as part of the price, along with five two-tank dives and one night dive, begins at $949 per person. A single tank dive goes for $45, a two-tank dive for $75, with a night dive costing $50. All rooms in the lodge are air-conditioned, and about half have TV and a telephone. On the premises is a bar (for residents and their guests only) and a Jacuzzi.

Divers from all over the world patronize the **Dive Centre,** at the Anchorage Hotel in Castle Comfort (☎ **767/448-2638**). A fully qualified PADI and NAUI staff awaits divers there. A single-tank dive costs $50; a double-tank dive, $65; and a one-tank night dive, $55. A unique whale and dolphin watch from 2pm to sunset is a popular feature, where all participants are actively engaged in trying to sight the faraway

Cheap Thrills: What to See & Do for Free (Well, Almost) on Dominica

- **Explore Jungle Jim Country.** In the Morne Trois Pitons National Park, you can explore one of the last island-based rain forests in the world. This lush, majestic blanket supports thousands of plants and animals. Precious and endangered wildlife are found in the area, which is the last refuge of the Sisserou or Imperial Parrot. There are more than 160 other bird species living in the rain forest as well, particularly in the forested region of Syndicate in the foothills of Morne Diabolotin. The trail to the summit of the mountain also starts in Syndicate. The tour to the top takes 4 to 6 hours. If you'd like a close encounter with the rain forest, consider making the Floral Gardens hotel your choice of accommodations (see page 210).

- **Take a River Dip.** Almost everywhere you go on the island you come across a river. The best places for swimming are under a waterfall, and there are dozens of them on the island. Almost all waterfalls have a refreshing pond at the base of them, ideal for a dip. The best places for a swim on the west coast are the Picard and Machoucherie Rivers. The finest spot on the east coast is White River, near the village of La Plaine. The source for this river is a boiling lake. For a lazy day on the river, float and clamber down the Layou River, which starts in the settlement of Belles in the rain forest and works its way down through the Layou flats to the west coast.

- **Kayak Off the Beaten Path.** There is no greater kayaking adventure in all the Caribbean than here in Dominica. It needn't cost a lot of money, either. Two persons can rent a kayak for a half-day, dividing the cost between them for only $12.50 each for a unique adventure around the rivers and coastline of the lushest island in the West Indies. **Nature Island Dive** in Roseau (☎ 767/449-8181) gives the best advice and offers rentals. You can combine bird watching, swimming, and snorkeling as you glide along. Consider Soufrière Bay, a marine reserve in southwest Dominica. You can frolic in the bubbling waters at Champagne near Pt. Michel, or follow the wall and be stunned by the coral reefs at Scotts Head. Off the west coast you can

plumes of pods of whales, herds of dolphins, and even schools of flying fish. The price for a 3½-hour experience of communal straining to catch sight of the animals is $45 per person. On the way home (and not before), rum punches are served. Celebrity participants of this experience in the past have included author Peter Benchley. With a pool, classrooms, a private dock, a mini-flotilla of dive boats, and a well-trained and alert staff, this is the most complete dive resort on Dominica.

SWIMMING The beaches may be lousy, but Dominica has some of the best river swimming in the Caribbean. It is said the little island has 365 rivers, one for every day of the year. The best bets for such activity are on the west coast at the **Picard** or the **Machoucherie Rivers.** On the east coast the finest swimming is at **White River.** All the rivers are unpolluted and you can do a little sunbathing, or perhaps bring along a picnic lunch to enjoy along their banks. Consider also the **Layou River** and its gorges. Layou is the island's largest river, ranging from tranquil beach-lined pools ideal for swimming to deep gorges and turbulent rapids.

discover the tranquil Caribbean waters with rainbow-hued fish along the beaches in Mero, Salisbury, and in the region of the Layou and Macoucherie Rivers.

- **Snorkel Over Flamboyant Colors.** The western side of the island, where nearly all of the snorkeling takes place, is the leeside, meaning the waters are tranquil. In all, there are some 30 separate and first-rate snorkeling areas immediately off the coast. Snorkelers can, for example, explore the underwater hot springs at Champagne and Toucari, or else the Coral Gardens off Salisbury, and they can meander along the southern shoreline of Scotts Head Beach and marvel at the outrageously flamboyant colors of more than 190 species of fish that call Dominica home. You'll see abundant marine life, prolific corals, and orange and yellow sponges, along with densely packed schools of rainbow-colored fish. The closeness of the reefs to shore makes snorkeling here among the best in the Caribbean, although it isn't a highly organized operation.

- **Bus Your Way Around the Island.** On most Caribbean islands we don't recommend buses; they're hot, inconvenient, and undependable. But Dominican buses—really minivans—afford great insights into local life. They're also a cheap way to get around. A trip between most towns costs only $3 one-way. These are privately-owned vehicles, and everybody comes aboard, often loaded with parcels. Some are taking their wares, including fresh vegetables, to market. One driver told us, "We don't consider visitors who ride buses strangers—we consider them friends." Packed into the tight confines of these minivans, you can set out for adventures in all directions, going to the Carib Indian reserve or stopping off to wander around the old port city of Portsmouth. These vans cruise the island like taxis. Just hail one when you see one and tell the driver where you want to go. They travel daily from about 6am to 8pm. On some vans you'll get to meet the most interesting chickens—live ones, that is. What a way to go!

WHALE- & DOLPHIN-WATCHING TRIPS Sperm whales, pilot whales, killer whales, and a large variety of dolphins can be seen in Dominica better than any other island in the Caribbean. A pod of sperm whales, for example, can often be spotted just yards from your boat since there are no laws in Dominica regarding the distance which you can go to "meet the whales." The best tours are offered by the **Anchorage Hotel,** at Castle Comfort (☎ **767/448-2638**), which features 4-hour trips for $40, with children under 12 going for half-price. The vessels leave the dock every Wednesday and Sunday at 2pm. Locals refer to these jaunts as "searching for Moby Dick."

6 Seeing the Sights

Those making day trips to Dominica from other Caribbean islands will want to see the ✪ **Carib Indian Reservation,** in the northeast. In 1903 Britain got the Caribs to agree to live on 3,700 acres of land. Hence, this is the last remaining turf of the once-hostile tribe for whom the Caribbean was named. Their look is Mongolian, and they are no longer "pure-blooded," as they have married outside their tribe. Today they survive by fishing, growing food, and weaving baskets and vertiver grass mats, which they sell to the outside world. They still make dugout canoes, too.

It's like going back in time when you explore ✪ **Morne Trois Pitons National Park,** a primordial rain forest. Mists rise gently over lush, dark-green growth, drifting up to blue-green peaks that have earned Dominica the title "Switzerland of the Caribbean." Framed by banks of giant ferns, rivers rush and tumble. Trees sprout orchids, and everything seems blanketed with some type of growth. Green sunlight filters down through trees, and roaring waterfalls create a blue mist.

One of the best starting points for a visit to the park is the village of **Laudat,** 7 miles from Roseau. Exploring the heart of Dominica is for serious botanists and only the most skilled hikers, who should never penetrate unmarked trails without a very experienced guide (see "Sports & Outdoor Pursuits," above).

Deep in the park is the **Emerald Pool Trail,** a ½-mile nature trail that forms a circuit loop on a footpath passing through the forest to a pool with a beautiful waterfall. Downpours are frequent in the rain forest, and at high elevations cold winds blow. It lies 3½ miles northeast of Pont Casse.

Five miles up from the **Roseau River Valley,** in the south-central sector of Dominica, **Trafalgar Falls** can be reached after you drive through the village of Trafalgar. Here, however, you have to approach on foot, as the slopes are too steep for vehicles. After a 20-minute walk past growths of ginger plants and vanilla orchids, you arrive at the base, where a trio of falls converge into a rock-strewn pool.

The **Sulphur Springs,** and the Boiling Lake east of Roseau as well, are evidence of the island's volcanic past. Jeeps or Land Rovers can get quite close. This seemingly bubbling pool of gray mud sometimes belches smelly sulfurous fumes—the odor is like rotten eggs. Only the very fit should attempt the 6-hour round-trip to **Boiling Lake,** the world's second-largest boiling lake. Go only with an experienced guide, as, according to reports, some tourists lost their lives in the **Valley of Desolation;** they stumbled and fell into the boiling waters.

Finally, **Titou Gorge** is a deep and narrow gorge where it's possible to swim under a waterfall. Later you can get warm again in a hot sulfur spring close by. Again, a visit here is best attempted only with an experienced guide (arranged at the tourist office). The guide will transport you to the gorge and will know if swimming is dangerous, which it can be after heavy rainfall.

On the northwestern coast, **Portsmouth** is Dominica's second-largest settlement. You can row up the Indian River in native canoes, visit the ruins of Fort Shirley in Cabrits National Park, and bathe at Sandy Beach on Douglas Bay and Prince Rupert Bay.

Cabrits National Park, on the northwestern coast, 2 miles south of Douglas Bay (☎ **767/448-2732**), is a 1,313-acre protected site containing mountain scenery, tropical forests, swampland, volcanic sand beaches, coral reefs, and the ruins of a fortified, 18th-century garrison of British, then French construction. The park's land area is a panoramic promontory formed by twin peaks of extinct volcanoes, overlooking beaches, with Douglas Bay on one side and Prince Rupert Bay across the headland. Entrance is EC$5.30 ($1.95).

7 Shopping

Store hours are usually Monday to Friday 8am to 5pm and Saturday 9am to 1pm.

In Roseau, the **Old Market Plaza,** of historical significance as a former slave-trading market and more recently the site of a Wednesday-, Friday-, and

Saturday-morning vegetable market, now houses three craft shops, each specializing in coconut, straw, and Carib craft products.

Tropicrafts Island Mats, 41 Queen Mary St. and Turkey Lane (☎ 767/448-2747), offers the well-known grass rugs handmade and woven in several intricate patterns at Tropicrafts' factory. They also sell handmade bags, shopping bags, and place mats, all appliquéd by hand. The handmade dolls are popular with collectors. The Dominican vertiver-grass mats are known throughout the world, and you can watch the weaving process during store hours. There's another outlet on Bay Street opposite Burroughs Square in Portsmouth (☎ 767/445-5956).

Caribana, 31 Cork St. (☎ 767/448-7340), displays Dominica's art, craft, and culture. This is the latest manifestation of the old Caribana Handicrafts, established by the late Iris Joseph, who is credited with creating the straw-weaving industry on the island. Caribana is operated by her granddaughter. The staff is usually pleased to explain the dyeing processes that turns the straw into one of three different earth tones.

Other outlets for crafts include **Dominica Pottery,** Bayfront Street at Kennedy Avenue in Roseau (no phone). A local priest runs this shop. An array of pottery made from local clays is on sale, as well as other handcrafts. A final place for crafts is **Balisier's,** 35 Great George St., in Roseau (no phone). A young and talented artist, Hilroy Fingol, is an expert in airbrush painting. The shop also has some of the most original T-shirts on the island, as well as an assortment of Carnival dolls and jewelry handmade by his family.

A medley of goods from all over the Caribbean is featured at the **Rainforest Shop,** 17 Old St., in Roseau (☎ 767/448-8834). Everything seems to be made of flamboyant colors, and many of the gifts and souvenirs are hand-painted. The shop honors the rainforest of Dominica and contributes one dollar from every purchase to protecting its fragile environment.

8 Dominica After Dark

Dominica's not very lively, but it does have some evening activity. A couple of the major hotels, such as the **Castaways Beach Hotel** at Mero (☎ 767/449-6244) and **Reigate Hall Hotel** on Mountain Road (☎ 767/448-4031), have entertainment on weekends, usually a combo or "jing ping" (traditional local music). In the winter season, the Castaways sponsors a weekend barbecue on the beach with live music. The **Anchorage Hotel** at Castle Comfort (☎ 767/448-2638) also has live entertainment and a good buffet on Thursday. Call for details.

The Warehouse, Checkhall Estate (☎ 767/449-1303), a 5-minute drive north of Roseau, adjacent to Canefield Airport, is the island's major dance club, a social magnet open on Saturday for the island's night owls and disco lovers. Recorded disco, reggae, and other music is played at loud volumes from 11pm to 5am. Admission is EC$10 ($3.70), and beer costs EC$4 ($1.50).

If you're seeking more action, such as it is, head for **Wykie's Tropical Bar,** 51 Old St. (☎ 767/448-8015), in Roseau. This is little more than a cramped hole in the wall, yet curiously enough it draws the power brokers of the island. Happy hour on Friday is the time to show up. You might be offered some black pudding or stewed chicken to go with your local tropical drink. A home-grown calypso band is likely to entertain. You'll definitely hear some "jing ping."

The Dominica Club, 49 High St. (☎ 767/448-2995), in Roseau, is another choice. They have two tennis courts, a lively bar, and live music on Friday night.

Other hot spots include **QClub,** corner of Bath Road and High Street in Roseau (☎ **767/448-2995**), which is the place to be on a Friday night when the joint jumps. Records, both local and American, are played till dawn breaks. If you get bored here, head for **Symes Zee's,** 34 King George V St. in Roseau (☎ **767/448-2494**), the domain of Symes Zee, the island's best blues man, gray hair or not. A local band entertains with blues, jazz, and reggae. Here's your chance to smoke a reasonably priced Cuban cigar.

The Dominican Republic

Sometimes called "the fairest land under heaven" because of its sugar-white beaches and mountainous terrain, the Dominican Republic has long attracted visitors not only for its natural beauty but for its rich colonial heritage. Its Latin flavor sharply contrasts with the character of many nearby islands, especially the British- and French-influenced ones. Often mistakenly thought of as "a poorer Puerto Rico," the Dominican Republic has its own distinctive cuisine and heritage. Five centuries of culture and tradition converge here.

There's also grinding poverty, which you can't help but see during your visit. Many Dominicans risk their lives to cross the 54-mile-wide Mona Passage and slip into Puerto Rico, and from there to the U.S. mainland. Crime, especially muggings and robbery of tourists, is on the rise.

As if this country didn't have enough problems, Hurricane Georges devastated the island in September 1998. The estimate of the death toll was never really known, as many were buried in the mud or carried away from the rivers. With the help of baseball slugging star Sammy Sosa, one of its native sons, and donations from all over the world, the country was slowly rebuilding in 1999. You should ask careful questions of your choice of hotel to make sure everything is back to normal.

In the heart of the Caribbean archipelago, the country has 870 miles of coral-edged coastline, about a third of it given to magnificent beaches. The republic occupies the eastern third of Hispaniola (Haiti has the rest). Columbus sighted this lush landmass in 1492 during his first voyage to the New World, and ruins of the first permanent European settlement in the Americas, founded in 1493, remain near Montecristi in the northeastern part of the island. The country has had a bloody history almost from the beginning, and it climaxed with the infamous reign of dictator Rafael Trujillo (1930–1961) and the civil wars that followed. Today the Dominican Republic is being rebuilt and restored, and it offers visitors a chance to enjoy the sun and sea as well as to learn about the history and politics of a developing society.

The Dominican Republic is one of the least expensive places in the West Indies to vacation. Too many hotels, too few guests, and underpaid workers keep costs down. Package deals are often available; refer back to chapter 2 for hints on how to find them. American and Canadian dollars are traded extremely favorably against the Dominican peso.

1 Essentials

VISITOR INFORMATION

Before your trip, go to **www.drl.com** on the Web or contact any of the following **Dominican Republic Tourist Information Centers:** 136 E. 57th St., Suite 803, New York, NY 10022 (☎ **888/374/6361** or 212/575-4966); 2355 Salzedo St., Suite 307, Coral Gables, FL 33134 (☎ **888/358-9594** or 305/444-4592; fax 305/444-4845); 2080 Crescent St., Montréal, PQ, H3A, 2B6, Canada (☎ **800/563-1611** or 514/499-1918; fax 514/499-1393); or 35 Church St., Unit 53, Toronto, Ontario M5E 1TE (☎ **888/494-5050** or 416/361-2130; fax 416/361-2130). Don't expect too many specifics.

In England there's an office at 20 Hand Court, High Holborn, W.C.1 (☎ **020/7723-1552;** fax 020/7723-9877).

GETTING THERE

American Airlines (☎ **800/433-7300**) offers the most frequent service, with at least a dozen flights daily from cities throughout North America to either Santo Domingo or Puerto Plata. Flights from hubs like New York's JFK, Miami International, or San Juan's Luís Muñoz Marin airports are usually nonstop. You can also make connections to the Dominican Republic from other cities through Miami. American also offers some good package deals.

If you're heading to one of the Dominican's smaller airports, your best bet is to catch a connecting flight with **American Eagle** (☎ **800/433-7300**), whose small-scale (up to a maximum of 64 passengers) planes depart every day from San Juan (with connecting flights from Mayagüez) for airports throughout the Dominican Republic, including Santo Domingo, Puerto Plata, La Romana, and Punta Cana.

Continental Airlines (☎ **800/525-0280** in the U.S.) maintains a daily flight between New Jersey's Newark airport and Santo Domingo.

TWA (☎ **800/221-2000** in the U.S.) flies nonstop every morning at 9:40am from New York's JFK to Santo Domingo, arriving there at 2:19pm local time, early enough to let you enjoy a midafternoon sunbath.

ALM (☎ **809/687-4569**) links Santo Domingo with Dutch St. Maarten and Curaçao.

Iberia (☎ **800/772-4642**) offers daily flights from Madrid to Santo Domingo, each making a brief stop in San Juan.

For information on flights into Casa de Campo/La Romana, see section 3 of this chapter.

A Traveler's Advisory: Arriving at Santo Domingo's Las Américas International Airport is confusing and chaotic. Customs officials tend to be rude and overworked and give you a very thorough check! Stolen luggage is not uncommon here; beware of "porters" who offer to help with your bags. Arrival at La Unión International Airport, 23 miles east of Puerto Plata on the north coast, is generally much smoother and safer, but you should still be cautious.

GETTING AROUND

This is not always easy if your hotel is in a remote location. The most convenient modes of transport are shuttle flights, taxis, rental cars, *públicos* (multi-passenger taxis), or *guaguas* (public buses).

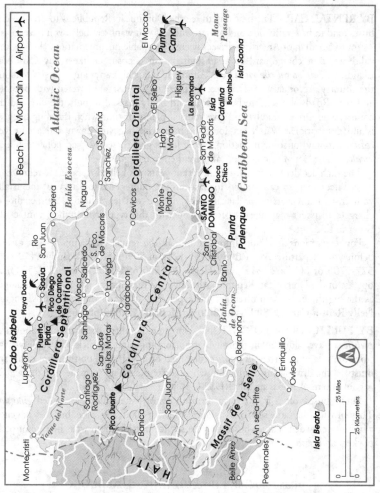

BY AIR   The quickest and easiest way to get across a difficult landscape is on one of the shuttle flights offered by **Air Santo Domingo** (☎ **809/687-4569**), flying from Santo Domingo to Puerto Plata, Punta Cana, La Romana, Samaná, and Santiago, among other towns. In general, each one-way flight costs about $50 a ticket.

BY TAXI   Taxis aren't metered, and determining the fare in advance (which you should do) may be difficult if you and your driver don't speak the same language. Taxis can be hailed in the streets, and you'll definitely find them at the major hotels and at the airport. The minimum fare within Santo Domingo is $6, but most drivers try to get more. In Santo Domingo the most reliable taxi companies are **Tecni-Taxi** (☎ **809/567-2010**) and **El Conde Taxi** (☎ **809/563-6131**). In Puerto Plata, call **Tecni-Taxi** (☎ **809/320-7621**). Don't get into an unmarked street taxi. Many visitors, particularly in Santo Domingo, have been assaulted and robbed by doing just that.

BY RENTAL CAR   The best way to see the Dominican Republic is to drive; island buses tend to be erratic, hot, and overcrowded. If you want seat belts, you have to ask.

Your Canadian or American driver's license is suitable documentation, along with a valid credit or charge card or a substantial cash deposit. Unlike many Caribbean islands, you *drive on the right* here. Although major highways are relatively smooth, the country's secondary roads, especially those in the east, are covered with potholes and ruts. Roads also tend to be badly lit and badly marked in both the city and the countryside. Drive carefully and give yourself plenty of time when traveling between island destinations. Watch out for policemen who flag you down and accuse you (often wrongly) of some infraction. Many locals give these low-paid policemen a $5 *regalo,* or gift "for your children," and are then free to go.

The high accident and theft rate in recent years has helped to raise car-rental rates here. Prices vary, so call around for last-minute quotes. Make sure you understand your insurance coverage (or lack thereof) before you leave home. Your credit- or charge-card issuer may already provide you with this type of insurance; contact the issuer to find out.

For reservations and more information, call the rental companies at least a week before your departure: **Avis** (☎ **800/331-1212** or 809/535-7191), **Budget** (☎ **800/527-0700** or 809/562-6812), and **Hertz** (☎ **800/654-3001** or 809/221-5333) all operate in the Dominican Republic. Although the cars may be not as well maintained as the big three, you can often get a cheaper deal at one of the local firms, notably **Nelly Rent-a-Car** (☎ **809/544-1800**) or **McBeal** (☎ **809/688-6518**).

BY PUBLIC TRANSPORTATION   Unmetered multi-passenger taxis known as *públicos* travel along main thoroughfares, stopping often to pick up people waving from the side of the street. A *público* is marked by a white seal on the front door. You must tell the driver your destination when you're picked up to make sure the *público* is going there. A ride is usually RD$2 (15¢).

Public buses, often in the form of minivans or panel trucks, are called *guaguas.* They provide the same service as *públicos* and cost about the same, but they're generally more crowded. Larger buses provide service outside the towns. Beware of pickpockets on board.

Fast Facts: The Dominican Republic

Currency   The Dominican monetary unit is the **peso (RD$),** made up of 100 centavos. Coin denominations are 1, 5, 10, 25, and 50 centavos, and 1 peso. Bill denominations are RD$5, RD$10, RD$20, RD$50, RD$100, RD$500, and RD$1,000. Price quotations in this chapter appear in American dollars or Dominican currency, depending on the policy of the establishment. The use of any currency other than Dominican pesos is technically illegal, but few seem to bother with this mandate. At press time, we got about RD$14.05 to U.S.$1.00 (in other words, RD$1 equals about U.S.7¢). Bank booths at the international airports and major hotels will change your currency at the prevailing free-market rate. You'll be given a receipt for the amount of foreign currency you've exchanged. If you have pesos left at the end of your trip, present this receipt at the Banco de Reservas booth at the airport, and you can trade in your pesos for American dollars.

Documents   To enter the Dominican Republic, citizens of the United States and Canada need only proof of citizenship, such as a passport or an original birth certificate. However, citizens may have trouble returning home without a passport—a reproduced birth certificate is not acceptable. Save yourself the hassle and just bring a passport. Upon your arrival at the airport in the Dominican Republic, you must purchase a tourist card for U.S.$10. You can avoid waiting in line by purchasing this card when checking in for your flight to the island.

Electricity   The country generally uses 110 volts AC (60 cycles), so adapters and transformers are usually not necessary for U.S.-made appliances.

Embassies   All embassies are in Santo Domingo, the capital. The Embassy of the **United States** is on Calle Cesar Nicholas Penson at the corner of Leopold Navarro (☎ **809/221-2171**); the Embassy of the **United Kingdom** is at Febrero 27 (☎ **809/472-7111**); and the Embassy of **Canada** is at Avenida Máximo Gómez 39 (☎ **809/685-1136**).

Language   The official language is Spanish; many people also speak some English.

Safety   The Dominican Republic has more than its fair share of crime (see "Getting There," above, for a warning about crime at airports). Avoid unmarked street taxis, especially in Santo Domingo; you could be targeted for assault and robbery. While strolling around the city, beware of hustlers selling various wares. Pickpockets and muggers are common here, and visitors are easy targets. Don't walk in Santo Domingo at night. Locals like to offer their services as guides, and it is often difficult to decline. Hiring an official guide from the tourist office is your best bet.

Taxes   A departure tax of U.S.$10 is assessed and must be paid in U.S. currency. The government imposes a 13% tax on hotel rooms, which usually is configured in conjunction with a 10% service charge that's automatically added onto your hotel bill for a total surcharge of 23%, a sum so staggering it helps support the country.

Time   Atlantic standard time is observed year-round. When New York and Miami are on eastern standard time and it's 6am, it's 7am in Santo Domingo. However, during daylight saving time, when it's noon on the U.S. east coast, it's noon in Santo Domingo too.

Tipping   In most restaurants and hotels, a 10% service charge is added to your check. Most people usually add 5% to 10% more, especially if the service has been good.

Weather   The average temperature is 77°F (25°C). August is the warmest month and January the coolest month, although even then it's warm enough to swim.

2 Santo Domingo

Bartholomeo Columbus, brother of Christopher, founded the city of New Isabella (later renamed Santo Domingo) on the southeastern Caribbean coast on August 4, 1496. It's the oldest city in the New World and the capital of the Dominican Republic. It has had a long, sometimes glorious, more often sad, history. At the peak of its power, Diego de Valásquez sailed from here to settle Cuba, Ponce de León went forth to conquer and settle Puerto Rico and Florida, and Cortés set out for Mexico. The city still reflects its long history today—French, Haitian, and especially Spanish.

SANTO DOMINGO ESSENTIALS

In Santo Domingo, **24-hour drugstore** service is provided by San Judas Tadeo, Avenida Independencia 57 (☎ **809/689-6664**). An emergency room operates at the **Centro Médico Universidad,** Avenida Máximo Gómez 68, on the corner of Pedro Enrique Urena (☎ **809/221-0171**). For the **police,** call ☎ **911.**

ACCOMMODATIONS YOU CAN AFFORD

Even the highest-priced hotels in Santo Domingo might be classified as medium-priced in most of the Caribbean. However, remember that taxes and service will be added to your bill, which will make the rates 23% higher. When making reservations, ask if these are included in the rates quoted—usually they aren't. And remember, all prices quoted are in U.S. dollars; if local prices are listed, the U.S. equivalent follows in parentheses.

Apart-Hotel Plaza Florida. Ave. Bolívar 203 (Calle Armando Rodriguez), Santo Domingo, República Dominicana. ☎ **809/541-3957.** Fax 809/540-5582. 32 units, all with kitchenette. A/C TV TEL. RD$575 ($40.80) single; RD$725 ($51.45) double. AE, MC, V.

Favored by business travelers from nearby Caribbean nations, this three-story hotel was built in 1978 in a modern commercial district near the larger (and more expensive) Hotel Commodoro. The small accommodations, all with kitchenettes, are simple, airy, and clean, with few frills, although the beds are comfortable with decent mattresses. Bathrooms don't have much room to spread out your stuff, and towels are skimpy. The result resembles something like an apartment complex, where residents tend to stay longer than conventional tourists, usually preparing at least breakfast in their rooms. About half the units have small balconies. There's a simple restaurant on site, serving Dominican specialties, but its management is separate from that of the hotel.

El Napolitano. Ave. George Washington 51 (between Calle Cambrunal and Calle del Número), Santo Domingo, República Dominicana. ☎ **809/687-1131.** Fax 809/687-6814. 72 units. A/C TV TEL. Year-round RD$1,130–RD$1,211 ($80.25–$86) single or double. AE, DC, MC, V.

El Napolitano is a safe haven and a good bargain along the Malecón, which is usually lively—and potentially dangerous—until the wee hours. Popular with Dominicans, the hotel rents comfortably furnished but simple units, many large enough for families. All accommodations open onto the sea. Mattresses are frequently renewed, and you'll probably get a good night's sleep. Bathrooms with rather thin towels are barely adequate in size but well maintained. There's a swimming pool on the second floor.

The restaurant, Da Luz, is open 24 hours a day and provides round-the-clock room service. Chefs specialize in seafood (especially lobster). There's a disco and a piano bar, plus a terrace casino, with both live and recorded music. If you like crowds, lots of action, and informality, El Napolitano may be for you.

Gran Hotel Lina. Aves. Máximo Gómez and 27 de Febrero, Santo Domingo, República Dominicana. ☎ **800/942-2461** or 809/563-5000. Fax 809/686-5521. www.barcelo.com. E-mail: h-lina@codetel.net.do. 217 units. A/C MINIBAR TV TEL. Year-round $105 single; $111 double. Extra person $28. Rates include breakfast. AE, DC, MC, V.

Rising 15 floors in the heart of the capital, the sterile, cinder-block Lina offers a wide range of services and facilities. All the rooms contain refrigerators, and at least 30% of the accommodations overlook the Caribbean. Bedrooms are comfortable and many of

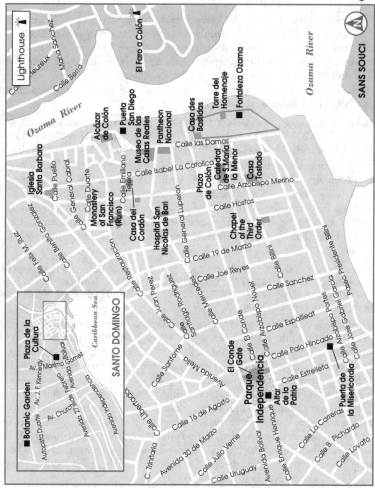

them quite spacious, with firm mattresses resting on sturdy beds, but the décor is in the standard motel style. Most units contain two double beds with a halo of reading lights. The best accommodations are on the 11th floor, as they have balconies. The tiled bathrooms have a combination shower and bathtub, along with spacious marble vanities to spread out your stuff.

The hotel boasts one of the best-known restaurants in the Caribbean (see "Great Deals on Dining," below), a cafeteria and snack bar, and a nightclub. Services include 24-hour room service and laundry, and facilities include a swimming pool, Jacuzzi, solarium, gym, sauna, and shopping arcade.

Hostal Nicolás Nader. Calle Admiral Luperón 251 (at Calle Duarte, 4 blocks west of calle Las Damas), Santo Domingo, República Dominicana. ☎ **809/687-6674.** 9 units. A/C. RD$750 ($53.25) single; RD$850 ($60.35) double. AE, V.

The family owners of this spacious hotel will proudly tell you that two former residents of this building were eventually elected president of the Dominican Republic.

Originally a private home in the 1930s, it provides clean and inviting lodgings, with battered, colonial furniture, some of them antiques. The guest rooms overlook either the street or a small Andalusian courtyard with cast-iron furniture. Most rooms have excellent twin beds with firm mattresses, although there are some with double beds. The walk-in closets are ideal for storing your clothing, and the combination baths (with both tub and shower) are a bit small but well maintained, with compact vanities. Breakfast is the only meal served.

Hotel Cervantes. Ave. Cervantes 202, Santo Domingo, República Dominicana. ☎ **809/ 688-2261.** Fax 809/686-5754. 170 units. A/C TV TEL. Year-round RD$558–RD$888 ($39.60–$63.05) single; RD$658–RD$983 ($46.70–$69.80) double. AE, DC, MC, V. Free parking.

Long a favorite among budget travelers, the family-oriented Cervantes, with a security guard on staff, offers comfortably furnished but small bedrooms with refrigerators. Most bedrooms are reasonably comfortable, although some mattresses need to be replaced. Baths are also a bit cramped, and towels are skimpy. It may not have the most tasteful decor in Santo Domingo, but is nevertheless clean and efficient and has a pleasant staff. The hotel has a swimming pool and is also known for its Bronco Steak House.

Hotel Palacio. Calle Duarte 106 (at Calle Solomé Ureña), Santo Domingo, República Dominicana. ☎ **809/682-4730.** Fax 809/687-5535. E-mail: h.palacio@codetel.net.do. 16 units, all with kitchenette. A/C TV TEL. $53–$72 single; $63–$71 double. Children 12 and under stay free in parents' room. AE, MC, V.

This severely dignified stone-and-stucco building is a stripped-down reminder of the grander aspects of the city's colonial past. It lies in the heart of Santo Domingo's historic zone, 2 blocks from the cathedral. Built in the 1600s, it functioned as the family home of a former president of the Dominican Republic, Buenaventura Báez, and still retains its original iron balconies and high ceilings. In the early 1990s kitchenettes were added to each of the bedrooms, and simple, warm-weather furniture was added as part of its transformation into a hotel. Since this was a private home, not all rooms are the same size. You can always request a more spacious unit, which is assigned on a first-come, first-served basis. Many bathrooms were tacked onto the rooms and tend to be small, but the plumbing works just fine. Your fellow guests are likely to be visiting business travelers from other parts of the Latin Caribbean and tourists. There's a small gym, with its own Jacuzzi on the rooftop.

Plaza Naco Hotel. In the Plaza Naco Mall, Ave. Presidente Gonzalez at Ave. Tiradentes (Apdo. Postal 30228), Santo Domingo, República Dominicana. ☎ **809/541-6226.** Fax 809/ 549-7743. 220 units. A/C TV TEL. Year-round $90 junior suite for 1 or 2; $130–$146 1-bedroom suite for up to 4. Rates include breakfast. AE, MC, V.

An ideal accommodation for business travelers or for visitors seeking a lot of space and facilities, the Plaza Naco offers handsomely decorated accommodations equipped with computer safe-lock doors, guest safes, kitchenettes, good beds, dining rooms, and hair dryers in the tiled baths. Each unit was renovated in 1998.

There's a good restaurant and a cafeteria, plus a gift shop. Those who want their own supplies for their suites can shop at the deli or the mini-market. Hotel guests are admitted free to the disco. There's also 24-hour room service, laundry, dry cleaning, bilingual secretarial and legal translation services, a rental-car desk, a tour desk, a sauna (with massage available), and a gym.

THE BEST ALL-INCLUSIVE DEAL

✪ **Capella Beach Resort.** Villas del Mar (Apdo. Postal 4750), Juan Dolio, Santo Domingo, República Dominicana. ☎ **800/924-5004** in the U.S., or 809/526-1080. Fax 809/526-1088.

E-mail: h.capella@codetel.com. 283 units. A/C TV TEL. Winter $147–$201 single; $170–$284 double. Off-season $108–$153 single; $144–$200 double. Rates are all-inclusive. $165 suite (EP) in summer, $250 (EP) in winter. AE, DC, MC, V.

Just 20 minutes from the International Airport of the Americas, this resort lies in the newly developed town of Villas del Mar. Architecturally, it resembles an exotic Andalusian town in southern Spain. It has its own beach, shared with Villas del Mar. Units come in three different sizes, the smallest being ranked standard, the medium size called superior, and the most spacious labeled deluxe. The smallest, standard rooms are in the front wing closer to Juan Dolio Beach. Here you'll find one king-size bed. The more superior rooms have two queen beds, but all are equipped with fine mattresses and are comfortable. Housekeeping is excellent. Bathrooms are medium in size with ample shelf space, good towels, and a hair dryer. There are 35 no-smoking rooms and special accommodations for persons with disabilities. The suites include six reserved for honeymooners, with private balconies, Jacuzzis, and sun decks. The best rooms are in the Renaissance club, which has extra service and amenities, including a complimentary continental breakfast.

There are three restaurants: Il Capellini, serving Italian fare; El Pescador, offering seafood; and the buffet-style El Batey de la Costa. Facilities include two swimming pools with swim-up bars, a water-sports center, evening tennis, a kid's club (ages 5 to 12), and a European spa facility.

GREAT DEALS ON DINING

✪ **El Conuco.** Calle Casimiro de Moya 152. ☎ **809/686-0129.** Main courses RD$50–RD$160 ($3.55–$11.35). Daily noon–2am. DOMINICAN/CRIOLLA.

Near the Jaragua Resort and Casino, close to the seafront avenue known as the Malecón, this well-managed and authentic restaurant gastronomically and visually celebrates the traditions of the Dominican Republic. Despite its urban location, it features many of the aesthetic traditions you'd have expected in the countryside. Amid thatched roofs and potted and hanging plants, you'll find original paintings, hand-woven baskets, battered license plates from virtually every corner of the country, and occasional bouts of either live or recorded merengue music. Menu items include all the staples of the traditional Dominican kitchen, including *la bandera* (stewed beef served with rice and beans), fresh fish, spicy versions of grilled chicken, and different preparations of stewed codfish. There are five separate dining areas, some air-conditioned, others open-air.

Fonda La Atarazana. Calle Atarazana 5. ☎ **809/689-2900.** Main courses RD$110–RD$225 ($7.80–$15.95). AE, DC, MC, V. Daily 11am–2am. CREOLE/INTERNATIONAL.

This patio restaurant offers regional food in a colonial atmosphere, with either live or recorded music for dancing. Just across from the Alcázar, it's a convenient stop if you're shopping and sightseeing in the old city. A cheap, good dish is *chicharrones de pollo*, tasty fried bits of Dominican chicken. Or you might try curried baby goat in a sherry sauce. Sometimes the chef cooks lobster Thermidor and Galician-style octopus. If you don't mind waiting half an hour, you can order the *sopa de ajo* (garlic soup). Many fans come here especially for the fricasseed pork chops.

✪ **La Bahía.** Ave. George Washington 1. ☎ **809/682-4022.** Main courses RD$70–RD$250 ($4.95–$17.75); fixed-price menu RD$150 ($10.65). AE, MC, V. Daily 9am–2am. SEAFOOD.

You'd never know that this unprepossessing place right on the Malecón serves some of the best, and freshest, seafood in the Dominican Republic. One predawn morning as we passed by, fishermen were waiting outside to sell the chef their latest catch. Rarely in the Caribbean will you find a restaurant with such a wide range of seafood dishes. For your appetizer, you might prefer *ceviche*—sea bass marinated in lime juice—or lobster cocktail. Soups usually contain big chunks of lobster as well as shrimp. Specialties include kingfish in coconut sauce, sea bass Ukrainian style, baked red snapper, and seafood in the pot. Conch is a special favorite with the chef. Desserts are superfluous. The restaurant will stay open until the last customer departs.

La Baguette. Calle Gustavo Meija Ricart 126. ☎ **809/565-6432.** Snacks and pastries RD$10–RD$55 (70¢–$3.90). MC, V. Mon–Sat 8:30am–8pm.

Don't expect fancy service and culinary chi-chi at this French bakery wanna-be. You'll stand up and place your order at the counter, then either carry your goodies away or sit at the limited number of utilitarian tables in the corner. Menu items lean toward the snack-food and tasty morsel category, and include brochettes of pork, chicken, and beef, and turnovers (*pastelitos*) stuffed with cheese or meat. There's quite an array of sweets and pastries—flan, tarts, cookies, slices of cake, and the house version of mango mousse.

✪ **La Canasta.** In the Melia Santo Domingo Hotel & Casino, Ave. George Washington 365. ☎ **809/221-6666.** Main courses RD$95–RD$305 ($6.75–$21.65). AE, DC, MC, V. Daily 8pm–6am. DOMINICAN/INTERNATIONAL.

The best late-night dining spot in the capital is set back from the Malecón, between the Omni Casino and the Omni Disco. It's not only economical but serves popular Dominican dishes culled from favorite recipes throughout the country, including *sancocho* (a typical stew with a variety of meats and yucca) and *mondongo* (tripe cooked with tomatoes and peppers). Other unusual dishes are goatmeat braised in a rum sauce, and pigs' feet vinaigrette Creole style. Canasta is locally known for its *pollo a la plancha,* grilled chicken flavored with fresh Dominican herbs. The late-night dining hours are perfectly suited to the young Dominican clientele the restaurant serves, many of whom frequent the discos in the wee hours.

Scherezade. Calle Roberto Pastoriza 226 (at Calle Lope de Vega). ☎ **809/227-2323.** Reservations recommended. Main courses RD$150–RD$400 ($10.65–$28.40). AE, MC, V. Daily noon–midnight. MEDITERRANEAN.

Its name (heroine of the Arabic legend of *A Thousand and One Nights*) and décor (a simulation of a Moorish palace) evoke the Middle East better than anything else in town. A main dining room is divided into two sections. The bustling kitchen makes a roster of international dishes that are ambitious and for the most part successful. Menu items include pastas, *osso bucco,* fresh fish, Turkish-style shish kebabs, and well-flavored versions of Lebanese dishes such as *tabouleh, tahini,* and roast lamb with Mediterranean herbs. The service is much better than we've typically found in Santo Domingo.

Spaghettissimo. 13 Paseo de Los Locubres. ☎ **809/565-3708.** Main courses RD$145–RD$365 ($10.30–$25.90). AE, DC, MC, V. Daily noon–3pm and 7–11pm. ITALIAN.

Convivial and unpretentious, this restaurant manages to convey the sense that a chef somewhere in a steamy kitchen will be genuinely disappointed if you don't manage to actually finish your pasta. You might begin your meal with a drink in the bar near the entrance, then segue into a simple but dignified dining room where part of the visual distraction derives from a generously appointed antipasti buffet (most of the selections are fish or grilled vegetables that have marinated succulently in olive oil and herbs). Starters might include shellfish, fish soup, *foie gras,* and the inevitable pastas such as penne with artichokes, which can be configured as main courses if you prefer.

Meats and fish are often grilled, well seasoned, and redolent of the traditions of far-away Italy.

Toscana. Calle Erik Leonard Ekman 34, in Arroyo Hondo. ☎ **809/563-2777.** Main courses RD$95–RD$315 ($6.75–$22.35). AE, MC, V. Daily noon–midnight. ITALIAN/INTERNATIONAL.

Perpetually friendly service and hefty portions of good, fresh food continue to make this a popular spot. Set in the Arroyo Hondo district, north of the colonial zone, this Italian restaurant, with two dining rooms, serves flavorful versions of pastas, raviolis, lobster, fresh fish, and squid. Reminders of Creole and Caribbean food creep into the menu, thanks to such dishes as a cold *ceviche* of snapper or grouper; red snapper served with onions, capers, and herbs; and the selection of rum-based drinks to wash down your otherwise all-Italian meal.

WORTH A SPLURGE

Mesón de la Cava. Avenida Mirador del Sur 1. ☎ **809/533-2818.** Reservations required. Main courses RD$125–RD$300 ($8.90–$21.30). AE, DC, MC, V. Daily noon–4pm and 6pm–1:30am. DOMINICAN/INTERNATIONAL.

Here you descend a perilous open-backed iron stairway into a cave. At first we thought this was a mere gimmicky club, but the cuisine is among the finest in the capital. This is an actual cave with stalactites and stalagmites. Recorded music is played to give the place a more festive ambience; merengue music is prominently featured along with Latin jazz, blues, and salsa. For an appetizer try the shrimp cocktail, onion soup, gazpacho, bisque of seafood, and especially the red snapper chowder. The chefs take justifiable pride in their meats, especially their gourmet beefsteak. But you can also order fresh fish. Try, if featured, the fresh sea bass in red sauce. Other dishes likely to appear on the menu include a tender tournedos perfectly prepared and a quite delectable *coq au vin* (chicken cooked in wine sauce).

Pappalapasta. Calle Dr. Baez 23. ☎ **809/689-4849.** Reservations recommended. Pastas RD$140–RD$225 ($9.95–$15.95); main courses RD$200–RD$300 ($14.20–$21.30). AE, DC, MC, V. Daily noon–3pm and 7pm–1am. ITALIAN/INTERNATIONAL.

Housed within an 80-year-old building that was once a private home, this restaurant is just a short walk from the presidential palace, and so is known for its chaotic lunch scene. The yellow dining rooms are accented with modern art, cut-glass windows, and varnished hardwoods. Here you can order from a variety of Italian dishes. Frankly, the staff is not as attentive as they should be, which is ironic considering the restaurant's high-powered clientele of lawyers and other professionals. The food, when it finally arrives, is far better than the service. Menu items might include dishes like sea bass grilled with Creole sauce or *meunière* (lightly floured and sautéed in butter); filet of beef with a brandy and mushroom-flavored cream sauce; red snapper with garlic, olives, and capers; and an assortment of pastas, gnocchi, and ravioli in savory sauces.

ALL-YOU-CAN-EAT LUNCH BUFFETS

✪ **El Alcázar.** In the Hotel Santo Domingo, Ave. Independencia at Ave. Abraham Lincoln. ☎ **809/221-1511.** Reservations required. Fixed-price lunch buffet RD$180 ($12.80). AE, DC, MC, V. Daily 11am–2pm. INTERNATIONAL.

The Dominican designer Oscar de la Renta created El Alcázar in a Moroccan motif, with aged mother-of-pearl, small mirrors, and lots of fabric. Dishes are always good, and sometimes excellent; well-made sauces add zest to the meals. The menu is likely to be Chinese one day, Mexican another day, Italian the next, although Monday is usually devoted to Dominican food. The presentation of the food and the service are two more reasons to dine here.

HITTING THE BEACHES

The Dominican Republic has some great beaches, but they aren't in Santo Domingo. The principal beach resort near the capital is at **Boca Chica,** less than 2 miles east of the international airport and about 19 miles from the center of Santo Domingo. Clear, shallow blue water leaves the fine white-sand beach, and there's a natural coral reef too. The east side of the beach, known as "St. Tropez," is popular with Europeans. In recent years the backdrop of the beach has become rather tacky, with an array of pizza and fast-food stands (some selling Dominican fried chicken), beach cottages, chaise longues, water sports concessions, and plastic beach tables.

Slightly better maintained is the narrow white-sand beach of **Juan Dolio,** lying a 20-minute drive east of Boca Chica. In recent years several resorts have located here, including the previously recommended Capella Beach Renaissance Resort. The beach used to be fairly uncrowded, but with all the resort hotels now lining it, it's likely to be as crowded as Boca Chica any day of the week. As for the pursuit of other outdoor activities, you need to venture outside the capital to such resorts as Puerto Plata or La Romana.

SPECTATOR SPORTS

BASEBALL   The national sport is baseball. The Dominican team is always a popular draw at the summer Olympics, and many of the country's native-born sons have gone on to the U.S. major leagues, including the Chicago Cubs' slugging superstar Sammy Sosa. October to February, games are played at stadiums in Santo Domingo and elsewhere. Check the local newspaper for schedules and locations of the nearest game.

HORSE RACING   Santo Domingo's racetrack, **Hipódromo V Centenario,** on avenida Las Américas (☎ 809/687-6060), schedules races daily. You can spend the day here and have lunch at the track's restaurant. Admission is free.

EXPLORING HISTORIC SANTO DOMINGO

Santo Domingo, a treasure trove of historic, sometimes-crumbling buildings, is undergoing a major government-sponsored restoration. The old town is still partially enclosed by remnants of its original city wall. The narrow streets, old stone buildings, and forts are like nothing else in the Caribbean, except Old San Juan. The only thing missing is the clank of the conquistadors' armor.

Old and modern Santo Domingo meet at the **Parque Independencia,** a big city square whose most prominent feature is its Altar de la Patria, a shrine dedicated to Duarte, Sanchez, and Mella, who are all buried here. These men led the country's fight for freedom from Haiti in 1844. As in provincial Spanish cities, the square is a popular family gathering point on Sunday afternoon. At the entrance to the plaza is **El Conde Gate,** named for the count (El Conde) de Penalva, the governor who resisted the forces of Admiral Penn, the leader of a British invasion. It was also the site of the March for Independence in 1844, and holds a special place in the hearts of Dominicans.

In the shadow of the Alcázar, **La Atarazana** is a fully restored section that centered around one of the New World's finest arsenals. It extends for a city block, a catacomb of shops, art galleries (both Haitian and Dominican paintings), boutiques, and some good regional and international restaurants.

Just behind river moorings is the oldest street in the New World, **Calle Las Damas** (Street of the Ladies). Some visitors assume that this was a bordello district, but actually it wasn't. Rather, the elegant ladies of the viceregal court used to promenade here in the evening. It's lined with colonial buildings.

Alcázar de Colón. Calle Emiliano Tejera (at the foot of Calle Las Damas). ☎ **809/689-4363.** Admission RD$20 ($1.40). Mon and Wed–Fri 9am–5pm, Sat 9am–4pm, Sun 9am–1pm.

The most outstanding structure in the old city is the Alcázar, a palace built for the son of Columbus, Diego, and his wife, the niece of Ferdinand, king of Spain. Diego became the colony's governor in 1509, and Santo Domingo rose as the hub of Spanish commerce and culture in America. Constructed of native coral limestone, it stands on the bluffs of the Ozama River. For more than 60 years it was the center of the Spanish court and entertained such distinguished visitors as Cortés, Ponce de León, and Balboa. The nearly two dozen rooms and open-air loggias are decorated with paintings and period tapestries, as well as 16th-century antiques.

Casa del Cordón (Cord House). At Calle Emiliano Tejera and Calle Isabel la Católica. No phone. Free admission. Tues–Sun 8:30am–4:30pm.

Near the Alcázar de Colón, the Cord House was named for the cord of the Franciscan order, which is carved above the door. Francisco de Garay, who came to Hispaniola with Columbus, built the casa in 1503–04, which makes it the oldest stone house in the western hemisphere. It once lodged the first royal audience of the New World, which performed as the Supreme Court of Justice for the island and the rest of the West Indies. On another occasion, in January 1586, the noble ladies of Santo Domingo gathered here to donate their jewelry as ransom demanded by Sir Francis Drake in return for his promise to leave the city.

✪ Catedral de Santa María la Menor. Calle Arzobispo Meriño (on the south side of Columbus Sq.). ☎ **809/689-1920.** Free admission. Cathedral, Mon–Sat 9am–4pm (Masses on Sun); Treasury, Mon–Sat 9am–4pm.

The oldest cathedral in the Americas was begun in 1514 and completed in 1540. With a gold coral limestone facade, it's a stunning example of the Spanish Renaissance style, with elements of Gothic and baroque. The cathedral, visited by Pope John Paul II in 1979 and again in 1984, was the center for a celebration of the 500th anniversary of the European Discovery of America in 1992. An excellent art collection of retables, ancient wood carvings, furnishings, funerary monuments, and silver and jewelry can be seen in the Treasury. On Sunday masses begin at 6am.

El Faro a Colón (Columbus Lighthouse). Ave. España (on the water side of Los Tres Ojos, near the airport in the Sans Souci district). ☎ **809/591-1492.** Admission RD$10 (70¢) adults, RD$5 (35¢) children 11 and under. Tues–Sun 10am–5pm.

Built in the shape of a pyramid cross, the towering El Faro a Colón monument is both a sightseeing attraction and a cultural center. In the heart of the structure is a chapel containing the Columbus tomb, and perhaps his mortal remains. The "bones" of Columbus were moved here from the Cathedral of Santa María la Menor (see above). (Other locations, including the Cathedral of Seville, also claim to possess the remains of the explorer.) Adjacent to the chapel is a series of museums representing more than 20 countries, plus a museum dedicated to the history of Columbus and the lighthouse itself. The most outstanding and unique feature is the lighting system, composed of 149 xenon Skytrack searchlights and a 70-kilowatt beam that circles out for nearly 44 miles. When illuminated, the lights project a gigantic cross in the sky that can be seen for miles beyond, even as far as Puerto Rico.

While the concept of the memorial dates back 140 years, the first stones were not laid until 1986 following the same design submitted in 1929 by J. L. Gleave, the winner of the worldwide contest held to choose an architect. The monumental lighthouse was inaugurated on October 6, 1992, the day Columbus's "remains" were transferred from the Santo Domingo cathedral, the oldest in the Americas. The multi-million-dollar monument stands 688 feet tall (taller than the Washington Monument) and 131 feet wide, with sloping sides from 56 feet at the top to 109 feet at the bottom.

Museo de las Casas Reales (Museum of the Royal Houses). Calle Las Damas (at Calle Las Mercedes). ☎ **809/682-4202.** Admission RD$10 (70¢). Tues–Sat 9am–4:45pm; Sun 10am–1pm.

Through artifacts, tapestries, maps, and re-created halls, including a courtroom, this museum traces Santo Domingo's history from 1492 to 1821. Gilded furniture, arms and armor, and other colonial artifacts make it the most interesting of all museums of Old Santo Domingo. It contains replicas of the three ships commanded by Columbus, and one exhibit is said to hold part of the ashes of the famed explorer. You can see, in addition to pre-Columbian art, the main artifacts of two galleons sunk in 1724 on their way from Spain to Mexico, along with remnants of another 18th-century Spanish ship, the *Concepción.*

OTHER SIGHTS

In total contrast to the colonial city, modern Santo Domingo dates from the Trujillo era. A city of broad, palm-shaded avenues, its seaside drive is called **Avenida George Washington,** more popularly known as the **Malecón.** This boulevard is filled with restaurants, as well as hotels and nightclubs. Use caution at night—there are pickpockets galore.

We also suggest a visit to the **Paseo de los Indios,** a sprawling 5-mile park with a restaurant, fountain displays, and a lake.

About a 20-minute drive from the heart of the city, off the Autopista de las Américas on the way to the airport and the beach at Boca Chica, is **Los Tres Ojos** or "The Three Eyes," which stare at you across the Ozama River from Old Santo Domingo. There's a trio of lagoons set in scenic caverns, with lots of stalactites and stalagmites. One lagoon is 40 feet deep, another 20 feet, and yet a third—known as the "Ladies Bath"—only 5 feet deep. A Dominican Tarzan will sometimes dive off the walls of the cavern into the deepest lagoon. The area is equipped with walkways.

Jardín Botánico. Ave. República de Colombia (at the corner of de los Proceres). ☎ **809/867-6211.** Admission RD$10 (70¢) adults, RD$5 (35¢) children. Tour by train RD$15 ($1.05) adults, RD$7 (50¢) children. Tues–Sun 9am–5pm.

Sprawled over 445 acres in the northern sector of the Arroyo Hondo, these are among the largest gardens of their kind in Latin America. They emphasize the flowers and lush vegetation native to the Dominican Republic, and require at least 2 hours to even begin to explore. A small, touristy-looking train makes a circuit through the park's major features, which include a Japanese Park, the Great Ravine, and a floral clock.

Museo de Arte Moderno. Plaza de la Cultura, Calle Pedro Henríquez Ureña. ☎ **809/ 685-2153.** Admission RD$20 ($1.40). Tues–Sat 9am–5pm.

The former site of the Trujillo mansion, plaza de la Cultura has been turned into a park and contains the Museum of Modern Art, which displays national and international works (the emphasis is, of course, on native-born talent).

Also in the center are the **National Library** (☎ **809/688-4086**) and the **National Theater** (☎ **809/687-3191**), which sponsor, among other events, folkloric dances, opera, outdoor jazz concerts, traveling art exhibits, classical ballet, and music concerts.

SHOPPING

The best buys are handcrafted native items, especially amber jewelry. Amber deposits, petrified tree resin that has fossilized over millions of years, are the national gem. Look for pieces of amber with trapped objects, such as insects and spiders, inside the enveloping material. Colors range from a bright yellow to black, but most of the gems are golden in tone. Fine-quality amber jewelry, along with lots of plastic fakes, is sold throughout the country.

A semiprecious stone of light blue (sometimes a dark-blue color), larimar is the Dominican turquoise. It often makes striking jewelry, and is sometimes mounted with wild boar's teeth.

Ever since the Dominicans presented John F. Kennedy with what became his favorite rocker, visitors have wanted to take home a rocking chair. To simplify transport, these rockers are often sold unassembled.

Other good buys include Dominican rum, hand-knit articles, macramé, ceramics, and crafts in native mahogany. Always haggle over the price, particularly in the open-air markets; no stallkeeper expects you to pay the first price asked. The best shopping streets are El Conde, the oldest and most traditional shop-flanked avenue, and avenida Mella.

In the colonial section, **La Atarazana** is filled with galleries and gift and jewelry stores, all charging inflated prices. Duty-free shops are found at the airport, in the capital at the **Centro de los Héroes,** and at both the Hotel Santo Domingo and the Hotel Embajador. Shopping hours are generally 9am to 12:30pm and 2 to 5pm Monday to Saturday.

Head first for the National Market, ✪ **El Mercado Modelo,** Avenida Mella, filled with stall after stall of crafts and spices, fruits, and vegetables. The merchants will be most eager to sell, and you can easily get lost in the crush. Remember to bargain. You'll see a lot of tortoise shell work here, but exercise caution, since many species, especially the hawksbill, are on the endangered-species list and could be impounded by U.S. Customs if discovered in your luggage. Rockers are for sale here, as are mahogany-ware, sandals, baskets, hats, clay braziers for grilling fish, and so on.

Ambar Marie, Caonabo 9, Gazcue (☎ **809/682-7539**), is a reliable source for amber. In case you're worried that the piece of amber you like may be plastic, you can be assured of the real thing at Ambar Marie, where you can even design your own setting for your chosen gem. Look especially for the beautiful amber necklaces, as well as the earrings and pins. Another reliable source is **Ambar Nacionale,** Calle Restauración 110 (☎ **809/686-5700**), around the corner from the Amber World Museum. This outlet hawks items for sale that include many stunning pieces of amber as well as coral and larimar. In general prices here are a bit less expensive than those at the more prestigious Amber World Museum. Look for some stunning jewelry fashioned from larimar or ancient amber and placed in silver settings.

In the colonial section of the old city, **Ambar Tres,** La Atarazana 3 (☎ **809/688-0474**), sells jewelry made from amber and black coral, as well as mahogany carvings, watercolors, oil paintings, and other Dominican products. **Amber World Museum,** 452 Arzobispo Meriño (☎ **809/682-3309**), lives up to its name. In the wake of the film *Jurassic Park,* more and more visitors are flocking to this display to see plants, butterflies, insects, and even scorpions fossilized in resin millions of years ago during the age of the dinosaurs. Although some of the display is not for sale, in an adjoining salon you can watch craftspeople at work, polishing and shaping raw bits of ancient amber for sale.

In the center of the most historical section of town is a well-known gallery, **Galería de Arte Nader,** Rafael Augusto Sanchez 22 (☎ **809/687-6674**), that sells so many Latin paintings that they're sometimes stacked in rows against the walls. Many of these paintings appear quite worthy, and works by some leading artists are displayed here. But others, especially those shipped in by the truckload from Haiti, seem to be mere tourist junk. In recent years, the focus has shifted away from Haiti. Today you get a more diversified collection of art, including some from such other countries as Colombia, Peru, Venezuela, and even Cuba.

Although the name implies that it's new, **Novo Atarazana,** La Atarazana 21 (☎ **809/689-0582**), is actually one of the longest-established shops in town. If you don't have time to survey a lot of shops looking for local art and crafts, you'll find a wide cross-section here. You can purchase pieces of amber, black coral, leather goods, wood carvings, and Haitian paintings.

Plaza Criolla, at the corner of Avenidas 27 de Febrero and Anacaona, is a modern shopping complex. Its shops are set amid gardens with tropical shrubbery and flowers, facing the Olympic Center. The architecture makes generous use of natural woods, and a covered wooden walkway links the stalls together.

SANTO DOMINGO AFTER DARK

La Guácara Taína, Calle Mirador, in Parque Mirador del Sur (☎ **809/533-1051**), is the best *discoteca* in the Dominican Republic. As you dance to the music within this underground cave, you might be worried that the reverberations of the state-of-the-art dance music might loosen one of the overhead rocks and send it crashing to the dance floor. Fortunately, that hasn't happened (or if it has, we haven't heard about it.) The site lies underground, within a verdant park surrounded by a middle-class neighborhood. The specialty is merengue, salsa, and other international sounds. Inside you'll find three bars, two dance floors, and banquettes and chairs nestled into irregularities within the rocky walls. Entrance is RD$150 ($10.65) per person.

Neon Discotheque, in the Hispaniola Hotel, Ave. Independencia (☎ **809/221-1511**), is one of the town's best dance clubs, offering Latin jazz with different guest stars each week. Disco dancing under flashing lights is one of the main reasons for its popularity. The clientele tends to be very young, and includes many university students. The management reserves the right to accept only "well-behaved" guests. A cover of RD$80 ($5.70) is imposed unless you're a guest of the hotel.

Omni Disco/Diamante Bar, in the Melia Santo Domingo Hotel & Casino, Ave. George Washington 361 (☎ **809/221-6666**), is a hot spot along the Malecón. Anyone could while away an intriguing evening by dividing his or her time between these two watering holes, both of which lie on the premises of this hotel. The Omni Disco is one of the most artfully decorated discos in town, with mirrors and gray, green, and blue decor that functions as background for the throbbing, pulsating recorded music. If you consider yourself older and a bit more sedate (at least by D.R. standards), avoid the place on Tuesday nights, when it's college night. After a while many visitors move on to the Diamante Bar, the showcase bar in the Sheraton's casino, in an annex building adjacent to the hotel itself. Here, live bands perform merengue, salsa, and more. Both bars are open daily from 8pm to 4am. The disco charges a cover of RD$60 ($4.25).

In the colonial zone, the best dance club is **Bachata Rosa,** La Atarazana 9 (☎ **809/ 688-0969**), with action on three floors.

Disco Free, Avenida Ortega y Gaset (☎ **809/565-8100**), which is open Thursday to Sunday only, is the country's leading gay dance club, and also has some of the best music in town. The club is known for its salsa and merengue.

Many other chic stops are in the big hotels.

Las Palmas, in the Hotel Santo Domingo, Ave. Independencia (☎ **809/221- 7111**), occupies premises originally decorated by Oscar de la Renta. Today it's best compared to a cross between a conventional bar and a disco, where the emphasis is on the bar trade between 6 and 9:30pm, and live music, such as salsa and merengue, from 9:30pm till closing time (4am). When someone isn't performing, large-screen TVs broadcast music videos beamed by satellite in from the U.S. mainland. Drink prices are reduced from 6 to 8pm.

Merengue Bar, in the Jaragua Renaissance Resort & Casino, Ave. George Washington 367 (☎ **809/221-2222**), has a party atmosphere that often spills out into the sophisticated Jaragua Casino. High-ceilinged and painted in dark, subtly-provocative colors, it includes a sprawling bar area, a sometimes overcrowded dance floor, and rows of banquettes and tables that face a brightly lit stage. Here, animated bands from as far away as the Philippines crank out high-energy sounds daily beginning at 4pm and going strong until the wee hours of the morning. The joint really gets jumping around 10pm, when this bar/nightclub seems to forget that it operates in a jangling casino.

Santo Domingo has several major casinos, all of which are open nightly till 4 or 5am. The most spectacular is the **Renaissance Jaragua Resort & Casino,** Ave. George Washington 367 (☎ **809/686-2222**), whose brightly flashing sign is the most dazzling light along the Malecón at night. The most glamorous casino in the country is fittingly housed in the capital's poshest hotel, and offers blackjack, baccarat, roulette, and slot machines. You can gamble in either Dominican pesos or U.S. dollars. Another casino is at the **Hispaniola Hotel,** Avenida Independencia (☎ **809/221-7111**). One of the most stylish casinos is the **Omni Casino,** in the Melia Santo Domingo Hotel & Casino, Ave. George Washington 361 (☎ **809/221-6666**). Its bilingual staff will help you play blackjack, craps, baccarat, and keno, among other games. There's also a piano bar.

3 Barahona Peninsula

True bargain hunters are deserting the high-priced resorts such as Casa de Campo at La Romana and those sprawling megahotels at Punta Cana. Instead, they're heading for more remote parts of the island nation, where tourist structures are just developing. There is no more remote corner than the Barahona Peninsula, often called "a closely guarded secret" in the travel industry.

You're certainly off the beaten track here. This seldom-visited southwestern region is still unspoiled, unlike the overly developed north coast around Puerto Plata. It's a 3-hour drive west of Santo Domingo. The peninsula's chief city is Barahona, whose locals are called *Barahoneros.* Even more remote is the tiny fishing village of Baoruco, some 15 miles of coastal scenery southwest of Barahona.

GETTING THERE & GETTING AROUND
If you don't have a car, call **Caribe Tours** (☎ 809/221-4422) in Santo Domingo. This agency runs a minibus to the peninsula daily, charging RD$50 ($3.55) per person round-trip.

Once here, you can rent a car in Barahona from **Challenger Rent-a-Car** (☎ 809/ 524-2457), which offers cars (often badly maintained) on a daily or weekly basis.

ACCOMMODATIONS & MEALS YOU CAN AFFORD

Hotel Caribe. Ave. Enriquillo, Barahona, República Dominicana. ☎ **809/524-4111.** Fax 809/524-4115. 31 units. A/C TV TEL. Year-round RD$406–RD$452 ($28.85–$32.10) single or double. Rates Mon–Thurs include breakfast. AE, MC, V.

Painted a shade of pale blue both inside and out, this three-story hotel lies a few steps from the larger Riviera Beach Hotel (see below). Unpretentious and carefully maintained by the Tesanos family, it occupies a strip of land near the sea, although anyone who wants to go swimming usually walks for 5 minutes to a more hospitable stretch of sand nearby. There's no pool, no tennis courts, and few other facilities. But the price represents extremely good value, the greeting is friendly, and the bedrooms offer comfortable retreats from the sun and sand. Furnishings are simple and basic, but mattresses are firm; the baths, though small, are well maintained.

There's a restaurant and bar on the premises (Punta Inglés), where main courses like grilled steaks and fried local fish range from RD$110 to RD$200 ($7.80 to $14.20).

THE BEST ALL-INCLUSIVE DEAL

✪ **Riviera Beach Hotel.** Ave. Enriquillo 6, Barahona, República Dominicana. ☎ **809/ 524-5111.** Fax 809/524-5798. 108 units. A/C TEL TV. Year-round $115 single; $170 double. Rates include all meals and drinks. AE, DC, MC, V.

This is the largest and most upscale hotel in Barahona. It encourages guests to check in as part of all-inclusive plans. Accented with touches of marble, it rises five stories above one of the best beaches in town. There's a generously proportioned swimming pool on the premises, a tennis court, and two restaurants, one (El Curro) specializing in a la carte dishes, the other (El Manglar) featuring an almost endless roster of buffets. The bedrooms are simple but comfortable, white-walled, and airy, each with a balcony but few other architectural pretensions. Most of the rooms are a bit small but beds are firm and comfortable, and the tiny bathrooms have decent plumbing and an adequate supply of towels.

A NEARBY PLACE TO STAY

Casa Bonita. Carretera de la Costa km 16, Baoruco (near Barahona), República Dominicana. ☎ **809/685-5184.** Fax 809/472-2163. E-mail: casa_bonita@hotmail.com. 12 bungalows. Winter $72–$78 single, $112–$122 double. Off-season $60–$70 single, $98–$112 double. Rates include breakfast and dinner. AE, MC, V.

Built around 1990 in the village of Baoruco, a 15-minute drive south of Barahona, this low-key, slow-paced cottage colony has accommodations that consist of a dozen earth-toned *casitas* whose architecture emulates the natural, simple outdoor life favored in this obscure corner of the D.R. The furnishings are simple, but the beds are good and room space is generous. Six accommodations contain air conditioning, and most of them open onto a view of the water or else the rain forest of the Sierra de Bahoruco. Bathrooms are small but adequate for the job. There's a swimming pool, a bar, a staff that speaks virtually no English, and both a river (the Baoruco) and a beach a short walk away. The food is a good reason to stay here. The chefs have their own secret recipes and will feed you well.

PRISTINE BEACHES & UNTAMED NATURE

"The southwest," as it's known, is filled in part with small coffee plantations and weekend homes of the upper class of Santo Domingo. The beaches here are white sand, set against a terrain that looks like rain forest in parts. The beaches are all but deserted, although we did spot Oscar de la Renta here one time surveying the land for a fashion layout for *Vogue*.

There's also a series of three government parks, among the most untamed in the Caribbean. **Parque Nacional Isla Cabritos** is one of three islands in the **Lago Enriquillo,** bordering Haiti. This is the largest lake in the Caribbean, 21 miles in length. At 144 feet below sea level, it's also the lowest point in the Caribbean. Because of the lack of rain, it's a rather barren place with a few cacti and gnarled plants. However, people visit in hopes of getting a look at the American crocodile, which was imported to the lake in the early 1930s from Florida.

To visit, contact the **Dirección Nacional de Parques** (☎ 809/221-5340), which escorts visitors to the island twice a day. Nearly a dozen passengers are taken on a small launch for the 20-minute ride across a passage. The island is also home to wild goats, poisonous scorpions, and iguanas. If you want to spot a croc, it's best to take the first boat leaving at 7am.

Another national park, **Parque Nacional Bahoruco,** doesn't have adequate facilities for visitors. However, the most intrepid explore **Parque Nacional Jaragua,** named for a Taíno Indian chief. This very arid land covers some 520 square miles, the largest in the Dominican Republic. It's covered with desert-like vegetation, including many species of birds. Pink flamingos also live here. The park embraces Lago Oviedo, a saltwater lake east of the town of Oviedo. Pink flamingos frequent this lake. You'll really need to take a guided tour to reach this park on the Haitian border. Only trucks and Jeeps can get through, and there are no tourist facilities.

4 La Romana & Altos de Chavón

On the southeast coast, La Romana was once a sleepy sugarcane town that also specialized in cattle raising, and unless one had business here with either industry, no tourist bothered with it. But then **Casa de Campo** (☎ 809/523-3333) was built on its outskirts, a tropical resort of refinement and luxury, and La Romana soon became known among the jet-set travelers. Casa de Campo today remains one of the most expensive resorts in the Caribbean, attracting the well-heeled who demand top service and amenities. There is no other place to stay in this area. (But don't give up—ask your travel agent about package deals. Casa de Campo can often be booked at surprising bargain rates.)

Just east of Casa de Campo is **Altos de Chavón,** a village built specially for artists. For the frugal traveler, Altos de Chavón remains the reason to visit. You can do so in a day, but leave Santo Domingo early in the morning in order to get back to the city by early evening.

GETTING THERE

The easiest air routing to Casa de Campo from almost anywhere in North America is through San Juan, Puerto Rico, on **American Eagle** (☎ 800/433-7300 in the U.S.). See "Getting There" in chapter 17 for details.

From Santo Domingo, you can drive here in about an hour and 20 minutes from the international airport, along Las Américas Highway. (Allow another hour if you're in the center of the city.) Of course, everything depends on traffic conditions. (Watch for speed traps—low-paid police officers openly solicit bribes whether you were speeding or not.)

LA ROMANA
GREAT DEALS ON DINING

Even if you can't afford to stay at Casa de Campo, you might want to enjoy a meal here, as some of its restaurants are moderate in price.

El Patio. In Casa de Campo. ☎ **809/523-3333.** Main courses RD$155–RD$330 ($11–$23.45); buffet RD$236 ($16.75). AE, DC, MC, V. Daily 7am–2:30pm and 3–10pm. CARIBBEAN/AMERICAN.

Originally designed as a disco, El Patio now contains a shield of lattices, banks of plants, and checkerboard tablecloths. Technically it's a glamorized bistro, specializing in all-you-can-eat buffets that are a remarkable value, considering the quality of the cookery and the first-class ingredients. You can also feast on selections from the constantly changing a la carte menu. Try such pleasing dishes as grilled snapper in a savory lime sauce or filet of salmon with a perfectly prepared vinaigrette. The fettuccine in seafood sauce is also good. If you like your dishes plainer, opt for half a roast chicken or else the classic beef tips in a mushroom and onion sauce.

✪ **Lago Grill.** In Casa de Campo. ☎ **809/523-3333.** Buffet RD$300 ($21.30) at lunch, RD$400 ($28.40) at dinner. AE, DC, MC, V. Daily 7–11am, noon–4pm, and 7–11pm. CARIBBEAN/AMERICAN.

The Lago Grill is ideal for breakfast; in fact, it has one of the best-stocked morning buffets in the country. Your view is of a lake, a sloping meadow, and the resort's private airport, with the sea in the distance. At the fresh-juice bar, an employee in colonial costume will extract juices in any combination you prefer from 25 different tropical fruits. Then you can select your ingredients for an omelet and an employee will whip it up while you wait. The buffet includes sandwiches, burgers, *sancocho* (the famous Dominican stew), and fresh conch chowder. There's also a well-stocked salad bar. The hotel also presents a changing array of dinner buffets here, including Chinese, Italian, or Dominican.

BEACHES & SPORTS GALORE AT CASA DE CAMPO

Casa de Campo has one of the most complete water-sports facilities in the Dominican Republic. If you can stay at the resort, which is fabulous, on a bargain package rate, great; if not, you can still take advantage of some of the resort's facilities. Reservations and information on any seaside activity can be arranged through the resort's concierge; call ☎ **809/523-3333.**

A large, palm-fringed sandy crescent, **Bayahibe** is a 20-minute launch trip or a 30-minute drive from La Romana. In addition, **La Minitas** is a tiny, but nice, immaculate beach and lagoon. Transportation is provided on the bus, or you can rent a horse-drawn buckboard. Finally, **Catalina** is a turquoise beach on a deserted island just 45 minutes away by motorboat. You can charter a boat for snorkeling. The resort maintains eight charter vessels, with a minimum of eight people required per outing. Wednesday to Monday, full-day snorkeling trips to Isla Catalina cost $28 per snorkeler.

Trail rides at Casa de Campo cost $20 for 1 hour, $40 for 2.

For **tennis** buffs, 13 clay courts at Casa de Campo are lit for night play. The courts are available daily from 7am to 10pm. Charges are $17 during the day or $20 at night.

ALTOS DE CHAVÓN: AN ARTISTS' COLONY

In 1976 a plateau 100 miles east of Santo Domingo was selected by Charles G. Bluhdorn, then chairman of Gulf + Western Industries, as the site for a remarkable project.

Dominican stonecutters, woodworkers, and ironsmiths began the task that would produce Altos de Chavón, today a flourishing Caribbean art center set above the canyon of the Río Chavón and the Caribbean Sea.

A walk down one of the cobblestone paths of Altos de Chavón reveals at every turn architecture reminiscent of another era. Coral block and terra-cotta brick buildings house artists' studios, craft workshops, galleries, stores, and restaurants. Mosaics of black river pebbles, sun-bleached coral, and red sandstone spread out to the plazas. The **Church of St. Stanislaus** is centered on the main plaza, with its fountain of the four lions, colonnade of obelisks, and panoramic views.

The **School of Design** at Altos de Chavón has offered a 2-year Associate in Applied Science degree, in the areas of communication, fashion, environmental studies, product design, and fine arts/illustration, since its inauguration in 1982. The school is affiliated with the Parsons School of Design in New York and Paris, providing local and international graduates with the opportunity to acquire the advanced skills needed for placement in design careers.

From around the world come artists-in-residence, the established and the aspiring. Altos de Chavón provides them with lodging, studio space, and a group exhibition at the culmination of their 3-month stay.

The **galleries** at Altos de Chavón offer a varied and engaging mix of exhibits. In three distinct spaces—the Principal Gallery, the Rincón Gallery, and the Loggia—the work of well-known and emerging Dominican and international artists is showcased. The gallery has a consignment space where finely crafted silk-screen and other multiple works are available for sale.

Altos de Chavón's *talleres* are craft ateliers, where local artisans have been trained to produce ceramic, silk-screen, and woven-fiber products. From the clay apothecary jars with carnival devil lids to the colored tapestries of Dominican houses, the richness of island myth and legend, folklore, and handcraft tradition is much in evidence. The posters, notecards, and printed T-shirts that come from the silk-screen workshops are among the most sophisticated in the Caribbean. All the products of Altos de Chavón's *talleres* are sold at **La Tienda,** the foundation village store.

Thousands of visitors annually view the Altos de Chavón **Regional Museum of Archaeology,** which houses the objects of Samuel Pion, an amateur archaeologist and collector of treasures from the vanished Taíno tribes, the island's first settlers. The timeless quality of some of the museum's objects makes them seem strangely contemporary in design—one discovers sculptural forms that recall the work of Brancusi or Arp. The museum is open daily 9am to 9pm.

At the heart of the village's performing-arts complex is the 5,000-seat open-air **amphitheater.** Since its inauguration over a decade ago by the late Frank Sinatra and Carlos Santana, the amphitheater has hosted renowned concerts, symphonies, theater, and festivals, including concerts by Julio Iglesias and Gloria Estefan. The annual Heineken Jazz Festival has brought together such diverse talents as Dizzy Gillespie, Toots Thielmans, Tania Maria, and Randy Brecker.

GREAT DEALS ON DINING

Café del Sol. Altos de Chavón. ☎ **809/523-3333,** ext. 2346. Pizza $8–$14. AE, MC, V. Daily 11am–11pm. ITALIAN.

The pizzas at this stone-floored indoor/outdoor cafe are the best on the south coast. The favorite seems to be *quattro stagioni,* made with tomato, mozzarella, mushrooms, artichoke hearts, cooked ham, and olives. You can also order such antipasti as a Mediterranean salad with tuna and ratatouille or a pasta primavera. The chef makes a

Cheap Thrills: What to See & Do for Free (Well, Almost) in the Dominican Republic

- **Explore the National Parks.** This island nation has 16 national parks and 7 nature reserves—unequalled in the Caribbean. Here you can mountain climb—Pico Durate in J. Armando Bermúdez National Park is the highest mountain in the West Indies at 10,700 feet—and cascade, an eco-sport involving climbing to the top of a waterfall, then rappelling down the middle of the cascade. In the southwestern tip of the country, Parque Nacional Jaragua is one of the largest in the Caribbean, with everything from offshore islands to inland deserts. Home to turtles and reptiles, it also has more than half of all the bird species found on the island. Dominican tourist offices will provide complete details about how to tour these parks on your own.

- **Call on the Crocs.** In the southwest part of the country, a rare collection of endangered American crocodiles still live around Lake Enriquillo, a vast body of saltwater that is the biggest lake in the West Indies. In the center of the lake is Parque Nacional Isla Cabritos or "Goat Island," home to the native American crocodile, as well as flocks of pink flamingos, roseate spoonbills, terns, herons, and other birdlife. Like the crocodile, the similarly endangerd rhinoceros iguana and the variegated shell turtle call the lake home. The drive down from Santo Domingo to the lake goes through the ocean-bordering town of Barahona and takes more than 3 hours. *Be duly warned:* This area is one of the hottest in the Caribbean, even in winter. But for some to see nature in the wild like this, it's worth a little heat and inconvenience.

- **Spend a Day in a "Medieval Village."** Alton de Chavón, on the southern coast near the chic resort of Casa de Campo, is without equal in the Caribbean. You can spend a delightful day here—it's free to enter—wandering around this re-creation of a 16th-century village created by an Italian set designer. It's a combination of a living museum and an artisans' colony. Some of the Caribbean's finest artisans can be seen at work here. There's a little bit of

soothing minestrone in the true Italian style, served with freshly made bread. To reach the cafe, climb a flight of stone steps to the rooftop of a building whose ground floor houses a jewelry shop.

El Sombrero. Altos de Chavón. ☎ **809/523-3333.** Reservations recommended. Main courses RD$155–RD$250 ($11–$17.75). AE, MC, V. Daily 6–11pm. MEXICAN.

In this thick-walled, colonial-style building, the jutting hand-hewn timbers and roughly textured plaster evoke a corner of Old Mexico. There's a scattering of dark, heavy furniture and an occasional genuine antique, but the main draw is the spicy cuisine. Most guests dine outside on the covered patio, within earshot of a group of wandering minstrels wearing sombreros. A margarita is an appropriate accompaniment to the nachos, enchiladas, black-bean soup, skillet-hot pork chops, grilled steaks, and brochettes.

La Piazzetta. Altos de Chavón. ☎ **809/523-3333.** Reservations required. Main courses RD$150–RD$354 ($10.65–$25.15). AE, MC, V. Daily 3–10pm. ITALIAN.

La Piazzetta snuggles in the 16th-century–style "village" set high above the Chavón River. Well-prepared Italian dinners might begin with an antipasto misto, followed everything, ranging from an ornate stone church to a Grecian-style amphitheater; there's even a museum with artifacts from the extinct Taíno Indians. Workshops, galleries, and studios can be visited, and the local shops hold equal fascination. There are also a lot of inexpensive dining places if you're staying over for lunch.

- **Explore Santo Domingo's Colonial Past.** Except for the historic core of Old San Juan, no other place in the Caribbean has as much history as the restored colonial zone of Santo Domingo, the heart of this ancient city. It's filled with attractions at every turn, including Calle Las Damas, one of the oldest and most beautiful streets in the New World, named for the ladies of the viceregal court who once lived here and used to promenade up and down.

- **Hang Out at Samaná.** The Samaná peninsula, along the east coast, was settled in the 1820s by thousands of escaped American slaves who established a new life here in little fishing villages. Samaná is just awakening to tourism, and a journey here will show you how the Caribbean used to be before the big developers moved in. The location, reached across rugged terrain, is 168 miles east of the airport at Puerto Plata. Las Terrenas on the north coast of the peninsula alone boasts 17 miles of virgin beach. You can meet and talk to many of the descendants of the runaway slaves, who still speak English.

- **Journey to the Dominican Alps.** Most visitors come to enjoy white sandy beaches. But for an offbeat adventure you can go inland to the resort towns of Jarabacoa and Constanza, the heartland of the "Dominican Alps." These resorts are unexpected on a tropical island. The evenings are cool up here. Evoking Switzerland, chalets instead of beachside homes dominate the landscape. Lying along 90 miles north of Santo Domingo, and easily reached by car, the beauty of the forests, the towering "Alps," and the rushing waterfalls await you.

with filet of sea bass with artichokes-and-black-olive sauce, chicken saltimbocca (with ham), or beef brochette with a walnut-and-arugula sauce. Your fellow diners are likely to be guests from the deluxe Casa de Campo nearby.

SHOPPING

The staff at **Bugambilia,** Altos de Chavón (☎ 809/523-3333, ext. 2355), one of the village's best shops, will explain the origins of dozens of ceramic figures on display. Women have been sculpted in positions ranging from bearing water to carrying flowers to posing as brides; the female figures are crafted in the industrial city of Santiago as part of a long tradition of presenting peasant women without faces. Look, however, for an expression of dignity in the bodies of the figurines. The largest are packed but not shipped. The store also has a winning collection of grotesque papier-mâché carnival masks.

At **Everett Designs,** Altos de Chavón (☎ 809/523-3333, ext. 8331), the designs here are so original that many visitors mistake this place for a museum. Each piece of jewelry is handcrafted in a mini-factory at the rear of the shop. Minnesota-born Bill Everett is the inspirational force for many of these pieces, which include Dominican larimar and amber, 17th-century Spanish pieces-of-eight from sunken galleons, and polished silver and gold.

5 Puerto Plata

Columbus intended to found a city at Puerto Plata and name it La Isabela. But a tempest detained him, and it wasn't until 1502 that Nicolás de Ovando founded Puerto Plata, or "port of silver," 130 miles northwest of Santo Domingo. The port became the last stop for ships going back to Europe, their holds laden with treasures taken from the New World.

Puerto Plata appeals to vacationers who may shun more expensive resorts, and some hotels boast a nearly full occupancy rate almost year-round. It's already casting a shadow on business at longer-established resorts throughout the Caribbean, especially in Puerto Rico.

Most of the hotels are not actually in Puerto Plata itself but are in a special tourist zone called **Playa Dorada.** The backers of this usually sun-drenched spot have poured vast amounts of money into a flat area between a pond and the curved and verdant shoreline. (It rains a lot in Puerto Plata during the winter, whereas the south is drier.) There are major hotels, a coterie of condominiums and villas, a Robert Trent Jones–designed golf course, and a riding stable with horses for each of the major properties.

PUERTO PLATA ESSENTIALS

GETTING THERE   The international airport is actually not in Puerto Plata but east of Playa Dorado on the road to Sosúa. For information about flights from North America, see "Getting There" at the beginning of this chapter.

From Santo Domingo, the 3½-hour drive directly north on Autopista Duarte passes through the lush Cibao Valley, home of the tobacco industry and Bermudez rum, and through Santiago de los Caballeros, the second-largest city in the country, 90 miles north of Santo Domingo.

GETTING AROUND   **Taxi service** is available; just be sure to agree with the driver on the fare before your trip starts, as the vehicles are not metered. You'll find taxis on Central Park at Puerto Plata. At night it's wise to rent your cab for a round-trip. If you go in the daytime by taxi to any of the other beach resorts or villages, check on reserving a vehicle for your return trip. Note that a taxi from Puerto Plata to Sosua will cost around RD$250 ($17.75) each way, and it will hold up to four occupants.

The cheapest way of getting around is on a *motoconcho,* found at the major corners of Puerto Plata and Sosúa. This motorcycle *concho* (taxi) offers a ride to practically anywhere in town. You can also go from Puerto Plata to Playa Dorada (site of most of the hotels). Fares range from RD$20 to RD$25 ($1.40 to $1.80).

For information on renting a car, see "Getting Around" at the beginning of this chapter. You might find that a motor scooter will be suitable for transportation in Puerto Plata or Sosúa, although the roads are potholed.

Minivans are another means of transport, especially if you're traveling outside town. They leave from Puerto Plata's Central Park and will take you all the way to Sosúa. Determine the fare before getting in. Usually a shared ride between Puerto Plata and Sosúa costs RD$15 ($1.05) per person. Service is daily from 6am to 9pm.

FAST FACTS   Round-the-clock drugstore service is offered by **Farmacía Deleyte,** Calle John F. Kennedy 89 (☎ **809/586-2583**). Emergency medical service is provided by **Clínica Dr. Brugal,** Calle José del Carmen Ariza 15 (☎ **809/586-2519**).

To summon the **police** in Puerto Plata, call ☎ **809/586-2331.** Tourist information is available in Puerto Plata at the **Office of Tourism,** Playa Long Beach (☎ **809/586-3676**).

ACCOMMODATIONS YOU CAN AFFORD

Hostal Jimessón. Calle John F. Kennedy 41, Puerto Plata, República Dominicana. ☎ **809/586-5131.** Fax 809/586-7313. 22 units. A/C. Year-round RD$300 ($21.30) single or double. Rates include morning coffee. AE, MC, V.

This is about as simple a hotel as we will recommend. It lies in the commercial heart of downtown Puerto Plata, in what was originally a rather grand wood-sided house whose vestiges of gingerbread trim still remain. The public rooms have high ceilings, remnants of a faded grandeur, and some unusual antiques. The bedrooms, however, lack the charm of the front rooms. In a cinder-block addition in back, they're small, anonymous, and somewhat cramped. Mattresses are well used, and bathrooms are tiny. There are almost no resort-style amenities to speak off, but the staff is polite and the price really can't be beat. No more than two occupants are ever allowed in any bedroom. Only coffee is served in the morning, but there are several cafes in the neighborhood, as well as the many inexpensive restaurants in town.

THE BEST ALL-INCLUSIVE DEALS

Caribbean Village Club on the Green. Playa Dorada, Puerto Plata, República Dominicana. ☎ **809/320-1111,** or 305/269-5909 in Miami. Fax 809/320-5386. 336 units. A/C TV TEL. Winter $130 per person double. Off-season $80 per person double. Rates include meals, beverages, and some water sports. AE, MC, V.

Upgraded in 1996 by a hotel chain, this modern low-rise property is near a cluster of competitors east of the airport, a 10-minute walk to the nearest good beach. The hotel offers comfortable but simple bedrooms, and the all-inclusive rates include three meals a day, all beverages, and some water sports. Surprisingly, their so-called suites aren't much different from the regular doubles—and don't cost any more. Accommodations are decorated in tropical Caribbean colors, with private safes, two queen-size beds with firm mattresses (some rooms have king-size beds), and medium-size bathrooms with good towels and excellent maintenance.

Standard Dominican and international food is offered at El Pilon, Italian pastas at Firenze, and fresh fish and seafood and local beef on the continental menu at La Miranda. At that last restaurant you may want to sample some of the excellent Chilean vintages, all at reasonable prices. Facilities include water sports, seven all-weather tennis courts, a gym, sauna, and swimming pool with swim-up bar.

Villas Doradas Beach Resort. Playa Dorada (Apdo. Postal 1370), Puerto Plata, República Dominicana. ☎ **809/320-3000.** Fax 809/320-4790. 244 units. A/C TV TEL. Year-round $60–$80 per person double. Rates are all-inclusive. AE, MC, V.

This collection of town houses east of the airport is arranged in landscaped clusters, usually around a courtyard. There's no beachfront here. Each unit is pleasantly furnished with louvered doors and windows. The units have sleek tropical styling with tile floors, rattan and bamboo furnishings, and wooden ceilings. Most of the bedrooms have either queen-size or twin beds, each with firm, frequently renewed mattresses. Many also have tiny kitchenettes and balconies or patios. Bathrooms are small but tidily arranged. We didn't get the impression that you'd get any personal service here.

A focal point of the resort is the restaurant Las Garzas, where shows entertain guests every evening beneath the soaring pine ceiling. The management also features barbecues around the pool area, where a net is sometimes set up for volleyball games. Of course, it would be tempting never to leave the shade of the cone-shaped thatch-roofed pool bar, which is one of the most popular parts of the whole resort. El Pescador is a fish restaurant open for dinner beside the beach, and Pancho serves Mexican dishes. For Chinese food, Jardín de Jade is another option. Facilities include a swimming pool, tennis, horseback riding, and kiddie pool, as well as sand beaches and golf facilities within walking distance.

GREAT DEALS ON DINING

Another World/Otro Mundo. Km. 7, Hwy. Puerto Plata–Sosúa. ☎ **809/320-4400** or 809/543-8019. Reservations recommended. Main courses RD$95–RD$300 ($6.75–$21.30). DC, MC, V. Daily 6pm–midnight. INTERNATIONAL.

This is the most unusual restaurant in Puerto Plata and even attracts diners from the nearby all-inclusive hotels. About a mile east of the Playa Dorada tourist zone, in a green-sided Victorian building, it has a benign resident ghost (which some readers claim to have spotted), an indoor/outdoor format accented with tropical touches, and an ersatz zoo whose residents (a tiger, monkeys, a honey bear, and wild birds) were all once abused before finding a home with the restaurant's kind-hearted owner. He is Stuart Ratner, a New York–born singer and actor who appeared in some productions during the 1970s with Barbra Streisand. ("I came here on holiday 15 years ago and never left," he explains.) Precede a meal here with the place's most popular drink, a "cocolobo, guaranteed to make you fly." It contains about four times the amount of alcohol in a "normal" cocktail. Follow with food that by local standards is almost incomprehensibly exotic, including frogs' legs, deep-water Caribbean crab, river prawns, chateaubriand, and beef Wellington. Also featured is fresh local fish, especially snapper. Live music is sometimes part of the entertainment.

Hemingway's Café. Playa Dorado Plaza. ☎ **809/320-2230.** Burgers RD$55–RD$88 ($3.90–$6.25); Mexican platters, steaks, and seafood RD$90–RD$250 ($6.40–$17.75). AE, MC, V. Daily noon–1:30am. INTERNATIONAL.

The most theme-conscious restaurant in Puerto Plata celebrates everybody's favorite red-blooded role model, Papa Ernesto. Inside, you'll find photographs of the writer fishing, drinking, womanizing, bullfighting, or whatever, and lots of rough-and-ready memorabilia that might make you think you're in Key West. Menu items include at least four kinds of burgers, grilled fish, two-fisted man-sized portions of New York strip steak or pepper steak, and a full complement of Mexican nachos, burritos, or tacos. Drinks include beers from virtually everywhere, priced from RD$35 ($2.50) per bottle. After around 9pm, a karaoke machine cranks out romantic or rock-and-roll favorites so that anyone can be a star.

Jardín de Jade. In the Villas Doradas Beach Resort, Playa Dorada. ☎ **809/586-3000.** Reservations recommended. Main courses RD$200–RD$325 ($14.20–$23.10). AE, DC, MC, V. Daily 7–11pm. CHINESE.

A high-ceilinged, airy, modern restaurant, Jardín de Jade offers the finest Chinese food in the area. Typical menu items include barbecued Peking duck, sautéed diced chicken in chile sauce, and fried crab claws. The chefs specialize in Cantonese and Szechuan cuisine. You've probably eaten these dishes before in better-prepared versions, but at least this restaurant provides a change of pace. Because it's located in a heavily booked resort, it has a captive audience, yet it remains solid and reliable. We haven't had good service here, though.

✪ **Porto Fino.** Ave. Las Hermanas Mirabal. ☎ **809/586-2858.** Main courses RD$50–RD$210 ($3.55–$14.90). AE, MC, V. Daily 10am–11pm. ITALIAN/DOMINICAN.

This popular restaurant, just across from the entrance of the Hotel Montemar in Puerto Plata, serves up generous helpings of parmesan breast of chicken, eggplant parmesan, ravioli, and pizzas, and such regional dishes as *arroz con pollo* (chicken with rice). You'll get off cheap if you order only pizza. Locals and visitors mingle freely here. This is a place to go for a casual meal in casual clothes.

Roma II. Calle Emilio Prud'homme 45 at the corner of Calle Beller. ☎ **809/586-3904.** Main courses RD$75–RD$285 ($5.30–$20.25); pizza RD$57–RD$175 ($4.05–$12.40). AE, MC, V. Daily 11am–midnight. INTERNATIONAL.

This air-conditioned restaurant in the corner of town is staffed by an engaging crew of well-mannered young employees who work hard to converse in English. You can order from 13 varieties of pizza, such as cheese, shrimp, and garlic. Seafood dishes include paella and several preparations of lobster and sea bass. The menu is unfussy, as is the preparation. Don't look for any new taste sensations (except for octopus vinaigrette, one of the chef's specialties). The meat dishes, such as filet steak, are less successful than the fish offerings.

BEACHES, WATER SPORTS & OTHER OUTDOOR PURSUITS

The north coast is a water-sports scene, although the sea here tends to be rough. Snorkeling is popular, and the windsurfing is among the best in the Caribbean. The resort of **Cabarete,** east of Puerto Plata, hosts an annual windsurfing tournament.

BEACHES   Although they face the sometimes turbulent waters of the Atlantic and it rains a lot in winter, beaches put the north coast, including the resort of Puerto Plata, on the tourist map.

The beaches at **Playa Dorada** are centered around the resort of Puerto Plata, which is called the "Amber Coast" because of all the deposits of amber which have been discovered here. Playa Dorada contains one of the most highly centralized concentrations of hotels on the north coast, so the beaches here, even though good, are likely to be crowded at any time of the year. They are lovely, with either soft beige or white powdery sand. The strand opens onto the Atlantic, and it's very popular for waterskiing and windsurfing. There are many concession stands along the beach renting equipment.

Another good choice in the area, **Luperón Beach** lies about a 60-minute drive to the west of Puerto Plata. It has wide powdery-white sand. It's more ideal for windsurfing, scuba diving, and snorkeling than it is for general swimming. Various water sports concessions can be found along the beach here, along with several snack bars. Luperón is set on a wide bay with palm trees in the backdrop that provide wonderful shade when the noonday sun becomes too fierce.

GOLF   Robert Trent Jones Jr. designed the par-72, 18-hole **Playa Dorada** championship golf course (☎ **809/320-3803**), which surrounds the resorts and runs along the coast. Even nongolfers can stop at the clubhouse for a drink or a snack to enjoy the views. It's best to make arrangements at the activities desk of your hotel. Greens fees are RD$450 ($31.95) for 18 holes. Another Jones design, **Playa Grande Golf Course** at Playa Grande, km. 9 carretera Rio San Juan-Cabrera (☎ **800/858-2258** or 809/223-0768), is generating a lot of excitement. Some pros have already hailed it as one of the best of the Caribbean's golf courses. Ten of its holes border the Atlantic, and many of these are also set atop dramatic cliffs overlooking the turbulent waters. When you're not concentrating on your game of golf, you can take in the panoramic views of the ocean and of Playa Grande Beach. The course is 4,888 yards, par 72, and greens fees are $50 year round, with carts costing $25.

SEEING THE SIGHTS

Fort San Felipe, the oldest fort in the New World, is a popular attraction. Philip II of Spain ordered its construction in 1564, a task that took 33 years to complete. Built with 8-foot-thick walls, the fort was virtually impenetrable, and the moat surrounding it was treacherous—the Spaniards sharpened swords and embedded them in coral below the surface of the water. The doors of the fort are only 4 feet high, another deterrent to swift passage. Fort San Felipe was used as a prison during Trujillo's rule. Standing at the end of the Malecón, the fort was restored in the early 1970s. Admission is RD$10 (70¢). It's open Thursday to Tuesday 8am to 4pm.

Isabel de Torres (no phone), a tower with a fort built when Trujillo was in power, affords a panoramic view of the Amber Coast from a point near the top, 2,595 feet above sea level. You reach the observation point by cable car (*teleférico*), a 7-minute ascent. Once here, you are also treated to 7 acres of botanical gardens. The round-trip costs RD$80 ($5.70) for adults, RD$20 ($1.40) for children 12 and under. The aerial ride is operated Thursday to Tuesday 8am to 5pm. There's often a long wait in line for the cable car, and at certain times it's closed for repairs, so check at your hotel before going there.

You can see a collection of rare amber specimens at the **Museum of Dominican Amber,** Calle Duarte 61 (☎ 809/586-2848). The museum, open Monday to Saturday 9am to 5pm, is near Puerto Plata's Central Park. Guided tours in English are offered. Admission is RD$20 ($1.40) for adults, RD$5 (35¢) for children.

The neoclassical house sheltering the Amber Museum also contains the densest collection of **boutiques** in Puerto Plata. Merchandise is literally packed into seven competing establishments. A generous percentage of the paintings are from neighboring Haiti, but the amber, larimar, and mahogany wood carvings are from the Dominican Republic. On the premises is also a patio bar.

SHOPPING

The **Plaza Turisol Complex,** the largest shopping center on the north coast, has about 80 different outlets. Each week, or so it seems, a new store opens. You may want to head here to get a sampling of the merchandise available in Puerto Plata before going to any specific recommendation. The plaza lies about 5 minutes from the centers of Puerto Plata and Playa Dorada, on the main road heading east. Nearby is a smaller shopping center, **Playa Dorada Plaza,** with about 20 shops, selling handcrafts, clothing, souvenirs, and gifts. Both centers are open daily 9am to 9pm.

The **Centro Artesanal,** Calle John F. Kennedy 3 (☎ 809/586-3724), is a non-profit school for the training of Dominican craftspeople, and it's also a promotion center for local crafts and jewelry. Selected student projects are for sale.

The **Plaza Isabela,** in Playa Dorada about 500 yards from the entrance to the Playa Dorada Hotel complex, is a collection of small specialty shops constructed in the Victorian gingerbread style, although much of its inventory has a Spanish inspiration and flair. Here you'll find the main branch of the Dominican Republic's premier jeweler, **Harrison's,** Plaza Isabela, Playa Dorada (☎ 809/586-3933), which specializes in platinum. Although there are almost two dozen branches of Harrison's in the Dominican Republic, the chain—at least as yet—has no outlets anywhere else in the world. Celebrities wearing the jewelry have included Madonna, Michael Jackson, Keith Richards of the Rolling Stones, and Patrick Swayze. It's possible to take a tour of this outlet. Any merchandise that sits for a year in a store is automatically marked down and placed in a special sale section. There's another branch of this store in the Playa Dorada Shopping Plaza (☎ 809/320-2219) in the Playa Dorada Hotel complex.

ROLLING THE DICE & OTHER AFTER-DARK DiVERSIONS

Allegro's Jack Tar Village, Playa Dorada (☎ 809/320-3800), joins the gaming and dancing flocks with a casino and disco. It's built in Spanish Mediterranean colonial style with a terra-cotta roof. Between bouts at the gaming tables, guests quench their thirst at one of five bars. There's also an entertainment center that includes a 90-seat European-style restaurant and a disco for 250 dancers. **Playa Dorada Casino,** in the Playa Dorada Hotel, Playa Dorada (☎ 809/586-3988), has an entrance flanked by columns that leads to an airy garden courtyard. Inside, mahogany gaming tables are reflected in the silver ceiling. No shorts are permitted inside the premises after 7pm, and beach attire is usually discouraged. Both are open daily until 5am.

The Playa Dorada Hotel complex contains about 20 hotels, 5 of which have discos that welcome anyone, resident or not. None of them charges a cover, and the almost-universal drink of choice, Presidente Beer, costs around RD$40 ($2.85) a bottle. As in any disco in a holiday resort, the clientele includes off-hours hotel employees, some local residents, and tourists. Three of the best are in the Playa Dorado Hotel complex: **Andromeda,** in the Hotel Heaven (☎ 809/320-5250), a high-voltage club off the hotel's lobby that opens nightly at 10pm; and **Crazy Moon,** in the Paradise Hotel (☎ 809/320-3663), outfitted in a colonial Caribbean style, with open-air balconies. You can also stop by **Crystal,** a ground-floor disco at the corner of Avenida Las Hermanas Mirabel and the Malecón (☎ 809/586-3752), which charges a cover of RD$100 ($7.10).

6 Sosúa

About 15 miles east of Puerto Plata is one of the finest beaches in the Dominican Republic, Sosúa beach, a strip of soft white sand more than half a mile wide in a cove sheltered by coral cliffs. The beach connects two communities, which together make up the town known as Sosúa. But, regrettably, you may not be allowed to enjoy a day on the beach in peace, as vendors and often beggars pursue visitors aggressively. To the east is our favorite beach, ✪ **Playa Grande,** a long stretch of white sand that has the consistency of powder. The swimming is safe in shallows close to shore. In summer the waters are calmer and more hospitable, and that's true anywhere along the north coast. Playa Grande beach is great for picnics, sunset watching, walking, and hanging out. It's rapidly being developed, and the Playa Grande Hotel is just one of many projects planned. Beachcombers delight in walking along this beach picking up driftwood or anything else that might have washed ashore.

At one end of the beach is **El Batey,** an area with residential streets, gardens, restaurants, shops, and hotels that can be visited by those who can tear themselves away from the beach. Real-estate transactions have been booming in El Batey and its environs, where many streets have been paved and villas constructed.

At the other end of Sosúa beach lies **Los Charamicos,** a sharp contrast to El Batey. Here you'll find tin-roofed shacks, vegetable stands, chickens scrabbling in the rubbish, and warm, friendly people. This community is a typical Latin American village, recognizable through the smells, sights, and sounds in the narrow, rambling streets.

Sosúa was founded in 1940 by European Jews seeking refuge from Hitler, when Trujillo invited 100,000 of them to settle in his country on a banana plantation. Actually, only 600 or so Jews were allowed to immigrate, and of those, only about a dozen or so remained. However, there are some 20 Jewish families living in Sosúa today, and for the most part they are engaged in the dairy and smoked-meat industry the refugees began during the war. Many of the Jews intermarried with Dominicans, and the town has taken on an increasingly Spanish flavor; women of the town are often seen wearing both the Star of David and the Virgin de Altagracia. Nowadays many German expatriates are also found in the town.

GETTING THERE

Taxis, charter buses, and *públicos* from Puerto Plata and Playa Dorada let passengers off at the stairs leading down from the highway to Sosúa beach. Take the *autopista* east for about 30 minutes from Puerto Playa. If you venture off the main highway, anticipate potholes that fall all the way to China.

ACCOMMODATIONS YOU CAN AFFORD

✪ **Hotel Sosúa.** Calle Dr. Alejo Martínez, El Batey, Sosúa, República Dominicana. ☎ 809/571-2683. Fax 809/571-2180. E-mail: hotel.sosua@net.do. 40 units. A/C TV TEL. Winter $40 single, $50 double. Off-season $30 single, $40 double. Rates include continental breakfast. AE, MC, V.

This place is one of the best choices for affordable accommodations in Sosúa. It's in a suburban community about a 2-minute drive from the center of town. Its simple and attractive layout includes a reception area designed to conceal a flagstone-rimmed pool from the street outside. The medium-size bedrooms are strung along a wing extending beside the pool and contain simple furniture that was for the most part crafted locally. The bedrooms contain ceiling fans, a mini-fridge, and an occasional pinewood balcony. Light furnishings, including good beds with firm mattresses, add a graceful note, but the bathrooms are only routine and a bit cramped. On the premises is a restaurant (Caballo Blanco, recommended below), a mini-gym, a bar, and a boutique selling the day-to-day necessities that tourists might need.

Hotel Yaroa. El Batey, Sosúa, República Dominicana. ☎ **809/571-2651.** Fax 809/571-3814. 24 units. A/C. Year-round $35–$45 single or double. MAP $10 extra. AE, MC, V.

The Yaroa is named after a long-ago native village. It encompasses views of dozens of leafy trees that ring its foundations. Inside you'll find an atrium illuminated by a skylight, lots of exposed wood and stone, and a well-designed garden ringing a sheltered swimming pool. Each bedroom has a Spanish-style *mirador* (sheltered balcony) with a planter filled with local ferns, pine louvers for privacy, terra-cotta floors, and airy space. Two of the accommodations are designed like private cabañas at poolside. You don't get a lot of style here, although the beds are moderately comfortable. Bathrooms are a bit old and sometimes you'll want (but not get) more hot water. Nonetheless, it's one of the bargains of the resort, attracting mainly beach buffs who are out partying most of the day and night instead of spending time in their hotel rooms. The on-site restaurant serves only breakfast and lunch, not dinner.

THE BEST ALL-INCLUSIVE DEALS

Casa Marina/Club Marina. La Playita, Sosúa, República Dominicana. ☎ **809/571-3690.** Fax 809/571-3110. 332 units. A/C TV TEL. Year-round Casa Marina $72 single; $150 double. Club Marina $70 single; $130 double. Rates are all-inclusive. AE, MC, V.

These twin hotels were erected in 1987 as part of the building boom that swept over Sosúa. Originally conceived as different entities, they were enlarged and combined in 1996. What's the difference between the two? Residents of the Club Marina's 32 bedrooms have to walk about 3 minutes to reach the resort's main cluster of dining, drinking, entertainment, and water-sports facilities at Playita Beach, a short drive from the center of Sosúa. By far the larger hotel is the Casa Marina, with units scattered among eight separate annexes. (Except for their views, over a pool or a garden, the units at the Club Marina are equivalent in virtually every way, but cost less because of their relative isolation from the heart of the resort's action.)

Throughout the complex, color schemes are brightly tropical, with locally made furniture and touches of rattan. Guest rooms are fairly compact with either twin beds or double ones, each with firm mattresses. The floors are tile, and an advantage are the mirrored closets with safes. Bathrooms are small, but maintenance and plumbing are good. If possible, opt for one of the rooms on the 10th or 11th floors where the views of the sea are panoramic. The big drawback here is massive group bookings.

Residents of both properties share access to three swimming pools, a medley of bars, and four restaurants (meals are included in the price). They include Luigi, an Italian restaurant; Seascape, a place for fish; El Batey, which serves Dominican food in mass-produced buffets; and Jalapeña, a Mexican *cantina*.

Punta Goleta Resort. Cabarete Rd., Cabarete, Sosúa, República Dominicana. ☎ **809/571-0700.** Fax 809/571-0707. 254 units. A/C TV. Winter $105 single; $155 double. Off-season $70 single; $100 double. Rates include all meals. AE, MC, V.

Built in 1986, and set on about 100 acres of sandy, palm-dotted soil, this all-inclusive resort makes it a point to include enough distractions to keep a guest busy. The resort is designed in a neo-Victorian theme, with gingerbread trim and pastel colors. The location is private without being isolated. Bedrooms are a bit cramped, but each one has a tropical motif, with decent beds (firm mattresses) and tiled baths that are tiny but well kept. There are two restaurants on the premises, one of which serves barbecued foods in a beachfront setting, and a disco, swimming pool, two tennis courts, and at least three different bars. Windsurfing is excellent in the waters offshore.

Sosúa by the Sea. Sosúa Beach, Sosúa (Apdo. Postal 361), Puerto Plata, República Dominicana. ☎ **809/571-3222.** Fax 809/571-3020. 81 units. A/C MINIBAR TV TEL. Year-round $92 double, $105 suite. AE, MC, V.

The blue-and-white main building here is softened with inviting wooden lattices. The pool area opens onto Sosúa Bay, and the resort stands on a coral cliff above the beach. From the open-air rooftop lounge you have a view of Mount Isabel de Torres. The accommodations lie along meandering paths through tropical gardens. Reached by elevator, the airy but rather basic bedrooms come with private safes. They are generous in size with light tropical furnishings, often cane, and quilted bedspreads over firm mattresses. Thoughtful extras include kitchenettes and wet bars. The oceanfront units open onto views but lack balconies, but the French windows allow the trade winds to drift in if you don't prefer air-conditioning. Baths are very routine and a bit cramped.

A formal restaurant, Sunset Place, serves both Dominican specialties and an international cuisine with live entertainment, and you can have lunch at the poolside bar and grill. The hotel has many amenities, including a massage parlor and a beauty salon.

GREAT DEALS ON DINING

Caballo Blanco. In the Hotel Sosúa, Calle Dr. Alejo Martínez, El Batey, Sosúa. ☎ **809/571-2683.** Main courses $8–$18. AE, MC, V. Daily 7am–6pm. DOMINICAN/ITALIAN.

This dining room overlooks a swimming pool and a small but pleasant garden. It serves a medley of inexpensive Italian wines, which go well with such dishes as melon slices with Italian ham, shellfish salads, tortellini, spaghetti (with either meat or shellfish sauce), paella (for two diners only), and veal parmigiana. If you want to divide your meal into pasta for an appetizer and a meat dish for a main course, the staff will acquiesce. Main courses include four different preparations of chicken, and your choice of beef filet prepared with cognac, with peppers, with mushrooms, or with ham and cheese, Cordon Bleu–style. These dishes are perfectly acceptable, even well prepared, if not imaginative.

Caribae. Camino Libre 70, Sosúa. ☎ **809/571-3138.** Main courses RD$130–RD$280 ($9.25–$19.90). Daily 5–10pm. AE, DC, MC, V. INTERNATIONAL.

Set within a few steps of Sosúa's police station, a short walk from the center of Sosúa, this restaurant occupies the open-sided premises of a high-ceilinged thatch-covered building that's set in the midst of a verdant garden that's studded with dozens of exotic shrubs and flowering trees. Part of its charm derives from the eco-sensitive efforts of owner Antonio Isa, a biological engineer who appreciates the good life he's created within an environment that stresses harmony of humans with nature. The decor consists of stone-topped tables supported by segments of thick natural logs, and views out over the garden. Ingredients include several kinds of herbs that the owners grow themselves, as well as copious amounts of shrimp they produce in their own shrimp farms. These farms, incidentally, can be toured as part of their eco-tourism endeavors. One of the most tasty dishes served here is a grilled combination platter of seafood, fillet of mahi-mahi or snapper, shrimp, and lobster. Salads here are meal-sized main courses, usually studded with shrimp or seafood. Wines are imported from Europe, California, or Chile. The perfect appetizer? Check out such *tapas* as smoked pork ribs served with tamarind sauce. Looking for something ethnic, simple, and satisfying? Consider a wholesome, time-tested version of *arroz con pollo* (chicken with rice) that's served with a generous helping of herb-flavored beans.

✪ **La Puntilla de Piergiorgio.** Calle La Puntilla. ☎ **809/571-2215.** Main courses RD$175–RD$295 ($12.40–$20.95). AE, MC, V. Daily noon–4pm and 6pm–midnight. ITALIAN.

Set a 10-minute walk west of Sosúa's center, this place serves the best Italian food in town, and attracts an animated clientele of Europeans looking for a change from too constant a diet of Creole and Dominican cuisine. Architecturally, the place might remind you of a garden-style veranda, permeated with Italian whimsy and perched over low cliffs at the edge of the sea. Everybody's drink of choice here seems to be mimosas, a homemade version that delectably precedes such dishes as veal cutlets milanese, spaghetti with marinara or clam sauce (or prepared Sicilian style with eggplant and tomatoes). Also, look for at least five different preparations of fresh fish, including a barbecued version that's especially succulent.

Morua Mai. Pedro Clisante 5, El Batey. No phone. Main courses RD$95–RD$275 ($6.75–$19.50). AE, MC, V. Daily 8am–midnight. CONTINENTAL/DOMINICAN.

The patio here, which faces a popular intersection in the center of town, is the closest thing to a European sidewalk cafe in town. Inside, where occasional live entertainment is an important attraction, is a high-ceilinged, double-decked, and stylish space filled with touches of neo-Victorian gingerbread, upholstered banquettes, and wicker furniture. Consider this place for a drink or cup of afternoon tea in the side courtyard, where a cabaña bar serves drinks from beneath a palm-thatched roof. Pasta, pizzas, and sandwiches, along with light meals, are served at lunch. Full dinners include such dishes as charcoal-grilled lobster, seafood platters, and lots of locally caught fish. An excellent paella is filled with lobster and shrimp. All meats and seafood are specially selected by the owner for freshness.

ECO-TOURING THE SOSÚA AREA

Caribae Tours, at the Caribae restaurant, Camino Libre 70, Sosúa (☎ 809/571-3138), is owned by biological engineer Antonio Isa, whose education and values emphatically stress the need for harmony between humans and the natural environment of the Dominican Republic's north shore. The most appealing of their trips involves a jeep and kayak tour of the upper reaches of the Yasica River valley, the north shore's most fertile. This full-day experience costs $65 per person, and includes tours of the organization's shrimp farms and the 20 riverside ponds they incorporate. There are also options for kayak riding, horseback riding, and guided commentary on an appropriate application of fertilizers and organic farming, particularly as it applies to the production of coffee and guava.

7 Samaná

Another offbeat destination, where prices are still affordable, Samaná is an undeveloped 30-mile-long peninsula located in the northeastern corner of the country. It's about as Casablanca as the Caribbean gets. Hiding out here is an international expatriate enclave of rampant individualists. It also has some of the finest white sandy beaches in the Dominican Republic. The best beach, **Las Terrenas,** lies on the north coast of the peninsula. At any minute you expect to encounter Robinson Crusoe here. Although the strand strip is narrow, it is filled with white sand set against a backdrop of palms. The beach is never crowded. About the only visitors you'll encounter are at sea: the several thousand humpback whales who swim in from Antarctica to birth their calves from January through March. The main town, **La Samaná,** lies on the southern side of the peninsula overlooking a bay. The north coast of the peninsula is more accessible by boat. The roads are a bit of a joke, better suited for donkeys than cars.

In 1824 the *Turtle Dove,* a sailing vessel, was blown ashore at Samaná. Dozens of American slaves from the Freeman Sisters' underground railway escaped to these shores. They settled in Samaná and today their offspring are waiting to greet you. Although Spanish is the major language, you can still hear some form of 19th-century English, and you'll see villages with names such as Philadelphia or Bethesda.

GETTING THERE

To reach Samaná from Sosúa, head east through Cabarete, a windsurfing town 8 miles east of Sosúa. In some ways Cabarete evokes Malibu, California, before it was overdeveloped. East of here lies Playa Grande, a long stretch of beach strip, among the best in the West Indies. After leaving Playa Grande, you still have 120 miles to go east before reaching remote Samaná. Allow about 3 hours, unless you're tempted by one of the beaches along the way.

It's also possible to fly here from Santo Domingo. A small carrier in Santo Domingo, **Air Santo Domingo** (☎ **809/683-8020**), has regularly scheduled flights to Samaná.

ACCOMMODATIONS & MEALS YOU CAN AFFORD

Cayo Levantado. Lomo de Puerto Escondido, Samaná, República Dominicana. ☎ **809/538-3141.** Fax 809/538-2764. 42 units. A/C TV TEL. Winter RD$1,150 ($81.65) single, RD$1,600 ($113.60) double; off-season RD$950 ($67.45) single, RD$1,500 ($106.50) double. Rates are all-inclusive. AE, MC, V.

Built in the mid-1990s and consisting of a main building and a cluster of *casitas* (bungalows) in a landscaped garden at the edge of the sea, this informal and unpretentious resort includes all food and drinks in one price. Within a 30-minute drive west of Samaná, it has two bars and two restaurants, beside the beach and in the hotel's main building, respectively, and a laid-back ambience. The accommodations are outfitted with wicker furniture and colorful, summery fabrics, each with a good bed and a medium-size bathroom. Each has a writing desk. There's a swimming pool on the premises and a sandy beach within a 3-minute walk from the hotel.

This is the more desirable of twin hotels charging the same rates for the same all-inclusive amenities. The affiliate is the **Hotel Cayacoa,** in Samaná (☎ **809/538-3131**), with 82 units that cost the same as those in the Levantado.

Hotel Tropic Banana. Las Terrenas, Provincia de Samaná, República Dominicana. ☎ **809/240-6110.** Fax 809/240-6112. 27 units. Year-round $45–$50 single; $60–$70 double. AE, MC, V.

On a pancake-flat 7-acre parcel of beachfront midway between the ocean and a range of rolling hills and mountains, this is one of the most escapist and otherworldly hotels in northeastern Hispaniola. Composed of an administrative headquarters and at least four white-and-yellow annexes, this place has a Swiss, French, and Dominican staff that will help you get away from it all and relax. There's an unpretentious French and Italian restaurant on the premises (open daily from breakfast to around midnight), a bar, a swimming pool, a tennis court, horses for beachfront gallops, and a car-rental kiosk. The accommodations have just enough furniture and amenities to be livable, but not enough to be plush. The rooms open to private porches and are cooled by ceiling fans and trade winds rather than air-conditioning. Bedrooms have firm mattresses and bathrooms, though small, are tidily maintained with a set of good towels.

The restaurant features Gallic/Caribbean and Italian food that's more stylish than you might have imagined. Try such creative dishes as fish carpaccio with passion fruit or squid salad flavored with fresh mint. It offers live music and merengue dancing at least 1 night a week.

The hotel lies in the town of **Las Terrenas,** with a population of around 8,000 people, set about 9 miles north of the larger town of Sánchez. From Sánchez, the drive is mountainous, requiring 30 minutes negotiating winding mountain roads. Las Terrenas lies 155 miles north of Santo Domingo. Despite that relatively short-sounding distance, the roads are awful, and require 5 hours of driving.

WORTH A SPLURGE

✪ **Villa Serena.** Apdo. Postal 51-1, Las Galeras, Samaná. ☎ **809/538-0000.** Fax 809/538-0009. 11 units. A/C. Year-round $105–$125 single; $115–$130 double. Half-board $23 extra. MC, V.

Some 26 miles east of the town of Samaná, beside the only road that runs along the edge of the peninsula, this hotel was built in the early 1990s along the lines of a rambling, two-story Victorian house with a wraparound balcony. Painted white with a blue-green roof and a large front garden, it sits above a rocky coastline, a 3-minute walk from a relatively uncrowded beach. The accommodations each have a private balcony and a decor that's different from its neighbors (Chinese, neoclassical gold-and-white, or Laura Ashley romantic). The more expensive rooms are air-conditioned; others have ceiling fans. The beds are most comfortable here, and the bathrooms are tidily kept. Conceived for honeymooners and anyone looking for a place to escape urban life, the site is quiet, isolated, and low-key, with little to do other than swim in the oval-shaped pool, visit the beach, read, and chat with other guests. Many guests order lunch from operators of small charcoal grills set up on the beach (simple platters of pork or fish). The in-house restaurant, however, is the best of the three or four mainstream restaurants in Las Galeras, opening every day for breakfast, lunch, and dinner.

EXPLORING A RAIN FOREST & WATCHING WHALES

You can ask your hotel staff about arrangements for day trips to **Los Haitisses,** a national park in nearby Sánchez. Ancient Taíno inscriptions still adorn the cave walls here. This remote, unspoiled rain forest has crystal lakes, mangrove swamps, and limestone knolls. This karst region comprises some 100 miles of mangrove estuaries and land. You can also visit **Las Terrenas,** a remote stretch of coastline with nearly deserted beaches that are only now being discovered, although some German tourists have found them.

Nature lovers also flock here to see some 3,000 **humpback whales** off the coast in winter. Many whale-watching expeditions come here in January and February.

Sportfishing off the coast is among the finest in the entire western hemisphere. The staff or owner of your hotel can put you in touch with local fishermen who will take you out.

12 Grenada

Grenada is famous for being invaded by the U.S. Marines in 1983, but the political troubles are long over on this sleepy island. Today it's a good place to relax in the midst of fairly friendly people and the lovely and popular white sands of Grand Anse Beach. Exploring the lush interior, especially Grand Etang National Park, also is worthwhile. Crisscrossed by nature trails and filled with dozens of secluded coves and sandy beaches, Grenada has moved beyond the 1980s and is now safe and secure. It's not necessarily for the serious party person—and definitely not for those seeking action at the casino. Instead, it attracts visitors who like snorkeling, sailing, fishing, and doing nothing more invigorating than lolling on a beach under the sun.

Because it shelters so many elegant inns and hotels, Grenada has long been known as an upmarket target for well-heeled visitors, some of whom arrive on yachts. However, in recent years it has developed a number of at least moderately priced inns and small hotels, even guest houses, which make traveling here much more possible than ever for the budget traveler. Even cheaper is the offshore island of Carriacou, which is—until it's discovered—one of the major bargains of the Caribbean.

Grenada has any number of inexpensive places to eat existing along-side the more expensive restaurants. Unlike many islands of the Caribbean, Grenada has abundant produce, so all the foodstuff doesn't have to be imported—hence, the lower costs in restaurants that rely on locally produced items.

The "Spice Island," Grenada (pronounced "Gre-*nay*-dah") is part of an independent three-island nation that also includes Carriacou, the largest of the Grenadines, and Petit Martinique. The southernmost of the Windward Islands, it lies 60 miles southwest of St. Vincent and about 90 miles north of Trinidad. An oval island, it's 21 miles long and about 12 miles wide, and is volcanic in origin.

The air on Grenada is full of the fragrance of spice and exotic fruits; the island has more spices per square mile than any other place in the world—cloves, cinnamon, mace, cocoa, tonka beans, ginger, and a third of the world's supply of nutmeg. "Drop a few seeds anywhere," the locals will tell you, "and you have an instant garden." The central area is like a jungle of palms, oleander, bougainvillea, purple and red hibiscus, crimson anthurium, bananas, breadfruit, birdsong, ferns, and palms.

Grenada has a **People to People** program that allows you to meet the doctor, the waiter, or the spice-basket maker. This free program matches visitors to the island with Grenadians who share similar interests. Just contact **New Trends Tours,** P.O. Box 797, St. George's, Grenada, W.I. (☎ **473/444-1236**), and request an introduction. Be sure to specify your interests and what you'd like to do on the island—play golf, have lunch, go to church—or specify the profession of the person you'd like to meet. If you're already on Grenada, stop by the New Trends Tours office.

1 Essentials

VISITOR INFORMATION

In the United States, the **Grenada Board of Tourism** (www.grenada.org) has an information office at 800 Second Ave., Suite 400K, New York, NY 10017 (☎ **800/927-9554** or 212/687-9554).

In Canada, contact the **Grenada Board of Tourism,** 439 University Ave., Suite 820, Toronto, ON M5G 1Y8 (☎ **416/595-1339**). In London, contact the **Grenada Board of Tourism,** 1 Collingham Gardens, Earl's Court, London, SW5 0HW (☎ **020/7370-5164**).

On the island, go to the **Grenada Board of Tourism,** The Carenage, in St. George's (☎ **473/440-2279**), open Monday to Friday 8am to 4pm. Maps, guides, and general information are available.

GETTING THERE

The **Point Salines International Airport** lies at the southwestern toe of Grenada. The airport is about 5 to 15 minutes by taxi from the major hotels.

American Airlines (☎ **800/433-7300**) offers a daily morning flight from Kennedy Airport in New York to Grenada. If you live in many cities of the southeast, such as Atlanta, the better connection is via Miami.

BWIA (☎ **800/292-1183**) has direct service from New York's Kennedy Airport on Thursday and Sunday. The rest of the week they fly from Kennedy to Grenada with stopovers in either Antigua, St. Lucia, or Barbados.

LIAT (☎ **800/468-0482** in the U.S. and Canada, or 268/462-0700) also has scheduled service between Barbados and Grenada (at least four flights daily, although they are sometimes canceled with little notice—we've often spent hours and hours waiting in the Barbados airport for a plane). Through either LIAT or BWIA, you can connect on Barbados with several international airlines, including British Airways, Air Canada, American Airlines, and Air France.

In addition, **British Airways** (☎ **0345/222-111** in England) flies to Grenada every Wednesday and Friday from London's Gatwick Airport, making a single stop at Antigua en route.

GETTING AROUND

BY TAXI   Taxi fares are set by the government. Most arriving visitors take a cab from the Point Salines International Airport to one of the hotels near St. George's, at a cost of $12. Add one-third to the fare from 6pm to 6am. You can also use most taxi drivers as a guide for a day's sightseeing, and the cost can be divided among three or four passengers. The price can be negotiated, depending on what you want to do.

BY RENTAL CAR   First, remember to *drive on the left.* A U.S., British, or Canadian driver's license is valid on Grenada; however, you must obtain a local permit, costing EC$30 ($11.10), before getting onto the roads. These permits can be obtained either from the car-rental companies or from the traffic department at The Carenage in St. George's.

Among the major U.S.-based car-rental firms, **Avis** (☎ **800/331-1212** or 473/440-3936) operates out of a Shell gasoline station on Lagoon Road, on the southern outskirts of Saint George's. Avis will agree to meet you at the airport, but requires at least 24-hour notice before its toll-free reservations service will guarantee availability. To get the best deal, it pays to shop around. Try **Dollar Rent-a-Car** at the Point Salines Airport (☎ **473/444-4786**). You might also try some local concerns such as **McIntyre Brothers Ltd.,** in the True Blue area (☎ **473/444-3944**).

A word of warning about local drivers: There's such a thing as Grenadian driving machismo; the drivers take blind corners with abandon. An extraordinary number of accidents are reported in the lively local paper. Gird yourself with nerves of steel, and be extra alert for children and roadside pedestrians while driving at night. Many foreign visitors, in fact, find any night-driving hazardous.

BY BUS Minivans, charging EC$1 to EC$6 (40¢ to $2.20), are the cheapest way to get around. The most popular run is between St. George's and Grand Anse Beach. Most minivans depart from Market Square or from the Esplanade area of St. George's.

SPECIAL EVENTS

Carnival time on Grenada is the second weekend of August, with colorful parades, music, and dancing. The festivities begin on a Friday, continuing practically nonstop to Tuesday. Steel bands and calypso groups perform at Queen's Park. Jouvert, one of the highlights of the festival, begins at 5am on Monday with a parade of Djab Djab/Djab Molassi, devil-costumed figures daubed with a black substance. (*Be warned:* Don't wear your good clothes to attend this event—you may get sticky from close body contact.) The carnival finale, a gigantic "jump-up," ends with a parade of bands from Tanteen through The Carenage into town.

Fast Facts: Grenada

Banks In St. George's, the capital, **Barclays** is at Church and Halifax streets (☎ **473/440-3232**); **Scotiabank,** on Halifax Street (☎ **473/440-3274**); the **National Commercial Bank (NCB),** at the corner of Halifax and Hillsborough streets (☎ **473/440-3566**); the **Grenada Bank of Commerce,** at the corner of Halifax and Cross streets (☎ **473/440-3521**); and the **Grenada Cooperative Bank,** on Church Street (☎ **473/440-2111**).

Currency The official currency is the **Eastern Caribbean dollar (EC$),** worth about 37¢ at press time. Always determine which dollars, EC or U.S., you're talking about when someone on Grenada quotes you a price. *Rates in this chapter are quoted in U.S. dollars unless otherwise noted.*

Documents A valid passport is required of U.S., British, and Canadian citizens entering Grenada, plus a return or ongoing ticket.

Electricity Electricity is 220–240 volts AC (50 cycles), so transformers and adapters will be needed for U.S.-made appliances.

Embassies & High Commissions Grenada, unlike many of its neighbors, has a **U.S. Embassy** at Point Salines at St. George's (☎ **473/444-1173**). It also has a **British High Commission,** on Church Street, St. George's (☎ **473/440-3536**).

Emergencies Dial ☎ **911** to summon the police, report a fire, or call an ambulance.

Language English is commonly spoken on this island of some 100,000 people, because of the long years of British influence. Creole English—a mixture of several African dialects, English, and French—is spoken informally by the majority.

Medical Care There is a general hospital, **St. George's Hospital** (☎ **473/440-2051**), with an X-ray department and operating room. Private doctors and nurses are available on call.

Pharmacies Try **Gittens Pharmacy,** Halifax Street, St. George's (☎ **473/440-2165**), open Monday, Tuesday, Wednesday, and Friday 8am to 6pm, Thursday 8am to 5pm, and Saturday 8am to 3pm.

Post Office The **General Post Office** is at The Pier, St. George's, open Monday to Friday 8am to 3:30pm.

Safety Street crime occurs here. Tourists have been victims of armed robbery in isolated areas, and thieves frequently steal U.S. passports and alien registration cards in addition to money. Muggings, purse-snatchings, and other robberies occur in areas near hotels, beaches, and restaurants, particularly after dark. Visitors should exercise appropriate caution when walking after dark, or rely on taxis. Visitors may wish to consult with local authorities, their hotels, and/or the U.S. Embassy for current information. Valuables left unattended on beaches are subject to theft. The loss or theft of a U.S. passport overseas should be reported to the local police and the nearest U.S. embassy or consulate. A lost or stolen birth certificate and/or driver's license generally cannot be replaced outside the United States.

Taxes   A 10% VAT (value-added tax) is imposed on food and beverages, and there's an 8% room tax. Upon leaving Grenada, you must fill out an immigration card and pay a departure tax of $14.

Telephone & Fax   International telephone service is available 24 hours a day from pay phones. Public telegraph, Telex, and fax services are also provided from The Carenage offices of **Grenada Telecommunications** (Grentel) in St. George's (☎ **473/440-1000** for all Grentel offices), open Monday to Friday 7:30am to 6pm, Saturday 7:30am to 1pm, and Sunday and holidays 10am to noon. To call another number on Grenada, dial all seven digits, as the island is divided among four telephone exchanges: 440, 442, 443, and 444. The most commonly used is 440.

Tipping   A 10% service charge is added to most restaurant and hotel bills.

Weather   Grenada has two distinct seasons, dry and rainy. The dry season is from January to May; the rest of the year is the rainy season, although the rainfall doesn't last long. The average temperature is 80°F (26.7°C). Because of constant trade winds, the humidity is seldom oppressive.

2 Accommodations You Can Afford

Don't forget that your hotel or inn will probably add a service charge to your bill—ask in advance about this. Also, there's an 8% government tax on food and beverage tabs.

Bailey's Inn. Spring (P.O. Box 82), St. George's, Grenada, W.I. ☎ **473/440-2912.** Fax 473/440-0532. 9 units. Year-round $20 single; $40 double. No credit cards.

This is about as simple a lodging as we will recommend, but if you adjust your expectations accordingly, you might appreciate its position on a hillside above the wharves, shops, and cheap restaurants of St. George's. It's a two-story building owned for four decades by Mrs. Muriel Bailey. The back-to-basics bedrooms are small and have white walls, angular wooden furnishings, ceiling fans, and floors, and tiny baths whose floors are covered either in tiles or carpeting. The beach (Grand Anse) lies within a 15-minute drive.

Camerhogne Park Hotel. Grand Anse (P.O. Box 378), St. George's, Grenada, W.I. ☎ **473/444-4587.** Fax 473/444-3111. 25 units. A/C TV TEL. Winter $55–$65 single or double. Off-season $45–$65 single or double. Apt., $90–$150 winter, $75–$130 off-season. AE, DC, MC, V.

About a 5-minute stroll over to the fabled sands of Grand Anse Beach, this family-owned and -operated hotel lies about a 10-minute drive to the international airport at Point Salines. The small rooms are simply but comfortably furnished and have more amenities than many comparably priced hotels, including both air-conditioning and ceiling fans and medium-sized baths. Most rooms have verandas as well. You'll get a 10% discount for stays of 6 or more nights. There's a restaurant, Cathy's Tavern, on the premises, that makes use of Grenadian produce when available. There's also a bar. The staff will help you arrange tours of the island and a car rental.

Cedars Inn. True Blue (P.O. Box 73), St. George's, Grenada, W.I. ☎ **800/223-6510** in the U.S., or 473/444-4641. Fax 473/444-4652. 20 units. A/C TV TEL. Winter $80–$90 single or double; $95–$105 apt. Off-season $60–$70 single or double; $65–$75 apt. Extra person $20; children 11 and under stay free in parents' room. MAP $30 per person extra. AE, DC, MC, V.

Conveniently located only minutes from both the international airport and Grenada's main attraction, Grand Anse Beach, this is a two-floor block of rooms and apartments. Each accommodation opens onto a private patio and contains a small private bath. The standard rooms are a bit cramped but with good beds, and the apartments are generous in size. The setting is in a tropical landscape, although the rooms themselves are in a very simple motel-type style. West Indian meals are served in the hotel restaurant, and guests can also enjoy the pool bar. There's a free shuttle to take guests to the airport.

✪ **La Sagesse Nature Center.** St. David's (P.O. Box 44), St. George's, Grenada, W.I. ☎ **473/444-6458.** Fax 473/444-6458. E-mail: tsnature@caribsurf.com. 6 units. MINIBAR TV TEL. Winter $60 single, $95–$105 double. Off-season $50 single, $75–$80 double. AE, MC, V.

On a sandy, tree-lined beach 10 miles from Point Salines International Airport, La Sagesse consists of a seaside guest house, restaurant, bar, art and pottery gallery, water sports, and satellite TV. Nearby are trails for hiking and exploring, a haven for wading and shore birds, hummingbirds, hawks, and ducks. Rivers, mangroves, and a salt pond sanctuary enhance the natural beauty of the place. The original Great House of what was once La Sagesse plantation contains two apartments, one with a fully equipped kitchen, and each with high ceilings and comfortable beds. Guests also have a choice of an attractive size two-bedroom beach cottage, with comfortable but well-used furnishings, and, as an added plus, a wraparound porch. The least desirable accommodations are two small, economy-priced bedrooms in back of the inn's patio restaurant. The restaurant/bar specializes in lobster, fresh fish, and salads. You must book early in winter.

Mamma's Lodge. Lagoon Rd. (P.O. Box 248), St. George's, Grenada, W.I. ☎ **473/440-1623.** Fax 473/440-4181. E-mail: dovetail@caribsurf.com. 10 units. Year-round $29.70 single; $42 double; $75 triple. Rates include breakfast. No credit cards.

This is the bargain on Grenada. Mamma's is named after the island's most celebrated cook (now deceased) who became famous in the press during the U.S. invasion of Grenada. Her restaurant, Mamma's (it's a 5-minute walk from here; see "Great Deals on Dining," below), became a hangout for U.S. service personnel. The lodge is about 5 minutes from Grand Anse Beach and about 3 minutes from St. George's. Built in the typical two-floor motel style, it's locally owned and managed. The somewhat cramped rooms are cooled by ceiling fans, and furnishings are rather sparse. Bathrooms are barely adequate for the job, but the place is clean and decent.

No Problem Apartment Hotel. True Blue (P.O. Box 280), St. George's, Grenada, W.I. ☎ **800/74-CHARMS** in the U.S., or 473/444-4634. Fax 473/444-2803. 20 units. A/C TV TEL. Winter $75–$85 single or double. Off-season $55–$65 single or double. Extra person $20. MAP $30 per person extra. AE, MC, V.

An all-suite hotel 5 minutes from Point Salines Airport and Grand Anse Beach, these small one-bedroom apartments are housed in a two-story motel unit. They offer one of the island's best deals at this price. The simply furnished suites open onto a swimming pool and bar area. Each is equipped with such amenities as a radio, satellite TV, phone, and alarm clock, good beds, as well as a fully equipped kitchenette. Babysitting can be arranged, and laundry service is provided. Thoughtful extras include a help-yourself coffee bar and free bicycles, plus a shuttle to and from the beach. There's also a reading room. The staff is one of the most helpful on the island.

St. Ann's Guest House. Paddock, St. George's, Grenada, W.I. ☎ **473/440-2717.** 12 units, 6 with bath. Year-round $20 single without bath, $25 single with bath; $30 double without bath, $40 double with bath; $50 triple with bath. Rates include breakfast. No credit cards.

On the outskirts of St. George's, this family-owned and -operated place is about as simple as you'd want to get. Yet, if you don't expect much, it offers one of the island's bargains. The atmosphere is homelike and inviting. The rooms, although comfortable, are very basic, with simple, much-used furniture. Baths are small. A regular bus runs into the city or to Grand Anse Beach (public transportation tends to be very crowded). Close to the Botanical Gardens and the yacht harbor, the guest house is also near a cinema and a supermarket where you can find the makings of a picnic lunch. Breakfast is included in the rates, and dinner can be provided upon request.

Tropicana Inn. Lagoon Rd., St. George's. ☎ **473/440-1586.** Fax 473/440-9797. www. cpscaribnet.com. E-mail: tropicana@cpsnet.com. 20 units. A/C TV TEL. Year-round $48–$59 single, $59–$71 double. AE, DC, MC, V.

A five-minute walk from the Carenage in St. George's, this relatively new hotel is ideal for those who'd like to be within walking distance of one of the Caribbean's most charming port cities rather than at the beach. There is no pool, but the prices are extremely reasonable. Accommodations in the front overlook the lagoon and one of the island's yacht services—and regrettably, a lot of traffic. Rooms in the back are more spacious but don't have any view at all. Amenities include air-conditioning, but the furnishings are rather basic and the baths are quite small, although the beds are good. The place can get quite lively at times, with buffets, barbecues, and entertainment. See "Grenada After Dark," below, for more details. Laundry, babysitting, and maid service are available. The resort is also family-friendly.

Wave Crest Holiday Apartments. P.O. Box 278, Grand Anse, St. George's, Grenada, W.I. ☎ **800/223-3463** in the U.S., or 473/444-4116. Fax 473/444-4847. 18 apts. A/C TV TEL. Winter $55–$60 single 1-bedroom apt.; $58–$68 double 1-bedroom apt.; $95 2-bedroom apt. for 4. Off-season $50–$55 single 1-bedroom apt., $55–$58 double 1-bedroom apt., $80 2-bedroom apt. for 4. Extra person $12–$15. AE, MC, V.

Set amid a hilly landscape on the outskirts of St. George's, this complex of four independent buildings (all with white walls, red roofs, and vaguely Mediterranean styling) was built in stages between 1980 and 1992. It was completely renovated in 1994 by owners and founders, John and Joyce DaBreo. The medium-size bedrooms have white walls, mahogany furniture (much of it built on the island), carpets laid over tile floors, and—in some cases—views of the ocean. Baths are like those in a standard roadside motel. It's a 7-minute walk to Grand Anse Beach, and a handful of inexpensive diners and bars are nearby. No meals other than breakfast are served.

WORTH A SPLURGE

✪ **Flamboyant Hotel.** P.O. Box 214, Grand Anse Beach, St. George's, Grenada, W.I. ☎ **473/444-4247.** Fax 473/444-1234. www.flamboyant.com. 40 units. A/C MINIBAR TV TEL. Winter $125–$135 single, $145–$160 double, $300–$400 2-bedroom unit for 4. Off-season $85–$105 single, $95–$115 double, $175–$255 2-bedroom unit for 4. Extra person $25–$40 each. MAP $40 extra per adult, $20 extra per child 11 and under. AE, DC, DISC, MC, V.

This hotel is a well-established staple here, and until its room count was surpassed by better-funded rivals, it was one of the larger hotels on the island. It occupies a hillside that slopes down to Grand Anse Beach, a neighborhood peppered with other resorts. It was designed as a complex of modern, red-roofed buildings punctuated with an outdoor swimming pool. The management conscientiously arranges parties, crab races, barbecues, dinner dances, and reggae bands several nights a week. Each medium-size accommodation has a loggia-style balcony overlooking the beach, cream-colored walls, tile floors, good beds, and floral-patterned curtains and upholsteries. The suites contain kitchenettes. Each unit has a somewhat cramped private bath, but maintenance is high. There's a mini-mart selling food supplies and a gift shop, and snorkeling equipment is lent free to residents.

True Blue Inn. Old Mill Ave., True Blue (P.O. Box 308), St. George's, Grenada, W.I. ☎ **800/742-4276** in the U.S., or 473/443-8783. Fax 473/444-1247. 7 units. A/C TV TEL. Winter $176.64 1-bedroom apt. for 1 or 2; $230.10 2-bedroom cottage for 4. Extra person $41.30. Off-season $88.50 single in 1-bedroom apt.; $106.20 1-bedroom apt. for 2; $147.50 2-bedroom cottage for 4. Extra person $29.50. AE, DC, MC, V.

On the south coast of Grenada, about 5 minutes by car from the Point Salines airport and Grand Anse Beach, this resort takes its name "blue" from an old indigo plantation that once stood on this spot. It's appropriately named even for today's site, because of the panoramic views of the blue waters of Prickly Bay. You can select one-bedroom apartments with verandas overlooking the bay, or two-bedroom cottages nestled in tropical gardens. Children can stay in the two cottages (but not in the one-bedroom apartments). The accommodations are tastefully furnished in pastels and tropical rattan pieces, with excellent beds, either king size or twin. Each unit has a fully equipped kitchen with gas stove and large refrigerator. You can scuba dive or snorkel from the hotel's own private dock, and there's also an on-site pool. Boaters frequent the hotel's restaurant and bar, serving an international and Caribbean menu.

3   Great Deals on Dining

The BoatYard. L'Anse-aux-Epines, Prickly Bay. ☎ **473/444-4662.** Main courses EC$25–EC$60 ($9.25–$22.20). AE, MC, V. Daily 8:30am–midnight. INTERNATIONAL.

A favorite hangout of the island's medical students, this restaurant is situated on the water overlooking the marina where the yachts are moored. Lunch consists of a Caribbean daily special, and may include stewed pork or Creole chicken served in a tomato-based sauce with rice. Some of the featured dishes include stewed and barbecued chicken, baked conch parmesan, and grilled steak; most are served with rice, salad, and fresh vegetables. Mexican specialties and Italian pastas also appear on the menu. On Friday nights a steel-drum band plays, and when they're done the sound system is cranked up for indoor-outdoor dancing to the wee hours.

Deyna's. Melville St., St. George's. ☎ **473/440-6795.** Main courses EC$15–EC$60 ($5.55–$22.20); lunch from EC$10.50 ($3.90). No credit cards. Mon–Sat 8am–9pm, Sun 10am–4pm. CREOLE.

This local dive has some true island flavor. It's not much on decor, but it has its faithful followers who come here often for lunch to order well-stuffed sandwiches. Otherwise, the lunch and dinner menus are much the same. Although Mamma's might do it better (see below), you can still dine well here, and eat as the islanders do. That means baked chicken, conch with breadfruit, and stewed fish, served with locally grown vegetables. Many dishes are given added zest by the use of various curries.

✪ Mamma's. Lagoon Rd., St. George's. ☎ **473/440-1459.** Reservations required a day in advance. Fixed-price meal EC$50 ($18.50). MC, V. Daily 8am–midnight. CREOLE. Mamma's lies on the road leading to Grenada Yacht Services.

Every trip to the Caribbean should include a visit to an establishment like this. Serving copious meals, the late Insley Wardally became famous during the U.S. intervention in Grenada, as U.S. servicemen and -women adopted her as their own island Mamma. Mrs. Wardally's daughter, Cleo, carries on, offering the likes of callaloo soup with coconut cream; shredded cold crab with lime juice; freshwater crayfish; fried conch; a casserole of cooked bananas, yams, and dasheen along with ripe baked plantain; and rôtis made of curry and yellow chickpeas, followed by sugar-apple ice cream. Mamma's seafoods are likely to include crab backs, octopus in a hot-and-spicy sauce, and even turtle steak, although the latter could be an endangered species. Mamma is also known for her "wild meats," including armadillo, opossum, monkey (yes, that's right), game birds, and even the endangered iguana. However, "wild things" are only available when Cleo can obtain them. The specialty drink of the house is rum punch—the ingredients are a secret. Dinner here must be reserved a day in advance so you'll be sure of having a choice of 22 different foods from Grenada.

✪ **Morne Fendue.** St. Patrick's. ☎ **473/442-9330.** Reservations required. Fixed-price lunch EC$45 ($16.45). No credit cards. Mon–Sat 12:30–3pm. CREOLE.

As you're touring north from the beach at Grand Anse, the late Betty Mascoll's Morne Fendue, 25 miles north of St. George's, is memorable. This 1912 plantation house, constructed the year she was born, is her ancestral home. It was built of carefully chiseled river rocks held together with a mixture of lime and molasses, as was the custom in that day. Although Miss Mascoll died in June of 1998, her loyal staff carries on in her tradition. Of course, they need time to prepare food for your arrival, so it's imperative to give them a call to let them know you're coming by. Lunch is likely to include yam and sweet-potato casserole, curried chicken with lots of hot spices, and a hotpot of pork and oxtail. Because this is very much a private home, tipping should be performed with the greatest tact. Nonetheless, the hardworking cook and maid seem genuinely appreciative of a gratuity. The staff is known for introducing guests to friends and neighbors on the long verandas beneath the hanging vines of her house.

The Nutmeg. The Carenage, St. George's. ☎ **473/440-2539.** Main courses at dinner EC$18–EC$55 ($6.65–$20.35); lunch EC$16–EC$45 ($5.90–$16.65). AE, DISC, MC, V. Mon–Sat 8am–11pm, Sun 2–11pm. SEAFOOD/CREOLE.

Right on the harbor, the Nutmeg is over the Sea Change Shop where you can pick up paperbacks and souvenirs. Another rendezvous point for the yachting set and a favorite with just about everybody, it's suitable for a snack or a full-fledged dinner. Its drinks are very good; try one of the Grenadian rum punches made with Angostura bitters, grated nutmeg, rum, lime juice, and syrup. An informal atmosphere prevails, as you're served your filet of fish with potato croquettes and string beans. There's always fresh fish, and usually callaloo or pumpkin soup. Lambi (that ubiquitous conch) is also done very well here. Lobster thermidor is the most expensive item on the menu. There's a small wine list with some California, German, and Italian selections. You can drop in just for a glass of beer to enjoy the sea view. Sometimes, however, you'll be asked to share a table.

Papa Hall's. At the Cot Bam Resort, Grand Anse. ☎ **473/444-2050.** Reservations recommended. Main courses EC$30–EC$50 ($11.10–$18.50); lunch EC$6–EC$30 ($2.20–$11.10). AE, MC, V. Daily 9am–11pm. CREOLE.

If you're looking for a casual atmosphere with lots of local color, then stop by for a drink and a bite to eat. If you order carefully, you can enjoy a meal at a sensible price, especially when the chef decides to run specials. The breakfast choices range in price from EC$15 to EC$19 ($5.55 to $7.05) and include not only the standard fare of eggs and bacon, but also West Indian favorites such as smoked herring, codfish, and other local fish served with tomatoes, onions, and fresh local vegetables. The lunch and dinner menus include favored choices like Creole fish, calypso chicken, and various curried dishes including beef, lamb, and lobster. If you're looking for rôtis, the selection consists of beef, fish, chicken, shrimp, vegetable, and lamb. Beverages include specialty juices made from seamoss or the bark of the mauby tree, and punches made from fresh local fruits, and even one made with peanut butter.

Pier 1. The Carenage. ☎ **473/440-9747.** Main courses EC$18–EC$28 ($6.65–$10.35). MC, V. Mon–Sat 8am–11pm. INTERNATIONAL/WEST INDIAN.

This place was originally built as a warehouse at the extreme tip of the northern edge of the Carenage, but when someone added a waterfront veranda to the boxy, unimaginative building, it was immediately transformed into the most desirable perch along the waterfront. The place is best suited for a midday pick-me-up, with or without alcohol, partly because of the cool breezes that blow in off the port. Drinks include U.S. bombers, mango daiquiris, and an especially potent concoction the owners refer to as "navy grog." Menu items include such West Indian fare as *lambi* (conch) chowder, sandwiches, and the most popular dish on the menu, lobster cooked in a coconut cream sauce. We wouldn't say it's the best cooking in town, but it's quite competent and you get good value here.

Rick's Café. Grand Anse Shopping Center. ☎ **473/444-4597.** Main courses EC$11–EC$25 ($4.05–$9.25). No credit cards. Tues–Thurs 11am–9:30pm, Fri–Sat 11am–10pm, Sun 4–9:30pm. AMERICAN.

The main dining area here is bordered on one side by an open kitchen, containing a stone oven and barbecue, and a 30-foot counter complete with stools on the other. The diner-style atmosphere (there's no table service) offers relatively inexpensive meals. They're not preset; you mix and match items to suit your own taste. For example, if you order barbecued chicken or ribs, you could pair it with a side order of fries or a potato served with your choice of toppings. If you're famished, consider a burger. The pizzas are served with a choice of the typical toppings; the most expensive option, a large with six toppings, costs EC$42 ($15.55). At the counter you can dine on banana splits, milkshakes, and 35 to 40 flavors of ice cream, including local favorites like passion fruit, coconut, rum raisin, and soursop.

4 Hitting the Beaches

There are 45 beaches on Grenada, the best of which are found in the southwestern part of the island. But the daddy of them all is ✪ **Grand Anse Beach,** 2 miles of sugar-white sand fronting a sheltered bay and extending into deep waters far offshore. This beach lies only a 10-minute ride from St. George's and is the site of the major resort hotels. The beach is lapped by a clear, gentle surf. If you wish to escape from the fierce heat of the noon-day sun, you can seek shade and relief under the coconut palms and sea-grape trees that form the backdrop for the beach. You can also do your shopping at the beach, as there is a Vendors Market about midway along the beach, where hawkers peddle coral jewelry, palm hats, straw baskets, and the inevitable T-shirts. You can even get your hair braided.

Grand Anse is really the stuff of dreams, and many visitors on short jaunts to Grenada never leave it to explore the interior of the island. It's that special! Protected from strong winds and currents, the waters here are relatively safe, which makes this beach a family favorite. The waters are populated with schools of rainbow-hued fish.

Water-skiing, parasailing, windsurfing, and scuba diving are here, available at watersports concessions and dive shops.

Adjoining Grand Anse, the beach at **Morne Rouge Bay** is less frequented but just as desirable, with its white sands bordering gin-clear waters. It forms a half-moon crescent and is noted for its calm waters and gentle surf, making it ideal for swimming. It also offers some of the best snorkeling in Grenada. Morne Rouge lies about a mile south of Grand Anse Bay and 3 miles south of St. George's. You can order light lunches at a small cafe on the beach.

Pink Gin Beach (don't you love the name?) lies near the airport at Point Salinas, bordering two large resorts, LaSOURCE and Rex Grenadian. It also has white sand and clear waters, ideal for swimming. When you get hungry you can patronize the Aquarium Beach Club with its alfresco dining by the water. Reef snorkeling is possible, and you can rent kayaks at a kiosk here.

If you like your waters more turbulent, you can visit dramatic **Pearl's Beach,** lying north of Grenville on the Atlantic coast. Here the sand is a light gray, but it stretches for miles and is lined with palm trees. You'll practically have the beach to yourself. Everybody else seemingly is at Grand Anse. The surf rises very high here.

Part of Levera National Park, **Levera Beach** is one of the most beautiful on Grenada. This beach lies at the northeastern tip of the island, its sands fronting the Atlantic, which most often means rough waters. Many locals come here for a picnic on the beach, especially on Sundays.

Also on Grenada's southern coast, **La Sagesse Beach** is part of La Sagesse Nature Center. Here the white sand is especially powdery. It is a lovely, tranquil part of the Spice Island, and you can go for nature walks. When it's time for lunch, you'll find a small dining room opening onto the beach.

5 Sports & Other Outdoor Pursuits

GOLF At the **Grenada Golf Course and Country Club,** Woodlands (☎ 473/444-4128), you'll find a 9-hole course, with greens fees of $16 for 9 holes, or $23 if you want to play 18 holes on the 9-hole course. The course is open Monday to Saturday from 8am to 7pm and on Sunday from 8am to 1:30pm. The course offers a view of both the Caribbean Sea and the Atlantic.

HIKING Because of its lushness and beauty, Grenada is one of the Caribbean's best islands for hiking. The best trails wind through **Grand Etang National Park and Forest Preserve** (☎ 473/440-6160 for information). You can take a self-guided nature trail around Crater Lake or go on a more elaborate jaunt, perhaps to the peak of Mount Qua Qua at 2,373 feet. The latter should be done with a guide, costing $25 per person for a 4-hour hike. You can also hike to Mount St. Catherine at 2,757 feet, but this should also be done with a guide, costing $35. For information about hikes, call **Telfor Bedeau Hiking Tours** at ☎ 473/442-6201 or **Arnold's Tours** at ☎ 473/440-0531.

SCUBA DIVING & SNORKELING Along with many other water sports, Grenada offers the diver an underwater world rich in submarine gardens, exotic fish, and coral formations, sometimes with underwater visibility stretching to 120 feet. Off the coast is the wreck of the ocean liner *Bianca C,* which is nearly 600 feet long. Novice divers might want to stick to the west coast of Grenada, whereas more experienced divers might search out the sights along the rougher Atlantic side.

Daddy Vic's Watersports, in the Grenada Renaissance, Grand Anse Beach (☎ 473/444-4371, ext. 638), is directly on the sands. The island's premier dive outfit, it offers night dives or two-tank dives for $65, and PADI instructors will offer an open-water certification program for $350 per person.

In addition, this is the best center for other water sports, offering snorkeling trips for $18 (1½ to 2 hours) or windsurfing with board rentals for $16 per hour. Sunfish rentals are $16 per hour, parasailing is $30 per 10 minutes, jet-skiing runs $44 per half hour, and waterskiing is $15 per run. Even deep-sea-fishing arrangements can be made.

Giving the center serious competition is **Grand Anse Aquatics,** at the Coyaba Beach Resort on Grand Anse Beach (☎ **473/444-7777**). Canadian-run, it's welcoming and inviting to divers, and there's a PADI instructor on site. The dive boat is well equipped with well-maintained gear. Both scuba diving and snorkeling jaunts to panoramic reefs and shipwrecks teaming with marine life are offered. A single dive costs $35, a resort course $75, or a night dive $55. A snorkeling trip can be arranged for $20 in winter or $15 in off-season. Diving instruction, including a resort course, is available.

If you'd rather strike out on your own, take a drive to Woburn and negotiate with a fisher for a ride to **Glovers Island,** an old whaling station, and snorkel away. Glovers Island is an uninhabited rock spit a few hundred yards offshore from the hamlet of Woburn.

Warning: Divers should know that Grenada doesn't have a decompression chamber. If you should get the bends, you'll have to take an excruciatingly painful air trip to Trinidad.

SAILING   Two large "party boats," designed for 120 and 250 passengers, respectively, operate out of St. George's harbor. The ***Rhum Runner*** and ***Rhum Runner II,*** c/o Best of Grenada, P.O. Box 188, St. George's, Grenada, W.I. (☎ **473/440-4FUN**), make shuttle-style trips, three times a day, with lots of emphasis on strong liquor, steelband music, and good times. Four-hour daytime tours, conducted every morning and afternoon, coincide with the arrival of cruise ships, but will carry independent travelers if space is available. Rides cost $20 per person and include snorkeling stops at reefs and beaches along the way. Evening tours are much more frequently attended by island locals, and are more bare-boned, louder, and usually less restrained. They cost $7.50 per person. Regardless of when you take it, your cruise will include rum, reggae music, and lots of hoopla.

TENNIS   The big resorts for the most part have tennis courts for their guests. But if you're staying at a small inn, you won't find such facilities. There are public courts, however, both at Grand Anse and in Tanteen in St. George's.

6 Exploring St. George's & Tropical Waterfalls

There's much to see here, both in the capital city of St. George's and around this lush island.

ST. GEORGE'S

The capital city of Grenada, **St. George's** is one of the most attractive ports in the West Indies. Its nearly landlocked inner harbor is actually the deep crater of a long-dead volcano—or so one is told.

In the town you'll see some of the most charming Georgian colonial buildings to be found in the Caribbean, still standing in spite of a devastating hurricane in 1955. The streets are mostly steep and narrow, which enhances the attractiveness of the ballast bricks, wrought-iron balconies, and red tiles of the sloping roofs. Many of the pastel warehouses date back to the 18th century. Frangipani and flamboyant trees add to the palette of color.

The port, which some have compared to Portofino, Italy, is flanked by old forts and bold headlands. Among the town's attractions is an 18th-century pink Anglican **church,** on Church Street, and the **Market Square** where colorfully attired farm women offer even more colorful produce for sale.

Fort George, on Church Street, built by the French, stands at the entrance to the bay, with subterranean passageways and old guardrooms and cells.

Everyone strolls along the waterfront of **The Carenage** or relaxes on its Pedestrian Plaza, with seats and hanging planters providing shade from the sun.

On this side of town, the **Grenada National Museum,** at the corner of Young and Monckton streets (☎ **473/440-3725**), is set in the foundations of an old French army barrack and prison built in 1704. Small but interesting, it houses finds from archaeological digs, including the petroglyphs, native fauna, the first telegraph installed on the island, a rum still, and memorabilia depicting Grenada's history. The most comprehensive exhibit traces the native culture of Grenada. One of the exhibits shows two bathtubs—the wooden barrel used by the fort's prisoners and the carved marble tub used by Joséphine Bonaparte during her adolescence on Martinique. The museum is open Monday to Friday 9am to 4:30pm and Saturday 10am to 1pm. Admission is $2.

The Outer Harbour is also called the **Esplanade.** It's connected to the Carenage by the Sendall Tunnel, which is cut through the promontory known as St. George's Point, dividing the two bodies of water.

You can take a drive up to Richmond Hill where **Fort Frederick** stands. The French began construction on the fort in 1779; however, after Grenada was returned to Britain, following the Treaty of Versailles in 1783, the English carried on the work until its completion in 1791. From its battlements you'll have a superb view of the harbor and of the yacht marina.

An afternoon tour of St. George's and its environs takes you into the mountains northeast of the capital. About a 15-minute drive delivers you to ✪ **Annandale Falls,** a tropical wonderland, where a cascade about 50-feet high falls into a basin. The overall beauty is almost Tahitian, and you can have a picnic surrounded by liana vines, elephant ears, and other tropical flora and spices. The **Annandale Falls Centre** (☎ **473/440-2452**) houses gift items, handcrafts, and samples of the indigenous spices of Grenada. Nearby, an improved trail leads to the falls, where you can enjoy a refreshing swim. Swimmers can use the changing cubicles at the falls free. The center is open daily 8am to 4pm.

A SPECTACULAR RAIN FOREST & MORE AROUND THE ISLAND

The next day you can head north out of St. George's along the western coast, taking in beaches, spice plantations, and the fishing villages that are so typical of Grenada.

You pass through **Gouyave,** a spice town, the center of the nutmeg and mace industry. Both spices are produced from a single fruit. Before reaching the village, you can stop at the Dougaldston Estate, where you'll witness the processing of nutmeg and mace.

At the **Grenada Cooperative Nutmeg Association** (☎ **473/444-8337**), near the entrance to Gouyave, huge quantities of the spice are aged, graded, and processed. Most of the work is done within the ocher walls of the factory, which sport such slogans as "Bring God's peace inside and leave the Devil's noise outside." Workers sit on stools in the natural light from the open windows of the aging factory and laboriously sort the raw nutmeg and its by-product, mace, into different baskets for grinding, peeling, and aging. It's open Monday to Friday 10am to 1pm and 2 to 4pm, costing $1.

Proceeding along the coast, you reach **Sauteurs,** at the northern tip of Grenada. This is the third-largest town on the island. It was from this great cliff that the Caribs leaped to their deaths instead of facing enslavement by the French.

To the east of Sauteurs is the palm-lined **Levera Beach,** an idyll of sand where the Atlantic meets the Caribbean. This is a great spot for a picnic lunch, but swimming can sometimes be dangerous. On the distant horizon you'll see some of the Grenadines.

Opened in 1994, the 450-acre **Levera National Park** has several white sandy beaches for swimming and snorkeling, although the surf is rough here where the Atlantic meets the Caribbean. It's also a hiker's paradise, and offshore are coral reefs and seagrass beds. The park contains a mangrove swamp, a lake, and a bird sanctuary. Perhaps you'll see a rare tropical parrot. Its interpretative center (☎ **473/442-1018**) is open Monday to Friday 8am to 4pm, Saturday 9am to 4pm, and Sunday 9am to 5pm.

Heading down the east coast of Grenada, you reach **Grenville,** the island's second city. If possible, pass through here on a Saturday morning when you'll enjoy the hubbub of the native fruit-and-vegetable market. There's also a fish market along the waterfront. A nutmeg factory here welcomes visitors.

From Grenville, you can cut inland into the heart of Grenada. Here you're in a world of luxuriant foliage, passing along nutmeg, banana, and cocoa plantations.

In the center of the island, reached along the major interior road between Grenville and St. George's, is ✪ **Grand Etang National Park,** containing the island's spectacular rain forest, which has been made more accessible by hiking trails. Beginning at the park's forest center, the Morne LeBaye Trail affords a short hike along which you can see the 2,309-foot Mount Sinai and the east coast. Down the **Grand Etang Road,** trails lead to the 2,373-foot summit of Mount Qua Qua and the Ridge, and the Lake Circle Trail, taking hikers on a 30-minute trek along Grand Etang Lake, the crater of an extinct volcano lying in the midst of a forest preserve and bird sanctuary. Among the birds you're likely to see are the yellow-billed cuckoo and the emerald-throated hummingbird. The park is also a playground for Mona monkeys. Covering 13 acres, the water is a cobalt blue. All three trails offer the opportunity to see a wide variety of Grenada's flora and fauna. Guides for the park trails are available, but they must be arranged for in advance. After a rainfall the trails can be very slippery (much of the rain falls on Grenada between June and November); hikers should wear sneakers or jogging shoes, and carry drinking water as well. The park's **Grand Etang Interpretation (Nature) Centre,** on the shores of Grand Etang Lake (☎ **473/440-6160**), is open Monday to Friday 8am to 4pm, featuring a video show about the park. An admission of $1 is charged.

You'll then begin your descent from the mountains. Along the way you'll pass hanging carpets of mountain ferns. Going through the tiny hamlets of Snug Corner and Beaulieu, you eventually come back to the capital.

On yet another day you can drive south from St. George's to the beaches and resorts spread along the already much-mentioned Grand Anse, which is one of the most beautiful beaches in the West Indies. Water taxis can also take you from the Carenage in St. George's to **Grand Anse.**

Point Salines, where the airport is located, is at the southwestern tip of the island, where a lighthouse stood for 56 years. A sculpture of the lighthouse has been constructed on the grounds just outside the airport terminal building. A panoramic view ranging from the northwest side of Grenada to the green hills in the east to the undulating plains in the south can be seen from a nearby hill.

Cheap Thrills: What to See & Do for Free (Well, Almost) on Grenada

- **Journey to Forgotten Petite Martinique.** In a 20-minute ride aboard the mailboat from Hillsborough on the island of Carriacou, you can be on an island that time forgot. The fare is only $5 one-way. This little, 486-acre dependency of Grenada is home to some 900 people. The island is really one large hill whose slopes run down to the coast. The eastern shore is rocky, but there are some fine beaches on the western, leeward side, which is more tranquil. It was first settled by the French, and many islanders still have names of French origin. The islanders have long supported themselves by boatbuilding, fishing, and a little smuggling. A visit here to this remote outpost is like a time capsule.

- **Visit the Caribbean's Kayak Capital.** A major attraction of visiting Carriacou, Grenada's sibling island, is to watch tiny, lightweight kayaks being made. Up at the hamlet of Windward, on the northern part of Carriacou, the island's formidable reputation for boat-building comes into sharp perspective. Here you'll see sturdy 70- and 80-foot schooners and sloops in the making, a tradition that goes back to Scottish settlers who came here in the 1800s. You can watch as builders work on their new craft without blueprints along the shoreline. Completion time for the average wooden boat: About 5 months with six good men.

- **Cool Off Under Concord Falls.** Just off the Coast Road, about 8 miles north of St. George's, are the Concord Falls, set in a lush landscape of bamboo, palms, mango, and breadfruit trees. Once here you can take wooden steps to the base of the 65-foot Concord Falls for photos, and, perhaps, a refreshing swim. These are actually a trio of waterfalls with a viewing platform and a small visitor's center. There's even a changing room where you can put on a bathing suit. In the dry months, usually January to May, you can actually stand under the waterfall, because the flow isn't too powerful then. It ranks as the most refreshing dip under a cascade on the island. To approach the two other waterfalls, you have to take an hour's hike through the rainforest. It's worth it. The third and final fall is the most panoramic of all, as water thunders down some 70 feet over massive boulders. Although this creates a pool at the base, no swimming is permitted here.

- **Visit Birds and Monkeys in Grand Etang National Park.** In the deep heart of mountainous Grenada is the Grand Etang National Park, encompassing a

Along the way you'll pass through the village of **Woburn,** which was featured in the film *Island in the Sun,* and go through the sugar belt of **Woodlands,** with its tiny sugarcane factory.

7 Shopping

Everybody who visits Grenada comes home with a basket of spices, better than any you're likely to find in your local supermarket. Wherever you go, you'll be besieged by spice vendors selling hand-woven panniers of palm leaf or straw filled with items grown on the island, including the inevitable nutmeg, as well as mace, cloves, cinnamon, bay leaf, vanilla, and ginger. The local stores also sell a lot of luxury imports, spine of mountains that dominate the interior of the island nation. The highest peaks are Mount Sinai at 2,309 feet and Mount Qua Qua at 2,373 feet. With miles of hiking trails, fishing streams, and panoramic lookout posts, this is one grand adventure for the hiker and Jungle Jim–type explorer. Our favorite trail (the visitor's center here will assist you) is the Seven Sisters Trail in the central mountains. It begins southwest of Grand Etang Lake and leads to a beautiful spot with seven waterfalls and reflecting pools. You're also surrounded by wild birds and other animals, including monkeys. Allow about three hours for hiking this trail, Grenada's most intriguing.

- **Buy Some Essence of Grenada.** No small wonder that Grenada is called the "Spice Island." It is the second largest producer of nutmeg in the world. At the Gouyave Nutmeg Processing Cooperative, in the little town of Gouyave (☎ 473/444-8337), for only $1 you can take a tour, climbing the narrow wooden stairs to the "drying floor" of the biggest processing factory on the island's western coast. Guides will show you the whole process of how nutmeg is produced from the time they are first received at the station until they are carefully graded by hand and bagged for shipment. Visitors can also take along some essence of Grenada with them in the form of jams, jellies, syrup, or plain ground nutmeg, all for sale here.

- **Stroll Around St. George's.** Of this there is little dispute: St. George's, the capital of Grenada, is the prettiest harbor town in the West Indies. It is stacked on an amphitheatrical hillside and filled with houses with red tin roofs, a picture postcard waiting to be photographed. Named after King George III of England, it is split into two main halves, the Carenage on the inner harbor and the Esplanade itself fronting the Caribbean. You can spend an entire day wandering around and taking in its beauty, including old warehouses overlooking the sea. There's a fish market to amuse when the catch is brought in at the end of the day, and the harbour itself is always filled with ferries, tour boats, and schooners. Cruise ships even dock here, and the whole place takes on a festive, fun atmosphere. When a windjammer appears in harbor, as they frequently do on weekends, the place takes on the aura of the 1800s.

mainly from England, at prices that are almost duty free. Grenada is no grand merchandise mart of the Caribbean like St. Thomas and St. Maarten, but you may locate some local handcrafts, gifts, and even art.

At **Arawak Islands,** Upper Belmont Road, St. George's (☎ 473/444-3577), look for at least nine different fragrances distilled from frangipani, wild lilies, cinnamon, nutmeg, and cloves; an all-natural insect repellent that some clients insist is the most effective (and safest) they've ever used; caffeine-free teas distilled from local plants; bitters that will perk up any rum-based drink; and soaps made in small batches and scented with nutmeg. Especially interesting is the root of the khus-khus plant which, when pulverized and stuffed into potpourri bags, will sweeten the scents emanating from musty closets in hot climes.

✪ **Spice Island Perfumes,** The Carenage (☎ 473/440-2006), is a little gem, a virtual treasure trove of perfumes made from the natural extracts of all those herbs and spices grown on Grenada. If you're a collector of exotic scents, this is your store. At least you'll smell different from everybody else. The workshop produces and sells perfumes, potpourri, and teas made from the locally grown flowers and spices. If you like, they'll spray you with a number of desired scents, including island flower, spice, frangipani, jasmine, patchouli, and wild orchid. The shop stands near the harbor entrance, close to the Ministry of Tourism and the public library.

Few other shops on Grenada convey as vivid an impression of the labor and detail that go into the manufacture of a yard of the boldly patterned batik cloth as **Art Fabrik,** Young Street, St. George's (☎ 473/440-0568). Your visit can combine a look at the showroom, where shirts, shifts, shorts, skirts, T-shirts, and virtually every other warm-weather garment you can think of, are sold. A quick visit to the studio is also worthwhile, partly as a means of seeing the hot wax applications and multiple dyeing rituals that go into the psychedelic patterns of the merchandise. If you fancy yourself a seamstress or couturier, or if you're just looking for upholstery fabric, you can buy it here by the bulky bolt.

Bon Voyage, The Carenage (☎ 473/440-4217), is the island's leading purveyor of diamonds, precious stones, and gold and silver jewelry, plus china and crystal that includes such world-renowned names as Wedgwood, Aynsley, Delft Blue, Royal Doulton, Royal Brierley, and Coalport. If you're going on to Aruba, St. Maarten, or St. Thomas, however, you may want to wait and make serious purchases there. Bon Voyage also sells sunglasses, scarves, and accessories.

Gift Remembered, Cross Street, St. George's (☎ 473/440-2482), in the center of town a block from the water, sells handcrafts, straw articles, jewelry, batiks, film, beach wear, postcards, high-quality T-shirts, books, and wood carvings. It's mainly for a sort of aimless shopping, but could come in handy if you promised to bring some remembrance back from the islands for a niece, nephew, or friend.

In the Grand Anse Beach area, you can break up your time in the sun with some handcraft purchases at **Imagine,** Grand Anse Shopping Centre (☎ 473/444-4028). The resort wear isn't the most fashionable we've ever seen, but it's ideal if you're seeking some minor gift item. This shop also offers excellent value in Caribbean handcrafts, all made of natural materials—dolls, ceramics, and straw items.

Sea Change Bookstore, The Carenage (☎ 473/440-3402), is cramped, crowded, and the staff here might remind you of the dissatisfied teachers who used to punish you during elementary school. But despite these drawbacks, it's the largest repository of pretty recent British and American newspapers on Grenada, piled untidily on overflowing shelves. There's also a collection of paperback books, island souvenirs, postcards, and film.

Tikal, Young Street, St. George's (☎ 473/440-2310), is located in an early 18th-century brick building off The Carenage, next to the museum. You'll find an array of tastefully chosen handcrafts from around the world, as well as the finest selection of crafts made on Grenada, including batiks, ceramics, wood carvings, paintings, straw work, and clothing. The owner, Jeanne Fisher, is the designer of the local crafts.

Yellow Poui Art Gallery, Cross Street, St. George's (☎ 473/440-3001), is a 2-minute walk from Market Square and the most interesting shop for souvenirs and artistic items. Here you can see oil paintings and watercolors, sculpture, prints, photography, rare antique maps, engravings, and woodcuts, with prices beginning at $10 and going up. There's also a comprehensive display of newly acquired works from Grenada, the Caribbean area, and other sources, shown in three rooms.

8 Grenada After Dark

The resort hotels provide regular evening entertainment, including steel bands, calypso, reggae, folk dancing, and limbo—even crab racing. Ask at your hotel desk to find out what's happening at the time of your visit.

The island's most popular nightspot is **Fantazia 2001,** Morne Rouge Beach (☎ **473/444-2288**). It's air-conditioned, with state-of-the-art equipment, good acoustics, and fantastic disco lights, and plays the best in regional and international sounds. Theme nights are frequent, ranging from "Oldie Goldies" to reggae nights. Live shows are presented on Friday and Saturday. Admission to the club costs EC$10 to EC$35 ($3.70 to $12.95) per person, depending on the entertainment.

One of our favorite bars is **The Aquarium** at Point Salines (☎ **473/444-1410**). You can also get delectable food here as well. A vaulted wooden roof shelters an array of bamboo stools, fake marble pillars, wooden tables, and a sprawl of decks, all open to the trade winds. You can enjoy the lights of St. George's Harbour here at night.

CatBam, Grand Anse Beach (☎ **473/444-2050**), offers dancing and dining and stays open late. Next to the Coyaba Beach Resort, it sells Carib beer and rôtis on its open terrace. Calypso and reggae waft on the wind. This is one of the best places on the island for a sundowner.

You can also try **Boatyard,** Prickly Bay, L'Anse aux Epines (☎ **473/444-4662**), down by the Marina. The time to show up is Friday night after 11pm when a local DJ spins dance music until dawn. **Casablanca,** Grand Anse (☎ **473/444-1631**), is the island's major sports bar. It is also a piano bar, where the customers are always telling the performer to "Play it again, Sam!" You can enjoy good music and good company, and watch games on a big TV screen.

Also consider the **Beachside Terrace** at the Flamboyant Hotel, Grand Anse (☎ **473/444-4247**), a laid-back spot featuring crab races on Monday nights (you can bet on your favorites), a live steel band on Wednesday and Saturday, and, our favorite, a beach barbecue with live calypso music on Friday nights.

Le Sucrier, Sugar Mill, Grand Anse (☎ **473/444-1068**), has comedy acts, golden oldies, and a disco scene, but only Wednesday through Saturday nights. A young local crowd, both visitors and residents, shows up any time after 9pm.

For those seeking culture, the 200-seat **Marryshow Folk Theatre,** Herbert Blaize Street near Bain Alley, St. George's (☎ **473/440-2451**), offers performances of Grenadian, American, and European folk music and drama, and West Indian interpretative folk dance. This is a project of the University of the West Indies School of Continuing Studies. Check with the Marryshow Theatre or the tourist office to see what's on. Tickets cost EC$15 to EC$20 ($5.60 to $7.40).

9 A Side Trip to Carriacou

Largest of the Grenadines, Carriacou, "land of many reefs," is populated by about 8,000 inhabitants, mainly of African descent, who are scattered over its 13 square miles of mountains, plains, and white-sand beaches. There's also a Scottish colony, and you'll see such names as MacFarland on the island. In the hamlet of Windward, on the east coast, villagers of mixed Scottish and African descent carry on the tradition of building wooden schooners. Large skeletons of boats in various stages of readiness line the beach where workers labor with the most rudimentary of tools, building the West Indian trade schooner fleet. If you stop for a visit, a master boatbuilder will let you climb the ladder and peer inside the shell, and will explain which wood came from which island, and why the boat was designed in its particular way. Much of the population, according to reputation, is involved in smuggling; otherwise, they're sailors, fisherfolk, shipwrights, and farmers.

ESSENTIALS

VISITOR INFORMATION   For information about the island, go to the **Carriacou Board of Tourism** in Hillsborough (☎ **473/443-7948**). Open Monday to Friday from 8am to noon and 1 to 4pm.

GETTING THERE   **Helen Air** (☎ **473/444-2266**) makes the short takeoff and landing (STOL) flight from Grenada's Point Salines International Airport to Carriacou's **Lauriston Airport** in about 25 minutes. It's also possible to fly **Airlines of Carriacou** (☎ **473/444-3549**), which has daily scheduled service not only to Carriacou but to St. Vincent and the Grenadines as well. There are two flights per day on both Monday and Friday. For reservations, contact a travel agent, LIAT, or Airlines of Carriacou itself at the Point Salines airport.

Ferries also run to Carriacou, including the *Osprey Express,* a hovercraft departing Thursday to Tuesday, taking 2 hours and costing $15 per person one way or else $28 round-trip. From the harbor at St. George's, the schooners, *Alexia II, Alexia III,* and *Adelaide B,* head for Carriacou daily except Monday and Thursday. These schooners carry both cargo and people, taking 4 hours and costing $7.50 one way or $12 round-trip.

ACCOMMODATIONS YOU CAN AFFORD

Carriacou is a beautiful but remote island that hasn't yet experienced the onslaughts of hotel developments that have, in many cases, disfigured the landscapes of some other islands.

Ade's Dream Guest House. Hillsborough, Carriacou, Grenada, W.I. ☎ **473/443-7317.** Fax 473/443-8435. 7 units, none with bath; 16 apts. TV. Year-round $25–$34 single or double; $49–$61 apt. for 2. AE, MC, V.

Pronounced "Oddy," these squeaky-clean rooms and apartments are above a grocery store in Carriacou's only town, Hillsborough. They're the bargain of the island, and could make a suitable overnight stop if you don't demand too much in the way of conveniences, although the self-contained apartments do have air-conditioning and ceiling fans. The apartments are worth the extra money, as each also has its own private balcony. You can watch the waves from these balconies and sleep to the sound of the surf. The bedrooms are basic, with shared bathing facilities similar to a school locker room. The facility lies at the edge of a good beach. A simple restaurant across the street serves three meals a day, and a water taxi is available for tours.

Cassada Bay Hotel. Belmont, Carriacou, Grenada, W.I. ☎ **473/443-7494.** Fax 473/443-7672. 15 units. Winter $65 cabin for 1 or 2. Off-season $50 cabin for 1 or 2. MC, V.

Formerly a research study center for a university marine-biology department, this property has been converted into a comfortable, secluded hotel. It occupies a prime hillside with panoramic views of uninhabited islands. Two cabins are made of rough-cut timber and have all-white paneled rooms with simple furniture, double bedrooms, living rooms, and verandas, all serviced by a maid. The bedrooms have insect screens, louvered windows, and ceiling fans. The restaurant serves traditional West Indian food, and there's an open-air bar terrace to watch the sun go down (with a rum punch made with local limes and flavored with freshly ground nutmeg). The area is ideal for beach buffs and snorkelers, and local boats take picnic-bound passengers for trips to nearby islands. There are two dive operations within easy reach, and Jeep rentals can be arranged. It's a 5-minute ride from the airport.

Hope's Inn. L'Esterre, Carriacou, Grenada, W.I. ☎ **473/443-7457.** 6 units, none with bath; 1 apt. Year-round $25 single; $29 double; $45 1-bedroom apt. for 2; $55 1-bedroom apt. for 3. No credit cards.

This is one of the cheapest yet acceptable inns you're likely to find in all of Carriacou or Grenada. Although none of the bedrooms has a private bathroom, the raffishly informal place seems to suit its position on an island rarely visited by outsiders. It was built in 1992 with white walls, a red roof, and ultra-simple amenities such as curtained showers in the hall. The accommodations come with the use of a fan (set on a stand, not hung from the ceiling). Only the apartment has its own private kitchen; residents of the simple bedrooms share two communal cooking areas. (Guests usually prepare their own meals, but some hire cooks.) There's a modest grocery store nearby for purchases of liquor, supplies, soft drinks, cigarettes, and groceries. The beach (L'Esterre Beach) begins about 50 feet from the hotel's foundations.

Scraper's Bay View Holiday Cottages. Tyrrel Bay, Carriacou, Grenada, W.I. ☎ **473/443-7403.** 6 units. Year-round $50 single or double. DISC, MC, V.

The administration of this 1970s hotel contributes a lot to its sense of somewhat disorganized fun. It consists of a main building and three white-sided outbuildings, flower gardens with picket fences and lots of hibiscus and oleander, and a restaurant that in its way is the best-known on the island.

You'll enjoy the bar (where rum punch is a specialty) and the rapid-fire dialogue of the owner, Scraper, whose real name is Stephen Gay. Scraper sometimes performs at his bar or restaurant. Don't expect the formality or services of a full-fledged resort here. If you appreciate nonstandard, aggressively informal hotels with a funky, strongly emphasized ethnic wit, this might be the place for you. The nearest beach is Tyrrel Bay, and the resort lies near the island's southern tip in the village of Harvey Vale.

VILLA RENTALS

Some of the island's most alluring accommodations are in privately owned houses, whose off-island owners surrender the keys to a local management company whenever they don't need access. **Down Island Villa Rentals,** Hillsborough, Carriacou, Grenada, W.I. (☎ **473/443-8182;** www.islandvillas.com; E-mail: islander@caribsurf. com), manages about 15 privately owned villas and apartments located in quiet residential spots. You need to book well ahead December to March. All the rentals are fully equipped homes with full kitchens and are built to take advantage of the trade winds. In winter, units range from $62 to $215 daily depending on their size, dropping in off-season to $50 to $185, plus $20 per extra person. Children 2 to 12 are housed for $10. Homes can accommodate from 2 to 6 guests. Villas are either on, over, or within walking distance of coves and beaches.

GREAT DEALS ON DINING

Scraper's. At Scraper's Bay View Holiday Cottages, Tyrrel Bay. ☎ **473/443-7403.** Main courses EC$16–EC$60 ($5.90–$22.20); lunch from EC$15 ($5.55). DISC, MC, V. Daily 7am–midnight. SEAFOOD.

At this previously recommended guest house, you can order some of the island's finest cuisine in relaxed, friendly surroundings where everybody gets to know everybody else. The decor is hardly elegant, but no one comes here for that. They visit for the good food and the low prices. Scraper's—actually Stephen Gay—makes the best conch on the island, and it's served either Creole style or with curry. Lobster is occasionally featured on the menu. All these seafood delectables are freshly caught that day. Local seasonings add the right touch to bring out the fresh flavor in the food. Begin with Scraper's callaloo soup. The restaurant is right on the beach, and guests have a choice of places for dining, not only inside, but alfresco on the beach if they desire. Three times a week there's a steel band for entertainment.

EXPLORING THE ISLAND

The best time to visit Carriacou is in August in time for its **regatta,** which was begun by J. Linton Rigg in 1965 with the work boats and schooners for which the Grenadines are famous. Now work boats, three-masted schooners, and miniature "sailboats" propelled by hand join the festivities. Banana boats docking at the pier are filled with people rather than bananas, and sailors from Bequia and Union Island camp on tiny Jack-a-Dan and Sandy Isle, only 20 minutes away by outboard motor from Hillsborough. The people of the Grenadines try their luck at the greased pole, footraces, and of course the sailing races. Music fills the air day and night, and impromptu parties are held. At the 3-day celebration, Big Drum dancers perform in the Market Square.

The **Big Drum dance** is part of the heritage of Carriacou brought from Africa and nurtured here more purely than perhaps on any other Caribbean island. The "Go Tambo," or Big Drum, is an integral part of such traditional events as stone feasts (marking the setting of a tombstone) and the accompanying rites. The feast, called *saraca,* and setting of the tombstone may be as long as 20 years after a death. Another event involving the Big Drum and *saracas* is the *maroon.* This can involve a dream interpretation, but it seems actually to be just a regular festivity, held in various places during the dry season, with dancing and feasting. A boat launching may also be accompanied by the Big Drum and the saraca and usually draws crowds of participants.

The **Carriacou Parang Festival** is usually held on the weekend closest to December 25. The festival serves to maintain the indigenous culture of the people of Carriacou. Bands are formed out of guitar, cuatro, bass drum, and violin.

Hillsborough is the chief port and administrative center, handling the commerce of the little island, which is based mainly on growing limes and cotton. The capital bustles on Monday when the produce arrives, then settles down again until "mail day" on Saturday. The capital is nestled in a mile-long crescent of white sand.

The **Carriacou Museum,** on Paterson Street in Hillsborough (☎ **473/443-8288**), opposite Grentel, has a display of Amerindian artifacts, European china, glass shards, and exhibits of African culture. In two small rooms, it preserves the history of Carriacou, which parallels that of its neighbor island, Grenada. It's open Monday to Friday 9:30am to 3:45pm and Saturday 10am to 2pm. Admission is EC$5 ($1.85) per person.

Guadeloupe consists of two islands separated by a narrow seawater channel known as the Rivière Salée. **Grande-Terre,** the eastern island, is typical of the charm of the Antilles, with its rolling hills and sugar plantations. **Basse-Terre,** to the west, is a rugged mountainous island, dominated by the 4,800-foot still-alive volcano La Soufrière. Its mountains are covered with tropical forests, impenetrable in many places. Bananas grown on plantations are the main crop. The island is ringed by beautiful beaches, which have attracted much tourism.

Like Martinique, Guadeloupe isn't the least expensive island in the West Indies. As in all French islands, the cost of dining in restaurants is usually high, though we've found some suitable budget selections. The island has its big expensive resorts, but it also offers a number of Relais Creoles, really like West Indian B&Bs, charging reasonable rates. Some visitors prefer renting a villa, a cottage, or an apartment with a kitchenette.

1 Essentials

VISITOR INFORMATION

For information before you go, call the **French Government Tourist Office** (☎ **800/391-4909** or 202/659-7779; www.francetourism. com).

The major tourist information office on Guadeloupe is the **Office Départemental du Tourisme,** Square de la Banque 5, in Pointe-à-Pitre (☎ **00590/82-09-30**).

GETTING THERE

Most flights into Guadeloupe are tied in with air connections to Martinique. See "Getting There" in chapter 15, Martinique.

Air Canada (☎ **800/268-7240** in Canada or 800/776-3000 in the U.S.), the national carrier of Canada, flies between Montréal and Guadeloupe (but not Martinique) every Saturday throughout the year. Otherwise, Air Canada routes passengers on one of their daily nonstop flights from Toronto to Barbados, where clients connect to other carriers (usually LIAT) to Guadeloupe.

GETTING AROUND

BY TAXI You'll find taxis when you arrive at the airport, but no limousines or buses. From 9pm to 7am, cabbies are legally entitled to charge you 40% more. In practice, either day or night, they charge you whatever they think the market will bear, though technically fares are regulated by the government. Always agree on the price before getting in. Approximate fares are 120F to 130F ($20.40 to $22.10) from the airport to Gosier hotels or 70F ($11.90) from the airport to Pointe-à-Pitre. **Radio taxis** can be called at ☎ **00590/82-99-88** (on Basse-Terre, ☎ **00590/81-79-70**).

If you're traveling with more than two people, it's possible to sightsee by taxi. Usually the concierge at your hotel will help you make this arrangement. Fares are usually negotiated but are around 800F ($136) per day.

BY RENTAL CAR   Having a car enables you to circumnavigate Basse-Terre, which is one of the most panoramic drives in the Caribbean. Car-rental kiosks at the airport are open to meet international flights. Rental rates at local companies might appear lower, depending on the agency, but several readers have complained of mechanical problems and billing irregularities and difficulties in resolving insurance disputes in the event of accidents. So we recommend reserving a car in advance through **Hertz** (☎ **800/654-3001** or 00590/21-09-35), **Avis** (☎ **800/331-1212** or 00590/21-13-54), or **Budget** (☎ **800/527-0700** or 00590/21-13-48), each of which is represented on the island and has its headquarters at the airport.

In addition to the rental rates, you'll have to pay a one-time airport surcharge of 100F ($17) and VAT (value-added tax) of 9.5%. Prices are usually 20% to 25% lower between March and early December.

Driving is on the right-hand side of the road. There are several gas stations along the island's main routes. Because of the distance between gas stations away from the capital, try not to let your gas gauge fall below the halfway mark.

BY BUS   Buses link almost every village with Pointe-à-Pitre. However, you may need to know some French to use the system. From Pointe-à-Pitre you can catch one of these jitney vans, either at the Gare Routière de Bergevin if you're going to Basse-Terre or at the Gare Routière de Mortenol if Grande-Terre is your destination. Service is daily from 5:30am to 7:30pm. The fare from the airport to the Pointe-à-Pitre terminal on rue Peynier is 7F ($1.20).

Fast Facts: Guadeloupe

Currency   The official monetary unit is the **French franc (F),** though some shops will take U.S. dollars. At press time, the exchange rate was 5.90F to U.S.$1 (1F = U.S. 17¢), the rate used to calculate the dollar values given in this chapter. As this is sure to fluctuate a bit, use this rate for general guidance only.

Customs   Items for personal use "in limited quantities" can be brought in tax free.

Documents   For stays of less than 21 days, U.S., British, or Canadian residents need a passport, plus a return or ongoing plane ticket.

Drugstores   The pharmacies carry French medicines, and most over-the-counter American drugs have French equivalents. Prescribed medicines can be bought if you have a prescription. At least one drugstore is always open, but the schedule is always changing. The tourist office can tell you what pharmacies are open at what time.

Electricity   The local electricity is 220 volts AC (50 cycles), meaning that those using U.S.-made appliances will need to bring a transformer and an adapter.

Guadeloupe

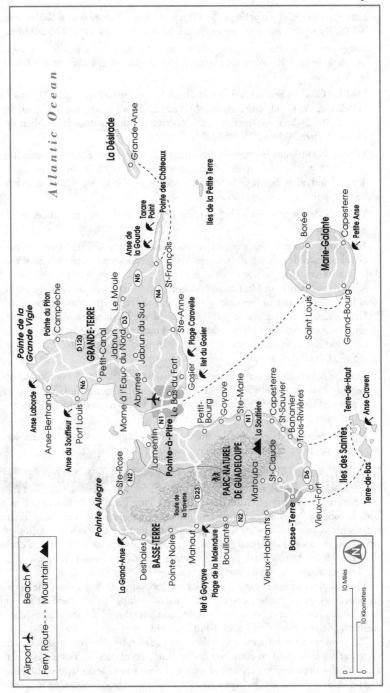

Emergencies   Call the **police** at ☎ **17;** report a **fire** or summon an **ambulance** at ☎ **18.** If the situation involving the police is less urgent, call ☎ **0590/93-00-66.**

Language   The official language is French, and Creole is the unofficial second language. English is spoken only in the major tourist centers, rarely in the countryside.

Medical Care   There are five modern hospitals on Guadeloupe, plus 23 clinics. Hotels and the Guadeloupe tourist office can assist in locating English-speaking doctors. A 24-hour emergency room operates at the **Centre Hôpitalier de Pointe-à-Pitre,** Abymes (☎ **0590/89-10-10**).

Safety   Guadeloupe is relatively free of serious crime. But don't go wandering alone at night on the streets of Pointe-à-Pitre; by nightfall they're relatively deserted and might be dangerous. Purse-snatching by fast-riding motorcyclists has been reported, so exercise caution.

Taxes   A departure tax is included in the airfares. Hotel taxes are included in all room rates.

Telephone   To call Guadeloupe from the United States, dial **011** (the international access code), then **590** (the area code for Guadeloupe), plus the rest of the local number, which will be in six digits.

St. Barts, French St. Martin, and offshore dependencies of Guadeloupe (such as Ile des Saints and La Desirade) are all directly linked to the phone network of Guadeloupe, so no telephone prefix is required when calling from Guadeloupe; simply dial the six-digit phone number of whomever you want to reach. If you call Martinique, however, you'll have to punch in the prefix for Martinique (0596), followed by a six-digit phone local number.

Time   Guadeloupe is on Atlantic standard time year-round, 1 hour ahead of eastern standard time (when it's 6am in New York, it's 7am on Guadeloupe). When daylight saving time is in effect in the U.S., clocks in New York and Guadeloupe show the same time.

Tips & Service   Hotels and restaurants usually add a 10% to 15% service charge. Most taxi drivers who own their own cars do not expect a tip.

2 Pointe-à-Pitre

The port and chief city of Guadeloupe, Pointe-à-Pitre lies on Grande-Terre. Having been burned and rebuilt many times, the port has emerged as a town lacking in character, with modern apartments and condominiums forming a high-rise backdrop over jerry-built shacks and industrial suburbs. The rather narrow streets are jammed during the day with a colorful crowd, creating a permanent traffic tie-up. However, at sunset the town becomes quiet again and almost deserted.

The real point of interest in Pointe-à-Pitre is shopping. It's best to visit the town in the morning—you can easily cover it in half a day—taking in the waterfront and outdoor market (the latter is livelier in the early hours). Be careful about walking alone on the nearly deserted streets of Pointe-à-Pitre at night.

The town center is **place de la Victoire,** a park shaded by palm trees and poincianas. Here you'll see some old sandbox trees said to have been planted by Victor Hugues, the mulatto who organized a revolutionary army of both whites and blacks to establish a dictatorship. In this square he kept a guillotine busy, and the death-dealing instrument still stood here (but not in use) until modern times.

With the recent completion of the **Centre St-Jean-Perse,** a $20-million project that had been on the drawing boards for many years, the waterfront of Pointe-à-Pitre has been transformed from a bastion of old warehouses and cruise-terminal buildings into an architectural complex comprising a hotel, 3 restaurants, 80 shops and boutiques, a bank, and the expanded headquarters of Guadeloupe's Port Authority.

Named for Saint-John Perse, the 20th-century poet and Nobel laureate who was born just a few blocks away, the center is tastefully designed in contemporary French Caribbean style, which blends with the traditional architecture of Pointe-à-Pitre. It offers an array of French Caribbean attractions: duty-free shops selling Guadeloupean rum and French perfume; small tropical gardens planted around the complex; and a location right near the open-air markets and small shops of this bustling port of call. For brochures, maps, and data on sightseeing, the Guadeloupe tourist office is just minutes away.

ACCOMMODATIONS YOU CAN AFFORD

Hôtel St-John Anchorage. Centre Saint-John-Perse, rue Frébaut (at the harbor-front), 97110 Pointe-à-Pitre, Guadeloupe, F.W.I. ☎ **0590/82-51-57.** Fax 0590/82-52-61. 44 units. A/C TV TEL. Year-round, 423F ($71.90) single; 523F ($88.90) double. Rates include continental breakfast. MC, V.

This hotel rises four stories above the harbor-front, near the quays. The small rooms are clean, simple, and furnished with locally-crafted mahogany pieces, with good beds. Very few have views over the sea. Once you check in, the staff might leave you alone until the end of your stay. There's a simple coffee shop/cafe on the street level. Stay here if you want to be in the capital and don't have convenient transportation to go elsewhere. To reach a beach, you'll have to travel 2 miles to the east to Le Bas du Fort and the Grosier area (see below).

GREAT DEALS ON DINING

Le Big Steak House. Rue Delgrès 2 (at quai Lardenoy). ☎ **0590/82-12-44.** Main courses 92F–128F ($15.65–$21.75). AE, MC, V. Mon–Sat noon–3pm. STEAKS/SEAFOOD.

Virtually every shopkeeper and office worker in Pointe-à-Pitre is familiar with this well-managed restaurant, since it offers some of the best midday meals in town. Decorated with wood paneling and a Wild West theme, it imports its meats twice a week from the French mainland and prepares them any way you prefer, usually with your choice of five sauces. Anyone who wants more than one sauce as a garnish is cheerfully obliged—examples are versions with mustard, shallots, peppercorns, and chives. Fish culled from local waters is also popular and includes red snapper cooked *en papillote* or grilled *daurade* with Creole sauce. A wide array of French wines is inventoried in the cellar. The place is popular with cruise-ship day-trippers, as it's virtually adjacent to the piers.

SHOPPING

Your best buys will be anything French—perfumes from Chanel, silk scarves from Hermès, cosmetics from Dior, and crystal from Lalique and Baccarat. Though they're expensive, we've found some of these items discounted as much as 30% below U.S. or Canadian prices (but not often). While most shops will accept U.S. dollars, they'll give these discounts only for purchases made by traveler's check. Purchases are duty free if brought directly from the store to the airplane. In addition to the places below, there are also duty-free shops at **Raizet Airport** (☎ **0590/21-14-66**) selling liquor, rums, perfumes, crystal, and cigarettes.

Most shops open at 9am, close at 1pm, then reopen between 3 and 6pm. They're closed on Saturday afternoon, Sunday, and holidays. When the cruise ships are in port, many eager shopkeepers stay open longer.

One of the best places to buy French perfumes, at prices often lower than those charged in Paris, is **Phoenicia,** rue Frébault 8 (☎ **0590/83-50-36**). The shop also has a good selection of imported cosmetics. U.S. traveler's checks will get you further discounts. Other leading perfume shops are **Au Bonheur des Dames,** 49 rue Frébault (☎ **0590/82-83-91**), which is also known for its skin-care products. **L'Artisan Parfumeur,** Center St-John Perse (☎ **0590/83-80-25**), carries not only top French perfumes but also leading American brands at discounted prices.

Rosébleu, rue Frébault 5 (☎ **0590/82-93-44**), sells fine crystal, fine porcelain, and tableware from all the grand chic names of Europe's leading porcelain manufacturers. These include Christofle, Kosta Buda, and Villeroy & Boch, always at prices 20% less than on the French mainland. **Vendôme,** rue Frébault 8–10 (☎ **0590/83-42-84**), has imported fashions for both men and women, as well as a large selection of gifts and perfumes, including the big names. Usually you can find someone who speaks English to sell you a Cardin watch.

If you're interested in French foodstuffs imported from France, including everything from cheese to chocolate, head for **Délice Shop,** rue Achille René-Boisneuf 45 (☎ **0590/82-98-24**). The **Distillerie Bellevue,** rue Bellevue-Damoiseau, 97160 Le Moule (☎ **0590/23-55-55**), produces "the essence of the island"—*rhum agricole,* a pure rum fermented from sugarcane juice. Once this rum was available in great abundance, but now only two distilleries process it. On the island, savvy locals say that the rum there (whose brand name is Rhum Damoiseau) is the only rum you can drink without suffering the devastation of a rum hangover the next morning (comparable to a gin hangover). You're allowed to taste the product.

If you're adventurous, you may want to seek out some native goods in little shops along the backstreets of Pointe-à-Pitre. Collector's items are the **straw hats (*salacos*)** made in Les Saintes islands. They look distinctly related to Chinese coolie hats and are usually well designed, often made of split bamboo. Native **doudou dolls** are also popular gift items.

Open-air stalls surround the **covered market** (Marché Couvert) at the corner of rue Frébault and rue Thiers. Here you can discover the many fruits, spices, and vegetables that are enjoyable just to view if not to taste. In madras turbans, Creole women make deals over their strings of fire-red pimientos. The bright fabrics they wear compete with the rich tones of oranges, papayas, bananas, mangos, and pineapples, and the sounds of an African-accented French fill the air.

MOVING ON TO THE "SOUTH RIVIERA"

Saint-John Perse once wrote about the fine times sailors had in Pointe-à-Pitre, as a stopover on the famous route du Rhum. But since that day is long gone, you may want to move on to the "South Riviera," along Grand-Terre's south coast from Pointe-à-Pitre to Pointe des Châteaux. This area has long stretches of white sands, though the beaches here aren't spectacular, and are often narrow and artificially created.

The first tourist complex you come to, just 2 miles east of Pointe-à-Pitre, is **Le Bas du Fort,** near Gosier. Here you can visit the **Aquarium de la Guadeloupe,** place Créole, Marina Bas-du-Fort (☎ **0590/90-92-38**), rated as one of the three most important of France and the largest and most modern in the Caribbean. Just off the highway near Bas-du-Fort Marina, the aquarium is home to tropical fish, coral, underwater plants, huge sharks, and other sea creatures. It's open daily 9am to 7pm. Admission is 38F ($6.45) for adults and 20F ($3.40) for children 12 and under.

3 Gosier

Some of the biggest and most important hotels of Guadeloupe are at this holiday center, with its nearly 5 miles of beach, stretching east from Pointe-à-Pitre.

For an excursion, you can climb to **Fort Fleur-d'Epée,** dating from the 18th century. Its dungeons and battlements are testaments to the ferocious fighting between the French and British armies seeking to control the island in 1794. The well-preserved ruins command the crown of a hill. From here you'll have good views over the bay of Pointe-à-Pitre, and on a clear day you can see the neighboring offshore islands of Marie-Galante and the Iles des Saintes.

ACCOMMODATIONS YOU CAN AFFORD

Canella Beach Residence. Pointe de la Verdure (B.P. 73), 97190 Gosier, Guadeloupe, F.W.I. ☎ **800/223-9815** or 00590/90-44-00. 146 units. A/C TV TEL. Winter 840F ($142.80) double; 1,050–1,400F ($178.50–$238) suite. Off-season 530F ($90.10) double; 710–970F ($120.70–$164.90) suite. Supplement of 70F ($11.90) in low season and 120F ($20.40) in high, for units with sea views. AE, DC, MC, V.

Near the Creole Beach Hotel and the tip of the Gosier peninsula, this resort evokes an apartment or condominium complex more than a hotel, as virtually everyone opts to prepare at least some of their own meals. Kitchenettes come as standard equipment in each of the summery-looking units, which are scattered amid a trio of three-story pink buildings. Interiors are monochromatically outfitted in wicker and varnished hardwoods, and many open onto views of the beach. Suites come in one-level or duplex form. Accommodations are medium in size, with sturdy beds and tidily maintained (though small) bathrooms. Look for lots of families—most from mainland France—who arrive for stays of at least a week or more. There's a pool and lots of pleasant corners and hideaways. The in-house restaurant, La Verandah, is appealing enough to be visited by residents of nearby hotels and is separately recommended below.

Hotel Le Clipper. Pointe de la Verdure, Gosier, Guadeloupe, F.W.I. ☎ **800/223-9815** in the U.S. and Canada, 212/476-9444 in New York City, or 00590/840-175. Fax 00590/843-815. E-mail: hleclipper@cgit.com. 88 units. A/C TV TEL. Mid-Dec to mid-Apr $131 single, $162 double. Off-season $86 single, $107 double. AE, MC, V.

One of Gosier's newest, and most theme-oriented, hotels was built to look like a five-story ocean liner rising from the sands adjacent to the much larger Hotel Salako. Each of the rooms has its own balcony, angled along the building's curved sides for a view over the sea, and contains a refrigerator, durable and practical wooden furniture, and a safe. Each bathroom has a round-sided window evocative of a porthole, and the bedrooms have oversized bay windows. On the premises is a pool, a bar, and a restaurant, and guests have access to tennis courts at a neighboring hotel. A good percentage of the guests check in as part of tour groups from the French mainland, often arriving with their children in tow.

✪ **Les Flamboyants.** Périnet, chemin des Phares et Balises, 97190 Gosier, Guadeloupe, F.W.I. ☎ **00590/84-14-11.** Fax 00590/84-53-56. 20 units, 10 with kitchenette. A/C. Winter 320–380F ($54.40–$64.60) single; 360–420F ($61.20–$71.40) double. Off-season, 260–320F ($44.20–$54.40) single; 300–360F ($51–$61.20) double. Rates include breakfast. MC, V.

Small scale and—at least in theory—more personalized than the massive hotels in the same neighborhood, this inn was developed around the core of a pink-sided Creole house in a pleasant garden. The main house was built just before World War II, and the various bungalows were constructed without much style in the mid-1970s, many with views over the seacoast and the offshore island, Islet du Gosier. The rooms with kitchenettes are the most expensive. Baths are cramped but generally adequate. Though there's a small pool, most guests opt for a 20-minute trek to the nearest beach, Plage du Gosier. The hotel offers discounts of around 15% for stays of a week or more.

L'Orchidée. Blvd. du Général-de-Gaulle 32, 97190 Gosier, Guadeloupe, F.W.I. ☎ **0590/ 84-54-20.** Fax 0590/84-54-90. 17 units, all with kitchenette; 2 apts. A/C TV TEL. Winter 550F ($93.50) single; 680F ($115.60) double; 750F ($127.50) apt. for 4; 900F ($153) apt. for 6. Off-season 300F ($51) single, 375F ($63.75) double; 500F ($85) apt. for 4; 550F ($93.50) apt. for 6. MC, V.

This four-story hotel rises next to the town hall, an easy walk from the beach and close to the resort's restaurants and shops. In its pale-blue wicker-furnished rooms you'll find a kitchenette with dishes and cookware, and some of the feeling of an apartment in an urban resort. Rooms are medium in size, with rather small bathrooms that are well maintained. There's no restaurant and no pool, but considering the nearby beach and the many attractions nearby, it's still a good choice. The staff is warm-hearted.

Sud Caraibes. Chemin de la Plage, Petit Havre, 97190 Gosier, Guadeloupe, F.W.I. ☎ **00590/85-96-02.** Fax 00590/85-80-39. 12 units. A/C. Winter 490F ($83.30) single, 790–890F ($134.30–$151.30) double. Off-season 300F ($51), 400F ($68) double. MC, V.

Part of this place's appeal (and the reason for its relatively low costs) is its location on the perimeter of the fishing village of Petit Havre, far removed from the shops, casinos, and bustle of Gosier. Opened in the mid-1980s, the resort has gradually developed a roster of guests who don't care much about its lack of resort amenities and appreciate the individual attention they get from the owners. Each room has rattan furniture and a private balcony, though except for a small refrigerator, none has any cooking facilities and there's no restaurant on-site (a mom-and-pop grocery store is within a 10-minute walk). There's a large rectangular pool and a poolside replica of a Creole cottage outfitted with a blue-and-white décor inspired by the traditions of Tunisia, with North African artifacts and ceramics. Many visitors opt for dips in the nearby sea, and serious sunbathing beside the above-mentioned pool. Other than breakfast, meals are not served on a regular basis, except by special arrangement.

GREAT DEALS ON DINING

La Véranda. In the Canella Beach Residence, Pointe de la Verdure, Gosier. ☎ **0590/ 90-44-00.** Reservations recommended. Lunch main courses 35–80F ($5.95–$13.60); dinner main courses 70–350F ($11.90–$59.50). AE, DC, MC, V. Daily noon–2pm and 7–10pm. FRENCH/CARIBBEAN.

In an indoor/outdoor beachfront building on the grounds of the Canella Beach Residence, this well-managed restaurant offers food that's better than you might imagine on first impression. It manages to import more Gallic *savoir-faire* than you might expect, too. Within the sound of the waves, you can enjoy dishes like steamed lobster with shallot butter, fricassee of chicken with freshwater crayfish, and snapper fillet with creamy onion sauce.

SHOPPING

Gosier is a good place to shop for souvenirs and some Haitian paintings. Try **Boutique de la Plage,** Blvd. Général de Gaulle (☎ 00590/84-52-51), which has all sorts of handcrafts. Many are quite junky but some are amusing. The island's best selection of Haitian art is found at **Centre d'Art Haitien,** Montauban 65 (☎ 00590/84-32-60).

ACCOMMODATIONS & DINING IN ST-FÉLIX

✪ **Chez Jeanne/La Nouvelle Table Créole.** In the Village Caraibes Carmelita, St-Félix.
☎ **0590/84-28-28.** Reservations recommended. Main courses 80–140F ($13.60–$23.80).
AE, DC, MC, V. Daily noon–3pm and Mon–Sat 7–9pm. CREOLE.

A 10-minute drive from Gosier on the coastal road to Ste-Anne and adjacent to a small apartment house that's under the same owners, this restaurant serves richly authentic Creole cuisine supervised, and in many cases personally prepared, by Mme Jeanne Carmelite, matriarch *extraordinaire*. Her versions of recipes handed down by her forebears are well seasoned, with a strong emphasis on grilled fish, steamed or stewed conch or octopus, goatmeat or pork stew, and court bouillons of fish. These are in addition to what's *de rigueur* as a part of any proper Creole meal, *accras de morue* and perhaps a *blaff* of chicken or seafood.

Madame Jeanne rents 16 simple rooms in the cement-sided apartment house next door, each with TV and phone and furnished in the simplest possible way. In high season, singles or doubles cost 620F ($105.40) with a kitchen or 420F ($71.40) without. In low season, singles or doubles rent for 400F ($68) with a kitchen or 250F ($42.50) without. The beach at Gosier is about 2 miles away.

4 Ste-Anne

About 9 miles east of Gosier, little Ste-Anne is a sugar town and a resort offering many fine sandy beaches and lodgings. It's the most charming of the villages of Guadeloupe, with its town hall in pastel colors, its church, and its principal square, place de la Victoire, where a statue of Schoelcher commemorates the abolition of slavery in 1848.

ACCOMMODATIONS YOU CAN AFFORD

Auberge du Grand Large. Route de la Plage, 97180 Ste-Anne, Guadeloupe, F.W.I.
☎ **0590/85-48-28.** Fax 0590/88-16-69. 10 bungalows, all with kitchenette. A/C TEL.
Winter, 600F ($102) bungalow for 1 or 2. Off-season, 350F ($59.50) bungalow for 1 or 2.
Extra person 100F ($17). MC, V.

This cottage colony is near the beachfront of Ste-Anne, close to the hamlet's center. Among the more unusual aspects is that each kitchenette is under the sheltering eaves of outdoor verandas guarded by shrubs and flowering vines and with views of the beach or a garden. Bedrooms and baths are small and routine, but the overall comfort is reasonable for the price. There's no pool and only a moderate number of amenities, but the independent travelers these bungalows attract don't seem to mind. You can rent a bungalow for a full week, and forgo the usual maid service, for 2,800F ($476) in high season or 2,100F ($357) in low.

La Barrière de Corail. Durivage, 97180 Ste-Anne, Guadeloupe, F.W.I. For information and reservations, write Mme Giroux, rue Bébian 4, 97110 Pointe-à-Pitre, Guadeloupe, F.W.I.
☎ **0590/88-20-03.** 27 bungalows, all with kitchenette. Winter, 300F ($51) bungalow for 1 or 2. Off-season, 200F ($34) bungalow for 1 or 2. Air-conditioning 20F ($3.40) per night. MC, V.

About ¾-mile from the center of Ste-Anne, adjacent to the Club Med Caravelle and close to clusters of equivalent (but more expensive) competitors, this is a complex of white cottages with corrugated (usually red) roofs and brown trim. The nearest beach is the one shared by the permissive and somewhat topless crowd at Club Med. Expect no frills here, but if you're looking for a woodsy back-to-the-earth kind of ambience and don't need amenities or maid service, one of these bungalows might be for you. The bedrooms, containing beds with well-used mattresses, are cramped, with tiny bathrooms and bare-bones kitchenettes, but few guests spend much time inside anyway. A handful of restaurants are within a brisk walk. No breakfast of any kind is served, and once you arrange for your rental you might not see any staff members for days at a time.

Mini-Beach. B.P. 77, 97180 Plage Ste-Anne, Guadeloupe, F.W.I. ☎ **0590/88-21-13.** Fax 0590/88-19-29. 6 units, 3 bungalows with kitchenette. A/C TEL. Winter, 550–700F ($93.50–$119) single or double or bungalow for 1 or 2. Off-season, 350–400F ($59.50–$68) single or double or bungalow for 1 or 2. Rates include breakfast. AE, V.

Beneath a canopy of trees near the isolated northern edge of Ste-Anne's beach, this small hotel is personally managed by the resident-owner Nicole Poinard. Opened in the early 1980s, it consists of a main building containing half a dozen tiny rooms, a restaurant, and three one-room bungalows close to the water's edge. Surprisingly, it's the rooms, not the bungalows, that sell out faster. Each accommodation features a different décor, with tropical accents and mosquito nets on the beds. There's no pool, no tennis courts, and no other resort-type amenities, but many guests enjoy the blasé, vaguely permissive ambience of this very French hotel. The restaurant has an open kitchen where diners can watch the chef (Philippe) at work preparing lobsters from a holding tank.

SHOPPING

All the rainbow colors of the Caribbean are for sale at **La Case à Soie** in Ste-Anne (☎ **0590/88-11-31**), known for its scarves in flamboyant colors and its flowing silk dresses.

5 St-François

Continuing east from Ste-Anne, you'll notice many old round towers named for Father Labat, the Dominican founder of the sugarcane industry. These towers were once used as cane-grinding mills. St-François, 25 miles east of Pointe-à-Pitre, used to be a sleepy fishing village, known for its native Creole restaurants. Then Air France discovered it and opened a Méridien hotel with a casino. That was followed by the promotional activities of J. F. Rozan, a native, who invested heavily to make St-François a jet-set resort. Now the once-sleepy village has first-class accommodations (and even some budget choices), as well as an airport available to private jets, a golf course, and a marina.

ACCOMMODATIONS YOU CAN AFFORD

Domaine de l'Anse des Rochers. L'Anse des Rochers, 97118 St-François, Guadeloupe, F.W.I. ☎ **0590/93-90-00.** Fax 0590/93-91-00. 356 studio apts. A/C TEL. Winter, 700F ($119) single, 975F ($165.75) double. Off-season 640F ($108.80) single, 715F ($121.55) double. AE, MC, V.

Except for a nearby hotel, this low-slung resort sits in an isolated position amid carefully landscaped grounds adjacent to the sea. Built in 1990, its somewhat cramped accommodations are in a network of detached bungalows or in a series of gingerbread-laced two-story annexes. Beds are good with firm mattresses, and baths don't really have enough room to spread out your stuff, though the plumbing is decent and maintenance is high. Each building is painted a different Creole-inspired color (green, pink, red, or yellow), and paths leading from each of them end up at the resort's pool. The overall effect is that of a small laid-back village that rocks to disco music after dark.

Every unit has a kitchenette, so most guests prepare their own breakfast and lunch from ingredients they buy at an on-site superette, then opt for a dinner in any of three on-site restaurants: Le Blanc-Mangé, focusing almost exclusively on buffets and open only for breakfast and dinner; La Ville Romaine, a French and Mediterranean bistro open daily for lunch and dinner; and Le Tilolo, an informal place for grilled fish and Creole food.

Golf Marine Club Hôtel. Ave. de l'Europe (B.P. 204), 97118 St-François, Guadeloupe, F.W.I. ☎ **0590/88-60-60.** Fax 0590/85-51-43. 74 units. A/C TV TEL. Winter, 600F ($102) single; 626F ($106.40) double. Off-season, 390–450F ($66.30–$76.50) single; 400–480F ($68–$81.60) double. No credit cards.

Critics of this hotel claim its name is deliberately misleading: The golf club it promises is a municipal course across the street; the marine facilities are within walking distance but not associated with the hotel in any way; and the nearest beach is a 5-minute walk away. Despite these caveats, the hotel is a good bet for simple bedrooms with good mattresses and tiny but tidy bathrooms. Some have balconies, but those facing the rear garden are quieter than those opening onto the busy main street of St-François. The staff isn't the most organized on the island, but once you've checked in, you might appreciate the low-key attitude. There's a bar and a simple bistro on-site, serving lunches and dinners.

GREAT DEALS ON DINING

L'Oursin Blanc. Route de la République, St-François. ☎ **0590/88-77-97.** Main courses 45–60F ($7.65–$10.20); fixed-price menu 65–135F ($11.05–$22.95). No credit cards. Daily noon–2:30pm and 6–10:30pm. SEAFOOD/CREOLE.

Outfitted rustically with a mariner's theme, this is a simple but good restaurant featuring fresh fish. There's a bar attached, if you feel like stopping in just for a thirst-quencher. After an apéritif, sit back and peruse the menu, including such dishes as *gratin de christophine* (similar to a squash), fricassee of conch, and a favorite local white fish caught off island, *coffre*, best grilled. You can also order grilled steaks and classic French dishes like mussels in a white-wine-and-butter sauce. But most diners come here for the Creole dishes, including flavorful stuffed crab backs and boudin Creole or blood sausage. Fresh island vegetables are used whenever possible.

6 An Excursion to the Eastern End

POINTE DES CHÂTEAUX

The Atlantic meets the Caribbean 7 miles east of St-François at Pointe des Châteaux, the easternmost tip of Grand-Terre. Here, where crashing waves sound around you, you'll see a cliff sculpted by the sea into castle-like formations, the erosion typical of France's Brittany coast. The view from here is splendid. At the top is a cross put there in the 19th century.

You might want to walk to **Pointe des Colibris,** the extreme end of Guadeloupe. From here you'll have a view of the northeastern sector of the island, and to the east a look at La Désirade, another island, which has the appearance of a huge vessel anchored far away. Among the **beaches** found in coves around here, Pointe Tarare is *au naturel.*

GREAT DEALS ON DINING

Restaurant Les Châteaux. Pointe des Châteaux. ☎ **0590/88-43-53.** Fixed-price menus 100–150F ($17–$25.50). Tues–Sun noon–2pm; Sat 7:30–10pm. CREOLE.

Many visitors make this gazebo-style restaurant the final destination of drives to the extreme eastern tip of Grande-Terre. Although some fixed-price meals are prohibitively expensive, many others cost only 100F ($17). Lunches are informal affairs where at least some guests may dine in bathing suits. Dinner, served only Saturday, is a bit more formal, but still has a barefoot kind of charm heightened by the isolation you might feel on flat, sandy, and scrub-covered Pointe des Châteaux. For savory local fare, try squid in Creole sauce, a court bouillon of fish (it's been simmering on the stove all day), several preparations of lobster, and an unusual *salade de coffre* from the tenderized and grilled flesh of a local fish (*le coffre*), whose armor is so tough local fishers compare it to a crustacean.

LE MOULE

To go back to Pointe-à-Pitre from Pointe des Châteaux, you can use an alternative route, N5 from St-François. After a 9-mile drive you reach the village of Le Moule, which was founded at the end of the 17th century and known long before Pointe-à-Pitre. It used to be a major shipping port for sugar. Now a tiny coastal fishing village, it never regained its importance after it and many other villages of Grand-Terre were devastated in the great hurricane of 1928. Because of its more than 10-mile-long crescent-shaped beach, it's developing as a holiday center. Modern hotels built along the beaches have opened to accommodate visitors.

Specialties of this Guadeloupean village are *palourdes,* the clams that thrive in the semi-salty mouths of freshwater rivers. Known for being more tender and less rubbery than saltwater clams, they often, even when fresh, have a distinct sulfur taste not unlike that of overpoached eggs. Local gastronomes prepare them with saffron and aged rum or cognac.

Nearby, the sea unearthed some skulls, grim reminders of the fierce battles fought among the Caribs, French, and English. It's called the **Beach of Skulls and Bones.**

Three miles from Le Moule heading toward Campêche, the **Edgar Clerc Archaeological Museum La Rosette,** Parc de la Rosette (☎ **0590/23-57-57**), shows a collection of both Carib and Arawak artifacts gathered from various islands of the Lesser Antilles. The museum is open Thursday to Tuesday 9am to 12:30pm and 2 to 5pm. Admission is 10F ($1.70).

To return to Pointe-à-Pitre, we suggest you use route D3 toward Abymes. The road winds around as you plunge deeply into Grand-Terre. As a curiosity, about halfway along the way a road will bring you to **Jabrun du Nord** and **Jabrun du Sud.** These two villages are inhabited by Caucasians with blond hair, said to be survivors of aristocrats slaughtered during the Revolution. Those members of their families who escaped found safety by hiding out in Les Grands Fonds. The most important family is named Matignon, and they gave their name to the colony known as Les Blancs Matignon. These citizens are said to be related to Prince Rainier of Monaco.

Pointe-à-Pitre lies only 10 miles from Les Grand Fonds.

7 Driving Around the Northern Coast of Grande-Terre

From Pointe-à-Pitre, head northeast toward Abymes, passing next through Morne à l'Eau. After 13 miles you'll reach **Petit Canal.** This is Guadeloupe's sugarcane country, and a sweet smell fills the air.

PORT LOUIS

Continuing northwest along the coast from Petit Canal, you come to Port Louis, well known for its beautiful beach, **Plage du Souffleur,** which we find best in spring, when the brilliant white sand is effectively shown off against a contrast of the flaming red poinciana. During the week the beach is an especially quiet spot. The little port town is asleep under a heavy sun and has some good restaurants.

GREAT DEALS ON DINING

✪ **Le Poisson d'Or.** Rue Sadi-Carnot 2, Port Louis. ☎ **0590/22-88-63.** Reservations required. Main courses 65–85F ($11.05–$14.45); fixed-price menu 85–150F ($14.45–$25.50). MC, V. Daily 11:30–4pm; dinner by reservation only. Drive northwest from Petit Canal along the coastal road. CREOLE.

You enter this white-sided Antillean house by walking down a narrow corridor and emerging into a rustic dining room lined with varnished pine. Despite the simple setting, the food is well prepared and satisfying. Don't even think of coming here at night without a reservation—you might find the place locked up and empty. Its true virtue, however, is evident during the lunch hour, when, depending on the season, it's likely to host a mix of locals and tourists from the French mainland. Try the stuffed crabs or the court bouillon, topped off by coconut ice cream, which is homemade and tastes it. The place is a fine choice for an experience with Creole cookery, complemented by a bottle of good wine.

ANSE BERTRAND

About 5 miles from Port Louis lies Anse Bertrand, the northernmost village of Guadeloupe. What's now a fishing village was the last refuge of the Carib tribes, and a reserve was once created here. Everything now, however, is sleepy.

GREAT DEALS ON DINING

✪ **Chez Prudence (Folie Plage).** Anse Laborde, 97121 Anse Bertrand, Guadeloupe, F.W.I. ☎ **0590/22-11-17.** Reservations not required for lunch, recommended for dinner. Main courses 70–153F ($11.90–$26); fixed-price menu 100–180F ($17–$30.60). AE. Daily noon–3pm and 7–10pm. CREOLE.

About a mile north of Anse Bertrand at Anse Laborde, this place is owned by Prudence Marcelin, a *cuisiniére patronne,* who enjoys much local acclaim for her Creole cookery. She draws people from all over the island, especially on Sunday, when this place is its most crowded. Island children frolic in the saltwater pool, and in between courses diners can shop for handcrafts, clothes, and souvenirs sold by a handful of nearby vendors. Her court bouillon is excellent, as is her goat or chicken colombo (curried). The *palourdes* (clams) are superb, and she makes a zesty sauce to serve with fish. She also rents half a dozen basic motel-style bungalows priced at 250F ($42.50) single or double.

CONTINUING AROUND THE NORTHERN TIP

From Anse Bertrand, you can drive along a graveled road heading for **Pointe de la Grande Vigie,** the northernmost tip of the island, which you reach after 4 miles of what we hope will be cautious driving. Park your car and walk carefully along a narrow lane that'll bring you to the northernmost rock of Guadeloupe. The view of the sweeping Atlantic from the top of rocky cliffs is remarkable—you stand at a distance of about 280 feet above the sea.

A 4-mile drive south on quite a good road will bring you to the **Porte d'Enfer** (Gateway to Hell). Once here, you'll find the sea rushing violently against two narrow cliffs. After this kind of awesome experience in the remote part of the island, you can head back, going either to Morne à l'Eau or Le Moule before connecting to the road taking you back to Pointe-à-Pitre.

8 Driving Around Basse-Terre

Leaving Pointe-à-Pitre on route N1, you can explore the lesser windward coast. After a mile and a half you cross the Rivière Salée at Pont de la Gabarre. This narrow strait separates Guadeloupe's two islands. For the next 4 miles the road runs straight through sugarcane fields.

At the sign, on a main crossing, turn right on N2 toward **Baie Mahault.** Leaving that town on the right, head for **Lamentin.** This village was settled by corsairs at the beginning of the 18th century, and scattered about are some colonial mansions.

STE-ROSE

From Lamentin, you can drive 6½ miles to Ste-Rose, where you'll find several good beaches. On your left, a small road leads to **Sofaia,** from which you'll have a panoramic view over the coast and forest preserve. The locals claim a sulfur spring here has curative powers.

ACCOMMODATIONS YOU CAN AFFORD

La Sucrerie du Comté. Comté de Loheac, 97115 Ste-Rose, Guadeloupe, F.W.I. ☎ **0590/28-60-17.** Fax 0590/28-65-63. 50 units. A/C. Winter, 480F ($81.60) single; 500F ($85) double. Off-season, 280F ($47.60) single; 320F ($54.40) double. Rates include breakfast. AE, MC, V.

Though you'll see the ruins of a 19th-century sugar factory (including a rusting locomotive) on these 8 acres of forested land overlooking the sea, most of the resort is modern (it opened in 1991). The medium-sized accommodations are in 26 pink-toned rectangular bungalows containing two units with ceiling fans; none has a TV or phone. Each cozy unit comes with rustic handmade furniture and a bay window overlooking the sea or a garden. The firm mattresses are sleep-producing; bathrooms are tiny but tidy. Scuba diving, snorkeling, and fishing can be arranged. There's a restaurant on site, open daily for lunch and dinner, and a bar beneath a veranda-style roof near the pool. The nearest major beach is Grand'Anse, a 10- to 15-minute drive from the hotel, but a small beach is within a 10-minute walk (the swimming isn't very good though).

GREAT DEALS ON DINING

✪ **Restaurant Clara.** On the waterfront, Ste-Rose. ☎ **0590/28-72-99.** Reservations recommended. Main courses 45–120F ($7.65–$20.40). MC, V. Mon–Tues and Thurs–Sat noon–2:30pm and 7–10pm, Sun noon–2:30pm. CREOLE.

Near the center of town is the culinary statement of Clara Lesueur, who lived for 12 years in Paris as a member of an experimental jazz dance troupe but returned to Guadeloupe, her home, and set up her breeze-cooled restaurant. Try for a table on the open patio, where palm trees complement the color scheme. Clara artfully melds the French style of fine dining with authentic Creole cookery. Specialties include *ouassous* (freshwater crayfish), brochette of swordfish, *palourdes* (small clams), several preparations of conch, sea-urchin omelets, and *crabes farcis* (red-orange crabs with a spicy filling). The sauce *chien* that's served with many of the dishes is a blend of hot peppers, garlic, lime juice, and secret things. The house drink is made with six local fruits and ample quantities of rum. Your dessert sherbet might be guava, soursop, or passion fruit.

DESHAIES & GRAND'ANSE

A few miles farther along you'll reach Pointe Allegre, the northernmost point of Basse-Terre. At **Clugny Beach,** you'll be at the site where the first settler landed on Guadeloupe.

A couple of miles farther will bring you to **Grand'Anse,** one of the best beaches on Guadeloupe. It's very large and still secluded, sheltered by many tropical trees.

At **Deshaies,** snorkeling and fishing are popular pastimes. The narrow road winds up and down and has a corniche look to it, with the blue sea underneath, the view of green mountains studded with colorful hamlets.

Some 9 miles from Deshaies, **Pointe Noire** comes into view. Its name comes from black volcanic rocks. Look for the odd polychrome cenotaph in town.

ACCOMMODATIONS YOU CAN AFFORD

Grand'Anse Hôtel. Grand'Anse, 97114 Trois-Rivières, Guadeloupe, F.W.I. ☎ **0590/ 92-92-21.** Fax 0590/92-93-69. 16 bungalows. A/C TV TEL. Winter, 400F ($68) single or double. Off-season 300–400F ($51–$68) single or double. Rates include breakfast. MC, V.

Built in the 1970s but renovated in 1996, this secluded hotel is removed from the tourist hordes but near the ferry piers of the hamlet of Trois-Rivières. Its beige interconnected bungalows are set in a garden with a view of the mountains and (in some cases) the sea. The small accommodations are mostly modern, with sliding glass doors, hints of French colonial styling, and mahogany furniture, including good beds. Its bar and Creole restaurant are well recommended. The closest beach, Plage Grand'Anse (black volcanic sand) is ¾ of a mile away, but the hotel has a rectangular pool. The staff is unpretentious and polite.

Résidence de la Pointe Batterie. 97126 Pointe Batterie Deshaies, Guadeloupe, F.W.I. ☎ **800/322-2223** in the U.S., or 0590/28-57-03. Fax 0590/28-57-28. 24 units, each with kitchenette. A/C TV TEL. Winter 890F ($151.30) 1-bedroom villa for up to 4 without pool; 1,300F ($221) 1-bedroom villa for up to 4 with pool; 1,420F ($241.40) 2-bedroom villa for up to 6 with pool. Off-season 540F ($91.80) 1-bedroom villa for up to 4 without pool; 690F ($117.30) 1-bedroom villa for up to 4 with pool; 890F ($151.30) 2-bedroom villa for up to 6 with pool. MC, V.

This is neither the most elegant nor the simplest villa compound on the island. Built in 1996 on steeply sloping land near the edge of the rain forest and the sea, it's an all-wood construction where the rooms are painted white, each with a veranda, and each constructed out of reddish termite-resistant wood from Guyana. Each contains an American-built kitchen, ceiling fans, good beds with firm mattresses, and summery furniture made from rattan, local hardwoods, and wicker. At the well-managed indoor-outdoor restaurant, Les Canons de la Baie, meals are served every day except Sunday night and all day Wednesday, with main courses at 70F to 150F ($11.90 to $25.50). The nearest beach, Grand'Anse, lies within a 3-minute drive. Be warned that you'll face a lot of hiking between your villa and the sea, thanks to a rugged terrain whose upper stretches afford very good views.

GREAT DEALS ON DINING

Chez Jacky. Anse Guyonneau, Pointe Noire. ☎ **0590/98-06-98.** Reservations recommended at dinner. Main courses 50–135F ($8.50–$22.95); fixed-price menu 65–120F ($11.05–$20.40). MC, V. Daily 9am–10pm. CREOLE.

Named after its owner, grande dame Creole matriarch Jacqueline Cabrion, this place has gained a loyal following since it opened in 1981. In a French-colonial house about 30 feet from the sea, it features lots of exposed wood, verdant plants, tropical furniture, and a bar that sometimes does a respectable business in its own right. Menu items

Cheap Thrills: What to See & Do for Free (Well, Almost) on Guadeloupe

- **Explore the Parc Naturel de Guadeloupe.** Basse-Terre has one of the largest and most spectacular parks in the Caribbean, the Parc Naturel de Guadeloupe. The 74,100-acre park has much to offer. A highlight is Chutes du Carbet, one of the tallest waterfalls in the Caribbean, with a drop of 800 feet. The park boasts 180 miles of marked trails through forests to lowlands, taking in rain forests and the wooded slopes of the 4,813-foot-high Soufrière volcano. You can hike for only 15 minutes or all day, encountering hot springs, rugged gorges, and rushing streams. Many locals bring a picnic lunch and a bottle of wine.

- **Spend a Day at Pointe des Châteaux.** At the eastern tip of Guadeloupe, Pointe des Châteaux is a rocky headland extending for almost a mile into the sea. It's one of the most dramatic coastlines in Guadeloupe, bordered by miles of white-sand beaches. Most of these are safe for swimming, except at the point where the waves of the turbulent Atlantic churn up the waters of the otherwise tranquil Caribbean Sea. There's a nudist enclave at Tarare, but most visitors run around in skimpy bikinis. You can also visit Grand Saline, a salt pond. If you're a birdwatcher, you will be enthralled at the hundreds of shorebirds who congregate here. The point also has varied vegetation, ranging from the Indian almond to cinnamon. Sometimes you can get a local boatman to take you to Iles de la Petit Terrace, two deserted islets offshore. You'll share the island with a colony of iguanas. The sandy beaches here are almost deserted.

- **Wander Around a Nostalgic, Almost Forgotten Town.** Most visitors assume Pointe-à-Pitre is the capital of Guadeloupe. The actual capital is Basse-Terre, a sleepy town of some 14,000 inhabitants, lying 20 miles from Pointe-à-Pitre. Founded in 1643, the town was constructed on a hill and is much lovelier than the larger city of Pointe-à-Pitre. Much of the antique flavor of the town is still in evidence, as evoked by its upper floors of shingle-wood tiles and clapboard buildings along narrow streets. Wrought-iron balconies still grace many buildings. For the most interesting views, seek out place du Champ d'Arbaud and the Jardin Pichon. At the harbor on the southern tier of town you can see Fort Delgrès, which once protected the island from the English. There are acres of ramparts to be walked with panoramic vistas.

- **See Where Columbus Was Peppered.** The sleepy little town of Ste-Marie, south of Petit-Bourg on the east coast of Basse-Terre, enjoyed its moment in history, for it was here Columbus first set foot on Guadeloupe in 1493. The people today are a lot friendlier than the cannibalistic Indians who greeted the great explorer, who was peppered with poison arrows. Columbus just had time to name the island for Spain's Virgin of Guadalupe before fleeing to friendlier places. A statue of Columbus in the town square honors him. The people are descended in the main from East Indian laborers imported to work on the plantations when a proclamation in 1848 freed the black slaves. Take time to visit the south of town and the Allée Dumanoir, a ½-mile stretch of road lined with towering palms that were planted in the 1800s by Pinel Dumanoir. His claim to fame was that he dramatized the French version of *Uncle Tom's Cabin*.

include colombo of conch, fricassee of conch or freshwater crayfish, several preparations of grilled fish, lobster, ragoût of lamb, and a dessert specialty of bananas flambé. Lighter fare includes a limited choice of sandwiches and salads, which tend to be offered only during daylight hours.

Le Karacoli. Grand'Anse (1¼ miles north of Deshaies). ☎ **0590/28-41-17.** Reservations recommended. Main courses 80–150F ($13.60–$25.50). MC, V. Daily noon–2pm; Fri–Sat 5–9:30pm. CREOLE.

It's the best-sign-posted restaurant in town, with at least three large signs indicating its position at the edge of the region's most famous beach. The setting is airy and tropical, with streaming sunlight, tables set outdoors in a garden, and a bar area sheltered by a combination of poured concrete and clapboards. No one will mind if you drop in just for a drink. If you want lunch, consider ordering such dishes as boudin Creole (blood pudding), stuffed crab backs, scallops prepared in the style of the chef, court bouillon of fish, fricassee of octopus, and fried chicken. Recently the restaurant has started serving dinner on weekends.

Les Gommiers. Rue Baudot, Pointe Noire. ☎ **0590/98-01-79.** Main courses 70–150F ($11.90–$25.50). AE, MC, V. Sun–Mon 11:30am–3pm, Tues–Sat 11:30am–3pm and 7–10pm. CREOLE.

Named after the large rubber trees (*les gommiers*) that grow nearby, this popular Creole restaurant serves well-flavored platters deriving from the culinary experience of Mme Josette Besplan. She established her restaurant in the 1960s, in a wood-and-concrete house across the busy road from Pointe Noire's local *collège* (high school). In a dining room lined with plants, you can order Creole staples like *accras de morue* (codfish), boudin Creole (blood pudding), fricassee of freshwater crayfish, seafood paella, and a custard-like dessert known as *flan coucou*. Dishes inspired by mainland France include filet of beef with Roquefort sauce and veal scallops.

ROUTE DE LA TRAVERSÉE

Four miles from Pointe Noire is **Mahaut.** On your left begins the **route de la Traversée,** the Transcoastal Highway. This is the best way to explore the scenic wonders of the **Parc Naturel de Guadeloupe,** passing through a tropical forest as you travel between the capital, Basse-Terre, and Pointe-à-Pitre.

Guadeloupe has set aside 74,100 acres, about one-fifth of its entire terrain, in the Parc Naturel. Reached by modern roads, this is a huge tract of mountains, tropical forests, and magnificent scenery. It's home to a variety of tame animals, including Titi (a raccoon adopted as the park's official mascot), and birds like the wood pigeon, turtledove, and thrush. Small exhibition huts, devoted to the volcano, the forest, or coffee, sugarcane, and rum, are scattered throughout the park. The park has no gates, no opening or closing hours, and no admission fee.

From Mahaut you climb slowly in a setting of giant ferns and luxuriant vegetation. Four miles after the fork, you reach **Les Deux Mamelles** (The Two Breasts), where you can park your car and go for a hike. Some of the trails are for experts only; others, such as the Pigeon Trail, will bring you to a summit of about 2,600 feet with a panoramic view. Expect to spend at least 3 hours going each way. Halfway along the trail you can stop at Forest House. From that point, many lanes, all sign-posted, branch off on trails that'll last anywhere from 20 minutes to 2 hours. Try to find the **Chute de l'Ecrevisse** (Crayfish Waterfall), a little pond of very cold water you'll discover after a quarter of a mile.

From the park, the main road descends toward pretentiously named **Versailles,** a hamlet about 5 miles from Pointe-à-Pitre. However, before taking this route, while still traveling between Pointe Noire and Mahaut on the west coast, you might consider the following luncheon stop.

GREAT DEALS ON DINING

Chez Vaneau. Mahaut/Pointe Noire. ☎ **0590/98-01-71.** Main courses 50–150F ($8.50–$25.50). AE, MC, V. Daily noon–4pm and 7–10:30pm. CREOLE.

In an isolated pocket of forest about 18 miles north of Pointe Noire, far from any of its neighbors, Chez Vaneau offers a wide breeze-filled veranda overlooking a gully, the sight of neighbors playing cards, and steaming Creole specialties. This is the well-established domain of Vaneau Desbonnes, who is assisted by his wife, Marie-Gracieuse, and their children. Specialties include oysters with a piquant sauce, crayfish bisque, ragoût of goat, fricassee of conch, different preparations of octopus, and roast pork. In 1995 they installed a saltwater tank to store lobsters, which are now featured heavily on the menu.

BOUILLANTE

If you don't take the route de la Traversée at this time but wish to continue exploring the west coast, you can head south from Mahaut until you reach **Bouillante.** This village is exciting for only one reason: You might encounter former French film star and part-time resident Brigitte Bardot.

Try not to miss seeing the small island called **Ilet à Goyave** or Ilet du Pigeon. Jacques Cousteau often explored the silent depths around it.

After a meal, you can explore around the village of Bouillante, known for its thermal springs. In some places if you scratch the ground for only a few inches you'll feel the heat.

GREAT DEALS ON DINING

✪ **Chez Loulouse.** Malendure Plage. ☎ **0590/98-70-34.** Reservations required for dinner. Main courses 50–200F ($8.50–$34); fixed-price menu 80F ($13.60). AE, MC, V. Daily noon–3:30pm and 7–10pm. CREOLE.

A good choice for lunch, Chez Loulouse is a staunchly matriarchal place with plenty of offhanded charm beside the sands of the well-known beach, opposite Pigeon Island. Many guests prefer their rum punches on the veranda, overlooking a scene of loaded boats preparing to depart and merchants hawking their wares. A quieter oasis is the equally colorful dining room, just past the bar. Beneath a ceiling of palm fronds is a wraparound series of Creole murals that seem to go well with the reggae music emanating loudly from the bar.

This is the creation of one of the most charming Creole matrons on this end of the island, Mme Loulouse Paisley-Carbon. Assisted by her children, she offers house-style Caribbean lobster, spicy versions of conch, octopus, *accras* (codfish), *gratin of christophine* (squash), and savory *colombos* (curries) of chicken or pork.

Le Rocher de Malendure. Malendure Plage, Pointe Batterie, 97125 Bouillante, Guadeloupe, F.W.I. ☎ **0590/98-70-84.** Reservations recommended. Main courses 78–350F ($13.25–$59.50). MC, V. Mon–Sat 11am–2pm and 7–10pm, Sun 11am–2pm. FRENCH/CREOLE.

Its position on a rocky peninsula 30 feet above the rich offshore reefs near Pigeon Island allows for great views over the land and seascape. Each table is sheltered from too direct a contact with the sun (and the rain) with a shed-style roof, whose placement on terraced terrain allows for greater feelings of privacy. This is the creative statement of Ghislaine Lesueur, who was born on Guadeloupe of Breton parents. Much of the cuisine is seafood caught in offshore waters, like grilled red snapper, fondues of fish, marinated marlin steaks, lobster, and conch. Meat dishes include veal in raspberry vinaigrette and filet of beef with any of three different sauces.

There are also 11 bungalows for rent, costing 350F ($59.50) single or double. Each small unit has a sea view and a simple kitchenette and a tiny bath, so many visitors cook most of their meals in-house.

VIEUX HABITANTS

The winding coast road brings you to Vieux Habitants (Old Settlers), one of the oldest villages on the island, founded in 1636. The name comes from the people who settled it. After serving in the employment of the West Indies Company, they retired here but preferred to call themselves inhabitants, so as not to be confused with slaves.

BASSE-TERRE

Another 10 miles of winding roads brings you to Basse-Terre, Guadeloupe's seat of government. The town lies between the water and La Soufrière, the volcano. Founded in 1634, it's the oldest town on the island and still has a lot of charm; its market squares are shaded by tamarind and palm trees.

The town suffered heavy destruction at the hands of British troops in 1691 and again in 1702. It was also the center of fierce fighting during the French Revolution, when the political changes that swept across Europe caused explosive tensions on Guadeloupe. As it did in the mainland of France, the guillotine claimed many lives on Guadeloupe during the infamous Reign of Terror.

In spite of the town's history, there isn't much to see in Basse-Terre except for a 17th-century **cathedral** and **Fort St-Charles,** which has guarded the city—not always well—since it was established.

ACCOMMODATIONS & DINING YOU CAN AFFORD

For rock-bottom rates, consider staying in the closest thing to a youth hostel, the **Centre de Vacances de C.G.O.S.H.,** Rivières-Sens, 97113 Gourbeyre, Guadeloupe, F.W.I. (☎ **0590/81-36-12**), within a 15-minute walk from the sleepy town of Basse-Terre and 5 minutes from Plage de Rivières Sens, a beach noted for its black sands. You don't have to be a member of a youth-hostel organization to stay here. There are 19 clapboard-covered bungalows built in the mid-1980s, and though they're far from luxurious, they're somewhat better than you might expect. Each bungalow, which can hold up to six, costs 452F ($76.85) per night. They have between four and six beds in an air-conditioned bedroom, two more beds in a living area, a terrace, a private bathroom, and a kitchenette. There's a pool, a simple restaurant, a bar, and a nearby marina. American Express, Diners Club, MasterCard, and Visa are accepted.

Hotel St-Georges. Rue Gratien, Parize, 97120 St-Claude, Guadeloupe, F.W.I. ☎ **00590/80-10-10.** Fax 0590/80-30-50. www.pro-wanadoo.fr/hotel.st.georges. E-mail: hotel-st-georges@wanadoo.fr. 40 units. A/C TV TEL. Year-round 660–690F ($112.20–$117.30) double; 890F ($151.30) suite. MAP 120F ($20.40) per person. AE, DC, MC, V.

This tastefully modern inn on a hill boasts views sweeping over the town and the sea. It's a series of three-story buildings configured into the shape of an L and centered around a large pool. Medium-size bedrooms are outfitted, Creole-style, with dark-grained and rattan furniture, beige-and-salmon floor tiles, good beds, and small bathrooms trimmed with touches of marble. Many guests are dignitaries visiting Guadeloupe from the French mainland and other Caribbean islands. Expect lots of amiable goodwill from the 20 or 30 students registered at the hotel training school associated with this place.

Lamasure, the name of the surrounding region, is the on-site restaurant open daily for lunch and dinner, charging 175F to 215F ($29.75 to $36.55) for fixed-price menus and 85F to 180F ($14.45 to $30.60) for main courses. Menu items are French-derived but concocted from Caribbean ingredients and include *Roi des Sources* (*ouassous,* or freshwater crayfish, with yellow bananas), confit of duckling with caramelized Caribbean spices, and fricassee of spiny lobster with pink peppercorns and ginger.

GREAT DEALS ON DINING

✪ L'Orangerie. Lieu-dit Desmarais, Basse-Terre. ☎ 00590/81-01-01. Reservations recommended. Main courses 109–145F ($18.55–$24.65); set-price lunch 130F ($22.10). Sun–Fri noon–2:30pm; Thurs–Sat 7–10pm. MC, V. CREOLE.

This is Basse-Terre's finest restaurant, always filled with representatives of the city's many legal offices, government agencies, hospitals, and cultural organizations. It occupies what was built in 1823 as the home of a slave-owning French aristocrat (the comte de Desmarets). Tables fill both the Creole-inspired interior and the verandas and are supervised by maître-d' Christophe Roubenne. The food, as prepared by award-winning Frenchman Christophe Moreau, is an upscale and modern interpretation of old Creole recipes. Examples are *gâteau* of octopus and smoked chicken, with rondelles of leeks marinated in starfruit-enhanced vinaigrette; moussaka of conch with a reduction of tomatoes, lentils, and smoked fish; lobster-stuffed veal filet with tagliatelle and a confit of ginger-infused vegetables; and beef filet roasted with black Jamaican pepper and flambéed with aged rum. Views from most of the tables encompass a sprawling French-Caribbean garden loaded with tropical fruit trees.

LA SOUFRIÈRE

The big attraction of Basse-Terre is the famous sulfur-puffing La Soufrière volcano, which is still alive but dormant—for the moment at least. Rising to a height of some 4,800 feet, it's flanked by banana plantations and lush foliage.

From the capital at Basse-Terre, you can drive to **St-Claude,** a suburb, 4 miles up the mountainside at a height of 1,900 feet. It has an elegant reputation for its perfect climate and tropical gardens.

Instead of going to St-Claude, you can head for **Matouba,** in an area of clear mountain springs. The only sound you're likely to hear at this idyllic place is of birds and the running water of dozens of springs. The village was settled long ago by Hindus.

From St-Claude, you can begin the climb up the narrow, winding road the Guadeloupeans say leads to hell—that is, **La Soufrière.** The road ends at a parking area at La Savane-à-Mulets, at an altitude of 3,300 feet. That is the ultimate point to be reached by car. Hikers are able to climb right to the mouth of the volcano. However, the appearance of ashes, mud, billowing smoke, and earthquake-like tremors in 1975 proved the old beast was still alive. No deaths were reported, but 75,000 inhabitants were relocated to Grande-Terre. The inhabitants of Basse-Terre still keep a watchful eye on the smoking giant.

Even in the parking lot you can feel the heat of the volcano merely by touching the ground. Steam emerges from fumaroles and sulfurous fumes from the volcano's burps. Of course, fumes come from its pit and mud caldrons as well.

GREAT DEALS ON DINING

Chez Paul de Matouba. Rivière Rouge. ☎ 0590/80-01-77. Main courses 55–150F ($9.35–$25.50); fixed-price menu 100F ($17). No credit cards. Daily noon–3pm. Follow the clearly marked signs—it's beside a gully close to the center of the village. CREOLE/INTERNATIONAL.

Up the Volcano

The mountainous terrain of Guadeloupe's Basse-Terre is some of the most beautiful in the entire Caribbean. Although the coastline of Basse-Terre is lined with beach resorts and fishing villages, the mountainous interior (about 20% of the landmass) is devoted almost completely to the protected terrain of a French national forest, the **Parc Naturel de Guadeloupe.** Near the park's southernmost tip rise the misty heights of one of the island's most distinctive natural features, the 4,812-foot volcanic peak of **La Soufrière.** Since recorded history on Guadeloupe began, the volcano has erupted in 1560, 1797, 1975, and 1976–77. Dozens of lava flows along its slopes attest to the potential violence that reigns in the volcano's core. Today its many pits and craters offer the rare ability for geologists and hikers to gaze down into the rumbling and smoking primeval forces that shaped the planet.

The park contains an intricate network of more than 200 miles of hiking trails, allowing physically fit hikers to visit a wealth of gorges, ravines, rain forests, rivers, and (at points north of La Soufrière) some of the highest waterfalls in the Caribbean. The watershed from the peak of La Soufrière pours rainwater down a ring of black sandy beaches along Basse-Terre's southern coastline.

Surprisingly, the trek up the mountainside isn't particularly strenuous, though you should wear a hat or some other form of sun protection. Most of your walk is through scrubland and, at higher elevations, rocky plateaux covered with moss and lichens. Total time expended round-trip, without accounting for admiration of the views, is about 3 hours.

Begin your walking tour to the volcano's summit from one of the highest-altitude parking lots on Guadeloupe, **Savane-à-Mulets.** Savane-à-Mulets has no amenities of any kind. Set on the volcano's western slope at about 3,400 feet above sea level, 3 miles west of the village of St-Claude, it marks the farthest point a conventional vehicle can proceed along route de la Soufrière. (The road between St-Claude and Savane-à-Mulets is very steep—put your transmission in low gear en route.) Park your car in the parking lot, then hike along a network of carefully marked trails toward the summit. If a wind is blowing, it'll probably clear away much of the mist that sometimes envelops the peak. Along the way you'll bypass a string of small craters and crevasses, many of them bubbling up mud and fumes. As you bypass each pit, the scent of sulfur and the radiant heat become very powerful. Of special note is the **South Crater** (Crater Sud), which spews lots of noise, steam, and sulfurous odors.

Be warned that a handful of hikers have had their valuables stolen during scattered incidents in this park. Lock anything extremely valuable in a safe back at your hotel, and carry minimal amounts of cash with you as you proceed on this itinerary. For more information about this and other hikes in the national park, contact the employees of the national park at ☎ **0590/80-24-25.**

You'll find good food in this family-run restaurant, which sits beside the banks of the small Rivière Rouge (Red River). The dining room on the second floor is enclosed by windows, allowing you to drink in the surrounding dark-green foliage of the mountains. The cookery is Creole, with crayfish dishes the specialty. Because of the influence of the region's early settlers, East Indian meals are also available. By all means, drink the Matouba mineral or spring water. What one diner called "an honest meal" might include stuffed crab, *colombo* (curried) of chicken, as well as an array of French, Creole, and Hindu specialties. You're likely to find the place overcrowded in winter with the tour-bus crowd.

THE WINDWARD COAST

From Basse-Terre to Pointe-à-Pitre, the road follows the east coast, called the Windward Coast. The country here is richer and greener than elsewhere on the island.

To reach **Trois Rivières** you have a choice of two routes. One goes along the coastline, coming eventually to Vieux Fort, from which you can see Les Saintes archipelago. The other heads across the hills, Monts Caraïbes.

Near the pier in Trois Rivières you'll see the pre-Columbian petroglyphs carved by the original inhabitants, the Arawaks. They're called merely Roches Gravées, or carved rocks. In this archaeological park, the rock engravings are of animal and human figures, dating most likely from A.D. 300 or 400. You'll also see specimens of plants, including cocoa, pimento, and banana, that the Arawaks cultivated long before the Europeans set foot on Guadeloupe. From Trois Rivières, you can take boats to Les Saintes.

After leaving Trois Rivières, continue on route 1. Passing through the village of Banaier, you turn on your left at Anse St-Sauveur to reach the famous **Chutes du Carbet,** a trio of waterfalls. The road to two of them is narrow, and winds over many steep hills and passes through banana plantations as you move deeper into a tropical forest.

After 3 miles, a lane, suitable only for hikers, brings you to **Zombie Pool.** Half a mile farther along, a fork to the left takes you to **Grand Etang,** or large pool. At a point 6 miles from the main road, a parking area is available, and you'll have to walk the rest of the way on an uneasy trail toward the second fall, Le Carbet. Expect to spend around 20 to 30 minutes, depending on how slippery the lane is. Then you'll be at the foot of this second fall, where the water drops from 230 feet. The waters here average 70°F (21°C), warm for a mountain spring.

The first fall is the most impressive, but it takes 2 hours of rough hiking to get here. The third fall is reached from Capesterre on the main road by climbing to Routhiers. This fall is less impressive in height, only 70 feet. When the Carbet water runs out of La Soufrière, it's almost boiling.

If you'd like to stop over along the Windward Coast before returning to Grande Terre, the area of Petit-Bourg, north of Ste-Marie and Goyave and directly southwest of Pointe-à-Pitre, makes the best stopover. To reach Vernou from Petit-Bourg, cut inland (west) along D23.

ACCOMMODATIONS YOU CAN AFFORD

Auberge de la Distillerie. Tabanon, C.D. 23, 97170 Petit-Bourg, Guadeloupe, F.W.I. ☎ **0590/94-25-91.** Fax 0590/94-11-91. 16 units. A/C TV TEL. Winter, 390–490F ($66.30–$83.30) single; 489–590F ($83.15–$100.30) double. Off-season, 350F ($59.50) single; 450F ($76.50) double. MAP 125F ($21.25) per person. AE, MC, V.

This inn attracts more of a hiking crowd than a beach-going one. Outfitted in a tropical-woodsy motif, it lies close to the entrance of the Parc Naturel, near the hamlet of Vernou, in a luxuriantly verdant setting. You'll have to drive about 15 minutes to reach the black sands of the nearest beach (Plage de Viard), but hiking trails through the volcanic oddities of Basse-Terre are nearby. On the premises is a bar (sometimes with live piano music) and an unpretentious restaurant serving mostly Creole cuisine. Each small accommodation contains a writing table, a good bed, a balcony with a hammock, and a radio, plus a tiny but tidy bath. Boating excursions can be arranged on the Lezard River, where a waterfall (Cascade aux Ecrevisses) is one of the primary attractions.

9 Hitting the Beaches

Chances are that your hotel will be right on a beach or no more than 20 minutes from a good one. Plenty of natural beaches dot the island, from the surf-brushed dark strands of western Basse-Terre to the long stretches of white sand encircling Grande-Terre. Public beaches are generally free, but some charge for parking. Unlike hotel beaches, they have few facilities. Hotels welcome nonguests, but charge for changing facilities, beach chairs, and towels.

Sunday is family day at the beach. Topless sunbathing is common at hotels, less so on village beaches.

Most of the best beaches lie between Gosier and St-François on Grande Terrace's southern coast. Most visitors go to the hotel beaches at Gosier. Since this is the site of the largest concentration of tourists, the hotels—adjacent to each other—are likely to be crowded. Stone jetties were constructed here to protect the beaches from erosion.

There's no shade at the **Creole Beach** fronting Creole Beach Hotel, though you can retreat to the bar there for a drink. The sands on this beach appear mainly on a stone jetty. A stone retaining-wall blocks access to the water. Nearby, the **Salako Beach** has more sand and is set against a backdrop of palms that offer some shade. Part of this beach also leads up to a jetty. This is a fine sandy beach, although a little too crowded at times, and it also contains a snack bar.

Also nearby, **Arawak Beach** is that cliché of a tropical beach with plenty of palm trees, beige sand, and shade. Like the other beaches, it's protected by jetties. Close at hand, **Callinago Beach** is smaller than Arawak's but still sought out for its pleasant crescent of beige sand and palms. **Ilet du Gosier** is a little speck of land lying off the shore of Gosier. It attracts mainly French tourists to its sand beaches where they sunbathe and swim in the buff.

Le Bas du Fort, 2 miles east of Pointe-à-Pitre and close to Gosier, is another frequented area. Its beaches, also protected by jetties, are shared by guests at the Hotels Fleu d'Epee and Marissol. This is a picture-postcard tropical beach with tranquil waters, plenty of sand, and palms for shade. There are hotel bars as well as snack bars, and vendors too, some of whom are rather aggressive.

Some of Grande-Terre's best beaches are in the Ste-Anne area, site of the Club Med that occupies one section of this beach. Just outside Ste-Anne, **Plage Caravelle** is one of the longest and prettiest strips of sand on the island. It's protected by reefs and is an ideal spot for snorkeling. Because this beach is heaped with white sand, it's generally crowded.

When the French visit the Antilles, they often like to go nude, and there's no finer nude beach than **Pointe Tarare,** east of St. François at Pointe des Châteaux, a 45-minute drive from Gosier. This is one of the island's most pristine beaches, but there's no shade to protect you from the fierce noonday sun. The water is usually tranquil, and you can also enjoy snorkeling. There's a good restaurant by the car park. The tourist office doesn't recommend women go here unaccompanied.

If you're not a nudist, you can enjoy the lovely strip of white sand at **Anse de la Gourde,** lying between St-François and Pointe des Châteaux. It has good sand but tends to become too popular on weekends.

The eastern coast of Grande-Terre is less desirable for swimming because it fronts the more turbulent Atlantic. Nonetheless, the sands at **La Moule** make for an idyllic beach because a reef protects the shoreline. There are also beach bars here—and the inevitable crowds, especially on weekends. You'll find a more secluded strip of sand north of here at **La Porte d'Enfer.**

There are two other excellent beaches on the northwestern coast, though you should be careful up here, since rough waters can make them exceedingly dangerous for swimming. One beach is at **Anse Laborde,** just outside the hamlet of Anse-Bertrand; another is **Anse du Souffleur,** at Port-Louis. We especially like the beach at Souffleur because of its flamboyant trees that bloom in summer. There are no facilities, but you can pick up supplies, including cold drinks, in the shops in the little village, then enjoy a picnic on the beach.

In Basse-Terre, a highly desirable beach is the **Grand'Anse,** just outside Deshaies, in the northwestern sector of the island, reached by heading west from Ste-Rose along N2. This is a secluded beach of soft, powdery sand facing tranquil waters and sheltered by palm trees. There's an area here for parking but no facilities. Another desirable beach is **Plage de la Malendure** lying on the west coast (the more tranquil side) of Basse-Terre across from Pigeon Island. This is a major center for scuba diving on the island. The sand tends to be dark on this beach, however.

If you want to escape the crowds you can seek out the spurs and shoulders produced by the mountains of Basse-Terre. In the northwest part of the island you'll find a string of fine sandy beaches. Favorites include **Plage de Cluny** near Pointe Allegre (though the waters can be treacherous), **Plage de la Tillette,** and **Plage de la Perle.**

South of Pointe Noire, also on the west coast, is **Plage de La Caraïbe,** with calm waters. There are picnic facilities, a shower, and toilets at this beach.

Other good beaches are found on the offshore islands, Iles des Saintes and Marie-Galante (see below).

10 Sports & Outdoor Pursuits

GOLF   Guadeloupe's only public golf course is the well-known ✪ **Golf de St-François** (☎ 00590/88-41-87), opposite the Hôtel Méridien. The course runs alongside an 800-acre lagoon where windsurfing, waterskiing, and sailing prevail. Designed by Robert Trent Jones Sr., it's a challenging 6,755-yard, par-71 course, with water traps on 6 of the 18 holes, not to mention massive bunkers, prevailing trade winds, and a particularly fiendish 400-yard, par-4 ninth hole. The par-5 sixth hole is the toughest hole on the course; its 450 yards must be negotiated in the constant easterly winds. Greens fees are 250F ($42.50) per day per person, which allows a full day of playing time. You can rent clubs for 100F ($17) a day; a cart costs 220F ($37.40) for 18 holes. This course is open daily from 7:30am to 6:30pm.

HIKING   The **Parc Naturel de Guadeloupe** contains the best hiking grounds in the Caribbean (see the "Up the Volcano" box earlier in this chapter). Marked trails cut through the park's deep foliage of rain forests until you come upon a waterfall or a cool mountain pool. The big excursion, of course, is around the volcano, La Soufrière. Hiking brochures are available from the tourist office. Hotel tour desks can arrange this activity. For information about this and other hikes in the national park, contact the **Organisation des Guides de Montagne de la Caraïbe,** Maison Forestière, Matouba (☎ 0590/94-29-11).

Warning: The annual precipitation on the higher slopes is 250 inches per year, so be prepared for downpours.

SAILING   Sailboats of varying sizes, crewed or bareboat, are plentiful. Information can be secured at any hotel desk. Sunfish sailing can be arranged at almost every beachfront hotel.

SCUBA DIVING   Scuba divers are drawn more to the waters off Guadeloupe than to any other point in the French-speaking islands. The allure is the relatively calm seas and **La Réserve Cousteau,** a kind of French national park with many intriguing dive sites, where the underwater environment is rigidly protected. Jacques Cousteau once described the waters off Guadeloupe's Pigeon Island as one of the world's 10 best diving spots. During a typical dive, sergeant majors become visible at a depth of 30 feet, spiny sea urchins and green parrotfish at 60 feet, and magnificent stands of finger, black, brain, and star coral at 80 feet. Despite the destruction of some branch coral in a 1995 hurricane, the reserve is still one of the most desirable underwater sites in the French-speaking world.

The most popular dive sites are Aquarium, Piscine, Jardin de Corail, Pointe Carrangue, Pointe Barracuda, and Jardin Japonais. Although scattered around the periphery of the island, many are in the bay of Petit Cul-de-Sac Marin, south of Rivière Salée, the channel separating the halves of Guadeloupe. North of the Salée is another bay, Grand Cul-de-Sac Marin, where the small islets of Fajou and Caret also boast fine diving.

The **Centre International de la Plongée (C.I.P.),** B.P. 4, Lieu-Dit Poirier, Malendure Plage, 97125 Pigeon, Bouillante, Guadeloupe, F.W.I. (☎ **00590/98-81-72**), is the island's most professional dive operation. In a wood-sided house on Malendure Plage, close to a well-known restaurant, Chez Loulouse, it's well-positioned at the edge of the Cousteau Underwater Reserve. Certified divers pay 220F ($37.40) for a one-tank dive. What the Americans usually refer to as a resort course for first-time divers (the French refer to it as a *baptême*) costs 280F ($47.60) and is conducted one-on-one with an instructor. Packages of 6 or 12 dives are offered for 1,100 and 2,000F ($187 and $340), respectively.

Nearby, **Les Heures Saines,** Rocher de Malendure, 97132 Pigeon-Malendure (☎ **00590/98-86-63**), has a trio of dive boats departing daily at 10am, 12:30pm, and 3pm for explorations of the waters in the reserve. With all equipment included, dives cost 250F ($42.50) each. Novices pay 280F ($47.60) for a *baptême.* Les Heures Saines maintains its own 11-room hotel, **Le Paradis Creole** (☎ **00590/98-71-62**), where motel-style accommodations rent for 400F to 600F ($68 to $102), breakfast included, depending on the season. Rooms, which are occupied almost exclusively by avid divers on holiday from the French mainland, are air-conditioned but contain few other real amenities.

A miniresort, **Le Jardin Tropical** (☎ **00590/98-77-23**), patronized almost exclusively by dive enthusiasts from France, lies adjacent to this school. The 16 rooms—each with air-conditioning and phone—rent for 556F ($94.50) per person, with breakfast, dinner, and two dives included, with lots of price breaks for divers who purchase accommodations as part of a hotel-dive package.

TENNIS   All the large resort hotels have tennis courts, many of them lit. If your hotel doesn't have courts, you can play at **St-François Plage,** in St-François, a durable but somewhat weathered facility that is often unused despite the fact that it's free. For information, contact **La Mairie** (Town Hall) of St-François at ☎ **00590/88-71-37.**

WINDSURFING & WATERSKIING   Each of the large-scale hotels on Guadeloupe provide facilities and instructions for both of these sports, but if you prefer to strike out on your own or your hotel doesn't provide it, head for the **Surfing Club,** Plage de St-François, St-François (☎ **00590/88-72-04**). Thirty-minute windsurfing lessons go for around 120F ($20.40) per hour, and rentals, depending on the size and make of the board you rent, average 150F ($25.50) per hour.

If you're interested in a more in-depth exposure to windsurfing or perhaps a week-long deep immersion in the sport, head for **UCPA** (Union National des Centres

Sportifs de Plein-Air), 97118 St-François (☎ 00590/88-64-80), a 60-room resort whose quarters are available only by the week and come with all meals. A week's sojourn, double occupancy, is 2,830F ($481.10) per person, including windsurfing, surfing and surfboard-riding, golf, and physical fitness.

11 Guadeloupe After Dark

Guadeloupeans claim the *beguine* was invented here, not on Martinique, and they dance the *beguine* as if they truly did own it. Of course, calypso and the merengue move rhythmically too—the islanders are known for their dancing.

Ask at your hotel where the folkloric **Ballets Guadeloupeans** will be appearing. This troupe makes frequent appearances at the big hotels, although they don't enjoy the fame of the **Ballets Martiniquais,** the troupe on Guadeloupe's neighbor island (see the box in chapter 15).

THE BAR & CLUB SCENE

Nighttime diversions in Guadeloupe tend to be seasonal, with winter being the busiest time. **Lele Bar** at the Hôtel Méridien in St-François (☎ 00590/88-51-00), is the island's most active, attracting Guadeloupeans along with visitors. **Le Figuier Vert,** Mare Gallaird in Gosier (☎ 00590/85-85-51), presents live jazz on most Friday and Saturday nights. At the marina, **Le Jardin Bresilien,** Bas-du-Fort (☎ 00590/90-99-31), is known for presenting live music. The island's dance clubs charge a uniform cover of 48F ($8.15), unless some special entertainment is presented.

If you'd like to dance the night away, head for **New Land,** route Riviera (☎ 00590/84-34-91); **Caraïbes 2,** Carrefour de Blanchard, Bas-du-Fort (☎ 00590/90-97-16); or **Le Plantation,** Gourbeyre (☎ 00590/81-23-37), the latter on Basse-Terre.

If you want to escape all the tourist joints and find some real local color, make it ✪ **Les Tortues,** off N2 near Bouillante (☎ 0590/98-82-83). It's sign-posted near the main road on Basse-Terre's western coast. This bar, closed all day Sunday and on Monday night, is a local hangout in the area, often filled with scuba divers downing Corsaire beer and telling tall tales of the deep. The bartender's specialty is ti punch made with the strongest rum on the island, the taste cut by lime juice and cane syrup. You can also dine here in this macho ambience, and the food is good, especially the fresh fish based on the catch of the day which might be marlin, kingfish, ray, snapper, or Caribbean lobster.

ROLLING THE DICE

One of the island's two gambling emporia, **Casino Gosier-les-Bains,** 43 Pointe de la Verdure (☎ 00590/84-79-68), in Gosier, is in the resort community. Although dress tends to be casually elegant, coat and tie for men aren't required. The bulk of the place is open nightly from 7:30pm to 3am (to 4am on Friday and Saturday), though an area containing only slot machines is open daily 10am to 3 or 4am, depending on the night of the week. There's no cover charge and no ID requested for admission to the area with the slot machines, but entrance to the gaming tables and roulette wheels costs 69F ($11.75) and requires the presentation of a photo ID.

A smaller casino, with fewer slot machines, is **Casino de la Marina,** avenue de l'Europe (☎ 00590/88-41-31), near the Hôtel Mèridien in St-François. Slot machines begin whirring every day at noon, continuing to 2am on Sunday to Thursday and to 3am on Friday and Saturday. The more interesting main core of the casino, containing tables devoted to blackjack, roulette, and chemin-de-fer, doesn't open until 8pm. Entrance costs 69F ($11.75). Dress codes are the same as those at the casino at Gosier-les-Bains, and both casinos contain bars.

12   Side Trips From Guadeloupe

✪ THE ILES DES SAINTES

A cluster of eight islands off the southern coast of Guadeloupe, the Iles des Saintes are certainly off the beaten track. The two main islands and six rocks are Terre-de-Haut, Terre-de-Bas, Ilet-à-Cabrit, La Coche, Les Augustins, Grand Ilet, Le Redonde, and Le Pâté. Only Terre-de-Haut (land of high), and to a lesser extent Terre-de-Bas (land below), attract visitors.

Some claim Les Saintes has one of the nicest bays in the world, a lilliput Rio de Janeiro with a sugarloaf. The isles, just 6 miles from the main island, were discovered by Columbus (who else?) on November 4, 1493, and he named them Los Santos.

The history of Les Saintes is very much the history of Guadeloupe itself. In years past, the islands have been heavily fortified, as if they were Guadeloupe's Gibraltar. The climate is very dry, and until the desalination plant opened, water was often rationed.

If you're planning a visit, **Terre-de-Haut** is the most interesting Saint to call on, and it's the only one with facilities for overnight guests. The population of Terre-de-Haut is mainly Caucasian fishermen or sailors and their families descended from Breton corsairs. The very skilled sailors maneuver large boats called *saintois,* and wear coolie-like headgear called a *salaco,* which is shallow and white with sun shades covered in cloth built on radiating ribs of thick bamboo. Frankly, the hats look like small parasols. If you want to take a photograph of these sailors, please make a polite request (in French; otherwise they won't know what you're talking about). Visitors often like to buy these hats (if they can find them) for use as beach wear.

Terre-de-Haut is a place for discovery and lovers of nature, many of whom stake out their exhibitionistic space on the nude beach at Anse Crawen.

Centre Nautique des Saintes, Plage de la Colline, at Bourg in Terre-de-Haut (☎ 0590/99-54-24) rents scuba diving gear and will direct you to the dozen or so top dive sights around the island.

GETTING THERE

BY PLANE   The fastest way to get there is by plane. The airport is a truncated landing strip accommodating nothing larger than 20-seat Twin Otters. **Air Guadeloupe** (☎ 0590/82-47-00 on Guadeloupe, or 0590/99-51-23 on Terre-de-Haut) has two round-trip flights daily from Pointe-à-Pitre, which take 15 minutes and cost around 360F ($61.20) per person round-trip.

BY FERRY   Most islanders reach Terre-de-Haut via one of the several ferries that travel from Guadeloupe daily. Visitors opt for one of the two boats that depart from Pointe-à-Pitre's Gare Maritime des Iles, on quai Gatine, across the street from the open-air market. The trip requires 60 minutes each way and costs 180F ($30.60) round-trip. The most popular departure time for Terre-de-Haut from Pointe-à-Pitre is 8am Monday to Saturday and 7am Sunday, with returns scheduled every afternoon at 4pm. Be at the ferryboat terminal at least 15 minutes prior to the anticipated departure.

Other ferries (two per day) also depart from Trois Rivières, and one additional ferry leaves daily from the island's capital of Basse-Terre. Transit from either of these last two cities requires 25 minutes each way and costs 100F ($17) round-trip.

For more information and last-minute departure schedules, contact **Frères Bru-dey** (☎ 0590/90-04-48) or **Trans Antilles Express,** Gare Maritime, quai Gatine, Pointe-à-Pitre (☎ 0590/83-12-45).

GETTING AROUND

On an island that doesn't have a single car-rental agency, you get about by walking or renting a bike or motor scooter from hotels and in town near the pier. **Localizé,** at Bourg in Terre-de-Haut (☎ **0590/99-51-99**), rents both motorboats and scooters.

There are also minibuses called **Taxis de l'Ile** (eight in all), which take six to eight passengers.

ACCOMMODATIONS YOU CAN AFFORD

Auberge Les Petits Saints aux Anacardiers. La Savane, 97137 Terre-de-Haut, Les Saintes, Guadeloupe, F.W.I. ☎ **0590/99-50-99.** Fax 0590/99-54-51. 12 units. A/C TV. Winter, 390–490F ($66.30–$83.30) single; 490–590F ($83.30–$100.30) double. Off-season, 350F ($59.50) single; 450F ($76.50) double. AE, MC, V.

Set in a hilltop garden a 5-minute walk from the nearest beach, this cost-conscious guest house occupies a 1970s building that was once the home of the island's mayor; it was transformed into a guest house in the early 1990s by expats from the French mainland. The small rooms are simple but appealing and comfortable, with new beds and very tiny baths. On the premises is a restaurant, on a terrace surrounded with plants, that serves health-conscious foods with an emphasis on fresh fish.

Hôtel La Saintoise. Place de la Mairie, 97137 Terre-de-Haut, Les Saintes, Guadeloupe, F.W.I. ☎ **0590/99-52-50.** 8 units. A/C. Year-round 280F ($47.60) single; 370F ($62.90) double. Rates include continental breakfast. MC, V.

From the 1960s, La Saintoise is a two-story building near the almond trees and wide-spread poinciana of the main square, near the ferry dock, across from the town hall. As in a small French village, the inn places tables and chairs on the sidewalk where you can sit and observe what action there is. The owner will welcome you and show you through the uncluttered lobby to one of his modest second-floor rooms, each with a small tiled bath. Housekeeping is good, beds have firm mattresses, and the comfort level is suitable. This is a friendly and unpretentious place.

Kanao. 97137 Terre-de-Haut, Les Saintes, Guadeloupe, F.W.I. ☎ **0590/99-51-36.** Fax 0590/99-55-04. 19 units, 3 bungalows with kitchenette. A/C TEL. Winter, 500–650F ($85–$110.50) double; 700–900F ($119–$153) bungalow for 2. Off-season, 300–400F ($51–$68) double; 500F ($85) bungalow for 2. Rates include continental breakfast. MC, V.

Named after the open-sided log canoes used by the Arawaks, this modern concrete-sided structure is on a little beach at Pointe Coquelet, about a 10-minute walk north of the town center. All the small accommodations have private showers in cramped baths and rather spartan furnishings, including narrow beds. Five have views of the sea and Anse Mire cove. Though very limited English is spoken, this still may be ideal for non–French speaking vacationers wanting to get away from it all. A garden with its own pool is near the hotel, and the hotel restaurant serves breakfast, lunch, and dinner.

GREAT DEALS ON DINING

Many French-speaking visitors used to come to Terre-de-Haut to eat roast iguana, the large but harmless lizard found on many of these islands. The species is now endangered, so we don't recommended you order this dish. Instead, you'll find conch (called *lambi*), Caribbean lobster, and fresh fish. For dessert, you can try the savory island specialty, *tournament d'amour* (agony of love), a coconut pastry available in the restaurants but best sampled from the barefoot children who sell the delicacy near the boat dock.

The island's most popular bar is **Nilce's Bar** at Bourg in Terre-de-Haut (☎ **0590/99-56-80**), which also serves good food. You're welcomed by Ghislain Laps and his wife, Nilce, who hails from Rio de Janeiro. Her fresh salads are among the island's best, and her fresh fish is truly excellent and never allowed to overcook. This is also the best place for people-watching, as you can see passengers disembarking or boarding the ferries to take them back to the mainland of Guadeloupe. In the late evening music is played until midnight, when local law dictates that Les Saintes quiets down. Nilce, a Brazilian chanteuse, will sometimes sing.

✪ **Chez Jeannine (Le Casse-Croûte).** Fond-de-Curé, Terre-de-Haut. ☎ **0590-99-53-37.** Reservations recommended for large groups only. Fixed-price 3-course meal 75F ($12.75). V. Daily 9–10am, noon–3pm, and 7pm–midnight. CREOLE.

The creative statement of Mme Jeannine Bairtran, originally from Guadeloupe, this restaurant is a 3-minute walk south of the town center in a simple Creole house decorated with modern Caribbean accessories. The fixed-price meal includes avocado stuffed with crabmeat, *gâteau de poissons* (literally fish cake), and several curry-enhanced stews (including one made with goat). Crayfish and grilled fish (the ubiquitous catch of the day) appear daily on the menu. Local vegetables are used. The ambience is that of a Creole bistro—in other words, a hut with nautical trappings and bright tablecloths.

Les Amandiers. Place de la Mairie, Terre-de-Haut. ☎ **0590/99-50-06.** Reservations recommended. Fixed-price menus 70–90F ($11.90–$15.30). AE, MC, V. Daily 8am–3pm and 6:30–9:30pm. CREOLE.

Across from the town hall on the main square of Bourg, this is the most traditional Creole bistro on Terre-de-Haut. A TV set (at loud volume) might provide entertainment in the bar. Monsieur and Mme Charlot Brudey are your hosts in this beige-painted building whose upper balconies sport tables and chairs for open-air dining. Conch (*lambi*) is prepared either in a fricassee or a colombo, a savory curry stew. Also available is a court bouillon of fish, a terrine of fish, and a seemingly endless supply of grilled crayfish, a staple of the island. The catch of the day is grilled the way you like it. You'll find an intriguing collection of stews, concocted from fish, bananas, and christophine (chayote). A knowledge of French would be helpful around here.

EXPLORING THE ISLAND

Terre-de-Haut's main settlement is **Bourg,** a single street following the curve of the fishing harbor. A charming hamlet, it has little houses with red or blue doorways, balconies, and Victorian gingerbread gewgaws. Donkeys are the beasts of burden, and everywhere you look are fish nets drying in the sunshine. You can also explore the ruins of **Fort Napoléon,** left over from those 17th-century wars, including the naval encounter known in European history books as the Battle of the Saints. You can see the barracks and prison cells, as well as the drawbridge and art museum. Occasionally you'll spot an iguana scurrying up the ramparts. Directly across the bay, atop Ilet-à-Cabrit, sits the fort named in honor of Empress Joséphine.

You can hike to **Le Grand Souffleur,** with its beautiful cliffs, and to **Le Chameau,** the highest point on the island, rising to a peak of 1,000 feet. You might also get a sailor to take you on his boat to the other main island, **Terre-de-Bas,** which has no accommodations.

The underwater world off Les Saintes has attracted scuba divers as renowned as Jacques Cousteau, but even the less experienced may explore its challenging depths and multicolored reefs. Intriguing underwater grottoes found near Fort Napoléon on Terre-de-Haut are also explored.

SHOPPING

Few come here to shop, but there's one offbeat choice at **Kaz an Nou Gallery** on Terre-de-Haut (☎ **0590/99-52-29**), where a local artist, Pascal Fay, carves miniature wooden house façades, all candy-colored and trimmed in gingerbread. His most popular reproduction graces the cover of the best-selling picture book *Caribbean Style*. Mr. Fay will point the way to the real house, a few blocks away, which has become a sightseeing attraction all on its own because of the book's popularity. The houses measure about 16 by 13 inches and sell for $100 to $400 each.

If you're looking for an authentic salako hat, compared to that of a Chinese coolie, head to **José Beaujour** at Terre-de-Bas (☎ **0590/99-80-20**). At **Mahogany Artisanat,** Bourg in Terre-de-Haut (☎ **0590/99-50-12**), you'll find Yves Cohen's batik and hand-painted T-shirts.

✪ MARIE-GALANTE

Full of rustic charm, this offshore dependency of Guadeloupe is an almost-perfect circle of about 60 square miles. Almost exclusively French-speaking, it lies 20 miles south of Guadeloupe's Grand-Terre.

Columbus noticed Marie-Galante before he did Guadelope, on November 3, 1493. He named it for his own vessel but didn't land here. In fact, it was 150 years later that the first European came ashore. The first French governor of the island was Constant d'Aubigné, father of the marquise de Maintenon. Several captains from the West Indies Company attempted settlement, but none of them succeeded. In 1674, Marie-Galante was given to the Crown, and from that point on its history was closely linked to that of Guadeloupe.

After 1816 the island settled down to a slumber so quiet you could almost hear the sugarcane growing on its plantations. Many windmills were built to crush the cane, and lots of tropical fruits were grown.

Now some 30,000 inhabitants live here and make their living from sugar and rum, the latter said to be the best in the Caribbean. The island's climate is rather dry, and there are many good beaches. Brilliantly white, one of these covers at least 5 miles. However, swimming can be dangerous in some places. The best beach is at **Petite Anse,** 6½ miles from **Grand-Bourg,** the main town that sports an 1845 baroque church. The 18th-century Grand'Anse rum distillery can be visited, as can the historic fishing hamlet of Vieux Fort.

GETTING THERE & GETTING AROUND

Air Guadeloupe (☎ **0590/82-74-00**) flies to Marie-Galante in just 20 minutes from Pointe-à-Pitre, landing at Les Basse Airport, about 2 miles from Grand-Bourg. Round-trip fare is 360F ($61.20).

Antilles Trans Express (**Exprès des Iles**), Gare Maritime, quai Gatine, Pointe-à-Pitre (☎ **0590/83-12-45** or 0590/91-13-43), operates boat service to the island with three daily round-trips between Point-à-Pitre and Grand-Bourg costing 170F ($28.90). Departures from Pointe-à-Pitre are daily at 8am, 12:30pm, and 5pm, with returns from Grand-Bourg at 6am, 9am, and 3:45pm.

A limited number of **taxis** are available at the airport, but negotiate a fare before you drive off.

ACCOMMODATIONS YOU CAN AFFORD

On the island are only a few accommodations, which, even if they aren't very up-to-date in amenities, are clean and hearty. At least the greetings are friendly. They may also be bewildering if you speak no French. You can also find lodgings as well as good meals at **Le Touloulou** (see "Great Deals on Dining," below).

Auberge de l'Arbre à Pain. Rue Jeanne-d'Arc 34, 97112 Grand-Bourg, Marie-Galante, Guadeloupe, F.W.I. ☎ **0590/97-73-69.** 7 units. A/C. Year-round, 250F ($42.50) single; 300F ($51) double. V. At the harbor, take the first street going toward the church.

Behind a clapboard façade close to the street, about a 5-minute stroll from the harborfront, this respected *auberge* was named after the half-dozen breadfruit trees (*les arbres à pain*) sheltering its courtyard and its simple but pleasant rooms from the blazing sun. Each room has uncomplicated furnishings and a private bath. You'll get a taste of Old France here. There's easy access to nearby beaches.

The hotel's restaurant is a favorite with many town residents. Meals are served daily from noon to 2pm and 7 to 11pm. Main courses cost 65F to 100F ($11.05 to $17) and include fresh fish and shellfish. Usually whatever's available includes a court bouillon of fish, a soufflé of sea urchins, and meat dishes following French culinary traditions. No reservations are required for the restaurant, although because the rooms are usually in demand throughout the winter, reservations for overnight stays are important.

GREAT DEALS ON DINING

Don't expect elaborate restaurants here, but you can often eat well, even if the choice for dining is housed in a shack.

In the center of Grand-Bourg you can dine right on the beach at **Le Neptune** (☎ **0590/97-96-90**) or **Côte Plage** (☎ **0590/97-76-25**). Naturally, the grilled fish is the way to go. In town itself, opt for **La Charette** (☎ **0590/97-79-78**). The island's best pizzas are made at **Pizzeria Le Moana & Crêperie** (☎ **0590/97-85-97**), also in the town center. The specialty is a pizza topped with shellfish. Only a 15-minute drive east from Grand-Bourg, **Tatie Zézette** (☎ **0590/97-36-02**) is known for its spicy seafood dishes. In St-Louis, in the northwestern part of the island, the place to go is a raffish little shack on the beach called **A Ka Pat** (☎ **0590/97-05-74**). Another good bet nearby, **Chez Henri** (☎ **0590/94-04-57**) is really a bar but it has an alfresco dining area. The grilled lobster and shrimp are special treats. Local vegetables like breadfruit and dasheen accompany the main courses.

Crêperie La Pergola. Plage de Petite Anse, Marie-Galante. ☎ **0590/97-32-63.** Crêpes 18F–35F ($3.05–$5.95). MC, V. Wed–Mon 7pm–1am. CRÊPES.

Most locals view this place as a Gallic-style fast-food joint, where a sweet or salted crêpe will provide a late-night pick-me-up. The setting combines aspects of both a bar and a cafe, and this noteworthy local hangout perks up with gossip and recorded music, including the island's only karaoke machine, every evening except Tuesday beginning around 9pm. Crêpes come in simple (with butter and a dusting of sugar) to complex (the kitchen sink that includes salted versions laden with ham, cheese, and vegetables) options.

Le Touloulou. Plage de Petite Anse, Marie-Galante, Guadeloupe, F.W.I. ☎ **0590/97-32-63.** Fax 0590/97-33-59. Main courses 45–150F ($7.65–$25.50); set menus 90–120F ($15.30–$20.40). MC, V. Tues–Sun noon–2:30pm, Tues–Sat 7–9:30pm. Closed Sept 15–Oct 15. CREOLE.

Its French-speaking owners will tell you, if you ask them *en français*, about how during one of the recent hurricanes the relatively rare bamboo walls of this 30-year-old house were blown away and later replaced with conventional boards. Adjacent to the beach, with a hardworking staff and a hyper-casual crowd, it specializes in shellfish and crayfish culled from local waters. If sea urchins or lobster is your passion, you'll find them in abundance, prepared virtually any way you want. Other standbys are a savory, and highly ethnic, version of *bébélé* (cow tripe enhanced with breadfruit, dumplings, and plantains), and conch served as fricassee or in puff pastry.

The inn has also added five basic units, each with air-conditioning and a small bath. These rooms offer little more than the simplest of comforts of the basic motel type, which means a decent bed and not much else, except those that have a small kitchenette. In winter, a double is 250F to 280F ($42.50 to $47.60), the latter price charged for a unit with kitchenette. A two-bedroom bungalow, suitable for four, rents for 400F ($68) and also has a kitchenette. Off-season, a double ranges from 220F to 280F ($37.40 to $47.60), with the bungalow renting for 350F ($59.50).

LA DESIRADE

The ubiquitous Columbus spotted this *terre désirée,* or sought-after land, after his Atlantic crossing in 1493. Named La Désirade, the island, 5 miles off the eastern tip of Guadeloupe, is less than 7 miles long and about 1½ miles wide. A single potholed road running along its length. This former leper colony is often visited on a day excursion.

The island has fewer than 1,700 inhabitants, including the descendants of Europeans exiled here by royal command. Tourism has hardly touched the place, if you can forget about those day-trippers. Most visitors opt to spend only a day on La Désirade, sunning or perhaps touring the island's barren expanses. There are, however, a handful of exceptionally simple guest houses charging from 300F ($51) for two. Don't expect anything grand.

The main hamlet is **Grand'Anse,** which has a small church with a presbytery and flower garden. **Le Souffleur** is a village where boats are constructed, and at **Baie Mahault** are the ruins of the old leper colony (including a barely recognizable chapel) from the early 18th century.

The best **beaches** are Souffleur, a tranquil oasis near the boat-building hamlet, and Baie Mahault, a small beach that's a Caribbean cliché of white sand and palm trees.

GETTING THERE & GETTING AROUND

Air Guadeloupe (☎ 00590/82-47-00) offers flights to La Désirade from Guadeloupe's Le Raizet Airport three times a week. The round-trip fare is 360F ($61.20) per person, and trip time is between 15 to 20 minutes each way. Unless a respectable number of passengers shows up for the flight, Air Guadeloupe might cancel it, leaving passengers to fend for themselves and find other means of transport.

As a result, some visitors opt to contact **Ailes Guadeloupiennes** (☎ 0590/82-24-66), a local aviation school whose pilots and planes are occasionally available for chartered flights from Guadeloupe to La Desirade. The one-way fare is 700F ($119), which can be divided among up to three passengers.

Most travelers opt to ride the **ferry** that leaves every day at 8am and 5pm (and sometimes at 3pm as well, depending on the season) from the wharves at St-François, near Guadeloupe's eastern tip. Return voyages include a daily departure at 3pm, allowing convenient access for day-trippers. Trip time is around 50 minutes each way, depending on conditions at sea. Round-trip passage costs 170F ($28.90) per person. Call ☎ **0590/83-12-45** for schedules.

On La Désirade, three or four **minibuses** run between the airport and the towns. To get around, you might negotiate with a local driver. **Bicycles** are also available at the hotels.

If you'd like to spend the night, call **L'Oasis** (☎ 00590/20-02-12) or **Le Mirage** (☎ 00590/20-01-08; fax 00590/20-07-45). Both are at Beauséjour, half a mile from the airport. Oasis has six plain rooms and charges 280F ($47.60) for a double, including breakfast. Built in 1990 of concrete, it's simple and boxy, lying a short walk from a good beach. A bit closer to the sea, Le Mirage offers seven rather drab rooms at 300F ($51) for a double, including breakfast. Built of concrete around the same time as Oasis, it offers a simple bar and restaurant.

Jamaica 14

Most visitors have a mental picture of Jamaica before they arrive: a boisterous culture of reggae and Rastafarianism, with white-sand beaches, tropical forests, rivers, mountains, and clear waterfalls. Jamaica's art, music, and cuisine (particularly jerk) are also remarkable.

Jamaica can be tranquil and intriguing, but there's no denying it's plagued by crime, drugs, and muggings. There's also palpable racial tension. But many visitors are unaffected—they're escorted from the airport to their heavily patrolled hotel grounds and venture out only on expensive organized tours. Those who want to see the real Jamaica, or at least to see the island in greater depth, had better be prepared for some hassle. Vendors on the beaches and in the markets can be particularly aggressive.

Most Jamaicans, in spite of their hard times, have unrelenting good humor and genuinely welcome visitors. Others harm the tourism business, so many visitors vow never to return. Jamaica's appealing aspects have to be weighed against its poverty and problems, the legacy of traumatic political upheavals that have characterized the island since the 1970s.

Should you go? By all means, yes. Be prudent and cautious, though—just as if you were visiting New York, Miami, or Los Angeles. But Jamaica is worth it! The island has fine hotels and a zesty cuisine, and is well-geared to couples who come to tie the knot or celebrate their honeymoon. As for sports, Jamaica boasts the best golf courses in the West Indies, and its landscape affords visitors lots of outdoor activities like rafting and serious hiking. The island also has some of the finest diving waters in the world, with an average diving depth of 35 to 95 feet. Visibility is usually 60 to 120 feet. Most of the diving is done on coral reefs, protected by underwater parks where fish, shells, coral, and sponges are plentiful. Experienced divers can also see wrecks, hedges, caves, drop-offs, and tunnels.

Jamaica is known for its all-inclusive resorts, most of which are expensive. But you can save money by staying at local B&Bs, small hotels, and guest houses. And if you steer clear of the pricey restaurants catering almost exclusively to tourists and eat where many Jamaicans do, you'll cut your meal costs by two-thirds, maybe a lot less. Every town from Kingston to Montego Bay to Negril has a jerk center, and you almost can't go wrong patronizing one of these local dives for a true taste of Jamaica. A jerk chicken or pork lunch runs about $6 in most places.

Jamaica

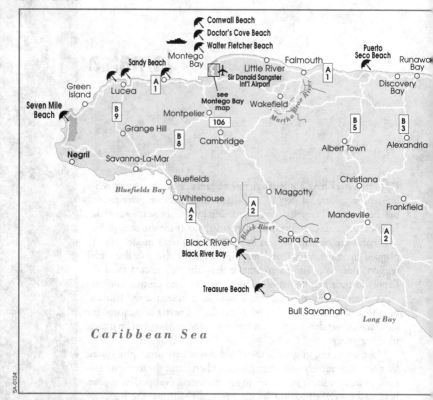

Jamaica lies 90 miles south of Cuba, with which it was chummy in the 1970s (when much of the world feared Jamaica was going Communist). It's the third largest of the Caribbean islands, with some 4,400 square miles of predominantly green land, a mountain ridge peaking at 7,400 feet above sea level, and many white-sand beaches with clear blue sea on the north coast.

1 Essentials

VISITOR INFORMATION

Before you go, you can obtain information from the **Jamaica Tourist Board** at the following U.S. addresses: 500 N. Michigan Ave., Suite 1030, Chicago, IL 60611 (☎ **312/527-1296**); 1320 S. Dixie Hwy., Suite 1101, Coral Gables, FL 33146 (☎ **305/665-0557**); 3440 Wilshire Blvd., Suite 805, Los Angeles, CA 90010 (☎ **213/384-1123**); and 801 Second Ave., New York, NY 10017 (☎ **212/856-9727**). In Atlanta, information can be obtained only by phone (☎ **770/452-7799**).

In **Canada,** contact 1 Eglinton Ave. E., Suite 616, Toronto, ON M4P 3A1 (☎ **416/482-7850**). Brits can call the **London** office: 1–2 Prince Consort Rd., London SW7 2BZ (☎ **020/7224-0505**).

Once on **Jamaica,** you'll find tourist board offices at 2 St. Lucia Ave., Kingston (☎ **876/929-9200**); Cornwall Beach, St. James, Montego Bay (☎ **876/952-4425**); Shop no. 29, Coral Seas Plaza, Negril, Westmoreland (☎ **876/957-4243**); in the

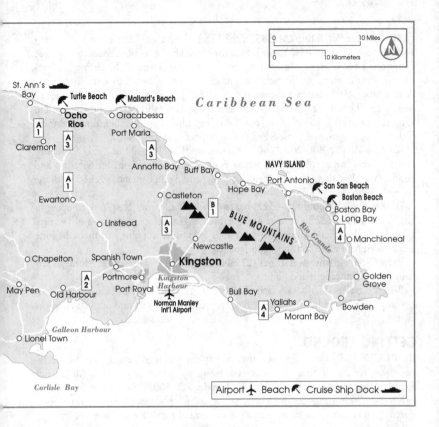

Ocean Village Shopping Centre, Ocho Rios, St. Ann (☎ 876/974-2582); in City Centre Plaza, Port Antonio (☎ 876/993-3051); and in Hendriks Building, 2 High St., Black River (☎ 876/965-2074).

The Internet address for Jamaica is **www.jamaicatravel.com**.

GETTING THERE

Before you book your own airfare, read the section on package tours in chapter 2—it can save you a bundle!

There are two **international airports** on Jamaica: Donald Sangster in Montego Bay (☎ 887/952-3124) and Norman Manley in Kingston (☎ 876/924-8235). The most popular flights to Jamaica are from New York and Miami. Remember to reconfirm all flights, going and returning, no later than 72 hours before departure. Flying time from Miami is 1¼ hours; from Los Angeles, 5½ hours; from Atlanta, 2½ hours; from Dallas, 3 hours; from Chicago and New York, 3½ hours; and from Toronto, 4 hours.

Some of the most convenient and popular routes to Jamaica are provided by **American Airlines** (☎ 800/433-7300 in the U.S.) via its hubs in New York and Miami. Throughout the year, three daily nonstop flights depart from New York's Kennedy Airport for Montego Bay, continuing on to Kingston. Return flights to New York from Jamaica usually depart from Montego Bay, touch down briefly in Kingston, then continue nonstop back to Kennedy. From Miami, at least two daily flights depart for Kingston and two daily flights for Montego Bay.

Air Jamaica (☎ 800/523-5585 in the U.S.), the national carrier, operates about 14 flights a week from New York's JFK, most of which stop at both Montego Bay and Kingston. They offer even more frequent flights from Miami. The airline has connecting service within Jamaica through its reservations network to a small independent airline, **Air Jamaica Express,** whose planes usually hold between 10 and 17 passengers. They fly from the island's international airports at Montego Bay and Kingston to small airports around the island, including Port Antonio, Boscobel (near Ocho Rios), Negril, and Tinson Pen (a tiny airport near Kingston).

Air Canada (☎ 800/268-7240 in Canada or 800/776-3000 in the U.S.) flies to Jamaica from Toronto. In winter, service is daily; off-season flights are Saturday and Sunday only. But all this is subject to change depending on demand, so check with the airline.

US Airways (☎ 800/428-4322) has two daily flights from New York stopping in Charlotte or Philadelphia to take on added passengers before continuing to Jamaica. Likewise, it also offers two daily flights out of Baltimore, stopping in either Charlotte or Philadelphia before continuing to Jamaica.

In addition, **Northwest Airlines** (☎ 800/225-2525) flies directly to Montego Bay daily from Minneapolis and Tampa.

British travelers usually take **British Airways** (☎ 0345/222-111), which has four nonstop flights weekly to Montego Bay and Kingston from London's Gatwick Airport.

GETTING AROUND

BY PLANE   Most travelers enter the country via Montego Bay. If you want to fly elsewhere, you'll need to use the island's domestic air service, provided by Air Jamaica Express. Reservations are handled by **Air Jamaica** (☎ 800/523-5585 in the U.S., or 876/923-8680 in Kingston and Montego Bay), which has consolidated its reservation system. You can also reserve before you leave home through a travel agent or through Air Jamaica.

Air Jamaica Express offers 30 scheduled flights daily, covering all the major resort areas. For example, there are 11 flights a day between Kingston and Montego Bay and 3 a day between Negril and Port Antonio. (Incidentally, Tinson Pen Airport in the heart of downtown Kingston is for domestic flights only.) Car-rental facilities are available only at the international airports at Kingston and Montego Bay.

Air SuperClub (☎ 876/940-7746) also provides shuttle service between Montego Bay and Ocho Rios and between Montego Bay and Negril. **Tropical Airlines** (☎ 876/968-2473 in Kingston or 876/979-3565 in Montego Bay) flies between Montego Bay and Kingston and also between Montego Bay and Cuba. Though travel to Cuba still has some serious restrictions, many Americans fly this route for a look at Castroland.

BY TAXI & BUS   Kingston has no city taxis with meters, so agree on a price before you get in. In Kingston and on the rest of the island, special taxis and buses for visitors are operated by **JUTA** (Jamaica Union of Travelers Association) and have the union's emblem on the side of the vehicle. All prices are controlled, and any local JUTA office will supply a list of rates. JUTA drivers handle nearly all the ground transportation, and some offer sightseeing tours.

BY RENTAL CAR   Jamaica is big enough, and public transportation unreliable enough, that a car is a necessity if you plan to do much independent sightseeing. In lieu of this, you can always take an organized tour to the major sights and spend the rest of the time on the beaches near your hotel.

Catch a Fire: Jamaica's Reggae Festivals

Jamaica comes alive to the pulsating sounds of reggae during August's **Reggae Sunsplash,** the world's largest annual reggae festival. This week-long music extravaganza features some of the most prominent reggae groups and artists, which in the past have included Ziggy Marley and the Melody Makers. Sunsplash takes place at different venues; check with the Jamaican Tourist Board for the latest details.

Some time during the second week of August a **Reggae Sunfest** is staged in Montego Bay. Usually this is a 4-day musical event, with some of the biggest names in reggae, both from Jamaica and worldwide, performing. Many local hotels are fully booked for the festivals, so advance reservations are necessary. The Jamaican Tourist Board's U.S. and Canadian offices can give you information about packages and group rates for the festivals. Call for information about Sunfest.

Other reggae concerts and festivals featuring top performers are held throughout the year on Jamaica. Ask the tourist board for details.

Depending on road conditions, driving time for the 50 miles from Montego Bay to Negril is 1½ hours; from Montego Bay to Ocho Rios, 1½ hours; from Ocho Rios to Port Antonio, 2½ hours; from Ocho Rios to Kingston, 2 hours.

Unfortunately, prices of car rentals on Jamaica have skyrocketed recently, making it one of the most expensive rental scenes in the Caribbean. There's also a 15% government tax on rentals. Equally unfortunate are the unfavorable insurance policies that apply to virtually every car-rental agency on Jamaica.

It's best to stick to branches of U.S.-based outfits. **Avis** (☎ **800/331-1212** in the U.S.) maintains offices at the international airports in both Montego Bay (☎ **876/952-4543**) and Kingston (☎ **876/924-8013**). The company's least-expensive car requires a 24-hour advance booking. There's also **Budget** (☎ **800/527-0700** or 876/952-3838 at the Montego Bay Airport, 876/924-8762 in Kingston); with Budget, a mandatory daily collision-damage waiver costs another $15. **Hertz** (☎ **800/654-3001** in the U.S.) operates branches at the airports at both Montego Bay (☎ **876/979-0438**) and Kingston (☎ **876/924-8028**). If you'd like to shop for a better deal with one of the local companies, try **Jamaica Car Rental** in Montego Bay (☎ **876/952-5586**) or in Ocho Rios (☎ **876/974-2505**).

In Montego Bay, some local options are **United Car Rentals,** 49 Gloucester Ave. (☎ **876/952-3077**), which rents Mazdas, Toyota Starlets, Hondas, and Suzuki Jeeps from $48 per day for a two-door car without air-conditioning. You can also try **Jamaica Car Rental,** 23 Gloucester Ave. (☎ **876/952-5586**), with a branch at the Sangster International Airport at Montego Bay (☎ **876/952-9496**). Daily rates begin at $70.

In Kingston, try **Island Car Rentals,** 17 Antigua Ave. (☎ **876/926-5991**), with a branch at Montego Bay's Sangster International Airport (☎ **876/952-5771**). It rents Hondas and Samurais, beginning at $115 daily in winter and $96 off-season.

Driving is on the left, and you should exercise more than your usual caution because of the unfamiliar terrain. Be especially cautious at night. Speed limits are 30 m.p.h. in town and 50 m.p.h. outside town. Gas is measured in the Imperial gallon (a British unit of measure that'll give you 25% more than a U.S. gallon), and the charge is payable only in Jamaican dollars; most stations don't accept credit cards. Your own valid driver's license from back home is acceptable for driving during short-term visits to Jamaica.

BY BIKE & SCOOTER   These can be rented in Montego Bay, and you'll need your valid driver's license. **Montego Honda/Bike Rentals,** 21 Gloucester Ave. (☎ **876/952-4984**), rents Honda scooters for $30 to $35 a day (24 hours), plus a $300 deposit. Bikes cost $10 a day, plus a $150 deposit. Deposits are refundable if the vehicles are returned in good shape. It's open daily 7:30am to 5pm.

Fast Facts: Jamaica

Banking Hours   Banks island-wide are open Monday to Friday 9am to 5pm.

Currency   The unit of currency on Jamaica is the **Jamaican dollar,** using the same symbol as the U.S. dollar ($). There's no fixed rate of exchange for the Jamaican dollar. Subject to market fluctuations, it's traded publicly. Visitors to Jamaica can pay for any goods in U.S. dollars. *Be careful!* Ask whether a price is being quoted in Jamaican or U.S. dollars. In this guide we've generally followed the price-quotation policy of the establishment, whether in Jamaican dollars or U.S. dollars. The symbol "J$" denotes prices in Jamaican dollars; the conversion into U.S. dollars follows in parentheses. When dollar figures stand alone, they're always U.S. currency.

Jamaican currency is issued in banknotes of J$10, J$20, J$50, J$100, and J$500. Coins are available in denominations of 5¢, 10¢, 25¢, 50¢, J$1, and J$5. Five-dollar banknotes and one-cent coins are also in circulation but increasingly rare. At press time (but subject to change), the exchange rate of Jamaican currency is J$36 to U.S.$1 (J$1 = about 2.8¢ U.S.). There are 58 Jamaican dollars in 1 pound sterling (J$1 = 1.7 pence).

There are Bank of Jamaica exchange bureaus at both international airports (Montego Bay and Kingston), at cruise-ship piers, and in most hotels.

Customs   Do *not* bring in or take out illegal drugs from Jamaica. Your luggage will be searched. Marijuana-sniffing police dogs are stationed at the airport. Otherwise, you can bring in most items intended for personal use.

Documents   U.S. and Canadian residents don't need passports, but must have proof of citizenship (or permanent residency) and a return or ongoing ticket. In lieu of a passport, an original birth certificate or a certified copy, plus photo ID, will do. Always double check, however, with the airline you're flying in case document requirements have changed. Other visitors, including British subjects, need passports, good for a maximum stay of 6 months. Immigration cards, needed for bank transactions and currency exchange, are given to visitors at the airport arrivals desks.

Drugs   You'll almost certainly be approached by someone selling *ganja* (marijuana), and, to be frank, that's why many travelers come here. However, know that drugs (including marijuana) are illegal here, and imprisonment is the penalty for possession. Don't smoke pot openly in public. Of course, hundreds of visitors do and get away with it, but you may be the one who gets caught. You should even give a thought as to whether the person selling to you might be a police informant. And above all, don't even consider bringing marijuana back home. The drug-sniffing dogs stationed at the Jamaican airports will check your luggage.

U.S. Customs agents, well aware of the drug situation, have also easily caught and arrested many who have tried to take a chance on bringing some home.

Drugstores   In Montego Bay, try **Overton Pharmacy,** 49 Union St., Overton Plaza (☎ **876/952-2699**); in Ocho Rios, **Great House Pharmacy,** Brown's Plaza (☎ **876/974-2352**); and in Kingston, **Moodie's Pharmacy,** in the New Kingston Shopping Centre (☎ **876/926-4174**). Prescriptions are accepted by local pharmacies only if issued by a Jamaican doctor. Hotels have doctors on call. If you need any particular medicine or treatment, bring evidence, such as a letter from your own physician.

Electricity   Most places have the standard 110 volts AC (60 cycles), as in the United States. However, some operate on 220 volts AC (50 cycles). If your hotel is on a different current from your U.S.-made appliance, ask for a transformer and adapter.

Embassies   Calling embassies or consulates in Jamaica is a challenge. Phones will ring and ring before being picked up, if they're answered at all. Extreme patience is needed to reach a live voice. The Embassy of the **United States** is at the Jamaica Mutual Life Centre, 2 Oxford Rd., Kingston 5 (☎ **876/929-4850**). The High Commission of **Canada** is in the Mutual Security Bank Building, 30–36 Knutsford Blvd., Kingston 5 (☎ **876/926-1500**), and there's a Canadian Consulate at 29 Gloucester Ave., Montego Bay (☎ **876/952-6198**). The High Commission of the **United Kingdom** is at 28 Trafalgar Rd., Kingston 10 (☎ **876/926-9050**).

Emergencies   For the **police** and air rescue, dial ☎ **119;** to report a **fire** or call an **ambulance,** dial ☎ **110.**

Hospitals   In Kingston, the **University Hospital** is at Mona (☎ **876/927-1620**); in Montego Bay, the **Cornwall Regional Hospital** is at Mount Salem (☎ **876/952-5100**); and in Port Antonio, the **Port Antonio General Hospital** is at Naylor's Hill (☎ **876/993-2646**).

Marriages   You can get a marriage license after 24 hours' residence on the island and then marry as soon as it can be arranged. You'll need your birth certificate and, where applicable, divorce documents or death certificates. All documents must be properly certified—ordinary photocopies won't be accepted. Most Jamaican hotels will make arrangements for your wedding and license. Otherwise, one of the offices of the Jamaica Tourist Board can assist you in meeting and making arrangements with a government marriage officer.

Nudity   Nude bathing is allowed at a number of hotels, clubs, and beaches (especially in Negril), but only where there are signs stating SWIMSUITS OPTIONAL. Elsewhere, the law won't allow even topless sunbathing.

Safety   Major hotels have security guards who protect the grounds, so most vacationers don't have any real problems. It's not wise to accept an invitation to see "the real Jamaica" from some stranger you meet on the beach. Exercise caution when traveling around Jamaica. Safeguard your valuables and never leave them unattended on a beach. Likewise, never leave luggage or other valuables in a car or even the trunk of a car. The U.S. State Department has issued a travel advisory about crime rates in Kingston, so don't go walking around alone at night. Caution is also advisable in many north-coast tourist areas, especially remote houses and isolated villas that can't afford security.

Shopping Hours   Hours vary widely, but as a general rule most stores are open Monday to Friday 8:30am to 4:30 or 5pm. Some shops are open Saturday until noon.

Taxes   The government imposes a 12% room tax. You'll be charged a J$750 ($21.40) departure tax at the airport, payable in either Jamaican dollars or in equivalent U.S. dollars. There's also a 15% government tax on rental cars and a 15% tax on all overseas telephone calls.

Time   Jamaica is on eastern standard time year-round. However, when the United States is on daylight saving time, at 6am in Miami it's 5am in Kingston.

Tipping   Tipping is customary. A general 10% or 15% is expected in hotels and restaurants on occasions when you would normally tip. Some places add a service charge to the bill. Tipping isn't allowed in the all-inclusive hotels.

Water   It's usually safe to drink piped-in water, island-wide, as it's filtered and chlorinated. But, as always, it's more prudent to drink bottled water if it's available.

Weather   Expect temperatures around 80° to 90°F on the coast. Winter is a little cooler. In the mountains it can get as low as 40°F. There is generally a breeze, which in winter is noticeably cool. The rainy periods in general are October and November (although it can extend into December) and May and June. Normally rain comes in short, sharp showers; then the sun shines.

TIPS ON FINDING AFFORDABLE ACCOMMODATIONS

CAMPING   Recent attacks against tourists have put a severe damper on many visitors' willingness to sleep in the Jamaican wild. Though you can, at your own risk, pitch a tent beneath any coconut palm, it's usually wiser (and in some cases much wiser) to stick to the limited number of bona-fide campsites scattered around the island.

A source of information about camping is the **Jamaica Alternative Tourism Camping and Hiking Association (JATCHA),** P.O. Box 216, Kingston 7, Jamaica, W.I. (☎ **876/702-0314**). This organization offers alternatives to traditional luxury resorts, which include lodgings in old plantation houses, run-down but respectable guest houses, and (in rare cases) outdoor camping under carefully controlled circumstances. For $15 you can get a pamphlet listing around 100 options. The organization also dispenses information to special-interest travelers like bird-watchers and botanists.

VILLA RENTALS   Certain villa rentals in the off-season (mid-April to mid-December) become quite reasonable, especially for families or groups who want to do their own cooking. Some of the best deals in the Ocho Rios area are offered by **Selective Vacation Services,** 154 Main St. (P.O. Box 335), Ocho Rios, Jamaica, W.I. (☎ **876/974-5187**). Available are two- and three-bedroom apartments and villas, and car rentals can also be arranged. In summer, the least expensive villa, a two-bedroom unit, begins at $1,700 per week, though this same villa will rent for $2,300 per week in winter.

Villa and condo rentals are also available from **Jamswi,** 135 Main St., Coconut Grove, Jamaica, W.I. (☎ **876/974-7114**). Its list of properties includes apartments, villa complexes, and even private villas. The lowest price off-season is $700 per week, rising to $800 and up per week in winter.

2 Montego Bay

On the northwestern coast of Jamaica, Montego Bay first attracted tourists in the 1940s, when Doctor's Cave Beach was popular with the wealthy who bathed in the warm water fed by mineral springs. Now it's Jamaica's second-largest city. In spite of the large influx of visitors, Montego Bay retains its own identity, with a thriving business and commercial center and cruise-ship piers, and it functions as the market town for most of western Jamaica. The history of Mo Bay, as the islanders call it, goes back to 1494, when it was discovered as an Arawak settlement.

Because Montego Bay has its own airport, the Donald Sangster International Airport, those who vacation here have little need to visit Kingston, the island's capital, unless they're seeking its cultural pleasures. Otherwise, you have everything in Mo Bay, the most cosmopolitan of Jamaica's resorts.

ACCOMMODATIONS YOU CAN AFFORD

Belvedere. 33 Gloucester Ave., Montego Bay, Jamaica, W.I. ☎ **800/814-2237** in the U.S., or 876/952-0593. Fax 876/979-0498. 27 units. A/C TEL. Winter $60–$70 single; $65–$75 double. Off-season $45–$55 single; $50–$60 double. AE, MC, V.

Simple and uncomplicated, this small hotel stands near Walter Fletcher Beach. Its modestly furnished rooms are small but have good beds. Facilities include a pool and a restaurant serving breakfast only. The beach is a 5-minute walk away, with shopping and restaurants nearby. On Tuesdays, the hotel hosts a manager's cocktail party with live entertainment featuring calypso music. A jazz band plays on the last Sunday of each month.

Blue Harbour Hotel. 6 Sewell Ave. (P.O. Box 212), Montego Bay, Jamaica, W.I. ☎ **876/952-5445.** Fax 876/952-8930. www.blueharbour-hotel.com. E-mail: robbyg@cwjamaica.com. 24 units. A/C. Winter $40–$64 single; $56–$72 double; $94 suite. Off-season $29–$48 single; $42–$58 double; $70–$75 suite. Children 11 and under stay free in parents' room. AE, DC, MC, V.

On a hillside overlooking the harbor, midway between the airport and town off the A1, this small hotel offers basic service in a friendly atmosphere. The standard rooms are simple, but the suites also contain TVs and kitchenettes. Mattresses are firm, and maintenance is generally quite acceptable. For dinner, the hotel offers the option of a dine-around plan that includes 10 Montego Bay restaurants (transportation provided). The facilities include a pool, an air-conditioned lounge, and a coffee shop serving breakfast and a light lunch. Tennis is nearby, and arrangements can be made for golf, deep-sea fishing, scuba diving, and island tours. The beach is a 5-minute walk from the hotel, which provides free transportation to/from the shore.

Ocean View Guest House. 26 Sunset Blvd. (P.O. Box 210), Montego Bay, Jamaica, W.I. ☎ **876/952-2662.** 12 units. Winter $35 single; $41–$43 double. Off-season $28 single; $34–$36 double. No credit cards.

Opened in the 1960s when the grandparents of the present owners began to rent extra rooms in their home, this super-bargain is half a mile west of the airport and the same distance from the public beach. You'll need a taxi to get here, though the owner sometimes provides transportation to/from the airport. The small rooms are supplemented with a small library and satellite TV room; all but two are air-conditioned, all have fans, and most open onto a veranda or the spacious front porch. It's quietest at the back. A few drawbacks: The mattresses are a bit tired, the baths really are cubicles, cleanliness and service are minimal, and the hotel doesn't take reservations (you'll have

Montego Bay

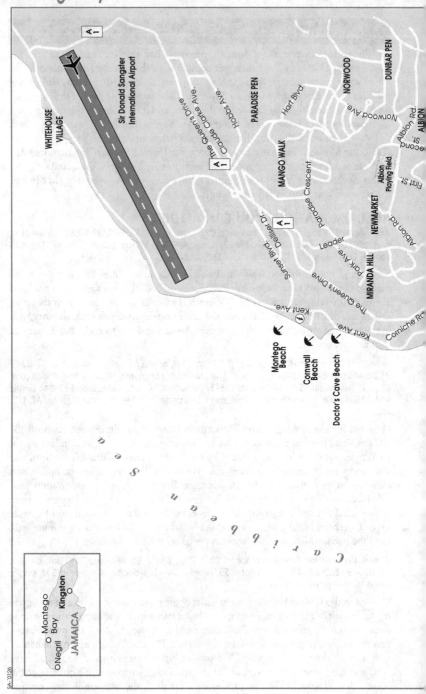

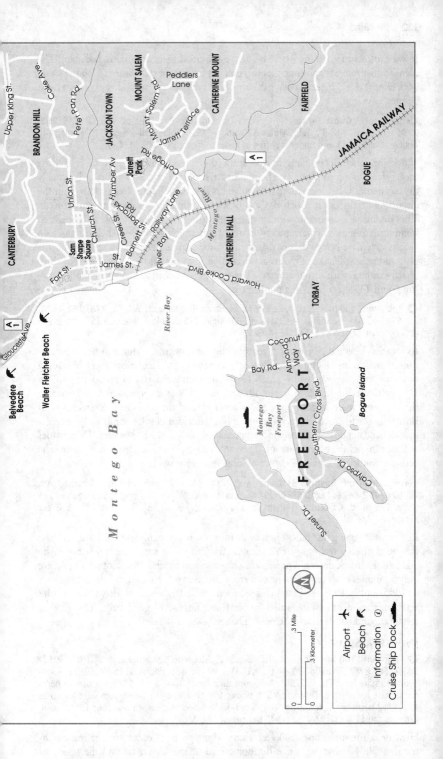

Montego Bay

BRANDON HILL

Upper King St.

Coke Ave.

Pete Pan Rd.

Peddlers
Lane

MOUNT SALEM

JACKSON TOWN

CATHERINE MOUNT

FAIRFIELD

Mount Salem Rd.

Cottage Rd.

Jarrett Terrace

JAMAICA RAILWAY

CANTERBURY

Union St.

Humber Av

Jarrett
Park

BOGUE

Church St.

Barracks
Rd.

Creek St.

Railway Lane

A
1

Sam
Sharpe
Square

Barnett St.

Montego River

Fort St.

St.
James St.

River Bay

CATHERINE HALL

Howard Cooke Blvd.

TORBAY

River Bay

Gloucester Ave.

A
1

Belvedere
Beach

Walter Fletcher Beach

Coconut Dr.

Bay Rd.

Almond Way

FREEPORT

Southern Cross Blvd.

Montego
Bay
Freeport

Bogue Island

M o n t e g o   B a y

Calypso Dr.

Sunset Dr.

N

.3 Mile

.3 Kilometer

0

0

Airport

Beach

Information

Cruise Ship Dock

to wait until you're on the island before you know if there are rooms available). The owner will arrange island tours, tennis, golf, and water sports. Dinners (T-bone steak, pork chops, roast chicken, fresh fish) are offered only to guests, and reservations must be made by 2pm.

✪ **Ridgeway Guest House.** 34 Queen's Dr., Montego Bay, Jamaica, W.I. ☎ **876/952-2709.** 10 units. A/C TV TEL. Winter $30 single; $50 double. Off-season $25 single; $40 double. Children 11 and under stay free in parents' room. DC, DISC, MC, V.

This hospitable B&B, far removed from the impersonal megaresorts (and their megaprices), is a great find. The helpful owners, Brenda and Bryan (Bryan is actually his last name, as he doesn't like to divulge his first name), offer free pickup from the airport and transport to Doctor's Cave Beach, a 15-minute walk or 5 minutes by car. The Bryans are constantly improving their property, a two-story white-painted building set among flowers and fruit trees from which guests may help themselves. Guests may have before-dinner drinks in the roof garden, enjoying a view of the airport and ocean. The large rooms are decorated in a tropical motif, with two or three queen-size beds with firm mattresses. The medium-size marble baths have modern fixtures, and TV is available in a public area.

✪ **Toby Inn.** 1 Kent Ave. (P.O. Box 467), Montego Bay, Jamaica, W.I. ☎ **876/952-4370.** Fax 876/952-6591. 65 units. A/C. Winter $65 single; $75 double. Off-season $55 single; $65 double. Extra person $25–$30. AE, MC, V.

Its location beside the busy main thoroughfare of downtown Montego Bay (and a 5-minute walk from Doctor's Cave Beach) is an advantage or a disadvantage, depending on how easy you want your access to the inexpensive bars and restaurants to be. Despite the traffic and crowds, the almond, mango, and grapefruit trees surrounding the two-story main building, a series of cottages, and the pool create a sense of rural isolation. You'll also find a restaurant serving Jamaican cuisine, a gift shop, a mini-gym, a bandstand for the rare concerts presented here, and a bar where a TV provides at least some of the entertainment. The rooms have either a terrace or a balcony. The beds are comfortable, with a choice of king, queen, or twin.

Verney Tropical Resort. 3 Leader Ave. (P.O. Box 18), Montego Bay, Jamaica, W.I. ☎ **876/952-8628.** Fax 876/979-2944. 25 units. A/C. Winter $45 single; $55 double; $75 triple; $95 quad. Off-season $40 single; $50 double; $60 triple; $80 quad. MAP $18 per person. AE, MC, V.

In a verdant setting just far enough away from the urban congestion of Montego Bay, this hotel offers a feeling of remote calm. You can still get to where the action is by taking a short trek downhill or head to one of several beaches (like Cornwall) that are only 5 minutes away on foot. The two-story structure was built on steeply sloping land in 1945, and in 1995 the pastel-colored rooms were freshened up. Each medium-size accommodation has white walls, simple furnishings, and good beds. The Kit-Kat restaurant and bar overlook the pool. The staff is usually gracious.

WORTH A SPLURGE

✪ **Richmond Hill Inn.** Union St. (P.O. Box 362), Montego Bay, Jamaica, W.I. ☎ **876/952-3859.** Fax 876/952-6106. 20 units. A/C TEL. Winter $85 single; $115 double; $198 1-bedroom suite for up to 4; $256 2-bedroom suite for up to 4; $290–$350 3-bedroom penthouse suite for up to 8. Off-season $75 single; $90 double; $168 1-bedroom suite for up to 4; $220 2-bedroom suite for up to 4; $250–$320 3-bedroom penthouse suite for up to 8. Extra person $27–$32; MAP $41–$48 per person. AE, MC, V.

High on a forested slope, 500 feet above Montego Bay's center, this is the much-restored site of what was once the homestead of the Dewar family (the scions of scotch). Little of that villa remains, but what you'll find is an eyrie ringed by urn-shaped concrete balustrades, a pool terrace suitable for sundowner cocktails, and comfortable, slightly fussy rooms with lace-trimmed curtains and homey bric-a-brac. Rooms come in a variety of sizes, from large to small, but all are comfortable with firm mattresses. Baths are small but tidy. If you're an avid beachlover, know in advance that the nearest beach (Doctor's Cave) is a 15-minute drive away. Maid and laundry service are provided, and there's both a bar and a restaurant (featuring vistas over the blinking lights of Montego Bay).

GREAT DEALS ON DINING

The Montego Bay area has some of the finest—and most expensive—dining on the island. But if you're watching your wallet and don't have a delicate stomach, you'll find that food is often sold right on the street. For example, on Kent Avenue you might try authentic jerk pork. Here you can get seasoned spareribs grilled over charcoal fires and sold with extra-hot sauce; order a Red Stripe beer to go with it. Cooked shrimp are also sold on the streets of Mo Bay; they don't look it, but they're very spicy, so be warned. If you have an efficiency unit with a kitchenette, you can cook fresh lobster or the catch of the day bought from Mo Bay fishers.

The Brewery. In Miranda Ridge Plaza, Gloucester Ave. ☎ **876/940-2433.** Main courses J$180–J$650 ($5.15–$18.55). AE, MC, V. Mon–Sat 11am–until, Sun noon–until. AMERICAN/JAMAICAN.

This restaurant/bar not only serves good food, but might also be your entertainment choice for the evening. It has extended its patio and built a roof over it so you can eat out regardless of the weather, with a view of the ocean. Burgers, salads, and sandwiches are available, and there's a nightly Jamaican dinner special, a freshly made soup of the day, and an excellent chicken gumbo. The chef is known for his pasta dishes, and you can also order classics like rib-eye steak and mesquite turkey. One night a week is devoted to shrimp mania, with a bevy of choices; another night ribs might be featured. Call ahead to find out what the special nights are and to learn if any entertainment is offered. The best time to come for drinks is the daily 4-to-6pm happy hour, when drinks made with local liquor are half price. If you're daring, you might want to try the bartender's special fire water—he won't disclose the ingredients, but promises it lives up to its name.

Le Chalet. 32 Gloucester Ave. ☎ **876/952-5240.** Main courses $3–$16 at lunch, $5–$16 at dinner. AE, MC, V. Mon–Sat 11am–10:30pm, Sun 4–10:30pm. INTERNATIONAL/JAMAICAN.

In the densest concentration of stores and souvenir shops on Montego Bay's tourist strip, this high-ceilinged restaurant lies across Gloucester Avenue from the sea and looks somewhat like a Howard Johnson's. The well-prepared food is served in copious portions: The lunch selection might include burgers, sandwiches, barbecued ribs, and salads, and the dinner selection chicken platters, steaks, fresh fish, and lobster, which seems to taste best here if prepared with Jamaican curry. The staff is articulate and helpful.

The Pelican. At the Pelican, Gloucester Ave. ☎ **876/952-3171.** Reservations recommended. Main courses $5–$25. AE, DC, MC, V. Daily 7am–11pm. JAMAICAN.

A Montego Bay landmark, the Pelican has been serving good food at reasonable prices for more than a quarter of a century. Most of the dishes are at the lower end of the price scale, unless you order shellfish. It's ideal for families, as it keeps long hours. Many diners come at lunch for one of the well-stuffed sandwiches, a juicy burger, or the barbecued chicken. You can also select from a wide array of Jamaican dishes, like stewed peas and rice, curried goat, Caribbean fish, fried chicken, and curried lobster. There's a meatless menu including dishes like a vegetable plate and vegetable chili. Sirloin and seafood are also available, and the soda fountain serves old-fashioned sundaes with real whipped cream, making it about the best kids' recommendation at the resort.

✪ **Pork Pit.** 27 Gloucester Ave. ☎ **876/952-1046.** 1 lb. jerk pork $11. No credit cards. Daily 11am–11:30pm. JAMAICAN.

The Pork Pit is the best place to go for the famous Jamaican jerk pork and jerk chicken, and the location is right in the heart of Montego Bay, near Walter Fletcher Beach. In fact, many beach buffs come over here for a big lunch. Picnic tables encircle the building, and everything is open-air and informal. The menu also includes steamed roast fish. A half-pound of jerk meat, served with a baked yam or baked potato and a bottle of Red Stripe, is usually sufficient for a meal.

WORTH A SPLURGE

The Native Restaurant. 29 Gloucester Ave. ☎ **876/979-2769.** Reservations recommended. Main courses J$270–J$1,100 ($7.70–$31.35). AE, MC, V. Daily 7:30am–10pm. JAMAICAN/INTERNATIONAL.

Open to the breezes, this casual restaurant with panoramic views serves some of the area's finest Jamaican dishes. Appetizers include jerk reggae chicken and ackee and saltfish or smoked marlin. This can be followed by old favorites like steamed fish or fried or jerk chicken. The most tropical offering is goat in a boat (a pineapple shell). A more recent specialty is Boononoonoos—billed as A Taste of Jamaica, it's a big platter with a little bit of everything; meats and several kinds of fish and vegetables. Although fresh desserts are prepared daily, you may prefer to finish with a Jamaican Blue Mountain coffee.

HITTING THE BEACHES

Cornwall Beach (☎ 876/952-3463) is a long stretch of white sand with dressing cabanas. Admission is $2 for adults and $1 for children, and a bar and cafeteria offer refreshments daily from 9am to 5pm. The grainy sand of this beach has made Cornwall a longtime favorite. Some of Jamaica's beaches are remote, but this one is near all the major hotels, especially the moderately priced and budget ones. In fact, you can generally walk here from your hotel. Regrettably, especially in winter, there isn't a lot of room for seclusion. Swimming is excellent and safe all year, though we've noticed the waters are coolest in January and February. However, parents should be careful their children don't venture out too far. The ocean bottom is shallow, gently sloping down to deeper waters. The beach is almost always occupied by guests of one of the nearby resorts; it doesn't seem to be popular with the Jamaicans themselves.

Across from the Doctor's Cave Beach Hotel, **Doctor's Cave Beach,** on Gloucester Avenue (☎ 876/952-2566), helped launch Mo Bay as a resort in the 1940s. Admission is $2 for adults and half price for children 12 and under. Dressing rooms, chairs, umbrellas, and rafts are available from 8:30am to 5pm daily. This is arguably the loveliest stretch of sand bordering Montego Bay and certainly one of the most inviting places to go swimming because of its gentle surf, golden sands, and fresh turquoise water. Sometimes schools of brilliantly colored tropical fish weave in and out of the waters, but usually there are so many people frolicking in the water it scares them away. The beach is an ideal spot for children. Even in winter the placid waters rarely become turbulent, unless a storm is brewing. Since the beach almost always gets crowded, especially in winter, you must go early to stake out a spot.

One of Jamaica's premier beaches, **Walter Fletcher Beach** (☎ 876/979-9447), in the heart of Mo Bay, is noted for its beauty and its tranquil waters, making it a favorite for families and both locals and visitors. Changing rooms and lifeguard service are available. The beach is open daily from 9am to 5pm, with an admission of $2 for adults and half price for children. Easy to reach, the beach is generally crowded in winter, less so in summer. You can have lunch here in a restaurant. Some people like to bring a picnic, but you must be careful not to litter or you will face a fine. Beachgoers show up in almost anything (or lack of anything), though nudity is prohibited.

Frankly, you may want to skip the public beaches and head for the **Rose Hall Beach Club** (☎ 876/953-2323), on the main road 11 miles east of Montego Bay. It's on half a mile of secure secluded white sand with crystal-clear water. The club offers a full restaurant, two beach bars, a covered pavilion, an open-air dance area, showers, rest rooms, and changing facilities, plus beach volleyball courts, various beach games, and a full water-sports program. There's also live entertainment. Admission fees are $8 for adults and $5 for children. This beach club, far better equipped than any of the beaches previously recommended, is open daily from 10am to 6pm.

SPORTS & OUTDOOR PURSUITS

DIVING, SNORKELING & OTHER WATER SPORTS   **Seaworld Resorts,** Rose Hall Main Road (☎ 876/953-2180), operates scuba-diving excursions, plus many other water sports, including sailing and windsurfing. Its scuba dives plunge to offshore coral reefs, among the most spectacular in the Caribbean. There are three certified dive guides, one dive boat, and all the necessary equipment for either inexperienced or certified divers. One-tank dives cost $35 and night dives are $50. In Montego Bay, the waters right on the beach are fine for snorkeling. However, it's more rewarding to go across the channel. Here Cayaba Reef, Seaworld Reef, and Royal Reef are full of barjacks, blue and brown chromis, yellow-headed wrasses, and spotlight parrot fish. You must have a guide to go here because the currents are strong and the wind picks up in the afternoon. If you're not staying at a resort offering snorkeling expeditions, Seaworld is your best bet; the charge of $25 per hour may be a bit steep, but the guides swim along with you, pointing out the various tropical fish.

GOLF   ✪ **Wyndham Rose Hall Golf & Beach Resort,** Rose Hall (☎ 876/953-2650), has a noted course with an unusual and challenging seaside and mountain layout. Its 8th hole skirts the water, then doglegs onto a promontory and a green thrusting 200 yards into the sea. The back 9 are the most scenic and interesting, rising up steep slopes and falling into deep ravines on Mount Zion. The 10th fairway abuts the family burial grounds of the Barretts of Wimpole Street, and the 14th passes the vacation home of singer Johnny Cash. The 300-foot-high 13th tee offers a rare panoramic view of the sea and the roof of the hotel, and the 15th is next to a 40-foot waterfall, once featured in a James Bond movie. A fully stocked pro shop, a clubhouse, and a professional staff are among the amenities. Nonguests of the Wyndham pay $80 for 18 holes and $60 for 9 holes; guests at the Wyndham are charged $70 for 18 holes and $50 for 9 holes. Mandatory cart rental is $33 for 18 holes, and the mandatory use of a caddy is another $14.

The excellent course at ✪ **Tryall** (☎ 876/956-5660), 12 miles from Montego Bay, is so regal it's often been the site of major golf tournaments, including the Jamaica Classic Annual and the Johnnie Walker Tournament. For 18 holes, guests of Tryall are charged $40 in spring, summer, and fall, or $80 in winter. Nonguests of Tryall pay a steep $150 year-round.

Half Moon, at Rose Hall (☎ 876/953-2560), features a championship course, designed by Robert Trent Jones, Sr. It has manicured and diversely shaped greens. For

18 holes nonguests pay $130 year-round; Half Moon hotel guests pay $100. Carts in any season cost $35 for 18 holes, and caddies (mandatory) are $15 in any season.

HORSEBACK RIDING A good program for equestrians is offered at the **Rocky Point Riding Stables,** at the Half Moon Club, Rose Hall, Montego Bay (☎ **876/953-2286**). Housed in the most beautiful barn and stables in Jamaica, built in the colonial Caribbean style in 1992, it offers around 30 horses and a helpful staff. A 90-minute beach or mountain ride costs $50, and a 2½-hour combination ride (including treks along hillsides, forest trails, and beaches, and ending with a salt-water swim) goes for $70.

RAFTING **Mountain Valley Rafting,** 31 Gloucester Ave. (☎ **876/956-4920**), offers rafting excursions on the Great River departing from the Lethe Plantation, about 10 miles south of Montego Bay. Rafts, composed of bamboo trunks with a raised dais to sit on, are available for $36 for up to two people. In some cases, a small child can accompany two adults on the same raft, although due caution should be exercised if you choose to do this. Trips last 45 minutes and operate daily from 8am to 5pm. Ask about pickup by taxi at the end of the rafting run to return you to your rented car. For $45 per person, a half-day experience will include transportation to/from your hotel, an hour's rafting, lunch, a garden tour of the Lethe property, and a taste of Jamaican liqueur.

TENNIS The **Half Moon Golf, Tennis, and Beach Club,** outside Montego Bay (☎ **876/953-2211**), has the finest tennis courts in the area. Its 13 state-of-the-art courts, 7 of which are lit for night games, attract tennis players from around the world. Lessons cost $20 to $30 per half hour or $35 to $55 per hour. Residents play free throughout the day or night. The pro shop, which accepts reservations for court times, is open daily from 7am to 9pm. If you want to play after those hours, you switch on the lights yourself. If you're not a guest of the hotel, you must buy a day pass ($50 per person) at the front desk. It'll allow you access to the resort's tennis courts, gym, sauna, Jacuzzi, pools, and beach facilities.

The **Wyndham Rose Hall Golf & Beach Resort,** Rose Hall (☎ **876/953-2650**), outside Montego Bay, is an outstanding tennis resort, though it's not the equal of Half Moon. Wyndham offers six hard-surface courts, each lit for night play. As a courtesy, nonguests are sometimes invited to play for free, but permission has to be obtained from the manager. You can't play unless you're invited. The resident pro charges $55 per hour for lessons, or $35 for 30 minutes.

SEEING THE SIGHTS
MEETING SOME FEATHERED FRIENDS

Rocklands Wildlife Station. Anchovy, St. James. ☎ **876/952-2009.** Admission J$300 ($8.55). Daily 2:30–5pm.

It's a unique experience to have a Jamaican doctor bird perch on your finger to drink syrup, to feed small doves and finches millet from your hand, and to watch dozens of other birds flying in for their evening meal. Don't take children 5 and under to this sanctuary, as they tend to bother the birds. Rocklands is about a mile outside Anchovy on the road from Montego Bay.

TOURING THE GREAT HOUSES

Occupied by plantation owners, the Great Houses of Jamaica were always built on high ground so they overlooked the plantation itself and provided a view of the next house in the distance. It was the custom for the owners to offer hospitality to travelers crossing the island by road; travelers were spotted by the lookout, and bed and food were given freely.

Barnett Estates and Bellfield Great House. Barnett Estates. ☎ **876/952-2382.** Admission $10. Daily 9:30am–5pm.

Once a private estate sprawled across 50,000 acres, this Great House has hosted everybody from President Kennedy to Churchill and even Queen Elizabeth II. Now anybody who pays admission can come in and take a look. The domain of the Kerr-Jarret family during 300 years of high society, this was once the seat of a massive sugar plantation. At its center is the 18th-century Bellfield Great House, a grand example of Georgian architecture (restored in 1994, but not as ornate as Rose Hall, below). Costumed guides offer narrated tours of the property. After the tour, drop in to the old Sugar Mill Bar for a tall rum punch.

Greenwood Great House. On A1, 14 miles east of Montego Bay. ☎ **876/953-1077.** Admission $12 adults, $6 children under 12. Daily 9am–6pm.

Some people find the 15-room Greenwood even more interesting than Rose Hall (below). Built on a hillside perch between 1780 and 1800, this Georgian house was the residence of Richard Barrett (cousin of poet Elizabeth Barrett Browning). She never visited Jamaica, but her father, an absentee planter who lived in England, once owned 84,000 acres and some 3,000 slaves. On display is the original library of the Barrett family, with rare books from 1697, along with oil paintings of the family, Wedgwood china, rare musical instruments, and a fine collection of antique furniture. The house is privately owned but open to the public.

✪ **Rose Hall Great House.** Rose Hall Hwy., 9 miles east of Montego Bay. ☎ **876/953-2323.** Admission $15 adults, $10 children. Daily 9am–5:15pm.

The subject of at least a dozen Gothic novels, the legendary Rose Hall was immortalized in H. G. deLisser's *White Witch of Rosehall.* It was built from 1778 to 1790 by John Palmer, a wealthy British planter, and was the centerpiece of a 6,600-acre plantation, with more than 2,000 slaves. However, it was Annie Palmer, wife of the builder's grandnephew, who became the focal point of fiction and fact. Called Infamous Annie, she was said to have dabbled in witchcraft, took slaves as lovers, and killed them off when they bored her. Servants called her the Obeah woman (*Obeah* is Jamaican for voodoo). Annie was said to have murdered several of her husbands while they slept and eventually suffered the same fate herself in a kind of poetic justice. Long in ruins, the house has now been restored and can be visited by the public. Annie's Pub is on the ground floor.

ORGANIZED TOURS & CRUISES

The **Croydon Plantation,** P.O. Box 1348, Catadupa, St. James (☎ 876/979-8267), is a 25-mile ride from Montego Bay and can be visited on a half-day tour from Montego Bay (or Negril) on Wednesday and Friday. Included in the $45 price are round-trip transportation from your hotel, a tour of the plantation, a taste of tropical fruits in season, and a barbecued-chicken lunch. Most hotel desks can arrange this tour.

For a plantation tour, go on a **Hilton High Day Tour,** through Beach View Plaza (☎ 876/952-3343). The tour includes round-trip transportation on a scenic drive through historic plantation areas. Your day starts at a plantation house with a continental breakfast. You can roam the plantation's 100 acres and visit the German village of Seaford town or St. Leonards village nearby. Calypso music is played throughout the day, and a Jamaican lunch is served at 1pm. The charge is $55 per person for the plantation tour, breakfast, lunch, and transportation. Tour days are Tuesday, Wednesday, Friday, and Sunday.

Day and evening cruises are offered aboard the *Calico,* a 55-foot gaff-rigged wooden ketch sailing from Margaritaville on the Montego Bay waterfront. An additional

vessel, *Calico B,* also carries another 40 passengers per boat ride. You can be transported to/from your hotel for either cruise. The day voyage, departing at 10am and
returning at 1pm, provides a day of sailing, sunning, and snorkeling (with equipment
supplied). The cruise costs $35 per person and is offered daily. On the *Calico's* evening
voyage, which goes for $25 per person and is offered Wednesday to Saturday from
5 to 7pm, cocktails and wine are served as you sail through sunset. For information and
reservations, call Capt. Bryan Langford at **North Coast Cruises** (☎ 876/952-5860).
A 3-day notice is recommended.

SHOPPING

When you go shopping in Montego Bay, be prepared for aggressive vendors. Since
selling a craft item may affect whether or not they put something in the stove that
night, there's often a feverish attempt to peddle goods to potential customers, all of
whom are viewed as rich. Therefore, prepare yourself for being pursued persistently. If
you want some item, also be prepared for some serious negotiation, as bargaining on
your part will lead to substantial discounts.

Warning: Some so-called duty-free prices are actually lower than stateside prices, but
then the government hits you with a 10% general consumption tax on all items. But
you can still find good duty-free items, including Swiss watches, Irish crystal, Italian
handbags, Indian silks, and liquors and liqueurs. Appleton's rums are an excellent
value. Tía Maria (coffee-flavored) and Rumona (rum-flavored) are the best liqueurs.
Khus Khus is the local perfume. Jamaican arts and crafts are available throughout the
resorts and at the Crafts Market (see below).

The main shopping areas are at **Montego Freeport,** within easy walking distance of
the pier; **City Centre,** where most of the duty-free shops are, aside from those at the
large hotels; and **Holiday Village Shopping Centre.**

SHOPPING CENTERS   The **Old Fort Craft Park,** a shopping complex with 180
vendors (all licensed by the Jamaica Tourist Board), fronts Howard Cooke Boulevard
(up from Gloucester Avenue in the heart of Montego Bay, on the site of Fort Montego). A market with a varied assortment of handcrafts, it's grazing country for both
souvenirs and more serious purchases. You'll see a selection of wall hangings, hand-
woven straw items, and wood sculpture. You can even get your hair braided. At the
Crafts Market, near Harbour Street in downtown Montego Bay, you can find the best
selection of handmade souvenirs, including straw hats and bags, wooden platters,
straw baskets, musical instruments, beads, carved objects, and toys. That *jipijapa* hat
is important if you're going to be out in the island sun.

One of the newest and most intriguing places for shopping is **Half Moon Plaza,**
set on the coastal road about 8 miles east of the commercial center of Montego Bay.
This upscale mini-mall caters to the shopping and gastronomic needs of residents of
one of the region's most elegant hotels, the Half Moon Club. On the premises are a
bank and about 25 shops arranged around a central courtyard and selling a wide
choice of carefully selected merchandise.

ARTS & CRAFTS   The **Ambiente Art Gallery,** 9 Fort St. (☎ 876/952-7919), is
housed in a 100-year-old clapboard cottage close to the road. The Austrian-born
owner, Maria Hitchins, is one of the *doyennes* of the Montego Bay art scene. She has
personally encouraged and developed scores of fine artworks and prints by local artists.
At **Blue Mountain Gems Workshop,** in the Holiday Village Shopping Centre
(☎ 876/953-2338), you can take a tour of the workshops to see the process of
jewelry creation, from raw stone to the finished product you can buy later. Wooden
jewelry, local carvings, and one-of-a-kind ceramic figurines are also sold.

Neville Budhai Paintings, Budhai's Art Gallery, Reading Main Road, Reading, 5 miles east of town on the way to Negril (☎ 876/979-2568), is the art center of a distinguished artist, Neville Budhai, the president and cofounder of the Western Jamaica Society of Fine Arts. He has a distinct style and captures the special flavor of the island and its people. The artist can sometimes be seen sketching or painting in Montego Bay or along the highways of rural Jamaica. **Things Jamaican,** 44 Fort St. (☎ 876/952-5605), is a showcase for the artisans of Jamaica. A wealth of products is displayed, even food and drink, including rums and liqueurs along with jerk seasoning and orange-pepper jelly. Look for Busha Browne's fine Jamaican sauces, especially spicy chutneys or planters' spicy piquant sauce. Other items for sale are wood sculpture, salad bowls, trays, and hand-woven baskets. Also look for reproductions of the Port Royal collection. Port Royal was buried by an earthquake and tidal wave in 1692. After resting underwater for 275 years, beautiful pewter items were recovered and are reproduced here. They include rat-tail spoons, a spoon with the heads of the monarchs William and Mary, and splay-footed lion rampant spoons. Many items were reproduced faithfully, right down to the pit marks and scratches.

FASHION   Klass Kraft Leather Sandals, 44 Fort St. (☎ 876/952-5782), next door to Things Jamaican, offers sandals and leather accessories made on location by a team of Jamaican craftspeople.

JEWELRY   Golden Nugget, 8 St. James Shopping Centre, Gloucester Ave. (☎ 876/952-7707), is a duty-free shop with an impressive collection of watches for both women and men and a fine assortment of jewelry, especially gold chains. The shop also carries leading brand-name cameras and a wide assortment of French perfumes.

MONTEGO BAY AFTER DARK

There's a lot more to do here at night than go to the dance clubs, but the area certainly has those, too. Much of the entertainment is offered at the various hotels.

Pier 1, Howard Cooke Boulevard (☎ 876/952-2452), already previewed as a dining option, might also be your choice for a night on the town. Friday night there's disco action from 10pm to 5am, with a J$300 ($8.55) cover charge and cheap Red Stripe beer. The **Cricket Club,** at the Wyndham Rose Hall (☎ 876/953-2650), is more than just a sports bar. It's a place where people go to meet and mingle with an international crowd. Televised sports, karaoke sing-alongs, tournament darts, and backgammon are all part of the fun. The club is open daily from 7pm to 1am, with no cover.

We've enjoyed the atmosphere of **Walter's,** 39 Gloucester Ave. (☎ 876/952-9391), which has an authentic Jamaican laid-back feel—complete with a constant flow of calypso and reggae music from as early as 10am daily until 2am. There's never a cover, and they have live bands on weekends. If you want to stick to what's more familiar, try **Witches Nightclub,** at the Holiday Inn Sunspree Resort (☎ 876/953-2485). Nonguests of the hotel can pick up a pass at the front desk for $50, allowing them all-inclusive privileges of the nightclub, a buffet, and all the drinks and dancing they can handle daily from 6pm to 2am. We found their policy to be a bit restrictive, but the house/disco/jazz music selection is as imaginative as what you'd find at a U.S. club.

Walter's is a Jamaican experience in Jamaica and Witches an American experience in Jamaica, but **Margueritaville,** Gloucester Avenue (☎ 876/952-4777), is a hybrid of the two. This place is entirely Jamaican in its feel—but be aware that you're as likely to hear country and western as you are reggae. The crowd, music, and fun include just about everything imaginable. There's a $3 nightly cover and $10 Saturday cover.

When you tire of your fellow visitors and want to escape to a place where time has stood still—the way Jamaica used to be—head for the appropriately named ✪ **Time 'n' Place,** just east of Falmouth (☎ 876/954-4371). From Montego Bay you'll spot the sign by the side of the road before you reach Falmouth: "If you got the time, then we got the place." This raffish beach bar opens onto an almost deserted 2-mile beach. Sit back and listen to the reggae from the local stations as you enjoy the friendly ambience. You can order the island's best daiquiris made from fresh local fruit or stick around for peppery jerk chicken or lobster. Time 'n' Place isn't as undiscovered as it once was: Fashion editors from *Vogue* swooped down and used it as a backdrop for beach fashion shots.

3 Negril

On the western tip of the island, this once-sleepy village has turned into a tourist mecca, with visitors drawn to its beaches along three well-protected bays: Long Bay, Bloody Bay (now Negril Harbour), and Orange Bay. It's 50 miles and about a 2-hour drive from Montego Bay's airport, along a winding road and past ruins of sugar estates and Great Houses. Negril became famous in the late 1960s when it attracted laid-back American and Canadian youths, who liked the idea of a place with no phones and no electricity; they rented modest little houses on the West End where the locals extended their hospitality. But today more sophisticated hotels and all-inclusive resorts like Hedonism II and Sandals Negril draw a better-heeled and less rowdy crowd, including Europeans.

There are really two Negrils: The **West End** is the site of many little eateries, such as Chicken Lavish, and cottages that still receive visitors. The other Negril is the **East End,** the first you approach on the road coming in from Montego Bay. Here are the upscale hotels, with some of the most panoramic beachfronts (such as Negril Gardens).

Chances are you'll stake out a favorite spot along Negril's famed ✪ **Seven Mile Beach.** You don't need to get up for anything, as somebody will be along to serve you. Perhaps it'll be the banana lady, with a basket of fruit perched on her head. Maybe the ice-cream man will set up a stand right under a coconut palm. Surely the beer lady will find you as she strolls along with a carton of Jamaican beer on her head, and hordes of young men will peddle illegal ganja whether you smoke it or not. At some point you'll want to explore **Booby Key** (or Cay), a tiny islet off the Negril coast. Once it was featured in the Walt Disney film *20,000 Leagues Under the Sea,* but now it's overrun with nudists from Hedonism II.

GETTING THERE

If you're going to Negril, you'll fly into **Donald Sangster Airport** in Montego Bay. Some hotels, particularly the all-inclusive resorts, will arrange for airport transfers from that point. Be sure to ask when you book.

If your hotel doesn't provide transfers, you can **fly** to Negril's small airport on the independent carrier **Air Jamaica Express,** booking your connection through Air Jamaica (☎ 800/523-5585 in the U.S.). The airfare is $45 one-way. Or you can take a **bus;** the fare is $20 for the 2-hour trip. We recommend **Tour Wise** (☎ 876/ 979-1027 in Montego Bay or 876/974-2323 in Ocho Rios) or **Caribic Vacations** (☎ 876/953-9874 in Montego Bay or 876/974-9106 in Ocho Rios). The bus will drop you off at your final destination once you reach Negril.

Or you can **rent a car** and make the 76-mile, 2-hour drive east of Montego Bay. Information on car rentals is given under "Getting There" at the beginning of this chapter. Or you can take a **taxi.** A typical one-way fare from Montego Bay to Ocho Rios is $50 to $60. Always negotiate and agree on a fare *before* getting into the taxi.

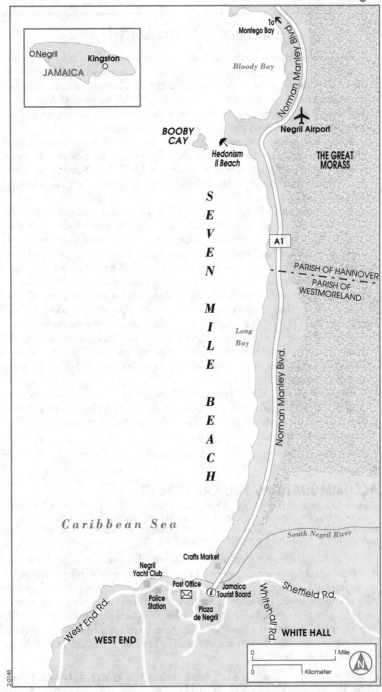

Ann Bonney & Her Dirty Dog

It was at Bloody Bay, off the coast of Negril, that one of the most notorious pirates of all time, Calico Jack Rackham, was finally captured in 1720. His is a name that'll live in infamy, along with Blackbeard's. He was captured with his lover Ann (also Anne) Bonney, the most famous female pirate of all time. (The bay isn't called bloody, however, because of these pirates. Whalers used to disembowel their catch here, turning the waters red with blood.)

After tracking her husband, a penniless ne'er-do-well sailor named James Bonney, to a brothel in the Virgin Islands, Ann slit his throat. However, she soon fell for Capt. Jack Rackham, who was known as Calico Jack. Some say he came by his nickname because of the colorful shirts he wore; others claim it was because of his undershorts.

Until he met this lady pirate, Calico Jack hadn't done so well as a pirate, but she inspired him to greatness. In a short time, they became the scourge of the West Indies. No vessel sailing the Caribbean Sea was too large or too small for them to attack and rob. Ann is said to have fought alongside the men, and was a much tougher customer than Calico Jack himself. With her cutlass and marlinspike, she was usually the first to board a captured vessel.

It was late in October, off the Negril coast, when Calico Jack and all the pirates were getting drunk on rum, that a British Navy sloop attacked. Calico Jack ran and hid, but Ann fought bravely. She flailed away with battle-ax and cutlass. Calico Jack and the other captured pirates were sentenced to be hanged. Ann, however, pleaded with the court that she was pregnant. Since British law didn't allow the killing of unborn children, she got off though her comrades were sentenced to death.

Her final advice to Calico Jack: "If you'd fought like a man, you wouldn't be hanged like the dirty dog you are." So much for a lover's parting words. Ann's father in Ireland bought her release, and she opened a gaming house in St. Thomas and prospered until the end.

ACCOMMODATIONS YOU CAN AFFORD

Banana Shout. West End Rd. (P.O. Box 4), Negril, Jamaica, W.I. ☎ or fax **876/957-0384.** www.negril.com/bananashout. E-mail: bananashout@yahoo.com. 7 cottages. Winter $50–$95 cottage for 1 or 2; $120 cottage for 4; $200 cottage for 8. Off-season $35–$55 cottage for 1 or 2; $70 cottage for 4; $160 cottage for 8. MC, V.

On 2½ acres of landscaped grounds with waterfalls, lily ponds, tropical flowers, and fruit trees, you'll find seven cottages with three units poised on a cliff overlooking the sea. In front of the property is a series of tiered decks with concrete steps leading down the rocks to the water. The garden cottages are across the road, with private access to the beach. Each of the secluded units contains a kitchenette, a good bed with firm mattress, a ceiling fan, and a small bath. The rooms are furnished with locally crafted pieces and artwork from Indonesia and Bali. The best deal at this hideaway is the cottage with the patio barbecue.

✪ **Blue Cave Castle.** Lighthouse Rd., Negril, Jamaica, W.I. ☎ **876/957-4845.** 10 units. Winter $50 single; $65 double. Off-season $35 single; $45 double. Extra person $10. No credit cards.

Filled with whimsy and fun, this little mock castle may be the Caribbean's best bargain. It's been featured by the Jamaica Tourist Board in its TV ads, and the 1997 Dallas Cowboy cheerleaders calendar was shot here. Battlements and turrets re-create medieval days, and the resort, covering an acre, is built over a cave. There are steps down to the cave from the garden, where wedding receptions are held regularly. The small guest rooms are decorated with handmade mahogany furniture and antique Turkish carpets covering the walls; only three are air-conditioned, but all have sea views, refrigerators, ceiling fans, good beds, balconies, and tiny baths. There's no pool, though you can swim off the cliffs in lieu of a beach. An on-site restaurant has closed, but guests interested in cooking can still use the kitchen. If a group of guests staying here would like a barbecue outside, it can be arranged.

Devine Destiny. Summerset Rd., West End (P.O. Box 117), Negril, Jamaica, W.I. ☎ **876/957-9184.** Fax 876/957-3846. www.negriljamaica.com. E-mail: devine.destiny@ cwjamaica.com. 44 units. TEL. Winter $77–$88 single or double; $180 suite. Off-season $58–$69 single or double; $125 suite. Children 11 and under stay free in parents' room. AE, MC, V.

About 550 yards from the West End cliffs, this funky retreat in a medley of styles is about a 20-minute walk from the beach; there's a shuttle to Seven Mile Beach if you don't want to walk. The two-story structure with a terra-cotta roof is surrounded by gardens where wedding receptions are often held. The motel-like rooms are furnished in a standard style, and though most are small, all are comfortable and boast refrigerators and patios or balconies; the baths are tiny. The suites are the best deal, with ceiling fans, kitchens, living rooms with pull-out beds, TVs, and patios. The most expensive rooms are air-conditioned. The restaurant serves simple fare three times a day, and there's a pool bar and a gazebo bar. Room service and baby-sitting are available, and the hotel has a TV room, sun deck, games room, gift shop, and tour desk.

Drumville Cove Resort. West End Rd. (P.O. Box 72), Negril, Jamaica, W.I. ☎ **876/957-4369.** Fax 876/929-7291. 25 units. Winter $90–$94 single; $103–$108 double; $85–$99 cottage. Off-season $36–$50 single; $54–$58 double; $54–$63 cottage. AE, MC, V.

The rooms are housed in cream-colored structures trimmed in brown overlooking the sea near the lighthouse, and the cottages are scattered around the property. All the medium-size rooms and cottages have radios, ceiling fans, and tiny baths, but only seven of the rooms and none of the cottages are air-conditioned; four rooms offer TVs. These basic lodgings are furnished with a mixture of wicker and hardwood and decorated with floral prints. The mattresses could use replacing, but the beds are generally comfortable. Included on the property is a restaurant serving Jamaican specialties with a few American dishes. The nearest beach is a 5-minute car ride away (the hotel provides transportation).

Home Sweet Home. West End Rd., Negril, Jamaica, W.I. ☎ or fax **800/925-7418** in the U.S., or ☎ 876/957-4478. 14 units. A/C. Winter $90–$100 single or double. Off-season $65–$80 single or double. Extra person $15; children 11 and under stay free in parents' room. AE, DC, MC, V.

On the cliff side, 1½ miles from the town center, this cozy down-home place at times seems to re-create Negril's 1960s hippie heyday. You may find your groove here, as writer Terry McMillan did when she visited many little inns while researching *How Stella Got Her Groove Back.* Home is a single pink concrete building with a garden with lots of greenery and flowering plants. There's also a pool and a Jacuzzi. All the cramped accommodations have ceiling fans, a routine bed, a radio and cassette player, and a balcony or veranda. There's a sun deck on the cliffs, and swimming, diving, and snorkeling are possible. A simple restaurant serves three inexpensive Jamaican-style meals a day.

Mirage Cottages. Lighthouse Rd., West End, Negril, Jamaica, W.I. ☎ **876/957-4471.** Fax 876/957-4414. 7 units. Winter $100 single or double; off-season $70 single or double. MC, V.

Daniel and Sylvia Grizzle, a Jamaican/French couple, direct this smooth operation, 2½ miles from the town center along the West End beach strip. The Grizzles have seven small cottages, set in 4½ acres of tropical gardens; all are well appointed, with ceiling fans, good beds, and tiny baths. Above the former restaurant are four units, and the other units are closer to the ocean. There are sunning areas, three access ladders to the sea, and a gazebo for relaxing in the shade. Although food is no longer served, you're but a short walk from about a dozen low-cost eateries.

Ocean Edge Resort Hotel. West End Rd. (P.O. Box 71), Negril, Jamaica, W.I. ☎ **876/957-4362.** Fax 876/957-0086. 28 units. TV TEL. Winter $80 single or double; $75 villa; $85 suite. Off-season $65 single or double; $55 villa; $70 suite. Children 11 and under stay free in parents' unit. AE, MC, V.

On a cliff on the West End Road across from Kaiser's Café, this hotel offers simple small accommodations in a laid-back atmosphere. They're modestly decorated in a tropical motif, with hardwood furnishings, decent beds, and a few pictures on the walls. If you must have air-conditioning, don't stay in one of the villa rooms cooled only by ceiling fans. The suite and villas have kitchenettes. Facilities include a pool, a Jacuzzi, and the Seven Seas restaurant, specializing in fresh seafood. The hotel provides transportation to/from the beach, a 5-minute drive away.

✪ **Rockhouse.** West End Rd. (P.O Box 24), Negril, Jamaica, W.I. ☎ and fax **876/957-4373.** 28 units. MINIBAR. Winter $100 studio; $165 villa. Off-season $85 studio; $120 villa. Extra person $25; children 11 and under stay free in parents' unit. AE, MC, V.

This boutique inn stands in stark contrast to the hedonistic all-inclusive resorts, evoking both a South Seas island retreat and an African village. A team of enterprising young Aussies recently restored and expanded this place, with thatched roofs capping stone-and-pine huts. The rooms have mini-bars, ceiling fans, and refrigerators. You'll really feel you're in Jamaica when you go to bed in a mosquito-draped four-poster (see the back cover of this guide for a peek at one of the rooms) or take a shower in the open air (mercifully, the toilet facilities are inside). One cottage is divided into two studios; other units contain queen-size beds; and four cottages have a sleeping loft with an extra queen-size bed. A quarter mile from the beach, Rockhouse has a ladder down to a cove where you can swim and snorkel; equipment is available for rent. After a refreshing dip in the cliff-side pool, you can dine in the open-sided restaurant pavilion serving spicy local fare three times a day. The restaurant and bar are quite fashionable. There's a rugged sense of individualism about the place.

Thrills. West End (P.O. Box 99, Negril Post Office), Westmoreland, Jamaica, W.I. ☎ **876/957-4390.** Fax 876/957-4153. 25 units. Winter $60 single; $65 double; $75 triple. Off-season $45 single; $50 double; $65 triple. MAP $21 per person. MC, V.

Southwest of Negril's center, on palm-dotted land sloping toward a rocky beach, this is a simple but well-managed resort. Its centerpiece is a hexagonal tower adjacent to a low-slung motel-like complex. Each rather small room is decorated with white walls, island-made mahogany furniture, louvered doors, and tiled floors. Baths are small but serviceable, with a minimum of towels. An in-house restaurant serves international cuisine. Beachlovers take a 10-minute drive (or a 20-minute walk) east to Negril's legendary beach. Snorkelers, however, find ample opportunities for pursuing their favorite sport off the low cliffs and caves along the coast. The resort has its own tennis courts, and a wide choice of dive shops and water-sports facilities is nearby.

WORTH A SPLURGE

Firefly Beach Cottages. Norman Manley Blvd. (P.O. Box 54), Negril, Jamaica, W.I. ☎ **800/477-9530** in the U.S., or 876/957-4358. Fax 876/957-3447. 19 units. Winter $104 single; $120 double; $135 2-bedroom apt. for 4; $160 1-bedroom apt. with 3 double beds for 6; $190 2-bedroom apt. for 8. Off-season $60 single; $88 double; $119 2-bedroom apt. for 4; $122 1-bedroom apt. with 3 double beds for 6; $132 2-bedroom apt. for 8. AE, MC, V.

With a lot of Jamaican flair, this is laid-back hodgepodge of several white concrete and wooden buildings. There's even a "penthouse" in the garden with sleeping lofts. In addition to these, there are various medium-size studios and cottages, including one large two-bedroom unit that can sleep up to eight in cramped conditions. Most of the units are cooled by air-conditioning and ceiling fans, and many beds are canopied; all rooms have verandas and kitchens. When they rent rooms with a view, they mean it: The hotel opens onto a stretch of clothing-optional beach. There's no restaurant, though many little eateries are within walking distance. And there's no pool, but the beach is nearby and you don't even have to put on your swimsuit to enjoy it.

Rock Cliff Hotel. West End Rd. (P.O. Box 67), Negril, Jamaica, W.I. ☎ **876/957-4331** or 876/957-4108. 31 units. A/C. Winter $115–$143 single; $132–$160 double; $330 2-bedroom suite for 6. Off-season $80–$92 single; $92–$103 double; $218 suite for 6. AE, MC, V.

This is one of the better of the dozens of raffish guest houses set among the palms and sea grapes west of Negril's center. Atop a low cliff overlooking the sea and popular with divers, it features a restaurant, two bars, and a Sunday-night all-you-can-eat lobster buffet. There's a pool, and you can inch your way down the cliff for dips offshore from the rocks, but sea bathers usually trek 2 miles to the nearest beach. The average-size rooms have mahogany furniture, good beds, pastel-colored draperies, and off-white walls, plus rather cramped baths. The suites contain kitchenettes. Maid service is included, and baby-sitting and laundry can be arranged. There's a Jacuzzi, volleyball and basketball courts, a kiosk for sundries and souvenirs, and a well-recommended PADI-affiliated dive shop.

GREAT DEALS ON DINING

✪ **Chicken Lavish.** West End Rd. ☎ **876/957-4410.** Main courses $5–$13. MC, V. Daily 10am–10pm. JAMAICAN.

We've found that Chicken Lavish, whose name we love, is the best of the low-budget eateries. Just show up on the doorstep and see what's cooking. Curried goat is a specialty, as is fresh fried fish. The red snapper is caught in local waters. But the main reason we've recommended the place is its namesake: Ask the chef to make his special Jamaican chicken. He'll tell you, and you may agree, that it's the best on the island. Dress as you would to clean up your backyard on a hot August day.

Choices. West End Rd. ☎ **876/957-4841.** Main courses $4.20–$11.20. No credit cards. Daily 7am–11pm. JAMAICAN.

This no-frills open-air restaurant offers a bustling atmosphere and simple local food in hearty portions. You'll pay about $5 to $6 for breakfast, which includes ackee and salt codfish prepared with Jamaican spices, onions, green peppers, and tomatoes. Daily soup specials may include pumpkin or red pea. For a real island experience, try the spicy jerk chicken, fish, or lobster. Other dishes may be stewed beef, curried goat, or a dish of oxtail. Most dishes come with salad and your choice of vegetable.

✪ **Cosmo's Seafood Restaurant & Bar.** Norman Manley Blvd. ☎ **876/957-4784.** Main courses J$200–J$620 ($5.70–$17.65). AE, MC, V. Daily 9am–10pm. SEAFOOD.

One of the best places to go for local seafood is centered around a Polynesian thatched bohío open to the sea and bordering the main beachfront. This is the rustic dining spot of Cosmo Brown, who entertains locals as well as visitors. You can order his famous conch soup, or conch in a number of other ways, including steamed or curried. He's also known for his savory kettle of curried goat, or you might prefer freshly caught seafood or fish, depending on what the catch turned up. The prices are among the most reasonable at the resort.

Hungry Lion. West End Rd. ☎ **876/957-4486.** Main courses $8.50–$18. No credit cards. Daily 5–10pm. JAMAICAN/INTERNATIONAL.

Some of the best seafood and vegetarian dishes are found at this laid-back alfresco hangout on the cliffs. The first floor of this green concrete-and-wood building has an open-air section with booths inside, but on the second floor it's all windows. Menus change daily, depending on what's available in the markets. About seven main courses are offered nightly; not only seafood and vegetarian platters, but many tasty chicken dishes as well, and even shepherd's pie, pasta primavera, grilled kingfish steak, and pan-fried snapper. Lobster is prepared in many ways, and everything is accompanied by rice and peas along with steamed vegetables. The homemade desserts are luscious, especially the pineapple-carrot cake, our favorite. You can visit the juice bar and sample the tropical punches. The restaurant may be closed for parts of September, October, and November; closings depend on the whim of the staff, so call to see if they're open before heading here.

Mariners Inn & Restaurant. West End Rd. ☎ **876/957-0392.** Pizzas $6.60–$10.20; main courses $14–$20; all-you-can-eat dinner buffet $11. AE, MC, V. Daily 8am–10:30pm. JAMAICAN/AMERICAN/CONTINENTAL.

Many people escaping from their all-inclusive dining rooms head here, looking for some authentic Jamaican flavor. The bar is shaped like a boat, and the adjoining restaurant is entered through a tropical garden. As you drink or dine, the sea breezes waft in. The one appetizer is a bacon-wrapped banana, not everybody's favorite way to begin a meal, but the food picks up considerably after that. The chef knows how to use curry effectively in the lobster and chicken dishes, and even the goat. The *coq au vin* (chicken in wine) has never been to France, so you're better off sticking to dishes like pan-fried snapper or fried chicken.

Margueritaville. Norman Manley Blvd. ☎ **876/957-4467.** Burgers and sandwiches $5.75–$7.75; main courses $7.75–$25.95. AE, MC, V. Daily 10am–11pm. AMERICAN/ INTERNATIONAL.

From this restaurant's open windows and veranda, it's only a short walk across the sand, past hundreds of sunbathers, to the sea. In the center of Negril, adjacent to the Beachcomber Hotel, this breeze-filled place combines a gift shop, an art gallery, and a bar. Look for at least 50 variations of margaritas. Menu items include burgers, sandwiches, lobster, grilled chicken and fish, and conch. Most of the paintings in the art gallery were executed by long-time resident American-born Geraldine Robbins. Every day around 9pm, live music is performed, usually loudly. Artists include local reggae stars Cowboys on Pebbles and Fathers & Sons, and on Saturday night, there's old-time Jamaican music known as mentho. Sunday and Wednesday, everyone can be a star, thanks to a karaoke setup.

The Pickled Parrot. West End Rd. ☎ **876/957-4864.** Main courses $5.95–$23.95. AE, MC, V. Daily 9am–midnight. MEXICAN/JAMAICAN/AMERICAN.

You know you'll have a night of fun at a place called the Pickled Parrot. The restaurant stands at the edge of a cliff and is open to the trade winds, and there's a rope swing and a water slide for fun outside. Slot machines inside add to the funky ambience. The cook claims he serves the best lobster fajitas in town (we agree). You can also order the usual burgers, sandwiches, and freshly made salads at lunch. Actually, you can order the full dinner menu at lunch if you like. They prepare a predictable array of burritos and nachos, but you might be tempted by the fresh fish, lobster Jamaican-style (also shrimp in the same method), and famous jerk chicken.

Restaurant Tan-Ya's/Calico Jack's. In the Sea Splash Resort, Norman Manley Blvd. ☎ **876/957-4041.** Reservations recommended. Main courses $10–$23; breakfast from $3; lunch $4–$7.50. AE, MC, V. Daily 11am–3pm and 6:30–10pm. JAMAICAN/INTERNATIONAL.

Within the thick white walls of the Sea Splash, these restaurants provide well-prepared food (however, on some occasions the food is slightly off the mark). Informal and affordable lunchtime food is served at Calico Jack's, whose tables are in an enlarged gazebo, near a bar and a pool. The gastronomic showcase is Tan-Ya's, whose specialties include lemon-flavored chicken, snapper with herb butter, three versions of lobster, smoked Jamaican lobster with fruit salsa, and deviled crab backs sautéed in butter.

Sweet Spice. 1 White Hall Rd. ☎ **876/957-4621.** Main courses $5.50–$14. MC, V. Daily 8:30am–11pm. JAMAICAN.

This is everybody's favorite mom-and-pop eatery, a hangout beloved by locals as well as scantily-clad visitors. The Whytes welcome guests warmly and serve them good food in an alfresco setting. The portions are large and most satisfying. You get what's on the stove or in the kettle that night, perhaps the fresh catch of the day or conch steak. The grilled chicken is done to perfection, and shrimp is teamed and served with garlic butter or cooked in coconut cream. A number of curry dishes tempt, like concoctions made with goat, lobster, and chicken. Meals come with freshly cooked Jamaica-grown vegetables. The fruit juices (in lieu of alcoholic beverages) are truly refreshing.

Tenby Beach Bar & Restaurant. West End Rd. ☎ **876/957-4372.** Reservations recommended. Main courses $6–$20. MC, V. Daily 8:30am–midnight. JAMAICAN/INTERNATIONAL.

This waterfront restaurant, decorated in cool tones of blue and white, is owned by the Lawrences, a native family who offer warm hospitality. You can get a variety of dishes, including stewed chicken with brown gravy (similar to chicken fricassee but a little spicier) or curried chicken and goat. The islanders recommend the seafood. You can order lobster in a variety of ways, like curried, grilled with butter sauce, with garlic, or Thermidor. If you don't see what you want on the menu, just ask—any reasonable request will be granted. The portions are huge and the atmosphere is inviting.

WORTH A SPLURGE

Xtabi. West End Rd. ☎ **876/957-4336.** Main courses $10–26; lunch $4.50–$15. AE, MC, V. Daily 8am–midnight. JAMAICAN/INTERNATIONAL.

The setting is formal and upmarket for laid-back Negril, though the prices are most affordable—if you read from the right side of the menu. Sitting on a cliff, near a series of caves where you can snorkel during the day, the octagonal Xtabi has a patio facing the ocean where you can dine under the stars. At lunch there's the usual burgers, grilled cheese, steak or club sandwiches, and salads. But at night, the chefs try harder and the setting is more dramatic. The lobster Thermidor is a sumptuous choice, as are the scampi grilled Jamaican-style and the batter-fried shrimp. The catch of the day can be steamed, fried, or grilled, and steak and chicken are prepared in a number of ways. For dessert, opt for the fruit salad or one of the homemade cakes, perhaps chocolate, lemon, or marble.

Cheap Thrills: What You Can See & Do for Free (Well, Almost) on Jamaica

- **Visit Cockpit Country.** Only 15 miles inland from Montego Bay on the south coast is the Caribbean's most primitive and undeveloped area. Nature created this harsh terrain with pitfalls and potholes carved in limestone, which evoked a cockpit where cock fights were staged. Once it was known as the Land of Look Behind, because English soldiers were always nervous when riding through here and looking over their shoulder. The region was settled by the fierce Maroons, fugitive slaves who refused to surrender to invading British troops and were in a state of constant war. The descendants of these historic freedom fighters continue to live in the area, just as ungoverned today as they were back then. No one pays taxes, for example. Head for their main hamlet at Accompong, where you can walk through the village and look at a few historic structures. You'll meet some of the Maroons, known as the island's finest herbalists.

- **Experience Market Day in Falmouth.** Lying 23 miles east of Montego Bay, this town, with its decaying Georgian architecture, is like a place time forgot. The best time to arrive is on Wednesday morning, when it hosts the country's biggest flea market, with hundreds of booths linking the marketplace and overflowing into the streets. Buyers from all over the island flock here to pick up bargains (later sold at inflated prices). Named after the British birthplace in Cornwall of Trelawny's parish's first governor, it still evokes a nostalgic atmosphere of the early 18th century. The most interesting buildings lie along Market Street near Water Square. Take time out to buy a loaf of *bammy* (cassava bread) and pick up the makings of a picnic.

- **Spend an Afternoon on Errol Flynn's Island.** The swashbuckling star who gave the world the expression "in like Flynn" may no longer be around, but his island—reached by a short boat ride—still lies off the coast of Port Antonio. Navy Island was once his hideaway. Of course, he didn't wear his famous green tights from *Robin Hood* here. Actually, according to reports, he didn't wear much at all. You can do the same when you visit the island if you go to its nudie beach, known as Trembly Knee Cove. There's also a non-nudie beach. The restaurant and bar feature plenty of posters of Flynn's movies. You'll have the entire island to roam.

ACCOMMODATIONS & DINING NEARBY

✪ **Coconuts.** Little Bay, Jamaica, W.I. ☎ **800/962-5548** in the U.S., or 876/997-5013. 10 cottages. Winter $695 per person per week cottage for 2. Off-season $595 per person per week cottage for 2. Children 13–17 $395 extra; 6–12 $295 extra; 5 and under $195 extra. Rates include all meals. MC, V.

In a fishing village on a quiet country road 8 miles east of Negril on the way to Savannah-La-Mar, this getaway offers a respite from the hustle and bustle of life. Guests stay in cedar-and-stone cottages that have their own private garden patios surrounded by flowers. Only two units have full baths; the rest have half baths. The philosophy here: In a climate as beautiful as Jamaica's, why lather up in an indoor cubicle when you can enjoy the garden and ocean views offered by the four totally private coral stone showers in the terraced gardens.

- **Swim in the Blue Lagoon.** Remember when model/actress Brooke Shields made an attempt to become a movie star? She came here to the Blue Lagoon outside Port Antonio to make a film of the same name in this calm protected cove. The water is so deep, nearly 20 feet or so, it turns a cobalt blue. There's almost no more scenic spot in all Jamaica, and it's fun to swim and think of Brooke. It's a great place for a picnic too. You can pick up plenty of the famous peppery delicacy, jerk pork, smoked at various shacks along the Boston Bay Beach.

- **Head for the Hellshire Hills.** Southwest of Kingston, reached along the coastal road, the limestone Hellshire Hills are different from the image of lush Jamaica. This is more like Arizona, a terrain of dry cacti and cassia growing in a semi-desert landscape. Many Kingstonians retreat here for the weekend to enjoy its beaches, where they're rarely disturbed by tourists. The backdrop for the Hellshire Hills is filled with salt ponds, mangroves, and undeveloped caves (some with petroglyphs). This is also snake country, including the endemic Jamaican boa, called the yellow snake. It often grows 6 to 8 feet long and is one of the largest in the Caribbean. However, it isn't poisonous. South of Port Henderson, you can take a marked hiking trail up to Rodney's Looking for the most panoramic overview of Kingston and the eastern coast.

- **Bite into Some Jerk Pork.** Wherever you go in Jamaica you'll encounter ramshackle stands selling jerk pork or jerk chicken. There's no more authentic Jamaican experience than to stop at one of these stands and order a lunch of jerk pork, preferably washed down with a Red Stripe beer. Jerk is a special way Jamaicans have of barbecuing highly spicy meats over a wood fire set in the ground. The Maroons who lived in the mountains are said to have developed this technique. What goes into the seasoning isn't clear, but the taste is definitely of peppers, pimiento, and ginger. The meat is cooked on slats of pimiento wood, giving it a unique flavor. You can also order jerk sausage, fish, and even lobster. As you place your order, the cook will haul out a machete and chop the meat into bite-size pieces for you and throw it into a paper bag.

Your stay includes the use of the saltwater pool and sporting equipment, including snorkeling and fishing gear. Island tours and excursions into Negril or Savannah-La-Mar can be arranged. Your meals consist of freshly caught fish and lobster, chicken, fresh local vegetables, and local fruits and juices you can enjoy at the seaside restaurant or on your private patio served by the staff. Price breaks are given to those traveling with a group.

HITTING THE BEACHES

Beloved by the hippies of the 1960s, ✪ **Seven Mile Beach** is still going strong but is no longer the paradise it was decades ago. Nudity, however, is just as prevalent, especially along the stretch near Cosmo's (see the dining recommendations, above). Resorts now line this beach, attracting an international crowd. Some of the resorts have built units opening directly onto the nude beaches.

The laid-back lifestyle and carefree ambience are evoked more by this beach than by any others. We'll go even farther: More than anywhere else in the Caribbean. On the western tip of the island, this white-sand beach with a palm tree backdrop stretches from Bloody Bay in Hanover to Negril Lighthouse in Westmoreland. Its aquamarine waters aren't polluted.

When you tire of the beach, you'll find all sorts of resorts, clubs, beach bars, open-air restaurants, and the like. The locals are very friendly, and vendors will try to sell you things. Chances are in a full day at the beach you'll be approached at least three times by young men wanting to sell you ganja.

Many of the big resorts have nude beaches as well, though these hotels are too expensive for us. The most exotic ambience is at Hedonism II, and the Grand Lido next door draws romantic couples and lots of over-25s. Nude beaches at each of these resorts are in separate and private areas of the property. Total nudity is required for strolling the beach, and security guards keep Peeping Toms at bay. Of course, photography isn't permitted. Most of the resorts also have a nude bar, a nude hot tub, and a nude pool. These resorts also have clothing mandatory sections: Hedonism II, for example, has a Nude Side and a Prude Side.

SCUBA DIVING & SNORKELING

The **Negril Scuba Centre,** in the Negril Beach Club Hotel, Norman Manley Boulevard (☎ **800/818-2963** or 876/957-9641), is the most modern, best-equipped facility. A professional staff of internationally certified scuba instructors and dive masters teach and guide divers to Negril's colorful coral reefs. Beginner's dive lessons are offered daily, as well as multiple-dive packages for certified divers. Full scuba certifications and specialty courses are also available.

A resort course, designed for first-timers with basic swimming abilities, includes all instruction, equipment, a lecture on water and diving safety, and one open-water dive. It begins at 10am daily and ends at 2pm, costing $75. A one-tank dive costs $30 per dive, plus $20 for equipment rental (not necessary if divers bring their own). More economical is a two-tank dive that must be completed in 1 day, costing $55, plus the optional $20 rental of equipment. This organization is PADI-registered, though it accepts all recognized certification cards.

One of the best-recommended dive facilities in Negril is **Scuba World,** a PADI-approved five-star dive shop at Orange Bay (☎ **876/957-6290**). It's open daily 8am to 5pm and offers a 4-day certification course for $350. A resort course for beginners costs $70, and a one-tank dive for certified divers goes for $30, plus $20 for the equipment rental. A two-tank dive costs $55, plus only $10 for equipment rental. More than 20 dive sites, including coral reefs and caves, are located at Poinciana.

In Negril, the best area for **snorkeling** is off the cliffs in the West End. The coral reef here is extremely lively with marine life at a depth of about 10 to 15 feet. The waters are so clear and sparkling that just by wading in and looking down you'll see lots of marine life. The fish are small but extremely colorful. Along West End Road are dozens of shops where you can rent snorkeling equipment for about $10 per day. There's no snorkeling on the beachfront.

NEGRIL AFTER DARK

Although smaller than Mo Bay, Negril isn't without spots to have a good time, though you're likely to spend most evenings enjoying the entertainment in your own resort. Fun places are easy to find, as nearly *everything* is on Norman Manley Boulevard, the only major road. We found **Alfred's** (☎ **876/957-4735**), a neat Jamaican experience with enough American fabric to make travelers feel welcome. There's no cover, and in addition to grabbing a drink, you can order a bite to eat until midnight. Particularly interesting is their beach party area. Not only do they have a bar on the beach, but they have a stage for live acts. Live reggae is presented on Tuesday, Friday, and Sunday, with live jazz on Monday and Thursday. Of course, you can boogie on the dance floor inside.

For more Jamaican/American nightclub experiences, try **De Buss** (☎ **876/957-4405**). The cover depends on special events or live acts, so call ahead to see what's planned.

4 Falmouth

This port town lies on the north coast of Jamaica, only about 23 miles east of Montego Bay. The Trelawny Beach Hotel originally put it on the tourist map (though we no longer recommend staying there). The Georgian town itself is interesting but ramshackle. There's talk about fixing it up for visitors, but no one has done it yet. If you leave your car at Water Square, you can explore the town in about an hour. The present courthouse was reconstructed from the early 19th-century building, and fishermen and -women still congregate on Seaboard Street. You'll pass the Customs Office and a parish church dating from the late 18th century. Later you can go on a shopping expedition outside town to Caribatik.

There's a dearth of accommodations in the area, so visitors usually seek lodgings in Montego Bay (above).

GREAT DEALS ON DINING
Glistening Waters Inn and Marina. Rock Falmouth (between Falmouth and the Trelawny Beach Hotel). ☎ **876/954-3229.** Main courses $8–$22. AE, MC, V. Daily 10am–9pm. SEAFOOD.

Residents of Montego Bay often make the 28-mile drive out here, along A1, just to sample the ambience of Old Jamaica. This well-recommended restaurant, with a veranda overlooking the lagoon, is housed in what was a private clubhouse of the aristocrats of nearby Trelawny. The furniture may remind you of a stage set for *Night of the Iguana.* Menu items usually include local fish dishes, like snapper or kingfish, served with *bammy* (a form of cassava bread). Other specialties are three lobster dishes, three preparations of shrimp, three conch viands, fried rice, and pork served as chops.

The waters of the lagoon contain a rare form of phosphorescent microbe that, when the waters are agitated, glows in the dark. Ask about evening booze cruises, costing $10 per person, including one drink. Departures are nightly at about 6:30pm.

RIVER RAFTING NEAR FALMOUTH
Rafting on the **Martha Brae** is an adventure. To reach the starting point from Falmouth, drive approximately 3 miles inland to **Martha Brae's Rafters Village** (☎ **876/952-0889**). The rafts are similar to those on the Río Grande, near Port Antonio, and cost $40 per raft, with two riders allowed on a raft, plus a small child if accompanied by an adult (but use precaution). The trips last 1¼ hours and operate daily from 9am to 4pm. You sit on a raised dais on bamboo logs. Along the way you can stop and order cool drinks or beer along the banks of the river. There's a bar, a restaurant, and two souvenir shops in the village.

SHOPPING
Two miles east of Falmouth on the north-coast road is ✪ **Caribatik Island Fabrics,** at Rock Wharf on the Luminous Lagoon (☎ **876/954-3314**). You'll recognize the place easily, as it has a huge sign painted across the building's side. This is the private

living and work domain of Keith Chandler, who opened the place with his late wife, Muriel, in 1970. Today the batiks created by Muriel Chandler before her death in 1990 are viewed as stylish and sensual garments by the chic boutiques in the U.S.

The shop has a full range of fabrics, scarves, garments, and wall hangings, some patterned after such themes as Jamaica's Doctor Bird and various endangered animal species. Muriel's gallery continues to sell a selection of her original batik paintings. Either Keith or a member of the staff will be glad to describe the intricate process of batiking during their open hours of 9am to 4pm Tuesday to Saturday. They're closed in September and on national holidays.

5 Runaway Bay

Once this resort was a mere western satellite of Ocho Rios. However, with the opening of some large resort hotels, plus a colony of smaller hostelries, Runaway Bay is now a destination in its own right.

This part of Jamaica's north coast has several distinctions: It was the first part of the island seen by Columbus, the site of the first Spanish settlement on the island, and the point of departure of the last Spaniards leaving Jamaica following their defeat by the British.

Jamaica's most complete equestrian center is the **Chukka Cove Farm and Resort,** at Richmond Llandovery, St. Ann (☎ 876/972-2506), less than 4 miles east of Runaway Bay. A 1-hour trail ride costs $30, and a 2-hour mountain ride goes for $40. The most popular ride is a 3-hour beach jaunt where, after riding over trails to the sea, you unpack your horse and swim in the surf. Refreshments are served as part of the $55 charge. A 6-hour beach ride, complete with picnic lunch, goes for $130. Polo lessons are also available, costing $50 for 30 minutes.

ACCOMMODATIONS YOU CAN AFFORD

Caribbean Isle Hotel. P.O. Box 119, Runaway Bay, St. Ann, Jamaica, W.I. ☎ **876/973-2364.** Fax 876/974-1706. 23 units. A/C. Winter $70 single; $100 double; $145 triple. Off-season $70 single; $85 double; $120 triple. AE, MC, V.

This hotel directly on the beach, a mile west of Runaway Bay, has 8 superior and 15 standard rooms, with personalized service in an informal atmosphere. The small tattered rooms have ocean views and tiny baths, and the so-called superior units have private balconies. The hotel has a TV in the bar-lounge and a dining room leading onto a sea-view patio. Meals are served from 7:30am to 11pm daily, with dinner including lobster, fish, shrimp, pork chops, chicken, and local dishes prepared on request. This place is mainly for beach buffs who like to spend most of their time in the outdoors and not much time in the rooms.

✪ **Runaway H.E.A.R.T. Country Club.** Ricketts Ave. (P.O. Box 98), Runaway Bay, St. Ann, Jamaica, W.I. ☎ **876/973-2671.** Fax 876/973-2693. 20 units. A/C TV TEL. Winter $111 single; $138 double. Off-season $99 single; $124 double. Rates include MAP. AE, MC, V.

The best-kept secret in Jamaica, this place is on the main road and wins hands down as the bargain of the north coast. One of Jamaica's few training and service institutions, the club and its adjacent academy are operated by the government to provide a high level of training for young Jamaicans interested in the hotel trade. The helpful staff made up of professionals and trainees offers the finest service of any hotel in the area. The good-size rooms are bright and airy and have either a king-size bed, a double bed, or twin beds. The baths have generous shelf space and good towels. The accommodations open onto private balconies with views of well-manicured tropical gardens or vistas of the bay and golf course. Laundry is available, and there's a pool and golf course.

Guests enjoy having a drink in the piano bar (ever had a cucumber daiquiri?) before heading for the dining room, the Cardiff Hall Restaurant, which serves Jamaican and continental dishes. Nonguests can also enjoy dinner, served nightly from 7 to 10pm; a well-prepared meal costs around $25. The academy has won awards for some of its dishes, including go-go banana chicken and curried codfish.

Tamarind Tree Hotel. P.O. Box 235, Runaway Bay, St. Ann, Jamaica, W.I. ☎ **876/973-4819.** Fax 876/973-2678. www.in-site-com-tamtree. E-mail: tamarindtree@cwjamaica.com. 16 units, 3 three-bedroom cottages with kitchenette. A/C TV TEL. Winter $62–$85 single or double. Off-season $60–$82 single or double. Year-round $187.50 cottage for up to 6. MC, V.

This small family-style hotel was named after a lavishly blossoming tamarind tree that once grew near its entrance. Red-roofed stucco buildings with awnings and pastel-trimmed balconies house cream-colored and carpeted rooms. The more appealing rooms are on the second floor, partly because of their greater access to cooling breezes. All are medium in size and comfortably furnished; baths are a bit small but contain ample towels. There's a pool terrace, and the nearest beach (Cardiff Hall) is within a 5-minute walk. Although the occupants of the cottages usually cook their meals in their lodgings, the simple Bird Wing restaurant serves breakfast and dinner. The Stinger is a disco whose drinks and recorded music relieve some of the evening monotony of this out-of-the-way hotel.

ACCOMMODATIONS & DINING NEARBY

Hotel and Gallery Joe James. Rio Bueno, Trelawny, Jamaica, W.I. ☎ **876/954-0048.** Fax 876/952-5911. 22 units. Winter $100–$135 single or double; from $175 suite. Off-season $89 single or double; $125 suite. Rates include breakfast. AE, DC, MC, V.

For a 4- or 5-year period in the 1970s, Joe James was a bright flame on the arts scene of Jamaica, with exhibits of his works in New York, Philadelphia, and Washington, D.C. Though his fame and press coverage have greatly diminished in recent years, he continues his endeavors in a concrete-sided compound of buildings set close to the shore of the sheltered harbor of Rio Bueno. Many visitors are fascinated by the show-room, loaded with large-scale paintings and wood carvings inspired by Jamaican and African themes. All the objects are for sale, and Mr. James is usually on the premises to explain his artistic theories.

Today, however, much of the place's income derives from the Lobster Bowl Restaurant, serving breakfast, lunch, and dinner daily. There's an outdoor terrace whose foundations were sunk into the harbor waters. Lunch platters include burgers, salads, sandwiches, and grilled fish. Evening meals are more copious and feature a choice of set menus comprised of grilled fish, broiled lobster, sirloin steak, or chicken, served with soup, salad, dessert, coffee, and Tía María as part of the all-inclusive price of $18 to $30. If you're just passing through the area, you'll find the restaurant open daily from 8am to 10pm.

In the late 1980s, Mr. James built an angular two-story concrete building containing small functional accommodations within a few steps of his showroom and the beach. All have ceiling fans; most have views over the bay and the massive industrial plant whose cranes and smokestacks rise on the opposite side of the harbor. Don't expect luxury: The primary allure lies in the low cost, the proximity to the studio of one of Jamaica's better-known artists, and the complete lack of pretension.

BEACHES & WATER SPORTS

The two best beaches at Runaway Bay are **Paradise Beach** and **Cardiffall Lot Public Beach.** Both have wide strips of white sand and are clean and well maintained. There's a great natural beauty to this part of Jamaica, and many visitors, especially Canadians, seek it out, preferring its more raffish look to the more publicized tourist meccas of Ocho Rios. You don't get a lot of facilities, however, so if you're going to the beach you'd better bring along whatever you need. Both of these beaches are ideal for a picnic. Even if you're staying in Ocho Rios, you may want to escape the crowds and come here.

The waters are calm almost all year, but somehow the noonday sun is fierce, and many visitors from far northern climes report massive sunburns on their first day. They literally turn their northern white bodies in lobster-red colors. Prevailing on-shore trade winds will often keep you cool, especially in the morning and late after-noon. In Ocho Rios some vendor will try to sell you something every 5 minutes. Here they'll let you alone.

Since there are no lifeguards, be especially careful if you're beaching it with children.

Runaway Bay offers some of the best areas for snorkeling. The reefs are close to shore and extremely lively with marine life, including enormous schools of tropical fish like blue chromis, trigger fish, small skate rays, and snapper. Since boats and fishing canoes can be a problem close to shore, you can go on a snorkeling excursion with the best diving facility at Runaway Bay. Try **Resort Divers** in Runaway Bay (☎ **876/974-5338**) along the beach. This five-star PADI facility takes you out to one of several protected reefs where the water currents aren't dangerous and where fishing boats are required to stay at least 200 yards away from snorkelers. Resort Divers also provides sportfishing jaunts as well as scuba-diving certification and equipment. A resort dive costs $75, with a one-tank dive going for $35 or a two-tank dive for $65. Parasailing is available at $40 per half hour.

EXPLORING THE AREA

Columbus Park Museum, on Queens Highway in Discovery Bay (☎ **876/973-2135**), is a large open area between the main coast road and the sea. You just pull off the road and walk among the fantastic collection of exhibits; admission is free. There's everything from a canoe made of a solid piece of cottonwood (the way Arawaks did it more than 5 centuries ago) to a stone cross that was placed on the Barrett estate at Retreat (9 miles east of Montego Bay) by Edward Barrett, brother of poet Elizabeth Barrett Browning. You'll see a tally, used to count bananas carried on men's heads from plantation to ship, as well as a planter's strongbox with a weighted lead base to prevent its theft. Other items are 18th-century cannons, a Spanish water cooler and calcifier, a fish pot made from bamboo, a corn husker, and a water wheel. Pimento trees, from which allspice is produced, dominate the park, which is open daily from 8:30am to 4:30pm.

You can also visit the **Seville Great House,** Heritage Park (☎ **876/972-2191**), open daily from 9am to 5pm, charging $4 for admission. Built in 1745 by the Eng-lish, the house contains a collection of artifacts once used by everybody from the Amerindians to African slaves. In all you're treated to an exhibit of 5-centuries worth of Jamaican history. Modest for a Great House, it has a wattle-and-daub construction. A small theater presents a 15-minute historical film about the house.

6 Ocho Rios

This north-coast resort is a 2-hour drive east of Montego Bay or west of Port Antonio. Ocho Rios was once a small banana and fishing port, but tourism became the leading industry long ago. This resort—short on charm—is now Jamaica's cruise-ship capital. The bay is dominated on one side by a bauxite-loading terminal and on the other by a range of hotels with sandy beaches fringed with palm trees.

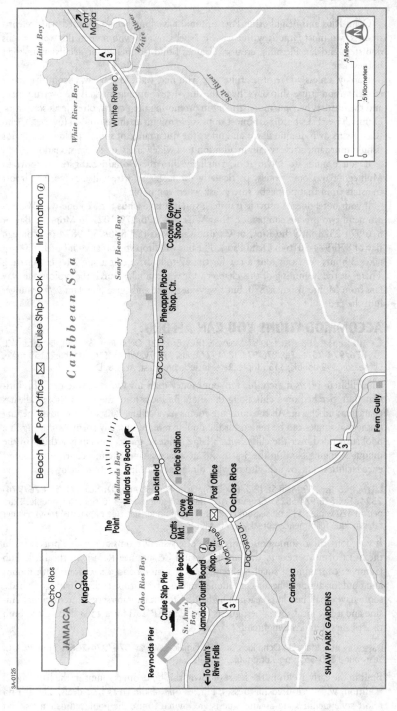

Ocho Rios

Beach 🏄 Post Office ⊠ Cruise Ship Dock ⚓ Information ⓘ

Caribbean Sea

Little Bay

White River Bay

Sandy Beach Bay

Mallards Bay

Ocho Rios Bay

St. Ann's Bay

White River ○

Salt River

White River

△3 Port Maria

△3

DaCosta Dr.

Coconut Grove Shop. Ctr.

Pineapple Place Shop. Ctr.

△3 Fern Gully

Mallards Bay Beach 🏄

■ Police Station

Buckfield

The Point

Cove Theatre

Crafts Mkt.

Shop. Ctr.

Turtle Beach 🏄

Cruise Ship Pier ⚓

Reynolds Pier ⚓

Jamaica Tourist Board

ⓘ

Main Street

Post Office ⊠

Ochos Rios ○

DaCosta Dr.

△3

Cariñosa

SHAW PARK GARDENS

← To Dunn's River Falls

JAMAICA

○ Ocho Rios

○ Kingston

N

0 .5 Miles

0 .5 Kilometers

SA-0125

345

Ocho Rios and neighboring Port Antonio have long been associated with celebrities. Its two most famous writers are Sir Noël Coward, who invited the world to his doorstep, and Ian Fleming, creator of James Bond (see below for details about their homes here).

Frankly, unless you're on a cruise ship, you may want to stay away from the major attractions on cruise-ship days. Even the duty-free shopping markets are overrun then, and the hustlers become more strident in promoting their crafts, often junk souvenirs. Dunn's River Falls becomes almost impossible to visit at those times. However, Ocho Rios has its own unique flavor and offers the usual range of sports, including a major fishing tournament every fall, in addition to a wide variety of accommodations.

If you're going to Ocho Rios, you'll fly into the **Donald Sangster Airport** in Montego Bay. Some hotels, particularly the larger resorts, will arrange for airport transfers from that point. Be sure to ask when you book.

If your hotel doesn't provide transfers, you can take a **bus** for $25 one-way. We recommend two private companies: **Tour Wise** (☎ **876/979-1027** in Montego Bay or 876/974-2323 in Ocho Rios) or **Caribic Vacations** (☎ **876/953-9874** in Montego Bay or 876/974-9016 in Ocho Rios). The bus will drop you off at your hotel. The trip takes 2 hours. You can **rent a car** for the 67-mile drive east along A1 (see "Getting There" at the beginning of this chapter). Or you can take a **taxi;** the typical one-way fare from Montego Bay is $70, but always negotiate and agree on a fare *before* you get into the taxi.

ACCOMMODATIONS YOU CAN AFFORD

✪ **Hibiscus Lodge Hotel.** 87 Main St. (P.O. Box 52), Ocho Rios, St. Ann, Jamaica, W.I. ☎ **876/974-2676.** Fax 876/974-1874. 27 units. A/C TV. Winter $105 double; $150 triple. Off-season $99 double; $135 triple. Rates include breakfast. AE, CB, DC, MC, V.

The Hibiscus offers more value for your money than any Ocho Rios resort. This intimate inn, perched on a cliff along the shore 3 blocks from the Ocho Rios Mall, has character and charm. All medium-size rooms have ceiling fans and verandas opening to the sea; singles can be rented for the double rate. After a day spent swimming in a pool suspended over the cliffs, with a large sundeck, guests can enjoy a drink in the unique swinging bar. On the 3-acre site are a Jacuzzi and a tennis court, plus conference facilities. The owners also provide dining at the Almond Tree (below).

Little Pub Inn. 59 Main St. (P.O. Box 256), Ocho Rios, St. Ann, Jamaica, W.I. ☎ **876/974-2324.** Fax 876/974-5825. 22 units. A/C TEL. Year-round $44–$70 single or double. Extra person $20 winter, $15 off-season; children 11 and under stay free in parents' room. Higher rates include full American breakfast. AE, MC, V.

If you don't mind some noise, this place offers small rooms at sensible prices. It's in the heart of town next to the Jamaica Grand Renaissance Resort, in the Little Pub Complex containing a small nightclub, slot machines, and a restaurant with indoor and outdoor dining. The air-conditioned rooms have a tropical décor with good beds; some have small bed lofts reached by ladder. The restaurant serves international cuisine and a few local specialties; guests receive a VIP card for a 15% discount at both the restaurant and the nightclub.

Parkway Inn. Main St., Ocho Rios, St. Ann, Jamaica, W.I. ☎ **876/974-2667.** 21 units. A/C. Year-round $60–$65 single or double. AE, MC, V.

Built in the early 1990s in the heart of town, this hotel offers rooms in the basic motel tradition, with well-used mattresses, but it's one of the area's best deals. Though no resort-style facilities are on site, guests are invited to use the pool, tennis courts, and water-sports facilities at the next-door Jamaica Grand Hotel and any of the Ocho Rios beaches (the nearest is a 10-minute walk away). There's a Chinese/Jamaican restaurant on the premises serving simple meals, plus a third-floor bar where guests can enjoy a grand view over the lights of Ocho Rios.

Pineapple Hotel. Pineapple Place (P.O. Box 263), Ocho Rios, St. Ann, Jamaica, W.I. ☎ **876/974-2727.** Fax 876/974-1706. 20 units. A/C. Year-round $60 single or double; $75 triple. Children 11 and under stay free in parents' room. AE, MC, V.

Next door to the Pineapple Place Shopping Centre, this hotel offers no frills, just tropically decorated quarters with tiny baths, decent beds, tile floors, and air-conditioning. TVs are available for $2 per day. The Pineapple Pizza Pub is on-site, serving a combination of cuisines with Italian, American, and Jamaican influences. There's a pool, and water sports can be arranged at the front desk. For a seaside romp, try Turtle Beach, a short walk away.

WORTH A SPLURGE

Turtle Beach Towers. DaCosta Dr. (P.O. Box 73), Ocho Rios, St. Ann, Jamaica, W.I. ☎ **800/223-9815** in the U.S. and Canada, or 876/974-2801. Fax 876/974-2806. 116 apts. A/C TEL. Winter $110–$125 studio apt.; $126–$155 1-bedroom apt.; $198–$212 2-bedroom apt. Off-season $82–$88 studio apt.; $88–$112 1-bedroom apt.; $132–$152 2-bedroom apt. Children 11 and under stay free in parents' apt. (no children in studio apts.). AE, MC, V.

In a commercial district opposite the cruise-ship pier, these medium-sized accommodations with equipped kitchenettes are housed in four high-rise towers offering apartment living with the bonus of daily maid service. Mattresses are firm, and maintenance is most acceptable. The property has a pool and tennis courts equipped for night play, in addition to the beach. Water sports can be arranged. Also on the premises is a restaurant serving Jamaican and international specialties for breakfast, lunch, and dinner. On Tuesday evening, there's a manager's complimentary rum-punch party.

ACCOMMODATIONS NEARBY

✪ **Jamel Jamaica Hotel.** 2 Richmond Estate, Priory P.A., St. Anne, Jamaica, W.I. ☎ **876/ 972-1031.** Fax 876/972-0714. 24 units. A/C TV TEL. Winter $55 single; $88 double; $99 triple; $110 1-bedroom suite for 2; $132 1-bedroom suite for 3; $176 2-bedroom suite for 4. Off-season $44 single; $66 double; $88 triple; $88 1-bedroom suite for 2; $99 1-bedroom suite for 3; $132 two-bedroom suite for 4. AE, DC, MC, V.

Some 7 miles west of Ocho Rios, this property lies on a windswept stretch of coastline. Despite its isolated locale, its designers managed to infuse it with some degree of drama, using hundreds of gallons of white paint, erecting urn-shaped balustrades separating pool terraces from the wild waterfront nearby, and landscaping with flowering shrubs and trees. Each medium-size accommodation features a balcony with a sea view, plus good beds and average-size baths. There's a restaurant and bar on the premises, but many guests cook in their kitchens or kitchenettes. (Cooking areas in the suites are larger and better equipped than those in the other rooms.) The entertainment includes disco evenings and calypso parties with live musicians. This is a good place for large families or couples.

GREAT DEALS ON DINING

Little Pub Restaurant. 59 Main St. ☎ **876/974-2324.** Reservations recommended. Main courses $13–$28. AE, MC, V. Daily 7pm–midnight. JAMAICAN/INTERNATIONAL.

Located in a redbrick courtyard with a fish pond and a waterfall surrounded by souvenir shops in the town center, this indoor-outdoor pub features a restaurant in the dinner-theater style. Top local and international artists are featured, as are Jamaican musical plays. No one will mind if you just enjoy a drink while seated on one of the barrel chairs. But if you want dinner, proceed to one of the linen-covered tables capped with cut flowers and candlelight. Menu items include barbecued chicken, stewed snapper, grilled kingfish, and the inevitable and overpriced lobster.

✪ **Ocho Rios Village Jerk Centre.** DaCosta Dr. ☎ **876/974-2549.** Jerk pork $3 for ¼ lb., $11 for 1 lb.; whole jerk chicken $14. MC, V. Daily 10am–11pm. JAMAICAN.

At this open-air restaurant, you can get the best jerk dishes on this part of the coast. When only a frosty Red Stripe beer can quench your thirst or the fiery taste of Jamaican jerk seasonings ease your stomach growls, head here. Don't dress up and don't expect anything fancy: It's the food that counts, and you'll find fresh daily specials posted on a chalkboard menu on the wall. If a cruise ship is in port, the place is likely to be swamped with passengers, so it's better to go in the evening. The food is hot and spicy but not too hot. Hot spices are presented on the side for those who want to go truly Jamaican. The barbecue ribs are especially good, and fresh fish is a delight, perfectly grilled. Try the red snapper. Vegetarian dishes are available on request, and if you don't drink beer you can wash it all down with natural fruit juices.

Parkway Restaurant. 60 DaCosta Dr. ☎ **876/974-2667.** Main courses $8–$20. AE, MC, V. Daily 8am–11:30pm. JAMAICAN.

This popular place in the commercial center couldn't have a plainer façade. Inside, it continues to be unpretentious, but many local families and members of the business community know they can get great-tasting inexpensive local dishes here. On clean linens, hungry diners are fed Jamaican-style chicken, curried goat, and filet of red snapper, and to top it off, banana-cream pie. Lobster and fresh fish are usually featured.

WORTH A SPLURGE

Almond Tree Restaurant. In the Hibiscus Lodge Hotel, 87 Main St. ☎ **876/974-2813.** Reservations recommended. Main courses $15.50–$37. AE, DC, MC, V. Daily 7am–2:30pm and 6–9:30pm. INTERNATIONAL.

The Almond Tree is a two-tiered patio restaurant with a tree growing through the roof, overlooking the Caribbean at this previously recommended resort 3 blocks from the Ocho Rios Mall. Lobster Thermidor is the most delectable item on the menu, but we also like the bouillabaisse (made with conch and lobster). Also excellent are the roast suckling pig, medallions of beef Anne Palmer, and a fondue *bourguignonne.* Jamaican plantation rice is a local specialty. The wine list offers a variety of vintages, including Spanish and Jamaican. Have an apéritif in the unique swinging bar (swinging chairs, that is).

SPORTS & OUTDOOR PURSUITS

BEACHES   The most idyllic sands are found at the often-overcrowded **Mallards Beach,** shared by hotel guests and cruise-ship passengers, but locals may steer you to the white sands of **Turtle Beach** in the south. Turtle Beach lies between the Renaissance Jamaica Grande and Club Jamaica. This is where the islanders themselves go to swim. The most frequented (and to be avoided when cruise ships are in port) is **Dunn's River Beach,** located below the famous falls. Another great spot is **Jamaica Grande's Beach,** which is open to the public. Parasailing is a favorite sport on this beach.

Many exhibitionistic couples check into the famous but pricey **Couples Resort,** known for its private *au naturel* island. A shuttle boat transports visitors offshore to this beautiful little island with a fine sandy beach. A bar, pool, and hot tub on the island are found just a few hundred yards offshore from Couples. Security guards keep the gawkers from bothering guests on this beach.

We always follow the trail of 007 and head for our favorite: ✪ **James Bond Beach** (☎ **876/975-3663**), east of Ocho Rios at Oracabessa Beach. Entrepreneur Chris Blackwell reopened writer Ian Fleming's former home, Goldeneye, and the master spy-thriller writer himself often used this beach. For $5, nonguests can enjoy its sand strip any day except Monday. Admission includes a free drink (beer or soda) and use of the changing room. There's also a water-sports rental center.

Under a thatched palm roof you can enjoy local specialties: Try the grilled fish and finish off with a local specialty, the *bammy* cake. You can also visit the bar just for drinks, like the Goldfinger (pineapple and orange juices mixed with rum), the Moonraker (a strawberry-flavored rum drink), or the 007 (for this you've got to take a chance, since the bartender refuses to divulge the ingredients).

GOLF **SuperClub's Runaway Golf Club,** at Runaway Bay near Ocho Rios on the north coast (☎ **876/973-4820**), charges no fee to guests who stay at any of Jamaica's affiliated SuperClubs. For nonguests, the price is $80 year-round. Any player can rent carts for $35 for 18 holes and clubs for $14 for 18 holes.

Sandals Golf & Country Club (☎ **876/975-0119**), a 15-minute ride from the center of the resort, is a 6,500-yard course, known for its panoramic scenery some 700 feet above sea level. From the center of Ocho Rios, travel along the main bypass for 2 miles until you reach Mile End Road, where you'll find a Texaco station. Turn right and drive for another 5 miles until you come to the Sandals course on your right. The 18-hole, par-71 course was designed by P. K. Saunders and opened in 1951 as the Upton Golf Club. Rolling terrain, lush vegetation, and flowers and fruit trees dominate the 120-acre course. A putting green and driving range are available. Sandals guests play free; otherwise, the cost is $50 for 9 holes or $70 for 18 holes.

SNORKELING & SCUBA DIVING The best outfitter is **Resort Divers Shop,** Main Street, Turtle Beach (☎ **876/974-6632**), at the Club Jamaica Resort. The skilled staff can hook you up for dive trips or snorkeling. The best spot for either of these sports is 200 yards offshore (you'll be transported there). A boat leaving daily at 1pm goes to Paradise Reef, where tropical fish are plentiful. Of course, bad weather can lead to a cancellation.

TENNIS **Ciboney Ocho Rios,** Main Street, Ocho Rios (☎ **876/974-1027**), focuses more on tennis than any other area resort. It offers three clay-surface and three hard-surface courts, all lit for nighttime play. Guests play free either day or night, but nonguests must call and make arrangements with the manager. A pro offers lessons for $25 an hour. Ciboney also sponsors twice-a-day clinics for both beginners and advanced players. Frequent guest tournaments are also staged, including handicapped doubles and mixed doubles.

Goldeneye at Oracabessa, St. Mary's (☎ **876/974-3354**), is not open to the public unless you rent one of the 11 units. Yet it's one of the most asked-about sights. Noël Coward was a frequent guest of Ian Fleming at Goldeneye, made fashionable in the 1950s. It was here in 1952 that the most famous secret agent in the world, 007, was born. Fleming built the house in 1946 and wrote each of the 13 original Bond books in it. Through the large gates with bronze pineapples on the top came a host of international celebs: Evelyn Waugh, Truman Capote, and Graham Greene. The house was closed and dilapidated for some time after the writer's death, but its present owner, British music publisher Christopher Blackwell, has restored the property. Though Fleming kept the place "just back to the basics," Blackwell sought the help of a designer to revamp the interior. With East Asia, including Timor, as the theme, the place now contains oversize bamboo sofas, totem-like Japanese obisps, and the like. Fleming's original desk, where 007 was born, remains. Look for the Esso (not Exxon) sign and take the narrow lane nearby going to the sea. Since you can't go inside, you might want to settle for a swim at James Bond Beach (see above).

EXPLORING THE AREA

A scenic drive south of Ocho Rios along the A3 takes you inland through **Fern Gully.** This was originally a riverbed, but now the main road winds up some 700 feet among a profusion of wild ferns, a tall rain forest, hardwood trees, and lianas. There are hundreds of varieties of ferns, and roadside stands offer fruit and vegetables, carved-wood souvenirs, and basketwork. The road runs for about 4 miles, and then at the top of the hill you come to a right turn onto a narrow road leading to **Golden Grove,** a small Jamaican community with a bauxite mine that is of no touristic interest.

Head west when you see the signs pointing to **Lyford,** a small community southwest of Ocho Rios. To approach it, take the A3 south (the Fern Gully Road) until you come to a small intersection directly north of Walkers Wood. Follow the signpost west to Lyford. You'll pass the remains of **Edinburgh Castle,** built in 1763, the lair of one of Jamaica's most infamous murderers, a Scot named Lewis Hutchinson who used to shoot passersby and toss their bodies into a deep pit. The authorities got wind of his activities, and although he tried to escape by canoe, he was captured by the navy under the command of Admiral Rodney and was hanged. Rather proud of his achievements (evidence of at least 43 murders was found), he left £100 and instructions for a memorial to be built. It never was, but the castle ruins remain.

Continue north on the A1 to **St. Ann's Bay,** the site of the first Spanish settlement on the island, where you can see the **statue of Christopher Columbus,** cast in his hometown of Genoa and erected near St. Ann's Hospital on the west side of town, close to the coast road. In the town are a number of Georgian buildings—the **Court House** near the parish church, built in 1866, is the most interesting.

Brimmer Hall Estate. Port Maria, St. Mary's. ☎ **876/994-2309.** Tours $15. Tours Mon–Fri 11am, 1:30pm, and 3pm.

Some 21 miles east of Ocho Rios, in the hills 2 miles from Port Maria, this 1817 estate is an ideal place to spend a day. You can relax beside the pool and sample a wide variety of brews and concoctions. The Plantation Tour Eating House offers typical Jamaican dishes for lunch, and the souvenir shop sells a good selection of ceramics, art, straw goods, wood carvings, rums, liqueurs, and cigars. All this is on a working plantation where you're driven around in a tractor-drawn jitney to see the tropical fruit trees and coffee plants and learn from the knowledgeable guides about the processes necessary to produce the fine fruits of the island.

Coyaba River Garden and Museum. Shaw Park Rd. ☎ **876/974-6235.** Admission $4.50 ages 13 and up; free for children 12 and under. Daily 8:30am–5pm. Take the Fern Gully–Kingston road, turn left at St. John's Anglican Church, and follow the signs to Coyaba, half a mile farther.

A mile from the center of Ocho Rios, at an elevation of 420 feet, this park and museum were built on the grounds of the former Shaw Park plantation. The word *coyaba* comes from the Arawak name for paradise. Coyaba is a Spanish-style museum with a river and gardens filled with native flora, a cut-stone courtyard, fountains, and a crafts shop and bar. The museum boasts a collection of artifacts from the Arawak, Spanish, and English settlements in the area.

✪ **Dunn's River Falls.** On A3. ☎ **876/974-2857.** Admission $6 adults, $3 children 2–11; free for children under 2. Daily 8:30am–5pm (8am–5pm on cruise-ship arrival days). From St. Ann's Bay, follow the A3 east back to Ocho Rios, and you'll pass Dunn's River Falls; there's plenty of parking.

For a charge, you can relax on the beach or climb with a guide to the top of the 600-foot falls. You can splash in the waters at the bottom of the falls or drop into the cool pools higher up between the cascades of water. The beach restaurant provides snacks and drinks, and dressing rooms are available. If you're planning to climb the falls, wear old tennis shoes to protect your feet from the sharp rocks and to prevent slipping.

Firefly. Grants Pen, in St. Mary, 20 miles east of Ocho Rios above Oracabessa. ☎ **876/997-7201.** Admission $10. Daily 8:30am–5:30pm.

Firefly was the home of Sir Noël Coward and his longtime companion, Graham Payn, who, as executor of Coward's estate, donated it to the Jamaica National Heritage Trust. The recently restored house is more or less as it was on the day Sir Noël died in 1973. His Hawaiian print shirts still hang in the closet of his austere bedroom, with its mahogany four-poster. The library contains a collection of his books, and the living room is warm and comfortable, with big armchairs and two grand pianos (he composed several famous tunes here). When the Queen Mother was entertained here, the lobster mousse Coward intended to serve melted, so, with a style and flair that was the stuff of legend, he opened a can of pea soup instead. Guests were housed at Blue Harbour, a villa closer to Port Maria, and included Evelyn Waugh, Sir Winston Churchill, Errol Flynn, Laurence Olivier, Vivien Leigh, Claudette Colbert, Katharine Hepburn, and Mary Martin. Paintings by the noted playwright, actor, author, and composer adorn the walls. An open patio looks out over the pool and the sea, and across the lawn, on his plain, flat, white-marble gravestone is inscribed simply: Sir Noël Coward, born December 16, 1899, died March 26, 1973.

Harmony Hall. Tower Isles on A3, 4 miles east of Ocho Rios. ☎ **876/975-4222.** Free admission. Gallery, Mon–Sat 10am–6pm; restaurant and cafe, daily 10am–10pm.

Harmony Hall was built near the end of the 19th century as the centerpiece of a sugar plantation. Today it has been restored and is now the focal point of an art gallery and restaurant that showcases the painting and sculpture of Jamaican artists as well as a tasteful array of arts and crafts. Among the featured gift items are Sharon McConnell's Starfish Oils, which contain natural additives harvested in Jamaica. The gallery shop also carries the Reggae to Wear line of sportswear, designed and made on Jamaica. Harmony Hall is also the setting for one of the best Italian restaurants along the coast, Toscaninni.

Prospect Plantation. On A3, 3 miles east of Ocho Rios, in St. Ann. ☎ **876/994-1058.** Tours $12 adults; free for children 12 and under; 1-hour horseback ride $20. Tours Mon–Sat at 10:30am, 2pm, and 3:30pm; Sun at 11am, 1:30pm, and 3pm.

This working plantation adjoins the 18-hole Prospect Mini Golf Course. A visit here is an educational, relaxing, and enjoyable experience. On your leisurely ride by covered jitney through the scenic beauty of Prospect, you'll readily see why this section of Jamaica is called the "garden parish" of the island. You can view the many trees planted by such visitors as Sir Winston Churchill, Dr. Henry Kissinger, Charlie Chaplin, Pierre Trudeau, and Sir Noël Coward. You'll learn about pimento (allspice), bananas, cassava, sugarcane, coffee, cocoa, coconut, pineapple, and the famous leucaena Tree of Life. And you'll see Jamaica's first hydroelectric plant and sample some of the exotic fruit and drinks. Horseback riding is available on three scenic trails at Prospect. The rides vary from 1 to 2¼ hours. Advance booking of 1 hour is necessary to reserve horses.

SHOPPING

For many, Ocho Rios provides an introduction to shopping Jamaica-style. After surviving the ordeal, some visitors may vow never to go shopping again. Hundreds of Jamaicans pour into town hoping to peddle something, often something they made, to cruise-ship passengers and other visitors. Be prepared for aggressive vendors and some fierce haggling. All vendors ask too much for an item at first, giving them the leeway to negotiate until the price reaches a more realistic level. Is shopping fun in Ocho Rios? A resounding no. Do cruise-ship passengers and land visitors indulge in it anyway? A decided yes.

SHOPPING CENTERS   There are seven main shopping plazas. We list them because they're here, not because we heartily recommend them. The **Ocean Village Shopping Centre** (☎ 876/974-2683) contains numerous boutiques, food stores, a bank, sundries purveyors, a pharmacy, travel agencies, service facilities, and what have you. East of Ocho Rios, the **Pineapple Place Shopping Centre** is a collection of shops in cedar-shingle-roofed cottages set amid tropical flowers.

The **Ocho Rios Craft Park** is a complex of some 150 stalls through which to browse. An eager seller will weave you a hat or a basket while you wait, or you can buy from the mix of ready-made hats, hampers, handbags, place mats, and lampshades. Other stands stock hand-embroidered goods and will make small items while you wait. Wood carvers work on bowls, ashtrays, wooden-head carvings, and statues chipped from lignum vitae, and make cups from local bamboo. The **Coconut Grove Shopping Plaza** is a collection of low-lying shops linked by walkways and shrubs. The merchandise consists mainly of local craft items. Many of your fellow shoppers may be cruise-ship passengers.

Island Plaza is a shopping complex in the heart of Ocho Rios. You can find some of the best Jamaican art here, all paintings by local artists. You can also buy local handmade crafts (be prepared to do some haggling over price and quality), carvings, ceramics, even kitchenware, and most definitely the inevitable T-shirts. **Mutual Security Plaza** contains some 30 shops.

SPECIALTY SHOPS   In general, the shopping is better in Montego Bay if you're going there. If not, wander the Ocho Rios crafts markets, though much of the merchandise has the same monotony. Among the places deserving special mention are these:

Swiss Stores, in the Ocean Village Shopping Centre (☎ 876/974-2519), sells all the big names in Swiss watches, like Juvenia, Tissot, Omega, Rolex, Patek Philippe, and Piaget. The Rolex watches are real, not those fakes touted by hustlers on the streets of Ocho Rios. The Swiss outlet also sells duty-free handcrafted jewelry.

One of the best bets for shopping is **Soni's Plaza**, 50 Main St., the address of all the shops recommended below. **Casa dé Oro** (☎ 876/974-5392) specializes in selling duty-free watches, fine jewelry, and classic perfumes. **Chulani's** (☎ 876/974-2421) sells a good assortment of quality watches, brand-name perfumes, and leather bags. Jewelry comes in a wide variety of 14-karat and 18-karat settings with diamonds, emeralds, rubies, and sapphires. **Gem Palace** (☎ 876/974-2850) is the place to go for diamond ring solitaires and tennis bracelets, as well as 14-karat gold chains and bracelets. **Taj Gift Centre** (☎ 876/974-9268) has a little bit of everything: Blue Mountain coffee, Jamaican cigars, hand-embroidered linen tablecloths, and Jamaican jewelry made from hematite, a mountain stone.

Mohan's (☎ 876/974-9270) offers one of the best selections of 14-karat and 18-karat gold chains, rings, bracelets, and earrings, as well as jewelry studded with precious gems like diamonds and rubies. **Soni's** (☎ 876/974-2303) dazzles with gold but also sells cameras, French perfumes, watches, china and crystal, linen tablecloths, and even standard Jamaican souvenirs. **Tajmahal** (☎ 876/974-6455) beats most competition with its name-brand watches, jewelry, and fragrances; it also has Paloma Picasso leather wear and porcelain by Lladró.

We generally ignore hotel gift shops, but the **Jamaica Inn Gift Shop** in the Jamaica Inn, Main Street (☎ 876/974-2514), is better than most, selling everything from Blue Mountain coffee to Walkers Wood products, and even guava jelly and jerk seasoning. If you're lucky, you'll find marmalade from an old family recipe, plus Upton Pimento Dram, a unique liqueur flavored with Jamaican allspice. Local handcrafts include musical instruments for kids, brightly painted tin country cottages, and intricate jigsaw puzzles of local scenes. The constantly replenished collection of antiques ranges from sterling silver collectibles to 18th-century teaspoons and serving pieces. The antique maps of the West Indies are among the finest in Jamaica. We recently bought a 1576 map of Jamaica for a surprisingly reasonable price.

OCHO RIOS AFTER DARK

The **Sports Bar** at the Little Pub Restaurant (see above) is open daily from 10pm to 3am, and Sunday is disco night. Most evenings are devoted to some form of entertainment, including karaoke, if you'd like to drop in.

Hotels often provide live entertainment to which nonguests are invited. Ask at your hotel desk where the action is on any given night. Otherwise, you may want to look in on **Silks Discothèque,** in the Shaw Park Hotel, Cutlass Bay (☎ 876/974-2552), which has a smallish dance floor and a sometimes-animated crowd of drinkers and dancers. If you're not a hotel guest, you can enter for an all-inclusive price of J$200 ($5.70).

If everything is in a name, then we recommend **Jamaic'N Me Crazy,** at the Jamaican Grande Hotel (☎ 876/974-2201). An all-inclusive club that will evoke more of a New York–nightclub memory than a Jamaican one, it charges nonguests $30 to cover everything you can shake or drink, daily from 10pm to 3am. They have the best lighting and sound system in Ocho Rios (and perhaps Jamaica), and the crowd can include anyone from the passing yachter to the curious tourist.

For more of the same without an overbearing Americanized atmosphere, try the **Acropolis,** 70 Main St. (☎ 876/974-2633). At least the adventurous traveler can rest assured this is a lot closer to an authentic Jamaican nightclub than Jamaic'N Me Crazy. Cover is required only on nights they have a live band, and it's rarely any higher than J$200 ($5.70).

7 Port Antonio

Port Antonio is a verdant and sleepy seaport on the northeast coast of Jamaica, 63 miles northeast of Kingston, where Tom Cruise filmed *Cocktail.* It has been called the Jamaica of 100 years ago. Port Antonio is the mecca of the titled and the wealthy, including European royalty and stars like Bruce Willis, Linda Evans, Raquel Welch, Whoopi Goldberg, Peter O'Toole, and Tommy Tune.

The bustling small town of Port Antonio is like many on the island: clean and tidy, with sidewalks around a market filled with vendors; tin-roofed shacks competing with old Georgian and modern brick-and-concrete buildings; and lots of people shopping, talking, laughing, and some just loafing. The market is a place to browse among local craftwork, spices, and fruits.

In bygone days, visitors arrived by banana boat and stayed at the Tichfield Hotel (which burned down) in a lush, tropical, unspoiled part of the island. Captain Bligh landed here in 1793 with the first breadfruit plants, and Port Antonio claims the ones grown in this area are the best on the island. Visitors still arrive by water—but now it's in cruise ships that moor close to Navy Island, and the passengers come ashore just for the day.

Navy Island and the long-gone Tichfield Hotel were owned for a short time by film star Errol Flynn. The story is that after suffering damage to his yacht, he put into Kingston for repairs, visited Port Antonio by motorbike, fell in love with the area, and in due course acquired Navy Island (some say he got it in a gambling game). Later he either sold (or lost) it and bought a nearby plantation, Comfort Castle, still owned by his widow, Patrice Wymore Flynn, who spends most of her time there. He was much loved and admired by the Jamaicans and was totally integrated into the community. They still talk of him in Port Antonio—his reputation for womanizing and drinking lives on.

GETTING THERE

If you're going to Ocho Rios, you'll fly into the **Donald Sangster Airport** in Montego Bay or the **Norman Manley International Airport** in Kingston. Some hotels, particularly the larger resorts, will arrange for airport transfers from that point. Be sure to ask when you book.

If your hotel doesn't provide transfers, you can **fly** to Port Antonio's small airport aboard the independent carrier **Air Jamaica Express,** booking your connection through Air Jamaica (☎ **800/523-5585** in the U.S.). The one-way airfare is $45 from Kingston or $60 from Montego Bay. Or you can take a **bus** for $25 one-way. We recommend two private companies: **Tour Wise** (☎ **876/979-1027**) and **Caribic Vacations** (☎ **876/953-9874**). The bus will drop you off at your hotel. The trip takes 2 hours, but for safety's sake, we recommend this option only if you fly into Montego Bay. You can **rent a car** for the 133-mile drive east along the A1 (see "Getting There" at the beginning of this chapter), but we don't advise this 4-hour drive for safety's sake, either from Montego Bay or from Kingston. Or you can take a **taxi;** the typical one-way fare from Montego Bay is $100, but always negotiate and agree on a fare *before* you get into the taxi.

ACCOMMODATIONS YOU CAN AFFORD

Bonnie View Plantation Hotel. Richmond Hill (P.O. Box 82), Port Antonio, Jamaica, W.I.
☎ **876/993-2752.** Fax 876/993-2862. 20 units. Winter $64–$72 single; $98–$114 double. Off-season $54–$62 single; $82–$104 double. MAP $24 per person. AE, DC, MC, V.

The two-story house containing this hotel is the subject of several local legends. Some claim it was built by an expat Englishman as a holiday home around 1900; others maintain it was the center of a large plantation and constructed around 1850. Other stories claim Errol Flynn owned it briefly and used it as a place to carouse. Regardless of the details, it's obvious that this building once boasted pretensions of grandeur and many of the graceful notes of the Old World. But today it's a battered remnant of its original self, with a much-renovated dining room, 15 rooms in the main house, and 5 in cabaña-style outbuildings in the garden. The somewhat tattered accommodations contain Jamaica-made furniture and often sagging mattresses and virtually no accessories, though a very limited number offer sea views. There's a smallish pool in back, a restaurant, and a bar. The nearest beach (Frenchman's Cove) is about a 20-minute drive away.

De Montevin Lodge. 21 Fort George St. (P.O. Box 85), Port Antonio, Jamaica, W.I. ☎ **876/993-2604.** 13 units, 3 with bathroom. $26 single without bathroom; $39 double without bathroom; $52 single or double with bathroom. AE.

This lodge, in the town center on Titchfield Hill, is an ornate yet somewhat shabby version of a Victorian gingerbread house. It stands on a narrow backstreet whose edges are lined with architectural reminders (some not well-preserved) of the colonial days. Cast-iron accents and elongated red-and-white balconies set a tone for the charm you find inside: cedar doors, art deco cupboards, a ceiling embellished with lacy plaster designs, and elaborate cove moldings. Don't expect modern amenities; your room might be a study of another, not-yet-renovated era. The hallway baths are adequate, but the furnishings are a bit spartan and frayed; the mattresses are often lumpy. Try to get an accommodation with a private side porch. The Little Reef Beach is a 5-minute walk away, and Frenchman's Cove and Boston Beach are a 15-minute drive away.

WORTH A SPLURGE

Navy Island Marina Resort. Navy Island (P.O. Box 188), Port Antonio, Jamaica, W.I. ☎ **876/993-2667.** 7 units. Year-round $80 double; $100 1-bedroom villa for 2; $130 1-bedroom villa for 3; $225 2-bedroom villa for 3; $250 2-bedroom villa for 4. Rates include breakfast. Children 11 and under stay free in parents' villa. AE, MC, V.

Jamaica's only private island getaway, this resort and marina is on that bit of paradise once owned by actor Errol Flynn. Today this cottage colony and yacht club is one of the best-kept secrets in the Caribbean. To reach the resort, you'll have to take a ferry from the dockyards of Port Antonio on West Street for a short ride across one of the most beautiful harbors of Jamaica. Hotel guests travel free.

Each accommodation is designed as a studio cottage or villa branching out from the main club. Ceiling fans and trade winds keep the cottages cool, and mosquito netting over the comfortable beds adds a plantation touch. Bathrooms are fairly small and routine, but at least the plumbing in this remote location is workable. One of the resort's beaches is a secluded clothing-optional stretch of sand known as Trembly Knee Cove. You can explore the island leisurely, whose grounds are dotted with hybrid hibiscus, bougainvillea, and palms (many of which were originally ordered planted by Flynn himself). At night, after enjoying drinks in the H.M.S. Bounty Bar, guests can dine in the Bounty (below). Facilities include a pool, two beaches, and snorkeling.

ACCOMMODATIONS NEARBY

✪ **Hotel Mocking Bird Hill.** Mocking Bird Hill (P.O. Box 254), Port Antonio, Jamaica, W.I. ☎ **876/993-7267.** Fax 876/993-7133. 10 units. Winter $150–$195 single or double. Off-season $120–$150 single or double. AE, MC, V.

A 6-mile drive east of Port Antonio, this hotel occupies the much-renovated premises of what was built in 1971 as the holiday home of an American family. In 1993 two imaginative women transformed the place into a blue-and-white enclave of good taste, reasonable prices, and ecological consciousness. About 600 feet above the coastline, on a hillside laden with tropical plants, the accommodations are simple but tasteful, and other than their ceiling fans, are devoid of electronic gadgets. They're tastefully furnished, with excellent beds in the best B&B tradition. Most of them are no-smoking. Much of the interior, including the restaurant (Mille Fleurs, below), is decorated with Ms. Walker's artworks, and as this hotel grows, the gallery aspect will probably be expanded. On the premises are a bar; a lounge with TV; a public phone; access to herbal massages, rafting tours, hiking treks, and classes in painting and papermaking; and sweeping views over the Blue Mountains and the Jamaican coastline.

GREAT DEALS ON DINING

Bounty. In the Navy Island Marina Resort, Navy Island. ☎ **876/993-2667.** Reservations recommended for dinner. Lunch or dinner $12–$20. AE, DC, DISC, MC, V. Daily 7am–10pm. JAMAICAN.

In Errol Flynn's former retreat (see above), the Bounty, reached by ferry across the Port Antonio harbor, is the perfect place for a romantic tryst at low prices. The kitchen is known for its convivial seafaring ambience, fresh fish, and down-home Jamaican cookery often appearing on the menu as daily specials. Come early so you can enjoy a drink, taking in the view from the bar. (Flynn used to have quite a few, all recorded in *My Wicked, Wicked Ways,* his autobiography.) The lunch and dinner menus are the same. Steak is prepared delectably in a variety of ways, as are lobster, shrimp, chicken, and crayfish.

✪ **De Montevin Lodge Restaurant.** 21 Fort George St. ☎ **876/993-2604.** Reservations recommended a day in advance. Fixed-price meal $12–$20. AE. Daily 12:30–2:30pm and 7–9:30pm. JAMAICAN/AMERICAN.

At this previously recommended lodge, start with pepperpot or pumpkin soup, follow with curried lobster or chicken Jamaican style with local vegetables, and finish with coconut or banana cream pie or bread pudding, washed down with coffee. We suggest an ice-cold Red Stripe beer with the meal. The menu changes according to the availability of fresh supplies, but the standard of cooking and the full Jamaican character of the meal are constant. If you'd like a special dish cooked, you can request it when you make reservations.

Yachtsman's Wharf. 16 West St. ☎ **876/993-3053.** Main courses $7–$15. No credit cards. Daily 7:30am–10pm. INTERNATIONAL.

This restaurant beneath a thatch-covered roof is at the end of an industrial pier, near the departure point for ferries to Navy Island. The rustic bar and restaurant is a favorite of the expat yachting set, and crews from many of the yachts have dined here and pinned their ensigns on the roughly textured planks and posts. It opens for breakfast and stays open all day. Menu items include the usual array of tropical drinks, burgers, seafood *ceviche,* curried chicken, and ackee with saltfish. Main dishes come with vegetables. Come for the setting, camaraderie, and good times—the food is only secondary.

WORTH A SPLURGE

✪ **Fern Hill Club.** Mile Gully Rd. ☎ **876/993-7374.** Reservations recommended. Lunch main courses $5–$10, dinner main courses $12–$20. AE, MC, V. Daily 7:30am–9:30pm. Head east on Allan Ave. INTERNATIONAL/JAMAICAN.

One of the finest dining spots in Port Antonio has a sweeping view of the rugged coastline—the sunset-watching here is the best at the resort. Specialties like jerk chicken, jerk pork, grilled lobster, and Creole fish are served. Depending on who's in the kitchen, the food can be quite satisfactory, though once in a while (especially off-season) it might be a bit of a letdown. There's a calypso band and piano music during the week and disco music on weekends.

DINING NEARBY

Mille Fleurs. In the Hotel Mocking Bird Hill, Port Antonio. ☎ **876/993-7267.** Reservations recommended. Fixed-price dinner $36; lunch platters $6.50–$17.90. MC, V. Daily 8:30am–10:30am, noon–2:30pm, and 7–9:30pm. INTERNATIONAL.

This restaurant (associated with the previously recommended hotel) is terraced into a verdant hillside about 600 feet above sea level with sweeping views over the Jamaican coastline and the faraway harbor of Port Antonio. Sheltered from the frequent rains but open on the sides for maximum access to cooling breezes, it features candlelit dinners, well-prepared food, and lots of New Age charm. Menu items at lunch include sandwiches, salads, grilled fish, and soups. Dinners are fixed-price three-course meals featuring wholesome stylish dishes derived from around the world. The restaurant has been acclaimed by *Gourmet* magazine. You may want to try the coconut-and-garlic soup, and the fish with spicy mango-shrimp sauce is a specialty. Breads and most jams are made on the premises. Some of the dishes are designed for vegetarians.

SPORTS & OUTDOOR PURSUITS

BEACHES   Port Antonio has several white-sand beaches, some free and some charging for use of facilities. The most famous is **San San Beach,** which has recently gone private, though guests of certain hotels are admitted with a pass. **Boston Beach** is free and often has light surfing; there are picnic tables as well as a restaurant and snack bar. Before heading here, stop nearby and get the makings for a picnic lunch at the most famous center for peppery jerk pork and chicken on Jamaica. These rustic shacks also sell the much rarer jerk sausage. The dish was said to originate with the Maroons who lived in the hills beyond and occasionally ventured out to harass plantation owners. The location is 11 miles east of Port Antonio and the Blue Lagoon.

Also free is **Fairy Hill Beach** (Winnifred), with no changing rooms or showers. **Frenchman's Cove Beach** attracts a chic crowd to its white-sand beach combined with a freshwater stream. Non-hotel guests are charged a fee. **Navy Island,** once Errol Flynn's hideaway, is a fine choice for swimming (one beach is clothing optional) and snorkeling (at **Crusoe's Beach**). Take the boat from the Navy Island dock on West Street across from the Exxon station. It's a 7-minute ride to the island, and a one-way fare is 30¢. The ferry runs 24 hours a day. The island is the setting for the Navy Island Marina Resort (see above).

RAFTING   Rafting started on the Río Grande as a means of transporting bananas from the plantations to the waiting freighters. In 1871 a Yankee skipper, Lorenzo Dow Baker, decided a seat on one of the rafts was better than walking, but it wasn't until Errol Flynn arrived that the rafts became popular as a tourist attraction. Flynn used to hire the craft for his friends, and he encouraged the rafters to race down the Río Grande. Bets were placed on the winner. Now bananas are transported by road, and the raft skipper makes one or maybe two trips a day down the waterway. If you want to take a raft trip, contact **Río Grande Attractions Limited,** c/o Rafter's Restaurant, St. Margaret's Bay (☎ **876/993-5778**).

The rafts, 33-feet long and only 4-feet wide, are propelled by stout bamboo poles. There's a raised double seat about two-thirds of the way back for the two passengers. The skipper stands in the front, trousers rolled up to his knees, the water washing his feet, and guides the craft down the lively river, about 8 miles between steep hills covered with coconut palms, banana plantations, and flowers, through limestone cliffs pitted with caves, through the Tunnel of Love, a narrow cleft in the rocks, then on to wider, gentler water.

The day starts at the Rafter's Restaurant, west of Port Antonio, at Burlington on St. Margaret's Bay. Trips last 2 to 2½ hours and are offered from 8am to 4pm daily at $45 per raft (suitable for two people). From the Rafter's Restaurant, a fully insured driver will take you in your rented car to the starting point at Grants Level or Berrydale, where you board your raft. The trip ends at the Rafter's Restaurant, where you collect

Climbing Blue Mountain

Jamaica has some of the most varied and unusual topography in the Caribbean, including a mountain range laced with rough rivers, streams, and waterfalls. The 192,000-acre **Blue Mountain–John Crow Mountain National Park** is maintained by the Jamaican government. The mountainsides are covered with coffee fields, producing a blended version that's among the leading exports of Jamaica. But for the nature enthusiast, the mountains reveal an astonishingly complex series of ecosystems that change radically as you climb from sea level into the fog-shrouded peaks.

The most popular climb begins at Whitfield Hall (see above). Reaching the summit of Blue Mountain Peak (3,000 feet above sea level) requires between 5 and 6 hours each way. En route, hikers pass through acres of coffee plantations and forest, where temperatures are cooler than you might expect and where high humidity encourages thick vegetation. Along the way, watch for an amazing array of bird life, including hummingbirds, warblers, rufous-throated solitaires, yellow-bellied sapsuckers, and Greater Antillean pewees.

The best preparation against the wide ranges of temperature you'll encounter is to dress in layers and bring bottled water. If you opt for a 2am departure to catch the sunrise from atop the peak, carry a flashlight as well. Sneakers are usually adequate, though many climbers bring hiking boots to Jamaica solely in anticipation of their trek up Blue Mountain. Be aware that even during the dry season (December to March), rainfall is common. During the rainy season (the rest of the year), these peaks can get up to 150 inches of rainfall, and fogs and mists are frequent.

You can always hike alone into the Jamaican wilderness, but considering the dangers of such an undertaking and the crime you might encounter, we don't advise it. A better bet is engaging one of Kingston's best specialists in eco-sensitive tours, **Sunventure Tours,** 30 Balmoral Ave., Kingston 10, Jamaica, W.I. (☎ **876/960-6685**). The staff can always arrange an individualized tour, but if you're interested in their mainstream offerings, here are two: The Blue Mountain Sunrise Tour is a camp-style overnight in one of Jamaica's most inaccessible areas. For $140 per person, participants are retrieved at their Kingston hotels and driven to an isolated ranger station, Wildflower Lodge, accessible only via four-wheel-drive vehicle. The two-stage hike begins at 4:30pm, and a simple mountaineer's supper is served at 6pm around a campfire at a ranger station near Portland Gap. At 3am, climbers hike by moonlight and flashlight to an aerie selected because of its view of the sunrise. Climbers stay aloft until about noon, then head back down for a return to their hotels by 4pm. There's also an excursion from Kingston Y's Waterfall on the Black River, in southern Jamaica's Elizabeth Parish. Participants congregate in Kingston at 6:30am for a transfer to a raft and boating party near the hamlet of Lacovia and an all-day waterborne excursion to a region of unusual ecological interest. Depending on the number of participants, fees range from $80 to $100 per person, including lunch.

your car, which has been returned by the driver. If you feel like it, take a picnic lunch, but bring enough for the skipper too.

SNORKELING & SCUBA DIVING   The best outfitter is **Lady Godiva's Dive Shop** in Dragon Bay (☎ **876/993-8988**), 7 miles from Port Antonio. Full dive equipment is available, and the service is provided daily. Technically, you can snorkel off most of the beaches in Port Antonio, but are likely to see much more farther offshore. The very best spot is San San Bay by Monkey Island. The reef is extremely active and full of exciting marine life. Lady Godiva offers two excursions daily to this spot for $10 per person. Snorkeling equipment costs $9 for a full day's rental.

EXPLORING THE AREA

Athenry Gardens and Cave of Nonsuch. Portland. ☎ **876/993-3740.** Admission (including a guide for gardens and cave) $5 adults, $2.50 children 11 and under. Daily 9am–5pm (last tour, 4:30pm). From Harbour St. in Port Antonio, turn south in front of the Anglican church onto Red Hassel Rd. and proceed about a mile to Breastworks community (fork in road); take the left fork, cross a narrow bridge, go immediately left after the bridge, and proceed about 3½ miles to the village of Nonsuch.

Twenty minutes from Port Antonio, it's an easy drive and an easy walk to see the stalagmites, stalactites, fossilized marine life, and evidence of Arawak civilization in Nonsuch. The cave is 1.5 million years old. From the Athenry Gardens, there are panoramic views over the island and the sea. The gardens are filled with coconut palms, flowers, and trees, and complete guided tours are given.

Crystal Springs. Buff Bay, Portland. ☎ **876/996-1400.** Admission J$100 ($2.85) adults, J$50 ($1.45) children. Daily 9am–5pm.

Crystal Springs is a tract of forested land whose borders were specified in 1655. Then it was attached to a nearby plantation whose Great House is now under separate (private) ownership. Visitors, however, can trek through the organization's 156 acres of forest, whose shelter is much beloved by bird- and wildlife. A simple restaurant is located on the premises. The series of cottages built in the early 1990s are usually rented to visiting ornithologists who don't care for the amenities or distractions of a traditional resort.

Folly Great House. On the outskirts of Port Antonio on the way to Trident Village, going east along the A4. Free admission.

This house was reputedly built in 1905 by Arthur Mitchell, an American millionaire, for his wife, Annie, daughter of Charles Tiffany, founder of the famous New York jewelry store. Sea water was used in the concrete mixtures of its foundations and mortar, and the house began to collapse only 11 years after they moved in. Because of the beautiful location, it's easy to see what a fine Great House it must have been.

Somerset Falls. 8 miles west of Port Antonio, just past Hope Bay on the A4. ☎ **876/913-0108.** Tour $3. Daily 9am–5pm.

Here the waters of the Daniels River pour down a deep gorge through a rain forest, with waterfalls and foaming cascades. You can take a short ride in an electric gondola to the hidden falls. A stop on the daily Grand Jamaica Tour from Ocho Rios, this is one of Jamaica's most historic sites; the falls were used by the Spanish before the English captured the island. At the falls, you can swim in the deep rock pools and buy sandwiches, light meals, soft drinks, beer, and liquor at the snack bar. The guided tour includes the gondola ride and a visit to both a cave and a freshwater fish farm.

8 Kingston

Kingston, the largest English-speaking city in the Caribbean with a population of more than 650,000, is the capital of Jamaica. It sits on the plain between Blue Mountain and the sea. The buildings are a mix of very modern, graceful, old, and plain ramshackle. It's a busy city, as you might expect, with a natural harbor that's the seventh largest in the world. The University of the West Indies has its campus on the edge of the city. The cultural center of Jamaica is here, along with industry, finance, and government. However, there's a terrible crime problem, and it's better to stay outside of the city.

NEARBY ACCOMMODATIONS YOU CAN AFFORD

Remember to ask if the 12% room tax is included in the rate quoted when you make your reservation. The rates listed below are year-round unless otherwise noted. All leading hotels in security-conscious Kingston have guards.

Pine Grove Mountain Chalets. Content Gap P.A., St. Andrew (for information, write Pine Grove Mountain Chalets, 62 Duke St., Kingston, Jamaica, W.I.). ☎ **876/977-8009.** Fax 876/977-8001. 17 units. Year-round $70 single or double. MAP $25 per person. MC, V.

This simple inn occupies what was a coffee plantation in the 1930s, with a view over misty hills and the lights of faraway Kingston, landscaped brick walkways, and topiary trees. The accommodations are in one-story motel-like units, each with basic amenities but good beds and small but tidy baths. Three contain slightly battered kitchenettes, for which there's no extra charge. Owners Ronald and Marcia Thwaites deliberately avoided the installation of air-conditioning in favor of the natural breezes. There's a restaurant, and hiking trips into the nearby mountains can be arranged.

Whitfield Hall. Halfway up Blue Mountain. Contact John Allgrove, 8 Armon Jones Crescent, Kingston 6, Jamaica, W.I. ☎ **876/927-0986** (preferably 7 to 9pm). 30 beds in 7 units, none with bathroom; 1 cottage with kitchen and bathroom. $14 per person in communal room; $55 per night in cottage for up to 4 (extra person, to a maximum of 8, $14). No credit cards. For directions, see below.

Offbeat Whitfield Hall is a high-altitude hostel about 6 miles from the hamlet of Mavis Bank. It's on a coffee plantation dating from 1776 and is the last inhabited house before you get to the peak at 7,402 feet. The main allure is the opportunity to see Blue Mountain from a hill-climber's viewpoint. The accommodations for 30 guests are in the bleakest dorm mode. Blankets and linen are provided, but personal items (towels, soap, and food) are not. There's a deep freezer and a refrigerator, as well as cooking facilities, crockery, and cutlery. You bring your own food and share the kitchen and the two baths. There's no restaurant. All water comes from a spring, and lighting is by kerosene lamps called Tilleys. A wood fire warms everyone—it gets cold in the mountains at night.

Most visitors come to see the sunrise from the summit of Blue Mountain, which means getting up at around 2 or 3am to walk the final distance along a bridle path through the forest. The route is clearly marked, and you need a good flashlight and warm clothing, along with hiking boots or strong shoes. It's a 3-hour walk each way. It's also possible to hire a mule or a horse to make the jaunt, accompanied by a guide, for $42 round-trip for the 13-mile journey.

To get here, you can drive to Mavis Bank, about 20 miles from Kingston. Head northeast along Old Hope Road to the suburb of Papine, then proceed to Gordon Town. At Gordon Town, turn right over the bridge near the police station and drive into the hills for some 10 miles until you reach Mavis Bank. As alternatives, Whitfield Hall will send a four-wheel-drive for you for $28, or you can walk. You can also get to Mavis Bank by bus from Kingston. Some people request they be picked up in Kingston by a Land Rover for $46 each way for up to six passengers; extra passengers pay $5.50.

GREAT DEALS ON DINING

✪ **Chelsea Jerk Centre.** 7 Chelsea Ave. ☎ **876/926-6322.** Reservations recommended. Jerk chicken J$400 ($11.40); 1 lb. jerk pork J$300 ($8.55). AE, MC, V. Mon–Thurs 11am–11pm, Fri–Sat 11am–midnight, Sun 1–10pm. JAMAICAN.

Between the New Kingston Shopping Centre and the Wyndham New Kingston Hotel, this is the city's most popular provider of the Jamaican delicacies jerk pork and jerk chicken. You can order food to take out or eat in the comfortably battered dining room. Though no appetizers are served, you can order a side portion of what the scrawled chalkboard refers to as Festival (fried cornmeal dumplings). On Friday nights, steamed fish is the specialty.

The Hot Pot. 2 Altamont Terrace. ☎ **876/929-3906.** Main courses $4–$6. MC, V. Daily 8am–10pm. JAMAICAN.

A short walk from the first-class Pegasus and Wyndham hotels, this uncomplicated Jamaican-run restaurant attracts an animated local crowd and serves simple but straightforward cuisine. In a red-and-white interior, near a view of a modest garden, you can drink Red Stripe beer or rum concoctions. Menu items include red-pea soup, beef stew, roast chicken, steaks, mutton, and fish.

✪ **Devonshire Restaurant/The Grogg Shoppe.** In Devon House, 26 Hope Rd. ☎ **876/929-7046.** Reservations recommended for Devonshire only. Dinner J$250–J$900 ($7.15–$25.65); lunch J$200–J$600 ($5.70–$17.10). AE, MC, V. Mon–Fri noon–3pm and 6–10pm, Sat 6–10pm. JAMAICAN/SEAFOOD/STEAK.

These two restaurants near New Kingston are in what were the brick-sided servants' quarters of Kingston's most-visited mansion, Devon House. The more formal of the two is the Devonshire, now a steak-and-seafood grill. You can eat on patios under the trees, in sight of the royal palms and the fountain in front of the historic Great House. Appetizers include a tidbit of jerk pork or a bowl of soup (perhaps Jamaican red-pea or pumpkin soup). Main dishes feature Jamaican ackee and saltfish, barbecued chicken, or steamed snapper. Also tasty are the unusual homemade ice creams made of local fruits, such as soursop. Blue Mountain tea or coffee is served. The bars for both restaurants serve 11 rum punches and 10 fruit punches. Especially popular is the Devon Duppy, combining virtually every variety of rum in the bartender's inventory. Many aficionados opt for these drinks on one of the Grogg Shoppe's two terraces.

HITTING THE BEACHES

You don't really come to Kingston for beaches, but there are some. To the southwest of the sprawling city are black sandy beaches at both **Hellshire Beach** and **Fort Clarence,** popular with locals on weekends. These beaches have changing rooms and heavy security, along with numerous food stands. The reggae concerts at Fort Clarence are legendary on the island. Just past Fort Clarence, the fisherman's beach at **Naggo Head** is an even hipper destination, or so Kingston beach buffs claim. After a swim in the refreshing waters, opt for one of the food stands selling fried fish and *bammy,* the latter made from cassava. The beach closest to the city (though it's not very good) is **Lime Cay,** on the outskirts of Kingston Harbour. The little island can be approached after a short boat ride from Morgan's Harbour at Port Royal.

SEEING THE SIGHTS

Even if you're staying at Ocho Rios or Port Antonio, you may want to visit Kingston for brief sightseeing and for trips to nearby Port Royal and Spanish Town.

IN TOWN   Downtown Kingston, the old part of the town, is centered around **Sir William Grant Park,** formerly Victoria Park, a showpiece of lawns, lights, and fountains. North of the park is the **Ward Theatre,** the oldest in the New World, where the traditional Jamaican pantomime is staged from December 26 to early April. To the east is **Coke Methodist Church,** and to the south, the equally historic **Kingston Parish Church.**

One of the major attractions, **Devon House,** 26 Hope Rd. (☎ **876/929-7029**), was built in 1881 by George Stiebel, a Jamaican who became one of the first black millionaires in the Caribbean. He made his fortune mining in Latin America. A striking classical building, the house has been restored to its original beauty by the Jamaican National Trust. The grounds contain craft shops, boutiques, two restaurants, shops selling the best ice cream in Jamaica (in exotic fruit flavors), and a bakery and pastry shop with Jamaican puddings and desserts. The main house also displays furniture of various periods and styles. Admission to the main house is J$110 ($3.15), and it's open Tuesday to Saturday 9:30am to 5pm. Admission to the grounds (including the shops and restaurants) is free. Almost next door to Devon House are the sentried gates of **Jamaica House,** residence of the prime minister, a fine white-columned building set well back from the road.

Continuing along Hope Road, at the crossroads of Lady Musgrave and King's House roads, turn left and you'll see a gate on the left with its own traffic light. This leads to **King's House,** the official residence of the governor-general of Jamaica, the queen's representative on the island. The outside and front lawn of the gracious residence, set in 200 acres of well-tended parkland, is sometimes open to viewing Monday to Friday from 10am to 5pm. The secretarial offices are housed next door in an old wooden building set on brick arches. In front of the house is a gigantic banyan tree in whose roots, legend says, *duppies* (as ghosts are called in Jamaica) take refuge when they're not living in the cotton trees.

Between Old Hope and Mona roads, a short distance from the Botanical Gardens, is the **University of the West Indies** (☎ **876/927-1660**), built in 1948 on the Mona Sugar Estate. Ruins of old mills, storehouses, and aquaducts are juxtaposed with modern buildings on what must be the world's most beautifully situated campus. The chapel, an old sugar-factory building, was transported stone by stone from Trelawny and rebuilt. The remains of the original sugar factory are well preserved and give a good idea of how sugar was made in slave days.

The **National Library of Jamaica** (formerly the West India Reference Library), Institute of Jamaica, 12 East St. (☎ **876/922-0620**), a storehouse of the history, culture, and traditions of Jamaica and the Caribbean, is the world's finest working library for West Indian studies. It has the most comprehensive, up-to-date, and balanced collection of materials on the region, including books, newspapers, photographs, maps, and prints. Exhibits highlight different aspects of Jamaica and West Indian life. It's open Monday to Thursday 9am to 5pm and Friday 9am to 4pm.

The **Bob Marley Museum** (formerly Tuff Gong Studio), 56 Hope Rd. (☎ **876/927-9152**), is the most-visited sight in Kingston, but if you're not a Bob Marley fan, it may not mean much to you. The clapboard house with its garden and high surrounding wall was the famous reggae singer's home and recording studio until his death. You can tour the singer's house and view assorted Marley memorabilia, and you might even catch a glimpse of his various children, who often frequent the grounds. The museum is open Monday to Saturday 9am to 4pm. Admission is J$350 ($10) for adults, J$175 ($5) for children 4 to 12; free for children 3 and under. It's reached by bus no. 70 or 75 from Halfway Tree, but take a cab to save yourself the hassle of dealing with Kingston public transportation.

IN PORT ROYAL   From West Beach Dock, Kingston, a ferry ride of 20 to 30 minutes will take you to Port Royal, which conjures up visions of swashbuckling pirates led by Henry Morgan, swilling grog in harbor taverns. This was once one of the New World's largest trading centers, with a reputation for being the wickedest city on earth. Blackbeard stopped here regularly on his Caribbean trips. But the whole thing came to an end at 11:43am on June 7, 1692, when a third of the town disappeared underwater during a devastating earthquake. Nowadays, Port Royal, with its memories of the past, has been designated by the government for redevelopment as a tourist destination.

Buccaneer Scuba Club, Morgan's Harbour, Port Royal, outside Kingston (☎ 876/967-8061), is one of Jamaica's leading dive and water-sports operators. It offers a wide range of dive sites to accommodate various divers' tastes, from the incredible Texas Wreck to the unspoiled beauty of the Turtle Reef. PADI courses are also available. A wide array of water sports are offered, including waterskiing, bodyboarding, ring-skiing, and even a banana boat ride. One-tank dives begin at $28, with a boat snorkeling trip costing $15, including equipment, for 1 hour.

As you drive along the Palisades, you arrive first at **St. Peter's Church.** It's usually closed, but you may persuade the caretaker, who lives opposite, to open it if you want to see the silver plate, said to be spoils captured by Henry Morgan from the cathedral in Panama. In the ill-kept graveyard is the tomb of Lewis Galdy, a Frenchman swallowed up and subsequently regurgitated by the 1692 earthquake.

Fort Charles (☎ 876/967-8438), the only one remaining of Port Royal's six forts, has withstood attack, earthquake, fire, and hurricane. Built in 1656 and later strengthened by Morgan for his own purposes, the fort was expanded and further armed in the 1700s, until its firepower boasted more than 100 cannons, covering both the land and the sea approaches. In 1779, Britain's naval hero, Horatio Lord Nelson, was commander of the fort and trod the wooden walkway inside the western parapet as he kept watch for the French invasion fleet. Scale models of the fort and ships of past eras are displayed. The fort is open daily from 9am to 5pm, charging J$140 ($4) admission.

Part of the complex, **Giddy House,** once the Royal Artillery storehouse, is another example of what the earth's movements can do. Walking across the tilted floor is an eerie and strangely disorienting experience.

IN SPANISH TOWN   From 1662 to 1872, Spanish Town was the capital of the island. Founded by the Spaniards as Villa de la Vega, it was sacked by Cromwell's men in 1655, and all traces of Roman Catholicism were obliterated. The English cathedral, surprisingly retaining a Spanish name, **St. Jago de la Vega,** was built in 1666 and rebuilt after being destroyed by a 1712 hurricane. As you drive into town from Kingston, the ancient cathedral, rebuilt in 1714, catches your eye with its brick tower and two-tiered wooden steeple, added in 1831. Since the cathedral was built on the foundation and remains of the old Spanish church, it's half-English and half-Spanish and displays two distinct styles: Romanesque and Gothic. Of cruciform design and built mostly of brick, the cathedral is one of the island's most interesting buildings. The black-and-white marble stones of the aisles are interspersed with ancient tombstones, and the walls are heavy with marble memorials that are almost a chronicle of Jamaica's history, dating back as far as 1662.

Beyond the cathedral, turn right and 2 blocks along you'll reach Constitution Street and the **Town Square.** This little square is surrounded by towering royal palms. On the west side is **King's House,** gutted by fire in 1925, though the façade has been restored. This was the residence of Jamaica's British governors until 1872, when the capital was transferred to Kingston. Many celebrated guests stayed here, among them Lord Nelson, Admiral Rodney, Captain Bligh of HMS *Bounty* fame, and King William IV.

Beyond the house is the **Jamaica People's Museum of Craft & Technology,** Old King's House, Constitution Square (☎ 876/922-0620), open Monday to Friday from 10am to 4pm. Admission is J$10 (30¢) for adults and J$5 (15¢) for children.

The garden contains examples of old farm machinery, an old water mill wheel, a hand-turned sugar mill, a fire engine, and other items. An outbuilding displays a museum of crafts and technology, together with a number of smaller agricultural implements. In the small archaeological museum are old prints, models, and maps of the town's grid layout from the 1700s.

The streets around the old Town Square contain many fine Georgian town houses intermixed with tin-roofed shacks. Nearby is the **market,** so busy in the morning you'll find it difficult, almost dangerous, to drive through. It provides, however, a bustling scene of Jamaican life.

SHOPPING

Cool arcades lead off from **King Street,** but everywhere you'll see a teeming mass of people going about their business. There are some beggars and the inevitable sales-people who sidle up and offer "hot stuff, mon," frequently touting highly polished brass lightly dipped in gold and offered at high prices as real gold. The hucksters do accept a polite but firm no, but don't let them keep you talking or you'll end up buying—they're very persuasive!

For many years, the richly evocative paintings of Haiti were viewed as the most valuable contribution to the arts in the Caribbean. There is on Jamaica, however, a rapidly growing perception of itself as one of the artistic leaders of the Third World. An articulate core of Caribbean critics is focusing the attention of the art world at large on the unusual, eclectic, and sometimes politically motivated paintings being produced on Jamaica.

The **Frame Centre Gallery,** 10 Tangerine Place (☎ **876/926-4644),** is one of Jamaica's most important galleries, and the founder and guiding force, Guy McIntosh, is widely respected as a patron of the Jamaican arts. Committed to presenting quality Jamaican art, it has three viewing areas and carries a varied collection of more than 300 works. The **Mutual Life Gallery,** in the Mutual Life Centre, 2 Oxford Rd. (☎ **876/ 926-9025**), is one of the country's most prominent galleries, the corporate headquarters of a major insurance company. After you pass a security check, you can climb to the corporation's mezzanine level for an insight into the changing face of Jamaican art. Exhibits change every 2 weeks.

The **Kingston Crafts Market,** at the west end of Harbour Street downtown, is a large covered area of individually owned stalls; you can reach the market through thoroughfares like Straw Avenue, Drummer's Lane, and Cheapside. All kinds of island crafts are sold: wooden plates and bowls, trays, ashtrays, mats, baskets, and pepperpots made from mahoe, the national wood of the island. Batik shirts and cotton shirts with gaudy designs are sold. Banners for wall decoration are inscribed with the Jamaican coat-of-arms, and wood masks often have elaborately carved faces. Here you can learn the art of bargaining and ask for a *brawta* (free bonus). However, be aware that, unlike in Haiti, bargaining is *not* a Jamaican tradition. Vendors will take something off the price, but not very much.

The **Shops at Devon House,** at Devon House, 26 Hope Rd. (☎ **876/929-7029**), are associated with one of Jamaica's most beautiful and historic mansions. These shops ring the borders of a 200-year-old courtyard once used by slaves and servants. Though about 10 shops operate from these premises, 4 of the largest are operated by Things Jamaican, a nationwide emporium dedicated to the enhancement of the country's handcrafts. Shops include the Cookery, offering island-made sauces and spices, and the Pottery, selling crockery and stoneware. Look for pewter knives and forks, based on designs of pewter items discovered in archaeological digs in the Port Royal area in

1965. Other outlets are a children's shop, a leather shop, and a stained-glass shop, as well as a gallery with paintings, ceramics, and sculpture.

9 Mandeville

The English town, Mandeville lies on a plateau more than 2,000 feet above the sea in the tropical highlands. The commercial part of the town is small and surrounded by a sprawling residential area popular with the large North American expat population mostly involved with the bauxite-mining industry. Much cooler than the coastal resorts, it's the best center from which to explore the entire island.

Shopping in the town is a pleasure, whether in the old center or in one of the modern complexes, such as **Grove Court.** The **market** in the center of town teems with life, particularly on weekends, when the country folk bus into town. The town has several interesting old buildings. The square-towered **church** built in 1820 has fine stained glass, and the little churchyard tells an interesting story of the past inhabitants of Mandeville. The **Court House,** built in 1816, is a fine old Georgian stone-and-wood building with a pillared portico reached by a sweeping double staircase. There's also **Marshall's Pen,** one of the Great Houses, in Mandeville.

ACCOMMODATIONS YOU CAN AFFORD

✪ **Hotel Astra.** 62 Ward Ave., Mandeville, Jamaica, W.I. ☎ **876/962-3725.** Fax 876/962-1461. www.access-ja.com/countrystyle. E-mail: comtours@cwjamaica.com. 22 units. TV TEL. Year-round $65 single or double; $150 suite. Rates include continental breakfast. AE, MC, V.

Our top choice for a stay in this area is the family-run Astra, operated by Diana McIntyre-Pike, known to her family and friends as Thunderbird. She's always coming to the rescue of guests, happily picking up people in her own car and taking them around to see the sights, and organizing introductions to island people. The accommodations are mainly in two buildings reached along open walkways. Units are spartan with well-worn beds, but they're well maintained and have basic comforts. There is a pool and a sauna, and the inn offers therapeutic massages. You can also spend the afternoon at the Manchester Country Club, where tennis and golf are available. Horses can be provided for cross-country treks.

The Country Fresh Restaurant offers excellent meals. Lunch or dinner offers a choice of a homemade soup like red pea or pumpkin, followed by local fish and chicken specialties. The kitchen is under the personal control of Diana, who's always collecting awards in Jamaican culinary competitions. Someone is on hand to explain the niceties of any Jamaican dish. A complete meal is $12 to $20, with some more expensive items like lobster and steak. Dinner is served from 6 to 9:30pm daily. Thursday is barbecue night, when guests and townsfolk gather around the pool to dine. The Revival Room is the bar, where everything including the stools is made from rum-soaked barrels. Try the family's own homemade liqueur and reviver, a pick-me-up made from Guinness, rum, egg, condensed milk, and nutmeg. It's open daily from 11am to 11pm.

Mandeville Hotel. 4 Hotel St. (P.O. Box 78), Mandeville, Jamaica, W.I. ☎ **876/962-2460.** Fax 876/962-0700. 56 units. TV TEL. Year-round $65–$125 single or double; from $95 suite. AE, MC, V.

This ornate hotel opened in the early 1900s and for a while housed part of the British military garrison. In the 1970s, the venerable hotel was replaced with a modern peach-colored building, which was completely refurbished in 1982. It lies in the heart of Mandeville, across from the police station. The rooms, which range from small to spacious, are furnished with Jamaican styling, often including a four-poster bed and mahogany furniture. The mattresses are a bit old but still comfortable. The baths are old fashioned but tidy. The hotel has an outdoor and indoor bar and a spacious lounge. Activity centers mainly around the pool and the coffee shop, where substantial meals are served at moderate prices. There are attractive gardens, and golf and tennis can be played at the nearby Manchester Country Club.

GREAT DEALS ON DINING

Mandeville Hotel. 4 Hotel St. ☎ **876/962-2460.** Reservations recommended. Main courses $12–$30. AE, MC, V. Daily 6:30am–9:30pm. JAMAICAN.

Close to the city center, near the police station, and popular with local businesspeople, the Mandeville Hotel offers a wide selection of sandwiches, plus milkshakes, tea, and coffee. In the restaurant the a la carte menu features Jamaican pepperpot soup, lobster Thermidor, fresh snapper, and kingfish. Potatoes and vegetables are included in the main-dish prices. There's no pretension to the homemade and basic food, almost like that served in the house of a typical Jamaican family. From the restaurant's dining room, you'll have a view of the hotel's pool and the green hills of central Jamaica.

EXPLORING THE AREA

Mandeville is the sort of place where you can become well acquainted with the people and feel like part of the community. One of the largest and driest **caves** on the island is at Oxford, about 9 miles northwest of Mandeville. Signs direct you to it after you leave Mile Gully, a village dominated by St. George's Church, some 175 years old.

The **Manchester Country Club,** Brumalia Road (☎ **876/962-2403**), is Jamaica's oldest golf course but has only nine holes. Beautiful vistas unfold from 2,201 feet above sea level. Greens fees are J$750 ($21.40), with caddy fees at J$500 ($14.25). The course also has a clubhouse. The club is also one of the best venues in central Jamaica for tennis.

Among the interesting attractions, **Marshall's Pen** is one of the Great Houses. A coffee plantation home some 200 years old, it has been restored and furnished in traditional style. In 1795 it was owned by one of the governors of Jamaica, the earl of Balcarres. It has been in the hands of the Sutton family since 1939; they farm the 300 acres and breed Jamaican Red Poll cattle. This is very much a private home and should be treated as such, though guided tours can be arranged. A contribution of $10 is requested for a minimum of four people. For information or an appointment to see the house, contact Ann or Robert Sutton, **Marshall's Pen,** Great House (P.O. Box 58), Mandeville, Jamaica, W.I. (☎ **876/904-5454**). Robert Sutton is coauthor of *Birds of Jamaica,* a photographic field guide published by Cambridge University Press.

10 The South Coast

Known as "Undiscovered Jamaica," the south coast attracts more foreign visitors every year and is a mecca for the budget traveler.

Local adventures are plentiful too. Among the most popular is South Coast Safaris' boat tour up the Black River—once a major logging conduit (and still home to freshwater crocodiles). Another favorite is the trip to the Y. S. Falls, where seven spectacular cascades tumble over rocks in the foothills of the Santa Cruz Mountains, just north of the town of Middle Quarters (famed for its spicy freshwater shrimp).

The south coast has been called the sunniest on Jamaica, and that's true. It also means the coast is the most arid. The Arawak lived here and were discovered by Columbus when he circumnavigated Jamaica in 1494. Five generations of Spaniards raised cattle on ranches on the broad savannas of St. Elizabeth, when not repelling French pirates.

To reach the south coast, head east from Negril, following the signposts to Savanna-La-Mar. This is Sheffield Road, and the highway isn't particularly good until it broadens into Route A2 at Savanna. After passing through the village of Bluefields, continue southeast to the small town of Black River, opening onto Black River Bay.

ACCOMMODATIONS YOU CAN AFFORD

Invercauld Great House & Hotel. 66 High St. (P.O. Box 12), Black River, St. Elizabeth, Jamaica, W.I. ☎ **876/965-2750.** Fax 876/965-2751. 48 units. TV TEL. Winter $48–$51 per person double; $62 per person suite. Off-season $44–$50 per person double; $54 per person suite. AE, MC, V.

In 1889, when Black River's port was one of the most important on Jamaica, a Scottish merchant imported most of the materials for the construction of this white-sided manor house. Today the renovated and much-enlarged house is a hotel. A few rooms are in the original high-ceilinged house; the rest are in a concrete outbuilding added in 1991. The rooms are clean and stripped down, usually with mahogany furniture made by local craftsmen, including the comfortable beds. All are air-conditioned except for two single rooms that have ceiling fans. On the premises is a concrete patio, a pool, a tennis court, and the conservatively dignified Willow restaurant. It's open daily for lunch and dinner, charging $20 to $24 for three-course meals of lobster, chicken, and fish.

✪ **Jake's.** Calabash Bay, Treasure Beach, St. Elizabeth, Jamaica, W.I. ☎ **800/OUTPOST** in the U.S., or 876/965-0635. Fax 876/965-0552. www.islandoutpost.com. E-mail: reservations@islandoutpost.com. 10 units. Year-round $95 single or double; $150 suite. AE, MC, V.

In a setting of cactus-studded hills in the arid southwest (in total contrast to the rest of tropically-lush Jamaica), this is a special haven, an ideal place for an off-the-record tryst. Perched on a cliffside overlooking the ocean, this complex of cottages is an explosion of colors, everything from funky purple to "toreador red." Each room is individually decorated, everything inspired by Sally Henzell, a Jamaican of British ancestry who's married to Perry Henzell, art director on *The Harder They Come,* that classic reggae film. Sally cites controversial Catalán architect Antoni Gaudí as her mentor in the creation of Jake's—especially in the generous use of cracked mosaic tile so familiar to Barcelona devotees. The rooms could contain anything Sally might've picked up at the flea market. But be warned: There's no air-conditioning and days are hot in the "desert." The fare is simple Jamaican, but it's tasty and good, made with fresh ingredients. Begin with the pepperpot soup and go on to the catch of the day, perfectly prepared.

Treasure Beach Hotel. Treasure Beach (P.O. Box 5), Black River, St. Elizabeth, Jamaica, W.I. ☎ **876/965-0110.** 36 units. A/C TEL. Winter $99 single; $110 double; $143 suite. Off-season $88 single; $99 double; $113.30 suite. Full board $27 per person. AE, MC, V.

Midway between Black River and Pedro Cross on a steep but lushly landscaped hillside above Treasure Beach, this white-sided hotel was built in the mid-1970s and renovated about a decade later. Although its staff is young and inexperienced, this is the largest and most elaborate hotel on Jamaica's south coast. Its centerpiece is a long and airy rattan-furnished bar whose windows look down the hillside to the beach and the hotel's 11 acres that flank it. Each unit has a ceiling fan and a veranda or patio, plus somewhat spartan rooms with well-used beds. Housekeeping is good, even if the furnishings are a bit tattered. Amenities include a freshwater pool and the Yabo restaurant, a simple affair with casual service open for breakfast, lunch, and dinner.

GREAT DEALS ON DINING

Bridge House Inn. 14 Crane Rd., Black River, St. Elizabeth, Jamaica, W.I. ☎ **876/ 965-2361.** Reservations recommended. Full meals $7–$18. MC, V. Daily 7:30am–3pm and 5–11pm. JAMAICAN.

This is an uncomplicated and very Jamaican restaurant in one of the town's few hotels, built in the early 1980s in a concrete beachfront motif in a grove of coconut palms and sea grapes. Guests include a cross-section of the region, as well as tourists. The menu includes complete dinners (fish, chicken, curried goat, oxtail, stewed beef, or lobster), served politely and efficiently by a staff of hardworking waiters. The chef has a secret recipe for pork chops that's so good people drive for miles around to sample it. A separate bar area dispenses drinks. Main dishes include soup, salad, and your choice of vegetables. Also on the premises are 14 rooms, some air-conditioned, and each with ceiling fan, TV, and simple furniture. Ten rooms are air-conditioned. In winter singles are priced at $33 and doubles $47, the prices lowered off-season to $25 single or $40 double.

THE ROAD TO ADVENTURE

The **Black River,** the longest stream on Jamaica, has mangrove trees, crocodiles in the wild, and the insectivorous bladderwort, plus hundreds of different species of bird including herons, ospreys, and many of the wading variety. You can indeed go on safari. The best tours are by **South Coast Safaris,** operating out of the town of Black River (☎ 876/965-2513 for reservations). The cost is $15; children 11 and under go for half price and those 2 and under go for free. Tours last about 1½ hours and cover 12 miles (6 miles upstream, 6 miles back) with a running commentary on the ecology and history of the Black River. Tours are at 9am, 11am, 12:30pm, 2pm, and 4pm daily. Specialized tours can be arranged for any number of groups, including bird-watchers, photographers, botanists, and natural-history buffs.

After leaving Black River, where you can find hotels and restaurants, you can continue north along the A2 to Mandeville or else go directly southeast to Treasure Beach. A2 north takes you to **Middle Quarters,** a village on the plains of the Great Morass, through which the Black River runs. Day visitors often stop here and order a local delicacy, pepper shrimps.

Just north of the town of Middle Quarters is **Y. S. Falls,** where seven waterfalls form crystal pools. Guests take a jitney and go through grazing lands and a horse paddock on the way to the falls, where they cool off in the waters and often enjoy a picnic lunch. After Middle Quarters, the road cuts east toward Mandeville along Bamboo Avenue, a scenic drive along 2 miles of highway covered with bamboo. Here you'll see a working plantation, Holland Estate, growing sugarcane, citrus, papaya, and mango.

If you've decided to take the southern-coast route to **Treasure Beach,** follow the signs to Treasure Beach directly southeast of Black River. The treasures here are seashells in many shapes and sizes. This is the site of the Treasure Beach Hotel (see above). To the east of Treasure Beach in Southfield is **Lovers' Leap,** a cliff plunging hundreds of feet into the sea. Two slave lovers reportedly jumped to their deaths here rather than be sold off to different masters.

Martinique 15

Martinique and Guadeloupe aren't French colonies, as many visitors assume, but the westernmost of France, meaning their inhabitants are full-fledged citizens of *la belle France,* a status they've enjoyed since 1946. Martinique has mountains dotted with lush vegetation, rain forests bursting with bamboo and breadfruit trees, and even a patch of desert in the south. But most visitors, including those from France, come just for the white-sand beaches.

In island boutiques you can buy that Hermès scarf you've always wanted, certainly a bottle of Chanel perfume, or even some Baccarat crystal. For breakfast, freshly baked croissants will arrive on your plate. French cheese is shipped in from Marseilles, and the Creole cuisine is among the most distinctive in the West Indies.

Napoléon's empress, Joséphine, was born on Martinique in 1763, the same year France relinquished rights to Canada in exchange for the French West Indies. The mistress of Louis XIV, Mme de Maintenon, also lived here, in the small fishing village of Le Prêcheur. Columbus was the first to chart Martinique. The French took possession in the name of Louis XIII in 1635 and then established sugarcane plantations and rum distilleries. In spite of some intrusions by British forces, the French have remained here ever since. In the beginning, the French imported slaves from Africa to work the plantations, but at the time of the French Revolution the practice began to decline on Martinique. It wasn't until the mid-19th century, however, that Victor Schoelcher, a Paris-born deputy from Alsace, successfully lobbied to abolish slavery.

On almond-shaped Martinique, the ground is mountainous, especially in the rain-forested northern part where Mount Pelée, a volcano, rises to 4,656 feet. In the center of the island the mountains are smaller, with Carbet Peak reaching a 3,960-foot summit. The high hills rising among the peaks or mountains are called *mornes.* The southern part of Martinique has only big hills, reaching peaks of 1,500 feet at Vauclin and 1,400 feet at Diamant. The irregular coastline provides five bays, dozens of coves, and miles of sandy beaches.

The climate is relatively mild, the average temperature in the 75°F-to-85°F range, but at higher elevations it's considerably cooler. The island is cooled by a wind the French called *alizé,* and rain is frequent but doesn't last very long. Late August to November might be called the rainy season; April to September are the hottest months.

The early Carib peoples, who gave Columbus such a hostile reception, called Martinique the "island of flowers," and indeed it has remained so. The vegetation is lush, and includes hibiscus, poinsettias, bougainvillea, coconut palms, and mango trees. Almost any fruit that can grow in the ground sprouts out of Martinique's soil—pineapples, avocados, bananas, papayas, and custard apples. Bird-watchers are often pleased at the number of hummingbirds, mountain whistlers, blackbirds, mongoose, and multicolored butterflies. After sunset there's a permanent concert of grasshoppers, frogs, and crickets.

However, all this lushness, tropical beauty, and French/Creole food come at a price. Martinique has a reputation for being one of the Caribbean's more expensive destinations, especially in the price of its food, a tradition it shares with mainland France. Its hotel and food prices are high. To beat the high cost of dining out, we suggest picnicking during the day and then splurging at dinner. Grocery stores are loaded with choice tidbits from mainland France, and a bottle of French wine will cost you less here than on the non-French islands in the Caribbean.

Taxis and automobile rentals are high, so try to stay at a place on the beach (or near a beach) so you won't have long, expensive commutes every day. True budget hotels are hard to find on Martinique, but we have several suggestions below.

1 Essentials

VISITOR INFORMATION

For information before you go, call the **French Government Tourist Office** (☎ **800/ 391-4909** or 202/659-7779; www.francetourism.com). In Canada, the **Martinique Tourist Office** is located at 2159 rue Mackay, Montréal, Quebec H3G 2J2 (☎ **800/ 361-9099** or 514/844-8566).

The **Office Départemental du Tourisme** is on boulevard Alfassa in Fort-de-France, across the waterfront boulevard from the harbor (☎ **0596/63-79-60**), open Monday to Friday from 8am to 5pm and Saturday from 8am to noon. The information desk at Lamentin Airport is open daily until the last flight comes in.

The Internet site for Martinique is **www.martinique.org**.

GETTING THERE

BY PLANE   Lamentin International Airport lies outside the village of Lamentin, a 15-minute taxi ride east of Fort-de-France and a 40-minute taxi ride northeast of the island's densest concentration of resort hotels (the Trois Islets peninsula). Most flights to Martinique require a transfer on a neighboring island—usually Puerto Rico, but occasionally Antigua. Direct or nonstop flights from the U.S. mainland are rare: Air France (below) offers only one flight per week, on Sunday, which leaves from Miami and stops at Martinique and Guadeloupe.

American Airlines (☎ **800/433-7300**) flies into its busy hub in San Juan, and from here passengers transfer to one of usually two daily **American Eagle** (same phone number) flights heading to Martinique and Guadeloupe. Taking off every day in the late afternoon, the American Eagle flights usually arrive at their destinations between 1½ hours and 2 hours later. Off-season, the evening flights are sometimes combined into a single flight. Return flights to San Juan usually depart separately from both islands twice a day. Consult an American Airlines reservations clerk about booking your hotel simultaneously with your flight, since substantial discounts sometimes apply if you handle both tasks at the same time.

Air France (☎ **800/237-2747**) flies from Miami to Martinique, sometimes with a touchdown in Guadeloupe en route, every Tuesday, Thursday, and Saturday. It also operates separate nonstop flights from Paris's Charles de Gaulle Airport, departing at least once a day or (in some cases, depending on the season and the day of the week)

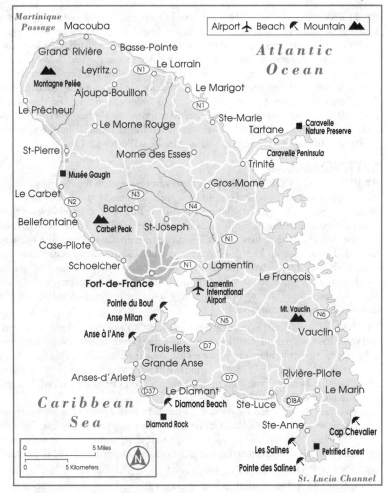

Airport ✈ Beach ⚓ Mountain ▲

Martinique Passage

Macouba
Grand' Rivière
Basse-Pointe
Le Lorrain
N1
Leyritz
▲ Montagne Pelée
Ajoupa-Bouillon
Le Marigot
Le Prêcheur
Le Morne Rouge
N1
Ste-Marie
Tartane
■ Caravelle Nature Preserve
St-Pierre
Morne des Esses
Caravelle Peninsula
Trinité
■ Musée Gaugin
Le Carbet
N2
Balata
N3
Gros-Morne
Bellefontaine
▲ Carbet Peak
St-Joseph
N4
Case-Pilote
N1
Schoelcher
N1
Lamentin
Le François
Fort-de-France
✈ Lamentin International Airport
Pointe du Bout ⚓
Anse Mitan ⚓
Mt. Vauclin ▲
N6
Anse à l'Ane ⚓
N5
Vauclin
Trois-Ilets
D7
Grande Anse
Anses-d'Arlets
D7
Rivière-Pilote
Caribbean Sea
D37
Le Diamant
⚓ Diamond Beach
Ste-Luce
D18A
Le Marin
■ Diamond Rock
Ste-Anne
⚓ Cap Chevalier
■ Petrified Forest
0   5 Miles
0   5 Kilometers
Les Salines
Pointe des Salines
St. Lucia Channel

Atlantic Ocean

twice a day. The airline also maintains three weekly flights from Port-au-Prince, Haiti, into Martinique, and three flights a week, depending on the season, between Cayenne, in French Guyana, and Martinique.

Antigua-based **LIAT** (☎ **800/468-0482** in the U.S. and Canada, 268/462-0700, or through the reservations department of American Airlines) flies from both its home base of Antigua, as well as from Barbados, to Martinique and Guadeloupe several times a day. Depending on the season, flights to these islands are either separate or combined into a single flight, with touchdowns en route. Both Antigua and Barbados are important air-terminus links for such larger carriers as American Airlines (see above).

Another option is flying **BWIA** (☎ **800/538-2942**), the national airline of Trinidad and Tobago, from either New York or Miami nonstop to both Barbados and Antigua and from there transferring onto a LIAT flight. **British Airways** (☎ **800/247-9297** in the U.S., or 0345/222-111 in England) flies separately to both Antigua and Barbados three times a week from London's Gatwick Airport. From either of those islands, LIAT connects to Martinique.

BY FERRY You can travel between Guadeloupe and Martinique by boat in a leisurely 3¾ hours with an intermediate stop in Dominica or Les Saintes. The trip is made on comfortable craft operated by **Exprès des Iles.** The company operates at least one ferryboat a day and, in some cases, two per day, between the French West Indies' two largest islands. Morning departures from Pointe-à-Pitre for Fort-de-France are usually at 8am, and departures from Fort-de-France for Pointe-à-Pitre are usually at 2pm. One-way fares are 340F to 535F ($57.80 to $90.95) round-trip. For details and reservations, contact **Exprès des Iles,** Gare Maritime, quai Gatine, 97110 Pointe-à-Pitre, Guadeloupe (☎ **0590-83-12-45**), or their office at Terminal Inter-Iles, Bassin de Radoub, 97200 Fort-de-France, Martinique (☎ **0596/63-12-11**).

GETTING AROUND

BY BUS & TAXI COLLECTIF Two types of buses operate on Martinique. Regular buses, *grands busses,* hold about 40 passengers and cost 5F to 8F (85¢ to $1.35) to go anywhere within the city limits of Fort-de-France. But to travel beyond that, *taxis collectifs* are used. These are privately owned minivans that traverse the island and bear the sign TC. Their routes are flexible and depend on passenger need. A one-way fare is 30F ($5.10) from Fort-de-France to Ste-Anne. *Taxis collectifs* depart from the heart of Fort-de-France from the parking lot of Pointe Simon. There's no phone number to call for information about this unpredictable means of transport, and there are no set schedules. Traveling in a *taxi collectif* is for the adventurous visitor—they're crowded and not very comfortable.

BY TAXI Travel by taxi is popular but expensive. Most of the cabs aren't metered, and you'll have to agree on the price of the ride *before* getting in. Most visitors arriving at Lamentin Airport head for one of the resorts along the peninsula of Pointe du Bout. To do so costs about 170F ($28.90) during the day or about 255F ($43.35) at night. Night fares are in effect from 7pm to 6am, when a 40% surcharge is added. You can call for a **radio taxi** at ☎ **0596/63-63-62.**

If you want to rent a taxi for the day, it's better to have a party of at least three or four people to keep costs low. Based on the size of the car, expect to pay from 700F to 850F ($119 to $144.50) and up for a 5-hour tour, depending on the itinerary you negotiate with the driver. Generally, four passengers are charged 200F ($34) per hour.

BY RENTAL CAR The scattered nature of Martinique's geography makes renting a car especially tempting. Martinique has several local rental agencies, but clients have complained of mechanical difficulties and billing irregularities. We recommend renting from one of America's big three (Hertz, Budget, and Avis). You must be 21 and have a valid driver's license, such as one from the United States or Canada, to rent a car for up to 20 days. After that, an International Driver's License is required.

Budget has offices at rue Félix-Eboué 12, in Fort-de-France (☎ **800/527-0700** in the U.S., or 0596/63-69-00); **Avis,** at rue Ernest-Deproge 4, in Fort-de-France (☎ **800/331-1212** in the U.S., or 0596/70-11-60); and **Hertz,** at Lamentin Airport (☎ **800/654-3001** or 0596/51-01-01). Prices are usually lower if you reserve a car in North America at least 2 business days before your arrival.

Remember that you'll be hit with a value-added tax (VAT) of 9.5% on top of the final car-rental bill. (VATs for some luxury goods on Martinique, including jewelry, can go as high as 14%.) Collision-damage waivers (CDWs), an excellent idea in a country where the populace drives somewhat recklessly, cost 60F to 127F ($10.20 to $21.60) per day, depending on the value of the car.

BY FERRY The least expensive way to go between quai d'Esnambuc in Fort-de-France and Pointe du Bout is by ferry (*vedette*), costing 30F ($5.10) round-trip or 15F ($2.55) each way. Schedules for the ferries, which usually run daily from 6am to midnight, are printed in the free visitor's guide *Choubouloute,* distributed by the tourist office. For information, call ☎ **0596/73-05-53.** If the weather is bad or the seas are rough, all ferry services may be canceled.

A smaller ferry runs between Fort-de-France and the small-scale unpretentious beach resorts of Anse Mitan and Anse-à-l'Ane, both across the bay and home to many two- and three-star hotels and several modest and unassuming Creole restaurants. A boat departs daily from quai d'Esnambuc in Fort-de-France at 30-minute intervals between 6am and 6:30pm. The trip takes only about 20 minutes. A one-way fare costs 20F ($3.40), a round-trip going for 30F ($5.10); for more information, call ☎ **0596/63-06-46.**

BY BICYCLE & MOTORBIKE   You can rent motor scooters from **Funny,** rue Ernest-Deproge 80, in Fort-de-France (☎ **0596/63-33-05**). The new 18-speed VTT (*velo tout terrain,* or all-terrain bike) is gradually making inroads from mainland France into the rugged countryside of Martinique, though there aren't many places to rent one. **St. Luce Location,** rue Schoelcher 14, St-Luce (☎ **0596/62-49-66**), about a 30-minute drive from Fort-de-France, rents scooters as well. A deposit of 3,500F ($595) is required. **Jacques-Henry Vartel,** VT Tilt, Anse Mitan (☎ **0596/66-01-01**), has moved away from rentals but operates bike tours around Martinique based on demand. Call for more information.

Fast Facts: Martinique

Banking Hours   Banks are open Monday to Friday 7:30am to noon and 2:30 to 4pm.

Consulate   The nearest U.S. consulate is on Barbados (see chapter 5).

Currency   The **French franc (F)** is the legal tender. Prices in this chapter are in both U.S. dollars and French francs. Currently, 1F is worth about 17¢ (5.90F = $1 U.S.). Banks give much better exchange rates than hotels, and there's a money-exchange service, **Change Caraïbes** (☎ **0596/42-17-11**), available at Lamentin Airport. Its downtown branch is at rue Ernest-Deproge 4 (☎ **0596/60-28-40**).

Customs   Items for personal use, such as tobacco, cameras, and film, are admitted without formalities or tax if not in excessive quantity.

Documents   U.S. and Canadian citizens need a valid passport. A return or ongoing ticket is also necessary. British subjects, Australians, and New Zealanders also need a valid passport.

Drugstores   Try the **Pharmacie de la Paix,** at the corner of rue Perrinon and rue Victor-Schoelcher in Fort-de-France (☎ **0596/71-94-83**), open Monday to Friday 7:15am to 6:15pm and Saturday 7:45am to 1pm.

Electricity   Electricity is 220 volts AC, 50 cycles, the same as that used on the French mainland. However, check with your hotel to see if it has converted the electrical voltage and outlets in the baths (some have). If it hasn't, bring your own transformer and adapter for U.S. appliances.

Emergencies   Call the **police** at ☎ **17,** report a **fire** at ☎ **18,** and summon an **ambulance** at ☎ **0596/75-15-75.**

Hospitals   There are 18 hospitals and clinics on the island, plus a 24-hour emergency room at **Hôpital Pierre Zobda Quikman,** Châteauboeuf, right outside Fort-de-France (☎ **0596/55-20-00**).

Languages French, the official language, is spoken by almost everyone. The local Creole patois uses words borrowed from France, England, Spain, and Africa. In the wake of increased tourism, English is occasionally spoken in the major hotels, restaurants, and tourist organizations—but don't count on driving around the countryside and asking for directions in English.

Safety Crime is hardly rampant on Martinique, yet there are still those who prey on unsuspecting tourists. Follow the usual precautions, especially in Fort-de-France and in the tourist-hotel belt of Pointe du Bout. It's wise to protect your valuables and never leave them unguarded on the beach.

Telephone To call Martinique from the United States, dial **011** (the international access code), then **596** (the country code for the Martinique), and finally the six-digit local number. When making a call from one place on Martinique to another on the island, you'll have to add a **0** (zero) to the country code (0596 for Martinique) and dial the four-digit country code plus the six-digit local number; in all, 10 digits for calls made on the island.

Time Martinique is on Atlantic standard time year-round, 1 hour earlier than eastern standard time except when daylight saving time is in effect. Then Martinique time is the same as that on the east coast of the United States.

Water Potable water is found throughout the island.

Weather The climate is relatively mild—temperatures are usually in the 75°F-to-85°F range.

TIPS FOR SAVING MONEY ON ACCOMMODATIONS

Often, family-run places are called **Relais Créoles**—a sort of French–West-Indian B&B. Though many are expensive, some are quite reasonable. However, don't expect the management to speak English, and be prepared to find your fellow guests are French travelers on a budget. Nevertheless, Relais Créoles represent some of the best values on Martinique.

Villa rentals, which can be arranged by the week or the month, are an option for families or groups. The **Villa Rental Service** of the Martinique Tourist Office (☎ **0596/63-79-60**) can arrange this type of vacation rental for you.

You can also contact **Gîtes de France,** B.P. 1122, 97209 Fort-de-France (☎ **0596/73-67-92**), which offers simple but comfortable studios and apartments in private homes. Also available are independent cottages as well as *chambres d'hôte* (B&B-style lodgings). Rates begin at 1,200F ($204) per week.

Camping can be done almost everywhere in the mountains, in the forests, and on the beaches, though indiscriminate camping isn't permitted. Only the French authorities can interpret what *indiscriminate* means. Comfortable camps with showers and toilets are located at **Nid Tropical,** at Anse-à-l'Ane near Trois-Ilets (☎ **0596/68-31-30**); one at **Vauclin,** on the southeast Atlantic coast (☎ **0596/74-40-40**); and one at **Pointe Marin,** near the Ste-Anne public beach (☎ **0596/76-72-79**). A nominal fee is charged for facilities. Between June and September, camping is allowed in other areas that have no facilities whatsoever. For more details, contact the **Office National des Forêts,** km 3.5, route de Moutte, Fort-de-France (☎ **0596/71-34-50**).

Recreational vehicles are an ideal way of discovering the natural and cultural riches along Martinique's nearly 500 miles of roadway. A recommended camping car operation is **West Indies Tours,** which offers campers outfitted with beds for four, a refrigerator, a shower, a sink, a 430-gallon water tank, a dining table, a stove, and a radio-cassette player. Weekly rates are $565, $645, and $735, depending on the season. Contact Michel Toula at West Indies Tours, Le François (☎ **0596/54-50-71**).

2 Fort-de-France

A *mélange* of New Orleans and Menton (French Riviera), Fort-de-France is the main town of Martinique, at the end of a large bay surrounded by evergreen hills. Iron-grill balconies overflowing with flowers are commonplace.

The proud people of Martinique are even more fascinating than the town, although today the Creole women are likely to be seen in jeans instead of traditional turbans and Empress Joséphine–style gowns, and they rarely wear those massive earrings that used to jounce and sway as they sauntered along. Narrow streets climb up the steep hills on which houses have been built to catch the overflow of the capital's more than 100,000 inhabitants.

ACCOMMODATIONS YOU CAN AFFORD

Rates are sometimes advertised in U.S. dollars, sometimes in French francs, and sometimes in a combination of both. Don't stay in town if you want a hotel near a beach (see the hotels listed below for beach resorts). If you do opt to stay in Fort-de-France, you'll have to take a ferry to reach the beaches at **Pointe du Bout** (see below).

Hôtel Malmaison. Rue de la Liberté 7, 97200 Fort-de-France, Martinique, F.W.I. ☎ **0596/ 63-90-85.** Fax 0596/60-03-93. 20 units. A/C TV TEL. Year-round 330F ($56.10) single, 360–380F ($61.20–$64.60) double. MC, V.

This inner-city hotel shows some of the battering it's received since it was built 60 years ago. It welcomes a crowd of business travelers from other parts of the Caribbean and off-island musicians playing at any of Martinique's resorts. Despite the building's age, the rooms, refurnished in 1997, are outfitted with modern furniture like comfortable beds, wooden tables, chairs, and armoires. Baths are quite small. The staff probably won't pay much attention to you after you've registered, but you'll have easy access to the bars and cheap restaurants of Fort-de-France.

Le Lafayette. Rue de la Liberté 5, 97200 Fort-de-France, Martinique, F.W.I. ☎ **0596/ 73-80-50.** Fax 0596/60-65-79. 24 units. A/C MINIBAR TV TEL. Year-round 350F ($59.50) single, 400F ($68) double. AE, MC, V.

You enter this modest downtown hotel, right on La Savane, through rue Victor-Hugo; the reception hall is up a few terra-cotta steps. The cramped and slightly dowdy rooms at this unpretentious hotel were partially renovated in 1992: Japanese wall tapestries decorate the walls, and most contain comfortable twin beds, with small white baths. The overall impression is neat but simple. This the oldest continuously operating hotel on Martinique, built in the 1940s. There's no restaurant, but several eateries are within a short walk.

ACCOMMODATIONS NEARBY

Martinique Cottages. B.P. 408, Jeanne d'Arc, Pays Mélé, 97232 Lamentin, Martinique, F.W.I. ☎ **0596/50-16-08.** Fax 0596/50-26-83. 8 cottages, all with kitchenette. TV TEL. Year-round 290F ($49.30) cottage for 1; 340F ($57.80) cottage for 2. AE, MC, V.

This place's only drawback is that the nearest beach (Plage Tartane or Plage de Ste-Luce) is a 15-minute drive away. Otherwise, you might be very happy in one of the eight pale-pink bungalows (built in 1988) that comprise this pleasant resort. The resident owners are the brother-sister team of Peggy and Jean-Marc Arnaud, who painted each bungalow roof a different color (green, red, or white) and who work hard at maintaining the garden around their buildings. Each medium-size bungalow contains one compact living unit with its own veranda, a ceiling fan, and locally made wooden furnishings, including good beds with firm mattresses. Baths are small but well maintained. The island's airport is a 5-minute drive away, and the cheap eateries of Fort-de-France are a 15-minute drive away. The on-site restaurant, La Plantation, might be a bit more expensive than you'd prefer, but the food is well prepared and the setting more stylish than the low cost of the accommodations might imply.

GREAT DEALS ON DINING

For the best food bargains, don't patronize the restaurants but go to **La Savane,** especially the eastern edge of the park along boulevard Chevalier Ste-Marthe. Here dozens of vendors nightly set up little trailers and light the fires to their grills. They serve surprisingly good food—and big portions too—from their stalls. They'll cook you succulent golden grilled chicken along with fresh conch, brochettes of lamb, and tasty herb-seasoned pork chops. Prices are remarkably low, and your evening can turn into a culinary adventure.

The Crew (L'Equipage). Rue Ernest-Deproges 42. ☎ **0596/73-04-14.** Main courses 75–120F ($12.75–$20.40). MC, V. Mon–Fri noon–3pm and 7–10pm, Sat noon–3pm. FRENCH/CREOLE.

In a wood-sided house built near the port 150 years ago, this restaurant is done in a nautical theme with wood trim. Styled after the kind of workaday brasserie you'd expect to find on the French mainland, it's in the heart of town, does a busy lunch trade with office workers and shopkeepers, and specializes in unfussy but traditional French and grilled cuisine. A choice of appetizers is included in the price of a main course. Menu items feature large platters of such items as escargots, mussels in white-wine sauce, steak tartare, chunky pâtés, grilled chicken, fish, steak, and even tripe.

Le Planteur. Rue de la Liberté 1. ☎ **0596/63-17-45.** Reservations recommended. Main courses 30–140F ($5.10–$23.80); set menus 80F ($13.60) and 180F ($30.60). AE, MC, V. Mon–Fri noon–2:30pm; daily 7–10:30pm. FRENCH/CREOLE.

Its growing number of local fans, as well as members of the island's business community, appreciate this restaurant's location on the southern edge of La Savane. Opened in 1997, it contains several somewhat idealized painted depictions of colonial Martinique, flowered linens with accents of red and white dressing up the small rectangular tables, and a staff who run around hysterically trying to be all things to all diners. Menu items are fresh and flavorful and may include hot *velouté* (soup) with shrimp and *giraumons* (a green-skinned tropical fruit with a succulent yellow core); *cassoulet* of minced conch; *daurade* filet with coconut; snapper *Belle Doudou,* with a sauce of tomatoes, onions, and chives; and *blanquette* (slow-simmered white stew) of shellfish.

✪ **Le Second Soufflé.** Rue Blénac 27. ☎ **0596/63-44-11.** Main courses 38–45F ($6.45–$7.65); fixed-price 4-course lunch or dinner 75F ($12.75). No credit cards. Mon–Fri 11am–3:30pm. VEGETARIAN.

This woodsy dining room close to Fort-de-France's cathedral prides itself on being Martinique's only vegetarian place that prepares its dishes exclusively from local ingredients. It employs a staff of health-conscious locals. You can admire a series of wall murals as you wait for medium- and large-sized platters of *crudités,* casseroles concocted from such vegetables as eggplant and christophine, vegetarian soups, and salads. Dessert might be a *fillet de tinain* (miniature green bananas) with chocolate sauce.

✪ **Marie-Sainte.** Rue Victor-Hugo 160. ☎ **0596/70-00-30.** Main courses 80–180F ($13.60–$30.60); fixed-price lunch 70F ($11.90). AE, V. Mon–Sat noon–4pm. CREOLE.

In its way, this is one of the most evocative restaurants in town, the kind of place you'd expect in remote areas of the island but not in the capital. Your host is Agnès Marie-Sainte, a venerable Creole cook whose recipes for *boudin Créole, daube de poisson,* and *colombo* of mutton were derived from her ancestors. Continuing the maternal links that have propelled Creole food through the ages, she's assisted by her daughter Jeannine Tésé. In a simple dining room that's likely to be crowded with locals, they offer fixed-price lunches with a strong emphasis on fresh fish (grilled or fried) and perhaps fricassee of conch, always accompanied by a medley of such *legumes de pays* as fresh beans, dasheen, breadfruit, and christophine. This is about as authentic as it gets and as inexpensive as you'll find for meals of such quality and authenticity.

SPORTS & OUTDOOR PURSUITS

If it's a beach you're looking for, take the ferry to **Pointe du Bout** (see section 3 for complete information). The island's only **golf course** is in Les Trois-Ilets, discussed in the next section.

Inexpensive guided hiking excursions are organized year-round by the personnel of the **Parc Naturel Régional de la Martinique,** Excollège Agricole de Tivoli, B.P. 437, 97200 Fort-de-France (☎ **0596/64-42-59**), and special excursions can be arranged for small groups. If you want to see the waters around Martinique, it's better to go on one of the **sailboat excursions** in the bay of Fort-de-France. Ask at your hotel desk what boats are taking passengers on cruises in Martinique waters. These vessels tend to change from season to season.

EXPLORING FORT-DE-FRANCE

At the center of the town lies a broad garden planted with many palms and mangos, **La Savane,** a handsome savannah with shops and cafes lining its sides. In the middle of this grand square stands a **statue of Joséphine,** Napoléon's little Creole, made of white marble by Vital Debray. With the grace of a Greek goddess, the statue poses in a Regency gown and looks toward Trois-Ilets, where she was born.

If you like masquerades and dancing in the streets, come in January or February to attend ✪ **Carnival,** or Vaval as it's known here. The event of the year, Carnival begins right after the New Year, as each village prepares costumes and floats. Weekend after weekend, frenzied celebrations take place, reaching fever pitch just before Lent. Fort-de-France is the focal point for Carnival, but the spirit permeates the whole island, as narrow streets are jammed with floats. On Ash Wednesday, the streets of Fort-de-France are filled with *diablesses,* or she-devils (portrayed by members of both sexes). Costumed in black and white, they crowd the streets to form King Carnival's funeral procession. As devils cavort and the rum flows, a funeral pyre is built at La Savane. When it's set afire, the dancing of the she-devils becomes frantic (many are thoroughly drunk at this point). Long past dusk, the cortège takes the coffin to its burial, ending Carnival until next year.

At any time of year, your next stop after La Savane should be the **St. Louis Roman Catholic Cathedral,** on rue Victor-Schoelcher, built in 1875. The religious centerpiece of the island, it's an extraordinary iron building, which someone once likened to a sort of Catholic railway station. A number of the island's former governors are buried beneath the choir loft.

A statue in front of the Palais de Justice is of the island's second main historical figure, **Victor Schoelcher** (you'll see his name a lot on Martinique). As mentioned, he worked to free the slaves more than a century ago. The **Bibliothèque Schoelcher,** rue de la Liberté 21 (☎ **0596/70-26-67**), also honors this popular hero. Functioning today as the island's central government-funded library, the elaborate structure was first displayed at the 1889 Paris Exposition. Back then the Romanesque portal in red and blue, the Egyptian lotus-petal columns, and even the turquoise tiles were imported piece by piece from Paris and reassembled here. Most of the books inside are in French, and it's one of the most stringently protected historic buildings in the French West Indies. It's open Monday 1 to 5:30pm, Tuesday to Thursday 8:30am to 5:30pm, Friday 8:30am to 5pm, and Saturday 8:30am to noon.

Guarding the port is **Fort St-Louis,** built in the Vauban style on a rocky promontory. In addition, **Fort Tartenson** and **Fort Desaix** stand on hills overlooking the port.

The **Musée Départemental de la Martinique,** rue de la Liberté 9 (☎ **0596/ 71-57-05**), the one bastion on Martinique that preserves its pre-Columbian past, has relics left from the early settlers, the Arawaks, and the Caribs. The era the museum celebrates is from 3,000 B.C. to A.D. 1635. Everything here stops shortly after the arrival of the first French colonials on the southern tip of Martinique in the early 1600s. It's mostly an ethnological museum that was enlarged and reorganized into a more dynamic and up-to-date place in 1997. The museum faces La Savane and is open Monday to Friday 8am to 5pm and Saturday 9am to noon, charging 15F ($2.55) for adults, 10F ($1.70) for students, and 5F (85¢) for children.

Sacré-Coeur de Balata Cathedral, at Balata, overlooking Fort-de-France, is a copy of the one looking down from Montmartre on Paris—and this one is just as incongruous, maybe more so. It's reached by going along route de la Trace (N3). Balata is 6 miles northwest of Fort-de-France.

A few minutes away on the N3, **Jardin de Balata** (☎ **0596/64-48-73**) is a tropical botanical park. The park was created by Jean-Philippe Thoze on land that the jungle was rapidly reclaiming around a Creole house that belonged to his grandmother. He has also restored the house, furnishing it with antiques and historic engravings. The garden contains flowers, shrubs, and trees growing in profusion and offering a vision of tropical splendor. Balata is open daily 9am to 5pm. Admission is 40F ($6.80) for adults and 15F ($2.55) for children 7 to 12; free for children under 6.

SHOPPING

Your best buys on Martinique are French luxury imports, such as perfumes, fashions, Vuitton luggage, Lalique crystal, or Limoges dinnerware. Sometimes (but don't count on it) prices are as much as 30% to 40% below those in the United States.

If you pay in dollars, store owners supposedly will give you a 20% discount; however, when you pay in dollars, the exchange rates vary considerably from store to store, and almost invariably they're far less favorable than the rate offered at one of the local banks. The net result is that you received a 20% discount, but then they take away from 9% to 15% on the dollar exchange, giving you a net savings of only 5% to 11%. You're better off shopping in the smaller stores, where prices are 8% to 12% lower on comparable items and paying in francs you've exchanged at a local bank.

The main shopping street in town is **rue Victor-Hugo.** The other two leading streets are **rue Schoelcher** and **rue St-Louis.** However, the most boutique-filled shopping streets are **rue Antione-Siger, rue Lamartine,** and **rue Moreau de Jones.** Here you'll find the latest French design fashions. Facing the tourist office and alongside **quai d'Esnambuc** is an open market where you can buy local handcrafts and souvenirs. Many of these are pretty tacky, however.

Far more interesting is the display of vegetables and fruit at the **open-air stalls along rue Isambert,** full of local flavor. You can't help but smell the **fish market** alongside the Levassor River. Gourmet chefs will find all sorts of spices in the open-air markets, or such goodies as tinned pâté or canned quail in the local *supermarchés*.

For the ubiquitous local fabric, madras, there are shops on every street with bolts and bolts of it, all colorful and inexpensive. So-called haute couture and resort wear are sold in many boutiques dotting downtown Fort-de-France. Try to postpone your shopping trip if a cruise ship is in town, to avoid the stampede.

Begin the Beguine

The sexy and rhythmic *beguine* was *not* an invention of Cole Porter. It's a dance of the islands—though exactly which island depends on whom you ask. Popular wisdom and the encyclopedia give the nod to Martinique. Guadeloupeans claim it for their own, and to watch them dance it you might be convinced. Of course, calypso and the *merengue* move rhythmically along too.

On Guadeloupe, the folkloric troupe **Ballets Guadeloupeans** makes frequent appearances at the big hotels, whirling and moving to the rhythms of island music in colorful costumes and well-choreographed routines. Some resorts, including the Club Med–Caravelle, use their weekly visit to set the theme for the evening with their restaurant, La Beguine, serving up a banquet of traditional island dishes to accompany the dance, music, and costumes.

Ask at your hotel where the Ballets Guadeloupeans will be appearing during your stay, as their schedule tends to vary as they tour the island. You can catch them as they rotate through the hotels Arawak, Salako, L'Auberge de le Vieille Tour, and Fleur d'Epée Novotel, as well as the Club Med–Caravelle. On the night of any of these performances, you can order a drink at the bar for 30F ($5.10) or more and witness the show, or partake of a hotel buffet for 180F ($30.60). Buffets usually start around 8pm, with the show beginning at 8:30pm. The troupe also performs on some cruise ships.

More famous than the dancers on Guadeloupe, however, is the touring group **Les Grands Ballets Martiniquais.** Everybody who goes to Martinique wants to see the show performed by this bouncy group of about two dozen dancers, along with musicians, singers, and choreographers. This most interesting program of folk dances in the Caribbean was launched in the early 1960s, and their performances of the traditional dances of Martinique have been acclaimed in Europe and the U.S. With a swoosh of gaily striped skirts and clever acting, the dancers capture all the exuberance of the island's soul. The group has toured abroad with great success, but they perform best on their home ground, presenting tableaux that tell of jealous brides and faithless husbands, demanding overseers and toiling cane cutters. Dressed in traditional costumes, the island women and men dance the spirited mazurka, which was brought from the ballrooms of Europe and, of course, the exotic beguine.

Les Grands Ballets Martiniquais perform Monday at the Hôtel Diamant-Novotel, Wednesday at the Novotel Carayou, Thursday at the Méridien Trois-Ilets, Friday at the Bakoua Beach, and Saturday at Hôtel La Batalière, but this can vary, so check locally. In addition, the troupe gives mini-performances aboard visiting cruise ships. The cost of dinner and the show is usually 260F ($44.20) per person. Most performances are at 8:30pm, with dinners at the hotels beginning at 7:30pm.

Whoever performs it for you, on whichever island, you'll soon realize the beguine is more than a dance—it's a way of life. See it for yourself, or dance it, if you think you can.

Cadet-Daniel, rue Antoine-Siger 72 (☎ **0596/71-41-48**), offers Lalique crystal and Christofle silver flatware, though by far the stars are the gleaming rows of 18-karat gold jewelry, some inset with precious and semi-precious stones. Most of it's manufactured in Martinique, and much of it is fashioned into traditional patterns inspired by the Créoles. The **Centre des Métiers d'Art,** rue Ernest-Deproges

(☎ **0596/70-25-01**), is an arts-and-crafts store adjacent to the tourist office. Inside is a mix of valuable and worthless local handmade artifacts, including bamboo, ceramics, painted fabrics, and patchwork quilts suitable for hanging.

The **Galeries Lafayette,** rue Victor-Schoelcher 10, near the cathedral (☎ **0596/71-38-66**), is a small-scale branch of the most famous department store in Paris. Specializing in fashion for men, women, and children, it also offers leather goods, jewelry, watches, and all the predictably famous names in French perfume and fashion. The store offers 20% off for purchases made with U.S. dollar traveler's checks or a credit or charge card.

La Case à Rhum, in the Galerie Marchande, rue de la Liberté 5 (☎ **0596/73-73-20**), is the place to go for the local brew. Aficionados consider Martinique rum to be one of the world's finest. This shop offers all the brands of rum manufactured on Martinique (at least 12), as well as several others famous for their age and taste. Bottles range from 35F to 5,400F ($5.95 to $918) for a connoisseur's delight—a bottle of rum distilled by the Bally Company in 1924 in the nearby hamlet of Carbet. They offer samples in small cups to prospective buyers. We suggest you try Clement, a dark mellow Old Mahogany, or a blood-red brown liqueur-like rum bottled by Bally.

La Galleria, route de Lamentin, is midway between Fort-de-France and the Lamentin Airport. This is the most upscale and elegant shopping complex on Martinique. On the premises are more than 60 vendors. You'll find a handful of cafes and simple restaurants to relieve your hunger pangs as you shop, as well as an outlet or two for the local pastries and sweets. **Paradise Island,** rue Ernest-Deproges 20 (☎ **0596/63-93-63**), features the most upscale collection of T-shirts on Martinique, each displayed as a kind of couture-conscious art form. Whatever you like will be available in about a dozen colors. The store also sells what it refers to as Les Polos, knit shirts with collars, priced at 229F to 329F ($38.95 to $55.95), a good value.

Roger Albert, rue Victor-Hugo 7–9 (☎ **0596/71-71-71**), is by far the largest emporium of luxury goods on Martinique, a department store for locals and cruise-ship passengers. It's one of five branches around Martinique, though this, a short walk from the waterfront, is by far the busiest. You'll find wristwatches (both fun and expensive), perfumes, sportswear by LaCoste and Tacchini, Lladró and Limoges porcelain, and crystal by Swarovski and such other manufacturers as Daum and Lalique. For anyone with a non-French passport, there are reductions of 20% off what a local resident would pay, plus discounts of an extra 20%, depending on seasonal discounts and promotions. Even better, the value-added tax isn't added to the price of your purchases.

FORT-DE-FRANCE AFTER DARK

The most exciting after-dark venue is a performance of the folkloric troupe **Les Grand Ballets Martiniquais** (see "Begin the Beguine," above).

Jazz sessions are a regular feature at **Westindies,** boulevard Alfassa (☎ **0596/63-63-77**). The popularity of dance clubs rise and fall almost monthly. Most of them charge a cover of 48F ($8.15), unless some special entertainment is presented. Current favorites, drawing both locals and visitors, are **L'Alibi,** Morne Tartenson (☎ **0596/63-45-15**), and **Zenith,** blvd. Allègre 24 (☎ **0596/60-20-22**). Another local hot spot is **Le Queen,** in the Hotel La Batellière, at Schoelcher, outside Fort-de-France (☎ **0596/61-49-49**).

For casino action, head for Martinique's new **Casino Batelière Plaza,** at Schoelcher (☎ **0596/61-91-51**), outside Fort-de-France. You'll need a passport and 70F ($11.90) to enter, plus a jacket and tie for men. You can play French baccarat, roulette, and blackjack. However, you can dispense with the formalities and the entrance fee to play the slots on the left as you enter. Slots are open Monday to Saturday from noon to 3am. The more formal gambling is daily from 8pm to 3am.

As for the gay scene, Martinique remains fairly conservative. However, the attitude of most Martinicans remains laissez-faire regarding your sleeping habits. Although you'll often see same-sex couples dancing together in the local discos, the only gay bar is **Daly's,** Route de Ravine Vilaine (☎ **0596/79-66-26**), in an affluent suburb of Fort-de-France. It's open only Friday and Saturday, offering two dance floors and both indoor and alfresco bars. Head out of Fort-de-France in the direction of St-Joseph and look for the signs.

3 Pointe du Bout & Les Trois-Ilets

Pointe du Bout is a narrow peninsula across the bay from Fort-de-France. It's the most developed resort area of Martinique, with at least four of the island's largest hotels, an impressive marina, about a dozen tennis courts, pools, and facilities for horseback riding and all kinds of water sports. There's also some independent restaurants, a casino, and boutiques. In nearby Trois-Ilets, the birthplace of Joséphine Bonaparte, is a Robert Trent Jones Sr.–designed golf course.

Except for the hillside that contains the Hôtel Bakoua, most of the district is flat and verdant, with gardens and rigidly monitored parking zones. All the hotels below are near the white-sand beaches of Pointe du Bout, and some of the smaller properties are convenient to the beaches of Anse Mitan.

GETTING THERE

If you're **driving** from Fort-de-France, take Route 1, along which you'll cross the plain of Lamentin—the industrial area of Fort-de-France and the site of the international airport. Often the air is filled with the fragrance of caramel because of the large sugarcane factories in the area. After 20 miles, you reach Trois-Ilets, Joséphine's hometown. Three miles farther on your right, take Route D38 to Pointe du Bout. For those who want to reach Pointe du Bout by sea, there's a **ferry service** (more fully described in "Getting Around," above) running all day long until midnight from the harborfront (quai d'Esnambuc) in downtown Fort-de-France. Round-trip fare is 30F ($5.10).

ACCOMMODATIONS YOU CAN AFFORD

Auberge de l'Anse Mitan. Anse Mitan, 97229 Trois-Ilets, Martinique, F.W.I. ☎ **0596/ 66-01-12.** Fax 0596/66-01-05. 25 units. A/C TEL. Winter 330F ($56.10) single; 420F ($71.40) double; 400F ($68) studio for 1 or 2. Off-season 280F ($47.60) single; 330F ($56.10) double; 300F ($51) studio for 1 or 2. Room (but not studio) rates include breakfast. AE, DC, MC, V.

Many people like this hotel's location at the isolated end of a road whose more commercial side is laden with restaurants and a bustling nighttime parade. The hotel was built in 1930 but has been renovated several times since by the hospitable Athanase family. Six of the units are studios with kitchens and TVs; all have private showers. The rooms are boxy but the beds comfortable; the baths are cramped but tidy, and towels are just adequate. You don't get a lot that's special here, but few object to the price.

Rivage Hôtel. Anse Mitan, 97229 Trois-Ilets, Martinique, F.W.I. ☎ **0596/66-00-53.** Fax 0596/66-06-56. www.pro.wanadoo.fr/rivagehotel. 18 units. A/C. Winter 360F ($61.20) single or double; 420F ($71.40) single or double with kitchen. Off-season 250F ($42.50) single or double; 300F ($51) single or double with kitchen. Extra person 100F ($17) in winter, 80F ($13.60) in off-season. Breakfast available only in winter 40F ($6.80). MC, V.

Across the road from the beach, this small hotel has units with either private kitchens or small refrigerators. There's a modest pool, but many visitors prefer the nearby sea. (As you swim, the lights of Fort-de-France twinkle across the bay from the faraway

Cheap Thrills: What to See & Do for Free (Well, Almost) on Martinique

- **Explore Fort-de-France.** There's no place like it in the Caribbean. The capital of Martinique is a little bit of Nice and a little bit of New Orleans but still unique unto itself. With its iron-grill balconies, narrow streets, and yacht-clogged harbor, it invites exploration. The heart of the city is La Savane, a large green park with playing fields, walks, and benches. The statue of Joséphine standing here was beheaded in 1991, probably because islanders felt she championed slavery. Near the harbor, at the edge of the park, you'll find stalls devoted to vendors selling their handmade crafts, including baskets, beads, bangles, wood carvings, and straw hats. You can also go shopping here, especially along boutique-loaded rue de la Liberté.

- **Find a Haven for Shutterbugs.** Martinique lends itself to photography, almost more than any other island in the Caribbean. That's why French fashion magazines often come here for shoots. Islanders don't mind being photographed, providing you ask first. Of course, if they don't consider themselves properly dressed they may turn down your request. The best sites are La Savane in Fort-de-France (see above); St-Pierre, the best place to photograph towering Mount Pelée; La Pagerie, with its decaying ruins of a sugar factory; and the rain forest, best photographed from panoramic overlooks along La Trace, a serpentine road winding through the entire forest. It scales the heights from Fort-de-France to towering Mount Rouge.

- **Traverse the Route de la Trace.** Cited as one of Martinique's most photographed places, this is one of the grand scenic routes of the French West Indies, going through the island's rain forest. From Fort-de-France, you can pick up the narrow Route de la Trace (or simply Trace). It heads north through the dense rain forests blanketing the island, part of the Regional Natural Park, going all the way to Deux-Choux, a tunnel on the north side of Pitons du Carbet, the spiked and scarped mountain covering the north and central regions. From every hairpin turn on this corkscrew highway, you'll be rewarded with sweeping views of the capital and its yacht-clogged harbor. The route ultimately leads to Mount Pelée, with its still-active volcano. On the final leg of the trip, the road descends slowly through a beautiful area of pineapple plantations. Once at Morne-Rouge, the route joins with the north

shoreline.) The boxy rooms, with cramped baths, would come as no surprise to motel-hopping motorists back in the days when Mamie and Ike were in the White House. The studios are more spacious. A barbecue pit set up in the garden is used by guests for cookout parties. There aren't many amenities here, though the bars, restaurants, and sporting facilities of Anse Mitan are just a short walk away.

GREAT DEALS ON DINING

Chez Fanny. Trois-Ilets, Anse Mitan. ☎ **0596/66-04-34.** Reservations recommended. Main courses 38–78F ($6.45–$13.25); set-price menus 120–150F ($20.40–$25.50). DC, MC, V. Thurs–Tues noon–3pm and 7–10pm. CREOLE/FRENCH.

On the ground floor of a four-story concrete building facing the sea, this restaurant is the domain of Creole chef Fanny Gallonde, who prepares well-received platters for cross-island road between the calm Caribbean Sea and the more turbulent Atlantic coast.

- **Have a Bottle of Rum & a Tour.** Martinique still has more than a dozen rhumeries, and you'll find acres still devoted to sugarcane. From January to June, the juice from this cane ends up in one of these rhumeries. It's boiled until it forms a thick syrup and then is distilled into one of the strongest drinks you'll likely ever encounter. It's generally toned down and softened before bottling. Nearly all rhumeries offer free tours and even a free drink. The most fascinating distillery to visit is at Ste-Marie (see below).

- **Explore the Village of Macouba.** At the northern tip of Martinique, between the towns of Grand-Rivière and Basse-Pointe, lies the village of Macouba (named after the Carib word for fish), overlooking Martinique Passage. If you're seeking an undiscovered village, head here. In the 17th century it was a thriving tobacco town, but prosperity has long passed it by. From its clifftop location you'll have one of the most panoramic views of the island, with the towering mountains as a backdrop. On a clear day you can see the island of Dominica, between Martinique and Guadeloupe. Here you can also visit the JM Distillery, which produces an excellent vintage rum. Macouba can be your starting point for a panoramic 6-mile drive along the Route du Grand-Rivière, passing groves of giant bamboo and cliffs curtained in vines.

- **Hike Through Martinique.** The northern part of the island is best for hiking, as it's covered by a rain forest guarded by towering volcanic Mount Pelée. The **Parc Naturel Régional de la Martinique** (☎ **0596/64-42-59**) organizes hiking tours. One goes along the east coast to the Caravelle Peninsula, with marked hiking trails along the beach out to the historic ruins of the Château Dubuc. In all, there are 30 hiking trails, each well marked and maintained. Most are designed for hikers to go on their own, as they're relatively safe. However, the most serious hiking tour, a 2-hour climb to Mount Pelée, should be done with a guide, as it's the most difficult, going through thick foliage and along overgrown trails. Fairly easy are hikes at Les Ombrages, a nature trail at Ajoupa-Bouillon, or along the Gorges de la Falaise, a ravine leading to a waterfall where guided canyoning is the local sport.

crowds that at lunchtime fill it to capacity. The décor is unpretentious, and the food includes a traditional roster of tried-and-true staples like *boudin* (blood sausage) Creole, codfish beignets (*accras de morue*), grilled or baked chicken, fricassee of shrimp, and grilled octopus. The menu also contains a short roster of dishes from the French mainland, including *coq au vin* (chicken in wine) and *boeuf bourguignonne*. The chef also makes a wicked cous cous spilling over with chicken, fresh vegetables, and chick peas.

Le Cantonnais. La Marina, Pointe du Bout. ☎ **0596/66-02-33.** Main courses 55–120F ($9.35–$20.40); fixed-price dinners 55–130F ($9.35–$22.10). AE, MC, V. Mon–Sat 6–11pm. CHINESE.

Amid a classic Chinese décor of red and gold, this moderately priced restaurant across from the Hôtel Méridien offers Asian food whose flavors and colors are sometimes a welcome change from a diet of Creole and Caribbean food. Try broiled shark fin, chicken with salted-bean sauce, or steamed ribs with black-bean sauce. The restaurant's sliced duckling with plum sauce is excellent. Soups include braised bird's nest with minced chicken and a soothing version of egg drop soup.

Pignon sur Mer. Anse-à-l'Ane. ☎ **0596/68-38-37.** Main courses 55–170F ($9.35–$28.90). MC, V. Tues–Sun 12:15–4pm; Tues–Sat 7–9:30pm. CREOLE.

Unpretentious, this small-scale Creole restaurant contains about 15 tables in a rustically dilapidated building beside the sea (it's a 12-minute drive from Pointe du Bout). Menu items are island-inspired and may include *délices du Pignon,* a platter of shellfish, or whatever grilled fish or shellfish were hauled in that day. *Lambi* (conch), shrimp, and crayfish are almost always available, and brochettes of chicken are filling and flavorful.

SPORTS & OUTDOOR PURSUITS

BEACHES   The clean white-sand beaches of **Pointe du Bout,** site of the major hotels, were created by developers and tend to be rather small. However, to the south are the golden-sand beaches at **Anse Mitan,** which have always welcomed visitors, including many snorkelers. The waters suffer from industrial usage, though, apparently, the pollution isn't severe enough to prevent you from going into the water. Most of the tourists who go to beaches are found at Pointe du Bout, and this is also the site of several marinas. The ferry from Fort de France unloads its passengers here, increasing the crowds. Even if you don't find a lot of space on the beach, with its semi-clear waters, you'll find toilets, phones, restaurants, and cafes galore. As a curiosity, you'll often see the French standing deep in the water conversing and smoking cigarettes. The beaches at Anse Mitan are far less crowded than Point du Bout's and are lovelier and more inviting, with cleaner waters. However, all isn't a rosy picture here. The steepness of Martinique's shoreline leaves much to be desired by swimmers and snorkelers. The water declines steeply into depths. No reefs ring the shores, and fish are rarely visible. Nonetheless, beaches here are ideal for sunbathing. The neighboring beach to Anse Mitan is **Anse-a-l'Ane,** an ideal place for a picnic with its white sand. There's also a little shell museum here of passing interest.

DIVING   The beachfront of the Hôtel Méridien (at Pointe du Bout) is the headquarters for the island's best dive outfit, **Espace Plongée Martinique** (☎ **0596/66-00-00**), which welcomes anyone who shows up, regardless of where they happen to be staying. Daily dive trips, depending on demand, leave from the Méridien's pier every day at 9am, returning at noon, and at 2:30pm, returning at 6pm. Popular dive sites within a reasonable boat ride, with enough diversity and variation in depth to appeal to divers of all degrees of proficiency, include La Baleine (The Whale) and Cap Solomon. A dive shop stocks everything you'll need. Depending on their level of proficiency, divers pay 220F to 250F ($37.40 to $42.50) per person, per session. However, pool instruction for novice divers (conducted in the Méridien's pool every day from 11:30am to noon) is free.

GOLF   In 1976, the famous golf-course designer Robert Trent Jones Sr. visited Martinique and left behind the 18-hole ✪ **Golf de l'Impératrice-Joséphine** at Trois-Ilets (☎ **0596/68-32-81**), a 5-minute drive from Pointe du Bout and about 18 miles from Fort-de-France. It's the only golf course on Martinique, and the greens slope from the birthplace of Empress Joséphine (for whom it's named) across rolling hills with scenic vistas down to the sea. Amenities include a pro shop, a bar, a restaurant, and three tennis courts. Greens fees are 270F ($45.90) per person for 18 holes.

HORSEBACK RIDING   The premier riding facility is **Ranch Jack,** Morne Habitué, Trois-Ilets (☎ **0596/68-37-69**). It offers morning horseback rides for both experienced and novice riders, at 350F ($59.50) per person for a 3½- to 4-hour ride. Jacques and Marlene Guinchard make daily promenades across the beaches and fields of Martinique, with a running explication of the history, fauna, and botany of the island. Cold drinks are included in the price, and transportation is usually free to and from the hotels of nearby Pointe du Bout. This is an ideal way to discover both botanical and geographical Martinique, and four to fifteen participants are needed to book a tour.

SNORKELING   Snorkeling equipment is usually available free to hotel guests, who quickly learn that coral, fish, and ferns abound in the waters around the Pointe du Bout hotels.

TENNIS   Tennis pros at Bathy's Club at the **Hôtel Méridien,** Pointe du Bout (☎ **0596/66-00-00**), usually allow nonguests to play for free if the courts are otherwise unoccupied, except at night, when the charge is almost always imposed. Or you can also play on one of the three courts on the grounds of **Golf de l'Impératrice-Joséphine** at Trois-Ilets (☎ **0596/68-32-81**). The setting is one of the most beautiful on Martinique. It costs 70F ($11.90) per hour to play. No racquet rentals.

WINDSURFING   A popular sport in the French West Indies, windsurfing (*la planche à voile*) is available at most of the large-scale hotels. One of the best equipped is the **Cabane des Sports,** the beachfront facilities at the Hotel Méridien, Pointe du Bout (☎ **0596/66-00-00**). Lessons cost 100F ($17) for 1 hour, and boards rent for about 60F ($10.20) an hour.

A VISIT TO JOSÉPHINE'S TROIS-ILETS

About 20 miles south of Fort-de-France is Trois-Ilets, a charming little village. Marie Josèphe Rose Tascher de La Pagerie was born here in 1763. At 17, this young woman known as Joséphine married Vicomte Alexandre de Beauharnais and bore two children, but she and her husband were jailed during France's Reign of Terror and he became one of its last victims when he was guillotined. Joséphine then went on to meet the rising Napoléon Bonaparte and become the empress of France from 1804 to 1809. Six years older than her husband, she pretended she'd lost her birth certificate so he wouldn't find out her true age. When she couldn't bear him a child, Napoléon divorced her, and she ended her days at Malmaison. Although many historians call her ruthless and selfish, she's still revered by some on Martinique as an uncommonly gracious lady. Others have less kind words—because Napoléon is said by some historians to have reinvented slavery, and many blame Joséphine's influence.

One mile outside the hamlet, turn left to La Pagerie, where the small **Musée de la Pagerie** (☎ **0596/68-33-06**), holding mementos relating to Joséphine, has been installed in the former estate kitchen. Along with her childhood bed in the kitchen, you'll see a passionate letter from Napoléon. The collection was compiled by Dr. Robert Rose-Rosette. Here Joséphine gossiped with her slaves and played the guitar.

Still remaining are the partially restored ruins of the Pagerié sugar mill and the church (in the village itself) where she was christened in 1763. The plantation was destroyed in a hurricane. The museum is open Tuesday to Friday 9am to 5:30pm and Saturday and Sunday 9am to 1pm and 2:30 to 5:30pm, charging 20F ($3.40) for admission.

A botanical garden, the **Parc des Floralies,** is adjacent to the golf course (above), as is the museum devoted to Joséphine (above).

The **Maison de la Canne,** Pointe Vatable (☎ **0596/68-32-04**), stands on the road to Trois-Ilets. (From Fort-de-France, you can take a taxi or shuttle bus to La Marina, Pointe du Bout; from here, an unnumbered bus heads for Pointe Vatable.) It was created in 1987 on the premises of an 18th-century distillery to house a permanent exhibit that tells the story of sugarcane and the sweeping role it played in the economic and cultural development of Martinique. Exhibits include models, tools, a miniature slave ship, an ancient cart tethered to life-size models of two oxen, and a restored carriage. Hostesses guide visitors through the exhibit. It's open Tuesday to Sunday 9am to 5:30pm, charging 20F ($3.40) for adults and 5F (85¢) for children 5 to 12 (free 4 and under).

SHOPPING

The **Marina complex** has a number of interesting boutiques. Several sell handcrafts and curios from Martinique. They're sometimes of good quality and are expensive, regrettably, particularly if you buy some of the batiks of natural silk and the enameled jewel boxes.

At Christmastime, many of the island's traditional foie gras and pastries are presented in crocks made by the island's largest earthenware factories, the **Poterie de Trois-Ilets,** Quartier Poterie, Trois-Ilets (☎ **0596/68-03-44**). At least 90% of its production is devoted to brick-making. However, one small-scale offshoot of the company devotes itself to producing earth-toned stoneware and pottery whose colors and shapes have contributed to the folklore of Martinique. In theory, the studios are open Monday to Saturday 7am to 2:30pm, but call before you set out to make sure they'll accept visitors.

POINTE DU BOUT AFTER DARK

Martinique has one of the dullest casinos in the French West Indies, **Casino Trois-Ilets** at Hotel Méridien Trois-Ilets, Pointe du Bout (☎ **0596/66-00-30**), open daily from 10pm to 3am, charging 70F ($11.90) for entrance to the room where roulette or blackjack is played. A picture ID is required. Entrance to the slot-machine room is free.

A mellow piano bar atmosphere is found at **L'Amphore,** in the rear of Le Bakoua hotel, at Pointe du Bout (☎ **0596/66-03-09**). Another piano bar is **Le Cotton Club** (☎ **0596/66-03-09**), at Trois-Ilets, taking its name from the once-fabled club in Harlem in New York.

4 The South Loop

We now leave Pointe du Bout and head south for more sun and beaches. Resort centers here include **Le Diamant** and **Ste-Anne.**

On the way to them from Trois-Ilets, you can follow a small curved road that brings you to **Anse-à-l'Ane, Grande Anse,** and **Anses d'Arlets.** At any of these places are small beaches, quite safe and usually not crowded.

ANSES D'ARLETS

This charming little village features a white-sand beach dotted with brightly painted *gommiers* (fishing boats), a good-size pier from which children swim and adults fish, a pretty steepled church, a bandstand for holiday concerts, and a smattering of modest dining spots. Rue du Président-Kennedy honors the slain American president.

The waters off Anses d'Arlets are a playground for scuba divers, with a wide variety of small tropical fish and colorful coral formations. The area itself has been for many years a choice spot for weekend second homes and is now beginning to develop touristically.

From Anses d'Arlets, D37 takes you to Diamant. The road offers much scenery.

LE DIAMANT

On the island's southwestern coastline, this village offers a good beach open to the prevailing southern winds. The village is named after one of Martinique's best-known geological oddities, **Le Rocher du Diamant (Diamond Rock),** a barren offshore island that juts upward from the sea to a height of 573 feet. Sometimes referred to as the Gibraltar of the Caribbean, it figured prominently in a daring British-led invasion in 1804, when British mariners carried a formidable amount of ammunition and 110 sailors to the top. Despite frequent artillery bombardments from the French-held coast, the garrison held out for 18 months, completely dominating the passage between the rock and the coastline of Martinique. Intrepid foreigners sometimes visit Diamond Rock, but the access across the strong currents of the channel is risky.

✪ **Diamond Beach,** on the Martinique mainland, offers a sandy bottom, verdant groves of swaying palms, and many surfing and bathing possibilities. The entire district has developed into a resort, scattered with generally small hotels, most of which consist of simple clusters of low-rise buildings with good landscaping and access to the beach.

ACCOMMODATIONS YOU CAN AFFORD

Chambre d'Hôte Diamant Noir. Anse Cafard, Dizac, 97233 Diamant, Martinique, F.W.I. ☎ **0596/76-41-25.** Fax 0596/76-28-89. www.sasi.fr/diamnoir. E-mail: diamnoir@sasi.fr. 9 units. Year-round 220–300F ($37.40–$51) single, 260–395F ($44.20–$67.15) double, 310–450F ($52.70–$76.50) triple. Rates include breakfast. No credit cards.

Much of the allure of this place derives from its charming owners, Dominique and Elléna Bertin. It consists of a 25-year-old main villa set in a sprawling well-maintained garden and a 1-year-old annex adjacent to the sea. The small rooms have little style and are basic, except for comfortable beds; the baths are a bit tiny but well maintained. It's about 1½ miles from Bourg Le Diamant, painted white with pink shutters, swathed in trailing strands of bougainvillea and ringed with fruit trees. Breakfast is the only meal served, but at least two restaurants are within an easy walk, and a communal kitchen is available for use by all guests.

Hôtel Relais Caraïbes. La Cherry, 97223 Diamant, Martinique, F.W.I. ☎ **0596/76-44-65.** Fax 0596/76-21-20. 15 units. A/C TV TEL. 450–650F ($76.50–$110.50) single, 550–800F ($93.50–$136) double, 700–1,200F ($119–$204) bungalow for 2. Rates include breakfast. MC, V. Closed May–Oct.

Despite its charm (some visitors define it as a tropical inn with an ocean view), the Caraïbes isn't as expensive as you might think after an initial glance. It consists of a main building (with a trio of small rooms above its restaurant) and a dozen medium-size bungalows scattered over carefully clipped lawns. Each bungalow offers a porch and a view from the clifftop location over the water to the jagged crags of Diamond Rock. (The rooms don't have ocean views.) They're decorated in an eclectic and rather modest style, each with a small salon, plus a sofa bed with a firm mattress and a tiny but tidy bath. Some guests prefer the standard rooms, which have a few graceful notes, like hand-painted headboards. Though privacy is assured by this inn's location about a mile from the main highway, the beach lies within a 5-minute walk. If you don't want to trek down to the beach, there's a pool perched along the clifftop.

L'Ecrin Bleu. Morne de la Croix, 97223 Le Diamant, Martinique, FWI. ☎ **0596/76-41-92.** Fax 0596/76-41-90. 20 units. A/C. Winter 450F ($76.50) single; 550F ($93.50) double. Off-season 250F ($42.50) single; 300F ($51) double. Rates include breakfast. AE, MC, V.

In the rocky hills above the hamlet of Bourg Le Diamant, this blue-and-white hotel was built in the early 1990s by the Tosatos from Marseilles. Isolated on virtually every side and composed of three buildings, it offers carefully decorated rooms with views sweeping out over the sea and the lofty heights of Diamond Rock. Though not large, they're nicely done in a simple French Antillean style, with fine mattresses and renovated baths that may lack space but not good maintenance. The beach is a 5-minute downhill walk away, there's a pool, and you have access to all kinds of scuba-related activities. The restaurant is open only for dinner, every night from 7pm until at least 10:30pm; French and Caribbean food, with an emphasis on lobster and shellfish, cost 85F to 150F ($14.45 to $25.50) for a fixed-price meal.

GREAT DEALS ON DINING

Chez Christiane. Rue Principale, Bourg Le Diamant. ☎ **0596/76-49-55.** Main courses 70–120F ($11.90–$20.40); set-menu 50F ($8.50). AE, DC, V. Mon–Sat 7–11pm. CREOLE.

On the main street of Bourg Le Diamant, amid a dining room decorated with varnished bamboo and slats of local hardwood, you can taste the Creole specialties of Christiane Ravin, a matron who has earned the respect of her colleagues after almost a dozen years at her trade. Every Friday night, live music plays in the dining room with an ambience more like a nightclub than a restaurant. Otherwise, it's a worthy choice for such menu items as fricassee of chicken or conch, curried shrimp, octopus with Creole sauce, and well-seasoned fillets of fish like freshly caught snapper.

LE MARIN

As you follow the road south to Trois-Rivières, you'll come to **Ste-Luce,** one of the island's most charming villages. Beautiful **beaches** surround the town, and it's the site of the **Forêt Montravail.** Continuing, you'll reach Rivière-Pilote, quite a large town, and **Le Marin,** at the bottom of a bay of the same name, 22 miles south of Fort-de-France.

Long a popular stop en route south, Le Marin is the site of one of Martinique's most historic monuments, a **Jesuit-style church** built in 1766. The town has become a sailing center, its marina sheltering the island's single largest yacht charter fleet. Also of interest is Le Marin's biennial **August fête,** a cultural extravaganza. For overnighting, the Auberge du Marin (below) is a good bet.

After passing Le Marin, you reach **Vauclin,** by going northeast; this is a fishing port and market town that's pre-Columbian. If you have time, stop in at the 18th-century **Chapel of the Holy Virgin.** Visitors like to make an excursion to **Mount Vauclin,** the highest point in southern Martinique, where you'll enjoy one of the most scenic panoramas in the West Indies.

ACCOMMODATIONS YOU CAN AFFORD

Auberge du Marin. Rue Osman-Duquesnay 21, 97290 Le Marin, Martinique, F.W.I. ☎ **0596/74-83-88.** Fax 0596/74-76-47. 5 units, 2 with bathroom. Year-round 200F ($34) single with or without bathroom; 250F ($42.50) double with or without bathroom. Rates include breakfast. MC.

This simple inn mimics the tradition of a *restaurant avec chambres,* which is well established in mainland France but not particularly common in the Antilles. Although most of the management's energies are devoted to running a restaurant (below), it maintains two no-frills rooms with cramped but serviceable showers on the street level and three larger rooms upstairs sharing a bathtub, shower, and toilet. The units without bath are much bigger and more comfortable than the rooms with bath, so the price is the same for both. Don't expect luxury or resort amenities, and Plage de Ste-Anne is 6 miles away. The advantages of this place are the low rates, the view of the marina from some rooms, the garden setting, and about the easiest access you can think of for a meal or a drink. The inn has a stunning collection of exotic masks, derived from Haiti, Ecuador, and Venezuela.

GREAT DEALS ON DINING

Auberge du Marin. Rue Osman-Duquesnay 21, Le Marin. ☎ **0596/74-83-88.** Main courses 62–140F ($10.55–$23.80); lunch *plat du jour* 45F ($7.65); fixed-price 3-course lunch or dinner 78F ($13.25). MC, V. Mon–Tues and Thurs–Sat noon–1:30pm and 7:30–9:30pm, Wed and Sun 7:30–9:30pm. Closed Sept. FRENCH/CREOLE.

This restaurant is the focal point of the *auberge* we recommended above for its simple rooms. Its staff is gruff and somewhat blasé, but the place will probably grow more likable as your meal progresses, and the relatively low tab will more than make up for the rustic setting. Decorated with artifacts and carved masks from Venezuela, Haiti, and Brazil, the restaurant is in the heart of Le Marin, overlooking a garden and a marina. The lunch *plat du jour* is a meal in itself, and the fixed-price meal (soup or salad, a main platter of meat or grilled fish, and dessert), is a bargain. The cuisine is French Creole and evocative of southwestern France. The chef makes a delectable *cassoulet* filled with white beans and meat products. His *magret* of duckling is excellent, as is his *confit* of duckling with flap mushrooms. He also prepares an old-fashioned version of sweetbreads.

STE-ANNE

From Le Marin, a 5-mile drive brings you to Ste-Anne, at the extreme southern tip of Martinique. This sleepy little village is known for **white-sand beaches.** The beaches here are white, while those to the north are more grayish. In many ways, the beaches at Les Salines are Martinique's finest. The climate is arid like parts of Arizona, and the beaches are almost always sunny, perhaps too much so during the fierce midday sun.

Holidays and weekends tend to be crowded, as many islanders and their families flock to this beach during those times. Regrettably, the beach isn't big enough to handle the hordes, and you'd be wise to seek out other beaches at this time.

The name of the beach comes from Étang des Salines, a large salt pond forming a backdrop to the strip of sand. Under no circumstances should you go under the manchineel trees here for protection in a rainfall. When it's sunny you can seek shade here. But when it rains, drops falling from this poisonous tree will be like acid on your tender skin. The trees are found mainly at the southeastern end of the beach.

Salines is the site of Martinique's only real **gay beach.** Drive to the far end of the parking lot, near the sign for Petite Anse des Salines. Here you'll find a trail leading through thick woods (although some of the sounds you're likely to hear coming from the woods aren't from local bird life!) to a sun-flooded beach often filled with naked gay men, with an occasional lesbian couple. Technically, there are no legal nudist beaches on Martinique, so it's possible you could be arrested here for going nude, although authorities don't seem to enforce this law. Throughout the island, however, the European custom of topless bathing isn't uncommon on any of the beaches of Martinique or even around hotel pools.

Ste-Anne opens onto views of the Ste-Lucia Canal, and nearby is the Petrified Savanna Forest, which the French call **Savane des Pétrifications.** It's a field of petrified volcanic boulders in the shape of logs. The eerie desert-like site, no-man's-land, is studded with cacti.

ACCOMMODATIONS YOU CAN AFFORD

La Dunette. 97227 Ste-Anne, Martinique, F.W.I. ☎ **0596/76-73-90.** Fax 0596/76-76-05. 18 units. A/C TV TEL. Winter 500F ($85) single; 600F ($102) double. Off-season 400F ($68) single; 500F ($85) double. Rates include continental breakfast. MC, V.

Beside the sea, this three-story stucco hotel appeals to those who appreciate its simplicity and its isolation from the more built-up resort areas. It's near the Club Med and the white-sand beaches of the Salines. Best defined as an unpretentious seaside inn with a summery decor, the hotel is accented by a garden filled with flowers and tropical plants. The furnishings are casual and modern, and though some rooms are quite small, each benefited from a complete renovation in 1993. The mattresses are renewed as needed, and the private baths, though small, are well maintained. Drinks are served every night on the terrace above the sea. The restaurant, open daily for lunch and dinner, is better than you might expect, thanks to the culinary finesse of the Tanzania-born owner Gerard Kambona. Main courses may include a succulent version of red snapper stuffed with sea urchins, or a wide selection of shellfish plucked from local waters.

GREAT DEALS ON DINING

✪ **Aux Filets Bleus.** Pointe Marin, Ste-Anne. ☎ **0596/76-73-42.** Reservations required. Fixed-price menu 59–260F ($10.05–$44.20). MC, V. Daily noon–3:30pm and 7–10:30pm. CREOLE/FRENCH.

This family-run blue-and-white restaurant is a 30-minute drive south of the airport. The seaside exposure of the alfresco dining room and its terrace makes you feel as if you're in an isolated tropical retreat, where the only sound is the splash of waves and the tinkling of ice in glasses. What appears to be a glass-covered reflecting pool set into the floor is actually a lobster tank, one of only a few on the island. You'll find one of the island's cheapest fixed-price menus here. Specialties include *bouillabaisse de la mer,* which is three types of fish covered with a tomato-and-onion sauce; crabmeat salad with a coulis of tomato, basil, and olive oil; *salade filets bleues,* with fresh crayfish, hearts of palm, avocados, fresh tomatoes, and whisky-laden cocktail sauce; and *pavé de daurade aux senteurs des îles* (white fish with a coriander-and-fennel sauce). You can go for a swim before or after your meal.

Poï et Virginie. Place de l'Eglise, rue du Bord-de-Mer, Ste-Anne. ☎ **0596/76-76-86.** Reservations recommended. Main courses 60–265F ($10.20–$45.05). AE, MC, V. Tues 7–9pm, Wed–Sun noon–2:30pm and 7–9:30pm. CREOLE.

From the outside, this restaurant looks like a ramshackle bungalow beside the beach. Inside, the décor is much more substantial, with terra-cotta floor tiles, primitive Haitian paintings, slowly spinning ceiling fans, and lots of roughly textured wood. If it isn't too hot or rainy, you might sit on a wooden deck whose foundations are sunk into the seabed and hear the waves splashing beneath your table. Menu choices include fresh local lobster, marinated raw conch, stuffed crab back, raw marinated fish, local fresh oysters, and grilled local fish. One fish dish is exceptional: grilled fresh fish with sauce Martiniquaise (vinaigrette with Martinique spices). The restaurant's name was inspired by a 19th-century romantic novel, *Paul et Virginie,* whose star-crossed protagonists were doomed to everlasting unrequited love.

5 The North Loop

As we swing north from Fort-de-France, our main targets are **Le Carbet, St-Pierre, Montagne Pelée,** and **Leyritz.** However, we'll sandwich in many stops along the way. From Fort-de-France there are three ways to head north to Montagne Pelée. The first way is to follow the N4 up to St-Joseph. Here you take the left fork for 3 miles after St-Joseph and turn onto the D15 toward Marigot.

Another way to Montagne Pelée is to take the N3 through the vegetation-rich mornes until you reach Le Morne Rouge. This road is known as the Route de la Trace and is now the center of the Parc Naturel de la Martinique. Yet a third route to reach Montagne Pelée is to follow N2 along the coast. Near Fort-de-France, the first town you reach is Schoelcher.

Farther along N2 you come to Case-Pilote, then Bellefontaine. This portion, along the most frequented tourist route on Martinique—that is, Fort-de-France to St-Pierre—will remind many a traveler of the French Riviera. Bellefontaine is a small fishing village with boats stretched along the beach. Note the many houses also built in the shape of boats.

LE CARBET

Leaving Bellefontaine, a 5-mile drive north will deliver you to Le Carbet. Columbus landed here in 1502, and the first French settlers arrived in 1635. In 1887, Gauguin lived here for 4 months before going on to Tahiti. You can stop for a swim at an Olympic-size pool set into the hills or watch the locals scrubbing clothes in a stream. The town lies on the bus route from Fort-de-France to St-Pierre.

The **Centre d'Art Musée Paul-Gauguin,** Anse Turin, Le Carbet (☎ **0596/ 78-22-66**), is near the beach represented in the artist's *Bord de Mer*. The landscape hasn't changed in 100 years. The museum, in a five-room building, commemorates the French artist's 1887 stay on Martinique, with books, prints, letters, and other memorabilia. There are also paintings by René Corail, sculpture by Hector Charpentier, and examples of the artwork of Zaffanella. Of special interest are faïence mosaics made of once-white pieces that turned pink, maroon, blue, and black in 1902 when the fires of Montagne Pelée devastated St-Pierre. There are also changing exhibits of works by local artists. The museum is open daily 9am to 5:30pm, with an admission of 20F ($3.40) for adults and 5F (85¢) for children under 8.

ST-PIERRE

In the early 1900s, St-Pierre was known as the Little Paris of the West Indies. Home to 30,000 inhabitants, it was the cultural and economic capital of Martinique. On May 7, 1902, the citizens read in their daily newspaper that Montagne Pelée didn't present any more risk to the population than Vesuvius did to the Neapolitans.

However, on May 8, 1902, at 8am, the southwest side of Montagne Pelée exploded into fire and lava. At 8:02am all 30,000 inhabitants were dead—that is, all except one. A convict in his underground cell was saved by the thickness of the walls. When islanders reached the site, the convict was paroled and left Martinique to tour in Barnum and Bailey's circus. St-Pierre never recovered its past splendor. Now it could be called the Pompeii of the West Indies. Ruins of the church, the theater, and some other buildings can be seen along the coast.

One of the best ways to get an overview of St-Pierre is riding a rubber-wheeled train, the **CV Paris Express** (☎ **0596/78-31-41**), which departs on tours from the base of the Musée Volcanologique. Tours cost 50F ($8.50) for adults and 25F ($4.25) for children and run Monday to Friday 10:30am to 1pm and 2:30 to 7pm. In theory, tours depart about once an hour, but they leave only when there are enough people to justify a trip.

The **Musée Volcanologique,** rue Victor-Hugo, St-Pierre (☎ **0596/78-10-32**), was created by American volcanologist Franck Alvard Perret, who turned the museum over to the city in 1933. Here in pictures and relics dug from the debris you can trace the story of what happened to St-Pierre. Dug from the lava is a clock that stopped at the exact moment the volcano erupted. The museum is open daily 9am to 5pm, with an admission of 10F ($1.70); free for children 7 and under.

GREAT DEALS ON DINING

La Factorerie. Quartier Fort, St-Pierre. ☎ **0596/78-12-53.** Reservations recommended. Main courses 72–150F ($12.25–$25.50). AE, MC, V. Daily noon–2pm. CREOLE.

This budget place is between St-Pierre and Le Prêcheur, near the ruins of a 19th-century church, the Eglise du Fort. It's a ramshackle-looking cottage in a grove of mango trees and coconut palms. At least some of the staff will have been trained at Martinique's nearby agricultural training school. The restaurant is a bit battered and serves only lunch, but if you're in the neighborhood around noon, it makes a good stop. You'll enjoy dishes like chicken with coconut, conch fricassee, chicken with prawns, freshwater crayfish served with piquant tomato sauce, colombo with chicken, and a dessert flan made with fresh coconuts and sweet potatoes.

LE PRÊCHEUR

From St-Pierre you can continue along the coast north to Le Prêcheur. Once the home of Mme de Maintenon, the mistress of Louis XIV, it's the last village along the northern coast of Martinique. Here you can see hot springs of volcanic origin and the **Tombeau des Caraïbes (Tomb of the Caribs),** where, according to legend, the collective suicide of many West Indian natives took place after they returned from a fishing expedition and found their homes pillaged by the French.

MONTAGNE PELÉE

A panoramic and winding road (N2) takes you through a **tropical rain forest.** The curves are of the hairpin variety, and the road is twisty and not always kept in good shape. However, you're rewarded with tropical flowers, baby ferns, plumed bamboo, and valleys so deeply green you'll think you're wearing cheap sunglasses.

The village of **Morne Rouge,** at the foot of Montagne Pelée, is a popular vacation spot for Martinicans. From here a narrow and unreliable road brings you to a level of 2,500 feet above sea level, 1,600 feet under the round summit of the volcano that destroyed St-Pierre. Montagne Pelée itself rises 4,575 feet above sea level.

If you're a trained mountain climber and don't mind 4 or 5 hours of hiking, you can scale the peak to Grand' Rivière. Realize that this is a mountain, that rain is frequent, and that temperatures drop very low. Tropical growth often hides deep crevices in the earth, and there are other dangers. So if you're really serious about this climb, you should hire an experienced guide. As for the volcano, its death-dealing reign in 1902 apparently satisfied it—at least for the time being.

On your descent from Montagne Pelée, drive down to **Ajoupa-Bouillon,** which some describe, with justification, as the most beautiful town on Martinique. Abounding in flowers and shrubbery with bright yellow and red leaves, this little village is the site of the remarkable **Gorges de la Falaise.** These are mini-canyons on the Falaise River up which you can travel to reach a waterfall.

GREAT DEALS ON DINING

Le Fromager. Route de Fonds-St-Denis, St-Pierre. ☎ **0596/78-19-07.** Reservations recommended. Fixed-price menus 100–150F ($17–$25.50); main courses 80–130F ($13.60–$22.10). AE, DC, MC, V. Daily noon–3pm. CREOLE/FRENCH.

About half a mile uphill (east) of the center of St-Pierre, this indoor-outdoor villa, owned by the René family, welcomes lunch guests with humor and charm that's half-French, half-Martinican. It has a sweeping view and resembles a covered open-air pavilion. Good-tasting menu items include marinated octopus, grilled conch or lobster, curried goat or chicken, and whatever grilled fish is available that day.

LEYRITZ

Continue east toward the coast, near the town of Basse-Pointe in northeastern Martinique. A mile before Basse-Pointe, turn left and follow a road that goes deep into sugarcane country to Leyritz, where you'll find one of the best-restored plantations on Martinique. Perhaps stop by for lunch.

ACCOMMODATIONS YOU CAN AFFORD

✪ **Hôtel Plantation de Leyritz.** 97218 Basse-Pointe, Martinique, F.W.I. ☎ **0596/ 78-53-92.** Fax 0596/78-92-44. www.fwinet.com/leyritz.htm. E-mail: hyleyritz@cgit.com. 67 units. A/C TV TEL. Winter 620F ($105.40) single, 700F ($119) double. Off-season 460F ($78.20) single, 520F ($88.40) double. Rates include continental breakfast. AE, MC, V.

This hotel, offering spa facilities, was built around 1700 by a plantation owner, Bordeaux-born Michel de Leyritz. It was the site of the 1974 swimming pool summit meeting between Presidents Gerald Ford and Valéry Giscard d'Estaing. Today you're likely to meet a stampede of cruise-ship passengers. It's a working banana plantation that has been restored to its original character. There are 16 acres of tropical gardens, and at the core is an 18th-century stone Great House. The owners have kept the best of the old, like the rugged stone walls (20-inches thick), beamed ceilings, and tile and flagstone floors. About half the accommodations are in small outbuildings scattered around the property; others are in a newer annex adjacent to the spa. The rooms come in a variety of sizes, ranging from spacious to small. Some have sundecks, and bed arrangements also vary throughout, ranging from twins to king-size beds, even singles. But the French mattresses are firm for your back, and the baths, though tiny, are tidy. Don't expect well-polished luxury—that's not the style here. Laundry service and an outdoor pool are pluses.

GREAT DEALS ON DINING

Hotel Plantation de Leyritz. Basse-Pointe. ☎ **0596/78-53-92.** Main courses 80–150F ($13.60–$25.50); fixed-price menu at lunch 127F ($21.60); fixed-price menu at dinner 150F ($25.50). AE, MC, V. Daily noon–2:30pm and 7–9:15pm. FRENCH.

The dining room is in a former rum distillery, incorporating the fresh spring water running down from the hillside. Eating here is dramatic at night, and the cuisine is authentically Creole. Tour-bus crowds predominate at lunch. Your lunch may be grilled chicken in coconut-milk sauce, along with *ouassous* (a freshwater crayfish that comes in herb sauce), sautéed breadfruit, and sautéed bananas. Dinner is more elaborate, with both French and Creole dishes, like duck with pineapple and *boudin* (blood pudding) Creole. Other good-tasting dishes are a colombo or curry of lamb, a fricassee of pork (or conch), *accras de morue* (codfish fritters), and a surprising dish of sauerkraut where shredded papaya is substituted for the traditional cabbage and the meat derives from sausages and from lardons (browned bacon and salt pork). You might want to begin your meal with the traditional planter's punch.

BASSE-POINTE

At the northernmost point on the island, Basse-Pointe is a land of pineapple and banana plantation fields, covering the Atlantic-side slopes of Mount Pelée volcano.

GREAT DEALS ON DINING

✪ **Chez Mally Edjam.** Route de la Côte Atlantique. ☎ **0596/78-51-18.** Reservations required. Main courses 70–180F ($11.90–$30.60); fixed-price menu 70F ($11.90). MC, V. Daily noon–3pm; dinner by special arrangement only. Closed mid-July to mid-Aug. FRENCH/CREOLE.

This local legend operates from a modest house beside the main road in the town center, 36 miles from Fort-de-France. Appreciating its exotic but genteel charm, many visitors prefer to drive all the way from Pointe du Bout to dine here instead of at the Leyritz Plantation. You sit at one of a handful of tables on the side porch, unless you prefer a seat in the somewhat more formal dining room.

Grandmotherly Mally Edjam (ably assisted by France-born Martine Hugé) is busy in the kitchen turning out her Creole delicacies. They know how to prepare all the dishes for which the island is known: stuffed land crab with hot seasoning, small pieces of conch in a tart shell, and a classic *colombo de porc* (the Creole version of pork curry). Equally acclaimed are the lobster vinaigrette, the papaya soufflé (which must be ordered in advance), and the highly original confitures (tiny portions of fresh island fruits, such as pineapple and guava, that have been preserved in a vanilla syrup).

GRAND' RIVIÈRE

After Basse-Pointe, the town you reach on your northward trek is Grand' Rivière. From here you must turn back, but before doing so you may want to stop at a good restaurant right at the entrance to the town.

GREAT DEALS ON DINING

Yva Chez Vava. Blvd. Charles-de-Gaulle. ☎ **0596/55-72-72.** Reservations recommended. Main courses 60–130F ($10.20–$22.10); fixed-price menu 80F ($13.60). AE, DC, MC, V. Daily noon–6pm. FRENCH/CREOLE.

West of Basse-Pointe, in a low-slung building painted the peachy-orange of a paw-paw fruit, Yva Chez Vava is a private home and restaurant. It represents the hard labor of three generations of Creole women. Infused with a simple country-inn style, it was opened in 1979 by a well-remembered, long-departed matron, Vava, whose daughter, Yva, is now assisted by her own daughter, Rosy. Local family recipes are the mainstay of this modest bistro. A la carte menu items include Creole soup, lobster, and various colombos or curries. Local delicacies have changed little since the days of Joséphine and her sugar fortune and include *z'habitants* (crayfish), *vivaneau* (red snapper), *tazard* (kingfish), and *accras de morue* (cod fritters).

STE-MARIE

Heading south along the coastal road, you'll pass Le Marigot to reach a sightseeing stop in the little town of Ste-Marie. The **Musée du Rhum St-James,** route de l'Union at the Saint James Distillery (☎ **0596/69-30-02**), displays engravings, antique tools and machines, and other exhibits tracing the history of sugarcane and rum from 1765 to the present. When inventories of rum are low and the distillery is functioning (February to July), guided tours of both the museum and its distillery are offered. Tours depart at 10am, 11:30am, 1pm, and 2:30pm, costing 20F ($3.40) per person, including a rum-tasting. Admission to the museum (open daily from 9am to 6pm, regardless of whether the distillery is functioning) is free. Samples of rum are available for purchase on site.

From here you can head out the north end of town and loop inland a bit for a stop at Morne des Esses or continue heading south straight to Trinité.

GREAT DEALS ON DINING

✪ **Restaurant La Découverte/Chez Tatie Simone.** Fôret la Philippe, Route du Marigot, Ste-Marie. ☎ **0596/69-44-04.** Reservations recommended. Main courses 80–160F ($13.60–$27.20). AE, DC, MC, V. Daily 11am–11pm. CREOLE.

Near the island's northeastern tip, 2½ miles north of Ste-Marie, this restaurant prepares superb versions of traditional Creole fare. The setting is a cement-sided house built in the early 1980s, the showcase for the cuisine of Auntie (Tatie) Simone Adelise. Formerly employed as a chef in a private home in France, she returned to her native Martinique to open this well-recommended restaurant. Assisted by her manager, Fritz, she prepares *boudin rouge* (blood sausages, in her case accented with habañera peppers and cinnamon); *boudin blanc* (sausages made from pulverized conch and spices); couscous with *fruits de mer* garnished with shrimp, crayfish, sea urchins, clams, and octopus; vegetable broth flavored with sea urchins and cognac; and a succulent array of grilled fish. After your meal, a member of the staff will propose you take a 40-minute promenade along a well-marked hiking trail dotted with signs that give the names of specific trees and plants. At its end you'll be rewarded with sweeping panoramas over sea and coast.

MORNE DES ESSES

This is the *vannerie* (basket-making) capital of Martinique, and you can pick up a sturdy straw food basket in any of the small village shops.

GREAT DEALS ON DINING

Le Colibri (The Hummingbird). Allée du Colibri. ☎ **0596/69-91-95.** Main courses 100–250F ($17–$42.50). AE, DC, MC, V. Daily noon–3pm and 7–10pm. CREOLE.

One of Martinique's oldest restaurants, this rustic-looking spot was opened by a well-respected matriarch, Mme Clotilde Paladino, who to an increasing degree is assisted by her daughters, Marie-José and Marie-Joseph, and her son, Joël. (Marie-José and Marie-Joseph are fraternal twins who bear a striking resemblance to each other, and the similarity of their names adds a charming but sometimes confusing spice to a meal here.) The site, which was enlarged and embellished in the mid-1990s with a series of paintings by local artists, is in the heart of town near the post office. The dining space is supplemented by two terraces, one of which overlooks a view of the busy kitchen. The cuisine is deeply rooted in Creole traditions and usually includes steaming bowls of callalou soup garnished with crabmeat, Creole-style *boudin* (blood sausage), *accras* of codfish, and less conventional fare like *buisson d'écrevisses* (stew of freshwater crayfish), chicken with coconut, conch tarts, avocado stuffed with crabmeat, and roast suckling pig. Especially appealing is a *salade de Colibri* loaded with seafood that some diners select as a main course and (when they're available) a *tourte des oursins* (sea urchin pie).

TRINITÉ

If you're in Mornes des Esses, continue south and then turn east, or from Ste-Marie head south along the coastal route (N1) to reach the small village of Trinité. The town is the gateway to the Carvalle peninsula, where the **Presqu'ile de la Carabelle Nature Preserve** offers excellent hiking and one of the only safe beaches for swimming on the Atlantic coast. This town would hardly merit a stopover were it not for the Hôtel Saint-Aubin.

ACCOMMODATIONS YOU CAN AFFORD

✪ **Saint-Aubin Hôtel.** 97220 Trinité, Martinique, F.W.I. ☎ **0596/69-34-77.** Fax 0596/ 69-41-14. 15 units. A/C TEL. Winter 320–360F ($54.40–$61.20) single; 480–580F ($81.60– $98.60) double. Off-season 300–340F ($51–$57.80) single; 380F ($64.60) double. Rates include continental breakfast. AE, DC, MC, V.

A former restaurant owner, Normandy-born Guy Forêt, has sunk his fortune into restoring this three-story Victorian and turning it into a three-star hostelry, one of the loveliest inns in the Caribbean. The house, painted a vivid pink with fancy gingerbread, was built in 1920 as a replacement for a much older house that was the seat of a large plantation. It sits on a hillside above sugarcane fields and Trinité's bay, 14½ miles from the airport, 19 miles from Fort-de-France, and 2 miles from the seaside village of Trinité itself. There are 800 yards of public beach, plus a pool. All the good-size rooms sport wall-to-wall carpeting and modern furniture, as well as views of either the garden or the sea. There are some family rooms as well. After dinner, you can relax on the veranda. The hotel restaurant and bar are reserved for use by hotel guests, with meals served only at dinner Monday to Saturday. Offerings may include avocado vinaigrette, Creole black pudding, grilled fresh fish, stuffed crab, and fish poached in court bouillon.

LE FRANÇOIS

Continuing your exploration of the east coast of Martinique, you can stop over in Le François to visit the **Musée Rhum Clement** at the Domaine de l'Acajou (☎ **0596/ 54-62-07**), about 1½ miles south of the village center. It's open daily from 9am to 6pm, charging an admission of 40F ($6.80). The distillery lies in the cellar of an 18th-century mansion with period furnishings. The house commemorates the summit meeting of Presidents Mitterrand and Bush in 1992. A Christopher Columbus exhibit is set up in caves, and other exhibits trace the institution of slavery in the islands. The museum is in a botanic park, and you could easily spend 2 or 3 hours exploring the exhibits and grounds.

Nevis 16

A local once said the best reason to go to Nevis was to practice the fine art of *limin'*—doing nothing. Limin' might still be the best reason to come to this small volcanic island. You can find lodging in one of the old plantation houses, now converted to inns, or in the small Antillean guest houses, and experience all the calm you want. And during the day you can head for reef-protected Pinney's Beach, a 3-mile strip of dark-gold sand set against a backdrop of palms, with panoramic views of St. Kitts.

Two miles south of St. Kitts, Nevis (*Nee*-vis) was sighted by Columbus in 1493. He called it Las Nieves, Spanish for "snows," because its mountains reminded him of the snow-capped range in the Pyrenees. When viewed from St. Kitts (see chapter 20), the island appears like a perfect cone, rising gradually to 3,232 feet. A saddle joins the tallest mountain to two smaller peaks, Saddle Hill (1,250 feet) in the south and Hurricane Hill (only 250 feet) in the north. Coral reefs rim the shore, and there's mile after mile of palm-shaded white-sand beaches.

Settled by the British in 1628, the island is famous as the birthplace of Alexander Hamilton, the American statesman who wrote many of the articles contained in the *Federalist Papers* and was Washington's secretary of the treasury. (He was killed by Aaron Burr in a duel.) Nevis is also the island on which Adm. Horatio Lord Nelson married a local woman, Frances Nisbet, in 1787. The historical facts are romanticized, but this episode is described in the late James Michener's best-seller *Caribbean*.

In the 18th century, this Queen of the Caribees was the leading spa of the West Indies, made so by its hot mineral springs. It was also once peppered with prosperous sugarcane estates, but they're gone now—many have been converted into some of the most intriguing hotels in the Caribbean. Sea island cotton is the chief crop today.

Though there has been sentiment for Nevis breaking away to form its own island nation, it's still part of a federation with neighboring St. Kitts. Nevis has great sibling rivalry with that island, both competing for upper-market tourists and doing very little to attract budget travelers—hence, prices on both islands tend to be high. Nevis also vies with St. Kitts as a banking island and is noted for its banking secrecy. Already some 10,000 offshore businesses are registered here, or more than one business for each inhabitant. In some cases, the operators of these businesses have never set foot on Nevis. More than half of these businesses, operating under strict secrecy laws, have opened since the mid-1990s.

As you drive around the island, through tiny villages like Gingerland (named for the spice it used to export), you'll reach the heavily wooded slopes of Nevis Peak, which offers views of the neighboring islands. On the Caribbean side, Charlestown, the capital, was fashionable in the 18th century, when sugar planters were carried around in carriages and sedan chairs. Houses are of locally quarried volcanic stone, encircled by West Indian fretted verandas. A town of wide, quiet streets, this port gets busy only when its major link to the world, the ferry from St. Kitts, docks at the harbor.

1 Essentials

VISITOR INFORMATION

Tourist information is available from the St. Kitts and Nevis tourist board's **stateside offices** at 414 E. 75th St., New York, NY 10021 (☎ **800/582-6208** or 212/535-1234); and 1464 Whippoorwill Way, Mountainside, NJ 07092 (☎ **208/233-6701**).

In **Canada,** an office is at 365 Bay St., Suite 806, Toronto, ON, M5H 2V1 (☎ **416/376-6707**), and in the **United Kingdom** at 10 Kensington Court, London, W8 5DL (☎ **0171/376-0881**).

The best source for information on the island is the **Tourist Bureau** on Main Street in Charlestown (☎ **020/7469-1042**).

The Internet address for both St. Kitts and Nevis is **www.stkitts-nevis.com**.

GETTING THERE

BY PLANE   You can fly to Nevis on **LIAT** (☎ **800/468-0482** in the U.S. and Canada, or 869/469-9333), which offers regularly scheduled service. Flights from St. Kitts and Antigua are usually nonstop, and flights from St. Thomas, St. Croix, San Juan, Barbados, and Caracas, Venezuela, usually require at least one stop before reaching Nevis. It's only a 7-minute hop from St. Kitts, and LIAT goes there daily at 6:40am and 2:05pm.

Nevis Express (☎ **869/469-9755**) operates a 12-passenger flight daily shuttle service of 10 departures each way between St. Kitts and Nevis. A round-trip ticket from St. Kitts to Nevis costs $40. Call for reservations and information. Any of North America's larger carriers, including **American Airlines** (☎ **800/433-7300**), can arrange ongoing passage to Nevis on LIAT through such hubs as Antigua, San Juan, or St. Maarten, connecting with your flight from North America.

The **Newcastle Airport** lies half a mile from Newcastle in the northern part of the island.

BY FERRY   You can use the interisland ferry service from St. Kitts to Charlestown on Nevis aboard the government passenger ferry **M.V. *Caribe Queen.*** It departs from each island between 7 and 7:30am on Monday, Tuesday, Wednesday, Friday, and Saturday, returning at 4 and 6pm (check the time at your hotel or the tourist office). The cost is $4 each way. You can also take an air-conditioned 110-passenger ferry, **M.V. *Spirit of Mount Nevis,*** which sails twice daily on Thursday and Sunday, costing $6 one-way. Call **Nevis Cruise Lines** at ☎ **869/469-9373** for more information.

GETTING AROUND

BY TAXI   Taxi drivers double as guides, and you'll find them waiting at the airport for the arrival of every plane. A taxi ride between Charlestown and Newcastle Airport costs EC$40 ($14.80); between Charlestown and Old Manor Estate, EC$30

($11.10); and from Charlestown to Pinney's Beach, EC$13 ($4.80). Between 10pm and 6am, 50% is added to the prices for Charlestown trips. Call ☎ **869/469-5621** for more information.

BY RENTAL CAR If you're prepared to face the winding, rocky, potholed roads of Nevis, you can arrange for a rental car from a local firm through your hotel. Or you can check with **Skeete's Car Rental,** Newcastle Village, near the airport (☎ **869/469-9458**).

To drive on Nevis you must obtain a permit from the traffic department, which costs EC$50 ($18.50) and is valid for a year. Car-rental companies will handle this for you. Remember, *drive on the left side of the road.*

Fast Facts: Nevis

Banking Hours Banks are open Monday to Saturday 8am to noon and most are also open Friday 3:30 to 5:30pm.

Currency The local currency is the **Eastern Caribbean dollar (EC$),** valued at about $2.70 to the U.S. dollar. Many prices, however, including those of hotels, are quoted in U.S. dollars. Always determine which "dollar" locals are talking about.

Customs You're allowed in duty-free with your personal belongings. Sometimes luggage is subjected to a drug check.

Drugstores Try **Evelyn's Drugstore,** Charlestown (☎ **869/469-5278**), open Monday to Friday 8am to 5:30pm (closes at 5pm on Thursday), Saturday 8am to 7pm, and Sunday 7 to 8pm only, to serve emergency needs.

Electricity As on St. Kitts, an electrical transformer and adapter will be needed for most U.S. and Canadian appliances, as the electricity is 230 volts AC (60 cycles). However, check with your hotel to see if it has converted its voltage and outlets.

Emergencies For the police, call ☎ **911.**

Entry Requirements U.S. and Canadian citizens can enter with proof of citizenship, such as a birth certificate with a raised seal. British subjects also need a passport, but not a visa. A return or ongoing ticket is also mandatory. Of course, if you clear customs in St. Kitts, you don't need to clear customs again in Nevis.

Hospitals A 24-hour emergency room operates at **Alexandra Hospital,** Government Road, in Charlestown (☎ **869/469-5473**).

Language English is the language of the island and is spoken with a decided West Indian patois.

Post Office The post office, on Main Street in Charlestown, is open Monday to Wednesday and Friday 8am to 3pm, Thursday 8 to 11am, and Saturday 8am to noon.

Safety Although crime is rare here, protect your valuables and never leave them unguarded on the beach.

Taxes The government imposes a 7% tax on hotel bills, plus a departure tax of EC$27 ($10) per person. You don't have to pay the departure tax on Nevis if you're returning to St. Kitts.

Telecommunications Telegrams and telexes can be sent from the **Cable & Wireless office,** Main Street, Charlestown (☎ **869/469-5000**). International telephone calls, including collect calls, can also be made from the cable office. It's open Monday to Friday 8am to 5pm and Saturday 8am to noon.

Time As with St. Kitts, Nevis is on Atlantic standard time year-round, which means it's usually 1 hour ahead of the U.S. east coast, except when the mainland goes on daylight saving time; then clocks are the same.

Tipping A 10% service charge is added to your hotel bill. In restaurants it's customary to tip 10% to 15% of the tab.

Water In the 1700s, Lord Nelson regularly brought his fleet to Nevis just to collect water, and Nevis still boasts of having Nelson spring water.

2 Accommodations You Can Afford

Jonathan's Villa Hotel. Mount Lily, Nevis, W.I. ☎ **869/469-9148.** Fax 809/469-9350. 10 units. TEL. Winter $60–$125 unit for 1 or 2. Off-season $50–$100 unit for 1 or 2. Extra person $15. AE, MC, V.

On the slopes of Mount Lily, an 8-minute drive from the airport, this family-owned hotel offers medium-size cottage and villa rooms with ceiling fans, radios, and tiny baths. They're furnished in a tropical motif, with wicker and colorful island prints. The family-style villa has a kitchenette. A restaurant specializes in West Indian cuisine, with vegetarian platters as well. The front desk staff can arrange outings for you, including island and rain-forest tours, nature hikes, and water sports. A 5-minute drive will take you to Herbert's Beach; other larger beaches, like Pinney's and Jones Bay, are a 10-minute drive away.

Lindale's Guest House. Main St. (P.O. Box 463), Charleston, Nevis, W.I. ☎ **869/469-5412.** 2 units. Year-round $60 single or double. Extra person $20. Rates include continental breakfast. No credit cards.

If you don't mind just the bare essentials, stay here. The house was built in 1963 and is a simple affair in the heart of Charlestown. The small rooms are clean, with equally small baths and ceiling fans. Mattresses were renewed in the late 1990s, and housekeeping is neat and tidy. Guests may use the phone in the office, and a TV is located in the main living room. Maude Cross owns and operates this tranquil abode, which was rebuilt after Hurricane Hugo wreaked its havoc. Children under 3 aren't accepted.

Meadville Cottages. Craddock Road (P.O. Box 66), Charlestown, Nevis, W.I. ☎ **869/469-5235.** 11 units. Winter $60 single; $80 double; $80 cottage for 2. Off-season $40 single; $60 double; $70 cottage for 2. Extra person $20. V.

The Meadville cottages, white concrete buildings on the outskirts of Charlestown in a commercial district, were opened in the mid-1980s. The amenities are few but the prices reasonable. The small rooms are simple with wall-to-wall carpeting, mahogany furniture, decent beds, and tiny baths. Some have kitchenettes and L-shaped verandas, but all have fans (at this elevation, you can usually count on refreshing trade winds). The cottages are near restaurants, shops, and Pinney's Beach.

Sea Spawn Guest House. Old Hospital Rd., Charlestown, Nevis, W.I. ☎ **869/469-5239.** Fax 869/469-5706. 18 units. Year-round, $35.10 single; $40.95–$58.50 double; $70.20 triple; $81.90 quad. Extra person $10. Children 11 and under stay free in parents' room. DISC, MC, V.

A 2-minute walk from Pinney's Beach, this is just about the island's most no-frills entry, but, hey, you didn't come here to hang out in your hotel room. You're assured of cleanliness and reasonable comfort, though, in this simple white two-story concrete building with verandas all around the upper and ground floors. The tiny rooms are a little bit grander than bunk style. Standing fans attempt to keep you cool. Baths are barely adequate, and plumbing isn't state of the art, but hearty types like it here. Guests share a communal kitchen for $5 a day, though the restaurant offers inexpensive local fare three meals a day.

✪ **Yamseed Inn.** Newcastle, Nevis, W.I. ☎ **869/469-9361.** 4 units. Year-round $100 single or double, 3-night minimum stay. Rates include full breakfast. No credit cards.

Built as a home in 1964, this charming yellow B&B is in the northernmost part of the island on a secluded beach offering panoramic views of St. Kitts. The spacious airy rooms are well appointed with antiques, Oriental rugs (including some from Nepal), and locally crafted headboards crowning comfortable beds with firm mattresses. Each has its own small but tidy bath and private entrance. Sybil Siegfried, who owns and operates the Yamseed, serves full breakfasts that include freshly baked multigrain and banana breads, homemade granola cereal, waffles, and fresh fruit. The Yamseed offers hammocks to laze away the days and beautiful surf to enjoy.

BEST OFF-SEASON BET

The Inn at Cades Bay. Cades Bay, Nevis, WI. ☎ **869/469-8139.** Fax 869/469-8129. www. cadesbayinn.com. E-mail: cadesbay@caribsurf.com. 16 units. A/C TV. Mid-Dec to mid-Apr $175 single or double; mid-Apr to mid-Dec $125 single or double. AE, MC, V.

Small, charming, and locally owned, this is the first hotel to open in Nevis since the blockbuster opening of the upscale Four Seasons in 1990. On the island's southern coast, occupying a quintet of salmon-colored one-story buildings, it's the creative statement of Eddy and Sheila Williams, who've already proven their skill thanks to the success of Eddy's restaurant in downtown Charlestown. Each medium-size accommodation contains a tray-shaped ceiling fashioned from pickled pine, a floor layered with terra-cotta Mexican tiles, off-white walls, ceiling fans, coffee-making facilities, hairdryers, and summery furniture. There's a long rectangular pool, shuttle bus service from the hotel to Eddy's restaurant, and a knowledgeable staff. The hotel's bar and restaurant, Tequila Sheila's, is separately recommended.

3 Great Deals on Dining

The local food is good. Suckling pig is roasted with many spices, and eggplant and avocado are used in a number of tasty ways. You may see turtle on some menus, but remember that this is an endangered species.

Beachcomber Restaurant & Bar. Pinney's Beach. ☎ **869/469-1192.** Reservations recommended. Burgers $8–$9; platters $15–$35. AE, MC, V. Daily 11am–9pm. Closed Sun–Wed off-season. INTERNATIONAL.

This open-air restaurant on the beach is ideal for dining, especially lunch at any time during the afternoon. Take a table on the veranda and let the trade winds cool you off. Watch for the changing specials. At lunch you might want to opt for the "Nevis burger," made with chopped mahi mahi or tuna and served on a sesame bun with cole slaw and fries. We also like to come here for a bowl of one of the soups, made fresh daily—especially tasty are the conch chowder and cream of pumpkin. For a main course, the Creole chicken is always spicy and filled with flavor, as is flying fish sautéed in curried beer batter. Locals are fond of the salt fish with Johnny cakes.

Callaloo Restaurant. Main St., Charlestown. ☎ **869/469-5389.** Sandwiches and salads EC$6–EC$12 ($2.20–$4.40); platters EC$20 ($7.40). AE, MC, V. Mon–Sat 11am–10pm. WEST INDIAN/INTERNATIONAL.

This likable and unpretentious local restaurant is set behind a tiny terrace on a street corner. Owned and operated by its Nevisian chef, Abdue Hill, it serves a loyal crowd in an air-conditioned, garden-inspired interior. Menu items include the usual: sandwiches and salads, burgers, locally styled preparations of steak and chicken, spareribs, stewed mutton, and grilled kingfish with rice, vegetables, and salad. No alcohol is served.

The Courtyard. Main St., Charlestown. ☎ **869/469-1854.** Main courses EC$15–EC$35 ($5.55–$12.95). No credit cards. Daily 6am–11pm. CARIBBEAN/INTERNATIONAL.

Near the main docks and the Customs House, this is a simple restaurant whose charms aren't fully realized until you explore the seating options. There's a West Indian bar on the ground floor and a dining room upstairs (used only when it threatens to rain). Most visitors head for the rear garden, where palms, almonds, and sea grape push up through holes in the crumbling concrete deck. Lunch platters include sandwiches, burgers, and fish-and-chips. Dinner is more elaborate; it's very tasty and well-prepared fare ranging from barbecued lobster to Creole-style shrimp. Fresh fish is invariably on the menu, and you can order it fried, stewed, or cooked Creole style with tomatoes, onions, and peppers. The proprietors boast that theirs is the best coffee on the island.

✪ **Eddy's.** Main St., Charlestown. ☎ **869/496-5958.** Main courses EC$28–EC$50 ($10.35–$18.50). AE, MC, V. Mon–Wed and Fri–Sat 11:45am–3pm and 7–9:30pm. INTERNATIONAL.

On the upper floor of a plank-sided Nevisian house in the center of Charlestown, this restaurant is open on three sides to the prevailing winds and its balcony juts out over the pedestrian traffic below. The airy interior contains a tucked-away bar, lattices and gingerbread, and lots of tropical color. The menu items, posted on one of several signs, are among the best prepared in town—perhaps try Eddy's fish cioppino with roasted garlic–mayonnaise croutons or juicy tandoori-sauced chicken. For a new twist on a traditional favorite, try the lime-glazed seafood kebabs with black-bean salsa. No one will mind if you arrive only for a drink at the corner bar, but you'll be missing out on a tasty meal.

✪ **Muriel's Cuisine.** Upper Happyhill Dr., Charlestown. ☎ **869/469-5920.** Reservations recommended. Dinner EC$25–EC$65 ($9.25–$24.05); lunch EC$15–EC$30 ($5.55–$11.10). AE, MC, V. Daily 8–10am and 11:30am–7pm. WEST INDIAN.

A 6-minute walk from Charlestown's waterfront, this restaurant is in the back of a concrete building whose front is devoted to a store, Limetree. Head here for a slice of real island life and for a West Indian cuisine that's typical of what the locals eat. Muriel's West Indian curries are the best in town, ranging from the simple goat or chicken to the more elaborate lobster. She also turns out some fabulous chicken and seafood rôtis and even a lobster Creole for those who want to get fancy. Her jerk pork or chicken would win the approval of a Jamaican, and her preparations of conch, stewed or curried, are worth the trip. If you want to go native all the way, ask for salt-fish or goatwater stew.

Newcastle Bay Marina Restaurant. Newcastle Marina, Charlestown. ☎ **869/469-9373.** Reservations recommended. Main courses EC$30–EC$37 ($11.10–$13.70); pizzas for 2 EC$35–EC$55 ($12.95–$20.35). AE, MC, V. Thurs–Tues 6–10pm. INTERNATIONAL.

This open-air restaurant on the water, housed in a concrete-block building with cathedral ceilings, is part of the Mount Nevis Beach Club. From the deck, you can take in a panoramic sea view. The informal cuisine is usually prepared with flair by the hard-working chef. Examples are a roster of meal-sized pizzas big enough for two (try the version with seafood) as well as chicken parmigiana with pasta, shrimp with salsa verde, and Mexican platters piled high with quesadillas, tacos, flautas, and spicy beef. The best way to begin a meal is with one of the colorful margaritas.

Prinderella's. Tamarind Bay. ☎ **869/469-1291.** Main courses $7–$25. MC, V. Daily 10am–midnight. INTERNATIONAL.

With a name like Prinderella's (an old joke based on spoonerisms), this place has to have some fun and whimsy. At its peak, as many as 60 diners can be accommodated, enjoying this popular local spot with lattice walls 15 feet from the water on the wharf. The menu ranges from burgers to lobster, and you can count on freshly made salads, homemade soups, and pasta dishes. Even some English pub food, like shepherd's pie and steak-and-kidney pie, appear on the menu, as does a homemade pâté. The safest bet? The fresh catch of the day, which somehow tastes better grilled—everything from flying fish to wahoo, mahi mahi, or yellowfin tuna.

Tequila Sheila's. Cades Bay. ☎ **869/469-8139.** Reservations recommended. Main courses EC$20–EC$35 ($7.40–$12.95) at lunch, EC$28–EC$60 ($10.35–$22.20) at dinner. Daily noon–3:30pm and 7–10pm. WEST INDIAN/INTERNATIONAL.

Named after one of its owners, a soft-spoken woman who isn't nearly as raucous as her name would imply, this restaurant is on the premises of the previously recommended Inn at Cades Bay. Set on a wooden platform less than 60 feet from the seafront, with a covered parapet but without walls, it offers panoramic views as far away as St. Kitts and a menu incorporating West Indian, Mexican, and international cuisine. Lunch menus include dishes like rôti, enchiladas, grilled or jerk chicken, and lobster que-sadillas. Dinner platters include vegetable-stuffed chicken, lobster, and New York strip steak with horseradish sauce or béarnaise sauce. Flying fish, wahoo, and mahi mahi are very fresh here and prepared as simply as possible—usually grilled with lemon juice and herbs. The bar, made from an overturned fishing boat, features margaritas, various brands of tequila, and the usual party-colored drinks.

4 Hitting the Beaches

Nevis's best beach—in fact, one of the best beaches in the Caribbean—is the reef-protected ✪ **Pinney's Beach,** which has gin-clear water, golden sands, and a gradual slope; it's just north of Charlestown on the west coast. You'll have 3 miles of sand (often virtually to yourself) that culminates in a sleepy lagoon against a backdrop of coconut palms. It's almost never crowded, and its calm, shallow waters are perfect for swimming. It's also ideal for wading, making it a family favorite. The Four Seasons Beach Resort lies in the middle of this beach. It's best to bring your own sports equipment; the hotels are stocked with limited gear that may be in use by its guests. You can go snorkeling or scuba diving here among damselfish, tangs, grunts, blue-headed wrasses, and parrot fish, among other species. The beach is especially beautiful in the late afternoon, when flocks of cattle egrets fly into its north end to roost at the freshwater pond at Nelson's Spring.

If your time on Nevis is limited, go to Pinney's. But if you're going to be around for a few more days, you might want to search out the other beaches, notably beige-sand **Oualie Beach,** known especially for its diving and snorkeling. The location is north of Pinney's and just south of Mosquito Bay. The beach is well maintained and rarely crowded; you can buy food and drink as well as rent water-sports equipment at the Oualie Beach Hotel.

Indian Castle Beach, at the very southern tip of Nevis, is rarely sought out. It has an active surf and a swath of fine-gray sand. Indian Castle is definitely for escapists—chances are you'll have the beach all to yourself except for an indigenous goat or two, who may be very social and interested in sharing your picnic lunch. **Newcastle Beach** is by the Nisbet Plantation, at the northernmost tip of the island on the channel that separates St. Kitts and Nevis. Snorkelers flock to this strip of soft, ecru sand set against a backdrop of coconut palms.

The beaches along the east coast aren't desirable. They front Long Head Bay in the north and White Bay in the south. These bays spill into the Atlantic ocean and are rocky and too rough for swimming, although rather dramatic to visit if you're sight-seeing. Of them all, **White Bay Beach** (sometimes called Windward Beach), in the southeastern section, east of Gingerland, is the most desirable. If you want some chillier Atlantic swimming, head here—but be careful, as the waters can suddenly turn turbulent.

5 Sports & Outdoor Pursuits

BOAT CHARTERS **Scuba Safaris,** an outfit that operates independently on the premises of the Oualie Beach Club (☎ 869/469-9518), offers boat charters to Banana Bay and Cockleshell Bay, which can make for a great day's outing, costing only $50 round-trip.

GOLF The ✪ **Four Seasons Golf Course,** Pinney's Beach (☎ 869/469-1111), has one of the world's most challenging and visually dramatic golf courses. Designed by Robert Trent Jones Jr. (who called it "the most scenic golf course I've ever designed"), this 18-hole championship golf course wraps around the resort and offers panoramic ocean and mountain views at every turn. The course is, in the words of one avid golfer, "reason enough to go to Nevis." But there's a high price tag. Guests of the hotel pay $125 for 18 holes, and nonguests are charged $150. Rental clubs are available, costing $40 for 18 holes.

HIKING & MOUNTAIN CLIMBING   Hikers can climb **Mount Nevis,** 3,232 feet up to the extinct volcanic crater, and enjoy a trek to the rain forest to watch for wild monkeys. This is strenuous and recommended only for the stout of heart. Ask your hotel to pack a picnic lunch and arrange a guide (charging about $35 per person). The hike takes about 5 hours, and once at the summit you'll be rewarded with views of Antigua, Saba, Statia, St. Kitts, Guadeloupe, and Montserrat. Of course, you've got to reach that summit, which means scrambling up near-vertical sections of the trail requiring handholds on not-always-reliable vines and roots. It's definitely not for acrophobes! Guides can be arranged at the **Nevis Historical and Conservation Society,** based at the Museum of Nevis History on Main Street in Charlestown (☎ **869/469-5786**).

Eco-Tours Nevis (☎ **869/469-2091** for reservations) offers three unique walking tours of the 36-mile island. Tours offer a wealth of fascinating and cultural history, reflecting the tropical climate and some 1,000 years of human activity. The expeditions explore the shore, tropical forests, and historic ruins. Each offers something for the experienced traveler or the first-time visitor and are taken at a leisurely pace, requiring only an average level of fitness.

The Eco-Ramble (2½ hours) takes place on the windswept east coast of Nevis, where sea, ruins, and mountains combine to provide a panorama. This tour covers the 18th-century New River and Coconut Walk Estates, where you'll experience the diverse ecology of Nevis, discover archaeological evidence of pre-Columbian Amerindian settlers, and explore the remains of the last working sugar factory. It's offered Monday and Friday at 9:30am and Wednesday at 3pm, costing $20 per person. The Mountravers Hike (2½ hours) takes a close look at Montraverse House, one of Nevis's hidden secrets. These spectacular ruins are the focus of an easy hike into the tropical forest–covered slopes of Nevis Peak. It's offered Tuesday and Saturday at 10am, costing $20 per person. The Historic Charlestown tour (1½ hours) takes you through the capital, with Gallows Bay and Jews Walk two of the reminders of Charlestown's rich and turbulent past. Called at various times "a sink of debauchery" and "a sleepy town with many of its buildings locked from day to day," Charlestown has survived 300 years of fire, earthquake, hurricanes, and warfare to become a charming Victorian-era West Indian town. It's offered Sunday at 3pm, costing $10 per person.

Shorts, socks, and closed shoes are suitable for all three tours. A hat is a welcome addition, and suitable casual attire is appreciated in Charlestown (no swimsuits). The Eco-Ramble is recommended for children over 12 years old. The other tours are not suitable for children. All walking tours are offered on a reservation-only basis.

HORSEBACK RIDING   Horseback riding is available at the **Nisbet Plantation Beach Club,** Newcastle (☎ **869/469-9325**). You can ride English saddle at $45 per person for 45 minutes. A guide takes you along mountain trails to visit sites of long-forgotten plantations.

SNORKELING & SCUBA DIVING   For **snorkeling,** head for Pinney's Beach. You might also try the waters of Fort Ashby, where the settlement of Jamestown is said to have slid into the sea; legend has it the church bells can still be heard and the undersea town can still be seen when conditions are just right. So far, no diver, to our knowledge, has ever found the conditions "just right."

For scuba divers, the best site on Nevis is the **Monkey Shoals,** 2 miles west of the Four Seasons. This is a beautiful reef starting at 40 feet, with dives up to 100 feet in depth. Angelfish, turtles, nurse sharks, and extensive soft coral can be found here. **The Caves** are on the south tip of Nevis, a 20-minute boat ride from the Four Seasons. A series of coral grottos with numerous squirrelfish, turtles, and needlefish make this an ideal dive for both certified and resort divers. **Champagne Garden,** a 5-minute boat ride from the Four Seasons, gets its name from bubbles created from an underwater sulfur vent. Because of the warm water temperature, large numbers of tropical fish are found here. Finally, **Coral Garden,** 2 miles west of the Four Seasons, is another beautiful coral reef with schools of Atlantic spadefish and large seafans. The reef is at a maximum depth of 70 feet and suitable for both certified and resort divers.

Scuba Safaris, Oualie Beach (☎ **869/469-9518**), on the island's north end, offers PADI scuba diving and snorkeling in an area rich in dive sites. It also offers resort and certification courses, dive packages, and equipment rental. A one-tank scuba dive costs $45; a two-tank dive, $80. Full certification courses cost $450 per person. Snorkeling trips cost $35 per person. Boat charters to Banana Bay and Cockleshell Bay, and other beaches are offered.

TENNIS   Some of the big hotels have tennis courts. But you must call in advance and see if nonguests are allowed to play (you might have to pay a fee). Outside of the posh Four Seasons, the best courts are at **Pinney's Beach hotel,** Pinney's Beach, just outside Charlestown (☎ **869/469-5207**); **Golden Rock,** Gingerland (☎ **869/469-9325**); and **Nisbet,** Newcastle Beach (☎ **869/469-9325**).

WINDSURFING   Often the waters here are ideal for this sport, especially for beginners and intermediates. **Windsurfing Nevis** at the Oualie Beach Hotel (☎ **869/469-9682**) offers the best equipment, costing $25 for 30 minutes.

6 Seeing the Sights

Negotiate with a taxi driver to take you around Nevis. The distance is only 20 miles, but you may find yourself taking a long time if you stop to see specific sights and talk to all the people who'll want to chat. A 3-hour sightseeing tour around the island will cost $60; the average taxi holds up to four people, so when the cost is sliced per passenger, it's a reasonable investment. No sightseeing bus companies operate on Nevis, but a number of individuals own buses they use for taxi service. Call **All Seasons Streamline Tours** at ☎ **869/469-5705** or 869/469-1138.

The major attraction is the **Museum of Nevis History,** in the house where Alexander Hamilton was born, on Main Street in Charlestown (☎ **869/469-5786**). Hamilton was the illegitimate son of a Scotsman and Rachel Fawcett, a Nevisian of Huguenot ancestry. The family immigrated to St. Croix and from there Alexander made his way to the North American colonies, where he became the first secretary of the U.S. Treasury. His picture, of course, appears on the U.S. $10 bill. The lava-stone house by the shore has been restored, and the museum, dedicated to the history and culture of Nevis, houses the island's archives. The museum is open Monday to Friday 8am to 4pm and Saturday 10am to noon. Admission is $2 for adults and $1 for children.

The **Eden Brown Estate,** about 1½ miles from New River, is said to be haunted. Once it was the home of a wealthy planter, whose daughter was to be married, but her husband-to-be was killed in a duel at the prenuptial feast. The mansion was then closed forever and left to the ravages of nature. A gray solid stone still stands. Only the most adventurous come here on a moonlit night.

At one time, Sephardic Jews who came from Brazil made up a quarter of the island's population, and it's believed that Jews introduced sugar production into the Leewards.

Outside the center of Charlestown, at the lower end of Government Road, the **Jewish Cemetery** has been restored and is the resting place of many of the early shopkeepers. Most of the tombstones date from 1690 to 1710.

A U.S. archaeological team believes an old stone building in partial ruin on Nevis is probably the oldest **Jewish synagogue** in the Caribbean, according to historian Dr. Vincent K. Hubbar, a resident of the island and author of *Swords, Ships, and Sugar: A History of Nevis to 1900*. Preliminary findings in 1993 traced the building's history to one of the two oldest Jewish settlements in the West Indies, Hubbard noted, and current work at the site plus historic documents in England establish its existence prior to 1650. The original function of the building site, adjacent to the government administration building in Charlestown, has been long forgotten. However, because of Nevis's relatively large Jewish population in the 17th century and its well-known Jewish cemetery, many scholars and historians believed a synagogue must have existed but didn't know exactly where.

One of the island's newest attractions is the 8-acre **Botanical Garden of Nevis** (☎ 869/469-3509), lying 3 miles south of Charlestown on the Montpelier Estate. Rain-forest plants grow in re-created Mayan ruins in a hillside site overlooking the Caribbean. The on-site restaurant serves an English tea with scones and double Devonshire cream. You can also order a ploughman's lunch (French bread, pickled onions, and cheese). If you patronize the restaurant and gift shop, the fee of $8 to the gardens is eliminated. The garden is open daily 10am to 6pm.

A bit incongruous for Nevis, **Caribbean Cove,** Stoney Grove (☎ 869/469-1286), is an amusement park that's just as popular with locals as visitors. A 2-acre multimillion-dollar facility, it was created by Joseph Murphy, a Philadelphia businessman, who wanted to create a slice of Walt Disney World. Among the attractions is an 18-hole miniature golf course loosely following the history of Nevis, focusing on times when pirates ruled the seas, complete with sculptured caves, waterfalls, a lagoon, blasting cannons, and even a simulated rain forest. A deli offers sandwiches as well as Philly cheese steaks in honor of Murphy's hometown. There's a gift shop, plus live entertainment, including bands, comedians, fashion shows, and a restaurant. Admission is $4, and hours are daily 10am to 10pm.

The **Nevis Jockey Club** organizes and sponsors thoroughbred races every month. Local horses as well as some brought over from other islands fill out a typical five-race card. If you want to have a glimpse at what horse racing must have been like a century or more ago, you'll find the Nevis races a memorable experience. For information, contact Richard Lupinacci, a Jockey Club officer and owner and operator of the Hermitage Plantation (☎ 869/469-3477).

7 Shopping

Normal store hours are Monday to Friday 8am to noon and 1 to 4pm, but on Thursday some places close in the afternoon and on Saturday some stay open to 8pm. Most are closed Sunday.

For original art, visit **Eva Wilkins's Studio,** Clay Ghaut, Gingerland (☎ 869/469-2673). The late Eva Wilkins became the island's most famous artist, the highlight of her life being when Prince Charles showed up to look at her work. Until her death in 1989, she painted island people, local flowers, and scenes of Nevis life. She worked in both black-and-white and color prints, which her custodians still sell today. Prints are available in some of the local shops, but her originals sell for $100 and more. Her former atelier can be visited, lying on the grounds of an old sugar-mill plantation her father owned near Montpelier.

Cheap Thrills: What You Can See & Do for Free (Well, Almost) on Nevis

- **Hike the Rain-Forest Trail.** One of the great nature walks in this part of the Caribbean begins at Stoney Hill at the top of Rawlins Road above Golden Rock Estate at Gingerland in the southeastern corner of the island, and winds its way through a rain-forest setting. The trail is relatively easy to walk as you pass by rich flora, including nutmeg trees and breadfruit and groves of cocoa. You'll also see rich bird life, including forest thrushes, yellow warblers, hummingbirds, tropical mockingbirds, black-crowned herons, and scaly breasted thrashers. It's possible to see wild monkeys too, especially between Golden Rock and Stoney Hill. Allow about 3 hours coming and going for this trail.

- **View a Nostalgic Sight.** Regrettably, a hurricane ruined an already ruined sight in Nevis: the decaying Bath Hotel (completed in 1778) in Bath Village, about half a mile from Charlestown. But nothing else conjures up the glory that was Nevis. Still emanating from the hillside, the thermal springs once attracted the elite from North America, with temperatures rising as high as 108°F (locals have reported miraculous cures). Guests drank and gambled in the hotel's casino. There are legends of entire plantation estates changing hands in its casino heyday, as well as a fair share of bloody duels of honor. When the hotel fell on bad days, it was turned into a brothel. It might be best to wander around and take in the sight without romping in the waters. There are plans for restoration, but nothing definite at the moment.

- **Drive Around the Island.** One of the great drives in this part of the Caribbean is around Nevis. Inland roads are rutted and best left to adventurers, but anybody can drive around the coast. The road is relatively good, unless tropical storms have caused highway damage. The most important

Hand-painted or tie-dyed cotton and batik clothing are featured at **Island Hopper,** in the T.D.C. Shopping Mall, Main St., Charlestown (☎ **869/469-0893**), which also has locations on St. Kitts and Antigua. From beach wraps to souvenirs, a wide selection of products is available. In a stone building about 200 feet from the wharf, near the marketplace, the **Nevis Handicraft Cooperative Society,** Cotton House, Charlestown (☎ **869/469-1746**), contains locally made gift items, like unusual objects of goatskin, local wines made from a variety of fruits grown on the island, hot-pepper sauce, guava cheese, jams, and jellies.

The Sandbox Tree, Evelyn's Villa, Charlestown (☎ **869/469-5662**), housed in a clapboard house built in 1836, is the most appealing gift shop on Nevis, with artwork from Haiti and Nevis, books for adults and children, hand-painted clothing, sheets, napkins, antique furniture, and spices, relishes, and exotic chutneys. It also sells 100% cotton hand–silk-screened fabrics and a complete line of clothing.

8 Nevis After Dark

Nightlife isn't the major reason to visit Nevis. Summer nights are quiet, but there's organized entertainment in winter, with steel bands often performing at the major island landmarks lie about this road, including Nisbet Plantation (now a hotel), former home of the wife of Lord Nelson. Vistas and panoramic ruins of the sugarcane plantation days greet you at nearly every turn. The trip evokes the days when not only sugarcane but sea island cotton flourished here. Time your trip so you can break up the drive, plus have lunch and lounge at Pinney's Beach.

- **Stroll Around Charlestown.** In colorful decay, the capital of Nevis is like a miniature West Indian port. Some Nevisians, however, hope it'll one day become the capital of their own nation—if Nevis ever breaks its association with St. Kitts. The biggest excitement here is when the ferries come in from St. Kitts. Otherwise, Charlestown is sleepy, and that's part of its charm. In about an hour you can wander around everywhere. After leaving the pier, turn right at the old Cotton House and Ginnery and stroll through the marketplace. This is best enjoyed in the morning. After that, you can make a left onto Prince William Street and follow it to Memorial Square, honoring the Nevis dead in the two world wars. After that, wander at will and perhaps browse through some handcraft shops.

- **Spend a Day at Pinney's Beach.** Many visitors in Nevis for an entire week spend every day on Pinney's Beach. It's one of the finest in the Caribbean, its reef-protected waters gin clear and idyllic for snorkeling or swimming. Rainbow-hued fish often can be seen up close to the shore. There are miles and miles of powdery sand, ideal for sunbathing or long walks. A sleepy lagoon lies through the palm trees at the sand strips windward edge. You'll think you've been miraculously delivered to the South Pacific. When you get bored (highly unlikely) you can also visit the nearby Alexander Hamilton Museum.

hotels. Most action takes place at the **Four Seasons Resort,** Pinney's Beach (☎ 869/469-1111), on Friday and Saturday. The **Old Manor Estate,** Gingerland (☎ 869/469-3445), often brings in a steel band on Friday. On Saturday, the action swings over to the **Golden Rock,** Gingerland (☎ 869/469-3346), where a string band enlivens the scene. Fridays and Saturdays can get raucous at **Eddy's** on Main Street (see above) when West Indian buffets are presented and live bands entertain.

The best place on a Wednesday night is **Pinney's Beach Hotel,** Pinney's Beach (☎ 869/469-5207), which stages a dinner and dance. The **Oualie Beach Hotel** at Oualie Beach (☎ 869/469-9735) offers a Saturday buffet at which time a live string band appears. Disco reigns supreme at **Tequila Sheila's** at Cades Bay (see above) on Saturday night.

One of the best beach bars on island is the **Beachcomber,** Pinney's Beach (☎ 869/469-1192), known for its happy hour and barbecues. Sometimes live bands appear. Another favorite in winter only is the **Sunset Terrace at Cliff Dwellers** on Tamarind Bay (☎ 869/469-0262). This is the best place for a sundowner, except you must take a not-always-reliable tram ride up the side of a sheer cliff. There's no more dramatic perch in all Nevis than this place for a tropical punch.

17

Puerto Rico

Puerto Rico boasts a vast array of sights, activities, and entertainment. You'll find hundreds of beaches, countless water sports, acres of golf courses, miles of tennis courts, casinos galore, more discos than any other place in the Caribbean, and shopping bargains to equal those of St. Thomas.

Lush Puerto Rico is some 1,000 miles southeast of the tip of Florida and offers 272 miles of Atlantic and Caribbean coastline. Its culture dates back 2,000 years. Old San Juan is its great historic center, with 500 years of recorded history, as reflected in its restored Spanish colonial architecture. There are 78 other cities and towns, each with a unique charm and flavor. The countryside is dotted with centuries-old coffee plantations, sugar estates, foreboding caves, and enormous boulders with mysterious petroglyphs carved by the Taíno (original settlers of the island). You can travel along colorful but often narrow and steep roads and meandering mountain trails leading to tropical settings. To see the real Puerto Rico, explore these back roads, leaving behind San Juan, especially the high-priced Condado Beach area.

Of all the Caribbean islands, Puerto Rico is the very best choice for budget travelers, with inexpensive *paradores* (government-sponsored inns), small guest houses, local inns, and mom-and-pop restaurants, many overlooking the sea. Any number of restaurants serve fresh fish and native Puerto Rican dishes. Following in the Spanish tradition, Puerto Rico also has the cafe, where you can enjoy a cup of coffee as well as a *comida criolla* (local dinner). Sometimes a dinner will cost only $12, or even less, at a roadside kiosk.

Keep in mind you can base yourself at one hotel and still do a lot of exploring elsewhere if you don't mind driving for a couple of hours. It's possible to branch out and see a lot of the island even if you're staying in San Juan.

1 Essentials

VISITOR INFORMATION

Out on the island, it's best to go to the local city hall for tourist information. Ask for a copy of *Qué Pasa,* the official visitors' guide.

For information before you leave, contact one of the following **Puerto Rico Tourism Company** offices: 575 Fifth Ave., New York, NY 10017 (☎ **800/223-6530** or 212/586-6262); 3575 W. Cahuenga Blvd., Suite 405, Los Angeles, CA 90068 (☎ **800/874-1230** or

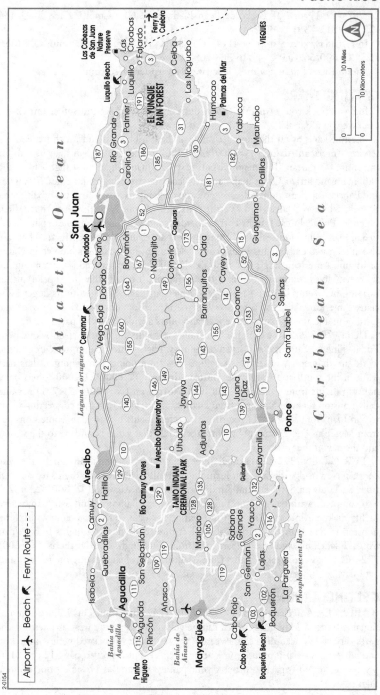

Puerto Rico

Airport ✈   Beach ◤   Ferry Route - - -

Atlantic Ocean

Las Cabezas de San Juan Nature Preserve
Las Croabas
Ferry to Culebra
Fajardo
Ceiba
Las Naguabo
Humacao
Palmas del Mar
VIEQUES

Luquillo Beach ◤
Luquillo
Palmer
Rio Grande
Carolina
EL YUNQUE RAIN FOREST
Yabucoa
Maunabo

Cerromar ◤
San Juan
Condado
Cataño
Bayamón
Naranjito
Comerío
Cidra
Caguas
Guayama
Palillas

Laguna Tortuguero
Vega Baja
Dorado

Arecibo
Arecibo Observatory
Utuado
Jayuya
Barranquitas
Coamo
Juana Diaz
Santa Isabel
Salinas
Ponce

Río Camuy Caves
TAINO INDIAN CEREMONIAL PARK
Adjuntas
Guánica
Guayanilla

Camuy
Hatillo
Isabela
Quebradillas
San Sebastián
Maricao
Sabana Grande
Yauco
Aguadilla
Añasco
San Germán
Lajas
La Parguera

Bahía de Aguadilla
Aguada
Rincón
Bahía de Añasco
Mayagüez
Cabo Rojo
Boquerón
Punta Higuero
Cabo Rojo ◤
Boquerón Beach ◤
Phosphorescent Bay

Caribbean Sea

10 Miles
10 Kilometers

Highways: 3, 52, 1, 2, 30, 31, 191, 187, 186, 185, 181, 182, 167, 164, 160, 155, 149, 156, 14, 153, 157, 143, 173, 15, 146, 140, 144, 139, 10, 129, 128, 135, 132, 116, 105, 119, 109, 111, 115, 102, 103

411

213/874-5991); or 901 Ponce de León Blvd., Suite 604, Coral Gables, FL 33134 (☎ **800/815-7391** or 305/445-9112).

In Canada you can stop by 41–43 Colbourne St., Suite 301, Toronto, ON M5E 1E3 (☎ **800/667-0394** or 416/368-2680).

Puerto Rico's Internet address is **www.discoverpuertorico.com**.

GETTING THERE

Before you book your own airfare, read the section on package tours in chapter 2—it can save you a bundle!

Puerto Rico is by far the most accessible of the Caribbean islands, with frequent air service. **American Airlines** (☎ **800/433-7300**) has designated San Juan its hub for the entire Caribbean. The major airport is in San Juan, where most flights from the U.S. mainland arrive. Other major airports serve the two other major cities, Mayagüez and Ponce. American alone offers 39 nonstop daily flights to San Juan from Baltimore, Boston, Chicago, Dallas–Fort Worth, Hartford, Miami, Newark, New York (JFK), Orlando, Philadelphia, Tampa, Fort Lauderdale, and Washington (Dulles), plus flights to San Juan from Montréal and Toronto with changes in Chicago or Miami. There are also at least two daily flights from Los Angeles to San Juan that touch down in Dallas or Miami. **American Eagle** (☎ **800/433-7300**) is the undisputed leader among the short-haul local commuter flights of the Caribbean. It usually flies in propeller planes carrying between 34 and 64 passengers. American Eagle, along with its larger associate, American Airlines, offers service to 37 destinations on 31 islands of the Caribbean and the Bahamas. American also offers a wide variety of packages.

Delta (☎ **800/241-4141**) has four nonstop flights from Atlanta on Monday to Friday, nine on Saturday, and seven on Sunday. Flights into Atlanta from around the world are frequent, with excellent connections from points throughout Delta's network in the south and southwest. **United Airlines** (☎ **800/221-2000**) offers daily nonstop flights from Chicago to San Juan. **Northwest** (☎ **800/447-4747**) has one daily nonstop flight to San Juan from Detroit, as well as at least one connecting flight to San Juan from Detroit. That airline also offers flights to San Juan, some nonstop, from Memphis and Minneapolis, with a schedule that varies according to the season and the day of the week.

TWA (☎ **800/892-4141**) offers three daily nonstop flights throughout the year between New York's JFK and San Juan. There are also daily nonstop flights to San Juan from St. Louis on Saturday and Sunday in winter. **US Airways** (☎ **800/428-4322**) also competes, with daily connecting flights between Baltimore and San Juan, where flights make an intermediate stop in Charlotte, North Carolina, before continuing nonstop to San Juan. The airline also offers three daily nonstop flights to San Juan from Philadelphia and one to San Juan from Pittsburgh. Finally, **Iberia** (☎ **800/772-9642**) has two weekly flights from Madrid to San Juan, leaving on Tuesday and Saturday.

GETTING AROUND

BY PLANE **American Eagle** (☎ **787/749-1747**) flies from Luís Muñoz International Airport to Mayagüez, which can be your gateway to the west of Puerto Rico. Fares vary widely according to the season, the restrictions associated with your ticket, and whatever special promotion might be in effect, but expect to pay $124 to $176 per person round-trip. Try to book your passage as early as possible prior to your flight.

BY CAR Some local car-rental agencies may tempt you with slashed prices, but if you're planning to tour the island, you won't find any local branches should you run into car trouble. And some of the agencies advertising low-cost deals don't take credit cards and want cash in advance. You also have to watch out for hidden extras and the insurance problems that sometimes proliferate among the smaller and not very well known firms.

The old reliables are **Avis** (☎ **800/331-1212** or 787/791-2500), **Budget** (☎ **800/527-0700** or 787/791-3685), or **Hertz** (☎ **800/654-3001** or 787/791-0840). Each offers minivan transport to its office and car depot from the San Juan airport. Be alert to the minimum age requirements for car rentals in Puerto Rico, as stringent rules apply: Both Avis and Hertz require renters be 25 or older; at Budget, renters 21 to 24 pay a $5 daily surcharge to the agreed-on rental fee. Alternatively, you can opt for a rental from **Kemwel Holiday Auto** (☎ **800/678-0678**). Kemwel's is willing to rent to drivers 21 to 24 for a supplement of $6 per day. However, such drivers must have had a license for at least two years. None of these companies rents Jeeps, four-wheel-drive vehicles, or convertibles.

Added security comes from an antitheft double-locking mechanism that has been installed in most of the rental cars available on Puerto Rico. Car theft is high here, so extra precaution is always needed. Distances are often posted in kilometers rather than miles (a kilometer is 0.62 miles), but speed limits are in miles per hour.

BY PUBLIC TRANSPORTATION   *Públicos* are cars or minibuses that provide low-cost transportation and are designated with the letter P or PD following the number on their license plates. They usually operate only during daylight hours, carry up to six passengers at a time, and charge rates that are loosely governed, with a baffling set of qualifiers, by the Public Service Commission.

Locals are adept at figuring out the *público* routes along rural highways and sometimes simply wave at a moving one they suspect might be headed in their direction. Unless you're extremely good at Spanish and know local roads and poorly marked byways well, your best bet is phoning either of the numbers below, describing where and when you want to go, and agreeing to the prearranged price between specific points. Then be prepared to wait. Although a *público* may be arranged between most of the towns and villages of Puerto Rico, by far the most popular routes are between San Juan and Ponce and San Juan and Mayagüez. Fares vary according to whether a *público* will make a detour to pick up or drop off a passenger at a specific locale. If you want to deviate from the predetermined routes, you'll pay more than if you wait for a *público* at vaguely designated points beside the main highway or at predefined points that include airports and even the main plaza of a town.

Information about *público* routes between San Juan and Mayagüez is available from **Lineas Sultana,** Calle Esteban González 898, Urbanización Santa Rita, Río Piedras (☎ **787/765-9377**). Information about *público* routes between San Juan and Ponce is available from **Choferes Unidos de Ponce,** Terminal de Carros Públicos, Calle Vive in Ponce (☎ **787/722-3275** or 787/764-0540). Fares from San Juan to Ponce are $20. Though prices are admittedly low, the routes are slow, with frequent stops, an often erratic routing, and lots of inconvenience.

SIGHTSEEING TOURS

If you want to see more of the island but don't want to rent a car or manage the inconveniences of public transportation, perhaps an organized tour is for you. **Castillo Sightseeing Tours & Travel Services,** 2413 Calle Laurel, Punta La Marias, Santurce (☎ **787/791-6195**), maintains offices at some of the capital's best-known hotels, like the Caribe Hilton, San Juan Marriott Resort, El San Juan Grand, El San Juan Towers, Embassy Suites, and Crowne Plaza Holiday Inn. Using six of their own air-conditioned buses, with access to others if demand warrants it, the company's tours include pickups and drop-offs at their hotels as an added convenience.

One of the most popular half-day tours departs most days of the week between 8:30 and 9am, lasts 4 to 5 hours, and costs $30 per person. Departing from San Juan, you'll travel along the northeastern part of the island to El Yunque rain forest. The company also offers a city tour of San Juan departing daily at 1 or 1:30pm. The 4-hour trip costs $32 per person and includes a stop at the Bacardi rum factory, where you're treated to a complimentary rum drink. The company also operates full-day snorkeling tours to the reefs near the coast of a deserted island off Puerto Rico's eastern edge aboard one of two sail- and motor-driven catamarans. With lunch, snorkeling gear, and piña coladas included, the price for the full day (7:45am to 5pm) is $69 per person.

For a day excursion to the area's best islands, beaches, reefs, and snorkeling, contact **Bill and Donna Henry** at the Puerto Del Rey Marina in Fajardo (☎ 787/860-4401). Bill has been sailing for 45 years, and their 50-foot boat *Gulfstar* was featured in Disney's *New Swiss Family Robinson,* where it was called the *Albatross.* They offer snorkeling trips from 10am to 5pm, with 2 to 6 passengers paying $75 each. A barbecue chicken meal is cooked onboard (Donna will prepare vegetarian or kosher food if notified). Sunset cruises for $55 per person are also offered, including drinks and hors d'oeuvres from 5 to 7pm. A minimum of 4 passengers must sign up for this.

Thanks to a protected historic core and a vivid sense of colonial history, few Caribbean cities lend themselves so gracefully to walking tours as San Juan. You can embark on these on your own, stopping and shopping en route. More comprehensive, however, are the 2-hour walks conducted by **Colonial Adventures,** 201 Calle Recinto Sur, Old San Juan (☎ 787/729-0114), for which you'll need a reservation. They're usually conducted Monday to Saturday at 10am, 2pm, and 4pm; begin and end at Pier 1, near the Plaza Darsena, in Old San Juan; and cost $20 per person.

GREAT DISCOUNTS THROUGH THE LELOLAI VIP PROGRAM

For $10, the cost of membership in Puerto Rico's ✪ **LeLoLai VIP (Value in Puerto Rico),** you can enjoy the equivalent of up to $250 in travel benefits. Admission to folkloric shows and discounts on guided tours of historic sites and natural attractions, as well as on lodgings, meals, shopping, sports activities, and more, add up to significant savings. Of course, most of the experiences linked to LeLoLai are of the touristy type, but participation in the program is a worthy investment nonetheless.

Once you're a member, the *paradores puertorriqueños,* the island's modestly priced network of country inns, will give you 10% to 20% lower room rates Monday to Thursday. Discounts of 10% to 20% are offered at many restaurants, from San Juan's toniest hotels to several *mesones gastronómicos,* government-sanctioned restaurants out on the island serving Puerto Rican fare. Shopping discounts are offered at many stores and boutiques and, best yet, you get 10% to 20% off at many island attractions.

The card also entitles you to free admission to some of the island's folkloric shows, the specific nature of which is often subject to the enthusiasm of the performers and the availability of the theater that presents it. The pass works for *Jolgorio,* presented every Wednesday at 8:30pm at the Caribe Terrace of the Caribe Hilton, though the specific details of that might change by the time of your arrival. For more information about this card and the details that apply to its use, call ☎ 787/723-3135 or go to the El Centro Convention Center at Ashford Avenue on the Condado. You can call for information before you leave home, especially about current offerings, but you can sign up for this program only once you reach Puerto Rico. Many hotel packages include participation in this program as part of their offerings.

SPECIAL EVENTS

Sanjuneros and visitors alike eagerly look forward to the annual **Casals Festival,** the Caribbean's most celebrated cultural event. June 1 to 20, the bill at San Juan's performing-arts center includes a glittering array of international guest conductors, orchestras, and soloists come to honor the memory of Pablo Casals, the renowned cellist who was born in Spain to a Puerto Rican mother. When Casals died in Puerto Rico in 1973 at age 97, the festival was 16 years old and attracting the same class of performers who appeared at the festival he founded in France after World War II. Ticket prices range from $20 to $40, with a 50% discount offered to students, seniors over 60, and persons with disabilities. Tickets are available through the performing-arts center in San Juan at ☎ **787/721-7727.**

And at **Carnival** time in early February, the island's celebrations feature float parades, dancing, and street parties. One of the most vibrant festivities is held in Ponce, known for its masqueraders wearing brightly painted horned masks. Live music includes the folk rhythms of the plena, which originated in Africa, and festivities include the crowning of a Carnival queen and the closing "burial of the sardine." For more information, call ☎ **787/840-4141.**

Fast Facts: Puerto Rico

American Express   American Express services are handled by **Travel Network,** at 1035 Ashford Ave., Condado (☎ **787/725-0960**). The office is open Monday to Friday 9am to 5pm and Saturday 9 to 11:30am.

Banks   Most major U.S. banks have branches in San Juan and are open Monday to Friday 8:30am to 2:30pm.

Currency   The **U.S. dollar** is the coin of the realm. Canadian currency is accepted by some big hotels in San Juan, although reluctantly.

Documents   Since Puerto Rico is part of the United States, American citizens don't need a passport or visa. Canadians, however, should carry some form of identification, such as a birth certificate. Citizens of the United Kingdom should have a passport.

Electricity   The electricity is 110 volts AC (60 cycles), as it is in the continental United States and Canada.

Emergencies   In an emergency, call ☎ **911.**

Language   English is understood at the big resorts and in most of San Juan. Out in the island, Spanish is still *numero uno.*

Safety   Use common sense and take precautions. Muggings are commonly reported on the Condado and Isla Verde beaches in San Juan, so you might want to confine your moonlit-beach nights to the fenced-in and guarded areas around some of the major hotels. The countryside of Puerto Rico is safer than San Juan, but caution is always the rule. Avoid narrow little country roads and isolated beaches, night or day.

Taxes   There's a government tax of 7% in regular hotels or 9% in hotels with casinos. The airport departure tax is included in the price of your ticket.

Time   Puerto Rico is on Atlantic standard time year-round, making it one hour ahead of U.S. eastern standard time. In winter when it's noon in Miami, it's 1pm in San Juan. But from April to late October (during daylight saving time on the east coast), Puerto Rico and the east coast keep the same time.

Tipping   Some hotels add a 10% service charge to your bill. If they don't, you're expected to tip for services rendered. Tip as you would in the United States (15% to 20%).

San Juan

PUERTO DE TIERRA

PARQUE MUÑOZ RIVERA
PARQUE SIXTO ESCOBAR

av. Muñoz Rivera
av. Ponce de León
av. Fernandez Juncos

Fuerte San Gerónimo

Ashford Avenue

Condado Beach

Laguna del Condado

Ashford Avenue

CONDADO

Aeropuerto de
Isla Grande

MIRAMAR

av. Ponce de León

av. Fernandez Juncos

U.S. Naval Res.

Expreso Luís Muñoz Rivera

calle Cerraá

calle Labra

calle Las Palmas

av. José de Die

c. del Parqu

calle Europ

Bahía de San Juan

Puente
Constitución

PARQUE CENTRAL

Caño de Martin Peña

av. J. F. Kennedy

Y.M.C.A.

Weather Puerto Rico is cooler than most of the other Caribbean islands because of its northeast trade winds. Sea, land, and mountain breezes also help keep the temperatures at a comfortable level. The climate is fairly stable all year, with an average temperature of 76°F. The only variants are found in the mountain regions, where the temperature fluctuates between 66° and 76°F, and on the north coast, where the temperature ranges from 70° to 80°F.

2 San Juan

San Juan, the capital of Puerto Rico, is a major city—actually an urban sprawl of several municipalities along the island's north coast. Its architecture ranges from classic colonial buildings that recall the Spanish empire to modern beachfront hotels reminiscent of Miami Beach.

San Juan breaks down into several divisions: **San Juan Island,** containing the city center and the old walled city (Old San Juan); **Santurce,** a large peninsula linked to San Juan Island by a causeway; **Condado,** a narrow peninsula stretching between San Juan Island and Santurce; **Puerto de Tierra,** the section east of Old San Juan that contains many government buildings; **Miramar,** a lagoon-front section south of Condado; and **Isla Verde,** detached from the rest of San Juan by an isthmus.

ESSENTIALS

ARRIVING If you're not traveling on a package deal that includes transfers to your hotel, you'll see lots of options after landing at San Juan's **Luís Muñoz Marín Airport**

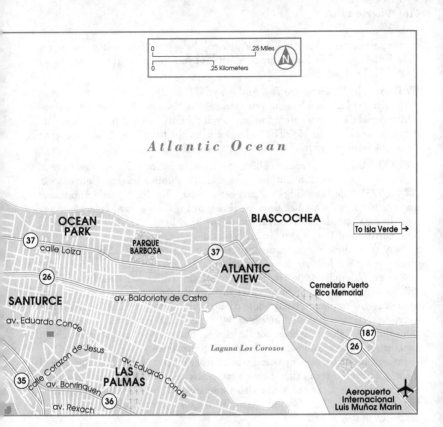

(☎ **787/791-1014**). A wide variety of vehicles refer to themselves as *limosinas* (their Spanish name).

One company with a sign-up desk in the arrivals hall of the international airport, near the American Airlines arrival facilities, is the **Airport Limousine Service** (☎ **787/791-4745**). It offers minivan transport from the airport to various neighborhoods of San Juan for prices that are lower than for similar routings offered by taxis. Whenever 8 to 10 passengers can be gathered, the fare for transport, with luggage, to any hotel in Isla Verde is $50 per van to the Condado or $60 per van to Old San Juan.

VISITOR INFORMATION Tourist information is available at the airport. Another office is at **La Casita,** Pier 1, Old San Juan (☎ **787/722-1709**).

FAST FACTS One of the most centrally located **drugstores** is the **Puerto Rico Drug Co.,** Calle San Francisco 157 (☎ **787/725-2202**), in Old San Juan; it's open Monday to Friday 7am to 9:30pm, Saturday 8am to 9:30pm and Sunday 8:30am to 7:30pm. **Walgreen's,** 1130 Ashford Ave., Condado (☎ **787/725-1510**), is a 24-hour pharmacy. In a **medical emergency,** call ☎ **787/721-2116. Ashford Memorial Community Hospital,** 1451 Ashford Ave. (☎ **787/721-2160**), maintains 24-hour emergency rooms.

GETTING AROUND
BY TROLLEY The best way to save your feet in Old San Juan is to board one of the free open-air trolleys that slowly make their way through the narrow, often

cobblestoned, streets. You can board at any point along the route (either side of the Calle Fortaleza or Calle San Jos are good bets), or you can go to either the marina or La Puntilla for departures.

BY BUS The **Metropolitan Bus Authority** (☎ 787/250-6064) operates buses in the greater San Juan area. Bus stops are marked by upright metal signs or yellow posts, reading *parada*. Bus terminals in San Juan are in the dock area and at Plaza de Colón. A typical fare is 25¢ to 50¢. The higher fee is for the faster buses that make fewer stops; call for more information about routes and schedules.

BY TAXI Except for a handful of high-profile tourist routes, public taxis are metered within San Juan—or should be. The island's **Public Service Commission** (☎ 787/751-5050) establishes flat rates between the Luís Muñoz Marin Airport and major tourist zones as follows: from the airport to any hotel in Isla Verde, $8; to any hotel in the Condado district, $12; and to any hotel in Old San Juan, $16. Tips of between 10% and 15% of that fare are expected.

Away from those routes, passengers traveling between most other destinations within greater San Juan are charged by meter readings. The initial charge is $1, plus 10¢ for each $1/10$ mile and 50¢ for every suitcase, with a minimum fare of $3. Call the PSC to request information or to report any irregularities. These rates apply to conventional *taxis turisticos,* usually white-painted vehicles with official logos on their doors. Owned by a medley of individual outfitters in San Juan, they maintain standards that are higher than those for the cheaper but more erratic and inconvenient *públicos* (see "Getting Around" in section 1 of this chapter).

Taxis are invariably lined up outside the entrance to most of the island's hotels, and if not, a staff member can almost always call one for you. But if you want to arrange a taxi on your own, call the **Mejor Cab Company** (☎ 787/723-2460). Transit by taxi to far-flung destinations within Puerto Rico must be individually negotiated with the driver, usually at a flat rate.

ACCOMMODATIONS YOU CAN AFFORD

Most hotels lie in Condado and Isla Verde, areas out by the airport that border the beach. Or you can stay in Old San Juan—but factor in the cost of daily transportation to the beach if that's where you want to go.

All hotel rooms in Puerto Rico are subject to a 7% to 9% tax, which isn't included in the rates listed below. Most hotels also impose a 10% service charge.

IN OLD SAN JUAN

Hotel Central. Calle San José 202, Old San Juan, PR 00901. ☎ **787-722-2751.** Fax 787/882-1030. 60 units. Year-round $49 single, $54 double. AE, DC, MC, V. Bus: Old Town trolley.

This is one of the most unusual hotels in the historic heart of Old San Juan. Its fans compare it to the kind of weather-beaten, rundown hotel that has staggered through revolutions, civil wars, and the changing tides of fashion. In fact, few other hotels on Puerto Rico will give you such a strong sense of nostalgia. Built in the 1930s and maintained by the same family ever since, it's adjacent to the Plaza de Armas. Don't expect amenities of any kind here: The small rooms have ceiling fans, minimalist (and rather old) furnishings, and tiny baths. A somewhat dingy cafeteria serves simple platters at lunch and dinner to local office workers. The nearest beach is a 20-minute ride away.

ON THE CONDADO

✪ **At Wind Chimes Inn.** 1750 Ashford Ave., Condado, San Juan, PR 00911. ☎ **800/946-3244** or ☎ 787/727-4153. Fax 787/726-5321. 13 units, 5 with bath; no suite. A/C TV TEL.

Winter $65–$95 double. Off-season $55–$85 double. Rates include continental breakfast. AE, DC, DISC, MC, V. Bus: B-21 or AS. Parking: $5.

This restored Spanish manor, 1 short block from the beach and 3½ miles from the airport, is one of the best Puerto Rican guest houses on the Condado. On entering a tropical patio, you'll find tile tables surrounded by palm trees and bougainvillea. There's plenty of space on the deck and a covered lounge for relaxing, socializing, and eating breakfast. Dozens of decorative wind chimes add melody to the daily breezes. The good-size rooms offer a choice of size, beds, and kitchens; all contain ceiling fans and air-conditioning. The beds have firm mattresses, and the baths, though small, are efficiently organized. The inn has recently added a pool.

Casa del Caribe. Calle Caribe 57, San Juan, PR 00907. ☎ **787/722-7139.** Fax 787/723-2575. 11 units. A/C TV TEL. Winter $65–$95 single or double. Off-season $45–$65 single; $55–$85 double. Rates include continental breakfast. AE, DISC, MC, V. Bus: B-21 or C-10. Parking: $5.

Don't expect the Ritz, but if you're looking for a bargain on the Condado, this is it. Formerly known as the Casablanca, this renovated guest house is in the heart of the Condado. Built in the 1940s, it was later expanded, then totally refurbished with a tropical décor late in 1995. A very Puerto Rican ambience has been created, with an emphasis on Latin hospitality and comfort. The cozy but small rooms have ceiling fans and air-conditioners, and most feature original Puerto Rican art. The baths have enough shelf room and plenty of medium-size towels. The front porch is a social center for guests. You can also cook out at a barbecue area. The beach is a 2-minute walk away, and the hotel is also within walking distance of some megaresorts with their casinos.

Embassy Condado. 1126 Seaview, Condado, San Juan, PR 00907. ☎ **787/725-8284.** 14 units. A/C TV. Winter $65–$115 single or double; $145 suite. Off-season $45–$85 single or double; $100–$120 suite. Extra person $15. AE, DISC, MC, V. Bus: B-21 or C-10.

This two-story guesthouse sits about a block inland from Condado Beach. On a quiet dead-end street surrounded by a residential neighborhood, it offers a relaxed atmosphere—you could live in a swimsuit or shorts for your entire stay. The all-white medium-size rooms have rattan furniture and tropical accessories, including good beds with firm mattresses. Each has a kitchenette or access to one, plus a small bath. The hotel features a rooftop sun deck and a restaurant (across the road) offering a view over the beach. Maid service is included, and baby-sitters can be arranged.

IN ISLA VERDE

Green Isle/Casa Mathiesen. Calle Uno 36, Villamar, Isla Verde, PR 00979. ☎ **800/677-8860** in the U.S., or 787/726-4330. Fax 787/268-2415. 44 units. A/C TV TEL. Year-round $42–$65 single or double. AE, DC, MC, V. Bus: B-21 or C-10.

Unassuming and somewhat battered by the tropical sun, this hotel stands across the busy avenue from the beach used by the larger and much more expensive Sands Hotel. Each of the simple low-slung rooms comes with a kitchenette and summery furniture that was upgraded in 1996, including replacement of mattresses. There's a small pool, though most guests prefer the nearby sea. No meals are served, but dozens of inexpensive hamburger joints are nearby.

IN OCEAN PARK

Beach Buoy Inn. 1853 McLeary, Ocean Park, San Juan, PR 00911. ☎ **800/221-8119** or 787/728-8119. Fax 787/268-0037. 15 units. A/C TV. Winter $80.50 single or double; $74.50–$86.25 efficiency. Off-season $70 single or double; $63–$73 efficiency. Children 11 and under stay free in parents' room. Rates include continental breakfast. AE, MC, V. Bus: B-21. Free parking.

About a block from the beach, this B&B deserves to be better known. Its small rooms aren't decorated as nicely as those at the At Wind Chimes (above), but they're clean and decent; the efficiencies have two double beds each. All have firm mattresses and some have small refrigerators; the baths are small and towels minimal. There's daily maid service. Though this place is a comfortable, snug nest, it's short on amenities: no restaurant, no bar, and no pool, but these are available nearby. The staff is especially helpful and friendly.

IN SANTURCE

Arcade Inn. 8 Taft St., Santurce, Condado, PR 00911. ☎ **787/725-0668.** Fax 787/728-7525. 20 units. A/C TV. Winter $60 single; $70 double. Off-season $55 single; $60 double. DC, MC, V. Bus: B-21.

This no-frills hotel has attracted families and college students traveling in groups since the 1960s. It's a stucco-covered building with vaguely Spanish colonial detailing on a residential street lined with similar buildings. The small accommodations each contain a small refrigerator and slightly battered furniture with well worn but still comfortable beds. The baths are cramped. There's no pool and very few amenities, but the beach is quite close.

WORTH A SPLURGE
On the Condado

Condado Lagoon Days Inn. Calle Clemenceau 6, Condado, San Juan, PR 00907. ☎ **800/858-7407** or 787/721-0170. Fax 787/724-4356. 50 units. A/C TV TEL. Winter $99 single; $109 double; $139–$149 suite. Off-season $79 single; $89 double; $139–$149 suite. Children stay free in parents' room. AE, DC, MC, V. Bus: B-21 and C-10.

Rising seven stories above a residential neighborhood across from the Convention Center is this family-oriented hotel, whose rooms were remodeled in 1996. The accommodations are small and not particularly imaginative in their décor, but usually contain comfortable king-size beds or two doubles and a small refrigerator, plus a small but tidy bath. Some have sofas that convert into beds for children. Although there are few frills (there is a pool), the bars, restaurants, and facilities of the Condado neighborhood are within walking distance. Baby-sitters can be arranged.

El Canario by the Lagoon Hotel. Calle Clemenceau 4, Condado, San Juan, PR 00907. ☎ **800/533-2649** in the U.S., or 787/722-5058. Fax 787/723-8590. www.canariohotels.com. E-mail: canariopr@aol.com. 40 units. A/C TV TEL. Winter $95 single; $100–$110 double. Off-season $75 single; $80–$90 double. Rates include continental breakfast and morning newspaper. AE, DC, DISC, MC, V. Bus: B-21 or C-10.

One of the area's better B&Bs, the European-style El Canario is in a residential neighborhood a short block from Condado Beach. It's very much in the Condado styling, evoking Miami Beach in the 1960s. The rooms are generous in size, with balconies. Most have large twin beds, each with a firm mattress. The baths are sleek and contemporary, with generous towels and enough rooms to spread out your stuff. Extras include in-room safes, free coffee in the lobby, a tour desk, and a self-service laundry. The staff can also make arrangements for you to have access to a nearby health club. If the hotel doesn't have room for you, it can book you into its sibling properties, El Canario Inn or El Canario by the Sea.

In Isla Verde

Casa de Playa Beach Hotel. Avenida Isla Verde 86, Isla Verde, San Juan, PR 00979. ☎ **800/916-2272** or 787/728-9779. Fax 787/727-1334. 21 units. A/C TV TEL. Winter $92 single; $103 double; $168 suite. Off-season $81 single; $92 double; $135 suite. Children 9 and under stay free in parents' room. Rates include continental breakfast. AE, DC, DISC, MC, V. Bus: B-21 or C-10.

Jutting out over the sand on the mile-long Isla Verde beach, this bargain oasis is a find. If you're less interested in being in the center of San Juan than you are in spending time on the beach, check out this modest choice. The hotel consists of two two-story peach-colored buildings, with a porch around the second floor and a small garden in front. Some rooms have small refrigerators. Furnishings are a bit modest and functional but comfortable nonetheless, with much-used but still firm mattresses. Rooms open onto tidily maintained small baths. Standard but inexpensive Italian food is served at a beach bar and restaurant, Fredo's. The staff will try to arrange baby-sitting. The hotel doesn't have everything—no pool, no room service—but the price is hard to beat in Isla Verde.

In Ocean Park

✪ **Hostería del Mar.** 1 Tapia St., Ocean Park, Santurce, San Juan, PR 00911. ☎ or fax **787/727-3302.** E-mail: hosteria@taribe.net. 21 units. Winter $64 single; $150 double; $175 apt. Off-season $54 single; $98 double; $150 apt. Children 11 and under stay free in parents' room. AE, DC, DISC, MC, V. Bus: T-1.

A few blocks from the Condado casinos are the white walls of this distinctive landmark, between Isla Verde and Condado in a residential seaside community. The hotel boasts medium-size ocean-view rooms with balconies from its second floor. On the floor below, the rooms open onto patios. The room style is invitingly tropical, with wicker furniture, good beds, pastel prints, and ceiling fans, plus small but efficient baths. There's no pool, but a full-service restaurant is known for its vegetarian, macrobiotic, and Puerto Rican plates, all freshly made. The hospitality is warm. Aficionados of select Caribbean inns would like to keep this one a secret.

Número Uno Guest House. Calle Santa Ana 1, Ocean Park, San Juan, PR 00911. ☎ **787/726-5010.** Fax 787/727-5482. 12 units. A/C. Winter $75–$145 single; $95–$165 double. Off-season $55–$90 single; $75–$110 double. Rates include continental breakfast. AE, MC, V. Bus: B-21.

In a prestigious residential neighborhood at the edge of the high-rise glitter of Isla Verde, this recently renovated small hotel has a well-trained English-speaking staff. There's a garden with palmettos and a pool, easy access to a sandy beach, and all the distractions of several megaresorts relatively close at hand. The accommodations, ranging from small to medium in size, have wicker or rattan furniture and a double, queen, or king-size bed. The baths are also medium in size, with plentiful towels and good plumbing. There's a bar and a very good restaurant serving a Caribbean fusion cuisine.

GAY-FRIENDLY PLACES TO STAY

As the gay capital of the Caribbean, San Juan offers a number of gay guest houses, catering to gay men and lesbians, though primarily to men. Here's the pick of the lot. Lesbians will find a welcoming environment at the Hostería del Mar (see above).

Atlantic Beach Hotel. 1 Vendig St., Condado, San Juan, PR 00907. ☎ **787/721-6900.** Fax 787/721-6917. 37 units. A/C TV TEL. Winter $93–$131 single; $109–$148 double. Off-season $76–$109 single; $93–$125 double. AE, DC, DISC, MC, V. Bus: B-21 or C-10.

On Condado Beach, this place is proud of its status as the best-known gay hotel on Puerto Rico. The five-story hotel, with vaguely art deco styling, is a friendly refuge, mostly for men. The rooms are outfitted with tropical fabrics and accessories and rattan furnishings. The ambience is a bit tatty and the mattresses look like they've received quite a workout, but, as one repeat visitor told us, "We stay here for the gay ambience, not expecting any grand comfort." Nonetheless, it's a clean and decent place and sometimes takes on the spirit of a house party. There's a simple snack-style bar and restaurant, with a Sunday-afternoon tea dance attracting many of the city's gay men.

Lavender Hill. Calle San Sebastian 254, Old San Juan, PR 00901. ☎ **787/722-5436.** 5 units, 3 with bathroom. Nov 15–Apr 15 $85 single or double without bathroom; $95 single or double with bathroom; $125 suite without bathroom, single or double occupancy. Apr 15–Nov 15, deduct $10 per unit for single occupancy or $15 per unit for double occupancy. Rates include breakfast. MC, V. Bus: Old San Juan Trolley.

This guest house occupies a three-story stone-sided house built in 1792 and renovated at regular intervals since. The common area contains a TV, a scattering of solid-looking antiques, and a view over a private courtyard. The small to medium rooms are outfitted in a conservative colonial style, with trim painted in "Old San Juan brown," and in the case of one of the suites (the one without a bath), access to a streetfront balcony hemmed in by French-inspired iron railings. Breakfast, served in an antique dining room, features fresh fruit, yogurt, and a choice of cooked items like omelets. Donald Campbell, your host, is a hip, youthful, and articulate New Yorker who knows well the gay-friendly charms of his adopted home.

Ocean Walk. 1 Atlantic Place, Condado, San Juan, PR 00911. ☎ **800/468-0615** or 787/728-0855. Fax 787/728-6434. www.cimarron.net/rd.html. 40 units, 5 apts. with kitchenette. TV TEL. Winter $60–$136 single; $66–$136 double; $131–$151 apt. Off-season $44–$93 single; $50–$93 double; $87–$104 apt. AE, DISC, MC, V. Bus: B-21 or C-10.

Built in the 1950s, this hotel caters to a mostly gay male crowd from all over the world. The accommodations are in three low-rise Spanish colonial–style buildings that ring the edges of a sun deck and pool. The beach is quite close, and on the premises are a bar and a simple restaurant open daily for breakfast and lunch. The accommodations are basic but comfortable, summery and airy, with air-conditioning or ceiling fans. The beds have well-used mattresses but are still reasonably comfortable, and the baths are tiny with not enough towels (you may have to request more from the maid).

BEST OFF-SEASON BETS

Some of the more expensive hotels, like those on beach-bordering Isla Verde, lower their rates substantially from mid-April to mid-December. Here's a great place to find an off-season bargain.

Comfort Inn Tanama Princess Hotel. 1 Joffre St., Condado, San Juan, PR 00907. ☎ **888/826-8621** or 787/724-4160. Fax 787/723-2282. 113 units. A/C MINIBAR TV TEL. Winter $91 single; $109 double. Off-season $81 single; $92 double. Prices include continental breakfast. Children 12 and under stay free in parents' room. AE, DC, DISC, MC, V. Bus: 21.

This hotel is a worthy middle-bracket choice for a stay on the Condado, with reasonable rates that are partly a function of the hotel's position about 2 blocks from the nearest beach. A seven-story beige-painted concrete tower, it was refurbished in 1998 and renamed as a reflection of its new management by the Comfort Inn chain. Most accommodations come with two double beds (ideal for families) with good mattresses and ceiling fans. Many open onto balconies with water views. Bathrooms are medium in size with spic-and-span maintenance and adequate towels. It's a relatively easy walk to any of the Condado casinos or to water-sports activities on the beach. In the lobby is a well-respected restaurant, Picayo (under separate management).

GREAT DEALS ON DINING
IN OLD SAN JUAN

Filled with rock 'n' roll memorabilia and loud rock music, the **Hard Rock Café,** Calle Recinto Sur 253 (☎ **787/724-7625;** Bus: A-7, T-1, or T-2), serves a "classic"

American cuisine—juicy burgers, well-stuffed sandwiches, fajitas, barbecued chicken, chili, and pork ribs. It's open daily 11:30am to midnight (bar open daily 11am to 2am).

Butterfly People Café. Calle Fortaleza 152. ☎ **787/723-2432.** Main courses $5.50–$13. AE, DC, MC, V. Mon–Sat 11am–5pm. Bus: Old Town trolley. CONTINENTAL/AMERICAN.

This butterfly venture with gossamer wings (see "Shopping," below) is on the second floor of a restored mansion in Old San Juan. Next to the world's largest gallery devoted to butterflies, you can dine in the cafe, which overlooks a patio and has 15 tables inside. The cuisine is tropical and light European fare made with fresh ingredients. You might begin with gazpacho or vichyssoise, follow with quiche or a daily special, and finish with chocolate mousse or the tantalizing raspberry chiffon pie with fresh raspberry sauce. Wherever you look, framed butterflies will confront you.

Café Berlin. Calle San Francisco 407. ☎ **787/722-5205.** Main courses $8.95–$16.95. AE, MC, V. Daily 9am–10pm. Bus: Old Town trolley. INTERNATIONAL/VEGETARIAN.

This indoor/outdoor cafe-style restaurant overlooking Plaza de Colón is a favorite of locals. No one is quite sure how it got its name, as this cafe isn't German; instead, it's known for its vegetarian dishes, including a specialty, an eggplant tofu sandwich with the works. You can also order chicken and turkey dishes, along with a delectable mahi mahi, salmon, shrimp, and quiche. You can make up various combinations of dishes. The cafe specializes in fresh bread, used in its tasty lunch sandwiches. You can also drop in for breakfast to sample homemade pastries.

El Buen Samaritano. Calle Luna 255 (near San Justo St.). ☎ **787/721-6184.** Platters and main courses $8–$15. No credit cards. Daily 7am–7pm. Bus: A5. PUERTO RICAN.

Only the most experimental visitors would venture in here, despite the fact that it provides insights into the subculture of this thriving inner-city neighborhood. In fact, we've included this authentic little eatery to answer the often-posed question, "Where do the locals dine?" It stands adjacent to City Hall's back door, on one of our favorite "backwater" streets in the Old Town. Almost no English is spoken; it's as Creole and ethnic as anything on the island and contains no more than four tables in a setting Hemingway would've praised. Everything is predictably filling and starchy, including roast pork with yellow rice and beans and red snapper fillet in pungent tomato sauce. The menu, which depends largely on what's available in the market, will be recited lethargically by a member of the family who owns this hole-in-the-wall. Except during the midday crush, no one will mind if you opt for just a cup of thick Puerto Rican coffee, a beer, or a soda.

El Patio de Sam. Calle San Sebastián 102 (across from the Iglesia de San José). ☎ **787/723-1149.** Sandwiches, burgers, salads $8.95–$12; main courses $10.95–$22.95. AE, DC, DISC, MC, V. Sun–Thurs 11am–midnight, Fri–Sat 11am–1:30am. Bus: A-7, T-1, or T-2. AMERICAN/PUERTO RICAN.

This is a popular gathering spot for American expats, newspeople, and shopkeepers, and is known for having the best burgers in San Juan. Even though the dining room isn't outdoors, it has been transformed into a patio. You'll swear you're dining alfresco: Every table is placed near a cluster of potted plants, and canvas panels and awnings cover the skylight. For a satisfying lunch, try the black bean soup, followed by the burger platter, and top it off with a key lime tart. Except for the hamburgers, some other items on the menu haven't met with favor among many visitors, who've written us that the food was overpriced and the service confused. Nevertheless, it remains Old Town's most popular dining room. They now have live entertainment, Tuesday to Saturday, with a guitarist playing Spanish music some nights, giving way to a classical pianist on other nights.

⭐ **La Bombonera.** Calle San Francisco 259. ☎ **787/722-0658.** Reservations recommended. American breakfast $7; main courses $6.55–$18. AE, DISC, MC, V. Daily 7:30am–8pm. Bus: M-2, M-3, or T-1. PUERTO RICAN.

This favorite, offering exceptional value at affordable prices, opened in 1902 and has been offering homemade pastries and coffee amid traditional colonial décor since. For decades it was a rendezvous for the island's literati and Old San Juan families, but now it has been discovered by visitors. The food is authentic and homemade. Its sandwiches are the thickest in town, and the regional dishes include rice with squid, roast leg of pork, and seafood *asopao*. For dessert, you might select apple, pineapple, or prune pie or one of many types of flan. Service is polite if a bit rushed, and the place fills up quickly at lunch.

La Mallorquina. Calle San Justo 207. ☎ **787/722-3261.** Reservations not accepted at lunch, recommended at dinner. Main courses $5.50–$10.50 at lunch, $13.95–$25.95 at dinner. AE, MC, V. Mon–Sat 11:30am–10pm. Bus: A-7, T-1, or 2. PUERTO RICAN.

San Juan's oldest restaurant opened in 1848, and it's in a three-story glassed-in courtyard with arches and antique wall clocks. Even if you've already eaten, you might want to stop by for a drink at the old-fashioned wooden bar. Begin your meal with garlic soup or gazpacho. The chef specializes in the typical Puerto Rican rice dish *asopao*, which you can have with chicken, shrimp, or lobster and shrimp. *Arroz con pollo* (rice with chicken) is almost as popular. Other recommended main courses are grilled pork chop with fried plantains, paella, beef tenderloin Puerto Rican style, and assorted seafood stewed in wine. Lunch is busy; dinners are sometimes quiet.

NoNo's. Calle San Sebastián 100 (at Calle Cristo). ☎ **787/725-7819.** Hamburgers and main courses $3.50–$10.95. AE, MC, V. Daily 11am–9pm. (Bar, daily 11am–4am.) Bus: Old Town trolley. AMERICAN/FAST FOOD.

In the heart of Old San Juan, NoNo's brings stateside food to those eager for a taste of the salads, mozzarella sticks, triple-decker sandwiches, chicken-fried steaks, hamburgers (here called NoNo burgers), and onion rings they've been missing. Most of the dishes are at the lower end of the price scale. You'll sit beneath a beamed ceiling in one of San Juan's oldest buildings, near a large and accommodating bar where folks seem only peripherally interested in the food.

In Condado

Cafe Mezzanine. In the Radisson Ambassador Plaza Hotel & Casino, 1369 Ashford Ave. ☎ **787/721-7300.** Main courses $6.95–$16.95; full American breakfast $6.25–$11.50. AE, DC, MC, V. Sun–Thurs 6:30am–10:30pm, Fri–Sat 6:30am–11:30pm. Bus: B-21 or C-10. INTERNATIONAL.

On the mezzanine level of one of the Condado's best hotels, this comfortable and cozy eatery for many years was the most famous Howard Johnson's in the Caribbean. It attracts some of the most prestigious politicians and financiers to its booths and tables (many luminaries live nearby and consider it their neighborhood diner). Depending on the time of day, you can be served pancakes, omelets, muffins, hash browns, and sausages; or you can order lunch and dinner foods like fish fries, teriyaki steaks, clam platters, and an array of sandwiches and burgers, as well as typical Puerto Rican dishes.

Caruso. 1104 Ashford Ave., Condado. ☎ **787/723-6876.** Main courses $6.75–$33; lunch platters $5–$10. AE, DC, MC, V. Daily noon–11pm. Bus: B-21 or C-10. ITALIAN.

The décor and the brisk efficiency of the staff might remind you of a neighborhood trattoria in New York City, and in fact Caruso's has become the neighborhood choice of many Condado residents who hail from New York. It's one of the most popular places around for pasta, partly because of its low prices and partly because of its simple but down-to-earth food. Menu items include fish fillet with caviar sauce, filet mignon, veal piccata, veal marsala, and grilled fish of the day. Most dishes are inexpensive, among the cheapest on the Condado, unless you order the expensive fish dishes.

Tony Roma's. In the Condado Plaza Hotel, 999 Ashford Ave. ☎ **787/721-1000,** ext. 2123. Main courses $7.50–$17.95. AE, DC, MC, V. Daily noon–midnight. Bus: B-21 or C-10. BARBECUE.

Efficient and unpretentious, this is Puerto Rico's busiest branch of the international chain. It's one of the least expensive restaurants in the Condado and is a fine choice if you're in the mood for spicy barbecued food (the honey barbecue isn't as fiery).

Via Appia. 1350 Ashford Ave., Condado. ☎ **787/725-8711.** Pizza $8.95–$14.95; main courses $9–$16; sandwiches $4–$6. AE, MC, V. Daily 11am–midnight. Bus: A-7. ITALIAN.

A favorite of *sanjuaneros* visiting Condado for the day, Via Appia offers food that's sometimes praiseworthy rather than merely passable. Its pizzas are the best in the neighborhood. Savory pasta dishes, like baked ziti, lasagne, and spaghetti with several of your favorite sauces, are also prepared. All of this can be washed down with sangría. During the day, freshly made salads or sandwiches are available.

ISLA VERDE

✪ **Metropol.** Ave. Isla Verde. ☎ **787/791-4046.** Main courses $5.50–$28.90. AE, MC, V. Daily 11am–7pm. Bus: A-7. CUBAN/PUERTO RICAN/INTERNATIONAL.

Metropol is the happiest blend of Cuban and Puerto Rican food we've ever discovered. The black-bean soup is among the island's finest, served in the classic Havana style with a side dish of rice and chopped onions. Endless garlic bread accompanies most dinners, likely to include Cornish game hen stuffed with Cuban rice and beans or marinated steak topped with a fried egg. Smoked chicken or chicken fried steak are also heartily recommended; the portions are huge. Plaintains, yucca, and all that good stuff accompany most dishes. Finish with a choice of thin or firm custard.

Panadería España Repostería. Centro Villamar, Isla Verde. ☎ **787/727-3860.** Sandwiches $3–$6. AE, DISC, MC, V. Daily 6am–10pm. Bus: B-21 or C-10. SANDWICHES/COFFEES.

The Panadería España makes San Juan's definitive Cuban sandwich—a cheap meal in itself. Consisting of sliced baked pork packed in crusty bread, it's about the only thing offered except for drinks and coffee dispensed from behind a much-used bar. There's also an assortment of gourmet items from Spain, arranged as punctuation marks on shelves set against an otherwise all-white décor. The place has been serving simple breakfasts, drinks, coffee, and Cuban sandwiches virtually every day since it opened around 1970.

✪ **Repostería Kassalta.** Calle McLeary 1966. ☎ **787/727-7340.** Full American breakfast $4.35; soups $5; sandwiches $3–$6. MC, V. Daily 6am–10pm. Bus: B-21 or C-10. SPANISH/PUERTO RICAN.

In a commercial neighborhood 4 miles east of Old San Juan, this is the most famous of San Juan's cafeteria/bakery/delicatessens because of its reasonable prices and eat-in and take-out foods. The cavernous room is flanked with modern sun-flooding windows and glass-fronted display cases filled with meats, sausages, and pastries. At one end of the room, patrons line up to place their order at a cash register, then carry their selections to one of the tables. It helps to know Spanish. Try a steaming bowl of the best *caldo gallego* in Puerto Rico—laden with collard greens, potatoes, and sausage slices and accompanied by hunks of bread, this soup makes a meal in itself. Also popular are Cuban sandwiches (made with sliced pork, cheese, and fried bread), steak sandwiches, octopus salad, and an assortment of omelets.

PICNIC FARE & WHERE TO EAT IT

Puerto Rico is usually ideal for picnicking year-round. The best place to fill a picnic basket is the **Repostería Kassalta** (see "In Ocean Park," earlier in this chapter), a cafeteria/bakery/deli with lots of goodies. Puerto Rican families often come here to order delicacies for their Sunday outings. The best places for a picnic are **Muñoz Marín Park,** along Las Américas Expressway, west of Avenida Piñero, and the **Botanical Gardens** operated by the University of Puerto Rico in the Río Piedras section.

HITTING THE BEACHES

Some public stretches of shoreline around San Juan are overcrowded, especially on Saturday and Sunday; others are practically deserted. If you find that secluded beach of your dreams, proceed with caution. On unguarded beaches you'll have no way to protect yourself or your valuables should you be approached by a robber or mugger, which has been known to happen. For more information about the island's many beaches, call the **Department of Sports and Recreation** at ☎ **787/721-2500.**

All beaches on Puerto Rico, even those fronting the top hotels, are open to the public, though you'll be charged for parking and use of *balneario* facilities, such as lockers and showers. Public beaches shut down on Monday; if Monday is a holiday, the beaches are open for the holiday but close Tuesday. Beach hours are 9am to 5pm in winter and to 6pm off-season. Major public beaches in the San Juan area have changing rooms and showers; Luquillo also has picnic tables.

Famous with beach buffs since the 1920s, ✪ **Condado Beach** put San Juan on the map as a resort. Backed up by high-rise hotels, it seems more like Miami Beach than any other in the Caribbean. From parasailing to sailing, all sorts of water sports can be booked at kiosks along the beach or at the activities desk of the various hotels. There are also plenty of outdoor bars and restaurants when you tire of the sands. People watching seems a favorite sport along these golden strands.

At the end of Puente Dos Hermanos, the westernmost corner of the Condado is the most popular strip. This section of the beach is small and shaded by palms, and a natural rock barrier calms the turbulence of the waters, making for safe swimming in gin-clear waters. The lagoon on the other side of the beach is ideal for windsurfing and kayaking. The lagoon runs east to west, and its waters are tranquil, with steady parallel winds.

A favorite of San Juaneros themselves, golden-sand **Isla Verde Beach** is also ideal for swimming, and it's lined with high-rise resorts and luxury condos. Isla Verde has picnic tables, so you can pick up the makings of a lunch and make it a day at the beach. This strip is also good for snorkeling because of its calm clear waters, and many kiosks will rent you equipment. Isla Verde Beach extends from the end of Ocean Park to the beginning of a section called Boca Cangrejos. The best beach at Isla Verde is at the Hotel El San Juan. Most sections of this long strip have separate names, like El Alambique, often the site of beach parties, and Punta El Medio, bordering the new Ritz-Carlton. If you go past the luxury hotels and expensive condos behind the Luís Muñoz Marín International Airport, you arrive at the major public beach at Isla Verde. Here you'll find a *balneario* with parking, showers, fast-food joints, and water-sports equipment. The sands here are whiter than the golden sands of the Condado and are lined with coconut palms, sea-grape trees, and even almond trees, all providing shade from the fierce sun.

The prettiest beach in the Greater San Juan area is **Ocean Park,** a mile-long wide stretch of fine golden sand in a residential neighborhood east of Condado. The waters are choppy but still quite swimmable. This beach is very popular with college students on weekends and also draws a big gay crowd (the other popular gay beach is nearby in front of the Atlantic Beach Hotel). Access to the beach at Ocean Park has been limited recently, but the best place to enter is from a section called El Ultimo Trolley. This area is also ideal for volleyball, paddleball, and other games. The easternmost portion, known as Punta Las Marias, is best for windsurfing.

Rivaling Condado and Isla Verde beaches, ✪ **Luquillo Public Beach** is the grandest in Puerto Rico and one of the most popular. It's 30 miles east of San Juan near the town of Luquillo. Here you'll find a mile-long half-moon bay set against a backdrop of coconut palms. This is another of the dozen or so balnearios of Puerto Rico. Saturday and Sunday are the worst times to go, as hordes of San Juaneros head here for fun in the sun. Water-sports kiosks are available, offering everything from windsurfing to sailing. Facilities include lifeguards, an emergency first-aid station, ample parking, showers, and toilets. You can easily have a local lunch here at one of the beach shacks offering cod fritters and tacos.

SPORTS & OUTDOOR PURSUITS

BAY CRUISES   For the best cruises of San Juan Bay, go to **Caribe Aquatic Adventures** (see "Scuba Diving," below). Bay cruises start at $20 per person. In relative comfort, you're taken on a panoramic sweep of the bay.

DEEP-SEA FISHING   It's top-notch! Allison tuna, white and blue marlin, sailfish, wahoo, dolphin (mahi mahi), mackerel, and tarpon are some of the fish you can catch in Puerto Rican waters, where 30 world records have been broken. Charter arrangements can be made through most major hotels and resorts.

Capt. Mike Benitez, who has chartered out of San Juan for more than 40 years, was listed in 1993 by the *Sports Fishing Tournament Guide* as one of the world's 15 most qualified sport-fishing captains. **Benitez Fishing Charters** can be contacted at P.O. Box 9066541, Puerto de Tierra, San Juan, PR 00906 (☎ **787/723-2292** to 9pm). The captain offers a 45-foot air-conditioned deluxe Hatteras, the *Sea Born*. Fishing tours for parties of up to six cost $450 for half a day and $750 for a full day, beverages and equipment included.

HORSE RACING   Great thoroughbreds and outstanding jockeys compete all year at **El Comandante,** Avenida 65 de Infantería, Route 3, kilometer 15.3, at Canovanas (☎ **787/724-6060**), Puerto Rico's only racetrack, a 20-minute drive east of the center of San Juan. Post time varies from 2:15 to 2:45pm on Monday, Wednesday, Friday, Saturday, and Sunday. Entrance to the clubhouse costs $3 per person, though no admission is charged for the grandstand.

SCUBA DIVING   In San Juan, head to **Caribe Aquatic Adventures,** P.O. Box 9024278, San Juan Station, San Juan, PR 00902 (☎ 787/724-1882 or 787/765-7444). Most of its activities revolve around its dive shop in the lobby of the Radisson Normandie. The company offers diving certification from both PADI and NAUI as part of 40-hour courses at $465 each. A resort course for first-time divers is $97. Also offered are local daily dives in San Juan or windsurfing (below) and a choice of full-day diving expeditions to various reefs off the east coast. If time is severely limited, the outfitter will take you to sites in San Juan where diving is best. But since the best sites for scuba diving are out on the island's coasts, the serious diver will have to commit to a full-day tour because of the transportation time involved.

SNORKELING   Snorkeling opportunities are better in the outlying portions of the island instead of in San Juan. However, if you're a confirmed snorkeler and don't have time to explore greater Puerto Rico, you'll find that most water-sports desks at the big San Juan hotels at Isla Verde and Condado can generally make arrangements for instruction and equipment rental and can lead you to the best places for snorkeling.

If your hotel doesn't have such services, you can contact **Caribe Aquatic Adventures** (see "Scuba Diving," above), which caters to both snorkelers and scuba divers. Other possibilities for equipment rentals are **Caribbean School of Aquatics,** Taft No. 1, Suite 10F, in San Juan (☎ 787/728-6606), and **Mundo Submarino,** Laguna Gardens Shopping Center, Isla Verde (☎ 787/791-5764). Snorkeling equipment generally costs $15. If you're snorkeling on your own in the San Juan area, one of the best places is the San Juan Bay marina near the Caribe Hilton.

TENNIS   In San Juan, the **Caribe Hilton & Casino,** Puerta de Tierra (☎ 787/721-0303), and the **Condado Plaza Hotel & Casino,** 999 Ashford Ave. (☎ 787/721-1000), have tennis courts. Nonguests can use these hotel courts if they make a reservation. There are 17 public courts, lit at night, at **San Juan Central Municipal Park** at Calle Cerra (exit on Route 2; ☎ 787/722-1646). Fees are $3 an hour 8am to 6pm here, going up to $4 per hour 6 to 10pm.

WINDSURFING   The sheltered waters of the Condado Lagoon in San Juan is a favorite spot. Throughout the island, many of the companies featuring snorkeling and scuba diving also offer windsurfing equipment and instruction, and dozens of hotels offer facilities on their own premises. One of the best places in San Juan to go windsurfing is at the Radisson Normandie, where **Caribe Aquatic Adventures** has its main branch (☎ 787/724-1882 or 787/765-7444). Board rentals cost $25 per hour, with a lesson costing $45.

STEPPING BACK IN TIME: SEEING OLD SAN JUAN

The streets are narrow and teeming with traffic, but a walk through Old San Juan (in Spanish, El Viejo San Juan) is like a stroll through 5 centuries of history. You can do it in less than a day. In a 7-square-block landmark area in the westernmost part of the city you can see many of Puerto Rico's chief historical attractions and do some shopping along the way.

The Spanish moved to Old San Juan in 1521, and the city played an important role as Spain's bastion of defense in the Caribbean. Once the city was called Puerto Rico (Rich Port), as the whole island was once called San Juan.

FORTS

The **city walls** around San Juan were built in 1630 to protect the town against both European invaders and Caribbean pirates, and indeed were part of one of the New World's most impregnable fortresses. Even today, they're an engineering marvel. At their top, notice the balconied buildings that served for centuries as hospitals and also residences of the island's governors. The thickness of the walls averages 20 feet at the base and 12 feet at the top, with an average height of 40 feet. Between Fort San Cristóbal and El Morro, bastions were erected at frequent intervals. The walls come into view as you approach from San Cristóbal on your way to El Morro. To get here, take the T-1 bus.

✪ **Castillo San Felipe del Morro.** At the end of Calle Norzagaray. ☎ **787/729-6960.** Admission (includes same-day admission to Fort San Cristóbal, below) $2 adults, $1 ages 13–17; free 12 and under. Daily 9am–5pm. Bus: A-5, B-21, or B-40.

Called El Morro, this fort, with some of the Caribbean's most dramatic views, stands on a rocky promontory dominating the entrance to San Juan Bay. Built in 1540, the original fort was a round tower, which you can still see deep inside the lower levels of the castle. More walls and cannon-firing positions were added, and by 1787 the fortification attained the complex design you see today. This fortress was attacked repeatedly by both the English and the Dutch. The National Park Service protects the fortifications of Old San Juan, which the United Nations has declared a World

Old San Juan

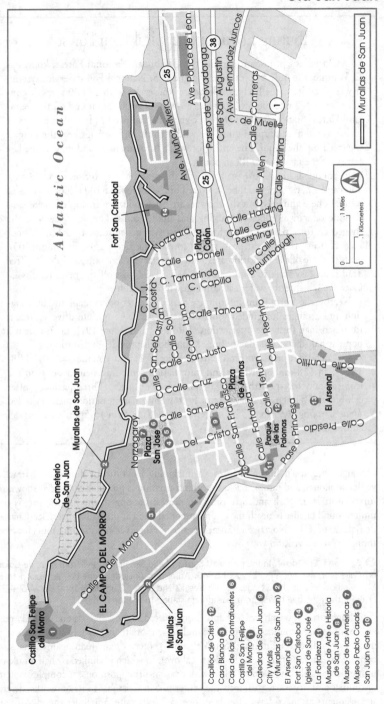

Atlantic Ocean

Fort San Cristobal

Castillo San Felipe del Morro

Murallas de San Juan

Cemeterio de San Juan

EL CAMPO DEL MORRO

Murallas de San Juan

Calle del Morro

Nozagaray

Plaza San José

Calle San Sebastián

Calle Sol

Calle Luna

Calle San Justo

Calle Tanca

Calle O'Donell

C. Tamarindo

C. Capilla

C. J. J. Acosta

Nozgara

Plaza Colón

Calle Harding

Calle Gen. Pershing

Calle Braumbaugh

Calle Recinto

Calle Cruz

Calle San Jose

Del Cristo

Calle San Francisco

Plaza de Armas

Calle Tetuan

Calle Fortaleza

Parque de las Palomas

Paseo Princesa

Calle Presidio

Calle Puntillo

El Arsenal

Ave. Muñoz Rivera

Ave. Ponce de León

Paseo de Covadonga

Calle San Augustin

C. Ave. Fernandez Juncos

Calle Contreras

Calle Allen

Calle Marina

C. de Muelle

25

25

38

1

Murallas de San Juan

.1 Miles

.1 Kilometers

0

0

Capilloa de Cristo 12
Casa Blanca 3
Casa de las Contrafuertes 6
Castillo San Felipe del Morro 1
Catedral de San Juan 9
City Walls (Murallas de San Juan) 2
El Arsenal 13
Fort San Cristobal 14
Iglesia de San José 4
La Fortaleza 11
Museo de Arte e Historia de San Juan 8
Museo de las Americas 7
Museo Pablo Casals 5
San Juan Gate 10

429

Touring El Yunque Tropical Rain Forest

Some 25 miles east of San Juan lies the **Caribbean National Forest,** known as **El Yunque,** the only tropical forest in the U.S. National Forest Service system. It was given its status by Pres. Theodore Roosevelt. With 28,000 acres, it contains some 240 tree species (only half a dozen of which are found on the mainland United States). In this world of cedars and satinwood (draped in tangles of vines), you'll hear chirping birds, see wild orchids, and perhaps hear the song of the tree frog, the coquí. The entire forest is a bird sanctuary and may be the last retreat of the rare Puerto Rican parrot.

El Yunque is high above sea level, and the peak of El Toro rises to 3,532 feet. You can be fairly sure you'll be showered on, as more than 100 billion gallons of rain falls here annually, but the showers are brief and there are lots of shelters. El Yunque offers a number of walking and hiking trails. The most scenic is the rugged El Toro, passing through four forest systems en route to the 3,532-foot Pico El Toro, the highest peak in the forest. The sign-posted El Yunque Trail leads to three of the recreation area's most spectacular lookouts, and the Big Tree Trail is an easy walk to panoramic La Mina Falls. Just off the main road is La Coca Falls, a sheet of water cascading down mossy cliffs.

Nearby, the Sierra Palm Interpretive Service Center offers maps and information and arranges for guided tours of the forest. A 45-minute drive southeast from San Juan (near the intersection of Route 3 and Route 191), El Yunque is a popular half-day or full-day outing. Major hotels provide guided tours.

El Portal Tropical Forest Center, Route 191, Rio Grande (☎ **787/888-1810**), an $18-million exhibit and information center, opened its doors in the tropical rain forest, with 10,000 square feet of space. Three pavilions offer exhibits and bilingual displays. Actor Jimmy Smits narrates a documentary called *Understanding the Forest.* The center is open daily 9am to 5pm, charging $3 admission.

Heritage Site. You'll find El Morro an intriguing labyrinth of dungeons, barracks, vaults, lookouts, and ramps. Background information is provided in a video shown to fort visitors in English and Spanish. The nearest parking to the historic fort is the underground facility beneath the Quincentennial Plaza at the Ballajá barracks (Cuartel de Ballajá) on Calle Norzagaray. Sometimes park rangers lead hour-long tours for free, though you can visit on your own.

✪ Fort San Cristóbal. In the northeast corner of Old San Juan (uphill from Plaza de Colón on Calle Norzagaray). ☎ **787/729-6960.** Admission (includes same-day admission to El Morro, above) $2 adults, $1 ages 13–17; free 12 and under. Daily 9am–5pm. Bus: A-5, B-21 or B-40; then the free trolley from Covadonga station to the top of the hill.

This huge fortress, begun in 1634 and re-engineered in the 1770s, is one of the largest ever built in the Americas by Spain. Its walls rise more than 150 feet above the sea, a marvel of military engineering. San Cristóbal protected San Juan against attackers coming by land as a partner to El Morro (above), to which it's linked by half a mile of monumental walls and bastions filled with cannon-firing positions. A complex system of tunnels and dry moats connects the center of San Cristóbal to its outworks, defensive elements arranged layer after layer over a 27-acre site. You'll get the idea if you look at the scale model displayed.

Like El Morro, the fort is administered and maintained by the National Park Service. Be sure to see the Garita del Diablo (Devil's Sentry Box), one of the oldest parts of San Cristóbal's defenses and famous in Puerto Rican legend. The devil himself, it's said, would snatch away sentinels at this lonely post at the edge of the sea. In 1898, the first shots of the Spanish-American War in Puerto Rico were fired by cannons atop San Cristóbal during an artillery duel with a U.S. Navy fleet. Check at the guard house at the entrance for the schedule of special activities. Sometimes park rangers lead hour-long tours for free, though you can visit on your own.

Fort San Jerónimo. Calle Rosales, east of the Caribe Hilton, at the entrance to Condado Bay. ☎ **787/724-1844.** Free admission. Wed–Sat 9am–3pm. Bus: T-1.

Completed in 1608, this fort was damaged in the 1797 English assault. Reconstructed in the closing year of the 18th century, it has now been taken over by the Institute of Puerto Rican Culture. Anyone wanting to see the view from the inside must call the Caribe Hilton; security here will open the gate to let you inside, but a special request has to be made.

CHURCHES

Capilla de Cristo. Calle del Cristo (directly west of Paseo de la Princesa). Free admission. Tues 10am–2pm. Bus: Old Town trolley.

The Cristo Chapel was built to commemorate what legend says was a miracle. In 1753, a young rider lost control of his horse in a race down this very street during the fiesta of St. John's Day and plunged over the precipice. Moved by the accident, the secretary of the city, Don Mateo Pratts, invoked Christ to save the youth and had the chapel built when his prayers were answered. Today it's a landmark in the old city and one of its best-known historical monuments. The chapel's gold-and-silver altar can be seen through its glass doors. Since the chapel is open only 1 day a week, most visitors have to settle for a view of its exterior.

Catedral de San Juan. Calle del Cristo 153 (at Caleta San Juan). ☎ **787/722-0861.** Free admission. Daily 8:30am–4pm. Bus: Old Town trolley.

San Juan Cathedral was begun in 1540 and has had a rough life. Restoration today has been extensive, so it hardly resembles the thatch-roofed structure that stood here until 1529, when it was wiped out by a hurricane. Hampered by lack of funds, the cathedral slowly added a circular staircase and two adjoining vaulted Gothic chambers. But then along came the Earl of Cumberland in 1598 to loot it and a hurricane in 1615 to blow off its roof. Since 1862, the cathedral has contained the wax-covered mummy of St. Pio, a Roman martyr persecuted and killed for his Christian faith. To the right of the mummy, you might notice a bizarre wooden statue of Mary with four swords stuck in her bosom. In 1908, the body of Ponce de León was disinterred from the nearby Iglesia de San José and placed here in a marble tomb near the transept, where it remains. Although the cathedral's great treasures, including gold and silver, were looted long ago, many beautiful stained-glass windows remain. The cathedral faces Plaza de las Monjas (the Nuns' Square), a shady spot where you can rest and cool off.

Iglesia de San José. Plaza de San José, Calle del Cristo. ☎ **787/725-7501.** Free admission. Church and Chapel of Belém, Mon–Wed and Fri 7am–3pm, Sat 8am–1pm. Bus: Old Town trolley.

Plans for this church were drawn up in 1523, and Dominican friars supervised its construction in 1532. Before entering, look for the statue of Ponce de León in the adjoining plaza—it was made from melted-down British cannons captured during Sir Ralph Abercromby's unsuccessful attack on San Juan in 1797.

Both the church and its monastery were closed by decree in 1838, and the property was confiscated by the royal treasury. Later, the Crown turned the convent into a military barracks. The Jesuits restored the badly damaged church. This was the place of worship for Ponce de León's descendants, who are buried under the family's coat-of-arms. The conquistador, killed by a poisoned arrow in Florida, was interred here until his removal to the Catedral de San Juan in 1908.

Though badly looted, the church still has some treasures, including *Christ of the Ponces,* a carved crucifix presented to Ponce de León; four oils by José Campéche, the 18th-century's leading Puerto Rican painter; and two large works by Francisco Oller, the stellar artist of the late 19th and early 20th century. Many miracles have been attributed to a painting in the Chapel of Belém, a 15th-century Flemish work called *The Virgin of Bethlehem.*

OTHER HISTORIC SIGHTS

San Juan Gate, Calle San Francisco and Calle Recinto Oeste, built around 1635, just north of La Fortaleza, several blocks downhill from the cathedral, was the main gate and entry point into San Juan—that is, if you arrived by ship in the 18th century. The gate is the only one remaining of the several that once pierced the fortifications of the old walled city. To get here, take the B-21 bus.

El Arsenal. La Puntilla. ☎ **787/724-0700.** Free admission. Wed–Sun 8:30am–4:30pm. Bus: B-21.

The Spaniards used shallow craft to patrol the lagoons and mangroves in and around San Juan. Needing a base for these vessels, they constructed El Arsenal in the 19th century. It was at this base they staged their last stand, flying the Spanish colors until the final Spaniard was removed in 1898, at the end of the Spanish-American War. Changing art exhibits are held in the building's three galleries.

Casa Blanca. Calle San Sebastián 1. ☎ **787/724-4102.** Admission $2. Tues–Sat 9am–noon and 1–4:30pm. Bus: B-21.

Ponce de León never lived here, though construction of the house—built in 1521—is sometimes attributed to him. The house was erected 2 years after the explorer's death, and work was ordered by his son-in-law, Juan García Troche. The parcel of land was given to Ponce de León as a reward for services rendered to the Crown. Descendants of the explorer lived in the house for about 2½ centuries until the Spanish government took it over in 1779 for use as a residence for military commanders. The U.S. government also used it as a home for army commanders. On the first floor, the Juan Ponce de León Museum is furnished with antiques, paintings, and artifacts from the 16th to the 18th century. In back is a garden with spraying fountains, offering an intimate and verdant respite from the monumental buildings of old San Juan.

La Fortaleza. Calle Fortaleza, overlooking San Juan Harbor. ☎ **787/721-7000,** ext. 2211. Free admission. 30-minute tours of the gardens and building (in English and Spanish) given hourly Mon–Fri 9am–4pm. Bus: B-21.

The office and residence of the governor of Puerto Rico is the oldest executive mansion in continuous use in the western hemisphere, and it has served as the island's seat of government for more than 3 centuries. Yet its history goes back farther, to 1533, when construction began on a fortress to protect San Juan's Spanish settlers during raids by Carib tribesmen and pirates. The original medieval towers remain, but as the edifice was subsequently enlarged into a palace, other modes of architecture and ornamentation were also incorporated, including baroque, Gothic, neoclassical, and Arabian. La Fortaleza has been designated a National Historic Site by the U.S. government. Informal but proper attire is required.

MUSEUMS

Museo de las Americas. Cuartel de Ballajá. ☎ **787/724-5052.** Free admission. Tues–Fri 10am–4pm, Sat–Sun 11am–5pm. Bus: Old Town trolley.

One of San Juan's major new museums, this showcases the artisans of North, South, and Central America, featuring everything from carved figureheads from New England whaling ships to dugout canoes carved by Carib Indians in Dominica. It's unique in Puerto Rico and well worth a visit. Also on display is a changing collection of paintings by artists from throughout the Spanish-speaking world, some of which are for sale, and a permanent collection called Puerto Rican *Santos,* which includes a collection of wood saints (carved wooden depictions of saints) donated by Dr. Ricardo Alegría.

Museo Pablo Casals. Plaza de San José, Calle San Sebastián 101. ☎ **787/723-9185.** Admission $1 adults, 50¢ children. Tues–Sat 9:30am–5pm. Bus: Old Town trolley.

Adjacent to the Iglesia de San José, this museum is devoted to the memorabilia left to the people of Puerto Rico by musician Pablo Casals. The maestro's cello is here, along with a library of videotapes (played on request) of some of his festival concerts. This small 18th-century house also contains manuscripts and photographs of Casals. The annual Casals Festival draws worldwide interest and attracts some of the greatest performing artists; it's still held during the first 2 weeks of June.

Museo de Arte e Historia de San Juan. Calle Norzagaray 150. ☎ **787/724-1875.** Free admission. Wed–Sun 10am–5pm. Bus: B-21 to Old San Juan terminal; then a trolley car from the terminal to the museum.

In a Spanish colonial building at the corner of Calle MacArthur, this cultural center was the city's main marketplace in the mid–19th century. Local art is displayed in the east and west galleries, and audiovisual materials reveal the city's history. Sometimes major cultural events are staged in the museum's large courtyard. English- and Spanish-language audiovisual shows are presented hourly Monday to Friday 9am to 4pm.

SHOPPING

U.S. citizens don't pay duty on items brought back to the U.S. And you can still find great bargains on Puerto Rico, where the competition among shopkeepers is fierce. Even though the U.S. Virgin Islands are duty-free, many readers report finding far lower prices on many items in San Juan than on St. Thomas.

The streets of **Old Town,** such as Calle San Francisco and Calle del Cristo, are the major venues for shopping. Note, however, that most stores in Old San Juan are closed on Sunday. The biggest and most up-to-date shopping plaza in the Caribbean Basin is **Plaza Las Americas,** in the financial district of Hato Rey, right off the Las Americas Expressway. The complex, with its fountains and advanced architecture, has more than 200 mostly upscale shops.

Native handcrafts can be good buys, like needlework, straw work, ceramics, hammocks, papier-mâché fruits and vegetables, and paintings and sculptures by Puerto Rican artists. Puerto Rican *santos* (saints) are sought by collectors. These carved wooden religious idols vary greatly in shape and size, and devout locals believe they have healing powers—often the ability to perform *milagros* (miracles). *Santos* arguably have been called Puerto Rico's greatest contribution to the plastic arts.

If you're interested in acquiring Puerto Rican art, there are many possibilities, especially these outlets. **Galería Botello,** Calle del Cristo 208 (☎ 787/723-2879), is a contemporary Latin American art gallery and a living tribute to the late Angel Botello, one of Puerto Rico's most outstanding artists. He was born in a small village in Galicia,

Spain, and after the Spanish Civil War fled to the Caribbean and spent 12 years in Haiti. His paintings and bronze sculptures are done in a style uniquely his own. This is his former home, and he restored the colonial mansion himself. Today it's a setting to display his paintings and sculptures as well as works by outstanding local artists and also a large collection of Puerto Rican antique *santos*. **Galería Palomas,** Calle del Cristo 207 (☎ 787/725-2660), rivals Galería Botello as the leading art gallery of Puerto Rico. Works range from $75 to $35,000, include some of the leading painters of the Latin American world, and are rotated every 2 to 3 weeks. The setting is a 17th-century colonial house. Of special note are works by such local artists as Homer, Moya, and Alicea.

San Juan is also a center for fashion. Try **Lindissima Shop,** Calle Fortaleza 300 (☎ 787/721-0550), an outlet offering a collection for women of contemporary sportswear and dresses for both daytime and evening. If you lack an outfit for a formal evening aboard ship, you're likely to find it here. **Nono Maldonado,** 1051 Ashford Ave. (☎ 787/721-0456), is named after its owner, a Puerto Rican designer who worked for many years as the fashion editor of *Esquire.* Selling both men's and women's clothing, it contains everything from socks to dinner jackets, as well as ready-to-wear versions of Maldonado's twice-a-year collections. Both ready-to-wear and couture are available. This is the designer's main store (midway between the Condado Plaza and the Ramada Hotel), but there's also a Maldonado boutique in the El San Juan Hotel in Isla Verde.

The **Polo/Ralph Lauren Factory Store,** Calle del Cristo 201 (☎ 787/722-2136), is as stylish as anything you'd expect from one of North America's leading clothiers. Even better, its prices are often 35% to 40% less than they'd be in the U.S. You can find even greater discounts on irregular or slightly damaged garments. The store occupies two floors of a pair of colonial buildings, with one upstairs room devoted to home furnishings. Men's sizes larger than a 42 waist are almost never in stock.

Barrachina's, Calle Fortaleza 104, between Calle del Cristo and Calle San José (☎ 787/725-7912), is a jewelry store and the birthplace, in 1963, of the piña colada. It's a favorite of cruise-ship passengers, offering one of the largest selections of jewelry, perfume, cigars, and gifts in San Juan. There's a patio for drinks where you can order—(what else?) a piña colada. There's also a Bacardi rum outlet selling bottles cheaper than stateside but at the same prices as the Bacardi distillery. You'll also find a costume-jewelry department, a gift shop, and a section for authentic silver jewelry, plus a restaurant.

Butterfly People, Calle Fortaleza 152 (☎ 787/723-2432), is a gallery/cafe in a handsomely restored building in Old San Juan. Butterflies, sold here in artfully arranged boxes, range from $20 for a single mounting to thousands of dollars for whole-wall murals. The butterflies are preserved and will last forever. The dimensional artwork is sold in limited editions and can be shipped worldwide. Most of these butterflies come from farms around the world, some of the most beautiful coming from Indonesia, Malaysia, and New Guinea. Tucked away on the same premises, with ownership by the daughter of the owner of the cafe, is **Malula Antiques.** Specializing in tribal art from the Moroccan sub-Sahara and Syria, it contains a sometimes startling collection of primitive and timeless crafts and accessories.

Galería Bóveda, Calle del Cristo 209 (☎ 787/725-0263), is a long narrow space crammed with exotic jewelry, clothing, greeting cards of images of life in Puerto Rico, some 100 handmade lamps, antiques, Mexican punched tin and glass, and art nouveau reproductions. **Olé,** Calle Fortaleza 105 (☎ 787/724-2445), deserves an Olé. Browsing this store is a learning experience. Practically everything comes from Puerto

Rico or Latin America. If you want a straw hat from Ecuador, hand-beaten Chilean silver, Christmas ornaments, or Puerto Rican *santos,* this is the place.

In a 200-year-old colonial building, ✪ **Puerto Rican Arts & Crafts,** Calle Fortaleza 204 (☎ 787/725-5596), is one of the premier outlets on the island for authentic artifacts. Of particular interest are papier-mâché carnival masks from Ponce, whose grotesque and colorful features were originally conceived to chase away evil spirits. Taíno designs inspired by ancient petroglyphs are incorporated into most of the sterling silver jewelry. There's an art gallery in back, with silk-screened serigraphs by local artists. You'll also find a gourmet Puerto Rican food section with coffee, rum, hot sauces, and more. A related specialty of this well-respected store involves the exhibition and sale of modern replicas of the Spanish colonial tradition of *santos.* They're laboriously carved by artisans in private studios around the island.

Now in its fourth decade, **Bared & Sons,** Calle Fortaleza 65, at the corner of Calle San Justo (☎ 787/724-4811), is the main outlet of a chain of at least 20 upscale jewelry stores on Puerto Rico. You'll find a worthy inventory of gems, gold, diamonds, and wristwatches on the street level. But the real value of this store is one floor up, where a monumental collection of porcelain and crystal is packed, in claustrophobic proximity, for display. It's a great source for hard-to-get and discontinued patterns (priced at around 20% less than at equivalent outlets stateside) from Christofle, Royal Doulton, Wedgwood, Limoges, Royal Copenhagen, Lalique, Lladró, Herend, Baccarat, and Daum.

The Gold Ounce, Plaza los Muchachos, Calle Fortaleza 201 (☎ 787/724-3102), is the direct factory outlet for the oldest jewelry factory on Puerto Rico, the Kury Company. Most of the output is shipped stateside. Don't expect a top-notch jeweler here: Many of the pieces are replicated in endless repetition. But don't overlook the place for 14-karat-gold ornaments. Some of the designs are charming, and prices are about 20% less than at retail stores in the U.S. In addition, the outlet has opened an art store, **Arts and More,** featuring regional works, plus a cigar store, **The Cigar Shop.**

200 Fortaleza, Calle Fortaleza 200, at the corner of Calle La Cruz (☎ 787/723-1989), is known as a leading cost-conscious place to buy fine jewelry in Old San Juan. This shop carries 14-karat Italian gold chains and bracelets that are measured, fitted, and sold by weight. You can buy watches or beautiful gems in modern settings in both 14- and 18-karat gold. The store recently expanded its collection to include 18-karat gold, emerald, ruby, diamond, and pearl jewelry, along with platinum bridal jewelry. **Yas Mar,** Calle Fortaleza 205 (☎ 787/724-1377), sells convincing fake diamonds for those who don't want to wear or can't afford the real thing. It also stocks real diamond chips, emeralds, sapphires, and rubies.

The town's best factory outlet for clothing is **London Fog,** Calle del Cristo 156 (☎ 787/722-4334). The last thing you need in steamy San Juan is an overcoat, but the prices here are usually very low—between 30% and 35% less than for equivalent garments on the U.S. mainland. Men's, women's, and children's garments are displayed on two floors of a colonial house. The best stop for linen is **The Linen House,** Calle Fortaleza 250 (☎ 787/721-4219), specializing in table linens, bed linens, and lace. Inventories include embroidered shower curtains selling from $35 each, and lace doilies, bun warmers, place mats, and tablecloths that seamstresses took weeks to complete. Some astonishingly beautiful items are available for around $30 each. The aluminum/pewter serving dishes have strikingly beautiful Spanish colonial designs. Prices here are sometimes 40% lower than in the U.S.

For Puerto Rican coffee and those hot spicy sauces of the Caribbean, head for **Spicy Caribbee,** Calle Cristo 154 (☎ 787/725-4690). This store sells the finest of Puerto

Rican coffee beans for about $10 per pound. It also offers moderately priced island handcrafts, plus other products from around the world, along with hot sauces and cookbooks featuring Puerto Rican recipes.

For travel guides, maps, and just something to read on the beach, there are two good bookstores. Try **Bell, Book & Candle,** 102 de Diego Ave., Santurce (☎ 787/728-5000), a large general-interest bookstore that carries fiction and classics in both Spanish and English, plus a huge selection of postcards. **The Book Store,** Calle San José 255 (☎ 787/724-1815), has Old Town's largest selection of titles. It sells a number of books on Puerto Rican culture and good touring maps of the island.

SAN JUAN AFTER DARK

THE PERFORMING ARTS   *Qué Pasa,* the official visitor's guide to Puerto Rico, lists cultural events, including music, dance, theater, film, and art exhibits. It's distributed free by the tourist office.

A major cultural venue in San Juan is the **Teatro Tapía,** Avenida Ponce de León (☎ 787/723-2079), across from Plaza de Colón. This is one of the oldest theaters in the western hemisphere, built about 1832. Much of Puerto Rican theater history is connected with the Tapía, named after the island's first prominent playwright, Alejandro Tapía y Rivera. Various productions, some musical, are staged here throughout the year, and include drama, dance, and cultural events. You'll have to call the box office (open Monday to Friday 10am to 6pm) for specific information. Tickets are generally $15 to $38.

THE CLUB & MUSIC SCENE   Modeled after an artist's rendition of the once-notorious city of Mesopotamia, **Babylon,** in El San Juan Hotel & Casino, 6063 Isla Verde Ave., Isla Verde (☎ 787/791-1000), boasts one of the Caribbean's best sound systems, a central dance floor, and a wraparound balcony where onlookers—from 25 to 45—can observe the fun. Its location in the most exciting hotel in San Juan allows guests the chance to visit the hotel's bars, intricately decorated lobby, and casino en route. The club is open Thursday to Saturday 9:30pm to 3am. Guests of the hotel enter free; otherwise, there's a $10 cover charge.

Cafe Matisse, Ashford Ave. (☎ 787/723-7910), is a hot spot for Latin sounds. Although it's also a restaurant, this place is best known as a bar where live music—often salsa—is usually part of the ambience. Depending on the night, you can also hear rumba, merengue, blues, jazz, or rock. It's open Tuesday to Saturday 5pm to around 2am or later, depending on the crowd. The only time a $3 cover is imposed is on a night when an expensive band is brought in.

Egipto, Avenida Roberto H. Todd 1 (☎ 787/725-4664), is a busy nightclub attracting upwardly mobile young singles. There's a dance floor well worn by years of boogying, though many visitors just come for drinks at the long bar. The décor is inspired by ancient Egypt and includes sphinxes and hieroglyphs. There's live music Thursday and Friday. Its transformation from a bar to a crowded disco usually begins around 10 or 11pm. It seems that everybody under 35 in San Juan has probably been to Egipto at least once, and many of them are regulars. You'll find the place in the Condado district, about 3 blocks south of Ashford Avenue. The club is open nightly 8pm to either 2am or 5am, depending on business. A $10 cover is charged.

Laser, Calle del Cruz 251 (☎ 787/725-7581), is in the heart of the old town near the corner of Calle Fortaleza. This disco is especially crowded when cruise ships pull into town. Once inside, you can wander over the three floors of its historic premises, listening to whatever music happens to be hot in New York at the time of your visit, with lots of merengue and salsa thrown in. The age of the crowd varies, but in general it's the 20s, 30s, and even 40s set. Usually, it's open daily 8pm to 4am. Women enter free after midnight on Saturday. A cover charge ranges from $6 to $10.

Millennium, in the Condado Plaza Hotel, 999 Ashford Ave. (☎ 787/721-1900), isn't the largest disco in San Juan, but in the opinion of many Condado-watchers, it's one of the favorites. Its entrance is adjacent to the main entrance ramp of the Condado Plaza, a mammoth structure known for its animated casino, sprawling format, and location at the beginning of the Condado. You'll find a pleasant and highly accommodating cigar bar and a great sound system projecting techno, latin merengues, and disco classics. The crowds tend to be in their late 20s and early 30s, but in the animated setting, folks in their 40s and 50s won't feel out of place. The club is open nightly 7pm to 2am, with most dance-a-holics arriving around 10:30pm. After 9pm, a $25 cover is charged.

Two of the most dramatic bars are at **El San Juan Hotel & Casino,** 6063 Isla Verde Ave., Isla Verde (☎ 787/791-1000). There's no more beautiful bar in the Caribbean than the ✪ **Palm Court,** which never closes. Most of the patrons are hotel guests, but discerning locals make up at least a quarter of the business. Set in an oval wrapped around a sunken bar area, amid marble and burnished mahogany, it offers a view of one of the world's largest chandeliers. After 9pm Monday to Saturday, live music, often salsa and merengue, emanates from an adjoining room (the El Chico Bar). The Palm Court Lobby at this elegant hotel now boasts the Caribbean's first Cigar Bar. Some of the most fashionable men and women can be seen puffing away in this chic rendezvous, while sipping a cognac. Although the bar is generally filled with visitors, it also attracts locals, especially men concluding high-powered business deals.

Violeta's, Calle Fortaleza 56 (2 blocks from the Gran Hotel Convento; ☎ 787/723-6804), is stylish and comfortable, occupying the ground floor of a 200-year-old beamed house. Because of its location in the old town, the bar draws an equal mixture of visitors and locals, usually in their 20s and 30s. Sometimes a pianist performs at the oversized grand piano. An open courtyard out back provides additional seating for sipping margaritas or other drinks.

THE GAY SCENE   The **Barefoot Bar,** Calle Vendig 2 (☎ 787/724-7230), is the hippest gay bar on Puerto Rico. It occupies a blue building whose terrace extends over the sands of the beach shared by the Marriott. At least 98% of the crowd are gay males and include a lot of whatever visiting employees from the local airlines and the cruise ships that happen to be in port. Simple lunches, consisting mostly of sandwiches and salads, are served noon to around 4pm; after that the food service ends in favor of drinking and dialogue.

The **Beach Bar,** in the Atlantic Beach Hotel, Calle Vendig 1 (☎ 787/721-6900), has the island's most popular tea dance on Sunday, and there's also a happy hour nightly, when many locals try to pick up a partner for the evening. The Barefoot Bar is just across the street. Together, they form a complex of bars and terraces that appeal to a crowd that's mostly male and mostly gay. A restaurant in the hotel serves breakfast and lunch 11am to 1am daily.

Cups, Calle San Mateo 1708, Santurce (☎ 787/268-3570), is a Latin tavern, the only place in San Juan that caters almost exclusively to lesbians. Men—of any sexual orientation—aren't particularly welcome. Although the club is open Wednesday to Sunday 7pm to 4am, entertainment like live music or cabaret is presented only on Wednesday at 9pm, Friday at 10pm, and Sunday at 8pm.

Eros, Ponce de León, Santurce 1257 (☎ 787/722-1131), is the town's most popular gay disco, with strippers and shows. Any gay man employed by one of the cruise lines that dock in San Juan's harbor overnight will almost invariably head here. It was renovated in 1996 in an ancient Greek/Egyptian motif and occupies two levels of a

Cheap Thrills: What to See & Do for Free (Well, Almost) on Puerto Rico

- **Seek Out the Secrets of Rum-Making.** This Bacardi distillery, the world's largest rum distillery, lies a short hop across San Juan Bay by ferry. It offers daily tours through its 127 acres and its plant, where 100,000 gallons are distilled daily. Complimentary rum drinks are offered at the beginning of the tour, and a well-stocked gift shop sells an assortment of items. The prices of Bacardi rums are better than those at home, and some rums not sold on the mainland also make excellent presents. It's open Monday to Saturday 9 to 10am and noon to 4pm; tours are given every 20 minutes. For more information, call ☎ 787/788-1500.

- **Stroll Along San Juan's Most Colorful Boulevard.** Streets around the world have become known for observing the passing scene. In Old San Juan, it's the Paseo de La Princesa, a 19th-century esplanade where Spanish colonial gentry once strolled and took the balmy Caribbean air. Its beauty shines again after a 2-year $2.8-million restoration. The paseo sweeps from the piers that welcome cruise ships past La Princesa, a restored former 1800s prison, around the old city walls beneath Casa Blanca (the ancestral home of the Ponce de León family), and continues to the entrance of the famed 16th-century El Morro. Outdoor tables with umbrellas are shaded by more than 20 trees, and delicious *criollo* dishes are dispensed from specially designed food carts with gaily colored awnings.

- **Find the Secret Beaches.** Some of Puerto Rico's most beautiful and isolated beaches lie on the southwestern coast. Stretching between Ponce, in the east, and Cabo Rojo, on Puerto Rico's extreme southwestern tip, they flank some of the least densely populated parts of the island. Drive west from Ponce along Highway 2, branching south along Route 116 to Guánica, the self-anointed gateway and capital of this string of secret beaches. Don't expect a lot—you're likely to see only a handful of simple bars, tacky luncheonettes, and gas stations. By far the most accessible and appealing beach is Caña Gorda, about a quarter-mile south of Guánica, at the edge of a legally protected marsh known for its rich bird life and thick reeds. It's a sprawling expanse of pale beige sand dotted with ramshackle-looking *bohios* (huts) crafted from tree branches and

building in an urban neighborhood in the Santurce district. Most of the crowd is in its late 20s. Rum-based drinks, merengue, and whatever music is favored in New York are popular, and most of the male/male flirting, dancing, and conversation begins after 10:30pm. It's open Wednesday to Sunday 9pm to 5am. A cover, including 2 free drinks, is imposed only on Friday and Saturday.

CASINOS Many visitors come to Puerto Rico on package deals and stay at one of the posh hotels at the Condado or Isla Verde just to gamble.

The casino generating all the excitement today is the 18,500-square-foot **Casino at the Ritz-Carlton,** 6961 State Rd., Isla Verde (☎ 787/253-1700), the largest facility of its kind on Puerto Rico. It combines the elegant décor of the 1940s with tropical fabrics and patterns. This is one of the Caribbean's plushest and most exclusive entertainment complexes. It features traditional games like blackjack, roulette, baccarat, craps, and slot machines.

palm fronds. Stray even farther west from Ponce, along coastal highways like 324, 304, and 323, and you'll pass beaches like Tamarindo, Manglillos, Rosado, and Playa Santa. Most westerly is Bahía Sucia, at the end of rutted and badly potholed roads.

- **Hike & Bird Watch in Guánica State Forest.** Directly west from Ponce is the Guánica State Forest, where you'll find the best-preserved subtropical ecosystem on the planet. The Cordillera Central cuts off the rain coming in, making this a dry region of cacti and bedrock. Some 50% of all the island's terrestrial bird species can be seen here, and some 750 plants and tree species grow in the area. UNESCO has named Guánica a World Biosphere Reserve.

- **Take the Caribbean's Most Spectacular Drive.** The 165-mile Ruta Panorámica runs across the top of the Cordillera Central, a panoramic mountain range with cool temperatures and lush forests. All 40 roads along the route are well marked. The drive links the western city of Mayagüez with Yabucoa in the southeast and can be traversed at either side. The highway stretches the entire length of Puerto Rico. Along this drive you'll see glimpses of rural Puerto Rico that've largely disappeared elsewhere. A detailed highway map will be provided by one of the tourist offices. Allow a solid 8 hours of driving nonstop. There are a number of paradors (government-sponsored guest houses, usually in remote areas) along the route.

- **Wander in the Carite Forest Preserve.** In southeastern Puerto Rico, lying off the Ponce Expressway near Cayey, Carite is a 6,000-acre reserve with a dwarf forest that was produced by the high humidity and moist soil. From several peaks you get panoramic views of Ponce and the Caribbean Sea. On one peak is Nuestra Madre, a Catholic spiritual meditation center that permits visitors to stroll the grounds. Fifty species of birds live in the Carite Forest Preserve, which also has a large natural pool called Charco Azul. A picnic area and campgrounds are shaded by eucalyptus and royal palms. The forest borders a lake of the same name. Entrances to the forest are signposted from the town of Cayey, which is reached after an hour's drive from Ponce or San Juan.

One of the splashiest of San Juan's casinos is at the **Wyndham Old San Juan Hotel & Casino,** Calle Brumbaugh 100 (☎ 787/721-5100), which turns some 80% of its lobby over to casino action. Five-card stud competes with some 240 slot machines and roulette tables. You can also try your luck at the **Caribe Hilton** (one of the better ones), Puerta de Tierra (☎ 787/721-0303); **El San Juan Hotel & Casino** on Isla Verde Avenue (☎ 787/791-1000) in Isla Verde (one of the most grand); and the **Condado Plaza Hotel & Casino,** 999 Ashford Ave. (☎ 787/721-1000). There are no passports to flash or admissions to pay, as in European casinos. The Stellaris Casino at the **San Juan Marriott Resort,** 1309 Ashford Ave. (☎ 787/722-7000), is one of the island's newest.

The **San Juan Grand Beach Hotel & Casino,** 187 Isla Verde Ave. (☎ 787/791-6100) in Isla Verde, is open continuously noon to 4am daily. This 10,000-square-foot gaming facility is an elegant rendezvous. One of its Murano chandeliers is longer than a bowling alley. The casino offers 207 slot machines, 16 blackjack tables, 3 dice tables, 4 roulette wheels, and a minibaccarat table.

Most casinos are open daily noon to 4pm and 8pm to 4am. Jackets for men are requested after 6pm.

3 Dorado

The name itself evokes a kind of magic. Along the north shore of Puerto Rico, about a 40-minute drive (22 miles) west of the capital, a world of luxury resorts and villa complexes unfolds. The big properties of the Hyatt Dorado Beach Hotel and Hyatt Regency Cerromar Beach Hotel sit on the choice white-sand beaches. These properties cost far more than even our most generous budget allows, but you can still spend a day in the area, enjoying the sands.

GREAT DEALS ON DINING

El Malecón. Rte. 693, km 8.2. ☎ **787/796-1645.** Main courses $7.25–$35.95. AE, MC, V. Daily 11am–11pm. PUERTO RICAN.

If you'd like to discover an unpretentious local place serving good Puerto Rican cuisine, then head for El Malecón, a simple concrete building 1 minute from a small shopping center. It has a cozy family ambience and is especially popular on weekends. Some members of the staff speak English, and the chef is best with fresh seafood, which most diners order. The chef might also prepare a variety of items not listed on the menu. Most of the dishes are at the lower end of the price scale; only the lobster is expensive.

SPORTS & OUTDOOR PURSUITS

GOLF The **Hyatt Resorts Puerto Rico** at Dorado (☎ 787/796-1234), with 72 holes of golf, offers the greatest number of options in the Caribbean. The 18-hole Robert Trent Jones Sr.–designed courses at the **Hyatt Regency Cerromar** and the **Hyatt Dorado Beach** match the finest anywhere. The two original courses—east and west (☎ 787/796-8961), both of which are associated with the Hyatt Dorado Beach Resort—were carved out of a jungle and offer tight fairways bordered by trees and forests, with lots of ocean holes. The somewhat newer and less frequently televised north and south courses (☎ 787/796-8915), which fall under the jurisdiction of the Hyatt Regency Cerromar, feature wide fairways with well-bunkered greens and an assortment of lakes, water traps, and tricky wind factors. Each of the four has a 72 par. The longest course is the south course at 7,047 yards.

Scheduling of tee-off times is almost always easier if you're a guest of one of the Hyatt resorts. For the north and south courses, Hyatt guests pay $65 for greens fees and nonguests pay $85. At the east and west courses, Hyatt guests pay $110 for greens fees and nonguests $160. Golf carts at any of the courses rent for $20, a fee that applies whether you play 9 or 18 holes. The north/south and the east/west courses each maintain separate pro shops, each with a bar and snack-style restaurant. Both are open daily 7am to dusk.

TENNIS Again, the twin Hyatt resorts of **Dorado** and **Cerromar** (☎ 787/796-1234) have the monopoly in this area, with a total of 17 courts between them. The charge is $15 an hour, rising to $18 from 6 to 10pm. Lessons are available for $60 per hour. Nonguests can't use the courts, however.

WINDSURFING & OTHER WATER SPORTS The best place on the island's north shore is along the well-maintained beachfront of the Hyatt Dorado Beach Hotel near the 10th hole of its east golf course. Here **Penfield Island Adventures**

(☎ **787/796-1234,** ext. 3200 or 787/796-2188) offers 90-minute **windsurfing lessons** for $60 each; board rentals cost $50 per half day. Well supplied with a wide array of Windsurfers, including some designed for beginners and children, the school benefits from the almost uninterrupted flow of the north shore's strong, steady winds and an experienced crew of instructors. A **kayaking/snorkeling** trip (☎ **787/796-4645**), departs daily at 9:15am and 11:45am, lasts 1½ hours, and costs $45. Two-tank boat **dives** go for $119 per person. **Waverunners,** fast, light boats designed for tight curves, can be rented for $60 per half hour for a single rider or $75 for two riders. A **Sunfish** rents for $45 for 1 hour or $65 for 2 hours.

4 Highlights in Northwestern Puerto Rico

Dubbed an ear to heaven, the **Arecibo Observatory** (☎ 787/878-2612) contains the world's largest and most sensitive radar/radiotelescope. The telescope features a 20-acre dish or radio mirror set in an ancient sinkhole. It's 1,000 feet in diameter and 167 feet deep and allows scientists to examine the ionosphere, the planets, and the moon with powerful radar signals and to monitor natural radio emissions from distant galaxies, pulsars, and quasars. It's being used by scientists as part of the Search for Extraterrestrial Intelligence (SETI). This research effort speculates that advanced civilizations elsewhere in the universe might also communicate via radio waves. The 10-year, $100-million search for life in space was launched on October 12, 1992, the 500-year anniversary of the New World's discovery by Columbus.

Unusually lush vegetation flourishes under the giant dish—ferns, wild orchids, and begonias. Assorted creatures like mongooses, lizards, and dragonflies have also taken refuge there. Suspended in outlandish fashion above the dish is a 600-ton platform that resembles a space station. Tours at $3.50 are available Wednesday to Friday noon to 4pm and Saturday and Sunday 9am to 4pm. There's a souvenir shop on the grounds. The observatory lies a 90-minute drive west of San Juan, outside the town of Arecibo. From Arecibo, it's a 35-minute drive via routes 22, 134, 635, and 625 (the site is sign-posted).

✪ **Río Camuy Cave Park,** 1⅓ hours west of San Juan on Route 129, at km 18.9 (☎ **787/898-3100**), contains the third-largest underground river in the world. It runs through a network of caves, canyons, and sinkholes that have been cut through the island's limestone base over the course of millions of years. Known to the pre-Columbian Taíno peoples, the caves came to the attention of speleologists in the 1950s and were opened to the public in 1986.

You first see a short film about the caves, then descend into the caverns in open-air trolleys. The trip takes you through a 200-foot-deep sinkhole and a chasm where tropical trees, ferns, and flowers flourish, along with birds and butterflies. The trolley then goes to the entrance of Clara Cave of Epalme, one of 16 in the Camuy caves network, where you begin a 45-minute walk, viewing the majestic series of rooms rich in stalagmites, stalactites, and huge natural sculptures. The park has added the Tres Pueblos Sinkhole and the Spiral Sinkhole to its slate of attractions. The caves are open Tuesday to Sunday 8am to 4pm. Tickets are $10 for adults or $7 for children 2 to 12; seniors pay $5. Parking is $2. For more information, phone the park.

5 Aguadilla

While big-spenders rush east from San Juan to pricey deluxe resorts, true budget travelers head for the west of Puerto Rico, where the living's easy, the beaches are among the island's finest, and the hotels and restaurants are often a bargain.

Reached along the north-coast road (Rte. 2), Aguadilla is about 2 to 2½ hours from the capital, depending on traffic (Sunday traffic is the worst). As you travel here, you'll be following in the footsteps of Columbus, who stepped onto Puerto Rican soil somewhere along the northern half of this coast during his 1493 voyage.

The area around Aguadilla is known for its beaches, shaded by coconut palms; they extend along northwestern Puerto Rico from Rincón (below) to the calm Crashboat Beach north of Aguadilla. The name Crashboat honors the vessels that used to leave from this beach to rescue fighter planes from the former Ramsey Air Force Base. At this popular public beach you'll find barbecues, simple restaurants and cafes, phones, picnic huts, playgrounds, showers, and toilets. Other beaches are around Borinquen Point, site of the former Ramey Air Force Base, now a civilian area being developed for tourism. From Punta Borinquen (its Spanish name), beaches stretch all the way to Isabela, which lies west of Quebradillas.

Be warned that waters off these beaches can be rough, especially from December to April. Although swimming isn't that great, the beaches draw windsurfers from around the world.

ACCOMMODATIONS YOU CAN AFFORD

Hacienda El Pedregal. Aguadilla Bay, off Rte. 111 (P.O. Box 4719), Aguadilla, PR 00605. ☎ **787/891-6068.** 27 units. A/C TV TEL. Year-round $62.15 single; $76.40 double. Extra person $10; children 11 and under stay free in parents' room. AE, MC, V.

At the highest point in Aguadilla, with the beach a 5-minute car ride away, this hacienda was the site of a former estate house. Now converted to receive guests, it consists of two white concrete-and-stucco buildings—one facing the ocean. The small rooms are simply but immaculately furnished, with good beds holding firm mattresses; some have balconies with a water view. The open-air restaurant and bar, El Boio Buesta de Sol, is reasonably priced, serving standard Puerto Rican fare at all three meals. There are two pools, one for adults, the other for children. There's a large parking area. Locals often hold weddings here on the green lush grounds.

SHOPPING

Aguadilla is the center of Puerto Rico's tiny lace-making industry, a craft imported here many centuries ago by immigrants from Spain, Holland, and Belgium.

El Hoz de Anero, Shopping Center B & M, Gate 5 near Ramey in Aguadilla (☎ 787/890-4690), carries Puerto Rican *santos* (saint figurines), including the nativity and three kings. Prices depend on the size and material used but start at $50. Wall hangings showing scenes from life in San Juan or Aguadilla are also featured, as are candle holders, picture frames, and hand-painted ceramic figures (not necessarily of local origin).

6 Rincón

At the island's westernmost point, Rincón, 6 miles north of Mayagüez, has one of the most exotic beaches on the island, which draws surfers from around the world. In and around this small fishing village are some unique accommodations.

If you rent a car at the San Juan airport, it'll take approximately 2½ hours to drive here via the busy northern Route 2 or 3 hours via the scenic mountain route (no. 52) to the south. We recommend the southern route through Ponce. In addition, there are 4 flights daily from San Juan to Mayagüez on **American Eagle** (☎ 800/433-7300). These flights take 40 minutes, and round-trip fares range from $85 to $133. From the Mayagüez airport, Rincón is a 30-minute drive to the north on Route 2 (go left or west at the intersection with Route 115).

ACCOMMODATIONS YOU CAN AFFORD

J. B. Hidden Village Hotel. Bo. Piedras Blancas, Sector Villarrubia, Aguada, PR 00602. ☎ **787/868-8686.** Fax 787/868-8701. 38 units. A/C TV TEL. Year-round $64.95 single; $82 double; $93–$129 semi-suite. AE, MC, V.

Named after the initials of its owners (Julio Bonilla, his wife, Jinnie, and their son, Julio Jr.), this isolated hotel opened in 1990. Half a mile east of nearby Aguada, on a side street running off Route 4414, it's nestled into a valley between three forested hillsides and offers a quiet refuge to vacationers who enjoy exploring the area's beaches. Each room, with views of the pool, contains furnishings in the basic motel style, and most are a bit small. The mattresses are relatively new. The restaurant offers a view over a neighboring ravine.

The Lazy Parrot. 413 Punta (P.O. Box 430), Rincón, PR 00677. ☎ **787/823-5654.** Fax 787/823-0224. E-mail: lazyparrot@coqui.net. 7 units. A/C TV. Year-round $65 single; $75 double, $95 quad. Extra person $5. AE, DISC, MC, V.

This extensively remodeled family-run inn is in a residential neighborhood a half-mile walk or drive from at least half a dozen beaches. The peach-colored accommodations have recently been upgraded and have small refrigerators; one room, with a bunk-bed arrangement, is ideal for families. As befits a former private home, rooms come in a variety of sizes. Some of the mattresses need renewing; others seem fairly new. A pool is scheduled to be installed at some point during the lifetime of this edition.

Even if you don't stay here, you may want to patronize the **Lazy Parrot Restaurant,** which offers good views from its main dining room, where your best bet is the catch of the day. It's more romantic at a table in the candlelit floral garden, where the coquí (tree frog), hummingbird, wild parrot, and butterflies can be seen year-round.

GREAT DEALS ON DINING

The Black Eagle. Rte. 413, km 1.0 interio, Barrio Ensenada. ☎ **787/823-3510.** Main courses $10–$18. AE, MC, V. Daily 11am–11pm. STEAKS/SEAFOOD.

This restaurant—the best in the neighborhood—serves up enormous portions of fresh seafood at low prices. It's in an isolated black-and-white house adjacent to the beach, about a quarter of a mile north of the center of Rincón, close to the Black Eagle marina (with which it's not associated). In the wood-paneled dining room, you might begin with a house special Black Eagle, a deceptively potent pink cocktail. Menu items include lobster or shrimp cocktail, a 32-ounce porterhouse steak (the restaurant's trademark dish), grilled lobster, pan-fried conch, and *asopao* of lobster or shrimp. All main courses come with salad, bread, and vegetables.

HITTING THE BEACHES & THE LINKS

One of Puerto Rico's most outstanding surfing beaches, comparable to the finest surfing spots in the world (according to competitors in the 1988 World Surfing Championship held here), is at **Punta Higuero,** on Route 413 near Rincón. In the winter especially, uninterrupted Atlantic swells with perfectly formed waves averaging 5 to 6 feet in height roll shoreward, and rideable swells sometimes reach 15 to 25 feet.

The **Punta Borinquén Golf Club,** Route 107 (☎ 787/890-2987), 2 miles north of Aguadilla's center and across the highway from the city's airport, was built by the U.S. government as part of the Ramey Air Force Base. Today, its 18 holes function as a public golf course, open daily 7am to 6:30pm. Greens fees cost $20 for an all-day pass, and rental of a golf cart that can carry two is $24 for 18 holes or $12 for 9 holes. Clubs can be rented for $10. The clubhouse contains a bar and a simple restaurant.

7 Mayagüez

Puerto Ricans have nicknamed their third-largest city the "Sultan of the West." This port city, 98 miles southwest of San Juan and not architecturally remarkable, was once the island's needlework capital. There are still craftspeople here who do fine embroidery.

Mayagüez is the honeymoon capital of Puerto Rico. The tradition dates from the 16th century, when, it's said, local fathers in need of husbands for their daughters (because of the scarcity of eligible young men) kidnapped young Spanish sailors who stopped here for provisions en route to South America.

GETTING THERE

American Eagle (☎ 800/433-7300) flies four times daily throughout the year between San Juan to Mayagüez. Flight time is 40 minutes, though there are often delays on the ground at either end. Depending on restrictions and the season you book your flight, round-trip fares range from $85 to $133 per person.

If you rent a car at the San Juan airport and want to drive to Mayagüez, the more efficient route is the northern one combining sections of the newly widened Route 22 with the older Route 2. Estimated driving time for locals is about 90 minutes but about 30 minutes longer for visitors. The southern route, combining the modern Route 52 with a transit across the outskirts of historic Ponce and a final access into Mayagüez via the southern section of Route 2, requires a total of about 3 hours and affords some worthwhile scenery across the island's mountainous interior.

ACCOMMODATIONS YOU CAN AFFORD

Hotel Parador El Sol. Calle Santiago Riera Palmer, 9 Este, Mayagüez, PR 00680. ☎ 787/834-0303. Fax 787/265-7567. 52 units. A/C TV TEL. Year-round $56–$72.05 single; $66.70–$92.75 double; $77.40–$93.45 triple. Rates include continental breakfast. AE, MC, V.

This concrete building from 1970 provides reasonable and hospitable accommodations, though it's geared to business travelers. It's 2 blocks from the landmark Plaza del Mercado in the heart of the city and is central to the shopping district and all western-region transportation and highways. Furnishings are no frills in the seven-floor restored hotel, but it offers up-to-date facilities, a restaurant, and a pool. Mattresses are firm and renewed as needed, and rooms range from small to medium in size; baths are small.

✪ **Parador Hacienda Juanita.** Rte. 105, km 23.5 (P.O. Box 777), Maricao, PR 00606. ☎ 800/443-0266 in the U.S. for reservations only, or 787/838-2550. Fax 787/838-2551. www.haciendajuanita.com. E-mail: juanita@caribe.net. 21 units. TEL. Winter $95 single; $123 double. Off-season $69.55 single; $80.25 double. Children 11 and under stay free in parents' room. AE, MC, V.

Named after one of its long-ago owners, a matriarch named Juanita, this parador was built in 1836 as part of a coffee plantation. It sits in relative isolation, surrounded by only a few neighboring buildings and the jungle, 2 miles west of the village of Maricao, beside Route 105 heading to Mayagüez. The pink-stucco house has a long veranda and a living room decorated with antique tools and artifacts of the coffee industry. The Luís Rivera family welcomes visitors and serves drinks and meals in the restaurant. The small rooms have ceiling fans, rocking chairs, and rustic furniture, though the beds are good, with firm mattresses. The baths are small but tidy, with thin towels. There's a pool, billiards table, and Ping-Pong table.

GREAT DEALS ON DINING

✪ **El Castillo.** In the Best Western Mayagüez Resort & Casino, Rte. 104. ☎ **787/832-3030.** Breakfast buffet $11.25. Mon–Sat buffet lunch $14; Sun brunch buffet $21.95; main courses $17.30–$20. AE, MC, V. Daily 6:30am–11pm. INTERNATIONAL/PUERTO RICAN.

This is the most professionally managed and large-scale dining room in western Puerto Rico, the main gastronomic outlet for the largest hotel and casino on this part of the island. Known as the venue for copious lunch buffets, it serves only a la carte items for dinner. These include such dishes as seafood stew served on linguine with marinara sauce, grilled salmon with mango-flavored Grand Marnier sauce, and sea bass fillets with a cilantro, white wine, and butter sauce. Steak and lobster are served on the same platter. The food has real flavor and flair.

La Casona de Juanita. In the Parador Hacienda Juanita, Rte. 105, km 23.5. ☎ **787/838-2550.** Main courses $9–$22.90. AE, MC, V. Sun–Thurs 8am–8pm, Fri–Sat 8am–10pm. PUERTO RICAN.

You'll find some of the best food and the most reasonable prices in the area at this previously reviewed parador. The regional cuisine is prepared with flair and zest. The chef makes at least three regional soups daily (the menu is the same for lunch or dinner); our favorite is the shrimp and rice. Look for the daily special or ask for one of the regular house specialties—corned beef and sweet banana pie, Puerto Rican–style beef stew, or local chicken, which can be breaded, fried, or roasted. Everything is served with rice, beans, and fried plantains. For dessert, make it guava shells with a native white cheese or homemade pumpkin custard pudding.

SEEING THE SIGHTS: SURFING BEACHES & TROPICAL GARDENS

Along the western coastal bends of Route 2, north of Mayagüez, lie the best **surfing beaches** in the Caribbean. Surfers from as far away as New Zealand come to ride the waves. You can also check out panoramic **Punta Higuero** beach, nearby on Route 413, near Rincón.

The chief sight is the ✪ **Tropical Agriculture Research Station** (☎ 787/831-3435), on Route 65 between Post Street and Route 108, adjacent to the University of Puerto Rico at Mayagüez campus and across from the **Parque de los Próceres (Patriots' Park).** At the administration office, ask for a free map of the tropical gardens, which contain a huge collection of tropical species useful to people, like cacao, fruit trees, spices, timbers, and ornamentals. The grounds are open Monday to Friday 7am to 5pm, and there's no admission charge.

Mayagüez might also be the jumping-off point for a visit by chartered boat to ✪ **Mona Island,** the Galápagos of the Caribbean, which enjoys many legends of pirate treasure and is known for its white-sand beaches and marine life. The island is virtually uninhabited, except for two policemen and a director of the institute of natural resources. The island attracts hunters seeking pigs and wild goats, along with big-game fishers. But mostly it's intriguing to anyone who wants to escape civilization. **Playa Sardinera** on Mona Island was a base for pirates. On one side of the island, at **Playa de Pajaros,** are caves where the Taíno left their mysterious hieroglyphs. Everything needed, including water, must be brought in, and everything, including garbage, must be taken out. For further information, call the **Puerto Rico Department of Natural Resources** at ☎ 787/723-1616.

Encantos Ecotours (☎ 787/272-0005) offers bare-bones but ecologically sensitive camping tours to Mona Island at sporadic intervals that vary according to demand. The experience includes ground transport to/from San Juan, sea transport departing from Cabo Rojo, use of camping and snorkeling gear, all meals (expect the equivalent of K-rations cooked over a campfire), and fees. Three nights and 4 days of outdoor life, which doesn't come without its share of discomforts and inconveniences, sells for around $600.

8 Boquerón & Cabo Rojo

Boquerón is Puerto Rico's Cape Cod, lying in the southwestern corner of the island and reached by heading south from Mayagüez along Route 102 (becoming 103) for 45 minutes or so, depending on the traffic. Once a tiny fishing village, Boquerón is now a center of tacky restaurants and low-cost beachside inns. It is, in fact, the cheapest place on Puerto Rico to go for a beachside vacation. It's not an elegant resort like Palmas del Mar, but Puerto Ricans, along with a scattering of foreign visitors, like the funky, often raffish, atmosphere of this laid-back retreat.

The big draw is ✪ **Boquerón Beach,** one of the island's best, ideal for swimming or windsurfing. It lies off Route 101 near the fishing village of Boquerón, at the head of a scenic bay stretching for 3 miles. The beaches are lined with coconut palms overlooking the coral-dotted waters (beach umbrellas aren't necessary). In the background stands the lush Boquerón Nature Reserve, one of Puerto Rico's important bird sanctuaries. The best sections along Boquerón Beach go by different names, including Los Pozos, Las Salinas, and Villa Taína. The waters are generally clear and most often calm, and the sands golden. Parking is $2 per car. For information about this beach, call ☎ **787/724-2500,** ext. 130 or 131. You can ask about the possibilities of renting two-room rustic cabins right on the beach. Snorkeling and scuba-diving equipment can be arranged at **Boquerón Dive Shop,** Main St., Boquerón (☎ **787/851-2155**).

Directly south of Boquerón is the fishing and resort community at **El Combate Beach.** Very popular with locals, especially on weekends, El Combate is picture-post-card perfect, set against a row of raffish fishing huts and an overcrowded jetty. There are camping facilities in the area and small kiosks that'll help you arrange water sports like windsurfing, snorkeling, and sailing. This area is the headquarters for the U.S. Fish and Wildlife's Caribbean refuges. A visitors' center provides information about regional wildlife refuges and local bird-watching trails.

Sleepy Boquerón is part of the municipality of Cabo Rojo. An additional attraction is the **Boquerón Lagoon,** a refuge for ducks and other birds. You can also shop here for crafts at various kiosks in the area.

A coastal mangrove forest and a salt farm sprawl along the southwest tip of the island. You can drive along a dirt road trenched with potholes to the end of the line, where the 19th-century Spanish colonial **Cabo Rojo Lighthouse** awaits. A former pirate hangout, this section—called Punta Jagüey—is one of the Caribbean's most beautiful spots, if you don't mind the rough ride to it. The lighthouse's squat hexagonal blue tower is now boarded up. But few come here just to view the lighthouse. Once here, you're treated to Puerto Rico's most panoramic view of the rugged coast and an inner lagoon with bays on either side. It's worth the detour.

ACCOMMODATIONS YOU CAN AFFORD
BOQUERÓN

At the tiny fishing village of Boquerón (now a vacation and water-sports center), the government of Puerto Rico offers beachside cabañas that sleep up to six, which is one of the best values on the island. Arrangements can be made by calling or contacting ✪ **Centro Vacacional Boquerón** (☎ **787/722-1551;** fax 787/722-0090). Beachside cabañas sleeping up to six rent for only $65.40 during the week or $130.80 Friday to Sunday (no credit cards). The cabañas have two bedrooms, a bath, and a kitchen, though they're sparsely furnished. At this price, you even have to provide your own bed linen and cooking utensils.

Parador Boquemar. 101 Rte. 307, Boquerón, PR 00622. ☎ **800/933-2158** or 787/ 851-2158. Fax 787/851-7600. 75 units. A/C TV. Year-round $59.55 single; $65–$79.80 double. AE, MC, V. From either Mayagüez or San Germán, take Rte. 102 into Cabo Rojo and then Rte. 100 south; turn right onto Rte. 101 and the hotel will be 2 blocks from the beach.

The Boquemar, built in the late 1980s, lies near Boquerón Beach in the southwest corner of the island, between Mayagüez and Ponce. The Boquemar rents small but comfortable rooms with modern furnishings and has a well-known restaurant (see below). Units are given a festive resort look with the use of rattan and tropical prints, and the baths are just big enough to do the job. The pool behind the hotel is popular with Puerto Rican families.

CABO ROJO

Hotel Joyuda Beach. Rte. 102, km 11.7, Cabo Rojo, PR 00623. ☎ **787/851-5650.** Fax 787/255-3750. 41 units. A/C TV TEL. Year-round $75–$85 single or double. 2 children 11 and under stay free in parents' room. AE, DISC, MC, V. Follow Rte. 102 south of Mayagüez to Joyuda.

On the beach in scenic Cabo Rojo, this 1989 hotel (often a favorite of Puerto Rican honeymooners) offers comfortably furnished rooms with small baths. It suffered massive damage during the 1998 hurricane but is now fully functional. This is a good center for touring such attractions as El Combate Beach and the Cabo Rojo Wildlife Refuge. Tennis and golf are just 5 minutes away, and sportfishing charters, windsurfing, and canoeing can be arranged. The restaurant is nothing more than a simple *cafetería,* serving snacks, drinks, and coffee, open daily during daylight hours or whenever the hotel thinks there's enough business. Room service is provided.

GREAT DEALS ON DINING

Boquerón has several restaurants known for their fresh fish and seafood (they're not strong on fruit and vegetables, except for plantains, rice, and beans). But you can eat well without going to a restaurant. At various **beach shacks** you can buy fresh oysters, a local delicacy. They're shucked right on the spot, and locals douse them with hot sauce. You can also buy skewers of chicken. For another local delicacy, finish off your meal with the incredibly delicious maize ice cream, made with sweet corn and dusted with paprika (don't knock it until you've tried it).

La Cascada. At the Parador Boquemar, 101 Rte. 307. ☎ **787/851-2158.** Main courses $10–$16. AE, MC, V. Daily 7:30am–noon and Thurs–Tues 4–10pm. PUERTO RICAN.

Known for its fresh seafood, this place is popular with San Juan families who flock to the beaches here on weekends and always schedule a dinner at La Cascada. The staff have their good and bad days and service is among the slowest on the coast, but you can get such great-tasting fresh fish you'll be willing to suffer the inconvenience. The red snapper can be broiled or fried and often is memorable. Begin with one of the salads, perhaps made of conch or octopus, then proceed to rice stew with lobster, shrimp in chili sauce, the chef's special rice with seafood and vegetables, or mashed green plantain stuffed with seafood, including lobster and shrimp. The meat dishes— shipped in frozen—aren't noteworthy, though the chicken stew isn't bad.

Tino's. Carretera 102, km 13.6, Joyuda/Cabo Rojo. ☎ **787/851-2976.** Main courses $12.95–$18.95. AE, DC, MC, V. Wed–Mon 11:30am–11pm. Drive 3½ miles south on Rte. 102. PUERTO RICAN.

One of the most appealing restaurants along this section of the coast occupies a simple beachfront building beside the highway and sports a clean tile-sheathed interior. It features fresh seafood and well-prepared roster of *mofongos,* a plantain dish. Seafood is brought in every day. Try the red snapper with Spanish sauce, zarzuela of shellfish, three versions of the rice dish *asopao,* and broiled or skewered shrimp. There are also flank steaks and filets from a charcoal brazier. The drink of choice is beer or any of the rum concoctions.

9 Ponce

Puerto Rico's second-largest city, Ponce—called the Pearl of the South—was named after Loíza Ponce de León, grandson of Juan Ponce de León. Today it's Puerto Rico's principal shipping port on the Caribbean, lying 75 miles west of San Juan. The city is well kept and attractive, as reflected by its many plazas, parks, and public buildings. There's something in its lingering air that suggests a provincial Mediterranean town. Look for the *rejas* (framed balconies) of the handsome colonial mansions.

Maps and information can be found at the **tourist office,** Fox Delicias Mall, on Plaza de las Delicias (☎ **787/840-5695**).

GETTING THERE

Ponce lies 75 miles southwest of San Juan and is reached by Route 52. Allow at least 1½ hours if you drive.

American Eagle (☎ **800/433-7300**) offers one daily flight between San Juan and Ponce (flight time is about 35 minutes) for $85 to $176 round-trip, depending on the ticket. However, prices are known to fluctuate, so call for last-minute details.

ACCOMMODATIONS YOU CAN AFFORD

Days Inn. Rte. 1, km 123.5, Mercedita, Ponce, PR 00715. ☎ **800/329-7466** or 787/841-1000. Fax 787/841-2560. 121 units. A/C TV TEL. Year-round $101.50 single; $111.50 double; $121.50 suite. Rates include continental breakfast. AE, DC, MC, V.

A 15-minute drive east of Ponce on Highway 52, opposite the Interamerican University, this hotel has modest rooms that are conservative and comfortable. This inn took a direct hit during the 1998 hurricane but should be up and running by the time of your arrival. The storm forced a massive renewal, so all the mattresses are good. The plumbing has been brought up-to-date in the small but well-maintained baths. The facilities include a courtyard pool, a children's wading pool, a Jacuzzi, a coin-operated laundry, an international restaurant, and a bar/disco.

Hotel Belgica. Calle Villa 122, Ponce, PR 00731. ☎ **787/844-3255.** 20 units. A/C TV. Year-round $55 single; $65 double. MC, V.

One of the best values in town, this boxy-looking hotel is a few steps from Ponce's main square. Built in 1911 and renovated several times since, it contains pale-green rooms that are bare-boned but relatively large—however, some don't have windows. If one of these assigned to you, don't worry about ventilation, as the air-conditioning system is strong. The baths are small, with a minimum of towels. No meals are served here, but considering the low prices and the fact that many cafes lie nearby, no one seems to mind.

Mary Lee's by the Sea. Rte. 333, km 6.7 (P.O. Box 394), Guánica, PR 00653. ☎ **787/821-3600.** 10 units. AC. Year-round $121 studio for 2, $121–$132 1-bedroom apt., $165–$176 2-bedroom apt., $192.50–$220 3-bedroom apt. Extra person $10. No credit cards.

Owned/operated by Michigan-born Mary Lee Alvarez, a fiercely independent former resident of Cuba and a self-described compulsive decorator, this is an informal collection of cottages, seafront houses, and apartments beside the coastal highway 4 miles east of Guánica. Two of the buildings are California-style houses; the rest are a confusing medley of other structures built since the 1970s. The entire compound is landscaped with flowering shrubs, trees, and vines.

To the north is the Guánica National Forest, a well-known sanctuary for birds and wildlife (see below). Picnic areas, trails, and campsites are located throughout the reserve. The hotel sits next to sandy beaches and a handful of uninhabited offshore cays. For the benefit of its nature-watching guests, the hotel maintains about half a dozen rental boats with putt-putt motors, two waterside sun decks, and several kayaks. A single visit by a maid each week is included in the price, though for an extra fee guests can arrange to have a maid come in daily. Each medium-size unit includes a modern kitchen, an outdoor barbecue pit, and a sense of privacy. Beds are most comfortable with firm mattresses, and the tidy but small baths have room to spread out your stuff.

Don't come here looking for nighttime activities or enforced conviviality: The place is quiet, secluded, and appropriate only for low-key vacationers seeking privacy and isolation with a companion and/or with nature. There isn't a bar or restaurant.

Melía. Calle Cristina 2, Ponce, PR 00731. ☎ **800/742-4276** in the U.S., or 787/842-0260. Fax 787/841-3602. www.home.coqui.net/melia. E-mail: melia@coqui.net. 78 units. A/C TV TEL. Year-round $70–$90 single; $75–$95 double. Rates include continental breakfast. AE, DC, MC, V. Parking $3.

A city hotel with southern hospitality, the Meliá, which has no connection with the international hotel chain, often attracts businesspeople. The location is a few steps from the Cathedral of Our Lady of Guadalupe and from the Parque de Bombas (the red-and-black firehouse). Though this old and somewhat tattered hotel was long ago outclassed by the Hilton, many of its admirers who could afford more upscale accommodations still prefer to stay here for its old-time atmosphere. The lobby floor and all stairs are covered with Spanish tiles of Moorish design. The desk clerks speak English. The small rooms are comfortably furnished and pleasant enough, and most have a balcony facing either busy Calle Cristina or the old plaza. In some rooms the mattresses are a bit tired, but others are new. Baths are very tiny, with a minimum of towels. Breakfast is served on a rooftop terrace with a good view of Ponce, and the Mark Restaurant thrives under separate management. You can park your car in the lot nearby.

GREAT DEALS ON DINING

✪ **El Ancla.** Avenida Hostos Final 9, Playa Ponce. ☎ **787/840-2450.** Main courses $10.95–$35. AE, DC, MC, V. Sun–Thurs 11am–10pm, Fri–Sat 11am–midnight. PUERTO RICAN/ SEAFOOD.

Opened by members of the Lugo family in 1978, this place ranks among Ponce's best restaurants. Much of its appeal derives from its location 2 miles south of the city center on soaring piers extending from the rocky coastline out over the surf. As you dine, the sound of the sea rises literally from beneath your feet. Menu items are prepared with real Puerto Rican zest and flavor. Three enduring specialties are the red snapper stuffed with lobster and shrimp and served with fried plantains or mashed potatoes, the salmon filet in caper sauce, and the seafood medley of lobster, shrimp, octopus, and conch. One corner of the menu is reserved for lobster, which tops the price scale. But you can dine here well and reasonably. The side orders are also delectable, including crabmeat rice or yuca in garlic. Every day a grand selection of desserts is made (ask your waiter what's featured).

Lupita's Mexican Restaurant. Calle Isabel 60. ☎ **787/848-8808.** Reservations required on weekends. Main courses $7–$28. AE, DC, MC, V. Sun–Thurs 11am–10pm, Fri–Sat 11am–2am. MEXICAN/PUERTO RICAN.

In a 19th-century building and its adjoining courtyard, a short walk from Ponce's main square, this is the creative statement of Hector de Castro. The specialties are tortilla soup, taco salads, grilled lobster tail with tostones, seafood fajitas, and burritos, tacos, and enchiladas with a wide choice of fillings. Some standard Puerto Rican dishes are offered as well. On Friday and Saturday 8pm to midnight, a mariachi band will probably provide entertainment.

SEEING THE SIGHTS

A $40-million project is restoring more than 1,000 buildings in town to their original early-1900s charm. Architectural styles that combine neoclassical with Ponce Creole and art deco give the town a distinctive ambience.

Any of the Ponceños will direct you to their ✪ **Museo de Arte de Ponce,** Avenida de las Americas 25 (☎ **787/848-0505**), which has a fine collection of European and Latin American art, the best on the island. Among the nearly 400 paintings, sculptures, and artworks are exceptional pre-Raphaelite and Italian baroque paintings. The building was designed by Edward Durell Stone, and it has been called the Parthenon of the Caribbean. It's open daily 10am to 5pm. Adults pay $4 and children 11 and under $1.

Most visitors head for the **Parque de Bombas,** Plaza de las Delicias (☎ **787/284-4141**), the main plaza of Ponce. The fantastic old black-and-red firehouse on the plaza, built for a fair in 1883, is open Wednesday to Monday 9:30am to 6pm. Around the corner from the firehouse, a trail leads you to the **Cathedral of Our Lady of Guadalupe,** Calle Concordia/Calle Union (☎ **787/842-0134**). Designed by architects Francisco Porrata Doría and Francisco Trublard, featuring a pipe organ installed in 1934, it remains an important place for prayer. It's open Monday to Friday 6am to 3:30pm and Saturday and Sunday 6am to noon and 3 to 8pm.

El Museo Castillo Serrallés, El Vigía 17 (☎ **787/259-1774**), the largest and most imposing building in Ponce, was built high on a hilltop by the Serrallés family (owners of a local rum distillery). This is one of the architectural gems of Puerto Rico and the best evidence of the wealth produced by the turn-of-the-century sugar boom. Guides will escort you through the Spanish Revival house, where Moorish and Andalusian details include panoramic courtyards, a baronial dining room, and a small cafe and souvenir shop. Hours are Tuesday to Sunday 10am to 5pm. Admission is $3 for adults, $2 for seniors over 62, and $1.50 for children 15 and under and students.

The oldest cemetery in the Antilles, excavated in 1975, is near Ponce on Route 503 at kilometer 2.7. The **Tibes Indian Ceremonial Center** (☎ **787/840-2255**) contains some 186 skeletons, dating from A.D. 300, as well as pre-Taíno plazas from A.D. 700. Guided tours in English and Spanish are conducted through the grounds. Shaded by trees are seven rectangular ball courts and two dance areas. The arrangements of stone points on the dance grounds, in line with the solstices and equinoxes, suggest a pre-Columbian Stonehenge. A re-created Taíno village includes not only the museum but also an exhibition hall where you can see a documentary about Tibes. The museum is open Wednesday to Sunday 9am to 4pm. Admission is $2 for adults and $1 for children.

Hacienda Buena Vista, Route 10, kilometer 16.8 (☎ **787/848-7020** or 787/722-5882), is a 30-minute drive north of Ponce. Built in 1833, it preserves an old way of life, with its whirring waterwheels and artifacts of 19th-century farm production. Once it was one of Puerto Rico's most successful plantations, producing coffee, corn, and citrus. It was a working coffee plantation until the 1950s, and 86 of the original 500 acres are still part of the estate. The rooms of the hacienda have been furnished with authentic pieces from the 1850s. Tours, lasting 2 hours, are Wednesday to Sunday at 8:30am, 10:30am, 1:30pm, and 3:30pm (in English only at 1:30pm). Reservations are required. Tours cost $5 for adults and $2 for children.

SHOPPING

If you feel a yen for shopping, head for the **Fox-Delicias Mall,** at the intersection of Calle Reina Isabel and Plaza de Las Delicias, the city's most innovative shopping center. The best outlet for souvenirs and artisan work is here: **El Palacio del Coquí Inc.** (☎ 787/841-0216). You can stop in merely for a reminder of your trip or else purchase something more substantial. The store is the best outlet at which to buy the grotesque masks (viewed as collectors' items) that are used at carnival time. Ask the owner to explain the importance and significance of these masks.

BEACHES & OUTDOOR PURSUITS

Ponce is a city—not a beach resort—and should be visited mainly for its sights. There's little in the way of organized sports, but a 10-minute drive west will take you to **Playa de Ponce,** a long strip of white sand opening onto the tranquil waters of the Caribbean. This beach is usually better for swimming than the Condado in San Juan.

Scuba divers can go to the best dive sites along the southern coast with **Gregory's Dive Center** (☎ 787/840-6424). The center can also make arrangements for fishing and sailing in the area. The city owns two **tennis complexes,** one at Poly Deportivos, with nine hard courts and another at Rambla with six courts. Both are open 9am to 10pm and lit for night play. You can play free.

To play golf, you have to go to **Aguirre Golf Course,** Route 705, Aguirre (☎ 787/853-4052), 30 miles east of Ponce (take Highway 52). This nine-hole course, open 7:30am to sunset daily, charges $15 greens fees Monday to Friday, going up to $18 on weekends and holidays. Another course, **Club Zeportivo,** Carretera 102, kilometer 15.4, Barrio Jogudas, Cabo Rojo (☎ 787/254-3748), lies 30 miles west of Ponce. This course is a nine-holer, open daily 7am to 6pm. Greens fees are $30 daily.

SIDE TRIPS TO GUANICA STATE FOREST & HISTORIC SAN GERMAN

GUANICA STATE FOREST   Heading directly west from Ponce, you reach ✪ **Guánica State Forest** (☎ 787/724-3724), which UNESCO has named a World Biosphere Reserve. Here you'll find the planet's best-preserved subtropical ecosystem. The Cordillera Central cuts off the rain coming in from the heavily showered northeast, making this a dry region of cacti and bedrock. Some 50% of all the island's terrestrial bird species can be seen here—you might even spot the Puerto Rican emerald-breasted hummingbird or the Puerto Rican nightjar, a local bird that was believed to be extinct until one was sighted locally. Some 750 plants and tree species grow in the area. To reach the forest, take Route 334 northeast of Guánica to the heart of the forest. A ranger station here will give you a booklet about hiking trails. The most interesting is the mile-long Cueva Trail, which gives you the most scenic look at the various types of vegetation. You might even encounter the endangered bufo lemur toad, once declared extinct but found to still be jumping in this area.

HISTORIC SAN GERMAN   Only an hour's drive from Ponce or Mayagüez and the beaches of the southern coast and just over 2 hours from San Juan, **San Germán,** Puerto Rico's second-oldest town, is a little museum piece. It was founded in 1512 and destroyed by the French in 1528. Rebuilt in 1570, it was named after Germain de

Foix, the second wife of King Ferdinand of Spain. Once the rival of San Juan, Sam Germán harbored many inhabitants who were engaged in piracy, pillaging the ships that sailed off the nearby coast. Indeed, many of today's residents are descended from the smugglers, poets, priests, and politicians who lived here.

Though the pirates and sugar plantations are long gone, the city retains many colorful reminders of those days. Today it has settled into a slumber, albeit one that has preserved the feel of the Spanish colonial era. Flowers brighten the patios here as they do in Seville. Also, as in a small Spanish town, many of the inhabitants stroll in the plaza in the early evening. Nicknamed Ciudad de las Lomas (City of the Hills), San Germán boasts scenery that provides a pleasant backdrop to a variety of architectural styles: Spanish colonial (1850s), criollo (1880s), neoclassical (1910s), art deco (1930s), and international (1960s). So significant are these buildings that San Germán is only the second Puerto Rican city (the other is San Juan) to be included in the National Register of Historic Places.

The city's 249 noteworthy historical treasures are within easy walking distance of one another. Regrettably, you must view most of them from the outside. If some actually are open, count yourself fortunate because they have no phones, keep no regular hours, and are staffed by volunteers who rarely show up.

One building you definitely can enter is the ✪ **Iglesia Porta Coeli (Gate of Heaven),** on a knoll at one end of town. Dating from 1606, this is the oldest church in the New World. Restored by the Institute of Puerto Rican Culture, it contains a museum of religious art with a collection of ancient *santos,* the carved figures of saints that have long been a major branch of Puerto Rican folk art. Look for the 17th-century portrait of St. Nicholas de Bari, the French Santa Claus. Inside, the original palmwood ceiling and tough, brown ausobo wood beams draw the eyes upward. Along the sides of the chapel are treasures gathered from all over the world, including early choral books from Santo Domingo, a primitive carving of Jesus, and 19th-century Señora de la Monserrate Black Madonna and Child statues. Further restoration work is now being done by Porta Coeli. It's open Tuesday to Sunday 9am to 4:15pm, and admission is $1. Call ☎ **787/264-4258** for more information.

Across the street, **The Tomás Vivoni House** is San Germán's most popular and widely recognized house. Named after the local architect who designed it, the home was built in 1913; it boasts a Queen Anne style, with a tower and gables that are key elements in the town's urban profile. Next door is the **Parque de Santo Domingo,** one of San Germán's two main plazas. Originally a marketplace, the plaza is now bordered with black iron and wooden park benches and features busts of some of the prominent figures in the town's history. The park also is the site of the Farmacia Martin, a Spanish colonial building converted to a pharmacy, which still operates today, and the Old City Hall.

The **San Germán de Auxerre Church** is the centerpiece of Plaza Mariano Quiñones, the town's other main plaza. Built in the 19th century, its wooden vault features a beautiful trompe l'oeil painting in blue and gray. The original pattern on the ceiling was restored in 1993. Nearby, the **Acosta y Forés** and **Juán Ortiz Perichi houses** are recognized as being among the most beautiful homes in Puerto Rico. The Acosta y Forés House, a stunning example of criollo architecture built in 1917, features traditional wood construction. Inside, the house has floor-to-ceiling stenciled designs painted over the walls of each room. Constructed in the 1920s and designed by Luis Pardo Fradera, the Juán Ortiz Perichi House is a fine example of Puerto Rican ornamental architecture. It features a multilevel design with a curved balcony and pitched roofs.

10 Exploring Northeastern Puerto Rico

Now that we've covered the western portion of Puerto Rico, we'll begin heading east from San Juan. From the capital, Route 3 leads toward the fishing town of Fajardo, where you'll turn north to Las Croabas, about 31 miles from the capital. You'll be near
✪ **Luquillo Beach,** one of the island's best and most popular public stretches of sand. See "Hitting the Beaches" under San Juan for more information.

In the Luquillo Mountains east of San Juan is another favorite escape from the capital—**El Yunque,** a tropical forest teeming with hundreds of species of plant and animal life (see the box earlier in this chapter).

ACCOMMODATIONS YOU CAN AFFORD NEAR EL YUNQUE

Some three dozen camping sites are located in parks ranging from Luquillo Beach to El Yunque National Forest. Tent sites are available at about $4 per person, though it's also possible to rent *casetas* (tiny cottages), lean-tos, huts, and even small trailers. Costs average $20 per night. Don't expect luxury; these are barebone and rustic. Sometimes a cold shower might be offered; at other times there's no running water or even a toilet. As such, these are recommended only for the most rugged campers.

For more information about the designated areas for camping, contact the **Department of Natural Resources** at ☎ 787/724-8774 or the **Recreation Department** at ☎ 787/722-1771.

Ceiba Country Inn. Rd. no. 977, km 1.2 (P.O. Box 1067), Ceiba, PR 00735. ☎ **787/885-0471.** 9 units. A/C TEL. Year-round $60 single; $70 double. Extra person $5. Rates include breakfast. AE, DISC, MC, V. Free parking.

If you're looking for an escape from the hustle and bustle of everyday life, then this is the place for you. This small B&B, built in 1951, is on the easternmost part of Puerto Rico, 4 miles west of Roosevelt Roads U.S. naval base, and to reach this little haven in the mountains you must rent a car. El Yunque is only 15 miles away. The small to medium-size rooms are on the bottom floor of a large old family home; two contain refrigerators. They're decorated in a tropical motif with flowered murals on the walls painted by a local artist. For a quiet evening cocktail, you may want to visit the small second-floor lounge.

TO THE LIGHTHOUSE: EXPLORING LAS CABEZAS DE SAN JUAN NATURE RESERVE

Better known as ✪ **El Faro** or **The Lighthouse,** this preserve in the northeastern corner of the island, north of Fajardo off Route 987, is one of the most beautiful and important areas on Puerto Rico—a number of ecosystems flourish in the vicinity.

Surrounded on three sides by the Atlantic Ocean, the 316-acre site encompasses forestland, mangroves, lagoons, beaches, cliffs, offshore cays, and coral reefs. El Faro serves as a research center for the scientific community. It's home to a vast array of flora and fauna, including sea turtles and other endangered species.

The nature reserve is open Wednesday to Sunday; reservations are required, so check by phone before going. For reservations throughout the week, call ☎ 787/722-5882; for reservations on Saturday and Sunday, call ☎ 787/860-2560 (reservations on weekends can be made only on the day of your intended visit). Admission is $5 for adults, $2 for children 11 and under, and $2.50 for seniors. Guided tours are conducted at 9:30am, 10am, 10:30am, and 2pm (in English at 2pm).

GREAT DEALS ON DINING IN FAJARDO

The sleepy town of Fajardo was established as a supply depot for the many pirates who plied the nearby waters. Today a host of private yachts bob at anchor in its harbor, and the many offshore cays provide naturalists with secluded beaches. From Fajardo, ferries make choppy but frequent runs to the offshore islands of Vieques and Culebra (see later in this chapter). Close by are the coral-bordered offshore islands, the most popular being Icacos, a favorite among snorkelers and divers. To get here, take Route 3 from the eastern outskirts of San Juan all the way to Fajardo.

Lolita's. Highway 3. ☎ **787/889-5770.** Main courses $11.95–$16.95. AE, DC, MC, V. Wed–Mon noon–midnight. MEXICAN.

On the western periphery of Fajardo, 2½ miles from the El Conquistador resort, this is the most popular independent restaurant around. The venue is Mexican and informal, the margaritas are cold, and the roster of fajitas, tacos, tortillas, empanadas, and burritos are among the most flavorful in town. Come here expecting a delay as you wait for an available table—if you do, you won't be alone, as many members of the staff at the deluxe El Conquistador and many locals will be there with you.

11 Two Island Drives

Puerto Rico is a relatively small island, barely 100 miles long and about 35 miles wide, but there's a wide variety of natural scenery. From your car you can see terrain ranging from the rain forests and lush mountains of El Yunque to the lime deposits of the north and the arid stretches along the south shore, where irrigation is necessary and cacti grow wild. Seasonal changes also transform the landscape: In November the sugarcane fields are in bloom, and in January and February the flowering trees along the roads are covered with red and orange blossoms. Springtime brings delicate pink flowers to the Puerto Rican oak and deep-red blossoms to the African tulip tree, while summer is a flamboyant time when the roadsides seem to be on fire with blooming flowers.

Puerto Rico has colorful but often narrow and steep roads. While driving on mountain roads, blow your horn before every turn; this will help to avoid an accident. Commercial road signs are forbidden, so make sure you take along a map and this guide to keep you abreast of restaurants, hotels, and possible points of interest. There are white roadside markers noting distances in kilometers (1 kilometer is equal to 0.62 miles) in black lettering. Speed limits are given in miles per hour.

Two programs that have helped the Puerto Rico Tourism Company successfully promote Puerto Rico as The Complete Island are the *paradores puertorriqueños* and the *mesones gastronómicos.*

The ***paradores puertorriqueños*** are a chain of privately owned/operated country inns under the auspices of the Commonwealth Development Company. These hostelries are easily identified by the Taíno grass hut that appears in their signs and logos. The Puerto Rico Tourism Company started the program in 1973, modeling it after Spain's parador system, though it's a poor cousin. Each *parador* is in a historic or particularly beautiful spot. They vary in size, but all share the virtues of affordability, hospitable staffs, and high standards of cleanliness.

The *paradores* are also known for their food—each serves Puerto Rican cuisine of excellent quality, with meals starting at $15. There are now *paradores* at locations throughout the island, many within an easy drive of San Juan. For reservations or further information, contact the **Paradores Puertorriqueños Reservation Office,** P.O. Box 902-3960, Old San Juan Station, San Juan, PR 00902 (☎ **800/443-0266** in the mainland U.S., 800/981-7575 in Puerto Rico, or 787/721-2884 in San Juan).

As you tour the island, you'll find few well-known restaurants, except for those in major hotels. However, there are plenty of roadside places and simple taverns. If you long for authentic island cuisine, you can rely on ***mesones gastronómicos*** (gastronomic inns). This established dining network, sanctioned by the Puerto Rico Tourism Company, highlights restaurants recognized for excellence in preparing and serving Puerto Rican specialties at modest prices. *Mesón gastronómico* status is limited to restaurants outside the San Juan area that are close to major island attractions.

What follows are two driving tours of the Puerto Rican countryside. The first will take you to the lush tropical forests and sandy beaches of eastern Puerto Rico, the second to the subterranean sights of Karst Country and on to the west and south coasts. They're both extended tours—the first takes about 2 days to complete and the second about 6 days—but Puerto Rico's small size and many roads will give you many places to pick up or leave the tour. In fact, there are several points where we give you the opportunity to cut your tour short and head back to San Juan.

Driving Tour 1
The Rain Forests & Beaches of the East

Start: San Juan.
Finish: San Juan.
Time: Allow about 2 days, though you may wish to stay longer at places along the way.
Best times: Any sunny day Monday to Friday.
Worst times: Saturday and Sunday, when the roads are often impossibly crowded.

This tour will take you through some of Puerto Rico's most spectacular natural scenery, including El Yunque Rain Forest and Luquillo Beach. You'll travel through the small towns of Trujillo Alto, Gurabo, Fajardo, Naguabo, Humacao, Yabucoa, San Lorenzo, and Caguas before returning to San Juan.

From Condado, signs point the way southeast to Route 1. Near Rio Piedras on your right, Route 3 is the famous highway most motorists take to visit Luquillo Beach and El Yunque. Route 1 naturally blends into Route 3, which is sometimes called Avenida 65 de Infantera after the Puerto Rican regiment that fought in World War II and the Korean War.

At the intersection of Route 3 and Route 181, head south toward Trujillo Alto. South of Trujillo Alto connect with Route 851, which continues until it comes to an intersection with Route 941. At this point get on Route 941, which runs southwesterly. To your right, you'll soon come to the first worthy stopover:

1. **Lake of Loíza,** surrounded by mountains. You may see local farmers (jíbaros) riding horses laden with products going to or from the marketplace. (Don't confuse Lake of Loíza with the northern coastal town of Loíza, known for its African heritage and its music.)

   Leave the town by heading east along Route 30. Before you approach the town of Juncos, signs point the way to Route 185, which will lead you to the small towns of Lomas. Continue north along Route 185, following the signs to the major artery of Route 3. Allow a leisurely hour of driving time for this trek after having left the lake.

   Once you've connected with Route 3, take it east toward El Yunque and then turn right (south) onto Route 191, which climbs into the forest surrounding El Yunque's peak and that of its taller sibling, El Toro. This is part of the Caribbean

National Forest, the most panoramic and dramatic part of the eastern drive through Puerto Rico.

After viewing the lake, continue on Route 941, which now swings in southeasterly through Puerto Rico's tobacco country to:

2. Gurabo. You'll know you're nearing the town by the sweet aroma of drying tobacco leaves. Part of the town of Gurabo is set on the side of a mountain, and the streets consist of steps.

Leave Gurabo by heading east on Route 30. Near Juncos, turn left onto Route 185 north, follow it up through Lomas, and then get on Route 186 south. This road offers views of the ocean beyond the mountains and valleys. At this point you'll be driving through the lower section of the Caribbean National Forest; the vegetation is dense, and you'll be surrounded by giant ferns. The brooks descending from the mountains become waterfalls on both sides of the road. At about 25 miles east of San Juan is:

3. ✪ El Yunque. Consisting of about 28,000 acres, this rare natural treasure is the only tropical rain forest in the U.S. National Forest system. Its Spanish name derives from its distinctive anvil shape. It lies in the Luquillo Mountains, a name that harks back to the benign Indian god *Yuquiyú*, who, according to ancient legend, ruled from the forest's mighty peaks and protected the Taíno, the island's original inhabitants. Today, El Yunque offers you close encounters of the natural kind, from picnics amid rare flora and fauna to hikes along the panoramic trails. If the outdoors appeals, give yourself at least a day to explore this natural wonderland.

Backtrack on Route 191 until you reach Route 3. Five miles east from the intersection is:

4. ✪ Luquillo Beach. Edged by a vast coconut grove, this crescent-shaped beach is not only the best on Puerto Rico but also one of the finest in the Caribbean. You pay $1 to enter with your car, and you can rent a locker, take a shower, and use the changing rooms. Luquillo Beach becomes crowded on weekends, so if possible, go on a weekday when you'll have more sand to yourself. Picnic tables are available as well.

The beach is open Tuesday to Sunday 9am to 5pm; it's closed Monday (if Monday is a holiday, the beach will be open Monday and closed Tuesday). Before entering the beach, you may want to stop at one of the roadside thatched huts that sell Puerto Rican snacks and pick up the makings of a picnic.

Not far from the beach is the Parador Martorell, where you can spend a restful night at the seaside (see below).

From Luquillo, return to Route 3 east and continue for another 15 minutes until the first exit to Fajardo. Make a left onto Route 194, heading toward the eastern shore. Turn left at the traffic light at the corner of the Monte Brisas Shopping Center; stay on this road until the next traffic light, turn right, and continue to the intersection with Route 987. Turn left onto Route 987 and continue north until reaching the entrance to:

5. ✪ Las Cabezas de San Juan Nature Reserve, better known as El Faro, or The Lighthouse, dating from 1882 and surrounded on three sides by the Atlantic Ocean. This northeast corner of Puerto Rico is one of the most beautiful areas. See "To the Lighthouse: Exploring Las Cabezas de San Juan Nature Reserve," above.

After visiting the reserve, you can take the same road back, heading south to Route 3. Then follow the highway signs south into:

6. **Fajardo,** a fishing port that was hotly contested during the Spanish-American War. Puerto Ricans are fond of giving nicknames to people and places—for many years, the residents of Fajardo have been called cariduros (the hard-faced ones). Don't let the label mislead you; the locals are very friendly. Sailors and fishers are attracted to the shores of Fajardo and nearby Las Croabas, with several seafood restaurants. If you have time, you can take a very satisfying trip by ferry from Fajardo to either Vieques or Culebra, small islands off the Puerto Rican coast that make urban troubles seem far away (see later in the chapter).

Continue south on Route 3, following the Caribbean coastline. At Cayo Lobos, just off the Fajardo port, the Atlantic meets the Caribbean. Here the vivid colors of the Caribbean seem subdued compared to those of the deep blue ocean.

Go through the town of Ceiba, near the Roosevelt Navy Base, until you reach:

7. **Naguabo Beach,** a 30-minute drive from Fajardo. Here you can have coffee and pastelillos de chapin, pastry turnovers that were used as tax payments during Spanish colonial days. At kilometer 70.9 of Route 3, take a brief detour to the town of Naguabo, but only if you wish to enjoy the town plaza's scented, shady laurel trees, imported from India. There isn't much else to see.

Continue south along Route 3, going through Humacao and its sugarcane fields. When the canes bloom during November and December, the tops of the fields change colors according to the time of day. Humacao itself isn't of much interest, but it has a *balneario*-equipped beach with changing facilities, lockers, and showers. From here you can detour to:

8. **Palmas del Mar,** a sprawling deluxe vacation resort. You can stop here or continue along Route 3 through Yabucoa, nestled amid some hills. The view along the road opens up at Cerro La Pandura, a mountain from which there's a panoramic outlook over giant boulders onto the Caribbean.

Directly to the west of Yabucoa you can connect to Route 182, heading west through some of the most dramatic scenery in Puerto Rico along the mountain chain of Cuchilla de Pandura. This road changes its number unexpectedly to Route 181 (but it's still the same road). After a sharp bend, it becomes Route 7740 (again, the same road), and before it reaches the mountain station of Cerro la Santa it becomes Route 184. Stay on Route 184, heading northwest and following the signs to Route 52, the major highway cutting across the heart of Puerto Rico. If you continue southwest on Route 52, you'll come to Ponce. But if you want to return to San Juan, where the driving tour began, go northeast, following the signs back into the heart of Puerto Rico's capital.

ACCOMMODATIONS YOU CAN AFFORD ALONG THE WAY

Parador Martorell. 6A Ocean Dr., Luquillo, PR 00773. ☎ **787/889-2710.** 11 units, 7 with bathroom. A/C TV. $65 single or double without bathroom, $75 single or double with bathroom. Rates include breakfast. MC, V. At km 36.2 along Rte. 3, turn toward the shore, then turn left and drive 4 short blocks.

Back in 1800, the Martorell family came to Puerto Rico from Spain and fell in love with the island. Their descendants own and operate this Luquillo *parador* near the island's most impressive beach. When you arrive, you'll enter an open courtyard, which will have to suffice for your alfresco outings, because there are no grounds. The main reason for staying here is Luquillo Beach, which has shady palm groves, crescent beaches, coral reefs for snorkeling and scuba diving, and a surfing area. Be advised that this parador could be better maintained and that the rather basic small rooms have displeased many readers. Not all units are air-conditioned. Breakfast always features plenty of freshly picked fruit and homemade breads and compotes.

Driving Tour 2
Western Puerto Rico & the Southwest Coast

Start: San Juan.
Finish: San Juan.
Time: Between 2 and 6 days, depending on how much of the itinerary you want to complete. The tour could run longer if you spend extra time at some of the stops along the way.
Best Times: Monday to Friday, any sunny day.
Worst Times: Weekends, when the roads are overcrowded with drivers from San Juan.

This tour begins with a foray into the famous Karst district of Puerto Rico. Along the way, you'll see the Taíno Indian Ceremonial Ball Park, Río Camuy Cave Park, and Arecibo Observatory. You'll then emerge from the island's interior to begin a round-about tour of the west and south coasts, taking in Guajataca Beach, Mayagüez, San Germán, Phosphorescent Bay, Ponce, Coamo, and numerous other towns and attractions.

A broad highway, Route 22 links San Juan with its western frontiers. The first major stop is the city of Arecibo, directly north of Karst Country. However, there's an interesting detour along the way. Take Highway 22 west from San Juan until you reach the intersection with Route 140, at which point you head south (sign-posted to the town of Jayuya). Unless you're in a hurry, you can allow a leisurely hour's drive from San Juan. But traffic is often heavy along Highway 22, since this is a major trucking route carrying supplies to and from the capital.

Route 140 will take you south through some of the most dramatic mountain scenery in Puerto Rico. At the intersection with Route 141, cut onto this highway and follow it south. It's sign-posted all the way to:

1. Jayuya, a village in the middle of the Cordillera Central and home to the **Parador Hacienda Gripinas,** a former coffee plantation where you can catch a very authentic and unique glimpse of the old days (see "Accommodations You Can Afford Along the Way," at the end of this tour).

  If you decide to make this restful side-trip, pick up the trail again by returning on Route 527 to Route 140, then travel west on Route 140 until you pass Lake Caonillas. Here turn onto Route 111 west and in 30 minutes you'll reach:

2. Utuado, a small mountain town boasting the **Parador La Casa Grande,** with accommodations, a restaurant, and a pool (see "Accommodations You Can Afford Along the Way," at the end of the tour).

  From Utuado, continue west for 20 minutes on Route 111 to kilometer 12.3, where you'll find the:

3. ✪ **Taíno Indian Ceremonial Center.** Archaeologists have dated this site to about 2 centuries before Europe's discovery of the New World. It's believed the Taíno chief Guarionex gathered his subjects on this site to celebrate rituals and practice sports. Set on a 13-acre field surrounded by trees, some 14 vertical monoliths with colorful petroglyphs are arranged around a central sacrificial stone monument. The ball complex also includes a museum, open daily 9am to 5pm; admission is free. There's also a gallery, Herencia Indigena, where you can buy Taíno relics at reasonable prices, including the sought-after *Cemis* (Taíno idols) and figures of the famous little frog, the coquí. The Taínos have long gone, and much that was here is gone with them. The site is of special interest to those with academic pursuits, but of only passing interest to the lay visitor. However, it makes a good stop along the route. You can walk around and stretch your legs before continuing with the tour.

Continue west on Route 111 for another 20 minutes to the town of Lares, then turn onto Route 129 north. Drive about 3 1/2 miles, then turn right onto Route 4456, and you'll soon reach the:

4. ✪ **Río Camuy Cave Park.** The world's third-largest underground river, Río Camuy runs through a network of caves, canyons, and sinkholes that have been cut through the island's limestone base over the course of millions of years. The caves, known to both the pre-Columbian Taíno peoples and local Puerto Rican farmers, came to the attention of speleologists in the 1950s. See "Highlights in Northwestern Puerto Rico," above, for more details.

After your tour of the caves, follow the signs northeast (it's sign-posted) to the hamlet of Bayaney along Route 134. This takes only 10 minutes. Pass through the town and continue along Route 134 north until you reach the intersection with Route 635 heading east toward the town of Esperanza. Before reaching the town, take a small road (Route 625) south for 10 minutes to the:

5. ✪ **Arecibo Observatory,** officially the National Astronomy and Ionosphere Center of Cornell University. This observatory has the world's largest and most sensitive radar/radiotelescope. It features a 20-acre dish or radio mirror set in an ancient sinkhole 1,000 feet in diameter and 167 feet deep, allowing scientists to examine the ionosphere, planets, and moon with powerful radar signals and to monitor natural radio emissions from distant galaxies, pulsars, and quasars. See "Highlights in Northwestern Puerto Rico," above, for more details.

When you're ready to leave the observatory, follow Route 625 north until reaching the town of Esperanza. From here, continue north on the same road (now called Route 635) toward Arecibo. Signs will point the way to Highway 22, the major traffic artery linking San Juan with the west. On the southern outskirts of Arecibo, you can either return east to San Juan if your time is limited or continue with the tour, this time heading west along Highway 22. This express highway from San Juan will come to an end on the western outskirts of Arecibo. At the point where Highway 22 terminates, pick up Route 2 and follow it west for about 30 minutes until you come to:

6. **Quebradillas.** Beautiful Guajataca Beach and two *paradores* are only a 15-mile trip from Arecibo along Route 2 in the vicinity of this small town near the sea. Guajataca is fine for sunning and collecting shells, but it's a *playa peligrosa* (dangerous unless you're a strong swimmer). **Parador El Guajataca** and **Parador Vistamar** are located fairly close to each other (see "Accommodations You Can Afford Along the Way," at the end of this tour).

Instead of continuing west along Route 2 to the dull city of Aguadilla, you can cut south from Quebradillas along Route 113, which in 30 minutes will take you to Lago de Guajataca, one of Puerto Rico's most beautiful lakes. After traversing its 2 1/2-mile shoreline, you'll see signposts pointing the way to the town of San Sebastián, a 15-minute drive west along Route 119. As you travel this region, you'll be on the northern border of the richest coffee-growing district.

Once you reach San Sebastián, follow Route 109 southwest to the town of La Parade and continue west along this route until reaching the slightly larger town of Añasco. This is an area of many coffee plantations, though they're private and not open to visitors.

Once at Añasco, you'll be just 30 minutes northeast of Mayagüez. To reach it, continue along Route 109 for about 10 minutes until you get back on the previously traveled Route 2. This will lead directly into the heart of:

7. Mayagüez, the Commonwealth's western port city (see above).

When you're ready to leave Mayagüez, continue southeast along Route 2 for 45 minutes until you reach:

8. ✪ San Germán, Puerto Rico's second-oldest town and a little museum piece included in the National Register of Historic Places (see "Ponce," above). On a knoll at one end of town stands the chapel of the:

9. ✪ Iglesia Porta Coeli (Gate of Heaven), one of the gems of the town's 249 noteworthy sites.

After visits to San Germán, and if you're now ready for some beaches, allow 40 minutes to travel on Route 102 west to Cabo Rojo, from which you can make a connection onto Route 307 heading south to:

10. Boquerón Beach, one of Puerto Rico's best beaches for swimming. There's a comfortable *parador* with a good restaurant only 2 blocks away. The beach also has facilities, including lockers and changing places, plus kiosks that rent water-sports equipment. For more information about **Parador Boquemar,** see "Accommodations You Can Afford Along the Way," at the end of this tour.

After time at the beach at Boquerón, you can discover more beaches in the east. From Boquerón, leave along Route 101 heading east and following the signs to the town of Lajas. Once at Lajas, get on Route 116 heading directly south. Once you reach the intersection with 304, get on this road and drive directly south to:

11. La Parguera, a small fishing village with the **Parador Vila Parguera** and the **Parador Posada Porlamar** (see "Accommodations You Can Afford Along the Way," at the end of this tour). If you have the good fortune to find yourself in La Parguera on a moonless night, go to:

12. Phosphorescent Bay. A boat leaves Villa Parguera pier nightly 7:30pm to 12:30am, depending on the demand, and heads for this small bay to the east (see below). Here a pitch-black night will facilitate a marvelous show, since you can see fish leave a luminous streak on the water's surface and watch the boat's wake glimmer in the dark. This phenomenon is produced by a large colony of dinoflagellates, a microscopic form of marine life that produces sparks of chemical light when their nesting is disturbed.

To travel on, take Route 304 up to Route 116 and drive west through Ensenada. At Guánica, you can turn south and follow Route 333 out to Caña Gorda Beach for lunch or a swim. While here, look for the cacti that flourish in this unusually dry region. Back on Route 116, drive north to Palomas, where you can take Route 2 into:

13. Ponce, the old colonial city with many interesting restaurants, inns, and sights (see above).

When you're ready to leave Ponce, take Route 1 east toward Guayama. At the town of San Isabel, you may want to take an interesting detour north along Route 153 to:

14. Coamo. Along the way to this town, you'll see signs pointing to the Baños de Coamo. Legend has it that these hot springs were the Fountain of Youth sought by Ponce de León. It's believed that the Taíno, during pre-Columbian times, held rituals and pilgrimages here as they sought health and well-being. Between 1847 and 1958, the site was a center for rest and relaxation for Puerto Ricans and others, some on their honeymoons, others in search of the curative powers of the geothermal springs. The baths are in poor condition—you can use them, but the experience is hardly special today.

After a look at the baths, you can backtrack. Instead of going all the way back to Route 1, you can get on the expressway (no. 52), heading east for a 40-minute drive to:

15. Guayama, a green and beautiful small town with steepled churches and the **Casa Cautiño Museum,** on the main plaza of town (☎ 787/864-0600). It's open Tuesday to Sunday 10am to 4pm, and admission is $1 for adults and 50¢ for seniors, students, and children 7 to 12 (free for 6 and under). This museum is in a turn-of-the-century mansion once occupied by the Cañuelo family. It contains all their original belongings and is a showplace for fine furnishings and pictures of the prize horses for which Guayama is famous. Just minutes from town is Arroyo Beach, a tranquil place to spend an afternoon but lacking facilities.

To begin the final leg back to San Juan, take Route 15 north. If you take this road in either spring or summer, you'll be surrounded by the brilliant colors of flowering trees. This route connects with express Highway 52 going north to San Juan, a trip of about an hour, depending on traffic.

ACCOMMODATIONS YOU CAN AFFORD ALONG THE WAY
AT JAYUYA

✪ **Parador Hacienda Gripiñas.** Rte. 527, km 2.5 (P.O. Box 387), Jayuya, PR 00664. ☎ **787/828-1717.** Fax 787/828-1719. 20 units. A/C TV TEL. Year-round $90–$95 single; $125 double. AE, MC, V. Rates include breakfast and dinner. From Jayuya, head east via Rte. 144; at the junction with Rte. 527, go south for 1½ miles.

A former coffee plantation about 2½ hours from San Juan, the Hacienda Gripiñas is reached by a long, narrow, and curvy road. The plantation ambience is everywhere—created by ceiling fans, splendid gardens, hammocks on a porch gallery where you can sit and enjoy a piña colada, and more than 20 acres of coffee-bearing bushes. You'll taste the homegrown product when you order the inn's aromatic brew.

Most of the modest rooms come with ceiling fans, and, though the rooms vary in size, they're kept neat as a pin. Badly needed renovations were completed in 1999. Mattresses are now firm again, and the baths, though small, are neatly arranged. For meals, stick to the restaurant's Puerto Rican dishes rather than its international cuisine. You can swim in the two chilly mountain pools (away from the main building), soak up the sun, or enjoy the nearby sights, like the Taíno Indian Ceremonial Ball Park at Utuado. Boating is possible 30 minutes away at Lake Caonillas. The *parador* is also near the Río Camuy Cave Park.

AT UTUADO

Parador La Casa Grande. P.O. Box 616, Caonillas, Utuado, PR 00761. ☎ **787/894-3939.** Fax 787/894-3900. www.hotelcasagrande.com. E-mail: parzan@coquie.net. 20 units. Year-round $85 single or double. AE, MC, V. From Utuado, head south via Rte. 111 until you reach Rte. 140; then head west until you come to the intersection with Rte. 612 and follow 612 south for about half a mile.

This *parador*, on 107 acres of a former coffee plantation in the mountainous heartland of the island about 2½ hours from San Juan, has been vastly improved since its takeover by Steven Weingarten and his wife, Marlene, who's a gourmet cook. Steven is still a practicing attorney in New York City, commuting to Puerto Rico on a regular basis. Each comfortably but simply furnished medium-size room has a ceiling fan, balcony, hammock, and mountain view, plus a good bed with a firm mattress. There's a pool, and nature trails are carved out of the jungle.

Marlene presides over Jungle Jane's Restaurant, which serves an array of delectably prepared international and Puerto Rican dishes. Even if you're not a guest, you can feast here daily from 7:30am to 9:30pm. It might make an ideal luncheon stop if you're touring in the area.

AT QUEBRADILLAS

Parador Vistamar. 6205 Rte. 113N (P.O. Box T-38), Quebradillas, PR 00678. ☎ **787/895-2065.** Fax 787/895-2294. 55 units. A/C TV TEL. Year-round $71–$105 single or double. Up to two children 12 and under stay free in parents' room. Extra person over age 12 costs $15.

AE, DC, MC, V. At Quebradillas, head northwest on Rte. 2, then go left at the junction with Rte. 113 for half a mile.

High atop a mountain, this 1970s *parador,* one of the largest on Puerto Rico, over-looks greenery and a seascape in the Guajataca area. The small rooms are comfortably furnished with good beds, but the overall look is a rather bland island-style motel. This is hardly a festive resort, but you get reasonable comfort at a decent price. There are gardens and intricate paths carved into the side of the mountain where you can enjoy the fragrance of the tropical flowers. Or you may choose to search for the calci-fied fossils that abound on the carved mountainside. For a unique experience, you can try your hand at freshwater fishing in the only river on Puerto Rico with green waters, just down the hill from the hotel. Flocks of rare tropical birds are frequently seen in the nearby mangroves.

A short drive from the hotel will bring you to the Punta Borinquén Golf Course. Tennis courts are just down the hill from the inn itself. Sightseeing trips to the nearby Arecibo are available. Another popular visit is to the plaza in Quebradillas, where you can tour the town in a horse-driven coach. Back at the hotel, prepare yourself for a typical Puerto Rican dinner or choose from the international menu in the dining room with its view of the ocean.

AT LA PARGUERA

Parador Posada Porlamar. Rte. 304 (P.O. Box 405), La Parguera, Lajas, PR 00667. ☎ 787/899-4015. 35 units. A/C TV TEL. Year-round $65 single; $75–$110 double. AE, MC, V. Drive west along Rte. 2 until you reach the junction of Rte. 116; then head south along Rte. 116 and Rte. 304.

Life in a simple fishing village plus all the modern conveniences you want in a vaca-tion are what you'll find here. The rooms are plain and, though neat, don't invite lin-gering; some are better than others, as they're larger and contain more recently renewed mattresses and in a few cases a balcony with a mini-bar, plus a small sitting room. The best are on the third floor. If possible, ask to look at a room before com-mitting yourself; of course, you can do that only when the hotel isn't full. Paradora Villa Parguera (below) has more style and flair. The area is famous for its Phosphores-cent Bay and good fishing, especially for snapper. If you like to collect seashells, you can beachcomb. Other collectors' items found here are fossilized crustacea and marine plants. If you want to fish, you can rent a boat at the nearby villages, and you can even cook your catch in a communal kitchen. The inn has added a pool and a dive shop and can arrange snorkeling, kayaking, windsurfing, waterskiing, and boat rides.

Parador Villa Parguera. 304 Main St. (P.O. Box 273), La Parguera, Lajas, PR 00667. ☎ 787/899-7777. Fax 787/899-6040. 62 units. A/C TV TEL. Year-round Sun–Thurs $86–$99 single or double; Fri–Sat (including half board) $325–$350 double-occupancy packages for 2 days. Two children 9 and under stay free in parents' room. AE, DC, MC, V. Drive west along Rte. 2 until you reach the junction with Rte. 116; then head south along Rte. 116 and Rte. 304.

The water in the nearby bay is too polluted for swimming, but guests here can still enjoy a view of the water and take a dip in the pool. This *parador*—a classic fish-ermen's inn—is known for its seafood dinners (the fish aren't caught in the bay), its comfortable and colorfully decorated rooms, and its location next to the phosphores-cent waters of one of the coast's best-known bays. The rooms have either a balcony or a terrace. Furnishings are in a tropical motif, with firm mattresses resting on good beds. Units range from small to medium.

Open daily noon to 5pm and 7:30 to 11pm, the spacious dining room offers daily specials, as well as chef's favorites like fish fillet stuffed with lobster and shrimp. Both international and Puerto Rican specialties are served. Nonguests are welcome. There's a play area for children. Because the inn is popular with the residents of San Juan on weekends, there's a special weekend package for a 2-night minimum stay; $325 to $350 covers the price of the double room, welcome drinks, breakfasts, dinners, flowers, and dancing with a free show.

12 Vieques

About 6 miles east of the big island of Puerto Rico lies Vieques (Bee-*ay*-kase), an island about twice the size of Manhattan with some 8,000 inhabitants and scores of palm-lined white-sand beaches. Since World War II, some two-thirds of the 21-mile-long island has belonged to the U.S. military. Much of the government-owned land is now leased for cattle grazing, and when there are no military maneuvers the public can visit the beaches, which are sometimes restricted. Being allowed use of the land doesn't, however, totally cover local discontent and protest at the presence of the navy and marine corps personnel on the island.

GETTING THERE

The **Puerto Rico Port Authority** (☎ 787/863-0852) operates two ferries a day from the eastern port of Fajardo to Vieques in about 45 to 60 minutes each way. The round-trip fare is $4 for adults and $2 for children 14 and under. Tickets on the morning ferry leaving on Saturday and Sunday sell out quickly, requiring passengers to be in line at the ticket window in Fajardo before 8am to be certain of a seat on the 9:30am boat. Otherwise, they must wait until the 3pm ferry. In Vieques call ☎ 787/741-8331 for more information.

   Vieques Airlink (☎ 787/722-3736) operates flights from Isla Grande Airport in San Juan. Five flights leave throughout the day, taking 20 minutes and costing $35. Service from San Juan is also provided by **Isla Nena Airlines** (☎ 787/791-5110).

GETTING AROUND

Public cabs or vans called *públicos* transport people around the island. **Island Car Rental,** Route 201 (in Florida ☎ 787/741-1666), is one of the two largest car-rental companies, with an inventory of stripped-down Suzukis that usually offer dependable, bare-bone transport to many of the island's beautiful but hard-to-reach beaches. Rates begin at $40 per day.

ACCOMMODATIONS YOU CAN AFFORD

✪ **Crow's Nest Guest House.** P.O. Box 1521, Barrio Florida, Vieques, PR 00765. ☎ **787/741-0033.** Fax 787/741-1294. 12 units. A/C. Year-round $60–$85 single or double; $150 suite. AE, MC, V.

Liz O'Dell, one of the most hospitable innkeepers on Vieques, runs this inviting little lodge on 5 hilltop acres with ocean views, with the nearest beach a 5-minute car ride away. There's also a pool. The units are housed in a pair of two-story buildings separated by a large patio and gardens overlooking the ocean. The rooms are decorated in a typical Caribbean motif with sitting areas, kitchenettes, ceiling fans, and reading lights over the good beds; all but two are air-conditioned. The baths are tidily maintained, with a generous amount of towels. The guest house operates a good restaurant, serving Puerto Rican and international dishes at breakfast and dinner. This is an adult retreat, and children under 12 are discouraged. Two locals will take you out fishing, and 2-hour horseback rides through the hills can be arranged.

✪ **La Casa del Francés.** P.O. Box 458, Barrio Esperanza, Vieques, PR 00765. ☎ **787/741-3751.** Fax 787/741-2330. 18 units. Winter $99 single or double. Off-season $75 single or double. MAP (available in winter only) $20 per person. AE, MC, V.

La Casa del Francés is about a 15-minute drive southeast of Isabel Segunda, just north of the center of Esperanza. Set in a field near the southern coastline, it has columns and an imposing façade. In the 1950s, it was acquired by Irving Greenblatt, who installed a pool and, with his partner, Frank Celeste, transformed 18 of its high-ceilinged rooms into an old-fashioned R&R oasis for his executives. The eclectic rooms are rather plain and the beds old, but there's plenty of space, except in the baths. Many of the rooms enjoy access to the two-story verandas ringing the white façade.

However, note that readers have had mixed reactions to this inn. Some praise it, while others have complained. If you don't like the personality of Mr. Greenblatt (and many readers don't), you really won't fit in here.

The $15 fixed-price dinners are attended by many island residents who enjoy the Italian, barbecue, or Puerto Rican buffets presented beneath a 200-year-old mahogany tree.

La Finca Caribe Guest House & Cottages. Rte. 995, km 2.2, Barrio Pilon (P.O. Box 1332), Vieques, PR 00765. ☎ 787/741-0495. www.lafinca.com. E-mail: info@lafinca.com. 6 units, none with bathroom; 2 cottages. Year-round $50 single, $65 double. Extra person $15. Cottage $625–$800 weekly 2 to 4 occupants. MC, V.

Formerly known as New Dawn's Caribbean Retreat & Guest House, this barebones place, on a forested hillside 3 miles from Sun Bay in the center of the island north of Esperanza, caters to budget-conscious travelers and youthful adventurers. The present owners, the Merwin family, have renamed it *finca,* which means "a rustic estate" in Spanish. The centerpiece of the property is a plywood-sided house built by a previous owner with student assistants in 1986. Today the guest house enjoys a spacious porch with hammocks and swinging chairs. The rooms are rustic and small, with thin mattresses. A series of outbuildings contains a bathhouse and communal kitchen. On a hill, the family-style two-story wooden cottage sleeps three to four comfortably; it comes with a kitchen, a bath, decks, and a living area. A casita, another cottage nestled in the garden, can accommodate three with its sleeping loft and queen bed. It has a private deck and its own kitchen. A nonchlorinated pool was installed, and bike rentals are available.

Water's Edge Guest House. P.O. Box 1374, Isabel Segunda, Vieques, PR 00765. ☎ 787/741-1128. Fax 787/741-0690. www.villagloria.com. 11 units. A/C TV. Winter $76.30 single, $92.65 double, $136.25 suite. Off-season, $65.40 single, $81.75 double, $98.10 suite. Children 11 and under stay free in parents' room. AE, MC, V.

Just north of town, this is one of the best-appointed guest houses on the island. Built of adobe cinderblock, stucco, and terra-cotta tile, it's a two-story building in a Mexican hacienda design. There's a second-floor deck for ocean-facing rooms. All the medium-size rooms are tastefully furnished, with ceiling fans and a small refrigerator. The mattresses are firm enough for a good night's sleep and the tiny baths adequate for the purpose. After new owners took over in 1998, the rooms were completely redone and brightened with Caribbean colors and mosquito netting over the beds. A good beach is only a few steps away, and there's a pool on site. You can have breakfast or dinner here at The Oasis at Water Edge, with complete meals in the evening at $10 to $15.

WORTH A SPLURGE

✪ **Hacienda Tamarindo.** Rte. 996 (P.O. Box 1569), Vieques, PR 00765. ☎ **787/741-8525.** Fax 787/741-3215. www.enchanted-isle.com/tamarindo. E-mail: hactam@sprynet. com. 16 units. Year-round $125–$150 single or double; $185 suite. AE, MC, V.

This is the only rival to the Inn on the Blue Horizon, and it's one charming hacienda—the creation of Linda and Burr Vail, who fled cold Vermont. It lies on a hill swept with trade winds, opening onto panoramic views of the Caribbean. An ancient tamarind tree, for which the inn takes its name, stands in the middle of the lobby, rising up three floors. Each of the rooms is individually decorated by Linda, an interior decorator who furnished them with original art, often antiques, and collectibles. They contain first-rate mattresses and good-size baths with a generous supply of fluffy towels; some baths offer Jacuzzis and private terraces. About half the rooms are air-conditioned; the others are cooled by trade winds. A full breakfast with tropical fruit is offered on the terrace on the floor above. For dinner all you have to do is stroll down the hill to the Inn on the Blue Horizon with its well-known Cafe Blu.

Children under 15 aren't permitted, as this is mainly an adult retreat. Box and pool-side picnic lunches are provided by the inn, and a well-stocked bar is available, operating on the honor system. A stroll past palms and mahogany trees will bring you to a freshwater pool where the view is panoramic.

✪ **Inn on the Blue Horizon.** Rte. 996 (P.O. Box 1556), Vieques, PR 00765. ☎ **787/741-3318.** Fax 787/741-0522. 9 units. E-mail: blue-inn@compuserve.com. Year-round $166–$225 single or double. AE, MC, V.

Although known mainly for its restaurant, Cafe Blu, the finest on the island (see below), this is also one of the leading inns on Vieques. It was created by two transplanted New Yorkers, Billy Knight and James Weis, who added four more rooms for a total of nine. The rooms are medium in size, opening onto views of the courtyard or the ocean. The beds are double, queen-size, or king-size. Each accommodation is individually decorated, often with antiques. Three of the rooms are in the main house, and the other six are in a trio of casitas. Seven of the units contain porches with oversized chairs for taking in that ocean view. Trade winds are sufficient to keep the rooms cooled, though two rooms in the main house are air-conditioned. The inn isn't suitable for children 13 and under.

GREAT DEALS ON DINING

✪ **Cafe Blu.** In the Inn on the Blue Horizon, Rte. 996. ☎ **787/741-3318.** Reservations required. Main courses $20–$24. AE, MC, V. Thurs–Mon 6–10pm. CONTINENTAL/CARIBBEAN.

At last Vieques has a restaurant that can compete in quality with some of the finer dining rooms of San Juan. Transplanted New Yorkers James Weis and Billy Knight have opened this charming eatery and hired creative Michael Glatz as its chef. He's a graduate of the Culinary Institute of America, with 18 years experience in fine restaurants before coming here. To get you going, try his couscous crab cakes with fresh baby spinach leaves, sprinkled with a sun-dried tomato lemon oil, or his mushroom papparedelle with shiitake mushrooms, fresh sage, and roasted garlic. Depending on what's available at the market, he's inspired to make a special soup every day. His main courses are equally distinguished, ranging from sweet spice pork tenderloin, pan seared and oven roasted with dark rum, to charcoal-grilled boneless chicken breast with curried pineapple-and-ginger chutney.

By all means come here for a drink. Its Blue Bar was named by *Newsweek* as one of the top bars in the world.

La Campesina. La Hueca. ☎ **787/741-1239.** Reservations recommended. Main courses $10–$20. MC, V. Wed–Sun 6–10pm. Closed Oct. INTERNATIONAL.

Designed to reflect indigenous dwellings, this unusual and excellent restaurant was built a few steps from one of the richest archeological deposits of Taíno artifacts in the Caribbean. It's on the southwestern end of the island (follow the coast road from Esperanza) in the untrammeled fishing village of La Hueca. In a room lined with baskets and weavings amid trailing vines of jasmine and flickering candles, you can enjoy a cuisine of distinctly tropical or uniquely Puerto Rican flair. Fresh herbs like cilantro, tasty varieties of local vegetables, and fruits like papaya, mango, and tamarind served in relishes and pastries, complement the menu. Nightly specials might include avocado rémoulade, conch fritters, lobster ravioli, local fish, and great steak.

Trade Winds. At the Trade Winds Guest House, Flamboyan 107C, Barrio Esperanza. ☎ **787/741-8666.** Reservations recommended. Meals $12–$24. AE, MC, V. Tues–Sat 7:30–10:30am and 6–9:30pm. STEAK/SEAFOOD.

You'll find this restaurant at the ocean esplanade on the south side of the island in the fishing village of Esperanza. It features the Topside Bar for relaxing with drinks with a view of the water, and the Upper Deck for open-air dining. Menu items include several shrimp dishes, Jamaican jerk beef, and fresh fish daily. The chef's specialty is grilled plantain with shrimp and lobster. A pasta of the day is also featured, served with a house or Caesar salad. Included in the price of a main dish are bread and butter, a salad, two fresh vegetables, and a choice of rice or potato.

HITTING THE BEACHES

On the south coast, **Esperanza,** once a center for the island's sugarcane industry and now a pretty little fishing village, lies near **Sun Bay (Sombe) public beach.** Sun Bay is a magnificent government-run crescent of sand. The fenced area has picnic tables, a bathhouse, and a parking lot. Admission is $1 per car.

Few of the island's 40-some beaches have even been named, but most have their loyal supporters—loyal, that is, until too many people learn about them, in which case the devotees can always find another good spot. The U.S. Navy named some of the strands, such as **Green Beach,** a beautiful clean stretch at the island's west end. **Red** and **Blue Beaches,** also with navy nomenclature, are great jumping-off points for snorkelers. Other popular beaches are **Navia, Half Moon, Orchid,** and **Silver,** but if you continue along the water, you may find your own nameless secluded cove with a fine strip of sand. **Mosquito Bay,** sometimes called Phosphorescent Bay because it glows with phosphorescence on moonless nights, is a short way east of Esperanza (see below).

THE LUMINOUS WATERS OF PHOSPHORESCENT BAY

One of the major attractions on the island is ✪ **Mosquito Bay,** also called **Phosphorescent Bay,** with its glowing waters produced by tiny bioluminescent organisms that live near the surface. These organisms dart away from boats, leaving eerie blue-white trails of phosphorescence. *The Vieques Times* wrote: "By any name the bay can be a magical, psychedelic experience, and few places in the world can even come close to the intensity of concentration of the dinoflagellates called pyrodiniums (whirling fire). They are tiny (1/500-inch) swimming creatures that light up like fireflies when disturbed, but nowhere are there so many fireflies. Here a gallon of bay water may contain almost three-quarter of a million." The ideal time to tour is on a cloudy, moonless night, and you should wear a swimsuit since it's possible to swim in these glowing waters.

Shannon Grasso (☎ 787/741-0720) operates trips aboard her *Luminosa I* and *Luminosa II* from La Casa del Francés (see above). These trips aren't offered around the time of the full moon. The charge for these trips is $20, and most jaunts last about 90 minutes.

SEEING THE SIGHTS

The Fort Conde de Morasol Museum, Magnolia 471 (☎ 787/741-1717), is the major man-made attraction on the island. In the 1840s, Count Mirasol convinced the

Spanish government to build a defensive fortress here. Today the carefully restored fort houses a museum of art and history celebrating the story of Vieques. There are Indian relics, displays of the Spanish conquest, and old flags of the Danes, British, and French. The French sugarcane planters and their African slaves are depicted, and there's even a bust of Simón Bolívar based on a visit to Puerto Rico by the great liberator. A unique collection of maps shows how the world's cartographers envisioned Vieques. Since the U.S. Navy occupies more than two-thirds of the island, its presence and controversial role are chronicled. The museum and fort are open Wednesday to Sunday 10am to 4pm, charging $1 for adults and 50¢ for children.

13 Culebra

A tranquil little island, Culebra lies in a mini-archipelago of 24 chunks of land, rocks, and cays in the sea, halfway between Puerto Rico and St. Thomas, U.S. Virgin Islands. Just 7 miles long and 3 miles wide, with nearly 2,000 residents, the inviting island is in U.S. territorial waters belonging to Puerto Rico, 18 miles away. This little-known year-round vacation spot in what was once called the Spanish Virgin Islands was settled as a Spanish colony in 1886, but like Puerto Rico and Vieques, it became part of the United States after the 1898 Spanish-American War. In fact, Culebra's only town, **Dewey,** was named for Adm. George Dewey, American hero of that war, although the locals call the fishing village **Puebla.**

For a long time, beginning in 1909, Culebra was used by the U.S. Navy as a gunnery range, and it even became a practice bomb site in World War II. In 1975, after years of protest over military abuse of the island's environment, the navy withdrew from Culebra, with the understanding that the island be kept as a nature preserve and habitat for the many rare species of birds, turtles, and fish that abound there.

GETTING THERE

From the port of Fajardo, the **Puerto Rico Port Authority** operates two ferries a day from the Puerto Rican mainland to Culebra, taking about an hour each way. The round-trip fare is $4.50 for adults and $1 for children 14 and under. For information and reservations, call ☎ **787/742-3161** on Culebra or ☎ **787/863-0705** in Fajardo.

Carib Air (☎ **800/981-0212** or 787/860-1660), located in Terminal B at Luís Muñoz Marín International Airport, flies four times a day to Culebra. A round-trip from here costs from $75.

ACCOMMODATIONS YOU CAN AFFORD

Club Seabourne. Fulladoza Rd. (P.O. Box 357), Culebra, PR 00775. ☎ **787/742-3169.** Fax 787/742-3176. www.culebra-island.com. 15 units. A/C. Year-round $105–$110 clubhouse double; $110 crow's nest; $125 studio villa; $135 cottage. Rates include continental breakfast. AE, MC, V. From Dewey, follow Fulladoza Rd. along the south side of the bay for 1½ miles.

Across the road from an inlet, about an 8-minute drive from town, is a concrete-and-wooden structure set in a garden of crotons and palms, lying at the mouth of one of the island's best harbors, Ensenada Honda. One of the island's few bonafide hotels, it offers eight villas, two cottages, one crow's nest, and four rooms inside the clubhouse. All units contain small refrigerators. The villas, set up as duplexes with staggered balconies and private entrances, are spacious and comfortable, opening onto views of Fulladosa Bay. Within each villa is one king-size bed and one twin bed, each with a comfortable mattress. The Crow's Nest is on the second floor of the clubhouse, with a queen-size bed, private entrance, and small balcony. Because of lush tropical landscaping, this nest doesn't offer much of a view. Each of the two rooms inside the clubhouse has a private patio, a queen-size bed, and an entry through the dining room. The two-bedroom cottage is the only unit with kitchen amenities. The cottage has a queen-size bed and two twin beds. Dive packages and water sports can be arranged at the office. The hotel has a large freshwater pool.

Flamenco Resort & Fishing Club. Pedro Marquez 10, Flamenco Beach (P.O. Box 183), Culebra, PR 00645. ☎ 787/742-3144. www.culebra-island.com. 29 units. A/C. Year-round $115 studio; $135 1-bedroom suite; $175 2-bedroom suite. MC, V.

This is the only guest house or hotel near the white sands of one of the region's best beaches, Flamenco Beach. The medium-size accommodations are arranged around spacious sitting rooms much like those in an informal beach house, and each has a kitchenette. The owner has studio apartments suitable for two and one-bedroom apartments also suitable for two. Mattresses are firm and frequently renewed; the baths are small with medium-size towels. You can opt to take day trips on a sailboat to one of the nearby islands, go snorkeling, and make fishing expeditions. Even if you're not a guest, consider a visit to the on-site Coconuts Beach Grill serving everything from burgers to freshly grilled local fish. Their tropical drinks are the island's best, especially their mango daiquiri.

GREAT DEALS ON DINING

Club Seabourne. Fulladoza Rd. ☎ **787/742-3169.** Reservations recommended. Main courses $5–$20. AE, MC, V. Daily 8–11am and 6–10pm. From Puebla, follow Fulladoza Rd. along the south side of the bay for 1½ miles. CARIBBEAN.

This is the major restaurant on the island. Overlooking Fulladoza Bay, the club's dining room features fresh lobster, shrimp, snapper, grouper, conch, steaks, and the occasional Puerto Rican specialty. Without ever rising to greatness, the cookery is always competent, the specialties tasty, especially if you stick to the seafood dishes. It also has a large patio with a nightly happy hour.

BEACHES & A WILDLIFE REFUGE

The four tracts of the **Culebra Wildlife Refuge,** plus 23 other offshore islands, are managed by the U.S. Fish and Wildlife Service. Culebra is one of the most important turtle-nesting sites in the Caribbean. Large seabird colonies, notably terns and boobies, are seen.

Culebra's **white-sand beaches** (especially **Flamenco Beach**), the clear waters, and long coral reefs invite swimmers, snorkelers, and scuba divers. The landscape ranges from scrub and cactus to poincianas, frangipanis, and coconut palms.

Culebrita, which means Little Culebra, is a mile-long coral-isle satellite of Culebra, known for its hilltop lighthouse, the oldest in the West Indies, or so it's said. A favorite goal of boaters and a venue for kayaking, it possesses one of Puerto Rico's better beaches on its north side. The islet is also known for its nature's aquariums or tide pools.

Saba 18

An extinct volcano, with no beaches or flat land, cone-shaped Saba is 5 square miles of rock carpeted in lush foliage like orchids (which grow in profusion), giant elephant ear, and Eucharist lilies. At its zenith, Mount Scenery, it reaches 2,900 feet. Under the sea, the volcanic walls that form Saba continue a sheer drop to great depths, making for some of the most panoramic dives in the Caribbean. Divers and hikers are increasingly attracted to the island, not the party person or gambler—and certainly not the beach-buff.

Unless you're a serious hiker or diver, you might confine your look at Saba to a day trip from St. Maarten. If you're a self-sufficient type who demands almost no artificial amusement, then sleepy Saba might be your hideaway. You can find reasonably priced lodgings and cut-rate meals all over the island. In other words, Saba is a bargain for those who appreciate its unique charms.

Saba is 150 miles east of Puerto Rico and 90 miles east of St. Croix. Most visitors fly over from the Dutch-held section of St. Maarten, 28 miles to the north.

1 Essentials

VISITOR INFORMATION

Before you go, you can get information at the **Saba Tourist Office,** P.O. Box 6322, Boca Raton, FL 33427 (☎ **800/722-2394** or 561/ 394-8580).

On the island, the **Saba Tourist Board** is at Lambees Place in the heart of Windwardside (☎ **599/4-62231**). It's open Monday to Thursday 8am to noon and 1 to 5pm and Friday 8am to noon and 1 to 4:30pm. The Internet address for Saba is **www.turq.com/saba**.

GETTING THERE

BY PLANE You can leave New York's JFK airport or Newark, New Jersey, in the morning and be at Captain's Quarters on Saba for dinner that night by taking a direct flight on either of the two airlines, **American Airlines** (☎ **800/433-7300** in the U.S.) flying out of JFK and **Continental Airlines** (☎ **800/231-0856**) flying out of Newark, that currently fly from the United States to **St. Maarten** (see chapters 17 and 22 for complete information and for other airlines with connections through San Juan). From Queen Juliana Airport there, you can take the 12-minute hop to Saba on **Winair (Windward Islands Airways International)** (☎ **599/4-62255**).

Arriving by air from St. Maarten, travelers step from Winair's 20-passenger planes onto the tarmac of the **Juancho E. Yrausquin Airport** (☎ **599/4-62255**). The airstrip is one of the shortest (if not the shortest) landing strips in the world, stretching only 1,312 feet along the aptly named Flat Point, one of the few level areas on the island.

Many guests at hotels on St. Maarten fly over to Saba on the morning flight, spend the day sightseeing, then return to St. Maarten on the afternoon flight. Winair connections can also be made on Saba to both St. Kitts and St. Eustatia.

GETTING AROUND

The traditional means of getting around on Saba is on foot. But we suggest that only the sturdy in heart and limb walk from The Bottom up to Windwardside. Many do, but you'd better have shoes that grip the ground, particularly after a recent rain.

BY TAXI   Taxis meet every flight. Up to four persons are allowed to share a cab, and there's no central number to call for service. The fare from the airport to Windwardside is $8 and $12.50 to The Bottom. A taxi from Windwardside to The Bottom is $6.50.

BY RENTAL CAR   None of the "big three" rental companies maintains a branch on Saba, partly because most visitors opt to get around by taxi. In the unlikely event you should dare to drive a car on Saba, locally operated companies include **Johnson's Rental,** Windwardside (☎ **599/4-62269**), renting about six Mazdas, starting at $40 per day and including a full tank of gas and unlimited mileage. Some insurance is included in the rates, but you might be held partly responsible for any financial costs in the event of an accident. Because of the very narrow roads and dozens of cliffs, it's crucial to exercise caution when driving.

Fast Facts: Saba

Banks   The main bank on the island is **Barclays,** Windwardside (☎ **599/4-62216**), open Monday to Friday 8:30am to 2pm.

Currency   Saba, like the other islands of the Netherlands Antilles, uses the **Netherlands Antilles guilder (NAf),** valued at 1.80NAf to U.S.$1. However, prices given here are in U.S. currency unless otherwise designated, since U.S. money is accepted by almost everybody.

Customs   You don't have to go through Customs when you land at Juancho E. Yrausquin Airport, as this is a free port.

Documents   The government requires that all U.S. and Canadian citizens show proof of citizenship, such as a passport or a birth certificate with a raised seal along with a government issued photo ID. A return or ongoing ticket must also be provided. U.K. citizens must have a valid passport.

Drugstore   Try **The Pharmacy,** The Bottom (☎ **599/4-63289**), open Monday to Friday 7:30am to 5:30pm.

Electricity   Saba uses 110 volts AC (60 cycles), so most U.S.-made appliances don't need transformers or adapters.

Medical Care   Saba's hospital complex is the **A. M. Edwards Medical Centre,** The Bottom (☎ **599/4-63289**).

Police   Call ☎ **599/4-63237.**

Safety Crime on this island, where everyone knows everyone else, is practically nonexistent. But who knows? A tourist might rob you. It would be wise to safeguard your valuables.

Taxes The government imposes an 8% tourist tax on hotel rooms. If you're returning to St. Maarten or flying over to St. Eustatius, you must pay a $5 departure tax. If you're going anywhere else, however, a $10 tax is imposed.

Telephone & Telegraph Cables and international telephone calls can be placed at **Antelecon,** The Bottom (☎ **599/4-63211**).

To call Saba from the United States, dial **011** (the international access code), then **599** (the country code for the Netherlands Antilles), and finally **4** (the area code for all Saba) and the five-digit local number. To make a call within Saba, only the five-digit local number is necessary.

Time Saba is on Atlantic standard time year-round, 1 hour earlier than eastern standard time. When the United States is on daylight saving time, clocks on Saba and the U.S. east coast read the same.

2 Accommodations You Can Afford

Cottage Club. Windwardside, Saba, N.A. ☎ **599/4-62486.** Fax 599/4-62476. E-mail: cottageclub@megatropic.com. 10 units. TV TEL. Winter, $115 studio apt. for 1 or 2. Off-season, $100 studio apt. for 1 or 2. Third and fourth person $20. MC, V.

This intimate hotel complex occupies about half an acre of steeply sloping and carefully landscaped terrain within a 2-minute walk of the capital's center. Only its lobby evokes a historic setting. Designed of local stone and set above the other buildings, it's the focal point for a collection of island antiques, lace curtains, and a round-sided pool. Each medium-size apartment contains a kitchenette, a semi-private patio, ceiling fans, a living-room area, and a queen-size bed with a firm mattress. They're contained in clapboard replicas of antique cottages—two studios per cottage—with red roofs, green shutters, white walls, and yellow trim. The interiors are breezy and comfortable. If you'd like a room with an ocean view, request no. 1 or 2. There's no bar or restaurant, but guests can buy groceries at a supermarket nearby; it'll deliver if requested. The owners are three Saban brothers (Gary, Mark, and Dean) whose extended families all seem to assist in the maintenance of the place.

✪ **Cranston's Antique Inn.** The Bottom, Saba, N.A. ☎ **599/4-63203.** Fax 599/4-63469. 6 units. Winter $129 single or double; off-season $99 single or double. A/C TV. AE, MC, V.

Everyone congregates for rum drinks and gossip on the front terrace of this inn near the village roadway, on the west coast north of Fort Bay. It's an old-fashioned house, more than 100 years old, and every room has antique four-posters with new mattresses. Mr. Cranston, the owner, will gladly rent you the room where Queen Juliana spent a holiday in 1955. The rooms are quite tiny, though the floral spreads jazz them up a bit. You come here for the old-time atmosphere and cheap prices, not for any grand style. The biggest improvement is that all rooms now have baths, but they're cramped, with rather thin towels. Mr. Cranston has a good island cook who makes use of locally grown spices. Island dishes are offered, including goat meat, roast pork from Saba pigs, red snapper, and broiled grouper. Meals begin at $15 to $20 and are served on a covered terrace in the garden or inside.

El Momo. Jimmy's Hill (P.O. Box 519), Windwardside, Saba, N.A. ☎ **599/4-62265.** Fax 599/4-62265. 5 cottages, 1 with bathroom. Year-round $30 single; $40 double. DC, MC, V.

A steep 10-minute trek up from Windwardside, this is Saba's least expensive accommodation. It's in a tropical garden and puts you close to nature in a fun, funky atmosphere. You'll soon get to know "the crew," including snakes, lizards, and iguanas. Angelica and Oliver, the mom and pop of the place, rent five small gingerbread cottages (really huts) that are merely sleeping rooms with platform beds. You may find the mattresses a bit thin, but tropical fabrics dress them up. *Warning:* The walls are rather thin too, so you might not want to plan an amorous adventure. The only room with bath is the honeymoon cottage; the rest share a communal area where guests hang a solar shower bag on hooks. One section is for those who like to take their shower out in the open with an audience; another offers a privacy wall. Ecotourists, backpackers, and scuba divers love the place. The small pool has a foot bridge, fancifully called "the only bridge on Saba." Simple meals are prepared, with advance notification, for guests, who pay around $9 for wholesome dinners. An honor bar on the premises provides beer and wine but no hard liquor.

The Gate House. Hells Gate, Saba, N.A. ☎ **599/4-62416,** or 708/354-9641 for reservations only. Fax 599/4-62415. www.members.aol.com/travelsaba/. E-mail: sabagate@ aol.com. 6 units. Winter $85 single; $95 double. Off-season, $75 single; $85 double. Rates include continental breakfast. DISC, MC, V. Closed Sept.

Its name derives from its position at the gateway to Saba, almost adjacent to the airport; it's the first hotel most visitors see on their way to other points around the island. It was built in 1990 as a concrete-sided replica of three two-story Saban townhouses set adjacent one to another. The units are small but nicely appointed and contain firm mattresses. Our preference is room no. 1 with its twin beds, louvered closet, and wicker love seat. Top-floor accommodations don't have private balconies, as the other rooms do, but share an encircling veranda looking out toward other islands. There's an oval pool. Your hosts are the American-Dutch partnership of Jim Seigel and Manuela Doey, who devote much of their attention to administering their restaurant (recommended below).

Scout's Place. Windwardside, Saba, N.A. ☎ **599/4-62205.** Fax 599/4-62388. 15 units. Winter, $65 single; $85 double; $100 apt. for 2. Off-season discounts of around 20%. Rates include continental breakfast. DISC, MC, V.

Set on the ledge of a hill in the village center, Scout's Place is hidden from the street. It's owned by Diana Medora, who makes guests feel right at home. With only 15 accommodations, it's still the second-largest inn on the island. The old house has a large covered but open-walled dining room, where every table has a sea view. It's an informal place, with an individual décor that might include Surinam hand-carvings, peacock chairs in red-and-black wicker, and silver samovars. The rooms open onto an interior courtyard filled with flowers, and each has a view of the sea. They're small and rather plain, except for the four-poster beds. Many have linoleum floors and tiny TVs. The best units are on the lower floor, as they contain French doors opening onto balconies fronting the ocean. The furniture is haphazard, and mattresses, though much used, are still comfortable. The baths are small, containing rather thin towels. The apartment with kitchenette is suitable for up to five occupants; an extra person is charged $20.

WORTH A SPLURGE

✪ **Juliana's Apartments.** Windwardside, Saba, N.A. ☎ **599/4-62269.** Fax 599/4-62389. 8 rms, 1 apt., 1 cottage. Winter $90 single; $115 double; $135 apt. or cottage. Off-season, $70 single; $90 double; $115 apt. or cottage. Extra person $20. Dive packages available. AE, MC, V.

Built in 1985 near the Captain's Quarters, this hostelry is set on a hillside. Modern and immaculate, the accommodations have balconies and access to a sun deck for lounging. All are simply but comfortably furnished and contain radios and good mattresses, though the beds are different, ranging from queen size to doubles. And all but room nos. 1 to 3 in the rear open onto beautiful Caribbean views. Ask for one of the trio of upper-level rooms (7, 8, or 9), as they offer the best views. The baths are small but adequate, with medium-sized towels. Housekeeping wins high marks here. Juliana's also offers a 2½-room apartment complete with kitchenette, and Flossie's Cottage, a renovated original Saban cottage (with two bedrooms, a spacious living room, a dining room, a color TV, and an equipped kitchen). There's also a recreation room and a pool. The complex contains a simple restaurant, Tropics Café, that's open daily except Sunday for breakfast and lunch and for dinner 4 nights a week.

3 Great Deals on Dining

At **Caribake Bakery/Deli,** Windwardside (☎ 599/4-625390), you'll find the island's best array of freshly baked breads, rolls, and sweets like pies and cakes. The staff also makes homemade soup, sandwiches, and even pizza daily. You can also pick up coffee and cold sodas. Daily lunch specials are offered 11:30am to 3pm for under $6. A deck and gazebo overlook Windwardside at Lambees Place next to the post office.

Guido's Pizzeria. Windwardside. ☎ **599/4-62230.** Main courses $7.50–$11; pizzas $5.50–$11. MC, V. Mon–Fri 6–10pm. AMERICAN/PIZZA.

Marcia Guido and her son, Giovanni, own this bustling pizzeria where you can find basic familiar food. The pizzas come with all the standard toppings, even anchovies, served on crusts that are made fresh daily. There's also spaghetti and meatballs, burgers, and meatball sandwiches. As you wait for your meal, you may want to try your hand at the pool table. On Friday and Saturday nights it's the hottest spot on the island (see below).

Lollipop's. St. John's. ☎ **599/4-63330.** Reservations recommended at dinner. Dinner (including soup/salad, main course, bread, dessert, coffee, free transport from/to your hotel) $18–$26; lunch $7–$14. MC, V. Daily 8am–11pm. CARIBBEAN.

Locals who gravitate here like the personality of owner Carmen Caines so much they've nicknamed her "Lollipop." She's warm and gracious and even has guests picked up at their hotel and delivered to her spot, then taken back. She presents her West Indian fare on an outdoor terrace as well as indoors, cooking whatever was good at the market that day (that usually means fresh grilled fish). She's known for her land crab and also prepares a wicked curried goat. Shrimp and lobster are also regularly featured. Lollipop is so sweet that after dinner you'll want to give her a kiss too!

Saba Chinese Bar & Restaurant (Moo Goo Gai Pan). Windwardside. ☎ **599/4-62353.** Main courses $7–$17. DISC, MC, V. Tues–Sun 11am–midnight. CHINESE.

Amid a cluster of residential buildings on a hillside above Windwardside, this place is operated by a family from Hong Kong. It offers some 120 dishes, an unpretentious décor of plastic tablecloths and folding chairs, and a cookery so popular many residents claim this to be their most frequented restaurant. Meals include an array of Cantonese and Indonesian specialties—lobster Cantonese, Chinese chicken with mushrooms, sweet-and-sour fish, conch chop suey, curry dishes, roast duck, and nasi goreng. If you've sampled the great Chinese restaurants of New York, San Francisco, and Hong Kong, you may find these dishes bland, but it's good change-of-pace fare.

Scout's Place. Windwardside. ☎ **599/4-62205.** Reservations required 2 to 3 hours in advance. Lunch $13; fixed-price dinner $17–$32. MC, V. Lunch daily at 12:30pm; dinner daily at 7:30pm. INTERNATIONAL.

This is a popular dining spot among day-trippers, but you should call or have your taxi driver stop by early and make a reservation for lunch or dinner for you. Dinner is more elaborate than lunch, with tables placed on an open-sided terrace, the ideal spot for a drink at sundown. The food is simple, good, and filling, and the prices are low. The sandwiches, the island's best, are made with freshly baked bread. Each day a selection of homemade soups is also offered, perhaps pumpkin or pigeon pea. Fresh seafood, ribs, and curried goat are specialties. Fresh local fruits and vegetables are used whenever possible. (If you care, this is the best place on the island to catch up on the latest gossip, especially the news that spreads among the expats.)

Sunset Bar & Restaurant. The Bottom. ☎ **599/4-63332.** Main courses $6–$14; lunch $4–$10. No credit cards. Daily 8am–2pm and 6pm–midnight. CARIBBEAN.

You'll enjoy West Indian specialties in a homelike atmosphere at this basic restaurant. For your main course you might want to go for something simple, such as the baked chicken served with rice and peas, potato salad, and your choice of local specialties. Other dishes include spareribs or pork chops with vegetables. The pastries and breads are home baked.

Cheap Thrills: What to See & Do for Free (Well, Almost) on Saba

- **Traverse "The Road."** Regardless of what road you travel in the Caribbean, there's nothing to compare with 19-mile-long "The Road." Its hairpin curves climb from the little airport up the steep, steep hillside to the lush interior of Saba. In days of yore, engineer after engineer came to the island and told Sabans they'd have to forget ever having a road on their volcanic mountain. Josephus Lambert Hassell, a local, had high hopes. In the 1930s, he began to take a correspondence course in engineering while he plotted and planned "The Road." Under his guidance, his fellow islanders built The Road over the next 2 decades or so. In recent years, it's been necessary to reconstruct The Road, but it's there waiting to thrill you. At the top of The Road stands Windwardside at 1,804 feet, Saba's second largest settlement and the island's midpoint.

- **Climb Mount Scenery.** There's no more aptly named mountain in the Caribbean, all 2,855 feet of it, reached by 1,064 concrete steps built into the mountainside. Mount Scenery is the island's central volcano and (mercifully) long extinct, and you reach it through a rain forest. Allow at least 3 hours to make this climb and bring along a jug of water. At the top you're rewarded with one of the most panoramic views in all the Caribbean. On a clear day you can view the neighboring islands of St. Kitts, St. Eustatius, St. Maarten, and St. Barthélemy. Along the way to the top of the mountain you'll be enthralled by such vegetation as begonias, orchids, mangoes, palms, red ferns, and especially the golden heliconias that often grow 6 feet tall.

- **Hike Around Saba.** The volcanic island has many hiking trails for the neophyte and the more experienced hiker. All are reached by paths leading off from "The Road." The tourist office will advise you about hiking and which trails are best and more scenic than others. Our favorite is the Crispeen Track, reached from Windwardside as the main road descends to the hamlet of St. John's. Here you'll encounter some of Saba's most panoramic views. Once at St. John's, the track heads northeast going through a narrow but dramatic gorge covered in thick tropical foliage. As you traverse this trail the vegetation grows more and more lush, taking in banana and citrus fields. As you reach the higher points of a section of the island called Rendezvous, the fields are no longer cultivated and resemble a rain forest, covered with such flora as philodendron, anthurium, and wild mammee. Hiking time to Rendezvous takes about an hour.

WORTH A SPLURGE

The Gate House. Hells Gate. ☎ **599/4-62416.** Reservations recommended. Fixed-price 3-course meal $25. MC, V. Thurs–Tues 6:30–9:30pm. Closed Sept. CARIBBEAN.

On one of the upper floors of a previously recommended hotel near the airport, this popular and lively place offers views encompassing the coastline, the hotel's pool, and the arrival and departure of virtually every plane that lands on the island. Staff members might derive from the U.S. mainland, Holland, or St. Vincent, depending on whomever happens to be here on the night of your arrival. The menu changes every

Diving to the Coral Gardens

Circling the entire island and including four offshore underwater mountains (seamounts), the **Saba Marine Park,** Fort Bay (☎ **599/4-63295**), preserves the island's coral reefs and marine life. The park is zoned for various pursuits. The all-purpose recreational zone includes Wells Bay Beach, Saba's only beach, but it's seasonal—it disappears with the winter seas, only to reappear in late spring. There are two anchorage zones for visiting yachts and Saba's only harbor. The five dive zones include a coastal area and four seamounts, a mile offshore. In these zones are more than two dozen marked and buoyed dive sites and a snorkeling trail. You plunge into a world of coral and sponges, swimming with parrotfish, doctorfish, and damselfish. The snorkel trail, however, isn't for the neophyte. It can be approached from Wells Bay Beach but only May through October. Depths of more than 1,500 feet are found between the island and the seamounts, which reach a minimum depth of 90 feet. There's a $3 per dive visitor fee. Funds are also raised through souvenir sales and donations. The park office at Fort Bay is open Monday to Friday 8am to 5pm, Saturday 8am to noon, and Sunday 10am to 2pm.

night, depending on what's available and on the chef's inspiration. Staples that virtually always appear are curried conch, coconut shrimp, and grilled flanksteak; items that come and go are pan-fried grouper, grilled mahi mahi with jerk sauce or with lemon-butter-garlic sauce, and grilled chicken with Creole sauce.

4 Sports & Outdoor Pursuits

Forget about beaches on Saba. If that's what you want, it's better to remain on the sands of St. Maarten.

HIKING   The island is as beautiful above the water as it is below. A favorite target for hikers is the top of ❂ **Mount Scenery,** a volcano that erupted 5,000 years ago. Allow half a day and take your time climbing the 1,064 sometimes-slippery concrete steps up to the cloud-reefed mountain. You'll pass along a nature reserve complete with a lush rain forest with palms, bromeliads, elephant ears, heliconia, mountain raspberries, lianas, and tree ferns. In her pumps, Queen Beatrix of the Netherlands climbed these steps and, on reaching the summit, declared: "This is the smallest and highest place in my kingdom." One of the inns will pack you a picnic lunch. The higher you climb, the cooler it grows, about a drop of 1°F every 328 feet; on a hot day this can be an incentive. The peak is 2,855 feet high.

SCUBA DIVING   Dive sites around Saba, all protected by the Saba Marine Park, have permanent moorings and range from shallow to deep. Divers see pinnacles, walls, ledges, overhangs, and reefs—all with abundant coral and sponge formations and a wide variety of reef and pelagic marine life. There's also a fully operational decompression chamber/hyperbaric facility located in the Fort Bay harbor.

❂ **Saba Deep Dive Center,** P.O. Box 22, Fort Bay, Saba, N.A. (☎ **599/4-63347**), is a full-service center offering scuba diving, snorkeling, equipment rental/repair, and tank fills. Whether you're 1 diver or 20, novice or experienced, Mike Myers and his staff of NAUI and PADI instructors and dive masters make an effort to provide personalized service and great diving. The **In Two Deep Restaurant** and the **Deep Boutique** offer air-conditioned comfort, a view of the harbor area and the Caribbean Sea, good food and drink, and a wide selection of clothes, swimwear, lotions, and sunglasses. The restaurant is open for breakfast and lunch. A certification course goes for $375. A single-tank dive costs $50 and a two-tank dive $90. Night dives are $65. The center is open daily 8am to 6pm.

Sea Saba Dive Center, Windwardside (☎ **599/4-62246**), has nine experienced instructors eager to share their knowledge of Saba Marine Park: famous deep and medium-depth pinnacles, walls, spur-and-groove formations, and giant boulder gardens. Their two 40-foot uncrowded boats are best suited for a comfortable day on Saba's waters. Daily boat dives are made between 9:30am and 1:30pm, allowing a relaxing interval for snorkeling. Courses range from resort through dive master. Extra day and night dives can be arranged. A one-tank dive costs $50 and a two-tank dive $90.

Saba Reef Divers, Fort Bay Harbour, Windwardside (☎ **599/4-62541**), is a PADI resort and ANDI training facility. The staff guides divers through the shoals, walls, shelves, reefs, pinnacles, and seamounts that surround the volcanic cone of the landmass of Saba, including the "Pinnacles" and Diamond Rock, where divers can spot barracuda, stingrays, grouper, and snapper. Tent Reef, a long underwater fault crisscrossed with crevasses and drop-offs ranging from 40 to 130 feet, is another unusual option for adventurous divers. Packages are available; a single-tank dive costs around $50 and a two-tank dive $90.

5 Seeing the Sights

Tidy white houses cling to the mountainside, and small family cemeteries adjoin each dwelling. Lace-curtained, gingerbread-trimmed cottages give a Disneyland aura.

The first Jeep arrived on Saba in 1947. Before that, Sabans went about on foot, climbing from village to village. Hundreds of steps had been chiseled out of the rock by the early Dutch settlers in 1640. Engineers told them it was impossible, but Sabans built a single cross-island road by hand. Filled with hairpin turns, it zigzags from Fort Bay, where a deep-water pier accommodates large tenders from cruise ships, to a height of 1,600 feet. Along the way it has fortress-like supporting walls.

Past storybook villages, the road goes over the crest to **The Bottom.** Derived from the Dutch word *botte* ("bowl-shaped"), this village is nestled on a plateau and surrounded by rocky volcanic domes. It occupies about the only bit of ground, 800 feet above the sea. It's also the official capital of Saba, a Dutch village of charm, with chimneys, gabled roofs, and gardens.

From The Bottom you can take a taxi up the hill to the mountain village of **Windwardside,** perched on the crest of two ravines at about 1,500 feet above sea level. This village of red-roofed houses, the second most-important on Saba, is the site of the two biggest inns and most of the shops.

From Windwardside you can climb steep steps cut in the rock to yet another village, **Hell's Gate,** teetering on the edge of a mountain. There's also a serpentine road from the airport to Hell's Gate, where you'll find the island's largest church. Only the most athletic climb from here to the lip of the volcanic crater.

If you don't want to explore the natural attractions of the island on your own, the **Saba Tourist Office,** P.O. Box 527, Windwardside (☎ **559/4-62231**), can arrange tours of the island's tropical rain forests. James ("Jim") Johnson (☎ **599/4-63307**), a fit 40-ish Sabian guide, conducts most of these tours and knows the terrain better than anyone else (he's sometimes difficult to reach, however). Johnson will point out orchids, golden heliconia, and other flora and fauna, as well as the rock formations

---

❓ Did You Know?

Saba has the highest per capita consumption of Heineken beer in the world.

---

and bromeliads you're likely to see. Tours can accommodate one to eight hikers and usually last about half a day; depending on your particular route and number of participants, the cost can be anywhere from $40 to $80. Actual prices are negotiated.

6 Shopping

After lunch you can go for a stroll in Windwardside and stop at the boutiques, which often look like someone's living room—and sometimes they are. Most stores are open Monday to Saturday 9am to noon and 2 to around 5:30pm; some are also open shorter hours on Sunday.

The traditional **drawn threadwork** of the island is famous. Sometimes this work, introduced by a local woman named Gertrude Johnson in the 1870s, is called Spanish work, because it was believed to have been perfected by nuns in Caracas. Selected threads are drawn and tied in a piece of linen to produce an ornamental pattern. It can be expensive if a quality linen has been used.

Try to go home with some **"Saba Spice,"** an aromatic blend of 150-proof cask rum, with such spices as fennel seed, cinnamon, cloves, and nutmeg, straight from someone's home brew. It's not for everyone (most find it too sweet), but it'll make an exotic bottle to show off at home.

Most streets in Windwardside have no names, but because it's so small shops are easy to find.

Ex-Manhattanite Jean Macbeth runs **Around the Bend,** at Scout's Place, Windwardside (☎ 599/4-62519), a classy little boutique featuring gifts, oddments, and what she calls "pretties," all one-of-a-kind. Charming locally made wooden Saba cottage wall plaques are sold along with magnets, switchplates, bright parrot and Toucan pinwheels, Caribbean perfumes, and spices. Naturally, there's a collection of hand-painted silk-screened T-shirts.

In recent years, the **Saba Artisan Foundation,** The Bottom (☎ 599/4-63260), has made a name for itself with its hand-screened resort fashions. The clothes are casual and colorful. Among the items sold are men's bush-jacket shirts, numerous styles of dresses and skirts, napkins, and place mats, as well as yard goods. Island motifs are used in many designs. Also popular are the famous Saban drawn-lace patterns. The fashions are designed, printed, sewn, and marketed by Sabans. Mail-order as well as wholesale-distributorship inquiries are invited.

Saba Tropical Arts, Windwardside (☎ 599/4-62373), is the place to go to watch hand silk-screening, and perhaps even buy some wares. Designer Mieke van Schadewijk has produced some catchy patterns, all of which are displayed at her workshop boutique.

7 Saba After Dark

If you're thinking about going to Saba to do some partying, you might want to think about another island. Saba is known for its tucked-away, relaxed, and calm atmosphere. However, don't be too dismayed; there's something to do at night.

Scout's Place, Windwardside (☎ 599/4-62205), is the place to hang out if you want to relax, enjoy a drink, and have a laugh, especially on weeknights. A hotel and restaurant, Scout's Place does moonlight as a local watering hole, entertaining guests, tourists, and locals alike with a distinct Saban/Caribbean atmosphere. You won't do much dancing (well, that depends on how much you've had to drink), but it's much better than the weeknight alternative—nothing. It's open daily, noon to around midnight (actual closing hours depend on business or the lack of it). There's no cover.

Normally a pizzeria, **Guido's,** Windwardside, near Scout's Place (☎ **599/ 4-62230**), serves simple food and drinks weeknights, but this becomes the most happening place on the island on Friday and Saturday nights, as this is really the only place to get a drink *and* boogie down. As a disco, it's known as Mountain High Club. They have a dance floor to shake on and a sound system to shake to—they even have a disco ball. Weeknights are similar to Scout's Place: a simple dining crowd. Hours are Monday to Thursday 6pm to midnight and Friday and Saturday 6pm to 2am. There's no cover.

19 | St. Eustatius

Often called Statia, this Dutch-held island is just an 8-square-mile pinpoint in the Netherlands Antilles, still basking in its 18th-century heritage as the "Golden Rock." One of the true backwaters of the West Indies, it's just awakening to tourism.

It might be best to visit first on a day-trip from St. Maarten to see if you'd like it for an extended stay. As Caribbean islands go, it's rather dull, with no nightlife, and the volcanic black-sand beaches aren't especially alluring. Some pleasant strips of beach exist on the Atlantic side, but the surf is dangerous for swimming.

If you're a hiker or a diver, the outlook improves considerably. You can hike around the base of **The Quill,** an extinct volcano on the southern end of the island. Wandering through a tropical forest, you encounter wild orchids, philodendron, heliconia, anthurium, fruit trees, ferns, wildlife, and birds, with the inevitable oleander, hibiscus, and bougainvillea.

The island's reefs are covered with corals and enveloped by marine life. At one dive site, known as **Crack in the Wall,** or sometimes "the Grand Canyon," pinnacle coral shoots up from the floor of the ocean. Darting among the reefs are barracudas, eagle rays, black-tip sharks, and other large ocean fish.

Statia is 150 miles east of Puerto Rico, 38 miles south of St. Maarten, and 17 miles southeast of Saba. The two extinct volcanoes, The Quill and **"Little Mountain,"** are linked by a sloping agricultural plain known as **De Cultuurvlakte,** where yams and sweet potatoes grow. Overlooking the Caribbean on the western edge of the plain, **Oranjestad** (Orange City) is the capital and the only village, consisting of both an Upper and Lower Town, connected by stone-paved, dogleg Fort Road.

Statia was sighted by Columbus in 1493, on his second voyage, and the island was claimed for the Netherlands by Jan Snouck in 1640. The island's history was turbulent before it settled down to peaceful slumber under Dutch protection; from 1650 to 1816 Statia changed flags 22 times! Once the trading hub of the Caribbean, Statia was a thriving market, both for goods and for slaves. Before the American Revolution the population of Statia didn't exceed 1,200, most of whom were slaves engaged in raising sugarcane. When war came and Britain blockaded the North American coast, Europe's trade was diverted to the Caribbean. Dutch neutrality lured many traders, which

Airport ✈ Beach ⚲ Mountain ▲▲

led to the construction of 1½ miles of warehouses in Lower Town. The American revolutionaries obtained gunpowder and ammunition through Statia—perhaps one of the first places anywhere to recognize as a country the newly declared United States of America.

The good news for the budget traveler is that rates here are often called "a steal."

1 Essentials

VISITOR INFORMATION

The U.S.-based representative of the St. Eustatia Tourist Bureau is **Classic Communications International,** P.O. Box 6322, Boca Raton, FL 33427 (☎ **800/ 722-2394** or 561/394-8580).

On the island the **Tourist Bureau** is at 3 Fort Oranjestraat (☎ **599/3-82213**), open Monday to Thursday 8am to noon and 1 to 5pm and Friday 8am to noon and 1 to 4:30pm.

The Internet address for Statia is **www.turq.com/statia**.

GETTING THERE

St. Eustatius can be reached from Dutch **St. Maarten's Queen Juliana Airport** via the 20-seat planes of **Windward Islands Airways International (Winair)** (☎ **599/ 5-54230** on St. Maarten). The five flights a day take only 20 minutes to hop the waters to Statia's **Franklin Delano Roosevelt Airport** (☎ **599/3-82362**). From here you can also make connections for flights to Saba or St. Kitts; two flights a day to Saba, and two a week to St. Kitts.

The little airline, launched in 1961, has an excellent safety record and has flown such passengers as David Rockefeller. Always reconfirm your return passage once you're on Statia.

GETTING AROUND

BY TAXI Taxis are your best bet. They meet all incoming flights, and on the way to the hotel your driver will offer himself as a guide during your stay on the island. Taxi rates are low, probably no more than $3.50 to $5 to your hotel from the airport. If you book a 2- to 3-hour tour (and in that time you should be able to cover all the sights), the cost is about $40 per vehicle. To summon a taxi, call **Rainbow Taxis** at ☎ **599/3-82811**, or **Josser Daniel** at ☎ **599/3-82358.**

BY RENTAL CAR Avis (☎ **800/331-1212** in the U.S., or 599/3-82421), offering unlimited mileage, is your best bet if you want to reserve a car in advance. Drivers must be 21 and present a valid license and credit card. Avis is located at the airport. You can also search for a cheaper deal at one of the local companies, although don't expect cars to be too well maintained. Try **Rainbow Car Rental** at ☎ **599/ 3-82811** or **Walter's** at ☎ **599/3-82719.** Walter's rents both cars and jeeps.

Fast Facts: St. Eustatius

Banks **Barclay's Bank,** Wilhelminastraat, Oranjestad (☎ **599/38-2392**), the only bank on the island, is open Monday to Thursday 8:30am to 3:30pm and Friday 8:30am to 12:30pm and 2 to 4:30pm. On weekends, most hotels will exchange money.

Currency The official unit of currency is the **Netherlands Antilles guilder (NAf),** exchanged at a rate of 1.80NAf to each U.S.$1, but nearly all places will quote you prices in U.S. dollars.

Customs There are no Customs duties since the island is a free port.

Documents U.S. and Canadian citizens need proof of citizenship, such as a passport or a birth certificate with a raised seal and a government-authorized photo ID, along with an ongoing ticket. If you're using a birth certificate or voter registration card, you'll also need some photo ID. British subjects need a valid passport.

Electricity It's the same as in the United States, 100 volts AC (60 cycles).

Language Dutch is the official language, but English is commonly spoken as well.

Medical Care A licensed physician is on duty at the **Queen Beatrix Medical Center,** 25 Princessweg in Oranjestad (☎ **599/3-82211**).

Safety Although crime is rare here, it's wise to secure your valuables and take the kind of discreet precautions you would anywhere. Don't leave valuables unguarded on the beach.

Taxes There's a $5 tax if you're returning to the Dutch-held islands of St. Maarten or Saba; if you're going elsewhere, the tax is $10. Hotels on Statia collect a 7% government tax.

Telephone & Telegraph   Ask for assistance at your hotel if you need to send a cable. St. Eustatius maintains a 24-hour-a-day telephone service-and sometimes it takes about that much time to get a call through!

To call Statia from the States, dial **011** (the international access code), then **599** (the country code for the Netherlands Antilles), and finally **3** (the area code for Statia) and the five-digit local number. To make a call within Statia, only the five-digit local number is necessary.

Time   St. Eustatius operates on Atlantic standard time year-round. Thus in winter, when the United States is on standard time, if it's 6pm in Oranjestad it's 5pm in New York. During daylight saving time in the United States the island keeps the same time as the U.S. east coast.

Tipping & Service   Tipping is at the visitor's discretion, although most hotels, guest houses, and restaurants include a 10% service charge.

Water   The water here is safe to drink.

Weather   The average daytime temperature ranges from 78° to 82°F. The annual rainfall is only 45 inches.

2 Accommodations You Can Afford

Don't expect deluxe hotels or high-rises—Statia is strictly for escapists. Sometimes guests are placed in private homes. A 15% service charge and 7% government tax are added to hotel bills.

Airport View Apartments. Golden Rock, St. Eustatius, N.A. ☎ **599/3-82474.** Fax 599/3-82517. 9 apts. A/C TV TEL. Year-round $66 apt. for 1 or 2. AE, MC, V.

Airport View Apartments has two locations: Most units are in the Golden Rock area near the airport and four others are on Princessweg in Upper Town, Oranjestad. The accommodations in the Golden Rock area all have compact refrigerators, coffeemakers, and baths. They consist of five one-bedroom apartments for one or two and four two-bedroom apartments for up to four. On the premises are a bar/restaurant and an outdoor patio with a swimming pool and barbecue facilities. In Upper Town, the accommodations consist of two three-bedroom units holding up to nine and two two-bedroom apartments for up to four. They all have kitchens, living rooms, cable TV, dining rooms, and small baths. You check into here for economy, not grand comfort.

Country Inn. Concordia, St. Eustatius, N.A. ☎ **599/3-82484.** Fax 599/3-82484. 6 units. A/C TV. Year-round $40 single; $55 double. Rates include breakfast. No credit cards.

This is about as basic a hotel as we're willing to recommend. Opened in the early 1990s, about a 5-minute walk from the airport and a reasonable stroll to several well-recommended beaches, it's in a residential neighborhood of weathered concrete buildings. Some of your neighbors might be docile cows and goats belonging to the owners, Wendell and Iris Pompier. Breakfast is included, but lunch or dinner can also be if you make arrangements in advance. Each small room contains a radio, an alarm clock, a small fridge, and a queen-size bed with a mattress that's likely in need of renewal. The baths are cubicles, the towels a bit thin. In all, it's a decent place to stay and a good value. A launderette and facilities for scuba diving are nearby.

Golden Era Hotel. Lower Town, Oranjestad, St. Eustatius, N.A. ☎ **599/3-82345.** Fax 599/3-82445. 20 units. Winter $70 single; $88 double; $104 triple. Off-season $60 single; $75 double; $90 triple. MAP $30 per person. AE, DISC, MC, V.

Directly on the water, this modern hotel is clean, serviceable, and comfortable, operated by Hubert Lijfrock and Roy Hooker. Eight accommodations don't have a water view, but the remaining rooms offer a full or partial exposure to the sea; the most stunning panorama is seen from room no. 205. All rooms are tasteful and spacious, with king or queen beds. Regrettably, the baths are so tiny it's hard to maneuver. Lunch and dinner are served daily. The fruit punch, with or without the rum, is delectable. The hotel also has a pool and a bar.

Kings Well Resort. Oranje Bay, Oranjestad, St. Eustatius, N.A. ☎ or fax **599/3-82538.** 8 units. TV. Winter $50–$65 single; $60–$90 double; $90 efficiency. Off-season $45–$60 single; $50–$75 double; $75 efficiency. Rates include breakfast. DISC, MC, V.

On the western (or Caribbean) side of the island, about half a mile north of Oranjestad, this simple secluded hotel occupies about two-thirds of an acre perched on an oceanfront cliff (your nearest neighbors are in the local cemetery). Construction began in 1994 and has progressed slowly ever since. Most views look to the southwest, ensuring colorful sunsets while you enjoy drinks served in the bar of the restaurant (reviewed below). The rooms are small and rather sparsely furnished, but each is somewhat different. Nos. 1 and 4 contain waterbeds; all beds are draped with mosquito netting over firm mattresses. The rooms in the rear are larger and face the sea, while those in front open onto a shared seaview balcony. The baths are small, with routine appointments. There are no room keys, so don't expect much security, and there's no pool. The owners are German-born Win Piechutzki, who designed the layout and many of the doors and windows, and his American wife, Laura.

Talk of the Town Hotel. L. E. Sadlerweg, Golden Rock, St. Eustatius, N.A. ☎ **599/3-82236.** Fax 599/3-82640. www.tradereps.com/tot/talk.html. E-mail: tottown@ megatropic. com. 20 units. A/C TV TEL. Year-round $73 single; $90 double. AE, DISC, MC, V.

Badly damaged by the 1998 hurricane but recovering, this inn lies in the hamlet of Golden Rock at the heart of the island. It's in a flat area between the hills in the north and the volcano (The Quill) to the south and is convenient to the airport and the historic capital at Oranjestad, but what beaches exist are a good trek away. There is, however, a pool on site. The rooms are generally spacious, with mattresses renewed after the hurricane, along with small baths that are well maintained (towels are a bit thin, however). You get no more comfort here than you would at a standard motel, but the price is right. Perhaps during the lifetime of this edition, the well-known restaurant that operated on this site will be functioning once again.

3 Great Deals on Dining

Blue Bead Bar & Restaurant. Bay Rd., Lower Town, Oranjestad. ☎ **599/38-2873.** Lunch main courses $6.50–$7; dinner main courses $12.50–$30. No credit cards. Daily 11:30am–2:30pm and 6–9:45pm. Bar daily 10am–10:30pm. INTERNATIONAL.

Occupying a wood-sided Antillean house painted in neon shades of blue and yellow, this restaurant beside the beach combines West Indian raffishness with a polite staff and cuisine that's well prepared by a crew of Dutch and California entrepreneurs. Menu items are international and whimsical and rely on culinary inspiration from around the world. Examples are grilled chicken salad, spicy Thai-style fish, beef skewers in peanut-based satay sauce, and grilled steaks and fish. The restaurant's name derives from the blue-glazed ceramic beads, originally used as money by Statia's slaves, that are sometimes washed up on the island's beaches after severe storms.

Chinese Bar and Restaurant. Prinses Weg, Oranjestad. ☎ **599/3-82389.** Main courses $7–$10. No credit cards. Mon–Sat noon–3pm and 7:30–11pm. CHINESE.

This place caters to locals and offers standard Chinese-restaurant fare, with a bit of local influence thrown in, including such dishes as curried shrimp. The atmosphere is very laid-back. For instance, even though the terrace isn't set up for dining, you can request to have your table moved there for an alfresco meal. The portions are hearty and range from the typical sweet-and-sour pork and a variety of shrimp dishes to chop suey and chow mein. This is the best place on the island for vegetarians.

Fruit Tree Restaurant. 484 Prinses Weg, Upper Town, Oranjestad. ☎ **599/3-82584.** Main courses $8.25–$9.90. No credit cards. Mon–Thurs 8am–9pm, Fri 8am–; Sat 6–9pm; Sun 7am–9pm. CARIBBEAN.

Authentically West Indian, this restaurant is one of the simplest on Statia, occupying a wood-sheathed antique house whose kitchens were built out of concrete block in recent times. Named after the fruit trees (mango, papaya, banana, and soursop) growing in its garden, the restaurant serves earthy and ethnic specialties that include roasted goat with Caribbean herbs, baked chicken, goatwater stew, braised oxtail, stewed beef, and fish. Most dishes are accompanied by peas and rice and cornmeal johnnycakes. No alcoholic drinks are served, though the management won't interfere if you bring a bottle of wine. Otherwise, preferred drinks are ginger beer, guava juice, sorrel juice, and lime juice. Vilma Rivers is the hardworking owner.

Kings Well Restaurant. Oranje Bay, Oranjestad. ☎ **599/38-2538.** Lunch platters $5–$12; dinner main courses $10–$18. DISC, MC, V. Daily 11:30am–2pm and 6–8:30pm. INTERNATIONAL.

This restaurant is more successful and more complete than the simple hotel in which it's housed (see above). It features wooden columns and panels, an open kitchen, and great sunset panoramas. Enjoy a fruity drink from the rustic bar before ordering lunch or dinner. Lunches feature deli-style sandwiches and a selection of platters from the dinner menu, which is more elaborate. Dishes might include grilled Colorado beefsteaks, fresh lobster, pan-fried grouper, or snapper with parsley-butter sauce, plus German meat dishes like Sauerbraten.

L'Etoile. 6 Van Rheeweg, northeast of Upper Town. ☎ **599/3-82299.** Reservations required. Main courses $10–$20. AE, MC, V. Mon–Fri 9am–1pm and 5–9pm, Sat 9am–1pm and 5–10pm. CREOLE.

Caren Henríquez has had this second-floor restaurant with a few simple tables for some time. She's well known on Statia for her local cuisine, but you don't run into too many tourists here. Favored main dishes are the ubiquitous "goat water" (a stew), stewed whelks, mountain crab, Caribbean-style lobster, and tasty spareribs. Caren is also known for her *pastechis*—deep-fried turnovers stuffed with meat. Expect a complete and very filling meal.

Stone Oven. 15 Faeschweg, Upper Town, Oranjestad. ☎ **599/3-82809.** Main courses $6–$12.50. No credit cards. Daily 10am–2pm and 5pm–"whenever." CREOLE.

A small house with a garden patio and a cozy Caribbean décor, this restaurant serves very simple food. To dine like many islanders do, you can try the bullfoot soup or the goatwater stew. For the less adventurous there are fried pork chops and beef stew. Most of the dishes are served with your choice of rice and peas, french fries, fried plantains, and sweet potatoes. Many know this place as a bar where people sometimes dance when the mood and the music are right. Most dishes are at the low end of the price scale.

Cheap Thrills: What to See & Do for Free (Well, Almost) on St. Eustatius

- **Catch Crabs at Night.** We're perfectly serious. If you're interested, you can join Statians in a crab hunt. The Quill's crater is the breeding ground for these large crustaceans—at night they emerge from their holes to forage, and that's when they're caught. Either with flashlights or relying on moonlight, crab hunters climb The Quill, catch a crab, and take the local delicacy home to prepare stuffed crab-back. Your hotel can usually hook you up with this activity.

- **Stroll Through Upper and Lower Towns.** Upper Town and Lower Town on the west coast facing the Leeward side are two parts of Oranjestad, the island's capital. Gradually many of Oranjestad's historic buildings are being restored. The ruins of Fort Orange, dating from 1636, are worth a visit. Presented in 1939 by Franklin Roosevelt to the people of Statia, a plaque in the parade grounds reads: "Here the sovereignty of the United States of America was first formally acknowledged to a national vessel by a foreign official." At the Historical Foundation Museum you can pick up a brochure outlining how you can tour both sections. Lower Town sits below Fort Oranjestraat and some steep cliffs and is reached from Upper Town on foot. Take the cobblestone Fort Road if you're walking between the two. Now these places look like ghost towns, but in the 18th century they were filled with warehouses doing a booming trade. As you walk along the water you'll see the crumbling ruins of this prosperous period. The sea is now reclaiming many of these abandoned warehouses.

- **Hike Up to The Quill.** There's no more dramatic walk in all Statia. Having last erupted some 4,000 years ago, The Quill is tranquil today. Lying at the southern end of Statia, it's a 2,000-foot-high extinct volcano with a lush rain forest inside its once-active crater. Five marked trails of varying difficulty lead up to the rim, each taking about 2 hours. Once you reach the summit, there are additional trails to follow if you have the time and stamina. To reach The Quill, we prefer "Quill Track I," the most direct route if you don't mind a steep climb. It starts on the south side of Oranjestad on Welfare Road, going up the western side of the rim of the crater to an elevation of 1,300 feet. Along the way you'll see some interesting vegetation, including pink poui. To look at the lush flora within the volcano is worth the climb.

4 Hitting the Beaches

Most of the beaches of Statia are small narrow strips of sand, either volcanic black or a dull mud-like gray. Regrettably, the preferred beaches are on the Atlantic side instead of the more tranquil Caribbean side, which means the waters are often too rough for swimming.

Beachcombers delight, however, in their search for the fabled **blue-glass beads** that were manufactured in the 1600s by a Dutch West Indies Company. These beads were used in lieu of money for the trading of such products as tobacco, cotton, and rum. They were even used to buy slaves. These beads—real collector's items—often are unearthed after a heavy rainfall or tropical storm.

On the Atlantic side, nearly always deserted **Zeelandia Beach** is 2 miles long and filled with either dark-beige or volcanic black sand. One tourist promotion speaks of its "exciting Atlantic surf and invigorating trade winds" but fails to warn of the dangerous undertow. Only one small section is safe for swimming. The beach is suitable, however, for wading, hiking, and sunbathing.

Orange Beach is also called Smoke Alley Beach. On the leeward side of the island, it lies directly off Lower Town. This is one of the small volcanic beaches on the southwest shore, with beige or black sands and waters suitable for a leisurely swim. You virtually have the beach to yourself until late afternoon, when locals start to arrive for a dip. Also on the leeward is **Crooks Castle Beach,** north of Oranjestad. The waters, filled with giant yellow sea fans, sea whips, and pillar coral, attract snorkelers, while beachcombers are drawn to the many blue beads that have been unearthed here.

On the southeast Atlantic side of the island, **Corre Corre Bay** has a strip of dark golden sand. It's about half an hour down Mountain Road and is worth the trip to get here, although the waters are often too churned up for comfortable swimming. Two bends north of this beach, the light-brown-sand **Lynch Bay Beach** is more sheltered from the wild swells of the Atlantic, especially along Concordia Bay. Nonetheless, the surf here is still almost always rough, plus there's a dangerous undertow; this beach is better used for sunbathing than swimming.

5 Sports & Outdoor Pursuits

HIKING   This is the most popular activity. Those with the stamina can climb the slopes of The Quill. The highest point on the island, The Quill's extinct volcanic cone harbors a crater filled with a dense tropical rain forest, containing towering kapok trees among other vegetation. A dozen or more species of wild orchids, some quite rare, grow here, and some 50 species of birdlife call it home, including the blue pigeon, a rare bird known to frequent the breadfruit and cottonwood trees here. Islanders once grew cocoa, coffee, and cinnamon in the crater's soil, but today bananas are the only crop. The tourist office (☎ 599/3-82433) will supply you with a list of a dozen trails with varying degrees of difficulty and can arrange for you to go with a guide whose fee is $20 or more (that has to be negotiated, of course).

WATER SPORTS   On the Atlantic side of the island, at Concordia Bay, the **surfing** is best. However, there's no lifeguard protection. **Snorkeling** is available through the Caribbean Sea to explore the remnants of an 18th-century man-of-war and the walls of warehouses, taverns, and ships that sank below the surface of Oranje Bay more than 200 years ago.

Dive Statia is a full PADI diving center on Fishermen's Beach in Lower Town (☎ 599/3-82435), offering everything from beginning instruction to dive master certification. Its professional staff guides divers of all levels of experience to spectacular walls, untouched coral reefs, and historic shipwrecks. Dive Statia offers one- and two-tank boat dives, costing $40 to $75, including equipment. Night dives and snorkel trips are also available.

Many adventurers come to Statia to enjoy waterskiing, but it's expensive. **Scubagua,** operating out of the Golden Era Hotel, Bay Road, Lower Town (☎ 599/3-82345), will hook you up with the sport for $90 per hour.

TENNIS   Statia maintains two courts at the **Community Center,** Rosemary Laan in Upper Town (☎ 599/3-82249), costing only $2 per hour. You'll have to bring your own rackets and balls, but there is a changing room.

6 Seeing the Sights

Oranjestad stands on a cliff looking out on a beach and the island's calm anchorage, where in the 18th century you might've seen 200 vessels offshore. **Fort Oranje** was built in 1636 and restored in honor of the 1976 U.S. Bicentennial celebration. Perched atop the cliffs, its terraced rampart is lined with the old cannons.

The **St. Eustatius Historical Foundation Museum,** Upper Town (☎ 599/ 3-82288), is also called the de Graaff House in honor of its former tenant, Johannes de Graaff. After British Admiral Rodney sacked Statia for its tribute to the United States, he installed his own headquarters in this 18th-century house. Today a museum, the house stands in a garden, with a 20th-century wing crafted from 17th-century bricks. There are exhibits on the process of sugar refining as well as shipping and commerce. Archaeological artifacts from the colonial period and a pair of beautiful 18th-century antique furnished rooms are also on view. There's a section devoted to the pre-Columbian period. In the wing annex is a massive piece of needlework by an American, Catherine Mary Williams, showing the flowers of Statia. The museum is open Monday to Friday 9am to 5pm and Saturday and Sunday 9am to noon; admission is $2 for adults and $1 for children.

A few steps away, a cluster of 18th-century buildings surrounding a quiet courtyard is called **Three Widows' Corner.** Nearby are the ruins of the first **Dutch Reformed church** on Kerkweg or Church Way. To reach it, turn west from Three Widows' Corner onto Kerkweg. Tilting headstones record the names of the characters in the island's past. The St. Eustatius Historical Foundation recently completed restoration of the church. Visitors may climb to the top level of the tower and see the bay as lookouts did many years before.

Once Statia had a large colony of Jewish traders, and you can explore the ruins of **Honen Dalim,** the second Jewish synagogue in the western hemisphere. Built around 1740 and damaged by a hurricane in 1772, it fell into disuse at the dawn of the 19th century. The synagogue stands beside Synagogpad, a narrow lane whose entrance faces Madam Theatre on the square. The walls of a *mikvah* (ritual bath) rise beside the **Jewish burial ground** on the edge of town. Most poignant is the memorial of David Haim Hezeciah de Lion, who died in 1760 at the age of 2 years, 8 months, 26 days; carved into the baroque surface is an angel releasing a tiny songbird from its cage.

You can also visit the **Lynch Plantation Museum** at Lynch Bay (☎ 599/3-82209), but you'll have to call to arrange a tour. Donations are accepted; otherwise admission is free. Locals still call this place the Berkel Family Plantation, though today it's a museum depicting life on Statia a century ago. The history of the island is shown in antiques, fishing and farming equipment, even pictures and old Bibles. Usually Ismael Berkel is on hand to show you around. This is a special sight because it's personal and still very much a place of residence instead of some deadly dull museum.

7 Shopping

At **Mazinga Giftshop,** Fort Oranje Straat, Upper Town (☎ 599/3-82253), you'll find an array of souvenirs—T-shirts, liquor, costume jewelry, 14-karat-gold jewelry, cards, drugstore items, beachwear, children's books, handbags, and paperback romances. You may have seen more exciting stores in your life, but this is without parallel for Statia. A selection of souvenirs and crafts, mainly toys, is found at the **Fun Shop,** Van Tonningenweg in Upper Town (☎ 599/3-82253), and you can also buy books and magazines at the **Paper Corner,** Van Tonningenweg, Upper Town (☎ 599/3-82208).

8 St. Eustatius After Dark

Las Vegas it isn't. Nightlife pickings here are among the slimmest in the Caribbean. Even though most visitors are satisfied by drinks and dinner, there are a few spots to wander after hours. Weekends are the best and busiest time to go out on Statia.

Check to see if there's any action at **Talk of the Town** (above), which often has live music on Sunday. **Exit Disco** (☎ 599/3-82543) at the Stone Oven Restaurant, 16A Feaschweg, Upper Town, Oranjestad, often has dancing and local bands on weekends, and you can also enjoy simple West Indian fare here. For local flavor, try **Cool Corner** (☎ 599/3-82523), across from the St. Eustatius Historical Foundation Museum, in the center of town.

20

St. Kitts

A volcanic island of the once-British Leewards, St. Kitts has become a resort mecca in recent years. Its major crop is sugar and has been since the 17th century. But tourism now overwhelms, as its southeastern peninsula, site of the best white-sand beaches, has been set aside for massive hotel and resort development. Most of the island's other beaches are of gray or black volcanic sand.

Though far more active and livelier than its companion island, Nevis (see chapter 16), St. Kitts is still fairly sleepy. But go now before its inherent Caribbean character changes forever. However, the island doesn't offer a wide range of accommodations, particularly on the lower end of the price scale. As for dining, if you avoid the high-priced resorts and eat at some of the little taverns where the locals go, you'll at least be able to keep food costs within reason.

The Caribs, the early settlers, called St. Kitts Liamuiga ("fertile isle"). Its mountain ranges reach up to nearly 4,000 feet, and in its interior are virgin rain forests, alive with hummingbirds and wild green vervet monkeys. The monkeys were brought in as pets by the early French settlers and turned loose in the forests when the island became British in 1783. These native African animals have proliferated and can be seen at the Estridge Estate Behavioral Research Institute. Another import, this one British, is the mongoose, brought in from India as an enemy of rats in the sugarcane fields. However, the mongooses and rats operate on different time cycles—the rats ravage while the mongooses sleep. Wild deer are found in the mountains. Sugarcane climbs right up the slopes, and there are palm-lined beaches around the island. As you travel around St. Kitts, you'll notice ruins of old mills and plantation houses. You'll also see an island rich in trees and other vegetation.

St. Kitts, 23 miles long and 6½ miles wide, rides the crest of that arc of islands known as the northerly Leeward group of the Lesser Antilles. It's separated from the associated state of Nevis by a 2-mile-wide strait, and its administrative capital is Basseterre.

1 Essentials

VISITOR INFORMATION

Tourist information is available from the tourist board's **stateside offices** at 414 E. 75th St., New York, NY 10021 (☎ **800/582-6208** or 212/535-1234).

St. Kitts

In **Canada,** an office is at 365 Bay St., Suite 806, Toronto, ON, M5H 2V1 (☎ **416/376-0881**), and in the **United Kingdom** at 10 Kensington Court, London, W8 5DL (☎ **020/7376-0881**).

On the island, the local tourist board operates at Pelican Mall, Bay Road in Basseterre (☎ **869/465-4040**), open Monday and Tuesday 8am to 4:30pm and Wednesday to Friday 8am to 4pm.

The Internet address for St. Kitts (and Nevis) is **www.stkitts-nevis.com.**

GETTING THERE

Dozens of daily flights on **American Airlines** (☎ **800/433-7300**) land in San Juan. From here, **American Eagle** (same phone) makes four daily nonstop flights into St. Kitts.

If you're already on St. Maarten and want to visit St. Kitts (with perhaps a side trip to Nevis), you can do so aboard one of the most remarkable little airlines in the Caribbean. Known by its nickname, **Winair (Windward Islands Airways International)** (☎ **869/465-8010**), it makes three to four flights a week from St. Maarten to St. Kitts, with easy connections to/from other Dutch islands like Saba and St. Eustatius and about a dozen other destinations throughout the Caribbean.

Another possibility involves transfers into St. Kitts or Nevis through Antigua, St. Maarten, or San Juan on the Antigua-based carrier, **LIAT** (☎ **800/468-0482** in the U.S. and Canada, or 869/465-8613). Likewise, LIAT can also be used for Canadians and British nationals, as the LIAT flies in from Antigua. **Air Canada**

A Taste of Sugarcane

At some point during your visit you should eat sugar directly from the cane. Any farmer will sell you a huge stalk, and there are sugarcane plantations all over the island. You strip off the hard exterior of the stalk, bite into it, chew on the tasty reeds, and swallow the juice. It's best with a glass of rum.

(☎ **800/776-3000**) flies from Toronto to Antigua and **British Airways** (☎ **800/ 247-9297** in the U.S., or 0345/222-111 in England) from London to Antigua.

GETTING AROUND

BY TAXI   Since most taxi drivers are also guides, this is the best means of getting around. You don't even have to find a driver at the airport—one will find you. They also wait outside the major hotels. Before heading out, however, you must agree on the price since taxis aren't metered. Also ask if the rates quoted to you are in U.S. dollars or the Eastern Caribbean dollar. To go from Robert L. Bradshaw International Airport to Basseterre costs about EC$16 ($5.90); to Sandy Point, EC$37 ($13.70) and up. For more information, call the **St. Kitts Taxi Association** at ☎ **869/465- 8487.**

BY RENTAL CAR   A U.S.-based rental firm maintaining a representative on St. Kitts is **Avis,** South Independence Square (☎ **800/331-1212** in the U.S., or 869/ 465-6507). It charges from $50 per day, $300 per week, plus $10 per day for collision damage, with a $250 deductible. Tax is 5% extra, and a week's rental allows a seventh day for free. The company offers free delivery service to either the airport or to any of the island's hotels, and drivers must be between ages 25 and 75. **Budget** at Golden Rock Airport (☎ **869/466-5585**) now offers comparable service, vehicles, and prices to Avis.

   Delisle Walwyn & Co., Liverpool Row, Basseterre (☎ **869/465-8449**), is a local company offering cars and jeeps. This might be your best deal on the island. You can also check two other local companies: **Sunshine,** Cayon Street in Basseterre and a kiosk at the Golden Rock Airport (☎ **869/465-2193**), and **TDC Rentals,** West Independence Square in Basseterre (☎ **869/465-2991**).

   Driving is on the left! You'll need a local driver's license, which can be obtained at the **Traffic Department,** on Cayon Street in Basseterre, for EC$50 ($18.50). Usually a member of the staff at your car-rental agency will drive you to the Traffic Department to get one.

Fast Facts: St. Kitts

Banking Hours   If you want to change your U.S. dollars into Eastern Caribbean dollars, you'll find banks open Monday to Thursday 8am to noon and Friday 8am to noon and 3 to 5pm.

Currency   The local currency is the **Eastern Caribbean dollar (EC$),** valued at about $2.70 to the U.S. dollar. Many prices, however, including those of hotels, are quoted in U.S. dollars. Always determine which "dollar" locals are talking about.

Customs   You're allowed in duty-free with your personal belongings. Sometimes luggage is subjected to a drug check.

Drugstores   Try **Parris Pharmacy,** Central Street at Basseterre (☎ **869/465-8569**), open Monday to Wednesday 8am to 5pm, Thursday 8am to 1pm, Friday 8am to 5:30pm, and Saturday 8am to 6pm. You can also try **City Drug,** Fort Street in Basseterre (☎ **869/465-2156**), open Monday to Wednesday and Friday to Saturday 8am to 7pm, Thursday 8am to 5pm, and Sunday 8 to 10am only.

Electricity   St. Kitts' electricity is 230 volts AC (60 cycles), so you'll need an adapter and a transformer for U.S.-made appliances.

Emergencies   Dial ☎ **911.**

Entry Requirements   U.S. and Canadian citizens can enter with proof of citizenship, such as a birth certificate with a raised seal accompanied by a government-issued photo ID. British subjects need a passport but not a visa.

Hospital   In Basseterre, there's a 24-hour emergency room at **Joseph N. France General Hospital,** Cayon Street (☎ **869/465-2551**).

Language   English is the language of the island and is spoken with a decided West Indian patois.

Police   In an emergency, call ☎ **911.**

Safety   This is still a fairly safe place to travel. Most crimes against tourists—and there aren't a lot—are robberies on Conaree Beach, so exercise the usual precautions. It would be wise to safeguard your valuables, and women should not go jogging alone along deserted roads.

Taxes   The government imposes a 7% tax on rooms and meals, plus another EC$27 ($10) airport departure tax (but not to go to Nevis).

Telecommunications   Telegrams and Telexes can be sent from **Skantel,** Cayon Street, Basseterre (☎ **869/465-1000**), Monday to Friday 8am to 6pm, Saturday 7:30am to 1pm, and Sunday and public holidays 6 to 8pm. International telephone calls, including collect calls, can also be made from this office.

Time   St. Kitts is on Atlantic standard time all year. This means that in winter when it's 6am in Basseterre, it's 5am in Miami or New York. When the U.S. goes on daylight saving time, St. Kitts and the East Coast mainland are on the same time.

Tipping   Most hotels and restaurants add a service charge of 10% to cover tipping. If not, tip 10% to 15%.

Water   The water on St. Kitts and Nevis is so good that baron de Rothschild's chemists selected St. Kitts as their only site in the Caribbean to distill and produce CSR (Cane Sugar Rothschild), a pure sugarcane liqueur.

Weather   St. Kitts lies in the tropics, and its warm climate is tempered by the trade winds. The average air temperature is 79°F, and the average water temperature is 80°F. Dry, mild weather is usually experienced from November to April; May to October it's hotter and rainier.

2 Accommodations You Can Afford

Blue Gables Bed and Breakfast. Canada Estates (P.O. Box 868), St. Peter's Parish, St. Kitts, W.I. ☎ or fax **869/466-7752.** 10 units. Winter $85 single; $100 double. Off-season $55 single; $70 double. Extra person $20. Rates include continental breakfast. MC, V.

If you'd like to go the B&B route, this is an ideal choice. It offers well-kept rooms, most often with queen-size beds with firm mattresses. The baths are small and the towels medium size. It's snug and cozy here, without a lot of amenities. A communal kitchen is shared by all, which cuts down on food costs. There's also a place where you can do your laundry. The owners are helpful, explaining St. Kitts and where to go and what to do.

Central Guest House. Central Market St., Basseterre, St. Kitts, W.I. ☎ **869/465-2278.** 10 units. TV. Year-round $30 single; $38–$45 double; $55 2-bedroom unit for 4; $65 3-bedroom unit for 6. No credit cards.

The owner said it all: "Don't oversell us, now. I don't want readers arriving here thinking it's the Ritz. Just say it's clean." Right in the heart of town, this is the least expensive place to stay on a pricey island. It's the address the islanders of the Caribbean select whenever they visit St. Kitts. The rooms are mere cubicles, but they come with and without a kitchenette. The mattresses are thin, as are the towels. It's best to ask to see a room before checking in. If you don't mind roughing it and really want to save money, you may appreciate this place.

Coconut Beach Club. Frigate Bay (P.O. Box 1198, Basseterre), St. Kitts, W.I. ☎ **800/ 345-0271** in the U.S., or 869/465-8597. Fax 869/466-7085. 60 units. Winter $100–$125 double; $150 studio suite; $175 1-bedroom apt. up to 4; $275 2-bedroom apt. up to 6. Off-season, $75–$90 double; $105 studio suite; $120 1-bedroom apt. up to 4; $190 2-bedroom apt. up to 6. AE, MC, V.

At the foot of a green mountain 3 miles east of Basseterre, this family-favorite resort is the only hotel on Caribbean Beach at Frigate Bay. Naturally the most sought-after units in this one- and two-bedroom condo complex are those opening directly onto the beach, with swimming, sailing, and water sports at your doorstep. There's also a pool, and it's just a short drive from an 18-hole golf course. The rooms are furnished in a Caribbean motif, the larger accommodations with kitchens. Units are time-shared, so there are no routine amenities. Most of them have decent mattresses and each has a medium-size bath with an adequate supply of towels. Accommodations house from two to six people; there are no singles rented as such. Guests can eat at the popular Banana Tree Restaurant, which features informal beachfront dining. Dinners at the cafe are particularly restful, and fresh grilled seafood is a specialty.

Gateway Inn. Frigate Bay (P.O. Box 1253, Basseterre), St. Kitts, W.I. ☎ **869/465-7155.** Fax 869/465-9322. 10 apts. A/C TV TEL. Winter $80 apt. for 2. Off-season $60 apt. for 2. Extra person $15. AE, MC, V.

Built by local entrepreneurs in the early 1990s, this self-catering complex has 10 medium-size apartments, each with a separate bedroom and living/dining area and a fully equipped kitchen. The furnishings include mostly rattan pieces with upholstery and curtains sporting a floral Caribbean motif. The place doesn't offer grand comfort but is good value for what you get. The baths are quite small with shower units. The complex is in a secluded position about an 11-minute walk to either the beach or the island's public golf course. Although there's no restaurant or bar, each apartment includes maid service. Laundry, baby-sitting, and water sports can be arranged on-site, and guests can shop at the mini-mart convenience store within walking distance.

Morgan Heights Condo Resort. Canada Estate (P.O. Box 735, Basseterre), St. Kitts, W.I. ☎ **869/465-8633.** Fax 869/465-2972. 14 units. AC MINIBAR TV TEL. Winter $85 2-bedroom condo; $125–$175 suite. Off-season $50 2-bedroom condo; $75–$105 suite. Extra person $20 in winter, $15 off-season. AE, DC, MC, V.

On a sandy offshore east coast island known as Canada Estate, this complex originally consisted of a quintet of two-bedroom apartments, each with wicker furniture, covered patios overlooking the Atlantic Ocean, and a kitchen. After its initial construction, the complex was enlarged with 10 suites. Units range from small to medium in size, but each is well maintained and fairly inviting, with good beds and small but tidy baths. In spite of its name, this place doesn't live up to its billing as a "resort," as it's really more for self-sufficient types with a minimum of assistance provided by the staff. Although there's a view of the water, the beach is a 10-minute drive away. A pool is on the grounds. In an open-sided outbuilding a short walk away is the simple Atlantic Club restaurant.

Palms Hotel. The Circus (P.O. Box 64), Basseterre, St. Kitts, W.I. ☎ **869/465-0800.** Fax 869/465-5889. 12 units. A/C TV TEL. Year-round $95 junior suite; $125 1-bedroom suite; $180 2-bedroom suite. AE, MC, V.

Occupying the upper floor of a two-story antique building surrounding the Circus, this hotel enjoys the most central location. Some of the rooms are accessible only via an outdoor veranda; others open off an enclosed hall inside the 200-year-old site. Though there's lots of hubbub in the square in the morning, after 4pm it quiets down considerably. No meals are served, but there's a small bar and cafe on the premises. The accommodations are high-ceilinged, spacious, and simply but comfortably furnished, with such amenities as coffeemakers and small fridges. The mattresses are in need of renewal. The baths are small, and the thin towels are kept at a minimum. The main drawback to this place is the slowness of the staff, whose languorous pace can be exasperating. Swimming is an option at Frigate Bay, a 5-minute drive from the hotel.

Rock Haven Bed & Breakfast. Box 821, Frigate Bay, St. Kitts, W.I. ☎ **869/465-5503.** Fax 869/466-6130. E-mail: blakekj@caribsurf.com. 2 units. TV TEL. Year-round, $85 double without kitchen, $95 double with kitchen. Rates include breakfast. AE, DC, MC, V.

Owners Judith and Keith Blake provide lots of charm at this 7-year-old private home. Both were born on St. Kitts and came back after years in Toronto, Canada, working as a dentist and a dietician, respectively. Although relatively new, the house was built with lots of Caribbean features that include decorative gingerbread, wide verandas, hardwood floors, and a location midway up one of the hills overlooking Frigate Bay Beach—high enough to benefit from the nearly constant ocean breezes. The larger of the two suites has a private patio and a kitchenette; the other doesn't have a kitchen but has reading areas and plenty of space for a cozy family holiday. Mattresses are first rate, and the medium-size baths contain plenty of fluffy towels with up-to-date plumbing. The Blakes recommend that guests have a car of their own, making access to the island's attractions a lot easier. Breakfast, the only meal served, is a high point of the day, served with a sense of personalized hospitality.

3 Great Deals on Dining

Most guests eat at their hotels; however, St. Kitts has a scattering of good restaurants where you're likely to have spiny lobster, crab back, pepperpot, breadfruit, and curried conch. The drink of the island is CSR (Cane Spirit Rothschild), a pure sugarcane liqueur developed by baron Edmond de Rothschild. Islanders mix it with Ting, a bubbly grapefruit soda.

The Atlantic Club. At the Morgan Heights Condo resorts, Canada Estate. ☎ **869/465-8633.** Reservations recommended for dinner. Main courses EC$15–EC$45 ($5.60–$16.70). AE, MC, V. Mon–Sat 11am–11pm. SEAFOOD/WEST INDIAN.

A Nevisian, Genford Gumbs, who worked at the deluxe Golden Lemon for 15 years, struck out on his own and opened this enterprise in the early 1990s next to his Morgan Heights Condominiums (recommended above). On the east coast, a

5-minute drive from the center of Basseterre and a 3-minute drive from the airport, it overlooks the Atlantic Ocean. The cuisine is West Indian, with some seafood like fresh fish, conch, and lobster usually available. The atmosphere is relaxed and casual, and the portions are large. A lot of locals show up on Saturday for the special, goatwater stew and souse. Some foreigners had better skip this treat and order the burgers, soups, salads, sandwiches, or Black Angus steaks.

Chef's Place. Upper Church St., Basseterre. ☎ **869/465-6176.** Reservations recommended for dinner. Lunch or dinner EC$20–EC$25 ($7.40–$9.25). No credit cards. Mon–Sat 8am–11pm. CARIBBEAN.

This small air-conditioned place is in the heart of Basseterre's business district. You can dine on the balcony overlooking the street. The breakfasts that include eggs, bacon, and pancakes are hearty. One of the specialties is the local version of jerk chicken. Another recommended dish, generally served on Saturday (a St. Kitts tradition), is goatwater stew and souse. Steamed fish, based on their catch of the day, is your best bet, unless you want to drop in on Friday to sample the local beloved specialty: pigtails and snout.

Glimbara Diner. In the Glimbara Guest House, Cayon St., Basseterre. ☎ **869/465-1786.** Main courses EC$12–EC$18 ($4.45–$6.65). AE, MC, V. Daily 7am–11pm. CARIBBEAN.

Don't expect grand cuisine from this workaday eatery. Opened in 1998 in a simple family-run guest house in the heart of town, it promises to become a local favorite, thanks to the hardworking staff and down-to-earth cuisine. It serves Creole cuisine that varies with the mood and inspiration of the cook, plus American-style combination platters, including hamburgers and hot dogs, which are usually served with fries and soda. Examples are large or small portions of the stew-like goatwater, pumpkin or bean soup, several kinds of fried or grilled fish which might be accompanied by coleslaw or green salad. Ask for a local fruit punch known as fairling or the bottled sugary grapefruit drink called Ting.

J's Place. Romney Grounds. ☎ **869/465-6264.** Main courses EC$20–EC$45 ($7.40–$16.65); lunch from EC$15 ($5.55). No credit cards. Daily 11am–7pm. CARIBBEAN.

Some of the best local food—cooked without fuss but filled with flavor—is found at this spot near the Brimstone Hill fortress. Most visitors to the fort stop off here for a reasonably priced lunch of burgers, sandwiches, and salads, including the "famous" lobster salad. Though the restaurant closes at 7pm, many habitués stop off here for an early dinner. In the late afternoon the menu expands, offering such regional favorites as goat and conch "water" (actually a stew), mutton with rice and peas, fried or steamed kingfish, and grilled Caribbean lobster.

P.J.'s Pizza. Next to Island Paradise Condominiums, Frigate Bay. ☎ **869/465-8373.** Main courses EC$15–EC$50 ($5.60–$18.50). AE, MC, V. Daily 5:30–11pm (times vary off-season). PIZZA/ITALIAN.

On 5 acres a short walk from the beach, this open-air casual place has been described even by its good-natured owner (Julie Dolma) as "a cinder-block gas station without the gas pumps." At night, metal storm shutters complete the "industrial building" look, but many visitors appreciate the joint for its good pizza. The owners are especially proud of their thin-baked spicy crust. Their specialty is a Mexican pizza with lettuce, tomatoes, refried beans, and sour cream. Another specialty is called garbage pie, which may sound unappetizing but is the local favorite, with just about everything the kitchen can throw on it. They also serve Italian onion soup, spicy sausage soup, and an array of made-at-home pastas.

Turtle Beach Bar & Grill. Southeastern Peninsula. ☎ **869/469-9086.** Reservations recommended. Main courses $10–$24. AE, MC, V. Daily noon–5pm. Follow the Kennedy Simmonds Hwy. over Basseterre's Southeastern Peninsula; then follow the signs. SEAFOOD.

Directly on the sands above Turtle Beach, this airy sun-flooded restaurant is a super lunch stop. Many patrons spend the hour before their meal swimming or snorkeling beside the offshore reef; others simply relax beneath the verandas or shade trees (hammocks are available), perhaps with a drink in hand. Scuba diving, ocean kayaking, windsurfing, and volleyball are available, and a flotilla of rental sailboats moor nearby. The menu specialties are familiar stuff, but prepared with an often scrumptious flavor. Typical dishes are stuffed broiled lobster, conch fritters, barbecued swordfish steak, prawn salads, and barbecued honey-mustard spareribs.

WORTH A SPLURGE

Fisherman's Wharf Seafood Restaurant and Bar. Fortlands, Basseterre. ☎ **869/465-6623.** Main courses $12–$28. AE, DISC, MC, V. Daily 7–11pm. SEAFOOD/CARIBBEAN.

At the west end of Basseterre Bay Road, the Fisherman's Wharf is between the sea and the white picket fence of the Ocean Terrace Inn. Near the busy buffet grill, hard-working chefs prepare fresh seafood. An employee will take your drink order, but you personally place your food orders at the buffet grill. It's a bit like eating at picnic tables, but the fresh fish selection is excellent, caught locally and grilled to order over St. Kitts chosha coals. Spicy conch chowder is a good starter; grilled lobster is an elegant main course, but you may prefer the grilled catch of the day, often snapper. Grilled swordfish steak is always a pleaser, as is the combination platter, with lobster, barbecued shrimp kebab, and calypso chicken breast.

Stonewalls. Princes St. ☎ **869/465-5248.** Main courses EC$38–EC$60 ($14.05–$22.20). AE, MC, V. Mon–Sat 5–11pm. CARIBBEAN/INTERNATIONAL.

Surrounded by ancient stone walls, this open-air bar in a tropical garden in Basseterre's historical zone is cozy and casual. In a garden setting with banana, plantain, lime, and bamboo trees, and climbing bougainvillea and elephant ears, Wendy and Garry Speckles present an innovative and constantly changing menu. The fare might be Caribbean, with fresh kingfish or tuna and zesty gumbo, or an authentic spicy Dhansak-style curry. Hot-off-the-wok stir-fries are served along with sizzling Jamaican-style jerk chicken. Appetizers might include piquant conch fritters. A small but carefully chosen wine list is available. The bar here is one of the most convivial places on the island.

4 Hitting the Beaches

Beaches are the primary concern of most visitors. The narrow peninsula in the southeast that contains the island's salt ponds also boasts the best white-sand beaches. All beaches, even those bordering hotels, are open to the public. However, if you use the beach facilities of a hotel, you must obtain permission first and will probably have to pay a small fee.

For years, it was necessary to take a boat to enjoy the beautiful unspoiled beaches of the southeast peninsula. But in 1989, the Dr. Kennedy Simmonds Highway, a 6-mile road beginning in the Frigate Bay area, opened. To traverse this road is one of the pleasures of a visit to St. Kitts. Not only will you take in some of the island's most beautiful scenery, but you'll also pass lagoon-like coves and fields of tall guinea grass. If the day is clear (and it usually is), you'll have a panoramic vista of Nevis.

Cheap Thrills: What to See & Do for Free (Well, Almost) on St. Kitts

- **Explore a Nostalgic Town.** The capital of St. Kitts, Basseterre, may have a French name, but it's evocative of its long control by Britain. On a wide bay in the southwest of the island, it invites the stroller interested in seeing glimpses of its often fading Georgian and Victorian architecture. The best place to begin is Independence Square, a public park with flowering gardens in the historic center. The square is surrounded on three sides by Georgian buildings, often in need of paint. You can view St. George's Anglican Church on Cayon Street, with its crenellated tower. The Circus hardly evokes Piccadilly, but its centerpiece is the Berkeley Memorial Clock, the island's Big Ben, a cast-iron Victorian clock tower with four faces and a fountain at its base. The town is also filled with shops and some art galleries. Finally, you can head down to the pier where the ferry departs for Nevis. It's best to go here on a Saturday morning for market day—the splendid array of tropical fruits and vegetables invites your camera.

- **Tour a Beer Factory.** Devotees claim that Carib Beer is the finest in the West Indies, though Jamaicans with their Red Stripe dispute the claim. Nonetheless, one of the few beer factories in the Caribbean open to the public can be toured free on St. Kitts. On the outskirts of town, **Carib Breweries St. Kitts Ltd.** (☎ **869/465-2309**) offers free tours Monday to Friday 10am to 2pm. This brewery produces 750,000 cases annually of not only Carib Beer but SKOL, Guinness, Royal Extra Stout, Giant Malt, and Vita Malt. At the end of the tour, you're offered a complimentary tasting, the cold beer an ideal drink on a hot day in St. Kitts.

- **Tour a Sugar Factory.** Near the Carib Brewery (above), the St. Kitts Sugar Manufacturing Corp. provides an insight into how important sugarcane was

The best beaches along the peninsula are **Frigate Bay, Friar's Bay, Sand Bank Bay, White House Bay, Cockleshell Bay,** and **Banana Bay.** Of all these, Sand Bank Bay gets our nod as the finest strip of sand.

Both **Cockleshell Bay** and **Banana Bay** also have their devotees. These two beaches run a distance of 2 miles, all with powder-white sands. So far, in spite of several attempts, this area isn't filled with high-rise resorts. **White House Bay** tends to be rocky, but the snorkeling is excellent, as it opens onto reefs surrounding a sunken tugboat from long ago. Schools of rainbow-hued fish swim around this tugboat, a stunning sight.

Friar's Bay is lovely, though its pristine qualities may be forever disturbed by the construction of a new Hyatt. Friar's has powder-fine sand as well, and many locals consider it their favorite. **Frigate Bay,** with its powder-white sand, is ideal for swimming as well as windsurfing and waterskiing.

As a curiosity, you may want to visit **Great Salt Pond** at the southern end of St. Kitts. This is an inland beach of soft white sand, opening onto the Atlantic Ocean in the north and the more tranquil Caribbean Sea in the south.

The beaches in the north of St. Kitts are numerous but are of gray volcanic sand and much less frequented than those of the southeast peninsula. Many beachcombers like to frequent them, and they can be ideal for sunbathing, but swimming is much and is to the island economy. The ideal months to visit are February to July, when the cane is harvested and brought here to begin the sugar-making process whereby raw cane is turned into bulk sugar. A very light liqueur, CSR, is also produced at this factory, and it's enjoyed with a local grapefruit drink, Ting. *Warning:* This drink can be addictive. Free tours are available, but you should call for an appointment at ☎ **869/465-8157.**

- **Picnic at Dieppe Bay.** Either at your hotel or at a deli in Basseterre, get the makings of a picnic lunch and head for Dieppe Bay in the far north of St. Kitts. The island has better beaches than this, but none has the drama of the volcanic sand here. In the startling sunlight, the black sand sparkles with gold flecks. The protection of an offshore reef makes for tranquil waters, and a lovely coconut grove provides welcome shade and becomes the ideal spot for your lunch. The major reason to come here is to take in the coastline of the fabled "Black Rocks," particularly dramatic formations of huge lava boulders.

- **See the Brimstone Hill Fortress.** The sightseeing highlight of the island, Brimstone Hill is named for the fume of sulfur that lingers around it and its fort 800 feet above the sea. From its peak you can enjoy a panoramic view of six Caribbean islands: volcanic Montserrat, Saba, Statia, St. Maarten, St. Barts, and St. Kitts's sibling island of Nevis. It took more than a century to erect this fort with its massive stone walls, which at some point are 12 feet thick. You can pack a picnic to spread out on a grassy hilltop after your tour of the 38-acre fortress. After a 1985 visit by Queen Elizabeth, the fort was officially designated a national park. From here, nature trails wind through an enveloping hardwood forest and savannah where the green vervet monkey might be spotted skittering about.

better in the southeast, as waters in the north, sweeping in from the Atlantic, can often be turbulent.

The best beach on the Atlantic side is **Conaree Bay,** with a narrow strip of gray-black sand. Bodysurfing is popular here. **Dieppe Bay,** also a black-sand beach on the north coast, is good for snorkeling and windsurfing but not for swimming. This is the site of the island's most famous inn, the Golden Lemon, which you might want to visit for lunch. *Warning:* If you should be on this beach during a tropical shower, do not seek shelter under the dreaded manicheel trees, which are poisonous. Rain falling off the leaves will feel like acid on your skin.

5 Sports & Outdoor Pursuits

BOATING   Most outfitters are found at Frigate Bay on the southeast peninsula. The best one to go to is provocatively named **Mr. X Watersports,** Frigate Bay (☎ **869/465-0673**). Here you can rent kayaks or arrange windsurfing for $15 an hour. You can also rent a Sunfish at $20 per hour or hook up with a snorkeling tour lasting 2 hours and costing $25 per person.

DIVING, SNORKELING & OTHER WATER SPORTS   Among the best diving spots is **Nagshead,** at the south tip of St. Kitts. This is an excellent shallow-water dive starting at 10 feet and extending to 70 feet. A variety of tropical fish, eaglerays, and lobster are found here. The site is ideal for certified divers. Another good spot is **Booby Shoals,** lying between Cow 'n' Calf Rocks and Booby Island, off the coast of St. Kitts. Booby Shoals has abundant sea life, including nurse sharks, lobster, and stingrays. Dives are up to 30 feet in depth, ideal for both certified and resort divers.

A variety of activities is offered by **Pro-Divers,** at Turtle Beach (☎ **869/465-3223** or 869/469-9086). You can swim, float, paddle, or go on scuba-diving and snorkeling expeditions from there. A two-tank dive costs $50 with your own equipment or $60 without equipment. Night dives are $50. A PADI certification is available for $300, and a resort course costs $75. Snorkeling trips lasting 3 hours are offered for $35 per person, and day trips to Nevis are $25 per person.

GOLF The ✪ **Royal St. Kitts Golf Course,** Frigate Bay (☎ **869/465-8339**), is an 18-hole championship golf course covering 160 acres. It's bound on the south by the Caribbean Sea and on the north by the Atlantic Ocean, featuring 10 water hazards. The course rating is 72 and can be 5,349, 6,033, 6,476, or 6,918 yards long, depending on which tees are being used. It's open daily from 7am to 7pm, charging $40 for greens fees for 18 holes. Cart rentals cost $50 for 18 holes, plus another $15 for clubs. A bar and restaurant opens daily at 7am.

HIKING Kris Tours at ☎ **869/465-4042** takes small groups into the crater of Mount Liamuiga. You are also led on hiking tours through a rain forest to enjoy the lushness of the island. If a group wants to, this outfitter will also conduct tours to Verchild's Mountain, which isn't a difficult trek. The cost of tours are $50 per person for a half day.

HORSEBACK RIDING The best stables are **Trinity Stable** at ☎ **869/465-3226.** They charge $35 for a half-day tour through a rain forest. You might also get to see the wild lushness of the North Frigate Bay area and the rather desolate Conaree Beach. You must call for a reservation and you'll be told where to meet and offered any advice, include what to wear.

6 Seeing the Sights

The British colonial town of **Basseterre** is built around a so-called **Circus,** the town's round square. A tall green Victorian clock stands in the center. After Brimstone Hill Fortress, this **Berkeley Memorial Clock** is the most photographed landmark of St. Kitts. In the old days, wealthy plantation owners and their families used to promenade here.

At some point, try to visit the **marketplace.** Here, country people bring baskets brimming with mangos, guavas, soursop, mammy apples, and wild strawberries and cherries just picked in the fields, and tropical flowers abound. Another major landmark is **Independence Square.** Once an active slave market, it's surrounded by private homes of Georgian architecture.

You can negotiate with a taxi driver to take you on a tour of the island for about $60 for a 3-hour trip, and most drivers are well versed in the lore of the island. Lunch can be arranged at the **Rawlins Plantation Inn** or the **Golden Lemon.** For more information, call the **St. Kitts Taxi Association,** The Circus, Basseterre (☎ **869/465-8487** during the day or 869/465-7818 at night).

The ✪ **Brimstone Hill Fortress** (☎ **869/465-6211**), 9 miles west of Basseterre, is the major stop on any tour of St. Kitts. This historic monument, among the Caribbean's largest and best preserved, is a complex of bastions, barracks, and other structures ingeniously adapted to the top and upper slopes of a steep-sided 800-foot

Into the Volcano

Mount Liamuiga was dubbed "Mount Misery" long ago, but it sputtered its last gasp around 1692. This dormant volcano on the northeast coast is one of the major highlights for hikers on St. Kitts today. The peak of the mountain often lies under a cloud cover.

The ascent to the volcano is usually made from the north end of St. Kitts at Belmont Estate. The trail winds through a rain forest and travels along deep ravines up to the rim of the crater at 2,625 feet. The actual peak is at 3,792 feet. Figure on 5 hours of rigorous hiking to complete the round-trip walk, with 10 hours required from hotel pickup to return.

The caldera itself has a depth of some 400 feet from its rim to the crater floor. Many hikers climb or crawl down into the dormant volcano. However, the trail is steep and slippery, so be careful. At the crater floor is a tiny lake along with volcanic rocks and various vegetation.

Greg's Safaris, P.O. Box Basseterre (☎ **869/465-4121**), offers guided hikes to the crater for $60 per person (a minimum of six participants needed), including breakfast and a picnic at the crater's rim. The same outfit also offers half-day rain-forest explorations for $35 per person.

hill. The fortress dates from 1690, when the British attempted to recapture Fort Charles from the French. In 1782, an invading force of 8,000 French troops bombarded it for a month before its small garrison, supplemented by local militia, surrendered. The fortress was returned to the British the following year, and they embarked on an intense program of building and reconstruction that resulted in the imposing military complex that came to be known as the "Gibraltar of the West Indies."

Today the fortress is the centerpiece of a national park of nature trails and a diverse range of plant and animal life, including the **green vervet monkey.** It's also a photographer's paradise, with views of mountains, fields, and the Caribbean Sea. On a clear day, you can see six neighboring islands. Visitors will enjoy self-guided tours among the many ruined or restored structures, including the barrack rooms at Fort George, which comprise an interesting museum. The gift shop stocks prints of rare maps and paintings of the Caribbean. Admission is $5, half price for children. The Brimstone Hill Fortress National Park is open daily 9:30am to 5:30pm.

In the old days, a large tamarind tree in the hamlet of **Half-Way Tree** marked the boundary between the British-held sector and the French half, and you can visit the site.

It was near the hamlet of **Old Road Town** that Sir Thomas Warner landed with the first band of settlers and established the first permanent colony to the northwest at Sandy Point. Sir Thomas's grave is in the cemetery of St. Thomas Church. A sign in the middle of Old Road Town points the way to **Carib Rock Drawings,** all the evidence that remains of the former inhabitants. The markings are on black boulders, and the pictographs date from prehistoric days.

Most visitors to St. Kitts or Nevis like to spend at least one day on the neighboring island. **LIAT** provides twice daily flights to and from Nevis. Make reservations at the LIAT office on Front Street in Basseterre (☎ **869/465-8613**) instead of at the airport. If you'd rather not fly, the government passenger ferry **M.V. _Caribe Queen_** departs from each island between 7 and 7:30am on Monday, Tuesday, Wednesday, Friday, and

Saturday, returning at 4 and 6pm (check the time at your hotel or the tourist office). The cost is $4 each way.

7 Shopping

The good buys here are in local handcrafts, including leather items made from goatskin, baskets, and coconut shells. Some good values are also to be found in clothing and fabrics, especially Sea Island cottons. Store hours vary, but are likely to be 8am to noon and 1 to 4pm Monday to Saturday.

If your time on the island is limited, head first for the **Pelican Shopping Mall,** containing some two dozen shops, banking services, a restaurant, and a philatelic bureau. Some major retail outlets in the Caribbean, including Little Switzerland, have branches at this mall. But don't confine all your shopping here. Check out the offerings along the quaintly named **Liverpool Row,** which has some unusual merchandise. **Fort Street** is also worth traversing.

Ashbury's, The Circus/Liverpool Row, Basseterre (☎ 869/465-8175), is a local branch of a chain of luxury-goods stores based on St. Maarten. This well-respected emporium sells discounted luxury goods including fragrances, fine porcelain, crystal by Baccarat, handbags by Fendi, watches, and jewelry. Prices are 25% to 30% below what you might pay in retail stores in North America, though the selection is similar to dozens of equivalent stores throughout the Caribbean.

Cameron Gallery, 10 N. Independence Sq., Basseterre (☎ 869/465-1617), is the island's leading gallery. Britisher Rosey Cameron-Smith displays her watercolors and limited-edition prints of scenes from St. Kitts and Nevis. In her work, she makes an effort to capture the essence of true West Indian life. Rosey is well known on the island for her paintings of Kittitian Carnival clowns, and she also produces greeting cards, postcards, and calendars, and displays the works of some 10 to 15 other artists.

Island Hopper, The Circus, Basseterre (☎ 869/465-1640), lies below the popular Ballahoo Restaurant. Island Hopper is one of St. Kitts's most patronized shops, with goods ranging from fashion to handcrafts. There's a lot of merchandise, both West Indian and international, on two floors. Notice the all-silk shift-style dresses from China, the array of batiks made on St. Kitts, and outfits suited for everything from formal to casual sportswear. Some 50% of the merchandise sold is from the islands, most of it from St. Kitts itself.

Kate Design, Mount Pleasant (☎ 869/465-7740), is set in an impeccably restored West Indian house, on a hillside below the Rawlins Plantation. This is the finest art gallery on St. Kitts. Virtually all the paintings are by English-born Kate Spencer, whose work is well known throughout North America and Europe. Her still-lifes, portraits, and paintings of island scenes range from $200 to $3,000 and have received critical acclaim. Also for sale are a series of Ms. Spencer's silk-screened scarves, each crafted from extra-heavy stone-washed silk.

The Linen and Gold Shop, in the Pelican Mall, Bay Road, Basseterre (☎ 869/465-9766), offers a limited selection of gold and silver jewelry, usually in bold modern designs. But the real appeal of this shop are the tablecloths and linens. Laboriously handcrafted in China from cotton and linen, they include everything from doilies to napkins to oversized tablecloths. The workmanship is as intricate as anything you'll find in the Caribbean. **The Palms,** in the Palms Arcade, Basseterre (☎ 869/465-2599), specializes in island "things," including handcrafts; larimar, sea opal, pottery, and amber jewelry; West Indies spices, teas, and perfumes; tropical clothes by Canadian designer John Warden; and Bali batiks by Kisha.

✪ **Romney Manor,** Old Road, 10 miles west of Basseterre (☎ **869/465-6253**), is the most unusual factory on St. Kitts. It was built around 1625 as a manor house for sugar baron Lord Romney, during the era when St. Kitts was the premier stronghold of British military might in the Caribbean. For years, it has been used as the head-quarters and manufacturing center for a local clothier, Caribelle Batik, whose tropical cottons sell widely to cruise-ship passengers and holiday-makers from at least three outlets in the eastern Caribbean. The range of merchandise consists of small items like scarves and separates, going on to caftans and dresses along with an extensive collection of wall hangings. In 1995, a tragic fire and hurricane completely gutted the building. The manor has now been rebuilt and extended. Consider a stop here if only to admire the 5 acres of lavish gardens, where 30 varieties of hibiscus, rare orchids, huge ferns, and a 250-year-old saman tree still draw horticultural enthusiasts. Entrance to the gardens is free.

8 St. Kitts After Dark

The **Ocean Terrace Inn's (O.T.I.) Fisherman's Wharf,** Fortlands, has a live band every Friday 8 to 10pm and a DJ from 10pm. The **Turtle Beach Bar and Grill,** Turtle Bay on the southeast peninsula, has a popular seafood buffet on Sunday with a live steel band 12:30 to 3pm; on Saturday it's beach disco time. There's no cover charge at the inn's Fisherman's Wharf or Turtle Beach Bar and Grill.

If you're in the mood to gamble, St. Kitts's only casino is at the **Jack Tar Village,** Frigate Bay (☎ **869/465-8651**). It's open to all visitors, who can try their luck at roulette, blackjack, poker, craps, and slot machines. The casino is open daily 10:30am to 2am. There's no cover charge.

A few other night spots come and go (mostly go). Currently, **Henry's Night Spot,** Dunn's Cottage, Lower Cayon Street, in Basseterre (☎ **869/465-3508**), is one of the island's most frequented dance clubs. **Bayembi Cultural Entertainment Bar & Café,** just off the Circus in Basseterre (☎ **869/466-5280**), couldn't look junkier, but it's a hot and happening place with a jazz guitarist on Wednesday and the inevitable karaoke on Saturday. Its daily happy hours pack everyone in at sunset. On Friday and Saturday, locals often head for **J's Place,** Romney Grounds across from Brimstone Hill (☎ **869/465-6264**). The place is often jumping until the early hours. Another fun joint is **Doo-Wop Days,** Memory Lane, Frigate Bay (☎ **869/465-1960**), painted in sherbet colors. The place looks like a junkyard, with its old 1940s photographs of such singers as Frank Sinatra or Chuck Berry. For a tasteful note, there are velvet Elvis paintings and pillows in the shape of guitars. Many nights there's live music, especially from doo-wop groups of yesterday like Ronn and the Rascals. Saturday is karaoke night.

21

St. Lucia

In recent years, St. Lucia (pronounced *Loo*-sha)—second largest of the Windward Islands—has become one of the most popular destinations in the Caribbean, with some of its finest resorts. The heaviest tourist development is concentrated in the northwest, between the capital of Castries and the northern end of the island. Here you'll find the string of white-sand beaches that put St. Lucia on world tourist maps.

The rest of the island remains relatively unspoiled, a checkerboard of green-mantled mountains, gentle valleys, banana plantations, a bubbling volcano, giant tree ferns, wild orchids, and fishing villages. There's a hint of the South Pacific about it, and a mixed French and British heritage.

In the 1990s, many luxurious and expensive all-inclusive resorts have been developed. Alas, there aren't that many inexpensive or even moderately priced properties, so you're going to have to search for bargains. Finding low-cost dining is also difficult. If you'd really like to see St. Lucia, contemplate an off-season visit when many hotels slash their prices by 40%.

St. Lucia lies some 20 miles from Martinique. This mountainous island of some 240 square miles has about 120,000 inhabitants. The capital, Castries, is built on the southern shore of a large, almost landlocked harbor surrounded by hills. The approach to the airport is very impressive.

1 Essentials

VISITOR INFORMATION

In the **United States,** the tourist information office is at 820 Second Ave., New York, NY 10017 (☎ **800/456-3984** or 212/867-2950). In the **United Kingdom,** information can be obtained at 421A Finchley Rd., London NW3 6HJ (☎ **020/7431-3675**).

On the island, the **St. Lucia Tourist Board** is located at Point Seraphine, Castries Harbour (☎ **758/452-4094**). In Soufrière the tourist office is on Bay Street (☎ **758/459-7200**).

The Internet address for St. Lucia is **www.st-lucia.com**.

GETTING THERE

Before you book your own airfare, read the section on package tours in chapter 2—it can save you a bundle!

The island maintains two separate airports whose locations cause endless confusion to most newcomers. Most international

Cape Moule-à-Chique ⑥
Diamond Mineral Baths/Botanical Gardens ③
Frigate Islands Nature Reserve ⑨
Gros Piton ⑤
Maria Islands Nature Reserve ⑦
Morne Fortune ②
Petit Piton ④
Pigeon Island National Historic Park ①
St. Lucia Rain Forest Reserve ⑧

Cariblue Beach
Pointe du Cap
Cap Estate
Pigeon Point. ①
Gros Islet
Anse Lavouette
Rodney Bay
Reduit Beach
Saint Lucia Channel
Choc Bay
Vigie Beach
Vigie Airport
La Toc Beach
Castries
Grande Anse Bay
Grand Anse
La Sorcière
Graand Cul de Sac Bay
②
Atlantic Ocean
Marigot Bay
Fort Charlotte
Roseau Bay
Roseau River
La Caye
L'Anse la Raye
Point la Ville
Fond d'or Bay
Dennery
Canaries
Canaries River
Anse Couchon
Anse Chastanet
Soufrière
③
La Soufrière
⑧
⑨
Fond River
Petit Piton
④
Anse des Pitons
Fond St. Jacques
Micoud
⑤
Gros Piton
Desruisseaux
Choiseul
Hewanorra International Airport
Savannes Bay
Maria Islands
⑦
Vieux Fort
Vieux Fort
⑥
Anse des Sables

0 5 Miles
0 5 Kilometers

Airport ✈ Beach 🏖 Mountain ▲▲▲

long-distance flights land at **Hewanorra International Airport** (☎ 758/454-6249) in the south, 45 miles from Castries. If you fly in here and you're booked into a hotel in the north, you'll have to spend about an hour and a half going along the potholed East Coast Highway. The average taxi ride costs $50 for up to four passengers. Flights from other parts of the Caribbean usually land at the somewhat antiquated **Vigie Field** (☎ 758/452-2596), in the island's northeast, whose location just outside Castries affords much more convenient access to the capital and most of the island's hotels.

You'll probably have to change planes somewhere else in the Caribbean to get to St. Lucia. **American Eagle** (☎ 800/433-7300 or 758/452-1820) serves both of the island's airports with nonstop flights from the airline's hub in San Juan. Connections from all parts of the North American mainland to the airline's enormous hub in San Juan are frequent and convenient. American also offers some good package deals.

Air Canada (☎ 800/268-7240 in Canada, 800/776-3000 in the U.S., or 758/454-6038) has a nonstop flight to St. Lucia that departs year-round on Saturday from Toronto. **LIAT** (☎ 800/468-0482 in the U.S. and Canada, or 758/452-3015) has small planes flying from many points throughout the Caribbean into Vigie Airport, near Castries. Points of origin include islands like Barbados, Antigua, St. Thomas, St. Maarten, and Martinique. Know in advance that LIAT flights tend to island-hop en route to St. Lucia.

Air Jamaica (☎ 800/523-5585 or 758/454-8869) serves the Hewanorra airport in St. Lucia with nonstop service from either JFK or Newark daily, except Wednesday and Friday. Another option is **BWIA** (☎ 800/292-1183 for North American reservations, or 758/452-3778), which has two flights weekly from JFK on Thursday and Sunday nonstop to Hewanorra, two weekly flights from Miami on Monday and Thursday, and two weekly flights from London's Gatwick Airport to Hewanorra on Tuesday and Sunday.

British Airways (☎ 800/247-9297 in the U.S., or 0345/222-111 in England) offers three flights a week from London's Gatwick Airport to St. Lucia's Hewanorra airport. All these touch down briefly on Antigua before continuing to St. Lucia.

GETTING AROUND

BY TAXI Taxis are ubiquitous on the island, and most drivers are eager to please. The drivers have to be quite experienced to cope with the narrow, hilly, switchback roads outside the capital. Special programs have trained them to serve as guides. Their cars are unmetered, but tariffs for all standard trips are fixed by the government. Always determine if the driver is quoting a rate in U.S. dollars or Eastern Caribbean dollars (EC$).

Most tours of the island cost $120 divided among four people. Some companies specialize in these tours, which can also be cut to a half day if that's your wish. Try **Barnard's Travel,** Micoud Street in Castries (☎ 758/452-2214), as well as **Explorer Adventure,** Micoud Street, in Castries (☎ 758/450-8356). You can call the latter about arranging a jeep safari for your party, or perhaps a trip to the rain forest followed by a barbecue lunch on the beach with some snorkeling and swimming.

BY RENTAL CAR First, *remember to drive on the left* and try to avoid some of the island's more obvious potholes. You'll need a St. Lucia driver's license, which can easily be purchased at either airport when you arrive or at the car-rental kiosks when you pick up your car. Present a valid driver's license from home to the counter attendant or government official and pay a fee of $12.

All three of the big U.S.-based rental companies maintain offices on St. Lucia: **Budget** (☎ 800/527-0700 or 758/452-0233), **Avis** (☎ 800/331-1212 or 758/452-2700), and **Hertz** (☎ 800/654-3001 or 758/452-0679). All three companies maintain offices at (or will deliver cars to) both of the island's airports. Each also has an office in Castries and, in some cases, at some of the island's major hotels.

You can sometimes get lower rates by booking through one of the local rental agencies where rates begin at $55 per day. Try **C.T.L. Rent-a-Car,** Grosislet Highway, Rodney Bay Marina (☎ 758/452-0732), which rents Suzuki Muritis or Suzuki Samurais. In addition, **Cool Breeze Car Rental,** New Development, Soufrière (☎ 758/454-7729), is also a good bet if you're staying in the south.

Drive carefully and honk your horn while going around the island's blind hairpin turns.

BY LOCAL BUS Minibuses (with names like "Lucian Love") and jitneys connect Castries with main towns like Soufrière and Vieux Fort. They're generally overcrowded and often filled with produce on the way to market. At least they're cheap, unlike taxis. Buses for Cap Estate, in the northern part of the island, leave from Jeremy Street in Castries, near the market. Buses going to Vieux Fort and Soufrière depart from Bridge Street in front of the department store.

Fast Facts: St. Lucia

Banking Hours Banks are open Monday to Thursday 8am to 1pm and Friday 8am to noon and 3 to 5pm.

Currency   The official monetary unit is the **Eastern Caribbean dollar (EC$).** It's about 37¢ in U.S. currency. Most of the prices quoted in this section will be in American dollars, as they're accepted by nearly all hotels, restaurants, and shops.

Customs   At either airport, Customs may be a hassle if there's the slightest suspicion, regardless of how ill-founded, you're carrying illegal drugs.

Documents   U.S., British, and Canadian citizens need a valid passport, plus an ongoing or return ticket.

Drugstore   The best is **William Pharmacy,** Williams Building, Bridge Street, in Castries (☎ **758/452-2797**), open Monday to Thursday 8am to 4:30am, Friday 8am to 5:30pm, and Saturday 8am to 1pm.

Electricity   Visitors from the U.S. will need to bring an adapter and transformer, as St. Lucia runs on 220–230 volts AC (50 cycles).

Emergency   Call the police at ☎ **999.**

Hospitals   There are 24-hour emergency rooms at **St. Jude's Hospital,** Vieux Fort (☎ **758/454-7671**), and **Victoria Hospital,** Hospital Road, Castries (☎ **758/452-2421**).

Language   Although English is the official tongue, St. Lucians probably don't speak it the way you do. Islanders also speak a French-Creole patois, similar to that heard on Martinique.

Safety   St. Lucia has its share of crime, like every place else these days. Use common sense and protect yourself and your valuables. If you've got it, don't flaunt it! Don't pick up hitchhikers if you're driving around the island. Of course, the use of narcotic drugs is illegal, and their possession or sale could lead to stiff fines or jail.

Taxes   The government imposes an 8% occupancy tax on hotel-room rentals, and there's an $11 departure tax for both airports.

Telephone   On the island, dial all seven digits of the local number. Faxes may be handed in at hotel desks or at the offices of **Cable & Wireless** in the NAS Building on the waterfront in Castries (☎ **758/452-3301**).

Time   St. Lucia is on Atlantic standard time year-round, placing it 1 hour ahead of New York or Miami. However, when the United States is on daylight saving time, St. Lucia matches the clocks of the U.S. east coast.

Tipping   Most hotels and restaurants simply add a 10% service charge.

Weather   This little island, lying in the path of the trade winds, has year-round temperatures of 70°F to 90°F.

2 Accommodations You Can Afford

Most of the leading hotels on this island are pretty pricey—you really have to look for the bargains. Once you reach your hotel, chances are you'll feel pretty isolated, but that's what many guests want. Many St. Lucian hostelries have kitchenettes where you can prepare simple meals. Prices are usually quoted in U.S. dollars. Don't forget the 8% hotel tax and the 10% service charge added to your bill.

Auberge Seraphine. Vigie Cove (Box 390), Castries. ☎ **758/453-2073.** Fax 758/451-7001. 22 units. A/C TV TEL. Year-round $70–$80 single; $85–$95 double; $115 for double occupancy of suite. AE, MC, V.

This two-story concrete-sided building painted cerulean blue and white is a 15-minute walk from Vigie Beach, overlooking the marina and the harbor of Castries. Owned/operated by the St. Lucia–born Joseph family, whose hotel skills derived from a long sojourn in England, the hotel offers well-maintained but very simple accommodations. They're generally spacious and decorated with bright colors, often tropical prints. The baths, though small, are clean and have a rack of medium-size towels. Most activities surround an open terrace whose surface is sheathed with terra-cotta tiles and which rings a small round-sided pool. Don't expect too many amenities, as the place's charm derives partly from its simplicity.

Bay Gardens. Rodney Bay (P.O. Box 1892), Castries, St. Lucia, W.I. ☎ **758/452-8060.** Fax 758/452-8059. 53 units. A/C TV TEL. Winter $95 single; $110 double; $120 suite. Off-season $75–$89 single; $94 double; $106 suite. Extra person $20; one child 11 and under stays free when sharing with 2 adults. AE, MC, V.

One of the newest small hotels, this choice lies on Rodney Bay 7 miles north of Castries, near Reduit Beach. The standard rooms are well furnished, with king-size or twin beds with good mattresses; they come with many extras, like electric kettles for making tea or coffee, mini-fridges, radios, and balconies or terraces. The most expensive doubles have Jacuzzis and showers, and the junior suites are the most elegant, with sitting areas and kitchenettes. The baths are small and rather routine, with shower stalls, but they're kept tidy. There are two pools and a heated Jacuzzi. For such a small hotel, the Bay Gardens has a good restaurant, offering continental and French dishes but with a dash of local herbs and spices. In fact, the restaurant is named Spices. Try the callaloo soup. The chef even caters to special diets, such as vegetarian. Live music is presented for dancing Wednesday to Saturday evenings. A Caribbean buffet is offered on Wednesday night.

✪ **Candyo Inn.** Rodney Bay (P.O. Box 386), Castries. ☎ **758/452-0712.** Fax 758/452-0774. 12 units. A/C TV TEL. Mid-Dec to mid-Apr $75 single or double; $90 suite. Mid-Apr to mid-Dec $60 double; $75 suite. AE, MC, V.

Amid the congestion of the fast-food restaurants and all-inclusive hotels flanking the edges of Rodney Bay, this is a two-story pink concrete hotel with a hardworking staff. There's a small pool and a simple bar on the premises, but most of the allure derives from the low rates, simple but comfortable rooms, and a location a 5-minute walk from the beach. The only meal served in the restaurant is breakfast, with an occasional light snack on special request. Each medium-size room contains white-painted furniture with flowered upholstery, a white-tile floor, a small private balcony, and a cramped bath. The best deal are the suites, as they boast sitting areas, baths with showers and tubs, and kitchenettes. The name of the hotel derives from an amalgam of the names of each of the owner's daughters, Candice and Yola.

Green Parrot. Red Tape Lane, Morne Fortune, St. Lucia, W.I. ☎ **758/452-3399.** Fax 758/453-2272. 60 units. A/C TEL. Winter $27.50–$64.80 single; $84.40–$90.90 double; $103.80–$110.30 triple. Off-season $25–59 single; $76.70–$82.60 double; $94.40–$110.30 triple. AE, MC, V.

About 1½ miles east of Castries, this inn operates the most famous restaurant on St. Lucia. But savvy bargain hunters have known for years it also offers some of the least expensive lodgings on the island. Built of stone and stucco, the complex overlooks Castries Harbour, and the small rooms are housed in units built up the hillside. The furnishings are more functional than stylish, but everything is clean and comfortable, with good mattresses. The small baths evoke an economy motel in the U.S. Try for a spacious room with a patio or, better yet, a balcony opening onto one of the most famous harbor views in the West Indies. The inn's shuttle takes guests on the 15-minute run between Castries and Vigie Beach. There's also a pool.

Kimatrai. Vieux Fort (P.O. Box 238), Castries, St. Lucia, W.I. ☎ **758/454-6328.** 17 units. A/C TV. Year-round $35 single; $45 double; $250 2-week rental of 1-bedroom apt. for 2; $280 2-week rental of 2-bedroom apt. for 4; $350–$400 2-week rental of 2- or 3-bedroom bungalow for 4 to 6. DISC, MC, V.

On the island's relatively undeveloped southeastern coast, just north of Vieux Fort, this hotel is about a quarter-mile from a beach whose surf is usually rougher than that of beaches on more sheltered regions of the island. But unless you'd planned to spend hours paddling in saltwater, that might not affect your appreciation of this otherwise very acceptable hotel too closely. The small rooms are outfitted with pastels and simple accessories, though the apartments and bungalows contain kitchenettes. Mattresses are a bit used but still comfortable, and the baths are routine. The staff is helpful. A plain restaurant serves Creole food at very reasonable prices. A car would make your stay here more appealing, especially because of its relative isolation.

Orange Grove Hotel. Grosislet Hwy. (P.O. Box GM 702), Castries, St. Lucia, W.I. ☎ **758/452-9040.** Fax 758/452-8094. 62 units. A/C TV. Year-round $50 single; $70 double; $83 suite. Children 11 and under stay free in parents' room. AE, MC, V.

This hilltop retreat, off the road leading to the super-expensive Windjammer Landing, has been recently renovated and improved, making it one of the island's most appealing choices. Formerly known as Bois d'Orange, it offers comfort and convenience—all at a good price. The beach is just 15 minutes away by car, and there's a shuttle bus daily. The suites are spacious and well furnished, though even the standard rooms are well appointed, with West Indian rattan furnishings and tropical prints to enliven the scene. The accommodations also have separate living and sitting areas, along with patios or balconies overlooking the view. The rooms have a king-size bed or two twin beds, each with a good mattress. There's a pool and a simple restaurant serving both Creole and international cuisine, and room service is available until 10pm.

Seaview Apartel. John Compton Hwy. (P.O. Box 527), Castries, St. Lucia, W.I. ☎ **758/452-4359.** Fax 758/451-6690. 3 units, 6 one-bedroom apts. with kitchenette. A/C TV TEL. Year-round $53 single or double; $59 apt. for 1 or 2. AE, MC, V.

Part of the reason the rates at this two-story motel-like place are so low is its position adjacent to Vigie Field. Though noises from the airport are sometimes bothersome during the day (but not during the night, when air traffic is reduced), noises from the coastal road nearby might present a problem for light sleepers. Otherwise, you might like the relative spaciousness of these units, and if you're interested in cooking, you'll appreciate the kitchenettes in the apartments. (Grocery stores, banks, laundries, shops, and a supermarket are a short walk away.) The small accommodations have off-white walls, rattan furniture, balconies, wall-to-wall carpeting that's moderately frayed, and easy access to the sea, just across the road. (Vigie Beach, a worthy place for swimming, is within a 10-minute walk.) The rooms have recently been renovated, but the new mattresses are still a bit thin, and the baths are as small as ever. The simple Seaview Restaurant serves Creole and Caribbean cuisine.

The Still Plantation & Beach Resort. P.O. Box 246, Soufrière, St. Lucia, W.I. ☎ **800/223-9815** in the U.S., or 758/459-7224. Fax 758/459-7301. 19 units. Year-round $50–60 single or double without kitchen; $60–$80 single or double with kitchen; $110 2-bedroom apt. for 5 (with kitchen). AE, MC, V.

The Still, a restaurant, has long been one of the most popular in the area, but in 1995, the owners opened a small inn right on the beach. Less than a mile east of Soufrière, it's on the grounds of a plantation growing citrus, cocoa, and copra. A freshwater pool landscaped into the lush tropical scene adds to the allure, and walks are possible in almost all directions. The cheapest rentals—four studio apartments—have no kitchens, but the others do. The most expensive one-bedroom units open onto a beach, and the site itself opens onto views of the towering Pitons nearby. Furnishings are of the standard motel variety with no special styling. The baths are tidily maintained, but a bit small, without enough shelf space.

WORTH A SPLURGE

✪ **Harmony Marina Suites.** Rodney Bay Lagoon (P.O. Box 155), Castries, St. Lucia, W.I. ☎ **758/452-0336.** Fax 758/452-8677. E-mail: harmony@candw.lc. 30 units. A/C TV TEL. Winter $127–$169 single or double. Off-season $105–$148 single or double. Extra person $20. AE, MC, V.

Between 1992 and 1993, this set of two-story buildings, a short walk from one of the island's finest beaches at Reduit, was renovated and upgraded and now offers well-maintained accommodations at reasonable rates. Eight of the suites contain kitchenettes, ideal for families on a budget, and come complete with coffeemakers, refrigerators, and a wet bar. The suites sit adjacent to a saltwater lagoon where boats find refuge from the rough waters of the open sea. Each of the units offers a patio or balcony with views of moored yachts, the lagoon, and surrounding hills. The suites are decorated in rattan, wicker, and florals. All suites, except the VIP/honeymoon units (eight of these), have sofa sleepers folding out to make a double bed in the living room. Each VIP suite features a double Jacuzzi, a four-poster queen-size bed on a pedestal, a sundeck, a bidet, and white rattan furnishings. Mattresses are frequently renewed here. The baths are small, of the routine motel variety.

3 Great Deals on Dining

As virtually every hotel on St. Lucia seems to be going all-inclusive, the independent restaurants have had to sail through rough waters. But there are quite a few, nevertheless, of varying quality. Most restaurants are open for lunch and dinner, unless otherwise noted. The big problem about dining out at night, as it is on nearly all Caribbean islands, is getting to that special hideaway and back again with adequate transportation across the dark potholed roads.

Bread Basket. Rodney Bay. ☎ **758/452-0647.** Breads and pastries EC$3–EC$6.50 ($1.10–$2.40); sandwiches EC$5.75–EC$12 ($2.15–$4.45); main courses EC$25–EC$65 ($9.25–$24.05). No credit cards. Mon–Sat 7am–5pm and 6–11pm, Sun 7am–noon. CONTINENTAL.

This small bakery offers homemade breads, pastries, and a wide selection of sandwiches. Overlooking the marina, it features alfresco dining on the deck where patrons can view million-dollar yachts and Pigeon Island. The forte here are the baked goods, from croissants to pies and cakes. This eatery serves full American breakfasts and light lunches with a few heartier specials, like stuffed crab backs and fish-and-chips. The sandwiches include roast beef, chicken, and tuna salad served on freshly baked bread. To finish your meal, try the baked cheesecake—the best on the island. Lately the Bread Basket has started serving dinner, mostly perfectly cooked steaks and succulent pastas.

Camilla's. 7 Bridge St., Soufrière, St. Lucia, W.I. ☎ **758/459-5379.** Main courses $10–$33. AE, MC, V. Mon–Sat 8am–11pm. WEST INDIAN.

A block inland from the waterfront and one floor above street level, this Caribbean-style restaurant serves unpretentious food. It's operated by a local matriarch, Camilla

Alcindor, who'll welcome you for coffee, a soda, or Perrier, or for full-fledged dinners that include Caribbean fish Creole, lobster Thermidor, and prime loin of beef with garlic sauce. The food is straightforward but with good flavor. Opt for the fish and shellfish instead of the beef, though the chicken curry is a savory choice. Lunches are considerably less elaborate and include an array of sandwiches, cold salads, omelets, and burgers. Our favorite tables are the pair that sit on a balcony overlooking the energetic activities in the street below. Otherwise, the inside tables can get a bit steamy on a hot night, as there's no air-conditioning.

Chak Chak Bolomé. Beanfield, Vieux Fort. ☎ **758/454-6260.** Main courses EC$18.50–EC$75 ($6.85–$27.75). AE, DISC, MC, V. Daily 9am–midnight. CARIBBEAN.

This simple restaurant, near the Hewanorra Airport, offers a savory West Indian cuisine. Don't expect to be pampered here. The meals are basic, with most of the main courses served with rice, vegetables, and salad. The menu features an assortment of curried stews and Creole-style fish. You can find sirloin steaks, pork and lamb chops, and baked chicken as well. For a quick bite, the restaurant also serves burgers and sandwiches. Customers may eat outside on a small patio, and on Friday and Saturday nights there's disco dancing from 8pm until closing. Look for the weekend specials, such as fish cakes or fish fingers. Want to go really local? Try the fish-head broth served with local green bananas.

The Hummingbird. At the Hummingbird Beach Resort, on the waterfront just north of the main wharf at Soufrière, St. Lucia, W.I. ☎ **758/459-7232.** Platters EC$40–EC$62 ($14.80–$22.95). AE, DC, MC, V. Daily noon–3:30 and 7–11pm. WEST INDIAN/INTERNATIONAL.

The resort that contains this outdoorsy beach-oriented restaurant consists of about half a dozen wood-sided buildings, each stained a dark shade of brown. This simple resort is most appropriately recommended for its restaurant, a raffish-looking veranda perched adjacent to the sands of Hummingbird Beach. Its cuisine focuses on such West Indian dishes as Creole-style conch, lobster, burgers, steaks, and fillets of both snapper and grouper, punctuated with American staples like burgers and BLTs. At the tiny gift shop you can buy batik items crafted by some members of the staff. Winter rates for the nine simply furnished rooms (seven of which have baths) are $55 to $65 for a single or double without bath; $130 to $140 for a double with bath; $145 for double occupancy of a suite; and $250 for a two-bedroom cottage. Between April and mid-December, rates for the categories noted above, respectively, are $40 to $50, $75, $95, and $150.

Key Largo. Rodney Heights. ☎ **758/452-0282.** Pizzas EC$20–EC$36 ($7.40–$13.30). AE, MC, V. Daily 6am–11pm. ITALIAN.

This local hangout serves only pizzas and salads in a casual environment. All pizzas come in one size (12 inches), served on a very thin crust with tomato sauce and mozzarella. The house specialties include the Union Jack (bacon, egg, sausage, and tomato slices) and the signature Key Largo (shrimp and artichokes). Featured on the salad menu are prawn and chicken options. Specialty coffees are served: espresso, cappuccino, and Key Largo coffee (with lime juice, dark rum, brown sugar, Kahlúa, and a frothy head of whipped milk). For a cooler, spirited drink, try the Caribbean punch.

J.J.'s. Marigot Bay Rd. ☎ **758/451-4076.** Main courses EC$35–EC$60 ($12.95–$22.20). MC, V. Daily 8am–midnight. SEAFOOD.

On a hill overlooking the bay, about a quarter mile from Marigot Bay Beach, this lively restaurant serves up seafood in many guises. The terrace provides outdoor dining with a view of the yachts as they come into the harbor. The starters include stuffed crab backs and fish cakes; the featured platter is the special mix of Creole-style

Cheap Thrills: What to See & Do for Free (Well, Almost) on St. Lucia

- **Shop at the Public Market.** As Caribbean capitals go, Castries is dull architecturally and has few sights to hold your interest—with one exception. The public market is one of the most fascinating in the West Indies, and it goes full blast every day except Sunday. It's most active on Friday and Saturday mornings. Not that you could miss it, but it lies a block from Columbus Square along Peynier Street, running down toward the water. Here you'll find rows of stalls under a covered market and out on the street. The array of color alone is astonishing, plus the display of fruits and vegetables, many of which may be unfamiliar. The varieties of bananas alone is daunting. By all means sample one. They're allowed to ripen on the tree and taste completely different from those picked green and sold at supermarkets in America. Many of the vendors are from neighboring islands or countries, including the Guianese, who for some reason always seem to be hawking electronics.

- **Spend a Day on Pigeon Island.** Few places in St. Lucia hold the allure of this island that's now linked to St. Lucia by a causeway between Gros Islet and Cap Estate. You can spend a day here, exploring the island, swimming at the beach, and hiking, especially on the grounds of Fort Rodney. You can still explore the grounds of scores of military buildings constructed by the English. The best climb is to the top of Fort Rodney, whose cannon installations evoke the naval conflicts of the English and French that eventually lead to British control of the island in 1814. Few small islands in the Caribbean have had such a turbulent history. You'll find caves once used by the cannibalistic Carib Indians. Pigeon Island was also the stamping grounds of some of the sea's most notorious pirates, including Jambe de Bois, or François Leclerc (Peg Leg). He attacked and captured several galleons in the mid-16th century.

- **Take the Waters at Diamond Falls.** The Soufrière Estate in the south of St. Lucia sprawls across 2,000 acres, a land grant made in 1713 by Louis XII. Today it's the Diamond Botanical Gardens and is still owned by the descendants of the original Devaux brothers, to whom the French king granted the land. Mrs. Joan Du Bouley Devaux has turned the area into a lush tropical Eden. Deep in the gardens is the Diamond Waterfall, created from water bubbling up from sulfur springs. Close to the falls, curative mineral baths are fed by these underground sulfur springs. You can slip into your swimsuit and bathe for half an hour for $2.50. For $3.75, you're given a private bath. As a young girl, Joséphine Bonaparte enjoyed these mineral baths while visiting her father's nearby plantation.

- **Explore the Scenic Outline at Morne Fortune.** To the south of Castries looms Morne Fortune, the inappropriately named "Hill of Good Luck" (no one ever had much luck here). It forms a stunning backdrop to the capital of Castries. Subjected to fierce battles, devastating hurricanes, and fires that have wiped it out, Morne Fortune today offers what many justifiably view as the most scenic lookout perch in the Caribbean. In the 18th century some of the most savage battles between the French and the British took place here. Today that's but a nostalgic memory as you wander about, looking at the beautifully planted private gardens, aflame with scarlet and purple bougainvillea. Former barracks, stables, and gun replacements are diverted to other purposes today, like Government House on Government House Road, the official residence of the governor-general of St. Lucia. It's one of the few examples of Victorian architecture remaining in St. Lucia (the once-rich heritage of Victorian buildings were destroyed by fires). As you take in the view, you'll see Vigie airport to the north and Pigeon Point beyond that. On a clear day you can see all the way to Martinique. To the south a view of the Pitons is possible.

- **Discover "Forgotten" Grande Anse.** The northeast coast is the least visited part of the island but contains the most dramatic rockbound shores interspersed with secret sandy coves. You can reach it via a bad road. The terrain is arid like parts of Arizona and is most unwelcoming, but fascinating nonetheless. Many locals tackle the road in a four-wheel-drive, especially the part from Desbarra to Grande Anse, where the road is the most bumpy. Here at Grande Anse live some rare bird species, notably the white-breasted thrasher. The only caution is to avoid a close encounter with a fer-de-lance, the only poisonous snake on the island. But visitors rarely report seeing one. Grande Anse with its series of beaches—one called Grande Anse, another Petite Anse, and a third Anse Louvet—is a nesting ground for sea turtles, including the hawksbill, the green turtle, the leatherback, and loggerhead. Nesting seasons last from February to October. Today the government has set Grande Anse aside as a nature reserve so it can never be developed.

- **Walk in a Rain Forest.** More than 12% of the forests covering St. Lucia, nearly 20,000 acres, is a government-protected rain forest, found in the interior highlands. In the south of this reserve is the Edmund Forest Reserve and the Quilesse Forest Reserve, site of a 7-mile-long Rain Forest Walk between the villages of Mahaut in the east leading to Fond St. Jacques in the west. This walk is one of the most dramatic in the Caribbean, taking in a quartet of St. Lucia's main bodies of water, Vieux Fort, Roseau, Canelles, and Troumasse (all rivers). In a good year, some 150 inches of rain fall on this reserve, and showers are frequent throughout the walk, so dress accordingly. There are various panoramic lookout points. You pass small hamlets as you go along country roads taking in the rich flora, including wild orchids perfuming the air. You'll also see bromelaids and anthuriums. Birdlife is evident everywhere, especially hummingbirds and purple-throated caribs. Count yourself lucky if you spot the rare and highly endangered St. Lucia parrot, known locally as a jacquot—it was hunted to near extinction for its meat.

squid and fish along with chicken. Of course there are other options, like curried chicken and grilled steaks. Prepared in a number of ways here, conch is especially tasty, as is either the grilled kingfish or tuna. For a place to dance and mingle with the locals, try J.J.'s on Friday and Saturday nights, when things get cranked up with live entertainment.

Razmataz! Rodney Bay Marina. ☎ **758/452-9800.** Reservations recommended. Main courses EC$24–EC$55 ($8.90–$20.35). MC, V. Fri–Wed 4pm until the last customer leaves. INDIAN.

Across from the Royal St. Lucian Hotel, this welcome entry into the island cuisine features delectable tandoori dishes among other offerings. It's in an original Caribbean colonial timbered building with lots of gingerbread decorated in a medley of colors and lying in a garden, a 2-minute walk from the beach. There's live music on weekends, and the owner is often the entertainer. A tempting array of starters greets you, from pieces of fresh local fish marinated in spicy yogurt and cooked in the tandoor to mulligatawny soup (made with lentils, herbs, and spices). Tandoori delights include shrimp, fresh fish like snapper or mahi mahi, chicken, and mixed grill, and you get the best assortment of vegetarian dishes on the island.

Restaurant Seraphine. Vigie Cove. ☎ **758/453-2073.** Lunch main courses EC$20–EC$25 ($7.40–$9.25); dinner main courses EC$50–EC$80 ($18.50–$29.60). AE, MC, V. Mon–Fri 6:30am–11pm; Sat–Sun 7–11pm. WEST INDIAN/INTERNATIONAL.

On the ground floor of the previously recommended hotel, this is a well-orchestrated West Indian restaurant a 15-minute walk from Vigie Beach. From its blue and white interior, views extend over a forested terrain sloping down to the harbor at Castries, arrival point for all manner of yachts and cruise ships. Menu items range from unpretentious salads and sandwiches to more complicated local and international dishes like grilled kingfish in white sauce, baked chicken, grouper with lime sauce, filet steak with pepper sauce, pork chops with cayenne pepper, and snapper in tomato- and pepper-based Creole sauce. The staff is friendly.

The Still. Soufrière. ☎ **758/459-7224.** Main courses EC$20–EC$45 ($7.40–$16.65). AE, DC, DISC, MC, V. Daily 8am–5pm. CREOLE.

The first thing you'll see as you drive up the hill from the harbor is a very old rum distillery on a platform of thick timbers, the home of this restaurant less than a mile east of Soufrière. The site is a working cocoa and citrus plantation that has been in the same St. Lucian family for four generations. The front blossoms with avocado and breadfruit trees, and a mahogany forest is a few steps away. The bar near the front veranda is furnished with tables cut from cross sections of mahogany tree trunks. A more formal and spacious dining room is nearby. Excellently prepared St. Lucian specialties are served here, depending on what's fresh at the market. Try to avoid the place when it's overrun with cruise-ship passengers or tour groups. There are far better restaurants on St. Lucia, but if it's lunchtime and you're near Diamond Falls, you don't have a lot of choices.

4 Hitting the Beaches

Since most of the island hotels are built right on the beach, you won't have far to go for swimming. All beaches are open to the public, even those along hotel properties. However, if you use any of the hotel's beach equipment, you must pay for it. We prefer the beaches along the western coast, as a rough surf on the windward (east) side makes swimming there potentially dangerous.

Leading beaches include **Pigeon Island** off the north shore, part of the Pigeon Island National Historic Park. The small beach here has white sand and picnic facilities. Pigeon Island is joined to the "mainland" of St. Lucia by a causeway, so it's easy to reach. Cleared of its natural growth long ago, the island has since been replanted with palm trees among other tropical trees and shrubs. The most frequented beach is **Reduit Beach** at Rodney Bay, a mile of soft beige sand fronting very clear waters, a 20-minute drive from Castries. Many water-sports kiosks can be found along the strip bordering Rex St. Lucian Hotel. With all its restaurants and bars, you'll find plenty of refueling stops.

Choc Bay is a long stretch of sand and palm trees on the northwestern coast, convenient to Castries and the big resorts. Its tranquil waters lure swimmers and especially families, including locals, who have small children. The 2-mile white-sand **Malabar Beach** runs parallel to the Vigie Airport runway, in Castries, to the Rendezvous resort. **Vigie Beach,** north of Castries Harbour, is also popular. It has fine sands, often a light beige in color, sloping gently into crystalline water. **La Toc Beach,** just south of Castries, opens onto a crescent-shaped bay containing golden sand.

Marigot Bay is the quintessential Caribbean cove, framed on three sides by steep emerald hills and skirted by palm trees. There are some small but secluded beaches here. The bay itself is an anchorage for some of the most expensive yachts in the Caribbean.

One of the most charming and hidden beaches of St. Lucia is the idyllic cove of **Anse Chastanet,** just north of Soufrière. This is a beach connoisseur's delight, with its dark sand and backdrop of lush green hills. Towering palms provide shade from the fierce noonday sun. Heading south on the windward side of the island is **Anse des Sables,** opening onto a shallow bay swept by tradewinds that make it great for windsurfing.

The dramatic crescent-shaped bay of **Anse des Pitons** is at the foot of and between the twin peaks of the Pitons, south of Soufrière. The white sand was imported by the Jalousie Hilton and spread over the beach's natural black sand; walk through the resort to get to it. It's popular with divers and snorkelers. While here, you can ask about a very special beach reached only by boat—the black volcanic sands and tranquil waters of **Anse Couchon.** With its shallow reefs, snorkeling possibilities, and picture-postcard charm, this beach has become a hideaway for lovers. It's south of Anse-le-Raye.

At the very southernmost tip of St. Lucia, the beach at **Vieux Fort** has miles of white sand and gin-clear waters. Reefs protect these waters, making them tranquil and ideal for swimming.

5 Sports & Outdoor Pursuits

BOATING The most dramatic trip offered is aboard the *Brig Unicorn* (☎ 758/452-6811), used in the filming of the famous *Roots* miniseries. Passengers sail to Soufrière and the twin peaks of the Pitons, among other natural attractions of the island. The vessel itself is 140 feet long. The cost of a full-day sail is $70. The ship is moored at Vigie Cove in Castries.

CAMPING Camping is now possible on St. Lucia courtesy of the **Environmental Educational Centre,** a division of the St. Lucia National Trust (☎ 758/452-5005). This reserve, opened in 1998, features 12 campsites (with many more to be added) along a beautiful stretch of beach on historic Anse Liberté in the fishing town of Canaries, 25 miles southwest of Castries and 8 miles north of Soufrière. Beachfront campsites are available for around $20 per night offering a view of the harbor and of

Martinique on a clear day. Each campsite features nearby community bathrooms and toilets, and community cooking areas dotted with 3 to 4 grills. Some cooking can be done at your campsite in each of the stone stoves provided, a feature designed to contain campfires. The reserve offers 5 miles of hiking trails, and staff members can give tours of the area and the rich emancipation history of the Anse Liberté, which literally translated means "freedom harbor." It was here that much of the Brigand (St. Lucian term for emancipation or "freedom fighters") activity was organized, and arms and supplies were stockpiled for the effort in the caves that can be found along a hike. Camping equipment is also available for rent.

GOLF   St. Lucia has a 9-hole golf course at the **Cap Estate Golf Club,** at the northern end of the island (☎ **758/450-8523**). Greens fees are $40 for 18 holes or $30 for 9 holes, and there are no caddies. Carts cost from $15 to $25, and clubs can be rented for $10. Hours are 8am to sunset daily.

HIKING   A tropical rain forest covers a large area in the southern half of St. Lucia, and the St. Lucia Forest & Lands Department has proven to be a wise guardian of this resource. One of the most popular trails is the **Barre De L'Isle Trail,** located almost in the center of St. Lucia, southeast of Marigot Bay; it's a fairly easy trail that's even recommended for children. This forest reserve divides the western and eastern halves of the island. A mile-long trail cuts through the reserve. There are four panoramic lookout points, offering a dramatic view of the sea where the Atlantic Ocean meets the Caribbean. It takes about an hour to walk this trail, which lies about a 30-minute ride from Castries. Guided hikes can usually be arranged through the major hotels or through the **Forest & Lands Department** (☎ 758/450-2231 or 758/450-2078).

HORSEBACK RIDING   North of Castries, you can rent a horse at **Cas-En-Bas.** To make arrangements, call René Trim (☎ **758/450-8273**). The cost is $40 for 1 hour; a 2-hour ride goes for $50. Ask about a picnic trip to the Atlantic, with a barbecue lunch and drink included, for $60. Departures on horseback are at 8:30am, 10am, 2pm, and 4pm.

PARASAILING   It's said that the most panoramic view of the northwest coast is sailing high over Rodney Bay. Parasailing is the key to this, and it's available at the water-sports kiosk at the **Hotel Rex St. Lucian** at Rodney Bay (☎ **758/452-8351**). The cost is $40.

SCUBA DIVING   In Soufrière, **Scuba St. Lucia,** in the Anse Chastanet Hotel (☎ **758/459-7000**), offers one of the world's top dive locations at a five-star PADI dive center. At the southern end of Anse Chastanet's ¼-mile-long, soft secluded beach, it features premier diving and comprehensive facilities for divers of all levels. Some of the most spectacular coral reefs of St. Lucia, many only 10 to 20 feet below the water surface from the beach, provide shelter for many marine denizens and a backdrop for schools of reef fish.

Many professional PADI instructors offer four dive programs a day. Photographic equipment is available for rent (film can be processed on the premises), and instruction is offered in picture taking, the price depending on the time and equipment involved. Experienced divers can rent the equipment they need on a per item basis. The packages include tanks, backpacks, and weight belts. PADI certification courses are available. A 2- to 3-hour introductory lesson is $75 and includes a short theory session, equipment familiarization, development of skills in shallow water, a tour of the reef, and all equipment. Single dives cost $35, and hours are 8am to 5:45pm daily.

Another full-service scuba center is available on St. Lucia's southwest coast at the new **Jalousie Hilton** at Soufrière (☎ **758/459-7666**), which offers competition for the longer established program at Anse Chastenet. The PADI center here offers dives in St. Lucia's National Marine Park; there are numerous shallow reefs near the shore. The diver certification program is available to hotel guests and other visitors age 12 or over. Prices range from a single dive for $55 to a certification course for $425. A daily resort course for $70 is offered Monday to Saturday for noncertified divers; it includes a supervised dive from the beach. All these prices include equipment, tax, and service charges.

Rosamond Trench Divers, at the Marigot Beach Club, Marigot Bay (☎ **758/ 451-4761**), is adjacent to the waters of the most famous bay on St. Lucia. The outfit takes both novices and experienced divers to shallow reefs or to some of the most challenging trenches in the Caribbean. A resort course designed for novices (it includes theory, a practice dive in sheltered waters, and one dive above a reef) costs $75. A one-tank dive for certified divers, all equipment included, goes for $50; a two-tank dive is $70, with night dives priced at $65. They also have a 6-dive package for $190 and a 10-dive package for $300.

TENNIS   The best place for tennis is the **St. Lucia Racquet Club,** adjacent to Club St. Lucia (☎ **758/450-0551**). It opened in 1991 and quickly became one of the finest tennis facilities in the Lesser Antilles. Its seven courts are maintained in state-of-the-art condition, and there's also a good pro shop. You must reserve 24 hours in advance. Guests of the hotel play for free; nonguests are charged EC$25 ($9.25) a day. To rent a tennis racquet costs EC$20 ($7.40) per hour.

If you're in the southern part of the island, a good new program is offered by the **Jalousie Hilton** at Soufrière (☎ **758/459-7666**). Vernon Lewis, the top-ranked player on St. Lucia and an 11-time Davis Cup singles winner, is the pro. You'll find four brand-new Laykold tennis courts, three of which are lit for night play. Guests of the hotel play for free (though they pay for lessons). Nonguests are welcomed and can play for EC$25 ($9.25) per hour.

WATER SPORTS   Unless you're interested in scuba (in which case you should head for the facilities at the Anse Chastenet Hotel), the best all-around water-sports center is **St. Lucian Watersports,** at the Rex St. Lucian Hotel (☎ **758/452-8351**). Water-skiing costs $12 for a 10- to 15-minute ride. Windsurfers can be rented for $15 for half an hour or $22 an hour. Snorkeling is free for hotel guests; nonguests pay $8 per hour, including equipment, and waterskiing is arranged for $12 for 15 minutes.

6 Seeing the Sights

Lovely little towns, beautiful beaches and bays, mineral baths, banana plantations—St. Lucia has all this and more. You can even visit a volcano.

Most hotel front desks will make arrangements for guided tours that take in all the major sights. For example, **Sunlink Tours,** Reduit Beach Avenue (☎ **758/452-8232**), offers many island tours, including full-day boat trips along the west coast of Soufrière, the Pitons, and the volcano for $80 per person. Plantation tours go for $56, and jeep safaris can be arranged for $80. One of the most popular jaunts is a rain-forest ramble for $55, and there's also a daily shopping tour for $20. The company has tour desks or representatives at most of the major hotels.

CASTRIES

The capital city has grown up around its **harbor,** which occupies the crater of an extinct volcano. Charter captains and the yachting set drift in here, and large cruise-ship wharves welcome vessels from around the world. Because it has been hit by several devastating fires that destroyed almost all the old buildings (most recently in 1948), the town has a look of newness, with glass-and-concrete (or steel) buildings replacing the French colonial or Victorian look typical of many West Indian capitals.

The **Saturday-morning market** in the old tin-roofed building on Jeremy Street in Castries is our favorite "people-watching" site on the island. The country women dress up in their traditional garb and cotton headdresses; the number of knotted points on top reveals their marital status (ask one of the locals to explain it). The luscious fresh fruits and vegetables of St. Lucia are sold as weather-beaten men sit close by playing warrie, a fast game using pebbles on a carved board. You can also pick up such St. Lucian handcrafts as baskets and unglazed pottery.

Beyond Government House lies **Morne Fortune,** which means "Hill of Good Luck," even though no one had much luck here, certainly not the battling French and British fighting for Fort Charlotte. The barracks and guard rooms changed nationalities many times. You can visit the 18th-century barracks to view the military cemetery, a small museum, the old powder magazine, and the "Four Apostles Battery" (a quartet of grim muzzle-loading cannons). The view of the harbor of Castries is panoramic: You can see north to Pigeon Island or south to the Pitons. To reach Morne Fortune, head east on Bridge Street.

PIGEON ISLAND NATIONAL LANDMARK

St. Lucia's first national park, the ✪ **Pigeon Island National Landmark,** was originally an island flanked by the Caribbean on one side and the Atlantic on the other. It's now joined to the mainland island by a causeway. On its west coast are two white-sand beaches. There's also a restaurant, Jambe de Bois, named after a wooden-legged pirate who once used the island as a hideout for his men.

Pigeon Island offers an **Interpretation Centre,** equipped with artifacts and a multimedia display on local history, ranging from the Amerindian occupation of A.D. 1000 to the Battle of the Saints, when Admiral Rodney's fleet set out from Pigeon Island and defeated Admiral De Grasse in 1782. The **Captain's Cellar Olde English Pub** lies under the center and is evocative of an 18th-century English bar.

Pigeon Island, only 44 acres in size, got its name from the red-neck pigeon or ramier that once made this island home. It's ideal for picnics, weddings, and nature walks. The park is open daily 9am to 5pm, charging an entrance fee of EC$10 ($3.70). For more information, call the **St. Lucia National Trust** at ☎ **758/452-5005.**

MARIGOT BAY

Movie crews, including those for Rex Harrison's *Dr. Doolittle* and Sophia Loren's *Fire Power,* have used this bay, one of the most beautiful in the Caribbean. Lying 8 miles south of Castries, it's narrow yet navigable by yachts of any size. Here Admiral Rodney camouflaged his ships with palm leaves while lying in wait for French frigates. The shore, lined with palms, remains relatively unspoiled, but some building sites have been sold. Again, it's a delightful spot for a picnic if you didn't take your food basket to Pigeon Island. A 24-hour ferry connects the bay's two sides.

RODNEY BAY

Reached after a 15-minute drive north of Castries, one of the most scenic bays in the Caribbean is named after Admiral Rodney. It's an 80-acre site set on a man-made lagoon. This has become a chic center for nightlife, hotels, and restaurants—in fact, it's the most active place on the island at night. Its marina is one of the top watersports centers in the Caribbean and a destination every December for the Atlantic Rally for Cruisers, when yachties who cross the Atlantic meet here and compare stories.

SOUFRIÈRE

This little fishing port, St. Lucia's second-largest settlement, is dominated by two pointed hills called ✪ **Petit Piton** and **Gros Piton.** The Pitons, volcanic cones rising to 2,460 and 2,619 feet, have become the very symbol of St. Lucia. Formed of lava and rock and once actively volcanic, they're now clothed in green vegetation. Their sheer rise from the sea makes them a landmark visible for miles around, and waves crash around their bases. It's recommended that you attempt to climb only Gros Piton, but to do so requires the permission of the **Forest and Lands Department** (☎ **758/450-2231**) and a knowledgeable guide.

Near Soufrière lies the famous "drive-in" volcano, ✪ **Mount Soufrière.** It's a rocky lunar landscape of bubbling mud and craters seething with fuming sulfur. You literally drive your car into an old (millions of years) crater and walk between the sulfur springs and pools of hissing steam. Entrance costs EC$3 ($1.10) per person and includes the services of your guide, who will point out the blackened waters, among the few of their kind in the Caribbean. Hours are daily 9am to 5pm; for more information call ☎ **758/459-5500.**

Nearby are the ✪ **Diamond Mineral Baths** (☎ **758/452-4759**), surrounded by a tropical arboretum. Constructed in 1784 on the orders of Louis XVI, whose doctors told him these waters were similar in mineral content to the waters at Aix-les-Bains, they were intended to provide recuperative effects for French soldiers fighting in the West Indies. Later destroyed, they were rebuilt after World War II. They have an average temperature of 106°F and lie near one of the geological attractions of the island, a waterfall that changes colors (from yellow to black to green to gray) several times a day. For EC$7 ($2.60), you can bathe and try out the recuperative effects for yourself.

From Soufrière in the southwest, the road winds toward **Fond St-Jacques,** where you'll have a good view of mountains and villages as you cut through St. Lucia's **Cape Moule-à-Chique** tropical rain forest. You'll also see the **Barre de l'Isle** divide.

7 Nature Reserves

The fertile volcanic soil of St. Lucia sustains a rich diversity of bird and animal life. Some of the richest troves for ornithologists are in protected precincts off the St. Lucian coast, in either of two national parks, Frigate Islands Nature Reserve and the Maria Islands Nature Reserve.

The **Fregate Islands** are a cluster of rocks a short distance offshore from Praslin Bay, midway up St. Lucia's eastern coastline. Barren except for tall grasses that seem to thrive in the salt spray, the islands were named after the scissor-tailed frigate birds (*Fregata magnificens*) that breed here every year between May and July. Large colonies of the graceful birds fly in well-choreographed formations over islands you can visit only under the closely supervised permission of government authorities. Many visitors believe the best way to admire the Fregate Islands (and respect their fragile ecosystems) is to walk along the nature trail the government has hacked along the clifftop of the St. Lucian mainland, about 150 feet inland from the shore. Even without binoculars, you'll be able to see the frigates wheeling overhead. You'll also enjoy eagle's-eye views of the unusual geology of the St. Lucian coast, which includes sea caves, dry ravines, a waterfall (which flows only during rainy season), and a strip of mangrove swamp.

The **Maria Islands** are larger and more arid and almost constantly exposed to salt-laden winds blowing up from the equator. Set to the east of the island's southernmost tip, off the town of Vieux Fort, they contain a strictly protected biodiversity. The approximately 30 acres of cactus-dotted land comprising the two largest islands (Maria

Major and Maria Minor) are home to more than 120 species of plants, lizards, butterflies, and snakes that are believed to be extinct in other parts of the world. These include the large ground lizard (*Zandolite*) and the nocturnal, nonvenomous kouwes (*Dromicus ornatus*) snake.

The Marias are also a bird refuge, populated by such species as the sooty tern, the bridled tern, the Caribbean martin, the red-billed tropicbird, and the brown noddy, which usually builds its nest under the protective thorns of prickly pear cactus.

If permission is granted, visitors will set foot in either park as part of a group that arrives by boat under the supervision of a qualified guide. The cost is $30 per person for the Frigates and $114 per person for the Marias, for guided tours that last a full day and include lunch for the Marias jaunt. These must be arranged through the staff of the **St. Lucia National Trust** (☎ 758/452-5005), who will supply further details.

8 Shopping

CASTRIES

Most of the shopping is in Castries, where the principal streets are **William Peter Boulevard** and **Bridge Street.** Many stores will sell you goods at duty-free prices (providing you don't take the merchandise with you from the store but have it delivered directly to the airport or cruise dock). There are some good (but not remarkable) buys in bone china, jewelry, perfume, watches, liquor, and crystal.

At **Noah's Arkade,** Jeremie Street (☎ 758/452-2523), many of the Caribbean handcrafts and gifts are routine tourist items, yet you'll often find something interesting if you browse. They sell local straw placemats, baskets, rugs, wall hangings, maracas, shell necklaces, locally made bowls, dolls dressed in banana leaves, and warri boards. Branches are found at Hewanorra International Airport and the Pointe Seraphine duty-free shopping mall (below).

POINTE SERAPHINE

Built for the cruise-ship passenger, Pointe Seraphine, in Castries, has the best collection of shops on the island, together with offices for car rentals, organized taxi service (for sightseeing), a bureau de change, a Philatelic Bureau, an Information Centre, and international telephones. Cruise ships berth right at the shopping center. Under red roofs in a Spanish-style setting, the complex requires you to present a cruise pass or an airline ticket to the shopkeeper when buying goods. Visitors can take away their purchases, except liquor and tobacco, which will be delivered to the airport. All shops in the complex keep the same hours. In winter, the center is open Monday to Friday 8am to 5pm and Saturday 8am to 2pm; off-season hours are Monday to Saturday 9am to 4pm. It's also open when cruise ships are in port.

Among the stores, you'll find a **Bennetton** (☎ 758/452-7685). In addition to T-shirts, tennis shirts, and shorts, there's an assortment of women's pants suits, men's business suits, and children's wear. Prices are about 20% lower than stateside. The inventory at **Little Switzerland** (☎ 758/452-7587) includes a broad-based array of luxury goods. Prices of the porcelain, crystal, wristwatches, and jewelry are usually around 25% less than those of equivalent goods in North American, but wise shoppers are usually alert to the special promotions (with savings of up to 40% below stateside retail prices) that influence the prices.

Though it doesn't even try to stock the porcelain, crystal, perfume, and luggage of Little Switzerland, **Colombian Emeralds** (☎ 758/453-7233) has a more diverse selection of watches and gemstones. There are two adjoining buildings, one of which sells only gold chains (14- and 18-karat) and watches; the other features a sophisticated array of precious and semiprecious stones. Gemstones are often reasonable in price. Of special value are the watches, which sometimes sell for up to 40% less than in North America. **Studio Images** (☎ 758/452-6883) offers a collection of designer fragrances, including some exotic locally made concoctions, often at prices representing 20% to 40% off stateside costs. The store also carries the latest brands of Sony electronics, plus leather accessories from Ted Lapidus as well as Samsonite luggage.

A wide collection of souvenirs is also sold. **The Land Shop** (☎ 758/452-7488) specializes in elegant handbags, garment bags, and briefcases. Prices are at least 25% less than in North America. Also available is a selection of shoes, but the inventory for women is more varied and interesting than the choices for men.

Oasis (☎ 758/452-1185) sells brand-name resort clothing and beach wear at duty-free prices. Look for Revo sunglasses, Reef and Naot footwear, Kipling bags, Gottex swimwear, and casual clothing by Gear. **Peer** (☎ 758/453-0815) stocks high-quality creative, colorful prints and embroidery designs on T-shirts, shorts, camp shirts, and more. There is a large range for children, as well as bags, caps, women's wear, and bright tropical prints. It's a good place to visit for a wearable souvenir or gift.

GABLEWOODS MALL

On Gros Islet Highway, 2 miles north of Castries, this mall contains three restaurants and one of the island's densest concentrations of shops. The best clothing and sundry shop is **Top Banana** (☎ 758/451-6389), selling beachwear, scuba and snorkeling equipment, gifts, inflatable rafts, and casual resort wear. Other branches of this store can be found at both the Rex St. Lucian Hotel and the Windjammer Hotel.

Made in St. Lucia (☎ 758/453-2788) sells only gifts and souvenirs made by local craftspersons in St. Lucia. The array of merchandise includes woodcarvings, clay cooking pots, sandals, a medley of spices and cooking sauces, a wide assortment of T-shirts, paintings, and such jewelry items as necklaces and "love beads" made from seeds and dried berries. Another worthwhile outlet is **Sea Island Cotton Shop** (☎ 758/451-6946), catering almost exclusively to visitors. This is one of the largest shops at the mall, offering an array of quality T-shirts, hand-painted souvenirs, Caribbean spices, beach and swimwear, and elegantly casual clothing.

NEAR CASTRIES

Bagshaws, La Toc (☎ 758/451-9249), just outside Castries, is the leading island hand-printer of silk-screen designs. The birds (look for the St. Lucia parrot), butterflies, and flowers of St. Lucia are incorporated into their original designs. The highlights are an extensive household line in vibrant prints on linen, as well as clothing and beachwear for both men and women, and the best T-shirt collection on St. Lucia. At La Toc Studios, the printing process can be viewed Monday to Friday. There are three other retail outlets: in the Pointe Seraphine duty-free shopping mall (☎ 758/452-7570), in Rodney Bay (☎ 758/452-9435), and at the "Best of St. Lucia" at Hewanorra International Airport, Vieux Fort (☎ 758/454-7784).

Caribelle Batik, Howelton House, 37 Old Victoria Rd., The Morne (☎ 758/452-3785), just a 5-minute drive from Castries, is where you can watch St. Lucian artists creating intricate patterns and colors through the ancient art of batik. You can also purchase batik in cotton, rayon, and silk, made up in casual and beach clothing, plus wall hangings and other gift items. Drinks are served in the Dyehouse Bar and Terrace in the renovated Victorian-era building.

Vincent Joseph Eudovic is a master artist and wood carver whose sculptures have gained increasing fame. You can view and buy his work at **Eudovic Art Studio,** Goodlands, Morne Fortune (☎ 758/452-2747; fax 758/459-0124). He usually carves his imaginative free-form sculptures from local tree roots, such as teak, mahogany, and red cedar. Ask to be taken to his private studio, where you'll see his own remarkable creations. Eudovic has recently added 10 simply furnished guest rooms, some with kitchenettes. These are among the bargains of the island, renting for $40 double without kitchenette or $50 double with kitchenette. Cooling is by ceiling fans, and each room has a private bath and cable TV. He accepts credit cards (AE, DISC, MC, V).

CHOISEUL

The coastal village of Choiseul, southwest of Castries, was named during St. Lucia's French-speaking regime and has ever since been the home of the descendants of Carib Indians whose bloodlines mingled long ago with African slaves. The village's artistic centerpiece is the **Choiseul Art & Craft Center,** La Fargue (☎ 758/459-3226), a government-funded retail outlet and training school that perpetuates the tradition of handmade Amerindian pottery and basketware. Look for place mats, handbags, and even artfully contrived bassinets, priced from EC$250 ($92.50) each, that might make a worthwhile present for parents-to-be.

9 St. Lucia After Dark

There isn't much except the entertainment offered by hotels. In winter, at least one hotel offers a steel band or calypso music every night. Otherwise, check to see what's happening at **Capone's** (☎ 758/452-0284) and **The Green Parrot** (☎ 758/452-3167), both in Castries.

Indies, at Rodney Bay (☎ 758/452-0727), is a split-floor dance club with a large wooden dancing area and stage. There's also a trio of bars, with smoking and no-smoking sections. The DJs keep the joint jumping, with both West Indian and international sounds, often American. The action gets going Wednesday, Friday, and Saturday, from 11pm to 4am. The cover ranges from EC$15 to EC$25 ($5.55 to $9.25). Indies has opened a bar around the side of the building called the Back Door, featuring alternative music and reggae. A sort of rock and sports bar, it serves snacks until 3am.

The Lime at Rodney Bay is a restaurant that operates **The Late Lime Night Club,** Reduit Beach (☎ 758/452-0761), offering entertainment Wednesday to Saturday, beginning at 10pm and lasting until the crowd folds. Wednesday, Friday, and Saturday are disco nights. Admission is EC$15 ($5.55).

If you'd like to go bar-hopping, begin at **Waves,** Choc Bay, Castries (☎ 758/451-3000), which is popular with both locals and visitors. Some nights a week there's live music or karaoke. **Banana Split,** on St. George's Street in Castries (☎ 758/450-8125), is another popular hangout that often offers live entertainment, as does **Shamrocks Pub,** Rodney Bay (☎ 758/452-8725). This Irish-style pub is especially popular among boaters and gets really lively on weekends.

St. Maarten & St. Martin

22

For an island boasting a big reputation for its restaurants, hotels, and energetic nightlife, St. Maarten/St. Martin is small—only 37 square miles, about half the area of the District of Columbia. The island is split between the Netherlands and France: **St. Maarten** is the Dutch half and **St. Martin** the French half. Legend has it that a gin-drinking Dutchman and a wine-guzzling Frenchman walked around the island to see how much territory each could earmark for his side in 1 day; the Frenchman outwalked the Dutchman, but the canny Dutchman got the more valuable piece of property.

The divided island is the smallest territory in the world shared by two sovereign states. The only way you know you're crossing an international border is when you see the sign bienvenue, partie française—attesting to the peaceful coexistence between the two nations on the island. The island was divided in 1648, and visitors still ascend Mount Concordia, near the border, where the agreement was reached. Even so, St. Maarten changed hands 16 times before it became permanently Dutch.

Returning visitors who've been "off island" for a long time are often surprised at the St. Maarten/St. Martin greeting them today. No longer a sleepy Caribbean backwater, it has become a boomtown. The 100% duty-free shopping has turned it into a shoppers' heaven, and the Dutch capital, Philipsburg, bustles with cruise-ship passengers who arrive by the hordes. Although Mother Nature rearranged them a bit, the 36 beaches of white sand remain unspoiled, and the clear turquoise waters are as enticing as ever. Sunshine is virtually guaranteed year-round, making all sorts of water sports and sailing possible. The nightlife is among the best in the Caribbean. But much has been lost to the bulldozer as well.

The Dutch side of the island, for the most part, is cheaper than the French side, especially its restaurants. Of course, they're not as good. And you'll find lots of deals, in package tours and villa rentals, so shop around and try never to pay the "rack" rate. Stay out of the swank places, book a guest house or a small inn, and avoid the upmarket French-style restaurants, and you'll probably fare all right in both St. Maarten and St. Martin.

Northernmost of the Netherlands Antilles, St. Maarten/St. Martin lies 144 miles southeast of Puerto Rico. A lush island, rimmed with bays and beaches, it has a year-round temperature of 80°F. The Dutch capital, **Philipsburg,** curves like a toy village along Great Bay. The

St. Maarten & St. Martin

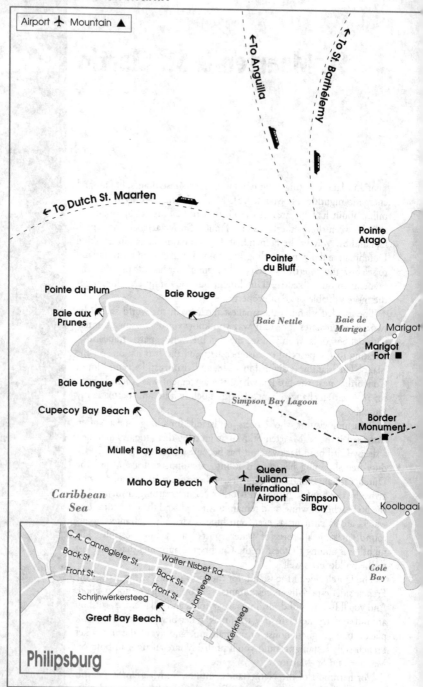

Airport ✈   Mountain ▲

← To Anguilla

← To St. Barthélemy

← To Dutch St. Maarten

Pointe Arago

Pointe du Bluff

Pointe du Plum

Baie Rouge

Baie aux Prunes

Baie Nettle

Baie de Marigot

Marigot

Marigot Fort ■

Baie Longue

Simpson Bay Lagoon

Border Monument ■

Cupecoy Bay Beach

Mullet Bay Beach

Maho Bay Beach

Queen Juliana International Airport

Simpson Bay

Koolbaai

Caribbean Sea

Cole Bay

C.A. Cannegieter St.

Back St.

Front St.

Walter Nisbet Rd.

Back St.

Front St.

Schrijnwerkersteeg

St. Jansteeg

Kerksteeg

Great Bay Beach

Philipsburg

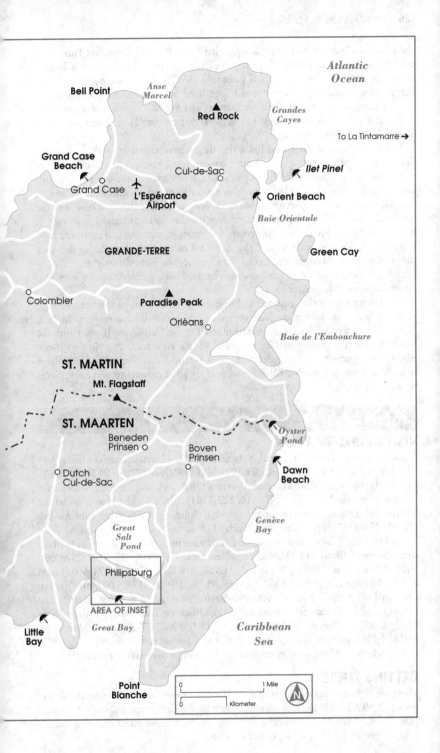

Atlantic Ocean

Bell Point

Anse Marcel

▲ Red Rock

Grandes Cayes

To La Tintamarre →

Grand Case Beach

Grand Case

Cul-de-Sac

✈ L'Espérance Airport

Ilet Pinel

Orient Beach

Baie Orientale

GRANDE-TERRE

Green Cay

Colombier

▲ Paradise Peak

Orléans

Baie de l'Embouchure

ST. MARTIN

▲ Mt. Flagstaff

ST. MAARTEN

Beneden Prinsen

Boven Prinsen

Oyster Pond

Dutch Cul-de-Sac

Dawn Beach

Genève Bay

Great Salt Pond

Philipsburg

AREA OF INSET

Little Bay

Great Bay

Caribbean Sea

Point Blanche

0   1 Mile

0   1 Kilometer

N

town lies on a narrow sand isthmus separating Great Bay and Great Salt Pond. The capital was founded in 1763 by Comdr. John Philips, a Scot in Dutch employ. To protect Great Bay, Fort Amsterdam was built in 1737. The main thoroughfare is busy Front Street, stretching for about a mile and lined with stores selling international merchandise, such as French designer fashions and Swedish crystal. More shops are dotted along the little lanes, known as *steegijes,* that connect Front Street with Back Street, another shoppers' delight.

The French side of the island has a slightly different character, with no dazzling sights and no spectacular nightlife. Even the sports scene here isn't as well organized as that on many Caribbean islands (though the Dutch side has golf and other diversions). Most people come to St. Martin to relax on its many white-sand beaches and to sample "France in the tropics." St. Martin not only has some of the best cuisine in the Caribbean but is filled with an extraordinary number of bistros and restaurants. It boasts a distinctly French air. Policemen, for example, wear *képis.* The towns have names like Colombier and Orléans, the streets are *rues,* and the French flag flies over the *gendarmerie* in **Marigot,** the capital. Its advocates cite it as distinctly more sophisticated, prosperous, and cosmopolitan than its neighboring *départements d'outre-mer,* Guadeloupe and Martinique.

Marigot isn't quite the same size as Philipsburg. It has none of the frenzied pace of the Dutch city, which is often overrun with cruise-ship passengers. In fact, Marigot looks like a French village transplanted to the Caribbean. If you climb the hill over this tiny port, you'll be rewarded with a view from the old fort there. About 20 minutes by car beyond Marigot is **Grand-Case,** a small fishing village that's an outpost of French civilization with many good restaurants and a few places to stay.

1 Essentials

VISITOR INFORMATION

If you're going to Dutch St. Maarten, contact the **St. Maarten Tourist Office,** 675 Third Ave., Suite 1806, New York, NY 10017 (☎ 800/786-2278 or 212/953-2084). In Canada, contact the **St. Maarten Tourist Office,** 243 Ellerslie Ave., Willowdale, Toronto, Ontario M2N 1Y5 (☎ 416/223-3501). Once on the island, go to the **Tourist Information Bureau,** in the Imperial Building at 23 Walter Nisbeth Rd. (☎ 599/5-22337), open Monday to Friday 8am to noon and 1 to 5pm.

For French St. Martin, you can obtain information from one of the **French Government Tourist Offices:** 444 Madison Ave., New York, NY 10022 (☎ 212/529-9069); 9454 Wilshire Blvd., Suite 715, Beverly Hills, CA 90212 (☎ 310/271-6665), and 676 N. Michigan Ave., Suite 3360, Chicago, IL 60611 (☎ 312/751-7800). You can also call France-on-Call at (☎ 900/990-0040 at the rate of 50¢ per minute. The tourist board on French St. Martin, called the **Office du Tourisme,** is at the port de Marigot, 97150 Marigot, St. Martin, F.W.I. (☎ 0590/87-57-21), open Monday to Friday 8:30am to 1pm and 2:30 to 5:30pm and Saturday 8am to noon.

The Internet address for both sections of the island is **www.st-martin.org**.

GETTING THERE

There are two airports on the island. St. Maarten's **Queen Juliana International Airport** (☎ 599/5-54211) is the second busiest in the Caribbean, topped only by San Juan, Puerto Rico. But you can also fly to the smaller **L'Espérance Airport** in Grand-Case on French St. Martin (☎ 0590/87-53-03).

American Airlines (☎ **800/433-7300** in the U.S.) offers more options and more frequent service into St. Maarten than any other airline—one daily nonstop flight from both New York's JFK and Miami. Additional nonstop daily flights into St. Maarten are offered by American and its local affiliate **American Eagle** (same toll-free number) from San Juan. Ask for one of the airline's tour operators, because you can usually save a lot of money by booking one of American's package tours.

Other air service is provided by **Continental Airlines** (☎ **800/231-0856**), offering daily flights out of its hub in Newark, New Jersey, and **LIAT** (☎ **800/468-0482** in the U.S. and Canada), with three flights out of San Juan. These latter flights stop first at Tortola (capital of the British Virgin Islands) before going on to St. Maarten. Even so, the trip usually takes only 90 minutes.

ALM Antillean Airlines (☎ **800/327-7230** in the U.S.) offers nonstop and once-daily direct service in winter to St. Maarten from the airline's home base on Curaçao. Off-season, there are two flights Sunday to Tuesday and again on Friday. **US Airways** (☎ **800/428-4322**) offers nonstop service from Baltimore on Saturday and Sunday and from Charlotte, North Carolina, on Sunday.

If you're coming from St. Barts, however, there are at least three airlines available to haul you and your possessions on the short route directly to French-speaking St. Martin. They include **Air Guadeloupe** (☎ **0590/87-10-36** on St. Martin) and its subsidiaries, **Air St-Martin** (☎ **0590/87-25-38**) and **Air St-Barthélemy** (☎ **0590/87-76-59**). Collectively, they maintain between 15 and 20 daily flights, each about 10 minutes long, from St. Barts, about a third of which land at L'Espérance. The cost of a one-way flight between St. Barts and French St. Martin on each of the three airlines mentioned above is 259F ($44.05) per person.

GETTING AROUND

BY TAXI   Since taxis are unmetered on both sides of the island, always agree on the rate before getting into an unmetered cab. Rate schedules are slightly different on the two sides. **St. Maarten taxis** have minimum fares for two passengers, and each additional passenger pays $2 extra. One piece of luggage per person is allowed free; each additional piece is 50¢. Fares are 25% higher between 10pm and midnight, and 50% higher between midnight and 6am. **St. Martin fares** are also for two passengers, but allow a supplement of about $1 for each suitcase or valise. These fares are in effect 7am to 10pm; after that, they go up by 25% until midnight, rising by 50% after midnight.

On the **Dutch side,** a typical fare from Queen Juliana Airport to the Maho Beach Hotel is $5; from Philipsburg to Queen Juliana Airport, $10. On the **French side,** taxi fares from Marigot to Grand-Case are $10, from Juliana Airport to Marigot and from Juliana Airport to La Samanna $14.

For late-night cab service on St. Maarten, call ☎ **599/5-54317.** A **Taxi Service & Information Center** operates at the port of Marigot (☎ **0590/87-56-54**) on the French side of the island.

BY MINIBUS   This is a reasonable means of transport on St. Maarten/St. Martin if you don't mind inconveniences, and at times overcrowding. Buses run daily 7am to midnight and serve most of the major locations on both sides of the island. The most popular run is from Philipsburg to Marigot on the French side. Privately owned and operated, minibuses tend to follow specific routes, with fares ranging from $1.15 to $2, depending on where you're going.

BY RENTAL CAR   Because of the island's size and diversity, car rentals are practical, particularly if you want to experience both the Dutch and the French sides. The taxi drivers' union strictly enforces a law that forbids anyone from picking up a car at the airport. As a result, every rental agency delivers cars directly to its customer's hotel (only if you've booked in advance), where an employee will complete the paperwork. If you prefer to rent your car on arrival, you can head for one of the tiny rental kiosks across the road from the airport, but beware of long lines. In recent years, policies against renting a car on the Dutch side to someone staying on the French have been less strict. But know in advance that the policy of car-rental outfits toward their counterparts on the opposite side of island seems about as changeable as the dishes at a local buffet. Check carefully before you go.

Bear in mind that **Budget** (☎ **800/527-0700** in the U.S., 599/5-54030 on the Dutch side, or 0590/87-38-22 on the French side), **Hertz** (☎ **800/654-3131** in the U.S., 599/5-54314 on the Dutch side, or 0590/87-40-68 on the French side), and **Avis** (☎ **800/331-1212** in the U.S., 599/5-52847 on the Dutch side, or 0590/87-50-60 on the French side) each maintain an office on both sides of the island. Another national chain represented is **National** (☎ **800/328-4567** in the U.S., 599/5-42168 in Cole Bay, or 599/5-96856 at Queen Juliana Airport). All these companies charge roughly equivalent rates, which are usually similar to rates at branches of the same company on the Dutch side.

All three major car-rental agencies require that renters be at least 25 years old. Your credit-card issuer may provide insurance coverage, so check before your trip; otherwise, it might be wise to buy the fairly cheap collision-damage waiver (CDW) when you rent.

BY BIKE OR SCOOTER Of course, it's far cheaper to get around the island by scooter or bike than by rented car. The best deal on such rentals is found at **Rent 2 Wheels,** Low Lands Road, Nettle Bay (☎ **0590/87-20-59**), just across the border on the French side. It rents scooters for 138F ($23.45) per day, with motorbikes beginning at 250F ($42.50).

Drive on the right-hand side (on both the French and Dutch sides of the island). Traffic jams are common near the island's major settlements, so be prepared to be patient. International road signs are observed, and there are no Customs formalities at the border between the island's political divisions.

Fast Facts: St. Maarten & St. Martin

Banking Hours On the Dutch side, most banks are open Monday to Thursday 8:30am to 1pm and Friday 8:30am to 1pm and 4 to 5pm. On the French side, they're also usually open every weekday afternoon 2 to 4 or 5pm, not only on Friday.

Currency The legal tender on the Dutch side is the **Netherlands Antilles guilder (NAf),** and the official rate at which the banks accept U.S. dollars is 1.80NAf for each U.S.$1. Regardless, U.S. dollars are easily and often eagerly accepted on St. Maarten. On the French side, the currency, officially at least, is the **French franc (F);** the current exchange rate is 5.90F to U.S.$1 (1F = 17¢ U.S.), but check the most up-to-date quotation at the time of your visit. Nevertheless, U.S. dollars seem to be preferred wherever you go. Since that seems to be true regardless of which side of the island you are on, prices in this chapter are given in U.S. currency unless otherwise designated.

Documents U.S., British, and Canadian citizens should have a passport, plus an ongoing or a return ticket and a confirmed hotel reservation.

Electricity   Dutch St. Maarten uses the same voltage (110 volts AC; 60 cycles) with the same electrical configurations as the United States, so adapters and transformers are not necessary. However, on French St. Martin transformers and adapters are necessary. To simplify things, many hotels on both sides of the island have installed built-in sockets suitable for both the European and North American forms of electrical currents.

Emergencies   On the Dutch side, call the **police** at ☎ **599/5-22222** or an **ambulance** at ☎ **599/5-22111.** On the French side, you can reach the **police** by dialing ☎ **17** or 0590/87-50-06. In case of **fire** dial ☎ **18.**

Hospitals   On the Dutch side, go to the **Medical Center,** Welegen Road, Cay Hill (☎ **599/5-31111**). On the French side, the local hospital is **Hospital de Marigot** in Marigot ☎ **0590/29-57-57** or 0590/29-57-48.

Language   The language on the St. Maarten side is officially Dutch, but most people speak English. The same is true for St. Martin, with English and French both widely spoken, though this is a French possession. A patois is spoken only by a small segment of the local populace.

Safety   Crime is on the rise on the island and, in fact, has become quite serious. If possible, avoid night driving—it's particularly unwise to drive on remote, unlit, back roads at night. Also, let that deserted, isolated beach remain so. You're safer in a crowd, though under no circumstances should you ever leave anything unguarded on the beach. The crime wave hitting Dutch St. Maarten also plagues French St. Martin.

Taxes & Service   There's no departure tax imposed for departures from Espérance Airport on the French side. However, for departures from Juliana Airport on the Dutch side, a departure tax of $20 is assessed ($6 if you're leaving the island for St. Eustatius or Saba).

On the Dutch side, an 8% government tax is added to hotel bills, and, in general, hotels also add a 10% or 15% service charge. If service has not been added (unlikely), it's customary to tip around 15% in restaurants. On the French side, your hotel is likely to add a 10% to 15% service charge to your bill to cover tipping. Likewise, most restaurant bills include the service charge.

Telephone   To call Dutch St. Maarten from the United States, dial **011** (the international access code), then **599** (the country code for the Netherlands Antilles), and finally **5** (the area code for Dutch St. Maarten) followed by the five-digit local number. To make a call within Dutch St. Maarten, you need only the five-digit local number. But if you're calling "long distance" from the Dutch side of the island to the French side of the island, dial **00,** followed by **590** (the international access code for French St. Martin), followed by the six-digit local number.

If you're on the French side of the island and want to call anyone on the Dutch side, you'll have to treat the call the same way you'd have handled a call to the Dutch side from the mainland of the United States: Dial **00,** followed by **599,** then **5,** followed by the five-digit local number. Know in advance that calls between the French and Dutch sides are considered long-distance calls and are much, much more expensive than you might have imagined considering the relatively short distances involved.

French St. Martin is linked to the Guadeloupe telephone system. To call French St. Martin from the United States, dial **011** (the international access code), then **590** (the country code for Guadeloupe), and then the six-digit local number. To make a call from French St. Martin to any point within French St. Martin, no codes are necessary—just dial the local six-digit French number.

Time   St. Maarten and St. Martin operate on Atlantic standard time year-round. Thus in winter when the United States is on standard time, if it's 6pm in Philipsburg it's 5pm in New York. During daylight saving time in the United States, the island and the U.S. east coast are on the same time.

Water   The water of St. Martin is safe to drink. In fact, most hotels serve desalinated water.

Weather   The island has a year-round temperature of about 80°F.

2 Accommodations You Can Afford

IN ST. MAARTEN

Remember, a government tax of 8% and a 10% to 15% service charge are added to your hotel bill. Ask about this when you book a room to save yourself a shock when you check out.

Calypso Guest House. Simpson Bay (P.O. Box 112), Philipsburg, St. Maarten, N.A. ☎ 599/5-54233. Fax 599/5-52881. 8 apts., all with kitchenette. A/C TV. Winter $92 apt. for 1; $100 apt. for 2; $160 2-bedroom apt. for 4. Off-season $57.50 apt. for 1; $92 apt. for 2; $120 2-bedroom apt. for 4. Extra person $15. AE, MC, V.

This is one of the smallest hotels on the island's Dutch side—a welcome contrast to the massive hotels that otherwise dominate the island. A 5-minute drive from both the airport (whose loud noises usually stop around dusk) and Simpson Bay Beach, it contains a plain but worthwhile restaurant, a bar, and rooms that are somewhat bigger (considering the low costs) than you might expect. The rooms have terra-cotta floor tiles, white walls, and simple (usually wicker) furnishings. That includes a good bed with a firm mattress and a small but tidy bath.

Caribbean Hotel. 90 Front St. (P.O. Box 236), Philipsburg, St. Maarten, N.A. ☎ 599/5-22028. 45 units. A/C TV TEL. Year-round $45 single; $65 double. AE, MC, V.

This hotel is popular with business travelers from other Caribbean islands, as well as cost-conscious vacationers looking for inexpensive lodgings in the heart of the Dutch capital, very close to the beach. It's in a three-story building with shops on the ground floor; climb a flight of steps to the second-floor reception area to register. The rooms, like the hotel's exterior, are outfitted in black and white with occasional touches of red and contain balconies with views over the back (which is quieter) or Front Street and the beach. They're small and have a sterile look but are clean, with decent but rather thin mattresses. The baths are cramped, with rather thin towels. At these great rates you don't get a lot of resort-type amenities—it's up to you to make your own fun. No meals are served on the premises, but many bars and cheap eateries are within walking distance.

Hotel L'Esperance. 4 Tiger Rd., Cay Hill, St. Maarten, N.A. ☎ 599/5-25355. Fax 599/5-24088. E-mail: esperanc@sintmaarten.net. 21 1-bedroom apts., 2 2-bedroom apts. A/C TV TEL. Winter $80 1-bedroom apt.; $120 2-bedroom apt. Off-season $60 1-bedroom apt.; $90 2-bedroom apt. Children 11 and under stay free in parents' apt. AE, DISC, MC, V.

The management exudes hospitality, as reflected by the bar operating on the honor system. This two-story white Mediterranean-style building is found in a residential area about 10 minutes from Philipsburg; you're a 10- to 15-minute walk from Belaire Beach, or about 10 to 15 minutes by car from the area's other good beaches. The lower apartments open onto patios, while the upper units have balconies. Each one-bedroom apartment comes with a living area, a dining area, and a refrigerator with a two-burner stove. The larger apartments have full kitchens where you can prepare your own meals, though there's a small restaurant serving mainly sandwiches and snacks. Guests often meet fellow guests at the bar. Because of its low cost and welcoming atmosphere, this is a haven for families, and baby-sitting can be arranged. A pool has been added.

Hotel Sylvia. 1 Leopard Rd., Cay Hill, St. Maarten, N.A. ☎ **599/5-23389.** 14 units. TV. Year-round $50–$60 single or double; $60 apt. No credit cards.

The rooms may be simple, but they're spotless. Near Philipsburg and only a 10-minute walk from the nearest beach, this two-story white concrete building is also quite close to some of St. Maarten's best restaurants and shopping. The rooms are decorated with somewhat worn carpeting and have either queen- or king-size beds with mattresses that could use replacing. Second-floor rooms open onto balconies. The rooms have air-conditioning, but the apartments, which have kitchens, are equipped with ceiling fans. The baths are cramped, with shower stalls and a small supply of thin towels. The restaurant serves three meals a day, a rather standard but affordable fare. Sylvia is more for adults; children aren't encouraged.

Joshua Rose Guest House. 7 Back St., Philipsburg, St. Maarten, N.A. ☎ **800/223-9815** in the U.S., or 599/5-24317. Fax 599/5-30080. E-mail: joshrose@sintmaarten.net. 14 units. A/C TV. Winter $50–$55 single; $70–$80 double. Off-season $40–$50 single; $50–$60 double. Children under 12 $10. AE, MC, V.

If you'd like to avoid transportation costs, you can stay in Philipsburg and walk wherever you need to go. This guest house on Back Street is perfect for that, only 1 block from the beach and within an easy walk of the leading entertainment, shopping, and restaurants. This family-owned facility rents small clean rooms with a vintage 1970s look. Some rooms open onto balconies with attractive mountain views. Don't expect much in the way of bedroom space, but units are suitable for one or two. The mattresses are comfortable, but the baths cramped and the towels thin. The hotel has a bar, plus a Chinese restaurant serving passable fare for lunch and dinner—at very low prices. However, if you really want to save money, you're invited to use the communal kitchen.

✪ **Sea Breeze Hotel.** 20 Cay Hill, St. Maarten, N.A. ☎ **599/5-26054.** Fax 599/5-26057. 30 units. A/C TV TEL. Winter $65 single; $75 double. Off-season $45 single; $55 double. Extra person $15. AE, DISC, MC, V.

It'll be a Dutch treat—at least for your wallet—if you stay here, far removed from the high prices of the megaresorts. This simple white concrete building is only 5 minutes from Philipsburg and a 5-minute walk from Belaire Beach. The small rooms are clean, comfortable, and plain but decently maintained, containing a firm mattress on the double or twin beds. The baths are a bit cramped with inadequate shelf space, but they're well cared for. To help you keep costs even lower, some accommodations have small kitchenettes; others contain just a refrigerator. The lower rooms have porches, and the upper units open onto balconies. There's a pool, a bar, and a simple restaurant serving three meals a day (other and better restaurants are within walking distance). Baby-sitting can be arranged.

Seaview Hotel & Casino. Front St. (P.O. Box 65), Philipsburg, St. Maarten, N.A. ☎ **599/5-22323.** Fax 599/5-24356. 45 units. A/C TV TEL. Winter $79–$99 single; $99–$130 double. Off-season $46–$54 single; $55–$66 double. AE, MC, V.

In the commercial heart of Philipsburg, this hotel might be ideal for easy access to the shops, bars, and restaurants of the Dutch side's capital. Set behind an anonymous-looking masonry façade, this place offers small but well-scrubbed accommodations, each with a comfortable bed with a recently renewed mattress. The baths are small, but are adequate in a typical roadside motel way. It's a favorite of business travelers from other Caribbean islands but is also a very good for a cost-conscious vacation on the beach. Breakfast is the only meal served, but all the restaurants of Philipsburg lie within a short walk.

WORTH A SPLURGE

Hotel La Châtelaine. Simpson Bay Beach (P.O. Box 2065), Philipsburg, St. Maarten, N.A. ☎ **599/5-54269.** Fax 599/5-53195. www.sint-maarten.com. E-mail: htlchtln@ sintmaarten.net. 12 apts., all with kitchenette. Winter $115–$175 1-bedroom apt. for 2; $235–$295 2-bedroom apt. for 2. Off-season $80–$110 1-bedroom apt. for 2; $165–$215 2-bedroom apt. for 2. Extra person $30 (up to 4 in a 1-bedroom apt., up to 6 in a 2-bedroom apt.). AE, MC, V.

This pink-sided apartment complex lies on an idyllic strip of white-sand beach. The only drawback is its proximity to the roar of the jets arriving and departing from the airport. (Luckily, air traffic is very light after 7pm.) The resort's focal point is a small but charming octagonal pool with a gazebo. Most visitors forsake the pool in favor of a chaise longue on the sands of nearby Simpson Bay. The hotel offers studio, one-bedroom, or two-bedroom apartments, the studios with kitchenettes and the others with complete kitchens. Some units can accommodate up to four by using living room couches for sleeping, and up to six can stay in a two-bedroom apartment with the addition of a roll-away bed (but that gets really crowded). Mattresses are a bit thin but fairly new, and all the baths are motel standard. Children 6 and under aren't accepted.

IN ST. MARTIN

Hotels on French St. Martin add a *taxe de séjour,* or government tax, and a 10% service charge. This visitors' tax on hotel rooms differs from hotel to hotel, depending on its classification, but the minimum is $3 a day.

Chez Martine. Blvd. de Grand-Case 140 (B.P. 637), 97150 St. Martin, F.W.I. ☎ **0590/ 87-51-59.** Fax 0590/87-87-30. 5 units. A/C. Winter 450F–550F ($76.50–$93.50) single or double. Off-season 350F–450F ($59.50–$76.50) single or double. Extra person 100F ($17). Rates include breakfast. AE, CB, DC, MC, V.

Chez Martine, one of Grand-Case's best-known restaurants, offers small guest rooms on the upper floor of its white two-story building at the edge of the bay, within easy walking distance of many other restaurants and bars. The furnishings include two single or two double beds, each with a good mattress and wicker headboard; wicker chairs; a small desk; and a sea view in some cases. The baths, though small, are adequate for the job and very well kept.

From May to September, the restaurant is open Monday to Saturday from noon to 2pm, and from 6 to 10:30pm. From December to April, the restaurant is open Monday to Saturday from noon to 3pm, and from 5:30 to 11pm. Main courses cost from 96F to 154F ($16.30 to $26.20).

Hévéa. Blvd. de Grand-Case 163, 97150 St. Martin, F.W.I. ☎ **0590/87-56-85.** Fax 0590/ 87-83-88. 5 units. A/C. Winter $58–$72 single; $80–$94 double; $122–$136 studio apt. with kitchen for 2. Off-season $44–$59 single; $55–$70 double; $92–$103 studio apt. with kitchen for 2. MC, V.

On sloping land across from the white sands of Grand-Case Beach, this small but charming guest house has named its accommodations after local flowers, shrubs, and trees. The setting is an old but much-renovated Creole house, with rooms surrounding a landscaped patio. The accommodations are small, but each contains carefully chosen antique artifacts and a fine twin or double bed with a good French mattress. Although none has a view of the sea, the relatively modest prices make this hotel a worthy and sometimes colorful choice. There's an expensive restaurant on the premises (Hévéa), open only for dinner. The cafes and restaurants of Grand-Case are a short walk away.

Jardins de Chevrise. Mont Vernon 52, 97150 St. Martin, F.W.I. ☎ **0590/87-37-79.** Fax 0590/87-38-03. 29 efficiency apts. with kitchenette. A/C TEL. Winter 570F ($96.90) single or double. Off-season 445F ($75.65) single or double. Extra person 100F ($17). MC, V.

These one-room apartments, each with a kitchenette, are in a series of two-story buildings connected by a network of pergolas surrounding an outdoor pool. The building is surrounded by palm trees and touched up with simple gingerbread trim. It's on a hillside overlooking Orient Bay in a subdivision of apartment buildings usually rented for weeks or months at a time. The apartments are clean, bright, and well maintained, with rattan furnishings, earth-toned upholstery in floral patterns, white walls, and tiled floors. In spite of the simple appointments, the beds are very good, with French mattresses; the baths are small but well maintained. A snack bar with limited offerings is beside the pool, but most visitors either cook in their rooms or dine out. Access to the beach at Orient Bay requires a rather steep descent down to the water.

La Résidence. Rue du Général-de-Gaulle (B.P. 679), Marigot, 97150 St. Martin, F.W.I. ☎ **800/423-4433** in the U.S., or 0590/87-70-37. Fax 0590/87-90-44. 21 units. A/C MINIBAR TV TEL. Year-round $72 single; $94 double. Rates include continental breakfast. AE, MC, V.

In the commercial center of town, La Résidence has a concrete façade enlivened with neo-Victorian gingerbread fretwork. Because of its location it's favored by business travelers. The small rooms are arranged around a landscaped central courtyard with a fish-shaped fountain. Each of the rooms contains a minimalist décor, and all but a few have sleeping lofts and a duplex design of mahogany-trimmed stairs and balustrades. The mattresses are a bit thin, but the general comfort level is acceptable. Room service is available. The hotel is known for its French and Creole restaurant (reviewed below), and a bar with a soaring tent serves drinks.

Le Cigalon. Rue Fichot 11, Marigot, 97150 St. Martin, F.W.I. ☎ **0590/87-08-19.** Fax 0590/87-79-84. 10 units. A/C. Year-round 230F ($39.10) single; 280F ($47.60) double; 330F ($56.10) triple. No credit cards.

This white-fronted Creole home with terraced pergolas lies in the heart of Marigot, on a quiet side street. The motel-like units are nothing to write home about, but they're a great value on this expensive island. Each is decorated with the utmost simplicity, usually with a handful of pictures, a bed with a good mattress, and a small modern writing table and chair, plus a tiny bath. The beach at Friar's Bay, a 10-minute car ride from the hotel, provides the closest site for swimming and sunbathing. A verdant garden surrounds the building, and Le Cigalon restaurant serves dinner every day December through April. The cuisine, steeped in Provençal traditions, includes traditional platters at 50F to 80F ($8.50 to $13.60). The owners are the Garabello family, who imbue the place with their personality and charm.

Le Royale Louisiana. Rue du Général-de-Gaulle, Marigot, 97150 St. Martin, F.W.I. ☎ **0590/87-86-51.** Fax 0590/87-96-49. 58 units. A/C TV TEL. Winter 350F ($59.50) single; 440F–490F ($74.80–$83.30) double; 610F–690F ($103.70–$117.30) duplex. Off-season 300F ($51) single; 410F ($69.70) double; 640F ($108.80) duplex. Rates include continental breakfast. AE, MC, V.

Occupying a prominent position in the center of Marigot, 10 miles north of the airport, this hotel is designed in a hip-roofed French-colonial Louisiana style; its rambling balconies are graced with ornate balustrades. Each small- to medium-size accommodation contains big sunny windows and modern furniture. Standard rooms have either king- or queen-size beds with good mattresses, and duplexes, ideal for families, have a bedroom and bath on the upper level and a sitting room with a foldout sofa on the lower floor. The baths are well maintained but a bit cramped. The restaurant serves a simple breakfast, plus salads and sandwiches at lunch, and the bar is open in the evening.

Marina Royale Hôtel. Marina La Royale (B.P. 176), 97150 St. Martin, F.W.I. ☎ **0590/ 87-52-46.** Fax 0590/87-92-88. 70 apts. A/C TV TEL. Year-round 400F ($68) studio with kitchenette for 1 or 2; 500F ($85) studio with kitchenette for 1 to 4; 600F ($102) duplex apt. with kitchenette for up to 6; 900F ($153) duplex apt. with kitchenette for up to 8. No credit cards.

This long two-story building sits at the edge of a marina at the seaward end of Marigot's rue du Général-de-Gaulle. It was built as a member of the Novotel chain, but since new owners took over in the 1990s, touches of rattan, floral curtains, white paint, and carpeting have been added. The rooms are bright and airy in the tropical motif, each with a fine French mattress; the baths are a bit cramped, lacking enough shelf space. Guests either cook in their apartments or try any of the many restaurants and snack bars of Marigot. No food or beverage facilities are at the hotel.

WORTH A SPLURGE

✪ **Hôtel Pavillon Beach.** Plage de Grand-Case (B.P. 5133), 97070 St. Martin, F.W.I. ☎ **0590/87-96-46.** Fax 0590/87-71-04. 17 units. A/C TV TEL. Winter 850F ($144.50) studio for 1; 950F ($161.50) studio for 2; 1,300F ($221) suite for 2. Off-season 450F ($76.50) studio for 1; 650F ($110.50) studio for 2; 850F ($144.50) suite for 2. Rates include continental breakfast. AE, MC, V.

This small two-story hotel lies a few feet from the edge of the sea, adjacent to Grand-Case Beach. Built in 1990, it's well designed and stylish, with decorative touches (tiles, urn-shaped balustrades, and kitchenettes) you might expect in more expensive lodgings. Each small accommodation has sliding glass doors with views over the water, wicker and rattan furnishings, a radio, and a safe. You can select a room on the ground floor and walk right onto the beach. Or you may prefer one of the upper-story accommodations—that way you can leave the shutters open to enjoy the trade winds. The kitchenettes are compact open-air affairs, each with a tiled countertop and wooden cabinet doors. This place doesn't offer much in the way of resort-type amenities: no pool, no bar, and no restaurant. Access to tennis courts and water sports can be arranged, and the many bars and restaurants of Grand-Case lie within a short walk.

3 Great Deals on Dining

IN ST. MAARTEN

A favorite for the partying crowd is **Everyt'ing Cool,** 95 Front St. in Philipsburg (☎ **599/5-31011**), though many do come just to eat. The place is known for its 81 varieties of both alcoholic and nonalcoholic piña coladas. You can come for the everyday party deal where you'll get a locker, a floating mattress, sports on the beach, and lunch and drinks all for $19.95. They close at 5pm daily.

✪ **Cheri's Café.** 45 Cinnamon Grove, Shopping Centre, Maho Beach. ☎ **599/5-53361.** Main courses $5.75–$19.75. MC, V. Daily 11am–midnight. AMERICAN.

The island hot spot, Cheri's was the winner of the *Caribbean Travel and Life* readers' pick for best bar in the West Indies. Known for its inexpensive food and live bands, it's by now an island institution. American expat Cheri Baston is the duenna of this open-air cafe serving some 400 meals a night. The place is really only a roof without walls, and it's not on a beach, but people flock to it anyway, devouring 18-ounce steaks or simple burgers. It's also possible to get grilled fresh fish platters. You can dine under the canopy or on a terrace under the stars. The bartender's special is a frozen "Straw Hat" made with vodka, coconut, tequila, pineapple and orange juice, and strawberry liqueur (and maybe even one more ingredient, we suspect, though nobody's talking).

✪ **Crocodile Express Café.** Casino Balcony, at the Pelican Resort Club, Simpson Bay. ☎ **599/5-42503.** Main courses $5.95–$13.75; sandwiches and salads $3.25–$9.50. DISC, MC, V. Daily 7:30am–11pm. DELI/GRILL/INTERNATIONAL.

Start the day overlooking Simpson Bay by enjoying extra-thick French toast made from homemade egg bread with fresh tropical fruits on top, or order eggs any style. There's continuous service throughout the day, beginning with breakfast and followed by lunch, with snacks in the afternoon. Many patrons file in for dinner as early as 6pm. Hearty deli fare includes well-stuffed sandwiches, but at night you might prefer grilled local fish or tasty kebabs. A specialty is grilled chicken breast West Indian style, marinated in tropical fruit juices and served with grilled onions. On Thursday it's all-you-can-eat barbecued chicken and ribs, costing $12.95. Meals are followed by home-baked pies and other desserts, and drinks include fresh mango or frozen passion fruit. On the beach Wednesdays 5 to 9pm there's a beach-party barbecue and a limbo show, with nail-dancing, fire-eating, magic, and steel-band music. The cost is $13.75 for the chicken-and-ribs dinner, and there's no cover.

Don Carlos Restaurant. Airport Rd., Simpson Bay. ☎ **599/5-53112.** Main courses $10.50–$28.50. AE, DC, DISC, MC, V. Daily 7:30am–10pm. MEXICAN/CARIBBEAN/INTERNATIONAL.

This down-home restaurant is just 5 minutes east of the airport, with a view of arriving and departing planes from the floor-to-ceiling windows. It serves breakfast, lunch, and dinner, providing consistently decent fare at reasonable prices. Owners Shenny and Carl Wagner invite you for a drink in their Pancho Villa Bar before your meal in their hacienda-style dining room with a multilingual staff. Quantity, instead of quality, is the rule here, but diners seem to view this as a "fun" choice.

The Greenhouse. Bobby's Marina (off Front St.), Philipsburg. ☎ **599/5-22941.** Main courses $8.95–$15.95. AE, MC, V. Daily 11am–1am. AMERICAN.

Open to a view of the harbor, the Greenhouse is filled with plants. As you dine, breezes filter through the open-air eatery. The menu features the catch of the day as well as burgers, pizza, and salads. Dinner specials might include fresh lobster Thermidor, Jamaican jerk pork, or salmon in light dill sauce. Some of the island's best steaks are served here, each cut certified Angus beef, including a New York strip, a T-bone, a porterhouse, or a filet mignon. The chef specializes in chicken, ranging from mango chicken to chicken parmigiana. Happy Hour is daily 4:30 to 7pm and features half-price appetizers and two-for-one drinks. The DJ not only spins out tunes but also gives prizes to Bingo champs and Trivia experts. There are also pool tables and video games to keep you entertained.

Indiana Beach. Simpson Bay. ☎ **0599/5-42797.** Reservations recommended. Lunch main courses $8–$15; dinner main courses $15–$25. AE, MC, V. Daily noon–3pm and 6–11pm. INTERNATIONAL.

The theme of this place revolves around the exploits and adventures of cinematic hero Indiana Jones as portrayed by Harrison Ford in the popular films. As such, you'll find a small forest of potted palms and plants; murals showing Temples of Doom and Egyptian hieroglyphs; and in the garden outside, caged birds, snakes, and a crocodile. Inside, you might think you've wandered over to the island's French side by accident, as you'll find a very French staff that isn't the least shy about imposing their language on English-speaking guests. The fare is always reliable and often superb. Menu items include a combination seafood platter; grilled snapper with mango sauce; grilled filet mignon with your choice of mushroom, pepper, or béarnaise sauce; and a selection of fish imported from the French mainland (grilled sea bass with fennel, Dover sole with butter sauce, or fresh tuna with béarnaise sauce). Looking for an appropriately racy cocktail? Consider the Indiana Beach, made with dark rum, Dubonnet, and passion fruit liqueurs.

✪ **Lynette's.** Simpson Bay Blvd. ☎ **599/5-52865.** Reservations recommended. Main courses $13.75–$32. AE, MC, V. Winter daily 11:30am–10:30pm. Off-season daily 6–10:30pm. WEST INDIAN.

This is the most noteworthy West Indian restaurant on St. Maarten. It's completely unpretentious, rich in local flavors and understated charm. St. Maarten–born Lynette Felix, along with Clayton Felix, are the creative forces here. The menu reads like a lexicon of tried-and-true Caribbean staples, like colombos (ragôuts) of goat and chicken, stuffed crab backs, curried seafood, and snapper fillet with green plantains and Creole sauce or garlic butter. An ideal lunch might be a brimming bowl of pumpkin (squash) soup followed by one of the main-course salads. The one made from herbed lobster, when available, is particularly succulent.

Ric's Place. 69 Front St., Phillipsburg. ☎ **0599/52-60-50.** Platters $3–$10.50. No credit cards. Daily 8am–11am and 11am–9pm. Closed 4 weeks Aug–Sept. AMERICAN/TEX-MEX.

This rough-and-ready sports bar stretches from Front Street all the way through to the beachfront, where guests sometimes go swimming or sunbathing before or after a meal. The décor includes the hundreds of commemorative T-shirts, baseball caps, and trucker's logos that well-wishing past diners have affixed to the walls—the resulting visual bombardment is complemented by the blare from the video screens on which replays of the previous night's football or baseball game are broadcast. Menu items include Tex-Mex specialties like burritos, taco salads, and enchiladas. More *norteamericano* are the overstuffed sandwiches and salads. The juicy burgers are the biggest on the island. The most popular drinks are vodka-laced lemonade and the several kinds of margaritas.

Shiv Sagar. 20 Front St., Philipsburg. ☎ **599/5-22299.** Reservations recommended. Main courses $14.75–$16.75. AE, DC, MC, V. Mon–Sat 11:30am–3pm and 6:30–10pm, Sun 11:30am–3pm. EAST INDIAN.

This restaurant opposite Barclay's Bank serves the island's only Indian cuisine. Because of its large selection of vegetarian dishes, it's also the best choice for noncarnivores. The cuisine roams freely through the East Indian kitchen, concentrating mainly on Mogul and Kashmiri specialties. Rôtis are prepared before diners in a traditional tandoori oven, and the curries are zesty and spicy. You can also order a number of unusual specialties—perhaps red snapper cooked in a blend of hot spices. The open-air bar out front is one of the friendliest on the island.

✪ **Turtle Pier Bar & Restaurant.** 114 Airport Rd., Simpson Bay. ☎ **599/5-52562.** Lunch main courses $6.50–$17.25; dinner main courses $11.95–$50. AE, DISC, MC, V. Daily 7:30am–10pm; bar remains open daily to 11 or 11:30pm. CARIBBEAN/INTERNATIONAL.

Less than a quarter-mile from the airport, on sunblasted scrubland adjacent to the lagoon, this restaurant offers well-prepared food, stiff drinks, and the added benefit of a 50-member menagerie (zoo) many diners interpret as an intriguing prelude before their meal. Members of the zoo include an aviary of birds, like colorful parrots that talk; turtles; rabbits; iguanas; monkeys; lobsters; and even a shark that swims nervously back and forth in a holding tank. Menu items include Creole-style grouper, roasted duck with either ginger or guavaberry sauce, conch fritters, stuffed christophene, and several preparations of lobster and burgers. A particularly popular burger is a "Turtle Pier," piling a beef patty atop an English muffin with lots of spinach, béarnaise sauce, and coleslaw. A particularly popular drink is a frozen colada. Wednesdays feature a live band and a $26 fixed-price dinner that includes a 1-pound lobster.

Village Café. In the Village Shopping Center, Front St., Philipsburg. ☎ **599/5-20361.** Sandwiches and main courses $4–$6. No credit cards. Daily 8:30am–5:30pm. WEST INDIAN.

Although many restaurants are very expensive on St. Maarten, you can dine inexpensively without resorting to fast-food joints. This small restaurant on the waterfront is a case in point. You can eat on the patio or inside amid a number of plants. If you arrive for breakfast, you can order ample but standard fare; the fresh pastries are best. Throughout the day you can sample various hot local dishes, including a special like chicken with rice and peas. Otherwise, there's an array of fresh salads and sandwiches served on fresh French bread. The ham-and-cheese special, for example, comes in a foot-long baguette that's ample enough for two—and only $3.75.

BEST FIXED-PRICE MENUS

Pelican Reef Restaurant and Seafood House. Waterfront Marina, at the Pelican Resort Club, Simpson Bay. ☎ **599/5-42503,** ext. 5950. Reservations recommended. Main courses $13.75–$29.95; fixed-price menus $17–$28. AE, DISC, MC, V. Daily 6:30–10:30pm. STEAK/SEAFOOD/INTERNATIONAL.

This American steakhouse not only serves what are reputed to be the island's best steaks, but also offers tasty chops and seafood. Hosts Marvin and Jean Rich offer fine, friendly service and good-quality ingredients, artfully served with a view over Simpson Bay. Signature dishes are a hearty slab of prime rib on the bone, grilled Argentinian style on a charcoal grill; whole Caribbean lobster, baked and stuffed; grilled fish fillet, perhaps red snapper, from local waters; rack of baby lamb; or a thick veal chop. Mention should be made of the El Gaucho steak, a chateaubriand cut from Argentina—a tasty treat because of its leanness and its uniquely rich flavor because the cattle were grass-fed on the pampas. Served grilled on a wooden plank, it's accompanied by a cognac-and-peppercorn sauce, vegetables, and steak fries. Save room for the conch fritters with two sauces and follow with a "chocolate island" or the frozen fantasy dessert. A special feature of the wine list is a "tasting" of fine armagnacs, unique because they're from single estates and both are made from 100% ugni blanc, a rare grape used only in the making of armagnacs and cognacs.

IN ST. MARTIN
IN & AROUND MARIGOT

Hévéa. Blvd. de Grand-Case 163. ☎ **0590/87-56-85.** Reservations required. Main courses 100F–210F ($17–$35.70); menu Creole (featuring West Indian items) 145F ($24.65). AE, MC, V. Daily 6:30–11pm. Closed Sept–Oct. FRENCH.

Normandy-born restaurateurs (a team headed by Annick Grasset) own this place, the most obviously French of any restaurant in Grand-Case. After storm damage in 1995, they reopened with Louis XV chairs, Norman artifacts, and candlelight. There are fewer than a dozen tables, so reservations are very important. The Caesar salad remains the best on the island. Opinion continues to be divided whether they do meat or fish dishes better. In honor of their Norman roots, the owners prepare classic French dishes like scallops *Dieppoise* (with cream-flavored mussel sauce); veal chops *Pays d'Auge,*

Cheap Thrills: What to See & Do for Free (Well, Almost) on St. Maarten & St. Martin

- **Chase After Butterflies.** Far from the crowds, you may want to seek out bucolic St. Martin. The little village of Orléans (also called the French Quarter) is the island's oldest French settlement. Its houses (called *cases*) are set in meadows that blossom with hibiscus, bougainvillea, and wisteria. On the road to Bayside and Galion is the charming **Butterfly Farm,** Route de Baie L'Embouchure (☎ **0590/87-31-21**), run by two Englishmen who created this Eden-like setting. Visitors are offered a rare insight into the amazing transformations between an egg and a butterfly. You'll learn all about these delicate creatures and meet such beauties as the Brazilian Blue Morpho and the Cambodian Wood Nymph. Morning visits are ideal.

- **Spend a Day at a Nudist Beach.** Many cruise-ship passengers, in St. Martin only for 2 or 3 hours, head immediately to the wild and wacky beach at Orient Bay, especially if they have a voyeuristic streak. This is one of the best-known clothing-optional beaches in the Caribbean, and most of the bodies on display are at the naturalist resort of Club Orient, at the middle of the beach. In the center are several local hangouts, often with bars and restaurants featuring live bands playing great music throughout the day. Our favorite spot is the open-air bar/restaurant **Kontiki** (☎ **0590/87-43-27**), where most patrons are clothed; the nudie area for the less inhibited drinker is a short stroll away. You can stick around for lunch, ordering reasonably good sushi or fresh lobster from saltwater holding tanks. After lunch you can rent a jet ski, go parasailing, or join in a hobie car race. Snorkeling equipment can be rented at various kiosks.

- **People-Watch in Philipsburg.** At Wathey Square (pronounced watty) in the center of the Dutch capital of St. Maarten you can sit and watch the world go by. This is the heartbeat of this thriving little town with its duty-free shops. It's filled with tourists and cruise-ship passengers, trinket peddlers, vendors, and all sorts of shops. That building across the street from the square with its white cupola dates from 1793 and has been everything from a jail to a fire station, but today it's the town hall and courthouse. Directly off the square is the town's largest collections of shops, restaurants, and cafes. Take any narrow alley leading to an arcade for an adventure. Once you reach these arcades you'll find flower-filled courtyards, more shops, and plenty of eateries. The town is filled with West Indian cottages decorated with a trim of gingerbread.

- **Visit Remote Ilet Pinel.** At the north end of Orient Bay on the Atlantic coast, Etang de la Parrière (technically part of mainland France) is the island's most beautiful cove, its sand banks filled with hundreds of ancient shells. Offshore here to the north is the remote Ilet Pinel, with fine white-sand beaches and reefs idyllic for snorkeling. Sometimes schools of rainbow-hued fish surround this island. The only inhabitants, other than visitors for the day, are wild goats feeding on the cacti and scrub brush. In an hour you can traverse the entire island. At Cul de Sac, the settlement on the French side, you can take a shuttle boat for $5 to take you over to this little bit of Eden.

made with apple brandy (Calvados) and cream; and *aiguillettes* of roasted duckling with honey sauce. You might also try the terrine of duck or *foie gras maison*. To remind you you're in the West Indies, there's a set-price all-Creole menu and a platter of West Indian smoked fish.

La Brasserie de Marigot. Rue du Général-de-Gaulle 11. ☎ **0590/87-94-43.** Main courses 45F–88F ($7.65–$14.95). AE, MC, V. Mon–Sat 7am–9pm, Sun 9am–4pm. FRENCH.

This is where the local French eat. It has a marble-and-brass décor and a sort of retro-1950s style, with green leather banquettes. Meals include pot-au-feu, stuffed snapper with conch, beef filet with mushroom sauce, veal with goat cheese, and even chicken on a spit and steak tartare. Naturally, you can order interesting terrines, and wine is sold by the glass, carafe, or bottle. The kitchen prepares a handful of Caribbean dishes as well, like swordfish in garlic sauce. The brasserie is air-conditioned, with sidewalk tables overlooking the pedestrian traffic outside. It also features the most glamorous "takeout" service in St. Martin.

Le Bar de la Mer. Rue Felix-Eboué 2. ☎ **590/87-81-79.** Pizzas, burgers, pastas, and salads 42F–78F ($7.15–$13.25); platters 76F–125F ($12.90–$21.25). AE, MC, V. Daily 8am–2am. INTERNATIONAL.

Its walls adorned with primitive Haitian paintings and its tables overlooking the food, vegetable, and handcrafts market of Marigot, this restaurant offers a menu of well-prepared dishes. There's a dish for virtually every budget and taste, including pastas, pizzas, grilled local fish, burgers, lobster, and barbecued ribs. Breakfast anyone? Mornings attract local merchants and office workers who appreciate the croissants, steaming cups of tea and coffee, and a tipple of wine or two as a means of jump-starting their day. Every night there's a barbecue on the beach, and live entertainment is most often featured.

Le Kontiki. Adjacent to the Hôtel La Plantation, Orient Bay Beach. ☎ **0590/87-43-27.** Main courses 88F–198F ($14.95–$33.65). AE, MC, V. Sat and Mon–Thurs noon–6pm, Fri noon–11pm, and Sun noon–8pm. FRENCH/ASIAN/INTERNATIONAL.

Decorated like a low-slung replica of a wood-sheathed Creole house, this beachfront bar, cafe, restaurant, and water-sports kiosk functions as the centerpiece for many tourists' days at the beach (part of which is nude). It's surrounded with about half a dozen thatch-covered cabañas for beach lovers and serves potent versions of rum-runners. The ambience is low-key, relaxed, and Gallic. The food includes lots of well-prepared seafood and grilled fish, as well as local versions of sushi—usually salmon, tuna, octopus, and squid. Jet skis and water scooters rent for $50 per half-hour session, and parachute waterskiing goes for $55 for a 15-minute *ballade*.

✪ **Rainbow Café.** Blvd. de Grand-Case 176, Grand-Case. ☎ **0590/87-55-80.** Reservations recommended. Main courses 105F–165F ($17.85–$28.05). AE, MC, V. Daily 6–11pm. Closed Sun Apr–Nov. FRENCH/INTERNATIONAL.

On the northeastern end of the row of restaurants lining both sides of the main road, this is a particularly worthy contender thriving under the direction of Dutch-born Fleur Radd and Buffalo, New York–born David Hendricks. The circa-1970s house opens onto views over the sea, and meals are served in an artfully simple dining room in shades of dark blue and white. Menu items evolve almost every evening, inspired by such dishes as snapper in parmesan-onion crust with tomato-flavored vinaigrette, and chicken breast marinated in lemongrass and ginger, with grilled balsamic-glazed vegetables. There's also salmon in puff pastry with spinach and citrus-dill butter sauce, and fricassee of scallops and shrimp with Caribbean chutney.

Restaurant La Résidence/La Petite Bouffe. In the Hotel La Résidence, Rue du Général-de-Gaulle. ☎ **0590/87-70-37.** Reservations recommended for dinner. La Résidence, set dinner 150F ($25.50). La Petite Bouffe, lunch platters 35F–55F ($5.95–$9.35). AE, MC, V. La Résidence Mon–Sat 6:30–10pm, Le Petite Bouffe Mon–Sat noon–2pm. FRENCH.

This open-air restaurant, associated with a previously recommended hotel, opens onto a view over the quiet interior passage of a complex of buildings near the Marina Royale. Lunch is served in an informal street-level annex, La Petite Bouffe, and more formal fixed-price dinners are offered at La Résidence upstairs. It's decorated with green-and-white tents and potted plants that contribute privacy to the dining tables. The menu includes a worthy version of an Antillean *soupe de poissons* (fish soup), like a Provençal bouillabaisse. You can also order a filet steak in green-peppercorn sauce flambéed in cognac, or snapper or grouper baked with olive oil and spices, plus dessert soufflés flavored with chocolate or Grand Marnier.

✪ **Yvette's.** Orléans. ☎ **0590/87-32-03.** Main courses $8.50–$27. No credit cards. Daily noon–2:30pm and 6–10pm. WEST INDIAN.

Owner Yvette Hyman-Connor prides herself on the simplicity of her "home cooking" and on the fact that she weathered the 1998 hurricanes with her business battered but intact. The setting is a part-wood, part-concrete white-sided house just off the main street running through the hamlet of Orléans, flanked with a dusty garden. Menu items are partly inspired by the cuisine of Aruba, where Ms. Hyman-Connor spent many years before returning to her native St. Martin. Know in advance that this place draws a lot of locals, many of whom wouldn't ever consider a meal at any of St. Martin's grander places. The most popular items are curried coconut-flavored chicken, stewed fresh conch with onions and fresh tomatoes, conch dumplings boiled in a conch shell in herb- and wine-scented water, and a lobster-and-shrimp combo with butter sauce. Consider prefacing a meal with one of the house special cocktails, a rum-based guavaberry or lime punch. If you'd like to sample really authentic Creole cuisine, you can do no better than Yvette's.

4 Hitting the Beaches

The island has 36 beautiful white-sand beaches, and it's fairly easy to find a part of the beach for yourself. Most beaches have recovered from the erosion caused by the 1995 hurricane. *Warning:* If it's too secluded, be careful. It's unwise to carry valuables to the beach; there have been reports of robberies on some remote strips.

Regardless of where you stay, you're never far from the water. If you're a beach sampler, you can often use the changing facilities at some of the bigger resorts for a small fee. Nudists should head for the French side of the island, though the Dutch side is getting more liberal about such things. Here's a rundown of the best, starting on the Dutch side of the island.

West of the airport, **Mullet Bay Beach** is filled with white sand and shaded by palm trees. Once it was the most crowded beach on the island, but St. Maarten's largest resort, Mullet Bay, remains closed at press time, enabling you to find your place in the sun today. Weekdays are best, as many locals flock here on weekends. Water-sports equipment can be rented at a kiosk here. North of the airport, **Maho Bay Beach,** at the Maho Beach Hotel and Casino, is shaded by palms and is ideal in many ways, if you don't mind the planes taking off and landing. This is one of the island's busiest beaches, buzzing with windsurfers. Food and drink can be bought at the hotel.

Stretching the length of Simpson Bay Village are the mile-long white sands of crescent-shaped **Simpson Bay Beach,** west of Philipsburg before you reach the airport. This beach is popular with windsurfers, and it's an ideal place for a stroll or a swim. Water-sports equipment rentals are available here, but there are no changing rooms or other facilities. **Great Bay Beach** is preferred if you're staying along Front Street in Philipsburg. This mile-long beach is sandy, but since it borders the busy capital, it may not be as clean as some of the more remote choices. On a clear day, you'll have a view of Saba. To the west, at the foot of Fort Amsterdam, is picturesque **Little Bay Beach**—but it, too, can be overrun with tourists. When you tire of the sands here, you can climb up to the site of Fort Amsterdam itself. Built in 1631, it was the first Dutch military outpost in the Caribbean. The Spanish captured it two years later, making it their most important bastion east of Puerto Rico. Only a few of the fort's walls remain, but the view is panoramic.

Dawn Beach is noted for its underwater tropical beauty, with some of the island's most beautiful reefs immediately offshore. Visitors talk ecstatically of its incredible sunrises. Dawn is suitable for swimming and offers year-round activities such as sand-castle-building contests and crab races. There's plenty of wave action for both surfers and windsurfers. The road to this beach is bumpy, but worth the effort. Nearby are the pearly white sands of **Oyster Pond Beach,** near the Oyster Pond Hotel northeast of Philipsburg. Bodysurfers like the rolling waves here.

Beyond the sprawling Mullet Beach Resort on the Dutch side, the popular **Cupecoy Bay Beach** is just north of the Dutch-French border, on the western side of the island. It's a string of three white-sand beaches set against a backdrop of caves, beautiful rock formations, and cliffs that provide morning shade. There are no restaurants, bars, or other facilities here, but locals come around with coolers of cold beer and soda. The beach has two parking lots, one near Cupecoy and Sapphire beach clubs, the other a short distance to the west. Parking costs $2. You must descend stone-carved steps to reach the sands. Cupecoy is also the island's major gay beach.

Top rating on St. Martin goes to **Baie Longue,** a beautiful beach that's rarely over-crowded. Chic and very expensive La Samanna opens onto this beachfront. Its reef-protected waters are ideal for snorkeling, but there's a strong undertow. Baie Longue is to the north of Cupecoy Beach, reached via the Lowlands Road. Don't leave any valuables in your car, as many break-ins have been reported along this occasionally dangerous stretch of highway. If you continue north along the highway, you'll reach another long and popular stretch of sand and jagged coral, **Baie Rouge.** Swimming is excellent here, and snorkelers are drawn to the rock formations at both ends of the beach. This intimate little spot is especially lovely in the morning. There are no changing facilities, but a local kiosk sells cold drinks.

Orient Beach is the island's only official nudist beach, so anything—or nothing—goes, in terms of attire. There's steady shore-side action here: bouncy Caribbean bands, refreshments of all kinds, water sports, and clothing, crafts, and jewelry vendors. Our favorite spot is the open-air bar/restaurant **Kontiki** (☎ **0590/87-43-27**), offering fresh lobster and reasonably good sushi for lunch. Club Orient, the nude resort, is at the end of the beach; voyeurs from cruise ships can always be spotted here. This is also a haven for windsurfers.

White-sand **Grand Case Beach** is right in the middle of the town of Grand Case and is likely to be crowded, especially on weekends. The waters are very calm here, making swimming excellent. A small but select beach, it has its own charm, with none of the carnival-like atmosphere of Orient Beach. Finally, for the most isolated and secluded beach of all, you have to leave St. Martin. **Ilet Pinel,** off the coast at Cul de Sac, is reached by a $5 boat ride off the northeast coast. Once on this islet, you'll find no residents (except wild goats), phones, or electricity. You will find fine white-sand beaches, reefs idyllic for snorkeling, and waters great for bodysurfing. There are even two beach bars: Pitou's and Karibuni. Both rent lounge chairs and serve dishes such as lobster, ribs, and grilled chicken.

5 Sports & Outdoor Pursuits

GOLF   The **Mullet Bay Resort** (☎ 599/5-52801, ext. 1850) on the Dutch side has an 18-hole course, one of the most challenging in the Caribbean, designed by Joseph Lee. Mullet Pond and Simpson Bay Lagoon provide both beauty and hazards. Greens fees are $62 for 9 holes or $108 for 18 holes. Clubs cost $21 for 9 holes or $26 for 18 holes.

HORSEBACK RIDING   **Crazy Acres,** Dr. J. H. Dela Fuente St., Cole Bay (☎ 599/5-42793), on the Dutch side, is your best get for riding expeditions. Two experienced escorts accompany a maximum of six people on the outings, which begin at 9:30am and 2:30pm Monday to Saturday and last 2½ hours. The price is $55 per person. Riders of all levels of experience are welcome. Reserve at least a day in advance; riding lessons are available.

SCUBA DIVING   Scuba diving is excellent around French St. Martin, with reef, wreck, night, cave, and drift diving; the depth of dives is 20 to 70 feet. Off the northeastern coast on the French side, dive sites include Ilet Pinel, for shallow diving; Green Key, a barrier reef; and Tintamarre, for sheltered coves and geologic faults. To the north, Anse Marcel and neighboring Anguilla are good choices. Most hotels will arrange for scuba excursions on request.

The island's premier dive operation is **Marine Time,** whose offices are based in the same building as L'Aventure, Chemin du Port, 97150 Marigot (☎ 0590/87-20-28). Operated from in front of the Market Dock in downtown Marigot by British-born Philip Baumann and his Mauritius-born colleague, Corine Mazurier, it offers morning and afternoon dives in deep and shallow water, wreck dives, and reef dives at $45 per dive. A resort course for first-timers with reasonable swimming skills is $80 and includes 60 to 90 minutes of instruction in a pool, then a one-tank dive above a coral reef. Full PADI certification costs $400, requires 5 days, and includes classroom training, sessions with a SCUBA tank in the safety of a pool, and three open-water dives. You can also arrange snorkeling trips with this outfitter, costing $25 for half a day or $75 for a full day, plus $10 for equipment rental.

You can also try **Blue Ocean Watersport & Dive Center,** BP 4079, Baie Nettlé, St. Martin (☎ 0590/87-89-73). A certified one-tank dive costs $45, including equipment. A PADI certification course is available for $350 and takes 4 to 5 days. Three one-tank dives are offered for $120 or five dives for $175. Snorkeling trips are more modestly priced at $30 and are conducted daily 1:30 to 4:30pm.

Dutch St. Maarten's crystal-clear bays and the countless coves make for good **snorkeling** and **scuba diving.** Underwater visibility reportedly runs from 75 to 125 feet. The biggest attraction for scuba divers is the 1801 British man-of-war, *HMS Proselyte,* which came to a watery grave on a reef a mile off the coast. Most of the big resort hotels have facilities for scuba diving, and their staff can provide information about underwater tours, for photography as well as for night diving.

The best water sports, and the best value, are found at **Pelican Watersports,** Pelican Resort and Casino, Simpson Bay (☎ 599/5-42640). Its PADI-instructed program features the most knowledgeable guides on the island, each one familiar with St. Maarten dive sites. Divers are taken out in custom-built 28- and 35-foot boats, and many return to claim they've been led to some of the best reef diving in the Caribbean. A single-tank dive costs $45 and a double-tank dive $90. Snorkeling trips can also be arranged, as can trips to nearby islands, including Saba, Anguilla, and St. Barts.

SNORKELING The calm waters ringing the shallow reefs and tiny coves found throughout the island make it a snorkeler's heaven. But the waters off the northeastern shores of French St. Martin have been classified as a regional underwater nature reserve, **Réserve Sous-Marine Régionale.** The area, comprising Flat Island (also known as Tintamarre), Pinel Islet, Green Key, Proselyte, and Petite Clef, is thus protected by official government decree. The use of harpoons is strictly forbidden. Snorkeling can be enjoyed individually or on sailing trips. Equipment can be rented at almost any hotel.

One of St. Martin's best-recommended sites for snorkeling, sunning, and generalized beach diversions is **Carib Watersports** (☎ **0590/87-51-87**), an independently operated clothing store, art gallery, and water-sports kiosk occupying a building on the beachfront of the Grand-Case Beach Club. Its French and American staff, supervised by Michigan-born Marla Welch, functions as a source of info on island activities and can confirm travel plans or schedules for leisure activities. It also rents paddleboats with parasols for $15 an hour, low-velocity motorized boats for $20 an hour, and chaise longues with beach umbrellas. Their main allure, however, is as a focal point for guided hour-long snorkeling trips to St. Martin's offshore reefs. The most visible of these are the waters surrounding Creole Rock, an offshore clump of reef-ringed boulders that are rich in underwater fauna. The cost of the experience, which departs every day at 2:30pm, with a return 2 hours later during high season (or whenever demand warrants it), costs $25 per person, all equipment included. Reservations are recommended.

TENNIS You can try the courts at most of the large resorts, but you must call first for a reservation. Preference, of course, is given to guests. On the Dutch side are three lit courts at the **Pelican Resort Club** at Simpson Bay (☎ **0599/54-25-03**); another three lit courts are at the **Divi Little Bay Beach Resort,** Little Bay Rd. (☎ **0599/52-54-10**); and yet another three courts are at the **Maho Beach Hotel,** Maho Bay (☎ **0599/55-21-15**). On the French side, the **Privilège Resort & Spa,** Anse Marcel (☎ **0590/87-38-38**), offers six lit courts; the **Hotel Mont Vernon,** Baie Orientale (☎ **0590/87-62-00**), has two lit courts; and the **Nettlé Beach Club,** Sandy Ground Rd. (☎ **0590/87-6-68**), has three lit tennis courts.

WATERSKIING & PARASAILING Most of French St. Martin's large beachfront hotels maintain facilities for waterskiing and parasailing, often from makeshift kiosks that operate from the sands of the hotel's beaches. Waterskiing averages $40 per 20-minute ride. Two independent operators are situated side-by-side on Orient Bay, close to the cluster of hotels near the Esmeralda Hotel: **Kon Tiki Watersports** (☎ **0590/87-46-89**) and **Bikini Beach Watersports** (☎ **0590/87-43-25**). High-velocity, highly maneuverable Water Scooters—also known as jet skis—rent for $40 to $45 per half-hour session, depending on what machine you rent; and parasailing, where you'll hang from a parachute while being towed behind a motorboat, costs $50 for a vertiginous 10-minute experience aloft.

Jet-skiing and waterskiing are also especially popular in Dutch St. Maarten. The unruffled waters of Simpson Bay Lagoon, the largest in the West Indies, are ideal for these sports.

WINDSURFING Because of prevailing winds and waters that are protected from violent waves by offshore reefs, most windsurfers gravitate to the strip of sand on the island's easternmost edge, most notably **Coconut Grove Beach, Orient Beach,** and to a lesser extent, **Dawn Beach,** all of which are in French St. Martin. The best of the several outfits that specialize in the sport is **Tropical Wave,** Coconut Grove, Le Galion Beach, Baie de l'Embouchure (☎ **0590/87-37-25**). Midway between Orient Beach and Oyster Pond, amid a sunblasted, scrub-covered landscape that's isolated from any of the island's big hotels, its combination of wind and calm waters is considered by windsurfing aficionados as almost ideal. Operated by American-born Patrick Turner, Tropical Wave is the island's leading sales agent for Mistral Windsurfers. They rent for $20 an hour, with instruction priced at $30 an hour.

In Dutch St. Maarten, visitors usually head to **Simpson Bay Lagoon.**

6 Cruises & Sightseeing Tours

DAY CRUISES

A popular pastime is a day of picnicking, sailing, snorkeling, and sightseeing aboard one of several boats providing the service. The sleek sailboats usually pack large wicker hampers full of victuals and stretch tarpaulins over sections of the deck to protect sunshy sailors.

In Dutch St. Maarten, *Random Wind* is a traditional clipper making day trips that circumnavigate the island, carrying 15 passengers at a cost of $70 per person, including a lunch bar and snorkeling. Reservations can be made at Simpson Bay Marina (☎ 0599/57-57-42). On Wednesday a breakfast cruise is available at $50 per person from 9am to 1pm. You get a real French breakfast, complete with mimosas. On Wednesday a sunset cruise costing $30 is offered from 5 to 6:30pm. Call for more information about these cruises.

Experienced skippers also make 1-day voyages to St. Barts in the French West Indies and to Saba, another of the Dutch Windwards in the Leewards; they stop long enough for passengers to familiarize themselves with the island ports, shop, and have lunch. To arrange a trip, ask at your hotel or at the **St. Maarten Tourist Bureau,** 23 Walter Nisbeth Rd. in Philipsburg (☎ 599/5-22337).

If you'd like to see some of the other islands nearby, the best deal is offered by *Voyager I* and *Voyager II.* There are daily sails to St. Barts costing $50 round-trip or to Saba, going for $60 round-trip. Children under 12 ride for half price. These trips are a good value and are well worth the time and money. For more details, call **Dockside Management** in Philipsburg (☎ 599/5-24096).

SIGHTSEEING TOURS

The only companies offering bus tours of the island are **Dutch Tours,** Cougar Road, 8 Unit One (☎ 599/5-23316), and **St. Maarten Sightseeing Tours** (☎ 599/5-53921), whose buses can accommodate between 22 and 52 people. They're only configured for large groups and are very difficult to prearrange.

In Dutch St. Maarten, you can also hire a taxi driver as your guide; a 2½-hour tour of the entire island costs $30 to $35 for up to two passengers and $7.50 to $10 for each additional passenger.

In French St. Martin, you can book 2-hour sightseeing trips around the island, either through **St. Martin's Taxi Service & Information Center** in Marigot (☎ 0590/87-56-54) or at any hotel desk. The cost is $50 for one or two passengers, plus $10 for each additional person.

7 Shopping

IN ST. MAARTEN

Not only is St. Maarten a free port, but there are also no local sales taxes. Prices are sometimes lower here than anywhere else in the Caribbean except St. Thomas, with which it's locked in a head-to-head race. However, you must be familiar with the prices of what you're looking for to know what actually is a bargain. On some items we've priced (fine liqueurs, cigarettes, Irish linen, German cameras, French perfumes) we've found prices 30% to 50% lower than in the United States or Canada. Many well-known shops on Curaçao have branches here, in case you're not going on to the ABC islands (Aruba, Bonaire, and Curaçao).

Except for the boutiques at resort hotels, the main shopping area is in the center of **Philipsburg.** Most of the shops are on two leading streets, **Front Street** (called Voorstraat in Dutch), which is closer to the bay, and **Back Street** (Achterstraat), which runs parallel to Front Street.

In general, the price marked on the merchandise is what you're supposed to pay. We're speaking of major retail outlets such as H. Stern, the jewelers, or Little Switzerland. At small, very personally-run shops, where the owner is on-site, some bargaining might be in order. Most shopkeepers will remind you their merchandise is already discounted, sometimes considerably, and they might add, "We've got to make some profit, now don't we?"

Antillean Liquors, Queen Juliana Airport (☎ **599/5-54267**), attracts the last-minute shopper. It has a complete assortment of liquor and liqueurs, as well as cigarettes and cigars. In general, prices are lower here than in other stores on the island, and the selection is larger. Many bottles are priced anywhere from 30% to 50% lower than in the U.S. The only local product sold is an island liqueur called Guavaberry, made from rum. The **Guavaberry Company,** 8–10 Front St. (☎ **599/5-22965**), sells the rare "island folk liqueur" of St. Maarten, which for centuries was made in private homes but is now available to everyone. Sold in square bottles, the product is made from rum that's given a unique flavor with rare berries usually grown in the hills in the center of the island. Don't confuse guavaberries with guavas—they're very different. The liqueur is aged and has a fruity, woody, almost bittersweet flavor. You can blend it with coconut for a unique guavaberry colada or pour a splash into a glass of icy champagne. Stop in at their shop and free-tasting house before you buy.

The **Caribbean Camera Centre,** 79 Front St. (☎ **599/5-25259**), has a wide range of merchandise, but it's always wise to know the prices charged back home. Cameras here may be among the lowest priced on St. Maarten; however, we've discovered better deals on St. Thomas if you're going there. At **Colombian Emeralds International,** Old Street (☎ **599/5-23933**), you'll find stones ranging from collector- to investment-quality. Unmounted duty-free emeralds from Colombia, as well as gold, diamond, ruby, and sapphire jewelry, will tempt you. Prices here are about the same as in other outlets of this famous chain throughout the Caribbean, and if you're seriously shopping for emeralds, this is the place. There are some huckster fly-by-night vendors around the island pawning fakes off on unsuspecting tourists; Colombian Emeralds offers the genuine item.

Little Europe, 80 Front St. (☎ **599/5-24371**), is an upscale purveyor of all the "finer things" in life. It's favored by cruise-ship passengers because its prices are inexpensive compared to North American boutiques. Inventory includes porcelain figurines by Hummel, jewelry, and watches by Concorde, Piaget, Corum, and Movado. **Little Switzerland,** 52 Front St. (☎ **599/5-23530**), is part of a chain of stores spread throughout the Caribbean. These fine-quality European imports are made even more attractive by the prices, often 25% or more lower than stateside. Elegant famous-name watches, china, crystal, and jewelry are for sale, plus perfume and accessories. Little Switzerland has the best overall selection of these items of any shop on the Dutch side.

The **Old Street Shopping Center,** with entrances on Front Street and Back Street (☎ **599/5-24712**), is 170 yards east of the courthouse. Its lion's-head fountain is the most photographed spot on St. Maarten. Built in a West Indian–Dutch style, it features more than two dozen shops and boutiques, including branches of such famous stores as Colombian Emeralds. Dining facilities include the Philipsburg Grill and Ribs Co. and Pizza Hut. The stores are open Monday to Saturday 9:30am to 6pm, but the Philipsburg Grill and Ribs Co. is open on Sunday too if a cruise ship docks.

The **New Amsterdam Store,** 66 Front St. (☎ 559/5-22787), is a tradition in the islands since 1925. This store opened in 1967 on Front Street. It's a general store with a little bit of everything—fine linen to fashion, footwear to swimwear, even porcelain. If your time is limited, you might want to visit this place first because it is so comprehensive. Prices are competitive with other stores in town touting similar merchandise. At the **Shipwreck Shop,** Front Street (☎ 599/5-22962), you'll find West Indian hammocks, beach towels, salad bowls, baskets, jewelry, T-shirts, postcards, books, and much more. It's also the home of wood carvings, native art, sea salt, cane sugar, and spices. If you're looking for gifts or handcrafts in general, this might be your best bet.

IN ST. MARTIN

Many day-trippers come over to Marigot from the Dutch side just to look at the collection of French-inspired boutiques and shopping arcades. Because it's also a duty-free port, you'll find some of the best shopping in the Caribbean here. There's a wide selection of European merchandise, much of it geared to the luxury trade, including crystal, perfumes, jewelry, and fashions, sometimes at 25% to 50% less than in the United States and Canada. There are also fine liqueurs, cognacs, and cigars. Whether you're seeking jewelry, perfume, or St-Tropez bikinis, you'll find it in one of the boutiques along **rue de la République** and **rue de la Liberté** in Marigot. Look especially for French luxury items, such as Lalique crystal, Vuitton bags (the real item, not the fakes seen worldwide), and Chanel perfume.

Prices are often quoted in U.S. dollars, and salespeople frequently speak English. Credit and charge cards and traveler's checks are generally accepted. When cruise ships are in port on Sunday and holidays, some of the larger shops open.

At harborside in Marigot there's a frisky **morning market** with vendors selling spices, fruit, shells, and local handcrafts. Shops here tend to be rather upscale, stocking mostly luxury items inspired by French fashions and tastes, catering to clients of the small but choice cruise ships that make a habit of docking offshore, especially in mid-winter.

At **Port La Royale,** the bustling center of everything, mornings are even more alive: Schooners unload produce from the neighboring islands, boats board guests for picnics on deserted beaches, a brigantine sets out on a sightseeing sail, and the owners of a dozen little dining spots get ready for the lunch crowd. The largest shopping arcade on St. Martin, it has many boutiques, some of which come and go with great rapidity. Another shopping complex, the **Galerie Périgourdine,** facing the post office, is a cluster of boutiques. Here you might pick up some designer wear for both men and women, including items from the collection of Ted Lapidus.

Act III, rue du Général de Gaulle 3 (☎ 0590/29-28-43), opened in 1994 and has almost always been cited as the most glamorous women's store in St. Martin. It prides itself on a higher percentage of evening gowns and chic cocktail dresses than any of its competitors, and limits its roster of bathing suits to a simple short-lived collection that appears only in the spring. Designers include Alaïa, Mugler, Versace, Lacroix, Cerruti, Gaultier, and others. The staff is accommodating and bilingual, and serves with tact and charm. **La Romana,** rue de la République 12 (☎ 0590/87-88-16), specializes in a roster of chic women's clothing. This store sells garments that are a bit less pretentious and more fun and lighthearted than those at its most visible competitor, Act III.

The motif is Italian rather than French. A small collection of menswear is also available, but overall, the focus is on garments for women.

Lipstick, Port La Royale, rue Kennedy (☎ **0590/87-73-24**), is the leading purveyor of women's cosmetics and skin-care products on French St. Martin, with a beauty parlor one floor above street level that's devoted to an intelligent and tasteful use of the store's impressive inventories. For sale are virtually every conceivable cosmetic or beauty aid made by such manufacturers as Chanel, Lancôme, Guerlain, Saint Laurent, Dior, and an emerging brand from Japan known as Shiseido. Hair removals, massages, manicures, pedicures, facials, and hair styling are available on the premises. The **Gingerbread & Mahogany Gallery,** 4–14 Marina Royale (☎ **0590/87-73-21**), is the finest gallery. Owner Simone Seitre scours Haiti four times a year to secure the best works of a cross-section of Haitian artists, both the "old master" and the talented amateur. One of the most knowledgeable purveyors of Haitian art in the Caribbean, this pan-European has promoted Haitian art at exhibits around the world. Even if you're not in the market for an expensive piece of art (the paintings come in all price ranges), you'll find dozens of charming and inexpensive handcrafts. The little gallery is a bit hard to find (on a narrow alleyway at the marina), but it's worth the search.

Little Switzerland, rue de la République (☎ **0590/87-50-03**), is the French outlet for this popular chain. As you travel throughout the islands, especially if you're on a cruise, you'll see branches of this store virtually everywhere. There's even another outlet on the Dutch side, but the merchandise is different here, with a concentration on French products. The widest array of duty-free luxury items in French St. Martin are displayed here, including French perfume and French leather goods. **Maneks,** rue de la République 24 (☎ **0590/87-54-91**), has a little bit of everything: video cameras, electronics, household appliances, liquors, gifts, souvenirs, Kodak film, watches, T-shirts, sunglasses, and pearls from Majorca. The staff even sells Cuban cigars, but these will have to be smoked abroad, as they can't be brought back into the United States.

✪ **Roland Richardson,** boulevard de France (☎ **0590/87-32-24**), welcomes visitors to his beautiful small gallery on the Marigot waterfront. A native of St. Martin, Mr. Richardson is recognized as one of the Caribbean's premier artists. His work encompasses oil, watercolor, pastel, charcoal, and etching. Called a "modern-day Gauguin," he's a gifted Impressionist painter known for his landscape, portraiture, and colorful still-life paintings. His work has been exhibited in more than 70 one-man and group shows in museums, major trade centers, and fine art galleries around the world, and is included in many fine private and public collections. Gallery hours are Monday to Friday 10am to 6pm and Saturday 9am to 2pm; the gallery is closed on Sunday. Special appointments are available.

8 St. Maarten & St. Martin After Dark

IN ST. MAARTEN

On the Dutch side of St. Maarten there are few real nightclubs. After-dark activities begin early here, as guests select their favorite nook for a sundowner, perhaps the garden patio of **Pasanggrahan,** a guest house at 15 Front Street, Philipsburg (☎ **599/5-23588**). Many hotels sponsor **beachside barbecues** (particularly in season) with steel bands, native music, and folk dancing. Outsiders are welcomed at most of these events, but call ahead to see if it's a private affair.

The most popular bar on the island is **Cheri's Café.** One of the new clubs to open is **Axum** at 7 Front St. in Philipsburg, a music hall, exhibition center, and popular bar, open Tuesday to Sunday from 9pm. The cover is $5 but could vary, depending on the

Look for the Green Flash

Visitors watch for the legendary **"green flash,"** an atmospheric phenomenon described by Ernest Hemingway—it sometimes occurs in these latitudes just as the sun drops below the horizon. Each evening, guests wait expectantly and have been known to break into a round of applause at a particularly spectacular sunset.

entertainment. Often featured are blues, reggae, and jazz, and even poetry readings. Axum is found above the St. Maarten Historical Museum. It has no phone but information is available from the Mosera Fine Arts Gallery next door at ☎ **0599/52-05-54.**

Most of the casinos are in the big hotels. **Casino Royale,** at the Maho Beach Hotel on Maho Bay (☎ **599/5-52115**), opened in 1975. It has 16 blackjack tables, 6 roulette wheels, and 3 craps and 3 Caribbean stud-poker tables. The casino offers baccarat, mini-baccarat, and a large collection of more than 250 slot machines. It's open daily 1pm to 4am. The Casino Royale Piano Bar is open nightly from 9:30pm, featuring the best of jazz, pop, and Caribbean music. There's no admission, and a snack buffet is complimentary. A popular casino is at the **Pelican Resort Club,** Simpson Bay (☎ **599/5-42503**), built to a Swiss design incorporating a panoramic view of Simpson Bay. The Las Vegas–style casino has 2 craps tables, 3 roulette tables, 9 blackjack tables, 2 stud-poker tables, and 120 slot machines. It's open daily 1pm to 3am.

The Roman-themed **Coliseum Casino,** on Front Street in Philipsburg (☎ **599/5-32102**), has taken several steps to attract gaming enthusiasts, especially "high rollers," and has the highest table limits ($1,000 maximum) on St. Maarten. On the management's approval, the Coliseum also offers credit lines for clients with a good credit rating at any U.S. casino. The Coliseum features about 225 slot machines, 4 blackjack tables, 3 poker tables, and 2 roulette wheels. The Coliseum is open daily from 11am to 3am.

Sports fans gravitate to **Lightning Casino,** Cole Bay (☎ **0599/54-32-90**), where on wide-screen TVs you can watch baseball or soccer games, boxing matches, hockey matches, and, of course, basketball and football, along with horse racing. This casino lies near the airport and will send a shuttle to pick you up, regardless of where you are on the island. Located at the **Pelican Resort Club** on Simpson Bay (☎ **0599/54-25-03**), is a Las Vegas–style casino offering blackjack, roulette, craps, and slot machines. Pelican also features horse racing, bingo, and sports night, with events broadcast via satellite. Nightly dancing on the Pelican Reef Terrace and island shows featuring Caribbean bands are often a feature here.

Also worth a visit 24 hours a day is the **Atlantis Casino** at beautiful Cupecoy Beach (☎ **0599/54-60-0**), only a short distance from Maho Bay and Mullet Bay. Atlantis was designed with an ancient nautical motif to evoke the lost continent. There's a private gaming room for higher-stakes baccarat, French roulette, chemin de fer, and seven-card poker.

IN ST. MARTIN

Some St. Martin hotels have dinner-dancing, piano-lounge music, and even discos. But the most popular after-dark pastime is leisurely dining.

Le Prive, rue de la République, in Marigot (☎ **0590/87-01-97**), is the most talked-about, most stylish, and most popular nightclub on the island's French side. Looking like an upscale yacht club, it's a high-energy multicultural disco where even 40-year-olds feel comfortable mingling with the island's young and energetic. The club has a state-of-the-art sound system and one of France's top DJs. The view of Marigot from its balcony is panoramic. The club is open daily 11pm to 4:30am, charging a cover of $10.

Le Club One, Auberge de la Mer, La Marina, Marigot (☎ **0590/87-98-41**), lies one floor above street level in a modern building facing the boats and yachts bobbing at anchor near the center of Marigot. Its fans, who descend on it every night from both sides of the island, view it as a Gallic/Caribbean version of a British pub, where views of the sea mingle with a polyglot of languages and recorded funk, reggae, and rap that encourages some folks to dance. Entrance is $8. Hours are nightly from 10pm to 1am.

The island attracts a lot of gay visitors, especially to its nude beaches, but there's little gay nightlife except for the **Pink Mango,** Residence Laguna Beach at Nettle Bay (☎ **0590/87-59-99**). This charming and rather small club lies behind the residence itself. To reach it, go to the far right section of this former hotel's parking lot, walk along the building, and keep to your left. When you see a rainbow flag, press a buzzer. Gay men of all ages flock here, and a few women too. The club opens nightly at 10pm but doesn't really get crowded until midnight. It keeps going until 3am or later.

23 St. Vincent & the Grenadines

One of the major Windward Islands, sleepy **St. Vincent** is only now awakening to tourism, which hasn't yet reached massive dimensions the way it has on nearby St. Lucia. Sailors and the yachting set have long known of St. Vincent and its satellite bays and beaches in the **Grenadines.**

Visit St. Vincent for its botanical beauty and the Grenadines for the best sailing waters in the Caribbean. Don't come for the nightlife, grand cuisine, or fabled beaches. There are some white-sand beaches near Kingstown on St. Vincent, but most of the others ringing the island are of black sand. The yachting crowd seems to view St. Vincent merely as a launching pad for the 60-mile string of the Grenadines, but there are enough attractions on the island to merit an exploration all on its own.

St. Vincent has any number of inexpensive inns and small West Indian taverns once you've paid the rather high airfare to reach it. The Grenadines, stamping ground of yachties, royalty, and high society (often British), are hardly what one thinks of first in contemplating a budget holiday in the sun. However, even here there are a few places to stay and keep costs affordable. If you'd like to visit the Grenadines, the one island in the chain that offers the widest range of affordable food and lodging is Bequia.

An emerald island 18 miles long and 11 miles wide, St. Vincent has fertile valleys, rich forests, lush jungles, rugged peaks, waterfalls, foam-whitened beaches, outstanding coral reefs (with what experts say is some of the world's clearest water), a volcano nestled in the sky and usually capped by its own private cloud, and 4,000 feet up, Crater Lake. Unspoiled by the worst fallout mass tourism sometimes brings, the islanders actually treat visitors like people: Met with courtesy, they respond with courtesy. British customs predominate, along with traces of Gallic cultural influences, but all with a distinct West Indian flair.

South of St. Vincent, the small chain of islands called the Grenadines extends for more than 40 miles and offers the finest yachting area in the eastern Caribbean. The islands are strung like a necklace of precious stones and have romantic-sounding names like Bequia, Mustique, Canouan, and Petit St. Vincent. We'll explore Bequia, Union and Palm Islands, and Mayreau. A few of the islands have accommodations, but many are so small and so completely undeveloped they attract only beachcombers and stray boaters. Populated by the descendants of African slaves and administered by St. Vincent, the Grenadines collectively add up to a land mass of 30 square miles.

Airport ✈
Beach 🏖
Mountain ▲

These bits of land, often dots on nautical charts, may lack natural resources, yet they're blessed with white-sand beaches, coral reefs, and their own kind of sleepy beauty. If you don't spend the night in the Grenadines, you should at least go over for the day to visit one of them and enjoy a picnic lunch (which your hotel will pack for you) on one of the long stretches of beach.

1 Essentials

VISITOR INFORMATION

In the United States, you can get information at the **St. Vincent and Grenadines Tourist Office,** 801 Second Ave., 21st Floor, New York, NY 10017 (☎ **800/729-1726** or 212/687-4981), or 6505 Cove Creek Place, Dallas, TX 75240 (☎ **800/235-3029** or 214/239-6451). Canadians can go to 32 Park Rd., Toronto, Ontario N4W 2N4 (☎ **416/924-5796**).

On St. Vincent, the local **Department of Tourism** is on Upper Bay Street, Government Administrative Centre, Kingstown (☎ **784/457-1502**).

The Internet address for St. Vincent and the Grenadines is **www.vincy.com.**

GETTING THERE

In the eastern Caribbean, St. Vincent—the gateway to the Grenadines (the individual islands are discussed later in this chapter)—lies 100 miles west of Barbados, where most visitors from North America fly first and then make connections to take them to St. Vincent's **E. T. Joshua Airport** and on to the Grenadines. For details on getting to

Barbados from North America, see chapter 5. However, the transfer through Barbados is no longer necessary, as **American Eagle** (☎ 800/433-7300 or 784/456-5000) has one flight daily from San Juan; getting here is more convenient than ever before.

Air Martinique (☎ 784/458-4528) runs once-daily service among Martinique, St. Lucia, St. Vincent, and Union Island.

Increasing numbers of visitors to St. Vincent prefer the dependable service of one of the best charter airlines in the Caribbean, **Mustique Airways** (☎ 784/458-4380). The airline makes frequent runs from St. Vincent to the major airports of the Grenadines. With advance warning, it will arrange specially chartered (and reasonably priced) transport for you and your party to and from many of the surrounding islands (like Grenada, Aruba, St. Lucia, Antigua, Barbados, Trinidad). The price of these chartered flights is less than you might expect and often matches the fares on conventional Caribbean airlines. Currently the airline owns seven small aircraft, none of which carry more than nine passengers.

GETTING AROUND

BY TAXI   The government sets the rates for fares, but taxis are unmetered; always ask the fare and agree on the charge before getting in. Figure on spending EC$15 to EC$20 ($5.55 to $7.40) to go from the E. T. Joshua Airport to your hotel, maybe more. You should tip about 12% of the fare.

If you don't want to drive yourself, you can also hire taxis to take you to the island's major attractions. Most drivers seem to be well-informed guides (it won't take you long to learn everything you need to know about St. Vincent). You'll spend EC$40 to EC$50 ($14.80 to $18.50) per hour for a car holding two to four passengers.

BY RENTAL CAR   Driving on St. Vincent is a bit of an adventure because of the narrow twisting roads. *Drive on the left.* To drive like a Vincentian, you'll soon learn to sound your horn a lot as you make the sharp curves and turns. If you present your valid U.S. or Canadian driver's license at the police department on Bay Street in Kingstown and pay an EC$40 ($14.80) fee, you'll obtain a temporary permit to drive.

The major car-rental companies don't have branches on St. Vincent. Rental cars cost EC$140 to EC$200 ($51.80 to $74) a day, but that must be determined on the spot. Contact **Kim's Rentals** (☎ 784/456-1884) or **Star Garage** (☎ 784/456-1743), both on Grenville Street in Kingstown.

BY BUS   Flamboyantly painted open buses travel the principal roads of St. Vincent, linking the major towns and villages. The price is low, depending on where you're going, and the experience will connect you with the people of the island. The central departure point is the bus terminal at the New Kingstown Fish Market. Fares range from EC$1 to EC$6 (40¢ to $2.20).

Fast Facts: St. Vincent & the Grenadines

Banking Hours   Most banks are open Monday to Thursday 8am to either 1 or 3pm and Friday either 8am to 5pm or 8am to 1pm and 3 to 5pm, depending on the bank.

Currency   The official currency of St. Vincent is the **Eastern Caribbean dollar (EC$),** worth about 37¢ in U.S. money. Most of the quotations in this chapter appear in U.S. dollars unless marked EC$. Most restaurants, shops, and hotels will accept payment in U.S. dollars or traveler's checks.

Documents British, Canadian, or U.S. citizens should have proof of identity and a return or ongoing airplane ticket. Passports or birth certificates with a photo ID are sufficient.

Drugstore On St. Vincent try **Deane's Pharmacy,** Halifax Street, Kingstown (☎ **784/457-2056**), open Monday to Friday 8:30am to 4:30pm and Saturday 8:30am to 12:30pm.

Electricity Electricity is 220 volts AC (50 cycles), so you'll need an adapter and a transformer. Some hotels have transformers, but it's best to bring your own.

Language English is the official language.

Medical Care There are two hospitals on St. Vincent, **Kingstown General Hospital,** Kingstown (☎ **784/456-1185**), and **Medical Associates Clinic,** Kingstown (☎ **784/457-2598**).

Post Office The **General Post Office,** on Halifax Street in Kingstown (☎ **784/456-1111**), is open Monday to Friday 8:30am to 3pm and Saturday 8:30 to 11:30am. There are sub–post offices in 56 districts throughout the country, including offices on the Grenadine islands of Bequia, Mustique, Canouan, Mayreau, and Union Island.

Safety St. Vincent and its neighboring islands of the Grenadines are still safe islands to visit. In Kingstown, the capital of St. Vincent, chances are you'll encounter little serious crime. However, take the usual precautions and never leave valuables unguarded.

Taxes The government imposes an airport departure tax of EC$30 ($11.10) per person. A 7% government occupancy tax is charged for all hotel accommodations.

Time Both St. Vincent and the Grenadines operate on Atlantic standard time year-round: When it's 6am on St. Vincent, it's 5am in Miami. During daylight saving time in the United States, St. Vincent keeps the same time as the U.S. east coast.

Tipping Hotels and restaurants add a 10% to 15% service charge, and the same percentage is customary to tip when the service charge isn't automatically added to the bill.

Weather The climate of St. Vincent is pleasantly cooled by the trade winds all year. The tropical temperature is in the 78° to 82°F range. The rainy season is May to November.

2 Accommodations You Can Afford

Don't expect high-rise resorts here, as everything is kept small. The places are comfortable, not fancy, and you usually get a lot of personal attention from the staff. Most hotels and restaurants add a 7% government tax and a 10% to 15% service charge to your bill; ask about this when you register.

✪ **Beachcombers Hotel.** Villa Beach (P.O. Box 126), Kingstown, St. Vincent, W.I. ☎ **784/458-4283.** Fax 784/458-4385. 13 units. TEL. Year-round $60 single; $83 double. AE, MC, V.

This relative newcomer, opened by Richard and Flora Gunn in a tropical garden right on the beach, immediately became a far more inviting choice than the traditional budget favorites, the Heron and Cobblestone. A pair of chalet-like buildings house the tastefully decorated accommodations, all cooled by ceiling fans, though a few rooms have air-conditioning. The standard of cleanliness and maintenance is the finest on the island. Try for room 1, 2, or 3, as they're not only the best rooms but also open onto the water. Two rooms have small kitchenettes. The baths are a bit cramped. The hotel has a health spa (Mrs. Gunn is a massage and beauty therapist). And, astonishingly for a B&B, the Beachcombers offers a steam room, sauna, and even facials and aromatherapy. The Beachbar & Restaurant, a favorite gathering place for locals, fronts an open terrace and serves an excellent cuisine. Daughter Cheryl, who mastered her cookery skills in England, is the chef.

Casa de Columbus. Indian Bay (P.O. Box 538), Kingstown, St. Vincent, W.I. ☎ **800/742-4276** or 784/458-4001. Fax 784/457-4777. E-mail: indianbay@casadecolumbus.com. 10 apts., some with kitchenette. A/C TEL. Year-round $65 1-bedroom apt. for 1; $75 1-bedroom apt. for 2; $90 2-bedroom apt. for 2 to 4. Extra person $10. Rates include breakfast. AE, MC, V.

Built in 1972 a few feet from the sea, in a residential neighborhood that's one of the most sought-after on St. Vincent, this is a modestly priced hotel that has been renovated several times. Don't expect personalized intimacy; the setting is anonymous but serviceable, with easy access to many neighboring resorts whose bars, restaurants, and sports facilities can sometimes be made available to you. You can swim on a narrow beach near the hotel's foundation, though a more desirable site might be Indian Bay Beach, whose sands are a 5-minute walk away. If you don't feel inspired to cook, you'll find a lattice-ringed Caribbean bistro, Sam's, on the premises, serving lunch from $10 and dinner from $15. The accommodations aren't frilly or fancy, but contain white walls, carpets, patterned draperies, wood furnishings, touches of rattan, and sometimes views over the offshore upscale resort of Young Island. The rooms are small and rather motel-like but offer good beds and rather tiny but tidily maintained baths. This is the place to be on Saturday night when the owners invite you to "Come and Drink Us Dry." For only EC$25 ($9.25) you can eat all you want at a buffet, drinks are included. Entertainment is from a live band.

✪ Cobblestone Inn. Bax St. (P.O. Box 867), Kingstown, St. Vincent, W.I. ☎ **784/456-1937.** Fax 784/456-1938. 20 units. A/C TEL. Year-round $60 single or double; $70 triple. AE, DC, DISC, MC, V.

Built as a warehouse for sugar and arrowroot in 1814, the core of this historic hotel is made of stone and brick. Today it's one of St. Vincent's most famous hotels, known for its labyrinth of passages, arches, and upper halls. To reach the high-ceilinged reception area, you pass from the waterfront through a stone tunnel into a chiseled courtyard. At the top of a massive sloping stone staircase, you're shown to one of the simple old-fashioned rooms. Most units contain TVs, and some have windows opening over the rooftops of town. Most of the rooms are small, though some are medium in size; the most spacious is no. 5, but it opens onto a noisy street. Mattresses are well worn but still comfortable, and the baths are very tiny, with thin towels. Meals are served on a third-floor eyrie high above the hotel's central courtyard. Rows of windows and rattan furnishings in its adjacent bar create one of the most frequented hideaways in town. You'll have to drive about 3 miles to the nearest beach.

Coconut Beach Inn. Indian Bay (P.O. Box 355), Kingstown, St. Vincent, W.I. ☎ or fax **784/457-4900.** 11 units. Year-round $45–$55 single; $65–$75 double. Rates include breakfast. AE, MC, V.

This owner-occupied inn/restaurant/bar lies 5 minutes (2 miles) south of the airport and a 5-minute drive from Kingstown. The hotel, which grew out of a villa built in the 1930s by one of the region's noted eccentrics, lies across the channel from the much more expensive Young Island. Its seaside setting makes it a good choice for swimming and sunbathing. Island tours, such as sailing the Grenadines, can be arranged, as can diving, snorkeling, and mountain climbing. Each small room is furnished in a modern style but contains a fairly good bed, though the mattresses look well used; the tiny baths have rather thin towels. A beach bar at water's edge serves tropical drinks, and an open-air restaurant opens onto a view of Indian Bay and features West Indian and Vincentian cooking prepared from local foods. Steaks, Cornish game hens, and hamburgers round out the fare.

Heron Hotel. Upper Bay St. (P.O. Box 226), Kingstown, St. Vincent, W.I. ☎ **784/457-1631.** Fax 784/457-1189. 13 units. A/C TEL. Year-round $45 single; $58.50 double, $62.50 suite. Rates include full breakfast. AE, MC, V.

This respectable but slightly run-down hotel is among the most historic buildings on St. Vincent. It was built of local stone and tropical hardwoods late in the 18th century as a warehouse, and later provided lodgings for colonial planters doing business along the then-teeming wharves of Kingstown. Operating in its present format since 1960, it occupies the second story of a building whose ground floor is devoted to shops. Some of the simple and rather small rooms overlook an inner courtyard; others face the streets. Room 15 is the largest. They have time-worn furnishings, including mattresses ready for retirement, rather garish floral draperies, single beds, and extremely cramped baths with thin towels. Though you don't get grand comfort, the price is extremely reasonable and the staff most hospitable. There's a restaurant whose busiest time of day is lunch. (The restaurant may close after dusk, so dinner reservations are important.)

WORTH A SPLURGE

Villa Lodge Hotel. P.O. Box 1191, Villa Point, St. Vincent, W.I. ☎ **784/458-4641.** Fax 784/457-4468. E-mail: villodge@caribsurf.com. 10 units. A/C TV TEL. Winter $120 single or double; $140 triple; $150 quad. Off-season $95 single; $105 double; $115 triple; $125 quad. AE, MC, V.

On the side of a residential hillside a few minutes southeast of the center of Kingstown and the E. T. Joshua Airport, this place is a favorite of visiting businesspeople. Because of its access to a beach and its well-mannered staff, it evokes the feeling of a modern villa. It's ringed with flowering tropical trees and shrubs growing in the gardens. The air-conditioned rooms have ceiling fans, king-size beds with firm mattresses, mini-fridges, hair dryers, good-size towels in the small baths, and comfortable rattan and local mahogany furniture. The hotel also rents eight apartments in its Breezeville Apartments complex, charging year-round prices of $130 double, $135 triple, and $145 quad.

There's a wood-sheathed bar on the second floor with a view of Young Island and the Grenadines, and a dining room where good food is served, usually from a fixed-price menu. There's also a bar and restaurant down by the pool. Services offered include room service, laundry, and baby-sitting.

BEST OFF-SEASON BET

Sunset Worldwide Sailing. P.O. Box 133, Blue Lagoon, St. Vincent, W.I. ☎ or fax **784/458-4308.** E-mail: sunsailsva@caribsurf.com. 19 units. A/C TV. Winter $100–$120 single or double. Off-season $76–$86 single or double. AE, MC, V.

A two-story grouping of rambling modern buildings crafted from local wood and stone, this hotel lies 4 miles from the airport on the main island road, opening onto a narrow black-sand curve of beach. There's a pleasantly breezy bar with open walls and lots of exposed planking, often filled with seafaring folk. As you relax, you'll overlook a moored armada of boats tied up at a nearby marina. A two-tiered pool, terraced into a hillside, offers two lagoon-shaped places to swim. Snorkeling, windsurfing, and daily departures on sailboats to Mustique and Bequia can be arranged. Each of the medium-sized high-ceilinged accommodations has a balcony, and about half the rooms are air-conditioned. They're well maintained and cared for, with ceramic tiled floors and good furnishings, including excellent beds with firm mattresses. The baths are in the standard motel style. Room service and laundry are available.

3 Great Deals on Dining

Unlike many Caribbean islands, many Vincentian hotels serve authentic West Indian cuisine. There are also a few independent eateries.

Aggie's. Grenville St., Kingstown. ☎ **809/456-2110.** Reservations recommended. Main courses EC$15–EC$45 ($5.55–$16.65). AE, MC, V. Daily 9am–4pm. WEST INDIAN/SEAFOOD.

On the island's southern end in Kingstown, this eatery provides a lively environment with warm hospitality. The matriarch who runs the place is Agatha Richards, affectionately called Aggie by her well-satisfied customers. This local hangout specializes in West Indian seafood at reasonable prices. What's in season determines which soups are offered (perhaps green pea, callaloo, or pumpkin); or try the fish or conch chowder. House specialties might include lobster, souse, conch, shrimp, fish, and whelk; or try the chicken, served baked or fried, or one of the curried beef and mutton dishes. A Creole buffet is featured at lunch noon to 3pm on Friday with your choice of three meats such as pork, chicken, and fish. It's Creole day on Saturday, with specialties like souse, Creole-style fish, and pilau.

Lime N' Pub Restaurant. Opposite Young Island at Villa. ☎ **784/458-4227.** Main courses EC$45–EC$140 ($16.65–$51.80). AE, DC, MC, V. Daily noon–midnight. WEST INDIAN/INDIAN.

This is one of the island's most popular restaurants, opposite the superexpensive Young Island Hotel, right on Young Island Channel. It's the most congenial pub on the island, with a wide selection of pub grub, including pizzas. There's even a live lobster pond. A local band enlivens the atmosphere a few times every week in winter. In the more formalized section of this indoor and alfresco restaurant, you can partake of some good West Indian food, along with some dishes from India or the international kitchen. The rôtis (Caribbean burritos) win high praise, but we gravitate to the fresh fish and lobster dishes. Coconut shrimp is generally excellent. Service is among the most hospitable on the island.

Basil's Bar & Restaurant. Bay St., Kingstown. ☎ **784/457-2713.** Reservations recommended. Main courses EC$37–EC$57 ($13.70–$21.10); lunch buffet EC$32 ($11.85). AE, MC, V. Mon–Sat 8am–10pm. SEAFOOD/INTERNATIONAL.

This brick-lined enclave is a less famous annex of the legendary Basil's Beach Bar on Mustique. It occupies an early 19th-century sugar warehouse, on the waterfront in Kingstown beneath the previously recommended Cobblestone Inn. The air-conditioned interior is accented with exposed stone and brick, soaring arches, and a rambling mahogany bar that remains open throughout the day. The food is quite creditable, but nowhere near as good as that enjoyed by Princess Margaret or Mick Jagger at Basil's other bar on Mustique. The menu could include lobster salad, shrimp in garlic butter, sandwiches, hamburgers, and barbecued chicken. Dinners feature grilled lobster, escargots, shrimp cocktail, grilled red snapper, and grilled filet mignon. You can order meals here throughout the day and late into the evening (until the last satisfied customer leaves).

Bounty. Egmont St., Kingstown. ☎ **784/456-1776.** Snacks and sandwiches EC$.75–EC$8 (30¢–$2.95); main courses EC$6–EC$15 ($2.20–$5.55). No credit cards. Mon–Fri 8am–5pm, Sat 8am–1:30pm. AMERICAN/WEST INDIAN.

In the redbrick Troutman Building, in the center of Kingstown, you'll find the extremely affordable Bounty serving the local workers (the true power-lunch venue is Basil's, above). A friendly staff greets you. Fill up on pastries of all kinds, rôtis (Caribbean burritos), hot dogs, hamburgers, and sandwiches, along with homemade soups. Fish-and-chips are also served, along with quiche and pizza. The cookery is just as simple as the surroundings, and the interesting collection of drinks includes passion fruit and golden apple. On-site is a gallery selling works by local artists.

Juliette's Restaurant. Egmont St., Kingstown. ☎ **784/457-1645.** Rôtis and sandwiches EC$5–EC$6 ($1.85–$2.20); fixed-price menus EC$11–EC$12 ($4.05–$4.45). No credit cards. Mon–Fri 8:30am–5pm, Sat 8:30am–2pm. WEST INDIAN.

Amid the capital's cluster of administrative buildings, across from the National Commercial Bank, this restaurant dispenses more lunches to office workers than any other in town. Though it's open early it doesn't serve breakfast, only snacks or lunch-type items. Meals are served in a clean dining area headed by a veteran of the restaurant trade, Juliette Campbell. (Ms. Campbell's husband is the island's well-known attorney general.) Menu items include soups, curried mutton, an array of fish, stewed chicken, stewed beef, and sandwiches. Many of the platters are garnished with fried plantains and rice. This is the type of cuisine you're likely to be served in a decent family-style boarding house in St. Vincent.

Pizza Party Chicken Roost. Arnos Vale. ☎ **784/456-4939.** Main courses EC$15–EC$60 ($5.60–$22.20). No credit cards. Daily 9am–11pm. INTERNATIONAL.

Overlooking Mustique and Bequia and across from the airport, this fast-food restaurant offers a wide range of specialties, from sandwiches and pizzas to steaks and lobster. The sandwiches extend from a simple egg and cheese to the more robust flying fish, and the burgers are made with a quarter pound of freshly ground local beef. You can also find stuffed whelk, conch fritters, and shark. The specialty pizzas consist of the jump-up carnival (ground beef, bacon, tomato sauce, oregano, and three cheeses), the Chicago tower (with everything, including sweet peppers and extra garlic), and the eastern special (curried chicken, pineapple, and mozzarella).

Rooftop Restaurant & Bar. Bay St., Kingstown. ☎ **784/457-2845.** Reservations recommended for dinner. Main courses EC$20–EC$50 ($7.40–$18.50); lunch platters EC$20 ($7.40). AE, DISC, MC, V. Mon–Sat 8:30am–10pm. WEST INDIAN/INTERNATIONAL.

This restaurant does a thriving business because of its well-prepared food and its location three stories above the center of Kingstown. After you climb some flights of stairs, you'll see a bar near the entrance, an indoor area decorated in earth tones, and a patio open to the breezes. Lunch stresses traditional Creole recipes using fresh fish, chicken, mutton, beef, and goat. Dinners are more international and include lobster, an excellent snapper with lemon-butter-and-garlic sauce, steak with onions and mushrooms, and several savory preparations of pork. Every Wednesday and Friday a karaoke singalong is featured, and Saturday is family night, with a barbecue along with a steel band in attendance after 6pm. In addition, 60 drinks are featured at the bar.

4 Hitting the Beaches

All beaches on St. Vincent are public, and many of the best ones border hotel properties, which you can patronize for drinks or lunch. Most of the resorts are in the south, where the beaches have golden-yellow sand. Young Island has the only beach of truly white sand on St. Vincent, but it's reserved for patrons of the expensive resort property. Many of the beaches in the north have sands of a lava-ash color. The safest swimming is on the leeward beaches; the surf on the windward or eastern beaches is often rough and can be quite dangerous.

Villa Beach, only a 10-minute drive from Kingstown, is the island's most frequented beach, although its sands are hardly large enough to accommodate the crowds who flock here. Weekends can be particularly bad. The narrow strip of sand fronts the better beach of Young Island. The tranquil Caribbean waters make swimming safe here. Dive shops and simple cafes dot the shoreline. Nearby **Indian Bay Beach** is similar to Villa Beach and also attracts lots of Vincentians on weekends. Monday to Thursday, however, you'll probably have plenty of room on the narrow strip. The sand here is slightly golden in color but tends to be rocky. The reef-protected tranquil waters are ideal for both swimming and snorkeling. You'll find both bars and restaurants here.

Heading north from Kingstown, you'll reach **Buccament Bay,** where the waters are clean, clear, and tranquil enough for swimming. This beach is very tiny, however, and its sand is of the black volcanic variety. In the same area, **Questelle's Bay Beach** (pronounced keet-*eels*) is also on the leeward, tranquil Caribbean side of the island. The black-sand beach, next to Camden Park, is very similar to Buccament Bay.

Only the most die-hard frequent the beaches on the east coast, or windward side. This is where the big breakers roll in from the Atlantic. Don't plan to go swimming in these rough waters—a beach picnic might be more appropriate. The best beaches, all with black volcanic sand, are found at **Kearton's Bay,** near the hamlet of Barrouallie, and at **Peter's Hope** and **Richmond,** all reached along the leeward highway running up the east coast of St. Vincent.

5 Sports & Outdoor Pursuits

FISHING   It's best to go to a local fisherman (or woman) for advice if you're interested in this sport, which your hotel can also arrange for you. The government of St. Vincent doesn't require visitors to take out a license. If you arrange things in time, it's sometimes possible to accompany the fishermen on a trip, perhaps 4 or 5 miles from shore. A modest fee should suffice. The fishing fleet leaves from the leeward coast at Barrouallie. They've been known to return to shore with everything from a 6-inch redfish to a 20-foot pilot whale.

HIKING   Exploring St. Vincent's hot volcano, **La Soufrière,** is an intriguing adventure. As you travel the island, you can't miss its cloud-capped splendor. This volcano has occasionally captured the attention of the world. The most recent eruption was in 1979, when it spewed ashes, lava, and hot mud that covered the vegetation on its slopes and forced thousands of Vincentians to flee its fury. Belching rocks and black curling smoke filled the blue Caribbean sky. Jets of steam spouted 20,000 feet into the air. About 17,000 people were evacuated from a 10-mile ring around the volcano.

Fortunately, the eruption was in the sparsely settled northern part of the island. The volcano lies away from most of the tourism and commercial centers, and even if it should erupt again, volcanologists don't consider it a danger to visitors lodged at beachside hotels along the leeward coast. At the rim of the crater you'll be rewarded with one of the most panoramic views in the Caribbean. That is, if the wind doesn't blow too hard and make you topple over into the crater itself! *Extreme caution is emphasized.* Looking inside, you can see the steam rising from the crater. The trail back down is much easier, we assure you.

Even if you're an experienced hiker, don't attempt to explore the volcano without a guide. And wear suitable hiking clothes and be sure you're in the best of health before making the arduous journey. The easiest route is the 3-mile-long eastern route leaving from Rabacca. Some people attempt this on their own. The more arduous trail, longer by half a mile, is the western trail from Chateaubelair, which definitely requires a guide. The round-trip to the crater takes about 5 hours.

The **St. Vincent Forestry Headquarters,** in the village of Campden Park, about 3 miles from Kingstown along the west coast (☎ **784/457-8594**), offers a pamphlet giving hiking data to La Soufrière. It's open Monday to Friday 8am to noon and 1 to 4pm. **HazEco Tours** (☎ **784/457-8634**) offers guided hikes up to La Soufrière, costing $100 per couple, including lunch.

If you don't want to face Soufrière, the best hikes are the **Vermont Nature Trails.** These marked trails (get a map at the tourist office) take you through a rain forest. You'll pass long-ago plantations that nature has reclaimed and enter a world of tropical fruit trees. If it's your lucky day, you might even see the rare St. Vincent parrot with its flamboyant plumage. Wear good hiking shoes and your anti-mosquito cologne. Call **Sailor's Wilderness Tours** in Kingstown at ☎ **784/457-1274** to get directions.

SNORKELING & SCUBA DIVING   The best area for snorkeling and scuba diving is the Villa/Young Island section on the southern end of the island.

Dive St. Vincent, on the Young Island Cut (☎ **784/457-4928**), has been owned/operated by a transplanted Texan, Bill Tewes, for more than a decade. The best dive company in the country, Dive St. Vincent now has two additional dive shops: **Dive Canouan,** at the Tamarind Beach Hotel on Canouan Island (☎ **784/458-8044**), and **Grenadines Dive,** at the Sunny Grenadines Hotel on Union Island (☎ **784/458-8138**). The shops have a total of six instructors and three dive masters, as well as seven dive boats. The chain of dive shops allows visitors to dive or be certified with a consistency of quality while sailing throughout St. Vincent and the Grenadines. All shops offer dive/snorkel trips as well as sightseeing day trips and dive instruction. Single-tank dives are $50 and two-tank dives $90, including all equipment and instructors and/or dive master guides. Dive packages are also available.

TENNIS   **Young Island Resort** on Young Island (☎ **784/458-4826**), and the **Grand View Beach Hotel** at Villa Point (☎ **784/458-4811**) have tennis courts.

6 Seeing the Sights

Special events include the week-long **Carnival** in early July, one of the largest in the eastern Caribbean, with steel-band and calypso competitions, along with the crowning of the king and queen of the carnival.

KINGSTOWN

Lush and tropical, the capital isn't as architecturally fascinating as St. George's on Grenada. Some English-style houses do exist, many looking as if they belonged in Penzance, Cornwall, instead of the Caribbean. However, you can still meet old-timers if you stroll on Upper Bay Street. White-haired and bearded, they load their boats with

Cheap Thrills: What to See & Do for Free (Well, Almost) on St. Vincent & the Grenadines

- **Hike Through a Lush Eden.** St. Vincent may not be much on beaches, but it's a hiker's paradise, filled with lush tropical forests and the volcanic La Soufrière. You can book the services of a guide through the tourist office or go it alone if you're skilled in handling yourself in the outdoors. The tourist office will provide you with a map. The best route to follow is the Vermont Nature Trails, a network of well-marked paths winding through a beautiful tropical rain forest. The ground beneath you will often be carpeted by huge ferns that look as if they're from the dawn of time, and you'll be shaded by a vast canopy of hardwood trees. Caribbean pine, 75-foot bamboo stands, and deep ravines are part of the landscape. Count yourself lucky if you see the endangered St. Vincent parrot.

- **Spend a Day on Bequia.** A scenic ride on an inexpensive government-owned mailboat will deliver you to the enchanting Grenadine island of Bequia, where time has seemingly stood still. Its capital is Port Elizabeth, one of the Caribbean's best sheltered harbors, 9 miles south of the parent island of St. Vincent. Part of the fun of going here is to meet and talk to some of the Bequinians, with their long tradition of seafaring and shipbuilding. There's not a lot to do here, and that's part of the fun. You can wander the port, soak up local color, enjoy a Creole lunch, and spend the rest of the day on the sandy beach.

- **Drive Through the Marriaqua Valley.** Also known as the Mesopotamia Valley, this rugged drive is one of the most dramatic in the Caribbean. It begins at the Vigie Highway, just east of the airport, and climbs northeast before heading north to the village of Mesopotamia. Along the way you'll pass rustic scenes like boys riding overburdened donkeys and farmers putting blue plastic on their crops to protect them from insects and wild birds. As you pass the fields of coconut, sweet corn, arrowroot, peanuts, and coconut palms, you'll know why this valley is called the breadbasket of St. Vincent. Surrounded by mountain ridges, the road opens onto a panoramic view of 3,180-foot Grand Bonhomme Mountain. Passing through deep tropical forests, you arrive at Montreal Gardens, 12 miles north of Kingstown. Here you can have lunch and go for a swim in the natural mineral springs.

- **Wander Kingstown.** Though often confused with the more famous Kingston, capital of Jamaica, this tiny town of some 25,000 Vincentians has its own unique personality. On the southwestern coast, it wraps itself around Kingstown Bay and is set against a backdrop of hills and ridges. A bustling port, it invites wandering and people watching. Most interest centers around the waterfront, where schooners from many other islands, including South America, unload their cargo. The best time to visit is Saturday morning, when the marketplace at the south end of town is at its most active. If you need a sightseeing goal, make it Fort Charlotte on the north side of the capital, lying at the end of a winding road on a promontory rising 650 feet above sea level. Originally used by the British to defend St. Vincent from the French, it was named for George III. At the fort you'll be rewarded with the most panoramic view of St. Vincent and the string of islands called the Grenadines.

produce grown on the mountain before heading to some secluded beach in the Grenadines. This is a chief port and gateway to the Grenadines, and you can also view the small boats and yachts that have dropped anchor here. The place is a magnet for charter sailors.

At the top of a winding road on the north side of Kingstown is **Fort Charlotte** (☎ **784/456-1165**), built on Johnson Point around the time of the American Revolution, enclosing one side of the bay. The ruins aren't much to inspect; the reason to come here is the view. The fort sits atop a steep promontory some 640 feet above the sea. From its citadel, you'll have a commanding sweep of the leeward shores to the north, Kingstown to the south, and the Grenadines beyond. On a clear day you can even see Grenada. Three cannons used to fight off French troops are still in place. You'll see a series of oil murals depicting the history of black Caribs. Admission is free, and it's open 24 hours.

The second major sight is the ✪ **Botanic Gardens,** on the north side of Kingstown at Montrose (☎ **784/457-1003**). Founded in 1765 by Gov. George Melville, they're the oldest botanical gardens in the West Indies. In this Windward Eden, you'll see 20 acres of such tropical exotics as teak, almond, cinnamon, nutmeg, cannonball, and mahogany; some trees are more than 2 centuries old. One of the breadfruit trees was reputedly among those original seedlings brought to this island by Captain Bligh in 1793. There's also a large *Spachea perforata* (Soufrière tree), a species believed to be unique to St. Vincent and not found in the wild since 1812. The gardens are open daily 6am to 6pm; admission is free.

✪ THE LEEWARD HIGHWAY

The leeward or west side of the island has the most dramatic scenery. North of Kingstown, you rise into lofty terrain before descending to the water again. There are views in all directions. Here you can see the massive **Carib Rock,** with a human face carving dating back to A.D. 600. This is one of the finest petroglyphs in the Caribbean.

Continuing north you reach **Barrouallie,** where there's a Carib stone altar. Even if you're not into fishing, you might want to spend some time in this whaling village, where some people still occasionally set out in brightly painted boats armed with harpoons, Moby Dick–style, to seek the elusive whale. But environmentalists should note that while Barrouallie may be one of the last few outposts in the world where whaling is carried on, Vincentians point out that it doesn't endanger an already endangered species since so few are caught each year. If one is caught, it's an occasion for festivities.

The leeward highway continues to **Chateaubelair,** the end of the line. Here you can swim at the attractive **Richmond Beach** before heading back to Kingstown. In the distance, the volcano, La Soufrière, looms menacingly in the mountains.

The adventurous set out from here to see the **Falls of Baleine,** 7½ miles north of Richmond Beach on the northern tip of the island, accessible only by boat. Baleine is a freshwater falls that comes from a stream in the volcanic hills. If you're interested in making the trip, check with the tourist office in Kingstown for tour information.

THE WINDWARD HIGHWAY

This road runs along the eastern Atlantic coast from Kingstown. Waves pound the surf, and panoramic seascapes are all along the rocky shores. If you want to go swimming along this often-dangerous coast, stick to the sandy spots, as they offer safer shores. Along this road you'll pass coconut and banana plantations and fields of arrowroot.

North of Georgetown lies the **Rabacca Dry River,** which shows the flow of lava from the volcano when it erupted at the beginning of the 20th century. The journey from Kingstown to here is only 24 miles, but it will seem like much longer. For those who want to go the final 11 miles along a rugged road to **Fancy,** the northern tip of the island, a Land Rover, jeep, or Moke will be needed.

MARRIQUA VALLEY

Sometimes known as the Mesopotamia Valley, this area is one of the lushest cultivated valleys in the eastern Caribbean. Surrounded by mountain ridges, the drive takes you through a landscape planted with nutmeg, cocoa, coconut, breadfruit, and bananas. The road begins at Vigie Highway, to the east of the E. T. Joshua Airport runway. At Montréal you'll come on natural mineral springs. Only rugged vehicles should make this trip.

Around Kingstown, you can also enjoy the **Queen's Drive,** a scenic loop into the high hills to the east of the capital. From here, the view is panoramic over Kingstown and its yacht-clogged harbor to the Grenadines in the distance.

7 Shopping

You don't come to St. Vincent to shop, but once here, you might pick up some of the Sea Island cotton fabrics and clothing that are specialties. In addition, Vincentian artisans make pottery, jewelry, and baskets that have souvenir value at least.

Since Kingstown consists of about 12 small blocks, you can walk and browse and see just about everything in a morning's shopping jaunt. Try to be in town for the colorful, noisy **Friday-morning market.** You might not purchase anything, but you'll surely enjoy the riot of color.

Juliette's Fashions, Back Street (☎ 784/456-1143), owned and operated by the same entrepreneur who runs Juliette's Restaurant, is the best-stocked and most glamorous women's clothing store on St. Vincent, but that's not saying a lot. Beneficiary of its owner's frequent buying trips to Miami and New York, it's one of the few outlets on the island to sell semiformal evening wear. At **Sprott Brothers, Homeworks,** Bay Street (☎ 784/457-1121), you can buy clothing designed by Vincentians, along with an array of fabrics, linens, and silk-screened T-shirts—even Caribbean-made furniture.

Noah's Arkade, Bay Street (☎ 784/457-1513), sells gifts from the West Indies, like wood carvings, T-shirts, and a wide range of books and souvenirs. Noah's has shops at the Frangipani Hotel in Bequia. **St. Vincent Philatelic Services,** Bonadie's Building, Bay Street (☎ 784/457-1911), is the Caribbean's largest operating bureau, and its issues are highly acclaimed by stamp collectors around the world. Stamp enthusiasts can visit or order by mail. The familiar **Y. de Lima,** Bay and Egmont streets (☎ 784/457-1681), is full of cameras, stereo equipment, toys, clocks, binoculars, and jewelry, the best selection on the island. Caribbean gold and silver jewelry are also featured.

Time for more shopping? The typical Caribbean duty-free goods are found at **Voyager,** Halifax Street (☎ 784/456-1686), including quality jewelry, French perfumes, leather goods, and Swiss watches. As you're leaving you can drop into **Carsyl Duty-Free Liquors** at the airport (☎ 784/457-2706), where you'll find liquor at prices often 40% off stateside prices. To add to your music collection, you can visit **Music World** at Egmont Street (☎ 784/547-1884), where you can listen to and buy the latest soca, reggae, and calypso music.

8 St. Vincent After Dark

The focus is mainly on the hotels, and activities are likely to include nighttime barbecues and dancing to steel bands. In season, at least one hotel seems to have something planned every night of the week. Beer is extremely cheap at all the places noted below.

During party nights when it rocks and rolls (usually Friday, Saturday, and Sunday), the **Aquatic Club,** adjacent to the departure point of the ferry from St. Vincent to Young Island (☎ 784/458-4205), is the loudest, most raucous nightspot on St. Vincent. On weekend nights, things heat up by 11pm and continue until as late as 3am. The other nights of the week the place functions just as a bar, with a spate of recorded music but without the high-volume live bands. Centered around an open-sided veranda and an outdoor deck, the place is open daily 9pm to 2 or 3am. For the Saturday-night dance, there's an entrance charge of EC$15 ($5.55); otherwise, there's no cover.

The Attic, in the Kentucky Building, at 1 Melville and Back sts. (☎ 784/457-2558), features jazz and easy-listening music. Music is live only on Friday and Saturday; Tuesday and Thursday it's recorded, and Wednesday is karaoke night. Fish and burgers are available. There's usually a cover of EC$10 ($3.70).

Emerald Valley Casino, Penniston Valley (☎ 784/456-7140), is not one of the Caribbean's glamorous casinos. This down-home nightspot offers a trio of roulette tables, three blackjack, and one Caribbean stud poker. You can also play craps here. There's a bar, and you can also order food. If you've got nothing else to do, you might consider a visit any time Wednesday to Monday 9pm to 3am.

The **Touch Entertainment Centre (TEC),** Grenville Street (☎ 784/457-1825), opposite KFC on the top floor of the Cambridge Building, is the best-known nightspot around. With advanced lighting, it's a soundproof air-conditioned environment, popular with tourists. Every Wednesday in summer is disco night, especially for the young and restless. Friday and Sunday nights the club has a house party with a DJ. Surprisingly, it isn't open on Saturday.

9 The Grenadines: Bequia, Union Island & Mayreau

GETTING THERE

BY PLANE Four of the Grenadines—Bequia, Mustique, Union Island, and Canouan—have small airports, the landing spots for flights on **Mustique Airways** (☎ 784/458-4380 on St. Vincent). Its planes are technically charters, though flights depart St. Vincent for Bequia daily at 8am. The cost is $43 round-trip.

BY BOAT The ideal way to go, of course, is to rent your own yacht, as many wealthy visitors do. But a far less expensive method of transport is to go on a mail, cargo, or passenger boat as the locals do, but you'll need time and patience. However, boats do run on schedules. The **government mailboat,** M/V *Baracuda* (☎ 784/456-5180), leaves St. Vincent on Monday and Thursday at 10:30am, stops at Bequia, Canouan, and Mayreau, and arrives at Union Island at about 3:45pm. On Tuesday and Friday, the boat leaves Union Island at about 6:30am, stops at Mayreau and Canouan, reaches Bequia at about 10:45am, and makes port at St. Vincent at noon. One-way fares from St. Vincent are: to Bequia, EC$10 ($3.70) Monday to Friday and EC$12 ($4.45) on weekends; to Canouan, EC$13 ($4.80); to Mayreau, EC$15 ($5.55); and to Union Island, EC$20 ($7.40).

You can also reach Bequia Monday to Saturday on the *Admiral I* and *II.* For information on these sea trips, inquire at the **Tourist Board,** Bay Street in Kingstown (☎ 784/457-1502).

BEQUIA

Only 7 square miles of land, Bequia (pronounced *beck*-wee) is the largest and northernmost island of the Grenadines (only 9 miles south of St. Vincent). It offers quiet lagoons, reefs, and long stretches of nearly deserted beaches. Descended from seafarers and other early adventurers, its population of some 6,000 will give you a friendly greeting if you pass them along the road. Of the inhabitants, 10% are of Scottish ancestry, who live mostly in the Mount Pleasant region. A feeling of relaxation and informality prevails.

GETTING AROUND

Rental cars, owned by local people, are available at the port, and you can hire a **taxi** at the dock to take you around or to your hotel if you're spending the night. Taxis are reasonably priced, but an even better bet are the so-called **dollar cabs,** which take you anywhere on the island for a small fee. They don't seem to have a regular schedule—you just flag one down.

Before going to your hotel, drop in at the circular **Tourist Information Centre,** Port Elizabeth (☎ 809/458-3286). Here you can ask for a driver who's familiar with the attractions of the island (all of them are). You should negotiate the fare in advance.

ACCOMMODATIONS YOU CAN AFFORD

✪ **Frangipani Hotel.** P.O. Box 1, Bequia, the Grenadines, St. Vincent, W.I. ☎ **784/458-3255.** Fax 784/458-3824. www.heraldsvg.com. E-mail: frangi@caribsurf.com. 15 units, 10 with bathroom. Winter $35 single without bathroom, $120–$130 single with bathroom; $55 double without bathroom, $130–$150 double with bathroom. Off-season $30 single without bathroom, $80–$100 single with bathroom; $40 double without bathroom, $90–$120 double with bathroom. Extra person $25. Children 12 and under $15. AE, DISC, MC, V.

The core of this pleasant guest house originated as the private home of a 19th-century sea captain. Since it became a hotel it has added accommodations that border a sloping tropical garden in back. The complex overlooks the island's most historic harbor, Admiralty Bay. The five rooms in the original house are smaller and much less glamorous (and cheaper) than the ones in the garden, which are handcrafted from local stone and hardwoods and have tile floors, carpets of woven hemp, wooden furniture (some made on St. Vincent), firm mattresses, and balconies. Most of the rooms have a small bath with a shower; otherwise, the hall baths are adequate and tidy. The in-house restaurant is open-sided and overlooks the yacht harbor. Guests can play tennis or arrange for scuba, sailboat rides, or other water sports nearby. (The nearest scuba outfitter, Sunsports, is fully accredited by PADI.) The hotel presents live music every Monday in winter and an outdoor barbecue every Thursday at 7:30pm, with a steel band.

Gingerbread. Belmont Walkaway, Admiralty Bay, Bequia, the Grenadines, St. Vincent, W.I. ☎ **784/458-3800.** Fax 784/458-3907. www.begos.com/gingerbread. 9 units. TV. Winter $140–$165 single or double; off-season $110–$125 single or double. MC, V.

About a minute's walk from the edge of Port Elizabeth, this is the gingerbread-accented architectural statement of a British entrepreneur who firmly believes in self-reliant holidays (each unit has a kitchen). The approach is formal, even a bit chilly. But if you're able to entertain yourself in a *laissez-faire* environment with a stiff dose of British reserve, you might find the place appealing. The units are simply but tastefully furnished with a re-interpretation of British living in the Caribbean tropics. Upstairs

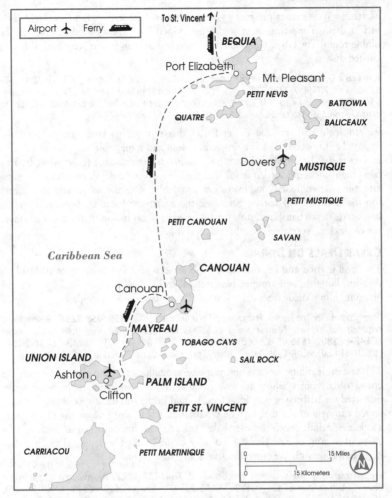

The Grenadines

Airport ✈   Ferry 🚢

To St. Vincent ↑

BEQUIA

Port Elizabeth
Mt. Pleasant
PETIT NEVIS
BATTOWIA
QUATRE
BALICEAUX

Dovers
MUSTIQUE

PETIT MUSTIQUE

PETIT CANOUAN
SAVAN

Caribbean Sea

CANOUAN

Canouan

MAYREAU
TOBAGO CAYS
SAIL ROCK

UNION ISLAND
Ashton
Clifton
PALM ISLAND

PETIT ST. VINCENT

CARRIACOU
PETIT MARTINIQUE

0   15 Miles
0   15 Kilometers
N

units have four-poster queen-sized beds, usually with draped mosquito netting; downstairs units have twin beds and lower ceilings but the same amenities. Mattresses are new and comfortable, and the baths, though small, are neatly arranged. Throughout are terra-cotta floor tiles from Italy, country-comfortable color schemes of blue and white, and a distinct sense that a sophisticated decorator performed some magic here. The Gingerbread restaurant is recommended separately. The hotel also has a tennis court.

Julie's and Isola's Guest House. P.O. Box 12, Port Elizabeth, Bequia, the Grenadines, St. Vincent, W.I. ☎ **784/458-3304.** Fax 784/458-3812. 20 units. Year-round $39 single; $65 double. Rates include half board. MC, V.

These twin places are owned by two of the most kindhearted hoteliers on the island, Julie and Isola McIntosh. Julie, a mason, laid many of the bricks for both hotels, which lie across the street from each other about a block from the water in the center of Port Elizabeth. Isola's Guest House is the more modern; Julie's is slightly older. The rooms tend to be hot, small, and noisy at times, but it's an enduring favorite nonetheless.

Mattresses have entertained many guests before you checked in, but there's still comfort in them. The baths are very cramped. Good West Indian food is served in the dining room. The bill of fare is likely to include pumpkin fritters, very fresh fish, and curried dishes.

Keegan's Guest House. Lower Bay, Bequia, the Grenadines, St. Vincent, W.I. ☎ **784/458-3530.** Fax 784/457-3313. 11 units. TV. Year-round $45–$55 single; $70–$85 double; $365–$490 per week apt. for 1 to 4. Room (but not apt.) rates include breakfast and dinner. Extra person $30. No credit cards.

Ringed with white-painted picket fences that separate its sandy garden from the unpaved road outside, this is a simple but clean and respectable guest house adjacent to Lower Bay Beach. Built in the early 1980s, it presents an angular white-fronted façade, an uncomplicated interior, and well-swept verandas. All rooms have ceiling fans, tile-covered floors, good mattresses, tiny baths, off-white walls, maid service, and (on the upper floors) narrow balconies; the apartment has a kitchenette. There's a kiosk-style beach bar. The simple food is based on West Indian traditions, with ample use of chicken, vegetables, conch, and local fish.

GREAT DEALS ON DINING

The food is good and healthful here—lobster, chicken, and steaks from such fish as dolphin, kingfish, and grouper, plus tropical fruits, fried plantain, and coconut and guava puddings made fresh daily. Even the beach bars are kept spotless.

Frangipani. In the Hotel Frangipani, Port Elizabeth. ☎ **809/458-3255.** Reservations required for dinner. Main courses EC$30–EC$70 ($11.10–$25.90); fixed-price dinner EC$45–EC$80 ($16.65–$29.60); breakfast EC$18 ($6.65); lunch EC$6–EC$40 ($2.20–$14.80). AE, MC, V. Daily 7:30am–5pm and 7–9pm. Closed Sept. CARIBBEAN.

This waterside dining room is one of the best restaurants on the island. The yachting crowd often comes ashore to dine here. With the exception of the juicy steaks imported for barbecues, only local food is used in the succulent specialties. Lunches, served throughout the day, include sandwiches, salads, and seafood platters. Dinner specialties include conch chowder, baked chicken with rice-and-coconut stuffing, lobster, and an array of fresh fish. A fixed-price menu is available at night. The Thursday-night barbecue with live entertainment is an island event.

Friendship Bay Resort. Port Elizabeth. ☎ **784/458-3222.** Reservations required for dinner. Main courses EC$35–EC$80 ($12.95–$29.60); lunch EC$20–EC$45 ($7.40–$16.65). AE, MC, V. Daily noon–3pm and 7:30–10pm. Closed Sept–Oct 15. INTERNATIONAL/WEST INDIAN.

Guests dine in a candlelit room high above a sweeping expanse of seafront on a hillside rich with the scent of frangipani and hibiscus. Lunch is served at the beach bar Spicy 'n Herby, but dinner is more elaborate. Meals are based on fresh ingredients and might include grilled lobster in season, curried beef, grilled or broiled fish (served Creole style with spicy sauce), shrimp curry, and charcoal-grilled steak flambé. Dishes are flavorsome and well prepared. An island highlight is the Friday- and Saturday-night jump-up and barbecue.

Gingerbread. Belmont Walkway, Admiralty Bay. ☎ **784/458-3800.** Reservations recommended for dinner. Lunch main courses $6–$12; dinner main courses $14–$18. MC, V. Daily 8am–9:30pm. INTERNATIONAL.

Associated with a previously recommended complex of self-contained apartments, this restaurant is cozy, calm, and more closely tuned to European models than many of its counterparts on Bequia. In a second-floor dining room overlooking a boardwalk, a garden, and the sea, you'll be served meals that include an array of grilled and baked fish; shellfish; and a broad selection of curries that include versions made with pork, fish, beef, and shrimp. The specialty drink of the place is a passionata, made with passion-fruit juice, rum, and selected island spices.

SEEING THE SIGHTS

Obviously, the **secluded beaches** are tops on everyone's list of Bequia's attractions. As you walk along the beaches, especially near Port Elizabeth, you'll see craftspeople building boats by hand, a method they learned from their ancestors. Whalers sometimes still set out from here in wooden boats with hand harpoons, just as they do from a port village on St. Vincent.

Dive Bequia, Gingerbread House, Admiralty Bay (P.O. Box 16), Bequia, St. Vincent, W.I. (☎ 784/458-3504), specializes in diving and snorkeling. Scuba dives cost $50 for one dive, $85 for two dives in the same day, and $400 for a 10-dive package. Introductory lessons go for $15 per person; a four-dive open-water certification course is $400. A snorkeling trip is $15 per person. These prices include all the necessary equipment.

The main harbor village, **Port Elizabeth** is known for its safe anchorage, **Admiralty Bay.** The bay was a haven in the 17th century for the British, French, and Spanish navies, as well as for pirates. Descendants of Captain Kydd (a.k.a. Kidd) still live on the island. Today the yachting set anchors here, often bringing a kind of excitement to the locals.

Frankly, after you leave Port Elizabeth there aren't many sights, and you'll probably have your driver, booked for the day, drop you off for a long, leisurely lunch and some time on a beach. However, you'll pass a fort with a harbor view and drive on to Industry Estates, which has a Beach House restaurant serving a fair lunch. At **Paget Farm,** you can wander into an old whaling village and maybe inspect a few jawbones left over from the catches of yesterday.

At **Moonhole,** a vacation and retirement community is built into the cliffs practically as a free-form sculpture. These are private homes, of course, and you're not to enter without permission. For a final look at Bequia, head up an 800-foot hill that the local people call **The Mountain.** From that perch, you'll have a 360° view of St. Vincent and the Grenadines to the south.

SHOPPING

This isn't a particularly good reason to come to Bequia, but there are some interesting stores. The best of the shops scattered along the water is **The Crab Hole,** next to the Plantation House, Admiralty Bay (☎ 784/458-3290), where they invite guests to visit their silk-screen factory in back. Later you can make purchases at their shop in front, including sterling-silver and 14-karat-gold jewelry.

At **Noah's Arkade,** in the Frangipani Hotel, Port Elizabeth (☎ 784/458-3424), island entrepreneur Lavinia Gunn sells Vincentian and Bequian batiks, scarves, hats, T-shirts, and a scattering of pottery. There are also dolls, place mats, baskets, and homemade jellies concocted from grapefruit, mango, and guava, plus West Indian cookbooks and books on tropical flowers and reef fish. This place stands a few steps from the terrace bar of the Frangipani Hotel.

Anyone on the island can show you the way to the workshops of **Sargeant's Model Boatshop Bequia,** Front Street, Port Elizabeth (☎ 784/458-3344), which lies west of the pier past the oil-storage facility. Sought out by yacht owners looking for a scale-model reproduction of their favorite vessel, Lawson Sargeant is the self-taught wood carver who established this business. The models are carved from a soft local wood called gumwood, then painted in brilliant colors of red, green, gray, or blue; whatever your fancy dictates. When a scale model of the royal family's yacht, *Britannia,* was commissioned in 1985, it required 5 weeks of work and meticulous blueprints and cost $10,000. You can pick up a model of a Bequia whaling boat for much less. The Sargeant family usually keeps 100 model boats in many shapes and sizes in inventory.

UNION ISLAND

Midway between Grenada and St. Vincent, Union Island is the southernmost of the Grenadines. It's known for its dramatic 900-foot peak, Mount Parnassus, which yachting people can often see from miles away. For those cruising in the area, Union is the port of entry for St. Vincent. Yachters are required to check with Customs upon entry.

Perhaps you'll sail into Union on a night when the locals are having a big drum dance, in which costumed islanders dance and chant to the beat of drums made of goatskin.

GETTING THERE

The island is reached either by chartered or scheduled aircraft, by cargo boat, by private yacht, or by mailboat (see "Getting There" at the beginning of this section). **Air Martinique** (☎ 784/458-4528) flies to Union Island from both Martinique and St. Vincent. **Mustique Airways** (☎ 784/458-4380 on St. Vincent) makes one flight per day to Union Island Monday to Thursday at a cost of $64 round-trip. Children under 12 fly half-price.

ACCOMMODATIONS YOU CAN AFFORD

Anchorage Yacht Club. Clifton, Union Island, The Grenadines, St. Vincent, W.I. ☎ **784/458-8221.** Fax 784/458-8365. 12 units. A/C. Winter $100 double; $150 bungalow or apt. Off-season $70 double; $80 bungalow or apt. Rates include continental breakfast. Extra person $35. MC, V.

This club occupies a prominent position a few steps from the bumpy airplane landing strip that services at least two nearby resorts (Petit St. Vincent and Palm Island) and about a half dozen small islands nearby. As such, something of an airline hub aura permeates the place as passengers shuttle between their airplanes and boats and the bar and restaurant here. Although at least two other hotels are nearby, this is the most important. It combines a three-fold function as a hotel, a restaurant, and a bar, with a busy marine-service facility (under different management) in the same compound. Each of the small rooms is set between a pair of airy verandas and has white-tile floors and simple, somewhat sun-bleached modern furniture, including good beds with firm mattresses. The baths are very small and towels a bit thin. The most popular units are the bungalows and cabañas beside the beach.

The yachting club meets in the wood-and-stone bar, where you can order meals for EC$80 ($29.60) and up. The menu might include fish soup, a wide array of fresh fish, and Creole versions of lamb, pork, and beef. Try the mango daiquiri. The bar is open all day and into the night, but meals are served daily: breakfast 7 to 10am, lunch noon to 3pm, and dinner to 10:30pm.

GREAT DEALS ON DINING

Lambi's Restaurant. Clifton Harbour, Union Island. ☎ **784/458-8549.** Fax 784/458-8395. Main courses all EC$30 ($11.10). 50-dish buffet EC$50 ($18.50). Daily 7am–midnight. MC, V. CREOLE/SEAFOOD.

Built partially on stilts into the sea on the waterfront in Clifton, this is the best place to sample the local cuisine. *Lambi* means conch in Creole patois, and naturally this is the specialty. You can order various other fresh fish platters as well, depending on the catch of the day. Lobster and crab are frequently available. You can also order the usual, like chicken, steaks, and lamb or pork chops, but all this is shipped in frozen. Fresh vegetables are used whenever possible. In winter, a steel band entertains nightly in the bar, and limbo dancers or even fire dancing will enthrall you.

Upstairs has been turned into a hotel of 41 rooms, Lambi's Guest House. Rooms are dorm-simple but come with two double beds and a tiny bath. There are ceiling fans, but no air-conditioning. Year-round prices are EC$50 ($18.50) single, EC$75 ($27.75) double, and EC$90 ($33.30) triple.

MAYREAU

A tiny cay, 1½ square miles of land in the Grenadines, Mayreau is a privately owned island shared by a hotel and a little hilltop village of about 170 inhabitants. It's on the route of the mailboat that plies the seas to and from St. Vincent, also visiting Canouan and Union Island. It's completely sleepy unless a cruise ship should anchor offshore and hustle its passengers over for a lobster barbecue on the beach.

ACCOMMODATIONS YOU CAN AFFORD

Dennis' Hideaway. Saline Bay, Mayreau Island, The Grenadines, St. Vincent, W.I. ☎ or fax **784/458-8594.** 2 units, neither with bathroom. Winter $50 single; $70 double. Off-season $40 single; $50 double. Rates include breakfast. AE, MC, V.

Most of the energy here goes into the restaurant and supermarket, though rooms are available to overnight guests. All electricity is produced by the complex's own generator. The isolation contributes to a neighborly sense of raffish fun. The tiny rooms have ceiling fans and simple but solid furniture, including well-worn mattresses. You're given some rather thin towels for the communal bath. Dennis will charm and entertain you while you enjoy lunch or dinner here; on some nights he even plays the guitar. The view alone would justify coming here, but the West Indian food is another good reason. Since there's water in all directions, seafood is naturally the choice on the bill of fare. The selection might include lobster, shrimp, or conch. For those who want meat, Dennis usually has lamb or pork chops. A steel band plays on Wednesday and Saturday, when bountiful buffets are featured.

24

Trinidad & Tobago

Trinidad, birthplace of calypso and the steel pan, used to be visited only by business travelers in Port-of-Spain. The islanders were more interested in its oil, natural gas, and steel industries than in tourism. But all that has changed now. Trinidad is a serious tourist destination, with a spruced-up capital and a renovated airport. The island's sophistication and cultural mélange, which is far greater than that of any other island in the southern Caribbean, is also a factor in increased tourist interest in Trinidad. Conversely, **Tobago,** its sibling island, is just as drowsy as ever—and that's its charm.

Charted by Columbus on his third voyage in 1498, Trinidad is named after the Holy Trinity he saw represented in three massive peaks on the southern coast. Through the years, the country has been peopled by immigrants from almost every corner of the world—Africa, the Middle East, Europe, India, China, and the Americas. It's against such a background that the island has become the fascinating mix of cultures, races, and creeds that it is today.

Trinidad, which is about the size of Delaware, and its neighbor island, tiny Tobago, 20 miles northeast, together form a nation popularly known as "T&T." The islands of the new country are the southernmost outposts of the West Indies. Trinidad lies only 7 miles from the Paria Peninsula in Venezuela, to which it was once connected in prehistoric times.

The Spanish settled the island, which the Native Amerindians had called Iere, or "land of the hummingbird." The Spaniards made their first permanent settlement in 1592 and held onto it longer than they did any of their other real estate in the Caribbean. The English captured Trinidad in 1797, and it remained British until the two-island nation declared its independence in 1962. The Republic of Trinidad and Tobago is a parliamentary democracy, with a president and a prime minister. The British influence is still clearly visible, from the strong presence of the British dialect to the islanders' fondness for cricket.

1 Essentials

VISITOR INFORMATION

Before you go, information about either Trinidad or Tobago is available by calling the **Tourism Hotline** at ☎ **888/595-4TNT.** You can also get information from the **Trinidad & Tobago Tourism Office** at

350 Fifth Ave., Suite 6316, New York, NY 10118 (☎ **800/748-4224**). Canadians are supplied information at **Taurus House,** 512 Duplex Ave., Toronto, Ontario M4R 2E3 (☎ **800/267-7600** or 416/485-7827). There's also an office in England at **International House,** 47 Chase Side, Enfield, Middlesex EN2 6NB2 (☎ **0181/367-3752**).

Once you're in Trinidad, you can get information from **TIDCO,** 10–14 Phillips St., Port-of-Spain (☎ **868/623-1932**). There's also an information desk at Piarco Airport (☎ **868/669-5196**). On Tobago, you can go to the **Tobago Division of Tourism,** N.I.B. Mall, Level 3, Scarborough (☎ **868/639-2125**). Tobago also maintains an information desk at its Crown Point Airport (☎ **868/639-0509**).

The Internet address for the islands is **www.tidco.co.tt**.

Fast Facts: Trinidad & Tobago

Banking Hours   Most banks are open Monday to Thursday 8am to 2pm and Friday 9am to noon and 3 to 5pm.

Currency   The **Trinidad and Tobago dollar (TT$)** is loosely pegged to the U.S. dollar at an exchange rate of about $1 U.S. = TT$6 (TT$1 = 16.6¢ U.S.). Ask what currency is being referred to when rates are quoted. We've used a combination of both in this chapter, depending on the establishment. U.S. and Canadian dollars are accepted for payment, particularly in Port-of-Spain. However, you'll usually do better by converting your Canadian or U.S. dollars into local currency. British pounds should be converted into the local currency. Unless otherwise specified, dollar quotations appearing in this chapter are in U.S. currency.

Customs   Readers have reported long delays in clearing customs on Trinidad. Personal effects are duty free, and visitors may bring in 200 cigarettes or 50 cigars plus 1 quart of "spirits."

Documents   Visitors arriving in Trinidad and Tobago should have an ongoing or return ticket from their point of embarkation. A visa isn't required for tourist/business stays of less than 6 weeks. You'll be asked to fill out an immigration card on your arrival, and the carbon copy of this should be saved, as it must be returned to immigration officials when you depart. Citizens of the United States, Britain, and Canada need passports to enter Trinidad and Tobago.

Electricity   The electricity is either 110 or 230 volts AC (60 cycles), so ask when making your hotel reservations if you'll need transformers and/or adapters.

Embassies & High Commissions   In Port-of-Spain on Trinidad, the **U.S. Embassy** is located at 7–9 Marli St., 15 Queen's Park West (☎ **868/622-6371**); the **Canadian High Commission** is located at Maple House, 3 Sweet Briar Rd., St. Clair (☎ **868/622-6232**); and the **British High Commission** is located at 19 St. Clair Ave., St. Clair (☎ **868/622-2748**).

Emergencies   Call the **police** at ☎ **999**. To report a **fire** or summon an **ambulance,** dial ☎ **990.**

Language   English is the official language, though you'll hear it spoken with many accents, including British. Hindi, Chinese, French, and Spanish are also spoken.

Safety   As a general rule, Tobago is safer than its larger neighbor, Trinidad. Crime does exist, but it's not of raging dimensions. If you can, avoid the downtown streets of Port-of-Spain at night, especially those around Independence Square, where muggings have been reported. Evening jaunts down Wilson Street and the Market of Scarborough are also discouraged. Visitors are open prey for pickpockets during Carnival time, so be alert during large street parties. It would also be wise to safeguard your valuables and never leave them unattended at the beach or even in a locked car.

Taxes The government imposes a 15% value-added tax (VAT) on room rates. It also imposes a departure tax of TT$85 ($13.60) on every passenger more than 5 years old.

Time Trinidad-and-Tobago time is the same as the U.S. east coast. But when the U.S. goes on daylight saving time, Trinidad and Tobago do not; then, when it's 6am in Miami, it's 7am in T&T.

Tipping The big hotels and restaurants add a 10% to 15% service charge to your final tab.

Weather Trinidad has a tropical climate all year, with constant trade winds maintaining mean temperatures of 84°F during the day, 74° at night, with a range of 70° to 90°F. The rainy season runs May to November, but it shouldn't deter you from visiting; the rain usually lasts no more than 2 hours before the sun comes out again. However, carry along plenty of insect repellent if you come then.

2 Trinidad

Trinidad is completely different from the other islands of the Caribbean, and that forms part of its charm and appeal. The island itself is 50 miles long and 40 miles wide. The limbo was born here, as were calypso and steel-drum music. Visitors in increasing numbers are drawn to this island of many rhythms.

Trinidad isn't for everyone, though. Because Port-of-Spain is one of the most bustling commercial centers in the Caribbean, more business travelers than tourists are drawn here. The island has beaches, but the best of them are far away from the capital. The city itself is hot, humid, and slightly on the dirty side, while the hilly suburbs are as charming as a southern city set in a tropical paradise.

Although Port-of-Spain, with its shopping centers, fast-food joints, modern hotels, and active nightlife, draws mixed reviews from readers, the countryside is calmer. Far removed from the traffic jams of the capital, you can explore the fauna and flora of the island. It's estimated there are some 700 varieties of orchids alone, plus 400 species of birds.

Prices on Trinidad are often lower than those on many other islands in the West Indies, such as Barbados. Port-of-Spain abounds in inexpensive inns and guest houses. Since most of the dining places cater to locals, dining prices reflect the low wages.

The people are part of the attraction on this island, the most cosmopolitan in the Caribbean. Trinidad's polyglot population includes Syrians, Chinese, Americans, Europeans, East Indians, Parsees, Madrasis, Venezuelans, and the last of the original Amerindians. You'll also find Hindustanis, Javanese, Lebanese, African descendants, and Creole mixtures. The main religions are Christianity, Hinduism, and Islam. In all, there are about 1.2 million inhabitants whose language is English, though you may hear speech in a strange argot, Trinibagianese.

Port-of-Spain, in the northwestern corner of the island, is the capital, with the largest concentration of the population, about 120,000 people. With the opening of

Caribbean Sea

Airport ✈ Beach ↖

its $2-million cruise-ship complex in Port-of-Spain, Trinidad now has become a major port of call for Caribbean cruise lines.

One of the most industrialized nations in the Caribbean and the third-largest exporter of oil in the Western Hemisphere, Trinidad is also blessed with the huge 114-acre Pitch Lake, from which comes most of the world's asphalt. Further, it's also the home of Angostura Bitters, the recipe for which is a closely guarded secret.

GETTING THERE

From North America, Trinidad is one of the most distant islands in the Caribbean. Because of the legendary toughness of Trinidadian Customs, it's preferable to arrive during the day (presumably when your stamina might be at its peak) if you can schedule it.

Trinidad is the transfer point for many passengers heading on to the beaches of Tobago. For information about getting to Tobago, refer to section 3 of this chapter.

Most passengers from eastern North America fly **American Airlines** (☎ 800/433-7300 or 868/664-4661), which has connections through New York. American also offers a daily nonstop flight to Trinidad from Miami, which is especially useful for transfers from the midwest and the west coast.

From New York, **BWIA** (☎ 800/538-2942 or 868/625-1010) offers one daily flight into Port-of-Spain, depending on the day of the week and the season. Several of these are nonstop; most touch down en route, usually on Barbados or Antigua, before continuing without a change of planes to Trinidad, the airline's home base. From

A Swirl of Color & Sound: The Carnival of Trinidad

Called "the world's most colorful festival," the Carnival of Trinidad is a spectacle of dazzling costumes and gaiety. Hundreds of bands of masqueraders parade through the cities on the Monday and Tuesday preceding Ash Wednesday, bringing traffic to a standstill. The island seems to explode with music, fun, and dancing.

Some of the Carnival costumes cost hundreds of dollars. For example, "bands" might depict the birds of Trinidad, such as the scarlet ibis and the keskidee; or a bevy of women might come out in the streets dressed as cats. Costumes are also satirical and comical.

Trinidad, of course, is the land of calypso, which grew out of the folk songs of the African–West Indian immigrants. The lyrics command great attention, as they're rich in satire and innuendo. The calypsonian is a poet-musician, and lyrics have often been capable of toppling politicians from office. In banter and bravado, the calypsonian gives voice to the sufferings and aspirations of his people. At Carnival time the artist sings his compositions to spectators in tents. There's one show a night at each of the calypso tents around town, from 8pm to midnight. Tickets for these are sold in the afternoon at most record shops.

Carnival parties, or fêtes, with three or four orchestras at each one, are public and advertised in the newspaper. For a really wild time, attend a party on Sunday night before Carnival Monday. To reserve tickets, contact the **National Carnival Committee,** Queen's Park Savannah, Port-of-Spain, Trinidad, W.I. (☎ **868/ 627-1358**). Hotels are booked months in advance, and most inns raise their prices—often considerably—at the time.

You can attend rehearsals of steel bands at their headquarters, called panyards, beginning about 7pm. Preliminary band competitions are held at the grandstand of Queen's Park Savannah in Port-of-Spain and at Skinner Park in San Fernando, beginning 2 weeks before Carnival.

Miami, BWIA usually offers a daily nonstop to Port-of-Spain, departing every afternoon and arriving on Trinidad in the early evening. Port-of-Spain is also serviced by as many as two additional flights per day, touching down on Barbados, Antigua, Grenada, and St. Lucia.

Air Canada (☎ **800/268-7240** in Canada, 800/776-3000 in the U.S., or 868/664-4065) offers two nonstop flights from Toronto to Port-of-Spain, one leaving Monday, the other Friday, with a return on Wednesday and Saturday.

GETTING AROUND

BY TAXI There are only unmetered taxis on Trinidad, and they're identified by their license plates, beginning with the letter *H*. There are also "pirate taxis"—private cars that cruise around and pick up passengers like a regular taxi. Maxi Taxis or vans can also be hailed on the street. A taxi ride from Piarco Airport into Port-of-Spain generally costs $20 ($30 after 10pm).

To avoid the anxiety of driving, you can rent taxis and local drivers for your sightseeing jaunts. Although it costs more, it alleviates the hassles of badly marked (or unmarked) roads and contact with the sometimes-bizarre local driving patterns; if a rented taxi and driver is too expensive, you can take an organized tour. Most drivers will serve as guides. Their rates, however, are based on route distances, so get an overall quotation and agree on the actual fare before setting off.

BY RENTAL CAR   Since the island is one of the world's largest exporters of asphalt, Trinidad's some 4,500 miles of roads are well paved. However, outback roads should be avoided during the rainy season as they're often narrow, twisting, and prone to washouts. Inquire about conditions, particularly if you're headed for the north coast.

The fierce traffic jams of Port-of-Spain are legendary, and night driving anywhere on the island is rather hazardous. If you're brave enough to set out on a venture via rental car, arm yourself with a good map and beware: The car will probably have a right-hand-mounted steering wheel; hence, *you'll drive on the left.* Visitors with a valid International Driver's License or a license from the United States, Canada, France, or the United Kingdom may drive without extra documentation for up to 3 months.

The major U.S.-based car-rental firms currently have no franchises on the island, so you have to make arrangements with a local firm (go over the terms and insurance agreements carefully). Count on spending about $40 to $60 per day or more, with unlimited mileage included.

Your best bet is one of the local car-rental firms maintaining offices at Piarco Airport. These include **Southern Sales Car Rentals** (☎ **868/669-2424**), **Econo-Car Rentals** (☎ **868/669-2342**), **Thrifty** (☎ **868/669-0602**), and **Auto Rentals** (☎ **868/669-2277**).

A word of warning: Although these local rental firms technically accept reservations, a car may not be waiting for you even if you reserve. Sometimes if a prospective renter shows up for an off-the-street booking, he or she gets the car you might have already reserved for a later pickup. The rule seems to be, a customer in hand is better than one that might—or might not—wing in later on a plane.

BY BUS   All the cities of Trinidad are linked by regular bus service from Port-of-Spain. Fares are low (about 50¢ for runs within the capital). However, the old buses are likely to be very overcrowded. Always try to avoid them at rush hours, and beware of pickpockets.

ACCOMMODATIONS YOU CAN AFFORD

The number of hotels is limited, and don't expect your Port-of-Spain room to open directly on a white-sand beach—the nearest beach is a long, costly taxi ride away. Don't forget that a 15% government tax and a 10% service charge will be added to your hotel and restaurant bills. All hotels raise their rates during Carnival (the week before Ash Wednesday).

Alicia's House. 7 Coblentz Gardens, St. Ann's, Port-of-Spain, Trinidad, W.I. ☎ **868/623-2802.** Fax 868/623-8560. 19 units. A/C TV TEL. Year-round, $30–$40 single; $38–$50 double; $58 triple; $78 quad. AE, MC, V.

This is a genteel guest house inspired by British models. It's in an upscale residential neighborhood, a short walk north of Queen's Park Savannah, the Botanical Gardens, and the dining and entertainment facilities of the Hilton Hotel. Locals claim Alicia's House sits on what used to be a sprawling plantation. During a slave uprising, the leaders of the revolt slaughtered 200 of their compatriots, which led to the closing of the property. Ghosts of those who were murdered are reputed to wander the streets of St. Ann's but shouldn't disturb your sleep.

The setting is a flat-roofed two- and three-story white-painted concrete building whose yard was neatly fenced in for privacy, with a ring-around garden and a pool in back. Ivan and Barbara Dara are your hosts (they named the place after their daughter, Alicia). The rooms contain wooden or rattan furniture, including good beds, small refrigerators, ceiling fans, white walls, wooden floors, and touches of homey bric-a-brac. They vary greatly in size, from small to large. The biggest one is named Admiral Rooney (not a naval commander but an island flower), with mahogany furniture and a giant tub. Alicia's Room is like a small apartment, with twin cherry-red sofas and large closets. The "Back Room" is tiny but airy and bright and offers a private spiral staircase going down to the pool. The baths are fitted in wherever possible and are immaculately maintained. Because of local zoning laws, no liquor is served on the premises, but guests are welcome to bring their own.

✪ **Blanchisseuse Beach Resort.** Blanchisseuse, Trinidad, W.I. ☎ 868/628-3731. Fax 868/628-3737. 15 units. Winter $66.55 single; $90.75 double. Off-season, $54.45 single; $78.65 double. Extra person $15. MC, V.

On the north coast, this beachfront property, owned by Fred and Barbara Zollna, who also operate Zollna House (see below), is set on 28 acres of rain forest at the Marianne River and its swimming lagoon. A place for those who seek solitude, it lures nature lovers with a free-flowing freshwater spring and natural pools, along with tropical plants and flowers. Coconut palms, coffee, and cocoa are cultivated throughout the estate, and birds, butterflies, and other forest creatures are abundant. In nesting season, leatherback turtles come to lay their eggs in the soft sand of the beach. The Blanchisseuse area is well known for its fishing, and you can fish off the beach or in the river. This place is recommended for its scenic setting in lush surroundings, not for its grand comforts. Nonetheless, the small rooms are neat and tidy, with comfortable beds and equally small baths. The Cocos Hut Restaurant, with its sliding roof, was formerly used for drying copra, coffee, or coconut. Today it serves local and international food, and there are also barbecue pits and rafts. A campsite is also available.

Carnetta's House. 28 Scotland Terrace, Andalusia, Maraval, Trinidad, W.I. ☎ 868/628-2732. Fax 868/628-7717. www.carnetta.com. e-mail: Carnetta@trinidad.net. 6 units. A/C TV TEL. Year-round $45–$50 single or double. AE, DC, MC, V.

This home is in the suburb of Andalusia in cool and scenic Maraval, about a 15-minute ride from the central business district and a 45-minute ride to Maracas Beach. It's owned by Winston and Carnetta Borrell, both keen naturalists (he was a former director of tourism) and both a wealth of information about touring the island. Winston is a grand gardener, filling his property with orchids, ginger lilies, and anthuriums, among other plant life. Carnetta grows her own herbs to produce some of the finest meals around. The rooms have floral themes and are furnished in a tropical style. For the most privacy, request a guest room on the upper floor. The others are on the ground level. Our preferred nest is "Le Flamboyant," opening onto the little inn's patio. Most of the rooms are medium in size, and each has a small and immaculately maintained bath.

✪ **La Maison Rustique.** 16 Rust St., St. Clair, Port-of-Spain, Trinidad, W.I. ☎ 868/622-1512. 6 units, 3 with bathroom; 1 studio cottage. Year-round $40 single without bathroom, $50 single with bathroom; $70 double with bathroom; $95 cottage. Children 9 and under stay free in parents' room. Rates include full breakfast. MC, V.

A great little Victorian B&B trimmed in gingerbread, this recommendation enjoys an in-the-heart location near Queen's Park Savannah. La Maison Rustique (which is far from rustic) allows you to sit on the veranda for a daily high tea. The delightful owner, Maureen Chin-Asiong, serves breakfast in a tea house and will cater to special diets if asked. She's a baker supreme—just taste her croissants and popovers—and a graduate of the Wilton School of Cake Decorating in Chicago. She'll even pack you a picnic basket if you're going touring for the day. The rooms are neat and homey, very comfortably furnished and immaculately maintained, with firm mattresses. The small baths have a shower stall. Guests in the rooms without bath will find the public baths adequate (there's rarely a line). The nearest beach is a 45-minute drive away, but guests may be admitted to a nearby country club.

Monique's Guest House. 114–116 Saddle Rd., Maraval, Trinidad, W.I. ☎ **868/628-3334.** Fax 809/622-3232. www.best-caribbean.com. E-mail: moniques@carib-link.ne. 20 units. A/C TEL. Year-round $50 single or double; $67.80 triple. MC, V.

In the lush Maraval Valley just an 8-minute (3-mile) drive north of the center of Port-of-Spain, Monique's offers 20 newly rebuilt bungalow-style rooms. Some are large enough to accommodate up to 4 people, and 10 rooms offer kitchenettes with their own porches and cable TVs. The biggest are units 25 and 26, which could possibly sleep up to 6, though that would be a bit crowded. One room is designed for elderly travelers or those with disabilities. Accommodations have open balconies so you can enjoy the tropical breezes and scenic hills. The baths are well organized and spotless. The air-conditioned dining room and bar offers a medley of local and international dishes, and Maracas Beach is only a 25-minute drive away. Mike and Monica Charbonné will be here to welcome you.

Surf's Country Inn. Blanchisseuse (P.O. Box 3429), Maraval, Trinidad, W.I. ☎ **868/669-2475.** 3 units. Year-round $60 single or double. Rates include breakfast. AE, MC, V.

This Spanish colonial inn overlooking the sea is set on a hillside a very short walk from the fishing village of Blanchisseuse. It's a small friendly place whose dining and drinking facilities are popular with locals. When he opened it in 1989, owner Andrew Hernandez conceived of it as only a restaurant, though over the years a trio of semi-detached outbuildings, each with private patio and views of the sea, was added. Each small accommodation is rustically outfitted with a ceiling fan, white walls, and red tile floors. Mattresses are firm and comfortable, and the tiny baths are well maintained. L'Anse Martin Beach is one of several secluded swimming areas a short walk from the hotel, and the nearby hamlet contains a handful of raffish bars and snack bars. Seafood is invariably featured as part of meals, which are served more or less continuously daily 9am to 10pm.

Tropical Hotel. 6 Rookery Nook, Maraval, Trinidad, W.I. ☎ **868/622-5815.** Fax 868/628-3174. 12 units. A/C TEL. Year-round $62.50 single; $75 double. AE, MC, V.

This hotel originated early in the 20th century as the centerpiece for the sugarcane plantation that surrounded it. (The setting is a short drive northwest of Port-of-Spain in the Maraval Valley and is a 45-minute ride to Maracas Beach.) Don't expect soaring columns and architecture like *Gone with the Wind*. Its design is vaguely Iberian, with walls made of stone and its red roof, and most of the overnight accommodations lie on the second floor. Mr. Lennox Lake, the owner, maintains a tile-ringed pool and restaurant. The rooms have white walls, carpeted floors, and nearly indestructible plastic chairs. The furnishings are a bit spartan and the mattresses a bit thin, and the color scheme evokes the psychedelic 1960s. The baths are small.

Zollna House. 12 Ramlogan Terrace, La Seiva, Maraval, Trinidad, W.I. ☎ **868/628-3731.** Fax 868/628-3737. 3 units, 2 with bathroom. Year-round $30 single without bathroom, $45 single with bathroom; $50 double without bathroom, $65 double with bathroom. Rates include American breakfast. MC, V.

On a hillside in the Maraval Valley with a view of Port-of-Spain and the Gulf of Paria, Zollna House is 2 miles from the capital. The two-story building has comfortably furnished rooms, two large porches, two indoor lounges, a beverage bar and games room, and dining areas on two floors, as well as a patio/barbecue set-up outdoors. The mattresses are well used but still comfortable, and the two rooms with bath have small private showers. The lush garden features flowering shrubs and fruit trees, home to a variety of birds. The house, white with black trim, is almost obscured by trees, but you can find it by going along Saddle Road, turning onto La Seiva Road, and going uphill for about a quarter of a mile. It's operated by Gottfried (Fred) Zollna, a German-American resident on Trinidad since 1965, and his Trinidadian wife, Barbara. They have a reputation for their easygoing hospitality and can advise on what to see and do. They also own a 35-foot yacht and often take their guests sailing in the Gulf of Paria. The Blanchisseuse Beach Resort on the north coast of Trinidad is also owned by the Zollnas.

WORTH A SPLURGE

✪ **Asa Wright Nature Centre and Lodge.** Spring Hill Estate, Arima, Trinidad, W.I. ☎ **800/426-7781** in the U.S., or 868/667-4655. Fax 868/667-4540. 25 units. Winter $155 single; $240 double. Off-season $120 single; $180 double. Rates include all meals, afternoon tea, and a welcoming rum punch. No credit cards.

There really isn't anything else like it in the Caribbean. Known to bird watchers throughout the world, this center sits on 196 acres of protected land at an elevation of 1,200 feet in the rain-forested northern mountain range of Trinidad, 10 miles north of Arima, beside Blanchisseuse Road. Hummingbirds, toucans, bellbirds, manakins, several varieties of tanagers, and the rare oilbird are all found on the property. Back-to-basics accommodations are available in the lodge's self-contained rooms, in guest rooms in the 1908 Edwardian main house, or in one of the cottages built on elevated ground above the main house. Even though they offer less privacy, we prefer the two guest rooms in the main house, as they have more atmosphere and are decorated with dark wood antiques and two king-size beds. Furnishings in the cottages are rather plain but comfortable. Mattresses are a bit thin, but the bird-watchers who "flock" here don't complain, as they're a hearty lot. Guided tours are available on the nature center's grounds, which contain several well-maintained trails, including a natural pool with a waterfall in which guests can swim in lieu of a beach that involves a 90-minute drive to the coast. Summer seminars are conducted with expert instructors in natural history, ornithology, and nature photography. The minimum age is 14 years if accompanied by an adult or 17 if unaccompanied.

For more information or to make reservations, call the above toll-free number or write **Caligo Ventures,** 156 Bedford Rd., Armonk, NY 10504.

GREAT DEALS ON DINING

The food should be better than it is, considering all the culinary backgrounds that have shaped the island, including West Indian, Chinese, French, and Indian. Stick to local specials like stuffed crabs or *chip-chip* (tiny clam-like shellfish), but skip the armadillo or opossum stewpots. Spicy Indian rôtis (Caribbean burritos) filled with vegetables or ground meat seem to be everyone's favorite lunch, and everyone's favorite drink is a fresh rum punch flavored with the home-produced Angostura Bitters. Except for a few fancy places, dress tends to be very casual.

For the fastest, cheapest lunch in town, try one of the rôtis mentioned. In Port-of-Spain you'll find them for sale at stalls on the street. Our favorite is **Nanny's Rôti Limited,** a funky little spot at the corner of Richmond and Sackville streets. One visitor called these rôtis a kind of "Indo-Caribbean tortilla stuffed with shrimp, beef, or chicken." For less than $5 you can order a rôti—a meal unto itself—along with a beer.

The Lounge. In the Chaconia Inn, 106 Saddle Rd., Maraval. ☎ **868/628-8603.** Main courses TT$30–TT$160 ($4.80–$25.60). AE, DC, MC, V. Daily 7am–10pm. INTERNATIONAL.

On the street level of a hotel, this conservatively decorated modern dining room offers international cuisine to a busy crowd of lunch and dinner patrons, who appreciate its straightforward cuisine. Dishes may not be innovative, but everything is market fresh.

You can order several preparations of fish, steak, shrimp, pork, and pasta dishes, as well as salads and a small choice of vegetarian dishes. Most are at the very low end of the price scale (above); only the fresh fish is expensive. On Saturday night, the Roof Garden Restaurant, on the hotel's uppermost floor, serves barbecued meals.

Rafters. 6A Warner St., Newtown. ☎ **868/628-9258.** Reservations recommended. Main courses TT$40–TT$125 ($6.40–$20); buffets from TT$100 ($16). AE, DC, MC, V. Mon–Fri 11:30am–10:30pm, Sat 6:30pm–11pm. SEAFOOD.

Rafters is a good-value dining choice housed in a century-old grocery shop in the central business district of a suburb of Port-of-Spain, a short walk off the Savannah. Wednesday to Saturday there are buffets, and you can also order from an a la carte menu devoted mainly to local seafood. The food is more plentiful than refined, but is a very good value. Buffets begin at 7pm. On Wednesday to Saturday there are carvery buffets. On the regular menu, house specialties include seafood Creole. You can also order U.S. choice beef steaks. In the lounge, a snack-and-sandwich menu is offered daily in a relaxed atmosphere, attracting folks of all ages and occupations.

Restaurant Singho. Long Circular Mall, Level 3, Port-of-Spain. ☎ **868/628-2077.** Main courses TT$85–TT$100 ($13.60–$16); Wed night buffet TT$100 ($16). AE, MC, V. Daily 11am–11pm. CHINESE.

This restaurant contains an almost mystically illuminated bar and aquarium. It's on the second floor of one of the capital's largest shopping malls, midway between the commercial center of Port-of-Spain and the Queen's Park Savannah. Many of its dishes are quite tasty and spicy. A la carte dishes include shrimp with oyster sauce, shark-fin soup, stewed or curried beef, almond pork, and spareribs with black-bean sauce. The takeout service is one of the best known in town. The Wednesday-night buffet has an enormous selection of main dishes, along with heaps of rice and fresh vegetables. Even dessert is included in the set price.

Woodford Café. 62 Tragarete Rd., New Town. ☎ **868/622-2233.** Main courses $3.50–$8.50. AE, MC, V. Mon–Sat 11am–10pm. TRINIDADIAN/WEST INDIAN.

In a conservative-looking West Indian house with jalousied windows overlooking a residential neighborhood, about a 5-minute walk southwest of the Savannah, this is a well-respected place where most of the food is richly steeped in local culinary traditions. Inside, you'll find a color scheme of peach and white, a hardworking staff, and at least 25 paintings, mostly by Trinidadian and Bajan artists. The most visible of these is an oversized triptych of a Trinidadian landscape by a local rising star on the arts scene, Peter Sheppherd. Menu items include at least a dozen vegetarian side dishes, any of which can be combined into an all-vegetarian meal. (Specific examples are red beans, lentils, black-eyed peas, stewed christophene, yams, macaroni pie, corn, salad, and several preparations of potatoes.) There's also a long array of slow-stewed meats and fish like curried conch or fish; stewed chicken, beef, pork, oxtail, and shrimp.

✪ **Veni Mangé.** 67A Ariapata Ave. ☎ **868/624-4597.** Reservations recommended. Main courses $5–$15. AE, MC, V. Daily 11:30am–3pm; Wed 7:30–10pm; Fri bar service only 6–11:30pm. CREOLE/INTERNATIONAL.

Built in the 1930s about a mile west of Port-of-Spain's center, Veni Mangé (whose name translates as "come and eat") is painted in coral tones and has louvered windows on hinges that ventilate the masses of potted plants. It was opened by two of the best-known women in Trinidad, Allyson Hennessy and her sister, Rosemary Hezekiah. Allyson, the Julia Child of Trinidad, hosts a daily TV talk show that's broadcast throughout Trinidad. Best described as a new generation of Creole women, both

Allyson and Rosemary (whose parents were English/Venezuelan and African-Caribbean/Chinese) entertain with their humor and charm.

Start with the bartender's special, a coral-colored fruit punch that's a luscious mix of papaya, guava, orange, and passion fruit juices. On some days they do an authentic calaloo soup, which, according to Trinidadian legend, can make a man propose marriage. Save room for one of the main courses, such as curried crab or West Indian hotpot (a variety of meat cooked Creole style), or perhaps a vegetable lentil loaf. The helpings are large, and if you still have room, order their pineapple upside-down cake, homemade soursop ice cream, or coconut mousse. Dinner is served only on Wednesday and is something of a social event among regulars. On Friday, the bar buzzes but no formal food is served, only snacks and finger foods.

HITTING THE BEACHES

Trinidad isn't thought of as beach country, yet it has more beach frontage than any other island in the West Indies. The only problem is that most of its beaches are undeveloped and in distant places, far removed from Port-of-Spain. The closest of the better beaches, **Maracas** (on the North Coast Road), is 18 miles from Port-of-Spain and a delight to visitors with its protected cove and quaint fishing village at one end. It's likely to be crowded, because many beach buffs, often locals, flock here for fun in the sun. There's another major drawback—a strong current, so be extremely careful. You'll find an array of snack bars and toilets. Chances are you'll be here for lunch. In addition to rôtis, one of the local seafood treats is a fish sandwich called "shark and bake." Sample it at Patsy's Shack or one of the other fast-food joints. At Patsy's you can also order one of the most refreshing fruit drinks on the island. It's called grenadillo and tastes very much like passion fruit.

Farther up the north coast is the **Las Cuevas Bay Beach,** which is far less crowded. Lying directly off the North Coast Road is a narrow strip of sand set against a backdrop of palm trees. There are changing rooms, and vendors come around selling the luscious tropical fruit juices of Trinidad. Las Cuevas is named after the underwater caves nearby.

To reach the other beaches, you'll have to range much farther afield, perhaps to **Blanchisseuse Bay** on the North Coast Road. See the previous recommendation of Blanchisseuse Beach Resort. This is a narrow strip of sand set against a palm-fringed backdrop, excellent for a picnic on the beach, though there are no facilities unless you're staying at the hotel. This is one of the best places in Trinidad for a beach picnic. You can also negotiate with one of the local fishers at anchor about taking you on an inexpensive boat ride along the coast, and maybe doing a little fishing as well. Also on the northeast coast is **Balandra Bay Beach.** This area is frequented by bodysurfers and sheltered by rocky outcroppings. But the waters generally aren't good for swimming.

Another beach worth a look is **Manzanilla Beach,** which lies along the east coast of Trinidad, north of Cocos Bay and south of Matura Bay. Because its waters open onto the often turbulent Atlantic on the windward side, it is not ideal for swimming. Nonetheless, it has some picnic facilities, and the view of the water is dramatic. The water here, however, is often muddied by the Orinoco River flowing in from South America. Many rich Trinidadians have their vacation homes here.

SPORTS & OUTDOOR PURSUITS

For serious golf and tennis holidays, we recommend you try another island.

GOLF　　The oldest golf club on the island, **St. Andrew's Golf Course,** Moka Estate (☎ **868/629-2314**), is in Maraval, about 2 miles from Port-of-Spain. This 18-hole course has been internationally acclaimed ever since it hosted the 1976 Hoerman Cup Golf Tournament. There's a full-service clubhouse on the premises. Greens fees are TT$250 ($40) for 18 holes. Clubs cost TT$80 ($12.80). It's open daily 6am to 6pm.

TENNIS The **Trinidad Hilton,** Lady Young Road (☎ **868/624-3211**), has the best courts on the island. These are two chevron courts lit for night pay. Reservations are recommended if you want to be assured of a court. The cost is $15 per half hour, but the courts are open only for hotel guests. At the **Trinidad Country Club,** Champs-Elysées, Maraval (☎ **868/622-3470**), six courts are available, and they're lit at night. You must buy a day pass for TT$30 ($4.80) and pay an additional TT$5 (80¢) per hour of play during the day or TT$10 ($1.60) per hour at night. There are public courts in Port-of-Spain on the grounds of the Prince's Building (ask at your hotel for directions to these).

SEEING THE SIGHTS

Sightseeing tours are offered by **The Travel Centre,** Uptown Mall, Edward Street, Port-of-Spain (☎ **868/623-5096**), in late-model sedans, with a trained driver-guide. Prices are quoted on a seat-in-car basis. Private arrangements will cost more. Several tours are offered regularly—the daily city tour, lasting 2 hours and costing $22 per person for two or $16 per person for three or more, will take you past (but not inside) the main points of interest of Port-of-Spain.

You'll see tropical splendor at its best on a Port-of-Spain/Maracas Bay/Saddle Road jaunt leaving at 1pm daily, lasting 3½ hours. The tour begins with a drive around Port-of-Spain, passing the main points of interest in town and then going on through the mountain scenery over the "Saddle" of the northern range to Maracas Bay, a popular beach. The cost is $35 per person for two or $25 per person if 3 or more. An Island Circle Tour is a 7- to 8-hour journey that includes a lunch stop (the tour price doesn't include lunch) and a welcome drink. Leaving at 9am daily, your car goes south along the west coast with a view of the Gulf of Paria, across the central plains, through Pointe-à-Pierre and San Fernando, and on eastward into rolling country overlooking sugarcane fields. Then you go down into the coconut plantations along the 14-mile-long Mayaro Beach for a swim and lunch before returning along Manzanilla Beach and back to the city. The cost is $75 per person for two or $55 per person for three or more.

An especially interesting trip is to the Caroni Swamp and Bird Sanctuary, a 4-hour trek by car and flat-bottomed boat into the sanctuary where you'll see rich Trinidad bird life. The tour guides recommend long pants and long-sleeved, casual attire along with lots of insect repellent. The cost is $75 per person for two or $55 per person for three or more.

PORT-OF-SPAIN One of the busiest harbors in the Caribbean, Trinidad's capital, Port-of-Spain, can be explored on foot. Start out at ✪ **Queen's Park Savannah,** on the northern edge of the city. Called the Savannah, it consists of 199 acres, complete with soccer, cricket, and rugby fields and vendors hawking coconut water. What's now the park was once a sugar plantation until it was swept by a fire in 1808 that destroyed hundreds of homes.

Among the Savannah's outstanding buildings is the pink-and-blue ✪ **Queen's Royal College,** containing a clock tower with Westminster chimes. Today a school for boys, it stands on Maraval Road at the corner of St. Clair Avenue. On the same road, the family home of the Roodal clan is affectionately called **"the gingerbread house"** by Trinidadians. It was built in the baroque style of the French Second Empire. In contrast, the family residence of the Strollmeyers was built in 1905 and is a copy of a German Rhenish castle. Nearby stands **Whitehall,** which was once a private mansion but today has been turned into the office of the prime minister of Trinidad and Tobago. In the Moorish style, it was erected in 1905 and served as the U.S. Army headquarters in World War II. These houses, including Hayes Court, the residence of the Anglican bishop of Trinidad, and others form what's known as **"the magnificent seven"** big mansions standing in a row.

On the south side of Memorial Park, a short distance from the Savannah and within walking distance of the major hotels, stands the **National Museum and Art Gallery,** 117 Frederick St. (☎ 868/623-5941), open Tuesday to Saturday 10am to 6pm. The free museum contains a representative exhibit of Trinidad artists, including an entire gallery devoted to Jean Michel Cazabon (1813–1888), permanent collections of artifacts giving a general overview of the island's history and culture, Amerindian archaeology, British historical documents, and a small natural-history exhibit including geology, corals, and insect collections. There's also a large display filled with costumes dedicated to the colorful culture of Carnival.

At the southern end of Frederick Street, the main artery of Port-of-Spain's shopping district, stands **Woodford Square.** The gaudy **Red House,** a large neo-Renaissance structure built in 1906, is the seat of the government of Trinidad and Tobago. Nearby stands **Holy Trinity Cathedral,** whose Gothic look may remind you of the churches of England. Inside, search out the marble monument to Sir Ralph Woodford made by the sculptor of Chantry.

Another of the town's important landmarks is **Independence Square,** dating from Spanish days. Now mainly a parking lot, it stretches across the southern part of the capital from the **Cathedral of the Immaculate Conception** to Wrightson Road. The Roman Catholic church was built in 1815 in the neo-Gothic style and consecrated in 1832. The cathedral has an outlet that leads to the **Central Market,** on Beetham Highway on the outskirts of Port-of-Spain. Here you can see all the spices and fruits for which Trinidad is known. It's one of the island's most colorful sights, made all the more so by the wide diversity of people who sell their wares here.

At the north of the Savannah, the **Royal Botanical Gardens** (☎ 868/622-4221) cover 70 acres and are open daily 9:30am to 6pm; admission is free. Once part of a sugar plantation, the park is filled with flowering plants, shrubs, and rare and beautiful trees, including an orchid house. Seek out the raw beef tree: An incision made in its bark is said to resemble rare, bleeding roast beef. Licensed guides will take you through and explain the luxuriant foliage to you. In the gardens is the **President's House,** official residence of the president of Trinidad and Tobago. Victorian in style, it was built in 1875.

Part of the gardens is the **Emperor Valley Zoo** (☎ 868/622-3530), in St. Clair, which shows a good selection of the fauna of Trinidad as well as some of the usual exotic animals from around the world. The star attractions are a family of mandrills, a reptile house, and open bird parks. You can take shady jungle walks through tropical vegetation. Adults pay TT$4 (65¢), children 3 to 12 are charged TT$2 (30¢), and children under 3 are admitted free. It's open daily 9:30am to 6pm.

AROUND THE ISLAND   For one of the most popular attractions in the area, the **Asa Wright Nature Centre,** see accommodations above.

On a peak 1,100 feet above Port-of-Spain, **Fort George** was built by Governor Sir Thomas Hislop in 1804 as a signal station in the days of the sailing ships. Once it could be reached only by hikers, but today it's accessible by an asphalt road. From its citadel, you can see the mountains of Venezuela. Locals refer to the climb up the winding road as "traveling up to heaven," since nature's bounty is at its greatest along this route. The drive is only 10 miles, but to play it safe, allow about 2 hours.

Pointe-a-Pierre Wild Fowl Trust, 42 Sandown Rd. Point Cumana (☎ 868/658-4230, ext. 2512), is a bird sanctuary a 2-hour drive south of Port-of-Spain. The setting is unlikely, near an industrial area of the state-owned Petrotrin oil refinery, with flames spouting from flare stacks in the sky. However, in this seemingly inhospitable clime, wildfowl flourish in a setting rich with luxuriant vegetation like crêpe myrtle, flamboyant soursop and mango trees, and even black sage bushes, said to be good for high blood pressure. In this setting live any number of birds, including endangered species like the toucan and purple gallinule. You can spot the yellow-billed jacana and plenty of Muscovies. The sanctuary sprawls across 26 acres. Adults pay TT$10 ($1.60) to enter. Ages 12 to 16 pay TT$5 (80¢), and ages 11 and under page TT$2 (30¢). Hours are Monday to Friday 8am to 5pm; Saturday and Sunday by appointment only 11am to 4pm.

Enhanced by the blue and purple hues of the sky at sunset, clouds of scarlet ibis—the national bird of Trinidad and Tobago—fly in from their feeding grounds to roost at the ✪ **Caroni Bird Sanctuary** (☎ **868/645-1305**). The 40-square-mile sanctuary is a big mangrove swamp interlaced with waterways and framed by mangrove trees. The setting couldn't be more idyllic, with blue, mauve, and white lilies; oysters growing on mangrove roots; and caimans resting on mudbanks. The sanctuary lies abut a half-hour drive (7 miles) south of Port-of-Spain.

Visitors are taken on a launch through these swamps to see the birds (bring along some insect repellent). For your exploration of this wonderland, the most reliable tour operator is **James Meddoo,** Bamboo Grove Settlement, 1 Butler Highway (☎ **868/662-7356**). Meddoo has toured the swamps for some 25 years. His tour leaves daily at 4pm, lasting 2½ hours and costing $10 per person or $5 for ages 5 to 14 (free for kids 4 and under).

The ✪ **Pitch Lake** lies on the west coast of Trinidad with the village of Le Brea on its north shore. To reach it from Port-of-Spain, take the Solomon Hocoy Highway for about a 2-hour drive, depending on traffic (which can be heavy around Port-of-Spain). At Le Brea, you'll find some bars and restaurants. One of the wonders of the world, with a surface like elephant skin, the lake is 300 feet deep at its center. It's possible to walk on its rough side, but we don't recommend you proceed far. Legend has it that the lake devoured a tribe of Chayma Amerindians, punishing them for eating humming-birds in which the souls of their ancestors reposed. The bitumen mined here has been used for paving highways throughout the world. This lake was formed millions of years ago, and it's believed that at one time it was a huge mud volcano into which muddy asphaltic oil seeped. Churned up and down by underground gases, the oil and mud eventually formed asphalt. According to legend, Sir Walter Raleigh discovered the lake in 1595 and used the asphalt to caulk his ships. Some say that no matter how much is dug out, the lake is fully replenished in a day, but actually the level of the lake drops at the rate of about 6 inches a year. A tour of 120 miles around the lake lasts 5 hours.

The ✪ **Saddle** is a humped pass on a ridge dividing the Maraval Valley and the Santa Cruz Valley. Along this circular run you'll see the luxuriant growth of the island, as reflected by grapefruit, papaya, cassava, and cocoa. Leaving Port-of-Spain by Saddle Road, going past the Trinidad Country Club, you pass through Maraval Village with its St. Andrew's Golf Course. The road rises to cross the ridge at the spot from which the Saddle gets its name. After going over the hump, you descend through Santa Cruz Valley, rich with giant bamboo, into San Juan, and back to the capital along Eastern Main Road or via Beetham Highway. You'll see panoramic views in every direction; this tour takes about 2 hours and covers 18 miles.

Nearly all cruise-ship passengers are hauled along Trinidad's "Skyline Highway," the **North Coast Road.** Starting at the Saddle, it winds for 7 miles across the Northern Range and down to Maracas Bay. At one point, 100 feet above the Caribbean, you'll see on a clear day as far away as Venezuela in the west or Tobago in the east, a sweep

Cheap Thrills: What to See & Do for Free (Well, Almost) on Trinidad & Tobago

- **Have a Close Encounter with Nature.** For getting close to nature, there's nothing in the Caribbean quite like the Asa Wright Nature Center and Lodge in Trinidad. Refer to "Accommodations You Can Afford" above if you'd like to stay here. But you can also visit just for the day. This 200-acre wildlife sanctuary lies in the island's rain-forested northern range, where it's not unusual to spot 20 to 30 species of birds before you've had your morning coffee. Commonly spotted are such species as the turquoise-billed toucan, chestnut woodpecker, white-bearded manakin, bearded bellbird, and rufous-browned pepperstrike. The center offers guided walks, and birding from the veranda of the center's main lodge is one of the world's most pleasant ornithological experiences.

- **Take Afternoon Tea at a Monastery Estate.** Evoking Trinidad's long British heritage, the quaint custom of afternoon tea in the Caribbean is still practiced at the Pax Guest House, on the Mount St. Benedict Monastery Estate (☎ **868/662-4084** for information and directions). Tea is served daily in the garden 3 to 6pm. Pax offers an assortment of international teas, homemade pastries, cakes, and breads. The guest house is situated on 600 acres of land that includes a rain forest, nature trails, tennis courts, and much more.

- **Limin' at a Funky Little Bar.** On the sleepy island of Tobago, a local told us that limin' (just doing nothing) is a favorite pastime. There's no better place to pursue this activity than the First Historical Cafe/Bar at Mile Marker 8 on the Windward Main Road in the Studley Park district en route to Charlotteville. The place doesn't even have a phone, but the roadside eatery lies in a typically Creole building with a backporch dining area. Painted in flamboyant colors, it rises above a cliff some 25 feet high. The walls are covered with boards inscribed with a specific piece of data about Tobago's history. Owner Kenneth Washington, who for decades was a public servant, is the bar's guiding light and main attraction. This is the best place to go to meet people on the island. By all means, opt for one of those fruit punches, the fruit plate, or a fish sandwich.

- **Take a Nostalgic Look at a Great House.** The ghost of Comte Charles Joseph de Lopinot, a French aristocrat, is said to still prowl the grounds of his former Great House, especially on a stormy night or when the moon is full.

of some 100 miles. Most visitors take this route to **Maracas Beach,** the most splendid on Trinidad. Enclosed by mountains, it has the expected charm of a Caribbean fantasy: white sands, swaying coconut palms, and crystal-clear water.

SHOPPING

One of the large **bazaars** of the Caribbean, Port-of-Spain has luxury items from all over the globe, including Irish linens, English china, Scandinavian crystal, French perfumes, Swiss watches, and Japanese cameras. Even more interesting are the **Asian bazaars,** where you can pick up items in brass. Reflecting the island's culture are calypso shirts (or dresses), sisal goods, woodwork, cascadura bracelets,

This historic complex is a restored cocoa-estate Great House, where the count used to live. He came to Trinidad at the dawn of the 19th century and selected this panoramic site to build his magnificent home. The restored estate has been turned into a museum, and a guide will show you through for free daily 10am to 6pm. You'll see displays of antiques, pottery, and other artifacts of the era. Sometimes small groups of musicians playing parang (traditional Christmas music with Spanish origins) roam through the property entertaining visitors. To reach the estate, take the Eastern Main from Port-of-Spain to Arouca. It's sign-posted from here, but there's no number to call for information.

- **Spend a Morning at Queen's Park Savannah.** What Piccadilly Circus is to London, this 199-acre park is to Trinidad's capital, Port-of-Spain. Here the major games are played: soccer, rugby, and cricket, in the British tradition. Here you can find the makings of a lunch, perhaps a rôti, an ear of roasted corn, and some sweet coconut water, all for sale from a local vendor in the park. The 3-mile perimeter of the Savannah has been called "the world's biggest roundabout." On Maraval Road you can take in seven imposing turn-of-the-century mansions, known as "the Magnificent Seven." Aside from the imposing residences and monuments, it's the life and the people who pass through this square every day that's reason enough to visit it.

- **Visit Remote "Little Tobago."** This islet lies a mile offshore from the little town on Speyside on the island of Tobago. The boat ride takes only about 20 minutes and can easily be arranged with one of the fishers. The crossing by boat is likely to be rough, as is the wet landing with its swells and whitecaps. But once you're on Little Tobago you'll see the effort is worth it. It's best to go in the early morning or late afternoon, when you'll see the biggest collection of wild birds, a total of 52 species. These include the magnificent frigatebird and even the sooty tern. Laughing gulls breed here from April to September. The islet is arid and hilly, but there's a network of marked trails, the longest of which is only half a mile. Our favorite is Sea View Trail, a short walk east along the lower tiers of the islet. Another interesting hike, taking about an hour, is along George Ride Trail, going through interior forests to a viewing platform facing across Alexander Bay. Along the way here you can say "hi" to the crested oropendola or the blue-crowned motmot.

silver jewelry in local motifs, and saris. For souvenir items, visitors often like to bring back figurines of limbo dancers, carnival masqueraders, or calypso singers.

Art Creators and Suppliers, Apt. 402, Aldegonda Park, 7 St. Ann's Rd., St. Ann's (☎ **868/624-4369**), lies in a banal apartment complex, but the paintings and sculptures sold are among the finest in the Caribbean. Karen De Lima Rosa Foster and Stella Beaubrun, the creative forces behind the gallery, are recognized for their knowledge of Trinidadian art. The works sold here are fairly priced samples of the best on Trinidad. Among the artistic giants are Glasgow, Robert Mackie, Boscoe Holder, Sundiata, Keith Ward, and Jackie Hinkson.

Gallery 1-2-3-4, in the Normandie Hotel, 10 Nook Ave., St. Anne's Village (☎ 868/625-5502), is more iconoclastic and less conservative than any other gallery on the island. This art center in the Normandie Hotel displays its paintings in a space of minimalist walls and careful lighting. The gallery opened in 1985 and since then has attracted the attention of the art world because of its wide selection of Caribbean artists.

The Market, 10 Nook Ave., St. Ann's (☎ 868/624-1181), is one of the most fashionable shopping complexes in Trinidad. It contains some 20 boutiques that represent some of the island's best jewelers, designers, and art dealers. You'll find a wide assortment of merchandise, including clothing, cosmetics, bags, shoes, china, decorative tableware, handcrafts, and designer jewelry and accessories. The complex forms an interconnected bridge among the Normandie Hotel and Restaurant, the restaurant La Fantasie, and a top-notch art emporium, Gallery 1-2-3-4.

Stecher's, in Excellent City Mall (☎ 868/623-5912), is the best bet for those luxury items we mentioned above. Stecher's sells crystal, watches, jewelry, perfumes, Georg Jensen silver, Lladró, Wedgwood, Royal Doulton, Royal Albert, Aynsley, Hutschenreuther china, and other in-bond items that can be delivered to Piarco International Airport on your departure. If you don't want to go downtown, you'll find branches at Long Circular Mall and West Mall, in residential areas of Port-of-Spain. You can also pay a last-minute call at their three tax-free airport branches—one outlet for famous perfumes, another for sunglasses, Cartier watches, lighters and pens, leather goods, Swarovski crystal, and local ceramics. A third branch sells tobacco and liquor. There's also a branch at the Cruise Ship Complex at the Port-of-Spain docks.

Y. De Lima, 23 Queen St. (☎ 868/623-1364), is another good store for duty-free cameras and watches, but its main focus is local jewelry. Its third-floor workroom will make whatever you want in jewelry or bronze work. You may emerge with anything from steel-drum earrings to a hibiscus-blossom broach. With any extra time remaining for shopping, check out some handcraft outlets, notably **The Boutique,** 43 Syndeham Ave., St. Ann's (☎ 868/624-3274). Among other wares, this is a showcase for batik silks created by Althea Bastien, one of Trinidad's finest artisans. Her fabric art is highly prized but reasonable in price. If you'd like to go home with some music of Trinidad, head for **Rhyner's Record Shop,** 54 Prince St. (☎ 868/623-5673), which has the best selection of soca and calypso recordings. There's also another branch at the airport.

TRINIDAD AFTER DARK

Mascamp Pub, French Street at Ariapata Avenue, on the western outskirts of Port-of-Spain (☎ 868/623-3745), is the only venue on Trinidad where calypso music from the island's greatest bands is presented continually throughout the year. Many similar places offer this music only during Carnival. It's rootsy, sometimes raucous, and generally high energy, recommended only to adventurous readers who love live musical performances with an ethnic slant. Though simple lunches are served here every weekday 11am to 2pm, for a cost of about TT$15 ($2.40), the place is far more recommendable and exciting as a nightspot. On Monday, Tuesday, and Thursday there's only a DJ, but live calypso and its modern variations are the almost exclusive format every Wednesday, Friday, Saturday, and Sunday. There's usually a $2 to $5 cover.

The **Trinidad Hilton,** Lady Young Road, Port-of-Spain (☎ 868/624-3211), stages a Poolside Fiesta show every Monday night, with a folkloric performance beginning at 7pm and continuing live until midnight. It features lots of live music, calypso, a steel band, and limbo. It's the most spectacular on Trinidad. The cover (including a buffet dinner with grills) is TT$140 ($22.40).

Other fun joints worth checking out include **Smokey & Bunty,** Western Main Road at Dengue Street in St. James (no phone). Self-billed as a sports bar, it's more a local hangout. If you have a rumor to spread in Port-of-Spain, get it going here. It's the local gossip center. As one habitué who comes here nightly said, "There's no better place in Trinidad for doing nothing." **Moon Over Bourbon Street,** Southern Landing, Westmall, Westmoorings (☎ 868/637-3488), offers live music on some nights, sometimes Trinidadian comedians on other occasions. It's got a long happy hour, and the place is fun, funky, and local, as is the **Blue Iguana,** Main Street, Chaguanas (no phone), which is the best place to go late at night when the clubs close and you're still in a party mood. It lies about half an hour west of Port-of-Spain, and opens at 10pm Wednesday to Sunday, seemingly closing when the last customer staggers out.

3 Tobago

Dubbed "the land of the hummingbird," Tobago lies 20 miles northeast of Trinidad, to which it's connected by frequent flights. It has long been known as a honeymooner's paradise. The physical beauty of Tobago is stunning, with its forests of breadfruit, mango, cocoa, and citrus, through which a chartreuse-colored iguana will suddenly dart.

Unlike bustling Trinidad, Tobago is sleepy, and Trinidadians come there, especially on weekends, to enjoy its wide sandy beaches. The legendary home of Daniel Defoe's *Robinson Crusoe,* Tobago is only 27 miles long and 7½ miles wide. The people are hospitable, and their villages are so tiny that they seem to blend with the landscape. Tobago's idyllic natural beauty makes it one of the greatest escapes in the Caribbean. It's for those who like a generous dose of sand, sun, and solitude in a mellow atmosphere.

Fish-shaped Tobago was probably sighted by Columbus in 1498 when he charted Trinidad, but the island was so tiny he paid no attention to it in his log. For the next 100 years it lay almost unexplored. In 1628, when Charles I of England gave it to one of his nobles, the earl of Pembroke, the maritime countries of Europe suddenly showed a belated interest. From then on, Tobago was fought over no fewer than 31 times by the Spanish, French, Dutch, and English, as well as marauding pirates and privateers.

After 1803, the island settled down to enjoy a sugar monopoly unbroken for decades. Great Houses were built, and in London it used to be said of a wealthy man that he was "as rich as a Tobago planter." The island's economy collapsed in 1884, and Tobago entered an acute depression. The ruling monopoly, Gillespie Brothers, declared itself bankrupt and went out of business. The British government made Tobago a ward of Trinidad in 1889, and the sugar industry was never revived.

The island's village-like capital lies on the southern coast and provides a scenic setting with its bay surrounded by a mountainside. **Scarborough,** which is also the main port, is a rather plain town, however. The local market, the Gun Bridge, the Powder Magazine, and Fort King George will provide a good day's worth of entertainment. Most of the shops are clustered in the streets around the market.

GETTING THERE

BY PLANE A recently established Trinidad-based airline, **Air Caribbean** (☎ 868/623-2500), maintains popular shuttle flights between Trinidad and Tobago, departing from Port-of-Spain every 2 hours daily 6am to 8pm. The final return to Trinidad departs from Tobago daily at 9pm. A round-trip ticket costs $75. Because the beaches of Tobago are a favorite of vacationing Trinidadians, shuttle flights on any airline between the two islands are almost always crowded, and on weekends, sometimes impossibly overbooked. Air Caribbean, however, operates extra flights on Friday, Sunday, and public holidays to meet traffic demands.

LIAT (☎ **800/468-0482** in the U.S. and Canada, or 868/639-0276) maintains one daily flight from Trinidad to Tobago. If you'd like to skip Trinidad completely, you can book a LIAT flight with direct service to Tobago from either Barbados or Grenada. **American Eagle** (☎ **800/433-7300**), the regional airline affiliate of American Airlines, operates daily round-trip flights between San Juan and Tobago. American Airlines also operates a daily nonstop flight between Miami and Trinidad; once at Trinidad, you can make a connecting flight into Tobago.

Tobago's small airport lies at Crown Point, near the island's southwestern tip.

BY BOAT It's possible to travel between Trinidad and Tobago by ferry service managed/operated by the **Port Authority of Trinidad and Tobago** (☎ **868/623-2901** in Port-of-Spain, 868/639-2417, or 868/639-2416 in Scarborough, Tobago). Call for departure times and more details. Ferries leave once a day (trip time is 5½ to 6 hours). The round-trip fare is TT$50 ($8) in economy or TT$60 ($9.60) in tourist.

GETTING AROUND

BY TAXI From the airport to your hotel, take an unmetered taxi, which will cost $8 to $36, depending on the location of your hotel. You can also arrange (or have your hotel do it for you) a sightseeing tour by taxi. Rates must be negotiated on an individual basis.

BY RENTAL CAR Contact **Tobago Travel,** Store Bay Road, Milford (☎ **868/639-8778**), where the average cost of a vehicle begins at $50 per day, with unlimited mileage, collision damage coverage, value-added tax, and comprehensive insurance, plus delivery if you're housed in a hotel near the airport. An international driver's license or your valid license from home entitles you to drive on the roads of Tobago. You must be 25 or over to rent a car. *Don't forget to drive on the left.*

BY BUS Inexpensive public buses travel from one end of the island to the other several times a day. Of course, expect an unscheduled stop at any passenger's doorstep, and never, never be in a hurry.

ACCOMMODATIONS YOU CAN AFFORD

The hotels of Tobago attract those who seek hideaways instead of high-rise resorts packed with activity. Sometimes to save money, it's best to take the MAP (breakfast and dinner) plan when reserving a room. There's a 15% value-added tax added to all hotel bills, and often a service charge of about 10%. Always ask if the VAT and service charge are included in the prices quoted to you.

Cocrico Inn. North St. at Commissioner St. (P.O. Box 287), Plymouth Village, Tobago, W.I. ☎ **800/223-9815** in the U.S., or 868/639-2961. Fax 868/639-6565. 16 units. Winter $50–$65 single; $60–$85 double; $105–$135 triple. Off-season $40–$55 single; $50–$70 double; $85–$120 triple. MAP $22 per person. AE, MC, V.

Built around 1978, this unpretentious L-shaped building is best known for its popular bar and restaurant. There's a pool, a paved-over sun terrace, and simple landscaping. In the center of Tobago's largest settlement, it's close to grocery stores and bars; Great Courtland Beach lies half a mile away, Turtle Beach is 1 mile away, and golf and tennis can be arranged within a reasonable distance. The rooms aren't very large but have white walls, wall-to-wall carpeting, wooden furnishings, and standing fans or ceiling fans; the more expensive doubles have kitchenettes. The furnishings are a bit drab, but

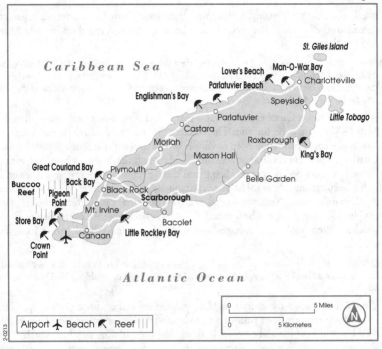

there's general comfort if you don't mind the stains on the otherwise clean carpeting. The staff is most hospitable and keeps the small baths decently maintained. The restaurant is a respectable diner-style place, its home-style cooking prepared with lots of local seafood and fresh produce.

The Golden Thistle. Store Bay Rd., Crown Point, Tobago, W.I. ☎ **868/639-8521.** Fax 868/639-8521. 36 units. A/C TV TEL. Winter $40 single; $60 double. Off-season, $35 single; $50 double. AE, MC, V.

This simple hotel is much appreciated by cost-conscious Europeans. Angela Williams, the kindly proprietor, welcomes a repeat clientele whose ages vary widely. It's on the island's western coast, about a 10-minute walk from Store Beach, in a well-tended garden perfumed with roses and flowering shrubs. The accommodations have kitchenettes, terrazzo or tile floors, large bathtubs, and white walls. They don't give you a lot of room but are generally comfortable, with decent mattresses. The baths are small, though two dozen contain tubs. There's a pool and a restaurant.

Harris Cottage. Bacolet, Scarborough, Tobago, W.I. ☎ **868/639-2111.** Fax 868/639-2226. 3 units. A/C TV. Year-round $35 single; $70 double. Rates include breakfast. MAP $15 per person. MC, V.

Its brick-sided construction marks this place distinctly from its many rather ramshackle guest house competitors. It lies about a mile from the center of Scarborough, in a fashionable residential neighborhood, a 4-minute walk from the white sands of Bacolet Beach. Built in the late 1980s and owned by Roger Harris, it offers cozy and family-oriented accommodations with carpeted floors, separate dressing areas, and morning breakfasts on the veranda. The rooms are genuinely comfortable, albeit small, as are the tidily maintained baths, and the rooms have fine mattresses. A garden surrounds the house, adding welcome touches of greenery. A rental car is available for $35 per day.

Man-O-War Bay Cottages. Charlotteville Estate, Charlotteville, Tobago, W.I. ☎ **868/660-4327.** Fax 868/660-4328. 9 cottages. Year-round $65 1-bedroom cottage; $80 2-bedroom cottage; $95 3-bedroom cottage; $130 4-bedroom cottage. For $12 a maid will clean the unit and prepare a meal. MC, V.

If you're seeking a Caribbean hideaway—that is, a cluster of beach cottages—then the Man-O-War might be for you. The cottages are a part of Charlotteville Estate, a 1,000-acre cocoa plantation open to visitors, who may wander through at will. Pat and Charles Turpin rent several cottages on a sandy beach. Each unit is complete with a kitchen, a good bed, a spacious living and dining room, a tiny private bath, and a porch opening onto the sea. The place is simplicity itself, so don't expect room phones or air conditioning. Near the colony is a coral reef that's ideal for snorkelers. The couple will also arrange a boat rental if you want to explore Lovers' Beach. Bird-watchers often book these cottages, and scuba diving and guided nature tours are available.

Store Bay Holiday Resort. Store Bay Rd., Crown Point, Tobago, W.I. ☎ **868/639-8810.** Fax 809/639-8810. 15 units. A/C. Year-round $45–$85 single or double; $95–$140 suite for up to 8. V.

This is an L-shaped motel-style building painted off-white with a green stripe. The rooms have recently been painted and redecorated, the mattresses have been much used but still have life and comfort in them, and the baths are tiny but tidy. For the most part, furnishings are a bit time-weary and a few carpets are well worn. Since there's a much-used kitchenette with a new refrigerator in each room, you might be tempted to cook your own meals. The rooms flank a pool, though you'll probably walk about 350 yards to reach the Store Bay Beach. No meals are served, but there are cafes and restaurants nearby.

WORTH A SPLURGE

✪ **Manta Lodge.** Speyside (P.O. Box 433), Speyside, Tobago, W.I. ☎ **868/660-5268.** Fax 868/660-5030. www.trinidad.net/tobagodive. E-mail: dive-manta@trinidad.net. 22 units. Winter $95–$135 single; $115–$170 double. Off-season $75–$110 single; $95–$145 double. Extra person $15. MAP $35 per person. AE, DC, MC, V.

One of the newer properties on the island, this complex caters to serious bird-watchers and even more serious divers. It overlooks a beach named for the monster manta rays islanders call "Tobago taxis." The mantas frequent the nearby dive sites. The lodge, built by Trinidad-born Sean Robinson, is a colonial-style concrete building across the road from the beach with a garden in front. The loft rooms are especially popular with divers, containing air-conditioning and a sundeck. The superior and more expensive rooms have verandas and air-conditioning, while the cheaper rooms are cooled by ceiling fans, though they have verandas as well. Surprisingly, the beds are the most sumptuous in Tobago, with the best linen and the finest mattresses. Amenities in the rooms include adequate desk space and roomy closets, along with medium-size tiled baths. Service and amenities are at a minimum, but ice may be obtained on request. There's a pool as well as a restaurant and bar serving island food and drink. Room service and baby-sitting are also available.

GREAT DEALS ON DINING

✪ **Jemma's Seaview Kitchen.** Speyside. ☎ **868/660-4066.** Reservations recommended. Main courses TT$60–TT$175 ($9.60–$28). MC, V. Sun–Fri 8am–9pm. TOBAGONIAN.

A short walk north of the hamlet of Speyside on Tobago's northeastern coast, this is one of the very few restaurants in the Caribbean designed as a tree house. Although the simple kitchen is firmly anchored to the shoreline, the dining area is set on a platform nailed to the massive branches of a 200-year-old almond tree leaning out over the water. Some 50 tables are available on a wooden deck that provides a roof-like structure for shelter from the rain. The owner is Mrs. Jemma Sealey, whose charming staff provides meals where soup or salad is included in the price of a main course. Lunch platters include shrimp, fish, and chicken, while dinners feature more elaborate portions of each of those, as well as steaks, curried lamb, grilled or curried kingfish, lamb chops, and lobster served grilled or Thermidor style. Most dishes are at the lower end of the price scale. No liquor is served (only fresh orange or pineapple juice).

Kiskadee Restaurant. In the Turtle Beach Hotel, Courtland Bay. ☎ **868/639-2851.** Reservations recommended for those not staying in the hotel. Main courses TT$90–TT$180 ($14.40–$28.80). AE, DISC, MC, V. Daily 7:30–10am, 1–2:30pm, and 7–10pm. CREOLE/CARIBBEAN.

Five miles from Scarborough, the Kiskadee is casual. Its tables overlook a tropical garden and the sea. Specialties include the catch of the day, steamed or grilled or in a curry. Other courses include baked chicken, sirloin steak, or Chinese-style stir-fry. The cooks pay special attention to the homemade soups, including kettles of pumpkin, calaloo, potato, and cucumber. The kitchen doesn't exactly extend itself in preparing these dishes, but the flavors are zesty and spicy.

Man Friday. In the Sandy Point Beach Club, Crown Point, Tobago, W.I. ☎ **868/639-9547.** Main courses TT$55–TT$120 ($8.80–$19.20); buffets and barbecues TT$65–TT$95 ($10.40–$15.20). AE, MC, V. Daily 7am–10pm. INTERNATIONAL.

What could be more a Caribbean cliché than this, an open-air restaurant on the beach beside a small waterfall? If you can forgive the glaring purple-and-turquoise décor, you can enjoy a medley of dishes. The Thai choices seem the most delectable, though fresh fish and a standard repertoire of pork, beef, and chicken dishes are also offered. Each day a different island specialty is featured. At lunch you can order "the usual": burgers, sandwiches, and shrimp and chicken dishes. Monday and Thursday are devoted to barbecues. Live music is presented Monday and Tuesday to Thursday. It's also a good place to head for your "sundowner."

Papillon. Buccoo Bay Rd., Buccoo Bay. ☎ **868/639-0275.** Reservations recommended. Main courses TT$80–TT$125 ($12.80–$20); lunch TT$40–TT$60 ($6.40–$9.60). AE, MC, V. Daily 7:30am–2:30pm and 7–11pm. SEAFOOD/INTERNATIONAL.

Near the Tobago Golf Club on the corner of Buccoo Bay Road and Mount Irvine, this restaurant offers international specialties with an emphasis on seafood, including kingfish steak, stuffed flying fish, and lobster Buccoo Bay (marinated in sherry and broiled with garlic, herbs, and butter sauce). The interior is adorned with pictures referring to the novel and film *Papillon,* a story about a convict who settles in the Caribbean. For a change of pace, try curried goat, beef Stroganoff, or grilled lamb and beef. There's a patio for alfresco dining.

The Village Restaurant. At Kariwak Village, Store Bay. ☎ **868/639-8442.** Reservations recommended. Fixed-price meals TT$50–TT$81 ($8–$12.95) at lunch, TT$94–TT$125 ($15.05–$20) at dinner. AE, MC, V. Daily 7:30am–9:30pm. INTERNATIONAL/WEST INDIAN.

At this restaurant where the menu changes daily, there are three eating areas, including two open-air thatched huts where you can enjoy dining by candlelight. At lunch the meal generally consists of a vegetable, a starch, and meat such as steak or chicken. If you want lighter fare, there are sandwiches and salads. Sunday to Thursday, the dinner menu consists of four courses, which might include fish broth, curried Caesar salad, baked chicken, and honey cake. Only fresh vegetables and fruits are served—no canned goods. Fresh herbs grown on Tobago enliven many dishes. With enough advance notice, special requests can be filled. A buffet is served on Friday and Saturday, costing TT$125 ($20); a band plays 9 to 11pm.

WORTH A SPLURGE

⭐ **The Cocoa House.** In Footprints Eco Resort, Golden Lane, Colloden Bay Rd. ☎ **868/860-0118.** Reservations recommended for lunch, required for dinner before 1pm on day of your intended arrival. Lunch main courses $6–$12; dinner main courses $16.50–$40. AE, MC, V. Daily 11:30–1:30pm and 6:30–9pm. WEST INDIAN/TOBAGONIAN.

Proud of its eco-sensitivity (waste water and paper trash are recycled here), this eating house is a worthy choice because of its allegiance to tried-and-true Tobagan food. It derives its name from its unusual design for a roof made of the fronds of the Timit Palm. During balmy evenings, the roof retracts, allowing views of the setting sun and—a bit later—of the moon and stars. Old-fashioned drying rooms for cocoa pods were designed with retractable roofs, allowing direct access of the sun as a means of drying the raw product. Menu items include a well-flavored roster of dishes like crabmeat or pork and dumplings; jerk versions of shrimp, chicken, port, and beef; duck with orange or pineapple sauce; and *pelau,* a French-inspired dish that combines rice, chicken, and beef.

The Steak Hut. In the Sandy Point Beach Village, Crown Point. ☎ **868/639-8533.** Reservations recommended. Main courses TT$60–TT$140 ($9.60–$22.40); breakfast TT$20–TT$35 ($3.20–$5.60); lunch TT$30–TT$65 ($4.80–$10.40). AE, MC, V. Daily 7:30–10:30, noon–5pm, and 7–9:45pm. STEAK/INTERNATIONAL.

On the island's southwestern side, the Steak Hut serves the best beef on the island, specializing in U.S. sirloin, T-bone, porterhouse, and tenderloin. The location, near the beach and pool of this hotel, is ideal, especially in the evening. The seafront restaurant also features local fish steaks—shark, flying fish, grouper, dolphin, barracuda, and kingfish. In addition to the good food, you often get entertainment: limbo on Tuesday night, old-time calypso on Wednesday, and soft romantic music on Sunday night.

HITTING THE BEACHES

On Tobago sands you can still feel like Robinson Crusoe in a solitary cove—at least for most of the week before the Trinidadians fly over to sample the sands on a Saturday.

A good beach, **Back Bay,** is within an 8-minute walk of the Mount Irvine Bay Hotel on Mount Irvine Bay. Along the way you'll pass a coconut plantation and an old cannon emplacement. Sometimes there can be dangerous currents here, but you can always enjoy exploring Rocky Point with its brilliantly colored parrot fish. In July and August, the surfing is the finest in Tobago, and it's also likely to be good in January and April. Snorkeling is generally excellent, even in winter. There are picnic tables, so get the makings for your picnic in Scarborough before coming here, though you can buy cold beer and drinks at an on-site snack bar.

Also try **Man-O-War Bay,** one of the finest natural harbors in the West Indies, at the opposite end of the island near the fishing village of Charlotteville. Once here, you'll come to a long sandy beach, and you can also enjoy a picnic at a government-run rest house. Sometimes the local fishers will come around hawking the day's catch. Many guests who have a kitchen or kitchenette in their living quarters buy fish and prepare it themselves for dinner. The fishers will clean the fish for you.

⭐ **Pigeon Point,** on the island's northwestern coast, is the best-known bathing area with a long coral beach. Thatched shelters provide changing rooms, as well as tables and benches for picnics. This beach is public but adjoins a former great coconut estate for which you pay TT$10 ($1.60) to enter the grounds, including the use of its facilities. Pigeon Point is a Caribbean cliché in that it's set against a backdrop of royal palms. This beach is becoming increasingly commercial with food kiosks and some crafts shops, plus a diving concession. You can generally rent paddleboats from one of the locals outfitters here to sail in the tranquil waters.

The true beach buff will want to head for **King's Bay Beach,** south of the town of Speyside in the northeast near the hamlet of Delaford (a sign between Roxborough and Speyside will direct you here). Against a backdrop of towering green hills, it's one of the island's best places for swimming. The grayish crescent-shaped beach is well protected here. Perhaps you'll resist the young men who offer themselves as guides to a local waterfall, but the climb and sight are worth the effort. Also approached from Roxborough on the north side of the island, **Parlatuvier Beach** is a classic half-moon crescent. The scene of villagers and fishing boats is like a picture postcard advertising Tobago. The setting is more bucolic than the swimming, however.

Lovers Beach in the northeast of the island is aptly named. On our last visit, a nude couple was making love so passionately they couldn't stop to excuse themselves on the arrival of our party. The remote beach lies near **Man O'War Bay** to the east of Charlotteville. This beach is accessible only by boat and is famous locally for its pink sand, formed by dozens of crushed seashells ages ago. If you want to visit it, local boatmen are willing to take you out for a fee to be negotiated. If you'd like to spend several hours here with a loved one, you can make arrangements to be picked up at an agreed-on time.

Great Courtyard Bay is known for its long expanse of tranquil, gin-clear waters, and is flanked by Turtle Beach, named for the sea creatures who nest here. Near Fort Bennett, Great Courtland Bay and Turtle Beach lie south of Plymouth, off the coast near the hamlet of Black Rock. This is one of the longest sandy beaches on the island and the site of several hotels, including a marina attracting visiting yachties. Beach lovers will also seek out **Bacelot Beach,** west of Scarborough and opening onto Bacelot Bay. It's a dark sandy beach with waters tranquil for swimming. This beach has seen its share of film crews, as it was used as a setting for the movies *Heaven Knows, Mr. Allison* and *Swiss Family Robinson.*

If you can't stand crowds and want the sands all to yourself, head for **Englishman's Bay Beach,** on the north coast, east of Plymouth and past the hamlets of Moriah and Castara. Here this lovely beach is virtually deserted. We don't know why: It's charming, secluded, and good for swimming. **Little Rockley Bay** is good for escapists, but not worth seeking out unless you're going to be on Tobago for several days. It lies west of the capital of Scarborough and is reached by taking the sign-posted Milford Road off the main highway. The beach here is rather craggy and not suited for either sunbathing or swimming. But beachcombers can be seen wandering its shoreline, and there's a panoramic view of Scarborough to be enjoyed from here.

SPORTS & OUTDOOR PURSUITS

BOATING   The **Rex Turtle Beach Hotel,** Great Courland Bay (☎ 868/639-2851), rents Aqua-finn sailboats and is a registered Mistral Sailing Centre. The cost is TT$85 ($13.60) an hour.

GOLF   Tobago is the proud possessor of an 18-hole, 6,800-yard golf course at Mount Irvine. Called the **Tobago Golf Club** (☎ 868/639-8871), it covers 150 breeze-swept acres and was featured in the *Wonderful World of Golf* TV series. Even beginners agree the course is friendly to golfers. As a guest of the Mount Irvine Bay Hotel, you're granted temporary membership, use of the clubhouse and facilities, and a 30% discount on greens fees. All well-heeled serious golfers should stay at the Mount

Irvine. However, the course is also open to nonguests, even those staying at some of Tobago's budget lodgings. Nonguests pay $48 for 18 holes or $30 for 9 holes. A cart can be rented for $36 for 18 holes or $20 for 9 holes, and clubs cost $15 for 18 holes or $10 for 9 holes.

SNORKELING, DIVING & MORE   The unspoiled reefs off Tobago teem with a great variety of marine life. Divers can swim through rocky canyons 60 to 130 feet deep, and underwater photographers can shoot pictures they won't find anywhere else. Snorkeling over the celebrated Buccoo Reef is one of the specialties of Tobago. Hotels routinely arrange for their guests to visit this underwater wonderland.

Wreck divers have a new adventure to enjoy with the sinking of the *Maverick*, a former ferry between Trinidad and Tobago. In 1997, the *Maverick* was sunk in 100 feet of water near Mount Irvine Bay Hotel on Tobago's southwest coast, making it accessible to divers. The ship lays the foundation for a new reef to support sea life, including resident and migrating fish as well as coral and sponges.

The **Rex Turtle Beach Hotel,** Courtland Bay (☎ 868/639-2851), is the best equipped for water sports. Activities here include sailing at TT$85 ($13.60) per hour and windsurfing at TT$100 ($16) per hour. You can also go waterskiing for TT$145 ($23.20) per half hour. **Dive Tobago,** Pigeon Point (P.O. Box 53), Scarborough, Tobago, W.I. (☎ 868/639-0202), is the oldest and most established dive operation, operated by Jay Young. It offers easy resort courses, single dives, and dive packages. Equipment is available to rent. It caters to the beginner as well as to the experienced diver. A basic resort course, taking half a day and ending in a 30-foot dive, costs $55, though for certification you must pay $300. Young is a certified PADI instructor. A one-tank dive goes for $40.

Tobago Dive Experience, at the Turtle Beach Hotel, Black Rock (☎ 868/639-7034), offers scuba dives, snorkeling, and boat trips. All dives are guided, with a boat following. Exciting drift dives are available for experienced divers. Manta rays are frequently seen 10 minutes from the shore, and there's rich marine life with zonal compaction. A one-tank dive costs $39 with no equipment or $46 with equipment; a two-tank dive costs from $70. A resort course costs $59.

Man Friday Diving, Charlotteville (☎ 868/660-4676), is a Danish-owned dive center with certified PADI instructors along with PADI dive masters. The location is right on the beach of Man-O-War Bay at the northernmost tip of Tobago. With more than 40 dive sites, they're always able to find suitable locations for diving, no matter what the water conditions are. Guided boat trips for certified divers go out twice a day except Sundays, at 9:30am and at 1pm. A resort course costs $75; a PADI open-water certification, $375. A one-tank dive costs $35, with a night dive going for $50.

TENNIS   The **Rex Turtle Beach Hotel** at Great Courtland Bay (☎ 868/639-2851) has two excellent tennis courts open to nonguests who are charged TT$30 ($4.80) per hour, though hotel guests play for free. The best courts, however, are at the **Mount Irvine Bay Hotel** (☎ 868/639-8871), where two good courts are available for TT$11.50 ($1.85) per half hour or TT$23 ($3.70) per hour.

SEEING THE SIGHTS

Tobago's capital, **Scarborough,** need claim your attention only briefly before you climb up the hill to **Fort King George,** about 430 feet above the town. Built by the English in 1779, it was later captured by the French. After that it jockeyed back and forth among various conquerors until nature decided to end it all in 1847, blowing off the roofs of its buildings. The cannons still mounted had a 3-mile range, and one is believed to have come from one of the ships of Sir Francis Drake (you can still see a replica of the *Tudor Rose*). One building used to house a powder magazine, and you can see the ruins of a military hospital. Artifacts are displayed in a gallery on the grounds.

If you'd like to get a close-up view of Tobago's exotic and often rare tropical birds, as well as a range of other island wildlife and lush tropical flora, **naturalist-led field trips** are the answer. The trips lead you to forest trails and coconut plantations, along rivers and past waterfalls. Each trip lasts about 2 to 3 hours, so you can take at least two per day if you like. One excursion goes to two nearby islands. The price per trip is $45 to $54 per person. For details, contact **Pat Turpin**, Man-O-War Bay Cottages, Charlotteville (☎ 868/660-4327 or 868/660-4328).

From Scarborough, you can drive northwest to **Plymouth,** Tobago's other town. Perched on a point at Plymouth is **Fort James,** which dates from 1768 when it was built by the British as a barracks. Now it's mainly in ruins. From Speyside, you can make arrangements with a local fisher to go to **Little Tobago,** a 450-acre offshore island where a bird sanctuary attracts ornithologists. Threatened with extinction in New Guinea, many birds, perhaps 50 species in all, were brought over to this little island in the early part of this century.

Off Pigeon Point lies ✪ **Buccoo Reef,** where sea gardens of coral and hundreds of fish can be seen in waist-deep water. This is the natural aquarium of Tobago. Nearly all the major hotels arrange boat trips to these acres of submarine gardens, which offer the best scuba diving and snorkeling. Even nonswimmers can wade knee-deep in the waters. Remember to protect your head and body from the tropical heat and to guard your feet against the sharp coral. After about half an hour at the reef, passengers reboard their boats and go over to **Nylon Pool,** with its crystal-clear waters. Here in this white-sand bottom, about a mile offshore, you can enjoy water only 3 or 4 feet deep. After a swim, you'll be returned to the Buccoo Village jetty in time for a goat and crab race.

Eco-consciousness on the island was enhanced by the opening of the **Franklyn Water Wheel and Nature Park** at Arnos Vale, Arnos Vale Estate, Franklyn Road (☎ 868/660-0815). This is the site of Tobago's best-preserved water wheel, which once helped provide power to a sugar estate. It has been rehabilitated, and the site offers walking trails and a restaurant. There's also an outdoor theater, and the old machinery itself is still in place for the most part. Walkways allow you to see the sights without upsetting Mother Nature. Many hiking trails are possible on the 12-acre estate, where you can see butterflies and iguanas, plus mango and citrus orchards—you can even pick your own fresh fruit. Admission is TT$10 ($1.60) for adults or TT$5 (80¢) for children. You can visit any time during the day and can gain entrance to the site as long as the restaurant is open (10pm).

SHOPPING

In Tobago's capital, **Scarborough,** you can visit the local market Monday to Saturday morning and listen to the sounds of a Creole patois. Scarborough's stores have a limited range of merchandise, more to tempt the browser than the serious shopper.

But if you're in town, you'll find **Farro's,** Wilson Road (☎ 868/639-2979), lying across from the marketplace. Here you can pick up the tastiest condiments on the island, which are packed into little straw baskets for you to carry back home. Sample the delectable lime marmalade, any of the hot sauces, the guava jelly, and most definitely the home-canned and -made chutney from the tamarind fruit. If you're seeking handcrafts, especially straw baskets, head for the **Souvenir & Gift Shop,** Port Mall (☎ 868/639-5632), also in Scarborough.

Cotton House Fashion Studio, Old Windward Road, in Bacolet (☎ 868/639-2727), is the island's best choices for "hands-on" appreciation of the fine art of batik. Batik is an Indonesian tradition where melted wax, brushed onto fabric, resists dyes on certain parts of the cloth, thereby creating unusual colors and designs. This outlet contains the largest collections of batik clothing and wall hangings on Tobago. Dying techniques are demonstrated to clients, who can try their skills at the art form free.

TOBAGO AFTER DARK

Your best bet for entertainment is at the **Mount Irvine Bay Hotel** at Mount Irvine Bay (☎ **868/639-8871**), where you might find some disco action or a steel band performing by the beach or poolside. The **Rex Turtle Beach Hotel,** Great Courtland Bay (☎ **868/639-2851**), is the place to be on Wednesday night, when it stages a Caribbean buffet dinner with cultural entertainment and dancing. You get real West Indian flavor here. Every Saturday a steel band is brought in to entertain at a barbecue dinner from 7 to 10pm.

The Grafton Beach Resort at Black Road owns one of the island's most charming bars, **Buccaneer's Beach Bar** (☎ **868/639-0191**), across from the resort. Here you'll find a wide wood terrace sheltered by a grove of almond trees. It evokes the feeling of a tree house, but the sea is right at your feet. Not only can you drink here, but you can also enjoy daily specials written on a surfboard—burgers, fried fish, and the like (don't expect the elegant beachside Creole cooking of Martinique). If your order gets too fancy, it's referred to the kitchens at Grafton Beach Resort itself. Even after the beach bar closes, you can stick around to see what's happening at the resort itself. Every night some cabaret-like entertainment is organized. If you can, catch the local troupe, Les Couteaux Cultural Group, which performs a version of Tobagonian history set to dance. They frequently appear here.

The best place for a sundowner is **Pigeon Point Bar** (☎ **868/639-8141**). Refer to our recommendation of the beach at Pigeon Point, above. Sit here, sip your drink, and watch for the legendary green flash that often happens in these parts when the sun goes down. Pan men might be playing on their steel drums to entertain you, and breakers unfurl on a distant reef. It's quite romantic.

Still want some local action? Drop in at **Bankers,** Store Bay Road at Crown Point (☎ **868/639-7173**), which is an active bar often with disco action. Here you'll hear the best on-island sounds of soca, reggae, or jazz. If you've been "bad," the DJ might order you to walk the gangplank into the pool. Disco parties are occasionally held at **Starting Gate,** Shirvan Road in Mount Irvine (☎ **868/639-0225**). Otherwise, this is one of the island's friendliest alfresco pubs. Drop in to see what's happening.

25

The U.S. Virgin Islands

The U.S. Virgin Islands are known for their sugar-white beaches, among the world's finest. The most developed island in the chain is **St. Thomas,** which has the Caribbean's largest concentration of shopping in its capital, Charlotte Amalie. With a population of some 50,000, St. Thomas isn't exactly a secluded tropical retreat; you'll hardly have its beaches to yourself. The place abounds in bars and restaurants, even fast-food joints, and has a vast selection of hotels in all price ranges, making it great for the budget traveler.

St. Croix is bigger but more tranquil. A favorite with cruise-ship passengers (as is St. Thomas), St. Croix touts its shopping and has more stores than most Caribbean islands, especially in and around Christiansted, though it's not the shopping mecca Charlotte Amalie is. Its major attraction is Buck Island, an offshore national park. The place is peppered with small inexpensive inns and condo, apartment, and villa rentals.

St. John, the smallest of the three islands, is also the most beautiful and the least developed. A few miles east of St. Thomas, it has only two big hotels but is known for its campgrounds. There are also several low-cost inns and a number of condo and villa rentals. Some two-thirds of the island is a national park. Even if you visit only for the day while based on St. Thomas, you'll want to sample the island's dream beach, Trunk Bay.

The U.S. Virgin Islands lie in two bodies of water: St. John is entirely in the Atlantic Ocean, St. Croix is entirely in the Caribbean Sea, and St. Thomas separates the Atlantic and the Caribbean. These islands, directly in the belt of the subtropical easterly trade winds, enjoy one of the world's most perfect year-round climates. At the eastern end of the Greater Antilles and the northern tip of the Lesser Antilles, the U.S. Virgins are some 60 miles east of Puerto Rico and 1,100 miles southeast of Miami.

1 Essentials

VISITOR INFORMATION

Before you go, contact the **U.S. Virgin Islands Division of Tourism,** 1270 Ave. of the Americas, New York, NY 10020 (☎ **212/332-2222**). Branch offices are at 225 Peachtree St. NE, Suite 260, Atlanta, GA 30303 (☎ **404/688-0906**); 500 N. Michigan Ave., Suite 2030, Chicago, IL 60611 (☎ **312/670-8784**); 2655 Le Jeune Rd., Suite

907, Coral Gables, FL 33134 (☎ **305/442-7200**); 3460 Wilshire Blvd., Suite 412, Los Angeles, CA 90010 (☎ **213/739-0138**); and 900 17th St. NW, Suite 500, Washington, DC 20006 (☎ **202/293-3707**).

Offices outside the United States are found in **Canada** at 3300 Bloor St. West, Suite 3120, Centre Tower, Toronto, ON M8X 2X3, Canada (☎ **416/233-1414**), and in **Britain** at 2 Cinnamon Row, Plantation Wharf, York Place, London SW11 3TW (☎ **020/7978-5262**).

The Internet address for the U.S. Virgin Islands is **www.usvi.net**.

GETTING THERE

While it's possible to fly directly to St. Croix from the mainland United States and even possible to fly from St. Thomas to St. Croix, you can't fly to St. John. The only way to get to St. John is by a ferry from either St. Thomas or Jost Van Dyke or Tortola in the British Virgin Islands.

TO ST. THOMAS OR ST. CROIX FROM THE U.S.   Nonstop flights to the U.S. Virgin Islands from either New York or Atlanta usually take 3¾ and 3½ hours, respectively. The flight time between St. Thomas and St. Croix is only 20 minutes. Flying to San Juan from mainland cities and changing planes may save you money over the APEX nonstop fare.

American Airlines (☎ **800/433-7300**) offers frequent service into St. Thomas and St. Croix from the U.S. mainland, with five daily flights from JFK to St. Thomas. Summer flights can vary; call for more information. Passengers originating in other parts of the world are usually routed to St. Thomas through American's hubs in Miami or San Juan, both of which offer nonstop service (often several times a day) to St. Thomas. Connections from Los Angeles or San Francisco to either St. Thomas or St. Croix are usually made through New York, San Juan, or Miami. One especially convenient nonstop flight from Miami, available only June to August, departs Miami at 5pm and continues to St. Croix, where the plane stays overnight. This late afternoon departure from Miami allows for connections to the U.S.V.I. from many other destinations within the U.S., including same-day connections from such remote places as Los Angeles. American can also arrange lots of great discount packages that include both airfare and hotel. Flights from Puerto Rico to the U.S. Virgin Islands are on American's partner, **American Eagle** (☎ **800/433-7300**), which has 13 nonstop flights daily.

Delta (☎ **800/221-1212**) in winter offers two daily nonstop flights between Atlanta and St. Thomas, the first departing in the morning and the second in the afternoon. The latter flight also provides an air link to St. Croix. In off-season, only one flight may be available. **TWA** (☎ **800/221-2000**) doesn't fly nonstop to any of the Virgin Islands but offers connections to other carriers through San Juan. TWA flies into San Juan 5 times daily from New York's JFK and twice daily from St. Louis with a touchdown in Miami. **US Airways** (☎ **800/428-4322**) has one flight nonstop from Philadelphia to St. Thomas.

Cape Air Airlines (☎ **800/352-0714**) began service between St. Thomas and Puerto Rico in the autumn of 1998. The Massachusetts-based airlines provides seven flights daily between 7am and 5pm. If needed, more frequent departures may be added.

TO ST. CROIX FROM ST. THOMAS   It's now easier than ever before to travel between St. Thomas and St. Croix. **American Eagle** (☎ **800/433-7300**) has 3 flights a day, costing $61 per person one-way. In addition, **Seaborne Seaplane** (☎ **340/**

773-6442), offers 10 or 11 round-trip flights daily, going for $55 per person one-way. Flight time is only 30 minutes.

Those who want to make the 40-mile crossing from St. Thomas to St. Croix by **hydrofoil** should call the new service at ☎ **340/776-7417.** A hydrofoil, *Katrun II,* departs twice daily from the harbor at Charlotte Amalie going to the harbor of Christiansted. The trip takes about an hour and costs $90 round trip.

A **ferry service** from St. Thomas to Puerto Rico, with a stop in St. John, is available once every 2 weeks, maybe more if demand merits it. The trip from Puerto Rico to Charlotte Amalie takes about 2 hours, costing $80 one-way or $100 round trip, including ground transportation to the San Juan airport or Condado. For more information, call ☎ **340/776-6282.**

TO ST. JOHN The easiest and most common way to get to St. John is by **ferry** (☎ **340/776-6282**), which leaves from the Red Hook landing pier on St. Thomas's eastern tip; the trip takes about 20 minutes each way. Beginning at 6:30am, boats depart more or less every hour, with minor exceptions throughout the day. The last ferry back to Red Hook departs from St. John's Cruz Bay at 11pm. Because of such frequent departures, even cruise-ship passengers temporarily anchored in Charlotte Amalie for only a short stay can visit St. John for a quickie island tour. The one-way fare is $3 for adults or $1 for children 10 and under. Schedules can change without notice, so call in advance before your intended departure.

To reach the ferry, take the **Vitran** bus from a point near Market Square (in Charlotte Amalie) directly to Red Hook. The cost is $1 per person each way. In addition, privately owned taxis will be willing to negotiate a price to carry you from virtually anywhere to the docks at Red Hook.

It's also possible to board a **boat** for St. John directly at the Charlotte Amalie waterfront for a cost of $7 each way. The ride takes 45 minutes. The boats depart from Charlotte Amalie at 9am and continue at intervals of between 1 and 2 hours until the last boat departs around 5:30pm. (The last boat to leave St. John's Cruz Bay for Charlotte Amalie departs at 3:45pm.) Call for more information.

Fast Facts: The U.S. Virgin Islands

Currency The **U.S. dollar** is the unit of currency in the Virgin Islands.

Customs Every U.S. resident can bring home $1,200 worth of duty-free purchases, including a gallon of alcoholic beverages per adult. If you go over the $1,200 limit, you pay a flat 5% duty, up to an additional $1,000. You can also mail home gifts valued at up to $100 per day, which you don't have to declare. (At other spots in the Caribbean, U.S. citizens are limited to $400 or $600 worth of merchandise and a single bottle of liquor.)

Documents U.S. and Canadian citizens are required to present some proof of citizenship to enter the Virgin Islands, such as a birth certificate with a raised seal along with a government-issued photo ID. A passport isn't strictly required, but carrying one is a good idea. Residents from other countries, including Britain, are required to carry a valid passport, and in some cases a visa. In other words, requirements are the same as for a foreigner entering mainland U.S. gateways.

Driving Remember to *drive on the left.* This comes as a surprise to many visitors, who expect that U.S. driving practices will hold here. Of course, you should also obey speed limits, which are 20 mph in towns, 35 mph outside.

Electricity It's the same as on the mainland: 120 volts AC (60 cycles). No transformer, adapter, or converter is needed for American appliances.

Mail The Virgin Islands are part of the U.S. Postal Service, so postage rates are the same as on the mainland.

Safety The U.S. Virgin Islands have more than their share of crime. St. John is safer than St. Thomas or St. Croix. But even on St. John there is crime—possessions that are left unattended are likely to be stolen. Travelers should exercise extreme caution both day and night when wandering the backstreets of Charlotte Amalie on St. Thomas and both Christiansted and Frederiksted on St. Croix. Muggings are commonplace. Avoid, if possible, night strolls or drives along quiet roads, and never go walking on the beaches at night.

Time The U.S. Virgins are on Atlantic standard time year-round, which places the islands an hour ahead of U.S. eastern standard time. When the U.S. east coast goes on daylight saving time, the Virgin Islands have the same time.

Tipping As a general rule, it's customary to tip 15% as in the U.S. Some hotels add a 10% to 15% surcharge to cover service, so check before you wind up paying twice.

Water There's ample water for showers and bathing in the Virgin Islands, but you are asked to conserve. Hotels will supply you with all your drinking water. Many visitors drink the local tap water with no harmful aftereffects. Others, more prudent or with more delicate stomachs, should stick to bottled water.

Weather From November to February, temperatures average about 77°F. The average temperature divergence is 5° to 7°F. Sometimes in August the temperature peaks in the high 80s, but the subtropical breezes keep it comfortably cool in the shade. The temperature in winter may drop into the low 60s, but this happens rarely.

2 St. Thomas

One of the two busiest cruise-ship harbors in the West Indies, St. Thomas is the second largest of the U.S. Virgins, about 40 miles north of St. Croix. St. Thomas, with the U.S. Virgins' capital at Charlotte Amalie, is about 12 miles long and 3 miles wide. The capital is also the shopping center of the Caribbean. Hotels on the north side of St. Thomas face the Atlantic and those on the south side front the calmer Caribbean.

St. Thomas is a boon for cruise-ship shoppers, who flood Main Street, the shopping center, basically 3 to 4 blocks long in the center of town. However, this center, which gets very crowded, is away from all beaches, major hotels, most restaurants, and entertainment facilities. At a hotel "out on the island," you can still find the seclusion you may be seeking.

If you're visiting in August, make sure you carry along mosquito repellent.

American Express is represented on St. Thomas by the **Caribbean Travel Agency/Tropic Tours,** 14AB The Guardian Building (☎ **340/774-1855**), a 5-minute drive east of Charlotte Amalie's center, opposite the entrance to the Havensight Shopping Mall (open Monday to Friday 8:30am to 5pm and Saturday 8:30am to noon). **Royal Roy Lester Schneider Hospital,** the largest on the island with the best-equipped emergency room, is at 48 Sugar Estate, Charlotte Amalie (☎ **340/776-8311**), a 5-minute drive east of the town's commercial center.

St. Thomas

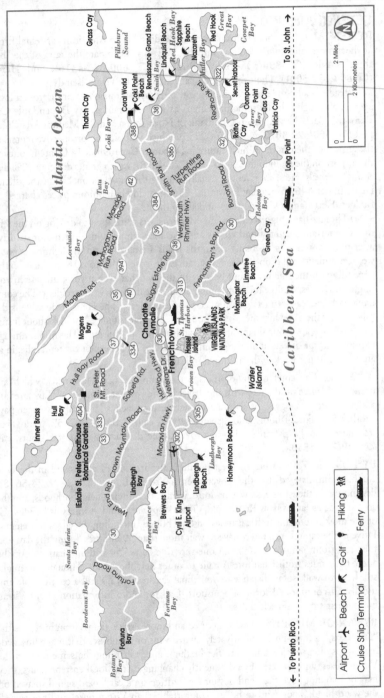

GETTING AROUND

BY RENTAL CAR   St. Thomas has many leading North American car-rental firms at the airport, and competition is stiff. Before you go, compare the rates of the "big three": **Avis** (☎ **800/331-1084**), **Budget** (☎ **800/626-4316**), and **Hertz** (☎ **800/654-3001**). There's no tax on car rentals in the Virgin Islands.

Instead of calling Hertz or Avis, you can often save money by renting from a local agency, although vehicles sometimes aren't as well maintained. Try **Dependable Car Rental,** 3901 B Altona, behind the Bank of Nova Scotia and the Medical Arts Complex (☎ **800/522-3076** or 340/774-2253), which will pick up prospective renters at the airport or their hotel. A final choice is **Discount Car Rental,** 14 Content, outside the airport on the main highway (☎ **340/776-4858**), which grants drivers a 12% discount on rivals' rates. Its rates are usually among the most reasonable on the island, beginning at $46.95 per day in winter. The firm closely monitors prices charged at Budget, Hertz, and Avis, and then undercuts them.

St. Thomas has a high accident rate: Many visitors aren't used to driving on the left, the hilly terrain shelters blind curves and entrance ramps, and some motorists drive after too many drinks. In many cases, the roads are narrow and the lighting is poor; we recommend collision-damage insurance. It costs $14 to $16 per day extra, depending on the fine print, but be alert to the fact that even if you purchase it, you might still be responsible for a whopping deductible if you have an accident. The company with the least-attractive insurance policies is Hertz. The Hertz deductible is the full value of the car, while the Avis or Budget deductible is only $250. Ask about insurance coverage and your financial responsibilities before you rent. The minimum age requirement for drivers at all three companies is 25. The cheapest car rentals begin at around $250 per week with unlimited mileage.

BY TAXI   The chief means of transport around the island are taxis, which are unmetered; agree on the fare with the driver before you get into the car. Taxi fares are $30 for two passengers for 2 hours of sightseeing; each additional passenger pays another $12. For 24-hour radio-dispatch service, call ☎ **340/774-7457.** Many taxis transport 8 to 12 passengers in vans to multiple destinations. For taxi tours, call ☎ **340/774-4550.**

BY BUS   St. Thomas has the best public transportation of any island in the U.S. chain. Administered by the government, **Vitran** buses (☎ **340/774-5678**), depending on their route, serve Charlotte Amalie, its outlying neighborhoods, and the countryside as far away as Red Hook. Vitran stops are found at intervals beside each of the most important traffic arteries on St. Thomas, including the edges of Veterans Drive in the capital. You rarely have to wait more than 30 minutes during the day, and they run from 5am to 10:40pm. A one-way ride costs 75¢ within Charlotte Amalie and $1 for rides from Charlotte Amalie to outer neighborhoods. Though you might still have to walk some distance to your final destination, it's still a comfortable and usually air-conditioned form of transport. Call for more information about Vitran buses, their stops, and schedules.

BY VAN OR MINIBUS   Less structured and more erratic than Vitran buses are the "taxi vans," a mini-flotilla of privately owned vans or minibuses that make unscheduled stops along major traffic arteries of the island. Charging the same rates as the Vitran buses, and operated by a frequently changing cast of local entrepreneurs, they may or may not have their end destination written on a cardboard sign displayed on the windshield. They tend to be less comfortable than Vitran buses and not as well maintained, but some residents opt for a ride if one happens to arrive near a Vitran stop at a convenient moment and if it's headed in the right direction. If you're in doubt, it's much better to stick to the Vitran buses.

ACCOMMODATIONS YOU CAN AFFORD

Nearly every beach has its own hotel, and St. Thomas may have more quaint inns than anyplace else in the Caribbean. There's an 8% government hotel tax.

Sometimes you can make a deal on an inexpensive condo or apartment rental that might not be as expensive as it sounds. We've found that **Calypso Realty,** P.O. Box 12178, St. Thomas, U.S.V.I. (☎ **800/747-4858**, or 340/774-1620), has the best deals. This agency is especially noted for its offerings at discount prices from April to mid-December. It features apartments, condos, houses, and villas, the apartments or small condos being cheaper, of course. A studio overlooking Pillsbury Sound often goes for $95 per night off-season or $135 per night in winter.

✪ **The Admiral's Inn.** Villa Olga (P.O. Box 306162), Frenchtown, Charlotte Amalie, St. Thomas, U.S.V.I. 00802. ☎ **800/544-0493** in the U.S., or 340/774-1376. Fax 340/774-8010. www.admirals-inn.com. E-mail: inn@admirals-inn.com. 16 units. A/C TV TEL. Winter $129–$159 single or double. Off-season $89–$109 single or double. Children 11 and under stay free in parents' room. Rates include continental breakfast. AE, DISC, MC, V.

On a peninsula in Frenchtown, near the western entrance to Charlotte Amalie's harbor, this famous inn was battered by recent hurricanes but is now up and running again. It often attracts divers and other travelers who aren't too particular about where they spend the night. Though the Admiral's Inn has had its share of admirers, it disappoints many readers, who complain about lack of security and a sometimes unhelpful staff. Luckily, units that were in bad need of refurbishment before the hurricane received much-needed facelifts. They contain one or two queen-sized beds with new mattresses, plus dressing areas flanking well-maintained tiled baths. Some units also have small refrigerators. A saltwater beach and sea pool lie a few paces from the lanai-style ocean-view units. There's a freshwater pool with a large sundeck, plus a poolside bar that remains open to guests in the morning and afternoon. You can have dinner at the Chart House Restaurant on the premises but not affiliated with the inn.

Bunker Hill Hotel. 7 Commandant Gade, Charlotte Amalie, St. Thomas, U.S.V.I. 00802. ☎ **340/774-8056.** Fax 340/774-3172. E-mail: bunkerhl@viaccess.com. 18 units. A/C TV TEL. Winter $80 single; $90 double; $95 suite. Off-season $59 single; $69 double; $79 suite. Rates include continental breakfast. AE, MC, V.

We recommend this only if the other hotels are booked up (as is often the case). This district is a bit questionable, so caution is advised—especially at night. This clean and centrally located guest lodge is suitable for anyone who'll sacrifice some comfort, like putting up with street noises, for economy's sake. Four rooms have balconies, and some offer a view of the lights of Charlotte Amalie and the sea. Despite some minor improvements, the furnishings in the small rooms are simple and often threadbare (the mattresses are well worn), and each has a small refrigerator. The baths are also exceedingly small. Guests share a communal kitchen, and on the premises is a deli serving soups, sandwiches, and drinks. The closest beach is Lindbergh Bay, a 15-minute drive away.

Danish Chalet Inn. 9E9J Nordsidevej (Solberg Rd.) (P.O. Box 4319), Charlotte Amalie, St. Thomas, U.S.V.I. 00803. ☎ **800/635-1531** in the U.S., or 340/774-5764. Fax 340/777-4886. www.vi-danish-chalet-inn.com. 11 units, 6 with bathroom. TEL. Winter $79 single or double without bathroom, $89–$99 single or double with bathroom. Off-season $64 single or double without bathroom, $74–$84 single or double with bathroom. Extra person $15. Rates include a continental breakfast. MC, V.

Above Charlotte Amalie on the western edge of the cruise-ship harbor, a 5-minute walk from the harborfront, this trio of buildings sits on a steeply inclined acre of land dotted with tropical shrubs and bougainvillea. The heart and soul of the place is the panoramic terrace, with a 180° view over the cruise ships and an honor bar. The small rooms are neat, clean, and colorful, all but the cheapest with refrigerators and air-conditioning; the others have ceiling fans. The mattresses are well worn but with some comfort still in them. The shared baths are generally adequate and well maintained; you rarely have to wait in line. The hotel has no pool, but it does have a semi-secluded Jacuzzi spa. The nearest beaches are Morningstar and Beachcomber, about a 4-minute drive away. Breakfast is the only meal served.

Galleon House. Government Hill (P.O. Box 6577), Charlotte Amalie, St. Thomas, U.S.V.I. 00804. ☎ **800/524-2052** in the U.S., or 340/774-6952. Fax 340/774-6952. www.st-thomas.com/galleonhouse/. 14 units, 12 with bathroom. A/C TV TEL. Winter $69 single without bathroom, $109 single with bathroom; $79 double without bathroom, $89–$119 double with bathroom. Off-season $49 single without bathroom, $69 single with bathroom; $59 double without bathroom, $79 double with bathroom. Rates include continental breakfast. AE, DISC, MC, V.

At the east end of Main Street, about a block from the main shopping area, Galleon House is reached after a difficult climb, especially in sweltering heat. Nevertheless, its rates are among the most competitive in town, if you don't mind a place operated without state-of-the-art maintenance and a staff attitude many readers have complained about. You walk up a long flight of stairs to reach a concrete terrace doubling as the reception area. The small rooms are scattered in several hillside buildings, each with a ceiling fan, a firm mattress, and so-so air-conditioning, plus a cramped bath. There's a small freshwater pool and a sundeck. Breakfast is served on a veranda overlooking the harbor, and Magens Beach is 15 minutes by car or taxi from the hotel.

Hotel Mafolie. 7091 Estate Mafolie, Mafolie Hill, Charlotte Amalie, St. Thomas, U.S.V.I. 00802. ☎ **800/225-7035** or 340/774-2790. Fax 340/774-4091. 22 units. A/C TV. Winter $81–$87 single; $93–$97 double; $135 mini-suite for up to 4. Off-season $65–$70 single; $75–$80 double; $105 mini-suite. Children 11 and under stay free in parents' room; children 12 and over $15 each. AE, MC, V.

An old favorite, with lots of fans and only a few detractors, the sprawling Mafolie is about 850 feet above Charlotte Amalie and offers a panoramic harbor view. It has bounced back after hurricane damage with major renovations that made it better than ever. Though the hotel attracts honeymooners, the ambience isn't the stuff of dreamy postcards, but the rooms are comfortable, with a rather uninspired décor. They may be small but not necessarily cramped, and the mattresses are fairly new and comfortable. The baths are like a cheap stateside motel's. Breakfast is served at the pool bar. The new restaurant, Lindy's, is home to a celebrated view of Charlotte Amalie harbor, a perfect backdrop for enjoying a drink and a Caribbean sunset. It offers alfresco dining Monday to Saturday, with an extensive menu specializing in shrimp, crab, and lobster dishes. The chefs seem to do crab the best—steamed and split and served with tangy mustard or cooked in herbs, spices, and garlic. Desserts might be Mary Russ's award-winning fruit tart, key lime pie, or chocolate chip–macadamia nut tart. A shuttle transports visitors to Magens Bay, about a 5-minute ride.

Island View Guesthouse. 11-C Contant (P.O. Box 1903), Charlotte Amalie, St. Thomas, U.S.V.I. 00803. ☎ **800/524-2023** for reservations only, or 340/774-4270. Fax 340/774-6167. www.st-thomas-com/islandviewguesthouse. E-mail: islandview@worldnet.att.net. 16 units, 14 with bathroom. TV TEL. Winter $60 single without bathroom, $90 single with bathroom; $65 double without bathroom, $95 double with bathroom; $10 suite. Off-season, $45 single without bathroom, $70 single with bathroom; $50 double without bathroom, $65 double with bathroom; $84 suite. Rates include continental breakfast. AE, MC, V. From airport, turn right onto Rte. 30; then cut left and continue to the unmarked Scott Free Rd., where you go left and look for the sign.

Island View is in a hilly neighborhood of private homes and villas about a 7-minute drive west of Charlotte Amalie and a 20-minute drive from the nearest beach at Magens Bay. Set 545 feet up Crown Mountain, it has sweeping views over the town and the harbor. Family-owned and -managed, it contains main-floor rooms (two without bath) and some poolside rooms, plus six units in an addition (three with kitchens and all with balconies). The rooms are cooled by breezes and fans, and the newer ones have optional air-conditioning. Furnishings are very basic, though a major restoration was completed in 1997, following damage from Hurricane Marilyn. The mattresses are relatively new and most comfortable, and baths are small but efficiently organized. A self-service open-air bar on the gallery operates on the honor system.

Sea Horse Cottages. Nazareth Bay (P.O. Box 302312), Charlotte Amalie, St. Thomas, U.S.V.I. 00803. ☎ **340/775-9231.** Fax 340/775-3590. 15 cottages. Winter $95 single or double; $140 cottage; $165 townhouse. Off-season $80 single or double; $105 cottage; $115 townhouse. Extra person $20. No credit cards.

The family-run Sea Horse overlooks Nazareth Bay on the southeastern side of the island near Red Hook, a commercial area where guests can go to restaurants and grocery stores. It has steps leading down the hillside from the pool to a tanning platform and a cove for swimming and snorkeling. The rooms contain teak furniture, twin beds with firm mattresses, and shuttered windows. Each cottage or townhouse is accented with dark ceiling beams and contains a complete kitchen. All the units have good-size baths with efficient plumbing. The airport is 9 miles away, but with the traffic the car ride may take about 45 minutes. Baby-sitting isn't difficult to arrange, and guests who enjoy water sports are sent to Secret Harbour nearby.

✪ **Simmonds House Inn.** 8A Estate Catherineberg, 00804 St. Thomas, U.S.V.I. ☎ **888/521-7044** or 340/776-7776. Fax 340/776-7075. 9 units. TEL. Winter $80 single; $110 double; $130–$150 suite. Off-season $70 single; $100 double; $100–$130 suite. AE, MC, V.

What's unusual about this hotel is its sense of historic charm and relatively low rates and the ease with which guests can walk about 10 minutes downhill and find themselves in the heart of Charlotte Amalie. The premises were built in the 1860s by the Simmonds family and later expanded and improved by the Petersen family, Danish emigrés and fishers. During a late 1990s renovation, fresh coats of pale yellow and green paint were applied to its exterior and improvements were made to the steeply sloping 1-acre garden dotted with venerable mango trees. The rooms are cozy and soothing, filled with a mix of genuine antiques and new but traditional furniture. Mattresses are state-of-the-art, and some of the beds are in the romantic plantation style with four posters. The baths are a bit small. In the back garden is a six-sided pool, and the 150-year-old kitchen is the site of breakfast every morning. No other formalized meals are served, unless you request that someone prepare and cook one of the fish you might've caught during a deep-sea expedition. There's a library and a small TV lounge as well.

Worth a Splurge

Best Western Carib Beach Resort. 70-C Lindbergh Bay, St. Thomas, U.S.V.I. 00801. ☎ **800/792-2742** in the U.S., or 340/774-2525. Fax 340/777-4131. 66 units. A/C TV. Winter $119–$139 single; $129–$159 double. Off-season $89–$129 single or double. Children 11 and under stay free in parents' room. AE, MC, V.

About a 3-minute walk from Lindbergh Bay with its good beach, this Best Western is recommendable for its affordable air-conditioned ocean-view rooms with private terraces. It's not the fanciest place on the island but is preferred to its sibling, the Emerald Beach. The rooms aren't large but are adequately comfortable, each with a refrigerator, one queen or two double beds with comfortable mattresses, and a small bath. This hotel is often a favorite with business travelers but is equally suitable for vacationers. There's a well-patronized pool, plus a restaurant and bar. Dinner is served only in winter; otherwise, guests are shuttled free to the Emerald Beach Resort.

Island Beachcomber Hotel. P.O. Box 302579, Lindbergh Bay, St. Thomas, U.S.V.I. 00803. ☎ **800/982-9898** in the U.S., or 340/774-5250. Fax 340/774-5615. 47 units. A/C TV TEL. Winter $125–$140 single; $130–$145 double. Off-season $95–$110 single; $100–$115 double. Children $20 extra. AE, DC, DISC, MC, V.

Near the airport, this rather standard hotel has long been known for its affordable rates and beach-party atmosphere. There's a Tahitian aura to the place, with tropical foliage, bird cages, bridges, and thatched umbrellas. The inn received a lot of publicity when *Caribbean Travel & Life* rated it as one of the 10 most affordable properties in the West Indies. The inn has been run by the same family for some four decades and enjoys a faithful clientele. The medium-size rooms are clean and well maintained, though their furnishings are a bit worn. They have louvered doors and jalousies, refrigerators, excellent lighting, and ceiling fans. The standard rooms contain two double beds, while the superiors are fitted with single king-size beds. Attracting locals as well as visitors, a decent beachfront restaurant serves a reasonably priced but standard cuisine. The beach bar can be fun if the crowd's right. Lounge chairs and rafts are free to guests. There's a free shuttle to town.

GREAT DEALS ON DINING

The cuisine on St. Thomas is among the top in the entire West Indies. But prices are high, and many of the best spots can be reached only by taxi. With a few exceptions, the finest and most charming restaurants aren't in Charlotte Amalie but out on the island. However, the town does offer the best options for budget travelers.

If you're in a villa, an apartment, or a condo rental, patronize the **Pueblo supermarkets.** You'll find them across from the Havensight Mall (where the cruise ships dock), at the Sub Base, and also at the Lockhart Gardens and Four Winds shopping centers.

IN CHARLOTTE AMALIE

✪ **Bumpa's.** 38-A Waterfront. ☎ **340/776-5674.** Main courses $4–$6.50. No credit cards. Daily 7am–6pm. Closed Sept. AMERICAN.

This open-air deli joint is on the second level of a little old West Indian house with a canvas-roof porch offering a panoramic harbor view. It isn't that special but is an ideal choice for a filling, low-priced breakfast or lunch. The shopping hordes find this a favorite refueling stop. The cook prepares a fresh soup for lunch, and you can also get sandwiches and freshly made salads. Many patrons stop in just to order Ben & Jerry's ice cream, one of the homemade pies, or a refreshing lemonade on a hot day.

Diamond Barrel. 18 Norre Gade. ☎ **340/774-5071.** Main courses $7–$13. No credit cards. Daily 6am–6pm. AMERICAN/WEST INDIAN.

This popular local eatery and hangout is active throughout the day. The décor (what there is of it) is appropriately nautical, with rattan pieces and murals of sealife. Breakfast is fairly standard, but at lunch you can sample good regional fare like the catch of the day and various chicken dishes. You might begin with the oxtail soup or whatever's in the kettle that day. If you want to go really local, opt for the stewed mutton or pickled pigs' feet, though you might settle more happily for the salmon patties. On site is a bakery providing fresh pastries and other baked goods. Expect cafeteria-style service with simple tables where you can eat your meal.

✪ **Gladys's Café.** Royal Dane Mall. ☎ **340/774-6604.** Reservations required for parties of 4 or more. Main courses $6.95–$12.95; breakfast $2.50–$6.95. AE, MC, V. Mon–Thurs and Sat 6:30am–4pm, Fri 6:30am–midnight, Sun 8am–2pm. WEST INDIAN/AMERICAN.

Antigua-born Gladys Isles worked at the Palm Passage for years as a waitress, but when she developed a following that demanded so much of her time, she decided to open her own place. Gladys is a warm, gracious woman who makes a visit here all the more special. Her cafe is housed in a 1700 pump house with a stonework courtyard that has a well (one of only three on the island) in the middle. Considering the portions, quality, and price, her breakfast is the best value in town. The lunch offerings are various sandwiches, salads, and fresh seafood, like excellent swordfish and dumplings. The house specialty is hot chicken salad made with pieces of sautéed breasts with red-wine vinegar, pine nuts, and dill weed, all nestled on a bed of lettuce. Dinner is served only on Friday, when a popular jazz band plays 8pm to midnight. Try a local lobster, shrimp, fresh pasta, fresh fish, or perfect steaks.

✪ **The Green House.** Veterans Dr. ☎ **340/774-7998.** Main courses $10.95–$23.95. AE, DISC, MC, V. Daily 11:30am–2am. AMERICAN/CARIBBEAN.

Fronted with big sunny windows, this waterfront restaurant attracts cruise-ship passengers who've shopped and need a place to drop. The food isn't the island's best but is satisfying if you're not too demanding. Many diners drop in during the afternoon to sample one of the tasty omelets, especially the Caribbean Creole three-egg concoction. The house specializes in chicken, often with exotic fruit flavors like mango-banana chicken and coconut chicken. Appetizers are often good enough to make a meal by themselves, ranging from conch fritters to stuffed jalapeño peppers. A kettle of soup is always on the stove. You can also make a meal of the fresh salads, perhaps Jamaican jerk chicken or pasta salad primavera. What's most popular on the menu? The big, juicy burgers made with Angus beef. There's also a wide selection of seafood and chef's specialties like slow-roasted and wood-smoked baby-back ribs. On Wednesday and Friday you can hear live reggae music; on other nights, it's the sounds selected by a DJ.

Hard Rock Cafe. In International Plaza, the Waterfront. ☎ **340/777-5555.** Main courses $8.99–$17.99. AE, MC, V. Mon–Sat 10am–9pm, Sun 10am–3pm. AMERICAN.

Occupying the second floor of a pink-sided mall whose big windows overlook the ships moored in the harbor, this restaurant is a member of the international chain that defines itself as the Smithsonian of Rock 'n' Roll. Entire walls are devoted to the memorabilia of John Lennon, Eric Clapton, Bob Marley, and others. Throughout most of the day the place functions as a restaurant, serving barbecued meats, salads, sandwiches, burgers (including a well-flavored veggie burger), fresh fish, steaks, and the best fajitas in the Virgin Islands. On Friday and Saturday a live band performs, at which time a small dance floor gets busy and the bar trade picks up considerably.

✪ **Little Bopeep.** Barberl Plaza. ☎ **340/774-1959.** Main courses $5.50–$11.95. No credit cards. Mon–Sat 7:30–11am (takeout only) and 11:30am–4pm. CARIBBEAN.

This little tavern serves up some of the best West Indian food on the island. The menu changes daily, and no one puts on any airs. Breakfast is strictly takeout, but it's the least expensive morning meal in town. You can order meat patties and sandwiches such as egg, bacon, and cheese. Lunch (the only main meal of the day served) gets more intriguing and a lot spicier, with jerk chicken (a secret recipe), curried chicken, and curried conch. Fried plantains accompany most dishes.

Pizza Amore. 18 Estate Thomas. ☎ **340/774-2822.** Meals $5–$23. No credit cards. Mon–Sat 11am–8pm, Sun 11am–5pm. PIZZA/SANDWICHES/SALADS.

This small pizzeria is decorated with an Italian motif, including posters of Italian coffees and wines. The booths, tables, and chairs are all made from maple, and the floor is brick. They serve New York–style pizza with a wide range of toppings. They also offer salads and sandwiches—salami, ham, and heros on French loaves. Round out your meal with an espresso or a cappuccino.

Tickles Dockside Pub. Crown Bay Marina. ☎ **340/776-1595.** Main courses $7–$21.50; lunch $7–$12. DC, MC, V. Daily 6am–10pm. AMERICAN.

Tickles is dedicated to the concept of comfort and reasonably priced food in a friendly atmosphere. Diners at this open-air restaurant can relax while watching the sailboats and cruise ships on the water. The menu offers a simple American fare of burgers (like a chicken burger) and sandwiches (like a Reuben made with your choice of ham, turkey, or corned beef, grilled with Tickles's special Russian dressing, Swiss cheese, and sauerkraut). Start with a plate of "gator eggs" (lightly breaded jalapeño peppers stuffed with cheese) or the "sweet lips" (strips of sweet fried chicken in the shape of lips with honey-mustard sauce). If you're in the mood for seafood, you may want to try the fish-and-chips, beer-battered white fish fried and served with Swiss-fried potatoes. Vegetarians delight in the burger made just for them, and the cooks also turn out an array of American classics like chicken Alfredo, prime ribs, baby-back ribs, and fried catfish.

Worth a Splurge

Randy's Wine Bar & Bistro. In Al Cohen's Plaza, 4002 Raphune Hill. ☎ **340/775-5001.** Main courses $15.95–$30.95; lunch $6.95–$12.95. AE, MC, V. Bistro, daily 9am–1am; deli, daily 9am–5pm. CONTINENTAL.

This is an oddity, catering to deli devotees (usually from New York), cigar aficionados, and bistro fans. As one local customer, who goes here every day, said to us, "It's anything you want it to be." The store sells a good selection of wines, along with the standard liquors and cigars. If you don't like the bistro wine list, you can buy a wine from the store and bring it into the bistro, though you'll pay a $5 corkage fee. The deli serves the usual sandwiches and salads, while the bistro dishes up a delectable cuisine, especially if you stick to the fresh fish, steak, and lobster. Look for the daily specials, like pork tenderloin in Dijon mustard sauce. At lunch you might want to try the portobello mushroom sandwich marinated in balsamic vinegar with basil mayonnaise, or the Carnegie Reuben with half a pound of meat. For dinner, shrimp scampi is always a favorite. Tuesday night brings out locals eager to sample the prime rib.

Zorba's Cafe. 1854 Hus, Government Hill. ☎ **340/776-0444.** Main courses $15–$25; lunch $8–$15. AE, MC, V. Mon–Thurs 10:30am–3:30pm and 6–10pm, Fri–Sat 10:30am–3:30pm and 6–10:30pm, Sun 6–10pm. GREEK.

If you're in the mood for Greek food, head here. Jimmy Boukas is the owner of this casual place in a 19th-century building at the heart of town. Guests may sit in the courtyard surrounded by banana and palm trees. We highly recommend the *spanikopita* (spinach-and-feta pie), the *moussaka* (eggplant casserole), and the gyros, but be sure to save room for the homemade baklava. On our recent rounds, we found the tastiest treats to be the Greek lemon chicken and the perfectly seasoned tender Greek-style lamb shanks.

At Frenchtown

Between the harbor and the airport on the outskirts of Charlotte Amalie, you'll find the **Frenchtown Deli,** in the Frenchtown Mall (☎ 340/776-7211). Home-baked breads, fresh salads, and beer, soda, and wine are sold. Some of the island's best and thickest sandwiches are served here, and their Green Mountain coffee is the best. Full-service breakfasts begin at $2.95, with lunches also starting at $2.95. Most dinners are $14.95 and that's for two, making this *the* bargain of St. Thomas. You can eat your dinner on the premises or else take it out. Hours are Monday to Friday 6am to 10pm, Saturday 6:30am to 5pm, and Sunday 9am to 5pm. It's a good place to stock up on supplies if you've rented a place with a kitchenette or would like the makings of a picnic.

Hook, Line & Sinker. 2 Honduras, Frenchtown. ☎ **340/776-9708.** Main courses $7.25–$20; lunch $6–$10; brunch (Sun) $6–$11. AE, MC, V. Mon–Sat 7–10am, 11:30am–4pm, and 6–10pm; Sun 10am–2:30pm. AMERICAN.

Both locals and visitors flock to this rendezvous, where they get friendly service, good food at reasonable prices, and a panoramic harbor view. The setting evokes a New England seaport village, and the restaurant has a pitched roof and skylights, along with wraparound French doors and windows. A *Cheers*-like crowd frequents the bar. Breakfast, except for Sunday brunch, is the standard old menu, but at lunch you can try everything from Caesar salad to various grilled chicken dishes. The dinner menu is usually a delight. The new chef devotes more time to preparing seafood than previous cooks did here—wait until you sample his mango-rum tuna, jerk swordfish inspired by Jamaica, or yellowtail in banana curry sauce or stuffed with mushrooms and red peppers and covered in garlic sauce. Locals call his soups outrageous: They're more like hearty stews, as exemplified by the sausage-and-potato combo.

In Red Hook

Duffy's Love Shack. 650 Red Hook Plaza, Rte. 38. ☎ **340/779-2080.** Main courses $9.25–$14. No credit cards. Daily 11am–2am. AMERICAN/CARIBBEAN.

This is a happening place if you like to mingle with locals. As the evening wears on, they become the entertainment, often dancing on tables or forming conga lines. Yes, it also serves food, a standard American cuisine given Caribbean flair and flavor. The restaurant is open-air with lots of bamboo and a thatched roof, the quintessential island look. Even the menu appears on a bamboo stick like an old-fashioned fan. Start with a Caribbean eggroll or black-bean cakes, then roll on to cowboy steak or voodoo pineapple chicken (in hot garlic-and-pineapple sauce). Surf and turf here translates as jerk tenderloin and mahi mahi. After 10pm, the stove-pot cookery is dropped and a late-night menu appears, mostly sandwiches. The bar business is huge, and the bartender is known for his lethal rum drinks.

Grateful Deli & Coffee Shop. 6500 Red Hook Plaza, Suite 125. ☎ **340/775-5160.** Sandwiches and burgers $5.95–$7.95. AE, MC, V. Mon–Sat 7am–6pm. AMERICAN DELI.

Across from the ferry dock, this is the most affordable joint for breakfast or dinner. The breakfast menu lists the usuals, but also designer omelets and glazed waffles with strawberries and whipped cream. Sometimes you can get low-cost regional fare at lunch, including stewed chicken with rice or vegetable lasagna, and even pumpkin or black-bean soup. But most people want one of the sandwiches, which are Red Hook's, or even the island's, finest—everything from Black Forest ham with Saga bleu cheese to a triple-decker club with pastrami, corned beef, and Swiss cheese. Each day 12 salads are made. You might also opt for the Greek pasta with feta cheese, olives, and sweet peppers.

Señor Pizza. Red Hook (across from St. John ferry dock). ☎ **340/775-3030.** Pizza $1.75 (slice) to $18 (supreme). No credit cards. Mon–Sat 11am–9pm, Sun noon–9pm. PIZZA.

Red Hook's best pizzas are served here; the generous slices are practically a lunch unto themselves. If you're staying in a place nearby, the staff will deliver, or you can settle into one of the on-site picnic tables. If you're not in the mood for pizza, try one of the tasty calzones.

Wok & Roll. 6200 Smith Bay, Red Hook. ☎ **340/775-6246.** Main courses $3.75–$9. No credit cards. Mon–Thurs 11am–10pm, Fri–Sat 11am–10:30pm, Sun 5–10pm. CHINESE.

Across from the dock for the St. John ferry, this small Chinese restaurant (below the Warehouse Bar) is housed in a cinder-block building with a blue roof. A patio seats about 25 people, but the majority of the business is takeout. The restaurant serves typical Asian dishes like chow mein and sweet-and-sour pork, along with specials like Shanghai spring rolls, shrimp in lobster sauce, and Hong Kong lo mein. The famous dish here is the crab Rangoon. Newly added to the menu is calamari in black bean sauce.

EN ROUTE TO THE EAST END

Polli's. Tillet Gardens, 4125 Anna's Retreat, Route 38, midway between Red Hook and Charlotte Amalie. ☎ **340/775-4550.** Lunch main courses $6–$13.95; dinner main courses $7–$14.95. AE, DC, MC, V. Mon–Thurs 11:30am–9:30pm; Fri–Sat 11:30am–10:30pm. TEX-MEX.

The setting for this likable restaurant is an open garden-style pavilion near a splashing fountain and adjacent to a collection of arts and crafts boutiques. Named and modeled after a similar restaurant in Hawaii, it features a roster of frozen margaritas and especially a golden margarita (with Cuervo Gold and Galliani liqueur; $5 each) that seems tailor-made to precede a Tex-Mex meal. Menu items are among the most savory and flavorful Mexican food on St. Thomas. Examples are fajitas (made with your choice of beef, chicken, seafood, or tofu); burritos supreme; seafood enchilada platters; fajita quesadillas; and some of the best-priced and juiciest steaks on the island. Children's plates, including tacos and cheese quesadillas or enchiladas, are also dished up.

AT BOLONGO & COWPET BAYS

Iggie's Restaurant. At the Bolongo Bay Beach Club, Bolongo Bay, 50 Estate Bolongo (Rte. 30). ☎ **340/775-1800.** Burgers and sandwiches $7.95–$9.95; main courses $9.95–$15.95. AE, MC, V. Daily noon–3pm and 6:30–10pm. AMERICAN/CONTINENTAL.

Sports fans and others patronize this action-packed seaside place—with giant TVs broadcasting the latest games, it's the island's best sports bar and grill. To make things even livelier, karaoke sing-alongs are staged. The place has indestructible furniture, lots of electronic action, and an aggressively informal crowd. Bring the kids along; no one will mind if they make a ruckus. The menu is geared to such kid favorites as burgers, oversized sandwiches, and pastas. It changes nightly, and often there's a theme name, such as "lobster night" or "Italian night." Most popular is "carnival night," when a West Indian all-you-can-eat buffet is served along with a limbo show. You can call to find out what the special theme nights are. Try one of the sudsy tropical drinks, like Iggie's Queen (coconut cream, crème de Noya, and rum), or the Ultimate Kamikazi, the ingredients of which are a secret.

Jerry's Beachfront Bar & Restaurant. In the Anchorage Condos (next to the St. Thomas Yacht Club), Cowpet Bay. ☎ **340/779-2462.** Reservations recommended in winter. Main courses $8–$15; set-price menu $21.95. AE, MC, V. Daily 10am–10pm, Sun brunch 11am–3pm. ITALIAN/SEAFOOD.

This is a refreshing waterside spot for a meal near the East End. The décor includes lots of exposed much-weathered wood, a color scheme of blue and white, and a large bar where nobody seems to mind dallying a bit before a table becomes available. The owners—veterans and survivors of several other popular waterfront eateries around the island—are proud of such lunch specialties as seafood bisque, soup of the day, parmesan sandwiches, hoagies, meatball heros, and Caesar salads. Evening meals are more elaborate and, in most cases, more leisurely. Look for well-prepared dishes like shrimp Sambuca, pasta bayou (with andouille sausages, shrimp, and smoked Gouda in creamy pink sauce), barbecued baby-back ribs, shrimp scampi, and both red and white versions of conch and scampi. Naturally, the drinks are potent enough to encourage you to linger.

ON THE NORTH COAST

✪ **Eunice's Terrace.** 6667 Smith Bay, Rte. 38. ☎ **340/775-3975.** Main courses $10.25–$29.95. AE, MC, V. Mon–Sat 11am–10pm, Sun 5–10pm. CARIBBEAN/AMERICAN.

A 30-minute taxi ride east of the airport is one of the best-known local restaurants, which went from a simple shack to a modern building. A collection of locals and visitors crowd in for generous platters of savory island food. A popular drink is the Queen Mary (tropical fruits laced with dark rum). This little restaurant made news around the world in January 1997 when President and Hillary Clinton dined here. They shared a conch appetizer; he then opted for a local fish (ole wife) while the First Lady had the grilled vegetable plate. Dinner specialties are conch fritters, broiled or fried fish (especially dolphin), sweet-potato pie, and a number of specials usually served with fungi, rice, or plantains. On the lunch menu are fishburgers, sandwiches, and daily specials like Virgin Islands doved pork or mutton. (Doving involves baking sliced meat while basting it with its own juices, tomato paste, Kitchen Bouquet, and island herbs.) Key lime pie is a favorite dessert.

IN & AROUND THE SUB BASE

Texas Pit BBQ. Sub Base. ☎ **340/776-9579.** Main courses $6–$10; combination platters $12–$15. No credit cards. Daily 6am–midnight. BARBECUE.

The owners hail from Texas, where they know not only how to barbecue but how to make a fiery sauce to wake up your palate . . . and everything else. This is just a take-away stand with no place to sit and eat, but locals flock here. It's been around for nearly two decades, and in spite of hurricanes is still going strong. Chicken, tender ribs, or Texas-style beef are dished up in cowboy-size portions, along with the usual accompaniments of rice, coleslaw, and potato salad. One local pronounced the ribs here the island's best, but we're still sampling other places before coming up with a final verdict.

NEAR MAFOLIE HILL

Ferrari's. Route 33/Crown Mountain Road. ☎ **340/774-6800.** Reservations recommended. Main courses $13–$30. AE, MC, V. Wed–Mon 5–10pm. ITALIAN.

Built in the 1950s on some of the island's highest terrain, in an isolated but panoramic spot whose view sweeps out over Magens Bay, this restaurant serves an assortment of well-prepared Italian-American foods. In polls conducted by the *USVI Daily News*, readers consistently vote this restaurant the best for value on the island. You might enjoy a drink or two amid the Chianti bottles and Italian flags of the bar area before heading on to a maroon-and-cream-colored dining room. Menu items include staples like spaghetti with seafood, Black Angus New York strip steak, veal scallopine, and chicken and eggplant parmigiana. All dishes are deftly handled by a skilled kitchen staff, most of whom have trained in Europe or the United States. The bar is open Wednesday to Monday 4 to 11:30pm.

Sibs Mountain Bar & Restaurant. Mafolie Hill. ☎ **340/774-8967.** Main courses $7–$22. AE, MC, V. Daily 5–10pm; bar daily 4pm–4am. AMERICAN.

Older residents of St. Thomas remember this place as a social fixture that was called Sibilly's Bar when it was first built of concrete and wood in 1927. In recent times, it received an update from new owners who added another dining area in back, hooked up some of the biggest TV screens on the island, and shortened its name to Sibs. Today, it combines an ongoing presentation of sports events with pool tables and electronic bar games. No one will mind if you stay in the front bar soaking up the sweaty athleticism of the place, but if you're hungry, a rear dining room offers a terrace and views that sweep out over the Charlotte Amalie. Menu items are generously proportioned and well seasoned and include burgers, some of the best ribs in St. Thomas, pastas, pizzas, and fresh fish.

PICNIC FARE & WHERE TO EAT IT

You can create a successful picnic with the culinary expertise of the **Cream and Crumb Shop,** Building 6, Havensight Mall (☎ **340/774-2499**), open daily 6:30am to 5pm. Located at the point where most cruise ships dock for day excursions onto St. Thomas, this cheerful modern shop is easy to miss amid the crush of tax-free jewelers and perfume shops. The thick deli sandwiches ($4.95 to $6.95), fresh salads (shrimp, chicken, potato, or crabmeat), and homemade pastries are all excellent. The shop also specializes in pizza and serves frozen yogurt and ice cream—these may not be the most practical picnic items, but they're still awfully good. With these ingredients, you can head for your favorite beach. We recommend **Magens Bay** not just for its beauty but for its picnic tables too. Other ideal spots are **Drake's Seat** or any of the secluded **high-altitude panoramas** along the island's western end.

HITTING THE BEACHES

Chances are, your hotel will be right on the beach or very close to one, and this is where you'll plop down on the sands for most of your stay. All the beaches in the Virgin Islands are public, and most lie anywhere from 2 to 5 miles from Charlotte Amalie.

THE NORTH SIDE Less than a mile long, ✪ **Magens Bay** lies between two mountains 3 miles north of the capital. Named one of the world's 10 most beautiful beaches, it charges $1 per person and $1 per car. The waters are calm and ideal for swimming; the bottom is flat and sandy, so this beach is better for swimming than snorkeling. Changing facilities are available, and snorkeling gear and lounge chairs can be rented, as can paddleboats and kayaks. There's no public transportation to reach it; from Charlotte Amalie, take Route 35 north all the way. The gates to the beach are open daily 6am to 6pm (after 4pm you'll need insect repellent). The beach is terribly overcrowded on cruise-ship days (which is virtually any day), but the crowds thin in midafternoon. If you'd like to flash your wares, as many locals do, you can follow a marked trail to **Little Magens Bay,** a separate beach reserved for nude bathers. This beach is especially popular with gay and lesbian visitors; it's also the preferred beach for President Clinton when he takes his annual vacation in St. Thomas (no, he doesn't go nude). Don't bring valuables to this beach and certainly don't leave anything of value in your parked car. There have been break-ins of cars and a few isolated muggings.

In the northeast near Coral World, **Coki Point Beach** is good but gets terribly crowded when cruise ships are in port. This beach is noted for its crystal-clear warm water, along with thousands of rainbow-hued fish swimming among the beautiful corals. This beach is of gently sloping white sand, ideal for swimming, and there's a panoramic view of offshore Thatch Cay. Snorkelers are attracted here, as are pick-pockets, so protect your valuables. Concessions here can arrange everything from waterskiing to parasailing. Locals sell small bags of fish food if you'd like to feed the sea creatures when you do your snorkeling. There's excellent snorkeling right offshore. An East End bus runs to Smith Bay and lets you off at the gate to Coral World and Coki.

Also on the north side is the **Renaissance Grand Beach Resort,** one of the island's most beautiful. Many water sports are available at this beach, which opens onto Smith Bay and is near Coral World. The beach lies right off Route 38 and fronts this deluxe resort.

THE SOUTH SIDE   On the south side near the Marriott Frenchman's Reef Beach Resort, **Morningstar** lies about 2 miles east of Charlotte Amalie. This is where you can wear your most daring swimwear, as do many of the habitués who flock here. They're often young people (a large percentage gay) who work on the cruise ships. You can rent sailboats, snorkeling equipment, and lounge chairs. The beach can easily be reached by a cliff-front elevator at Frenchman's Reef.

Limetree Beach is set against a backdrop of sea grape trees and shady palms. It lures those who want a serene spread of sand where they can bask in the sun and even feed hibiscus blossoms to iguanas. You can rent snorkeling gear, lounge and beach chairs, and towels. Cool drinks are served, including a Limetree green piña colada. There's no public transportation, but the beach can easily be reached by taxi from Charlotte Amalie.

Brewer's Bay is one of the island's most popular beaches, lying in the southwest near the University of the Virgin Islands (students often come here to swim between classes). This beach of white coral sand is almost as long as the beach at Magens Bay. Unfortunately, this is not the place to come for snorkeling. Light meals and drinks are served at stands along the beach. From Charlotte Amalie, take the Fortuna bus heading west. Get off at the edge of Brewers Bay, across from the Reichhold Center, the cultural center of St. Thomas.

Lindbergh Beach, with a lifeguard, toilet facilities, and a bathhouse, lies at the Island Beachcomber Hotel and is used extensively by the locals, who sometimes stage political rallies here as well as carnival parties. Drinks, such as piña coladas, are served on the beach. It's not good for snorkeling. Take the Fortuna bus route west from Charlotte Amalie.

THE EAST END   Small and special, **Secret Harbour** lies near a collection of condos whose owners you'll meet on the beach. With its white sand and coconut palms, it's a living cliché of Caribbean charm. The snorkeling near the rocks is some of the best on the island. No public transportation stops here, but it's an easy taxi ride east of Charlotte Amalie heading toward Red Hook.

One of the finest on St. Thomas, ✪ **Sapphire Beach** is set against the backdrop of the desirable Doubletree Sapphire Beach Resort & Marina, where you can have lunch or order drinks. Windsurfers like it a lot, and snorkeling gear and lounge chairs can be rented. A large reef is found close to the shore, and there are good views of offshore cays and St. John. The beach of fine white coral sand opens onto beautiful bay views. To reach it, you can take the East End bus from Charlotte Amalie, going via Red Hook. Ask to be let off at the entrance to Sapphire Bay; it's not too far to walk from here to the water.

Although not long, **Lindquist Beach** is one of the island's prettiest, with a lovely strip of white sand. It lies between the Sugar Bay Beach Resort and the Sapphire Beach Resort.

High Society on the High Seas: The Best Day Cruises

The biggest charter business in the Caribbean is done by Virgin Islanders. On St. Thomas most of the business centers around the Red Hook and Yacht Haven marinas.

The easiest way to go to sea is to charter a yacht, with captain, for the day from *Yacht Nightwind,* Sapphire Marina (☎ 340/775-4110, 24 hours) for only $95 per person. You're granted a full-day sail starting with continental breakfast and including a champagne buffet lunch and an open bar aboard this 50-foot yawl. You're also given free snorkeling equipment and instruction and you visit St. John and the outer islands.

New Horizons, 6501 Red Hook Plaza, Suite 16, Red Hook (☎ 340/775-1171), offers windborne excursions amid the cays and reefs of the Virgin Islands. This two-masted 63-foot ketch has circumnavigated the globe and been used as a design prototype for other boats. Owned/operated by Canadian Tim Krygsveld, it contains a hot-water shower, serves a specialty drink called a New Horizons Nooner (with a melon-liqueur base), and carries a complete line of snorkeling equipment for adults and children. A full-day excursion, with a hot Italian buffet and an open bar, is $90 per person; children 2 to 12, when accompanied by an adult, cost $45. Excursions depart daily, weather permitting, from the Doubletree Sapphire Beach Resort & Marina. Call ahead for reservations and information. The outfitter has recently expanded with another vessel, *New Horizons II,* a 44-foot custom-made speedboat taking you to some of the most scenic highlights of the British Virgin Islands, costing $110 for adults or $85 for children (2 to 12) for the all-day trip. *New Horizons* also operates **Power Trips** next door, renting out 25-foot Wellcrafts for $245 per day for up to eight people. The boats have fuel-efficient engines and can make it to any of the 10 islands in the vicinity

The setting is so photogenic many films and TV commercials have used this beach as a backdrop. It's not likely to be crowded, as it's not very well known.

SPORTS & OUTDOOR PURSUITS

FITNESS CENTERS   The most reasonably priced club on the island is the **Bayside Fitness Center,** 7140 Bolongo (☎ 340/693-2600), part of the Bolongo Beach complex. The club offers weights, cardio, treadmills, and a sauna. The cost of a day pass is $10 for nonguests; otherwise free to guests of the Bolongo complex. Hours are Monday to Friday 6am to 9pm and Saturday and Sunday 8am to 5pm.

GOLF   On the north shore, **Mahogany Run,** Mahogany Run Road (☎ 800/253-7103 or 340/775-6006), is an 18-hole, par-70 course that President Clinton pronounced very challenging. This beautiful course rises and drops like a roller coaster on its journey to the sea, where cliffs and crashing sea waves are the ultimate hazards at the 13th and 14th holes. Greens fees are $85 for 18 holes, reduced to $75 in the late afternoon, depending on the daylight available. Carts cost $15 year-round.

HORSE & PONY TOURS   **Half Moon Stables** (☎ 340/777-6088) offers hour-long guided horse and pony tours of the East End, exploring areas of the island rarely seen from safari tour buses or rental cars. Riders go along a secluded trail winding through lush green hills to a pebble-covered beach. The cost is $45 per person hourly. Western or English saddles are available.

of St. Thomas. The outfitter also offers dive and fishing equipment and will supply a captain upon request.

You can avoid the crowds by sailing aboard the *Fantasy* (☎ **340/775-5652;** fax 340/775-6256), which is docked at 6700 Sapphire Village, no. 253, and departs from the American Yacht Harbor at Red Hook at 9:30am daily. It sails to St. John and nearby islands, allowing a maximum of six passengers to go swimming, snorkeling, beachcombing, and trolling. Snorkel gear with expert instruction is provided, as is a champagne lunch. An underwater camera is available. The cost of a full-day trip is $95 per person. A full-day trip to Jost Van Dyke is also offered for $95 per person, including a B.V.I. Customs charge of $15 (no lunch). A half-day sail, morning or afternoon, lasts 3 hours and costs $65. Sunset tours are also popular, with an open bar and hors d'oeuvres, costing $50 per person.

Remember Grace Kelly and Bing Crosby crooning a duet in *High Society?* The *True Love,* 6501 Red Hook Plaza, Suite 54 (☎ **340/779-6547,** 24 hours), a sleek coast guard–certified 54-foot Malabar schooner, is the very same yacht featured in the classic 1956 film. No longer just for lovers, the craft sails daily from the Doubletree Sapphire Marina for $95 per person. Included in the price is a gourmet lunch, open bar, snorkeling equipment, and lessons.

⭕ **American Yacht Harbor,** Red Hook (☎ **340/775-6454**), offers both bareboat and fully crewed charters. It does so from a colorful yacht-filled harbor set against a backdrop of Heritage Gade, a reproduction of a Caribbean village. The harbor is home to numerous boat companies, including day-trippers, fishing boats, and sailing charters. There are also four restaurants on the property, serving everything from continental to Caribbean cuisine.

KAYAK TOURS Virgin Island Ecotours (☎ **340/779-2155** for information) offers 2½-hour kayak trips through a mangrove lagoon on the southern coastline. The tour, which costs $50 per person, is led by professional naturalists who allow enough time for 30 minutes of snorkeling.

SCUBA DIVING & SNORKELING With 30 spectacular reefs just off St. Thomas, the U.S. Virgins are rated as one of the most beautiful areas in the world by *Skin Diver* magazine.

The ⭕ **St. Thomas Diving Club,** 7147 Bolongo Bay (☎ **800/538-7348** or 340/776-2381), is a full-service, PADI five-star IDC center, the best on the island. An open-water certification course, including four scuba dives, costs $385. An advanced open-water certification course, including five dives that can be accomplished in 2 days, goes for $275. Every Thursday, participants are taken on an all-day scuba excursion that includes a two-tank dive to the wreck of the *HMS Rhone* in the British Virgin Islands, costing $110. A scuba tour of the 350-foot wreck of the *Witshoal* is featured every Saturday for experienced divers only. You can also enjoy local snorkeling for $30.

DIVE IN!, in the Doubletree Sapphire Beach Resort & Marina, Smith Bay Road, Route 36 (☎ **800/524-2090** or 340/775-6100), is a complete diving center offering some of the finest diving services in the U.S. Virgin Islands, including professional instruction (beginner to advanced), daily beach and boat dives, custom dive packages, underwater photography and videotapes, snorkeling trips, and a full-service PADI dive center. An introductory course costs $60, with a one-tank dive going for $55 and two-tank dives for $70. A six-dive pass is $195.

TENNIS The best tennis on the island is at the ✪ **Wyndham Sugar Bay Beach Club,** 6500 Estate Smith Bay (☎ **340/777-7100**), which has the Virgin Island's first stadium tennis court, seating 220, plus six additional Laykold courts lit at night. The cost is $8 an hour. There's also a pro shop.

Another good resort for tennis is the **Bolongo Bay Beach Resort,** Bolongo Bay (☎ **340/775-1800**), which has two tennis courts that are lit until 10pm. They're free to members and hotel guests, but cost $10 for nonguests. At the **Marriott Frenchman's Reef Tennis Courts,** Flamboyant Point (☎ **340/776-8500,** ext. 444), four courts are available, and nonguests are charged $10 an hour per court. Lights stay on until 10pm.

WINDSURFING This increasingly popular sport is available at the major resort hotels and at some public beaches, including Brewer's Bay, Morningstar Beach, and Limetree Beach. The **Renaissance Grand Beach Resort,** Smith Bay Road, Route 38 (☎ **340/775-1510**), is the major hotel offering windsurfing, with rentals costing $20 per hour.

SEEING THE SIGHTS
CHARLOTTE AMALIE

The capital of St. Thomas, Charlotte Amalie, where most visitors begin their sight-seeing on this small island, has all the color and charm of an authentic Caribbean waterfront town. In days of yore, seafarers from all over the globe flocked to this old-world Danish town, as did pirates and members of the Confederacy, who used the port during the American Civil War. (Sadly, St. Thomas was the biggest slave market in the world.)

The old warehouses once used for storing pirate goods still stand and, for the most part, house today's shops. In fact, the main streets (called *Gade,* because of the islands' Danish heritage) are now a virtual shopping mall and usually packed. (See "Shopping" for our specific recommendations.) Sandwiched among these shops are a few historic buildings, most of which can be covered on foot in about 2 hours.

Before starting your tour, stop off in the so-called **Grand Hotel,** near Emancipation Park. No longer a hotel, it contains, along with shops, a **visitor center,** Tolbod Gade 1 (☎ **340/774-8784**), that's open Monday to Friday 8am to 5pm and Saturday 8am to noon.

Fort Christian. In the town center. ☎ **340/776-4566.** Free admission. Mon–Fri 8:30am–4:30pm.

Most visitors explore Charlotte Amalie to shop rather than to look at historic buildings; however, they can't miss this imposing structure dating from 1672 and dominating the center of town. Named after the Danish king, Christian V, the fort has been everything from a governor's residence to a jail. The fort became a National Historic Landmark in 1977 but still functioned as a police station, court, and jail until 1983. Now a museum, the fort houses displays detailing the history of the island culture and its people, including the Danish settlement. Cultural workshops and turn-of-the-century furnishings are just some of the exhibits. A museum shop features local crafts, maps, and prints.

Seven Arches Museum. Government Hill. ☎ **340/774-9295.** Admission $5. Tues–Sat 10am–3pm or by appointment.

Browsers and gapers like to flood in here to take a look at the private home of long-time residents Philibert Fluck and Barbara Demaras. This is an 18th-century Danish house, completely restored to its original condition and furnished with West Indian antiques. You can walk through the yellow ballast arches and visit the great room with its view of the busiest harbor in the Caribbean. There are night-blooming cacti and iguanas on the roof of the slave quarters. The admission includes a cold tropical drink served in a walled garden filled with flowers.

Synagogue of Beracha Veshalom Vegmiluth Hasidim. 15 Crystal Gade. ☎ **340/774-4312.** Free admission. Mon–Fri 9am–4pm.

Its name in English means "Blessing, Peace, and Loving Deeds," and it's the oldest synagogue in continued use under the American flag and the second oldest in the Western Hemisphere. It still maintains the tradition of sand on the floor, commemorating the exodus from Egypt. Erected in 1833 by Sephardic Jews, it was built of local stone along with ballast brick from Denmark and mortar made of molasses and sand. Next door, the **Weibel Museum** showcases 300 years of Jewish history. It keeps the same hours.

ELSEWHERE ON THE ISLAND

West of Charlotte Amalie, Route 30 (Veterans Drive) will take you to **Frenchtown** (turn left at the sign to the Admirals Inn). This was settled by French-speaking people who were uprooted when the Swedes invaded and took over their homeland on St. Barts. Some of the people who live here today are the direct descendants of those long-ago immigrants.

This colorful village, many of whose residents engage in fishing, contains several interesting restaurants and taverns. Now that Charlotte Amalie has been deemed a dangerous place to be at night, Frenchtown has picked up the business, and it's the best choice for nighttime dancing, entertainment, and drinking.

✪ **Coral World Marine Park & Underwater Observatory.** 6450 Coki Point. ☎ **340/775-1555.** Admission $18 adults, $9 ages 3–12. Daily 9am–5:30pm.

This aquarium, a 20-minute drive from downtown off Route 38, is St. Thomas's number-one attraction, set in a 4½-acre park. It was destroyed by Hurricane Marilyn in 1995 but was rebuilt. The marine complex features a three-story underwater observation tower 100 feet offshore. Through windows you'll see sponges, fish, coral, and other underwater life in its natural state. In the Marine Gardens Aquarium, saltwater tanks display everything from sea horses to sea urchins. An 80,000-gallon reef tank features exotic marine life of the Caribbean; another tank is devoted to sea predators, with circling sharks and giant moray eels, among other creatures. The entrance is hidden behind a waterfall of cascading water.

The latest addition to the park is a semi-submersible that lets you enjoy the panoramic view and the underwater feeling of a submarine without truly submerging. Coral World's guests can take advantage of adjacent Coki Point Beach for snorkel rental, scuba lessons, or simply swimming and relaxing. Lockers and showers are available.

Also included in the marine park are a cafe, duty-free shops, and a tropical nature trail. Activities include daily fish and shark feedings and exotic bird shows.

Paradise Point Tramway. ☎ **340/774-9809.** Admission $12 per person round-trip, children half-price. Daily 9am–5pm.

This tramway, opened in 1994, affords visitors a dramatic view of Charlotte Amalie harbor on a ride to a 697-foot peak, though you'll pay dearly for the privilege. The tram operates four cars, each with a 10-person capacity, for the 15-minute round-trip ride. The tramways, similar to those used at ski resorts, transport customers from the Havensight area to Paradise Point, where riders disembark to visit shops and a popular restaurant and bar.

Estate St. Peter Greathouse Botanical Gardens. At the corner of Rte. 40 (6A St. Peter Mountain Rd.) and Barrett Hill Rd. ☎ **340/774-4999.** Admission $8 adults, $4 children. Daily 9am–4pm.

This estate consists of 11 acres at the foot of volcanic peaks on the northern rim of the island. It's laced with self-guided nature walks that'll acquaint you with some 200 varieties of plants and trees from all over the world, like an umbrella plant from Madagascar. From a panoramic deck you can see some 20 of the Virgin Islands, including Hans Lollick, an uninhabited island between Thatched Cay and Madahl Point. The house itself is worth a visit, its interior filled with art by locals.

A SUBMARINE RIDE

A major attraction is the ✪ *Atlantis* **submarine** (☎ **340/776-5650**), which takes you on a 1-hour voyage to depths of 90 feet, unfolding a world of exotic marine life. You'll gaze on coral reefs and sponge gardens through 2-foot windows in the air-conditioned sub, which carries 30 passengers. To board the submarine, you take a surface boat from the West Indies Dock, right outside Charlotte Amalie, to the *Atlantis,* which lies near Buck Island (the St. Thomas version, not the more famous Buck Island near St. Croix). The fare is $72 per person, or $36 ages 4 to 17. Children 3 and under aren't permitted. The *Atlantis* operates daily November to April and Tuesday to Saturday May to October. Hours and days vary depending on the arrival of cruise ships. Reservations are imperative: Get tickets at the Havensight Shopping Mall, Building 6, or call the number above.

SHOPPING

Shoppers not only have the benefits of St. Thomas's liberal duty-free allowances but also find well-known brand names at savings of up to 40% off U.S. mainland prices. However, to find true value, you often have to plow through a lot of junk. Many items—binoculars, stereos, watches, cameras—can be matched in price at your hometown discount store. Therefore, you need to know the prices back home to determine if you're making a savings.

Most of the shops, some of which occupy former pirate warehouses, are open Monday to Saturday 9am to 5pm; some stay open later. Nearly all stores close on Sunday and major holidays, unless a cruise ship is in port. Friday is the biggest cruise-ship visiting day at Charlotte Amalie (one day we counted eight at one time), so try to avoid shopping then.

Nearly all the major shopping on St. Thomas is along the harbor of Charlotte Amalie. Cruise-ship passengers mainly shop at the **Havensight Mall,** where they disembark at the eastern edge of Charlotte Amalie. The principal shopping street is **Main Street** or **Dronningens Gade** (its old Danish name). North of this street is another merchandise-loaded street called **Back Street** or **Vimmelskaft.**

Many shops are also spread along the **Waterfront Highway** (also called **Kyst Vejen**). Between these major streets or boulevards are a series of side streets, walkways, and alleys, all filled with shops. Major shopping streets are **Tolbod Gade, Raadets Gade, Royal Dane Mall, Palm Passage, Storervaer Gade,** and **Strand Gade.**

All the major stores on St. Thomas are located by number on an excellent map in the publication *St. Thomas This Week,* distributed free to all arriving plane and boat passengers.

It's illegal for most street vendors to ply their trades outside a designated area called **Vendors Plaza,** at the corner of Veterans Drive and Tolbod Gade. Hundreds converge at 7:30am, remaining here usually no later than 5:30pm, Monday to Saturday. (Very few remain in place on Sunday, unless a cruise ship is scheduled to arrive.)

When you completely tire of French perfumes and Swiss watches, head for **Market Square** as it's called locally, or more formally, **Rothschild Francis Square.** Here, under a Victorian tin roof, locals with machetes will slice open fresh coconuts for you so you can drink the milk, and women wearing bandanas will sell ackee, cassava, or breadfruit they harvested themselves.

ART The **Gallery Camille Pissarro,** Caribbean Cultural Centre, 14 Dronningens Gade (☎ 340/774-4621), lies in the house where Pissarro, dean of Impressionism, was born on July 10, 1830. This art's gallery—reached by climbing a flight of stairs—honors the illustrious painter. In three high-ceilinged rooms you'll discover all the available Pissarro paintings relating to the islands, which were created from 1852 to 1856. Many prints and note cards of local artists are also available, and the gallery also sells original batiks, alive in vibrant colors.

The ✪ **Jim Tillett Art Gallery & Silk Screen Print Studio,** Tillett Gardens, 4126 Anna's Retreat, Tutu (☎ 340/775-1929), is reached by following Route 38 east from Charlotte Amalie. Since 1959 Tillett Gardens, once an old Danish farm, has been the island's arts-and-crafts center. Including an art gallery and a screen-printing studio, this tropical compound is a series of buildings housing studios, galleries, and an outdoor garden restaurant and bar. Prints in the galleries start as low as $10. The best work of local artists is displayed here—originals in oils, watercolors, and acrylics. The Tillett prints on fine canvas are all one of a kind, and the famous Tillett maps on fine canvas are priced from $30. If you're not interested in buying any art, perhaps you'd prefer watching the daily iguana feedings in the garden.

The **Mango Tango Art Gallery,** Al Cohen's Plaza, Raphune Hill, Rte. 38 (☎ 340/777-3060), is one of the largest art galleries in St. Thomas, with close contacts with about half a dozen internationally recognized artists. Except for prints and posters, which are cheaper, original artworks begin at $200. Represented are internationally reputed artists who spend at least part of their year in the Virgin Islands, many of them sailing during breaks from their studio time. Well-known examples are Don Dahlke, Max Johnson, Anne Miller, David Millard, Dana Wylder, and Shari Erickson.

The **Native Arts and Crafts Cooperative,** Tarbor 1 (☎ 340/777-1153), is the largest arts-and-crafts emporium in the U.S. Virgin Islands, combining the output of 90 artisans into one sprawling shop. Contained in the former headquarters of the U.S. District Court, a 19th-century brick building adjacent to Charlotte Amalie's tourist information office, it specializes in items small enough to be packed in a suitcase or trunk that almost never need to be shipped. Examples are spice racks, paper towel racks, lamps crafted from conch shells, salad utensils and bowls, crocheted goods, and straw goods.

BAGS **Coki,** Compass Point Marina (☎ 340/775-6560), has a factory at Compass Point Marina amidst a little restaurant row, so you might want to combine a gastronomic tour with a shopping expedition. From the factory's expansive cutting board come some of the most popular varieties of shoulder tote bags in the Virgin Islands. These include pieces of canvas and elegant cotton prints converted to beach bags, zip-top bags, and drawstring bags. All Coki bags are 100% cotton, stitched with polyester sailmaker's thread.

BOOKSTORES The **Dockside Bookshop,** Havensight Mall (☎ 340/774-4937), is the place to go if you need a beach read. Head for this well-stocked store near the cruise-ship dock, east of Charlotte Amalie. The shop has the best selection of books on island lore, as well as a variety of general reading selections.

BRIC-A-BRAC   **Carson Company Antiques,** Royal Dane Mall, off Main St. (☎ 340/774-6175), invites browsers. Its clutter and eclecticism might appeal to you, especially if you appreciate small spaces loaded with merchandise, tasteless and otherwise, from virtually everywhere. Much of it is calibrated to appeal to the tastes of cruise-ship passengers looking for bric-a-brac that usually accumulates on shelves back on the U.S. mainland. Bakelite jewelry is cheap and cheerful, and the African artifacts are often interesting.

ELECTRONICS   ✪ **Royal Caribbean,** 33 Main St. (☎ 340/776-4110), is the largest camera and electronics store in the Caribbean. This store and its outlets carry Nikon, Minolta, Pentax, Canon, and Panasonic products. It's a good source for watches, including brand names like Seiko, Movado, Corum, Fendi, and Zodiac. They also have a complete collection of Philippe Charriol watches, jewelry, and leather bags, and a wide selection of Mikimoto pearls, 14- and 18-karat jewelry, and Lladró figurines. There's another branch at Havensight Mall (☎ 340/776-8890).

EROTIC ACCESSORIES   **Lover's Lane,** Raadets Gade 33 (☎ 340/777-9616), is for erotic tastes. Despite the fact that this store expends a lot of effort to present its merchandise as items to be enjoyed within marital respectability, some of it is pretty earthy and raunchy. That doesn't prevent a visit here from being amusing and even a lot of fun. Day visitors from cruise ships sometimes make a visit here a required stop, usually to perk up the sometime tame roster of shipboard activities. One floor above street level of a building beside Veteran's Drive, the shop sells provocative lingerie; edible panties; inflatable men, women, and sheep; massage aids of every conceivable type; the largest inventory of electric or battery-operated vibrators in the Virgin Islands; and all the lace, leather, or latex you'll ever need.

FASHION   **Cosmopolitan,** Drakes Passage and the waterfront (☎ 340/776-2040), has been in business since 1973. Its shoe salon features Bally of Switzerland, and Bally handbags are a popular addition. In swimwear, it offers one of the best selections of Gottex of Israel for women and Gottex, Hom, Lahco of Switzerland, and Fila for men. A menswear section offers Paul & Shark from Italy and Burma Bibas sports shirts. The shop also features ties by Gianni Versace and Pancaldi of Italy (priced at least 30% less than on the U.S. mainland) and Nautica sportswear for men discounted at 10%.

FRAGRANCES   **Tropicana Perfume Shoppe,** 2 Main St. (☎ 800/233-7948 or 340/774-0010), at the beginning of Main Street, is billed as the largest perfumery in the world. It offers all the famous names in perfumes, skin care, and cosmetics. They carry Lancôme and La Prairie among other products, and men will also find Europe's best colognes and aftershave lotions.

GIFTS & LIQUORS   **Al Cohen's Discount Liquors,** Long Bay Road (☎ 340/774-3690), occupies a big warehouse at Havensight, across from the West Indian Company docks where cruise-ship passengers disembark. You can make purchases from one of the island's biggest storehouses of liquor and wine. The wine department is especially impressive. The quarters have been recently expanded and remodeled, and there are now more brands and items on sale than ever before. You can also purchase fragrances, T-shirts, and souvenirs.

   ✪ **A. H. Riise Gift & Liquor Stores,** 37 Main St. at A. H. Riise Gift & Liquor Mall (perfume and liquor branch stores at the Havensight Mall) (☎ 800/524-2037 or 304/776-2303), is St. Thomas's oldest outlet for luxury items like jewelry, crystal, china, and perfumes. It also offers the widest sampling of liquors and liqueurs on the island. Everything is displayed in a 19th-century Danish warehouse, extending from Main Street to the waterfront. The store boasts a collection of fine jewelry and watches from Europe's leading craftspeople, like Vacheron Constantin, Bulgari, Omega, and Gucci, as well as a wide selection of Greek gold, platinum, and precious gemstone jewelry.

Imported cigars are stored in a climate-controlled walk-in humidor. Delivery to cruise ships and the airport is free. A. H. Riise offers a vast selection of fragrances for both men and women, along with the world's best-known names in cosmetics and treatment products. Waterford, Lalique, Baccarat, and Rosenthal, among others, are featured in the china and crystal department. Specialty shops in the complex sell Caribbean gifts, books, clothing, food, art prints, note cards, and designer sunglasses.

Caribbean Marketplace, Havensight Mall (Building III) (☎ **340/776-5400**), offers the best selections of island handcrafts, in addition to some distinctively Caribbean food items, including Sunny Caribbee products, a vast array of condiments (ranging from spicy peppercorns to nutmeg mustard). There's also a wide selection of Sunny Caribbee's botanical products. Other items range from steel-pan drums from Trinidad to wooden Jamaican jigsaw puzzles, from Indonesian batiks to bikinis from the Cayman Islands. Do not expect very attentive service.

Down Island Traders, Veterans Drive (☎ **340/776-4641**), offers a taste of the Caribbean. The aroma of spices will lead you to these markets, which have Charlotte Amalie's most attractive array of spices, teas, seasoning, candies, jellies, jams, and condiments, most of which are packaged from natural Caribbean products. The owner carries a line of local cookbooks, as well as silk-screened T-shirts and bags, Haitian metal sculpture, handmade jewelry, Caribbean folk art, and children's gifts. Be sure to ask for the collection of tropical coconut-mango bath and body products and the Calypso Spa Sun Care line.

JEWELRY **Blue Carib Gems and Rocks,** 2 Back St., behind Little Switzerland (☎ **340/774-8525**), has unique items. For a decade, the owners of this shop scoured the Caribbean for gemstones, and these stones have been brought directly from the mines to you. The raw stones are cut, polished, and then fashioned into jewelry by the lost-wax process. On one side of the premises you can see the craftspeople at work, and on the other view their finished products. A lifetime guarantee is given on all handcrafted jewelry. Since the items are locally made, they're duty free and not included in the $1,200 Customs exemption.

✪ **Cardow Jewelers,** 39 Main St. (☎ **340/776-1140**), is often called the Tiffany's of the Caribbean. This outlet boasts the world's largest selection of fine jewelry. This fabulous shop, where more than 20,000 rings are displayed, offers savings because of its worldwide direct buying, large turnover, and duty-free prices. Unusual and traditional designs are offered in diamonds, emeralds, rubies, sapphires, Brazilian stones, and pearls. Cardow has a whole wall of Italian gold chains and also features antique-coin jewelry. The Treasure Cove, a discount area in the store, has cases of fine gold jewelry all priced under $200.

LEATHER GOODS **The Leather Shop,** 1 Main St. (☎ **340/776-0290**), sells the best selection from Italian designers like Fendi, Longchamp, De Vecchi, Furla, and Il Bisonte. There are many styles of handbags, belts, wallets, briefcases, and attaché cases. Some of these are very expensive, of course, but there's less-expensive merchandise like backpacks, carry-ons, and Mola bags from Colombia. If you're looking for a bargain, ask them to direct you to the outlet store on Back Street, selling closeouts at prices sometimes 50% off U.S. mainland tags.

ST. THOMAS AFTER DARK

St. Thomas has more nightlife than any other of the Virgin Islands, but it's not as extensive as you might think. The big resort hotels offer the most varied programs.

Cheap Thrills: What to See & Do for Free (Well, Almost) on the U.S. Virgin Islands

- **Spend a Day on Honeymoon Beach.** The fourth-largest of the U.S. Virgins, with 500 acres of land, Water Isle off the coast of St. Thomas is only half a mile long. Visitors head out here to spend the day on **Honeymoon Beach,** where they swim, snorkel, sail, waterski, or just sunbathe on the palm-shaded beach and order lunch or a drink from the beach bar. The U.S. government, previous owner of Water Isle, has transferred it to the U.S.V.I. government and has spent some $3 million cleaning and sprucing it up. The island lies about ¼ mile out in the harbor of Charlotte Amalie. It was once a part of the peninsula of St. Thomas but a channel was cut through it, allowing U.S. submarines to reach their base in a bay to the west. A ferry, **Launch with Larry** (☎ 340/775-8073), runs between Crown Bay Marina and Water Island several times a day. Crown Bay Marina is part of the St. Thomas submarine base.

- **Escape to Hassel Island.** Despite the maritime mob scene at Charlotte Amalie in St. Thomas, the harbor's nearest and most visible island, **Hassel Island,** is almost completely deserted—its membership in the National Parks network prohibits most forms of development. There are no hotels or services of any kind, and swimming is limited to narrow rocky beaches. Even so, many visitors hire a boat to drop them off for an hour or two of relief from the cruise-ship congestion. One company that makes the trip is **Launch with Larry** (☎ 340/690-8073). A hike along part of the island's shoreline provides a different perspective on the hustle and bustle of Charlotte Amalie. You'll need to make arrangements in advance with the skipper who drops you off for your return trip. We recommend bringing your own drinking water and food if you plan to spend more than 3 hours. The round-trip fare costs only $5, well worth it to escape the hordes for a day.

- **Snorkel on St. John.** The coastline of St. John measures nearly 50 miles, including an equal number of bays, a few odd cays, and many secluded coves. Many of its bays and beaches aren't reachable by land because of the rugged terrain. But some of the best spots are accessible, including the north shore bays at Hawksnest, Trunk, Maho, Leinster, and Cinnamon. All of St. John is in the Atlantic, which means its waters are more turbulent than other islands opening onto the Caribbean Sea. On St. John's east coast or windward side, the winds are stronger and the waves bigger. But the leeward or western side is

St. Thomas might be the most cosmopolitan of the Virgin Islands, but it's no longer the gay paradise it was in the 1960s and 1970s—the action has shifted mainly to San Juan. The major gay scene in the U.S. Virgins is in Frederiksted on St. Croix. That doesn't mean gays and lesbians aren't attracted to St. Thomas. They are, but many of the clubs that used to cater exclusively to them are gone. Today there are pockets of gays who attend predominantly straight places.

THE PERFORMING ARTS The **Reichhold Center for the Arts,** University of the Virgin Islands, 2 John Brewer's Bay (☎ 340/693-1550), the premier venue in the Caribbean, lies west of Charlotte Amalie. Call the theater or check with the tourist office to see what's on at the time of your visit. The lobby displays a frequently changing free exhibit of paintings and sculptures by Caribbean artists. A calmer and more suited for snorkelers. If you have time to snorkel on only one bay, make it Leinster Bay, home to Watermelon Cay. Surrounded by gin-clear tranquil waters, it invites you to explore its world of sponges in tropical hues, giant sea stars, and perhaps the odd turtle swimming by along with an occasional nurse shark or schools of blue tangs and fields of sea fans.

- **Have a Close Encounter of the Wildlife Kind.** One of the most rarely visited parts of St. Croix, the island's southwestern tip is composed of salt marshes, tidal pools, and low vegetation inhabited by birds, turtles, and other wildlife. More than 3 miles of ecologically protected coast lie between Sandy Point (the island's westerly tip) and the shallow waters of the Westend Saltpond. Home to colonies of green and hawksbill turtles, the site is also a resting ground for leatherback turtles. It's one of only two such places in U.S. waters. The site is also home to thousands of birds, including herons, brown pelicans, Caribbean martins, black-necked stilts, and white-crowned pigeons. Sandy Point gave its name to a rare form of orchids, a brown and/or purple variety. Part of the continued viability of the site as a wildlife refuge depends on its inaccessibility, except on Saturday and Sunday 6am to 6pm. The site is most easily reached by driving to the end of Route 66 (Melvin Evans highway) and continuing down a gravel road. Earthwatch, a nonprofit organization staffed mostly by volunteers working cooperatively with advisors from universities around the world, maintains a monitoring program here. For inquiries about guided weekend visits to the site, call the St. Croix Environmental Association at ☎ **340/773-1989.**

- **Visit the Easternmost Point of the United States.** Diehards get up before sunrise to see the sun come up over Point Udall, a rocky promontory that's the easternmost point of the United States, jutting into the Caribbean Sea. But considering the climb via a rutted dirt road, you may want to wait until the sun comes up before heading here. Once at the top, you'll be rewarded with one of the most panoramic views in the U.S. Virgin Islands. On the way to the lookout point, you'll see the Castle, a local architectural oddity. It looks like the St. Croix version of the Taj Mahal. Its occupant is mysterious, known locally only as the Contessa. Point Udall is reached along Route 82 (it's signposted).

Japanese-inspired amphitheater is set into a natural valley, with seating space for 1,196. The smell of gardenias adds to the beauty of the performances. Several repertory companies of music, dance, and drama perform here. Performances begin at 8pm (call the theater to check), and tickets run $12 to $40.

THE BAR, CLUB & MUSIC SCENE The ✪ **Bar at Paradise Point,** Paradise Point (☎ **340/777-4540**), is best for a sundowner. Any savvy insider will tell you to head here for your sunset watching. It's 740 feet above sea level across from the cruise-ship dock, providing excellent photo ops and sunset views. There's a tram you can ride up the hill. Get the bartender to serve you a Bushwacker (his specialty)—you'll have to guess what's in it. Sometimes a one-man steel band is on hand to serenade the sunset watchers, who after a few of those painkillers don't know if the sun has set or not. You can also order inexpensive food here, such as barbecued ribs, hot dogs, and hamburgers, beginning at $4. It opens at 11am daily; closing time varies depending on business. Happy hour with discounted drinks begins at 5pm, with no set cut-off time.

Bakkeroe's, at Marriott's French Reef, Estate Bakkeroe (☎ **340/776-8500**), has been vastly improved and upgraded. Nightly it offers a classic pop and rock venue with a large stage and the island's finest sound system. Mirrored balls create that 1940s ambience, and there's a long stretch of bar. Local acts alternate with DJs, and karaoke is inevitably featured. The place gets going nightly at 9pm and generally stays open until the last customers stagger out.

Baywinds, at the Renaissance Grand Beach Resort, Smith Bay Road (☎ **340/775-1510**), is one of the most romantic places to be in the evening. This is a posh tradewind-cooled poolside club where loving couples dance at the side of the luxurious pool as moonlight glitters like diamonds off the ocean in the background. Music ranges from jazz to pop. The club is open nightly with live music and dinner 6pm to midnight.

Dungeon Bar, Bluebeard's Hill (☎ **340/774-1600**), overlooks the yacht harbor and offers piano-bar entertainment nightly. It's a popular gathering spot for both guests and visitors. You can dance 8pm to midnight on Thursday and 8pm to 1am on Saturday. Entertainment varies from month to month, but a steel band comes in on some nights and other nights are devoted to karaoke (Monday) or jazz (Wednesday). Drink specialties are named after Bluebeard himself—Bluebeard's wench, cooler, and ghost. There's no cover, and it's open Tuesday to Friday 4pm to midnight and Saturday to Monday 4pm to 1am.

Epernay, rue de St-Barthélemy, Frenchtown (☎ **340/774-5348**), is adjacent to Alexander's Restaurant. This stylish watering hole with a view of the ocean adds a touch of Europe to the neighborhood. You can order glasses of at least six brands of champagne and vintage wines by the glass. Appetizers cost $6 to $10 and include sushi and caviar. You can also order main courses, plus tempting desserts, such as chocolate-dipped strawberries. It's open Monday to Wednesday 11:30am to 11pm and Thursday to Saturday 11:30am to midnight.

Fat Tuesday, 26A Royal Dane Mall (☎ **340/777-8676**), is on the waterfront in downtown Charlotte Amalie. This spot serves up frozen concoctions: In the party-like atmosphere, patrons enjoy specialties like the Tropical Itch (a frozen punch made with bourbon and 151-proof rum) or the Moko Jumbi Juice (made with vodka, bourbon 151-proof rum, and banana and cocoa liqueurs). There's also a variety of beers, highballs, and shooters (like the Head Butt, containing Jagermeister, Bailey's, and amaretto). Each night the bar has special events, like Monday-night football or T.G.I.F. night. There's no cover, and hours are daily 10am to midnight or even 1am (perhaps later on Friday and Saturday).

The Green House, Veterans Drive (☎ **340/774-7998**), is directly on the waterfront. This is one of the few nightspots we recommend in the heart of Charlotte Amalie. You can park nearby and walk to the entrance. Each night a different entertainment is featured, ranging from reggae to disco. There's no cover except on Wednesday and Friday, when a $5 charge is imposed to cover the cost of live reggae music.

Larry's Hideaway, 10 Hull Bay (☎ **340/777-1898**), has a laid-back atmosphere. Many local fans like to hideaway here on lazy Sunday afternoons especially. The atmosphere is still funky, and it's a cheap place to eat if you devour the hot dogs and hamburgers served until 3:45pm. After 5pm, you can order affordable main courses in the restaurant, including the catch of the day and the chef's pork stew.

Latitude 18, Red Hook Marina (☎ **340/779-2495**), is the hot spot on the east coast where the ferries depart for St. John. Its interior ceiling is adorned with boat sails. It's both a restaurant and bar, opening nightly at 6pm. Live entertainment is regularly featured, especially on Tuesday and Saturday. This spot is especially popular with locals.

Martini's in Frenchtown (☎ **340/714-2145**) is the newest and hottest club to open in St. Thomas. The bar and club feature the best martinis on the island, along with a mix of R&B, classic Motown, and contemporary music. It features live entertainment Thursday to Saturday, when a $5 cover is imposed. The club is generally open daily 6pm to 12:30am, but hours can vary, so call to be sure.

Turtle Rock Bar, in the Mangrove Restaurant at the Wyndham Sugar Bay Beach Club, 6500 Estate Smith Bay (☎ **340/777-7100**), is a few minutes' drive west of Red Hook. This popular bar presents live music, steel bands, and karaoke. There's space to dance, but most patrons just sway and listen to the steel-pan bands that play from 2pm to closing every night or the more elaborate bands that play on Tuesday, Sunday, and some other nights. Thursday night is karaoke night. If you're hungry, burgers, salads, steaks, and grilled fish are available at the Mangrove Restaurant a few steps away. There's no cover, and happy hour (when most drinks are half price) is 4 to 6pm every night.

Walter's Livingroom, 3 Trompeter Gade (☎ **340/774-5025**), is dimly and rather flatteringly lit. This two-level watering hole attracts locals, often gay men, in season, drawing more off-island visitors in winter. Located about 100 yards from the island's famous synagogue, in a clapboard townhouse built around 1935, Walter's cellar bar features an intimate atmosphere with music from the 1950s, 1960s, and 1970s.

3 St. John

The smallest and least populated of the U.S. Virgin Islands, St. John is known for its lush unspoiled beauty. More than half its land, as well as its shoreline, was set aside and protected in 1956 as the Virgin Islands National Park.

Ringed by a rocky coastline, crescent-shaped bays, and white-sand beaches, the island contains an array of bird and wildlife that's the envy of ornithologists and zoologists around the world. Miles of serpentine hiking trails lead to spectacular views and the ruins of 18th-century Danish plantations. Mysterious geometric petroglyphs incised into boulders and cliffs can be pointed out by island guides; of unknown age and origin, the figures have never been deciphered.

The boating set seeks out its dozens of sheltered coves for anchorages and swimming. The hundreds of coral gardens surrounding St. John's perimeter are protected as rigorously as the land surface by the National Park Service. Any attempt to damage or remove coral from these waters is punishable by large and strictly enforced fines.

About 3 to 5 miles east of St. Thomas, St. John lies just across Pillsbury Sound. The island is about 7 miles long and 3 miles wide, with a total land area of some 20 square miles.

The **St. John Tourist Office** (☎ **340/776-6450**) is located near the Battery, a 1735 fort that's a short walk from where the ferry from St. Thomas docks. It's open Monday to Friday 8am to noon and 1 to 5pm. If you have Internet access, head to **www.stjohnusvi.com**.

In a medical emergency, dial ☎ **911.** Otherwise, go to **St. John Myrah Keating Smith Community Health Clinic,** 28 Sussanaberg (☎ **340/693-8900**), reached along Route 10, 7 miles east of Cruz Bay. A leading drugstore is **St. John Drugcenter,** in the Boulon Shopping Center, Cruz Bay (☎ **340/776-6353**), which also sells film, cameras, magazines, and books; it's open Monday to Saturday 9am to 6pm and Sunday 10am to 2pm.

GETTING AROUND

BY PUBLIC TRANSPORTATION   The most popular way to get around is by local **Vitran** service, the same company that runs bus service on St. Thomas. Buses now run between Cruz Bay and Coral Bay, costing $1 for adults and 75¢ for children (4 and under free). A **surrey-style taxi** is more fun however (☎ **340/693-7530**). Typical fares are $4 to Trunk Bay, $5.50 to Cinnamon Bay, or $10 to Mahoe Bay. Between midnight and 6am fares are increased by 40%. Call for more information.

BY CAR OR JEEP   The roads are undeveloped and uncluttered, and offer panoramic vistas. Because of these views, many visitors opt to rent a car (sometimes with four-wheel drive) to tour the island. You might consider one of the open-sided jeep-like vehicles. Most people need a car for only a day or two. During the busiest periods of midwinter, there's sometimes a shortage of cars, so try to reserve early.

Just remember that the island has only two gas stations. (A third gas station on the island dispenses gas only to government vehicles.) Because of the distance between gas stations, it's never a good idea to drive around St. John with less than half a tank.

The two largest car-rental agencies on St. John are **Hertz** (☎ **800/654-3001** or 340/693-7580) and **Avis** (☎ **800/331-1212** or 340/776-6374); Budget isn't represented. If you're a Budget fan, you can rent a car from its fleet on St. Thomas, then take the vehicle over to St. John by car ferry. If you want a local firm, try **St. John Car Rental,** across from the post office in Cruz Bay (☎ **340/776-6103**). Its stock is limited to Jeep Wranglers, Jeep Cherokees, and Suzuki Sidekicks.

ACCOMMODATIONS YOU CAN AFFORD

The choice of accommodations on St. John is limited, and that's how most people would like to keep it. And except for the campgrounds recommended below, the tabs at most of the establishments here are far beyond the pocketbook of the average traveler. However, the following places will provide you a low-cost holiday on St. John.

The Inn at Tamarind Court. South Shore Rd. (P.O. Box 350), Cruz Bay, St. John, U.S.V.I. 00831. ☎ **800/221-1637** or 340/776-6378. Fax 340/776-6722. www.tamarindcourt .com. E-mail: tamarind@worldnet.att.net. 23 units, 13 with bathroom. Winter $48 single without bathroom; $88 double with bathroom; $118 apt.; $138 suite. Off-season, $38 single without bathroom; $68 double with bathroom; $98 apt.; $118 suite. Rates include continental breakfast. AE, DISC, MC, V.

Right outside Cruz Bay but still within walking distance of the ferry dock, this modest place consists of a small hotel (where the no-smoking rooms have been renovated) and an even simpler West Indian inn. The rooms are small, evoking those in a little country motel, most often with twin beds, each with a firm mattress. The baths at the inn are shared, while in the hotel all rooms have a small bath. The social life here revolves around the courtyard bar/restaurant, Pa Pa Bulls (see below). From the hotel, you can walk to shuttles taking you to the beaches; the staff will advise.

✪ **St. John Inn.** P.O. Box 37, Crux Bay, St. John, U.S.V.I. 00831. ☎ **800/666-7688** in the U.S. or 340/693-8688. 12 units. A/C TV TEL. Winter $95–$175 single or double. Off-season $60–$120 single or double. Extra person $15. Rates include a continental breakfast. AE, DC, DISC, MC, V.

The old Cruz Inn, once the budget staple of the island, has been given a new lease on life and reincarnated as the St. John Inn. Though its rates have gone up, it has been

St. John

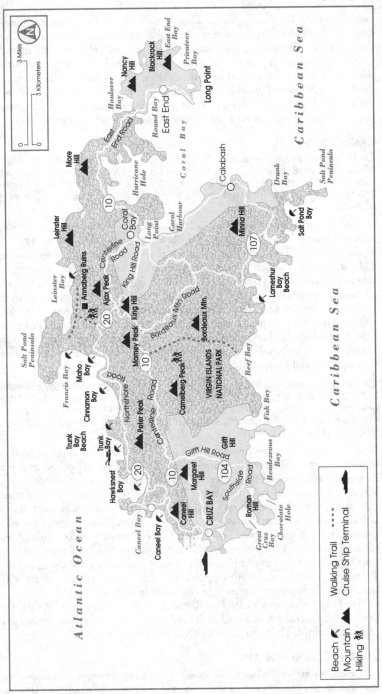

Beach 🏖
Mountain ▲
Hiking 🚶

Walking Trail - - - -
Cruise Ship Terminal

much improved. Overlooking Enighed Pond, the inn is only a few blocks from the Cruz Bay Dock area. Guests can now stay in accommodations evoking a light, airy California feel. The small to medium-size rooms have wrought-iron beds and new mattresses, handcrafted pine armoires, and a touch of Ralph Lauren flair. The junior suites contain full sofa beds and kitchenettes along with sitting areas. The baths are small but with renewed plumbing. Guests meet one another by the hotel pool or at the bar. The inn offers a 43-foot motor yacht, *Hollywood Waltz,* for daily excursions to private snorkeling spots on the coast or private beaches on uninhabited islands.

CAMPGROUNDS

✪ **Cinnamon Bay Campground.** P.O. Box 720, Cruz Bay, St. John, U.S.V.I. 00831. ☎ **800/539-9998** in the U.S., or 340/776-6330. Fax 340/776-6458. 126 units, none with bathroom. Winter $95–$105 cottage for 1 or 2; $75 tent site; $17 bare site. Off-season $63–$68 cottage for 1 or 2; $48 tent site; $17 bare site (5-day minimum). Extra person $15. AE, MC, V.

Opened by the National Park Service in 1964, this campground is the most complete in the Caribbean. The site is directly on the beach, and thousands of acres of tropical vegetation surround you. You have a choice of three ways of sleeping: tents, cottages, and bare sites. At the bare sites, nothing is provided except general facilities. The canvas tents are 10 by 14 feet with a floor, and a number of facilities are offered, like all cooking equipment; even your linen is changed weekly. The cottages are 15 by 15 feet, a screened room with two concrete walls and two screen walls. They contain four twin beds with thin mattresses, and two cots can be added; cooking facilities are also supplied. Lavatories and cool-water showers are in separate buildings nearby. Camping is limited to a 2-week period in any given year. Near the road is a camp center office, with a grocery and a cafeteria (dinners for $15).

✪ **Maho Bay.** P.O. Box 310, Cruz Bay, St. John, U.S.V.I. 00831. ☎ **800/392-9004**, 212/472-9453 in New York City, or 340/776-6226. Fax 340/776-6504, or 212/816-6210 in New York City. 114 tent cottages, none with bathroom. Winter $105 tent cottage for 1 or 2 (minimum stay of 7 nights required). Off-season $60 tent cottage for 1 or 2 (no minimum stay). Extra occupant $15. MC, V.

Maho Bay is an interesting concept in ecological vacationing, where you camp close to nature but with considerable comfort. Defined as a deluxe campground an 8-mile drive northeast from Cruz Bay, it's set on a hillside above the beach surrounded by the Virgin Islands National Park. To preserve the existing ground cover, all 114 tent cottages are built on platforms above a thickly wooded slope. Utility lines and pipes are hidden under wooden boardwalks and stairs. The tent cottages are covered with canvas and screens. Each unit has two movable twin beds with thin mattresses, a couch, electric lamps and outlets, a dining table, chairs, a propane stove, and an ice chest (cooler). That's not all—you're furnished linen, thin towels, and cooking and eating utensils. There's a store where you can buy supplies. You can do your own cooking or eat at the camp's outdoor restaurant. Guests share communal bathhouses.

Maho Bay has an open-air Pavilion Restaurant serving breakfast and dinner. The Pavilion also functions as an amphitheater and community center where various programs are featured. The camp has an excellent water-sports program.

VILLA & CONDO RENTALS

Villa vacations are on the rise on St. John. These private homes and condos deliver spaciousness and comfort, as well as privacy, and come with fully equipped kitchens, dining areas, bedrooms, and such amenities as VCRs and patio grills. Rentals go from large multiroom resort homes to simply decorated one-bedroom condos. Villa rentals year-round typically run from about $1,295 to $2,000 per week, an affordable option for multiple couples or families looking for a large house. Condos generally range from $185 to $285 per night per unit. However, in the off-season you can get substantial reductions, perhaps $110 to $175 per night or $770 to $1,225 per week.

For information on privately owned villas and condos on St. John, call ☎ **800/USVI-INFO.** You can also try **Caribbean Villas & Resort Management** (☎ **800/338-0987** in the U.S., or 340/776-6152) or **Villa Portfolio Management** (☎ **800/858-7989** or 340/693-9100).

Serendi Vacation Condos. P.O. Box 293, Cruz Bay, St. John, U.S.V.I. 00831. ☎ or fax **340/776-6646.** 10 apts., all with kitchenette. TEL. Winter $105 studio apt. for 1 or 2; $155 1-bedroom apt. for 2. Off-season $85 studio apt. for 1 or 2; $110 1-bedroom apt. for 2. Extra person $20; children 3–10 $10 each; children 2 and under stay free in their parents' apt. MC, V.

Set on sloping land on a hillside above Cruz Bay, these condos with angular lines and concrete verandas are shielded by masses of shrubbery. Each unit has slightly dated furniture, concrete latticework, a ceiling fan, a radio, and a terrace or balcony, plus a double or twin beds, each with a good mattress. The baths are in good order. Maid service is usually not included as part of a rental here. Tennis courts and water sports are nearby. A gas-heated barbecue grill on the grounds is available. Costs here are especially attractive for vacationers who include extra guests in their plans.

WORTH A SPLURGE

Estate Concordia Studios. 20–27 Estate Concordia, Coral Bay, St. John, U.S.V.I. 00830. ☎ **800/392-9004** in the U.S. and Canada, or 212/472-9453 in New York City. Fax 212/861-6210 in New York City. 9 units, 11 eco-tents. Winter $135–$190 studio for 1 or 2; $110–$120 eco-tent for 2. Off-season $95–$150 studio for 1 or 2; $70 eco-tent for 2. Extra person $25 in winter, $15 off-season. MC, V.

Opened in 1993, this environmentally correct 51-acre development project was widely praised for its integration with the local ecosystem. The elevated structures were designed to coexist with the stunning southern edge of St. John. Nestled on a low cliff above a salt pond, surrounded by hundreds of acres of pristine national park, the secluded location is recommended for those with a rental vehicle. Each building was designed to protect mature trees and is connected to its neighbors with boardwalks. The nine studios are contained in six postmodern cottages. Each comes with a kitchen, bath, balcony, and ceiling fan. Some units have an extra bedroom or a larger-than-expected private bath. Sofa beds have recently been replaced with regular queen-size beds with firm new mattresses. A newer addition are eco-tents, which are solar- and wind-powered, with large screened-in windows to create a "tree house" atmosphere. There are two twin beds in each room, one or two thin twin mattresses on a loft platform, and a queen-size fold-out couch, allowing the tent cottages to sleep 5 or 6 comfortably. Each kitchen comes with a stove and a running-water sink. Each tent has a toilet and private shower.

Estate Concordia also features a hillside swimming pool and guest laundry facilities. On-site management assists with activity suggestions.

✪ **Harmony.** P.O. Box 310, Cruz Bay, St. John, U.S.V.I. 00831. ☎ **800/392-9004** in the U.S. and Canada, 212/472-9453 in New York City, or 340/776-6226. Fax 340/776-6504, or 212/861-6210 in New York City. E-mail: mahony@maho.org. 12 units. Winter $165–$195 studio for 1 or 2. Off-season $105–$135 studio for 1 or 2. Extra person $25. 7-night minimum stay in winter. DISC, MC, V.

Built on a hillside above the Maho Bay Campground, this is a cluster of 12 luxury studios in 6 two-story houses with views sweeping down to the sea. Designed to combine both ecological technology and comfort, it's one of the few resorts in the Caribbean to operate exclusively on sun and wind power. Most of the building materials are derived from recycled materials, including reconstituted plastic and glass containers, newsprint, old tires, and scrap lumber. The managers and staff are committed to offering educational experiences as well as the services of a small-scale resort. Guests are asked to share their experience of living in an ecologically sensitive resort. They're taught to operate a user-friendly computer telling them how their unit's energy is being spent and to give their assessments of the experimental appliances, furnishings, and supplies.

Studios contain queen-size sleep sofas and/or twin beds, small tile baths, kitchenettes, dining area, and an outdoor terrace. Mattresses are a bit thin for some tastes, but still have comfort in them. Guests can walk a short distance downhill to the restaurant, grocery store, and water-sports facilities at the Maho Bay campground.

GREAT DEALS ON DINING

✪ La Tapa. Centerline Rd., across from Scotia Bank, Cruz Bay. ☎ 340/693-7755. Reservations recommended. Tapas $4–$5; main courses $15–$25. AE, MC, V. Mon–Sat 6–10pm. INTERNATIONAL.

One of our favorite restaurants in Cruz Bay occupies a raffish-looking building serving the cuisine its sophisticated owner, Alex Ewald, learned about during the time she spent living in Japan, Scotland, and Argentina. Featured here is a great selection of *tapas*, the bite-sized morsels of fish, meat, or marinated vegetables the Spanish produce in large numbers for consumption with pitchers of sangria. There's a tiny bar, with no more than five stools; a two-tiered dining room; and lots of original paintings (the place is also an art gallery for emerging local artists, with the paintings for sale). Menu items are thoughtful and well conceived, like quick-seared tuna with a Basque-inspired relish of onions, peppers, garlic, and herbs; filet mignon with gorgonzola, caramelized onions, and port; and linguine with shrimp, red peppers, and leeks in peanut sauce.

The Lime Inn. In the Lemon Tree Mall, Konges Gade, Cruz Bay. ☎ 340/776-6425. Reservations recommended. Main courses $6.25–$20; lunch $3.95–$9.95. AE, MC, V. Mon–Fri 11:30am–3pm and 5:30–10pm, Sat 5:30–10pm. Closed 3 weeks in July. SEAFOOD.

This lively open-air restaurant is located at the Lemon Tree Mall in the heart of Cruz Bay. It's known for its fresh-grilled Caribbean-style lobster as well as its grilled seafood ranging from shrimp to the fresh catch of the day. If you're not in the mood for seafood, try one of the daily chicken and pasta specials or one of the grilled steaks. For a combination of both land and sea, the Lime Inn offers a tender grilled filet mignon stuffed with crabmeat. The most popular night of the week here is Wednesday, when the Lime Inn offers an all-you-can-eat, peel-and-eat shrimp feast for $17.95.

Luscious Licks. Cruz Bay. ☎ 340/693-8400. Main courses $5–$8. No credit cards. Mon–Sat 10am–4pm. VEGETARIAN/VEGAN.

On the eastern side of the island at Cruz Bay, next to Mongoose Junction, this eatery offers open-air dining with a view of the water. The walls are appointed with small chalkboards, which have various quotations and pithy everyday sayings written on them. The menu offers a varied selection of vegetarian dishes—from soups, such as split pea, to the house specialty, the stroller (a flour tortilla filled with hummus, bean sprouts, carrots, avocado, broccoli, tahini, and yogurt). Diners may enjoy the pita sandwiches with fillings ranging from Swiss cheese to hummus, tabbouleh, or marinated tofu. Your drink comes from the vegetable and fruit juice bar. For a finish, try a selection from the ice-cream bar located off the patio, featuring Ben and Jerry's creamy concoctions.

Mongoose Deli/Global Village Restaurant. Mongoose Junction. ☎ **340/693-8677.** Sandwiches in deli $5–$9; lunch main courses in restaurant $6–$10; dinner main courses in restaurant $16–$24. AE, MC, V. Deli daily 7am–8pm; restaurant daily 8:30am–10pm; bar daily 11:30am–midnight or later, depending on business. AMERICAN.

Despite a setting that's soothing, woodsy, and very tropical, you'll get hints of the culinary traditions of California and just a whiff of New Age thinking at this popular deli/outdoor restaurant. If you're stocking up for a beach picnic or are hungry for an overstuffed sandwich, the takeaway service at the deli provides one of the best options on St. John. There's a cluster of wooden tables near the deli if you prefer to eat on-site, and breads—including sourdough and multigrain—are baked fresh every day. More substantial, more esoteric fare is served in the restaurant, where the vegetation of a tropical forest extends up to the restaurant's deck and where a high roof and a lack of walls give the impression of eating outdoors. You can always precede or end a meal at the center-stage bar. Perennially popular drinks are rum and fruit-based painkillers, costing $5.50, which are among the 20 frozen drinks available. Menu items at lunch include quesadillas, burgers, grilled chicken, and blackened tuna sandwiches. Menu items at dinner focus more on fresh grilled or sautéed fish, often served with a salsa made from local fruits; margarita-marinated shrimp; mahi-mahi with a cashew crust, and lots of vegetarian options as well.

Olive'r Twist. Cruz Bay. ☎ **340/693-9200.** Main courses $12–$14, lunch from $8. AE, MC, V. Mon–Fri 11:30am–5pm, daily 5–10pm. Bar daily 4pm–2am. INTERNATIONAL.

Cruz Bay's newest hangout is a hip and happy-go-lucky place that can be a lot of fun thanks to the humor of the men from Boston and New Jersey who opened it in 1997. It promotes itself as a "Bar/Lounge and porch," and a "place for fine lounging with good food." Within 200 yards of the public docks, it's a pavilion open on two sides, with lots of comfortable chairs, touches of wrought iron, and a bar that dispenses the largest and most potent martinis in St. John. Drinks accompany such standard menu items as burgers, fish with homemade chips, blackened mahi mahi, chicken of the day, and rib-eye steak. This is also one of the best venues on the island for nightlife, offering jazz every Tuesday and disco every Friday.

Pa Pa Bulls. In the Inn at Tamarind Court, South Shore Rd. ☎ **340/693-8955.** Reservations recommended. Breakfast $4.25–$10; lunch $3–$7.50; dinner $9–$14. AE, DISC, MC, V. Tues–Sun 7am–9:30pm. SOUTHWESTERN.

On the west end of Cruz Bay, this restaurant, in one of the island's few budget inns, offers casual foods in comfortable surroundings that draw both visitors and locals alike. Diners enjoy meals amid a setting of palm trees and tropical flowers in a courtyard with a fountain. You can begin your day with breakfast, ordering light fare or even steak and eggs. The menu leans heavily to the Southwest for its inspiration. Its smoked ribs are the island's finest, as are the barbecue specialties. It's not just for meat eaters, as a vegetarian platter is also featured nightly. Live music is presented Wednesday and Friday. Wednesday is also the time for crab races, followed by crab specials to eat.

Seabreeze Café. 4F Little Plantation, on Salt Pond Rd., Coral Bay. ☎ **340/693-5824.** Main courses $9–$12; standard breakfast $2.25; lunch specials $3–$6; Sun brunch $5.25. No credit cards. Mon–Sat 6:30am–2am, Sun 9am–2am. AMERICAN/CARIBBEAN.

This local hangout, which keeps the longest hours on the island, is in a green concrete building in the country and has a patio where you can watch the ocean and mountains. Dinner service technically stops after 9pm, but if you speak sweetly to the bartender, she might feed you. Most of the food is American, but with Caribbean overtones. It's really standard fare, but the price is right, and there's plenty of local color. Breakfast often attracts workers heading for their jobs. At lunch, you get the usual burgers, plus steak sandwiches. Fresh fish dishes, depending on what's available, appear on the dinner menu. Pizzas are often served, and Sunday is usually Mexican night with live music.

✪ **Shipwreck Landing.** 34 Freeman's Ground, Rte. 107, Coral Bay. ☎ **340/693-5640.** Reservations requested. Main courses $9.75–$15.25; lunch from $5.75–$10.75. AE, MC, V. Daily 11am–10pm. (Bar, daily 11am–11pm.) SEAFOOD/CONTINENTAL.

Eight miles east of Cruz Bay on the road to Salt Pond Beach, Shipwreck Landing is run by Pat and Dennis Rizzo. You dine amid palms and tropical plants on a veranda overlooking the sea, and the intimate bar specializes in tropical frozen drinks. Lunch isn't ignored here, and there's a lot more than sandwiches, salads, and burgers—try pan-seared blackened snapper in Cajun spices or conch fritters to get you going. The chef shines brighter at night though, offering a pasta of the day along with such specialties as a rather tantalizing Caribbean blackened shrimp. A lot of the fare is routine, like New York strip steak and fish and chips, but the grilled mahi mahi in lime butter is worth the trip. Entertainment, including jazz and reggae, is featured Friday to Sunday nights, with no cover charge.

✪ **Vie's Snack Shack.** East End Rd. ☎ **340/693-5033.** Main courses $4.95–$6.50. No credit cards. Tues–Sat 10am–5pm. WEST INDIAN.

Vie's, 12½ miles east of Cruz Bay, looks like little more than a plywood-sided hut. Nonetheless, its charming and gregarious owner is known as one of the best local chefs on St. John—her garlic chicken is famous. She also serves conch fritters, johnnycakes, island-style beef pâtés, and coconut and pineapple tarts. Don't leave without a glass of homemade limeade made from home-grown limes. The place is open most days, but as Vie says, "Some days, we might not be here at all"—so you'd better call before you head out.

Woody's Seafood Saloon. Cruz Bay. ☎ **340/779-4625.** Main courses $7.95–$15; lunch $5–$7.95. AE, DC, MC, V. Mon–Thurs 11am–1am, Fri–Sun 11am–2am. SEAFOOD/ AMERICAN.

Just 50 yards from the ferry dock, this local dive and hangout at Cruz Bay is more famous for its beers on tap than for its cuisine. A mix of local fishers, taxi drivers, tour guides, aimless on-island drifters, and an occasional husband and wife show up here to sample the spicy conch fritters and mingle with the islanders. Shrimp appears in various styles, and you can usually order fresh fish and other dishes, including blackened shark, drunken shellfish, and mussels and clams steamed in beer. But fancy cookery is just not the style of this place. You can always get a burger here, reggae on Wednesday, and, as a patron said, "a little bit of everything and anything" on a Saturday night.

WORTH A SPLURGE

✪ **Pusser's.** Wharfside Village, Cruz Bay. ☎ **340/693-8489.** Reservations recommended. Main courses $11.95–$21.95; pizzas $9.95–$11.95. AE, MC, V. Daily 11am–10pm. INTERNATIONAL/CARIBBEAN/PIZZA.

A double-decker air-conditioned store and pub in Cruz Bay, Pusser's overlooks the harbor and is near the ferry dock. These stores are unique to the Caribbean, and they serve Pusser's Rum, a blend of five West Indian rums the Royal Navy has served to its men for 3 centuries. You face a choice of three bars: the Beach Bar (where you can enjoy food while still in your swimsuit), the Oyster Bar (the main dining area), and the Crow's Nest. The same food is served at each bar. Here you can enjoy traditional English fare, including steak and ale. Try the jerk tuna fillet, the jerk chicken with tomato-basil sauce over penne, or the spaghetti with lobster cooked in rum, wine, lemon juice, and garlic. Caribbean lobster is the eternal favorite, or you might be seized with island fever and order the chicken Tropical (coconut-encrusted, pan-seared chicken served with rum-and-banana sauce with macadamia nuts). Finish your meal with Pusser's famous "mud pie." The food is satisfying, competent, and not a lot more, but after all that Pusser rum, will you notice?

✪ Serafina's Seaside Bistro. Route 107, Coral Bay. ☎ **340/693-5630.** Reservations recommended. Main courses $15.25–$22.75. AE, MC, V. Tues–Sat 5:30–9pm. INTERNATIONAL.

Named after a favorite aunt of the Italian-born entrepreneur who founded the place, this restaurant occupies a brick-floored pavilion, without walls, whose tables overlook the waters of Coral Bay, about 8 miles from Cruz Bay. Because it faces east (away from the sunset), locals claim it as the best site in the neighborhood for full-moon watching, in which event, one or two of the place's painkillers (Pusser's rum, tropical juices, and nutmeg; $4 each) go down nicely. The food is exceedingly well prepared, with a bit of flair and zest. Menu items include fresh snapper Creole, black angus New York strip steak, pork filet *au poivre*, and both a fish and a pasta of the day. During our visit, the selection was cheese tortellini with shrimp, fresh vegetables, romano cheese, and basil-lemon sauce.

HITTING THE BEACHES

The best one, hands down, is ✪ **Trunk Bay,** the biggest attraction on St. John and a beach collector's find. To miss its great white sweep would be like touring Europe and skipping Paris. This beach, with its picture-perfect shoreline of white sand, is often cited as one of the loveliest in the Caribbean. Diving, snorkeling, swimming, and sailing are ideal here. Trouble is, even though it's a beautiful stretch of sand, the word is out. It's likely to be overcrowded, and there are pickpockets. The beach has lifeguards and offers rentals, such as snorkel gear. Beginning snorkelers in particular are attracted to its underwater trail near the shore (described under "Water Sports" below). It costs $4 per person for travelers over 16 who visit Trunk Bay.

If you're coming from St. Thomas, both taxis and "safari buses" to Trunk Bay meet the ferry from Red Hook when it docks at Cruz Bay.

As mentioned, **Caneel Bay,** the stamping ground of the rich and famous, has seven beautiful beaches on its 170 acres. Among them is **Hawksnest Beach,** a little gem of white sand, beloved by St. Johnians. The beach is a bit narrow and windy, but beautiful, as filmmakers long ago discovered. It is lined with seagrape trees. Close to the road are barbecue grills, and there are portable toilets. Technically the government grants the right of access to all the beaches in the U.S. Virgin Islands. However, access across private land is not granted. Therefore six of the beaches, including Hawksnest Beach, can only be reached by private boat. The seventh beach, **Caneel Bay** Beach, is easy to reach from the main entrance of the resort. A staff member at the Caneel Bay gatehouse will provide directions. Safari buses and taxis from Cruz Bay will take you along North Shore Road.

The campgrounds of **Cinnamon Bay** (see above) have their own beach, where forest rangers sometimes have to remind visitors to put their swimming trunks back on. Changing rooms and showers are available. Cinnamon Bay is our particular favorite, a beautiful strip of white sand with hiking trails, great windsurfing, ruins, and feral donkeys (don't feed or pet them!). You can rent water-sports equipment on this beach. Snorkeling is especially popular, as you'll often see big schools of purple triggerfish as you take a look below water. Cinnamon Bay is better in the morning or at midday, as afternoons are likely to be windy. After beaching it, you can take a nature trail that is marked, with signs identifying the flora. It loops through a tropical forest on even turf before becoming steep as it leads straight up to Centerline Road. Immediately to the east of Cinnamon Bay, **Maho Bay Beach** also borders campgrounds. As you lie on the beach, you can take in a whole hillside of pitched tents. This is also a popular beach, often with the campers themselves, as it has white sands.

Salt Pond Bay is known to locals but often missed by visitors. The remote bay here is tranquil but the beach somewhat rocky. The location is on the panoramic coast in the southeast, adjacent to Coral Bay and Trunk Bay, and the beach lies a short walk down the hill from a parking lot. Be extra careful, however, if you park in this lot, as cars have recently been broken into. Facilities are meager here but include an outhouse and a scattering of tattered picnic tables. The snorkeling is good, and the bay here has some fascinating tidal pools. The Ram Head Trail beginning here and winding for a mile leads to a panoramic belvedere overlooking the bay.

If you want to escape the crowds of Trunk Bay, head for **Lameshur Bay Beach,** along the rugged south coast, west of the beach at Salt Pond Bay. This is one of the island's most remote beaches. It's reached after taking a bumpy dirt road. Once here the sands are beautiful and the snorkeling is excellent as you swim among rainbow-hued fish. When you tire of the beach, you can explore the ruins nearby of an old plantation estate that was destroyed in a slave revolt. The ruins are found after a 5-minute stroll down the road here past the beach.

Francis Bay Beach and **Watermelon Cay Beach** are just a few more of the beaches encountered as visitors continue eastward along St. John's gently curving coastline. Powdered with sugary-white sand, the beach at ✪ **Leinster Bay** is another haven for those seeking the solace of a private sunny retreat. If not solitarily soaking up the sun's rays, vacationers can swim in the bay's shallow water and snorkel in the company of an occasional turtle or stingray among the spectacular and colorful coral reef.

Does St. John have a nude beach? Not officially. But **Solomon Bay Beach** is a contender, though park rangers of late have sometimes patrolled the beach asking those in the buff to put their swimwear back on. The beach is reached by leaving Cruz Bay on Route 20 and turning left at the Park Service sign, about ¼ mile past the Visitors Center. You can park at the end of a cul-de-sac and then walk along a trail for about 15 minutes leading to the sea. This is one of the lovely beaches of the island, filled with white sand. Go early and you'll practically have the beach to yourself.

SPORTS & OUTDOOR PURSUITS

Don't visit St. John expecting to play golf. Come for some of the best snorkeling, scuba diving, swimming, fishing, hiking, sailing, and underwater photography in the Caribbean, the centerpiece of the island being Virgin Islands National Park. The island is known for its coral-sand beaches, winding mountain roads, hidden coves, and trails that lead past old, bush-covered sugarcane plantations.

BOAT CHARTERS   You can take half- and full-day boat charters, including trips to the Baths at Virgin Gorda on Tuesday. The cost of this full-day adventure is $85. On Wednesday and Friday an "Around St. John Snorkel Excursion" costs $50 per person. Call **Vacation Vistas and Motor Yachts** at ☎ **340/776-6462** for more details.

HIKING   St. John's **Virgin Islands National Park** is laced with a wide choice of clearly marked **walking paths.** At least 20 of these originate from North Shore Road (Route 20) or from the island's main east-west artery, Centerline Road (Route 10). Each is marked at its starting point with a preplanned itinerary; the walks can last anywhere from 10 minutes to 2 hours.

Another series of hikes traversing the more arid eastern section of St. John originate at clearly marked points along the island's southeastern tip, off Route 107. Many of the trails wind through the grounds of 18th-century plantations, often past ruined schoolhouses, rum distilleries, molasses factories, and Great Houses, many of which are covered with lush, encroaching vines and trees.

Because of the island's semi-wild state, with terrain ranging from arid and dry (in the east) to moist and semitropical (in the northwest), many hikers and trekkers consider a visit here among the most rewarding in the Virgin Islands. The island boasts more than 800 species of plants, 160 species of birds, and more than 20 hiking trails maintained in fine form by the island's crew of park rangers.

Maps of the island's hiking trails are available from the national park headquarters at Cruz Bay, but one of our favorite tours requires only about a half-mile stroll (about 30 minutes, round-trip, not including stops to admire the views) and departs from clearly marked points along the island's north coast, near the junction of routes 10 and 20. Identified by the National Park Service as Trail no. 10, the **Annaberg Historic Trail** is a self-guided tour that includes the partially restored ruins of a manor house built during the 1700s and overlooking the island's north coast. Signs along the way give historical and botanical data. To visit the ruins costs $4 per person for those over 16.

If you want to prolong your hiking experience, the **Leinster Bay Trail** (Trail no. 11) begins near the point where Trail no. 10 ends, leading past mangrove swamps and coral inlets rich with plant and marine life, often with markers identifying some of the plants and animals.

The **National Park Service** (☎ 340/776-6330 or 340/776-6201) provides a number of ranger-led activities in the park. One of the most popular is the 2½-mile **Reef Bay Hike.** A park ranger leads the hike down the Reef Bay Trail interpreting the natural and cultural history along the way. Included is a stop at the only known petroglyphs on the island and a tour of the sugar mill ruins. Reservations are required for this hike and can be made by phone. Tours are conducted at 10am on Monday and Thursday, costing $15 per person. Visitors are encouraged to stop by the **Cruz Bay Visitor Center** where you can pick up the park brochure, which includes a map of the park, and the *Virgin Islands National Park News,* which has the latest information on activities in the park.

WATER SPORTS   The most complete line of water sports available on St. John is offered at the **Cinnamon Bay Watersports Center** on Cinnamon Bay Beach (☎ 340/776-6330). For the adventurous, there's windsurfing, kayaking, and sailing.

The **windsurfing** here is some of the best anywhere, for either the beginner or the expert. High-quality equipment is available for all levels, even for kids. You can rent a board for $12 an hour; a 2-hour introductory lesson costs $40. Want to paddle to a secluded beach, explore a nearby island with an old Danish ruin, or jump overboard anytime you like for snorkeling or splashing? Then try a sit-on-top **kayak;** one- and two-person kayaks are available for rent for $10 to $17 per hour. You can also sail away in a 12- or 14-foot Hobie monohull **sailboat,** which can be rented for $20 to $30 per hour.

Snorkeling equipment can be rented from the Watersports Beach Shop for $4, plus a $25 deposit. Two of the best snorkeling spots around St. John are **Leinster Bay** and **Haulover Bay.** Leinster Bay offers some of the best snorkeling in the U.S. Virgins. With calm, clear, and usually uncrowded waters, the bay is filled with an abundance of sea life, especially brilliantly hued tropical fish in rainbow colors. Visibility is usually excellent. Haulover Bay is a favorite among the locals. It is often deserted, and the waters are often clearer than in other spots around St. John. The ledges, walls, and nooks here are set very close together, making the bay a lot of fun for anyone with a little bit of experience.

Divers can ask about scuba packages at **Low Key Watersports,** Wharfside Village (☎ **800/835-7718** or 340/693-8999). All wreck dives are two-tank/two-location dives. A one-tank dive costs $55 per person, with night dives going for $65. Snorkel tours are also available at $25 to $35 per person, and parasailing is possible at $50. The center uses its own custom-built dive boats and also offers and specializes in water-sports gear, including masks, fins, snorkels, and "dive skins." It also arranges day sailing charters, kayaking tours, and deep-sea sport fishing.

Cruz Bay Watersports, P.O. Box 252, Palm Plaza, St. John, U.S.V.I. 00831 (☎ **800/835-7730** or 340/776-6234), is a PADI and NAUI five-star diving center on St. John. Certifications can be arranged through a dive master, for $350. Certification classes start daily, as well as two-tank reef dives with all the dive gear for $75. Beginner scuba lessons start at $75, and wreck dives (Wednesday and Friday), night dives, and dive packages are available at accommodations that range from budget to first class. Snorkel tours are available daily as well as trips to the British Virgin Islands (bring your passport), the latter costing $80, including food and beverages.

At Trunk Bay, you can take the ✪ **National Park Underwater Trail** (☎ **340/776-6201**), stretching for 650 feet, allowing you to identify what you see, everything from false coral to colonial anemones. You'll pass lavender sea fans and schools of silversides. Equipment rental costs $4, with a $25 refundable deposit, and rangers are on hand to provide information. If time is limited, try to visit the **Annaberg Ruins** on Leinster Bay Road, where the Danes maintained a thriving plantation and sugar mill after 1718. It's located off North Shore Road east of Trunk Bay on the north shore. Admission is $4 for those over 16. On certain days of the week (dates vary) guided walks of the area are given by park rangers.

Trunk Bay is one of the world's most beautiful beaches. It's also the site of one of the world's first marked underwater trails (bring your mask, snorkel, and fins). It lies to the east of Cruz Bay along North Shore Road. **Fort Berg** (also called Fortsberg), at Coral Bay, dating from 1717, played a disastrous role during the 1733 slave revolt—it served as the base for soldiers who brutally crushed the rebellion.

SHOPPING

Compared to shopping on St. Thomas, St. John's shopping isn't much, but what's here is intriguing. The boutiques and shops of Cruz Bay are individualized and quite special. Most of the shops are clustered at **Mongoose Junction,** in a woodsy area beside the roadway, about a 5-minute walk from the ferry dock. We've already recommended restaurants in this complex (see above), and it also contains shops of merit.

Before you set sail for St. Thomas, you'll want to visit the recently expanded **Wharfside Village,** just a few steps from the ferry-departure point on the waterfront, opening onto Cruz Bay. Here in this complex of courtyards, alleys, and shady patios is a mishmash of all sorts of boutiques, along with some restaurants, fast-food joints, and bars.

The most fun shopping on the island is to the beating of drums and the flash of flamboyant sarongs swaying in the breeze, as you get a whiff of the fragrant spices and aromas of St. John. All this takes place on ✪ **St. John Saturday,** a feast for the senses. Sponsored on the last Saturday of every month, this day-long event begins early in the morning in the center of town and spills across the park. Vendors hawk handmade items, ranging from jewelry to handcrafts, even clothing, and especially food made from local ingredients. One woman vendor concocts soothing salves from recipes passed on by her ancestors; another designs and makes porcelain earrings, and yet another flavors chicken and burgers with her own secret hickory barbecue sauce that's so good it should be bottled (get Paul Newman on the phone). One vendor hollows out and carves gourds from local calabash trees.

Bamboula, Mongoose Junction (☎ **340/693-8699**), has an unusual and very appealing collection of gifts from the Caribbean, Haiti, India, Indonesia, and Central Africa. Its exoticism is unexpected and very pleasant. The store has added clothing for both men and women under its own label—hand-batiked soft cottons and rayons made for comfort in a hot climate. Many locally crafted items, ideal as gifts, are also sold. **The Canvas Factory,** Mongoose Junction (☎ **340/776-6196**), produces its own handmade, rugged, and colorful canvas bags in the factory at Mongoose Junction. Their products range from sailing hats to soft-sided luggage. **The Clothing Studio,** Mongoose Junction (☎ **340/776-6585**), is the Caribbean's oldest hand-painted clothing studio, in operation since 1978. You can watch talented artists create original designs on fine tropical clothing, including swimwear and daytime and evening clothing, mainly for babies and women.

Coconut Coast Studios, Frank Bay (☎ **340/776-6944**), lies a 5-minute stroll from the heart of Cruz Bay (follow along the waterfront bypassing Gallows Point). This will lead you to the studio of Elaine Estern and Lucinda Schutt, two of the best watercolorists on the island. Especially known for her Caribbean landscapes, Elaine is the official artist for Westin Resorts, St. John; Lucinda is the artist for Caneel Bay. **Donald Schnell Studio,** Mongoose Junction (☎ **340/776-6420**), is a studio and gallery where Mr. Schnell and his assistants have created one of the Caribbean's finest collections of handmade pottery, sculpture, and blown glass. The staff can be seen working daily and are especially noted for their rough-textured coral work. Water fountains are a specialty item, as are house signs and coral-pottery dinnerware. The studio will mail works all over the world; go in and discuss any particular design you may have in mind.

Fabric Mill, Mongoose Junction (☎ **340/776-6194**), features silk-screened and batik fabrics from around the world. Vibrant rugs and bed, bathroom, and table linens add the perfect touch to your home if you like a Caribbean flair. Whimsical soft sculpture, sarongs, and handbags are also made in this studio shop. **Pusser's of the West Indies,** Wharfside Village, Cruz Bay (☎ **340/693-8489**), is a link in the famous chain that was previously recommended for food and drink. The store offers a large collection of classically designed old-world travel and adventure clothing along with unusual accessories. Clothing for women, men, and children is displayed, along with T-shirts emblazoned with the Pusser's emblem.

R and I Patton Goldsmithing, Mongoose Junction (☎ **340/776-6548**), on the island since 1973, is one of the oldest businesses here, and three-quarters of the merchandise is made on St. John. It has a large selection of island-designed jewelry in sterling silver, gold, and precious stones. Also featured are the works of goldsmiths from outstanding American studios, plus Spanish coins.

ST. JOHN AFTER DARK

Bring a good book. After dark, St. John is no St. Thomas, and everybody here seems to want to keep it that way. Most people are content to have a long leisurely dinner and then head for bed.

Among the popular bars of Cruz Bay, **Pusser's** (above) at Wharfside Village has the most convivial atmosphere. The **Caneel Bay Bar,** at the Caneel Bay Resort (☎ **340/776-6111**), presents live music nightly 8:30 to 11pm. The most popular drinks are a Cool Caneel (local rum with sugar, lime, and anisette) and the trademark of the house, a Plantation Freeze (lime and orange juice with three kinds of rum, bitters, and nutmeg).

The two places recommended above are very touristy. If you'd like to go where the locals go for drinking and gossiping, try **JJ's Texas Coast Café,** Cruz Bay (☎ **340/776-6908**), across the park from the ferry dock. Your Texan host, JJ Gewels, makes everybody feel welcome—at least if he likes you. The Tex-Mex food is the island's best, and the margaritas are deservedly called lethal. Also at Cruz Bay, check out the action at **Fred's** (☎ **340/776-6363**), across from The Lime Inn. The most laid-back bar on the island, it brings in island bands on Wednesday, Friday, and Sunday, and is also the best place to go to dance, at least on those nights. It's just a little hole-in-the-wall and can get crowded fast.

The best sports bar on the island is **Skinny Legs,** Emmaus, Coral Bay, beyond the fire station (☎ **340/779-4982**). It's only a shack made out of tin and wood, but it serves the best hamburgers on St. John. The chili dogs aren't bad either. The yachting crowd likes to hang out here, and it often seems like the richer they are, the poorer they dress—many of them look as if they're refugees, though in fact they've disembarked from $1.5-million yachts. The bar has a satellite dish to televise major sporting events. Live music is presented at least once a week; otherwise it's the dartboard or horseshoe pits for you.

Morgan's Mango, though primarily a restaurant, is also one of the hottest watering holes along the island, lying in Cruz Bay across from the national park dock (☎ **340/693-8141**). Thursday is margarita night, when a soft rock duo plays. Count yourself lucky if you get in on a crowded night in winter. The place became famous locally when it turned away actor Harrison Ford, who was vacationing at Caneel Bay.

As a final option, check out **Sea Breeze,** 4F Little Plantation, Coral Bay on Salt Pond Road (☎ **340/693-5824**), where you can not only drink and enjoy live entertainment but also can order three meals a day. Each night a different chef demonstrates his/her specialties. The Sunday brunch 9am to 2pm is an island highlight. A local dive and popular hangout, this place is very laid-back. Try the barbecued beef sandwich, the best on the island.

4 St. Croix

Even though seven flags have flown over St. Croix, it's the nearly 2½ centuries of Danish influence that still permeate the island and its architecture.

At the east end of St. Croix—which, incidentally, is the easternmost point of the United States—the terrain is rocky and arid. The west end is more lush, with a rain forest of mango and mahogany, tree ferns, and dangling lianas. Rolling hills and upland pastures characterize the area lying between the two extremes. African tulips are just one of the species of flowers that add a splash of color to the landscape, which is dotted with stately towers that once supported grinding mills. The island is 84 square miles.

St. Croix has some of the best beaches in the Virgin Islands and ideal weather. It doesn't have the nightlife of St. Thomas, nor would its permanent residents want that.

The **American Express** representative is **Southerland,** Chandler's Wharf, Gallows Bay (☎ **800/260-2603** or 340/773-9500). For medical care, try the **St. Croix Hospital,** 6 Diamond Bay, Christiansted (☎ **340/778-6311**).

GETTING AROUND

BY TAXI   At Alexander Hamilton Airport you'll find official taxi rates posted. Per person rates require a minimum of two passengers; a single person pays double the

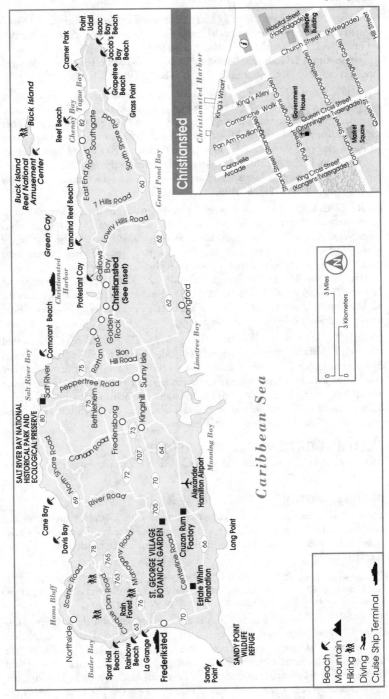

St. Croix

Christiansted

Hospital Street (Hospitalgade)
Steeple Building
Church Street (Kirkegade)
Hill Street

Christiansted Harbor

King's Wharf
King's Alley
Comanche Walk
Government House
Pan Am Pavillion
Strand Street (Strandgade)
King Street (Kongens Gade)
Queen Cross Street (Dronningens Tvaergade)
Company Street (Compagniets Gade)
Queen St. (Dronningens Gade)
Caravelle Arcade
Market Square
King Cross Street (Kongens Tvaergade)

N

3 Miles
0
3 Kilometers
0

Point Udall
Isaac Bay Beach
Jacob's Bay Beach
Cramer Park
Grapetree Beach
Reef Beach
Grass Point
Chenay Bay
Tague Bay
82
Southgate
Reef Beach
East End Road
South Shore Rd.
Great Pond Bay
Buck Island
Buck Island Reef National Amusement Center
Green Cay
Tamarind Reef Beach
7 Hills Road
Lowry Hills Road
60
Christiansted Harbor
Cormorant Beach
Protestant Cay
Gallows Bay
Christiansted (See Inset)
62
Salt River Bay
Salt River
SALT RIVER BAY NATIONAL HISTORICAL PARK AND ECOLOGICAL PRESERVE
80
Golden Rock
Sion Hill Road
Longford
62
Limetree Bay
75
Pepperttree Road
Sunny Isle
75
Bethlehem
Fredensborg
Kingshill
73
Canaan Road
707
64
72
70
Manning Bay
North Shore Road
69
River Road
705
Alexander Hamilton Airport
Caribbean Sea
Cane Bay
Davis Bay
78
765
ST. GEORGE VILLAGE BOTANICAL GARDEN
Cruzan Rum Factory
66
Long Point
Hams Bluff
Scenic Road
Creque Dam Road
763
Mahogany Road
76
Centerline Road
Estate Whim Plantation
70
Northside
Sprat Hall Beach
Rain Forest
63
Rainbow Beach
La Grange
Frederiksted
70
Butler Bay
SANDY POINT WILDLIFE REFUGE
Sandy Point

Beach
Mountain
Hiking
Diving
Cruise Ship Terminal

639

posted fares. Expect to pay about $12 for one or two riders from the airport to Christiansted and about $10 for one or two from the airport to Frederiksted. As the cabs are unmetered, agree on the rate before you get in.

The **St. Croix Taxicab Association** at ☎ **340/778-1088** offers door-to-door service. You can also call **Caribbean Taxi** at ☎ **340/773-9799.**

BY BUS   Air-conditioned buses run between Christiansted and Frederiksted about every 30 minutes daily from 5:30am to 9pm. Beginning at Tide Village, to the east of Christiansted, buses go along Route 75 to the Golden Rock Shopping Center. Then they make their way to Route 70, with stopovers at the Sunny Isle Shopping Center, La Reine Shopping Center, St. George Village Botanical Garden, and Whim Plantation Museum, before reaching Frederiksted. Bus service is also available from the airport to each of the two towns. Fares are $1 or 55¢ for senior citizens. For more information, call ☎ **340/778-0898.**

BY RENTAL CAR   Okay, we've warned you: The roads are often disastrous. Sometimes the government smoothes them out before the big season begins, but don't count on it. Car-rental rates on St. Croix are reasonable. However, because of the island's higher than usual accident rate (which is partly because many visitors aren't used to *driving on the left*), insurance costs are higher than on the mainland.

Avis (☎ **800/331-2112**), **Budget** (☎ **888/227-3359** or 340/778-9636), and **Hertz** (☎ **800/654-3001** or 340/778-1402) all maintain their headquarters at the island's airport; look for their kiosks near the baggage claim areas. Not to beat a dead horse, but do remember: *Driving is on the left.*

BY BIKE   **St. Croix Bike and Tours,** 5035 Cotton Valley, Christiansted (☎ **340/773-5004**), offers bike rentals and guided bicycle tours. The outfitter rents 21-speed mountain bikes, which are suitable for the rugged terrain of St. Croix. They also feature a 12-mile historical-ecotour of moderate exertion level along the rolling western coast and a 14-mile ridgeline tropical mountain bike tour for the experienced biker or fitness buff. Guides are knowledgeable about the social, political, and natural history of the island. Call for more information.

ACCOMMODATIONS YOU CAN AFFORD

All rooms are subject to an 8% hotel room tax, which is *not* included in the rates given below.

IN CHRISTIANSTED

The trick is to reserve one of the cheaper rooms at Club Comanche instead of the most expensive. If you do, you'll be nailing down one of the bargain rooms of Christiansted. But even this traditional budget leader doesn't match the deal offered by the Breakfast Club.

✪ **Breakfast Club.** 18 Queen Cross St., 00820 Christiansted, U.S.V.I. ☎ **340/773-7383.** Fax 340/773-8642. E-mail: reservations@the-breakfast-club.christiansted.vi.us. 9 units. Year-round $45 single; $55 double. Rates include breakfast. AE, V. Free parking.

The best value of any B&B in St. Croix is this comfortable but architecturally undistinguished hotel that combined a circa-1950s compound of efficiency apartments with a traditional-looking stone house rebuilt from a ruin in the 1930s. Each of the units has a kitchenette, a cypress-sheathed ceiling, white walls, a beige tile floor, and simple summery furniture, including good beds with firm mattresses. The baths are small and adequately maintained, with a nice set of towels. The centerpiece of the place is the hot tub that's set on a raised deck, where impromptu parties are likely to develop. Toby Chapin, the Ohio-born owner, labors over one of the most generous and appealing breakfasts on the island—the menu lists at least nine choices, the most popular of which are banana pancakes and chiles rellenos.

Club Comanche. 1 Strand St., Christiansted, St. Croix, U.S.V.I. 00820. ☎ **800/524-2066** or 340/773-0210. Fax 340/713-9145. www.usvi.net_hotel_comanche.html. E-mail: comanche@islands.vi. 45 units. A/C TV TEL. Winter $65–$120 single or double; $170 suite. Off-season $65–$104 single or double; $105 suite. AE, DC, V.

Right on the Christiansted waterfront, this is a famous old West Indian inn, based around a 250-year-old Danish-inspired main house, once the home of Alexander Hamilton. Extensively remodeled over the years, some of its small to medium-sized rooms have slanted ceilings with carved four-poster beds, old chests, and mahogany mirrors. Reached by a covered bridge, a more modern addition passes over a shopping street to the waterside. Some rooms are at poolside or harborfront buildings. Since accommodations come in such a wide range of styles and sizes, your opinion of this place is likely to be influenced entirely by your room assignment. Most of the units face the pool instead of the ocean. Since the hurricanes, all the mattresses have been replaced, and beds are most comfortable, often king sized. The baths remain small but have been renewed. The club also offers the most popular restaurant in Christiansted. Four minutes by ferry will take you to the beach at Hotel on the Cay.

○ **Holger Danske.** 1200 King Cross St., Christiansted, St. Croix, U.S.V.I. 00821. ☎ **800/528-1234** or 340/773-3600. Fax 340/773-8828. 44 units. A/C TV TEL. Winter $89–$130 single; $94–$140 double. Off-season $64–$110 single; $69–$130 double. AE, DC, DISC, MC, V.

This is one of the best bets in town for the budget traveler. Freshly remodeled and refurbished, right in the heart of Christiansted, it's a Best Western. The inn provides pleasantly furnished but small accommodations, each with a private furnished balcony and a fridge. Following hurricane damage, the rooms have been renewed, with fresh mattresses and rejuvenated plumbing. Some units also offer efficiency kitchens. It has a pool patio and a garden path walkway, but only the superior rooms open onto the harbor and its offshore cay. Water sports and other activities are near at hand, as are a bevy of shops and restaurants. The nearest beach is a 4-minute ferry ride away.

King Christian Hotel. 59 King St. (P.O. Box 3619), Christiansted, St. Croix, U.S.V.I. 00824. ☎ **800/524-2012** in the U.S., or 340/773-6330. Fax 809/773-9411. E-mail: kchotel@ viaccess.net. 39 units. A/C TV TEL. Winter $95 economy single, $125 superior single; $100 economy double, $135 superior double. Off-season $80 economy single, $100 superior single; $85 economy double, $107 superior double. AE, DC, DISC, MC, V.

This hotel is directly on the waterfront. Each of its front rooms has two double beds, a refrigerator, a room safe, and private balcony overlooking the harbor. No-frills economy-wing rooms have two single beds or one double but no view or balcony. Rooms are either small or medium size, and under new management all units have been redone, with fresh mattresses on the comfortable beds, new rugs and draperies, and renewed bath fixtures. You can relax on the sundeck or shaded patio or in the freshwater pool. The staff will make arrangements for golf, tennis, horseback riding, and sightseeing tours, and there's a beach just a few hundred yards across the harbor, reached by ferry. Mile Mark Charters water-sports center offers daily trips to Buck Island's famous snorkeling trail as well as a complete line of water sports.

King's Alley Hotel. 57 King St., Christiansted, St. Croix, U.S.V.I. 00820. ☎ **800/843-3574** or 340/773-0103. Fax 340/773-4431. 35 units. A/C TV TEL. Winter $99–$148 single; $109–$158 double. Off-season $89–$144 single; $94–$154 double. AE, DC, MC, V.

The King's Alley Hotel stands at water's edge, near Christiansted Harbor's yacht basin, a 4-minute ferry ride to the nearest beach at Hotel on the Cay. The inn is furnished with a distinct Mediterranean flair, and many of its small to medium-size rooms overlook its pool terrace surrounded by tropical plants. The galleries opening off the rooms are almost spacious enough for entertaining. All rooms have twin or king-size beds with good mattresses, and the newly added deluxe units contain four-poster mahogany beds. The medium-size baths are very comfortable, with good lighting. Right outside your door are boutiques and restaurants. Breakfast can be ordered if you walk over to one of the nearby cafes.

✪ **Kronegade Inn.** 1112 Western Suburb, Christiansted, St. Croix, U.S.V.I. 00820. ☎ **340/692-9590.** Fax 340/692-9591. 16 units. A/C TV TEL. Winter $85 suite for 1 or 2; $107 2-bedroom suite. Off-season $75 suite for 1 or 2; $95 2-bedroom suite. AE, MC, V.

Opened in 1994, this small inn in Christiansted offers a certain "down-home" charm at reasonable rates. Some guests call it the "best kept secret in Christiansted." The inn offers 12 suites or apartments, each with full kitchen, radio, and ceiling fan. The beds are most comfortable with firm mattresses, and baths, though small, are tidily maintained. The nearest beach is at the offshore Hotel on the Cay, a 4-minute ferry ride away, where Kronegade guests are allowed to use the beach and facilities. The décor is in a tropical motif with white rattan furnishings. The inn doesn't offer food service, but a number of restaurants and cafes are nearby.

✪ **Pink Fancy.** 27 Prince St., Christiansted, St. Croix, U.S.V.I. 00820. ☎ **800/524-2045** in the U.S., or 340/773-8460. Fax 340/773-6448. www.pinkfancy.com 13 units. A/C TV TEL. Winter $65–$90 single; $75–$120 double. Off-season $65–$75 single; $65–$90 double. Children 11 and under stay free in parents' room. Extra person $15. Rates include continental breakfast. AE, MC, V.

The Pink Fancy was restored and turned into this small private hotel 1 block from the Annapolis Sailing School. The oldest part of the four-building complex is a 1780 Danish townhouse, now one of the historic places of St. Croix. Years ago the building was a private club for wealthy planters. Fame came when Jane Gottlieb, the Ziegfeld Follies star, opened it as a hotel in 1948. In the 1950s, the hotel became a mecca for writers and artists, including, among others, Noël Coward. The efficiency rooms, with ceiling fans, are in four buildings clustered around the pool. Guest rooms have a bright tropical feeling, with ceiling fans, floral prints, and rattan furnishings, including good mattresses on the king or twin beds. The baths are medium in size with a combination shower and tub. You get more atmosphere here than anywhere else in town, and guests quickly get to know each other around the bar. Other than the complimentary breakfast and a 24-hour complimentary bar, you're on your own for meals.

BEST OFF-SEASON BET

Club St. Croix. 3280 Estate Golden Rock (Route 70), Christiansted, St. Croix, U.S.V.I. 00820. ☎ **800/524-2025** or 340/773-4800. Fax 340/773-8726. 54 units. A/C TV TEL. Winter efficiencies and junior suites $150 double; 1-bedroom apt. for up to 4, $195; 2-bedroom apts. for up to 6, $245. Off-season efficiencies and junior suites $110 double; 1-bedroom apt. for up to 4 $150; 2-bedroom apts. for up to 6, $160. AE, MC, V.

Adjacent to its own beach, about a quarter-mile north of Christiansted's center, this is a well-managed upscale apartment complex. Each unit has its own kitchenette and between one and two separate bedrooms. Built in the late 1970s and reconstructed in an upgraded form in the wake of Hurricane Hugo in 1989, it's a site for clean and partially tiled private apartments that afford privacy and the ever-present option of saving money on meals you prepare yourself on-site. Each contains both rattan and wicker furnishings including glass-topped tables, excellent beds with firm mattresses, uphol-steries whose tropical colors were inspired by a Caribbean summer, and views over Buck Island and the glittering lights of Christiansted. The small baths are exceedingly well maintained, with quality fixtures. Breezes restaurant is open daily for lunch and dinner. There's a pool and three tennis courts on the premises, as well as a private dock and a bar.

AT FREDERIKSTED

Cottages by the Sea. 127A Smithfield, Frederiksted, St. Croix, U.S.V.I. 00840. ☎ 800/323-7252 or 340/772-1753. Fax 340/772-1753. 22 units. A/C TV. Winter $95–$115 cottage for 1 or 2; $175 villa for 4. Off-season $70–$95 cottage for 1 or 2; $140 villa for 4. Extra person $20 in winter, $15 off-season. AE, DISC, MC, V.

These isolated cottages are on the water right outside Frederiksted, about 6 miles from the airport. In 1998, *Caribbean Travel & Life* voted this the best bargain of the U.S. Virgins. The enterprise was launched with 4 cottages back in the late 1970s and has increased to 20. The managers, Vicki McFee and Richard Mercure, like to keep it quiet so no children under the age of 8 are allowed. Some cottages are made of cinder blocks and others of wood. The timeworn interiors include paneling, and all cottages have air-conditioning, TVs, and private patios. The look is a bit spartan but reason-ably comfortable. Most rooms have king-size or twin beds, with freshly renewed mat-tresses, along with tight, compact baths. Maintenance is excellent, however. There are big patios out front where guests can grill their dinners. Water sports have to be arranged elsewhere, but guests are welcome to go snorkeling in the waters just outside the grounds.

On the Beach Resort. Frederiksted Beach (P.O. Box 1908), Frederiksted, St. Croix, U.S.V.I. 00841. ☎ **800/524-2018** or 340/772-1205. Fax 340/772-1757. www.gaytravel.com/onthebeach. E-mail: onthebeach@virginisland.net. 23 units. Winter $125–$303 single or double. Off-season $70–$180 single or double. Rates include continental breakfast. AE, DISC, MC, V.

The best-known gay hotel in Frederiksted, this small place lies half a mile from the town's shopping and dining facilities. Catering to both gays and lesbians, or anyone else for that matter, the hotel offers comfortably furnished but small rooms, all with kitchenettes, good mattresses, and tiny private baths. Units have a lot of thoughtful extras, like VCRs, computer hook-ups, private safes, ironing boards and irons, coolers, and hair dryers. There are two freshwater pools, a hot tub, and a beachfront patio. The resort's restaurant is one of the best in Frederiksted.

WORTH A SPLURGE

Sprat Hall Plantation. Rte. 63 (P.O. Box 695), Frederiksted, St. Croix, U.S.V.I. 00841. ☎ **800/843-3584** or 340/772-0305. Fax 340/772-2880. 17 units. A/C TV. Winter $110–$120 single; $120–$130 double; $150 suite; $200 cottage; $150 Great House room. Off-season $90–$100 single; $100–$110 double; $130 suite; $200 cottage; $130 Great House room. No credit cards.

This resort, 1 mile north of Frederiksted, is the oldest plantation Great House (and the only French-built plantation house left intact) in the Virgin Islands. Dating from St. Croix's French occupation of 1650 to 1690, it's set on 20 acres, with private white-sand beaches. The plantation has room for about 40 people, depending on how many guests use the cottage units, which all have radios.

The units in the Great House have been designated for nonsmokers because of the value of the antiques. An annex was built in the 1940s, and each of its units has simple furnishings and a view of the sea. If you prefer your Caribbean living old-fashioned and homey, ask for a room in the Great House. The cottages aren't very romantic but have been remodeled and refurnished with queen-size beds with good mattresses; you'll find greater comfort elsewhere on the island, though nothing that even comes close to matching the history and legacy of this place. You can be assured of good food, at the Beach Restaurant during the lunch hour or in the Sprat Hall Restaurant. Guests are requested to dress with decorum—no jeans or T-shirts, please. Only guests of the hotel and/or their invited guests can attend dinners. On the grounds is a worthwhile equestrian stable (see below). The Hurd and Young families run the operation and offer hiking and bird-watching, as well as snorkeling, swimming, and shore fishing. Jetskiing and waterskiing can be arranged.

GREAT DEALS ON DINING
IN & AROUND CHRISTIANSTED

The Bombay Club. 5A King St. ☎ **340/773-1838.** Reservations recommended. Main courses $10–$18. MC, V. Mon–Fri 11am–10pm, Sat–Sun 6–10pm. INTERNATIONAL.

The owners have managed to squeeze much miscellany into what has become one of the most enduring restaurants in Christiansted. It's concealed from the street by the brick foundations of an 18th-century planter's townhouse. You enter through a low stone tunnel and eventually find yourself near its bar and the courtyard that contains many of its tables. The food, while not overly fancy, is plentiful, flavorful, and reasonably priced. Menu items include the catch of the day, regional dishes like conch, veal dishes, beef filet, and pasta. The island's best fresh lobster pasta is served here. The catch of the day mentioned is likely to be wahoo, tuna, or dolphin.

Cheeseburgers in Paradise. 57 Southgate. ☎ **340/773-1119.** Main courses $6.50–$8.50. MC, V. Daily 11am–11pm (bar open later). WEST INDIAN.

Three miles outside of Christiansted, this restaurant isn't owned by Jimmy Buffett but does make the best burgers on island. You get almost a half pound of meat with all the fixin's. A margarita accompanies many a burger plate. Cheeseburgers aren't all: You get an array of burritos, freshly made salads, a tasty grilled chicken sandwich, and daily specials. The pizza oven is heated up on Thursday. Dinners run the gamut from barbecued ribs to stir-fry. The fresh fish dishes are excellent, and the chef has a winning way with chicken and cooks a big prime rib on Saturday. Live music is presented Thursday to Sunday.

Comanche Club. 1 Strand St. ☎ **340/773-2665.** Reservations recommended. Main courses $9.95–$18; lunch from $12. AE, MC, V. Mon–Sat 11:30am–2:30pm and 5:30–9:30pm. CARIBBEAN/CONTINENTAL.

One of the island's most popular restaurants, Comanche is relaxed yet elegant. The specialties are eclectic—everything from fish and conch chowder to shark cakes. Each night a different special is featured. There's also a good selection of Cruzan dishes, one for every night of the week. Salads and a cold buffet are traditionally featured; the Comanche curries have won over devotees. Island fish are generally sautéed with lemon butter and capers; typical West Indian dishes include conch Creole with fungi. You can also order standard international dishes like filet mignon with béarnaise sauce.

The Hideaway. At the Hibiscus Beach Hotel, La Grande Princesse. ☎ **340/773-4042.** Reservations recommended. Main courses $10–$20; lunch $6–$10. AE, DISC, MC, V. Daily 7am–10pm. AMERICAN.

Three miles west of Christiansted, this open-air restaurant fronts one of the island's best beaches. Even if you don't go here for dinner, you might want to patronize it at lunch. It's a true hideaway, known for serving one of the island's best breakfasts, including good stuff like eggs Benedict and salmon with sour cream. The chef also makes one of the island's best omelets. At lunch, you get the usual burgers and sandwiches, as well as hot main-dish specialties. At night, the menu is considerably upgraded, based on the market that day. You can usually get fresh fish prepared as you like it, along with lobster (sometimes available). The baby-back ribs are a winner, and chicken and beef are prepared in interesting ways. On Wednesday, it's beach barbecue time, all-you-can-eat for $15. And on Tuesday it's all the tacos you can eat for only $5.

Junie's Bar and Restaurant. 132 Peter's Rest. ☎ **340/773-2801.** Lunch main courses $6–$9; dinner main courses $7–$20. AE, DC, DISC, MC, V. Mon–Sat 10am–11pm; Sun 11am–8pm. WEST INDIAN/SEAFOOD.

A favorite of locals and particularly the island's taxi drivers, this restaurant occupies a white-painted cement building about a half-mile south of Christiansted's main core. The wooden tables, metal chairs, bowls of cut flowers, and well-scrubbed kind of simplicity add to the appeal. Your hosts, Junie Allen and her daughter Denise, prepare a flavorful but basic medley of West Indian staples, including a roster of drinks you might not have tasted before. Examples are sea moss, a kind of eggnog flavored with pulverized seaweed; mauby, fermented from rainwater and tree bark; and ginger beer. Good-tasting menu items include boiled fish, conch, or lobster in butter sauce; stewed goat; Creole-style lobster; and pork chops with greens and yams. Desserts feature carrot cake, cheesecake, and key lime pie.

Harbormaster Restaurant. At the Hotel on the Cay, Protestant Cay. ☎ **340/773-2035.** Main courses $5.75–$15.50; breakfast from $2.75. AE, DISC, MC, V. Mon–Fri 8am–5pm, Tues 7–9:30pm. AMERICAN.

A 4-minute ferry ride across the harbor from Christiansted, this is where guests at the local town inns head for a day at the beach (it's the nearest, best beach). While here, you don't want to go back into Christiansted for lunch, so the hotel has decided to accommodate its many day visitors by offering this quite acceptable restaurant. The cookery isn't the island's best, but it's good. Of course, you get the usual array of salad platters, sandwiches, omelets, and burgers. But many main dishes are more elaborate and appealing, especially the grilled fillet of dolphin (or swordfish); the conch in lemon, garlic, and butter sauce; and the barbecued ribs. The chef also prepares a good dinner, but only 1 night a week: the Tuesday evening West Indian barbecue. You pay $23 for all-you-can-eat and are entertained by steel band music.

Harvey's. 11B Company St. ☎ **340/773-3433.** Main courses $7–$10. No credit cards. Mon–Sat 11:30am–5pm. CARIBBEAN/CONTINENTAL.

Forget the plastic and the flowery tablecloths that give this place the aura of a 1950s time warp, and try to grab one of its dozen or so tables. If you do, you can enjoy the thoroughly zesty cooking of island matriarch Sarah Harvey, who takes joy in her work and definitely aims to fill your stomach with her basic but hearty fare. Try one of her homemade soups, especially the callaloo or chicken. She'll even serve you conch in butter sauce as an appetizer. For a main dish you might choose from barbecue chicken, barbecue spareribs, boiled fillet of snapper, and even lobster when they can get it. Fungi comes with just about everything. For dessert, try one of her delectable tarts made from guava, pineapple, or coconut.

✪ **Luncheria.** In the Apothecary Hall Courtyard, 2111 Company St. ☎ **340/773-4247.** Main courses $5–$7.75. No credit cards. Mon–Fri 11am–9pm, Sat noon–9pm. MEXICAN/CUBAN/PUERTO RICAN.

In a historic courtyard in the center of town, this Mexican restaurant offers some of the best dining values on the island. You get the usual tacos, tostadas, burritos, nachos, and enchiladas. Specialties include chicken fajitas, enchiladas verde, and arroz con pollo (spiced chicken with brown rice). Daily specials feature both low-calorie and vegetarian choices, and the chef's refried beans are lard free. Whole-wheat tortillas are offered. Check the board for daily specials, and know that the salsa bar is complimentary, ranging from mild to hot sauce, plus jalapeños. Some Cuban and Puerto Rican dishes have appeared on the menu, like zesty chicken curry, black-bean soup, and roast pork. The bartender makes the island's best margaritas. However, the $1 cheap version is referred to as "ethyl" or "jet fuel" by locals.

Marina Bar & Grill. At the Kings Landing Yacht Club. ☎ **340/773-0103.** Main courses $5.50–$10. AE, MC, V. Daily 7am–9pm. CARIBBEAN/CONTINENTAL.

Some in-the-know boaters head here for their morning pick-me-up, a spicy Bloody Mary to get their blood circulating. You can join them for breakfast, which is rather standard fare, with bagels, muffins, and eggs as you like them. Lunch is also a bit standard; many opt for one of the burgers, even a veggie burger. The best bet is one of the daily specials. In the evening the menu perks up, and fresh fish is the best item to order. Your dinner is often accompanied by steel drum music. If you show up Monday night you can get in on the crab races. Locals are fond of dining here, sitting on the waterfront watching the seaplane land.

✪ **Nolan's Tavern.** 5A Estate St. Peter, Christiansted East. ☎ **340/773-6660.** Reservations recommended only for groups of 6 or more. Burgers $7–$8.50; main courses $12.75–$16.25. AE, DISC, MC, V. Kitchens daily 5–9pm; bar at 3pm. INTERNATIONAL/WEST INDIAN.

It's the first place people in the know think of when you ask them for a cozy Antillean tavern with absolutely no social pretensions. It's 2 miles east of Christiansted's harbor front, across from the Pearl B. Larsen School. Your host is Nolan Joseph, a Trinidad-born chef who makes a special point of welcoming guests and offering "tasty food and good service." No one will mind if you stop in just for a drink. Mr. Joseph, referred to by some diners as "King Conch," prepares the mollusk in at least half a dozen ways, including versions with curry, Creole sauce, and garlic-pineapple sauce. He reportedly experimented for 3 months to perfect a means of tenderizing the tough mollusk without artificial chemicals, and you'll be able to assess his progress. His ribs are also worthy. Many guests come here to fill up on steak, ribs, and chicken.

✪ **Paradise Café.** 53B Company St. (at Queen Cross St.). ☎ **340/773-2985.** Breakfast $3.50–$7.50; lunch $4–$8; dinner $13–$22. MC, V. Mon–Sat 7:30am–3pm and 5–10pm. DELI/AMERICAN.

Across from Government House, this local dive won many friends as Camille's. Now with a new owner and a name change, the place remains a draw for savvy locals seeking good food and great value. Its brick walls and beamed ceiling were originally part of an 18th-century Great House. New York deli food is served during the day. Enjoy the savory homemade soups or a choice of freshly made salads to which you may add grilled chicken or grilled fish. Daily luncheon specials are also a feature. At breakfast you can select from an assortment of omelets, even steak and eggs if you have a hearty appetite. Dinners are more elaborate and very good tasting, especially the 12-ounce New York strip steak or one of the freshly made pasta specialties.

Percy's Place. In the Apothecary Hall Courtyard, Company St. ☎ **340/773-8666.** Main courses $6.75–$8.50. No credit cards. Daily 11:30am–3pm. MEDITERRANEAN/GREEK/CARIBBEAN.

This local hangout is a good inexpensive place for lunch if you're spending the day shopping in Christiansted. The food doesn't exactly explode with color and flavor but is quite good. A wide variety of cuisines is offered, happily blending the Mediterranean and the Caribbean. Dining is in air-conditioned rooms or else in the courtyard with an open-air porch for sunlovers and smokers. The pastas are quite decent, including some in pesto sauce. A variety of soups are homemade daily, and you can also get some of the town's best sandwiches. Call 2 days in advance and the chef will prepare his locally celebrated West Indian red bean soup made with red beans, pumpkin, and sweet potatoes. Locals come from miles around to order bowl after bowl of this soup.

Stixx on the Waterfront. 39 Strand St. ☎ **340/773-5157.** Reservations recommended. Main courses $10–$30; lunches from $5.50; all-you-can-eat Sun brunch $10. AE, MC, V. Daily 7am–10pm. INTERNATIONAL/AMERICAN.

This rustic eatery is on the waterfront in downtown Christiansted. This two-story place at the Pan Am Pavilion has a deck extending out over the harbor, and it has been said that this restaurant sells more lobster than anywhere else on the island, thus making it the house specialty. The good-tasting menu is varied from chicken to seafood. Stixx is also known for its stuffed mushrooms, the swordfish served with a mango salsa, and grilled vegetables over angel-hair pasta, with surf-and-turf specials once or twice a week.

WORTH A SPLURGE

✪ **South Shore Café.** Junction of Rtes 62 and 624. ☎ **340/773-9311.** Reservations required. Main courses $14.75–$21.75. V. Mid-Dec to Apr Wed–Sun 6–9pm; May to mid-Dec Thurs–Sun 6–9pm. AMERICAN.

Set in a breezy building on an isolated inland region ("in the middle of nowhere") 2 miles southeast of Christiansted, this is a charming and intensely personalized restaurant whose décor reflects the family-style dining that has helped make the place a success since its debut. Diane Scheuber is the owner. Her decorating quirks (including a collection of umbrellas—her trademark—hanging from the ceiling of the lattice-trimmed dining room) add a funky note to what are usually well-turned-out meals with a rural North American twist. Excellent examples are ravioli stuffed with sweet potatoes and spring onions, tomato-based Sicilian clam chowder, baked Brie with Cruzan rum sauce, local grilled fish with herb-flavored butter sauce, and homemade grilled chicken lasagna with sun-dried tomatoes and sherry-flavored cream sauce.

IN & AROUND FREDERIKSTED

✪ **Blue Moon.** 17 Strand St. ☎ **340/772-2222.** Main courses $14–$18.50. AE, DISC, MC, V. Tues–Fri 11:30am–2pm, Tues–Sat 6–9:30pm, Sun 11am–2pm and 6–9pm. Closed Aug. INTERNATIONAL/CAJUN.

The best little bistro in Frederiksted becomes a hip spot during Sunday brunch and on Friday nights, when it offers entertainment. A favorite of all visiting jazz musicians, the bistro is in a 200-year-old stone house on the waterfront. For more than a decade, it's been going strong, building up a savvy local following. Tourists have now discovered but not ruined it. It's decorated with funky, homemade art from the U.S., including a garbage-can-lid restaurant sign. It has a very casual, cafe-like atmosphere. Begin with the "lunar pie," with feta cheese, cream cheese, onions, mushrooms, and celery in phyllo pastry. Or else opt for the artichoke-and-spinach dip. This could be followed by the catch of the day or, on occasion, Maine lobster. The clams in garlic sauce are also from Maine. Vegetarians opt for the spinach fettuccine, and there's the usual array of steak and chicken dishes. Save room for the yummy guava pie for dessert.

Dowies. 111 Market St. ☎ **340/772-0845.** Breakfasts $3.75–$5.50; lunch platters $3.75–$8.50. MC, V. Tues–Sat 7:30am–2pm. CARIBBEAN/AMERICAN.

Buck Island: Unspoiled Nature & World-Class Snorkeling

The crystal-clear waters and the white coral sand of ✪ **Buck Island,** a satellite of St. Croix, are legendary. Some visitors, including Arthur Frommer, have called it the single most important attraction of the Caribbean. In years past, the island was frequented by the swashbuckling likes of Morgan, LaFitte, Blackbeard, and even Captain Kidd. Now the **National Park Service** has marked an underwater snorkeling trail in the waters offshore, attracting a new generation of seafarers. The park covers about 850 acres, including the land area, which has a sandy beach with picnic tables and barbecue pits, as well as rest rooms and a small changing room. There are two major underwater trails for snorkeling on the reef, plus many other labyrinths and grottoes for more serious divers.

You can also take a **hiking trail** through the tropical vegetation covering the island. Despite the fact that access to Buck Island is only via chartered tours and boat trips, this is one of the most-visited rock spits in the Caribbean.

Only ⅓ mile wide and a mile long, Buck Island lies 1½ miles off the northeastern coast of St. Croix. A barrier reef shelters many reef fish, including queen angelfish and smooth trunkfish. The attempt to return the presently uninhabited Buck Island to nature has been successful—even endangered brown pelicans are producing young here. Small boats run between St. Croix and Buck Island, and snorkeling equipment is supplied. You head out in the morning, and nearly all charters allow for 1½ hours of snorkeling and swimming. You can have a memorable ramble through sun-flooded and shallow waters off the rocky coast. Circumnavigating the island on foot will take about 2 hours. Buck Island's trails meander from several points along its coast to its sun-flooded summit, affording views over nearby St. Croix.

A couple of warnings: Bring protection from the sun's sometimes merciless rays; and even more important, don't rush to touch every plant you see. The island's western

Its regulars appreciate this place for its complete lack of pretense, its hearty portions, and its West Indian format. Sheltered from the sun and rain with a corrugated tin roof, with tables set on a bed of gravel in the open air, this local diner occupies a prominent position in the heart of Frederiksted. Actually, it's a bit more elegant then the Formica-sheathed countertops you might've expected: Madras-patterned tablecloths cover most surfaces, and diners can choose from a cosmopolitan choice of American and West Indian food. Breakfast includes omelets (meat, vegetarian, and seafood); as well as French toast and any imaginable kind of eggs. On Friday and Saturday, an additional option is a Cruzan breakfast with saltfish, johnnycakes, and banana fritters. Lunches include platters of grilled fish, served with beans, rice, and stewed greens; a prize-winning version of fish pudding; bullfoot soup; stewed conch in butter sauce; grilled or jerk chicken meatloaf plates; and sandwiches. After around 2:30pm, everyone goes home and the place is shut up tight.

Turtle's Deli. 625 Strand St. ☎ **340/772-3676.** Sandwiches $5.50–$7.50. No credit cards. Mon–Sat 10am–4:30pm. DELI.

This is the only seafront deli on St. Croix, and so lots of the folk who buy the over-stuffed sandwiches sold here make a beeline for the handful of outdoor tables sitting atop the wharf at its back side. Thomas Kash, who was born in the Midwest but whose edge has groves of poisonous machineel trees, whose leaves, bark, and fruit cause extreme irritation if they come into contact with human skin.

Buck Island's greatest attraction is its **underwater snorkeling trail,** which rings part of the island. Equipped with a face mask, swim fins, and a snorkel, you'll be treated to some of the Caribbean's most beautiful underwater views. Plan on spending at least two-thirds of a day at this extremely famous ecological site.

Mile Mark Watersports, in the King Christian Hotel, 59 King's Wharf, Christiansted (☎ **800/523-DIVE** or 340/773-2628), conducts twice-daily tours of Buck Island. They offer two ways to reach the reefs. One is a half-day tour aboard a glass-bottom boat departing from the King Christian Hotel. Tours are daily 9:30am to 1pm and 1:30 to 5pm, costing $35 per person, all snorkeling equipment included. A more romantic half-day journey is aboard one of the company's sailboats, which, for $45 per person, offers the sea breezes and the thrill of harnessing the wind's power to reach the reef. A full-day tour, offered daily 10am to 4pm on the company's 40-foot catamaran, can take up to 20 participants to Buck Island's reefs. Included in the tour are a West Indian barbecue picnic on the isolated sands of Buck Island's beaches and plenty of opportunities for snorkeling. The full-day tour costs $70.

Captain Heinz (☎ **340/773-3161** or 340/773-4041) is an Austrian-born skipper with more than 25 years of sailing experience. His trimaran, *Teroro II,* leaves Green Cay Marina H Dock at 9am and 2pm, never filled with more than 24 passengers. The snorkeling trip costs $50 in the morning or $45 in the afternoon, all gear and safety equipment provided. The captain is not only a skilled sailor but also a considerate host. He'll even take you around the outer reef, which the other guides don't, for an unforgettable underwater experience.

deli follows New York City models, serves salads, baked-on-site bread, bagels, lox, and cold cuts, as well as pastries and munchies. The place is especially good at packing boxed picnics. During the lifetime of this edition, a more formal bistro, the Café du Soleil, might open upstairs from this deli; at this writing it was closed because of the owner's self-defined burnout and the devastation of the 1998 hurricanes.

Sprat Hall Beach Restaurant. Rte. 63. ☎ **340/772-5855.** Lunch $7–$15. No credit cards. Daily 10am–4pm (hot food 11:30am–2:30pm). CARIBBEAN.

One mile north of Frederiksted, this is an informal spot on the western coast near Sprat Hall Plantation. It's the best place on the island to combine lunch and a swim. Try such local dishes as conch chowder, pumpkin fritters, tannia soup, and fried fish of the day. These dishes have authentic island flavor, perhaps more so than any other place on the island. If you'd like more standard fare, they also do salads and burgers. The bread is home-baked daily. The place is directed by Cruzan-born Joyce Merwin Hurd and her husband, Jim, who charge $2 for use of the showers and changing rooms.

Vel's. 16A King St. ☎ **340/772-2160.** Main courses $6.50–$10. No credit cards. Mon–Sat 11am–8:30pm. PUERTO RICAN/WEST INDIAN.

Savvy local foodies, even the island governor, will steer you to this place if you're seeking down-home West Indian cookery. Val, a native of Puerto Rico, is the owner, and she does her own cooking. Does she ever know how to rattle those pots and pans. She also prepares a daily special; perhaps it'll be her classic arroz con pollo (chicken and rice) at the time of your visit. She does a really tasty pork, as well as a savory beef stew, and somehow gets the best fish caught on the island. She also prepares a "mean" conch. The place is so popular that some residents from St. Thomas come over here just to dine.

Villa Morales. Plot 82C, off Route 70, Estate Whim. ☎ **340/772-0556.** Reservations recommended. Main courses $6–$28. AE, MC, V. Tues–Wed 11am–6pm; Thurs–Sat 11am–10pm. PUERTO RICAN.

Set inland from the sea in a rambling building from the 1950s that lies about 2 miles from Frederiksted, this is one of the premier Puerto Rican restaurants in St. Croix. You can choose between indoor and outdoor seating areas, including a cozy bar lined with the memorabilia collected by several generations of the Puerto Rican family that maintains the place. No one will mind if you come just to drink, but if you want a meal, platters will invariably be garnished with beans and rice. Look for a broad cross section of Hispanic tastes. Savory examples are fried snapper with white rice and beans, stewed conch, roasted or stewed goat, stewed beef, and bacon-enriched barbecued fried chicken. Most of the dishes are at the lower end of the price scale. About once a month, the owners transform the place into a dance hall, bringing in live salsa and merengue bands, with entrance fees of between $5 and $12, depending on how well-known the band is.

HITTING THE BEACHES

Beaches are St. Croix's big attraction. The drawback is that getting to them from Christiansted, home to most of the hotels, isn't always easy. It can also be expensive, especially if you want to go back and forth every day of your stay. Of course, you can always rent one of those housekeeping condos right on the water.

We highly recommend **Davis Bay** and ✪ **Cane Bay**—they're the type of beaches you'd expect to find on a Caribbean island, with palms, white sand, and good swimming and snorkeling. These are north shore beaches, and the waters aren't always tranquil. The snorkeling is truly spectacular, however, and you'll see elkhorn and brain corals some 250 yards off the "Cane Bay Wall." Cane Bay adjoins Route 80 on the north shore. Snorkelers and divers are attracted to this beach, with its rolling waves, coral gardens, and drop-off wall. No reefs guard the approach to Davis Beach, which draws bodysurfers but doesn't have changing facilities. It's in the vicinity of the Carambola Beach Resort.

In Christiansted, if you want to beach it, head for the **Hotel on the Cay.** You'll have to take a ferry to this palm-shaded island with its beach of white sand. **Cramer Park,** at the northeastern end of the island, is a special public park operated by the Department of Agriculture. Lined with sea grape trees, the beach also has a picnic area, a restaurant, and a bar.

Windsurfers like **Reef Beach,** which opens onto Teague Bay along Route 82, East End Road, a half-hour ride from Christiansted. Food can be ordered at Duggan's Reef. On Route 63, a short ride north of Frederiksted, **Rainbow Beach** beckons with its white sand and ideal snorkeling conditions. In the vicinity, also on Route 63, about 5 minutes north of Frederiksted, **La Grange** is another good beach. Lounge chairs can be rented, and there's a bar nearby.

At the **Cormorant Beach Club** about 5 miles west of Christiansted, some 1,200 feet of white sands are shaded by palm trees attracting a gay crowd. Since a living reef lies just off the shore, snorkeling conditions are ideal. **Grapetree Beach** offers about the same footage of clean white sand on the eastern tip of the island (Route 60). Follow the South Shore Road to reach it. Water sports are popular here.

Two more beaches on St. Croix are **Buccaneer Beach,** 2 miles west of Christiansted, and **Sandy Point,** directly south of Frederiksted, the largest beach in all the U.S. Virgin Islands. Its waters are shallow and calm, perfect for swimming. Jutting out from southwestern St. Croix like a small peninsula, Sandy Point is reached by taking the Melvin Evans Highway (Route 66) west from the Alexander Hamilton Airport.

For the adventurer, there's an array of beaches at the East End of the island, but without a four-wheel drive it is very difficult to get here. Once you do you'll practically have the place to yourself. The best beach here is **Isaac Bay Beach,** its white sands ideal for snorkeling, swimming or sunbathing.

The most celebrated beach in St. Croix is offshore ✪ **Buck Island,** part of the U.S. National Park network. Reached by boat, Buck Island is actually a volcanic islet surrounded by some of the most stunning underwater coral gardens in the Caribbean. The beaches here are beautiful, filled with white sand against a backdrop of vegetation, but the snorkeling is even more acclaimed. The elkhorn coral here are among the most massive specimens on earth. The white-sand beaches lie mainly on the southwest and west coasts. These shores line an interior filled with such plants as cactus, wild frangipani, or pigeonwood. There are picnic areas on Buck Island if you want to bring provisions and make a day of it. Boat departures are from Kings Wharf in Christiansted, the ride taking half an hour.

SPORTS & OUTDOOR PURSUITS

GOLF   St. Croix has the best golfing in the U.S. Virgins. In fact, guests staying on St. John and St. Thomas often fly over for a day's round on the island's two 18-hole and one 9-hole golf courses.

The ✪ **Carambola Golf Course,** on the northeast side of St. Croix (☎ 340/778-5638), was designed by Robert Trent Jones Sr., who called it "the loveliest course I ever designed." The course, formerly the Fountain Valley and the site of "Shell's Wonderful World of Golf," has been likened to a botanical garden. Its collection of par-3 holes is known to golfing authorities as the best in the tropics. Carambola's course record of 65 was set by Jim Levine in 1993. Greens fees are $70 per person for a day in winter ($48 in summer), which allows you to play as many holes as you like. Golf cart rentals are mandatory and cost $13 for 18 holes.

The other major course, at **The Buccaneer,** Gallows Bay (☎ 340/773-2100, ext. 738), 2 miles east of Christiansted, is a challenging 5,810-yard, 18-hole course with panoramic vistas that allow the player to knock the ball over rolling hills right to the edge of the Caribbean. Nonguests of this deluxe resort pay $55 in winter or $45 off-season, including use of a cart.

A final course is the **Reef,** at Teague Bay (☎ 340/773-8844), a 3,100-yard, 9-hole course, charging greens fees of $10, with carts renting for $5 to $7. On the east end of the island, its longest hole is a 579-yard par 5.

HIKING   The **St. Croix Environmental Association,** 6 Company St. (☎ 340/773-1989), in Christiansted, offers regularly scheduled hikes from December to March. In addition to in-season hikes, their programs include lectures, slide shows, and films on environmental issues. Prices for events vary, and contributions are accepted.

HORSEBACK RIDING   Specializing in nature tours, **Paul and Jill's Equestrian Stables,** Sprat Hall Plantation, Route 58 (☎ 340/772-2880), is the largest equestrian stable in the Virgin Islands. Set on the sprawling grounds of the island's oldest plantation Great House, it's operated by Paul Wojcie and his wife, Jill Hurd, one of the daughters of the original founders. The stables are known throughout the Caribbean for the quality of the horses and the scenic trail rides through the forests, past ruins of abandoned 18th-century plantations and sugar mills, to the tops of the hills of St. Croix's western end. All tours are accompanied by the operators, who give running commentaries on island fauna, history, and riding techniques. Beginners and experienced riders alike are welcome.

A 2-hour trail ride costs $50 per person. Tours usually depart daily in winter at 10am and 4pm, and off-season at 5pm, with slight variations according to demand. Reservations at least a day in advance are important.

TENNIS Some authorities rate the tennis at the ✪ **Buccaneer,** Gallows Bay (☎ **340/773-2100,** ext. 736) as the best in the Caribbean. This resort offers a choice of eight courts, two lit for night games, all open to the public. Nonguests pay $8 per person per hour; however, you must call to reserve a court. A tennis pro is available for lessons, and there's also a pro shop.

A notable selection of recently restored courts can also be found at the **Sunterra Resorts Carambola Golf Club** at Kingshill (☎ **340/778-3800**), which has five clay courts open to guests of the hotel, who play for free. Courts are no longer lit for night games; both a pro shop and a tennis pro offering lessons are available.

WATER SPORTS Sponge life, black-coral trees (the finest in the West Indies), and steep drop-offs into water near the shoreline have made St. Croix a diver's dream.

✪ **Buck Island,** with an underwater visibility of more than 100 feet, is the site of an underwater nature trail, and it's the major diving target (see the box "Buck Island: Unspoiled Nature & World-Class Snorkeling," earlier in this chapter). All the minor and major agencies offer scuba and snorkeling tours to Buck Island. St. Croix is home to the largest living reef in the Caribbean, including the fabled north-shore **wall** that begins in 25 to 30 feet of water and drops, sometimes straight down, to 13,200 feet. There are 22 moored sites, allowing the dive boats to tie up without damaging the reef. Favorite scuba-diving sites include the historic **Salt River Canyon,** the gorgeous coral gardens of **Scotch Banks,** and **Eagle Ray,** the latter so named because of the rays that cruise along the wall there. **Pavilions** is yet another good dive site, with a virgin coral reef that's in pristine shape.

Dive St. Croix, 59 King's Wharf (☎ **800/523-DIVE** in the U.S., or 340/773-2628; fax 340/773-7400), operates the 38-foot dive boat *Reliance.* The staff offers complete instruction from resort courses through full certification, as well as night dives. A resort course is $80, with a two-tank dive going for $75. Scuba trips to Buck Island are offered for $65, and dive packages begin at $250 for five dives.

V.I. Divers Ltd., in the Pan Am Pavilion on Christiansted's waterfront (☎ **800/544-5911** or 340/773-6045), is the oldest (opened 1971) and one of the best dive operations on the island. In fact, *Rodales Scuba Diving* magazine rated its staff as among the top 10 worldwide. A full-service PADI five-star facility, it offers daily two-tank boat dives, guided snorkeling trips to Green Cay, night dives, and a full range of scuba-training programs from introductory dives through dive master. Introductory dives, which require no experience, are $75 for a two-tank dive, including all instruction and equipment. The outfitter offers a six-dive package for $205 and a 10-dive package for $330. A two-tank boat or beach dive is priced at $75, with night dives going for $60. A 2-hour guided snorkel tour costs $75, or $35 for the boat snorkeling trip to Green Cay.

The best place for the increasingly popular sport of windsurfing is the **St. Croix Water Sports Center** (☎ **340/773-7060**), on a small offshore island in Christiansted Harbor and part of the Hotel on the Cay. They give lessons and are open daily 10am to 5pm. Windsurfing rentals are $25 per hour. They also offer Sea Doos, which seat two and can be rented for $45 to $55 per half hour, parasailing for $65 per person, and snorkeling equipment for $20 per day.

St. Croix Water Sports (above) now offers an ideal way for visitors to view the island's aquatic life without getting wet. *Oceanique,* a semi-submersible vessel acting as part submarine and part cruiser, carries visitors on one-hour excursions through Christiansted harbor and along Protestant Cay. The inch-thick windows lining the vessel's underwater observation room provide views of St. Croix's marine life in a cool and dry environment. The cruiser, one of only two of its kind in the world, is especially popular with children and non-swimmers. Day and night excursions are available for $25 for adults and $15 for children.

SEEING THE SIGHTS

Taxi tours are the ideal way to explore the island. For one or two passengers, the cost is often $40 for 2 hours or $60 for 3 hours. All prices should be negotiated and agreed on in advance. For more information, call the **St. Croix Taxi Association** at ☎ 340/778-1088.

THE RAIN FOREST

Unlike the rest of St. Croix, a verdant parcel in the island's western district is covered with dense forest, a botanical landscape very different from the scrub-covered hills on other parts of the island. Set amid the sparsely populated terrain of the island's northwestern corner, north of Frederiksted, the area grows thick with mahogany trees, kapok (silk-cotton) trees, turpentine (red birch) trees, samaan (rain) trees, and all kinds of ferns and vines. Sweet limes, mangos, hog plums, and breadfruit trees, which have sown themselves in the wild since the plantation era, are woven among the forest's larger trees. Bird life includes crested hummingbirds, pearly-eyed thrashers, green-throated caribs, yellow warblers, and perky banana quits.

Although the district isn't technically a tropical rain forest, it's known by virtually everyone as the Rain Forest. How best to experience its botanical charms? Some visitors opt to drive along Route 76 (also known as Mahogany Road), stopping the car beside any of the footpaths meandering off the highway into dry riverbeds and glens on either side. (It's advisable to stick to the best worn of the footpaths to avoid losing your way and to retrace your steps after a few moments of admiring the local botany.)

Equally feasible is a hike beside those highways of the island's western sector where few cars ever venture. Three of the most viable are the **Creque Dam Road** (Routes 58/78), the **Scenic Road** (Route 78), and the **Western Scenic Road** (Routes 63/78). Consider beginning your trek near the junction of Creque Dam Road and Scenic Road. (Though passable by cars, it's likely you'll see only a few along these roads during your entire walking tour.)

Your trek will cover a broad triangular swath, beginning at the above-mentioned junction, heading north and then west along Scenic Road. The road will first rise and then descend toward the coastal lighthouse of the island's extreme northwestern tip, **Hamm's Bluff.** Most trekkers decide to retrace their steps after about 45 minutes of northwesterly walking, returning to their parked cars after admiring the land and seascapes. Real diehards, however, can continue trekking all the way to the coastline, head south along the coastal road (Butler Bay Road), then head east along Creque Dam Road to their parked car at the junction of Creque Dam Road and Scenic Road. Embark on this longer expedition only if you're really prepared for a prolonged trek (about 5 hours) and some serious nature-watching.

CHRISTIANSTED

The picture-book harbor town of the Caribbean, ✪ **Christiansted** is a handsomely restored (or at least in the process of being restored) Danish port. On the northeastern shore of the island, on a coral-bound bay, the town is filled with Danish buildings erected by prosperous merchants in the booming 18th century. These red-roofed structures are often washed in pink, ocher, or yellow. Arcades over the sidewalks make ideal shaded colonnades for shoppers. The whole area around the harbor front has been designated a historic site, including **Government House,** which is looked after by the National Park Service.

You can begin at the **visitors' bureau,** Queen Cross Street (☎ 340/773-0495), a yellow-sided building with a cedar-capped roof near the harbor front. It was built as the Old Scalehouse in 1856 to replace a similar structure that burned down. In its heyday, all taxable goods leaving and entering the harbor were weighed here. The scales that once stood here could accurately weigh barrels of sugar and molasses weighing up to 1,600 pounds each.

Steeple Building. On the waterfront off Hospital St. ☎ 340/773-1460. Admission $2 (also includes admission to Fort Christiansvaern, below). Daily 8am–5pm.

This building's full name is the Church of Lord God of Sabaoth, and it was completed in 1753 as St. Croix's first Lutheran church, now a major island attraction. It too stands near the harborfront, reached by going along Hospital Street. It was embellished with a steeple in 1794 to 1796, and today houses exhibits relating to island history and culture. The building was deconsecrated in 1831 and served at various times as a bakery, a hospital, and a school.

Fort Christiansvaern. ☎ 340/773-1460. Admission included in the ticket to the Steeple Building (above). Mon–Thurs 8am–5pm, Fri–Sat 9am–5pm.

This fortress overlooking the harbor is the best-preserved colonial fortification in the Virgin Islands. The fort is maintained as a historic monument by the National Park Service, and its original four-pronged star-shaped design was in accordance with the most advanced military planning of its era.

St. Croix Aquarium. Caravelle Arcade. ☎ 340/773-8995. Admission $4.50 adults, $2 children. Tues–Sat 11am–4pm.

This aquarium moved here from Frederiksted and has expanded with many exhibits, including one devoted to night creatures. In all, it houses some 40 species of marine animals and more than 100 species of invertebrates. With constant rotation, each creature can adjust easily back to its natural habitat, as hundreds pass through the tanks each year. A touch pond contains starfish, sea cucumbers, brittle stars, and pencil urchins. The aquarium allows you to become familiar with marine life before you see it while scuba diving or snorkeling.

FREDERIKSTED

This former Danish settlement at the western end of the island, about 17 miles from Christiansted, is a sleepy port town that comes to life only when a cruise ship docks at its shoreline. In 1994, a 1,500-foot pier opened to accommodate the largest cruise ships. The pier facility is designed to accommodate two large cruise vessels and two mini–cruise ships simultaneously.

Frederiksted was destroyed by a fire in 1879, and the citizens rebuilt it with wood frames and clapboards on top of the old Danish stone and yellow-brick foundations.

Most visitors begin their tour at russet-colored **Fort Frederik,** next to the cruise-ship pier (☎ 340/772-2021). Some historians claim this was the first fort to sound a foreign salute to the U.S. flag, in 1776. It was here on July 3, 1848, that Gov.-Gen. Peter von Scholten emancipated the slaves in the Danish West Indies. The fort, at the northern end of Frederiksted, has been restored to its 1840 appearance and is today a national historic landmark. In 1998, a bust was unveiled here of General Buddhoe, the young black man who led the insurrection of slaves into town to demand their freedom on July 3, 1848. You can explore the courtyard and stables, and a local history museum has been installed in what was once the Garrison Room. Admission is free, and it's open Monday to Saturday 8:30am to 4:30pm.

Just south of the fort, the Customs House is an 18th-century building with a 19th-century two-story gallery. Here you can go into the **visitors' bureau** at Strand Street (☎ 340/772-0357) and pick up a free map of the town.

AROUND THE ISLAND

North of Frederiksted you can drop in at **Sprat Hall,** the island's oldest plantation, or continue along to the rain forest, which covers about 15 acres, including the 150-foot-high **Creque Dam.** The terrain is private property, but the owner lets visitors go inside to explore. Most visitors come here to see the jagged estuary of the northern coastline's **Salt River.** The Salt River was where Columbus landed on November 14, 1493, the only known site where the explorer ever landed on what's now U.S. territory. Marking the 500th anniversary of Columbus's arrival, then-Pres. George Bush signed a bill creating the 912-acre **Salt River Bay National Historical Park and Ecological Preserve.** The landmass encompasses the site of the original Carib village explored by Columbus and his men, including the only ceremonial ball court ever discovered in the Lesser Antilles. The park contains the largest mangrove forest in the Virgin Islands, sheltering many endangered animals and plants, plus an underwater canyon attracting scuba divers from around the world.

At the Carib settlement, Columbus's men liberated several Taíno women and children who were being held as slaves. On the way back to their vessels, the Spaniards faced a canoe filled with hostile Caribs, armed with poison-tipped arrows. One Spanish soldier was killed, and perhaps six Caribs were either slain or captured. This is the first documented case of hostility between invading Europeans and the Native Americans. Sailing away, Columbus named this part of St. Croix Cape of the Arrows.

The **St. Croix Environmental Association,** 3 Arawak Building, Gallows Bay (☎ 340/773-1989), conducts tours of the area and can be called for details. Tours cost $15 for adults and $10 for children under 10.

St. George Village Botanical Garden of St. Croix. 127 Estate St., Kingshill. ☎ **340/692-2874.** Admission $5 adults, $1 children 12 and under; donations welcome. Nov–May daily 9am–5pm; June–Oct Tues–Sat 9am–4pm.

Just north of Centerline Road, 4 miles east of Frederiksted at Estate St. George, is a veritable 16-acre Eden of tropical trees, shrubs, vines, and flowers. Built around the ruins of a 19th-century sugarcane workers' village, the garden is a feast for the eye and the camera, from the entrance drive bordered by royal palms and bougainvillea to the towering kapok and tamarind trees. There's a gift shop and rest rooms, and self-guided walking-tour maps are available at the entrance to the garden's Great Hall.

Cruzan Rum Factory. W. Airport Rd., Rte. 64. ☎ **340/692-2280.** Admission $4. Tours Mon–Fri 9–11:30am and 1–4:15pm.

This factory distills the famous Virgin Islands rum, which is considered by residents to be the finest in the world. Guided tours depart from the visitors' pavilion; call for reservations and information. There's also a gift shop.

Estate Whim Plantation Museum. Centerline Rd. ☎ **340/772-0598.** Admission $6 adults, $1 children. June–Oct Tues–Sat 10am–3pm; Nov–May Mon–Sat 10am–4pm.

About 2 miles east of Frederiksted, this museum was restored by the St. Croix Landmarks Society and is unique among the many sugar plantations whose ruins dot St. Croix. This Great House is different from most in that it's composed of only three rooms. With 3-foot-thick walls made of stone, coral, and molasses, the house resembles a luxurious European château.

A division of Baker Furniture Company used the Whim Plantation's collection of models for one of its most successful reproductions, the Whim Museum–West Indies Collection. A showroom in the museum sells these reproductions, plus others from the Caribbean, including pineapple-motif four-poster beds, cane-bottomed planters' chairs with built-in leg rests, and Caribbean adaptations of Empire-era chairs with cane-bottomed seats.

Also on the museum's premises is a woodworking shop (featuring tools and techniques from the 18th century), the estate's original kitchen, a museum store, and servant's quarters. The ruins of the plantation's sugar-processing plant, complete with a restored windmill, remain.

SHOPPING

In **Christiansted,** where the core of our shopping recommendations are found, the emphasis is on hole-in-the-wall boutiques selling one-of-a-kind merchandise; the selection of handmade items is especially strong. Knowing it can't compete with Charlotte Amalie, Christiansted has forged its own creative statement and has now become *the* chic spot for merchandise in the Caribbean. All the shops are within half a mile or so.

Following the hurricanes of 1995, a major redevelopment of the waterfront at Christiansted was launched. The **King's Alley Complex** (☎ 340/778-8135) opened as a pink-sided compound, filled with the densest concentration of shopping options on St. Croix. The $1.2-million project was built on a 50-foot strip of land from Strand Street to King Street, the town's main thoroughfare. It bustles with merchants, vendors, and restaurants.

The Coconut Vine, Pan Am Pavilion, Strand Street (☎ 340/773-1991), is a little boutique, one of the most colorful and popular on the island. A storefront on the Pan Am Pavilion opens to a world of color and style. Hand-painted batiks for both men and women are the specialty for this tropical shop. **Crucian Gold,** 59 King's Wharf (☎ 340/773-5241), offers unique gold creations of island-born Brian Bishop. He designs all the gold jewelry himself, and less expensive versions of his work come in sterling silver. The most popular item is the Crucian bracelet, which contains a True Lovers' Knot in its design. The outlet also sells hand-tied knots (bound in gold wire), rings, pendants, and earrings.

Elegant Illusions Copy Jewelry, 55 King St. (☎ 340/773-2727), a branch of a hugely successful chain based in California, sells convincing copy jewelry. The lookalikes range from $9 to $1,000 and include credible copies of the baroque and antique jewelry your great-grandmother might have worn. If you want the real thing, you can go next door to **King Alley Jewelry** (☎ 340/773-4746), owned by the same company and specializing in fine designer jewelry, including Tiffany and Cartier.

✪ **Folk Art Traders,** Strand Street (☎ 340/773-1900), is a gem. Since 1985, the operators of this store have traveled throughout the Caribbean (in the bush) to acquire a unique collection of local art and folk-art treasures, not only carnival masks, pottery, ceramics, and original paintings, but also hand-wrought jewelry. The assortment is wide-ranging, including batiks from Barbados and high-quality iron sculpture from

Haiti. There's nothing else like it in the Virgin Islands. **From the Gecko,** 1233 Queen Cross St. (☎ **340/778-9433**), is a hip and eclectic clothier/gift shop. You can find anything from hand-painted U.S.V.I. cottons and silks to the old West Indian staple, batiks. Items will give you gift ideas. We found the Indonesian collection among the most imaginative in the U.S.V.I.—everything from ornate candleholders to banana leaf knapsacks.

About 60% of the merchandise in **Gone Tropical,** 5 Company St. (☎ **340/773-4696**), is made in Indonesia (usually Bali). The prices of new, semi-antique, or antique sofas, beds, chests, tables, mirrors, and decorative carvings are the same as or less than those of similar pieces you might've bought new at more conventional furniture stores. The store also sells worthy art objects (which can be shipped wherever you want), as well as jewelry, batiks, candles, and baskets. **Little Switzerland,** 1 Strand St. (☎ **340/773-1976**), has branches throughout the Caribbean and is the island's best source for crystal, figurines, watches, china, perfume, flatware, leather, and lots of fine jewelry. It specializes in all the big names, such as Paloma Picasso leather goods. For luxuries like a Rolex watch, an Omega, or heirloom crystal like Lalique, Swarovski, and Baccarat, this is the place. At least a few items are said to sell for up to 30% less than on the U.S. mainland, but don't take anyone's word for that unless you've checked prices carefully.

Many Hands, 21 Pan Am Pavilion, Strand Street (☎ **340/773-1990**), sells Virgin Islands handcrafts exclusively. The merchandise includes West Indian spices and teas, shellwork, stained glass, hand-painted china, pottery, and handmade jewelry. Their collection of local paintings is intriguing, as is their year-round Christmas tree. **The Royal Poinciana,** 1111 Strand St. (☎ **340/773-9892**), is the most interesting gift shop on St. Croix. In what looks like an antique apothecary, you'll find such Caribbean-inspired items as hot sauces (fire water), seasoning blends for gumbos, island herbal teas, Antillean coffees, and a scented array of soaps, toiletries, lotions, and shampoos. There's also a selection of museum-reproduction greeting cards and calendars as well as fun and educational gifts for children.

Sonya Ltd., 1 Company St. (☎ **340/778-8605**), is the domain of Sonya Hough, the matriarch of a cult following of locals who wouldn't leave home without wearing one of her bracelets. She's most famous for her sterling-silver or gold (from 14- to 24-karat) interpretations of the C-clasp bracelet. Locals communicate discreet messages by how it's worn: If the cup of the C is turned toward your heart, it means you're emotionally committed. If the cup of the C is turned outward, it means you're available to whomever strikes your fancy. She also sells rings, earrings, and necklaces. **Urban Threadz/Urban Kidz,** 52C Company St. (☎ **340/773-2883**), is the most comprehensive clothing store in Christiansted's historic core, with a big-city scale and appeal that's different from the tropicalboutique aura of nearby T-shirt shops. It's the store where islanders prefer to shop, because of the clothing's hip urban styles. Men's garments are on the street level and women's upstairs, and the inventory includes everything from Bermuda shorts to lightweight summer blazers and men's suits. They carry Calvin Klein, Nautica, and Oakley, among others.

Waterfront Larimar Mines, The Boardwalk/King's Walk (☎ **340/692-9000**), sells the largest selection of the Caribbean's own gemstone, **larimar.** Everything sold in this shop is produced by the largest manufacturer of larimar gold settings in the world. Discovered in the 1970s, larimar is a pale-blue pectolyte prized for its sky-blue color. It's extracted from mines in only one mountain in the world, on the southwestern edge of the Dominican Republic, near the Haitian border. **The White House,** King's Alley Walk (☎ **340/773-9222**), takes a stand against those who appear only in black. Going against a trend, this outlet lives up to its name. Everything is white or off-white—nothing darker than beige is allowed on the premises. The style of clothing for women ranges from dressy to casual and breezy.

ST. CROIX AFTER DARK

St. Croix doesn't have the nightlife of St. Thomas, so to find the action, you might have to hotel- or bar-hop or consult *St. Croix This Week.*

Try to catch a performance of the **Quadrille Dancers,** the cultural treat of St. Croix. Their dances have changed little since plantation days; the women wear long dresses, white gloves, and turbans, and the men are attired in flamboyant shirts, sashes, and tight black trousers. When you've learned their steps, you're invited to join the dancers on the floor. Ask at your hotel if and where they're performing.

The big nightlife news on St. Croix is the opening of the casino at the **Divi Carina Bay Resort** (☎ 340/773-3616 for information), which should be up and running by 2000. The island's first casino will feature 275 slot machines and 12 table games.

THE PERFORMING ARTS The 1,100-seat **Island Center,** Sunny Isle (☎ 340/778-5272), half a mile north of Sunny Isle, continues to attract big-name entertainers to St. Croix. Its program is widely varied, ranging from jazz, nostalgia, and musical revues to Broadway plays. Consult *St. Croix This Week* or call the center to see what's being presented. The Caribbean Community Theatre and Courtyard Players perform regularly. Call for performance times. Tickets run $5 to $25.

BARS & CLUBS **Blue Moon,** 17 Strand St. (☎ 340/772-2222), is a little dive that's also a good bistro, the hottest and hippest spot in Frederiksted on Friday nights, when a five-piece ensemble provides the entertainment. The good news is that there's no cover, so you'll have to spend money only on drinks. Stick around to try some of the food from an eclectic menu that samples flavors from the Bayou Country to Asia. Closed in August.

The Marina Bar, in the King's Alley Hotel, King's Alley/The Waterfront (☎ 340/773-0103), occupies a panoramic position on the waterfront, on a shaded terrace overlooking the sea and Protestant Cay. Although the place remains open throughout the day, the real festivities begin right after the last seaplane departs for St. Thomas (around 5:30pm) and continue energetically to 8:30pm. Sunset-colored cocktails made with rum, mangos, bananas, papaya, and grenadine are the libations of choice. You can stave off hunger pangs with burgers, sandwiches, and West Indian–style platters. The bar has live entertainment most nights, usually steel bands. On Monday you can bet on crab races.

Mt. Pellier Hut Domino Club, Montpellier (☎ 340/772-9914), is a one-of-a-kind club. It came into being as a battered snack shack established to serve players of a never-ending domino game. Gradually it grew into a drinking and entertainment center, although the game is still going strong. Today, the bar charges $1 to view a beer-drinking pig (Miss Piggy) and has a one-man band, Piro, who plays on Sunday. The bartender will also serve you a lethal rum-based Mamma Wanna. The **Terrace Lounge,** in the Buccaneer, Rte. 82, Estate Shoys (☎ 340/773-2100), is for a grand night on the town. Every night this lounge off the main dining room of one of St. Croix's most upscale resorts welcomes some of the Caribbean's finest entertainers, often including a full band. Call to see what's happening.

The ✪ **Cormorant Beach Club Bar,** 4126 La Grande Princesse (☎ 340/778-8920), has gone gay. One of the island's most romantic bars is along La Grande Princesse northwest of Christiansted, opening onto one of the island's best beaches. It's a Caribbean cliché, but that's why people often come to the islands in the first place, to enjoy tropical drinks in a moonlit setting with palm trees swaying in the night winds. Guests—usually gay men—sit at tables overlooking the ocean or around an open-centered mahogany bar, surrounded by an enlarged gazebo, wicker love seats, comfortable chairs, and soft lighting. Excellent tropical drinks are mixed, including the house specialty, a Cormorant cooler made with champagne, pineapple juice, and Triple Sec.

2 Plus 2 Disco, along the La Grande Princesse (☎ **340/773-3710**), is a real Caribbean disco. This joint features the regional sounds of the islands, not only calypso and reggae, but also salsa, rhythm and blues, and soca (a hybrid of calypso and reggae). Usually you get a sweaty DJ selecting the music, except on weekends, when local bands are brought in. Not fancy or large, the disco has a black-tile dance floor with a simple lighting system. Come here for Saturday Night Fever. Hours are Tuesday to Sunday 8:30pm to 2am and Friday and Saturday 8pm to either 5 or 6am. A cover of $7 is imposed when there's live entertainment.

Appendix: The Islands & the Islanders

Golden beaches shaded by palm trees and crystalline waters teeming with colorful sea creatures—it's all just a few hours' flight from the east coast of the United States. Dubbed the "Eighth Continent of the World," the Caribbean islands have an amazing variety of terrain that ranges from thick rain forests to haunting volcanoes, from white- to black-sand beaches. Spicy food, spicier music, and the leisurely lifestyle of the islands draw millions of visitors each year, all hoping to find that perfect place in the sun.

1 From Salsa to Reggae: The Musical Heritage of the Caribbean

The gutsy, aggressive beat of African music was brought in with the slave ships—it drowned out the harpsichord music wafting from the master's house soon enough. Over the years, it spawned many musical forms, including calypso and reggae, which usually spring to mind for most people when the music of the Caribbean is mentioned.

The major "music islands" of the Caribbean are Jamaica and Puerto Rico, and to a lesser extent the Dominican Republic, Trinidad, and Barbados.

The best time to enjoy the music and dancing of the Caribbean is during **Carnival.** On islands with strong Roman Catholic ties, this is similar to Mardi Gras in New Orleans. For some islands, carnival lasts from Epiphany (January 6) to Ash Wednesday, with parades and dancing in the streets, especially on each Sunday before Lent. On other islands, festivals, fiestas, and special days (many held in summer) take the place of carnival. For example, Barbados holds a festival celebrating the end of the sugarcane harvest.

At least some of the instruments used in traditional Puerto Rican music had their origins with the Taíno peoples. Most noteworthy is the *guicharo,* or *guiro,* a notched, hollowed-out gourd whose form was almost directly adapted from pre-Columbian days. At least four different stringed instruments were adapted from the six-string Spanish classical guitar: the *requinto,* the *bordonua,* the *cuatro,* and the *tiple,* each of which produces a unique tone and pitch. The most popular of these is the cuatro, a guitar-like instrument with 10 strings (arranged into 5 pairs).

Also used on the island are such percussion instruments as *tambours* (hollowed tree trunks covered with stretched-out animal skin), *maracas* (gourds filled with pebbles or dried beans and mounted on handles), and a host of different drums whose original designs were brought from Africa by the islands' slaves. All these instruments have a place in a rich variety of folk music with roots in the cultural melting pot of the island's Spanish, African, and native Taíno traditions.

SALSA

The major music coming out of Puerto Rico now is **salsa,** literally translated as the "sauce" that makes parties happen. Originally developed in the Puerto Rican community of New York, it draws heavily on the musical roots of the Cuban and the African-Caribbean experience. Highly danceable, its rhythms are hot, urban, sophisticated, and very compelling. Salsa bands employ a huge array of percussion instruments, including maracas, bongos, timbales, conga drums, and claves—and, to add the *jíbaro* (hillbilly) touch, a clanging cow bell. Of course, it also takes a bass, a horn section, a chorus, and a lead vocalist to get the combination right.

REGGAE & SKA

The roots of Jamaica's unique **reggae** music can be found in an early form of Jamaican music called *mento,* brought to the island from Africa by slaves and reminiscent of the rhythm and blues that in the mid–20th century swept across North America. It was usually accompanied by hip-rolling dances known as bubbling, with highly suggestive lyrics to match.

In the late 1950s Jamaican musicians combined boogie-woogie with rhythm and blues to form a short-lived but vibrant music named **ska.** It was the politicization of ska by Rastafarians that led to the creation of reggae.

Sometimes referred to as the heartbeat of Jamaica, reggae is the island's most distinctive musical form, as closely linked to Jamaica as soul is to Detroit, jazz to New Orleans, and blues to Chicago. The term *reggae* is best defined as "coming from the people." It has influenced the music of international stars like the Rolling Stones, Eric Clapton, and Paul Simon. Most notably, it propelled a street-smart kid from Kingston named Bob Marley onto the world scene. Today the recording studios of Kingston churn out hundreds of reggae albums every year.

One of the most recent adaptations of reggae is **soca,** which is more upbeat and less politicized. Aficionados say that reggae makes you think, while soca makes you dance. The music is fun, infectious, and spontaneous, perfect for partying, and often imbued with the humor and wry attitudes of Jamaican urban dwellers.

After 1965, the influx of Jamaican immigrants to the potboiling pressures of North America's ghettos had a profound influence on popular music. Such Jamaican-born stars as Clive Campbell, combining the Jamaican gift for the spoken word with reggae rhythms and high electronic amplification, developed the roots of what eventually became known as rap.

CALYPSO

Some purists point out that **calypso** music is really a product of Trinidad, though it remains very popular in Jamaica (and also Barbados). Calypso, which originated on Trinidad, is a mixture—basically African but with African-Spanish rhythms, English verses, and traces of French structure. The words to calypso tunes were originally (and sometimes still are) spontaneous improvisations based on all sorts of subjects—love, sex, politics, whatever.

2 A Taste of the Islands

Chefs throughout the Caribbean prepare a presentable American and continental cuisine, but in recent years, even the kitchens of the deluxe hotels have placed a greater emphasis on local dishes. We've had many memorable meals in the cheap, authentic, local spots on each island—you really don't have to splurge in a so-called gourmet restaurant at some deluxe resort to savor the best flavors of the islands, and we'll share some terrific finds with you.

And what's on the menu? Well, first off, you'll enjoy an abundance of fruit in the islands. Most breakfasts include a platter of freshly sliced fruit. Coconut is used in everything from breads to soups. Soursop ice cream appears on some menus, and guava might turn up in anything from juice to cheese. Papaya is called paw paw, and it will most often be your melon choice at breakfast. Mango is ubiquitous, used not only in chutney but also in drinks and desserts. The avocado, most often called "pears," is used in fresh seafood salads and often stuffed with fresh crabmeat.

By now, most visitors know that plantain (which is similar to a banana but red in color) is not eaten raw. It's usually served as a cooked side dish, the way Americans serve french fries. Puerto Ricans eat dried plantains, called *tostones,* instead of potato chips. Plantains can also be served mashed or boiled, and they turn up in many desserts, especially when mixed with coconut and pineapple.

Two staples of the Caribbean islands have always been rice and pigeon peas. Balls of cornmeal, called fungi, often accompany a salt-pork main dish known as *mauffay.* Sometimes these cornmeal concoctions will appear on the menus of local restaurants as *coo coo.*

One of the most common vegetables in the islands is christophine (sometimes called *foo foo*), a green, prickly gourd that tastes somewhat like zucchini. Breadfruit, introduced to the islands by Captain Bligh (of *Mutiny on the Bounty* fame) is green and round and used like a potato. Potatoes and yams are also local favorites. The leaf-like callaloo is one of the best-known vegetables in the West Indies. It's like spinach and is often served with crab, salt pork, and fresh fish (with floating fungi as a garnish).

In a true local restaurant in the Caribbean, you'll see hot peppers placed on the table. (Be sparing.) A selection of hot-pepper pastes is called *sambal.*

And, of course, aside from tropical fruit, seafood is the staple of island cuisine. Throughout the islands, warm-water **lobster** is the king of the sea and the most sought after—and most expensive—main course to order. The "catch of the day" is most likely to be **red snapper** or **grouper,** but could also be shark or barracuda.

We urge you to be cautious in eating **barracuda,** which have been known to contain copper deposits. Fish caught north of Antigua and also along the Cayman Islands and Cuba are said to be at risk, though the barracuda in south-lying Barbados are fine and usually very healthy. **Dolphin** may also appear on the menu, but—never fear—this dolphin is a fish, not Flipper.

Distilled easily from sugarcane, **rum** played a major role in the history of the West Indies. Today the rusted machinery and tumbledown ruins of distilleries are tourist stops on dozens of Caribbean islands.

While **planter's punch** is the most popular drink in the islands, the average bar in the Caribbean is likely to offer a bewildering array of rum-based drinks. *One word of caution though:* Be alert to your limits, especially if you're driving. Sure, these frosty drinks are pastel-colored and come with cute umbrellas, but they'll get you drunk on very short notice because of their elevated sugar content as well as the hot climate.

Don't think that the only **beer** you'll be able to find will be imported from Milwaukee or Holland. Of course, Heineken is ubiquitous, as is Amstel, especially in the Dutch islands, but Red Stripe from Jamaica is a famous local brand.

Water is generally safe throughout the islands, but many tourists get sick from drinking it simply because it's different from the water they're accustomed to. If it's available, order bottled water.

SPECIALTIES OF THE ISLANDS

ANTIGUA & BARBUDA   At most restaurants and in most resorts catering to tourists, you get typical American or continental fare. But look for local food, which tends to be spicy, with sauces often based on Creole recipes or East Indian curry dishes—that means pepperpot stew, spareribs, curried goat, and the like. A British heritage lingers in some of the island's blander dishes. If fresh seafood is on the menu, go for it.

ARUBA   A few of Aruba's restaurants serve *rijsttafel,* the Indonesian "rice table," or *nasi goreng,* a mini-rijsttafel. In addition, many Chinese restaurants operate in Oranjestad. Aruban specialties are beginning to appear on menus. Although we don't always find them suited to the tropics, these include *keshi yena,* Edam cheese filled with a mixture of chicken or beef and flavored with onions, pickles, tomatoes, olives, and raisins. *Sopito de pisca* is a savory fish chowder made with a bouquet of spices. *Funchi,* like a cornmeal pudding of the Deep South, accompanies many regional dishes. *Pastechi* is a meat-stuffed turnover, and *cala* is a bean fritter.

BARBADOS   The famous flying fish appears on every menu, and when prepared right, it's a delicacy—moist and succulent, nutlike in flavor, approaching the subtlety of brook trout. Bajans boil it, steam it, bake it, stew it, fry it, and stuff it.

Try the sea urchin, or *oursin,* which you may have already sampled on Martinique and Guadeloupe. Bajans often call these urchins "sea eggs." Crab-in-the-back is another specialty, as is *langouste,* the Bajan lobster. Dolphin and salt fish cakes are other popular items. Yams, sweet potatoes, and eddoes (similar to yams) are typical vegetables. Luscious Bajan fruits include papaya, passion fruit, and mango.

If you hear that any hotel or restaurant is having a *cohobblopot* (or more commonly, a Bajan buffet), head right over! This is a Bajan term that means to "cook up," and it inevitably will produce an array of local dishes.

BONAIRE   Bonaire's food is generally acceptable, though nearly everything has to be imported. Your best bet is fresh-caught fish and an occasional *rijsttafel,* the traditional Indonesian "rice table," or local dishes. Popular foods are conch cutlet or stew, pickled conch, red snapper, tuna, wahoo, dolphin, fungi (a thick cornmeal pudding), rice, beans, sate (marinated meat with curried mayonnaise), goat stew, and Dutch cheeses.

BRITISH VIRGIN ISLANDS   The food is relatively simple and straightforward, with fresh fish the best item on the menu. Most other items, including meat and poultry, are shipped in frozen. In most major restaurants and hotels, American or continental cuisine prevails. For a taste of the islands, seek out the local dives (we recommend several good bets in that chapter). Locals give colorful names to the various fish brought home for dinner, everything from "ole wife" to "doctors." "Porgies and grunts," along with yellowtail, kingfish, and bonito, show up on many tables. Fish is usually boiled in a lime-flavored brew seasoned with hot peppers and herbs, and is commonly served with a Creole sauce of peppers, tomatoes, and onions, among other ingredients. Salt fish and rice is another low-cost dish, the fish flavored with onion, tomatoes, garlic, and green pepper.

Conch Creole is a tasty brew, flavored with onions, garlic, spices, hot peppers, and salt pork. A favorite local dish is chicken and rice, made with Spanish peppers. Curried goat, the longtime "classic" West Indian dinner, is made with herbs, including cardamom pods and onions. The famous johnnycakes that accompany many of these fish and meat dishes are fried in deep fat or baked.

CAYMAN ISLANDS American and continental cooking predominate, although there is also a cuisine known as Caymanian, which features specialties made from turtle. (Environmental groups in the U.S. consider this species to be endangered; however, in the Cayman Islands it is bred for food, as opposed to being caught in the wild at sea.) Fresh fish is the star, and conch is used in many ways. Local lobster is in season from late summer through January. Since most restaurants have to rely on imported ingredients, prices tend to be high.

CURAÇAO The basic cuisine is Dutch, but there are many specialty items, particularly Latin American and Indonesian. The cuisine strikes many visitors as heavy for the tropics, so you may want to have a light lunch and order the more filling concoctions, such as *rijsttafel*, in the evening. You'll want to finish your meals with Curaçao, the orange-based liqueur that made the island famous.

Ertwensoep, the well-known Dutch pea soup, is a popular dish, as is *keshi yena*, which is Edam cheese stuffed with meat and then baked. *Funchi*, a cornmeal pudding, accompanies many local dishes. *Sopito*, fish soup often made with coconut water, is an especially good local dish, and conch is featured in curries and many other dishes.

DOMINICA The local delicacy is the fine flesh of the *crapaud* (a frog), called "mountain chicken." Freshwater crayfish is another specialty, as is *tee-tee-ree*, fried cakes made from tiny fish. Stuffed crab back is usually a delight—the backs of red and black land crabs are stuffed with delicate crabmeat and Creole seasonings. The fresh fruit juices of the island are lovely, and no one lets a day go by without at least one rum punch.

DOMINICAN REPUBLIC The national dish is *sancocho*, a thick stew made with meats (maybe seven kinds), vegetables, and herbs, especially marjoram. Another national favorite is *chicharrones de pollo*, pieces of fried chicken and fried green bananas flavored with pungent spices. One of the most typical dishes is *la bandera* (the flag), made with red beans, white rice, and stewed meat. Johnnycakes and *mangu*, a plaintain-like dish, are frequently eaten. Johnnycakes can be bought on the street corner or at the beach, but you must ask for them as *vaniqueques*.

A good local beer is called Presidente. Wines are imported, so prices tend to run high. Dominican coffee compares favorably with that of Colombia and Brazil.

GRENADA We've found food on Grenada better than on the other British Windward Islands. Many of the chefs are European or European-trained, and local cooks are also on hand to prepare Grenadian specialties, such as conch (called *lambi* here), lobster, callaloo soup (with greens and crab), and soursop or avocado ice cream. Turtle steaks appear on many menus, although this is an endangered species. The national dish, called "oil down," consists of breadfruit and salt pork covered with dasheen leaves and steamed in coconut milk (it's not the favorite of every visitor). Some 22 kinds of fish, including fresh tuna, dolphin, and barracuda, are caught off the island's shores, and most are good for eating. Naturally, the spices of the island, such as nutmeg, are used plentifully. Meals are often served family style in an open-air setting with a view of the sea.

GUADELOUPE The Creole cuisine of Guadeloupe is similar to Martinique's, and we think it's the best in the Caribbean. The island's chefs have been called "seasoned sorcerers." Having African roots, Creole cooking is based on seafood. Out in the country, every cook has his or her own herb garden, since the cuisine makes great use of herbs and spices. Except in the major hotels, most restaurants are family run, offering real homemade cooking. Best of all, you usually get to dine alfresco.

Stuffed, stewed, skewered, or broiled spiny lobsters, as well as clams, conchs, oysters, and octopus, are presented to you with French taste and subtlety. Every good chef knows how to make *colombo,* a spicy rich stew of poultry, pork, or beef served with rice, herbs, sauces, and a variety of seeds. Another Creole favorite is *calalou* (callaloo in English), a soup flavored with savory herbs. Yet another traditional French Caribbean dish is *blaff,* fresh seafood poached in clear stock and usually seasoned with hot peppers.

JAMAICA There is great emphasis on seafood here. Rock lobster appears on every menu—grilled, Thermidor, cold, and hot. *Saltfish* and *ackee,* the national dish, is a concoction of salt cod and a brightly colored vegetable that tastes something like scrambled eggs. *Escovitch* (marinated fish) is usually fried and then simmered in vinegar with onions and peppers. Curried mutton and goat are popular, as is pepperpot stew, all highly seasoned.

Jerk pork is found in country areas, where it's barbecued slowly over wood fires until crisp and brown. Rice and peas (really red beans) are usually served with onions, spices, and salt pork. Vegetables are exotic: breadfruit, imported by Captain Bligh in 1723; callaloo, rather like spinach, used in pepperpot soup; *cho-cho,* served boiled or stuffed; and green bananas and plantains, fried or boiled and served with almost everything. Then there's pumpkin, which goes into a soup or is served on the side, boiled and mashed with butter. Sweet potatoes appear with main courses, but there's also a sweet-potato pudding made with sugar and coconut milk, flavored with cinnamon, nutmeg, and vanilla.

You'll come across dishes with really odd names: *stamp and go* are saltfish cakes eaten as appetizers; *dip and fall back* is a salty stew with bananas and dumplings; and *rundown* is mackerel cooked in coconut milk, often eaten for breakfast. For the really adventurous, *manish water,* a soup made from goat offal and tripe, is said to increase virility. Patties (meat pies) —the best on the island are at Montego Bay—are another staple snack. Boiled corn, roast yams, roast saltfish, fried fish, soups, and fruits are all sold at roadside stands.

Tea is used to describe any nonalcoholic drink in Jamaica, a tradition dating back to plantation days. Fish tea is actually a bowl of hot soup made from freshly caught fish. *Skyjuice,* a favorite on hot afternoons, is sold by street vendors from not-always-sanitary carts. It consists of shaved ice with sugar-laden fruit syrup and is sold in small plastic bags with a straw. Coconut water is a refreshing drink, especially when you stop to have a local vendor chop open a fresh coconut.

Rum punches are everywhere, and the local beer is Red Stripe. The island produces many liqueurs, the most famous being Tía Maria, made from coffee beans. *Bellywash,* the local name for limeade, will supply the extra liquid you may need to counteract the heat. Blue Mountain coffee is the best, but tea, cocoa, and milk are usually available to round off a meal.

MARTINIQUE   See Guadeloupe, above.

PUERTO RICO   Although Puerto Rican cooking has similarities to Cuban, Spanish, and Mexican cuisine, it has its own unique style, using such indigenous ingredients as cilantro, papaya, cacao, nispero, apio, plantains, and yampee.

Lunch and dinner generally begin with sizzling hot appetizers such as *bacalaitos* (crunchy cold fritters), *surullitos* (sweet, plump cornmeal fingers), and *empanadillas* (crescent-shaped turnovers filled with lobster, crab, conch, or beef). Next, a bowl of steaming *asopao* (a hearty gumbo soup with rice and chicken or shellfish) may be followed by *lechón asado* (roast suckling pig), *pollo en vino dulce* (succulent chicken in wine), or *bacalao* (dried salted cod mixed with various roots and tubers and fried). No matter the selection, main dishes are served with salted *tostones* (deep-fried plantains, or green bananas) and plentiful portions of rice and beans.

The aroma that wafts from kitchens throughout Puerto Rico comes from *adobo* and *sofrito*—blends of herbs and spices that give many of the native foods their distinctive taste and color. *Adobo,* made from peppercorns, oregano, garlic, salt, olive oil, and lime juice or vinegar, is rubbed into meats before they are roasted. *Sofrito,* a potpourri of onions, garlic, and peppers browned in olive oil or lard and colored with *achiote* (annatto seeds), imparts a bright yellow color to the island's rice, soups, and stews. Dessert is usually *flan* (custard) or perhaps *nisperos de batata* (sweet-potato balls made with coconut, cloves, and cinnamon), or guava jelly and *queso blanco* (white cheese).

SABA   No one visits Saba for the food. Caribbean and continental dishes prevail, and there are no really outstanding local dishes. Most of the food is imported.

ST. EUSTATIUS   You won't find this Dutch island written up in gourmet cookbooks. Most of the food is imported, and restaurants are adequate, not exciting. Some restaurants make a stab at preparing a French cuisine with generally frozen ingredients. Local bistros serve some regional cooking such as stewed conch, salt fish with johnnycakes, or curried goat.

NEVIS & ST. KITTS   On Nevis, the local food is good. Suckling pig is roasted with many spices, and eggplant is used in a number of tasty ways, as is avocado. (You may see turtle on some menus, but remember that this is an endangered species.)

On St. Kitts, most guests eat at their hotels, but the island has a number of good restaurants where you can find spiny lobster, crab back, pepperpot stew, breadfruit, and curried conch. The drink of the island is CSR (Cane Spirit Rothschild), a pure sugarcane liqueur developed by Baron Edmond de Rothschild. Islanders mix it with Ting, a bubbly grapefruit soda.

ST. LUCIA   It's best to dine in one of St. Lucia's little character-loaded restaurants (we make suggestions in that chapter). The local food is excellent and reflects the years of French and British occupation. St. Lucia's marketplace offers the ingredients for local dishes, including callaloo soup (fresh greens, dumplings, and salted beef), *pouile dudon* (a sweet, zesty chicken dish), and breadfruit cooked on open hot coals. Pumpkin soup, flying fish, lobster, and *tablette* (a coconut sugar candy that resembles white coral) round out the menu choices.

ST. MAARTEN & ST. MARTIN   This island, part Dutch, part French, has a truly excellent cuisine, in spite of its heavy reliance on imported ingredients. Here you'll find classic French cuisine, as well as American and continental, with a touch of West Indian spice and flavors. All the French classics are served, including frogs' legs and escargots, but Caribbean offerings, inspired by Martinique, include *crabes farcis* (stuffed crab), *blaff* (seafood poached and seasoned with peppers), and curried *colombo* (a stew with chicken, mutton, or goat). Nearby Anguilla supplies a never-ending basket of spiny lobsters, the most delectable dish on the island. Dutch specialties are rare, although there's plenty of tasty Dutch beer. A lot of good French wine, served either by the bottle or the carafe, is also shipped into the island.

ST. VINCENT & THE GRENADINES   Most dining takes place in the hotels, although there are a scattering of local bistros serving such West Indian food as local fish Creole style and callaloo soup. But mostly locals try to serve what they've heard foreigners like, including frozen steak flown in from Chicago, frozen shrimp from South America, and frozen french fries from who-knows-where. Local bartenders take pride in the variety of their rum punches as well as their lethal effects.

TRINIDAD & TOBAGO   The food on these islands is as varied and cosmopolitan as the islanders themselves. Red-hot curries testify to Trinidad's strong East Indian influence, and some Chinese dishes are about as good here as any you'll find in Hong Kong. Creole and Spanish fare, as well as French, are also to be enjoyed. A typical savory offering is a *rôti,* a king-size crêpe, highly spiced and filled with chicken, shellfish, or meat. Of course, you may prefer to skip such local delicacies as opossum stew and fried armadillo. Naturally, your fresh rum punch will have a dash of Angostura Bitters. On Trinidad, there's a tendency to deep-fry everything—you can avoid this by careful menu selections.

Tobago has fewer dining choices than Trinidad. On Tobago, your best bet are local fish dishes, such as stuffed kingfish in Creole sauce. Local crayfish is also good, and lobster appears on some menus, perhaps stuffed into a crêpe. One island favorite that appears frequently is seafood casserole with ginger wine. Some typical Tobago dishes include baby shark marinated in lime and rum and conch stewed with coconut and rum.

U.S. VIRGIN ISLANDS   Although a lot of the food is imported and frozen (often from Miami or Puerto Rico), St. Thomas, and to a lesser extent St. Croix and St. John, serve some of the finest American and continental cuisine in the Caribbean. A whole range of ethnic restaurants exist too, including Chinese and Mexican. Italian food is commonplace.

The most famous soup of the islands is kallaloo, or *callaloo,* made in an infinite number of ways from a leafy green vegetable similar to spinach. This soup is flavored with salt beef, pig mouth, pig tail, ham bone, fresh fish, crabs, or perhaps conch, along with okra, onions, and spices. Many soups are sweetened with sugar, and putting fruits in soups is common. The classic *red-bean soup,* made with pork or ham, various spices, and tomatoes, is sugared to taste. *Tannia* soup is made from the root of the so-called Purple Elephant Ear. Salt-fat meat and ham, along with tomatoes, onions, and spices, are added to the *tannias.*

Souse is an old-time favorite made with the feet, head, and tongue of the pig, and flavored with a lime-based sauce and various spices. Salt-fish salad is traditionally served on Holy Thursday or Good Friday, as well as at other times. It's made with boneless salt fish, potatoes, onions, boiled eggs, and an oil-and-vinegar dressing. *Herring gundy* is an old-time island favorite made with salt herring, potatoes, onions, sweet and hot green peppers, olives, diced beets, raw carrots, herbs, and boiled eggs.

Seasoned rice is popular with Virgin Islanders, who often serve several starches at one meal. Most often rice is flavored with ham or salt pork, tomatoes, garlic, onion, and shortening. *Fungi* is a simple cornmeal dumpling that can be made more interesting with the addition of various ingredients, such as okra. Sweet fungi becomes a dessert, with sugar, milk, cinnamon, and raisins.

Okra (often spelled ochroe in the islands) is a mainstay vegetable, often accompanying beef, fish, or chicken. It's fried in an iron skillet after being flavored with hot pepper, tomatoes, onions, garlic, and bacon fat or butter. *Accra,* another popular dish, is made with okra, black-eyed peas, salt, and pepper. It's dropped into boiling fat and fried until golden brown. The classic vegetable dish—some families serve it every night—is peas and rice, made with pigeon peas flavored with ham or salt meat, onion, tomatoes, herbs, and sometimes slices of pumpkins.

For dessert, sweet-potato pone is a classic, made with sugar, eggs, butter, milk, salt, cinnamon, raisins, and chopped almonds. The exotic fruits of the islands lend themselves to various homemade ice creams, including mango. Orange-rose sherbet is made by pounding rose petals into a paste and flavoring it with sugar and orange juice. Guava ice cream is a delectable flavor, as are soursop, banana, and papaya. Sometimes dumplings are served for dessert, made with guava, peach, plum, gooseberry, or cherry, and certainly apple.

Index

See also Accommodations index, below.
Page numbers in *italics* refer to maps.

General Index

General Index

ACCOMMODATIONS

Accommodations Index

FROMMER'S® COMPLETE TRAVEL GUIDES

Alaska
Amsterdam
Arizona
Atlanta
Australia
Austria
Bahamas
Barcelona, Madrid & Seville
Beijing
Belgium, Holland & Luxembourg
Bermuda
Boston
Budapest & the Best of Hungary
California
Canada
Cancún, Cozumel &
  the Yucatán
Cape Cod, Nantucket & Martha's Vineyard
Caribbean
Caribbean Cruises & Ports of Call
Caribbean Ports of Call
Carolinas & Georgia
Chicago
China
Colorado
Costa Rica
Denmark
Denver, Boulder & Colorado Springs
England
Europe
Florida
France
Germany
Greece
Greek Islands
Hawaii
Hong Kong
Honolulu, Waikiki & Oahu
Ireland
Israel
Italy
Jamaica & Barbados
Japan
Las Vegas
London
Los Angeles
Maryland & Delaware
Maui
Mexico
Miami & the Keys

Montana & Wyoming
Montréal & Québec City
Munich & the Bavarian Alps
Nashville & Memphis
Nepal
New England
New Mexico
New Orleans
New York City
Nova Scotia, New Brunswick &
  Prince Edward Island
Oregon
Paris
Philadelphia & the
  Amish Country
Portugal
Prague & the Best of the Czech Republic
Provence & the Riviera
Puerto Rico
Rome
San Antonio & Austin
San Diego
San Francisco
Santa Fe, Taos &
  Albuquerque
Scandinavia
Scotland
Seattle & Portland
Singapore & Malaysia
South Africa
Southeast Asia
South Pacific
Spain
Sweden
Switzerland
Thailand
Tokyo
Toronto
Tuscany & Umbria
USA
Utah
Vancouver & Victoria
Vermont, New Hampshire
  & Maine
Vienna & the Danube Valley
Virgin Islands
Virginia
Walt Disney World & Orlando
Washington, D.C.
Washington State

FROMMER'S® DOLLAR-A-DAY GUIDES

Australia from $50 a Day	Hawaii from $70 a Day	New Zealand from $50 a Day
California from $60 a Day	Ireland from $50 a Day	Paris from $85 a Day
Caribbean from $70 a Day	Israel from $45 a Day	San Francisco from $60 a Day
England from $70 a Day	Italy from $70 a Day	Washington, D.C.,
Europe from $60 a Day	London from $85 a Day	from $60 a Day
Florida from $60 a Day	New York from $80 a Day	

FROMMER'S® PORTABLE GUIDES

Acapulco, Ixtapa & Zihuatanejo	Dublin	Puerto Vallarta, Manzanillo & Guadalajara
Alaska Cruises & Ports of Call	Hawaii: The Big Island	San Diego
Bahamas	Las Vegas	San Francisco
Baja & Los Cabos	London	Sydney
Berlin	Maine Coast	Tampa & St. Petersburg
California Wine Country	Maui	Venice
Charleston & Savannah	New Orleans	Washington, D.C.
Chicago	New York City	
	Paris	

FROMMER'S® NATIONAL PARK GUIDES

Family Vacations in the National Parks	National Parks of the American West	Yellowstone & Grand Teton
Grand Canyon	Rocky Mountain	Yosemite & Sequoia/ Kings Canyon
		Zion & Bryce Canyon

FROMMER'S® GREAT OUTDOOR GUIDES

New England	Southern California & Baja
Northern California	Washington & Oregon

FROMMER'S® MEMORABLE WALKS

Chicago	New York	San Francisco
London	Paris	Washington D.C.

FROMMER'S® IRREVERENT GUIDES

Amsterdam	London	New Orleans	Seattle & Portland
Boston	Los Angeles	Paris	Vancouver
Chicago	Manhattan	San Francisco	Walt Disney World
Las Vegas			Washington, D.C.

FROMMER'S® BEST-LOVED DRIVING TOURS

America	Florida	Ireland	Scotland
Britain	France	Italy	Spain
California	Germany	New England	Western Europe

THE UNOFFICIAL GUIDES®

Bed & Breakfast in
New England
Bed & Breakfast in
the Northwest
Beyond Disney
Branson, Missouri
California with Kids
Chicago

Cruises
Disneyland
Florida with Kids
The Great Smoky &
Blue Ridge
Mountains
Inside Disney
Las Vegas

London
Miami & the Keys
Mini Las Vegas
Mini-Mickey
New Orleans
New York City
Paris
San Francisco

Skiing in the West
Walt Disney World
Walt Disney World
for Grown-ups
Walt Disney World
for Kids
Washington, D.C.

SPECIAL-INTEREST TITLES

Born to Shop: France
Born to Shop: Hong Kong
Born to Shop: Italy
Born to Shop: New York
Born to Shop: Paris
Frommer's Britain's Best Bike Rides
The Civil War Trust's Official Guide
to the Civil War Discovery Trail
Frommer's Caribbean Hideaways
Frommer's Europe's Greatest Driving Tours
Frommer's Food Lover's Companion to France
Frommer's Food Lover's Companion to Italy
Frommer's Gay & Lesbian Europe
Israel Past & Present
Monks' Guide to California

Monks' Guide to New York City
The Moon
New York City with Kids
Unforgettable Weekends
Outside Magazine's Guide
to Family Vacations
Places Rated Almanac
Retirement Places Rated
Road Atlas Britain
Road Atlas Europe
Washington, D.C., with Kids
Wonderful Weekends from Boston
Wonderful Weekends from New York City
Wonderful Weekends from San Francisco
Wonderful Weekends from Los Angeles

WHEREVER YOU TRAVEL, *H*ELP IS NEVER FAR AWAY.

From planning your trip to providing travel assistance along the way, American Express® Travel Service Offices are always there to help you do more.

Caribbean

BAHAMAS
Playtours (R)
303 Shirley St.
Nassau
(242) 322-2931

BARBADOS
Barbados International Travel Service
Horizon House
McGregor St.
(246) 431-2423

BRITISH VIRGIN ISLANDS
Travel Plan Ltd. (R)
Romasco Place
Road Town
Tortola
(284) 494-6239

U.S. VIRGIN ISLANDS
Southerland Tours (R)
Chandlers Wharf
Gallows Bay
St. Croix
(340) 773-9500

CAYMAN ISLANDS
Cayman Travel Services, Ltd. (R)
Shedden Rd., Elizabethan Sq.
George Town
Grand Cayman
(345) 949-8755/5400

JAMAICA
Grace Kennedy Travel Ltd. (R)
19-21 Knutsford Blvd.
Kingston 5
(876) 929-6290

MARTINIQUE
Roger Albert Voyages (R)
7 Rue Victor Hugo
Fort de France
(596) 71-71-71/71-42-20

PUERTO RICO
Travel Network (R)
1035 Ashford Ave.
Condado Area
San Juan
(787) 725-0960

ST. KITTS
Kantours (R)
Liverpool Row
Basseterre
(869) 465-2098

ST. MAARTEN
S.E.L. Maduro & Sons, (W.I.) Inc. (R)
Emmaplein Bldg. One
Philipsburg
(599)(5) 22678

do more AMERICAN EXPRESS

Travel

www.americanexpress.com/travel

American Express Travel Service Offices are found in central locations throughout the Caribbean.